MANCHESTER
WITHDRAWN
UNIVERSITY LIBRARY
AF841768

NICHOLLS, MONTGOMERY, AND KNOWLES ON

THE LAW OF EXTRADITION AND MUTUAL ASSISTANCE

NICHOLLS, MONTGOMERY, AND KNOWLES ON

THE LAW OF EXTRADITION AND MUTUAL ASSISTANCE

THIRD EDITION

Clive Nicholls QC
Clare Montgomery QC
Julian B. Knowles QC
Anand Doobay
Mark Summers

OXFORD
UNIVERSITY PRESS

OXFORD
UNIVERSITY PRESS

Great Clarendon Street, Oxford, OX2 6DP,
United Kingdom

Oxford University Press is a department of the University of Oxford.
It furthers the University's objective of excellence in research, scholarship,
and education by publishing worldwide. Oxford is a registered trade mark of
Oxford University Press in the UK and in certain other countries

© Clive Nicholls, Clare Montgomery, Julian B. Knowles, Anand Doobay, Mark Summers 2013

The moral rights of the authors have been asserted

Third edition published in 2013

Impression: 1

All rights reserved. No part of this publication may be reproduced, stored in a retrieval system, or transmitted, in any form or by any means, without the prior permission in writing of Oxford University Press, or as expressly permitted by law, by licence or under terms agreed with the appropriate reprographics rights organization. Enquiries concerning reproduction outside the scope of the above should be sent to the Rights Department, Oxford University Press, at the address above

You must not circulate this work in any other form
and you must impose this same condition on any acquirer

Crown copyright material is reproduced under Class Licence
Number C01P0000148 with the permission of OPSI
and the Queen's Printer for Scotland

British Library Cataloguing in Publication Data
Data available

ISBN 978–0–19–969281–1

Printed in Great Britain by
CPI Group (UK) Ltd, Croydon, CR0 4YY

Links to third party websites are provided by Oxford in good faith and
for information only. Oxford disclaims any responsibility for the materials
contained in any third party website referenced in this work.

MANCHESTER
METROPOLITAN
16 MAY 2014
UNIVERSITY LIBRARY

This book is dedicated to our families

PREFACE

Extradition law has developed in range and complexity in a way that we doubt anyone foresaw 10 years ago, when the first edition of this book was published. The European arrest warrant (EAW) scheme and the expansion of the EU have contributed to a deluge of cases which the courts have sometimes struggled to cope with. The figures in Appendix D to the Home Office's 2011 Extradition Review show that in 2004, 24 people were surrendered under EAWs. By 2010, that figure had increased to 1068, an increase of over 4000%. The courts' task in dealing with these cases has not been helped by the Extradition Act 2003, which must rank as one of the most badly drafted Acts in recent memory.

As far as the UK's extradition relations with the US are concerned, since 2007, when our second edition appeared, it has been a case of *plus ça change plus c'est la même chose.* In 2007 the case of the so-called 'NatWest 3' was causing controversy. As their alleged crime was largely committed in the UK, many people thought that they ought to have been tried in the UK, rather than being extradited to the US. In 2012, Gary McKinnon's case and other cases in which the US exercised what some see (rightly or wrongly) as an exorbitant long-arm jurisdiction generated headlines. The case of Julian Assange also stimulated considerable interest and debate during 2011/12, and at the time of writing remains unresolved.

Against this background, we are not going to try and predict where extradition law will go next. In October 2012 the Government announced its intention to withdraw the UK from all EU criminal justice measures passed before the Lisbon Treaty, including the EAW Framework Decision. We suspect that the Government will find that this process may not be as easy as it has imagined, and that withdrawal might have unintended consequences that it has not yet appreciated.

The writing team for this edition has been joined by Mark Summers and Anand Doobay, and their work has ensured that this edition of *N, M & K* is the best yet. Mark and Anand are hugely distinguished extradition and MLA practitioners; Anand was one of the Panel which produced the 2011 Extradition Review and Mark has been involved in many high profile cases including, most recently, the Julian Assange case.

We have attempted to state the law as at November 2012, when the text was completed. However, the writing schedule necessarily involved in a book of this length was such that some sections were completed earlier in the year. We have noted relevant dates where necessary, but the up-to-date legislative position should always be checked, given the rapid pace of change in this area of the law.

A note on terminology

Consistently with previous editions of this book, we have continued to refer to the person whose return is requested as 'the defendant'. This term is less clumsy than 'the requested person', and less old-fashioned (and more accurate) than the traditional description of him/her as 'the fugitive criminal', although both of these terms continue to be used in the cases. Also, although the EAW scheme uses the term 'surrender' rather than 'extradition', and there are conceptual differences between the two processes, we have continued to refer to the process under the scheme as 'extradition', as the Extradition Act 2003 does.

Clive Nicholls QC
3 Raymond Buldings, Gray's Inn

Clare Montgomery QC

Julian B. Knowles QC

Mark Summers
Matrix Chambers, Gray's Inn

Anand Doobay
Peters & Peters Solicitors LLP, London EC4

3 December 2012

CONTENTS

TABLE OF CASES

CYPRUS

GERMANY

GREECE

ITALY

POLAND

PORTUGAL

SPAIN

TABLE OF LEGISLATION

STATUTES

STATUTORY INSTRUMENTS

EU Legislation

TABLE OF TREATIES, CONVENTIONS, AND OTHER INTERNATIONAL INSTRUMENTS

OTHER JURISDICTIONS

Albania

Poland

Republic of Ireland

United States

Part I

EXTRADITION

1

INTRODUCTION AND OVERVIEW

A. Definition of Extradition

Extradition has been defined to be:[1] **1.01**

> Extradition is the formal name given to a process whereby one sovereign state, 'the requesting state', asks another sovereign state, 'the requested state', to return to the requesting state someone present in the requested state ... in order that the subject of the request may be brought to trial on criminal charges in the requesting state. The process also applies where the subject of the request has escaped from lawful custody in the requesting state and is found in the requested state.

Laws governing extradition seek to reconcile two objectives that are of concern to states that recognize the rule of law. One objective is to give effect to the principle that, in the ordinary way, persons in one state who are credibly accused of committing serious crimes triable in another state should be surrendered to that other state to answer for their alleged misdeeds. The second objective is to protect those whose surrender is sought against such surrender in circumstances where they would suffer injustice or oppression.[2] States ordinarily seek to provide safeguards against the surrender of those within their borders in such circumstances.[3] **1.02**

Extradition should be distinguished from deportation, which involves the country in which the person is present initiating the removal process.[4] Essentially, extradition involves three elements: an act of sovereignty on the part of two states; a request by one state to another state for the delivery to it of an alleged criminal; and the delivery of the person requested for the purposes of trial or punishment in the territory of the requesting state. Deportation is, in most cases, a unilateral act taken by the deporting state in order to expel an undesired alien. The **1.03**

---

[1] *R v Evans ex p Pinochet Ugarte*, 28 October 1998, CO/4074/98, para 3, per Lord Bingham of Cornhill CJ.

[2] *Knowles v Government of the United States of America* [2006] UKPC 38, para 12.

[3] The principal UK statute governing extradition, the Extradition Act 2003 (EA 2003), contains a number of such safeguards and these are examined in detail below: see para 5.32 and para 6.22.

[4] *R v Governor of Brixton Prison ex p Soblen* [1963] QB 243; *R v Staines Magistrates' Court ex p Westfallen* [1998] 1 WLR 652; *Caddoux v Bow Street Magistrates' Court* [2004] EWHC 642 (Admin), para 11.

purpose of deportation is achieved when the alien leaves the deporting state's territory; unlike extradition, the destination of the deportee is irrelevant to the purpose of deportation.[5]

1.04 In *Norris v Government of the United States of America (No 2)* [2010] 2 AC 487, para 5, Lord Phillips observed that public international law does not impose a general duty upon countries to accede to requests for extradition. Obligations to extradite typically arise out of bilateral treaties. None the less, a number of international criminal Conventions have been concluded that impose on states an obligation to extradite or prosecute in respect of certain offences,[6] or which limit the grounds upon which a state can refuse to extradite, reflecting increasing international cooperation in the fight against crime.

1.05 Extradition from the UK is governed by the Extradition Act 2003 (EA 2003). In order to understand the operation of the EA 2003 it is necessary to examine in outline the history of extradition in the UK and the provisions of some of its statutory predecessors.

B. History of Extradition Legislation in the UK[7]

1.06 The practice of extradition originated in ancient civilizations as a matter of courtesy and goodwill between sovereigns. One of the earliest recorded treaties providing for the mutual return of criminals dates to 1280 BC between Ramses II, the Pharaoh of Egypt, and King Hattusli III of the Hittites.[8]

1.07 The history of extradition within the British Isles can be traced back to 1174 when Henry II of England and William of Scotland agreed to the delivery up of fugitive offenders. Similar agreements were reached in 1303 between Edward I and Philip of France, and in 1496 between Henry VII and the Duke of Burgundy.

1.08 The modern law of extradition started to develop in the eighteenth and nineteenth centuries when Great Britain began to negotiate extradition treaties with foreign states. The development of extradition procedures in the nineteenth century was the result of new forms of transport and communication, namely, the railway, the steamship, the telegraph, and telephone. Between them, these facilitated both the movement of criminals and their subsequent detection. Until that time, only five extradition treaties had been concluded by England between 1174 and 1794.[9]

---

[5] *Mohammed v President of the Republic of South Africa* 2001 (3) SALR 893 (CC), para 29. The Constitutional Court held that deportation of the appellant to the United States to face trial for capital murder charges in the absence of any undertakings that the death penalty would not be imposed violated his right to life under the South African Constitution. Extradition and the death penalty are examined at para 7.82.

[6] See, for example, the UN Convention Against Torture and and Cruel, Inhuman or Degrading Treatment or Punishments 1984 (UNTS Vol 1465, p 85). Article 7(1) provides: 'The State Party in the territory under whose jurisdiction a person alleged to have committed any [offence of torture] is found, shall ..., if it does not extradite him, submit the case to its competent authorities for the purpose of prosecution.'

[7] See *A Review of the United Kingdom's Extradition Arrangements*, Home Office, September 2011 (hereafter '2011 Extradition Review'), Part 3; available at <http://www.homeoffice.gov.uk>.

[8] IA Shearer, *Extradition in International Law* (Manchester University Press, 1971), p 5; Kai I Rebane, 'Extradition and Individual Rights: The Need for an International Criminal Court to Safeguard Individual Rights', 19 *Fordham Int'l LJ* 1636, 1645 (1996).

[9] E. Clarke: *A Treatise Upon The Law of Extradition* (4th edn, 1903), pp 18–22. Sir Edward Clarke was Treasury counsel in the late nineteenth century and was involved in many of the leading cases under the Extradition Act 1870. His *Treatise* is one of the most authoritative expositions of the history and origins of extradition in the UK. See also: HC Biron and KE Chalmers, *Law and Practice of Extradition* (1903); E Hartley Booth, *British Extradition Law and Procedure* (1980), Vol I.

Great Britain's extradition relationship with the United States of America began in 1794 with the 'Treaty of Amity, Commerce and Navigation with Great Britain' (the Jay Treaty).[10] The Jay Treaty provided for either government to deliver persons charged with murder or forgery to the other government 'on requisition', but only on evidence of criminality that would justify apprehending and trying the defendant in the country where he was located if the offence had been committed there. However, the Jay Treaty provided no specific procedure for extradition.[11] **1.09**

Great Britain signed an extradition treaty with France in 1842, and the Webster-Ashburton Treaty with the United States was signed in 1843.[12] The latter was entitled: **1.10**

> A Treaty to Settle and Define the Boundaries between the Territories of the United States and the Possessions of Her Britannic Majesty in North America, for the Final Suppression of the African Slave Trade, and for the Giving Up of Criminals Fugitive from Justice, in Certain Cases.

The extradition arrangements contained in the Anglo-French Treaty and the Webster-Ashburton Treaty were given the force of law by two Acts of Parliament in 1843.[13] These Acts permitted extradition only for a limited number of serious crimes[14] but were notable in that they contained the requirement for dual criminality, that is, the requirement that the alleged conduct should amount to a crime in both the requesting and requested state. Dual criminality remained a feature of extradition legislation until the incorporation of the European arrest warrant in Part 1 of the EA 2003. **1.11**

Extradition to foreign states[15]

In 1868 a Select Committee inquired into the state of treaty relationships concerning extradition, and its recommendations were the model for what became the EA 1870. The purpose of this Act was to provide the procedural machinery for the surrender of defendants under any treaty then in force with a foreign state (ie a state outside the Empire) and any that might be concluded after its enactment. **1.12**

Each extradition treaty set out the arrangements for extradition with the foreign state and the conditions under which extradition would be granted. Section 2 of the EA 1870 provided that, where such an arrangement had been made, Her Majesty might by Order in Council direct that the 1870 Act apply in the case of that foreign state, subject to the limitations contained in the Order in Council. Once an extradition treaty had been concluded with a foreign state, an Order in Council under s 2 was made applying the 1870 Act and extradition to that foreign state became available. Between 1870 and 1932 the EA 1870 was supplemented by other extradition Acts. **1.13**

In *Re Nielsen* [1984] 1 AC 606, 616 Lord Diplock observed: **1.14**

> The jurisdiction conferred upon the Bow Street magistrate by the Acts of 1870 to 1932 is the widest that he may lawfully exercise upon applications for extradition of fugitive criminals from foreign states. His jurisdiction cannot be extended beyond that maximum but it may be limited, in the case of fugitive criminals from a particular foreign state, by the terms of the extradition treaty with that state.

---

10 *R (Norris) v Secretary of State for the Home Department* [2006] EWHC 280 (Admin), para 20.

11 Benjamin N Bedrick, 'United States Extradition Process: Changes in Law to Address Constitutional Infirmity', 15 *Dick J Int'l L* 385, 387 (1997).

12 JF Stephen, *History of the Criminal Law of England* (1883), Vol 2, p 66.

13 6 & 7 Vict. c75 and c76.

14 *Ex p Windsor* (1865) 10 Cox CC 118; *Re Tivnan* (1864) 9 Cox CC 522.

15 2011 Extradition Review, paras 3.16–3.35.

1.15 In *Government of the Federal Republic of Germany v Sotiriadis* [1975] AC 1, 24 Lord Diplock explained the relationship between the EA 1870 and bilateral extradition treaties:

> The Act was passed to enable effect to be given in the United Kingdom to extradition treaties with foreign states made by the Crown in the exercise of its prerogative. Since effect may not be given under the Act to treaties which are not in conformity with its provisions, one finds the main provisions of the Act reflected in the extradition treaties; though, since such treaties are reciprocal, the language in which they are expressed may not follow the precise wording of the Act itself and the treaty may also contain restrictions upon the surrender of fugitive criminals additional to those provided in the Act itself.
>
> The underlying policy of the Act is to assimilate, so far as this is practicable, the procedure for the extradition of persons to stand their trial for crimes which they are accused of having committed in foreign states to the procedure for the committal for trial in England of persons charged with what would have been the corresponding indictable offences had they been committed here instead of abroad.

1.16 The EA 1870 made fugitive criminals liable to surrender for 'extradition crimes'. These were defined in s 26 to be crimes which, if they had been committed in England or within English jurisdiction, would be one of the crimes described in the First Schedule to the Act. The First Schedule (in its original form) contained a generic list of 19 offences for which extradition would be granted. Extradition could not be granted for offences not falling within the list.[16] As new crimes were created, the list had to be amended to enable extradition to take place for these crimes.[17]

Extradition within the Commonwealth[18]

1.17 Historically extradition within the Empire (later the Commonwealth) was governed by separate legislation from that which governed extradition to foreign states. The existence of the Empire meant that extradition between Great Britain and its dominions did not depend upon the existence of treaty relationships. In 1881 Parliament enacted the Fugitive Offenders Act 1881 to govern the return of defendants between the various parts of the Empire. The Act continued in force until the 1960s, when the independence of many former colonies required a review of the law.

1.18 In 1966 the Commonwealth Law Ministers met in London in order to review arrangements for extradition within the Commonwealth in the light of the constitutional changes that had taken place since the passing of the Fugitive Offenders Act 1881. The meeting considered that Commonwealth extradition arrangements should be based upon reciprocity and substantially uniform legislation incorporating certain features then commonly found in extradition treaties, for example a list of returnable offences, the establishment of a prima facie case before return, and restrictions on the return of political offenders.

1.19 The meeting accordingly formulated a Scheme setting out principles which could form the basis of legislation within the Commonwealth and recommended that effect should be given to the Scheme in each Commonwealth country. The 'Scheme relating to the Rendition of Fugitive Offenders within the Commonwealth' (sometimes referred to as the London Scheme) was published in 1966.[19]

---

[16] *Re Counhaye* (1873) LR 8 QB 410; *R v Secretary of State for the Home Department ex p Gilmore* [1999] QB 611.

[17] See for example *R v Bow Street Metropolitan Stipendiary Magistrate ex p Government of the United States of America* [2000] 2 AC 216 (whether offences created by the Computer Misuse Act 1990 were extradition crimes).

[18] 2011 Extradition Review, paras 3.36–3.42.

[19] Cmnd 3008.

The Fugitive Offenders Act 1967 was enacted to give effect to the London Scheme in the UK. The 1967 Act permitted extradition for offences against the law of the requesting Commonwealth country punishable with more than 12 months' imprisonment which fell within the general descriptions in Sch 1 to the Act.[20] The 1967 Act continued in force until its repeal by the EA 1989. **1.20**

Proposals for reform[21]

In 1974 and 1984 Home Office working parties considered the operation of the EA 1870. Whilst the 1974 Report did not result in any changes to the law, by 1984 the need for reform had been recognized, in particular because of problems of compatibility between the English common law system and continental civil law jurisdictions. The 1984 Report[22] was followed in 1985 by a Green Paper on Extradition[23] and then by a White Paper.[24] **1.21**

The Criminal Justice Bill 1986 contained provisions relating to extradition, however these were removed when the Bill had to be passed in shortened form because of the 1987 general election. Part I of the Criminal Justice Act 1988 contained provisions relating to extradition which were never brought into force. **1.22**

The Extradition Act 1989[25]

The EA 1989 came into force on 27 September 1989. It was a consolidation of three earlier pieces of legislation: Part I of the Criminal Justice Act 1988, the Fugitive Offenders Act 1967, and the EA 1870 (as amended). The earlier Acts were repealed.[26] **1.23**

Part III of the EA 1989 contained the machinery for processing requests for extradition from foreign states with whom the UK had general extradition arrangements (in practice, those signatories to the European Convention on Extradition 1957 which were designated in an Order in Council under s 4); designated Commonwealth countries; and colonies. One of the principal features of Part III of the EA 1989 was the removal of the need in all cases for the requesting state to prove a prima facie case by admissible evidence. Whilst this requirement was retained in Commonwealth and colony cases, it was removed in respect of requests from the UK's European treaty partners. **1.24**

A distinct extradition scheme was contained in Sch 1 to the Act. The provisions of Sch 1 were largely derived from the EA 1870 and governed the processing of requests from foreign states with whom there was an extant treaty embodied in an Order in Council made under s 2 of the EA 1870 (principally the United States of America). The requirement for a prima facie case was retained in Sch 1 cases. **1.25**

C. Background to the Enactment of the Extradition Act 2003[27]

The origins of the EA 2003 lie in the domestic and European developments in international criminal law which took place during the 1990s. In 1997 a domestic review commenced to **1.26**

---

[20] *Government of Canada v Aronson* [1990] 1 AC 579.

[21] 2011 Extradition Review, paras 3.62–3.68.

[22] *A Review of the Law and Practice of Extradition in the United Kingdom; the Report of an Interdepartmental Working Party*, published by the Home Office.

[23] Cmnd 9421.

[24] Cmnd 9658.

[25] 2011 Extradition Review, paras 3.69–3.70.

[26] For a detailed account of the operation of the EA 1989 see C Nicholls QC, C Montgomery QC, and JB Knowles, *The Law of Extradition and Mutual Assistance* (1st edn, 2002).

[27] 2011 Extradition Review, Part 4.

consider the legislative requirements of two European Union Conventions on Extradition signed in 1995[28] and 1996.[29] The review developed extensively following the Tampere Special European Council in October 1999. The Treaty of Amsterdam, signed on 2 October 1997, aimed to establish the EU as an area of freedom, security, and justice.[30] The implementation of the treaty was discussed at the Cardiff European Council in June 1998, and again at Tampere. The conclusion at Tampere was that mutual recognition of judicial decisions should become the cornerstone of judicial cooperation in both criminal and civil matters within the EU.[31]

1.27 In October 1998 Spain made a request for the extradition of the former Chilean President and dictator General Augusto Pinochet whilst he was on a visit to the UK. The crimes alleged included torture and murder committed following the *coup d'etat* in 1973 during which Pinochet seized power. Pinochet was arrested and the extradition proceedings which followed lasted until March 2000, when the Secretary of State allowed Pinochet to return to Chile on the grounds of ill-health.[32] The Pinochet case focused world attention on the UK's extradition arrangements and caused the Government a significant degree of political embarrassment as it found itself caught in a struggle between Chile and Spain, its former colonial master. On 2 March 2000, the day Pinochet returned to Chile, the Home Secretary announced in the House of Commons that a wide-ranging review of the UK's extradition legislation was to be carried out.[33]

1.28 The Government set out its proposals to reform the law in a consultation document, 'The Law on Extradition: A Review' in March 2001.[34] In para 1 the Government set out the purpose of the Review:

> Crime, particularly serious and organized crime, is increasingly international in nature, and criminals can flee justice by crossing borders with increasing ease. Improved judicial co-operation between nations is needed to tackle this development; this review of the United Kingdom's extradition law and procedure is designed to contribute to that process. Extradition is an important tool in dealing with international crime: no one should be able to escape justice simply by crossing a border. The law should provide a quick and effective framework to extradite a person to the country where they are accused or have been convicted of a serious crime, providing that this does not breach their fundamental human rights.

1.29 The Review contained 47 recommendations which were intended to modernize arrangements between the UK and its extradition partners. They included creating a four-level framework with countries being designated for each tier by way of an Order in Council; a simple fast-track extradition procedure for member States of the European Union; retention of current arrangements for non-European Union states with modifications to reduce the duplication and complexity of extradition procedures; a single avenue of appeal for all extradition cases; and accession to the 1995 and 1996 European Union Conventions on Extradition.

1.30 The proposals in the Review were overtaken by the events of 11 September 2001 and the onset of the so-called war against terror in Western Europe and the United States of America. The fear of terrorism provided added political impetus for speeding up the extradition of criminal suspects. The Review was also overtaken by progress in respect of extradition to other EU member

---

[28] Convention on simplified extradition between the Member States of the European Union, OJ No C78 of 30.3.95, p 1.

[29] Convention relating to extradition between the Member States of the European Union, OJ No C313 of 23.10.96, p 11.

[30] Official Journal C 340, 10 November 1997.

[31] See further para 15.11.

[32] *R v Secretary of State for the Home Department ex p Kingdom of Belgium*, 15 February 2000 CO/236/00.

[33] *Hansard*, HC vol 345, cols 572–575 (2 March 2000).

[34] 2011 Extradition Review, paras 3.97–3.100.

States, in particular the Council Framework Decision (following Tampere) of 13 June 2002 on the European arrest warrant and the surrender procedures between member States.[35]

The Extradition Bill was published in draft form on 27 June 2002 and was open to public consultation until 30 September 2002. The Bill was introduced in Parliament on 14 November 2002 and received Royal Assent on 20 November 2003.[36] During the debate on the Bill's Second Reading, the Minister of State set out the Government's case for reform:[37] **1.31**

> This important Bill will bring what are essentially 19th-century extradition arrangements into the very different world of the 21st century. The main legislation that it will replace is the Extradition Act 1989, which, of course, was a consolidation measure that included large chunks of the Extradition Act 1870. The 1870 legislation effectively still governs our bilateral extradition arrangements.
>
> Our extradition arrangements are in urgent need of reform. On average, it takes 18 months to extradite someone from the UK and, in many cases, much longer. The system allows the fugitive to raise the same—arguably, often spurious—points time and again, and to mount numerous legal challenges. Even when—as has happened many times—an individual appeals all the way to the House of Lords following the committal hearing, he can, once the Secretary of State has considered the case, appeal all the way again on exactly the same grounds.

The EA 2003 came into force on 1 January 2004 in relation to extradition requests made on or after that date.[38] **1.32**

D. Outline of the Extradition Act 2003

The main features of the procedure established by the EA 2003 are: **1.33**

- A system where each of the UK's extradition partners is in one of two categories. Each country is designated by an order for a particular category. It is therefore be possible for a country to move from one category to the other when appropriate, depending on the extradition procedures that the UK negotiates with each extradition partner.[39]
- The adoption of the framework decision of the Council of the European Union made on 13 June 2002 on the European arrest warrant and the surrender procedures between member States (the EAW Framework Decision) creating a fast-track extradition arrangement within the EU and Gibraltar.[40]
- Retention of the current arrangements for extradition with non-EU countries with modifications to reduce duplication and complexity.
- A significant reduction of the Secretary of State's role.
- A simplification of the rules governing the authentication of foreign documents.
- The abolition of the requirement to provide prima facie evidence in certain cases.
- A simplified single avenue of appeal for all cases.

---

35 2002/584/JHA. The EAW is considered in Ch 15.

36 *Hansard:* HC Vol 394 col 164 (1R); Vol 396 col 39 (2R) (PM) (MR); Vol 402 col 161 (3R); HL Vol 646 col 814 (1R); Vol 647 cols 852 (2R); 954 (MfA); Vol 648 col GC 117 (Comm); Vol 649 cols GC 1, 287, 353 (Comm); Vol 650 cols GC 113, GC 173 (Comm); Vol 651 cols GC 53, GC 105 (Comm); Vol 652 col GC 1 (Comm); Vol 654 cols 21, 101, 375 (Rep); Vol 654 col 1410 (3R); HC Vol 413 col 430 (PM; MR and Lords' Amendments); HL Vol 654 col 1904 (Commons' Amendments).

37 Vol 396 col 39.

38 Extradition Act 2003 (Commencement and Savings) Order 2003 (SI 2003/3103); *R (Government of the United States of America) v Senior District Judge, Bow Street Magistrates' Court* [2006] EWHC 2256 (Admin). Commencement is dealt with below at para 1.47.

39 *R (Oliver) v Secretary of State for the Home Department* [2006] EWHC 1847 (Admin), paras 10–15.

40 2002/584/JHA. The text of the EAW Framework Decision is at App E4, and is dealt with in detail in Ch 15.

1.34 The EA 2003 is divided into five Parts and four Schedules:

1.35 Part 1: contains the fast-track extradition arrangements for Category 1 territories.[41] These have been transposed into UK law from the EAW Framework Decision. Part 1 provides the legislative framework for incoming warrants from Category 1 territories. The countries in relation to which Part 1 applies are those designated by the Extradition Act 2003 (Designation of Part 1 Territories) Order 2003, as amended.[42]

1.36 Part 2: contains the procedure for extradition for countries with which the UK has bilateral treaty arrangements (Category 2 territories). Part 2 provides the legislative framework for incoming requests from such territories. Part 2 applies to those countries designated by the Extradition Act 2003 (Designation of Part 2 Territories) Order 2003, as amended.[43]

1.37 Part 3: covers the procedure for applying for a warrant for extradition to the UK from Category 1 territories. Part 3 provides the legislative framework for outgoing warrants to Category 1 territories. Requests to Category 2 territories continue to be made under the Royal Prerogative.

1.38 Part 4: outlines the powers supplementary to the Police and Criminal Evidence Act 1984 (PACE) available to the police in extradition cases. Part 4 was placed in the Act following the decision of the House of Lords in the case of *R v Commissioner of Police for the Metropolis ex p Rottman* [2002] 2 AC 692, which held that the powers contained in Part II of PACE did not apply in relation to offences committed abroad.

1.39 Part 5: contains miscellaneous provisions such as those that will apply for British overseas territories and the power to repeal the existing legislation. It also confers order-making powers on the Secretary of State.

1.40 Schedule 1: contains provisions relating to re-extradition (see ss 186–189).

1.41 Schedule 2: contains the list of conduct which to which a EAW can apply (see s 64(2)(b) and s 215(1)).

1.42 Schedule 3: contains amendments to other statutes.

1.43 Schedule 4: contains repeals.

1.44 In *Norris v Government of the United States of America (No 2)* [2010] 2 AC 487, para 3, Lord Phillips of Worth Matravers gave a succinct summary of the scheme of the EA 2003.

1.45 The 2003 Act created a new extradition regime that was intended to simplify the process. Under the new regime considerations that were for the Secretary of State are transferred to the court, and these include the compatibility of extradition with Convention rights. Part 1 of the 2003 Act deals with extradition to 'Category 1 territories'. These are, in effect, members of the European Union which operate the European Arrest Warrant. Part 2 deals with extradition to Category 2 territories that have been designated by order of the Secretary of State. Under both Part 1 and Part 2 procedures the appropriate judge has to carry out an extradition hearing at which he considers whether there exists any of the prescribed statutory bars to extradition.

---

[41] The terms Part 1/Category 1 territories and Part 2/Category 2 territories are used interchangeably in this book.

[42] SI 2003/3333. For a list of Part 1 territories, see App E7.

[43] SI 2003/3334. For a list of Part 2 territories, see App E7.

Criticism of the EA 2003

The EA 2003 has not received especially good notices.[44] One striking feature is its extraordinary length and complexity, certainly by comparison with earlier extradition legislation. However, its detailed structure has not brought clarity. In *Office of the King's Prosecutor, Brussels v Cando Armas* [2005] 1 WLR 1389, paras 24 and 31, Stanley Burnton J said the court had not found it easy to construe the EA 2003. In *Dabas v High Court of Justice, Madrid* [2007] 2 AC 1, para 25, Lord Hope of Craighead commented on the difficulties the EA 2003 had thrown up and said that the problem with Part 1 in particular was that it 'tries to do too much'. In *Government of Germany v Kleinschmidt* [2005] 3 All 759, para 52, Sedley LJ commented that some of the problems in the Act had been caused by haste in its composition.[45] **1.46**

E. Commencement Provisions

The EA 2003 came into force on 1 January 2004, in accordance with the Extradition Act 2003 (Commencement and Savings) Order 2003, as amended ('the Commencement Order').[46] **1.47**

Article 3 of the Commencement Order (as substituted by the Extradition Act 2003 (Commencement and Savings) (Amendment No 2) Order 2003 (SI 2003/3312)) provides that the coming into force of the Act shall not apply for the purposes of any request for extradition, whether made under any of the provisions of the EA 1989 or of the Backing of Warrants (Republic of Ireland) Act 1965 or otherwise, which is received by the relevant authority in the UK on or before 31 December 2003. Article 4 provides that the coming into force of the Act shall not apply for the purposes of an extradition made from or to the UK on or before 31 December 2003. **1.48**

The EA 2003 therefore applies to all extradition requests received on or after 1 January 2004. Requests received prior to that date and not withdrawn are to be dealt with under the EA 1989. Defendants extradited to or from the UK prior to that date will be dealt with under the EA 1989. **1.49**

In *R (Government of the United States of America) v Senior District Judge, Bow Street Magistrates' Court* [2006] EWHC 2256 (Admin) the defendants' extradition was sought for offences of fraud and a number of indictments were issued against them in the United States. A request for their extradition was made in March 2003 and then withdrawn in April 2004. Their extradition was then sought again in October 2004, after the EA 2003 had come into force and the order made which removed the need for the United States to supply prima facie evidence.[47] **1.50**

The defendants argued before the Administrative Court inter alia that, on its true construction, the Commencement Order did not apply to the United States' extradition request because (a) the subject matter of the request was the same as that of the request made before 31 December 2003; (b) alternatively, the United States Government had, in bad faith, withdrawn its 2003 request with the intention of making a new request after 31 December 2003. On the question of construction of the Commencement Order, the Court said at paras 97–99:[48] **1.51**

> ... [the defendants'] primary case ... is that, on true construction of the Commencement Order, these proceedings relate to a request for extradition received before 31st December

[44] See Spencer, 'Implementing the European Arrest Warrant: A Tale of How Not to Do It', (2009) 30(3) *Statute Law Review* 184.

[45] A problem anticipated by some commentators: see JB Knowles, 'More Haste Less Justice', The Times, 9 October 2001.

[46] SI 2003/3103.

[47] See para 6.35.

[48] An alternative submission based on abuse of process was also rejected at paras 105–109. Abuse of process is dealt with at para 5.120.

> 2003. They submit that if a request is made in 2003, withdrawn and then submitted in essentially the same terms after 2004, the proceedings which are initiated in response to the latter request are, for the purpose of the Commencement Order, brought in respect of a request for expedition made before 31 December 2003.
>
> [Counsel] recognised, in his submissions, that it is possible to withdraw a request for extradition and then to make a fresh request, provided that the motivation for so doing is not such as to make the exercise an abuse of process. If his primary submission is correct, it must follow that where a request made before 31st December 2003 is withdrawn, a fresh request in relation to the same alleged conduct must be dealt with in accordance with the provisions of the 1989 Act.
>
> We do not find this an acceptable construction of the Commencement Order. It is simply inaccurate, in such circumstances, to suggest that the new proceedings relate to a request made before 31st December 2003. The construction of the Commencement Order suggested is not a natural one. Nor, on the face of it, is there any reason to give the Order such a construction. The Order is a mechanical provision bringing the 2003 Act into effect. The saving in relation to requests made before 31 December 2003 is naturally read as addressing the position of existing proceedings. It has no application once a request is withdrawn and the proceedings come to an end.

1.52 At paras 101–103 the Court dealt with the defendants' alternative submissions:

> Their alternative case proceeds on the assumption that if a request made prior to 31st December 2003 is withdrawn 'in good faith' because the requesting State has decided not to proceed with it, but then, perhaps because of some change of circumstances, the State decides to make a fresh request after that date, the proceedings that are initiated in response to the fresh request will be governed by the 2003 Act. If, however, the requesting State withdraws a request that has been made under the old regime 'in bad faith', with the intention of making a fresh request after 31 December 2003, it is submitted that the consequent proceedings fall to be treated, for the purposes of the Commencement Order, as relating to the request made before 31 December 2003. Thus it is suggested that the manner in which the Commencement Order applies depends upon the motive that has led the requesting State to withdraw the first request and subsequently to make a fresh request.
>
> We can deal with this submission shortly. The suggested approach to the construction of the Commencement Order is extraordinary. We can see no basis for finding that the Order operates in this bizarre manner.

F. The Home Office Review of the UK's Extradition Arrangements 2011[49]

1.53 On 8 September 2010 the Home Secretary announced that the Government had commissioned a review of the UK's extradition arrangements.[50] The Review fulfilled the Coalition Government's promise to review the EA 2003 in its programme for government[51] published after the general election in 2010. The Review Panel, presided over by Scott Baker LJ,[52] was asked to consider five issues in particular:

- the operation of the European arrest warrant, including the way in which its optional safeguards contained in the European Union Framework Decision on the European arrest warrant have been transposed into the law of the United Kingdom;
- whether the forum bar[53] to extradition should be brought into force;

[49] Referred to in this book as 'the 2011 Extradition Review'.
[50] *Hansard*, 8 September 2010, col 15WS.
[51] Page 14, available at <http://www.direct.gov.uk>.
[52] The other members of the Review Panel were David Perry QC and Anand Doobay.
[53] EA 2003, ss 19B and 83A, dealt with at para 5.91 and 6.31.

- whether the United States/United Kingdom Extradition Treaty 2003 is unbalanced;
- whether requesting States should be required to provide prima facie evidence;
- the breadth of the Home Secretary's discretion in extradition.

The 2011 Extradition Review was published on 30 September 2011. On these five issues the Review did not recommend any substantial amendments to the law. The Review also considered a number of additional issues including: appeals on questions of fact;[54] other causes of delay for appeals;[55] training;[56] regional extradition courts;[57] and provisional arrest.[58] The Review's findings are noted in this book in relation to the relevant topic. **1.54**

In October 2012 the Government published its response to the 2011 Extradition Review.[59] The Government accepted all of the Review's recommendations, except in relation to the forum bar. Whereas the Review had recommended that the forum bar not be enacted,[60] the Government announced its intention to bring the relevant provisions of the EA 2003 into force. **1.55**

G. Extradition and the United States of America

The UK's extradition relationship with the United States deserves particular attention because of its political importance and the volume of extradition traffic between the two countries. The extradition relationship between the United States and the UK was considered in detail in Chapter 7 of the 2011 Extradition Review. **1.56**

The United States achieved independence from Great Britain in 1776. Extradition relations between the two countries began in 1794 with the 'Treaty of Amity, Commerce and Navigation with Great Britain' (Jay's Treaty). The Webster-Ashburton Treaty was signed in 1843. Article X of this Treaty provided: **1.57**

> It is agreed that the United States and Her Britannic Majesty shall, upon mutual requisitions by them, or their Ministers, Officers, or authorities, respectively made, deliver up to justice, all persons who, being charged with the crime of murder, or assault with intent to commit murder, or Piracy, or arson, or robbery, or Forgery, or the utterance of forged paper, committed within the jurisdiction of either, shall seek an asylum, or shall be found, within the territories of the other: Provided, that this shall only be done upon such evidence of criminality as, according to the laws of the place where the fugitive or person so charged, shall be found, would justify his apprehension and commitment for trial, if the crime or offense had there been committed: And the respective Judges and other Magistrates of the two Governments, shall have power, jurisdiction, and authority, upon complaint made under oath, to issue a warrant for the apprehension of the fugitive or person so charged, that he may be brought before such Judges or other Magistrates, respectively, to the end that the evidence of criminality may be heard and considered; and if, on such hearing, the evidence be deemed sufficient to sustain the charge it shall be the duty of the examining Judge or Magistrate, to certify the same to the proper Executive Authority, that a warrant may issue for the surrender of such fugitive. The expense of such apprehension and delivery shall be borne and defrayed by the Party who makes the requisition, and receives the fugitive.

54 Para 11.82.
55 Para 11.83.
56 Para 11.88.
57 Para 11.89.
58 Para 11.90.
59 Cm 8458.
60 2011 Extradition Review, paras 6.77–6.80.

1.58 The 1842 Treaty was supplemented by further treaties in 1889,[61] 1900,[62] and 1905.[63] A new extradition treaty was signed in 1931.[64] In 1972 the Treaty on Extradition between the Government of the United States of America and the Government of the United Kingdom of Great Britain and Northern Ireland[65] was signed. It was not until 1976 that this treaty was ratified by the United States, and it came into force in January 1977. It was amended by the Supplementary Extradition Treaty of 1985,[66] which came into force in December 1985.

1.59 Between 1870 and 1989 extradition from the UK to the United States was governed by the EA 1870, as amended, and the 1972 and 1985 extradition treaties. After the coming into force of the EA 1989, extradition was governed by Sch 1 of the EA 1989.

1.60 In accordance with Article IX of the 1972 Treaty, Sch 1 required the United States to supply prima facie evidence, that is evidence sufficient to warrant the committal for trial of the defendant if the offence of which he is accused had been committed in the territory of the UK. The symmetrical arrangement provided for by Article IX required the UK to supply evidence of probable cause to the United States in order to secure a defendant's extradition to the UK.

1.61 On 31 March 2003 the Treaty on Extradition between the Government of the United States of America and the Government of the United Kingdom of Great Britain and Northern Ireland[67] was signed by both governments. After considerable delay in ratification by the United States the Treaty was finally ratified on 30 September 2006, and the 1972 Treaty, as amended ceased to have effect, subject to the transitional provisions in the new Treaty.[68]

1.62 The 2003 UK/US Extradition Treaty has proved unprecedentedly controversial. The case of the so-called 'NatWest 3' in 2006[69] focused attention on the UK's extradition relationship with the United States and, in particular, on the removal of the United States' evidential burden in cases under the EA 2003. Many observers objected that the defendants were being extradited for a crime which in their view ought to have been tried in the UK.[70]

1.63 In the face of public and parliamentary[71] protest the NatWest 3 were extradited to the United States in July 2006 for alleged fraud offences connected with the failed Enron energy company. Many observers viewed the case as the unfortunate product of a flawed extradition scheme in the UK and an over-zealous prosecution in the United States.[72] There was also criticism that the UK's Treaty arrangements with the United States were unbalanced, in that the UK is required to supply more to the United States by way of evidence in order to secure extradition than the United States does in order to secure extradition from the UK.[73]

---

[61] USTS 139; C 5972.
[62] USTS 391; Cd 598.
[63] USTS 458; Cd 3344.
[64] USTS 849.
[65] Cmnd 6723.
[66] Cm 294.
[67] Cm 5821.
[68] cf *Ahmad v Government of the United States of America* [2006] EWHC 2927 (Admin), para 12.
[69] *R (Bermingham) v Director of the Serious Fraud Office* [2006] EWHC 200 (Admin).
[70] Paras 4 and 5 of Sch 13 to the Police and Justice Act 2006 amended the EA 2003 by providing a bar to extradition where the alleged crime would be better tried in the UK. These sections of the EA 2003, ss 13A and 83B, are not yet in force: para 5.91 and para 6.31. Although the 2011 Extradition Review recommended that they not be brought into force, in October 2012 the Government announced that it did not accept this recommendation and would bring the forum bars into force.
[71] HC Deb Vol 448 col 1396.
[72] JB Knowles, 'The Long Arm of the Law', Counsel Magazine, August 2006.
[73] *R (Norris) v Secretary of State for the Home Department* [2006] EWHC 280 (Admin).

In March 2012 the House of Commons Home Affairs Select Committee reported on the Treaty,[74] and in para 1 of its Report summarized some of the concerns that had been expressed about it. 1.64

One of the first commitments made by the Coalition Government was to review the operation of the EA 2003 and the US–UK Extradition Treaty to make sure that they are even-handed. This commitment was made in the context of widespread political concern about the operation of the UK's extradition arrangements with the USA. Representatives of both Coalition Parties had expressed reservations about the operation of the Treaty while in opposition. Opening an emergency debate called in 2006 by the Liberal Democrats shortly before the extradition of the 'NatWest Three',[75] the Rt Hon Nick Clegg MP said: 1.65

> We on the Liberal Democrat Benches have objected to the extradition arrangements with the USA ever since the text of the new treaty was published in May 2003. [...] the extradition treaty and its enactment through the Extradition Act 2003 is manifestly unfair to British citizens.

During the same debate, the Rt Hon Dominic Grieve MP (then the shadow Attorney General), expressed reservations about the new standard of information required by the Treaty—which he described in relation to one case as 'very scanty indeed'—and described the lack of forum provisions in the 2003 Act as 'a serious flaw'. The Rt Hon David Blunkett MP, who was Home Secretary when the Treaty was signed, told us that although the 2003 Treaty was in principle an improvement over previous treaties, 'the practice has been very different'.

The most controversial aspect of the 2003 Treaty is Article 8. This has the effect of relieving the United States of the obligation of supplying evidence to the UK in order to secure extradition whilst at the same time requiring the UK to supply to the United States, where it seeks a defendant's extradition 'such information as would provide a reasonable basis to believe that the person sought committed the offense for which extradition is requested'.[76] 1.66

In order that the UK could comply with Article 8, the United States was designated by the Secretary of State pursuant to s 84(7) of the EA 2003 as a Category 2 territory which does not need to supply evidence at the extradition hearing[77] by virtue of Article 3 of the Extradition Act 2003 (Designation of Part 2 Territories) Order 2003.[78] In draft form, the Order was considered by the House of Commons Third Standing Committee on delegated legislation on 15 December 2003, and by the House of Lords on the following day. Assurances were given on behalf of the Government that, subject to an inevitable measure of delay before the United States could or would ratify it, the 2003 Treaty would complete the appropriate processes leading to ratification in early 2004. Nevertheless, an amendment to the statutory instrument was moved by Lord Goodhart QC, inviting the Government to withdraw the draft Order and lay a new draft Order deleting the reference to the United States in para 3 of the Order. This amendment was defeated by 120 votes to 50. Accordingly the United States remains a designated territory for the purposes of s 84(7).[79] 1.67

The Secretary of State's decision to continue to include the United States in the list of countries in Article 3 of the Extradition Act 2003 (Designation of Part 2 Territories) Order 2003[80] 1.68

---

74 HC 644, Twentieth Report of Session 2010–2012.

75 *R (Bermingham) v Director of the Serious Fraud Office* [2006] EWHC 200 (Admin).

76 Art 8(3)(c).

77 Para 6.36.

78 SI 2003/3334.

79 In October 2006 House of Lords' amendments to the Police and Justice Bill, which would have had the effect of de-designating the United States, were defeated in the House of Commons: HC Deb, 24 October 2006, Col. 1389. Cf Police and Justice Act 2006, s 43.

80 SI 2003/3334.

despite the contended-for asymmetry in the 2003 Treaty, and the fact that it had not at the time come into force, was unsuccessfully challenged in *R (Norris) v Secretary of State for the Home Department* [2006] EWHC 280 (Admin). Judge LJ said at para 45:

> In a wide-ranging reform of the law relating to extradition, Parliament chose to give the Secretary of State power to make orders which, subject to affirmative resolutions in both Houses of Parliament, permitted the Government of the United Kingdom to afford other states, including United States, greater assistance in the extradition process than that provided in the 1972 Treaty, and simultaneously altered, and indeed reduced the protective provisions formerly available to United Kingdom citizens. The necessary affirmative resolutions were then passed. The protective conditions in the 1972 Treaty, and in particular art IX, cannot obstruct, or hinder, or postpone the application of the 2003 Act, or defer the impact of the new legislative structure. The Act itself does not provide that the wide powers granted to the Secretary of State may not be exercised, or that he should postpone making designation orders, or delay the enforcement of those orders until reciprocity is achieved.

1.69 The 2011 Extradition Review rejected criticisms of the 2003 Treaty,[81] and concluded that there is no imbalance in the UK's arrangement with the United States and no unfairness in the way in which it operates in the UK.[82] The Review concluded at paras 7.86–7.87:

> The United States and the United Kingdom have similar but different legal systems. In the United States the Fourth Amendment to the Constitution ensures that arrest may only lawfully take place if the probable cause test is satisfied; in the United Kingdom the test is reasonable suspicion. In each case it is necessary to demonstrate to a judge an objective basis for the arrest. There is no practical difference between the two tests and the 2003 Treaty does not operate in an unbalanced manner. Nor is there any basis to conclude that extradition from the United Kingdom to the US operates unfairly or oppressively.
>
> For these reasons we have concluded that there is no basis for seeking to renegotiate the 2003 Treaty.

1.70 By contrast, the House of Commons Home Affairs Committee said in its March 2012 Report:[83]

> Concern about the operation of the current extradition arrangements between the USA and the UK should not be allowed to obscure the fundamental point that it is firmly in our national interest to have effective, fair and balanced extradition arrangements with the United States and our other international partners. Criminals must not be allowed to evade British justice by fleeing the country; nor should the UK become a safe haven for those who have committed crimes in other territories. The development of the internet and the rise of international terrorism and organised crime mean that extradition is now more important than ever in the fight against crime. While the Committee has serious misgivings about some aspects of the current arrangements, we are firmly convinced that an effective extradition agreement with the USA is appropriate and clearly in our national interest.

---

[81] Part 7.

[82] Paras 7.81, 7.86, 7.87.

[83] HC 644, Twentieth Report of Session 2010–2012, para 8.

2

LIABILITY TO EXTRADITION; EXTRADITION OFFENCES

The first part of this chapter examines the circumstances in which a person becomes liable to extradition under the EA 2003 as either an accused person or a person who has been convicted and is unlawfully at large following his conviction. **2.01**

The second part of this chapter considers the important topic of extradition offences. These are the offences for which extradition from the UK can be granted. Whilst there are some similarities with the way in which extradition offences were defined in Part III of the EA 1989, the scheme established by the EA 2003 contains a number of significant differences. **2.02**

A. Liability to Extradition

Introduction

The purpose of extradition is to secure the return for trial or punishment of those accused or convicted of crimes.[1] Extradition should not be granted merely to secure the return for questioning of those who are suspected of committing crimes. Accordingly, only a person who is accused of the commission of an extradition offence or who has been convicted of such an offence is properly liable to extradition under the EA 2003. **2.03**

Extradition requests are frequently made for the return of defendants who are unaware of their convictions and who, if returned, have a right to be re-tried. This is because trials in absentia are commonplace in many civil law jurisdictions. Under the EA 1989 defendants in this category had to be treated as accused persons even though they had already been convicted and sentenced. This could give rise to difficulties.[2] The position was further complicated by the Secretary of State's duty to specify in his authority to proceed whether the defendant was **2.04**

[1] *Re Ismail* [1999] AC 320, 326; *Hilali v Central Court of Criminal Proceedings Number 5 of the National Court of Madrid* [2006] EWHC 1239 (Admin), para 54; *Assange v Swedish Prosecution Authority* [2011] EWHC Admin 2849, para 129.

[2] See for example EA 1989, s 35(2); *Lodhi v Governor of HMP Brixton* [2001] EWHC (Admin) 178, para 54.

accused or convicted. If the Secretary of State placed the defendant into the wrong category then the district judge was required to discharge him.[3]

2.05 Thus under the EA 1989 the classification of defendants as either accused or convicted was not entirely straightforward. One difficulty was that neither term was defined in the Act. It remained a question of fact whether, in a given case, a defendant was properly regarded as being accused of an offence rather than merely suspected of it.[4]

2.06 Liability to extradition under the EA 2003 remains dependent on the defendant being accused or convicted in the requesting state. However, the Act has attempted to remove some of the difficulties which beset the earlier legislative regime by relieving the Secretary of State of the duty of specifying the defendant's status in the requesting state, and by specifying with greater precision than the EA 1989 did how a defendant who has been convicted in his absence is to be dealt with.[5] The onus is now on the requesting state to state explicitly whether the defendant is sought as an accused or convicted person.[6]

2.07 It is most convenient to consider Category 1 and 2 territories separately.

Liability to return to a Category 1 territory

2.08 Section 2 of the EA 2003 requires the judicial authority of the Category 1 territory to supply an arrest warrant containing either the information specified in s 2(2)(a) or the information specified in s 2(2)(b). These paragraphs deal respectively with accused and convicted persons.

Accused persons

2.09 Section 2(2) of the EA 2003 contains the requirement that there be a statement of the defendant's status. Section 2(2)(a) requires the warrant to contain the statement referred to in s 2(3) and the information referred to in s 2(4)[7] in cases where extradition is sought for the purposes of trying the defendant. The statement referred to in s 2(3) concerns the defendant's status in the requesting state and is intended to make clear that the defendant is properly to be regarded as an accused person. Section 2(3) requires that the warrant should specify:

(a) that the person in respect of whom the warrant is issued is accused in the Category 1 territory of the offence specified in the warrant; and
(b) that the Part 1 warrant is issued with a view to his arrest and extradition to the Category 1 territory for the purposes of being prosecuted for the offence.[8]

2.10 The leading decision on when a person is 'accused' for the purposes of extradition is *Re Ismail* [1999] AC 320, a case under the EA 1989; the House of Lords rejected the appellant's submission that he was not an accused person—and so not liable to extradition—because he had not been formally charged with an offence in Germany. Lord Steyn said at pp 325–326:

> It is common ground that mere suspicion that an individual has committed offences is insufficient to place him in the category of 'accused' persons. It is also common ground that it is not enough that he is in the traditional phrase 'wanted by the police to help them with their

[3] *R (Guisto) v Governor of HM Brixton Prison* [2004] 1 AC 101.
[4] *Re Ismail* [1999] AC 320.
[5] cf EA 2003, ss 20 and 86.
[6] EA 2003, ss 2(2) and 70(4).
[7] This includes particulars of identity and particulars of the circumstances in which the person is alleged to have committed the offence and particulars of the offence. If the warrant is deficient as to these particulars then it is not a Part 1 warrant within the meaning of the EA 2003 and the defendant will fall to be discharged: para 4.11.
[8] This wording is included in the pro forma warrant in the Annex to the EAW Framework Decision: cf *Asztaslos v Szekszard City Court, Hungary* [2010] EWHC 237 (Admin), paras 14–15.

> inquiries.' Something more is required ... For my part I am satisfied that the Divisional Court in this case posed the right test by addressing the broad question whether the competent authorities in the foreign jurisdiction had taken a step which can fairly be described as the commencement of a prosecution.

The approach to the meaning of the term 'accused' in the EA 2003 is the same as the approach set out in *Re Ismail [1999] AC 320*.[9] In *Asztaslos v Szekszard City Court, Hungary* [2010] EWHC 237 (Admin), para 19, Aikens LJ said: **2.11**

> The effect of Lord Steyn's analysis [in *Re Ismail* [1999] AC 320], as applied to s 2(3)(a) and (b) must be as follows: first, the phrases '... is accused ... of the commission of an offence' in para (a), and 'for the purpose of being prosecuted' in para (b), are not to be treated as terms of art. Secondly, it is a question of fact whether the surrender sought is of an accused person and for the purpose of the requested person being prosecuted. Thirdly, it would be wrong to approach the construction of the phrases 'accused' and 'for the purposes of being prosecuted' solely from the perspective of English (or Scottish or Northern Irish) criminal procedure; in particular from the point of view of the formal acts of the laying of an information or the preferring of an indictment. Fourthly, it is necessary to adopt a purposive construction of the words 'accused ... of the commission of an offence' and 'for the purpose of being prosecuted' to accommodate the differences between legal systems. Lastly, the question of whether a person is 'accused' and is to be surrendered 'for the purpose of being prosecuted' will require an intense focus on the facts in each case.

As the Administrative Court noted in *Assange v Swedish Prosecution Authority* [2011] EWHC 2849, para 134, the requirement in the EA 2003 that the EAW state that the person is accused is not to be found in the EAW Framework Decision, whereas the requirement that surrender be sought for the purposes of prosecution is contained in Article 1. **2.12**

Since the EA 2003 was enacted, the courts have had to consider the issue of whether the request for extradition is made for the purpose of the requested person being prosecuted for an offence as an accused person, or for the purpose only of conducting an investigation to see whether that person will be prosecuted. If an EAW has been issued by a requesting state as an 'accusation case' warrant, but its purpose is, in fact, the surrender of the requested person for the purpose of conducting an investigation to see whether that person should be prosecuted, it is not a legitimate purpose and so the warrant is not an EAW within the meaning of s 2(2) and (3). Accordingly, Part 1 of the Act will not apply to it.[10] **2.13**

In a number of cases the courts have had to look at detailed provisions relating to foreign criminal procedure in order to determine the defendant's status. This is plainly contrary to what the EAW Framework Decision and the EA 2003 were intended to achieve. In *Thompson v France* [2008] EWHC 2787 (Admin), para 39, Aikens J said: **2.14**

> District Judges who have to deal with applications for European arrest warrants on an almost daily basis, must not be put in the position where the court may have to consider detailed evidence about criminal procedures in other European countries for the purpose of the deciding whether or not the statutory requirements in section 2(3)(b) of the Act are fulfilled. If the objectives of speed and simplicity in the procedure of cross-border arrest and surrender within the EU are to be achieved, the solution, in my view, is clear. When a requesting authority issues a European arrest warrant with a request to the United Kingdom, the precise English-language wording in the head of the pro forma warrant annexed to the Framework Decision should be used. Furthermore, care should be taken to ensure that there is nothing in the body of warrant

[9] *Office of the King's Prosecutor, Brussels v Cando Armas* [2006] 2 AC 1, para 24; *Dabas v High Court of Justice, Madrid, Spain* [2006] EWHC 971 (Admin), para 12.

[10] *Office of the King's Prosecutor, Brussels v Cando Armas* [2006] 2 AC 1, paras 28 and 54.

that detracts from that unequivocal statement. The liaison magistrate in the requesting state and the liaison authority in the United Kingdom can ensure that this is done. In that way, the objective of paragraph 5 of the recitals to the Framework Decision and Part 1 of the Act, viz the introduction of a new simplified system of arrest and surrender between judicial authorities, can be fulfilled.

2.15 In deciding whether a person is 'accused' for the purposes of the EA 2003, the warrant must be construed as a whole.[11] Although it is unnecessary for the warrant to use the precise words used by s 2(3) (or s 2(4)),[12] the documentation should nevertheless be drafted so as to produce clarity.[13] In *Judicial Authority of the Court of First Instance, Hasselt, Belgium v Bartlett* [2010] EWHC 1390 (Admin), Toulson LJ said at para 52 that the EAW in that case complied with s 2(3) even though the warrant did not contain the word 'accused'. He applied the approach in *Asztaslos v Szekszard City Court, Hungary* [2010] EWHC 237 (Admin) of examining the warrant without regard to evidence extraneous to the EAW to see if it was clear. He then adopted what Jack J had said in *Dabas v High Court of Madrid* [2006] EWHC 971 (Admin):

> If [a person] is wanted for prosecution, and the warrant later describes the offence and sets out its circumstances and gives the statutory provision which he is alleged to have infringed, it is very difficult to see how be can be described other than as an 'accused' even if there is no statement using that word. The subject of such a European arrest warrant is clearly more than a suspect or someone who is wanted for questioning.

2.16 In *Assange v Swedish Prosecution Authority* [2011] EWHC 2849 (Admin), para 152, the Court adopted another approach to the question of whether the defendant had moved from a mere suspect to an accused person:

> As it is common ground that a criminal investigation about someone's conduct is not sufficient to make a person an accused, a further way of addressing this broad question is to ask whether the case against him has moved from where he can be seen only as a suspect where proof may be lacking or whether there is an accusation against him supported by proof ... Plainly this is a case which has moved from suspicion to accusation supported by proof.

2.17 In *Dabas v High Court of Justice, Madrid, Spain* [2006] EWHC 971 (Admin), the appellant challenged the formulation on the EAW which requested he be 'arrested and surrendered for the purposes of conducting a criminal prosecution or executing a custodial sentence or detention order'. He argued this did not constitute the wording required by s 2(3), and hence the warrant did not comply with s 2(2)(a). In rejecting this argument Latham LJ said at para 14:[14]

> In the present case, whilst I accept that the proforma wording in the preamble to the warrant is not necessarily determinative of the issue of whether or not the requirements of s 2(2)(a), (b) have been met, it seems to me that the court could only properly conclude that they did not mean what they say if the context throws clear doubt upon their prima facie meaning.[15]

2.18 A defendant who has been convicted in his absence but who can set aside the conviction as of right and be re-tried may nevertheless be be an accused person.[16] In *Calderelli v Judge for*

[11] *Harvey v Judicial Authority Of Portugal – Tribunal Judicial De Albufeira* [2007] EWHC 3282 (Admin), para 10.

[12] *Office of the King's Prosecutor, Belgium v Cando Armas* [2006] 2 AC 1, paras 43–44.

[13] *Vey v Office of the Public Prosecutor of the County Court of Montluçon* [2006] EWHC 760 (Admin), para 31.

[14] See also *Boudhiba v Central Examining Court No 5 of the National Court of Justice Madrid, Spain* [2006] EWHC 167 (Admin), para 21.

[15] See *Asztaslos v Szekszard City Court, Hungary* [2010] EWHC 237 (Admin), paras 20–38, for the circumstances in which the court will consider extraneous evidence.

[16] *In Re Coppin* LR 2 Ch App 47.

Preliminary Investigations of the Court of Naples [2008] 1 WLR 1724 the House of Lords held that a defendant who had been convicted in his absence and who did not have an unqualified right of appeal was properly characterized as an accused person. On the other hand, it may be appropriate to regard such defendants as convicted persons, as some member states do. In *Istanek v District Court of Prerov* [2011] EWHC 1498 (Admin), paras 21–23, the Administrative Court set out three propositions relevant where it is argued that a defendant has been wrongly categorized as either accused or convicted in the EAW: (i) the EA 2003 has to operate in relation to warrants from different jurisdictions where the principles and procedures of the criminal courts often differ, both from each other and certainly—most of them being civil law jurisdictions—from the criminal process in England; (ii) accordingly the statements and information prescribed to be given by s 2(3)–(6) of the EA 2003 will in every case reflect local practice; it is possible that what one state regards as an accusation case will in another be treated as a conviction case. The material before the court showed that there is no consensus across the European Union as to the approach to be taken within the EAW scheme to convictions in absence where the individual enjoys an unqualified right of re-trial; (iii) it must be inherent in the scheme that UK courts, in deciding whether the fugitive's extradition is sought on a valid EAW within the meaning of s 2 of the EA 2003, will go on the basis of the statements in the warrant, and will properly categorize the relevant facts according to the procedures and law of the requesting state.

To what extent can the court 'go behind' the warrant and look at extrinsic evidence tendered by the defendant for the purpose of showing that he is not accused, but still only subject to an investigative process? The authorities bearing on this question were considered in *Asztaslos v Szekszard City Court, Hungary* [2010] EWHC 237 (Admin), paras 20–38.[17] At paras 21–22, Aikens LJ noted that although in *Dabas v High Court of Justice, Madrid* [2007] 2 AC 31, para 50, Lord Hope of Craighead had said that a warrant which did not contain the statements referred to in s 2(2) could not be 'eked out by extraneous information', that had not been the approach of the courts in all cases. At para 38 he summarized what he considered to be the effect of the authorities, as follows. The court will look at the warrant as a whole to see whether it is an 'accusation case' warrant or a 'conviction case' warrant. It will not confine itself to the wording on the first page of the warrant, which may well be equivocal. In the case of an 'accusation case' warrant, issued under Part 1 of the EA 2003, the court has to be satisfied, looking at the warrant as a whole, that the requested person is an 'accused' within s 2(3)(a) of the EA 2003. Similarly, the court will look at the wording of the warrant as a whole to decide whether the warrant indicates, unequivocally, that the purpose of the warrant is for the purpose of the requested person being prosecuted for the offences identified. The court must construe the words in s 2(3)(a) and (b) in a cosmopolitan sense and not just in terms of the stages of English criminal procedure. If the warrant uses the phrases that are used in the English-language version of the EAW annexed to the EAW Framework Decision, there should be no (or very little scope) for argument on the purpose of the warrant. Only if the wording of the warrant is equivocal should the court consider examining extrinsic evidence to decide on the purpose of the warrant. But it should not look at extrinsic material to introduce a possible doubt as to the purpose where it is clear on the face of the warrant itself. Consideration of extrinsic factual **2.19**

[17] *Harvey v Judicial Authority of Portugal – Tribunal Judicial de Albufeira* [2007] EWHC 3282; *Vey v The Office of the Public Prosecutor of the County Court of Montluçon* [2006] EWHC 760 (Admin); *Paschayan v Government of Switzerland* [2008] EWHC 388 (Admin); *McCormack v Tribunal de Grande Instance, Quimper, France* [2008] EWHC 1453; *Thompson v Public Prosecutor of Boulogne sur mer* [2008] EWHC 2787 (Admin); *Johnson v State Prosecutor at the Tribunal de Grande Instance de Lille and Stevens v Judicial Authority of the Government of France* [2009] EWHC 2830 (Admin); *R(Trenk) v District Court in Plzen-Mesto, Czech Republic* [2009] EWCH 1132 (Admin).

or expert evidence to ascertain the purpose of the warrant should be a last resort and it is to be discouraged. The introduction of such evidence is contrary to the aspiration of the EAW Framework Decision, which is to introduce clarity and simplicity into the surrender procedure between member States of the EU. Therefore the introduction of extrinsic factual and expert evidence is to be discouraged, except in exceptional cases.

2.20 In *Assange v Swedish Prosecution Authority* [2011] EWHC 2849 (Admin), para 147, the Administrative Court declined to consider whether the principles set out in *Asztaslos v Szekszard City Court, Hungary* [2010] EWHC 237 (Admin), paras 20–38, were correct, but agreed that cases where evidence extraneous to the EAW is admitted 'should be very few and far between'.

Convicted persons

2.21 Where the extradition of a convicted person is sought, s 2(2)(b) requires the warrant to contain the statement referred to in s 2(5)[18]and the information in s 2(6).[19] The statement referred to in s 2(5) is one that the person in respect of whom the Part 1 warrant has been issued has been convicted of an offence specified in the warrant by a court in the Category 1 territory and the Part 1 warrant is issued for the purpose of his arrest and extradition to the Category 1 territory for the purpose of being sentenced for the offence or of serving a sentence of imprisonment or another form of detention imposed in respect of the offence. This statement is not a mere formality but forms an important part of the extradition procedure under the EA 2003, although the precise words in the EA 2003 need not be used.[20]

2.22 If the defendant is specified as having been convicted, the judge at the extradition hearing has to determine whether the defendant was convicted in his presence.[21] If not, the person must be discharged unless the conditions in s 20 are made out. These conditions are intended to ensure that the defendant will be treated fairly in the requesting state. They are considered in more detail at para 5.96.

Liability to return to a Category 2 territory

2.23 Return to Category 2 territories is also based upon the defendant's status as an accused or convicted person.

2.24 An extradition request made by a Category 2 territory must be made to the Secretary of State and must be 'valid' as defined by s 70(3). As amended by para 1(2) of Sch 13 to the Police and Justice Act 2006, s 70(3) provides that in order to be valid the request must contain the statement referred to in s 70(4) or s 70(4A) and must be made in the 'approved way', as defined by 70(7).

2.25 The statement in s 70(4), as amended is one that the person is accused in the Category 2 territory of the commission of an offence specified in the request, and the request is made with a view to his arrest and extradition to the Category 2 territory for the purpose of being prosecuted for the offence.

2.26 The statement in s 70(4A) is one that the person has been convicted of an offence specified in the request by a court in the Category 2 territory, and the request is made with a view to his arrest and extradition to the Category 2 territory for the purpose of being sentenced for the offence, or of serving a sentence of imprisonment or another form of detention imposed in respect of the offence.[22]

---

18 As amended by Sch 13, para 1, to the Police and Justice Act 2006.

19 This includes particulars of the person's identity and particulars of the conviction.

20 *Office of the King's Prosecutor, Belgium v Cando Armas* [2006] 2 AC 1, paras 43–44, para 57.

21 s 20(1).

22 The amendments to s 70 made by Sch 13, para 1, to the Police and Justice Act 2006 removed the need for the request to state that the defendant is unlawfully at large. This requirement had on occasion caused problems: *R (Bleta) v Secretary of State for the Home Department* [2005] 1 WLR 3194.

Section 70, as amended by para 17 of Sch 13 to the Police and Justice Act 2006, provides that if the request is valid the Secretary of State must, subject to s 70(2),[23] issue his certificate under s 70. The s 70 certificate must certify that the request is made in the approved way and identify the order by which the requesting state is designated as a Category 2 territory. The Secretary of State's decision to certify a request is susceptible to judicial review notwithstanding the terms of s 116 of the EA 2003.[24] **2.27**

There is no requirement for the Secretary of State to specify whether the defendant is accused or convicted, nor the English offence constituted by equivalent conduct.[25] Thus, the sort of problems which arose in *Re Farinha* [1992] Imm 174 (defective authority to proceed) and *R (Guisto) v Governor of HM Brixton Prison* [2003] UKHL 19 (defendant wrongly categorized) are unlikely to arise under the EA 2003. **2.28**

Where the defendant is specified as having been convicted the judge at the extradition hearing has to determine whether the defendant was convicted in his presence (s 85(1)). If not, the person must be discharged unless the conditions in s 85 are made out. These conditions, which are analogous to those in s 20, are designed to ensure that the defendant will be treated fairly in the requesting state. They are considered in more detail at para 5.96 and para 6.61. **2.29**

B. Extradition Offences

Introduction

The concept of an extradition offence[26] is fundamental to extradition law. This is because only those accused or convicted of such offences in the requesting state can be extradited. One of the principal questions to be decided by the judge at the extradition hearing is whether the defendant is accused or has been convicted of an extradition offence in the requesting state.[27] **2.30**

Under the EA 1989 the term 'extradition crime' bore different meanings in Part III and Sch 1 cases.[28] In cases dealt with under EA 1989, Sch 1, it was necessary to consult the Order in Council made under the EA 1870 in order to determine whether or not the alleged offence was an extradition crime. This was sometimes a difficult issue to resolve.[29] **2.31**

To some extent the EA 2003 simplifies the concept of extradition offences and establishes the same basic definitions in relation to Category 1 and Category 2 territories, which are analogous to the definition in s 2 of the EA 1989. However, some important differences remain. **2.32**

One particularly important change from the EA 1989 regime should be noted at the outset. Whereas, under the old law, dual criminality had to be satisfied in all cases, that is, the alleged conduct had to be an offence under the law of the requesting state and, had it been committed in the UK, an offence there,[30] the EA 2003 removes dual criminality in relation to Category 1 **2.33**

---

23 s 70(2), inserted by para 17 of Sch 13 to the Police and Justice Act 2006, entitles the Secretary of State not to issue a certificate if the defendant is a refugee: see para 4.122.

24 *Akaroglu v Government of Romania* [2007] EWHC 367 (Admin), para 38.

25 *Akaroglu v Government of Romania* [2007] EWHC 367 (Admin), para 21.

26 The term 'extradition crime' was used in the EA 1870 and EA 1989.

27 EA 2003, ss 10(2) and 78(4)(b).

28 cf EA 1989, s 2 (Part III cases) and EA 1989, Sch 1, para 20 (Sch 1 cases).

29 See for example *R v Secretary of State for the Home Department ex p Gilmore* [1999] QB 611 (whether conspiracy to defraud is an extradition crime).

30 EA 1989, s 2(1).

territories which are part of the EAW scheme in relation to the offences specified in the EAW and listed in Sch 2. Accordingly, for the first time, defendants can be extradited from the UK for conduct that would not be criminal under UK law if committed there.

Extradition offences in relation to Category 1 territories

2.34 The EA 2003 provides separate definitions of 'extradition offence' in ss 64 and 65 for persons not sentenced for their offence and those who have been sentenced, respectively. Each section provides for different definitions of extradition offence depending on the circumstances and type of offence.

Expressions used in ss 64 and 65

2.35 Some of the basic terms used in ss 64 and 65 are defined in s 66. An 'appropriate authority' of a Category 1 territory is a judicial authority of the territory which the appropriate judge believes has the function of issuing arrest warrants in that territory.[31] The 'law of a territory' is the general criminal law of the territory.[32] The 'relevant part of the UK' is the part of the UK in which the relevant proceedings are taking place (s 66(4)). The relevant proceedings are the proceedings in which it is necessary to decide whether conduct constitutes an extradition offence.[33]

2.36 Sections 64 and 65 refer to 'conduct'. This means the conduct of which the defendant is accused or has been convicted which is referred to in s 2(4) and s 2(5) of the EA 2003 which must be included in a Part 1 warrant.[34] If the judge requires further information to determine whether or not the conduct alleged in the warrant amounts to an extradition crime then he may request it, provided that he is satisfied that the warrant is a Part 1 warrant.[35] Where dual criminality is required it is the conduct for which extradition is sought, not any narrative that may be included in the Part 1 warrant simply by way of background, that must satisfy the test of double criminality.[36]

Extradition offences: person not sentenced for offence

2.37 The definition of extradition offence in s 64 applies in relation to conduct of a person where:

(a) he is accused in a Category 1 territory of the commission of an offence constituted by the conduct, or
(b) he is alleged to be unlawfully at large[37] after conviction by a court in a Category 1 territory of an offence constituted by the conduct and he has not been sentenced for the offence.

EAW Framework list offences

2.38 Section 64(2) defines an extradition offence in relation to requests made using an EAW and gives effect to Article 2(2) of the EAW Framework Decision. The following conditions must each be satisfied:

(a) the conduct must occur in the Category 1 territory and no part of it must occur in the UK;

---

[31] EA 2003, s 66(2).
[32] EA 2003, s 66(3).
[33] EA 2003, s 66(5).
[34] *Dabas v High Court of Justice, Madrid, Spain* [2006] EWHC 971 (Admin), para 20.
[35] *Dabas v High Court of Justice, Madrid, Spain* [2007] 2 AC 31, paras 50–51.
[36] *Dabas v High Court of Justice, Madrid, Spain* [2007] 2 AC 31, para 48.
[37] By EA 2003, s 68A, a person is alleged to be unlawfully at large after conviction of an offence if he is alleged to have been convicted of it, and (b) his extradition is sought for the purpose of his being sentenced for the offence or of his serving a sentence of imprisonment or another form of detention imposed in respect of the offence. Section 68A applies for the purposes of Part 1, other than s 14 and s 63 (s 68A(3)).

(b) a certificate issued by an appropriate authority of the Category 1 territory must show that the conduct falls within the European framework list;
(c) the certificate must show that the conduct is punishable under the law of the Category 1 territory with imprisonment or another form of detention for a term of three years or a greater punishment.

The European framework list is defined by s 215(1) to be the list of conduct contained in Sch 2 to the EA 2003. The Secretary of State may, by order, amend Sch 2 for the purpose of ensuring that the list of conduct set out in the Schedule corresponds to the list of conduct set out in Article 2(2) of the EAW Framework Decision (s 215(3)).[38] **2.39**

The list of conduct in Sch 2 is identical to the offences specified in Article 2 of the EAW Framework Decision, namely: **2.40**

1. Participation in a criminal organization.
2. Terrorism.
3. Trafficking in human beings.
4. Sexual exploitation of children and child pornography.
5. Illicit trafficking in narcotic drugs and psychotropic substances.
6. Illicit trafficking in weapons, munitions, and explosives.
7. Corruption.
8. Fraud, including that affecting the financial interests of the European Communities within the meaning of the Convention of 26 July 1995 on the protection of the European Communities' financial interests.
9. Laundering of the proceeds of crime.
10. Counterfeiting currency, including of the euro.
11. Computer-related crime.
12. Environmental crime, including illicit trafficking in endangered animal species and in endangered plant species and varieties.
13. Facilitation of unauthorized entry and residence.
14. Murder, grievous bodily injury.
15. Illicit trade in human organs and tissue.
16. Kidnapping, illegal restraint, and hostage-taking.
17. Racism and xenophobia.
18. Organized or armed robbery.
19. Illicit trafficking in cultural goods, including antiques and works of art.
20. Swindling.
21. Racketeering and extortion.
22. Counterfeiting and piracy of products.
23. Forgery of administrative documents and trafficking therein.
24. Forgery of means of payment.
25. Illicit trafficking in hormonal substances and other growth promoters.
26. Illicit trafficking in nuclear or radioactive materials.
27. Trafficking in stolen vehicles.
28. Rape.
29. Arson.
30. Crimes within the jurisdiction of the International Criminal Court.

---

[38] 2002/584/JHA. The text of the EAW Framework Decision is at App E4, and is dealt with in Ch 15.

31. Unlawful seizure of aircraft/ships.
32. Sabotage.

2.41 As explained at para 2.40, the definition in s 64(2) does not require the conduct to be a criminal offence in the UK. It is sufficient if it is criminal in the requesting state and the conditions in sub-paras (a), (b), and (c) of s 64(2) are satisfied. In *Office of King's Prosecutor v Cando Armas* [2006] 2 AC 1, para 5, Lord Bingham of Cornhill explained the purpose of the European framework list:

> These are not so much specific offences as kinds of criminal conduct, described in very general terms. Some of these, such as murder and armed robbery, are likely to feature, expressed in rather similar terms, in any developed criminal code. Others, such as corruption, racism, xenophobia, swindling and extortion, may find different expression in different codes. Included in the list, and relevant to this case, are the offences of trafficking in human beings, facilitation of unauthorised entry and residence and forgery of administrative documents. Underlying the list is an unstated assumption that offences of this character will feature in the criminal codes of all member states.[39]

2.42 Section 64(2) requires there to be 'a certificate' attesting to the specified matters in s 64(2)(b) and (c). In *Dabas v High Court of Justice, Madrid* [2007] 2 AC 31, the appellant contended that the certificate had to be contained in a separate document and that the EAW could not itself constitute the certificate. The House of Lords rejected the appellant's contention. Lord Bingham of Cornhill said at para 3 that interpreting s 64(2) in isolation he would conclude that a separate certificate was required. However, the section had to be interpreted in the context of the EAW Framework Decision to which Part 1 of the EA 2003 gives effect. One of the purposes of the Framework Decision is to reduce complexity and delay in extradition procedures. Thus, he concluded at para 8:

> The short question is whether this arrest warrant, complying with the formal requirements of the Framework Decision, is invalid under the 2003 Act because there is no separate certificate, and no express certification, to the effect specified in section 64(2)(b) and (c). If it is, the effect of the Act would be to introduce a requirement not found in the Framework Decision and thereby to impede, to some extent, achievement of the purpose of the Framework Decision, by reintroducing an element of technicality which the Framework Decision is intended to banish and by frustrating the intention that a warrant in common form should be uniformly acceptable in all member states. Happily, as I think, the House is not driven to that conclusion, since I consider that the Spanish judge, by signing the warrant, has given his authority to and thereby vouched the accuracy of its contents. Thus the warrant is in substance if not in form a certification by the judge. It would be inconsistent with the trust and respect assumed to exist between judicial authorities to insist on any additional verification, which would impede the process of surrender but do nothing to protect the rights of the appellant.[40]

2.43 In determining whether the alleged conduct properly falls within the list of Framework offences, the appropriate judge should ordinarily accept the classification of the issuing judicial authority unless there is an obvious inconsistency which shows the conduct alleged does not amount to an offence under the law of that state.[41] This is consistent with Article 2(2) of the

[39] The broad and ill-defined nature of these categories led to concerns about how the EAW would operate in practice: *House of Commons Home Affairs Committee*, Extradition Bill, First Report of Session 2002–2003, HC 138, paras 20–32.

[40] cf *Palar v Court of First Instance Brussels* [2005] EWHC 915, para 11 (Admin), where Laws LJ doubted, obiter, that the EAW could constitute the certificate required by s 64(2).

[41] *Assange v Swedish Prosecuting Authority* [2011] EWHC 2849 (Admin), para 112, approving the approach of the District Court of Amsterdam in Decision LJN BO 7884; cf *Minister of Justice, Equality and Law Reform v Desjatnikvos* [2008] IESC 53 (Irish Supreme Court); *Minister of Justice v Tighe* [2010] IESC 61.

Framework Decision, which provides that the offences in the list are to be regarded 'as they are defined by the law of the issuing Member State'.

Other territorial offences

Section 64(3) defines an extradition offence where the conduct occurs in the territory of the requesting state and it falls outside the list of Framework offences.[42] It gives effect to Articles 2(4) and 4(1) of the EAW Framework Decision, which permit member States to preserve the requirement of dual criminality for offences other than those specified in the framework list. Conduct also constitutes an extradition offence in relation to a Category 1 territory if: **2.44**

(a) the conduct occurs in the Category 1 territory;[43]
(b) the conduct would constitute an offence under the law of the relevant part of the UK if it occurred in that part of the UK;
(c) the conduct is punishable under the law of the Category 1 territory with imprisonment or another form of detention for a term of 12 months or a greater punishment (however it is described in the law).

By requiring that the conduct be an offence in both the requesting state and in the UK, s 64(3) preserves dual criminality. There are two distinct forms of dual criminality. One involves considering whether the juristic elements of the foreign offence correspond to the juristic elements of the UK offence.[44] The other approach involves considering whether the defendant's alleged actual conduct would constitute an offence in the UK if committed there.[45] In *Norris v Government of the United States of America* [2008] 1 AC 920, para 65, the House of Lords said that: **2.45**

> ... it is useful to stand back from the detail and recognise the essential choice that the legislature makes in deciding just what the double criminality principle requires. It is possible to define the crimes for which extradition is to be sought and ordered (extradition crimes) in terms either of conduct or of the elements of the foreign offence. That is the fundamental choice. The court can be required to make the comparison and to look for the necessary correspondence either between the offence abroad (for which the accused's extradition is sought) and an offence here, or between the conduct alleged against the accused abroad and an offence here. For convenience these may be called respectively the offence test and the conduct test. It need hardly be pointed out that if the offence test is adopted the requested state will invariably have to examine the legal ingredients of the foreign offence to ensure that there is no mismatch between it and the supposedly corresponding domestic offence. If, however, the conduct test is adopted, it will be necessary to decide, as a subsidiary question, where, within the documents emanating from the requesting state, the description of the relevant conduct is to be found.

At para 91 of *Norris v Government of the United States of America* [2008] 1 AC 920 the House of Lords held that s 137(2) of the EA 2003 (the equivalent provision to s 63(3) in Part 2 cases) imposes the conduct test, and requires the court to consider whether the conduct alleged against the defendant in the requesting state would amount to an offence in the UK:[46] **2.46**

---

42 *Convery v Government of the Kingdom of the Netherlands* [2005] EWHC 566 (Admin).

43 Only some of the conduct need occur in the territory. It need not all take place there: *Office of the King's Prosecutor v Cando Armas* [2006] 2 AC 1, para 17, para 30; *Tesler v Government of the United States Of America* [2011] EWHC 52 (Admin), paras 19–38.

44 This was the approach to dual criminality in the Fugitive Offenders Act 1967: *Government of Canada v Aronson* [1990] 1 AC 579.

45 This was the approach to dual criminality in the EA 1870: *Re Nielsen* [1984] 1 AC 606, and the EA 1989: *R v Governor of Brixton Prison ex p Hill* [1999] QB 886.

46 The approach to dual criminality under the EA 2003 is the same in Part 1 and Part 2 cases: *Norris v Government of the United States of America* [2008] 1 AC 920, paras 78 and 91.

> ... the conduct test should be applied consistently throughout the 2003 Act, the conduct relevant under Part 2 of the Act being that described in the documents constituting the request (the equivalent of the arrest warrant under Part 1), ignoring in both cases mere narrative background but taking account of such allegations as are relevant to the description of the corresponding United Kingdom offence.

2.47 This decision was foreshadowed by what Lord Bingham of Cornhill said in *Office of the King's Prosecutor v Cando Armas* [2006] 2 AC 1, para 16, in connection with s 65(2)(a) of the EA 2003:[47]

> I would accept the submission of ... the prosecutor that 'the conduct' in section 65 means the conduct complained of or relied on in the warrant. Such a reading is consistent with the language and purpose of the Framework Decision, obviates the need for an undesirable inquiry into the niceties of a foreign law ... and is consistent, so far as that is relevant, with the earlier decision of the House in *In re Nielsen*[48] ...

2.48 When considering the conduct in the warrant, a narrative of events prior in date to the conduct relied on will not be objectionable if it is included merely in order to set the scene, to identify the people with whom the person concerned was associating, for example, and their backgrounds and associates. Information of that kind is relevant and admissible to enable inferences to be drawn as to the nature of the offence constituted by the conduct for which extradition is sought. But it is the conduct for which extradition is sought, not any narrative that may be included in the Part 1 warrant simply by way of background, that must satisfy the test of double criminality.[49] As to mens rea, it is unnecessary for the warrant to identify or specify in terms the relevant mens rea of the English offence. It is sufficient if it can be inferred by the court from the conduct that is spelled out in the warrant and further information.[50]

2.49 In *Dabas v High Court of Justice, Madrid* [2007] 2 AC 31 the House of Lords considered two questions relating to extradition offences under s 64(3): (i) whether section 64(3) requires that the court be satisfied that the conduct relied on constitutes an offence under the law of the requesting state and whether, for that purpose, the text of the relevant law must be set out in the EAW or otherwise made available to the court; and (ii) whether, in a case where section 64(3) of the EA 2003 applies, and where part of the conduct complained of did not constitute an offence under English law at the time it occurred, the court may none the less order extradition based upon the part of the conduct which would have constituted an offence under English law.[51]

2.50 Lord Hope of Craighead dealt with the first question at paras 53–55. Having noted that Article 8(1)(d) of the EAW Framework Decision required an EAW merely to contain details of 'the nature and legal classification of the offence', s 2(4)(c) of the EA 2003 required no more than that. Consistently with that requirement, he said that the judge need not examine the text of the foreign law in order to decide whether the conditions set out in s 64(3) are satisfied:[52]

> None of the conditions set out in section 64(3) require an analysis of the foreign law for the judge to decide under section 10(2) whether they are satisfied. Section 64(3)(c) directs

[47] s 65 rather than s 64 because *Cando Armas* was a conviction case rather than an accusation case.

[48] [1984] 1 AC 606.

[49] *Dabas v High Court of Justice, Madrid* [2007] 2 AC 31, para 48.

[50] *Zak v Regional Court of Bydgoszsz, Poland* [2008] EWHC 470 (Admin), para 16; *Huburn v Provincial Court of Malaga, Spain* [2012] EWHC 897 (Admin), para 5.

[51] Section 64(3), like its analogue under the EA 1989, requires that for the purposes of dual criminality the conduct complained of must have been a criminal offence in the UK (had it been committed there) at the time it was committed: *R v Bow Street Metropoitan Stipendiary Magistrate ex p Pinochet (No 3)* [2000] 1 AC 147, 196; *Dabas v High Court of Justice, Madrid* [2007] 2 AC 31, para 46.

[52] *Office of the King's Prosecutor, Brussels v Cando Armas* [2006] 2 AC 1, para 30.

attention to the question of punishment. All the judge needs to examine this question are particulars of the sentence which may be imposed under the law of the category 1 territory in respect of the offence if the person is convicted of it. Those are among the particulars which the warrant must contain if it is to be dealt with as a Part 1 warrant: see section 2(4)(d). This consistent with article 8(1)(f) of the Framework Decision which requires only that information be given as to the penalty imposed, if there is a final judgment, or the prescribed scale of penalties for the offence under the law of the issuing member state. There is no requirement here that the text of the law which gives rise to that punishment must be made available. The requested person's article 5 and article 6 Convention rights are sufficiently protected by the procedures that are laid down in Part 1 of the 2003 Act.[53]

As to the second question, at para 51 Lord Hope of Craighead said that a judge may conclude that the test in s 64(3) is not satisfied because part of the conduct which is said to constitute the offence mentioned in the Part 1 warrant occurred before it constituted an offence under the law of the relevant part of the UK if it occurred there. He said the question then, was whether in that situation the judge has no alternative other than to order the person's discharge under s 10(3). The answer is 'no'. Lord Hope of Craighead concluded that in that situation it would be open to the judge in such circumstances to ask that the scope of the warrant be limited to a period that would enable the test of double criminality to be satisfied. If this is not practicable, it would be open to him to make this clear in the order that he issued when answering the question in s 10(2) in the affirmative. He also said[54] that if a judge conducting an extradition hearing found that the information presented to him was insufficient to enable him to decide whether or not the offence specified in the Part 1 warrant was an extradition offence within the meaning of s 64(2) or s 64(3) he could request further information from the appropriate authority of the Category 1 territory under articles 10(5) and 15(2) of the EAW Framework Decision. However, Lord Hope emphasized that the judge must first be satisfied that the warrant was a Part 1 warrant within the meaning of s 2(2), and that a warrant which did not contain the statements referred to in that subsection could not be 'eked out' by extraneous information.[55] **2.51**

Extra-territorial offences

Section 64(4), (5), and (6) deals with the situation where the alleged conduct constitutes an extra-territorial offence against the law of the requesting state.[56] **2.52**

Under s 64(4) the conduct is an extradition offence if: **2.53**

(a) the conduct occurs outside the Category 1 territory;[57]
(b) the conduct is punishable under the law of the Category 1 territory with imprisonment or another form of detention for a term of 12 months or a greater punishment (however it is described in that law);
(c) in corresponding circumstances equivalent conduct would constitute an extra-territorial offence under the law of the relevant part of the UK punishable with imprisonment or another form of detention for a term of 12 months or a greater punishment.

---

53 Para 55.
54 Para 49.
55 cf *Asztaslos v Szekszard City Court, Hungary* [2010] EWHC 237 (Admin), paras 20–38. The circumstances in which the judge can consider information outside the warrant are dealt with at para 2.21.
56 *Taylor v Public Prosecutors Office, Berlin, Germany* [2012] EWHC 475 (Admin), paras 21–26.
57 This must mean entirely outside the Category 1 territory, otherwise the case will fall within s 64(3): *Office of the King's Prosecutor, Brussels v Cando Armas* [2006] 2 AC 1, para 17.

2.54 Section 64(5) provides that conduct also constitutes an extradition offence in relation to the Category 1 territory if:

(a) the conduct occurs outside the Category 1 territory and no part of it occurs in the UK;
(b) the conduct would constitute an offence under the law of the relevant part of the UK punishable with imprisonment or another form of detention for a term of 12 months or a greater punishment if it occurred in that part of the UK;
(c) the conduct is so punishable under the law of the Category 1 territory (however it is described in that law).

2.55 Special provision is made in the EA 2003 for war crimes, genocide, and so on. Section 64(6) provides that the conduct also constitutes an extradition offence in relation to the Category 1 territory if:

(a) the conduct occurs outside the Category 1 territory and no part of it occurs in the UK;
(b) the conduct is punishable under the law of the Category 1 territory with imprisonment or another form of detention for a term of 12 months or a greater punishment (however it is described in that law);
(c) the conduct constitutes or if committed in the UK would constitute an offence mentioned in s 64(7).

2.56 The offences mentioned in s 64(7) (in relation to England and Wales) are an offence under ss 51 or 58 of the International Criminal Court Act 2001 (genocide, crimes against humanity, and war crimes); an offence under ss 52 or 59 of that Act (conduct ancillary to genocide, and so on committed outside the jurisdiction); an ancillary offence, as defined in ss 55 or 62 of that Act, in relation to an offence falling within para (a) or (b) of s 64(7).

2.57 Section 64(8) deals with fiscal offences. It provides that in relation to s 64(3)(b), (4)(c), and (5)(b) if the conduct relates to a tax or duty, it is immaterial that the law of the relevant part of the UK does not impose the same kind of tax or duty or does not contain rules of the same kind as those of the law of the Category 1 territory. Also, if the conduct relates to customs or exchange, it is immaterial that the law of the relevant part of the UK does not contain rules of the same kind as those of the law of the Category 1 territory.

Extradition offences: person sentenced for the offence

2.58 Section 65 defines the different types of conduct that constitute an extradition offence in respect of Category 1 territories in cases where the defendant has been convicted and sentenced for the offence and is alleged to be unlawfully at large (s 65(1)).

EAW Framework list offences

2.59 In relation to EAW countries, s 65(2) provides that the conduct constitutes an extradition offence in relation to the Category 1 territory if:

(a) the conduct occurs in the Category 1 territory and no part of it occurs in the UK;
(b) a certificate[58] issued by an appropriate authority of the Category 1 territory shows that the conduct falls within the European framework list in Sch 2;
(c) the certificate shows that a sentence of imprisonment or another form of detention for a term of 12 months or a greater punishment has been imposed in the Category 1 territory in respect of the conduct.

---

58 On the requirement for a certificate, see para 2.42.

Non-Framework list offences

2.60 Section 65(3) defines extradition offences in relation to offences that are territorial offences in the requesting state. In relation to offences committed within the requesting state, the conduct also constitutes an extradition offence if:

(a) the conduct occurs in the Category 1 territory;
(b) the conduct would constitute an offence under the law of the relevant part of the UK if it occurred in that part of the UK;
(c) a sentence of imprisonment or another form of detention for a term of four months or a greater punishment has been imposed in the Category 1 territory in respect of the conduct.

2.61 Sections 65(2) and 65(3) were considered by the House of Lords in *Office of the King's Prosecutor, Brussels v Cando Armas* [2006] 2 AC 1. The defendant was convicted in Brussels in his absence and sentenced to five years' imprisonment for directing, from London, the systematic illegal immigration of Ecuadorean citizens into Europe through Brussels. He was subsequently arrested in the UK on the authority of an EAW and his extradition sought by Belgium under Part 1 of the EA 2003. The warrant identified three offences from the framework offences list contained in Sch 2 to the EA 2003, as constituting the conduct for which surrender was sought, namely, (i) people trafficking; (ii) facilitating unauthorized entry and residence; and (iii) forgery of administrative documents.

2.62 When the matter came before the magistrates' court the district judge held that the defendant's conduct did not constitute an extradition offence within the meaning of s 65 since part of the conduct relied on had occurred in the UK and was accordingly excluded by s 65(2)(a), and s 65(3) did not apply since the relevant conduct had not occurred exclusively in Belgium.

2.63 The Administrative Court, allowing the Prosecutor's appeal, concluded that the conduct described in s 65(2)–(6) as constituting the extradition offences did not mean 'all the conduct' but only such conduct as constituted the criminal offence under the law of the state issuing the warrant; that s 65(3)–(6) were not confined to non-framework offences; and that the conduct alleged in the warrant was therefore capable of constituting extradition offences within s 65(2).

2.64 The House of Lords dismissed the defendant's appeal. It held that the distinct categories of case set out in s 65(2)–(6) for which surrender might be sought provided a cumulative list in which a condition applicable to one category might also be applicable to another. Although s 65(2) alone referred to Framework offences in respect of which the double criminality requirement was dispensed with, the conduct specified in s 65(3)–(6) might also include those offences where the relevant requirement of double criminality was met.

2.65 The House held that 'conduct' for the purposes of s 65 was that complained of or relied on in the warrant and that it occurred 'in' the requesting state irrespective of the physical presence of the defendant so long as the intended effect of his actions was felt there. While s 65(2) expressly required that no part of the relevant conduct should take place in the UK, no such qualification was intended in respect of s 65(3), for which it was sufficient that some, but not all, of the conduct occurred in the requesting state.[59]

2.66 Since the warrant alleged that part of the defendant's conduct had taken place in the UK, s 65(2) did not apply; however, since his conduct, constituting the Framework offences, had

[59] *Office of the King's Prosecutor, Brussels v Cando Armas* [2006] 2 AC 1, paras 17 and 49; *R (Bermingham) v Director of the Serious Fraud Office* [2006] EWHC 200 (Admin), paras 82–84.

occurred partly in Belgium, s 65(3) was applicable. Accordingly, the House of Lords remitted the case to the district judge to continue the hearing.

Extra-territorial offences

2.67 For offences committed outside of the requesting state, s 65(4), (5) and (6) apply. Section 65(4) states that conduct also constitutes an extradition offence in relation to the Category 1 territory if:

(a) the conduct occurs outside the Category 1 territory;
(b) a sentence of imprisonment or another form of detention for a term of four months or a greater punishment has been imposed in the Category 1 territory in respect of the conduct;
(c) in corresponding circumstances equivalent conduct would constitute an extra-territorial offence under the law of the relevant part of the UK punishable with imprisonment or another form of detention for a term of 12 months or a greater punishment.

2.68 Section 65(5) provides that the conduct also constitutes an extradition offence in relation to the Category 1 territory if:

(a) the conduct occurs outside the Category 1 territory and no part of it occurs in the UK;
(b) the conduct would constitute an offence under the law of the relevant part of the UK punishable with imprisonment or another form of detention for a term of 12 months or a greater punishment if it occurred in that part of the UK;
(c) a sentence of imprisonment or another form of detention for a term of four months or a greater punishment has been imposed in the Category 1 territory in respect of the conduct.

2.69 Special provision for war crimes and so on is made in s 66(6) and (7). These are in pari materia with s 65(6) and (7) in relation to persons not sentenced for their offence.

2.70 Section 65(8) contains provisions in relation to fiscal offences which are also in pari materia with those in s 65(8) in relation to accused persons.

Extradition offences in relation to Category 2 territories

2.71 Sections 137 and 138 define 'extradition offence' in relation to Category 2 territories for persons not sentenced for their offence and persons so sentenced, respectively.

2.72 The references in these two sections to 'relevant part of the UK' is to the part of the UK in which the extradition hearing took place, if the question of whether conduct constitutes an extradition offence is to be decided by the Secretary of State (for example, where he has to decide whether to give consent under s 129(4)), and in any other case, to the part of the UK where the proceedings in which it is necessary to decide that question are taking place.[60]

2.73 In Part 2 cases, by s 78(2)(c), the judge must be satisfied that the documents sent to him by the Secretary of State include particulars of the offence specified in the request, in other words, the conduct of which he is accused or has been convicted. In *Dudko v Government of the Russian Federation* [2010] EWHC 1125 (Admin), paras 15–16, the High Court noted that the wording of s 78(2)(c) is much narrower than the similar requirement in s 2(4)(c). Thomas LJ said that s 78(4)(c) should be read as encompassing the more comprehensive phraseology used in s 2(4)(c) because it would have been an odd result if Parliament had intended that the request

[60] EA 2003, ss 137(8) and 138(8).

of persons to be extradited to EU countries required particulars of the offence that were more onerous than the requirements of those to be extradited to other countries.[61]

Extradition offences: person not sentenced for offence

The definition of extradition offence in s 137 applies in relation to conduct of a person if: **2.74**

(a) he is accused in a Category 2 territory of the commission of an offence constituted by the conduct, or
(b) he is alleged to be unlawfully at large after conviction by a court in a Category 2 territory of an offence constituted by the conduct and he has not been sentenced for the offence.

Section 137(2) applies to conduct committed within the territory of the requesting state. Such conduct is an extradition offence if: **2.75**

(a) the conduct occurs in the Category 2 territory;[62]
(b) the conduct would constitute an offence under the law of the relevant part of the UK punishable with imprisonment or another form of detention for a term of 12 months or a greater punishment if it occurred in that part of the UK;
(c) the conduct is so punishable under the law of the Category 2 territory (however it is described in that law).

Sections 137(3), (4), and (5) define extradition offences where the conduct alleged is extra-territorial. **2.76**

Section 137(3) provides that conduct also constitutes an extradition offence in relation to the Category 2 territory if: **2.77**

(a) the conduct occurs outside the Category 2 territory;
(b) the conduct is punishable under the law of the Category 2 territory with imprisonment or another form of detention for a term of 12 months or a greater punishment (however it is described in that law);
(c) in corresponding circumstances equivalent conduct would constitute an extra-territorial offence under the law of the relevant part of the UK punishable with imprisonment or another form of detention for a term of 12 months or a greater punishment.

Section 137(4) provides that conduct also constitutes an extradition offence in relation to the Category 2 territory if: **2.78**

(a) the conduct occurs outside the Category 2 territory and no part of it occurs in the UK;
(b) the conduct would constitute an offence under the law of the relevant part of the UK punishable with imprisonment or another form of detention for a term of 12 months or a greater punishment if it occurred in that part of the UK;
(c) the conduct is so punishable under the law of the Category 2 territory (however it is described in that law).

---

[61] *Government of the United Arab Emirates v Allen* [2012] EWHC 1712 (Admin), para 15; *Jethwa v Government of the United States of America* [2012] EWHC 31 (Admin), para 19.

[62] The conduct does not have to be committed entirely within the Category 2 territory. It is sufficient if only part of it occurred there: *R (Bermingham) v Director of the Serious Fraud Office* [2006] EWHC 200 (Admin), paras 81–85; *Tesler v Government of the United States Of America* [2011] EWHC 52 (Admin), paras 19–38.

2.79 Section 137(5) makes provision for war crimes, and so on. It provides that conduct also constitutes an extradition offence in relation to the Category 2 territory if these conditions are satisfied:

(a) the conduct occurs outside the Category 2 territory and no part of it occurs in the UK;
(b) the conduct is punishable under the law of the Category 2 territory with imprisonment for a term of 12 months or another form of detention or a greater punishment (however it is described in that law);
(c) the conduct constitutes or if committed in the UK would constitute an offence mentioned in s 137(6).

2.80 The offences mentioned in s 137(6) in relation to England and Wales are: an offence under ss 51 or 58 of the International Criminal Court Act 2001 (genocide, crimes against humanity, and war crimes); an offence under ss 52 or 59 of that Act (conduct ancillary to genocide, etc committed outside the jurisdiction); an ancillary offence, as defined in ss 55 or 62 of that Act, in relation to an offence falling within s 137(6)(a) or (b) of the EA 2003.

2.81 Section 137(7) provides an important exclusion for military offences under the law of the requesting state. If the conduct constitutes an offence under the military law of the requesting Category 2 territory but does not constitute an offence under the general criminal law of the relevant part of the UK, it does not constitute an extradition crime.

Extradition offences: person sentenced for the offence

2.82 The definitions in s 138 apply in relation to conduct of a person if he is alleged to be unlawfully at large after conviction by a court in a Category 2 territory of an offence constituted by the conduct, and he has been sentenced for the offence (s 138(1)).

2.83 Section 138(2) relates to territorial offences and provides that the conduct constitutes an extradition offence in relation to the Category 2 territory if:

(a) the conduct occurs in the Category 2 territory;
(b) the conduct would constitute an offence under the law of the relevant part of the UK punishable with imprisonment or another form of detention for a term of 12 months or a greater punishment if it occurred in that part of the UK;
(c) a sentence of imprisonment or another form of detention for a term of four months or a greater punishment has been imposed in the Category 2 territory in respect of the conduct.

2.84 Extra-territorial offences are dealt with in s 138(3), (4) and (5). The conduct constitutes an extradition offence in relation to the Category 2 territory if:

(a) the conduct occurs outside the Category 2 territory;
(b) a sentence of imprisonment or another form of detention for a term of four months or a greater punishment has been imposed in the Category 2 territory in respect of the conduct;
(c) in corresponding circumstances equivalent conduct would constitute an extra-territorial offence under the law of the relevant part of the UK punishable with imprisonment or another form of detention for a term of 12 months or a greater punishment.

2.85 Section 138(4) provides that conduct also constitutes an extradition offence in relation to the Category 2 territory if:

(a) the conduct occurs outside the Category 2 territory and no part of it occurs in the UK;

(b) the conduct would constitute an offence under the law of the relevant part of the UK punishable with imprisonment or another form of detention for a term of 12 months or a greater punishment if it occurred in that part of the UK;
(c) a sentence of imprisonment or another form of detention for a term of four months or a greater punishment has been imposed in the Category 2 territory in respect of the conduct.

Section 138(5) and (6) contains provisions relating to war crimes in similar terms to s 138(5) and (6). **2.86**

Section 138(7) excludes military offences in the same terms as s 137(7). **2.87**

Temporal issues

The concept of extradition offences in the EA 2003 raises two issues in relation to the time when the conduct was committed. **2.88**

(a) Is a defendant liable to be extradited for an offence committed before the EA 2003 came into force?
(b) Except in EAW cases, is he liable to be extradited for conduct which was not an offence in the UK at the time it was committed, but which has become an offence by the date of the extradition request?

The first issue was considered in *R v Secretary of State for the Home Department ex p Hill* [1999] QB 886 in relation to the EA 1989. The applicant argued that the Act only applied to offences committed after 27 September 1989, the date of its commencement. The Divisional Court rejected this submission. Hooper J held that as a matter of statutory construction, the definition of extradition crime in s 2(1) included conduct committed before the Act came into force, and that it was not necessary to consider the Government's submissions that because the 1989 Act was a procedural Act, the presumption against non-retroactive application did not apply. **2.89**

The same reasoning is applicable to the EA 2003. It follows that extradition will not be prohibited under the EA 2003 merely because the alleged offence took place before the Act came into force. The EA 2003 applies to all extradition requests received on or after 1 January 2004.[63] **2.90**

The second question was one of the many issues considered by the House of Lords in *R v Metropolitan Stipendiary Magistrate ex p Pinochet (No 3)* [2000] AC 147. A number of the allegations of torture made against General Pinochet were not criminal in the UK at the time they were committed because s 134 of the Criminal Justice Act 1988 had not yet come into force. The House of Lords held that the conduct to be considered under Part III must have been a crime in the UK at the time it was committed and that it was not sufficient that it be a crime at the time the request for extradition is made. **2.91**

The EA 2003 uses the same tense structure in its definitions of extradition offences as s 2(1) of the EA 1989—'... if it occurred ...' and '... if committed ...'—and so the reasoning of the House of Lords would seem to be equally applicable to the EA 2003. Therefore, where dual criminality is required, in order to constitute an extradition offence, the alleged conduct must have been criminal in the UK at the time it was committed.[64] **2.92**

---

[63] Para 1.47; *R (Government of the United States of America) v Senior District Judge, Bow Street Magistrates' Court* [2006] EWHC 2256 (Admin).
[64] *Dabas v High Court of Justice, Madrid* [2007] 2 AC 31, para 46.

2.93 Section 196 contains special provisions in relation to genocide, war crimes, and the other crimes against humanity specified in s 196(2). Section 196(3) provides that the defendant cannot object to extradition under the EA 2003 on the grounds that he could not have been punished for the offence under the law in force at the time when and in the place where he is alleged to have committed the act of which he is accused or been convicted.

3

CATEGORIZATION OF TERRITORIES; TERRITORIAL SCOPE OF THE EXTRADITION ACT 2003

A. Categorization of Territories

Introduction

3.01 Historically English extradition law provided different schemes of extradition for different categories of requesting country. In broad terms these categories were foreign states;[1] colonies; and designated Commonwealth countries.[2] The EA 1870 governed extradition from the UK to foreign states, and the Fugitive Offenders Act 1881 (replaced by the Fugitive Offenders Act 1967) governed extradition within the Empire and later the Commonwealth.

3.02 The EA 1989 repealed the EA 1870 and the Fugitive Offenders Act 1967. Under the EA 1989 requests for extradition by European countries,[3] designated Commonwealth countries, and colonies were dealt with under Part III of the 1989 Act. Requests made by countries in relation to whom an Order in Council made under the EA 1870 was in force (principally the United States of America) were dealt with under Sch 1 to the 1989 Act, the provisions of which were derived from the EA 1870.

3.03 In addition to the differing evidential requirements in Part III and Sch 1 cases, there were also differences between European Part III cases, where no evidence was required[4] and Commonwealth Part III cases, where admissible evidence sufficient to amount to a prima facie case was required.[5]

---

[1] See the EA 1870 and EA 1989, s 3.

[2] See Fugitive Offenders Act 1967, the EA 1989, s 5, and *R v Governor of Brixton Prison ex p Kahan* [1989] QB 716.

[3] For these purposes, signatories to the European Convention on Extradition 1957 designated in an Order in Council made under the EA 1989, s 4.

[4] See for example *R v Bow Street Metropolitan Stipendiary Magistrate ex p Pinochet (No 3)* [2000] 1 AC 147; *In re Evans* [1994] 1 WLR 1006.

[5] See for example *R (Saifi) v Governor of HM Prison Brixton* [2001] 1 WLR 1134.

3.04 The EA 2003 largely removes these complexities by designating extradition partners as either Category 1 or Category 2 territories.[6] Claims for extradition by Category 1 territories are dealt with under Part 1, while requests for extradition by Category 2 territories are dealt with under Part 2.

Category 1 territories

3.05 Category 1 territories are territories designated for the purposes of Part 1 by order (s 1(1)). In the Act, references to Category 1 territories are to the territories designated for the purposes of Part 1 (s 1(2)).

3.06 The EA 2003 does not provide any guidance as to which countries are to be designated as Category 1 territories. The only restriction is contained in s 1(3), which provides that a territory may not be designated for the purposes of Part 1 if a person found guilty in the territory of a criminal offence may be sentenced to death for the offence under the general criminal law of the territory. When the Government presented the Extradition Bill to the House of Lords the Minister of State said:[7]

> It is the Government's intention, as we have indicated, that the only countries that should be subject to Part 1 procedures are precisely the ones covered by the official Opposition amendment—the member states of the European Union plus Norway and Iceland. However I do not think that it would be wise to limit the future quite as tightly as that amendment would indicate. It would limit the room for manoeuvre of our successors if they decided that there were good reasons to bring before Parliament the case for putting a non-European country into Part 1. My noble and learned friend Lord Bassam trailed that point by referring to Australia, New Zealand and Canada. Although we currently have no intention of doing that, it is not outside the bounds of possibility ... [W]e have not really given much thought to criteria because there is no current intention to add to designation. That does not mean to say that we believe that there should be a rigid set of criteria, but one might at least have to reflect on possible principles.

3.07 The EA 2003 came into force on 1 January 2004. At that date only seven member States had complied with Article 34 of the EAW Framework Decision, which required that member States should take the necessary measures to comply with its provisions by 31 December 2003. These states were Belgium, Denmark, Finland, Ireland, Portugal, Spain, and Sweden. Thus these seven were designated by the Secretary of State as Category 1 territories pursuant to s 1 of the Act. That was effected by the Extradition Act 2003 (Designation of Part 1 Territories) Order 2003.[8]

3.08 As and when other member States implemented the EAW Framework Decision in their own domestic laws, the Secretary of State proceeded to designate them as Category 1 territories under s 1 of the EA 2003.[9]

3.09 At the time of writing (November 2012) the Extradition Act 2003 (Designation of Part 1 Territories) Order 2003[10] designates the following territories, which are the other 26 member States of the European Union and Gibraltar, as Category 1 territories:

> Austria, Belgium, Bulgaria, Cyprus, Czech Republic, Denmark, Estonia, Finland, France, Germany, Gibraltar, Greece, Hungary, Ireland, Italy, Latvia, Lithuania, Luxembourg, Malta, The Netherlands, Poland, Portugal, Romania, Slovakia, Slovenia, Spain, Sweden.

---

[6] Also referred to in the EA 2003 and this book as Part 1 and Part 2 territories: see App E5.

[7] 3 June 2003, *Hansard* 648, col GC167.

[8] SI 2003/3333: see App E5.

[9] See Extradition Act 2003 (Amendment to Designations) Order 2004 (SI 2004/1898) for Austria, Cyprus, France, Hungary, Latvia, Lithuania, Luxembourg, Malta, the Netherlands, Poland, and Slovenia; the Extradition Act 2003 (Amendment to Designations) Order 2005 (SI 2005/365) for the Czech Republic, Estonia, Germany, Greece, and Slovakia; and the Extradition Act 2003 (Amendment to Designations) Order 2005 (SI 2005/2036) for Italy.

[10] SI 2003/3333, as amended.

The Secretary of State has a wide discretion as which states should be designated as Category 1 territories. On 18 July 2005 in a case concerned with the proposed extradition to Spain of a man called Darkanzali, the Second Senate of the German Federal Constitutional Court declared the German European Arrest Warrant Act (*Europäisches Haftbefehlgesetz*) unconstitutional and void in its entirety. In *R (Oliver) v Secretary of State for the Home Department* [2006] EWHC 1847 (Admin) the applicant challenged the refusal by the Secretary of State to re-designate Germany as a Category 2 state following the Federal Constitutional Court's decision. The applicant argued that the only proper response open to the Secretary of State was for him to re-designate Germany as a Category 2 territory. In rejecting this submission Laws LJ said at para 31: **3.10**

> I do not say there might not come a point at which, all else having failed, a Member State's proper and lawful response to another's repudiation of the EAW system (in relation to its own nationals) would be to withdraw co-operation. But for the domestic court to conclude that such a point had been reached, if it were ever right for it do so, would require an overwhelming case. Here, amending legislation remains under consideration in Germany. We cannot begin to say that such a point has been reached ... the nature of the United Kingdom's response to the *Darkanzali* decision was a matter for the judgment of the Secretary of State; and in the exercise of that judgment his present decision not to re-designate ... could not be faulted.

Category 2 territories

Category 2 territories are those designated for the purposes of Part 2 of the EA 2003 by Order in Council (s 69(1)). In the Act, references to Category 2 territories are to those so designated (s 69(2)). **3.11**

At the time of writing (November 2012) the Extradition Act 2003 (Designation of Part 2 Territories) Order 2003[11] designates the following as Category 2 territories: **3.12**

> Albania, Algeria, Andorra, Antigua and Barbuda, Argentina, Armenia, Australia, Azerbaijan, The Bahamas, Bangladesh, Barbados, Belize, Bolivia, Bosnia and Herzegovina, Botswana, Brazil, Brunei, Canada, Chile, Colombia, Cook Islands, Croatia, Cuba, Dominica, Ecuador, El Salvador, Fiji, The Gambia, Georgia, Ghana, Grenada, Guatemala, Guyana, Hong Kong Special Administrative Region, Haiti, Iceland, India, Iraq, Israel, Jamaica, Kenya, Kiribati, Lesotho, Liberia, Libya, Liechtenstein, Macedonia, FYR, Malawi, Malaysia, Maldives, Mauritius, Mexico, Moldova, Monaco, Montenegro, Nauru, New Zealand, Nicaragua, Nigeria, Norway, Panama, Papua New Guinea, Paraguay, Peru, Russian Federation, Saint Christopher and Nevis, Saint Lucia, Saint Vincent and the Grenadines, San Marino, Serbia, Seychelles, Sierra Leone, Singapore, Solomon Islands, South Africa, Sri Lanka, Swaziland, Switzerland, Tanzania, Thailand, Tonga, Trinidad and Tobago, Turkey, Tuvalu, Uganda, Ukraine, Uruguay, the United Arab Emirates, the United States of America, Vanuatu, Western Samoa, Zambia, Zimbabwe.

Parties to international Conventions

The UK is a signatory to a number of international Conventions which place it under an obligation to criminalize certain types of conduct which have come to be known as 'international crimes'.[12] Specifically, the UK is required by these Conventions either to prosecute or extradite those accused of such offences who are found within its jurisdiction. Where a request for extradition for such an offence is made by a Category 1 or 2 territory then no difficulty arises in giving effect to this obligation to extradite. However, in order to fulfil this obligation in respect **3.13**

[11] SI 2003/3334, as amended: see App E5.

[12] See generally *R v Metropolitan Stipendiary Magistrate ex p Pinochet Ugarte (No 3)* [2000] AC 147; *Lodhi v Governor of HMP Brixton* [2001] EWHC (Admin) 178.

of a requesting state which has not been designated under the EA 2003 but which is a party to the relevant international criminal Conventions, s 193 allows for it to be designated by order for the purposes of that section.

3.14 The effect of designation is that the requesting territory is regarded as Category 2 territory, and the EA 2003 applies to it subject to the amendments in s 193(3)(a) and as if the conduct that constituted an extradition offence for the purposes of Part 2 were the conduct specified in the designating order.

3.15 The Extradition Act 2003 (Parties to International Conventions) Order 2005[13] has been made under s 193(1). Article 2 provides that each territory listed in column 1 of the Schedule to the Order (not being a Category 1 or Category 2 territory) is designated under s 193(1). In relation to any such territory, the conduct in respect of which the EA 2003 has effect by virtue of s 193(3)(b) is conduct to which the international Convention specified in relation to that territory in column 2 of the Schedule applies and specified in relation to that territory in column 3 of the Schedule.

Special extradition arrangements

3.16 The EA 2003 contains provisions in s 194 which allow a suspect to be extradited even if the requesting state is not a Category 1 or Category 2 territory. The agreement in such a case is known as a 'special extradition arrangement'.

3.17 Section 194 applies if the Secretary of State believes that arrangements have been made between the UK and another territory (which is not a Category 1 or 2 territory) for the extradition of a person to that territory (s 194(1)).

3.18 Where it applies, under s 194(2) the Secretary of State can issue a certificate to that effect. If he does so, the EA 2003 applies with the modifications in s 194(4) as if the requesting state were a Category 2 territory.

3.19 A certificate issued under s 194(2) is conclusive as to the existence of the conditions in s 194(1) (s 194(5)): see *Brown v Governor of HMP Belmarsh* [2007] EWHC 498 (Admin).

B. Jurisdictional Scope of the EA 2003; British Overseas Territories; The Republic of Ireland

Introduction

3.20 Extradition law in the UK is complicated by the fact that the UK is responsible for the extradition arrangements of British possessions including the Channel Islands, the Isle of Man, and British overseas territories. This section considers the application of the EA 2003 in this context.

3.21 Before the EA 2003 came into force, extradition from colonies to other countries and colonies was governed by a mixture of pre-EA 1989 legislation and provisions in the EA 1989 itself. The applicable law depended upon the identity of the colony and of the requesting state, and the result was an unwieldy tangle of legislation.

3.22 Although the EA 2003 simplifies the law considerably, it is nevertheless important to have a proper understanding of the UK's constitutional structure in order to understand its provisions.

[13] SI 2005/46.

The United Kingdom, Channel Islands, and the Isle of Man

The UK consists of England, Scotland, Wales, and Northern Ireland.[14] Section 226 limits the operation of parts of the EA 2003 to certain parts of the UK. Sections 157–160, 166–168, 171, 173, and 205 do not extend to Scotland (s 226(1)). Sections 154, 198, 200, and 201 extend to England and Wales only. Sections 183 and 199 extend to Scotland only. Sections 184 and 185 extend to Northern Ireland only. **3.23**

The Channel Islands consist of Jersey, Guernsey, Alderney, and Sark. They are not part of the UK[15] although the UK has responsibility for their external affairs. **3.24**

Similarly, the Isle of Man is not part of the UK although it became vested in the Crown in 1765.[16] The UK, the Isle of Man, and the Channel Islands together make up the British Islands.[17] **3.25**

Section 222 states that an Order in Council may provide that the EA 2003 extend to the Channel Islands or the Isle of Man with such modifications, if any, as are specified in the Order. **3.26**

Article 2 of the Extradition Act 2003 (Commencement and Savings) (Amendment) Order 2003[18] provides that the coming into force of the repeal of the EA 1989 by s 218(b) of, and Sch 4 to, the EA 2003 shall not apply for the purposes of the Bailiwick of Jersey, the Bailiwick of Guernsey, the Isle of Man; or any of the British overseas territories with the exception of Gibraltar, until such time as any provision which is made for (or by) the dependency or territory in question (whether under ss 177, 178, or 222 of the Act or otherwise) and which has the effect of replacing the provisions of the EA 1989 comes into force. **3.27**

In the case of Gibraltar the European Arrest Warrant Ordinance 2004 implements the EAW scheme but the EA 1989 applies in relation to all other British overseas territories. **3.28**

In Jersey, the Extradition (Jersey) Law 2004 (which mirrors the EA 2003) is in force. The Isle of Man has consulted on a draft bill and expressed an intention to enact a similar law. **3.29**

British overseas territories

Sections 177 and 178 of the EA 2003 deal with extradition to and from 'British overseas territories'. These territories, formerly known as dependent territories or colonies, are those specified in Sch 6 to the British Nationality Act 1981, as amended (see British Overseas Territories Act 2002, s 1(1) and 1(1)), namely: **3.30**

> Anguilla, Bermuda, British Antarctic Territory, British Indian Ocean Territory, Cayman Islands, Falkland Islands, Gibraltar, Montserrat, Pitcairn, Henderson, Ducie and Oeno Islands, St. Helena, Ascension and Tristan da Cunha, South Georgia and the South Sandwich Islands, the Sovereign Base Areas of Akrotiri and Dhekelia (ie the areas mentioned in section 2(1) of the Cyprus Act 1960), Turks and Caicos Islands, and the Virgin Islands.

In these territories, the EA 1989 will continue to apply until such time as fresh legislation is made by or for them under the enabling provisions in the EA 2003 to replace the EA 1989. The Extradition (Overseas Territories) Order 2002[19] extends with certain modifications, the provisions of the EA 1989 relating to extradition between the UK and Commonwealth countries **3.31**

---

14 Royal and Parliamentary Titles Act 1927, s 2(2); Interpretation Act 1978, Sch 1.
15 *Calvin's Case* 7 Co Rep 1, 21.
16 Isle of Man Purchase Act 1765.
17 Interpretation Act 1978, Sch 1.
18 SI 2003/3258.
19 SI 2002/1823, as amended.

or the British overseas territories to all the British overseas territories except Gibraltar. It also applies those provisions as appropriate so as to regulate extradition between the territories and the Republic of Ireland and the territories and the UK itself.

3.32 The enabling provisions in the EA 2003 are examined in the following paragraphs.

Extradition from British overseas territories

3.33 Section 177 applies in relation to extradition from British overseas territories to Category 1 and 2 territories (s 177(1)(a) and (c)), and to extradition from British overseas territories to the UK (s 177(1)(b)), and to the Channel Islands and to the Isle of Man (s 177(1)(d)).

3.34 Section 177(2) states that an Order in Council may provide for any provision of the EA 2003 applicable to extradition from the UK to apply to extradition from British overseas territories to Category 1 territories and the UK.

3.35 Section 177(3) states that an Order in Council may provide for any provision of the EA 2003 applicable to extradition from the UK to a Category 2 territory to apply to extradition from British overseas territories to a Category 2 territory, the Channel Islands, and the Isle of Man.

Extradition to British overseas territories

3.36 Section 178 deals with extradition to British overseas territories from Category 1 and Category 2 territories (s 178(1)(a) and (c)), and to extradition to British overseas territories from the UK (s 178(1)(b)), and the Channel Islands and the Isle of Man (s 178(1)(d)).

3.37 Section 178(2) states that an Order in Council may provide for any provision of the EA 2003 applicable to extradition to the UK to apply to extradition to British overseas territories from Category 1 territories and the UK.

3.38 Section 178(3) states that an Order in Council may provide for any provision of the EA 2003 applicable to extradition to the UK from a Category 2 territory to apply to extradition to British overseas territories from Category 2 territories, the Channel Islands, and the Isle of Man.

The Republic of Ireland

3.39 The UK and the Republic of Ireland are neighbours with close ties. Thus there are no immigration controls between Ireland and the UK. Also, the provisions for extradition between the UK and the Republic of Ireland have historically been much more simple and domesticated than the extradition procedures which applied to other foreign states. Ireland was almost treated as part of the UK, and vice versa, for the purposes of extradition.

3.40 Ireland was excluded from the EA 1989 by virtue of s 3(2)(iv) of that Act, and extradition between the UK and the Republic was governed instead by the Backing of Warrants (Republic of Ireland) Act 1965.[20] This Act allowed for the surrender of persons in accordance with a reciprocal system for backing and enforcing warrants between the two countries.

3.41 Ireland is a member of the EU and has been designated as a Category 1 territory. Accordingly return to Ireland is now governed by Part 1 of the EA 2003. The Backing of Warrants (Republic of Ireland) Act 1965 is repealed by EA 2003, s 218(a) and Sch 3.

---

20 *R v Governor of Belmarsh Prison ex p Gilligan* [2001] 1 AC 34.

C. Return within the British Islands

Return to Scotland and Northern Ireland from England and Wales

Although England and Scotland form part of the UK,[21] legally they are distinct countries.[22] In *Stuart v Stuart and Moore* (1861) 4 Macq 1, 49 Lord Campbell LC said: **3.42**

> . . . as to judicial jurisdiction, Scotland and England, although politically under the same Crown, and under the supreme sway of one legislature, are to be considered as independent foreign countries, unconnected with each other.

Equally, it is obvious that the public interest requires that the authorities on either side of the border within the UK should cooperate with each other with the minimum of formality in the investigation and prosecution of crime. **3.43**

Return from England and Wales to Scotland (and vice versa) is governed by a system of mutually enforceable arrest warrants. A warrant issued in England, Wales, or Northern Ireland for the arrest of a person charged with an offence may (without any endorsement) be executed in Scotland by any constable of any police force of the country of issue or of the country of execution as well as by any other persons within the directions in the warrant.[23] **3.44**

Similarly, a warrant issued in Scotland or Northern Ireland for the arrest of a person charged with an offence may (without any endorsement) be executed in England or Wales by any constable of any police force of the country of issue or of the country of execution as well as by any other persons within the directions in the warrant.[24] **3.45**

A warrant issued in England or Wales or Scotland, for the arrest of a person charged with an offence may (without any endorsement) be executed in Northern Ireland by any constable of any police force of the country of issue or of the country of execution as well as by any other persons within the directions in the warrant.[25] **3.46**

A person arrested in pursuance of a warrant must be taken, as soon as reasonably practicable, to any place to which he is committed by, or may be conveyed under, the warrant. **3.47**

Return from England to the Isle of Man, Guernsey, Jersey, Alderney, and Sark

As explained above, these islands are not part of the UK and they have a distinct legal system. A backing of warrants system operates to secure the return of criminal defendants. Section 13 of the Indictable Offences Act 1848 allows warrants issued in England to be endorsed and executed in the Isle of Man, Guernsey, Jersey, Alderney, and Sark, and vice versa.[26] **3.48**

---

[21] Union with Scotland Act 1706.

[22] *R v Manchester Stipendiary Magistrate ex p Granada Television Ltd* [2001] 1 AC 300, 304; *Stuart v Stuart and Moore* (1861) 4 Macq 1, 49.

[23] Criminal Justice and Public Order Act 1994, s 136(1).

[24] Criminal Justice and Public Order Act 1994, s 136(2).

[25] Criminal Justice and Public Order Act 1994, s 136(3).

[26] *Bryce-Richards v Attorney General of Jersey* [2003] EWHC 3365 (Admin). An Irish case concerning a person convicted and sentenced in Jersey who then absconded and fled to Ireland after being transferred to an open prison in England considers how the backing of a warrants system operates between Jersey and England (*Minister for Justice, Equality and Law Reform v Breen* [2008] IEHC 54).

4

INITIAL STAGES OF THE EXTRADITION PROCESS

A. Introduction

4.01 This chapter examines the provisions of the EA 2003 which deal with arrest, legal aid, bail, and the initial hearing in the magistrates' court. It also examines relevant parts of the Codes of Practice relating to Part 4 issued by the Secretary of State under s 173.[1] The Codes contain provisions relating to the detention and treatment of suspects arrested under the EA 2003.[2]

B. Arrest for the Purposes of Extradition

Introduction

4.02 The process of extradition begins with arrest. In the case of Category 1 territories there are two ways a defendant can be arrested. These are dealt with in ss 3–6. The first method is arrest under a 'Part 1 warrant' (defined in s 2(1)) which has been certified by a designated authority pursuant to s 2(7). The second method is arrest without a warrant under s 5. This is known as 'provisional arrest'.

4.03 The powers of arrest for the purposes of extradition to Category 2 territories are contained in ss 71–75. There are two methods of arrest, both of which require a warrant. The first method requires the Secretary of State to have received a valid request[3] for extradition to a Category 2

1 <http://www.homeoffice.gov.uk/publications/police/operational-policing/extradition-codes-of-practice>.
2 See para 4.62.
3 As defined in EA 2003, s 70(3).

territory under s 71. Once the request has been sent to an appropriate judge under s 72(1) the judge may then issue an arrest warrant under s 72(2). The second method, known as 'provisional arrest', takes place where a judge issues a warrant under s 74 before an extradition request has been received. This method is utilized where there are reasons to believe that the defendant would flee from the UK if he were alerted to the possibility of proceedings and the requesting state asks the UK to arrest the defendant before it submits its extradition request.

4.04 A Code of Practice, Code B, issued under s 173, contains detailed guidance about the procedures which should be followed upon and after arrest, and this guidance should be read alongside this chapter.

Arrest in Category 1 cases

Arrest under a Part 1 warrant

4.05 The process of arrest under a Part 1 warrant commences when the authority designated for the purpose under s 2(9) receives a Part 1 warrant in respect of a person. Sections 203 and 204 permit the warrant to be sent by fax or other electronic means (eg as an e-mail document).[4]

4.06 The Extradition Act 2003 (Part 1 Designated Authorities) Order 2003,[5] as amended, designates the Serious Organized Crime Agency (SOCA) and the Crown Agent of the Crown Office in Scotland as designated authorities, which allows both these bodies to certify Part 1 warrants in the UK.[6]

4.07 A Part 1 warrant is defined by s 2(2) to be an arrest warrant which is issued by a 'judicial authority' of a Category 1 territory and which contains either:

(a) in the case of a defendant accused of an offence, the statement referred to in s 2(3) and the information referred to in s 2(4), or
(b) in the case of a defendant who has been convicted, the statement referred to in s 2(5) and the information referred to in s 2(6).

4.08 Who, or what, are the 'judicial authorities' referred to in s 2 of the EA 2003? In many Category 1 territories, warrants are issued by persons or entities that are not independent of the Executive or the parties and thus would not generally regarded as 'judicial' in the normal (to common-law eyes) sense of that term. Article 6 of the EAW Framework Decision leaves it to each member State to determine who shall be its relevant judicial authority. The term 'judicial authority' in s 2 is not defined in the EA 2003, and was considered by the UK Supreme Court in *Assange v The Swedish Prosecution Authority* [2012] UKSC 22. The appellant was arrested on an EAW issued by the Swedish Prosecution Authority. He contended that the warrant had not been

4 EA 2003, s 212, contains provisions relating to Art 95 alerts issued before 1 January 2004. An Art 95 alert is an alert issued pursuant to Art 95 of the Convention implementing the Schengen Agreement of 14 June 1985: see para 21.37. The alert is intended as mechanism for ensuring the quick arrest of a fugitive offender within the state parties to the Agreement. Where an alert has been issued, s 212 provides that the alert should act as a Part 1 warrant, and that the EA 2003 should operate with the specified amendments.

5 SI 2003/3190.

6 SOCA is a national law enforcement agency under Home Office sponsorship which was established by s 1 of the Serious Organised Crime and Police Act 2005. It operates within the UK and collaborates (through its network of international offices) with many foreign law enforcement and intelligence agencies. It is also the UK Central Bureau of Interpol: see Chapter 21. On 1 April 2006 SOCA took over the functions of the National Criminal Intelligence Service (NCIS), which was formerly the designated authority for England and Wales. The Extradition Act 2003 (Part 1 Designated Authorities) Order 2003 was accordingly amended by the Serious Organised Crime and Police Act 2005 (Consequential and Supplementary Amendments to Secondary Legislation) Order 2006 (SI 2006/594) with effect from that date. SOCA is due to be incorporated into the new National Crime Agency (NCA) in 2013: <http://www.official-documents.gov.uk/document/cm80/8097/8097.pdf>.

issued by a judicial authority within the meaning of s 2 of the EA 2003. A majority of the UK Supreme Court held that the term 'judicial authority' in Part 1 of the EA 2003 bears the same meaning as it bears in the EAW Framework Decision, and that as used in the EAW Framework Decision, it includes public prosecutors.[7]

The statement referred to in s 2(3) is one that the person in respect of whom the Part 1 warrant is issued is accused in the Category 1 territory of the commission of an offence specified in the warrant, and the Part 1 warrant is issued with a view to his arrest and extradition to the Category 1 territory for the purpose of being prosecuted for the offence. This provision is considered in Chapter 2.[8] **4.09**

The information referred to in s 2(4) is: **4.10**

(a) particulars of the person's identity (s 2(4)(a));
(b) particulars of any other warrant issued in the Category 1 territory for the person's arrest in respect of the offence (s 2(4)(b));
(c) particulars of the circumstances in which the person is alleged to have committed the offence, including the conduct alleged to constitute the offence and the time and place at which he is alleged to have committed the offence, and any provision of the law of the Category 1 territory under which the conduct is alleged to constitute an offence (s 2(4)(c));
(d) particulars of the sentence which may be imposed under the law of the Category 1 territory in respect of the offence if the person is convicted of it (s 2(4)(d)).

If the warrant fails to contain these particulars then it is not a warrant within the meaning of Part 1 and so any extradition order founded upon it is liable to be quashed.[9] In *Office of the King's Prosecutor, Brussels v Cando Armas* [2006] 2 AC at para 28 Lord Hope of Craighead said: **4.11**

> If the warrant does not conform to the requirements set out in section 2, it will not be a Part 1 warrant within the meaning of that section and Part 1 of the Act will not apply to it. And if the offence that it describes is not an extradition offence within the meaning of section 64 or 65, as the case may be, the judge must order the person's discharge: section 10(3). In either of these two situations there is no way back for the judicial authority of a category 1 territory.

The provisions of s 2(4) are derived from Article 8(1) of the EAW Framework Decision and are subject to the common-law presumption that the EA 2003 was intended to be read consistently with the United Kingdom's international obligations under the EAW Framework Decision. But this presumption is subject always to the will of Parliament as expressed in the language of the EA 2003 read in the light of such other interpretative canons and material as may be relevant and admissible.[10] **4.12**

The requirements imposed by s 2(4) have generated a considerable amount of case law. The applicable principles can be summarized as follows. **4.13**

[7] In some member States, EAWs are issued by the Ministry of Justice, in particular in conviction cases. In *Ministry of Justice v Bucnys* [2012] EWHC 2771 (Admin) the High Court held that a Ministry of Justice may, or may not, qualify as a 'judicial authority' within the meaning of s 2, depending on the legal arrangements in the country for the issuing of EAWs. The UK Supreme Court will hear an appeal in that case in May 2013.

[8] Para 2.09.

[9] *Dabas v High Court of Justice, Madrid* [2007] 2 AC 31, para 50; *Vey v Office of the Public Prosecutor of the County Court of Montlucon* [2006] EWHC 760 (Admin); *Boudhiba v Central Examining Court No 5 of the National Court of Justice Madrid Spain* [2006] EWHC 167 (Admin); *Von Der Pahlen v Leoben High Court* [2006] All ER (D) 310 (June).

[10] *Assange v The Swedish Prosecution Authority* [2012] UKSC 22, para 217.

4.14 Section 2(4)(b) requires particulars to be given in the Part 1 warrant of any other warrant issued in the Category 1 territory for the arrest of the person in respect of the offence specified in the warrant. This refers to any domestic warrant on which the Part 1 warrant is based. It does not require particulars of any other warrant issued for the purposes of extradition.[11]

4.15 Section 2(4)(c) requires the warrant to be drafted with clarity.[12] However, it does not require the circumstances of the offence to be set out in great detail. It would be contrary to the purpose of the EAW scheme if too much detail were required.[13] Providing that the description in the warrant of the facts relied upon as constituting an extradition offence identifies such an offence and when and where it is alleged to have been committed, it is not necessary or appropriate to subject it to the requirements of specificity accorded to the particulars of a count in an indictment or an allegation in a civil pleading in the UK. However, a broad omnibus description of the alleged criminal conduct such as 'obtaining property by deception' will not suffice.[14] The warrant must contain enough information to enable the requested person to understand with a reasonable degree of certainty the substance of the allegations against him, namely, what he is said to have done, when and where, and also, in a case where knowledge of particular matters is an essential ingredient of the offence, sufficient information to enable him to understand why it is said that he had the necessary knowledge.[15] When considering a warrant, allowance should be made for the fact that the description of the offence was likely originally to have been set out in a different language and then translated into English.[16] The court should adopt an appropriate degree of strictness and vigilance when construing the warrant to ensure fairness, without getting caught up in fine points of technicality as to the precise meaning of words used in it.[17] A balance must be struck between the need, on the one hand, for an adequate description to inform the person of what is alleged, and on the other, the object of simplifying extradition procedures. The person sought by the warrant needs to know what offence he is said to have committed and to have an idea of the nature and extent of the allegations against him in relation to that offence. The amount of detail which is required depends on the nature of the offence. Where dual criminality is involved, the detail must also be sufficient to enable the transposition exercise to take place.[18] Section 2(4)(c) requires the description of the conduct to be correct, fair, and accurate. In an appropriately clear case the court may quash a warrant if the conduct is set out in a way which is misleading (eg, if it alleges an offence which cannot succeed as a matter of law in the requesting state).[19] Section 2(4)(c) requires the location of the offence to be specified clearly.[20] The term 'time' in s 2(4)(c) does not require the EAW to specify a

---

[11] *Louca v Public Prosecutor in Beilefeld, Germany* [2009] 1 WLR 2550, para 16, disapproving *Ruiz v Central Court of Criminal Proceedings No 5 of the National Court* [2007] 1 WLR 2798, paras 10–27.

[12] *Vey v Office of the Public Prosecutor of the County Court of Montluçon* [2006] EWHC 760 (Admin), paras 32–35; *Haynes v Court of Magistrates – A Maltese Judicial Authority* [2007] EWHC 2651 (Admin).

[13] *Taylor v Public Prosecutors Office, Berlin, Germany* [2012] EWHC 475 (Admin), para 11.

[14] *Dara v Public Prosecutor's Office, Marburg, Germany* [2007] EWHC 1678, para 5.

[15] *Dhar v National Office of the Public Prosecution Service for the Netherlands* [2012] EWHC 697 (Admin), para 117.

[16] *Fofana and Belise v Deputy Prosecutor Thubin Tribunal De Grande Instance De Meaux, France* [2006] EWHC 744 (Admin), para 39; *Lubomir Balint v Municipal Court in Prague, Czech Republic* [2011] EWHC 498 (Admin).

[17] *Sidlauskaite v Prosecutor General's Office of the Republic of Lithuania* [2006] EWHC 3486 (Admin), para 10.

[18] *Ektor v National Public Prosecutor of Holland* [2007] EWHC 3106 (Admin), para 7; *Kopycki v Provincial Court in Lodz, Poland* [2012] EWHC 744 (Admin), para 7.

[19] *Criminal Court at the National High Court, 1st Division v Murua* [2010] EWHC 2609 (Admin), para 58; cf *R (Castillo) v Kingdom of Spain* [2005] 1 WLR 1043.

[20] *R (Pillar) v Bow Street Magistrates' Court* [2006] EWHC 1886 (Admin), para 19.

precise date.[21] Section 2(4)(c) does not require the text of the foreign law to be set out.[22] It is not necessary for the court to examine the warrant to see how the pleaded conduct violates the foreign law.[23] However, the warrant must identify specifically the relevant provision of the foreign law.[24] Errors on the face of the warrant which are obviously merely typographical do not affect the validity of the warrant unless they are material and cause prejudice.[25]

Section 2(4)(d) requires that the warrant should contain particulars of the sentence which may be imposed under the law of the Category 1 territory in respect of the offence if the person is convicted of it. The rationale behind this provision is so that the appropriate judge can determine whether the punishability condition in the requesting state in s 64 or s 65 is made out.[26] However, it is not sufficient simply for the warrant to specify that imprisonment in excess of 12 months may be imposed; it must state the specific figure for the offence in question.[27] **4.16**

The 'statement in s 2(5)' referred to in s 2(2) is a statement that the person in respect of whom the Part 1 warrant is issued has been convicted[28] by a court in the Category 1 territory, and the Part 1 warrant is issued with a view to his arrest and extradition to the Category 1 territory for the purpose of being sentenced for the offence or of serving a sentence of imprisonment or another form of detention imposed in respect of the offence. **4.17**

The information contained in s 2(6) in relation to a convicted defendant is: **4.18**

(a) particulars of the person's identity (s 2(6)(a));
(b) particulars of the conviction (s 2(6)(b));
(c) particulars of any other warrant issued in the Category 1 territory for the person's arrest in respect of the offence (s 2(6)(c));
(d) particulars of the sentence which may be imposed under the law of the Category 1 territory in respect of the offence, if the person has not been sentenced for the offence (s 2(6)(d));
(e) particulars of the sentence which has been imposed under the law of the Category 1 territory in respect of the offence, if the person has been sentenced for the offence (s 2(6)(e)).

A warrant which fails to satisfy these criteria is not a Part 1 warrant for the purposes of the EA 2003.[29] **4.19**

Section 2(6)(b) does not necessarily require the date of the conviction to be specified. It is sufficient if there is sufficient other information in the EAW which enables the fact and circumstances of conviction to be ascertained.[30] Neither the EAW Framework Decision nor the EA **4.20**

---

21 *Crean v Government of Ireland* [2007] EWHC 814 (Admin), para 17; *Aryantash v Tribunal De Grand Instance, Lille, France* [2008] EWHC 2115 (Admin); *Skrzypczak v Circuit Court In Poznan* [2011] EWHC 1194 (Admin), para 21.

22 *Dabas v High Court of Justice, Madrid* [2007] 2 AC 31, para 53.

23 *Cebelis v The Prosecutor General's Office of the Republic of Lithuania* [2006] EWHC 3201 (Admin), para 9; *Dabas v High Court of Justice, Madrid* [2007] 2 AC 31, para 53.

24 *Hunt v Court of First Instance, Antwerp* [2006] EWHC 165 (Admin), para 17; *Hall v Government of Germany* [2006] EWHC 462 (Admin).

25 *Aryantash v Tribunal De Grand Instance, Lille, France* [2008] EWHC 2115 (Admin).

26 *Sidorowicz v Circuit Court Of Zielona Gora, Poland* [2012] EWHC 205 (Admin), para 9.

27 *Srama v District Court in Bydgoszcz, Poland* [2010] EWHC 3320 (Admin), para 21.

28 As amended by para 1 of Sch 13 to the Police and Justice Act 2006.

29 *Zakowski v Regional Court in Szczecin, Poland* [2008] EWHC (Admin) 1389, paras 3–4.

30 *Howell v Deputy Attorney General Court of Appeal of Douai, France* [2012] EWHC 150 (Admin), para 24; *Wozniuk v Regional Court in Bialystok* [2010] EWHC 3138 (Admin), para 9; cf *Sandi v Craiova Court of Romania* [2009] EWHC 3079 (Admin), para 30.

2003 specify that there must inevitably be a particular piece of information such as the date of conviction or sentence supporting the arrest warrant. The question is to be looked at in the round and without unnecessary technicality, but it is necessary that the totality of the information must give the necessary particulars of conviction so as to inform the defendant to enable him to know what he is going back to and what defences he might have, in both the UK and abroad.[31] The matter has to be assessed by reference to the EAW read as a whole.[32]

4.21 Section 2(6)(c) requires particulars to be given in the EAW of any other warrant issued in the Category 1 territory for the arrest of the person in respect of the offence specified in the EAW. This refers to any domestic warrant on which the EAW is based. It does not require particulars of any other EAW.[33]

4.22 Section 2(6)(e) does not require the warrant to state whether the sentence of imprisonment was suspended. It is sufficient to state the date upon which the sentence was imposed, as opposed to condescending to further detail as to whether that sentence was suspended or not.[34] This is because all the requested state needs to know is the length of the sentence in order to determine whether or not it falls within the scope of the EAW scheme.[35] Nor, where a defendant has been sentenced in respect of several different offences, does s 2(6)(e) require the warrant to state the overall effect of the sentences.[36] It is also sufficient compliance with s 2(6)(e), where the defendant has been convicted of more than one offence, for the warrant to specify the total sentence,[37] unless one of the offences is not an extradition offence and the court is unable to determine that sentences of sufficient length have been imposed for the offences which are extradition offences.[38] Thus, where a warrant states that a sentence has been imposed for offences which include an offence which is not an extradition offence, then it is not invalidated.[39] A warrant is not invalidated by reason of it incorrectly stating the remaining part of the sentence to be served.[40]

4.23 The designated authority may issue a certificate under s 2 if it believes that the authority which issued the Part 1 warrant is a judicial authority of the Category 1 territory, and that it has the function of issuing arrest warrants in the territory. As discussed above,[41] in many civil law jurisdictions, public prosecutors and other non-judicial officers have the power to issue arrest warrants.[42] It follows that a certificate may not be issued under s 2(7) unless the warrant has been issued by a judicial authority which has the power to issue an EAW. Where the designated authority issues a certificate it must certify that the authority which issued the Part 1 warrant is a judicial authority of the Category 1 territory, and that it has the function of issuing arrest warrants in the territory.

---

31 *R (Denis) v Regional Court in Warsaw* [2010] EWHC 3507 (Admin), para 18.

32 *Bader v Penal Division of the Veszprem County Court, Hungary* [2011] EWHC (Admin) 436, para 27.

33 *Louca v Public Prosecutor in Bielefeld, Germany* [2009] 1 WLR 2550 , para 16, disapproving *Ruiz v Central Court of Criminal Proceedings No 5 of the National Court* [2007] 1 WLR 2798, paras 10–27; *Office of Public Prosecutor of Hamburg, Germany v Hughes* [2009] EWHC 279 (Admin), para 6.

34 *Bulkowski v Regional Court of Elblag Poland* [2012] EWHC 381 (Admin), paras 18–22; *Kuchta v District Court of Czestochowa* [2010] EWHC 432 (Admin), para 8.

35 EA 2003, ss 64–65; *Bulkowski v Regional Court of Elblag, Poland* [2012] EWHC 381 (Admin), paras 20–22; *Pilecki v Circuit Court of Legnica, Poland* [2008] 1 WLR 325, paras 27–28; *Thompson v Public Prosecutor of Boulogne Sur Mer* [2008] EWHC 2787 (Admin), paras 26–27.

36 *Bartkowiak v Judicial Authority of Poland* [2012] EWHC 333 (Admin), para 15.

37 *Trepac v Presiding Judge County Court in Trencin, Slovak Republic* [2006] EWHC (Admin), para 15.

38 *Wiercinski v Second Criminal Division of the Circuit in Olsztyn, Poland* [2008] EWHC 200 (Admin).

39 *Kucera v District Court Of Karvina* [2008] EWHC 414 (Admin), paras 55–56.

40 *Pietrzak v Regional Court in Wloclawek, Poland* [2008] EWHC 2138 (Admin).

41 Para 4.08.

42 *Assange v The Swedish Prosecution Authority* [2012] UKSC 22.

Where a certificate has been issued under s 2(7), the person in respect of whom it has been issued can be arrested under s 3. The authority for the arrest is the Part 1 warrant and not the certificate. The warrant may be executed by a constable or a customs officer in any part of the UK (s 3(2)). The warrant may also be executed by a service policeman, subject to the conditions in s 3(3) and (4). **4.24**

Section 4 contains certain procedural safeguards for a person arrested under a Part 1 warrant. If neither the warrant nor a copy of it was shown to the person at the time of his arrest, and he asks to be shown the warrant, the warrant or a copy of it must be shown to him as soon as practicable after his request (s 4(2)). The person must be brought as soon as practicable before the 'appropriate judge' (s 4(3)). In England and Wales the appropriate judge is a district judge (Magistrates' Courts) designated for the purposes of Part 1 by the Lord Chancellor (s 67(1)). **4.25**

Section 4(4) provides that if either s 4(2) or (3) is not complied with the person must be taken to be discharged. A person arrested under the warrant must be treated as continuing in legal custody until he is brought before the appropriate judge under s 4(3) or he is taken to be discharged under s 4(4). **4.26**

Section 4(3) and (4) were considered in *Nikonovs v Governor of Brixton Prison* [2006] 1 All ER 927. The claimant was the subject of an EAW. The claimant was arrested at his home in Lincolnshire shortly before midday on Friday 16 September 2005. Those responsible for conveying the claimant to court were under the mistaken impression that Bow Street Magistrates' Court would be closed over the weekend and informed the police that the claimant would not be collected until the Monday. In fact the court was open on the Saturday. In the event, the claimant was not brought before the district judge at Bow Street until the afternoon of Monday 19 September. **4.27**

An application was made for his discharge under EA 2003, s 4(5). Among the issues before the court was whether the claimant had been brought before an appropriate judge as soon as practicable. In allowing the application for *habeas corpus*, Scott Baker LJ said at paras 21–22: **4.28**

> Whether or not the claimant was brought before the judge at Bow Street as soon as practicable is a question of fact.[43] Two points should be noted. First the criterion is practicable rather than the more elastic reasonably practicable. Second, the draftsman has chosen the practicability rather than the more precise criterion of a specified period as, for example, 48 hours in s 6(3) of the 2003 Act. There will no doubt be cases at the margins where views could reasonably differ whether the applicant was indeed brought before the appropriate judge as soon as practicable. But that is not this case. The only reason why Mr Nikonovs was not brought before the court on Saturday 17 September was because GSL Court Services were under the mistaken impression that the Bow Street court was closed on that day. No one suggests it was not practicable to bring him to London that day. He could have been brought to Bow Street and the district judge was very unhappy that he was not. He was not, in the event, brought before District Judge Wickham at Bow Street until 14.00 hrs on the Monday afternoon. In these circumstances I have no hesitation in concluding that the applicant was not brought before an appropriate judge as soon as practicable . . . District Judge Wickham should have directed Mr Nikonovs' release under s 4(5) because he was not brought before an appropriate judge as soon as practicable and was therefore no longer being lawfully held. For these reasons, therefore, it was in my judgment appropriate to grant a writ of *habeas corpus*.

Section 4(3) requires police officers to take all the steps which are practicable to effect a transfer as soon as possible after the arrest of a person under Part 1 of the EA 2003. The most basic step **4.29**

---

[43] On an application for *habeas corpus* following a ruling pursuant to s 4(5), the High Court's task is to determine whether the district judge's factual determination was reasonable: *Atlinski v Her Majesty's Prison Wandsworth* [2009] EWHC 2713 (Admin), para 11.

to be taken is to contact the courier services to ascertain the first time that they can undertake such a transfer.[44]

Provisional arrest

4.30 The provisional arrest powers in Part 1 of the EA 2003 permit arrest without a warrant in extradition cases.

4.31 Section 3(1) provides that a constable, a customs officer, or a service policeman, may arrest a person without a warrant if he has reason to believe that a Part 1 warrant has been or will be issued in respect of the person by an authority of a Category 1 territory, and that the authority is a judicial authority of the Category 1 territory and has the function of issuing arrest warrants in the territory.

4.32 A constable or a customs officer can arrest the person under s 5(1) in any part of the UK (s 5(2)). A service policeman may also carry out an arrest under s 5(1) subject to the conditions in s 5(3) and (4).

4.33 A person arrested under s 5 must be dealt with speedily. Within 48 hours of arrest he must be brought before the appropriate judge (s 6(2)(a)) and the documents specified in s 6(4) must also be produced to the judge within the same period (s 6(2)(b)). These documents are a Part 1 warrant in respect of the person and a certificate under s 2 in respect of the warrant.

4.34 If s 6(2) is not complied with the person must be taken to be discharged. The person must be treated as continuing in legal custody until he is brought before the appropriate judge under s 6(2) or he is taken to be discharged under s 6(5).

Arrest in Category 2 cases

4.35 The powers of arrest in Category 2 cases are contained in ss 71–75. There are two methods of arrest, which will be considered separately.

Arrest following receipt of Secretary of State's certificate (s 70)

4.36 This method is analogous to the procedure under the EA 1989 whereby a defendant could be arrested following receipt of an authority to proceed under s 8(1)(a) of the EA 1989.

4.37 Where, under s 70, the Secretary of State receives a valid request (as defined in s 70(3)) for extradition from a Category 2 territory then he must, subject to s 70(2), issue a certificate under s 70(1).[45] The certificate must be sent to the appropriate judge together with the documents specified in s 70(9). Section 203 permits faxed documents to be used as if they were original documents. More than one s 70 certificate can be issued to certify supplemental material sent by the requesting state after the initial request.[46]

4.38 Section 70(2)[47] permits the Secretary of State to refuse to certify a request where the defendant is a refugee. It is intended to prevent extradition proceedings that are bound to result in a finding by the judge that extradition is barred under s 81. It provides that the Secretary of State may refuse to issue a certificate under s 70 if he has power under s 126 to order that proceedings on the request be deferred; the person whose extradition is requested has been recorded by the Secretary of State as a refugee within the meaning of the Refugee Convention; or the person whose extradition is requested has been granted leave to enter or remain in the UK on

[44] *Atlinski v Her Majesty's Prison Wandsworth* [2009] EWHC 2713 (Admin), para 21.

[45] The Secretary of State's decision to certify can be challenged by way of judicial review: *Akaroglu v Government of Romania* [2007] EWHC 367 (Admin), para 38.

[46] *R (Edwards) v Secretary of State for the Home Department* [2012] EWHC 1660 (Admin).

[47] Inserted by para 17 of Sch 13 to the Police and Justice Act 2006.

the ground that it would be a breach of Article 2 or 3 of the European Convention on Human Rights to remove him to the territory to which extradition is requested. Although s 70(2) uses the word 'may', that does not confer any real discretion on the Secretary of State in a case where refugee status has been granted to the person in question, and where that status is not under active reconsideration by the Secretary of State. In such a case the Secretary of State *must* refuse to certify the request.[48]

Section 70(3)[49] provides that an extradition request is valid if it contains the statement referred to in s 70(4) or s 70(4A) and it is made in the approved way. The statement in s 70(4)[50] is one that the person is accused in the Category 2 territory of the commission of an offence specified in the request, and the request is made with a view to his arrest and extradition to the Category 2 territory for the purpose of being prosecuted for the offence. The statement in s 70(4A)[51] is that the person has been convicted of an offence specified in the request by a court in the Category 2 territory, and the request is made with a view to his arrest and extradition to the Category 2 territory for the purpose of being sentenced for the offence or of serving a sentence of imprisonment or another form of detention imposed in respect of the offence. **4.39**

A request for extradition to a Category 2 territory which is a British overseas territory is made in the approved way if it is made by or on behalf of the person administering the territory (s 70(5)). A request for extradition to a Category 2 territory which is the Hong Kong SAR is made in the approved way if it is made by or on behalf of the government (s 70(6)). **4.40**

A request for extradition to any other Category 2 territory is made in the approved way if it is made by an authority of the territory which the Secretary of State believes has the function of making requests for extradition in that territory, or by a person recognized by the Secretary of State as a diplomatic or consular representative of the territory (s 70(7)). **4.41**

The certificate issued under s 70 must certify that the request is made in the approved way and must identify the order by which the requesting state is designated as a Category 2 territory (s 70(8)).[52] The certificate is not required to state whether the individual is being sought as an accused or a convicted person.[53] **4.42**

Once the appropriate judge has received the documents mentioned in s 70(9)[54] (namely, the request and the certificate) he may issue an arrest warrant if the conditions in s 71(2) are satisfied, namely, if it appears to him that: **4.43**

(a) the offence in respect of which extradition is requested is an extradition offence, and
(b) where required, there is evidence falling within s 71(3).

Section 71(3) specifies the evidence required to justify a warrant being issued, namely: **4.44**

(a) in accusation cases, evidence that would justify the issue of a warrant for the arrest of a person accused of the offence within the judge's jurisdiction, if the person whose extradition is requested is accused of the commission of the offence;
(b) in conviction cases, evidence that would justify the issue of a warrant for the arrest of a person unlawfully at large after conviction of the offence within the judge's jurisdiction,

48 *District Court of Ostroleka v Dytlow* [2009] EWHC 1009 (Admin), para 13.
49 As amended by para 1 of Sch 13 to the Police and Justice Act 2006.
50 As amended by para 1 of Sch 13 to the Police and Justice Act 2006.
51 Inserted by para 1 of Sch 13 to the Police and Justice Act 2006.
52 As amended by para 17 of Sch 13 to the Police and Justice Act 2006.
53 *Akaroglu v Government of Romania* [2007] EWHC 367 (Admin), para 21.
54 As amended by para 17 of Sch 13 to the Police and Justice Act 2006.

if the person whose extradition is requested is alleged to be unlawfully at large after conviction of the offence.

4.45 The evidentiary threshold for the grant of an arrest warrant is low. In *R v Weil* (1882) 9 QB 701, 705 it was said that 'very little evidence will do'. Nonetheless, evidence in the proper sense is required. However, s 71(4) introduces an important modification of s 71(2) and (3) in the case of Category 2 territories which have been designated for the purposes of s 71 by an order made by the Secretary of State. In such cases, s 71(2) and (3) have effect as if 'evidence' reads 'information'. Section 71(4) mirrors ss 8(3) and (3A) of the EA 1989, which removed the requirement for 'evidence' in certain cases, and reversed the decision in *Re Dokleja*, 31 January 1994, CO/523/93, in which it had been held that 'allegations, assertions, and hints' were insufficient to justify the grant of an arrest warrant.

4.46 As at June 2012 the following countries have been designated for the purposes of s 71(4) by the Extradition Act 2003 (Designation of Part 2 Territories) Order 2003,[55] Article 3, as amended:

> Albania, Andorra, Armenia, Australia, Azerbaijan, Bosnia and Herzegovina, Canada, Croatia, Georgia, Hong Kong SAR, Iceland, Israel, Liechtenstein, Macedonia, FYR, Moldova, New Zealand, Norway, Russian Federation, Serbia and Montenegro, South Africa, Switzerland, Turkey, Ukraine, the United States of America.[56]

4.47 Once the warrant has been issued it may be executed in the manner provided for in s 71(5), (6), and (7). The warrant issued under this section may be executed in any part of the UK (s 71(7)). The warrant may be executed by any person to whom it is directed or by any constable or customs officer (s 71(5)(a)). It may also be executed even if neither the warrant nor a copy of it is in the possession of the person executing it at the time of the arrest (s 71(5)(b)).

4.48 If a warrant issued under this section in respect of a person is directed to a service policeman, it may only be executed in any place where the service policeman would have power to arrest the person under the appropriate service law (defined in s 71(8)) if the person had committed an offence under that law.

Proceedings after arrest

4.49 Section 72 provides safeguards for the arrested person following his arrest. If neither the warrant nor a copy of it was shown to the person at the time of his arrest, the warrant or a copy of it must be shown to him as soon as practicable after his arrest (s 72(2)).

4.50 After his arrest the person must be brought as soon as practicable before the appropriate judge (s 72(3)). In England and Wales the appropriate judge is a district judge (Magistrates' Courts) designated for the purposes of Part 2 by the Lord Chief Justice in consultation with the Lord Chancellor (s 139(1)). However, this requirement does not apply if the person is granted bail by a constable following his arrest, or the Secretary of State decides under s 126 that the request for the person's extradition is not to be proceeded with (s 72(4)).

4.51 If either s 72(2) or (3) is not complied with and the person applies to the judge to be discharged, then the judge must order his discharge (s 72(5)).[57]

---

[55] SI 2003/3334: see App E5.

[56] Subject to the revocation in the Police and Justice Act 2006, s 43(1) (not in force at the time of writing).

[57] cf EA 2003, s 4(4); *Nikonovs v Governor of Brixton Prison* [2006] 1 All ER 927; *Atlinski v Her Majesty's Prison Wandsworth* [2009] EWHC 2713 (Admin).

When the person first appears or is brought before the appropriate judge, the judge must (s 72(7)): **4.52**

(a) inform him of the contents of the request for his extradition;
(b) give him the required information about consent;
(c) remand him in custody or on bail.[58] If the judge remands the person in custody he may later grant bail (s 72(9)).

The required information about consent is defined by s 72(8) as information that: **4.53**

(a) the person may consent to his extradition to the Category 2 territory to which his extradition is requested;
(b) an explanation of the effect of consent and the procedure that will apply if he gives consent;
(c) that consent must be given in writing and is irrevocable.

Consent is dealt with in detail at Chapter 11. **4.54**

Provisional arrest under s 74

A provisional warrant is an emergency procedure for taking a person into custody. Hence, the issue of a provisional warrant is a relatively informal process. Although it is a preliminary step in the extradition process, at that stage the defendant is not, strictly, subject to extradition at all, and may never become so.[59] **4.55**

An application for a provisional warrant is generally made ex parte and those applying for the warrant are therefore under a duty to make full and frank disclosure to the court of all matters that are material to the judge's decision whether to grant the warrant.[60] More than one provisional warrant can be issued and be in force at the same time if new material comes to light to justify additional warrants.[61] The court has a discretion to hear representations from the defendant before issuing a warrant, although in practice the defendant and/or his legal representatives are seldom present at the hearing.[62] **4.56**

Section 73 empowers a justice of the peace to issue a provisional warrant if the conditions in the section are satisfied. Section 73 applies if the justice is satisfied on information in writing and on oath that a person who is within s 73(2) is (or is believed to be) either in or on his way to the UK. A person is within s 73(2) if he is accused in a Category 2 territory of the commission of an offence or he is alleged to be unlawfully at large after conviction of an offence by a court in a Category 2 territory. **4.57**

The justice of the peace may issue a warrant for the arrest of the person under s 73(3) if it appears to him that the offence of which the person is accused or has been convicted is an extradition offence, and there is written evidence falling within s 73(4). This is evidence that: **4.58**

(a) would justify the issue of a warrant for the arrest of a person accused of the offence within the justice's jurisdiction, if the person in respect of whom the warrant is sought is accused of the commission of the offence; and

[58] *Asliturk v HMP Wandsworth* [2010] EWHC 1720 (Admin).
[59] cf *R v Governor of Pentonville ex p Osman (No 3)* [1990] 1 WLR 878, 887; *Government of the Federal Republic of Germany v Sotiriadis* [1975] AC 1, 25.
[60] *Government of United States of America v Gavin Tollman*, 14 September 2006, Case E-1/05 (Ontario Superior Court of Justice); cf *R v Lewes Crown Court ex p Hill* (1991) 93 Cr App R 60.
[61] *R v Evans ex p Pinochet Ugarte*, The Times, 3 November 1998.
[62] *R v West London Stipendiary Magistrate ex p Klahn* [1979] 1 WLR 933.

(b) would justify the issue of a warrant for the arrest of a person unlawfully at large after conviction of the offence within the justice's jurisdiction, if the person in respect of whom the warrant is sought is alleged to be unlawfully at large after conviction of the offence.

4.59 However, if the Category 2 territory is designated for the purposes of s 73 by order made by the Secretary of State, s 73(3) and (4) have effect as if 'evidence' reads 'information' (s 73(5)). As at June 2012 the following countries have been designated by the Extradition Act 2003 (Designation of Part 2 Territories) Order 2003,[63] Article 3, as amended:

> Albania, Andorra, Armenia, Australia, Azerbaijan, Bosnia and Herzegovina, Canada, Croatia, Georgia, Hong Kong SAR, Iceland, Israel, Liechtenstein, Macedonia, FYR, Moldova, New Zealand, Norway, Romania, Russian Federation, Serbia and Montenegro, South Africa, Switzerland, Turkey, Ukraine, the United States of America.

4.60 A provisional warrant can be executed in any part of the UK (s 73(8)) by any person to whom it is directed or by any constable or customs officer (s 73(6)(a)). It may be executed even if neither the warrant nor a copy of it is in the possession of the person executing it at the time of the arrest (s 73(6)(b)).

4.61 If the provisional warrant is directed to a service policeman, it may be executed in any place where the service policeman would have power to arrest the person under the appropriate service law if the person had committed an offence under that law (s 73(7)).

C. Arrest and Detention of Extradition Defendants

Codes of Practice (s 173)

4.62 There was a lack of clarity about the status of persons arrested for the purposes of extradition under the EA 1989. Although they were cautioned on arrest and were taken to a police station as if they were ordinary criminal arrestees, their detention was not covered in terms by the Codes of Practice issued under the Police and Criminal Evidence Act 1984, and much was done on an ad hoc basis.

4.63 The EA 2003 removed much of this ambiguity by putting a range of police powers on a statutory footing for the first time in Part 4. These are considered in detail in Chapter 13. The status of extradition detainees is clarified, and their rights are defined, both in the statute and in the Codes of Practice issued under s 173.

4.64 Section 171 applies in relation to cases where a person is arrested under an extradition arrest power at a police station, or is taken to a police station after being arrested elsewhere under an extradition arrest power, or is detained at a police station after being arrested under an extradition arrest power. The extradition arrest powers are defined in s 174(2).

4.65 In relation to cases under s 171 the Secretary of State may by order apply the provisions mentioned in s 172(3) with specified modifications, namely, the following sections of the Police and Criminal Evidence Act 1984: s 54 (searches of detained persons); s 55 (intimate searches); s 56 (right to have someone informed when arrested); s 58 (access to legal advice).

4.66 Section 173 of the EA 2003 requires the Secretary of State to issue Codes of Practice in connection with the exercise of the powers conferred by Part 4, including the seizure and retention of evidence. The Codes are designed to provide guidance for officers in the handling of extradition

---

[63] SI 2003/3334: see App E5.

cases and the operation of police powers under the EA 2003. A failure by a constable to comply with a provision of the Codes does not of itself make him liable to criminal or civil proceedings (s 173(6)). The Codes are admissible in evidence in proceedings under the EA 2003 and must be taken into account by a judge or court in determining any question to which it appears to the judge or the court to be relevant (s 173(7)).

The Codes of Practice were laid before Parliament on 2 December 2003 and came into force on 1 January 2004.[64] The Codes are: **4.67**

Code B—Searches, seizure, retention, use and delivery of property
Code C—Arrest and detention and treatment of detained persons
Code D—Identification of persons

The Codes, which apply to police officers operating in England, Wales, and Northern Ireland and customs officers operating throughout the UK (para 1.12) must be readily available at all police stations for consultation by police officers, detained persons, and members of the public, and each police station in England, Wales, and Northern Ireland has been provided with a copy of them (paras 1.9 and 1.10). **4.68**

Caution on arrest

Code C, para 2.1 provides that an officer arresting a person under any of the powers in the EA 2003 must administer a caution in the following terms: **4.69**

> You do not have to say anything, but anything you do say may be given in evidence.

The arresting officer must take all reasonable steps to ensure that the person understands that they are being arrested and why they are being arrested. If necessary, the procedure should be repeated at the police station in the presence of an interpreter if there are language difficulties (para 2.6). Copies of relevant documents should also be served on the arrested person (para 2.4). **4.70**

Rights of the detainee

Code C specifies the rights which the detainee has whilst in police custody. These include the right to have someone informed of his arrest, the right to consult privately with a solicitor and to be told that free independent legal advice is available. **4.71**

Annex B to Code C contains a checklist of duties for the custody officer in extradition cases. These include ensuring that the detainee understands why he has been arrested, explaining the extradition process to him, ensuring that he is aware of his right to legal advice and to advice from his consulate or Embassy. **4.72**

Custody records

Code C, para 3 requires a custody record be opened and maintained as in a domestic criminal case. **4.73**

Treatment generally

Code C, paras 7–11 apply the relevant provisions of Code C issued under s 66 of the Police and Criminal Evidence Act 1984 relating to the right not to be held incommunicado, the right to legal advice, and so on. **4.74**

---

[64] Extradition Act 2003 (Police Powers: Codes of Practice) Order 2003 (SI 2003/3336). The Codes of Practice are available on the Home Office website at <http://www.homeoffice.gov.uk/publications/police/operational-policing/extradition-codes-of-practice>.

D. Legal Aid[65]

4.75 Legal aid is available for those arrested for the purposes of extradition proceedings. EA 2003, s 182, amends s 12 of the Access to Justice Act 1999 to include proceedings under the EA 2003 within the definition of 'criminal proceedings' in s 12(2) (s 12(2)(c)). This means that extradition proceedings qualify for criminal legal aid funding in accordance with the relevant regulations.[66]

4.76 Legal aid for counsel in the magistrates' court can be obtained under reg 12 of the Criminal Defence Service (General) (No 2) Regulations 2001[67] where the court is of the opinion that, because of circumstances which make the proceedings unusually grave or difficult, representation by both a solicitor and an advocate would be desirable.

E. Bail

4.77 The effect of ss 7(9), 8(1)(d), (2), 9(1), (4), (5), 72(9), 74(7)(c), (9), and 77(1) of the EA 2003 is that the defendant can be granted bail at any stage of the extradition proceedings in the magistrates' court.[68]

4.78 Section 198 of the EA 2003 makes a number of amendments to the Bail Act 1976 in respect of extradition proceedings. The effect of these is as follows.

Right to bail for extradition defendants

4.79 The most important change made by s 198 is that a defendant arrested for the purposes of extradition under the EA 2003 has the same right to bail under s 4 of the Bail Act 1976 as a domestic criminal defendant, except where he is alleged to be unlawfully at large after conviction of the offence in the requesting state.

4.80 Section 198 amends the Bail Act 1976 as follows:

(a) the exclusion of extradition proceedings in the Bail Act 1976, s 4(2), is deleted by s 198(4);
(b) s 4(2A), inserted by s 198(5), provides that the right to bail in s 4 applies when a defendant appears or is brought before a court in the course of or in connection with extradition proceedings in respect of the offence, or he applies to a court for bail or for a variation of the conditions of bail in connection with the proceedings;
(c) however, s 4(2B), also inserted by s 198(5), provides that s 4(2A) does not apply if the person is alleged to be unlawfully at large after conviction of the offence.

---

65 See *Stopyra v District Court of Lublin, Poland* [2012] EWHC 1787 (Admin), where the High Court described a number of problems relating to the grant of legal aid in extradition cases. The Court concluded that the current legal aid system is incompatible with the UK's obligations under the EAW Framework Decision and contrary to principles of justice in that it does not result in decision on legal aid being made within a proper timeframe. The Court said that the UK must put in place a legal aid system for EAWs which ensures that requested persons have speedy access to legal representation within a timeframe which is compatible with ensuring compliance with the time limits laid down in the Articles 11 and 17 of the EAW Framework Decision and which is consonant with the principles of justice. See also *Kozluk v Circuit Court Lublin* [2009] EWHC 3523 (Admin); *R (Jeziorowski) v District Court in Torun, Poland* [2010] EWHC 2112 (Admin); *Marusinski v Regional Court of Piatrkow, Poland* [2011] EWHC 1296 (Admin).

66 See <http://www.legalservices.gov.uk/docs/news/focus_cds14.pdf>.

67 SI 2001/1437.

68 *Asliturk v HMP Wandsworth* [2010] EWHC 1720 (Admin).

Powers of arrest in relation to absent defendants

Section 198(9) amends s 7 of the Bail Act 1976 and confers the power to arrest without a warrant where an extradition defendant has absconded. **4.81**

Reasons for refusing bail in extradition cases

Section 198(12) amends para 1, Sch 1 of the Bail Act 1976 so that the exceptions to the right to bail in Sch 1 apply when the judge is considering whether to grant bail in extradition proceedings. The most common exceptions are those in para 2, namely, that there are substantial grounds for believing that the defendant, if released on bail would fail to surrender to custody; commit an offence on bail; or interfere with witnesses. **4.82**

Section 198(13) inserts an additional ground for refusing bail in extradition proceedings. Paragraph 2B of Sch 1 provides that the defendant need not be granted bail in extradition proceedings if: **4.83**

(a) the conduct constituting the offence would, if carried out by the defendant in England and Wales, constitute an indictable offence or an offence triable either way; and
(b) it appears to the court that the defendant was on bail on the date of the offence.

Prosecution appeal against grant of bail

Section 200 of the EA 2003 amends s 1 of the Bail (Amendment) Act 1993 by inserting s 1(1A), which provides for a right of appeal by the prosecution (ie the person acting on behalf of the territory to which extradition is sought)[69] to the Crown Court against a grant of bail. Para 28 of Sch 13 to the Police and Justice Act 2006[70] substitutes the High Court for the Crown Court in s 1(1A), from 15 January 2007. **4.84**

Bail in the High Court

The inherent power of the High Court to entertain an application in relation to bail where a magistrates' court has granted or withheld bail, or has varied the conditions of bail, was abolished by s 17(2) of the Criminal Justice Act 2003. However, the power was re-introduced by s 22(1A) of the Criminal Justice Act 1967, inserted by Sch 13, para 27 of the Police and Justice Act 2006, with effect from 15 January 2007. **4.85**

The Administrative Court may also grant bail as an interim remedy where there are ongoing extradition proceedings before it. This is because, by s 17(6) of the Criminal Justice Act 2003, nothing in s 17 affects any other power of the High Court to grant or withhold bail or to vary the conditions of bail, or any right of a person to apply for a writ of *habeas corpus* or any other prerogative remedy. **4.86**

F. Role of the Crown Prosecution Service in Extradition Proceedings[71]

The Director of Public Prosecutions is the head of the Crown Prosecution Service (CPS). On 5 July 1996 the Attorney General formally assigned responsibility for extradition to the Director of Public Prosecutions under s 3(2)(g) of the Prosecution of Offences Act 1985. The CPS (and counsel instructed by it) represents the requesting state in nearly all extradition cases. **4.87**

[69] EA 2003, s 200(9).
[70] With effect from 15 January 2007.
[71] See generally *Government of Germany v Kleinschmidt* [2005] 3 All ER 759; *R (Raissi) v Secretary of State for the Home Department* [2008] 1 QB 836.

4.88 In *R v Director of Public Prosecutions ex p Thom* [1995] COD 194 the Divisional Court held that the role of the CPS under the EA 1989 was that of a private solicitor to the requesting state. Consequently, many of the CPS's powers, such as its power to discontinue proceedings under s 23(3) of the Prosecution of Offences Act 1985, do not apply in extradition cases.[72] In *R (Raissi) v Secretary of State for the Home Department* [2008] 1 QB 836, paras 135–140, the Court of Appeal made a number of observations about the CPS's role in extradition proceedings: (i) the CPS does not act as a prosecutor in extradition proceedings, but as a lawyer on behalf of a foreign client whose instructions it is generally bound to follow; (ii) however, the CPS must not act unquestioningly on its instructions. If a conflict arises between those instructions and its duty to the court then its duty is to withdraw from the case; (iii) the CPS's duty to the court includes a duty to ensure that the requesting state complies with its duty of disclosure. The CPS has a duty to disclose evidence about which it knows and which destroys or severely undermines the evidence on which the requesting state relies (including in relation to bail).[73]

4.89 The EA 2003 amends the Prosecution of Offences Act 1985 and provides a statutory basis for the CPS's conduct of extradition proceedings. Section 190(2) inserts s 3(2)(ea) and (eb) into the 1985 Act. This provides that it shall be the duty of the DPP to have the conduct of any extradition proceedings and to give, to such extent as he considers appropriate, and to such persons as he considers appropriate, advice on any matters relating to extradition proceedings or proposed extradition proceedings.[74]

4.90 Section 3(2A) of the 1985 Act, inserted by s 191(3), makes clear that s 3(2)(ea) does not require the DPP to have the conduct of proceedings where the requesting state asks him not to do so. This preserves the right of requesting states to retain private solicitors.

G. Determination of Preliminary Issues

4.91 The EA 2003 provides for a system of initial hearings in Category 1 cases at which the judge is required to dispose of preliminary issues relating to the defendant's identity and to set a date for the extradition hearing at which the substantive issues arising in the case are to be determined in accordance with the EA 2003.[75] In Category 2 cases identity and other preliminary issues are determined during the extradition hearing itself.[76]

The approach of the judge and the parties to extradition proceedings

4.92 In *R (Government of the United States of America) v Senior District Judge, Bow Street Magistrates' Court* [2006] EWHC 2256 (Admin) the Administrative Court made a number of observations about the way extradition proceedings should be conducted. The remarks were made in the context of a case in which there had been a dozen hearings over an 18-month period concerning a number of preliminary issues. The Government sought judicial review in order inter alia to secure an order that the extradition hearing should commence.

72 *Government of the United States of America v Tollman* [2008] EWHC 184 (Admin), para 145.

73 *Knowles v Government of the United States of America* [2007] 1 WLR 47, paras 34–35. Disclosure is considered at para 6.49.

74 In *R (Government of the United States of America) v The Senior District Judge, Bow Street Magistrates' Court* [2006] EWHC 2256 (Admin), para 124, the Administrative Court suggested that s 190 enables the CPS legitimately to assist a foreign state with the drafting of an extradition request.

75 EA 2003, ss 7–8.

76 EA 2003, s 78; cf *Asliturk v HMP Wandsworth* [2010] EWHC 1720 (Admin).

The Court made the following observations in paras 75–79: **4.93**

- Extradition proceedings are criminal proceedings, albeit of a special kind. The judge should apply the normal rules of criminal evidence and procedure to the extent that these are appropriate having regard to the specifics of the statutory schemes in Part 1 and Part 2.[77]
- The Criminal Procedures Rules 2005[78] apply to extradition hearings to the extent that they contain provisions relevant to such hearings.[79] The Rules impose upon the court a duty to manage the case[80] and upon the parties a duty to assist the court,[81] so that the overriding objective is achieved.[82] The Rules codify what were the pre-existing duties of the court and the parties.
- It may appear to be in the interests of a party resisting extradition to delay the extradition procedure. It is, however, the duty of the parties and those acting for them to cooperate in ensuring that extradition procedures comply as closely as possible with the statutory time limits. The timetables set out in Parts 1 and 2 of the EA 2003 should be complied with and extensions of time granted only in exceptional circumstances where the interests of justice so require.
- It will usually be desirable to hold a case management conference in advance of the extradition hearing to identify any issues that are likely to arise and so that the judge can give directions designed to ensure that these issues can be addressed without causing delay.

Initial hearings in Category 1 cases

Sections 7 and 8 specify the judge's duties at the initial hearing. **4.94**

Identity

Where the defendant has been arrested under a Part 1 warrant and brought before the judge under s 4(3), or the defendant has been provisionally arrested under s 5 and the documents received from the requesting state and produced to the judge, then the judge must hold a hearing to determine the questions arising under s 7 (s 7(1)). **4.95**

Under s 7 the judge is required to decide on a balance of probabilities (s 7(3)) whether the person before him is the person in respect of whom the Part 1 warrant was issued (s 7(2)). If he answers this question negatively then the defendant must be discharged (s 7(4)). If he answers the question affirmatively then he must proceed to decide the issues arising under s 8. There is no right of appeal by the appellant against a decision under s 7(2). The right of appeal lies only against an order of extradition.[83] **4.96**

Proving the defendant's identity in extradition matters is generally straightforward. For example, in *Savvas v Government of Italy* [2004] EWHC 1233 (Admin) the unusual nature of the surname of the person sought and the person in the dock and the fact they lived in the same London Borough were held to be sufficient to establish that the two people were in fact the **4.97**

---

77 *R v Governor of Brixton Prison ex p Levin* [1997] AC 741, 746–747.

78 Now the Criminal Procedure Rules 2012.

79 See Part 17 of the Rules. Note that the majority of the rules in Part 17 apply only in relation to extradition requests received before 31 December 2003, that is requests dealt with under the EA 1989.

80 Crim Proc R 3.2.

81 Crim Proc R 3.3.

82 In *Hubner v District Court of Prostejov* [2009] EWHC 2929 (Admin) the Administrative Court rejected the argument that the overriding objective enables the Court to refuse extradition on the grounds that the alleged extradition offence is trivial (in that case, theft of £20 of petrol). At para 7 the Court said that a court must, in the exercise of all its procedural powers, including those given by legislation, have in mind the overriding obligation to deal with cases justly, but that this cannot affect the way in which the substantive law is interpreted.

83 EA 2003, s 26; *Nikonovs v Governor of Brixton Prison* [2006] 1 All ER 927, paras 9–15; *Hilali v Central Court of Criminal Proceedings Number 5 of the National Court of Madrid* [2006] EWHC 1239 (Admin), para 19.

same. If a photograph has been supplied the judge is entitled to compare this with the person in the dock in order to determine whether they are the same person. Thus, in the vast majority of cases, identity is not in issue. Arresting police officers usually establish identity at the time of the arrest (by asking questions to elicit the suspect's name, date of birth, etc). Any conversation with the arrested person is ordinarily admissible as evidence in the extradition proceedings. Where identity is in issue the police carry out further checks and, where possible, conduct biometric testing. Admissions or statements by the person on arrest or in court may also be sufficient evidence of identity.[84]

4.98 Where the appropriate judge has decided the question of identity then a subsequent judge before whom the matter comes does not have jurisdiction to re-open the issue. The appropriate route of challenge is by way of judicial review.[85]

The power to adjourn

4.99 Section 7(6) provides that in England and Wales the judge has the same powers (as nearly as may be) as a magistrates' court would have if the proceedings were the summary trial of an information against the person. One of these powers is the power to adjourn proceedings.[86] It follows that the judge has the power to adjourn the initial inquiry until such time as the parties are in a position to adduce evidence about the defendant's identity.[87] In most cases there is no issue as to identity, however it is a matter which goes to the court's jurisdiction and, where it is in issue, the defendant is entitled to adduce evidence about it.[88]

Matters arising under s 8

4.100 If the judge decides that it is more likely than not that the person in the dock is the person to whom the Part 1 warrant relates, then he is required by s 7(5) to proceed under s 8. Section 8(1) requires the judge to do the following:

(a) fix a date on which the extradition hearing is to begin;
(b) inform the defendant of the contents of the Part 1 warrant;
(c) give the defendant the required information about consent;[89]
(d) remand the defendant in custody or on bail.

4.101 One of the purposes of the EA 2003 is to speed up the extradition process. To this end, the Act imposes time limits in a number of places.[90] Section 8(4) provides that the date for the extradition hearing which the judge is required to set by s 8(1)(a) must not be later than the end of the permitted period, which is 21 days starting with the date of the arrest referred to in s 7(1)

---

[84] *Re Bradshar*, CO/301/83; *Re Rodriguez*, 15 November 1984, CO/952/84; *Re Mullin*, 31 July 1992, CO/341/92; *Hilali v Central Court of Criminal Proceedings Number 5 of the National Court of Madrid* [2006] EWHC 1239 (Admin), para 18.

[85] *Stanczk v Circuit Court in Katowice* [2010] EWHC 3651 (Admin); *Hilali v Central Court of Criminal Proceedings Number 5 of the National Court of Madrid* [2006] EWHC 1239 (Admin), paras 19 and 20.

[86] Magistrates' Courts Act 1980, s 10(1). A decision concerning adjournment can be challenged by way of judicial review: *Olah v Regional Court in Plzen, Czech Republic* [2008] EWHC 2701; *R (Ras) v City Of Westminster Magistrates' Court* [2011] EWHC 562 (Admin).

[87] *Jeziorowski v Poland* [2010] EWHC 2112 (Admin).

[88] *Re Anthony*, 27 June 1995, CO/1657/94.

[89] Consent to extradition is considered in Chapter 11.

[90] Article 17 of the EAW Framework Decision specifies the period within which an EAW should be executed. The general rule is that a European arrest warrant is to be dealt with and executed as a matter of urgency. In cases where the requested person consents to surrender, the final decision on execution should be taken within a period of 10 days after consent has been given. In other cases, the final decision on execution should be taken within a period of 60 days after the arrest of the requested person, although this period may be extended by a further 30 days.

(a) or (b). However, s 8(5) provides that if, before the date fixed under s 8(1)(a) for the start of the hearing, a party to the proceedings applies to the judge for a later date to be fixed, and the judge believes there are exceptional circumstances, he may fix a later date. More than one extension can be granted.

In considering whether to grant an extension under these provisions the judge should keep in mind the requirements of Article 5(4) of the European Convention on Human Rights because he is required to act compatibly with the defendant's Convention rights as defined in the Human Rights Act 1998.[91] Article 5(4) guarantees detained persons the right to adequate time and facilities for the preparation of a challenge to the legality of their detention.[92] It follows that the judge must interpret the 'exceptional circumstances' criterion in s 8(5) so as not to infringe the defendant's right under the Convention to have sufficient time to gather evidence in support of his defence. **4.102**

The required information about consent referred to in s 8(1) is defined by s 8(3) to be: **4.103**

(a) the information that the defendant may consent to his extradition to the Category 1 territory in which the Part 1 warrant was issued;
(b) an explanation of the effect of consent and the procedure that will apply if he gives consent;
(c) that consent must be given before the judge and is irrevocable.

Preliminary hearings in Category 2 cases

Hearing following arrest under provisional warrant

Where a defendant has been arrested under a provisional warrant then s 74 applies. If neither the warrant nor a copy of it was shown to the defendant at the time of his arrest, the warrant or a copy of it must be shown to him as soon as practicable after his arrest (s 74(2)). The defendant must be brought before the appropriate judge as soon as practicable (s 74(3)). If either of these requirements is not complied with and the person applies to the judge to be discharged, the judge must order his discharge (s 74(5)).[93] However, if the defendant is granted bail by the police, or the Secretary of State decides under s 126 that the request is not to be proceeded with, then there is no requirement to produce the defendant before a judge (s 74(4)(a)). **4.104**

When the defendant first appears or is brought before the appropriate judge, the judge must, in accordance with s 74(7): **4.105**

(a) inform him that he is accused of the commission of an offence in a Category 2 territory or that he is alleged to be unlawfully at large after conviction of an offence by a court in a Category 2 territory;
(b) give him the required information about consent;[94]
(c) remand him in custody or on bail.

The required information about consent is defined by s 74(7) to be information: **4.106**

(a) that the person may consent to his extradition to the Category 2 territory in which he is accused of the commission of an offence or is alleged to have been convicted of an offence;

---

91 Human Rights Act 1998, s 6(1).

92 *Farmakopoulos v Belgium* (1992) 16 EHRR 187.

93 *Nikonovs v Governor of Brixton Prison* [2006] 1 All ER 927; *Atlinski v Her Majesty's Prison Wandsworth* [2009] EWHC 2713 (Admin).

94 Consent is considered in Chapter 11.

(b) containing an explanation of the effect of consent and the procedure that will apply if he gives consent;
(c) that consent must be given in writing and is irrevocable.

4.107 If the judge remands the defendant in custody he may later grant bail (s 74(8)).

4.108 Under the EA 1989 the period during which a defendant could be detained under a provisional warrant was limited.[95] The EA 2003 provides a similar restriction. Section 74(10) provides that the judge must order the person's discharge if the documents referred to in s 70(9) (request, etc) are not received by him within the 'required period'. This is defined in s 74(11) to be:

(a) 45 days starting with the day on which the person was arrested, or
(b) if the Category 2 territory is designated by order made by the Secretary of State for the purposes of s 74, any longer period permitted by the order.

4.109 The Extradition Act 2003 (Designation of Part 2 Territories) Order 2003,[96] Article 4, as amended, designates the following territories for the purposes of s 74(11)(b) with the relevant longer period for each territory following in brackets:[97]

> Argentina (65 days); Bolivia (65 days); Brazil (65 days); Chile (65 days); Colombia (65 days); Cuba (65 days); El Salvador (65 days); Guatemala (95 days); Haiti (65 days); Hong Kong Special Administrative Region (65 days); Iraq (65 days); Liberia (95 days); Libya (65 days); Mexico (65 days); Monaco (65 days); Nicaragua (65 days); Panama (95 days); Paraguay (95 days); Peru (95 days); San Marino (65 days); Thailand (65 days); the United Arab Emirates (65 days); the United States of America (65 days).

4.110 Once the documents specified in s 70(9) have been received, the judge must fix a date on which the extradition hearing is to begin, in accordance with s 76(1) and (2). The date fixed must not be later than the end of the permitted period, which is two months starting with the date on which the judge receives the documents (s 76(3)). However, if before the date fixed under s 76(2) a party to the proceedings applies to the judge for a later date to be fixed and the judge believes there are exceptional circumstances, he may fix a later date (s 76(4)). If the extradition hearing does not begin on or before the date fixed under this section and the person applies to the judge to be discharged, the judge must order his discharge (s 76(5)).

4.111 Section 78 requires the appropriate judge in Category 2 cases to determine a number of issues relating to the service of documents and the defendant's identity before he begins to consider questions relating to extradition offences and the bars to extradition. Unlike in Category 1 cases, these issues are considered following the commencement of the extradition hearing.[98]

H. The Secretary of State's Role at the Beginning of the Extradition Process[99]

4.112 Under the EA 1989 extradition from the UK was an executive act. As well as deciding whether to order extradition at the end of judicial proceedings, the Secretary of State was also required to decide whether to allow proceedings to commence at all. The mechanism by which he

95 *Quentin v Governor of Brixton Prison* [1998] COD 193; *Re Abdullah*, 2 May 1997, CO/1440/97.
96 SI 2003/3334.
97 The time periods are generally derived from the period specified in the extradition treaty with the state concerned: see App E5.
98 Para 6.12.
99 2011 Extradition Review, Part 9.

signified his consent was by issuing an authority to proceed under s 7 of the EA 1989 or an order to proceed under para 4(2) of Sch 1. He had a discretion whether or not to issue an authority to proceed, and in taking the decision he was required to consider a variety of factors including whether the offence was a political offence, whether interests of the UK would be harmed if the request was allowed to proceed, and whether he would in fact order extradition in due course.[100]

The authority to proceed was the foundation of the district judge's jurisdiction at committal. The Secretary of State was required to specify the English offences which it appeared to him were constituted by the foreign conduct, and the district judge had no jurisdiction to commit for any offence not included on the authority to proceed.[101] Any defect in the authority to proceed rendered the committal unlawful.[102] **4.113**

In practice, the Secretary of State very seldom refused to issue an authority to proceed and the courts discouraged challenges by the applicant to his decision to issue an authority to proceed.[103] **4.114**

The Home Office Consultation Paper of March 2001 made the case for reducing the Secretary of State's role in extradition proceedings, and for removing it altogether in some cases.[104] These proposals are largely reflected in the EA 2003. In the following paragraphs the Secretary of State's role at the beginning of the extradition process is examined. **4.115**

Category 1 cases

The EA 2003 removes the Secretary of State entirely from the process in Category 1 cases save in exceptional cases. The Part 1 warrant is received by the designated authority under s 2(1), and forwarded directly to the appropriate judge if the formalities required by s 2 are complied with. The Extradition Act 2003 (Part 1 Designated Authorities) Order 2003,[105] as amended, designates SOCA and the Crown Agent of the Crown Office in Scotland as designated authorities. **4.116**

Competing claims (s 179)

The Secretary of State can become involved in a Category 1 case if he is required to exercise his powers under s 179 to regulate competing claims to extradition under Part 1 and Part 2. These powers are considered at para 8.45. **4.117**

National security cases (s 208)

The Secretary of State may intervene to stop extradition proceedings on national security grounds. Section 208 is intended to prevent the extradition of members of the intelligence services including the Security Service (MI5), the Secret Intelligence Service (MI6), and GCHQ, for offences committed in the course of their work. **4.118**

Section 208 applies if the Secretary of State believes that the conditions in s 208(2)–(4) are satisfied in relation to a person. The first condition is that the defendant's extradition is sought **4.119**

---

100 *R v Chief Metropolitan Stipendiary Magistrate ex p Government of Denmark* (1983) 79 Cr AppR 1, 11; 2011 Extradition Review, para 3.89

101 *In Re Nielsen* [1984] AC 606, 619.

102 *Re Farinha* [1992] Imm LR 174.

103 *Government of United States of America v Bowe* [1990] 1 AC 500; *R v Governor of Brixton Prison ex p Kahan* [1989] QB 716; *R v Secretary of State for the Home Department ex p Pinochet Ugarte*, 27 May 1999 (CO/1786/99).

104 Paras 80 and 81.

105 SI 2003/3190.

or will be sought under Part 1 or Part 2 in respect of an offence. The second condition is that, in engaging in the conduct constituting the offence, the person was acting for the purpose of assisting in the exercise of a function conferred or imposed by or under an enactment, or as a result of an authorization given by the Secretary of State the person is not liable under the criminal law of any part of the UK for the conduct constituting (or alleged to constitute) the offence. The third condition is that the person's extradition in respect of the offence would be against the interests of national security.

4.120 Where he considers these conditions are satisfied, the Secretary of State may certify as such under s 208(5). Where he issues such a certificate he may direct that a Part 1 warrant issued in respect of the person and in respect of the offence is not to be proceeded with, or direct that a request for the person's extradition in respect of the offence is not to be proceeded with and/or he may order his discharge (s 208(6) and (7)). Section 208(8) contains procedural provisions for giving effect to any directions given by the Secretary of State on national security grounds.

Category 2 cases

4.121 The Secretary of State also has a limited role in Category 2 cases.

Section 70 certificate

4.122 Where the Secretary of State receives a valid request from a Category 2 territory, then he must (subject to s 70(2) and s 126) issue a certificate under s 70(1) containing the statement required by s 70(8). Section 70(2), as amended by Sch 13 to the Police and Justice Act 2006, enables the Secretary of State to refuse to issue a certificate where the person sought is a refugee. If the Secretary of State issues his certificate, he then must send the request, the certificate, and a copy of the relevant order to the appropriate judge (s 70(9)).

4.123 The Secretary of State's decision to certify an extradition request under s 70 can be challenged by way of judicial review.[106]

Competing extradition requests

4.124 Section 126 deals with competing extradition requests. It applies if:

(a) the Secretary of State receives a valid request for a person's extradition to a Category 2 territory;
(b) the person is in the UK;

and before the person is extradited in pursuance of the request or discharged, the Secretary of State receives another valid request for the person's extradition.

4.125 Where these conditions are satisfied the Secretary of State may do one of two things.

(a) If neither of the requests has been disposed of, he can order proceedings (or further proceedings) on one of the requests to be deferred until the other one has been disposed of.
(b) Alternatively, if an order for extradition in pursuance of the request under consideration has been made, he can order the person's extradition to be deferred until the other request has been disposed of.

---

106 *Akaroglu v Government of Romania* [2007] EWHC 367 (Admin), *R (Bleta) v Secretary of State for the Home Department* [2005] 1 WLR 3194.

In taking these decisions, s 126(3) requires the Secretary of State to take into account the relative seriousness of the offences concerned; the place where each offence was committed (or was alleged to have been committed); the date when each request was received; and whether, in the case of each offence, the person is accused of its commission (but not alleged to have been convicted) or is alleged to be unlawfully at large after conviction. These powers are considered further at para 8.49. **4.126**

National security

The Secretary of State can also intervene in Part 2 cases on national security grounds under s 208. **4.127**

5

THE EXTRADITION HEARING IN CATEGORY 1 CASES

A. Introduction

In this chapter the appropriate judge's duties and functions in an extradition hearing under Part 1 of the EA 2003 are considered. This is the hearing at which the appropriate judge[1] must decide whether to order the extradition of the defendant in respect of whom a Part 1 warrant has been issued (s 68(1)).[2] Some of the sections of the EA 2003 considered in this chapter in relation to Part 1 cases have equivalent provisions in Part 2. Therefore, some parts of this chapter are also relevant in Part 2 cases, and appropriate cross-references are given in Chapter 6, which examines the extradition hearing in Part 2 cases. **5.01**

[1] In England and Wales the appropriate judge is a district judge (Magistrates' Courts) designated for the purposes of Part 1 by the Lord Chief Justice after consulting with the Lord Chancellor (s 67(1)(a), as amended). Part 1 and Part 2 of the EA 2003 are both structured so that the appropriate judge must decide a sequential series of issues before the extradition order can be made. This raises the question of whether, one judge having commenced hearing a case, he must continue to do so. S 67(3A) and s 139(3A), inserted by para 13 of Sch 13 to the Police and Justice Act 2006, provide that the use of the expression 'the judge' in a section containing a previous reference to 'the appropriate judge' or 'the judge' does not in itself require both references to be read as referring to the same individual.

[2] The equivalent hearings under the EA 1989 were known as 'committal hearings'.

The scheme under the EA 1989[3]

5.02 Extradition proceedings under the EA 1989 involved a three-stage process. First, there were committal proceedings before the district judge. The district judge's functions at committal were relatively circumscribed. His task was principally to assess the evidence (where a prima facie case had to be proved under Part III or Sch 1), or decide whether the conduct alleged was an extradition crime in cases where no evidence was required. If the defendant sought to rely on s 6 (discrimination on grounds of race, etc) or another statutory bar then the judge was required to determine whether they were applicable.

5.03 Lord Templeman described the process in European cases under the EA 1989 in *In re Evans* [1994] 1 WLR 1006, 1010–1111:

> There are thus six steps in the extradition of a suspect from the United Kingdom. First, the foreign court must consider that a charge of serious crime has been properly laid against the suspect on the basis of information which justifies the issue of a warrant for his arrest. Secondly, the administration of the foreign country must consider that the charge, the law of the foreign country and the circumstances justify a request for extradition in accordance with the provisions of the Convention. Thirdly, the foreign state must identify the suspect, authenticate the foreign warrant for his arrest, give particulars of the alleged conduct which constitutes the offence and produce a translation of the relevant foreign law which establishes the offence and makes it punishable by 12 months' imprisonment or more. Fourthly, the Secretary of State must satisfy himself that the request is in order. The Secretary of State must then satisfy himself that equivalent conduct in the United Kingdom would constitute an offence under the law of the United Kingdom punishable by 12 months' imprisonment or more. The Secretary of State may then issue an authority to proceed and must identify and specify the relevant law of the United Kingdom. Fifthly, the metropolitan magistrate sitting as a court of committal must be satisfied, after he has heard representations, that the alleged conduct would constitute a serious offence in the foreign state and in the United Kingdom. In other words the magistrate must be satisfied that a charge of serious crime offensive in the foreign country and offensive in the United Kingdom has been properly laid against the accused. The suspect can then be committed and the magistrate must certify the offence against the law of the United Kingdom which would be constituted by his conduct. Sixthly, subject to any *habeas corpus* proceedings, the Secretary of State may enforce extradition.

5.04 If the defendant was committed by the district judge to await the Secretary of State's decision on his extradition, the second stage was for him to apply to the High Court for a writ of *habeas corpus ad subjiciendum*. In his application he could challenge decisions taken by the district judge during the committal proceedings. The High Court also enjoyed an original jurisdiction to discharge the defendant on the grounds set out in s 6 and s 11 (triviality, delay, and bad faith).

5.05 Finally, if the High Court dismissed the application for *habeas corpus*, the Secretary of State had to consider whether to order return under s 12. He enjoyed a broad discretion, but was precluded from doing so on the grounds set out in s 12; following the coming into force of the Human Rights Act 1998, if it would be contrary to the defendant's Convention rights as defined in s 1 of that Act;[4] or if it would be otherwise 'wrong, unjust or oppressive' to extradite the defendant.[5]

The scheme under the EA 2003

5.06 The scheme contained in the EA 2003 represents a fundamentally different approach as compared with the EA 1989. Virtually all of the issues arising in connection with the extradition

---

[3] 2011 Extradition Review, para 3.69 et seq.
[4] Human Rights Act 1998, s 6(1).
[5] *Atkinson v Government of the United States of America* [1971] AC 197, 232.

request now have to be decided by the appropriate judge. There is a right of appeal to the High Court against the judge's decision to order or refuse extradition, however the original jurisdiction that the High Court enjoyed under ss 6 and 11(3) of the EA 1989 has been removed. The High Court's function in appeals under the EA 2003 is to act as a court of appeal from the appropriate judge's decision. Appeals are considered in Chapter 9. The Secretary of State has virtually no role to play in Category 1 cases, and only a limited role in Category 2 cases.[6]

B. Extradition Hearings under Part 1: A Summary

Part 1 of the EA 2003 is intended to achieve speedy and simple extradition, as envisaged in the EAW Framework Decision.[7] Those sections of Part 1 of the EA 2003 which implement the EAW Framework Decision should be interpreted in light of it so as to give effect to it, not because of the Community law interpretive obligation requiring states to interpret their domestic law to be consistent with Community law,[8] or because of the European Communities Act 1972,[9] but because of the analogous common-law rule which presumes that Parliament intends to legislate consistently with the UK's international obligations.[10] In *Office of the King's Prosecutor v Cando Armas* [2006] 2 AC 1, Lord Bingham of Cornhill said at para 8:[11] **5.07**

> Part 1 of the 2003 Act did not effect a simple or straightforward transposition, and it did not on the whole use the language of the Framework Decision. But its interpretation must be approached on the twin assumptions that Parliament did not intend the provisions of Part 1 to be inconsistent with the Framework Decision and that, while Parliament might properly provide for a greater measure of cooperation by the United Kingdom than the Decision required, it did not intend to provide for less.

[6] Para 4.107, para 4.116, para 4.121, and para 8.04.

[7] *Hilali v Central Court of Criminal Proceedings Number 5 of the National Court of Madrid* [2006] EWHC 1239 (Admin), para 3. The EA 2003 and Part 1 in particular has been criticized for the quality of its drafting and complexity: see Spencer, 'Implementing the European Arrest Warrant: A Tale of How Not To Do It' (2009) 30(3) Statute Law Review 184.

[8] Which, at the European level, includes Framework Decisions: *Criminal Proceedings against Pupino* (Case C-105/03) [2006] QB 83; cf *Assange v The Swedish Prosecution Authority* [2012] UKSC 22, para 202, para 217.

[9] The EAW Framework Decision, the Court of Justice's decision in *Criminal Proceedings against Pupino* (Case C-105/03) [2006] QB 83, and the European legal principle of conforming interpretation are not part of UK law under the European Communities Act 1972: *Assange v The Swedish Prosecution Authority* [2012] UKSC 22, para 217.

[10] *Assange v The Swedish Prosecution Authority* [2012] UKSC 22 *per* Lord Phillips at para 10 and para 77; Lord Brown at para 98; Lord Kerr at para 112; Lord Dyson at paras 122–123; Lord Mance at paras 201–218.

[11] Lord Hope of Craighead at para 24 of *Office of the King's Prosecutor v Cando Armas* [2006] 2 AC 1 adopted what might appear to be a conflicting approach. He expressed the view that the task of interpreting Part 1 so as to give effect to the EAW Framework Decision should be approached on the assumption that, where there were differences, these were regarded by Parliament as a necessary protection against an unlawful infringement on the right to liberty. Both Lord Bingham and Lord Hope in *Dabas v High Court of Justice in Madrid, Spain* [2007] 2 AC 31 returned to this topic after the Grand Chamber of the Court of Justice of the European Communities had commented on it when giving a preliminary ruling in *Criminal Proceedings against Pupino* ECAS ELR (Case C-105/03) [2006] QB 83. Lord Hope, after citing from *Pupino*, referred with approval to Lord Bingham's statement in *Cando Armas* and remarked that the imposition of additional formalities not found in the EAW Framework Decision by one member State to suit its own purposes would tend to frustrate the objectives of the Decision. See also *Assange v The Swedish Prosecution Authority* [2012] UKSC 22, para 7, paras 204–205; *Caldarelli v Judge for Preliminary Investigations of the Court of Naples, Italy* [2008] 1 WLR 1724, para 23; *Dabas v High Court of Justice in Madrid, Spain* [2007] 2 AC 31, para 35.

5.08 The steps in an extradition hearing in a Category 1 case can be summarized as follows:

(a) The appropriate judge must first decide whether the offence specified in the Part 1 warrant is an extradition offence (s 10(2)).
(b) If it is not, then the defendant has to be discharged.
(c) If it is, the judge must go on to consider whether any of the bars to extradition specified in s 11 are applicable.
(d) If none of them are, and the defendant is alleged to be unlawfully at large after conviction, the judge must then consider whether the defendant falls to be discharged under s 20 (convictions in absence).
(e) If s 20 does not apply, or the restrictions in it are not made out, the judge must then consider whether extradition would violate the defendant's rights under the Human Rights Act 1998 (s 21).
(f) If it would not, he must order the defendant's extradition to the requesting Category 1 territory.
(g) The extradition hearing is then at an end. Subject to any appeal by the defendant to the High Court or the Supreme Court, he is liable to be extradited.

5.09 Part 1 thus prescribes both the questions the judge has to decide and the order in which he has to decide them. In *Raffile v Government of the United States of America* [2005] 1 All ER 889 the Administrative Court held that the judge is able to re-open questions that he has already decided if issues are raised later in the proceedings which affect them.[12]

C. The Judge's Powers at the Extradition Hearing

5.10 Section 9(1) of the EA 2003 provides that in England and Wales at the extradition hearing the appropriate judge has the same powers (as nearly as may be) as a magistrates' court would have if the proceedings were the summary trial of an information against the person in respect of whom the Part 1 warrant was issued. This provision applies the general powers of a magistrates' court in Part I of the Magistrates Courts' Act 1980.

5.11 Where the judge adjourns the extradition hearing he must remand the person in custody or on bail (s 9(4)). If the defendant is remanded in custody he may later be granted bail (s 9(5)).[13]

5.12 The judge is entitled to adjourn the extradition hearing and call for further information from the requesting state if necessary.[14] Decisions about adjournments should be challenged by way of judicial review, rather than as part of the statutory appeals process.[15]

---

[12] See para 6.08.

[13] Bail is dealt with at para 4.77.

[14] *Dabas v High Court of Justice in Madrid, Spain* [2007] 2 AC 31, para 49; *Vey v Office of the Public Prosecutor of the County Court of Montluçon* [2006] EWHC 760 (Admin), para 16; *R (Government of the United States of America) v Senior District Judge, Bow Street Magistrates' Court* [2006] EWHC 2256 (Admin), para 89.

[15] *Ras v City of Westminster Magistrates' Court* [2011] EWHC 562 (Admin); *R (Slavik) v District Court of Nitra, Slovak Republic* [2011] EWHC 265 (Admin); *R (Koniak) v Regional Court for Warsaw, Poland* [2010] EWHC 3501 (Admin); *Kaminski and others v Judicial Authority of Poland* [2010] EWHC 2772 (Admin); *R (Roszas) v Baranya County Court, Hungary* [2010] EWHC 1265 (Admin); *Olah v Regional Court in Plzen, Czech Republic* [2008] EWHC 2701 (Admin); *Slator v Bow Street Magistrates' Court* [2006] EWHC 2628 (Admin); *R (Handa) v Bow Street Magistrates' Court* [2004] EWHC 3116.

D. Burden and Standard of Proof

Section 206 contains general provisions relating to the burden and standard of proof. **5.13**

Section 206(1) applies if, in proceedings under the EA 2003, a question arises as to burden or standard of proof (for example, in relation to whether the defendant deliberately absented himself from his trial).[16] By s 206(2), the question must be decided by applying any enactment or rule of law that would apply if the proceedings were proceedings for an offence. Any enactment or rule of law so applied must be applied as if the person whose extradition is sought (or who has been extradited) were accused of an offence and the Category 1 or Category 2 territory concerned were the prosecution.[17] **5.14**

Standard of proof in relation to identity

In Part 1 cases, s 7(3) provides that the judge is to decide the question of whether the person arrested is the person mentioned in the Part 1 warrant on the balance of probabilities.[18] **5.15**

E. Authentication of Documents

Authentication refers to the form of the documents used in extradition proceedings. Only documents that are in the form prescribed in the EA 2003 are authenticated and so receivable in evidence. The process of authentication under s 202 makes potentially admissible in evidence in extradition proceedings documents containing written statements of fact, notwithstanding that under English rules of evidence what appears in the statement would only be admissible in the form of oral testimony given on oath by the maker of the statement. The purpose of s 202 is to obviate the necessity of bringing witnesses from the requesting state to give oral evidence in the extradition proceedings.[19] However, authentication does not, by itself, make the contents of the document admissible in evidence. In cases where evidence is required then the contents of the document must still be admissible according to the ordinary rules of evidence, read together with the hearsay provisions in Part 2 cases.[20] **5.16**

Section 202(1) provides that a Part 1 warrant may be received in evidence in proceedings under the EA 2003. Sections 203 and 204 permit faxed or electronic copies to be used also. **5.17**

By s 202(2) and (3), any other document issued in a Category 1 or Category 2 territory may be received in evidence if it is duly authenticated. Section 202(4), as amended by para 26 to Sch 13 to the Police and Justice Act 2006, provides that a document issued in a Category 1 or Category 2 territory is duly authenticated if (and only if) it purports to be signed by a judge, magistrate, or officer of the territory; it purports to be certified, whether by seal or otherwise, by the Ministry or Department of the territory responsible for justice or for foreign affairs; or **5.18**

---

16 *B v District Court in Trutnov* [2011] EWHC 963 (Admin); *Benko v Hungary* [2009] EWHC 3530; *Murtati v Albania* [2008] EWHC 2856.

17 *Kociukow v District Court of Bialystok III Penal Division* [2006] EWHC 56 (Admin), para 9 (applying s 206 in the context of abuse of process).

18 *Savvas v Government of Italy* [2004] EWHC 1233 (Admin). S 78(5) is the equivalent provision in Part 2 cases. The question of identity in Part 2 cases is dealt with at para 6.17.

19 *Friesel v Government of the United States of America* [2009] EWHC 1659 (Admin), para 33; *Savvas v Government of Italy* [2004] EWHC 1233 (Admin), para 9; *Dowse v Governor of Pentonville Prison* [1983] 2 AC 464 (considering the analogous provision in the EA 1870).

20 *Fernandes v Governor of HM Prison Brixton* [2004] EWHC 2207 (Admin), para 47. Hearsay is considered at para 6.53.

it purports to be authenticated by the oath or affirmation of a witness. In the last case, the oath must be given in court in the UK and not the requesting state.[21]

5.19 In *Schtraks v Government of Israel* [1964] AC 556, 582 the House of Lords held that material submitted by the defendant in support of his religious persecution submissions did not have to be authenticated as required by the EA 1870. Section 202(5) of the EA 2003 provides that the authentication requirements in s 202(2) and (3) do not prevent a document that is not duly authenticated from being received in evidence in proceedings under the EA 2003. This preserves the right of the defendant to rely on unauthenticated material (eg, reports produced by human rights organizations) in support of an extraneous considerations argument under ss 13 or 81, or a human rights argument under ss 21 or 87.[22] Generalized country reports are, however, likely to be of little value by themselves in establishing that the defendant is at risk of having his Convention rights violated in the requesting state.[23]

F. Charges and Multiple Offences

English charges

5.20 The almost invariable practice under the EA 1989 was for the requesting state to supply a list of the English offences which it alleged were constituted by equivalent conduct. In *R v Bow Street Magistrates' Court ex p Kline*, 30 June 1999, CO/813/99, the Court explained:

> Although there is nothing in the statute or any subordinate legislation which requires it, it is the practice for the Government to set out in the form of what are described as charges the offences which would have been committed in England and Wales as a result of the allegations in an accusation case or the conviction in a conviction case.

5.21 In *R v Governor of Pentonville Prison ex p Osman* [1990 1 WLR 277, 302 Lloyd LJ observed:

> The practice in extradition cases has been that the English 'offences' are stated in the authority to proceed in very general terms. The magistrate is not, of course, concerned with whether the offence is made out in foreign law. He is concerned solely with whether the evidence would support committal for trial in England, if the conduct complained of had taken place in England: see *In re Nielsen* [1984] AC 606. So the magistrate is furnished at the commencement of the hearing with a schedule of charges based on the alleged conduct and formulated in accordance with English law. The schedule of charges is frequently amended in the course of the hearing.

5.22 The same practice has continued in extradition hearings under the EA 2003 in cases where the requesting state is required to demonstrate dual criminality,[24] notwithstanding that there is no longer an authority to proceed.

5.23 In *Charron v Government of the United States* [2000] 1 WLR 1793 the Privy Council held in a case involving the Bahamas Extradition Act 1994 (in similar form to the EA 1989) that a failure to supply a list of charges would only invalidate the committal if the defendant could demonstrate that he had been prejudiced by a lack of particulars.

---

[21] *Re Majeed Ahmed*, 14 July 1983, CO/85/1983.

[22] *Hilali v Central Court of Criminal Proceedings Number 5 of the National Court of Madrid* [2006] EWHC 1239 (Admin), para 63.

[23] *Miklis v Deputy Prosecutor General of Lithuania* [2006] EWHC (Admin) 1032, paras 8 and 11.

[24] *Boudhiba v Central Examining Court No 5 of the National Court of Justice, Madrid* [2006] EWHC 167 (Admin), paras 31–32 (English charges provided to assist the appropriate judge in the event the Government was required to demonstrate dual criminality); *Fofana v Deputy Prosecutor Thubin Tribunal de Grande Instance de Meaux, France* [2006] EWHC 744 (Admin), para 5.

The charges are prepared by the CPS (or counsel instructed by it) for the use of the court and the defendant as an aid to identifying, in English law terms, the precise conduct of which the defendant is accused or has been convicted in the requesting state. It is important to recognize, however, that the charges have no formal status as such in the extradition process. The judge's task under s 10 (in Part 1 cases) and s 78(4)(b) (in Part 2 cases) is to determine whether the conduct amounts to an extradition offence as defined in the EA 2003 irrespective of whether it is one of the offences specified on the list of English charges.[25] He is not limited to determining whether the conduct in the Part 1 warrant (or the extradition request in Part 2 cases) amounts to the extradition offences in the list of charges.[26] Nor can the form of the English charges, by themselves, determine the question of whether extradition is barred on the grounds of *autrefois convict* or *acquit*.[27] **5.24**

Multiple offences

In an extradition hearing the appropriate judge must apply the relevant statutory provisions in respect of each of the offences contained in the Part 1 warrant (or extradition request in Part 2 cases). Section 207 provides that the Secretary of State may by order provide for the Act to have effect with specified modifications in relation to a case where a Part 1 warrant is issued in respect of more than one offence or a request for extradition is made in respect of more than one offence. **5.25**

The Extradition Act 2003 (Multiple Offences) Order 2003[28] has been made under s 207. Article 2(2) provides that the Act is to have effect with the modifications specified in the Schedule to the Order in relation to a case where the Part 1 warrant or extradition request contains more than one offence. **5.26**

Accordingly, the following chapters should be read subject to the modifications contained in the Schedule to the Order where the extradition hearing is concerned with multiple offences. The Order is contained in Appendix E6. **5.27**

G. Is the Offence Specified in the Part 1 Warrant an Extradition Offence?

Extradition offences were considered in Chapter 2. Section 10(2) provides that if a person in respect of whom a Part 1 warrant has been issued appears at the extradition hearing, the appropriate judge must decide whether the offence specified in the Part 1 warrant is an extradition offence. The appropriate judge is required to consider the particulars of conduct on the warrant and to determine whether it amounts to an extradition offence within the definitions set out in ss 64–66.[29] **5.28**

Where dual criminality is required in order for the foreign offence to be an extradition offence, the appropriate judge must carry out a transposition exercise on the conduct specified in the warrant in accordance with the relevant definition of extradition offence in the EA 2003.[30] The **5.29**

---

25 *R v Bow Street Magistrates' Court ex p Kline*, 30 June 1999, CO/813/99.

26 cf *Re Nielsen* [1984] AC 606 (magistrate could only commit in respect of the offences specified on the order to proceed issued under the EA 1870).

27 EA 2003, ss 12 and 80; *Boudhiba v Central Examining Court No 5 of the National Court of Justice, Madrid* [2006] EWHC 167 (Admin), paras 31–32; *Fofana v Deputy Prosecutor Thubin Tribunal de Grande Instance de Meaux, France* [2006] EWHC 744 (Admin).

28 SI 2003/3150: see App E6.

29 *Office of the King's Prosecutor v Cando Armas* [2006] 2 AC 1, para 16.

30 *Dabas v High Court of Justice, Madrid, Spain* [2006] EWHC 971 (Admin), para 31, where Latham LJ emphasized that it was the conduct set out in the warrant and not the English charge which had to be examined in order to determine whether the conduct alleged is an extradition offence.

idea behind the process of transposition was explained in *R v Governor of Pentonville Prison ex p Tarling* (1980) 70 Cr App R 77, 136:

> In considering the jurisdiction aspect it is necessary to suppose that England is substituted for Singapore as regards all the circumstances of the case connected with the latter country, and to examine the question whether upon that hypothesis and upon the evidence adduced the English courts would have jurisdiction to try the offences charged.

5.30 The speech of Lord Hope of Craighead in *R v Metropolitan Stipendiary Magistrate ex p Pinochet (No 3)* [2000] AC 147, 229–240 is a useful illustration, against a complicated factual and legal background, of how the question of whether the alleged conduct amounts to an extradition offence is to be determined.

5.31 As discussed in Chapter 4, s 2(4)(c) requires the Part 1 warrant to contain particulars of the alleged offences.[31] If the Part 1 warrant does not contain sufficiently clear allegations of conduct then the judge may not be able properly to conclude that the conduct alleged is an extradition offence. Also, if the conduct has not been adequately set out, or the other particulars of the Part 1 warrant required by s 2 are absent, the warrant will fail to be a Part 1 warrant within the meaning of the EA 2003 and thus the foundation for the judge's jurisdiction to order extradition will be absent.[32]

H. Bars to Extradition

5.32 The appropriate judge is precluded from ordering extradition if he is satisfied that any of the specified bars to extradition is applicable. The original bars to extradition in the EA 2003 were contained in s 11(1)(a)–(h) and defined in ss 12–19. Paragraphs 3 and 4 of Sch 13 to the Police and Justice Act 2006 introduce two new bars to extradition, namely a restriction on extradition following the defendant's transfer from the International Criminal Court, and a restriction on extradition in cases where a trial in the UK would be more appropriate. These bars to extradition are defined in ss 19A and 19B respectively, and inserted into the EA 2003 by paras 3 and 4.

The rule against double jeopardy (s 12)

5.33 Section 12 provides a bar to return where extradition would violate the rule against double jeopardy, also known as *ne bis in idem*. The purpose of this provision is to stop a defendant from being prosecuted twice for the same offence in different jurisdictions. It gives effect to Article 3(2) of the EAW Framework Decision.[33] *Ne bis in idem* is a fundamental principle of law whose origins can be traced at least to 355BC, when Demosthenes reasoned that 'the laws forbid the same man to be tried twice on the same issue'.[34]

5.34 The defendant's return to a Category 1 country is barred by reason of the rule against double jeopardy if and only if it appears that he would be entitled to be discharged under any rule of law relating to previous acquittal or conviction on the assumption:

(a) that the conduct constituting the extradition offence constituted an offence in the part of the UK where the judge exercises jurisdiction;
(b) that the person were charged with the extradition offence in that part of the UK.

---

[31] Para 4.15.

[32] *Dabas v High Court of Justice, Madrid, Spain* [2007] 2 AC 31, para 50; *Office of the King's Prosecutor, Brussels v Cando Armas* [2006] 2 AC at para 28; para 4.11.

[33] See also, Article 4 of Protocol 7 to the ECHR; Article 50 of the EU Charter on Fundamental Rights; and the Schengen Convention, Article 54.

[34] Hunter, *The Rule Against Double Jeopardy*, (1984) Journal of Legal History 5.

A defendant can rely on s 12 in circumstances where, if he were charged in the UK with the conduct for which his extradition is being sought, he could plead *autrefois acquit* or *autrefois convict* in the narrow sense in which the pleas were stated by the House of Lords in *Connelly v Director of Public Prosecutions* [1964] AC 125 and *Director of Public Prosecutions v Humphreys* [1977] AC 1, that is where precisely the same offence is charged in the later proceedings. **5.35**

Section 12 is also engaged where the requesting state seeks to prosecute the defendant for an offence, the facts of which are so closely related to an offence for which he has already been prosecuted that it would be abuse of process to prosecute him a second time.[35] **5.36**

Where, in the requesting state, the defendant is acquitted at trial but his acquittal is set aside on appeal, then it will not be a breach of double jeopardy principles to seek his extradition to re-try him.[36] **5.37**

Extraneous considerations (s 13)

The jurisdiction to decline to extradite a defendant because he is accused or has been convicted of a political offence was a long-standing principle of extradition law before the enactment of the EA 2003.[37] From the nineteenth century onwards, when much of Europe was in a state of political upheaval, Parliament and the courts were anxious to ensure that extradition was not used as a tool of political repression. In *R v Governor of Pentonville Prison ex p Cheng* [1973] AC 931, 944, Lord Diplock said that s 3(1) of the EA 1870 (no extradition for political offences): **5.38**

> ... contemplated that a foreign government in its eagerness to revenge itself upon a political opponent might attempt to misuse an extradition treaty for this purpose.

During the twentieth century, extradition treaties came to include bars to extradition where there was a risk that the defendant would suffer discrimination in the requesting state on the grounds of his race, religion, nationality, or political opinions.[38] **5.39**

The growth of international terrorism in the latter part of the twentieth century resulted in legislation which reduced the scope of the political offence exception, and produced a hardening in the attitude of courts to those who sought refugee status after committing acts of violence.[39] For example, the Suppression of Terrorism Act 1978 deemed a range of violent offences including murder and kidnapping not to be political offences for the purposes of extradition, and **5.40**

---

[35] A species of abuse of process recognized in *Beedie* [1998] QB 356. For its application in the extradition context, see *Zdinjak v Republic Of Croatia* [2012] EWHC 1554 (Admin), para 9; *Voros v The District Courts of Sopron, Gyor and Zalaegerszeg, Hungary* [2012] EWHC 518 (Admin), para 26; *Maxwell King v Government of the United States of America* [2006] EWHC 3033 (Admin), para 25; *Fofana v Deputy Prosecutor Thubin Tribunal de Grande Instance de Meaux, France* [2006] EWHC 744 (Admin), para 79; cf *Bohning v Government of the United States of America* [2005] EWHC 2613, para 21; *Caddoux v Bow Street Magistrates' Court* [2004] EWHC 642 (Admin), para 17. Article 3(2) of the EAW Framework decision dealing with *ne bis in idem* is in similar terms to Article 54 of the Schengen Convention. The European Court of Justice said in *Gozutok* and *Brugge* [2003] ECRI 5689 (C-87/01 and C-385/01) and *Van Esbroeck* (C-436/04), 9 March 2006, that Article 54 must be interpreted as meaning that the relevant criterion for the purposes of the application of that article is identity of the material acts, understood as the existence of a set of facts which are inextricably linked together, irrespective of the legal classification given to them or the legal interest protected. See also Opinion of Advocate General Kokott, 8 September 2011, Case, C-17/10, *Toshiba Corporation and Others*; Case C-467/04, *Gasparini and Others* [2006] ECR I-9199, para 54; Case C-150/05 *Van Straaten* [2006] ECR I-9327, paras 41, 47, and 48; Case C-367/05 *Kraaijenbrink* [2007] ECR I-6619, paras 26 and 28; Case C-261/09 *Mantello* [2010] ECR I-11477 para 39.

[36] *Re Oncel* [2001] EWHC (Admin) 1142, paras 14–15.

[37] *Re Castioni* [1891] 1 QB 149; *In re Meunier* [1894] 2 QB 415. See 2011 Extradition Review, para 3.29.

[38] See for example Art 3 of the European Convention on Extradition 1957.

[39] *T v Secretary of State for the Home Department* [1996] AC 742.

they were therefore excluded from the scope of the protection given by s 6(1)(a) of the EA 1989 (no extradition for political offences).

5.41 In the EA 2003 Parliament took this process to its conclusion by removing entirely the political offence exception to extradition for both Category 1 and Category 2 countries.

5.42 However, although it is no longer open to a defendant to argue that he should not be extradited because he is accused of a political offence, extradition remains barred in Part 1 cases where there is a risk that the defendant will be persecuted on one or more of the grounds specified in s 13.[40] These are known as 'extraneous considerations'.

5.43 Section 13 is in similar terms to EA 1989, s 6(1)(c) and (d), which in turn were derived from provisions in the Fugitive Offenders Act 1967. Section 13 provides that a person's extradition to a Category 1 territory is barred by reason of extraneous considerations if and only if it appears that:

(a) the Part 1 warrant issued in respect of him (though purporting to be issued on account of the extradition offence) is in fact issued for the purpose of prosecuting or punishing him on account of his race, religion, nationality, gender, sexual orientation, or political opinions (s 13(a));
(b) if extradited he might be prejudiced at his trial or punished, detained, or restricted in his personal liberty by reason of his race, religion, nationality, gender, sexual orientation, or political opinions (s 13(b)).

5.44 In order to rely on s 13 it is not sufficient for the defendant to show that there is some general risk of prejudice to him. Section 13(a) and 13(b) require there to be a causal link between the issue of the warrant, or the likely prejudice, and one of the stated grounds.[41] The defendant bears the burden of showing that s 13 applies. The defendant is able to rely on material to show the necessary risk of prejudice whether or not it is authenticated as required by the EA 2003.[42]

5.45 Section 13(a) requires the court to assess the state of mind of the prosecuting authority responsible for making the request at the time the request is made so as to establish whether or not its purpose was to punish for discriminatory reasons.[43]

5.46 In relation to s 13(b), which is concerned with what may happen in the future, the defendant does not need to show that it is more likely than not that he will be prejudiced. It is sufficient if he can establish that there is a 'reasonable chance' or 'serious possibility' of prejudice. In *Fernandez v Government of Singapore* [1981] 1 WLR 987 the House of Lords considered the provisions of s 4(1)(c) of the Fugitive Offenders Act 1967 which were in similar terms to s 13(b). It was suggested that the defendant had to establish the defence on a balance of

[40] Sections 79 and 81 are the analogous provisions in Part 2 cases: see para 6.25; *R(Ahsan) v Director of Public Prosecutions and Government of the United States* [2008] EWHC 666 (Admin), paras 129–141; *McKinnon v Secretary of State for the Home Department* [2007] EWHC 762 (Admin), paras 16–17.

[41] *McKenzie v Judge of Instruction No 9 Palma De Mallorca Spain – A Spanish Judicial Authority* [2008] EWHC 3187 (Admin), para 42; *Hilali v Central Court of Criminal Proceedings Number 5 of the National Court of Madrid* [2006] EWHC 1239 (Admin), para 62; *Lodhi v Governor of HM Prison Brixton* [2001] EWHC (Admin) 178, para 89 et seq.

[42] EA 2003, s 202(5); *Miklis v Deputy Prosecutor General of Lithuania* [2006] EWHC 1032 (Admin), paras 8 and 11; *Hilali v Central Court of Criminal Proceedings Number 5 of the National Court of Madrid* [2006] EWHC 1239 (Admin), para 63; *Dabas v High Court of Justice, Madrid, Spain* [2006] EWHC 971 (Admin), paras 35–39; cf *Schtraks v Government of Israel* [1964] AC 556, 582.

[43] *Slepcik v Governor of HM Prison Brixton* [2004] EWHC 1224 (Admin), para 23.

probabilities. This contention was rejected by Lord Diplock at p 994, who emphasized the much lower burden on the defendant:[44]

> My Lords, bearing in mind the relative gravity of the consequences of the court's expectation being falsified either in one way or in the other, I do not think that the test of the applicability of paragraph (c) is that the court must be satisfied that it is more likely than not that the fugitive will be detained or restricted if he is returned. A lesser degree of likelihood is, in my view, sufficient; and I would not quarrel with the way in which the test was stated by the magistrate or with the alternative way in which it was expressed by the Divisional Court. 'A reasonable chance,' 'substantial grounds for thinking,' 'a serious possibility'. I see no significant difference between these various ways of describing the degree of likelihood of the detention or restriction of the fugitive on his return which justifies the court in giving effect to the provisions of section 4(1)(c).

The *Fernandez* test is applicable in relation to s 13(b).[45] **5.47**

Section 13 reflects the grounds for claiming refugee status under Article 1A(2) of the Convention and Protocol relating to the Status of Refugees 1951[46] and 1967, where the form of persecution concerned is prosecution.[47] This provides that persecution on the grounds of 'race, religion, nationality, membership of a particular social group or political opinion' is grounds for claiming refugee status. It follows that some of the case law arising in the asylum context is relevant to s 13.[48] **5.48**

The principles concerning prosecution on the grounds of political opinion were comprehensively reviewed by the Immigration Appeal Tribunal presided over by Collins J in *Emilia Gomez v Secretary of State for the Home Department* [2000] INLR 549. The principles can be summarized as follows. A broad purposive construction should be given to the political opinion ground (para 21). In particular the word 'political' should be given a broad meaning (paras 27 and 40).[49] It is not necessary to show the prosecutor's *only* motive is political persecution: it is sufficient if political reasons form part of his motivation (para 22). It is generally the existence of a group of opponents that concerns a government or other persecutor sufficient to provoke oppression (para 23). In order to show persecution on account of political opinion it is not necessary to show political action or activity (para 24). Political opinions may be those expressed by the persecuted person or may be those imputed to him by the persecuting government (para 26). It is not appropriate to maintain a rigid distinction between political opinions on the one hand and economic opinions on the other (para 43). **5.49**

In *Iqbal*[50] the Asylum and Immigration Tribunal summarized how asylum claims, based on a fear of prosecution amounting to persecution, should be dealt with. It provides a useful **5.50**

---

44 The focus on the inquiry is on the situation in the requesting state at the time it is considered by the Court, rather than on what the situation may have been in the past: *Zdinjak v Republic of Croatia* [2012] EWHC 1554 (Admin), para 21 and 22; *Travica v Croatia* [2004] EWHC (Admin) 2747; *Spanovic v Croatia* [2009] EWHC (Admin) 723.

45 *McKenzie v Judge of Instruction No 9 Palma De Mallorca Spain – A Spanish Judicial Authority* [2008] EWHC 3187 (Admin), para 42; *Hilali v Central Court of Criminal Proceedings No 5* [2006] EWHC 1239, para 62.

46 Cmd 9171.

47 Cmd 3906. See United Nations High Commissioner for Refugees, *Handbook on Procedures and Criteria for Determining Refugee Status*, paras 56–60; *Macdonald's Immigration Law and Practice*, para 12.50. See also 2011 Extradition Review, para 9.43 et seq.

48 See *R v Immigration Appeal Tribunal ex p Shah* [1999] 2 AC 629 (persecution on grounds of gender); *Z v Secretary of State for the Home Department* [2002] EWCA Civ 952; *Egan v Canada* (1995) 29 CRR (2d) 79; *NAGL v Minister for Home Affairs* (2000) (2) SA 1 (persecution on grounds of sexual orientation).

49 *Asliturk v Governor of HM Prison Holloway* [2002] EWHC 2326 (Admin).

50 *Iqbal (Muzafar)* [2002] UKIAT 02239. See also *Fazilat* [2002] UKIAT 00973 and *HD (Iran)* [2004] UKIAT 00209. *Iqbal (Muzafar)* [2002] UKIAT 02239 was approved in *Hariri v Secretary of State for the Home Department* [2003] EWCA Civ 807 and *Batayav v Secretary of State for the Home Department* [2003] EWCA Civ 1489.

approach to claims in extradition cases under s 13 of the EA 2003. In summary: (1) although it is not the purpose of the asylum determination process to judge guilt or innocence, nonetheless a factual evaluation as to whether there is a real risk that the claimant faces injustice rather than justice must be made; (2) whether prosecution amounts to persecution is a question of fact, and all relevant circumstances must be considered on a case-by-case basis; (3) the criminal justice process in the country of origin must be looked at as a whole, with possible harms considered cumulatively and not separately; (4) whether prosecution amounts to persecution must be analysed by reference to international human rights norms; (5) prosecution does not amount to persecution unless likely failures in the fair-trial process go beyond shortcomings and pose a threat to the very existence of the right to a fair trial; (6) when considering whether there is a general risk of persecution to any person subjected to the criminal law process in a given country, it is important to establish the scale of relevant human rights violations, particularly in relation to mistreatment in detention and the right to a fair trial, and, using Article 3 of the ECHR as a benchmark, it is useful to ask whether the level of human rights abuse rises to the level of a consistent pattern of gross, flagrant, or mass violations of human rights.

5.51 Section 13 is concerned with the treatment which the defendant might receive at the hands of the state. In other words, s 13(b) is directed at the criminal process; it is not concerned with general restrictions that apply quite independently of and which are unaffected by the criminal process.[51] Thus, a defendant who is at risk of assault from fellow prisoners because, for example, of his nationality, falls outside s 13,[52] although such a case may raise an issue under Article 3 of the ECHR.[53]

Passage of time (s 14)

5.52 Section 14 provides a bar to extradition in Part 1 cases where, because of the passage of time, it would no longer be right to extradite the defendant.[54] Section 14 provides that a person's extradition to a Category 1 territory is barred by reason of the passage of time if (and only if) it appears that it would be unjust or oppressive to extradite him by reason of the passage of time since he is alleged to have (a) committed the extradition offence (where he is accused of its commission), or (b) become unlawfully at large (where he is alleged to have been convicted of it).

5.53 Section 14 is similar but not identical to s 11(3)(b) of the EA 1989, which was derived from s 8(3) of the Fugitive Offenders Act 1967.[55] These provisions gave rise to a considerable amount of case law, much of which is relevant to s 14. However, consideration of s 14 necessitates a fact-specific inquiry. In *Steblins v Government of Latvia* [2006] EWHC 1272 (Admin), para 13, Scott Baker LJ commented that 'authorities are of very limited value when considering the facts of individual cases'.[56] In *Austins v Government of Spain* [2004] EWHC 2693 (Admin), para 16, Laws LJ commented that 'in the end the matter is one of judgment, if not impression'.[57] Although in *La Torre v Republic of Italy* [2007] EWHC 1370, para 37, Laws LJ said that 'an overall judgment on the merits is required, unshackled by rules with too sharp edges', this approach cannot be taken too far; in *Gomes v Republic of Trinidad and Tobago* [2009] 1 WLR 1038, para 26, the House of Lords said that s 14 is an area of the law 'where a substantial measure of clarity and certainty is required'. The relevant principles are as follows.

---

51 *Zadvornovs v Riga City Vidzene Suburb Court Latvia* [2011] EWHC 1257 (Admin), para 5.

52 *Holman v Regional Court In Warsaw Poland* [2012] EWHC 1503 (Admin), para 13.

53 Para 7.39.

54 Sections 79 and 82 are the analogous provisions in Part 2 cases: see para 6.27.

55 See *Union of India v Narang* [1978] AC 278.

56 For the approach in recent cases see, for example, *Gudzelak v Judicial Authority in Krosno, Poland* [2012] EWCH 1764 (Admin); *Rexha v Office of the Prosecutor attached to the Court in Rome* [2012] EWHC 1274 (Admin); *Clark v Government of United States of America* [2012] EWHC 957 (Admin).

57 *Parasiliti-Mollica v Court of Appeal of Reggio Calabria* [2010] EWHC 2722 (Admin), paras 32–33.

In *Kakis v Government of the Republic of Cyprus* [1978] 1 WLR 779, 782–783, Lord Diplock said: **5.54**

> 'Unjust' I regard as directed primarily to the risk of prejudice to the accused in the conduct of the trial itself, 'oppressive' as directed to hardship to the accused resulting from changes in his circumstances that have occurred during the period to be taken into consideration; but there is room for overlapping, and between them they would cover all cases where to return him would not be fair. Delay in the commencement or conduct of extradition proceedings which is brought about by the accused himself by fleeing the country, concealing his whereabouts or evading arrest cannot, in my view, be relied upon as a ground for holding it to be either unjust or oppressive to return him. Any difficulties that he may encounter in the conduct of his defence in consequence of the delay due to such causes are of his own choice and making. Save in the most exceptional circumstances it would be neither unjust nor oppressive that he should be required to accept them.
>
> As respects delay which is not brought about by the acts of the accused himself, however, the question of where responsibility lies for the delay is not generally relevant. What matters is not so much the cause of such delay as its effect; or, rather, the effects of those events which would not have happened before the trial of the accused if it had taken place with ordinary promptitude. So where the application for discharge under section 8(3) is based upon the 'passage of time' under paragraph (b) and not on absence of good faith under paragraph (c), the court is not normally concerned with what could be an invidious task of considering whether mere inaction of the requisitioning government or its prosecuting authorities which resulted in delay was blameworthy or otherwise. Your Lordships have no occasion to do so in the instant case.

The relevant period runs from the date of the alleged offence to the date of the challenge, which is not necessarily the date of the extradition hearing.[58] The court is required to ascertain the facts relied upon by the defendant as giving rise to injustice or oppression. The standard of proof in relation to injustice and oppression is the balance of probabilities and the burden of proof lies on the defendant.[59] Where necessary, the court is entitled to look at any evidence given by the defendant and to form a view whether, in reality, it lacks any real credibility.[60] Where the issue of delay under s 14 is raised, even if it is unsupported by evidence, then the appropriate judge should decide the issue.[61] **5.55**

In *Gomes v Republic of Trinidad and Tobago* [2009] 1 WLR 1038 Lord Brown referred to the paragraphs from *Kakis v Government of the Republic of Cyprus* [1978] 1 WLR 779, 782–783 quoted at para 5.54 above as 'Diplock para 1' and 'Diplock para 2' respectively. He said at para 29 that the rule in Diplock para 1 that delay in the commencement or conduct of extradition proceedings which is brought about by the accused himself cannot be relied upon as giving rise to injustice or oppression, should be strictly applied. But, he said, there may be 'most exceptional circumstances' in which, despite the accused's responsibility for the delay, the court will nevertheless find the s 14 bar established.[62] It is for the requesting state to show, to the criminal standard of proof, that the defendant is disentitled to rely on the bar by reason of any passage **5.56**

---

[58] *Gomes v Government of Trinidad* [2009] 1 WLR 1038, para 38; *Kakis v Government of Cyprus* [1978] 1 WLR 779, 782; *R v Governor of Pentonville Prison ex p Tarling* [1979] 1 WLR 1417, 1425; *Re Davies* [1998] COD 1.

[59] EA 2003, s 206; *Kociukow v District Court of Bialystok III Penal Division* [2006] EWHC 56 (Admin), para 9; *Union of India v Narang* [1978] AC 278, 293–294. Where it is alleged that the defendant fled then this must be proved by the requesting state to the criminal standard: *Gomes v Republic of Trinidad and Tobago* [2009] 1 WLR 1038, para 27; *Filipek-Kwasny v Polish Judicial Authority* [2012] EWHC 25 (Admin), para 17.

[60] *Sirvelis v Government of Lithuania* [2005] EWHC 2611 (Admin), para 25.

[61] *An Chen v Government of Romania* [2006] EWHC 1752 (Admin), para 27.

[62] He gave as an example *In re Davies* [1998] COD 30, where the defendant became unfit to plead during the relevant time.

of time for which he is responsible.[63] In *Gomes v Republic of Trinidad and Tobago* [2009] 1 WLR 1038, para 26, Lord Brown said where a defendant flees then 'it simply does not lie in his mouth' to suggest that the requesting state should share responsibility for ensuing delay in bringing him to justice because of some subsequent supposed fault on their part (eg mere inaction through pressure of work and limited resources). Only a deliberate decision by the requesting state communicated to the defendant not to pursue the case against him, or some other circumstance which would similarly justify a sense of security on his part notwithstanding his own flight from justice, could allow him properly to assert that the effects of further delay were not 'of his own choice and making'.

5.57 If the requesting government can be shown to have been inexcusably dilatory in taking steps to bring the defendant to justice, then this may serve to establish the necessary injustice and oppressiveness, whereas the issue may be left in some doubt if the only known fact relates to the passage of time.[64] A sense of false security engendered in the defendant is also a relevant consideration. If the actions of the government have led him to believe that he will not be extradited then it may be oppressive if the government then proceeds to try to do so.[65]

5.58 A refusal to return the defendant must be based on injustice or oppression caused by the passage of time as it operated in the circumstances of the particular case to give to that particular passage of time a quality or significance which leads to the conclusion that return would be unjust or oppressive.[66] In other words, delay must have operated as the 'cradle of events' giving rise to injustice or oppression in order for s 14 to be engaged.[67] The test for injustice is a high one.[68]

5.59 With regard to the concept of injustice, in *Gomes v Republic of Trinidad and Tobago* [2009] 1 WLR 1038, para 32, the House of Lords referred with approval to the judgment of the Privy Council delivered by Lord Bingham in *Knowles v Government of the United States of America* [2007] 1 WLR 47, para 31, where the Board approved the Divisional Court's judgment in *Woodcock v Government of New Zealand* [2004] 1 WLR 1979 from which it extracted and endorsed the propositions:

> First, the question is not whether it would be unjust or oppressive to try the accused but whether … it would be unjust or oppressive to extradite him (para 20). Secondly, if the court of the requesting state is bound to conclude that a fair trial is impossible, it would be unjust or oppressive for the requested state to return him (para 21). But, thirdly, the court of the requested state must have regard to the safeguards which exist under the domestic law of the requesting state to protect a defendant against a trial rendered unjust or oppressive by the passage of time (paras 21–22). Fourthly, no rule of thumb can be applied to determine whether the passage of time has rendered a fair trial no longer possible: much will turn on the particular case (paras 14–16, 23–25). Fifthly, 'there can be no cut-off point beyond which extradition must inevitably be regarded as unjust or oppressive' (para 29).

---

63 *Gomes v Republic of Trinidad and Tobago* [2009] 1 WLR 1038, para 27; *Filipek-Kwasny v Polish Judicial Authority* [2012] EWHC 25 (Admin), para 17.

64 *Kakis v Government of Cyprus* [1978] 1 WLR 779, 785 per Lord Fraser. The conflict between this passage in Lord Fraser's speech that of Lord Diplock at p 783—where he appeared to suggest that dilatoriness on the part of the requesting state was not a relevant factor— was explained by Woolf LJ in *R v Governor of Brixton Prison ex p Osman (No 4)* [1992] 1 All ER 579, 587. Inexcusable delay by the government is relevant in borderline cases: *Hunt v Court of First Instance Antwerp* [2006] EWHC 165 (Admin), para 24; *Re Boente* [2006] All ER (D) 30 (Jul), subject always to the requirement emphasized in *Gomes v Republic of Trinidad and Tobago* [2009] 1 WLR 1038, para 26, that the defendant has not caused the delay.

65 *Kakis v Government of Cyprus* [1978] 1 WLR 779, 790 *per* Lord Scarman; *Holmes v Government of Portugal* [2004] EWHC 2875 (Admin).

66 *Kakis v Government of Cyprus* [1978] 1 WLR 779, 785; *Union of India* v *Narang*, [1978] AC 278, 290.

67 *Kakis v Government of Cyprus* [1978] 1 WLR 779, 790.

68 *Gomes v Republic of Trinidad and Tobago* [2009] 1 WLR 1038, para 36.

5.60 The second of these propositions requires consideration of whether a fair trial is impossible, and in *Gomes v Republic of Trinidad and Tobago* [2009] 1 WLR 1038, para 33, Lord Brown said that is the essential question underlying any application for a s 14[69] bar on the ground that the passage of time has made it unjust to extradite the accused, rather than whether there is a mere risk of prejudice. However, it does not require the defendant to establish a 'flagrant denial of justice'.[70]

5.61 The third proposition requires the requested state to have regard to the domestic safeguards in the law of the requesting state. This is because the domestic court of the requesting state has obvious advantages in deciding whether or not a fair trial is now possible, including a clearer picture of what evidence is available and the issues likely to arise. However, in the absence of an abuse of process jurisdiction similar to that possessed by courts in the UK, the courts there will have to reach a conclusion on whether a fair trial would now be possible in the requesting state.[71] In relation to Council of Europe countries, they are bound by Article 6 of the ECHR and should readily be assumed to be capable of protecting the defendant against an unjust trial.[72] In all cases, there should be a general presumption that justice will be done despite the passage of time, and the burden should be on the defendant to establish that the contrary is the case.[73]

5.62 In considering an application for a bar under s 14 on the basis of loss of evidence, the judge must assess the strength of the defendant's complaint by analysing the extent to which missing evidence is likely to undermine the case the prosecution seeks to adduce or to assist the defence. He should bear in mind that lost evidence is likely to hamper the prosecution as much as the defence and that trial processes in the requesting state are equipped to deal with most of the complaints on which applications for a stay are founded. There must exist some basis for concluding that he is in a worse and not in a better position in consequence of the lack of availability of witnesses or documents. There must be some foundation, other than mere assertion, for concluding that evidence no longer available might have undermined the prosecution or supported the defence.[74]

5.63 The oppression limb of s 14 allows the court to consider a wide variety of factors. The graver the offence then the higher the threshold of oppression.[75] Whilst no exhaustive list can be given, factors which have been held to give rise to oppression include changes in the defendant's situation during the relevant time; the effect of return on the defendant's own life and that of his family;[76] and health issues.[77] Extradition by its nature involves a degree of disruption which

---

69 Section 82 of the EA 2003 in Part 2 cases.

70 *Gomes v Republic of Trinidad and Tobago* [2009] 1 WLR 1038, para 36.

71 *Gomes v Republic of Trinidad and Tobago* [2009] 1 WLR 1038, para 35; *Government of the United States v Tollman* [2008] EWHC 184 (Admin), paras 60–65.

72 In so far as Keene LJ's judgment in *Lisowski v Regional Court of Bialystok (Poland)* [2006] Extradition LR 272, para 26 suggests the contrary, it should not be followed: *Gomes v Republic of Trinidad and Tobago* [2009] 1 WLR 1038, para 35.

73 *Gomes v Republic of Trinidad and Tobago* [2009] 1 WLR 1038, para 36.

74 *Government of the United States of America v Tollman* [2008] EWHC 184 (Admin), paras 47–50, para 68.

75 *Kakis v Government of the Republic of Cyprus* [1978] 1 WLR 779, 784.

76 *Government of the United States of America v Tollman* [2008] EWHC 184 (Admin), paras 47–50, para 110; *Hunt v Court of First Instance, Antwerp* [2006] EWHC 165 (Admin); *Cookeson v Government of Australia* [2001] EWHC (Admin) 149 (serious psychiatric illness of defendant's adult son of whom he was principal carer); *Re Ashley-Riddle*, 22 November 1993, CO/216/93 (oppression to school-age son); cf *Filipczak v Provincial Court (5th Crim District) Warsaw Praga, Poland* [2006] All ER (D) 233 (Oct).

77 *R (Warren) v Secretary of State for the Home Department* [2003] EWHC 1177 (Admin); *Re Davies* [1998] COD 1; *R v Secretary of State for the Home Department ex p Kingdom of Belgium*, 15 February 2000, CO/236/00. The extradition of someone who is seriously ill may also raise issues under Arts 2 or 3 of the European Convention on Human Rights: para 7.38.

does not, by itself, make the defendant's return necessarily oppressive.[78] Thus, what is required is some particular factor which makes return oppressive. The test of oppression will not easily be satisfied: hardship, a comparatively commonplace consequence of an order for extradition, is not enough.[79]

5.64 Although the length of the delay is a relevant factor in determining the question of injustice or oppression, there is no cut-off point beyond which extradition must inevitably be regarded as unjust or oppressive.[80] Nevertheless, in some extreme cases the delay has been so protracted that the court has been ready virtually to assume that it has given rise to injustice and oppression, especially where the prosecuting authorities have been at fault.[81]

Age (s 15)

5.65 Section 15 introduces a new bar to extradition based on the defendant's age. It gives effect to Article 3(3) of the EAW Framework Decision. Extradition of a person who would have been under the age of criminal responsibility at the time the alleged offence was committed is now prohibited.

5.66 The defendant's extradition to a Category 1 territory is barred by reason of his age if (and only if) it would be conclusively presumed because of his age that he could not be guilty of the extradition offence on the assumption:

(a) that the conduct constituting the extradition offence constituted an offence in the part of the UK where the judge exercises jurisdiction;
(b) that the person carried out the conduct when the extradition offence was committed (or alleged to be committed);
(c) that the person carried out the conduct in the part of the UK where the judge exercises jurisdiction.

5.67 These assumptions require the court to assume that the offence was committed by the defendant in the UK and that the conduct amounts to an offence in the UK. The question then is whether the defendant would conclusively presumed not to be guilty on the grounds of his age.

5.68 In England and Wales it is conclusively presumed that no child under the age of ten years can be guilty of any offence.[82]

Hostage-taking considerations (s 16)

5.69 Section 16 provides a new bar to extradition, derived from Article 9 of the International Convention against the Taking of Hostages.[83] Article 9(1)(b)(ii) of the Convention provides:

> A request for the extradition of an alleged offender, pursuant to this Convention, shall not be granted if the requested State Party has substantial grounds for believing ... that the person's position may be prejudiced ... for the reason that communication with him by the appropriate authorities of the State entitled to exercise rights of protection cannot be effected.

[78] *Steblins v Government of Latvia* [2006] EWHC 1272 (Admin), para 13.
[79] *Gomes v Republic of Trinidad and Tobago* [2009] 1 WLR 1038, para 36.
[80] *Dziedzic v Government of Germany* [2006] EWHC 1750 (Admin), para 9.
[81] cf *Woodcock v Government of New Zealand* [2004] 1 WLR 1979, para 29.
[82] Children and Young Persons Act 1933, s 50.
[83] Opened for signature at New York on 18 December 1979: <http://www.unodc.org/unodc/terrorism_convention_hostages.html>.

A person's extradition to a Category 1 territory is barred by reason of hostage-taking considerations if (and only if) the territory is a party to the Hostage-taking Convention and it appears that: **5.70**

(a) if extradited he might be prejudiced at his trial because communication between him and the 'appropriate authorities' would not be possible;
(b) the act or omission constituting the extradition offence also constitutes an offence under s 1 of the Taking of Hostages Act 1982 or an attempt to commit such an offence.

The appropriate authorities are the authorities of the territory which are entitled to exercise rights of protection in relation to him, ie the relevant consular authorities.[84] **5.71**

Specialty (s 17)

Specialty (also called 'speciality') is a rule of extradition law that is intended to ensure that a person extradited is not dealt with in the requesting state for any offence other than that for which he was extradited. The term derives from the French '*spécialité*' which means 'particularity'.[85] Although the EA 2003 refers in s 17 and s 95 to 'speciality', in this work the 'time-honoured' word specialty will be used.[86] **5.72**

In its absolute form, specialty requires that the defendant only be tried for the offence for which his extradition was granted. However the rule as stated has been widely relaxed in modern extradition legislation, including the EA 2003. That relaxation is reflected in the fact that under the EA 2003 the requesting state may be permitted to deal with the defendant for offences other than those for which he was returned which are disclosed by the facts upon which his surrender was based.[87] Also, the requesting state may be permitted to seek from the requested state its consent to try the defendant for another offence not covered by its original request, provided that the offence is extraditable. **5.73**

Section 17(1) of the EA 2003 incorporates specialty protection for defendants whose return is sought by a Category 1 territory. Section 17(1) provides that the defendant's extradition to a Category 1 territory is barred by reason of specialty if (and only if) there are no 'specialty arrangements' with the Category 1 territory. **5.74**

Section 17(2) provides that there are specialty arrangements with a Category 1 territory if, under the law of that territory, or arrangements made between it and the UK, a person who is extradited to the territory from the UK may be dealt with in the territory for an offence committed before his extradition only if either the offence falls within s 17(3), or the condition in s 17(4) is satisfied.[88] **5.75**

Thus, the protections required by s 17 can be provided by the domestic law or practice of the foreign state. For example, in *ex p Bouvier* (1872) 12 Cox CC 303 it was held that a circular instruction issued to the law officers in France contained sufficient legal provisions guaranteeing specialty protection. **5.76**

[84] See Vienna Convention on Consular Relations 1963 (United Nations, Treaty Series, Vol 596, p261), Article 36.
[85] Feller, 'Reflections on the Nature of the Specialty Principle in Extradition Relations', (1977) 12 *Israel Law Rev* 466.
[86] *Hilali v Central Court of Criminal Proceedings Number 5 of the National Court of Madrid* [2006] EWHC 1239 (Admin), para 45.
[87] EA 2003, ss 17 and 95.
[88] *Virciglio v Judicial Authority of the Graz High Court, Austria* [2006] All ER (D) 44 (Oct).

5.77 The specialty protections required by s 17 may also be contained in the extradition arrangements between the UK and the foreign state.

5.78 The offence falls within s 17(3) if it falls into one of the following categories:

(a) it is an offence in respect of which the person is extradited;
(b) it is an extradition offence disclosed by the same facts as that offence;
(c) it is an extradition offence in respect of which the appropriate judge gives his consent under s 55;
(d) it is an offence which is not punishable with imprisonment or another form of detention;
(e) it is an offence in respect of which the person will not be detained in connection with his trial, sentence or appeal;
(f) it is an offence in respect of which the person waives the right that he would have (but for s 17(3)(f)) not to be dealt with for the offence.

5.79 The conditions in s 17(4) are that the defendant is given the opportunity to leave the Category 1 territory and he does not do so before the end of 45 days starting with the day he arrives in the Category 1 territory, or he does leave before the end of the permitted period and returns there. Thus, once the defendant has been extradited to the Category 1 territory and dealt with there for the offences for which he was extradited, once he is free to leave the territory, if he does not do so within 45 days the territory is free to try him for any offence.

5.80 The Court must be satisfied that there are adequate specialty arrangements in place.[89] The burden is on the defendant to show that there are no such arrangements, on a balance of probabilities.[90] The existence of an express treaty provision is generally sufficient to satisfy the court that specialty arrangements exist. In *Hilali v Central Court of Criminal Proceedings Number 5 of the National Court of Madrid* [2006] EWHC 1239 (Admin) the issue was raised on appeal whether there are practical and effective arrangements in Spain to ensure that the defendant would only be tried for the offence for which he was extradited or other offences disclosed by the same facts. At para 52 Scott Baker LJ said:

> It seems to us a surprising submission that Spain is likely to act in breach of the international obligations to which it has signed up. There is no evidence before us that it has done so in the past and in these circumstances we would need compelling evidence that it is likely to do so in the future. By Article 34 of the Framework Decision Member States were requested to take the necessary measures to comply with its provisions by 31 December 2003. It is not suggested that Spain has failed to meet this implementation provision. It seems to us therefore that it is to be inferred that the specialty arrangements referred to in s 17(2) of the 2003 Act are in place.[91]

5.81 The EAW Framework Decision contains specialty provisions in Article 27(2),[92] which were cosidered by the Court of Justice of the European Union in *Leymann and Pustovarov*, Case C-388/08 PPU, 1 December 2008. L and P were suspected of illegally importing drugs into

[89] *Arain v Government of Germany* [2006] EWHC 1702 (Admin), para 19; *Welsh and Thresher v Secretary of State for the Home Department* [2006] 3 All ER 204, para 135; *R (Allison) v Secretary of State for the Home Department* [2001] EWHC (Admin) 506, paras 22–24. *Welsh and Thresher* contains a detailed analysis of the specialty issue in relation to the United States, a Category 2 territory, and is considered in detail at para 8.18 in relation to s 95.

[90] *Kucera v District Court of Karvina, Czech Republic* [2009] 1 WLR 806, paras 59–62; *Hilali v Central Court of Criminal Proceedings Number 5 of the National Court of Madrid* [2006] EWHC 1239 (Admin), para 51.

[91] *Ruiz Jaso v Central Criminal Court No 2, Madrid* [2007] EWHC 2983 (Admin), paras 63–70.

[92] Article 27(2) provides: '. . . a person surrendered may not be prosecuted, sentenced, or otherwise deprived of his or her liberty for an offence committed prior to his or her surrender other than that for which he or she was sentenced.' See also European Convention on Extradition 1957, Art 14.

Finland with a view to selling them. The Finnish authorities sent an EAW to the Polish authorities in the case of L and to the Spanish authorities in the case of P. The warrants stated that they were suspected of committing a serious drug-trafficking offence, between 1 January 2005 and 31 March 2006 in the case of L and between 19 and 25 February 2006 in the case of P. According to the arrest warrants, the offence related to a large quantity of amphetamines. The arrest warrant for P also mentioned two separate offences. L and P were surrendered to the Finnish authorities on the basis of those arrest warrants and were remanded in custody. Some months later, the indictment against L and P stated that the serious drug-trafficking offence concerned not amphetamines but hashish and had been committed between 15 and 26 February 2006. A new arrest warrant with those alterations was sent to the Spanish authorities, but they did not give their consent until much later. L and P were meanwhile both convicted at first instance and sentenced to imprisonment for that offence and, in the case of P for the two separate offences. Before the appeal court and then the Supreme Court L and P argued that they had been convicted for an offence other than that for which they had been surrendered, contrary to the specialty rule in Article 27(2) of the EAW Framework Decision.

On a referral on a preliminary question to the Court of Justice, the Court said that the EAW Framework Decision has the objective of creating a judicial area of freedom, security, and justice on the basis of mutual recognition and of speeding up judicial cooperation. The specialty rule, which is linked to sovereignty, has a number of exceptions. In particular, a person may be prosecuted for another offence if the judicial authorities of the member State executing the arrest warrant give their consent. However, to require that consent for every amendment to the description of the facts would go beyond what is implied by the specialty rule and would interfere with the objective of the Framework Decision. Alterations may be made to the description of the facts in the course of the proceedings and may describe more precisely or amend the ingredients of the offence. To determine whether or not another offence is concerned, it must be ascertained whether the ingredients of the offences as defined in the European arrest warrant are still present in the later procedural document and whether there is a sufficient correspondence between the information stated in the two documents. Alterations to the circumstances of time and place are allowed under certain conditions. In a case such as that of L and P in which the offence is still punishable by imprisonment for a maximum period of at least three years, and still comes under the rubric 'illegal trafficking in narcotic drugs' in the EAW Framework Decision, a change to the class of narcotics concerned, in this case hashish instead of amphetamines, was not in itself capable of characterizing another offence. The Supreme Court also asked whether the exception to the specialty rule where the criminal proceedings do not give rise to a measure restricting personal liberty applies in the case of a person such as P, who was in custody for the two separate offences of which he was accused. The Court explained that the exception applies as long as no measure restricting personal liberty is taken against the person for the 'offence other' than that for which he has been surrendered. If that person is ultimately sentenced to imprisonment for the 'other offence', consent must be sought and obtained before the sentence is enforced. The EAW Framework Decision does not, however, prevent the person surrendered from being subjected to a measure restricting personal liberty before consent is obtained, where that restriction is justified in law by other charges mentioned in the EAW. **5.82**

As was explained at para 1.17, for historical reasons the UK does not generally have extradition treaty relationships with other Commonwealth countries. In order to ensure that extradition to such territories does not fail for want of specialty protection, s 17(6) provides that specialty arrangements may be made with Commonwealth countries or British overseas territories for a particular case or more generally. **5.83**

Section 17(7) provides that a certificate issued by the Secretary of State confirming the existence of such arrangements with a Commonwealth country or British overseas territory and **5.84** stating the terms of the arrangement is conclusive. A conclusive certificate may only be issued by the Secretary of State in relation to Commonwealth countries and British overseas territories. Although arrangements may be made with other territories, any certificate will not be conclusive, and the court therefore has jurisdiction to enquire into the effectiveness of the arrangements and whether they provide the protections required by s 17(3) and (4).[93]

Extradition barred by reason of earlier extradition to the UK (ss 18 and 19)

5.85 Sections 18 and 19 prohibit the defendant's extradition under certain circumstances where he has already been extradited to the UK from a Category 1 territory (s 18) or non-Category 1 territory (s 19). The prohibition on re-extradition is closely related to the rule on specialty.[94] Article 28 of the EAW Framework Decision provides:

> ... a person who has been surrendered pursuant to a European arrest warrant shall not be extradited to a third State without the consent of the competent authority which surrendered the person.

5.86 A person's extradition to a Category 1 territory is barred by reason of his earlier extradition to the UK from another Category 1 territory if and only if (s 18):

(a) the person was extradited to the UK from another Category 1 territory (the extraditing territory);
(b) under arrangements between the UK and the extraditing territory, that territory's consent is required to the person's extradition from the UK to the Category 1 territory in respect of the extradition offence under consideration;[95]
(c) that consent has not been given on behalf of the extraditing territory and the arrangements do not treat it as having been given.

5.87 A person's extradition to a Category 1 territory is barred by reason of his earlier extradition to the UK from a non-Category 1 territory if and only if (s 19):

(a) the person was extradited to the UK from a territory that is not a Category 1 territory (the extraditing territory);
(b) under arrangements between the UK and the extraditing territory, that territory's consent is required to the person's being dealt with in the UK in respect of the extradition offence under consideration;
(c) consent has not been given on behalf of the extraditing territory to the person's extradition from the UK to the Category 1 territory in respect of the extradition offence under consideration.

Extradition barred by reason of return from the ICC (s 19A)

5.88 Para 3(1) of Sch 13 to the Police and Criminal Justice Act 2006 inserted a new bar to extradition in s 11(i) and s 19A of the EA 2003. Section 11(i) provides that the appropriate judge must decide whether extradition is barred by reason of the defendant's earlier transfer to the UK by the ICC.

5.89 Section 19A provides that the defendant's extradition to a Category 1 territory is barred by reason of his earlier transfer by the ICC if (and only if) he was transferred to the UK to serve a sentence imposed by the Court; under arrangements between the UK and the Court, the

[93] *R v Secretary of State for the Home Department, ex p Launder (No 2)* [1998] QB 944.
[94] *R v Secretary of State for the Home Department ex p Johnson* [1999] QB 1174.
[95] For example EAW Framework Decision, Art 28; European Convention on Extradition, Art 15.

consent of the Presidency of the Court is required to the person's extradition from the United Kingdom to the Category 1 territory in respect of the extradition offence under consideration and that consent has not been given.

Section 19A(1) does not apply if the person has served the sentence imposed by the Court and has subsequently remained voluntarily in the UK for more than 30 days, or left the UK and returned to it. **5.90**

Extradition barred because UK more appropriate forum for trial (s 19B)

The case of the 'NatWest 3' in 2006[96] caused controversy in part because in the view of many the UK rather than the United States was the proper forum for the defendants' trial. Although their judicial review challenge to the failure by the SFO to prosecute them was rejected by the High Court, in the view of some the case exposed the risk of injustice where a crime that has been committed (in whole or in large part) in the UK results in an extradition request from a foreign state which has jurisdiction to try the defendant for the alleged conduct. **5.91**

Concern about the NatWest 3 case led Parliament to include provisions in the Police and Justice Act 2006 which amend the EA 2003 to allow the appropriate judge to consider where the defendant's trial should take place, where there is a choice of venue available. Paragraph 3(2) of Sch 13 to the Police and Justice Act 2006 inserts s 11(j) and s 19B into the EA 2003, and these allow the appropriate judge to refuse extradition where the UK would be a more suitable venue for trial.[97] However, the 2011 Extradition Review considered the forum provisions in Part 5 and recommended against enacting them. In contrast, in March 2012 the House of Commons Home Affairs Select Committee recommended that the forum provisions in the EA 2003 be brought into force, and in October 2012 the Governer said it would do so.[98] **5.92**

Section 11(j) is entitled 'Forum'. Section 19B provides that the defendant's extradition to a Category 1 territory ('the requesting territory') is barred by reason of forum if (and only if) it appears that a significant part of the conduct alleged to constitute the extradition offence is conduct in the UK, and in view of that and all the other circumstances, it would not be in the interests of justice for the person to be tried for the offence in the requesting territory.[99] **5.93**

Section 19B(2) provides that for the purposes of s 19B(1)(b) the judge must take into account whether the relevant prosecution authorities in the UK have decided not to take proceedings against the person in respect of the conduct in question. **5.94**

Section 19B does not apply if the defendant is alleged to be unlawfully at large after conviction of the extradition offence (s 19B(3)). **5.95**

---

96 *R (Bermingham) v Director of the Serious Fraud Office* [2006] EWHC 200 (Admin); see para 1.62.

97 Para 3 also inserts s 83A for Part 2 cases, in similar terms to s 19B. These provisions were not in force at the time of writing (August 2012). Para 6 of Sch 13 to the Police and Justice Act 2006 provides that an order bringing the provisions into force is not to be made within the period of 12 months beginning with the day on which the Act was passed (8 November 2006). If after the end of that period a resolution is made by each House of Parliament that the provisions should come into force, the Secretary of State shall make an order under s 53 bringing the paragraphs (or paragraph) into force (para 6(2)). An order made by virtue of para 6(2) must bring the provisions in question into force no later than one month after the day on which the resolutions referred to in that sub-paragraph are made or, if they are made on different days, the day on which the later resolution is made.

98 20th Report, 27 March 2012; <http://www.publications.parliament.uk>.

99 For a discussion of how forum conflicts within the EU should be addressed, including an analysis of the Council Framework Decision of 30 November 2009 on the prevention and settlement of conflicts of exercise of jurisdiction in criminal proceedings, 2009/948/JHA, (L 328/42, 15 December 2009), see *Williams v Public Prosecutor – Lille Court of First Instance, France* [2012] EWHC 2128 (Admin); cf *R (Bermingham) v Director of the Serious Fraud Office* [2006] EWHC 200 (Admin), paras 57–78.

I. Other Grounds for Refusing Extradition

Convictions in absence (s 20)

5.96 Trials *in absentia* are commonplace in civil law jurisdictions despite the risk of unfairness arising from a trial where the defendant is absent.[100] Section 6(2) of the EA 1989 provided a bar to return where a defendant had been convicted in his absence and it was not in the interests of justice to return him. Section 20 of the EA 2003 removes this generalized test and replaces it with an inquiry into whether the defendant deliberately absented himself from his trial. If he did so then he is not able to rely on that fact to avoid extradition.[101]

5.97 It is obviously unjust to imprison a defendant on the basis of a conviction obtained in his absence at a trial he could not have attended, without him being able to re-open the case against him. In *Othman v United Kingdom*, Application No 8139/09, para 259, the European Court of Human Rights cited such a situation as being a rare example of a 'flagrant denial of justice' which would be sufficient to bar extradition under Article 6 of the ECHR.[102] Section 20 is intended to ensure that a defendant who has been convicted in his absence but who did not have an opportunity to appear at his trial (eg, because he was unaware of it) is not extradited unless he is guaranteed a fair trial in his presence in the Category 1 requesting state. The judge is required to proceed under s 20 if the defendant is alleged to be unlawfully at large after conviction of an extradition offence (s 11(4)).The effect of s 20 is that if a defendant was convicted in his absence and if he did not deliberately absent himself from his trial, and if he would not be entitled to a re-trial or, on appeal, a review amounting to a re-trial, then the court must discharge him.[103]

5.98 The first question to be decided under s 20 is whether the defendant was convicted in his presence (s 20(1)). If he was, then the inquiry under s 20 is at an end and the judge must proceed under s 21 (s 20(2)). If the judge decides that the defendant was convicted in his absence he must then decide whether the defendant 'deliberately' absented himself from his trial (s 20(3)). If the judge decides that he did so, he must proceed under s 21 (s 20(4)).[104]

5.99 The burden of showing that the defendant deliberately absented himself lies on the requesting state, which must prove it to the criminal standard.[105] In order to deliberately absent himself from his trial within the meaning of s 20(3), the defendant must be fully informed of the consequences if he absents himself. In *Czekala v District Court in Bydgoszcz* [2010] EWHC 1895 (Admin), para 31, King J said that the authorities were to the effect:

> ... that to make a finding that the Appellant deliberately absented himself from his trial the court must satisfy itself that the Requested Person has made a clear conscious decision not to attend his trial foreseeing that the consequence of this decision will be that the trial takes place in his absence. Normally, such a decision can only be properly said to have been taken where the Requested Person is aware of the date and place of the hearing since only then will the Requested Person reasonably foresee that his conduct will have the consequence of him not

---

100 *Re Peci*, 5 November 1999, CO/1368/99; *R v Governor of Brixton Prison ex p Caborn-Waterfield* [1960] 2 QB 498; *R v Governor of Pentonville Prison ex p Zezza* [1983] 1 AC 46; *Lodhi v Governor of HM Prison Brixton* [2001] EWHC 178; *Re Foy*, 14 April 2000, CO/3969/99.

101 Section 85 is the equivalent provision in Part 2 cases.

102 Para 7.69.

103 *Deputy Public Prosecutor of the Court of Appeal of Montpellier v Wade* [2006] EWHC 1909 (Admin), para 5; *Virciglio v Judicial Authority of the Graz High Court, Austria* [2006] All ER (D) 44 (Oct).

104 cf *Mariotti v Government of Italy* [2005] EWHC 2745 (Admin).

105 EA 2003, s 206; *Nebak v Regional Court Bydgoszcz, Poland* [2012] EWHC 417 (Admin), para 7; *Mitoi v Government of Romania* [2006] EWHC 1977 (Admin).

being present at his trial. Nevertheless, if the Requested Person's conduct clearly and unequivocally demonstrates that the Requested Person does not intend to take part in his forthcoming trial, the court may infer that the Requested Person has deliberately absented himself.[106]

If the judge decides that the defendant did not deliberately absent himself he must decide whether he would be entitled to a re-trial or (on appeal) to a review amounting to a re-trial.[107] This may require the judge to hear expert evidence of foreign law. In *Mucelli v Secretary of State for the Home Department* [2012] EWHC 95 (Admin), para 50, the High Court commented that courts must resist the temptation to offer their own interpretation of foreign law. Neither they nor the English lawyers involved can have a full understanding of the context of foreign constitutional and statutory instruments or judicial decisions. The experts have that understanding. Their views may be in conflict and the court may have to reconcile them, but should not do so primarily through its own interpretation of the foreign law materials. **5.100**

Although s 20(5) uses the word 'entitled', an undertaking by the requesting state that the defendant will be given a re-trial may be sufficient, even if he is not guaranteed a re-trial as a matter of law.[108] However, *Bohm v Romanian Judicial Authority* [2011] EWHC 2671, para 5, Irwin J said that in relation to the issue of re-trial, if the answer as the defendant's entitlement was 'no' or 'perhaps' or 'in certain circumstances', that would not be enough to meet the statutory test and the defendant in those circumstances must be discharged. In other words, the court must be sure that the right to a re-trial or a review on appeal exists.[109] **5.101**

If the judge decides that the defendant would be entitled to a re-trial then he must proceed under s 21. If the judge decides that question in the negative he must order the person's discharge. **5.102**

Section 20(8) specifies the ingredients of a re-trial sufficient for the purposes of s 20(5). The judge should not regard as a re-trial or (on appeal) a review amounting to a re-trial, any proceedings that do not include provision for: **5.103**

(a) the suspect to be present at the re-trial;
(b) the suspect to have like rights to hear and examine witnesses as he would have done at the original trial;
(c) the suspect to have the same right to publicly funded legal services as any suspect or defendant.

The High Court has considered the right to a re-trial in a number of Albanian cases under Part 2 of the EA 2003, the relevant provisions of Albanian law having proved troublesome. In *Government of Albania v Bleta* [2005] 1 WLR 3576, the High Court upheld the district judge's decision to discharge the defendant. The extradition request from the Albanian authorities provided an 'official guarantee' for the re-trial of Bleta 'with reference to the present Albanian criminal legislation ...'. In their letter the Albanian authorities referred to a number of articles in their Constitution and the Criminal Procedure Code. However, the defendant submitted that Article 147 Criminal Procedure Code only contained the possibility of an appeal. That was conditional and fell short of the required entitlement to a review amounting to a re-trial. Article 427 on appeals did not provide an entitlement to a re-trial. Pill LJ (with whom Cox J agreed) held that, despite making all allowances for matters such as translation difficulties, and despite accepting the good faith of the guarantee, there were 'too many open ends and **5.104**

---

106 *Nebak v Regional Court Bydgoszcz, Poland* [2012] EWHC 417 (Admin), para 8; *Deputy Public Prosecutor of the Court of Appeal of Montpellier v Wade* [2006] EWHC 1909 (Admin), para 15.

107 EA 2003, s 20(5).

108 *Lodhi v Governor of HM Prison Brixton* [2001] EWHC (Admin) 178; *Re Peci*, 5 November 1999, CO/1368/99.

109 *Mucelli v Secretary of State for the Home Department* [2012] EWHC 95 (Admin), para 32.

insufficient clarity' to be able to conclude that s 85(5) was satisfied. Signatures of the European Convention on Human Rights or the UN covenants, in themselves, did not amount to sufficient assurance in the circumstances.

5.105 In *Mucelli v Government of Albania* [2008] 1 WLR 2437, the High Court dismissed the defendant's appeal as being out of time, but, in an obiter dictum at para 26, the Court did consider the merits of the appeal and said that an examination of the detailed provisions of the Code of Criminal Procedure cast real doubt on the effectiveness of the guarantee of a re-trial which the Albanian authorities had offered. Richards LJ concluded that the position was too uncertain to enable the court to conclude, on the strength of the guarantee provided, that the appellant would be entitled to a re-trial on his return.

5.106 However, in *Bogdani v Government of Albania* [2008] EWHC 2065 (Admin) Pill LJ (with whom Rafferty J agreed) upheld the decision of the district judge that on return to Albania the appellant would be entitled to a re-trial or review on appeal. The district judge had a letter from the Albanian Minister of Justice relating to Article 147(2) confirming that an extradited person could exercise the right under it within ten days from the date of being handed over to the Albanian authorities and that the Ministry of Justice 'was legally entitled to decide on respecting the conditions imposed by the foreign state that in this case relates to the right of retrial of the subject tried in absence'.

5.107 But, in *R (Bulla) v Secretary of State for the Home Department* [2010] EWHC 3506 (Admin) Sullivan LJ reverted to the approach of in *Government of Albania v Bleta* [2005] 1 WLR 3576 and *Mucelli v Government of Albania* [2008] 1 WLR 2437. On appeal, Sullivan LJ noted the difficulties of interpretation in extradition cases, but said at para 12 that even making due allowances for such difficulties a great deal had been lost, and there were too many loose ends, and Albania's status as a signatory to the ECHR was insufficient to satisfy the requirement in s 85 that the defendant be entitled to a re-trial as of right.

5.108 In *Mucelli v Secretary of State for the Home Department* [2012] EWHC 95 (Admin), paras 48–56, the High Court again reviewed the position, including recent expert evidence and cases before the European Court of Human Rights relating to rights of re-trial in Albania, and concluded that there is a right to re-trial under Albanian law for a defendant convicted in his absence, sufficient to satisfy s 85 of the EA 2003.

Human rights (s 21)

5.109 Section 21 prohibits the judge from ordering extradition where to do so would be incompatible with the defendant's Convention rights within the meaning of the Human Rights Act 1998. This topic is dealt with separately in Chapter 7.

Physical or mental condition (s 25)

5.110 Extradition of a defendant who is seriously ill may be unfair or oppressive.[110] Section 25 gives the appropriate judge the power to discharge the defendant on the grounds of his physical or mental condition, at any stage of the proceedings. Alternatively, the judge can adjourn the proceedings pending the defendant's recovery.[111]

---

110 *Dewani v Government of the Republic of South Africa* [2012] EWHC 842 (Admin); *United States of America v Tollman* [2008] 3 All ER 150, paras 162–172; *R (Warren) v Secretary of State for the Home Department* [2003] EWHC 1177 (Admin); *Re Davies* [1998] COD 30; cf *R v Secretary of State for the Home Department ex p Kingdom of Belgium*, 15 February 2000, CO/236/00. Extradition of a person who is physically or mentally ill may also violate Art 3 of the ECHR if the illness is sufficiently severe: para 7.38.

111 Section 91 is the equivalent provision in Part 2 cases.

Section 25 applies if at any time in the extradition hearing it appears to the judge that the condition in s 25(2) is satisfied (s 25(1)). This condition is that the physical or mental condition of the person in respect of whom the Part 1 warrant is issued is such that it would be unjust or oppressive to extradite him. **5.111**

Section 25 and s 91 were new provisions in the EA 2003. They were intended to safeguard those whose physical or mental health means that extradition would result in unfairness or oppression to them. They empower the appropriate judge either to discharge the defendant (without prejudice to the requesting state's ability to re-submit its request in the event of the defendant's recovery), or to adjourn the hearing if there is a real prospect of recovery within a reasonable time. These bars first appeared in the EA 2003 to deal with the problem which emerged during the *Pinochet* case in 1999–2000 under the EA 1989.[112] Following his committal in October 1999, General Pinochet suffered a number of strokes and became unfit to stand trial, although this was disputed by the requesting state and others. The Secretary of State thus had to consider contested medical evidence concerning General Pinochet's fitness to stand trial, resulting in him being drawn into judicial review proceedings.[113] **5.112**

As a consequence, during the passing of what became the EA 2003, Parliament decided that it was inappropriate for matters of health to be left for determination by the Executive, and so s 25 and s 91 were included in the EA 2003 in order to ensure that health matters would, in the future, be decided by a court. **5.113**

Section 25 and s 91 are a recognition that ill-health is a proper basis to delay or deny extradition. They require the court to look at the fairness of the extradition proceedings if a person is unfit (for example whether he can adequately defend himself in the proceedings), as well as the consequences of extradition if it were to be granted, for example whether the defendant could fairly defend himself at trial, or whether extradition would cause a deterioration in his health or a threat to his life. **5.114**

Section 25 gives effect to Article 23(4) of the EAW Framework Decision, which provides: **5.115**

> Surrender may exceptionally be temporarily postponed for serious humanitarian reasons, for example if there are substantial grounds for believing that it would manifestly endanger the requested person's life or health.

It is established that the EA 2003 must be construed in a manner which gives effect to the EAW Framework Decision.[114] Section 25 should therefore be construed in a manner that gives effect to the important protection contained in Article 23(4).[115] The Commission proposal, COM (2001)522 Final, which formed the *travaux preparatoire* for the EAW Framework Decision, noted that this provision was concerned with: **5.116**

> ... concrete situations in which the European arrest warrant should not be executed on account of the practical situation of the person, and in particular his health. It can be deferred until the person's situation has improved. The warrant will then have to be executed as soon as possible.

---

112 *Dewani v Government of the Republic of South Africa* [2012] EWHC 842 (Admin), para 66.

113 *R v Secretary of State ex p Kingdom of Belgium*, 15 February 2000, CO/236/2000.

114 *Assange v The Swedish Prosecution Authority* [2012] UKSC 22, paras 10, 77, 98, 112, 122–123, 201–218.

115 The point was left open in *Dewani v Government of the Republic of South Africa* [2012] EWHC 842 (Admin), paras 66–74, but it is obvious that s 25 has to be interpreted in light of the EAW Framework Decision. Section 91 should be interpreted in the same manner. It cannot be the case that Parliament intended a lesser degree of protection for defendants who are facing extradition to non-EU states; cf *Dudko v Government of the Russian Federation* [2010] EWHC 1125 (Admin), para 16.

The use of the word 'humanitarian' in Article 23(4) assists in the approach that should be adopted to the interpretation of s 25 and to the words 'unjust or oppressive'. The term 'humanitarian' most commonly connotes having concern for, or helping to improve, the welfare and happiness of people; alternatively it pertains to the alleviation of human suffering, seeking to promote human welfare as a primary or pre-eminent good, and acting, or disposed to act, on this basis rather than for pragmatic or strategic reasons. In the context of s 25, the terms 'unjust' and 'oppressive' must therefore be interpreted to cover any case where it would be harsh, wrong, or unfair to extradite the defendant given his illness. In *Dewani v Government of the Republic of South Africa* [2012] EWHC 842 (Admin) the district judge had sent the defendant's case to the Secretary of State notwithstanding the agreed medical evidence that he was unfit to stand trial, and that extradition would further harm him to the point that he could become psychotic and/or permanently unfit to stand trial and would be at high risk of committing suicide. The High Court held that the judge should have adjourned the extradition hearing to allow the defendant time to recover.

5.117 The terms 'unjust and oppressive' are used in s 25 and in other places in the EA 2003, and have appeared in extradition legislation since the nineteenth century.[116] However, Parliament intended its own test in relation to s 25 and s 91, and courts in applying these sections should not be distracted by observations that the threshold of oppression is high, or that the graver the charge the higher the bar,[117] as this inevitably risks taking the eye of the parties and the court off the statutory test by drawing the court into the consideration of the facts of the other cases. The term 'unjust or oppressive' requires regard to be had to all the relevant circumstances, including the fact that extradition is ordinarily likely to cause stress and hardship; neither of those is sufficient.[118] The court should keep its eye on the question posed by s 25 and s 91. The question is not how ill the defendant is, *per se*, but whether by reason of his illness it would be unjust or oppressive to extradite him.[119]

5.118 The court's decision in relation to s 25 must be made on the basis of what is known at the time the court considers the matter. This is because s 25 is expressed in the present tense, so that health must be considered as it stands at the time the court considers the issue, together with the foreseeable consequences for the defendant's health should extradition occur.

5.119 Where the defendant is unfit to stand trial then it will almost inevitably be unjust or oppressive to extradite him whilst he remains unfit.[120] Where there is a risk that the courts of the requesting state may reach a contrary conclusion then, *a fortiori*, it will be unjust or oppressive to extradite the defendant.[121]

Abuse of process and bad faith

Background

5.120 Unfortunately requesting states sometimes abuse their right to seek extradition. Extradition requests can be made for improper reasons or pursued in a vexatious or oppressive manner. To say that an extradition request is an abuse of process, or that it is made in bad faith, is not necessarily to impugn the good faith of the high sovereign authorities who make the request

116 Fugitive Offenders Act 1881, s 10.

117 *Government of Croatia v Spanovic* [2007] 1770 (Admin); *Tajik v Government of the United States of America* [2008] EWHC (Admin).

118 *Dewani v Government of the Republic of South Africa* [2012] EWHC 842 (Admin), para 73.

119 *Boudhiba v Central Examining Court No.5 of the National Court of Justice, Madrid, Spain* [2006] EWHC 167 (Admin), para 65; *Prancs v Rezekne Court of Latvia* [2006] All ER (D) 28 (Oct).

120 *R (Warren) v Secretary of State for the Home Department* [2003] EWHC 1177 (Admin), paras 26–28.

121 *United States of America v Tollman* [2008] 3 All ER 150, paras 162–172.

on behalf of the state.[122] Extradition requests are the product of criminal investigations and so can become infected with the corruption or dishonesty of witnesses, police, or prosecutors. In *Atkinson v Government of the United States of America* [1971] AC 197, 232 Lord Reid said:

> Extradition may be requested either because the man is accused of an extradition crime or because he has been convicted in the foreign country of an extradition crime. It is not unknown for convictions to be obtained in a few foreign countries by improper means, and it would be intolerable if a man so convicted had to be surrendered. Parliament can never have so intended when the 1870 Act was passed.

There have been numerous cases in which the requesting state has sought extradition in circumstances where it would have been an affront to justice to return the defendant.[123]

The High Court had a statutory jurisdiction under s 11(3)(c) of the EA 1989 in Part III cases to discharge a defendant where it concluded that the accusation against him was not made in good faith in the interests of justice. However, other than that, prior to the Human Rights Act 1998, abuse of process or bad faith on the part of the requesting state was not a matter that the courts would consider. It was a matter for the Secretary of State to consider at the order for return stage when he had to consider whether extradition would be 'wrong, unjust or oppressive'.[124]

The Human Rights Act 1998 produced an important change to the law in this area. In *R (Kashamu) v Governor of Brixton Prison* [2002] QB 887 the applicants contended that following the incorporation of Article 5(4) of the European Convention on Human Rights, the court of committal had jurisdiction to determine whether extradition proceedings against them amounted to an abuse of process. They argued that the absence of any judicial abuse of process jurisdiction was inconsistent with Article 5(4), which requires the 'lawfulness' of detention (inter alia for the purposes of extradition under Article 5(1)(f)) to be 'speedily' decided by a 'court'. In this context, 'lawfulness' does not just mean domestic lawfulness, but also means lawfulness in the Convention sense, that is non-arbitrary detention.[125] The applicants argued that detention arising from bad faith or abuse of power, in particular, rendered the detention arbitrary and hence unlawful under the Convention. Consequently, they contended that the effect of incorporation of Article 5(4) into domestic law was to confer such an abuse of process jurisdiction on the court of committal. **5.121**

The Administrative Court upheld the applicants' arguments, holding that the Strasbourg jurisprudence meant that, in order to comply with the requirements in Article 5(4), the magistrates' **5.122**

122 *R (Saifi) v Governor of HM Prison Brixton* [2001] 1 WLR 1134, para 63. However, in *Symeou v Public Prosecutor's Office at the Court of Appeals, Patras, Greece* [2009] 1 WLR 2384, paras 33–34, the High Court held that misconduct by the police did not engage the court's abuse of process jurisdiction in Part 1 cases, and that the wrongdoing had to be at the level of the prosecuting authorities. This is an unjustifiable distinction; given the purpose of the abuse of process jurisdiction in extradition cases is to protect the integrity of the process, it is hard to see why wrongdoing by some officials but not others which all feed into the extradition request should engage the court's abuse of process jurisdiction.

123 *Sofia City Court v Atanasova-Kalaidzhieva* [2011] EWHC 2335 (Admin) (Bulgaria: prosecutor acting in bad faith); *Government of Russian Federation v Temerko*, 23 December 2005 (Senior District Judge) (Russia: extradition sought for political reasons); *Government of Russian Federation v Zakaev*, 13 November 2003 (Russia: extradition sought for political reasons); *Re Asliturk* [2002] EWHC 2326 (Admin) (Turkey: extradition sought for political reasons); *Re Sutej* [2003] EWHC 1940 (Switzerland: bad faith by complainant); *R (Saifi) v Governor of HM Prison Brixton* [2001] 1 WLR 1134 (India: improper pressure brought to bear on only witness against the defendant); *Re Murat Calis*, 19 November 1993 (CO/2757/92) (Turkey: bad faith by complainant).

124 *In re Schmidt* [1995] 1 AC 399; *R v Governor of Pentonville Prison ex p Sinclair* [1991] 2 AC 64; *Atkinson v Government of the United States of America* [1971] AC 197.

125 *R v Governor of Brockhill Prison ex p Evans* [2001] AC 19, 38.

court hearing the committal proceedings had jurisdiction to determine the question of whether a fugitive's detention was lawful. The Court said that the district judge's obligation under s 6(1) of the Human Rights Act 1998 Act to act compatibly with the Convention required him to make a determination under Article 5(4) as to whether the detention was lawful by English domestic law, complied with the general requirements of the Convention and was not arbitrary. Rose LJ said at paras 32–34:

> What is in issue in the present case is whether, when lawful extradition procedures are being used, a resultant detention may be unlawful by virtue of abuse of the court's process. The magistrates' court, rather than the High Court, is, in my judgment, the appropriate tribunal for hearing evidence and submissions, finding facts relevant to abuse and doing so speedily. Furthermore, as it seems to me, the district judge's obligation under section 6(1) of the Human Rights Act 1998 to act compatibly with Convention rights requires him to make a determination under Article 5(4). It seems to me that ... he must consider whether the detention is lawful by English domestic law, complies with the general requirements of the Convention and is not open to criticism for arbitrariness ... What is pertinent here in the present cases is solely whether the detention is unlawful by English domestic law and/or arbitrary, because of bad faith or deliberate abuse of the English courts' procedure.

Abuse of process under the EA 2003

5.123 In *R (Bermingham) v Director of the Serious Fraud Office* [2006] EWHC 200 (Admin), para 96, Laws LJ held that the appropriate judge conducting an extradition hearing under Part 2 of the EA 2003 has a discretion to stay proceedings as an abuse of process in order to ensure that 'the [extradition] regime's integrity' is not usurped by abuse of process. At para 100 he said:

> The prosecutor must act in good faith. Thus if he knew he had no real case, but was pressing the extradition request for some collateral motive and accordingly tailored the choice of documents accompanying the request, there might be a good submission of abuse of process. Again, if he knew he could not (or perhaps, could not without great difficulty) make out a *prima facie* case and so deliberately delayed the extradition process until the 1989 Act had been safely superseded by the 2003 Act, that also might be held to be abusive.

5.124 In *R (Government of the United States of America) v Senior District Judge, Bow Street Magistrates' Court* [2006] EWHC 2256 (Admin), para 82, the Administrative Court approved the observations on abuse of process in *R (Bermingham) v Director of the Serious Fraud Office* [2006] EWHC 200 (Admin). The Court applied to extradition proceedings the statement made by Bingham LJ in *R v Liverpool Stipendiary Magistrate ex p Ellison* [1990] RTR 220 in relation to conventional criminal proceedings:

> If any criminal court at any time has cause to suspect that a prosecutor may be manipulating or using the procedures of the court in order to oppress or unfairly to prejudice a defendant before the court, I have no doubt that it is the duty of the court to inquire into the situation and ensure that its procedure is not being abused. Usually no doubt such inquiry will be prompted by a complaint on the part of the defendant. But the duty of the court in my view exists even in the absence of a complaint.

5.125 In *McKinnon v Government of the United States of America* [2008] 1 WLR 1739, para 8, Lord Brown said:

> The district judge also has jurisdiction to consider whether the extradition proceedings constituted an abuse of process so as to protect the integrity of the statutory regime

The abuse of process jurisdiction established in *R (Government of the United States of America) v Senior District Judge, Bow Street Magistrates' Court* [2006] EWHC 2256 (Admin) and *R (Bermingham) v Director of the Serious Fraud Office* [2006] EWHC 200 (Admin) is equally applicable to hearings under Part 1.[126] Hence, persons arrested for the purposes of proceedings under both Parts 1 and 2 of the EA 2003 can seek to stay the extradition proceedings against them on the grounds that they are an abuse of process.

The test for abuse of process

Abuse of process can arise in extradition proceedings either because of some forensic unfairness in the hearing itself, or because of some more fundamental breach of the principles of justice or the rule of law.[127] In *R (Bermingham) v Director of the Serious Fraud Office* [2007] QB 727, para 100, Laws LJ gave, as examples of abuse of process, the failure of a prosecutor to exercise good faith by pressing a request when he knows he has no real case, or the deliberate delay of the extradition process to gain the advantage of the EA 2003. The rationale for the existence of the power to protect the statutory regime's integrity is to protect the court from manipulation by invoking procedures which might oppress or unfairly prejudice a defendant.[128] In *United States of America v Cobb* [2001] 1 SCR 587, para 35, Arbour J of the Supreme Court of Canada emphasized that: **5.126**

> The Requesting State is a party to judicial proceedings before a Canadian court and is subject to the application of rules and remedies that serve to control the conduct of the parties who turn to the courts for assistance ... litigants are protected from unfair, abusive proceedings through the doctrine of abuse of process, which bars litigants – and not only the State – from pursuing frivolous or vexatious proceedings, or otherwise abusing the process of the courts.

In *Larosa v Her Majesty the Queen and the United States of America* 166 CCC (3d) 449, para 52, the Ontario Court of Appeal interpreted the decision in *United States of America v Cobb* [2001] 1 SCR 587[129] as recognizing a jurisdiction to stay proceedings in two related but different situations: (i) where the actual conduct of the hearing produces unfairness; and (ii) where proceeding with the committal hearing would amount to an abuse of process or breach principles of fundamental justice. As to the latter species of abuse of process, in *McKinnon v Government of the United States of America* [2008] 1 WLR 1739, para 33, where the suggestion was that the United States had tried to force the defendant not to contest his extradition by the threat of a longer sentence, Lord Brown said that the questions to be considered were whether there had been an attempt to interfere with the due process of the court; whether undue pressure had been placed on the defendant to forego due legal process in the UK by the requesting state so as to disentitle it from pursuing extradition proceedings; whether extradition would violate those fundamental principles of justice which underlie the community's sense of fair play and decency; and whether the defendant, following extradition, would pay an unconscionable price having insisted on exercising his rights under English law. **5.127**

In *Symeou v Public Prosecutor's Office at the Court of Appeals, Patras, Greece* [2009] 1 WLR 2384, paras 33–34, the High Court held that misconduct by the police did not engage the court's abuse of process jurisdiction in Part 1 cases, and that the wrongdoing had to be at the level of the prosecuting authorities.[130] This is an unjustifiable distinction; given the purpose of the abuse of process jurisdiction in extradition cases is to protect the integrity of the process, it is difficult to see why wrongdoing by some officials but not others, all of which may feed into an **5.128**

---

126 *R (Government of the United States of America) v Senior District Judge, Bow Street Magistrates' Court* [2006] EWHC 2256 (Admin) was decided with a Part 1 case, *R (Central Examining Court, Criminal Court of the National Court, Madrid) v Bow Street Magistrates' Court.*

127 cf *Beckford* [1996] 1 Cr App R 94, 101.

128 *Office of Prosecutor General of Turin v Barone* [2010] EWHC 3004 (Admin), para 18.

129 See also *United States v Shulman* [2001] 1 SCR 616.

130 cf *Khan v Government of the United States of America* [2010] EWHC 1127 (Admin), para 9, where *Symeou v Public Prosecutor's Office at the Court of Appeals, Patras, Greece* [2009] 1 WLR 2384 was applied in a Part 2 case.

extradition request, should engage the court's abuse of process jurisdiction. The proper question is whether the conduct complained of goes simply to the admissibility of the evidence, in which case it can properly be left for determination by the courts of the requesting state, or whether it is of such a nature that to base an extradition request upon it can be said to undermine fundamental principles of justice.

5.129 In *Khan v Government of the United States Of America* [2010] EWHC 1127 (Admin), para 9, the High Court emphasized the residual nature of abuse of process in extradition cases and said that the focus of the enquiry is whether there has been an abuse of the requested state's duty to extradite those who are properly requested and who are unable to raise any of the statutory bars to extradition in the EA 2003.

When is the issue of abuse of process to be determined?

5.130 In ordinary criminal proceedings abuse of process operates as a plea in bar and is generally determined at the outset of proceedings.[131] The same procedure does not necessarily apply in extradition cases. In *R (Government of the United States of America) v Senior District Judge, Bow Street Magistrates' Court* [2006] EWHC 2256 (Admin) the defendant sought to raise the issue *in limine* prior to the commencement of the extradition hearings. The Court said that this was the wrong approach and that where the issue of abuse of process is raised it should be decided as one of the issues arising during the extradition hearing. At para 80 the Court said:

> The 2003 Act makes express provision for extradition to be refused when the request is motivated by 'extraneous circumstances' that under English law would constitute an abuse of process and for these and human rights issues to be considered as part of the extradition hearing. Where extradition is challenged on grounds, such as abuse of process, which are not dealt with expressly under the Act they should none the less normally be considered within the extradition hearing. The 2003 Act lays down special rules in relation to extradition that are designed to ensure that extradition proceedings are concluded with expedition. This objective will be torpedoed if allegations of abuse of process are pursued outside the statutory regime.

The court's approach where abuse of process is raised

5.131 In *R (Government of the United States of America) v Senior District Judge, Bow Street Magistrates' Court* [2006] EWHC 2256 (Admin), paras 83–93 the Administrative Court gave general guidance on the approach to be adopted by the appropriate judge where the defendant raises the issue of abuse of process:

> The 2003 Act places a duty on the judge to decide a large number of matters before acceding to a request for extradition. To these should be added the duty to decide whether the process is being abused, if put on enquiry as to the possibility of this. The judge will usually, though not inevitably, be put on enquiry as to the possibility of abuse of process by allegations made by the person whose extradition is sought.
>
> ... Where an allegation of abuse of process is made, the first step must be to insist on the conduct alleged to constitute the abuse being identified with particularity. The judge must then consider whether the conduct, if established, is capable of amounting to an abuse of process. If it is, he must next consider whether there are reasonable grounds for believing that such conduct may have occurred. If there are, then the judge should not accede to the request for extradition unless he has satisfied himself that such abuse has not occurred ...

[131] *R v Aldershot Youth Court ex p A* [1997] 3 Archbold News 2; Practice Direction (Criminal Proceedings: Consolidation) [2002] 1 WLR 2870, para IV.36.

Sovereign, diplomatic, and consular immunity

The defendant may in an appropriate case claim diplomatic or sovereign immunity from arrest or detention for the purposes of extradition proceedings.[132] **5.132**

Section 1 and Sch 1 of the Diplomatic Privileges Act 1964 incorporates the provisions of the Vienna Convention on Diplomatic Relations 1961 into UK law. The Convention confers absolute immunity from arrest for diplomats, members of their families, and their immediate households. Thus, persons falling into this category cannot lawfully be arrested for the purposes of extradition unless their immunity is waived. Section 4 of the Diplomatic Privileges Act 1964 provides that where any question arises whether or not any person is entitled to any privilege or immunity under the Act a certificate issued by the Secretary of State under the Act stating any fact relating to that question is conclusive evidence of that fact. The burden is on the defendant to produce the certificate.[133] **5.133**

Section 20(1)(a) of the State Immunity Act 1978 confers the same immunity *mutatis mutandis* on visiting heads of state. Thus a head of state is immune from arrest while visiting the UK.[134] **5.134**

As a matter of customary international law, members of special missions[135] are immune from arrest whilst in the UK.[136] **5.135**

Ministers of foreign states whose position requires them to travel internationally in order to represent their state (eg, Ministers of Foreign Affairs) are immune from the criminal jurisdiction of the UK as a matter of customary international law.[137] **5.136**

The Pinochet case

The immunity from arrest and prosecution of a former head of state for offences committed whilst he was in office was one of the issues considered by House of Lords in *R v Metropolitan Stipendiary Magistrate ex p Pinochet Ugarte* (No 1) [2000] AC 61 and *R v Metropolitan Stipendiary Magistrates ex p Pinochet Ugarte* (No 3) [2000] AC 147. General Pinochet seized power in Chile in 1973. Following the *coup d'etat* there was widespread torture and murder of political opponents and others. Pinochet left office in 1990. In October 1998 he was arrested on a provisional warrant issued at Bow Street Magistrates' Court at the request of a Spanish prosecuting magistrate, and his extradition was requested by Spain. He claimed immunity from criminal proceedings as a former head of state, and the Divisional Court upheld this plea.[138] The Government of Spain appealed to the House of Lords. **5.137**

In *R v Metropolitan Stipendiary Magistrate ex p Pinochet Ugarte (No 1)* [2000] AC 61 the House of Lords held by a majority of three to two that General Pinochet was not entitled to immunity *ratione personae* as a former head of state. That decision was set aside in *R v Metropolitan* **5.138**

---

132 cf EAW Framework Decision, Art 20.

133 *Re Osman (No 2)*, 21 December 1988.

134 In *R (Alamieyeseigha) v Crown Prosecution Service* [2005] EWHC 2704 (Admin) the applicant was the Governor and Chief Executive of Bayelsa State, a constituent part of the Federal Republic of Nigeria. He was arrested in the UK and charged with money laundering. He claimed state immunity. The High Court rejected his claim on the grounds that the head of a state which is part of a federal state is not entitled to immunity; only the head of the federal state was immune.

135 Convention on Special Missions of 8 December 1969.

136 *Bat v The Investigating Judge of the German Federal Court* [2011] EWHC 2029 (Admin).

137 *Democratic Republic of Congo v Belgium*, 14 February 2002; Fox, *The Law of State Immunity*, (OUP, Oxford 2008), Chapter 12; Warbrick, *Immunity and International Crimes in English Law*, (2004) 53 ICLQ 769. Attempts by political activists to obtain arrest warrants for visiting ministers from foreign states to whom they objected (in particular, Israel), led to the enactment of s 153 of the Police Reform and Social Responsibility Act 2011, which provides that arrest warrants for crimes of universal jurisdiction can only be issued with the consent of the DPP.

138 *R v Evans ex p Pinochet Ugarte*, The Times, 3 November 1998.

Stipendiary Magistrate ex p Pinochet Ugarte (No 2) [2000] AC 119 following the revelation that one of the majority, Lord Hoffmann, was the Chairman of Amnesty International, one of the parties to the litigation. A re-hearing was ordered.

5.139 In *R v Metropolitan Stipendiary Magistrate ex p Pinochet Ugarte (No 3)* [2000] AC 147 the majority of the House of Lords held that Pinochet was entitled to immunity in respect of most of the alleged crimes. In summary, they held that a former head of state had immunity from the criminal jurisdiction of the UK for acts done in his official capacity as head of state pursuant to s 20 of the State Immunity Act 1978, read with Article 39(2) of Sch 1 to the Diplomatic Privileges Act 1964. However, because torture was an international crime against humanity, after the coming into effect of the United Nations International Convention against Torture and other Cruel, Inhuman or Degrading Treatment or Punishment 1984, there had been a universal jurisdiction in all the Convention state parties to either extradite or punish a public official who committed torture. Therefore, in the light of that universal jurisdiction, state parties could not have intended that an immunity for ex-heads of state for official acts of torture would survive their ratification of the Convention. The UK, Spain, and Chile had ratified the Convention by 8 December 1998 and so Pinochet had no immunity from extradition for offences of torture or conspiracy to torture alleged to have occurred after 8 December 1988 and the extradition could proceed on those charges.[139]

5.140 In October 1999 General Pinochet was committed at Bow Street Magistrates' Court under s 9 of the EA 1989 to await the Secretary of State's decision whether to return him to Spain under s 12. An application for *habeas corpus* was made to the High Court. This application was overtaken by events when, in February 2000, the Secretary of State decided that General Pinochet's health was such that it would be wrong to order his return to Spain to face trial. Accordingly, the order of committal was cancelled and General Pinochet returned to Chile. Criminal proceedings continued against him there in one form or another until his death on 10 December 2006.[140]

5.141 The *Pinochet* case raised a number of legal and political issues.[141] As discussed at para 1.27, the controversy it generated gave added impetus to the UK Government's review of extradition law which led to enactment of the EA 2003.

---

[139] cf *Jones v Kingdom of Saudi Arabia* [2006] UKHL 26 (officials enjoy immunity from civil proceedings for torture).

[140] The other decisions in the *Pinochet* case were: *ex p Amnesty International*, The Times, 11 December 1998 (Amnesty International refused injunction pending the the Secretary of State's decision whether or not to issue an authority to proceed); *R v Secretary of State for the Home Department ex p Pinochet Ugarte*, 27 May 1999 (CO/1786/99) (permission to seek judicial review of the Secretary of State's decision to issue an authority to proceed refused on grounds of alternative remedies and prematurity); *In re Pinochet Ugarte*, The Times, 16 February 2000 (not appropriate to join interested parties to extradition *habeas corpus* proceedings); *R v Secretary of State for the Home Department ex p Kingdom of Belgium*, 15 February 2000 (CO/236/00) (Secretary of State acted unfairly in refusing to disclose Senator Pinochet's medical report to requesting states). cf *R v Secretary of State for the Home Department ex p Kingdom of Belgium*, 15 February 2000 (CO/236/00).

[141] See Woodhouse (ed), *The Pinochet Case: A Legal and Constitutional Analysis* (Hart Publishing, 2000). Among the many law review articles on the case are Byers, 'The law and politics of the Pinochet case', (2000) 10 Duke Jour Comp Int'l Law 415; Nicholls, 'Reflections on Pinochet', (2000) 41 Va J Int'l Law 140; Turns, 'Pinochet's fallout: jurisdiction and immunity for criminal violations of international law', (2000) 20 LS 566; Perera, 'Ex parte Pinochet and the concept of state immunity: some reflections', (1999) 25 CLB 647; Boister and Burchill, 'The implications of the Pinochet decisions for the extradition or prosecution of former South African heads of state for crimes committed under apartheid', (1999) 11 RADIC 619; Caplan, 'The Pinochet case—a personal view', (2000) 144 SJ 372; Malleson, 'Judicial bias and disqualification after *Pinochet (No 2)*' (2000) 63 MLR 119; Tierney, 'The extradition case against Pinochet Ugarte', (1999) 5 *EPL* 500; Warbrick, 'Extradition law aspects of *Pinochet No 3*', (1999) 48 ICLQ 958; Bianchi, 'Immunity versus human rights: the Pinochet case', (1999) 10 EJIL 237; Wedgewood, 'International criminal law and Augusto Pinochet', (2000) 40 Va J Int'l Law 829.

The House of Lords' reasoning was doubted by the International Court of Justice in *Democratic Republic of Congo v Belgium*, 14 February 2002.[142] The Congo requested the Court to declare that the Kingdom of Belgium should annul the international arrest warrant issued on 11 April 2000 by a Belgian investigating judge against the Minister for Foreign Affairs in office in the Congo, seeking his provisional detention pending a request for extradition to Belgium for alleged crimes against humanity. The Congo argued that as a Foreign Minister he was immune from criminal jurisdiction. In reliance on *R v Metropolitan Stipendiary Magistrates ex p Pinochet Ugarte (No 3)* [2000] AC 147, Belgium argued that any immunity enjoyed by a Minister for Foreign Affairs could not protect him if he was accused of crimes against humanity. **5.142**

The Court said it was unable to deduce any rule of international law in the form of an exception to the rule according immunity from criminal jurisdiction and inviolability to incumbent Ministers for Foreign Affairs, where they are suspected of having committed war crimes or crimes against humanity. Thus the Court concluded that most serving ministers will have immunity from arrest, and former ministers have immunity for all official acts committed in office. **5.143**

J. Competing Part 1 Warrants

Where two Part 1 warrants have been issued in respect of a defendant then the appropriate judge must decide which of them is to take precedence in accordance with s 44. **5.144**

If a Part 1 warrant and an extradition request under Part 2 has been sent to the UK for execution then it is for the Secretary of State to decide which of them should be dealt with first under s 179. This power is considered at para 8.43. **5.145**

Section 44 applies if at any time in the relevant period the conditions in s 44(3) are satisfied in relation to a person in respect of whom a Part 1 warrant has been issued. These conditions are that: **5.146**

(a) the judge is informed that another Part 1 warrant has been issued in respect of the person;
(b) the other warrant falls to be dealt with by the judge or by a judge who is the appropriate judge in another part of the UK;
(c) the other warrant has not been disposed of.

For these purposes the relevant period is the period starting when the person is first brought before the appropriate judge following his arrest under Part 1 and ending when the person is extradited in pursuance of the warrant or discharged (s 44(2)). **5.147**

Where s 44 applies the judge may do one of two things. He may: **5.148**

(a) order further proceedings on the warrant under consideration to be deferred until the other warrant has been disposed of, if the warrant under consideration has not been disposed of;
(b) order the person's extradition in pursuance of the warrant under consideration to be deferred until the other warrant has been disposed of, if an order for his extradition in pursuance of the warrant under consideration has been made.

142 <http://www.icj-cij.org>.

5.149 If the judge makes an order under s 44(4) and the person is not already remanded in custody or on bail, the judge must remand the person in custody or on bail (s 44(5)). If the judge remands the person in custody he may later grant bail (s 44(6)).

5.150 In considering what order to make under s 44(4) the judge must take account in particular of the following matters:

(a) the relative seriousness of the offences concerned;
(b) the place where each offence was committed (or was alleged to have been committed);
(c) the date on which each warrant was issued;
(d) whether, in the case of each offence, the person is accused of its commission (but not alleged to have been convicted) or is alleged to be unlawfully at large after conviction.

K. Deferral of Extradition Hearing for Domestic Proceedings

Defendant charged with an offence

5.151 Section 22 applies if at any time during a Part 1 extradition hearing the judge is informed that the defendant has been charged with an offence in the UK. The judge must adjourn the extradition hearing until one of the following occurs (s 22(2)):

(a) the charge is disposed of;
(b) the charge is withdrawn;
(c) proceedings in respect of the charge are discontinued;
(d) an order is made for the charge to lie on the file (or its Scottish equivalent).

5.152 If the defendant is sentenced to imprisonment or another form of detention then the judge may adjourn the extradition hearing until the sentence has been served (s 22(3)).

5.153 In some cases the domestic proceedings may relate to the offence for which extradition has been requested. This may raise double jeopardy issues. Accordingly, s 22(4) provides that if the extradition hearing is adjourned under s 22(2) and the judge has already decided the double jeopardy question under s 11, the judge must decide that question again after the resumption of the hearing.

Defendant sentenced to imprisonment

5.154 Section 23 applies if during the extradition hearing the judge is informed that the defendant has been sentenced to imprisonment or another form of detention in the UK. The judge may then adjourn the extradition hearing until the sentence has been served (s 23(2)). Section 23(3), inserted by para 7 of Sch 13 to the Police and Justice Act 2006, permits the period of remand to be up to six months.

5.155 Prior to the enactment of s 197A of the 6A 2003 by the Police and Justice Act 2006, Sch 13, para 25, there was no power under UK law to interrupt or terminate a sentence of imprisonment for the purposes of extradition.[143] Nevertheless, the judge should normally adjourn the extradition hearing where the defendant's release date is so far in the future that the answer to the question of whether a bar to extradition may be in existence at that point is uncertain. In *R (Slator) v Bow Street Magistrates' Court* [2006] EWHC 2628 (Admin) the defendant, who was a serving prisoner, challenged the appropriate judge's refusal to adjourn an extradition hearing

[143] *R (Handa) v Bow Street Magistrates' Court* [2004] EWHC 3116 (Admin).

in 2005 in circumstances where his earliest release date was in 2008. In allowing the application for judicial review Wilkie J said at paras 14–18:

> It is acknowledged that it must inevitably be a matter of degree at what point, if at all, is it too long before the extradition order takes effect to enable a sensible assessment under section 11 and section 21 to be undertaken ... although it must be a matter of fact and degree, in our judgment where the district judge is being invited to express his satisfaction over matters under section 11 and section 21 in respect of the ultimate extradition of a person which cannot take place for in excess of three years, then it is simply irrational for him to consider that he could properly do so at that distance in time.

L. Costs

The EA 2003 introduces, for the first time, a power to award costs against a person whose extradition is ordered. **5.156**

Section 60(2) provides that where an order for extradition is made under Part 1 the appropriate judge may make such order as he considers just and reasonable with regard to the costs to be paid by the person. The order for costs must specify their amount, and may name the person to whom they are to be paid (s 60(4)). **5.157**

Where the defendant is discharged then an order for costs in his favour can be made under s 61(5). An order under s 61(5) is an order for a payment of the appropriate amount to be made to the person out of money provided by Parliament. Section 61(6) provides that the appropriate amount is such amount as the judge or court making the order considers reasonably sufficient to compensate the person in whose favour the order is made for any expenses properly incurred by him in the proceedings under this Part. Section 61(7) confers a power to reduce this amount in appropriate circumstances. **5.158**

The practice under the EA 1989 was to award a successful defendant the whole of his costs out of central funds under s 16 of the Prosecution of Offences Act 1985. **5.159**

6

THE EXTRADITION HEARING IN CATEGORY 2 CASES

A. Introduction

In this chapter the appropriate judge's duties and functions in an extradition hearing under Part 2 of the EA 2003 are considered. This is the hearing at which the appropriate judge is to deal with a request for extradition to a Category 2 territory (s 140(1)). **6.01**

As in Category 1 cases, in England and Wales the appropriate judge is a district judge (Magistrates' Courts) designated for the purposes of Part 2 by the Lord Chief Justice after consulting the Lord Chancellor (s 139(1)(a), as amended). **6.02**

The judge's functions in a Part 2 extradition hearing are, or may be, more elaborate than in a Part 1 hearing. This is because s 84 preserves the requirement for the requesting state to present prima facie evidence, except where the requesting Category 2 territory has been designated by the Secretary of State in an order made under s 84(7). **6.03**

Many of the provisions of Part 2, in particular the bars to extradition, are similar to the equivalent provisions in Part 1. Therefore in this chapter cross-reference will be made to the relevant parts of Chapter 5 (Category 1 cases) where appropriate. **6.04**

B. Extradition Hearings under Part 2: A Summary

6.05 In *R (Government of the United States of America) v Senior District Judge, Bow Street Magistrates' Court* [2006] EWHC 2256 (Admin) the Administrative Court made a number of general remarks on the way in which extradition proceedings should be conducted in the context of a case which had become enmeshed in preliminary issues. The Court's observations are set out at paras 4.92–4.93.

6.06 The steps in an extradition hearing in a Category 2 case can be summarized as follows:

(a) The judge must first decide whether the documents sent to him by the Secretary of State include the documents and information specified in s 78(2). If they do not, then the defendant must be discharged (s 78(3)).

(b) If the documents are in order the judge must decide the following questions (s 78(4)):
   (i) whether, on a balance of probabilities, the person appearing or brought before him is the person whose extradition is requested;
   (ii) whether the offence specified in the request is an extradition offence;
   (iii) whether copies of the documents sent to the judge by the Secretary of State have been served on the defendant.

(c) If the judge decides these questions affirmatively he must then go on to decide whether any of the bars to extradition in s 79 are applicable. If one or more of them is applicable then the defendant must be discharged (s 79(3)).

(d) If there are no applicable bars to extradition under s 79:
   (i) and the person is accused of the commission of the extradition offence but is not alleged to be unlawfully at large after conviction of it, the judge must proceed under s 84 (s 79(4)). This requires the judge to decide whether there is a prima facie case, unless the requesting state has been designated by the Secretary of State under s 84(7). In that case, the judge is required to proceed under s 87;
   (ii) and the person is accused of the commission of the extradition offence and is alleged to be unlawfully at large after conviction of the extradition offence, the judge must proceed under s 85 (s 79(5)). This requires the judge to decide if the defendant was convicted in his absence and, if so, whether he will receive a re-trial. If he will, the judge must proceed under s 86. This is in similar terms to s 84.

(e) If the issues arising under the sections mentioned above are decided adversely to the defendant, the judge must then decide under s 87 whether extradition would be compatible with the defendant's Convention rights within the meaning of the Human Rights Act 1998.

(f) If it would not be so compatible, the defendant must be discharged (s 87(2)). If it would be so compatible, the judge must send the case to the Secretary of State for his decision whether the defendant is to be extradited (s 87(3)).

6.07 The extradition hearing is then at an end. The Secretary of State's role in Category 2 cases is considered in Chapter 8.

6.08 Both Parts 1 and 2 of the EA 2003 are densely structured and set out in detail both the questions the appropriate judge has to decide and the order in which he has to decide them. In *Raffile v Government of the United States of America* [2005] 1 All ER 889 the Administrative Court considered whether the judge could consider the questions 'out of turn'. At para 33 Pitchford J said:

> Having made his decision under s 87, the district judge was then faced for the first time with an application from counsel to address him on other matters, specifically, the passage of time.

The district judge held that he could not do so since he had already made his decision on that issue in the absence of submissions made at the appropriate time. The procedure in which he was engaged was a staged progress through the relevant sections, each of which was dependent upon a decision previously made. He could not be expected to reopen those decisions at such a late stage of the hearing. In fact, passage of time under s 79(1)(c) was three steps back in the procedure. Two of those steps involved decisions made under ss 84 and 85 which were uncontested; while, on the other hand, s 79, to which the district judge's attention was being redirected, created statutory bars to extradition. If it was the case that, as a result of misunderstanding or neglect, counsel had failed to advance submissions at the appropriate time, it is my view that those submissions should have been heard and, if necessary, the district judge's previous decisions reopened for that purpose. Not to do so was capable of resulting in procedural unfairness, and, at worst, injustice.

C. The Judge's Powers at the Extradition Hearing

In England and Wales, at the extradition hearing the appropriate judge has the same powers (as nearly as may be) as a magistrates' court would have if the proceedings were the summary trial of an information against the person whose extradition is requested. This provision applies the general powers of a magistrates' court in Part I of the Magistrates' Courts Act 1980. Where the judge adjourns the extradition hearing he must remand the person in custody or on bail (s 77(4)). If the defendant is remanded in custody he may later be granted bail (s 77(5)). **6.09**

D. Burden and Standard of Proof

This is dealt with in s 206: see para 5.13. **6.10**

E. Authentication

This is dealt with in s 202: see para 5.16. **6.11**

F. The Initial Stages of the Extradition Hearing

The EA 2003 provides for an initial hearing in Category 1 cases at which the issue of identity is to be determined.[1] In Category 2 cases this issue and other preliminary matters are determined following the commencement of the extradition hearing itself. **6.12**

Sufficiency of documents

The Secretary of State's certificate under s 70 has already been considered in para 4.122. Section 70(1) requires the Secretary of State to issue his certificate where he receives a valid extradition request which has been made in the approved way as defined in s 70(5), s 70(6), and s 70(7), subject to the exception provided for in s 70(2).[2] If he issues his certificate he is then required by s 70(9)[3] to send the request and the certificate to the appropriate judge. **6.13**

1 Para 4.91.
2 As amended by Police and Justice Act 2006, Sch 13, para 17.
3 As amended by Police and Justice Act 2006, Sch 13, para 17.

6.14 By s 78(2) the first task for the appropriate judge at the extradition hearing is to determine that the documents sent to him by the Secretary of State include the documents and information required by s 78(2), namely the documents referred to in section 70(9) (ie the request and the s 70 certificate; particulars of the person whose extradition is requested; particulars of the offence specified in the request;[4] in the case of a person accused of an offence, a warrant for his arrest issued in the Category 2 territory; in the case of a person alleged to be unlawfully at large after conviction of an offence, a certificate issued in the Category 2 territory of the conviction and (if he has been sentenced) of the sentence).

6.15 If the documents are deficient then the defendant must be discharged.

The s 78(4) questions

6.16 Assuming that the paperwork is in order, the judge must go on to decide the three questions specified in s 78(4).

6.17 The first question is whether, on a balance of probabilities (s 78(5)), the person appearing or brought before the judge is the person whose extradition is requested (s 78(4)(a)). Proving identity in extradition cases is a relatively straightforward matter: see para 4.95.

6.18 The second question is whether the offence specified in the request is an extradition offence (s 78(4)(b)). This is dealt with below under para 6.21.

6.19 The third question is whether copies of the documents sent to the judge by the Secretary of State have been served on the person (s 78(4)(c)). This should have happened well before the extradition hearing commences, although it does not always do so. Prior to its amendment by para 17 of Sch 13 to the Police and Justice Act 2006, s 70(9) required the Secretary of State to send a copy of the relevant Order in Council to the appropriate judge. In *Government of Germany v Kleinschmidt* [2005] 3 All ER 759 the Order in Council was not served on the defendants prior to the commencement of the extradition hearing and the judge refused the government's application to serve it on them at the hearing, holding that it was too late to do so. In allowing the government's appeal, Beatson J declined to interpret s 78(4)(c) so as to require service of the Order in Council prior to the commencement of the extradition hearing. He said that if late service risked causing prejudice then the proper remedy would be to grant an adjournment.[5] In practice, responsibility for service of the documents referred to in s 70(9) lies with the CPS on behalf of the requesting state.[6]

G. English Charges and Multiple Offences

6.20 Where a request for extradition relates to more than one offence then provisions within the EA 2003 are to be read as modified by the Extradition Act 2003 (Multiple Offences) Order 2003.[7] In *Tappin v Government of the United States of America* [2012] EWHC 22 (Admin), paras 43–44, the Administrative Court stated three principles relating to allegations of multiple

[4] In *Dudko v The Government of the Russian Federation* EWHC 1125 (Admin) the court said that s 78(2)(c) should be read as including the more comprehensive phraseology used in s 2(4)(c) in Part 1 cases. Section 2(4)(c) requires the arrest warrant to contain particulars of the circumstances in which the person is alleged to have committed the offence, including the conduct alleged to constitute the offence, the time, and place at which he is alleged to have committed the offence and any provision of the law of the Category 1 territory under which the conduct is alleged to constitute an offence. See also *Jethwa v Government of the United States of America* [2012] EWHC 31 (Admin), para 19.

[5] Paras 31 and 32.

[6] Paras 47 and 55.

[7] SI 2003/3150: see App E6 and para 5.20.

offences in the extradition request: (i) each offence in the request needs to be considered separately; (ii) each offence in the request need not be assigned a reciprocal offence under English law; (iii) where the alleged conduct relevant to a number of the offences in a request is closely interconnected, it matters not that it would not be charged in England in the same manner as in the requesting state.

H. Is the Offence in the Request an Extradition Offence?

Extradition offences in Category 2 cases were considered at para 2.71. The district judge is required to consider the particulars of the defendant's alleged conduct as described in the request and to determine whether it amounts to an extradition offence within the definitions set out in ss 137–138. In order to determine whether the requesting state has satisfied the dual criminality test for the offence alleged, the court must look at the conduct alleged against the defendant and then analyse whether it constitutes an offence in the UK. The conduct is that described in the documents constituting the request, ignoring mere narrative background, but taking account of such allegations as are relevant to the description of the corresponding UK offence.[8] **6.21**

I. Bars to Extradition

The judge's next task is to determine whether any of the bars to extradition in s 79 are applicable. These are the rule against double jeopardy; extraneous considerations; the passage of time; hostage-taking considerations; and forum.[9] **6.22**

Rule against double jeopardy (s 80)

A person's extradition to a Category 2 territory is barred by reason of the rule against double jeopardy if (and only if) it appears that he would be entitled to be discharged under any rule of law relating to previous acquittal or conviction if he were charged with the extradition offence in the part of the UK where the judge exercises his jurisdiction. These rules include, but are not limited to, those cases where a plea in bar of *autrefois convict* or *autrefois acquit* may be raised by a defendant as of right, which are only available where the later alleged offence is the same as the earlier both in fact and law. But the law also recognizes a broader discretionary jurisdiction to stop a prosecution based on substantially the same facts as were relied on against the defendant in an earlier prosecution. Such a second prosecution will generally be an abuse of the process, but may be permissible in special circumstances where it will not be so characterized. Both the narrow plea in bar and the wider jurisdiction to stop a second prosecution as abusive are embraced within the double jeopardy rule as applied by s 80 to extradition proceedings under Part 2 of the EA 2003.[10] Where the broader test is in issue, it is necessary to consider whether an English court would stay on grounds of abuse of process the proposed foreign proceedings against the defendant if they were brought in the UK. This requires consideration not only of **6.23**

---

8 *Norris v Government of the United States of America* [2008] 1 AC 920, para 91; *Tappin v Government of the United States of America* [2012] EWHC 22 (Admin), para 30; *Elbeyati v Federation of Bosnia and Herzegovina* [2011] EWHC 625 (Admin), para 6; *Tesler v Government of the United States of America* [2011] EWHC 52 (Admin); *R (Bermingham) v Director of the Serious Fraud Office* [2006] EWHC 200 (Admin), paras 81–85.

9 Inserted by para 5 of Sch 13 to the Police and Justice Act 2006 (not in force at the time of writing, June 2012).

10 *Zdinjak v Republic of Croatia* [2012] EWHC 1554 (Admin), para 9; *John v Government of the United States of America* [2006] EWHC 3512 (Admin), para 17.

whether the second prosecution arises out of the same or substantially the same facts as the first, but also of whether the second set of charges which the requesting state seeks to pursue should have been pursued at the time of the first prosecution.[11]

6.24 Section 80 is virtually identical to s 6(3) of the EA 1989 but is in a different form to s 12, the equivalent provision in Part 1: see para 5.34.

Extraneous considerations (s 81)

6.25 A person's extradition to a Category 2 territory is barred by reason of extraneous considerations if (and only if) it appears that:

(a) the request for his extradition (though purporting to be made on account of the extradition offence) is in fact made for the purpose of prosecuting or punishing him on account of his race, religion, nationality, gender, sexual orientation, or political opinions or;
(b) if extradited he might be prejudiced at his trial or punished, detained or restricted in his personal liberty by reason of his race, religion, nationality, gender, sexual orientation, or political opinions.

6.26 This section is identical to s 13, considered at para 5.38.[12]

Passage of time (s 82)

6.27 This provision is similar to s 14 in Category 1 cases; see para 5.52.

6.28 Section 82 provides that a person's extradition is barred by the passage of time if (and only if) it appears that it would be unjust or oppressive to extradite him by reason of the passage of time since he is alleged to have committed the extradition offence (where he is accused of its commission), or become unlawfully at large (where he is alleged to have been convicted of it).

Hostage-taking considerations (s 83)

6.29 A person's extradition to a Category 2 territory is barred by reason of hostage-taking considerations if (and only if) the territory is a party to the International Convention against the Taking of Hostages opened for signature at New York on 18 December 1979 and it appears that:

(a) if extradited, he might be prejudiced at his trial because communication between him and the appropriate authorities would not be possible, and
(b) the act or omission constituting the extradition offence also constitutes an offence under s 1 of the Taking of Hostages Act 1982 or an attempt to commit such an offence.

6.30 This provision is identical to s 16, applicable in Category 1 cases.[13]

Forum (s 83A)

6.31 Section 83A is inserted by para 5 of Sch 13 to the Police and Justice Act 2006. A person's extradition to a Category 2 territory ('the requesting territory') is barred by reason of forum if (and only if) it appears that a significant part of the conduct alleged to constitute the extradition offence is conduct in the UK, and in view of that and all the other circumstances, it would

---

[11] *Jones v Government of the United States* [2012] EWHC 2332 (Admin); *Maxwell-King v Government of the United States of America* [2006] EWHC 3033 (Admin), para 25.

[12] *Tamarevichute v The Russian Federation* [2008] EWHC 534 (Admin), para 12; *R (Ahsan) v Director of Public Prosecutions* [2008] EWHC 666 (Admin), paras 129–141; *McKinnon v Government of the United States of America* [2007] EWHC 475 (Admin), paras 16–17.

[13] Para 5.69.

not be in the interests of justice for the person to be tried for the offence in the requesting territory.

For the purposes of 83A(1)(b) (interests of justice) the judge must take into account whether the relevant prosecution authorities in the UK have decided not to take proceedings against the person in respect of the conduct in question. **6.32**

Section 83A does not apply if the person is alleged to be unlawfully at large after conviction of the extradition offence. **6.33**

Section 83A is in similar terms to s 19B, considered at para 5.91.[14] **6.34**

J. Prima Facie Evidence[15]

Under the EA 1989 evidence sufficient to amount to a prima facie case was required in Sch 1 cases (principally requests from the United States of America), and in cases under Part III, unless the requesting state was designated in an Order in Council under ss 9(4) and (8). In practice, this meant that designated Commonwealth countries, colonies, and the Hong Kong Special Administrative Region were required to adduce prima facie evidence, whereas signatories to the European Convention on Extradition 1957 were not so required. **6.35**

Although the policy of the EA 2003 is to simplify and remove evidential requirements where possible, prima facie evidence is required in Category 2 cases by virtue of ss 84(1) and 86(1) unless the requesting Category 2 territory has been designated by the Secretary of State in an order under s 84(7) or s 86(7). At the time of writing (June 2012) the following countries have been designated for these purposes by the Extradition Act 2003 (Designation of Part 2 Territories) Order 2003,[16] Article 3: **6.36**

> Albania, Andorra, Armenia, Australia, Azerbaijan, Bosnia and Herzegovina, Canada, Croatia, Georgia, Iceland, Israel, Liechtenstein, Macedonia, FYR, Moldova, New Zealand, Norway, Russian Federation, Serbia and Montenegro, South Africa, Switzerland, Turkey, Ukraine, the United States of America.[17]

Accordingly, it is not necessary for these territories to prove a prima facie case against the defendant. **6.37**

However, where evidence is required, the rules of evidence are simplified by ss 84(2) and 86(2), which give the judge discretion to admit hearsay evidence.[18] **6.38**

---

[14] S 83A is not in force at the time of writing (June 2012). Para 6 of Sch 13 to the Police and Justice Act 2006 provides that an order bringing the provisions into force is not to be made within the period of 12 months beginning with the day on which the Act was passed (8 November 2006). If after the end of that period a resolution is made by each House of Parliament that the provisions should come into force, the Secretary of State shall make an order under s 53 bringing the paragraphs (or paragraph) into force (para 6(2)). An order made by virtue of para 6(2) must bring the provisions in question into force no later than one month after the day on which the resolutions referred to in that sub-paragraph are made or, if they are made on different days, the day on which the later resolution is made. The 2011 Extradition Review did not recommend that the forum provisions be brought into force: see Part 6. However, in October 2012 the Government announced its intention to bring the forum bars into force: Cm 8458.

[15] See generally 2011 Extradition Review, Part 8.

[16] SI 2003/3334: see App E5.

[17] The United States of America's designation is revoked by the Police and Justice Act 2006, s 43(1), from a date to be appointed: s 53(1)(a). The revocation is not in force at the time of writing (June 2012). The proposal to de-designate the United States of America arose out of the controversy regarding the 2003 UK/US Extradition Treaty: see para 1.67 and the 2011 Extradition Review, para 8.68.

[18] Para 6.53.

The test for a prima facie case

6.39 Sections 84(1) and 86(1) provide that if the judge is required to proceed under s 84 or 86 he must decide whether there is evidence which would be sufficient to make a case requiring an answer by the defendant if the proceedings were the summary trial of an information against him.

6.40 The reference to 'the summary trial of an information' makes clear that the evidence has to be admissible under ordinary criminal rules of evidence, subject to the provisions of ss 84(2)–(4) and 86(2)–(4). In *R (Government of the United States of America) v Senior District Judge, Bow Street Magistrates' Court* [2006] EWHC 2256 (Admin), para 76, the Court said:

> Extradition proceedings are criminal proceedings, albeit of a very special kind. The judge should apply the normal rules of criminal evidence and procedure to the extent that these are appropriate having regard to the specifics of the statutory schemes in Part 1 and Part 2.

6.41 The test to be applied by the appropriate judge in determining whether there is a case to answer is the *Galbraith* [1981] 1 WLR 1039, 1042 test namely, whether the prosecution evidence, taken at its highest, is such that no jury properly directed could properly convict upon it. This was held to be the correct test for extradition cases by the House of Lords in *R v Governor of Pentonville Prison ex p Alves* [1993] AC 284, 290, 292. Lord Goff of Chieveley observed that it became the practice during the twentieth century after the case of *Zossenheim* (1903) 20 TLR 121 for the magistrate to take into account evidence tendered on behalf of the defendant in extradition proceedings when deciding whether there was a case to answer. Even though the judge is required to behave as if he were conducting a summary trial, in deciding whether there is a prima facie case, he is required to have regard to evidence called on behalf of the defendant.

6.42 In *R v Governor of Brixton Prison ex p Gross* [1999] QB 538 the Divisional Court held that the amendments made to the EA 1989 by the Criminal Justice and Public Order Act 1994 (which introduced the language of summary trials) had not altered this practice. It follows that the defendant is entitled to give evidence and call witnesses in extradition hearings where evidence is required.[19]

6.43 The mechanics of the process the judge has to go through in deciding whether or not a prima facie case has been established were explained by Lloyd LJ in *R v Governor of Pentonville Prison ex p Osman* [1990] 1 WLR 277, 299:

> ... it was the magistrate's duty to consider the evidence as a whole, and to reject any evidence which he considered worthless. In that sense it was his duty to weigh up the evidence. But it was not his duty to weigh the evidence. He was neither entitled nor obliged to determine the amount of weight to be attached to any evidence, or to compare one witness with another. That would be for the jury at the trial.

Form of evidence and issues as to admissibility

6.44 The evidence in extradition cases generally consists of a combination of one or more of the following forms of evidence:

(a) Written documentary evidence from the requesting state, for example a statement from a witness, translated in an admissible fashion,[20] and duly authenticated in accordance

[19] cf *R v Governor of Pentonville Prison ex p Alves* [1993] AC 284, 292; *Re Tomlins*, 18 November 1994, CO/1257/94; *R (Saifi) v Governor of Brixton Prison* [2001] 1 WLR 1134.

[20] *R v Governor of Brixton Prison ex p Saifi* [2001] 1 WLR 1134; *Lodhi v Governor of HM Prison Brixton* [2001] EWHC (Admin) 178; *R v Governor of Brixton Prison ex p Lennon* [1963] Crim LR 41; *Kruger v Governor of Northward Prison* [1996] CILR 157.

with EA 2003, s 202. The process of authentication under s 202 makes potentially admissible in evidence in extradition proceedings documents containing written statements of fact, notwithstanding that under English laws of evidence what appears in the statement would only be admissible in the form of oral testimony given on oath by the maker of the statement. The purpose of s 202 is to obviate the necessity of bringing witnesses from the requesting state to give oral evidence in the extradition proceedings.[21] It should be noted that s 202 permits authenticated 'documents' to be received in evidence. This represents a loosening of the former requirements under the EA 1989, Sch 1, para 12, which provided that only certain types of document, namely authenticated 'depositions and statements on oath', could be received in evidence.[22] However, authenticated documents from the requesting state are not necessarily admissible in evidence. They are receivable (ie, capable of being received) in evidence and only admissible to the extent that what is contained within them complies with English rules of evidence.[23] The foreign state's documents do not have to be in any particular form. Section s 84(2) of the EA 2003 does not require that something which on its face is a statement within the ordinary meaning of that term should take the exact form of a statement made for the express purpose of prosecution in the UK.[24] The requesting state is able to rely on a statement made by a co-accused implicating the defendant notwithstanding that he would not be a competent witness at the time the statement was made.[25] The press are entitled to inspect and take copies of documentary evidence in extradition proceedings.[26]

(b) Live evidence.[27] Witnesses who appear in person may be cross-examined,[28] and the old practice of recording their evidence in the form of a deposition under the Magistrates' Courts Act 1980 has continued even though the procedure now is that of a summary trial. Where properly authenticated evidence is presented, however, there is no duty on the requesting state to make the witness available for cross-examination.[29]

(c) Written evidence in the form required by s 9 of the Criminal Justice Act 1967, read by consent. Section 9 is applied to extradition proceedings by EA 2003, s 205(2)(a).

(d) Formal admissions (ie, agreed facts) under s 10 of the Criminal Justice Act 1967, which is applied to extradition proceedings by EA 2003, s 205(2)(b).

The exclusion of evidence in extradition proceedings

Whilst the evidence tendered by the requesting state must in general comply with the ordinary rules of evidence, failure to observe English procedural rules relating to evidence does not necessarily render the evidence inadmissible.[30] **6.45**

---

[21] *Savvas v The Government of Italy* [2004] EWHC 1233 (Admin), para 9; *Dowse v Governor of Pentonville Prison* [1983] 2 AC 464 (considering the analogous provision in the EA 1870).

[22] *R (Government of the United States of America v Bow Street Magistrates' Court* [2002] EWHC 1144 (Admin).

[23] *Fernandez v Governor of HMP Brixton* [2004] EWHC 2207 (Admin), para 47; *R v Governor of Pentonville Prison ex p Kirby* [1979] 2 All ER 1094, 1099.

[24] *Tudor v United Arab Emirates* [2012] EWHC 1098 (Admin), para 17.

[25] *Tudor v United Arab Emirates* [2012] EWHC 1098 (Admin), paras 18–21.

[26] *Guardian News and Media Limited v City of Westminster Magistrates' Court* [2012] EWCA Civ 420.

[27] *R v Governor of Pentonville Prison ex p Herbage* (No 3) (1987) 84 Cr App R 149.

[28] cf *Fernandes v Governor of Brixton Prison* [2004] EWHC 2007.

[29] *Dowse v Governor of Pentonville Prison* [1983] 2 AC 464; *R v Governor of Brixton Prison ex p Caldough* [1961] 1 WLR 464; *R v Secretary of State for India ex p Ezekiel* [1941] 2 KB 169.

[30] *R v Governor of Pentonville Prison ex p Schneider* (1981) 73 Cr App R 200, 211–212.

6.46 The following have been characterized as rules of practice whose breach does not render evidence inadmissible in extradition proceedings: rules relating to the identification of witnesses;[31] rules relating to anonymous witnesses;[32] rules relating to the interviewing of witnesses;[33] and rules relating to memory-refreshing documents.[34]

6.47 Section 78 of the Police and Criminal Evidence Act 1984 applies to extradition proceedings.[35] However, evidence should only be excluded under s 78 where it has been obtained in a way which outrages 'civilized values'.[36] This test imposes a high threshold, and cases where it is appropriate to exclude evidence are likely to be rare.[37]

6.48 In *R (Saifi) v Governor of Brixton Prison* [2001] 1 WLR 1134 the Divisional Court said in relation to s 78:

> Section 78 confers a power in terms wide enough for its exercise on the court's own motion. The power is to be exercised whenever an issue appears as to whether the court could conclude that the evidence should not be admitted. The concept of a burden of proof has no part to play in such circumstances. No doubt it is for that reason that there is no express provision as to the burden of proof, and we see no basis for implying such a burden. The prosecution desiring to adduce and the defence seeking to exclude evidence will each seek to persuade the court about impact on fairness. We regard the position as neutral and see no reason why section 78 should be understood as requiring the court to consider upon whom the burden of proof rests …
>
> Under section 78 any circumstance which can reasonably have a bearing on fairness should be considered. The weight to be attached to an individual circumstance may increase or decrease because of the presence of other related or unrelated circumstances. The preponderance of all the circumstances may show that the admission of the evidence would have such an adverse effect on fairness as to require its exclusion.
>
> The absence from section 78 of words suggesting that facts are to be established or proved to any particular standard is, in our judgment, deliberate. It leaves the matter open and untrammelled by rigid evidential considerations.

Disclosure

6.49 During the 1990s there were significant developments in the common law relating to the prosecution duty of disclosure in criminal cases.[38] However, these developments left open the question of the extent of the duty of disclosure in criminal cases. That there should be such a duty is consistent with the need for a fair hearing: if the requesting state is in possession of

---

31 *R v Governor of Pentonville Prison ex p Voets* [1986] 1 WLR 470.

32 *R (Al-Fawwaz) v Governor of HM Prison Brixton* [2002] 1 AC 556.

33 *Beese v Governor of Ashford Remand Centre* [1973] 1 WLR 1426.

34 *R v Governor of Gloucester Prison ex p Miller* [1979] 2 All ER 1103. Criminal Justice Act 2003, s 139, has replaced the common-law rules relating to memory-refreshing documents.

35 *R (Saifi) v Governor of HM Prison Brixton* [2001] 1 WLR 1134; *Re Proulx* [2000] 1 All ER 57; but cf *Wellington v Governor of Her Majesty's Prison Belmarsh* [2004] EWHC 418 (Admin), para 17 where Mitting J doubted, obiter, that s 78 of PACE applied to proceedings under Sch 1 of the EA 1989. It is submitted that *Saifi* and *Proulx* represent the law both in relation to the EA 1989 and the EA 2003 and that s 78 applies to proceedings under the EA 2003 because: (i) s 78 applies to criminal proceedings; (ii) extradition proceedings are criminal proceedings (*R (Government of the United States of America) v Senior District Judge, Bow Street Magistrates' Court* [2006] EWHC 2256 (Admin), para 76); (iii) under Part 2 of the EA 2003 the judge's task is to consider whether the evidence would be sufficient to call for an answer if the matter were the trial of summary proceedings (s 86(1)); and (iv) s 78 applies in summary trials (*Halawa v Federation Against Copyright Theft* [1995] 1 Cr App R 21).

36 *R v Governor of Brixton Prison ex p Levin* [1997] AC 741, 748.

37 *Nnamdi v Governor of HMP Brixton* [2001] EWHC (Admin) 112, para 10; *Re Proulx* [2000] 1 All ER 57.

38 *Ward* [1993] 1 WLR 619; *Keane* [1994] 1 WLR 746.

exculpatory or potentially exculpatory material then considerations of fairness suggest that the material should be disclosed. On the other hand, to impose too rigorous a duty of disclosure on the requesting state would risk turning extradition proceedings into a criminal trial even though the defendant is entitled to a fair trial in the requesting state following his return as a condition of being extradited.

The case law on this issue has not always been consistent. In *R v Governor of Pentonville Prison ex p Lee* [1993] 1 WLR 1294 the Divisional Court held that it was for the requesting state alone to decide what material should be placed before the magistrate and that it was not under a duty to comply with any request for other material, including unused material, which might be requested by the defence.[39] Ognall J said that provided that there was compliance with the terms of the EA 1989, fairness was not a criterion relevant to the function of the committing court.[40] The correctness of this dictum was doubted by Pill LJ in *R v Governor of Brixton Prison ex p Kashamu*, 6 October 2000 (CO/2141/2000), where the committal was quashed because of serious non-disclosure by the Government of the United States of America. However, the Court did not state authoritatively the extent of the government's duty of disclosure in extradition cases. Later cases seemed to affirm the correctness of Ognall J's observations in *R v Governor of Pentonville Prison ex p Lee* [1993] 1 WLR 1294.[41] **6.50**

The law now appears to be settled as a result of the decision in *Wellington v Governor of Her Majesty's Prison Belmarsh* [2004] EWHC 418 (Admin).[42] Mitting J summarized at para 26 the principles of disclosure as they apply in extradition cases where the requesting state is required to adduce evidence. The principles are as follows. It is for the requesting state alone to determine the evidence upon which it relies to seek an extradition order. The requesting state is not under any general duty of disclosure similar to that imposed on the prosecution at any stage in domestic criminal proceedings. The court conducting the extradition hearing has the right to protect its process from abuse and the requesting state has a duty not to abuse that process. That is no different from saying that the requesting state must fulfil the duty of candour which it has always had in making applications for extradition. In fulfilment of that duty, the requesting state must disclose any evidence which would render worthless the evidence on which it relies to seek committal. It is for the person subject to the extradition process to establish that the requesting state is abusing the process of the court. The requested state may be given power to request further evidence under the relevant extradition treaty[43] but, in the absence of evidence of abuse, the court is entitled to, and should generally, refuse to request the UK authorities to exercise that power or to adjourn to permit it to be exercised. In *R (Raissi) v Secretary of State for the Home Department* [2008] 1 QB 836, paras 139–140, the Court of Appeal said that the duty of candour in relation to disclosure extends to bail hearings. **6.51**

In *R (Government of the United States of America) v Senior District Judge, Bow Street Magistrates' Court* [2006] EWHC 2256 (Admin) the Administrative Court considered the issue of disclosure in connection with abuse of process applications. The defendants had raised an abuse issue **6.52**

[39] *Lodhi v Governor of HMP Brixton* [2001] EWHC (Admin) 178, paras 114 and 115; *Serbeh v Governor of HMP Brixton* [2002] EWHC (Admin) 2396.

[40] *R v Governor of Pentonville Prison ex p Lee* [1993] 1 WLR 1294, 1300.

[41] *Lodhi v Governor of HMP Brixton* [2001] EWHC (Admin) 178, paras 114 and 115.

[42] Approved by the Judicial Committee of the Privy Council in *Knowles v Government of the United States* [2006] UKPC 38.

[43] For example Art 10 of the Treaty on Extradition between the Government of the United States of America and the Government of the United Kingdom of Great Britain and Northern Ireland (Cm 5821) provides: 'If the Requested State requires additional information to enable a decision to be taken on the request for extradition, the Requesting State shall respond to the request within such time as the Requested State requires.' cf EAW Framework Decision, Art 15(2).

at the outset of proceedings and the judge had made a disclosure order against the government which had led to a multiplicity of further hearings.[44] The Court said at paras 85–93:

> Both our civil and our criminal procedures have complex rules in relation to disclosure of documents. In each of the cases before us the persons whose extradition is being sought have persuaded the judge that he should make an order for disclosure. We do not consider that this was the appropriate course to take. Neither the rules governing disclosure in a civil action, nor those governing disclosure in a criminal trial can be applied to an extradition hearing. Furthermore, those rules form part of an adversarial process which differs from extradition proceedings. Where an order for disclosure is made, it requires one party to disclose documents to the other, not to the court. But where extradition is sought, the court is under a duty to satisfy itself that all the requirements for making the order are satisfied and that none of the bars to making the order exists.
>
> There is a further objection to ordering disclosure. The order will be made either against a judicial authority within the European Union or against a foreign Sovereign State that is requesting the Secretary of State to comply with treaty obligations. In neither case would it be appropriate to order discovery. Were it appropriate to make such an order, the only sanction for a failure to comply with it would be to reject the request for extradition. That fact points the way to the appropriate course that the court should take where there are grounds for believing that an abuse of process has occurred.
>
> ... The appropriate course for the judge to take if he has reason to believe that an abuse of process may have occurred is to call upon the judicial authority that has issued the arrest warrant, or the State seeking extradition in a Part 2 case, for whatever information or evidence the judge requires in order to determine whether an abuse of process has occurred or not. The information and evidence obtained should be made available to the party contesting extradition. We agree with Mr Gordon that the standards required by Article 13 of the ECHR should apply to the extradition proceedings. Equality of arms requires that, in normal circumstances, the party contesting extradition should be aware of, and thus able to comment on, the material upon which the court will be basing its decision.
>
> What if the judicial authority or the requesting State is only prepared to provide the court with the information or evidence on terms that it is not shown to the party contesting extradition ?... If the judge concludes that fairness requires that the material be disclosed, but the requesting authority or State is not prepared to agree to this, then the appropriate course will be for the judge to hold that fair process is impossible, that to grant the application for extradition in the circumstances would involve an abuse of process, and to discharge the person whose extradition is sought.

Hearsay evidence

6.53 The rule at common law was that hearsay evidence was inadmissible in criminal proceedings, subject to certain recognised exceptions (eg, *res gestae*). The rule rendered inadmissible any statement other than one made by a person giving oral evidence in the proceedings as evidence of any fact or opinion stated.[45]

6.54 In extradition cases where the requesting state was required to adduce evidence, first-hand hearsay evidence was permissible to the extent that the requesting state was entitled to rely upon the authenticated written statements of witnesses contained in the extradition request and was not required to call those witnesses to give oral evidence in the proceedings.[46] However, second-hand hearsay was not admissible.[47] Sections 84(2) and 86(2) of the EA 2003 remove

[44] Abuse of process is considered at para 5.120.

[45] *Subramaniam v Public Prosecutor* [1956] 1 WLR 956, 969; *Sharp* [1988] 1 WLR 7.

[46] *Dowse v Governor of Pentonville Prison* [1983] 2 AC 464; *R v Governor of Brixton Prison ex p Caldough* [1961] 1 WLR 464; *R v Secretary of State for India ex p Ezekiel* [1941] 2 KB 169.

[47] *R v Governor of Pentonville Prison ex p Kirby* [1979] 2 All ER 1094.

this restriction. They give the judge a discretion to treat a statement made by a person in a document as admissible evidence of a fact if the statement is made by the person to a police officer or another person charged with the duty of investigating offences or charging offenders; and direct oral evidence by the person of the fact would be admissible. Sections 84(4) and 86(4) provide that a summary in a document of a statement made by a person must be treated as a statement made by the person in the document for the purposes of ss 84(2) and 86(2). Thus, under the EA 2003 both first-hand hearsay and second-hand hearsay are now potentially admissible. Sections 84 and 86 contain the *lex specialis* in relation to hearsay evidence in extradition proceedings. The provisions of the Criminal Justice Act 2003, Part 2, Chapter 2, relating to hearsay apply to criminal proceedings in the strict sense, that is, proceedings before magistrates and juries, and do not apply in extradition proceedings.[48]

6.55 The effect of EA 2003, ss 84 and 86 can be illustrated by the following example. If the evidence in the request includes a police report in which the police officer records the witness, W, as telling him that D committed the crime, then the judge has a discretion to admit the statement as evidence that D committed the crime because the statement was made to a police officer and direct oral evidence at trial from W that D committed the crime would be admissible. However, if the report recorded W as telling the officer that A told him that D committed the crime then this would not be admissible. This is because although the statement was made to a police officer, evidence from W at trial about what A told him would not be admissible in order to show that D committed the offence because it would be hearsay.

6.56 Sections 84(3) and 86(3) require the judge to have regard to certain matters before admitting a statement under s 84(2) or 86(2). The judge must have regard to the nature and source of the document; to whether or not, having regard to the nature and source of the document and to any other circumstances that appear to the judge to be relevant, it is likely that the document is authentic; to the extent to which the statement appears to supply evidence which would not be readily available if the statement were not treated as being admissible evidence of the fact; to the relevance of the evidence that the statement appears to supply to any issue likely to have to be determined by the judge in deciding the question in ss 84(1) and 86(1); and to any risk that the admission or exclusion of the statement will result in unfairness to the person whose extradition is sought, having regard in particular to whether it is likely to be possible to controvert the statement if the person making it does not attend to give oral evidence.

6.57 Section 84 was considered by the Administrative Court in *Government of India v Bow Street Magistrates' Court* [2006] All ER (D) 51 (Nov). The government sought the defendant's extradition in relation to alleged offences of fraud. An important part of the case against him was an affidavit by V, a police superintendent, which set out in some detail a synopsis of the case. Two paragraphs recited content from, and the conclusions of, a report from a firm of chartered accountants to support a prima facie case of fraud. The government argued at the extradition hearing that those paragraphs were admissible as either: (i) amounting to a statement by a person whose direct oral evidence would be admissible and which had been made to a police officer for the purposes of s 84(2); or (ii) amounting to a summary of such evidence within the meaning of s 84(4). The district judge ruled the material inadmissible on the basis that it did not constitute 'first hand hearsay' for the purposes of s 84(2), nor was it a summary by an intended witness of his own evidence. The district judge ordered the defendant's discharge and the government appealed.

6.58 On the appeal, issues arose as to how the government could establish that a statement had been made to a police officer or another person charged with the duty of investigating offences or

[48] *Friesel v Government of the United States of America* [2009] EWHC 1659 (Admin), para 33.

charging offenders so as to come within s 84(2) and whether, even if the district judge had been right to rule the evidence inadmissible, the matter should, nevertheless, be remitted to him on the basis that any difficulty was one of technicality rather than of substance.

6.59 The Administrative Court ruled that where it was apparent on the face of a document that it purported to be made by a police officer or another person charged with the duty of investigating offences or charging offenders, then, unless there was some proper basis upon which that could be doubted, the court was entitled to rely on the face of the document. However, the affidavit was not a 'statement', nor was it a 'summary' for the purposes of s 84(4). The impugned paragraphs did not purport to be a statement by the firm of accountants, let alone a witness from that firm, but appeared to be part summary and part narrative of the accountant's report by V in a way that did not make it clear how it could be a full summary of that report. Accordingly, the Court held that the district judge had correctly ruled that the paragraphs in question did not provide evidence upon which he could rely to answer the question posed by s 84(1).

6.60 However, the Court held that given the seriousness of the fraud alleged, the government should be given the opportunity to provide a secure basis upon which the district judge could determine the question of extradition and it accordingly remitted the case to the district judge. The Court commented, *per curiam*, that having regard to s 84(4), a 'summary' of the evidence of a person who is capable of giving admissible evidence for the purposes of s 84(2) may be made by a person giving that summary as hearsay.

K. Convictions in Absence

6.61 Where the defendant is alleged to be unlawfully at large after conviction of the extradition offence, the judge must proceed under s 85. This section is intended to ensure that a defendant who has been convicted *in absentia* will be treated fairly in the requesting state by being re-tried in his presence.

6.62 Section 85 is in similar terms to s 20: see para 5.96. The burden of showing pursuant to s 85(3) that a defendant deliberately absented himself from his trial lies on the government, which must satisfy the burden to the criminal standard.[49]

L. Human Rights

6.63 Section 87 prohibits the judge from ordering extradition where to do so would be incompatible with the defendant's Convention rights within the meaning of the Human Rights Act 1998. This topic is dealt with separately in Chapter 7.

M. Other Bars to Extradition

Physical or mental condition

6.64 Section 91 provides a bar to extradition where the judge is satisfied it would be unjust or oppressive to return the defendant because of his physical or mental condition. It is in similar terms to s 25 in Part 1 cases, see para 5.110.[50]

---

[49] *Mitoi v Government of Romania* [2006] EWHC 1977 (Admin).
[50] *Dewani v Government of the Republic of South Africa* [2012] EWHC 842 (Admin).

Bad faith/abuse of process

This is considered at para 5.120.[51] **6.65**

Sovereign and diplomatic immunity

This is considered at para 5.132. **6.66**

N. Deferral of Proceedings under Part 2

Sections 88–90 deal with the situation where the defendant becomes subject to other extradition proceedings or criminal proceedings in the UK. The appropriate judge has power to adjourn the hearing until the other proceedings are disposed of. **6.67**

Person charged with offence in the UK (s 88)

If the judge is informed during the extradition hearing that the defendant has been charged with an offence in the UK he must adjourn the extradition hearing until one of the following events occurs (s 88(1) and (2)): **6.68**

(a) the charge is disposed of;
(b) the charge is withdrawn;
(c) proceedings in respect of the charge are discontinued;
(d) an order is made for the charge to lie on the file (or the Scots equivalent).

If a sentence of imprisonment or another form of detention is imposed in respect of the offence charged, the judge may adjourn the extradition hearing until the sentence has been served. **6.69**

If before he adjourns the extradition hearing under s 88(2) the judge has decided under s 79 whether the defendant's extradition is barred by reason of the rule against double jeopardy, the judge must decide that question again after the resumption of the hearing (s 88(4)). **6.70**

Person serving sentence in the UK (s 89)

If the judge is informed at any time in the extradition hearing that the person is serving a sentence of imprisonment or another form of detention in the UK then he may adjourn the extradition hearing until the sentence has been served (s 89).[52] Section 89(3), inserted by para 7 of Sch 13 to the Police and Justice Act 2006, allows for a period of remand in custody for up to six months. **6.71**

Competing extradition claims (s 90)

The Secretary of State has power under ss 126 and 179 to regulate competing requests by ordering that one set of proceedings be deferred until the conclusion of the other. These powers are considered at paras 8.45 and 8.49. **6.72**

Section 90 prescribes the appropriate judge's function where the Secretary of State has exercised his powers. Section 90 applies if at any time in the extradition hearing the judge is informed that the conditions in s 90(2) or (3) are met. The conditions in s 90(2) are that: **6.73**

(a) the Secretary of State has received another valid request for the person's extradition to a Category 2 territory;

---

[51] *Stepp v Government of the United States of America* [2006] EWHC 1033 (Admin); *R (Bermingham) v Director of the Serious Fraud Office* [2006] EWHC 200, paras 91–100; *R (Government of the United States of America) v Senior District Judge, Bow Street Magistrates' Court* [2006] EWHC 2256 (Admin), paras 83–93.

[52] *R (Handa) v Bow Street Magistrates' Court* [2004] EWHC 3116.

(b) the other request has not been disposed of;
(c) the Secretary of State has made an order under s 126(2) for further proceedings on the request under consideration to be deferred until the other request has been disposed of.

6.74 The conditions in s 90(3) are that:

(a) a certificate has been issued under s 2 in respect of a Part 1 warrant issued in respect of the person;
(b) the warrant has not been disposed of;
(c) the Secretary of State has made an order under s 179(2) for further proceedings on the request to be deferred until the warrant has been disposed of.

6.75 Where the judge orders a deferral he must remand the defendant in custody or on bail. If the remand is in custody the judge may later grant bail.

O. Costs

6.76 Section 133 provides for costs to be awarded against a defendant whose extradition is ordered under Part 2. Section 134 allows for an award of costs in favour of a person who is discharged. They are identical to ss 60 and 61 in Part 1 cases, considered at para 5.156.

7

EXTRADITION AND HUMAN RIGHTS

A. Introduction

This chapter examines the relationship between extradition under the EA 2003 and the European Convention on Human Rights ('the ECHR'). It also considers the substantive content of the Convention rights relevant to extradition.[1] **7.01**

Human rights principles impact upon the extradition process in two main ways. First, as a public authority under the Human Rights Act 1998, a court dealing with an extradition case must act compatibly with the defendant's Convention rights[2] in the manner in which it deals with the matter.[3] Secondly, a defendant cannot be extradited if to do so would violate his Convention rights. Section 21 of the EA 2003 (in Part 1 cases) and s 87 (in Part 2 cases) prohibit the appropriate judge from ordering the defendant's extradition (or sending the case to the Secretary of State) where extradition would be incompatible with the defendant's Convention rights.[4] An important principle underlying the operation of these two sections is that the UK will incur liability under the ECHR if it extradites a defendant in circumstances which expose him to a risk of treatment in the requesting state which is prohibited under the ECHR (in particular, by Articles 2 and 3) even if the requesting state is not itself a signatory to the ECHR.[5] In other words, although the obligations imposed by the ECHR relate **7.02**

---

[1] The House of Commons and House of Lords Joint Committee on Human Rights examined the human rights implications of the Extradition Bill in the Twentieth Report of its 2001–2002 session (26 July 2002, HC 1140). In June 2011 the Committee's Fifteenth Report of its 2010–2011 session addressed *The Human Rights Implications of UK Extradition Policy*. The 2011 Extradition Review dealt with human rights at para 5.29 et seq.

[2] Defined in the Human Rights Act 1998, s 1.

[3] Human Rights Act 1998, s 6(1); *R (Kashamu) v Governor of Brixton Prison* [2002] QB 887, para 32.

[4] *Norris v Government of the United States of America (No 2)* [2010] 2 AC 487, para 1.

[5] *Al-Saadoon and Mufdhi v United Kingdom*, Application no. 61498/08, paras 123–125; *Soering v United Kingdom* (1989) 11 EHRR 439. In *Norris v Government of the United States of America (No 2)* [2010] 2 AC 487, para 99, Lord Phillips indicated that it was this situation that s 87 was mainly intended to address: 'To my mind section 87 is designed essentially to cater to the occasional "foreign case" where (principally although not exclusively) Article 2 or 3 rights may be at stake.' In *Ullah v Secretary of State for the Home Department* [2004] 2 AC 323, paras 7–9, Lord Bingham used the term 'foreign cases' to mean those cases where it is not claimed that the state complained of has violated the defendant's ECHR rights within its own territory, but where it is said that

primarily to the manner in which its signatories treat those who are within their jurisdiction, decisions of the European Court of Human Rights have established that extradition is capable of infringing Convention obligations by reason of the treatment that the individual is likely to receive in the country to which he is extradited.

7.03 Before considering the substantive content of the relevant Convention rights it is useful to examine some of the key provisions of the Human Rights Act 1998.

B. Outline of the Human Rights Act 1998

7.04 The long title of the Human Rights Act 1998 declares that it is 'An Act to give further effect to rights and freedoms guaranteed under the European Convention on Human Rights …'. This makes clear that even before the 1998 Act came into force the ECHR already had an effect in domestic law. Courts sought to interpret ambiguous legislation consistently with the ECHR.[6] They also sought to exercise judicial discretion consistently with the ECHR and to develop the common law in a manner not inconsistent with it.[7] Although ministers and other public authorities had no duty to exercise discretionary powers in a manner consistent with the Convention,[8] the human rights involved were relevant to the question of whether the authority had acted reasonably and taken all relevant matters into account when exercising its powers.[9]

7.05 The Human Rights Act 1998 imposes a number of duties on courts and public authorities so as to give further effect to certain Convention rights in domestic law. A detailed discussion of the history and effect of the Human Rights Act 1998 is outside the scope of this work.[10] The following is a summary of its more important provisions.

Convention rights

7.06 Section 1 provides which rights under the ECHR are to be given further effect in domestic law. These are Articles 2–12 and 14 of the Convention, Articles 1–3 of the First Protocol, and Article 1 of Protocol No 13, in each case read with Articles 16–18 of the Convention. These are referred to in the Human Rights Act 1998 as 'Convention rights', and the appropriate judge's task under ss 21 and 87 of the EA 2003 is to determine whether extradition is compatible with these rights.

Duty of courts to take ECHR into account

7.07 Section 2 provides that a court or tribunal determining a question which has arisen in connection with a Convention right must take into account any judgment or decision of the European Court of Human Rights; any opinion of the Commission given in a report adopted under Article 31 of the Convention; any decision of the Commission in connection with Article 26 or 27(2) of the Convention; or any decision of the Committee of Ministers taken under Article 46 of the Convention, so far as, in the opinion of the court or tribunal, it is relevant to the proceedings in which that question has arisen.

---

the conduct of the state in removing a person from its territory to another territory will lead to a violation of the person's ECHR rights in that other territory. When he used the term 'domestic cases' he meant cases concerning claims based on the ECHR where a state is said to have acted within its own territory in a way which infringes the enjoyment of an ECHR right within that territory.

[6] *JH Rayner (Mincing Lane) Ltd v Department of Trade and Industry* [1990] AC 418.

[7] *Sultan Khan* [1997] AC 558.

[8] *R v Secretary of State for the Home Department ex p Brind* [1991] 1 AC 696.

[9] *R v Ministry of Defence ex p Smith* [1996] QB 517; *R v Lord Saville of Newdigate ex p B* [2000] 1 WLR 1855.

[10] For a detailed account see Clayton and Tomlinson, *The Law of Human Rights* (2nd edn, Oxford, 2009).

Section 2 does not mean that domestic courts are bound by decisions of the European Court of Human Rights.[11] They merely have to be taken into account.[12] Nevertheless, the House of Lords has said that English courts should follow clear and consistent jurisprudence of the Strasbourg Court in the absence of some special reason.[13] The meaning of s 2(1) was authoritatively expounded by Lord Bingham of Cornhill, in reasoning with which all other members of the House agreed, in *R (Ullah) v Special Adjudicator* [2005] 2 AC 323, para 20: **7.08**

> In determining the present question, the House is required by s 2(1) of the Human Rights Act 1998 to take into account any relevant Strasbourg case law. While such case law is not strictly binding, it has been held that courts should, in the absence of some special circumstances, follow any clear and constant jurisprudence of the Strasbourg Court ... This reflects the fact that the Convention is an international instrument, the correct interpretation of which can be authoritatively expounded only by the Strasbourg Court. From this it follows that a national court subject to a duty such as that imposed by s 2 should not without strong reason dilute or weaken the effect of the Strasbourg case law. It is indeed unlawful under s 6 of the 1998 Act for a public authority, including a court, to act in a way which is incompatible with a convention right. It is of course open to member states to provide for rights more generous than those guaranteed by the convention, but such provision should not be the product of interpretation of the convention by national courts, since the meaning of the convention should be uniform throughout the states party to it. The duty of national courts is to keep pace with the Strasbourg jurisprudence as it evolves over time: no more, but certainly no less.

Consistently with this approach, in *Secretary of State for the Home Department v AF (No 3)* [2009] 3 WLR 74 the House of Lords held itself bound to apply a clear statement of principle by the Grand Chamber of the European Court of Human Rights in respect of the precise issue that was before the Committee. However, in *R v Horncastle* [2010] 2 AC 373, para 11, the Supreme Court said: **7.09**

> The requirement to 'take into account' the Strasbourg jurisprudence will normally result in this Court applying principles that are clearly established by the Strasbourg Court. There will, however, be rare occasions where this court has concerns as to whether a decision of the Strasbourg Court sufficiently appreciates or accommodates particular aspects of our domestic process. In such circumstances it is open to this court to decline to follow the Strasbourg decision, giving reasons for adopting this course. This is likely to give the Strasbourg Court the opportunity to reconsider the particular aspect of the decision that is in issue, so that there takes place what may prove to be a valuable dialogue between this court and the Strasbourg Court.

Duty of courts to interpret legislation compatibly with Convention rights

Section 3(1) provides that so far as it is possible to do so, primary legislation and subordinate legislation (whenever enacted)[14] must be read and given effect in a way which is compatible with Convention rights. This interpretative obligation goes beyond the previous rules which **7.10**

---

[11] *Stare decisis* itself does not apply to decisions of the Court or Commission because of the interpretive approach adopted by the Convention organs. They interpret the Convention as a 'living instrument' in the light of modern standards. Its meaning is therefore capable of evolving over time: *Tyrer v United Kingdom* (1978) 2 EHRR 1.

[12] During the debate on the Human Rights Bill in Parliament the Lord Chancellor said that domestic courts may 'depart from existing Strasbourg decisions and upon occasion it might well be appropriate to do so, and it is possible they might give a successful lead to Strasbourg'. However, he added that 'where it is relevant we would of course expect our courts to apply Convention jurisprudence and its principles to the cases before them': 583 HL Official Reports (5 Series), cols 514–515, 18 November 1997.

[13] *R v Spear* [2003] 1 AC 734, paras 12 and 92.

[14] s 3(2)(a).

permitted courts to take the Convention into account when resolving an ambiguity in a statutory provision.

7.11 Section 3(1) requires courts to strive for compatibility, if necessary by reading down over-broad legislation or reading necessary safeguards into an Act.[15] It may involve giving a meaning to a statutory provision which it would not ordinarily bear[16] if necessary by jettisoning particular words in a section,[17] or by implying words into a section.[18] If a higher court cannot properly construe a statute so as to be compatible then the court may make a declaration of incompatibility under s 4.

7.12 In *R v A (No 2)* [2002] 1 AC 45, para 44 Lord Steyn explained the effect of s 3:[19]

> In accordance with the will of Parliament as reflected in section 3 it will sometimes be necessary to adopt an interpretation which linguistically may appear strained. The techniques to be used will not only involve the reading down of express language in a statute but also the implication of provisions. A declaration of incompatibility is a measure of last resort. It must be avoided unless it is plainly impossible to do so.

7.13 In *Lukaszewski v The District Court in Torun, Poland* [2012] UKSC 20, para 38, the Supreme Court said that the interpretive obligation imposed by s 3 of the Human Rights Act 1998:

> … may involve reading in words, provided that they are 'compatible with the underlying thrust of the legislation' and do not go against 'the grain of the legislation' …[20]

7.14 The obligation in s 3(1) applies to all courts and tribunals. Lower courts are thus no longer bound by a previous construction which has been given to existing legislation by a higher court if, in the opinion of the inferior court, this construction would lead to a result which would be incompatible with the Convention rights.[21]

Duty on public authorities to act compatibly with Convention rights

7.15 Section 6(1) makes it unlawful for a 'public authority' to act in a way which is incompatible with a Convention right. Section 6(3) defines public authorities as including a court or tribunal, and any person certain of whose functions are functions of a public nature.[22] An appropriate judge presiding over an extradition hearing under the EA 2003 is therefore a public authority. The Secretary of State is also a public authority. This means that the Secretary of State cannot maintain an order for extradition under Part 2 of the EA 2003 if this would violate the defendant's Convention rights, even though his right of appeal under the EA 2003 has been exhausted.[23]

---

15 cf *Attorney General of Gambia v Momodou Jobe* [1984] AC 689, 702.

16 *Webb v EMO Air Cargo (UK) Ltd (No 2)* [1995] 1 WLR 1454.

17 *O'Brien v Sim-Chem Ltd* [1980] 1 WLR 1011, 1017.

18 *Jones v Kingdom of Saudi Arabia* [2006] UKHL 26, para 39; *Vasquez and O'Neil v R* [1994] 1 WLR 1304, 1314.

19 For a full discussion of the effect of s 3, see *Ghaidan v Godin-Mendoza* [2004] 2 AC 557, paras 25–34; *Sheldrake v Director of Public Prosecutions* [2005] 1 AC 264, para 24. See also *Connolly v Director of Public Prosecutions* [2008] 1 WLR 276, para 18.

20 Accordingly, the Supreme Court held that the absolute time limits for filing and serving a notice of appeal against the appropriate judge's decision in the EA 2003 were to be read as subject to a power in exceptional circumstances to extend time to avoid a breach of the defendant's Convention rights: see para 9.29.

21 *R v Offen* [2001] 1 WLR 253; *R v A (No 2)* [2002] 1 AC 45; *Lambert* [2001] 3 WLR 206.

22 *Aston Cantlow and Wilmcote with Billesley Parochial Church Council v Wallbank* [2004] 1 AC 546.

23 *R (Vatoci) v Secretary of State for the Home Department* [2012] EWHC 1356 (Admin); *Mucelli (No.2)*; *Hoxhaj and Gjoka v Government of Albania* [2012] EWHC 95 (Admin); *R (Greer aka Bailey) v The Serious Organised Crime Agency* [2011] EWHC 446 (Admin); *R (Mann) v Serious Organised Crime Agency* [2010] EWHC 1760 (Admin); *R (Mann) v City of Westminster Magistrates' Court* [2010] EWHC 48 (Admin); *Atkinson v Commissioner of the Metropolitan Police Force* [2009] EWHC 2661 (Admin); *R (McKinnon) v Secretary of State for Home Affairs* [2009] EWHC 2021 (Admin); *McKinnon v Government of the United States* [2007] EWHC 762 (Admin).

Remedies for violations of Convention rights

Section 7 allows a person who claims that a public authority acts (or proposes to act) in a way which is made unlawful by s 6(1) to bring proceedings against the authority in respect of the act and to rely on the Convention. Section 195 of the EA 2003 provides that the appropriate judge is the only appropriate tribunal in relation to proceedings under s 7(1)(a) of the Human Rights Act 1998 if the proceedings relate to extradition under Part 1 or Part 2 of the EA 2003. Section 9 of the Human Rights Act 1998 provides that in respect of judicial acts the proceedings in s 7 can only be brought by way of appeal. **7.16**

C. Extradition and Convention Rights

Introduction

The ECHR specifically permits extradition and detention pending extradition. Article 5(1)(f), which defines the circumstances in which the state can lawfully detain an individual, provides: **7.17**

> 5(1) Everyone has the right to liberty and security of person. No-one shall be deprived of his liberty save in the following cases and in accordance with a procedure prescribed by law …
>
> …
>
> (f) the lawful arrest or detention of a person to prevent his effecting an unauthorised entry into the country or of a person against whom action is being taken with a view to deportation or extradition.

Thus, the ECHR does not prevent cooperation between states, within the framework of extradition treaties, for the purpose of bringing fugitive offenders to justice, provided that it does not interfere with any specific rights recognized in the Convention.[24] **7.18**

As explained at para 7.02, extradition proceedings under the EA 2003 may raise issues under the ECHR where the domestic extradition process is conducted in a way which may result in a violation of the Convention,[25] or there is a risk that extradition itself will breach one or more of the defendant's Convention rights.[26] **7.19**

The interaction of extradition law with human rights law first emerged in the context of Article 3. The principle that extradition could raise issues under Article 3 in a way that engaged the responsibility of the extraditing state was first authoritatively stated by the European Court of Human Rights in *Soering v United Kingdom* (1989) 11 EHRR 439. The question whether extradition could raise issues, in other words, potentially infringe, other Articles of the Convention was considered by the House of Lords in *R (Ullah) v Special Adjudicator* [2004] 2 AC 323. The House of Lords, reversing the Court of Appeal, held that it could. However, Lord Bingham of Cornhill said at para 24: **7.20**

> While the Strasbourg jurisprudence does not preclude reliance on articles other than Article 3 as a ground for resisting extradition or expulsion, it makes it quite clear that successful reliance demands presentation of a very strong case. In relation to Article 3, it is necessary to show strong grounds for believing that the person, if returned, faces a real risk of being subjected to torture or to inhuman or degrading treatment or punishment … Where reliance is placed on

---

[24] *Ocalan v Turkey* (2003) 37 EHRR 10, para 89.

[25] Human Rights Act 1998, s 6; *(Al-Fawwaz) v Governor of Brixton Prison* [2001] 1 WLR 1234, paras 58–62.

[26] EA 2003, ss 21 and 87.

> Article 6 it must be shown that a person has suffered or risks suffering a flagrant denial of a fair trial in the receiving state ... Successful reliance on Article 5 would have to meet no less exacting a test. The lack of success of applicants relying on Articles 2, 5 and 6 before the Strasbourg Court highlights the difficulty of meeting the stringent test which that court imposes.[27] This difficulty will not be less where reliance is placed on articles such as 8 or 9, which provide for the striking of a balance between the right of the individual and the wider interests of the community even in a case where a serious interference is shown. This is not a balance which the Strasbourg Court ought ordinarily to strike in the first instance, nor is it a balance which that court is well placed to assess in the absence of representations by the receiving state whose laws, institutions or practices are the subject of criticism. On the other hand, the removing state will always have what will usually be strong grounds for justifying its own conduct: the great importance of operating firm and orderly immigration control in an expulsion case; the great desirability of honouring extradition treaties made with other states.

7.21 Thus, extradition may raise issues under a number of different Articles of the ECHR. The following paragraphs examine Articles 2, 3, 5, 6, 8, and Article 1 of Protocol 13 in detail.

Article 2: right to life

7.22 Article 2 provides:

> 2(1) Everyone's right to life shall be protected by law. No one shall be deprived of his life intentionally save in the execution of a sentence of a court following his conviction of a crime for which this penalty is provided by law.
>
> (2) Deprivation of life shall not be regarded as inflicted in contravention of this article when it results from the use of force which is no more than absolutely necessary:
>
> (a) in defence of any person from unlawful violence;
>
> (b) in order to effect a lawful arrest or to prevent the escape of a person lawfully detained;
>
> (c) in action lawfully taken for the purpose of quelling a riot or insurrection.

7.23 Article 2 protects the individual's right to life. It places a positive duty on the state to safeguard the lives of those within its jurisdiction and a negative duty to refrain from the unlawful taking of life.[28] Extradition in circumstances which put the defendant's life in jeopardy may therefore violate Article 2.

7.24 Even though Article 2 on its face permits the imposition of the death penalty, the Sixth Protocol to the ECHR, which came into force in 1985, prohibits the imposition of a death sentence and the carrying out of such a sentence in peacetime, while Protocol No 13 to the ECHR, adopted by the Council of Europe in 2002, requires state parties to abolish the death penalty in *all* circumstances, including in time of war or of imminent threat of war. In *Al-Saadoon and Mufdhi v United Kingdom*, Application No 61498/08, para 120, the European Court of Human Rights concluded that imposition of the death penalty would violate Article 3 of the ECHR, notwithstanding the terms of Article 2, because of the adoption of Protocol No 13 by all but two Council of Europe States. Article 1 of Protocol No 13 is one of the Convention rights in the Human Rights Act 1998. Thus, no-one can lawfully be extradited from the UK on a charge which potentially carries a death sentence if there is a real risk of the death penalty being imposed.[29]

---

[27] cf *Ahmad and Aswat v Government of the United States of America* [2006] EWHC 2927 (Admin), para 23, where it was conceded that extradition of a defendant to the United States who would be liable to detention at Guantanamo Bay pursuant to Military Order No 1 would be incompatible with Arts 3, 5, and 6.

[28] *Osman v United Kingdom* (1988) 29 EHRR 245. As well as imposing an obligation on the state not to take life, Art 2 also requires that domestic law provide a mechanism whereby the circumstances of a deprivation of life by the agents of a state can receive public and independent scrutiny: *R (Amin) v Secretary of State for the Home Department* [2004] 2 AC 653; *R (Wright) v Secretary of State* [2001] UKHRR 1399.

[29] *Al-Saadoon and Mufdhi v United Kingdom*, Application no. 61498/08, paras 123–125. See para 7.90.

The test applied by the Strasbourg bodies in assessing whether extradition would give rise to a violation of Article 2 has evolved over time. Initially, the Commission held that in relation to claims under Article 2 there needed to be an 'almost certainty' of the applicant being killed in the requesting state before a violation of Article 2 could be established.[30] However, in later cases the Court has applied a 'real risk' test akin to that applied in relation to Article 3.[31] **7.25**

In *Maclean v High Court, Dublin* [2008] EWCA 547 (Admin) Richards LJ said (without deciding the issue) that it will be a breach of Article 2 for a state to extradite a person if there is known to be a real (or real and immediate) risk to his life in the receiving country. Where the risk to life is from non-state agents, it is necessary to show in addition a lack of reasonable protection in the receiving country.[32] He said at para 10: **7.26**

> The adoption of essentially the same test in relation to Article 2 as in relation to Article 3 has obvious attractions to it. It is very unsatisfactory to apply a higher threshold in the case of a risk to life than in a case where the risk is of less serious harm (albeit sufficiently serious to fall within Article 3). True, the point may be devoid of practical significance since *Launder* shows that Article 3 can be relied on even where the risk is to life; but it is strange to have to rely on Article 3 where the subject matter falls more naturally under Article 2.

The Strasbourg Court has applied the 'real risk' test in a number of subsequent cases, and this can now be regarded as the appropriate test in assessing whether extradition would violate Article 2.[33] **7.27**

Article 3: prohibition of torture and inhuman treatment

Article 3 provides that: **7.28**

> No-one shall be subjected to torture or inhuman and degrading treatment or punishment.

Article 3 is one of the shortest provisions in the Convention. However, that brevity should not belie the importance of Article 3. The European Court of Human Rights has repeatedly stressed that the protection afforded by Article 3 ranks among the most important guaranteed by the ECHR.[34] The fact that the defendant is accused of serious crimes, or that there are national security reasons for seeking his removal, are irrelevant. The protection provided by Article 3 is absolute.[35] Indeed, the prohibition on torture is not just a prohibition contained in the ECHR, but is also part of customary international law, and is considered to be *jus cogens*.[36] **7.29**

'Torture' encompasses deliberately inflicted inhuman treatment which causes very severe and cruel suffering, whether physical or mental.[37] In determining whether the necessary threshold **7.30**

---

30 *Launder v United Kingdom*, Application No 27279/95. The defendant's claim that that he would, if returned, be tortured in Hong Kong was also rejected under the 'real risk' standard applicable in relation to Article 3. See also, *R v Secretary of State for the Home Department ex p Launder* [1997] 1 WLR 839; *R v Secretary of State for the Home Department ex p Launder (No 2)* [1998] QB 994.

31 *Bader v Sweden*, Application No 13284/04, para 42, para 48.

32 *R (Bagdanavicius) v Secretary of State for the Home Department* [2005] 2 AC 668, para 24.

33 *Al-Saadoon and Mufdhi v United Kingdom*, Application No 61498/08, para 123; *Hakizimana v Sweden*, Application No 37913/05; *SR v Sweden*, Application No 62806/00; *Ismaili v Germany*, Application No 58128/00; *Kaboulov v Ukraine*, Application No 41015/04.

34 *Al-Saadoon and Mufdhi v United Kingdom*, Application No 61498/08, para 122.

35 *Chahal v United Kingdom* (1996) 23 EHRR 413, para 80.

36 *A v Secretary of State for the Home Department (No 2)* [2006] 2 AC 221, paras 30–33; *Prosecutor v Furundzija*, 10 December 1998, case no. IT-95-17/I-T (ICTY); *Prosecutor v Delacic and others*, 16 November 1998, case no IT-96-21-T, para 454 (ICTY); *Prosecutor v Kunarac*, 22 February 2001, case no IT-96-23, para 466 (ICTY).

37 *Ireland v United Kingdom* (1978) 2 EHRR 25. Unlike, for example, the definition of torture in Article 1 of the UN Convention against Torture and Other Cruel, Inhuman or Degrading Treatment or Punishment 1984, under Article 3, to qualify as torture, the treatment in question need only reach the relevant level of severity

of severity has been crossed all the circumstances must be taken into account, including the nature and context of the treatment or punishment, the manner and method of its execution, its duration, its physical and mental effects, and the sex, age, and state of health of the victim. In *Dikme v Turkey* (Application No 20869/92) where the applicant had been beaten, suffered electric shocks and other ill-treatment in police custody, the Court said at paras 94–96 that whether the severity of the treatment amounted to torture:

> ... depends on all the circumstances of the case, such as the duration of the treatment, its physical and/or mental effects and, in some cases, the victim's sex, age and state of health ...
>
> In the instant case the first applicant undeniably lived in a permanent state of physical pain and anxiety owing to his uncertainty about his fate and to the blows repeatedly inflicted on him during the lengthy interrogation sessions to which he was subjected throughout his time in police custody. The Court considers that such treatment was intentionally meted out to the first applicant by agents of the State in the performance of their duties, with the aim of extracting a confession or information about the offences of which he was suspected.
>
> In those circumstances the Court finds that the violence inflicted on the first applicant, taken as a whole and having regard to its purpose and duration, was particularly serious and cruel and was capable of causing 'severe' pain and suffering. It therefore amounted to torture within the meaning of Article 3 of the Convention.

7.31 Mistreatment falling short of torture must reach a minimum level of severity to breach Article 3.[38] Again, in determining whether the threshold has been crossed, all the relevant circumstances must be taken into account. These include the nature and context of the treatment or punishment; the manner and method of its execution; its duration; its physical or mental effects; and, in some cases, the sex, age, and state of health of the victim.[39] In *Al-Saadoon and Mufdhi v United Kingdom*, Application No 61498/08, para 121, the Court said:

> In accordance with its constant case-law, ill-treatment must attain a minimum level of severity if it is to fall within the scope of Article 3. The assessment of this minimum depends on all the circumstances of the case, such as the duration of the treatment, its physical or mental effects and, in some cases, the sex, age and state of health of the victim. The Court has considered treatment to be 'inhuman' because, *inter alia*, it was premeditated, was applied for hours at a stretch and caused either actual bodily injury or intense physical or mental suffering. It has deemed treatment to be 'degrading' because it was such as to arouse in the victims feelings of fear, anguish and inferiority capable of humiliating and debasing them. In considering whether a punishment or treatment was 'degrading' within the meaning of Article 3, the Court will have regard to whether its object was to humiliate and debase the person concerned and whether, as far as the consequences are concerned, it adversely affected his or her personality in a manner incompatible with Article 3. However, the absence of any such purpose cannot conclusively rule out a finding of a violation of Article 3. In order for a punishment or treatment associated with it to be 'inhuman' or 'degrading', the suffering or humiliation involved must go beyond that inevitable element of suffering or humiliation connected with a given form of legitimate treatment or punishment.[40]

7.32 Article 3 makes it unlawful for the UK to extradite an individual to a country where he is foreseeably at real risk of being treated in a manner prohibited by Article 3.[41] The defendant has to establish that there are 'substantial grounds for believing that there is a real risk of ill-treatment'

---

and need not be inflicted for any particular purpose, such as to secure information or a confession, although in practice the Court looks for such a purpose before characterizing treatment as torture.

[38] *Tyrer v United Kingdom* (1978) 2 EHRR 1, paras 29, 80.

[39] *Soering v United Kingdom* (1989) 11 EHRR 439, para 100.

[40] *Pretty v United Kingdom*, Application No 2346/02, para 52.

[41] *R (Ullah) v Special Adjudicator* [2003] 1 WLR 770, para 47; *Soering v United Kingdom* (1989) 11 EHRR 439.

of the requisite degree of severity in the receiving state.[42] A real risk is more than a mere possibility but is less than a 'greater probability than not' that an event will occur.[43] The European Court of Human Rights has been very cautious in finding that removal from the territory of a state party to the ECHR would be contrary to Article 3. Save for cases involving the death penalty, it has even more rarely found that there would be a violation of Article 3 if an applicant were to be removed to a state which has a long history of respect for democracy, human rights, and the rule of law.[44]

The burden of establishing an Article 3 claim lies on the defendant.[45] The material point in time for the assessment of risk is the date of the Court's consideration of the case.[46] The Court is able to take into account all the material placed before it as well as information obtained of its own motion.[47] An applicant may be able to establish a breach of Article 3 either by referring to evidence specific to his own circumstances or by reference to evidence applicable to a class of which he is a member. In the second category of case the applicant will only be able to demonstrate substantial grounds for believing that there is such a real risk if he can point to a consistent pattern of gross and systematic violation of rights under Article 3. However, the fact that human rights violations take place is not, of itself, evidence that a particular individual is at risk of being subjected to those human rights violations in the country in question. Much will depend upon the extent to which the violations are systemic, their frequency, and the extent to which the particular individual in question can be said to be specifically vulnerable by reason of a characteristic which would expose him to human rights abuse.[48] Where a defendant has been tortured in the requesting state in the past this will not of itself establish that extradition will breach Article 3, but it demands a detailed and careful consideration by the court as to future risk.[49] A court should not refuse extradition as a means of punishing the requesting state for any past failures, unless they can be shown to have a bearing on future risk.[50] **7.33**

In *Soering v United Kingdom* (1989) 11 EHRR 439 the European Court of Human Rights held that the defendant's extradition to Virginia on charges of capital murder would violate Article 3, not because of the risk of the imposition of the death penalty *per se*, but because of the risk that the defendant would be held for a number of years on death row before being executed, thereby undergoing significant psychological suffering while awaiting execution.[51] This case was one of the first decisions to establish that the responsibility of the extraditing state could be engaged under the ECHR for treatment imposed by a receiving state which was not a signatory to the ECHR. In 2008, in *Al-Saadoon and Mufdhi v United Kingdom*, Application No 61498/08, para 120, the Court held that the coming into force of Protocol No 13 to the Convention, outlawing the death penalty in all circumstances, meant that there was no longer **7.34**

42 *Al-Saadoon and Mufdhi* v *United Kingdom*, Application No 61498/08, para 123; *Chahal v United Kingdom* (1996) 23 EHRR 413, para 74; *Soering v United Kingdom* (1989) 11 EHRR 439, para 91.

43 *R (Lodhi) v Secretary of State for the Home Department* [2010] EWHC 567 (Admin), para 10.

44 *Harkins and Edwards v United Kingdom*, Application Nos 9146/07 and 32650/07, para 131.

45 *Aziz v Secretary of State for the Home Department* [2003] EWCA Civ 118, para 19.

46 *Chahal v United Kingdom* (1996) 23 EHRR 413, para 97.

47 *Mamatkulov and Askarov v Turkey*, Application Nos 46827/99 and 46951/99, paras 67–69.

48 *Miklis v The Deputy Prosecutor General of Lithuania* [2006] EWHC 1032 (Admin), para 11; *Batayav v Secretary of State for the Home Department* [2003] EWCA Civ 1489, para 7; *Hariri v Secretary of State for the Home Department* [2003] EWCA Civ 807, para 8. In *R (Lodhi) v Secretary of State for the Home Department* [2010] EWHC 567 (Admin) the High Court upheld an Article 3 challenge on the basis of evidence about conditions generally in the UAE, and evidence relating to risks to the defendant personally.

49 *Konuksever v Government of Turkey* [2012] EWHC 2166 (Admin), para 58.

50 *Wilby v Municipal Court, Prague* [2012] EWHC 1006 (Admin), para 34; *R (Berners) v Westminster Magistrates' Court* [2010] EWHC 1010 Admin, para 23.

51 cf *Pratt and Morgan v Attorney-General of Jamaica* [1994] 2 AC 1.

any bar to interpreting the prohibition in Article 3 as including the death penalty. Accordingly, extradition where there is a real risk of the imposition of death penalty will violate Article 3.

7.35 In *R (Wellington) v Secretary of State for the Home Department* [2009] 1 AC 335, a majority[52] of the House of Lords adopted a 'relativist' approach to Article 3 in extradition cases, and held that treatment which in other contexts might infringe Article 3 would not do so where it was imposed following extradition, having regard to the need for countries to give effect to extradition treaties. Lord Brown, on the other hand, preferred an absolutist approach to what constitutes inhuman or degrading treatment. He held that if the treatment or punishment likely to be faced by an individual if extradited to the requesting country and then tried, convicted, and sentenced for the crimes in question would be inhuman or degrading for Article 3 purposes in a domestic context, the treatment or punishment would count as inhuman or degrading in a foreign context, whether as a likely consequence of extradition or for any other reason.[53]

7.36 In *Harkins and Edwards v United Kingdom*, Application Nos 9146/07 and 32650/07, paras 119–128, the European Court of Human Rights rejected the view of the majority in *R (Wellington) v Secretary of State for the Home Department* [2009] 1 AC 335 and held that Article 3 is absolute and that the reasons for the person's removal are not to be taken into account in determining whether the threshold of prohibited treatment has been crossed. However, the Court went on to hold that extradition to face a mandatory sentence of life imprisonment without the possibility of parole does not violate Article 3. The Court emphasized that the absolute nature of Article 3 does not mean that any form of ill-treatment will act as a bar to removal from a state party to the ECHR. It noted that it has repeatedly stated that the ECHR does not purport to be a means of requiring state parties to impose ECHR standards on other states. Thus, treatment which might violate Article 3 because of an act or omission of a state party to the ECHR might not attain the minimum level of severity which is required for there to be a violation of Article 3 in an expulsion or extradition case.[54]

7.37 Extradition defendants frequently resist extradition on the basis of prison conditions in the requesting state, or the treatment which they allege they will receive there.[55] Where there is a risk of the defendant being detained in poor prison conditions in the requesting state then extradition may violate Article 3 if it can be shown that the minimum threshold of severity is passed. The focus of the inquiry is on the effect of the conditions on the individual.[56] In the context of the ill-treatment of prisoners, the following factors, among others, have been decisive in the Strasbourg Court's conclusion that there has been a violation of Article 3: the presence of premeditation;[57] that the measure may have been calculated to break the applicant's resistance or will;[58] an intention to debase or humiliate an applicant, or, if there was no such intention, the fact that the measure was implemented in a manner which nonetheless caused

---

52 Lord Hoffmann, Baroness Hale, and Lord Carswell at paras 22, 24, 36, 48, 51–52, 56–57, 58.

53 Paragraphs 85–87. Lord Scott agreed with Lord Brown: para 40.

54 For example, the negligence of a state party to the Convention in providing appropriate medical care within its jurisdiction has, on occasion, led the Court to find a violation of Article 3, but such violations have not been so readily established in the extra-territorial context: cf, for example, *Aleksanyan v Russia*, Application No 46468/06, paras 145–158, and *N v United Kingdom*, Application No 26565/05.

55 *Pisarek v the Regional Court in Elblag 11* [2010] EWHC 877 (Admin); *Targosinski v Judicial Authority of Poland* [2011] EWHC 312 (Admin); *Palczynski v District Court in Zamosc* [2011] EWHC 445 (Admin); *Tworkowski v Judicial Authority of Poland* [2011] EWHC 1502 (Admin); *Slowinski v Judicial Authority of Poland* [2011] EWHC 1548 (Admin); *Nogalski v the Judicial Authority of Poland* [2011] EWHC 1963 (Admin); *Tamarevichute v The Russian Federation* [2008] EWHC 534 (Admin).

56 *Deya v Government of Kenya* [2008] EWHC 2914 (Admin), para 53.

57 *Ireland v the United Kingdom* (1978) 2 EHRR 25, para 167.

58 *Ilaşcu v Moldova and Russia*, Application No 48787/99, para 446.

feelings of fear, anguish, or inferiority;[59] the absence of any specific justification for the measure imposed;[60] the arbitrary punitive nature of the measure;[61] the length of time for which the measure was imposed;[62] the fact that there has been a degree of distress or hardship of an intensity exceeding the unavoidable level of suffering inherent in detention.[63] All of these elements depend closely upon the facts of the case and so will not be readily established prospectively in an extradition context.[64]

The extradition of a defendant who is physically or mentally ill may violate Article 3 if his illness is sufficiently severe and will be exacerbated by extradition.[65] Extradition of a person who is at a very high risk of suicide may violate Article 3.[66] Article 3 may also be violated if there is a significant risk that the defendant will be subjected to a grossly disproportionate sentence.[67] **7.38**

Article 3 will not only be violated where there is a real risk of ill-treatment by state officials in the requesting state. If there is a risk of ill-treatment by private individuals in the requesting state then extradition may violate Article 3 if it can be shown that the risks are significant and the requesting state cannot or will not obviate them.[68] **7.39**

Where the requesting state is a signatory to the ECHR then the starting point for any inquiry for the purpose of making a decision under s 21 or s 87 of the EA 2003 is the presumption that the requesting state is able to, and will, fulfil its obligations under the ECHR. In Part 1 cases in particular, given the underlying objective of the EAW scheme, that presumption will not easily be displaced. However, it is capable of being rebutted by clear and cogent evidence which establishes that, in any particular case, extradition would not be compatible with the defendant's Convention rights.[69] **7.40**

Requesting states frequently give assurances to the UK that the defendant will not be ill-treated on his return, or will be treated in a particular way if he is returned (eg, detained in a particular **7.41**

---

[59] *Jalloh v Germany*, Application No 54810/00, para 82; *Peers v Greece*, Application No 28524/95, para 75.

[60] *Van der Ven v the Netherlands*, Application No 50901/99, paras 61–62; *Iwańczuk v Poland*, Application No 25196/94, para 58.

[61] *Yancov v Bulgaria*, Application 39084/97, para 117.

[62] *Ireland v the United Kingdom* (1978) 2 EHRR 25, para 92.

[63] *Mathew v the Netherlands*, Application No 24919/03, paras 197–205.

[64] *Harkins and Edwards v United Kingdom*, Application Nos 9146/07 and 32650/07, para 130.

[65] *McKinnon v Secretary of State for the Home Department* [2009] EWHC 2021 (Admin), paras 67–71; *Pretty v United Kingdom*, Application No 2346/02, para 52

[66] *Dewani v Government of the Republic of South Africa* [2012] EWHC 842 (Admin); *Wrobel v Judicial Authority of Poland* [2011] EWHC 374 (Admin); *Sbar v The Court of Bologna* [2010] EWHC 1184 (Admin); *Jansons v Latvia* [2009] EWHC 1845 (Admin). In *J v Secretary of State* [2005] EWCA Civ 629, paras 25–32 identified six factors relevant in deportation cases to the question whether there was a real risk of a violation of Article 3.

[67] *Harkins and Edwards v United Kingdom*, Application Nos 9146/07 and 32650/07, para 133.

[68] *Stopyra v District Court o Lublin, Poland* [2012] EWHC 1787 (Admin), para 76; *Maclean v The High Court of Dublin, Ireland* [2008] EWCA 547 (Admin); *R (Bagdanavicius) v Secretary of State for the Home Department* [2005] 2 AC 668; *Horvath v Secretary of State for the Home Department* [2001] 1 AC 489.

[69] *Agius v Court of Magistrates, Malta* [2011] EWHC 759 (Admin), para 18; *Targosinski v Judicial Authority of Poland* [2011] EWHC 312 (Admin), para 11; *R (Elayathamby) v Secretary of State* [2011] EWHC 2182 (Admin), para 42; *Boudhiba v Central Examining Court No 5 of the National Court of Justice in Madrid* [2007] 1 WLR 124, para 48; *Hilali v The Central Court of Criminal Proceedings No 5 of the National Court, Madrid* [2006] EWHC 1239 (Admin), para 77; *MSS v Belgium and Greece*, Application No 300696/09, para 359; cf *Gomes v Government of the Republic of Trinidad and Tobago* [2009] 1 WLR 1038, para 35, overruling on this point *Lisowski v Regional Court of Bialystok, Poland* [2006] EWHC 3227 (Admin). Membership of the Council of Europe is not, of course, a complete answer, as *R (on the application of Bulla) v Secretary of State for the Home Department* [2010] EWHC 3506 (Admin) demonstrates. Where there are reliable reports that the authorities have resorted to, or tolerated, practices contrary to the principles of the Convention, membership is no answer: *MSS v Belgium*, ECHR, Grand Chamber, 21 January 2011.

prison). In its examination of whether an applicant faces a real risk of ill-treatment in the country to which he is to be returned, the Strasbourg Court considers both the general human rights situation in that country and the particular characteristics of the applicant. If assurances have been given, then they constitute a relevant factor which the Court considers. There is a presumption that a country will honour the assurances that it gives.[70] However, assurances are not in themselves sufficient to ensure adequate protection against the risk of ill-treatment. There is an obligation on the requested state to examine whether assurances provide, in their practical application, a sufficient guarantee that the applicant will be protected against the risk of ill-treatment. The weight to be given to assurances from the requesting state receiving depends, in each case, on the circumstances prevailing at the material time. In assessing the practical application of assurances and determining what weight is to be given to them, the preliminary question is whether the general human rights situation in the receiving state excludes accepting any assurances whatsoever. However, it will only be in rare cases that the general situation in a country will mean that no weight at all can be given to assurances. More usually, the Court assesses first, the quality of assurances given and, second, whether, in light of the receiving state's practices they can be relied upon.[71]

Article 5: right to liberty and security

7.42 Article 5 contains a number of different provisions relevant to a defendant detained for the purposes of extradition. Article 5 may be engaged in the extradition process either because: (i) the domestic extradition process is conducted in a manner which violates one or more of its provisions;[72] and/or (ii) because the extradition of the defendant to the foreign state will result in a serious violation of Article 5. In the latter situation extradition will only violate Article 5 if there is a flagrant breach, which is a high threshold. In *Othman v United Kingdom*, Application No 8139/09, para 233, the European Court of Human Rights said:[73]

> The Court therefore considers that ... it is possible for Article 5 to apply in an expulsion case. Hence, the Court considers that a Contracting State would be in violation of Article 5 if it removed an applicant to a State where he or she was at real risk of a flagrant breach of that Article. However, as with Article 6, a high threshold must apply. A flagrant breach of Article 5 would occur only if, for example, the receiving State arbitrarily detained an applicant for many years without any intention of bringing him or her to trial. A flagrant breach of Article 5 might also occur if an applicant would be at risk of being imprisoned for a substantial period in the receiving State, having previously been convicted after a flagrantly unfair trial.

Article 5(1)(f)

7.43 Article 5(1)(f) permits the state to detain a person 'against whom action is being taken with a view to deportation or extradition'. This right is subject to implied limitations. In particular, the detention must be lawful under domestic law and must not be arbitrary or disproportionate. In *Saadi v United Kingdom* (2008) 47 EHRR 17, para 67, the Strasbourg Court said that where the lawfulness of detention is in issue, including the question whether 'a procedure prescribed by law' has been followed, the ECHR refers essentially to national law and lays down the obligation to conform to the substantive and procedural rules of national law. Compliance with national law is not, however, sufficient: Article 5(1) requires in addition that any deprivation of

---

[70] *Ahmad and Aswat v The Government of the United States of America* [2007] HRLR 8, para 101; *Serbeh v Governor of HMP Brixton* [2002] EWHC 2356 (Admin), para 40.

[71] *Othman v United Kingdom*, Application No 8139/09, paras 183–198. For the approach of UK domestic courts, see *RB (Algeria) v Secretary of State* [2010] 2 AC 110, para 23.

[72] *R (Kashamu) v Governor of Brixton Prison* [2002] QB 887.

[73] The Court did not follow the suggestion it had made in an earlier case, *Tomic v United Kingdom*, Application No 17837/03, that Article 5 did not apply in expulsion cases.

liberty should be in keeping with the purpose of protecting the individual from arbitrariness. In *R v Governor of Brockhill Prison ex p Evans* [2001] 2 AC 19, 38, Lord Hope of Craighead summarized the relevant principles:

> The jurisprudence of the European Court of Human Rights indicates that there are various aspects to Article 5(1) which must be satisfied in order to show that the detention is lawful for the purposes of that article. The first question is whether the detention is lawful under domestic law. Any detention which is unlawful in domestic law will automatically be unlawful under Article 5(1). It will thus give rise to an enforceable right to compensation under Article 5(5), the provisions of which are not discretionary but mandatory. The second question is whether, assuming that the detention is lawful under domestic law, it nevertheless complies with the general requirements of the Convention. These are based upon the principle that any restriction on human rights and fundamental freedoms must be prescribed by law: see Articles 8 to 11 of the Convention. They include the requirements that the domestic law must be sufficiently accessible to the individual and that it must be sufficiently precise to enable the individual to foresee the consequences of the restriction ... The third question is whether, again assuming that the detention is lawful under domestic law, it is nevertheless open to criticism on the ground that it is arbitrary because, for example, it was resorted to in bad faith or was not proportionate ...

It follows that, for detention to be lawful, the state must act in good faith.[74] Thus detention for the purposes of disguised extradition may violate Article 5(1)(f).[75] **7.44**

Detention for the purposes of extradition is justified only so long as the deportation or extradition proceedings remain in progress and it will cease to be justified if such proceedings are not prosecuted with due diligence. In *Lynas v Switzerland* (1976) 6 DR 141 the Commission said:[76] **7.45**

> Article 5(1)(f) clearly permits the Commission to decide on the lawfulness of the detention of a person against whom action is being taken with a view to extradition ... The wording of both the French and English texts makes it clear that only the existence of extradition proceedings justifies deprivation of liberty in such a case. It follows that if for example the proceedings are not conducted with the requisite diligence or if the detention results from some misuse of authority it ceases to be justifiable under Article 5(1)(f). Within these limits the Commission might therefore have cause to consider the length of time spent in detention pending extradition from the point of view of the above cited provision.

However, delays caused by a defendant's utilization of all available avenues of appeal will not violate Article 5(1)(f) provided the authorities have not demonstrated a lack of diligence.[77] **7.46**

Article 5(1)(f) refers to 'lawful arrest or detention' pursuant to a procedure 'prescribed by law'. The meaning of these terms was examined in *Day v Italy*, Application No 34573/97. The applicant was an American citizen arrested and detained in Italy pursuant to a request from the United States. He alleged that his arrest and detention were neither 'lawful' within the meaning of the Convention nor governed by a procedure 'prescribed by law'. The Commission stated: **7.47**

> The Commission recalls that when requiring that a detention be 'lawful' and in compliance with a 'procedure prescribed by law' the Convention essentially refers back to national law and states the obligation to conform to the substantive and procedural rules thereof. It further

74 *Bozano v France* (1987) 9 EHRR 297; *Quinn v France* (1995) 21 EHRR 529.

75 *Öcalan v Turkey* (2003) 37 EHRR 10. See Liu, European Court of Human Rights rules that the continued detention after a judicial decision directing release and the subsequent detention with a view to extradition constituted violations of Art 5(1) of the ECHR, (1997) 10 New York Int'l Law Rev 137. Disguised extradition is considered at para 12.69.

76 *Bordovskiy v Russia*, Application No 49491/99, 8 February 2005, para 50.

77 *Osman v United Kingdom*, Application No 15933/89 (second application).

requires that any deprivation of liberty should be consistent with the overall purpose of Article 5, namely to protect individuals from arbitrariness ... If detention is to be 'lawful', including the observance of a procedure prescribed by law, it must essentially comply with national law and the substantive and procedural rules thereof ... Article 5(1)(f) does not require the Commission to provide its own interpretation on questions of national law concerning the legality of the detention or extradition. The scope of the Commission's review is limited to examining whether there was a legal basis for the detention and whether the decision of the courts on the question of lawfulness could be described as arbitrary in the light of the facts of the case ...

7.48 The use of unlawfully obtained evidence in extradition proceedings may, in exceptional circumstances, result in a violation of Article 5(1)(f). In *Chinoy v United Kingdom*, Application No 15199/89, the applicant was sought by the United States for conspiring to possess cocaine with intent to distribute, conspiring to launder drugs money, and knowingly laundering drugs money. Much of the evidence against him had been obtained by United States investigators in France, possibly in breach of French law. He argued that the requirements of Article 5 excluded the possibility of detention for extradition solely on the basis of evidence which, although not unlawful in domestic terms, is considered unlawful under the domestic law of a third state and which may have been obtained in violation of that state's sovereignty, and which is considered to be in violation of the Convention. The Commission analysed the problem in the following way:

> The question therefore arises as to what extent the alleged unlawfulness of evidence falls to be considered under Article 5(1)(f) of the Convention. The European Court of Human Rights has held, in the context of Article 5(1)(e) of the Convention: 'On the question whether the detention is "lawful" including whether it complies with "a procedure prescribed by law", the Convention refers back essentially to national law and lays down the obligation to conform to the substantive and procedural rules thereof. However, it requires in addition that any deprivation of liberty should be consistent with the purpose of Article 5, namely to protect individuals from arbitrariness.' ... There is no indication in the present case that the procedural or substantive rules of domestic law were infringed. Moreover, although the domestic courts appear, in the absence of evidence to the contrary, to have accepted as admitted that the recording of the evidence was in fact in violation of French law and/or of the Convention, the Commission has already found that this cannot be accepted as the final conclusion, either as to French law or as to the Convention. Moreover, the domestic courts considered that breaches of French law and/or the Convention 'could carry no more weight than breaches of English law'. The Commission finds no indication of arbitrariness in the decision of the United Kingdom courts to admit evidence which may have been obtained, and appears to have been accepted by the domestic courts as having been obtained, in breach of French law and/or the Convention. It follows that at all relevant times the applicant's detention was covered by Article 5(1)(f) of the Convention and this part of the application is therefore manifestly ill-founded.

7.49 Thus although the Commission rejected the complaint on the facts, it left open the possibility that an extradition based on illegally obtained evidence could breach Article 5(1)(f). However it is likely that extreme facts would need to exist before a breach would be found.[78]

Article 5(3)

7.50 Article 5(3) requires that a defendant be eligible for bail where he is detained under Article 5(1)(c).[79] Article 5(3) also requires that an extradition defendant be eligible for bail. This is because, although on its face Article 5(1)(c) excludes extradition proceedings (the Convention ground

[78] *R (Ullah) v Special Adjudicator* [2004] 2 AC 323, para 24.
[79] *R (O) v Harrow Crown Court* [2006] All ER 1157.

for detention in such cases being Article 5(1)(f)), in *Osman v United Kingdom*, Application No 15933/89, the Commission stated:

> ... given the primordial importance of the right to liberty ensured by Article 5(1) of the Convention, the Commission may examine whether the refusal of bail to an individual, even if his detention falls within Article 5(1)(f) of the Convention, could be said to be unreasonable or arbitrary, thus affecting the general notion of lawfulness, which is a common thread throughout the provisions of Article 5(1) of the Convention.

The European Court of Human Rights has recognized a number of grounds which can, in principle, justify a refusal of bail. Pre-trial detention may be compatible with the defendant's right to release under Article 5(3) if, were the defendant released, he would fail to attend trial;[80] interfere with evidence or witnesses, or otherwise obstruct the course of justice;[81] or commit a serious offence.[82] Detention may also be justified if it is necessary for the purposes of the investigation into the defendant's case;[83] if his release would result in a disturbance to public order;[84] or if it is necessary for the defendant's own protection. **7.51**

These grounds are merely *capable* of justifying pre-trial detention. Whether they will *in fact* justify such detention in a particular case depends on the circumstances of the individual case, namely, the strength of the evidence that the risk to be averted by the detention is indeed a real risk; the length of the detention; and the persuasiveness of the arguments put forward to justify it.[85] It is essentially on the basis of the reasons given in these decisions and of the facts mentioned by the applicant in his applications for release that the European Court of Human Rights will decide whether or not there has been a violation of Article 5(3).[86] **7.52**

The extradition of a defendant who has been convicted in his absence in the requesting state and who will not be eligible for bail as a consequence does not, for this reason alone, violate Article 5. In *Government of Romania v Ceaucescu* [2006] EWHC 2615 (Admin) the defendant left Romania when he became aware that he was under investigation in respect of allegations of corruption. At that time he had not been charged with any offence. He was convicted in his absence. At that time he was living in the UK and received no notice of the commencement of a prosecution or the date of trial. He was sentenced to five years' imprisonment. **7.53**

At the extradition hearing, the district judge found that if the respondent were to be extradited to Romania there would be no possibility of his being granted bail pending trial, which she concluded would involve a breach of Article 5(3), and that it would not be 'just and proportionate' to extradite him in the light of the violation of those rights. She therefore discharged him pursuant to s 87 of the EA 2003. **7.54**

The Government of Romania appealed. It submitted that the district judge was wrong to apply the provisions of Article 5(3) rather than Article 5(1)(a) and that she had failed to apply the cor- **7.55**

80 *Wemhoff v Germany* (1987) 1 EHRR 55, para 14; *Matznetter v Austria* (1969) 1 EHRR 198, para 8; *Stögmüller v Austria* (1969) 1 EHRR 155, para 15; *B v Austria* (1990) 13 EHRR 20, para 41; *Letellier v France* (1991) 14 EHRR 83, paras 40–43; *Kemmache v France (No 3)* (1994) 19 EHRR 349, para 52.

81 *Clooth v Belgium* (1991) 14 EHRR 717, paras 43–44.

82 *Matznetter v Austria* (1969) 1 EHRR 198, para 9.

83 *Clooth v Belgium* (1991) 14 EHRR 717, paras 43–44.

84 *Tomasi v France* (1992) 15 EHRR 1, para 91.

85 *Ilijkov v Bulgaria* [2001] ECHR 33977/96, paras 84–85. The European Court attaches particular importance to the standard of reasoning in bail decisions: *Ringeisen v Austria* (1971) 1 EHRR 455; *Letellier v France* (1991) 14 EHRR 83.

86 *Letellier v France* (1991) 14 EHRR 83, paras 40–43.

rect test when assessing and characterizing a breach of Article 5. In allowing the government's appeal, Maurice Kay LJ said at para 11:

> From the moment of conviction at the original trial the relevant part of Article 5 became Article 5(1)(a), rather than Article 5(1)(c) and Article 5(3). Under section 87 of the Extradition Act 2003 the District Judge is concerned with compatibility with Convention Rights, neither more nor less. Broader considerations of justice arise, for example, when there is an issue as to the passage of time under Article 82 but section 87, the provision in play in the present case, gives a person no rights beyond those set out in the Convention. In my judgment, the District Judge was wrong to treat this as a case under Article 5(1)(a) and Article 5(3). Those provisions do not apply following conviction by a competent court and it is not for the court in this country to seek to enlarge Convention Rights by analogy.

7.56 As to the test to be applied in determining whether or not extradition would breach Article 5, Maurice Kay LJ adopted the 'flagrancy' test propounded by Lord Bingham of Cornhill in *R (Ullah) v Special Adjudicator* [2004] 2 AC 323, para 24:[87]

> It is apparent from the passage in her judgment ... that the District Judge decided that it would not be 'just and appropriate' to extradite the respondent in the light of a perceived violation of his rights under Article 5(3) ... The correct test in relation to whether extradition was barred under section 87 by reason of incompatibility with Convention Rights is not one of what is 'just and proportionate' or one based on a 'balancing of the issues'. The test is one of 'flagrant breach' ... Accordingly, even if the District Judge had been correct to identify a breach of Article 5, her decision would have been flawed by a failure to apply the 'flagrant breach' test.

7.57 In *Neave v Court Of Rome, Italy* [2012] EWHC 358 (Admin), paras 28–37, the Administrative Court rejected a challenge under Article 5 in relation to the extradition of defendants to Italy where there was a possibility that they would be held for some months before the prosecutor decided to 'charge' them and send them for trial.

Article 5(4)

7.58 Article 5(4) provides that:

> ... everyone who is deprived of his liberty by arrest or detention shall be entitled to take proceedings by which the lawfulness of his detention shall be decided speedily by a court and his release ordered if his detention is not lawful.

7.59 Article 5(4) requires that a detained person has the right to challenge his detention before a court according to a procedure that is fair. The European Court has held that the reference to a 'court' in Article 5(4) guarantees certain procedural rights for the defendant.[88] Where the conduct relied on as justifying detention is criminal in nature (in that it could give rise to criminal charges) the procedural guarantees should not be markedly inferior to those under Article 6. The procedure adopted must ensure equal treatment between the parties and it must be 'truly adversarial' which requires, where necessary, disclosure of relevant documents.[89] The defendant must have the opportunity to take legal advice prior to the hearing, and representation at the hearing where this is necessary to make it an effective hearing.[90] The defendant must

---

[87] The same test as that applied by the ECHR: *Othman v United Kingdom*, Application No 8139/09, para 233.

[88] *De Wilde v Belgium (No 1)* (1971) 1 EHRR 373 paras 76–79.

[89] *Lamy v Belgium* (1989) 11 EHRR 529, para 29; *Sanchez-Reisse v Switzerland* (1986) 9 EHRR 71; *R v Governor of Brixton Prison ex p Kashamu*, 6 October 2000, CO/2141/2000. Disclosure in extradition cases is considered at para 6.49.

[90] *Zamir v United Kingdom* (1983) 40 DR 42.

also be given time and facilities for the preparation of his case and the time must not be so short as to restrict the tangibility and availability of the remedy.[91]

These principles mean that a defendant in extradition proceedings must have a reasonable opportunity of presenting his case to the court under conditions 'which do not place him at a substantial disadvantage vis-à-vis his opponent'.[92] **7.60**

The incorporation of Article 5(4) into domestic law by the Human Rights Act 1998 had an important effect in extradition law. Prior to the enactment of the Human Rights Act 1998 it was well-settled that neither the court of committal nor the High Court had jurisdiction to discharge a defendant in extradition proceedings on the grounds of abuse of process.[93] However, in *R (Kashamu) v Governor of Brixton Prison* [2002] QB 887, a case under the EA 1989, the Administrative Court said that detention arising from an act of bad faith or an abuse of power by a requesting state meant that the detention would be arbitrary and thus unlawful under the Convention.[94] Rose LJ held that in order to comply with Article 5(4), the court hearing committal proceedings was required to have jurisdiction to determine the question of whether a fugitive's detention was lawful in the Convention sense, ie not arbitrary.[95] As a consequence, he held that a court hearing extradition proceedings had jurisdiction to consider whether or not the extradition proceedings were an abuse of process. **7.61**

The abuse of process jurisdiction applies equally to those who are on bail in extradition proceedings. This is because for fundamental extradition purposes, including the right to apply for *habeas corpus*, such defendants are effectively in custody and have to be treated as such.[96] **7.62**

Abuse of process under the EA 2003 is discussed at para 5.120. **7.63**

Article 6: right to fair trial

Article 6(1) provides: **7.64**

> In the determination of his civil rights and obligations or of any criminal charges against him, everyone is entitled to a fair and public hearing within a reasonable time by an independent and impartial tribunal established by law. Judgment shall be pronounced publicly but the press and public may be excluded from all or part of the trial in the interests of morals, public order or national security in a democratic society, where the interests of juveniles or the protection of the private life of the parties so require, or to the extent strictly necessary in the opinion of the court in special circumstances where publicity would prejudice the interests of justice.

Article 6(2) provides that everyone charged with a criminal offence shall be presumed innocent until proved guilty according to law and Article 6(3) sets out a number of specific guarantees applicable in criminal cases. **7.65**

Prior to the decision of the Supreme Court in *Lukaszewski v The District Court in Torun, Poland* [2012] UKSC 20, the orthodox view was that Article 6 did not apply to the conduct of extradition proceedings. In a number of decisions, the European Commission on Human Rights and the European Court of Human Rights had said that Article 6 only applies to the full process **7.66**

---

91 *Farmakopoulous v Belgium* (1992) 16 EHRR 187 at para 51 (Commission Report).

92 *Neumeister v Austria* 1 EHRR 91, para 22; *Delcourt v Belgium* 1 EHRR 355; *Borgers v Belgium* 15 EHRR 92, paras 26–28; *Jespers v Belgium* 27 DR 61, paras 51–56; *Bendenoun v France* (1994) 18 EHRR 54, para 52.

93 *Atkinson v Government of the United States of America* [1971] AC 197; *R v Governor of Pentonville Prison ex p Sinclair* [1991] 2 AC 64; *R v Governor of Pentonville Prison ex p Alves* [1993] AC 284, 294; *In re Schmidt* [1995] 1 AC 399.

94 *Re Darren Hayes*, 9 October 2000, CO/1339/2000.

95 *R v Governor of Brockhill Prison ex p Evans* [2001] AC 19, 38.

96 *R v Secretary of State ex p Launder (No 2)* [1998] QB 994, 1011.

of the examination of an individual's guilt or innocence of an offence, and not the mere process of determining whether a person can be extradited to another country.[97] In other words, the domestic extradition process does not have to offer all the guarantees in Article 6(3), for example, the right to cross-examine witnesses.[98] In relation to the question whether extradition involves the determination of civil rights or obligations so as to engage Article 6(1), in *Mamatkulov and Askarov v Turkey* (2005) 41 EHRR 494, in the context of complaints about the fairness of Turkish extradition proceedings, the European Court of Human Rights reiterated, at para 82, that decisions regarding the entry, stay, and deportation of aliens do not concern the determination of an applicant's civil rights or obligations or of a criminal charge against him, within the meaning of Article 6(1) of the Convention.

7.67 In *Lukaszewski v The District Court in Torun, Poland* [2012] UKSC 20, para 31, the UK Supreme Court said that the Strasbourg case law demonstrated that the Commission and the Court had stood firm against any suggestion that extradition as such involves the determination of a criminal charge, or entitles the person affected to the procedural guarantees provided in the determination of such a charge under Article 6(1) or Article 6(3). However, the Supreme Court also noted that the Strasbourg cases had all involved the extradition of aliens. Noting that a British citizen has the right (recognized at least since the time of Blackstone) to enter and remain in the UK, and that extradition potentially affects that right, Lord Mance said at paras 32–33 in respect of one of the appellants, Mr Halligen:

> 32. In these circumstances, Mr Halligen enjoyed a common (or 'civil') law right to enter and remain in the United Kingdom as and when he pleased. The next question is whether proceedings under the Extradition Act 2003, in that they may affect his freedom to remain in the United Kingdom at least for the duration of American criminal proceedings, involve 'the determination' of that civil right. The 2003 Act has the authority of Parliament, and to that extent Mr Halligen's right to remain in the United Kingdom is potentially qualified. But under the Act it is only through domestic extradition proceedings that this right can be affected and suspended for the purpose and period of any American proceedings and of any sentence which might thereafter be passed on him, if found guilty. In so far as it may be suspended, the extradition proceedings determine whether Mr Halligen may continue to enjoy his common law right for whatever proves to be the relevant period. A claim to extradite him does not involve the determination of a criminal charge, and he is not entitled to any full process of examination of his guilt or innocence, or to the procedural guarantees which would attend that. But he is entitled to a fair determination as to his common law right to remain within the jurisdiction.
>
> 33. In these circumstances, it follows in my view that the extradition proceedings against Mr Halligen fall within Article 6(1).

7.68 It follows that extradition proceedings under the EA 2003 in respect of UK citizens are governed by Article 6(1), and so must comply with the procedural requirements contained within it.

7.69 Extradition will be incompatible with the defendant's Article 6 rights if there is a real risk[99] that he will suffer a 'flagrant denial of justice' in the requesting state.[100] In *Othman v United*

---

97 *R (Al Fawwaz) v Governor of Brixton Prison* [2002] AC 556, para 87; *Salgado v Spain*, Application No 65964/01; *EGM v Luxembourg*, Application No 24015/94; *GK and BJF v The Netherlands*, Application No 12543/86; *Kirkwood v United Kingdom* (1984) 37 DR 158; *H v Spain* (1983) 37 DR 93; *X v Belgium*, Application No 7256/75.

98 *R (Al Fawwaz) v Governor of Brixton Prison* [2002] AC 556, para 87; *R (Al-Fawwaz) v Governor of HM Prison Brixton* [2001] 1 WLR 1234, para 59; *Lodhi v Governor of HM Prison Brixton* [2001] EWHC (Admin) 178.

99 This means 'a risk which is substantial and not merely fanciful; and it may be established by something less than proof of a 51% probability': *Brown v Government of Rwanda* [2009] EWHC 770 (Admin), para 34.

100 *R (Ullah) v Special Adjudicator* [2004] 2 AC 323, para 24; *Drozd and Janousek v France* (1992) 14 EHRR 745, para 110; *Soering v United Kingdom* (1989) 11 EHRR 439, para 113.

Kingdom [2012] ECHR 56, paras 258–260, the Strasbourg Court discussed the 'flagrant denial of justice' test. The Court said that a flagrant denial of justice goes beyond mere irregularities or lack of safeguards in the trial procedures. Such a denial only exists where the breach of the principles of fair trial guaranteed by Article 6 is so fundamental as to amount to a nullification of the very essence of the right.[101] At para 259, the Court gave the following examples of matters which might amount to a flagrant denial of justice: a conviction *in absentia* with no possibility subsequently to obtain a fresh determination of the merits of the charge; a trial which is summary in nature and conducted with a total disregard for the rights of the defence; detention without any access to an independent and impartial tribunal to have the legality the detention reviewed; and the deliberate and systematic refusal of access to a lawyer, especially for an individual detained in a foreign country.

The test of 'flagrancy' is obviously a high one which will only exceptionally be satisfied.[102] However, it was held to have been met in *Brown v Government of Rwanda* [2009] EWHC 770 (Admin). The defendants' extradition was sought by Rwanda for their alleged involvement in the 1994 genocide. The Government of Rwanda proposed that they be tried in the High Court of Rwanda, a court of criminal jurisdiction established in 2004. Allowing the defendants' appeal, Laws LJ and Sullivan LJ held that the defendants would suffer a flagrant denial of justice if they were extradited to Rwanda because of the problems they would face in calling defence evidence and because of potential interference by the Executive in the trial process. Another case where the test was satisfied was *Othman v United Kingdom*, Application No 8139/09, where one of the principal issues was whether the use of evidence at the applicant's proposed trial which might have been obtained by the torture of third persons would amount to a flagrant denial of justice. At paras 264–267 the European Court of Human Rights said that no legal system based upon the rule of law could countenance the admission of evidence obtained by such a barbaric practice as torture and, accordingly, that the admission of torture evidence at a trial is manifestly contrary, not just to the provisions of Article 6, but to the most basic international standards of a fair trial and thus amounts to a flagrant denial of justice. Because there was a real risk[103] that the witnesses in question had been tortured into incriminating the applicant, the Court held that his return to Jordan would violate Article 6.[104] **7.70**

Evidence obtained by torture aside, it will seldom be the case that the use of a particular type of evidence, or the requesting state's rules of evidence, will justify the conclusion that the defendant's trial will be a flagrant denial of justice.[105] **7.71**

When the requesting state is a signatory to the ECHR and a member of the EU it will, in general, be very difficult to show that there is a real risk of a total denial of Article 6 rights.[106] However, being a signatory to the ECHR may not of itself be sufficient to protect against a flagrant violation of Article 6 where an analysis of domestic law and practice leads to the conclusion that there is a real risk of such a violation. In *R (Bulla) v Secretary of State for the Home Department* **7.72**

[101] See also *RB (Algeria) v Secretary of State* [2010] 2 AC 110, paras 133–142, 195–203, 243–249, 258–261; *Dudko v Government of the Russian Federation* [2010] EWHC 1125 (Admin), para 36.

[102] *Drew v Region Court Kielce Poland* [2012] EWHC 3073 (Admin); *RB (Algeria) v Secretary of State* [2010] 2 AC 110, paras 7–8.

[103] Agreeing with the minority of the House of Lords in *A v Secretary of State for the Home Department (No 2)* [2006] 2 AC 221, the Court said at para 274 that it was not necessary for the applicant to show that it was more likely than not that the evidence had been obtained by torture.

[104] cf *R (Ramda) v Secretary of State for the Home Department* [2002] EWHC 1278 (Admin).

[105] *R (Ramda) v Secretary of State for the Home Department* [2002] EWHC 1278 (Admin), para 22; *R v Home Secretary ex p Elliot* [2001] EWHC (Admin) 559, para 11; *R (Abdullah) v Secretary of State* [2001] EWHC (Admin) 263; cf *Okendeji v Government of the Commonwealth of Australia* [2005] EWHC 471 (Admin).

[106] *Symeou v Public Prosecutor's Office at the Court of Appeals, Patros, Greece* [2009] 1 WLR 2384, para 66.

[2010] EWHC 3506 (Admin) the High Court concluded that despite Albania's membership of the Council of Europe, the evidence showed there was a possibility that the defendant might not be able to re-open his conviction *in absentia*, and thus a real risk of a flagrant violation of Article 6 of the ECHR if he were to be extradited.

Article 8: respect for private and family life

7.73 Article 8 provides:

> 8(1) Everyone has the right to respect for his private and family life, his home and his correspondence.
>
> (2) There shall be no interference by a public authority with the exercise of this right except such as is in accordance with the law and is necessary in a democratic society in the interests of national security, public safety or the economic well-being of the country, for the prevention of disorder or crime, for the protection of health or morals, or for the protection of the rights and freedoms of others.

7.74 The concept of private life in Article 8 is broadly defined.[107] It includes not only personal information, but also an individual's relationships with others, including (in certain circumstances) business relationships. Family life extends beyond the formal relationships created by marriage, and includes, for example, relationships between a parent and an illegitimate child.[108]

7.75 A criminal prosecution constitutes an 'interference by a public authority' for the purposes of Article 8(2).[109] Extradition also represents an interference with the defendant's right to respect for his private and family life.[110] The mere threat of a prosecution may be sufficient if it directly interferes with the defendant's private life.[111]

7.76 The judge at the extradition hearing is required by s 21 (Part 1 cases) and s 87 (Part 2 cases) to consider whether extradition would be compatible with the defendant's rights under Article 8 of the ECHR. In order for extradition to be compatible with Article 8(1), it must satisfy the conditions in Article 8(2), namely: (i) it must take place in accordance with law; (ii) it must be necessary in a democratic society, in the sense of being proportionate; and (iii) it must take place for one of the specified purposes in Article 8(2). Of these conditions, (i) and (iii) will always be satisfied. The issue will be whether extradition is proportionate to the legitimate aim which it seeks to achieve, namely the prevention of crime.[112] In *Norris v Government of the United States of America (No 2)* [2010] 2 AC 487 the Requesting State contended that the legitimate aim, or pressing social need, which is engaged is the honouring of extradition arrangements, which are an important aspect of the prevention of crime, and that this aim weighs heavily in the scales and that the circumstances in which interference with Article 8 rights will not be proportionate to it will be exceptional. At para 56 Lord Phillips said:

> The reality is that only if some quite exceptionally compelling feature, or combination of features, is present that interference with family life consequent upon extradition will be other than proportionate to the objective that extradition serves ... I can see no reason why the district judge should not, when considering a challenge to extradition founded on Article 8, explain his rejection of such a challenge, where appropriate, by remarking that there was nothing out of the ordinary or exceptional in the consequences that extradition would have

107 *Niemietz v Germany* 16 EHRR 97, para 29.

108 *Marckx v Belgium* 2 EHRR 330.

109 *Laskey v United Kingdom* (1997) 24 EHRR 39; *Dudgeon v United Kingdom* (1981) 4 EHRR 149.

110 *Norris v Government of the United States of America (No 2)* [2010] 2 AC 487, para 9; *R (Bermingham) v Director of the Serious Fraud Office* [2006] EWHC 200 (Admin), para 118.

111 *Norris v Ireland* 13 EHRR 186.

112 *Norris v Government of the United States of America (No 2)* [2010] 2 AC 487, para 9.

> for the family life of the person resisting extradition. 'Exceptional circumstances' is a phrase that says little about the nature of the circumstances. Instead of saying that interference with Article 8 rights can only outweigh the importance of extradition in exceptional circumstances it is more accurate and more helpful to say that the consequences of interference with Article 8 rights must be exceptionally serious before this can outweigh the importance of extradition. A judge should not be criticised if, as part of his process of reasoning, he considers how, if at all, the nature and extent of the impact of extradition on family life would differ from the normal consequences of extradition.

In *HH v Deputy Prosecutor of the Italian Republic, Genoa* [2012] UKSC 25, para 8, Lady Hale derived seven propositions from the judgments in *Norris v Government of the United States of America (No 2)* [2010] 2 AC 487: (i) there may be a closer analogy between extradition and the domestic criminal process than between extradition and deportation or expulsion, but the court has still to examine carefully the way in which it will interfere with family life; (ii) there is no test of exceptionality in either context; (iii) the question is always whether the interference with the private and family lives of the defendant and other members of his family is outweighed by the public interest in extradition; (iv) there is a constant and weighty public interest in extradition: that people accused of crimes should be brought to trial; that people convicted of crimes should serve their sentences; that the UK should honour its treaty obligations to other countries; and that there should be no 'safe havens' to which either can flee in the belief that they will not be sent back; (v) that public interest will always carry great weight, but the weight to be attached to it in the particular case does vary according to the nature and seriousness of the crime or crimes involved; (vi) the delay since the crimes were committed may both diminish the weight to be attached to the public interest and increase the impact upon private and family life; (vii) hence it is likely that the public interest in extradition will outweigh the Article 8 rights of the family unless the consequences of the interference with family life will be exceptionally severe.[113] **7.77**

In *Norris v Government of the United States of America (No 2)* [2010] 2 AC 487, paras 64–65, Lord Phillips said that when considering the impact of extradition on family life, the question did not fall to be considered simply from the viewpoint of the defendant, and that the effect of extradition on innocent members of the defendant's family could be a particularly cogent consideration.[114] If extradition for an offence of no great gravity were sought in relation to someone who had sole responsibility for an incapacitated family member, he said that this combination of circumstances might well lead a judge to discharge the defendant under s 87 of the EA 2003. **7.78**

The Supreme Court considered the relevance of Article 8 family life issues, and in particular the impact of extradition on children, in the conjoined appeals of *HH v Deputy Prosecutor of the Italian Republic, Genoa* [2012] UKSC 25. In one of the cases, an Italian court had issued an EAW in respect of both parents of three children aged 11, 8, and 3, the parents having been convicted of a series of drug-trafficking offences. The parents were both British nationals. In the other, a Polish court had issued EAWs in respect of the mother of five children aged 21, 17, 13, 8, and 3, who was accused of offences of dishonesty. The parents were both Polish nationals who had been living in the UK since 2002, after the alleged offences were committed. At **7.79**

[113] There is no Strasbourg case in which Article 8 interests have prevailed against the legitimate aims of extradition, which were recognized by the court in *Launder v United Kingdom* (1997) 25 EHRR CD 67 and *Aronica v Germany*, Application No 72032/01. The European Court of Human Rights has recently stated that only in exceptional circumstances will an applicant's private or family life outweigh the legitimate aim pursued by extradition: *King v United Kingdom*, Application No 9742/07, para 29; *Babar Ahmad v United Kingdom* (2010) 51 EHRR SE97, para 172.

[114] *Beoku-Betts v Secretary of State for the Home Department* [2009] AC 115, para 64.

para 1, Lady Hale said that: 'No-one seriously disputes that the impact upon the younger children of the removal of their primary carers and attachment figures will be devastating.' The issue before the Supreme Court was the relevance of their interests in the extradition proceedings, and whether the approach in *Norris v Government of the United States of America (No 2)* [2010] 2 AC 487 had to be modified in light of the decision in *ZH (Tanzania) v Secretary of State for the Home Department* [2011] 2 AC 166. In that case, the mother of children who had been born in the UK and were British citizens faced expulsion from the UK to Tanzania, which would have the practical consequence that her children would also have to go to Tanzania with her. The judgments in *ZH* made it clear that in considering Article 8 in any case in which the rights of a child are involved, the best interests of the child must be a primary consideration. They may be outweighed by countervailing factors, but they are of primary importance. The importance of the child's best interests is not to be devalued by something for which he is in no way responsible, such as the suspicion that he may have been deliberately conceived in order to strengthen the parents' case.[115]

7.80 In *HH v Deputy Prosecutor of the Italian Republic, Genoa* [2012] UKSC 25, Lady Hale said at paras 29–32 that the approach of the court to Article 8 rights should not be 'radically different' as between extradition and expulsion cases. The countervailing public interest arguments may be different, in particular because extradition is an obligation owed by the requested state to the requesting state, but the balancing process involves asking the central question, namely whether the interference is 'necessary in a democratic society' in the sense of being a proportionate response to that legitimate aim. In all cases, there must be a careful analysis under Article 8 of the potential effects of extradition on the children concerned.[116] At paras 30 and 34 Lady Hale said that in answering the question under s 21 (or s 87) whether extradition would be compatible with Convention rights:

> 30. ... the court would be well advised to adopt the same structured approach to an Article 8 case as would be applied by the Strasbourg Court. First, it asks whether there is or will be an interference with the right to respect for private and family life. Second, it asks whether that interference is in accordance with the law and pursues one or more of the legitimate aims within those listed in Article 8.2. Third, it asks whether the interference is 'necessary in a democratic society' in the sense of being a proportionate response to that legitimate aim. In answering that all-important question it will weigh the nature and gravity of the interference against the importance of the aims pursued. In other words, the balancing exercise is the same in each context: what may differ [between extradition and expulsion cases] are the nature and weight of the interests to be put into each side of the scale.
>
> 34. One thing is clear. It is not enough to dismiss these cases in a simple way—by accepting that the children's interests will always be harmed by separation from their sole or primary carer but also accepting that the public interest in extradition is almost always strong enough to outweigh it. There is no substitute for the careful examination envisaged by Lord Hope in *Norris* ...[117]

7.81 Article 8 may also exceptionally impact on the extradition process in relation to evidence gathering. Article 8 imposes strict standards on the regulation and supervision of evidence-gathering techniques. The right to privacy under Article 8 may be violated by intrusive surveillance, for

[115] *HH v Deputy Prosecutor of the Italian Republic, Genoa* [2012] UKSC 25, para 15.

[116] At paras 82–86 Lady Hale gave guidance as to the sort of evidence the court should have before it including, if necessary, the need for involvement of outside agencies.

[117] *Norris v Government of the United States of America (No 2)* [2010] 2 AC 487, para 89: '... decisions of the Strasbourg Court have repeatedly shown that an intense focus on the rights of the individual is necessary when striking the balance that proportionality requires. I do not think that there are any grounds for treating extradition cases as falling into a special category which diminishes the need to examine carefully the way the process will interfere with the individual's right to respect for his family life.'

example, telephone intercepts or the use of listening and tracking devices.[118] However, where the requesting state seeks to rely in extradition proceedings on evidence obtained in breach of Article 8 it does not automatically fall to be excluded under s 78 of the Police and Criminal Evidence Act 1984,[119] nor will the extradition breach Article 5(1)(f) of the ECHR.[120]

Protocol No 13 to the ECHR (death penalty)

As noted at para 7.22, Article 2 of the ECHR, on its face, specifically preserves the death penalty. However, the Sixth Protocol to the Convention required state parties to abolish the death penalty in peacetime.[121] The UK ratified the Sixth Protocol in 1999 and it formed one of the Convention rights in Sch 1 to the Human Rights Act 1998. **7.82**

Subsequently, the Parliamentary Assembly of the Council of Europe established a practice whereby it required from states wishing to become a member of the Council of Europe a commitment that they apply an immediate moratorium on executions, that they delete the death penalty from their national legislation, and that they sign and ratify the Sixth Protocol. The Parliamentary Assembly also put pressure on countries which failed or risked failing to meet the commitments they had undertaken upon accession to the Council of Europe. More generally, the Assembly took the step in 1994 of inviting all member States who had not yet done so, to sign and ratify Protocol No 6 without delay.[122] **7.83**

This fundamental objective to abolish the death penalty was also affirmed by the Second Summit of Heads of State and Government of member States of the Council of Europe held in Strasbourg in October 1997. In the Summit's Final Declaration, the Heads of State and Government called for the 'universal abolition of the death penalty and [insisted] on the maintenance, in the meantime, of existing moratoria on executions in Europe'. For its part, the Committee of Ministers of the Council of Europe indicated that it 'share[d] the Parliamentary Assembly's strong convictions against recourse to the death penalty and its determination to do all in its power to ensure that capital executions cease to take place'. The Committee of Ministers subsequently adopted a Declaration 'For a European Death Penalty-Free Area'. **7.84**

In the meantime, significant related developments in other fora had taken place. In June 1998, the EU adopted 'Guidelines to EU Policy Toward Third Countries on the Death Penalty' which, inter alia, stated the EU's opposition to the death penalty in all cases. Within the framework of the UN, a Second Optional Protocol to the International Covenant on Civil and Political Rights, aiming at the abolition of the death penalty, was adopted in 1989. Also, for a number of years, the UN Commission on Human Rights has regularly adopted Resolutions which call for the establishment of moratoria on executions, with a view to completely abolishing the death penalty. Also, capital punishment was excluded from the penalties that the International Criminal Court and the International Criminal Tribunals for the Former Yugoslavia and Rwanda are authorized to impose. **7.85**

The specific issue of the abolition within the Council of Europe of the death penalty also in respect of acts committed in time of war or of imminent threat of war should therefore be seen **7.86**

---

118 *Klass v Germany* (1978) 2 EHRR 214; *Malone v United Kingdom* (1984) 7 EHRR 14.

119 *R v Governor of Brixton Prison ex p Levin* [1997] AC 741; *Khan* [1997] AC 558. Nor does the use of such evidence at trial automatically lead to such unfairness that Art 6 is breached: *Khan v United Kingdom* (2000) 8 BHRC 310.

120 *Chinoy v United Kingdom*, Application No 15199/89.

121 Article 1 of the Sixth Protocol provides: 'The death penalty shall be abolished. No one shall be condemned to such penalty or executed.' However, Article 2 provides: 'A State may make provision in its law for the death penalty in respect of acts committed in time of war or of imminent threat of war ...'.

122 Resolution 1044 (1994) on the abolition of capital punishment.

against the background of these wider developments concerning the abolition of the death penalty. It was raised for the first time by the Parliamentary Assembly in Recommendation 1246 (1994), in which it recommended that the Committee of Ministers draw up an additional protocol to the Convention, abolishing the death penalty both in peacetime and in wartime.

7.87 While the Council of Europe's Steering Committee for Human Rights, by a large majority, was in favour of drawing up such an additional protocol, the Committee of Ministers at the time considered that the political priority was to obtain and maintain moratoria on executions, to be consolidated by complete abolition of the death penalty. A significant further step was made at the European Ministerial Conference on Human Rights, held in Rome in November 2000 on the occasion of the 50th anniversary of the ECHR, which pronounced itself clearly in favour of the abolition of the death penalty in time of war. In Resolution II adopted by the Conference, the few member states that had not yet abolished the death penalty nor ratified the Sixth Protocol were urgently requested to ratify it as soon as possible and, in the meantime, to respect the moratoria on executions. In the same Resolution, the Conference invited the Committee of Ministers 'to consider the feasibility of a new additional protocol to the Convention which would exclude the possibility of maintaining the death penalty in respect of acts committed in time of war or of imminent threat of war'.[123] The Conference also invited member states which still had the death penalty for such acts to consider its abolition.

7.88 The Government of Sweden presented a proposal for an additional protocol to the Convention at the 733rd meeting of the Ministers' Deputies in December 2000. The proposed protocol concerned the abolition of the death penalty in time of war, as in time of peace. The Committee of Ministers adopted the text of the Protocol on 21 February 2002 at the 784th meeting of the Ministers' Deputies and opened it for signature by member States of the Council of Europe, in Vilnius, on 3 May 2002.

7.89 Protocol No 13 to the ECHR requires state parties to abolish the death penalty in time of war. Article 1 provides that: 'The death penalty shall be abolished. No-one shall be condemned to such penalty or executed', and by Article 2 no derogation is permissible under Article 15 of the ECHR. At the time of writing (August 2012), Protocol No 13 has been signed by all member States of the Council of Europe with the exception of Armenia and Poland.

7.90 The impact of the coming into force of Protocol No 13 on the status of the death penalty within the ECHR was profound. In *Öcalan v Turkey* (2003) 37 EHRR 10, para 198, the European Court said that it could not exclude, in the light of the developments in state practice on capital punishment during the 1990s, that state parties to the Convention had agreed through their practice to modify the second sentence in Article 2(1) in so far as it permits capital punishment in peacetime. The Court said it could also be argued that the implementation of the death penalty can be regarded as inhuman and degrading treatment contrary to Article 3, although it did not reach a final conclusion. However, by 2010 when the Court came to consider *Al-Saadoon and Mufdhi v United Kingdom*, Application No 61498/08, it concluded at para 120:

> It can be seen, therefore, that the Grand Chamber in *Öcalan* did not exclude that Article 2 had already been amended so as to remove the exception permitting the death penalty. Moreover, as noted above, the position has evolved since then. All but two of the Member States have now signed Protocol No. 13 and all but three of the States which have signed have ratified it. These figures, together with consistent State practice in observing the moratorium on capital punishment, are strongly indicative that Article 2 has been amended so as to prohibit the death penalty in all circumstances. Against this background, the Court does not consider that the

[123] Paragraph 14 of Resolution II.

> wording of the second sentence of Article 2(1) continues to act as a bar to its interpreting the words 'inhuman or degrading treatment or punishment' in Article 3 as including the death penalty.

The UK's ratification, first, of the Sixth Protocol and then of Protocol No 13 has had two principal consequences. First, it required the UK to abolish the death penalty for all offences.[124] Secondly, ratification resulted in the UK acquiring a new international obligation not to subject those under its control to a risk either of being sentenced to death or being executed either by extraditing them or returning them.[125] In 2004, Article 1 of Protocol No 13 was substituted for Article 1 of the Sixth Protocol as one of the Convention rights in the Human Rights Act 1998.[126] **7.91**

Accordingly, extradition from the UK is not permissible where there is a real risk that the defendant will be sentenced to death, irrespective of whether the sentence is likely to be carried out. This follows from the wording of Article 1 of Protocol No 13, which prohibits both the sentencing of prisoners to death *and* the carrying out of the execution. The Sixth Protocol thus precludes extradition for capital offences to states where the death penalty is mandatory for those offences.[127] **7.92**

However, there is a tension between this prohibition and the provisions of the EA 2003. Section 94 provides: **7.93**

> 94(1) The Secretary of State must not order a person's extradition to a category 2 territory if he could be, will be or has been sentenced to death for the offence concerned in the category 2 territory.
>
> (2) Subsection (1) does not apply if the Secretary of State receives a written assurance which he considers adequate that a sentence of death:
>
> (a) will not be imposed, or
>
> (b) will not be carried out (if imposed).

Given that Article 1 of Protocol No 13 prohibits the sentencing of any person to death irrespective of whether or not the sentence will be carried out, it is difficult to see how the Secretary of State would be acting compatibly with Article 1 of Protocol 13 if he were to accept an undertaking that a person would be sentenced to death but not executed. **7.94**

Hence, in order for extradition to be compatible with Article 3 and Article 1 of Protocol No 13, the Secretary of State must receive a written assurance that the death penalty will not be imposed in the requesting state.[128] The effectiveness of any such undertaking must be critically scrutinized[129] and, ideally, there should be evidence of the undertaking's effectiveness in the **7.95**

---

124 The death penalty for murder was suspended in 1965 by the Murder (Abolition of the Death Penalty) Act 1965. The Act was introduced to Parliament as a private member's bill. It provides that charges of capital murder at the time it was passed were to be treated as charges of simple murder and all sentences of death were to be commuted to sentences of life imprisonment. The Act also contained a 'sunset clause', which stated that the Act would be repealed unless renewed by Parliament within five years. This was done in 1969 and the Act was made permanent. The Act did not affect the death penalty for the other offences for which it was then available, namely high treason; piracy with violence (ie, piracy with intent to kill or cause grievous bodily harm); arson in the royal dockyards; and espionage, as well as capital offences under military law. The death penalty was abolished for all offences by the Crime and Disorder Act 1998, s 36, and the Human Rights Act 1998, s 21(5).

125 *Soering v United Kingdom* (1989) 11 EHRR 439 did not prohibit extradition on capital charges *per se*, but held that where execution would be preceded by long incarceration on death row then extradition was prohibited by Article 3 because of the suffering which the defendant would undergo during this period.

126 Human Rights Act 1998 (Amendment) Order 2004 (SI 2004/1574).

127 For example Trinidad and Tobago: see *Charles Matthews v The State* [2005] 1 AC 433.

128 *R (St John) v Governor of Brixton Prison* [2002] QB 613; *Minister of Justice v Burns* [2001] SCC 7.

129 See House of Commons and House of Lords Joint Committee on Human Rights, 20th Report, 26 July 2002, para 28.

domestic law of the requesting state.[130] English courts have jurisdiction to scrutinize the effectiveness of undertakings given by foreign states in relation to extradition,[131] including those concerning the death penalty.[132] Only where it is clear that the undertaking provides adequate protection for the defendant should the Secretary of State accept it under s 94(2).[133]

7.96 The United States is the UK's most important extradition partner and the industrialized world's chief executioner.[134] Given the growing worldwide rejection of the death penalty[135] and the reluctance of abolitionist states to extradite for capital offences there is, unsurprisingly, considerable literature on the tensions between extradition and capital punishment in the United States.[136]

---

[130] *R v Secretary of State for the Home Department ex p Launder (No 2)* [1998] QB 994.

[131] *Ahmad and Aswat v Government of the United States of America* [2006] EWHC 2927 (Admin) (undertaking that the defendant would not be sent to Guantanamo Bay).

[132] *R (St John) v Governor of Brixton Prison* [2002] QB 613, para 64.

[133] In the United States, undertakings are given by the Department of Justice on behalf of the Federal Government. However, capital punishment is mostly imposed by individual states at the instance of the local district attorney. There have been cases where, despite the fact that the Federal Government has requested a state not to carry out an execution, the execution has proceeded regardless: see *Paraguay v United States* (the *Breard* case), 9 April 1998 (ICJ); Koh, 'Paying "Decent Respect" to World Opinion on the Death Penalty' 35(5) UC Davis Law Review, 1085–1131; Rieter, 'Interim measures by the World Court to suspend the execution of an individual: the *Breard* case' NQHR 1998, 16(4), 475–494; *Germany v United States of America* [1999] ICJ Rep 9 (ICJ); Feria Tinta, 'Due process and the right to life in the context of the Vienna Convention on Consular Relations: arguing the *LaGrand* case' (2001) 12 EJIL 363.

[134] In 2012 there were 42 executions in the United States: see <http://www.amnesty.org>.

[135] More than two-thirds of the world's states have now abolished the death penalty in law or practice: see <http://www.amnesty.org.uk>.

[136] See especially Nanda, 'Bases for refusing international extradition requests—capital punishment and torture' (2000) 23 *Fordham Int'l Law Jour* 1369; Williams, 'Extradition to a state that imposes the death penalty' (1990) 28 *Can YBIL* 117; Pinkard, 'The death penalty for drug kingpins' (1999) 24 *Vermont Law Rev* 1; Schabas, 'International law and the abolition of the death penalty: recent developments' (1998) 4 *ILSA Jour Int'l Law* 535; De Witt, 'Extradition enigma: Italy and human rights v America and the death penalty' (1998) 47 *Cath Uni Law Rev* 535; McGarvey, 'Missed opportunity? The affirmation of the death penalty in the AEDPA: extradition scenarios' (1998) 24 *Jour of Legislation* 99.

8

THE ROLE OF THE SECRETARY OF STATE; DEFERRAL OF EXTRADITION

A. Introduction

In Chapters 4 and 5 the Secretary of State's limited role at the beginning of the extradition process in Category 2 cases was considered. This chapter examines his role in Category 2 cases after the extradition hearing has taken place, when he has to decide whether to order extradition. **8.01**

One of the major changes to the extradition regime effected by the EA 2003 is the substantially reduced role of the Secretary of State. He is no longer required to consider whether extradition would be wrong, unjust, or oppressive before ordering return.[1] His principal task under the EA 2003 is to consider whether any of the restrictions on extradition or reasons for deferring extradition in ss 94–96A are made out. The main part of this chapter analyses these provisions. **8.02**

This chapter also considers the Secretary of State's and appropriate judge's duty to regulate competing extradition claims; their obligations where an extradition defendant is the subject of domestic criminal proceedings; and their powers where the defendant has claimed asylum in the UK. **8.03**

B. The Secretary of State's Decision after the Extradition Hearing under Part 2

As explained at para 5.06, in Part 1 cases the Secretary of State is unlikely to have a role in the extradition case once the appropriate judge has made an order that the defendant be extradited **8.04**

[1] cf EA 1989, s 12; *Atkinson v Government of the United States of America* [1971] AC 197, 232.

under s 21. If no national security issue under s 208 arises, once the extradition order has been made by the appropriate judge under s 21(3) then, subject to any appeal, the defendant is liable to be extradited.

8.05 In Part 2 cases, if the appropriate judge decides that there are no bars to extradition then he is required to send the case to the Secretary of State for his decision whether the defendant is to be extradited (s 87(3)). Section 93 then applies. Section 93(2) provides that the Secretary of State must decide whether he is prohibited from ordering the defendant's extradition under s 94 (death penalty); s 95 (specialty); s 96 (earlier extradition to the UK from other territory); or s 96A (earlier transfer to the UK from the ICC).[2] The Secretary of State may rely on diplomatic notes when considering the death penalty and specialty.[3]

8.06 If the Secretary of State decides that any of these restrictions is applicable then he must order the defendant's discharge (s 93(3)). Otherwise, he must order the defendant to be extradited unless he is informed that the request has been withdrawn; he makes an order under s 126(2) or 179(2) for further proceedings on the request to be deferred and the person is discharged under s 180; or he orders discharge under s 208.

Representations to the Secretary of State

8.07 Under s 13 of the EA 1989 the defendant had the right to make written representations to the Secretary of State setting out why an order for return should not be made in his case. The process of making representations could be a complex one. The Secretary of State was under a duty to consider representations fairly and, where necessary, to provide adequate disclosure to interested parties to enable them to make further representations.[4] He was also under a duty to keep his order for return under continuous review and to revisit it if further relevant information came to light.[5]

8.08 The EA 2003 reduces the Secretary of State's burden by simplifying the questions he has to address following the appropriate judge's decision. Also, s 93(5) provides that he is not required to consider any representations received by him after the end of the 'permitted period'. By s 93(6), as amended by para 18(2) of Sch 13 to the Police and Justice Act 2006, this is the period of four weeks starting with the 'appropriate day'. The 'appropriate day' is defined in s 102. In most cases, it will be the day on which the appropriate judge makes his decision (s 102(7)).

8.09 Section 93(7), inserted by para 18(3) of Sch 13 to the Police and Justice Act 2006, provides that in the case of a person who has consented under s 127 to his extradition, the Secretary of State is not required to wait until the end of the permitted period before ordering the person's extradition, or to consider any representations received after the order is made.

Death penalty (s 94)

8.10 Section 94 provides that the Secretary of State must not order a person's extradition to a Category 2 territory if he could be, will be, or has been sentenced to death for the offence concerned in the Category 2 territory (s 94(1)). However, s 94(1) does not apply if the Secretary of State receives a written assurance which he considers adequate that a sentence of death will not be imposed, or will not be carried out (if imposed).

---

[2] Inserted by para 3(4) of Sch 13 to the Police and Justice Act 2006.

[3] The status and effect of diplomatic notes were considered in *Ahmad and Aswat v Government of the United States of America* [2006] EWHC 2927 (Admin) and by the European Court of Human Rights in *Othman (Abu Qatada) v United Kingdom* 32 BHRC 62.

[4] *R v Secretary of State for the Home Department ex p Ramda* [2002] EWHC 1272 (Admin); *R v Secretary of State for the Home Department ex p Kingdom of Belgium*, 15 February 2000, CO/236/00.

[5] *R v Secretary of State for the Home Department ex p Launder* [1997] 1 WLR 839, 852.

This section is considered in detail at paras 7.93–7.95. 8.11

Specialty (s 95)[6]

As explained at para 5.72, specialty is a rule of extradition law that is intended to ensure that a person extradited is not dealt with in the requesting state for any offence other than that for which he was extradited.[7] 8.12

In Category 1 cases it is for the appropriate judge to determine whether the defendant has adequate specialty protection under the law of the requesting state. If he does not then the judge is bound to order his discharge.[8] However in Category 2 cases it is for the Secretary of State to determine whether the defendant has adequate specialty protection. 8.13

Section 95(1) provides that the Secretary of State must not order the defendant's extradition to a Category 2 territory if there are no specialty arrangements with the Category 2 territory, unless the defendant consented to his extradition under s 127 before his case was sent to the Secretary of State (s 95(2)). 8.14

Section 95(3) defines when there are specialty arrangements. There are specialty arrangements with a Category 2 territory if (and only if) under the law of that territory or arrangements made between it and the UK, a person who is extradited to the territory from the UK may be dealt with in the territory for an offence committed before his extradition only if the offence is one falling within s 95(4), or he is first given an opportunity to leave the territory.[9] 8.15

The offences in s 95(4) are the offence in respect of which the person is extradited; an extradition offence disclosed by the same facts as that offence, other than one in respect of which a sentence of death could be imposed; an extradition offence in respect of which the Secretary of State consents to the person being dealt with; and an offence in respect of which the person waives the right that he would have (but for s 95(4)(d)) not to be dealt with for the offence. 8.16

Section 95 requires the protection of the defendant in the law of the requesting state against re-surrender to another jurisdiction. This is a form of 'dealing with' prohibited by s 95.[10] 8.17

Specialty and the United States

The approach of the United States' courts to specialty was considered in detail in *Welsh and Thresher v Secretary of State for the Home Department* [2006] EWHC 156 (Admin).[11] The United States sought the extradition of the defendants from the UK on conspiracy charges and substantive charges arising out of an advanced fee fraud committed largely on United States residents. 8.18

---

[6] The EA 2003 refers to 'speciality' however this work continues to use the 'time-honoured' word 'specialty': *Hilali v Central Court of Criminal Proceedings Number 5 of the National Court of Madrid* [2006] EWHC 1239 (Admin), para 45.

[7] An alleged breach of specialty which takes place after extradition can only be dealt with by means of a diplomatic protest and cannot found a judicial action in the UK: *R (on the application of Farid Hilali) v The City of Westminster Magistrates' Court* [2008] EWHC 2892 (Admin).

[8] s 17.

[9] Specialty is dealt with in detail at para 5.72. The court in *Selami Cokaj v Secretary of State for the Home Department and another* [2007] EWHC 238 (Admin) considered the specialty arrangements with Albania (which is a party to the European Convention on Extradition 1957) finding that they satisfied s 95(3).

[10] *R v Secretary of State for the Home Department ex p Launder (No 2)* [1998] QB 994, 100.

[11] Applied in *R (Bermingham) v Director of the Serious Fraud Office* [2006] EWHC 200 (Admin), para 134. Also applied by the Irish High Court, see *Attorney General v Russell* [2006] IEHC 164. See also *Ahmad v Government of the United States of America* [2006] EWHC 2927 (Admin), para 75. The Court of Appeal considered the specialty rule as it relates to the treaty between the UK and the United States in the context of a committal for contempt following extradition from the United States to the UK for allegations of fraud (*OB v Director of the Serious Fraud Office* [2012] 3 All ER 1017).

Their extradition was ordered by the Secretary of State. The defendants submitted, inter alia, that the United States would breach the specialty rule because (i) it would permit a superseding indictment to be returned against them alleging conduct which did not form part of the extradition request, it would not permit them to leave the United States before doing so, and it would not obtain the consent of the Secretary of State before doing so; (ii) the United States courts would permit the extradition offence to be proved by evidence relating to offences upon which extradition had been expressly refused; (iii) if convicted, the defendants would be sentenced, that is dealt with, for money laundering offences for which extradition had been refused as the relevant United States sentencing guidelines would use the facts of those offences to increase the sentences which the appellants would receive for the extradition offences; and (iv) undertakings offered by the United States Government affirming its commitment to the rule of specialty were ineffective and irrelevant.

8.19 The Court explained the general approach to s 95:[12]

> The effect of s 95 is to impose a prohibition on extradition where the conditions it contains are not met. In my judgment, it does require the English courts to reach their own view as to whether or not the practice in the United States of America amounts to 'dealing with' someone, which includes punishing him, in a way prohibited by s 95. It does not permit the United Kingdom simply to say that a practice is not regarded as falling foul of the specialty doctrine by the United States of America and therefore does not fall foul of the prohibition in the 2003 Act. It is not permissible simply to adopt the United States of America's view of what offences are being punished.
>
> However, the language of the 2003 Act has to be applied to many treaties and foreign justice systems which will differ from each other as well as from those of the United Kingdom. It is not intended, I believe, to require the imposition of peculiarly English or United Kingdom sentencing practices before extradition can occur. Reaching an answer on the scope of 'deal with' in relation to extradition and punishment demands a purposive and flexible approach, which must be capable of accommodating the reasonable range of sentencing practices and values which other countries adopt. The recognition of important technical requirements is not the same as the erection of technical hurdles wherever ingenuity can manage it. A court may properly be reluctant to adopt a construction of the 2003 Act which would allow those who flee a jurisdiction to gain an unwarranted reward for their flight, because of the routine and justifiable sentencing practices of the jurisdiction which they seek to evade.

8.20 In rejecting the defendants' appeal, the Administrative Court held that on the true construction of s 95, the consent of the Secretary of State, where required under s 95(4)(c), had to be expressly given. Although absence of such a consent to a prosecution for which it was necessary would mean that the trial would be in breach of the specialty rule, having reviewed the relevant case law the Court concluded there was no basis for supposing that the requirement for consent would be ignored by the United States authorities.[13]

8.21 The Court also rejected the defendants' complaints about the use of evidence relating to offences for which extradition had been refused. The Court held that the specialty rule was not breached in circumstances where the United States courts permitted the extradition offence to be proved by evidence relating to offences upon which extradition had been expressly refused. The specialty rule did not limit the evidence which could be admitted to prove the extradition offence and the rules which governed admissibility of evidence were those of the trial state.[14]

[12] Paras 135 and 136.
[13] Para 87.
[14] Paras 88, 89, 99.

In relation to specialty and sentencing, the Court said that the EA 2003 had not been intended to bring about profound changes in extradition arrangements in a way which would add a novel and significant hindrance to extradition and so it could not have been intended to halt extraditions to the United States on the basis of a sentencing practice which its case law suggested had been in place since before its independence.[15] Accordingly, the absence of an arrangement which would prevent the extradited person being punished for the extradition offence in the way he could be under the United States sentencing guidelines did not show that the requisite arrangement for s 95 was not in place.[16] Such a person was not being 'dealt with' within the scope of that phrase in the EA 2003 for an offence for which he had not been or could not have been extradited. He was being 'dealt with' for that very offence by reference to conduct which was relevant to the gravity of the way in which he committed the offence or to the offending behaviour revealed by it.[17] It has also been argued that as some US states do not appear to allow a defendant to argue a breach of specialty then this means that section 95 is not satisfied.[18] However, in *Calder v Her Majesty's Advocate*,[19] the Scottish High Court of Justiciary held that even if this is the legal position in some US states, a remedy is open to the defendant as if there is an alleged breach of specialty as he can proceed by writ of *habeas corpus*. **8.22**

Specialty and Commonwealth countries and British overseas territories

Arrangements made with a Category 2 territory which is a Commonwealth country or a British overseas territory may be made for a particular case, or more generally (s 95(5)). A certificate issued by or under the authority of the Secretary of State confirming the existence of arrangements with a Category 2 territory which is a Commonwealth country or a British overseas territory and stating the terms of the arrangements is conclusive evidence of those matters (s 95(6)).[20] **8.23**

Specialty arrangements may also be made with other territories, and a certificate will not be conclusive because s 95(6) only applies in relation to Commonwealth countries and British overseas territories. In such a case the court has jurisdiction to enquire into the effectiveness of the arrangements and whether they provide the protection required by s 95(3) and (4).[21] **8.24**

Earlier extradition to the UK from other territory (s 96)

Section 96(1) provides that the Secretary of State must not order a person's extradition to a Category 2 territory if: **8.25**

(a) the person was extradited to the UK from another territory (the extraditing territory);
(b) under arrangements between the UK and the extraditing territory, that territory's consent is required to the person's extradition from the UK to the Category 2 territory in respect of the extradition offence under consideration;
(c) that consent has not been given on behalf of the extraditing territory.

A problem relating to re-extradition arose in *R v Secretary of State for the Home Department ex p Akbar*, 31 July 1996 (CO/1707/96). The defendant had been extradited to the UK from France in respect of certain offences. The United States requested his extradition and the **8.26**

[15] Para 137.
[16] Para 138.
[17] Para 142.
[18] *Stepp v Government of the United States of America and another* [2006] EWHC 1033 (Admin).
[19] [2006] HCJAC 71 at para 23.
[20] cf EA 1989, s 6(4) and (7).
[21] *R v Secretary of State for the Home Department, ex parte Launder (No 2)* [1998] QB 994, 1003–6; *Aswat v Government of the United States of America* [2006] EWHC 2927 (Admin), para 62.

French Government was asked to consent to re-extradition under Article 15 of the European Convention on Extradition 1957. Consent was not immediately forthcoming, and the Secretary of State proposed to extradite the defendant without waiting for consent. It was argued for the Secretary of State that Article 15 of the European Convention on Extradition 1957 had no application because the request for extradition was being made under Sch 1 to the EA 1989, which has no relevant provision, and nor does the extradition treaty between the UK and the United States. This argument was rejected by the Divisional Court:

> It seems to me that, having regard to principles of international comity, firstly the Secretary of State would not wish that the applicant should be returned to the United States against the wishes of the French government; equally the United States government would not wish to cause the Secretary of State the embarrassment of acting against the wishes of the French government; and the French government for its part would not wish, except for sound reasons, to refuse consent to re-extradition for a serious offence committed by the applicant in the United States which has come to light since it originally returned the applicant to the United Kingdom in 1993.

Earlier return to the UK from the ICC (s 96A)

8.27 Section 96A of the EA 2003 is inserted by para 3(4) of Sch 13 to the Police and Justice Act 2006. It provides that the Secretary of State must not order a person's extradition to a Category 2 territory if he was transferred to the UK to serve a sentence imposed by the ICC; under arrangements between the UK and the Court, the consent of the Presidency of the Court is required to the person's extradition from the UK to the Category 2 territory in respect of the extradition offence under consideration; and that consent has not been given (s 96A(1)).

8.28 Section 96A(1) does not apply if the person has served the sentence imposed by the Court and has subsequently remained voluntarily in the UK for more than 30 days, or left the UK and returned to it.

The Secretary of State and human rights

8.29 The scheme of the EA 2003 in Category 2 cases is that it is for the appropriate judge to decide under s 87 whether extradition is prohibited because it would be incompatible with the defendant's Convention rights, and it is then for the Secretary of State to consider whether ss 94–96 prohibit extradition.

8.30 The question of whether the Secretary of State is also required to consider human rights issues falling outside the scope of ss 94–96 was considered by Laws LJ in *R (Bermingham) v Director of the Serious Fraud Office* [2006] EWHC 200 (Admin), paras 151–152:

> ... little if anything was said at the hearing about the potential impact of the Convention rights upon the Secretary of State's functions under the 2003 Act. It is, however, to be noted that in the context of those functions there is no analogue to s 87; and as I have shown unless the Secretary of State is prohibited from ordering the person's extradition by any of the three matters specified in s 93(2), s 93(4) requires him, subject to certain exceptions, to order the person's extradition to the territory of the requesting state. The three matters are the death penalty (s 94), specialty (s 95), and earlier extradition to the United Kingdom from another territory (s 96). While these—notably the first—may run into ECHR territory, it would appear that the Secretary of State has no free standing duty or discretion to consider the Convention rights and fashion his extradition decision accordingly.
>
> It may well be said, however, that by force of s 6 of the [Human Rights Act 1998] the Secretary of State must not order a person's extradition if that would violate his Convention rights; and the price of compatibility with the ECHR is that the 2003 Act must have recognised as much. In these proceedings we have heard no argument upon such an issue, and I am very far from

suggesting that it should be canvassed now. The true position may very well be that a defendant's Convention rights are sufficiently protected by s 87 read with ss 103(5) and 104(4). Section 103(5) postpones the hearing of any appeal against the judge's decision until after the Secretary of State has made his decision. I have already set out s 104(4). It would appear that if any new facts emerged after the case was sent to the Secretary of State which bear on the Defendant's Convention rights, they can be raised on an appeal against the judge which will be heard after the Secretary of State's decision.[22]

In Part 2 cases, there will be a short period after the conclusion of an unsuccessful appeal by the defendant or, if no appeal is lodged, after the decision of the Secretary of State to order extradition before the defendant is physically extradited.[23] The defendant may believe that during this period there has been a material change of circumstances, which mean his human rights would be violated if he is extradited. If so then he can make representations to the Secretary of State claiming that it would be a breach of the Human Rights Act 1998 for the Secretary of State to maintain his extradition order and the Secretary of State is bound to consider the representations.[24] **8.31**

In *McKinnon v Secretary of State for Home Affairs*[25] the High Court stated:[26] **8.32**

> The Secretary of State has accepted that he has an implied power to withdraw any extradition order where, as here, something new has arisen exceptionally between the exhaustion of the statutory remedies under the 2003 Act of the person whose extradition is sought and his actual removal. This proposition has the authority of the first judgment of the Divisional Court [2007] EWHC 762 (Admin) at 61 to 63. The basis for this implied power is s 6 of the Human Rights Act 1998, which renders it unlawful for the Secretary of State, as a public authority, to act in a way which is incompatible with a Convention right. It follows that the 'something new' must be evidence that that person's Convention rights would be infringed by his extradition. The Secretary of State also accepts that his decision in such circumstances is susceptible of judicial review ... In my judgment, it follows from the basis of the implied power of the Secretary of State that is the subject of these proceedings that the question for the court is not whether the Secretary of State properly exercised her discretion, or reached a sustainable decision, but whether objectively the evidence before the Secretary of State established a real risk that the Claimant's extradition would infringe his Convention rights, and in particular his right not to be subjected to treatment that would contravene Article 3.

---

22 The Court also adopted this position in *Nisbet v Secretary of State and others* [2007] EWHC 1768 (Admin): 'The position is that as a public authority the First Respondent [the Secretary of State] is bound by s 6 of the Human Rights Act 1998, but he is not required to consider afresh whether the Appellant's extradition was incompatible with his Convention rights. That was a matter for consideration by the district judge who was best placed to consider the evidence relied upon in relation to human rights. In this instance no such material had been put forward. In those circumstances—if no material is put forward to the district judge in the first instance or if it has been considered at first instance, but an Appellant wants to rely on it at appeal—it is open to him to raise, on appeal, matters of that sort.'

23 See paras 10.42–10.62 for the time limits within which extradition should take place. See also *R (Tajik) v The city of Westminister Magistrates' Court and others* [2012] EWHC 3347 (Admin).

24 The 2011 Extradition Review has recommended that this situation should not be dealt with by the Secretary of State but that it should be possible to make an application to the High Court which would determine whether extradition should still take place (see paras 9.24–9.40 of the 2011 Extradition Review which set out the Review's analysis and detailed recommendation). The Government has responded by agreeing that, where a supervening event occurs after the end of the extradition process raising human rights considerations, these should be for the Administrative Court to consider rather than the Secretary of State (Cmnd 8458). At the time of writing no amendments have been made to the EA 2003 to implement this change.

25 [2009] EWHC 2021 (Admin).

26 Para 64, per Stanley Burnton LJ.

C. The Secretary of State's Decision

Procedure

8.33 Where the Secretary of State orders the defendant's extradition under Part 2 he must inform the defendant of the order; inform him in ordinary language that he has a right of appeal to the High Court (unless the defendant has consented to his extradition under s 127); and inform a person acting on behalf of the Category 2 territory of the order (s 100(1)). The Secretary of State can provide this information by sending a letter by fax or post to the solicitors acting for the defendant. The Secretary of State can communicate in English even if the defendant cannot understand English.[27] The letter can also be sent by email and it will be deemed to have been delivered when it is received regardless of whether it is opened and read on that day.[28]

8.34 If the Secretary of State has received an assurance concerning the death penalty as mentioned in s 94(2), he must give the defendant a copy of the assurance when he informs him under s 100(1) of the order (s 100(3)).

8.35 If the Secretary of State orders the defendant's discharge he must inform him of the order and inform a person acting on behalf of the Category 2 territory of the order (s 100(4)).

8.36 Orders for extradition or discharge under s 93, and an order for discharge under s 123, must be made under the hand of the Secretary of State, a Minister of State, a Parliamentary Under-Secretary of State, or a senior official (s 101(1) and (3)). 'Senior officials' are members of the Senior Civil Service and members of the Senior Management Structure of Her Majesty's Diplomatic Service.

Time limits

8.37 In keeping with the EA 2003's underlying policy of speeding up extradition, Part 2 imposes a timetable within which the Secretary of State must take his decision on return.

8.38 Section 99 applies if the appropriate judge sends a case to the Secretary of State under Part 2 for his decision whether the defendant is to be extradited, and within the 'required period' the Secretary of State does not make an order for his extradition or discharge. Then, if the defendant applies to the appropriate judge, the judge must order his discharge (s 99(2), as amended by para 19(2) of Sch 13 to the Police and Justice Act 2006).

8.39 However if, before the required period ends, the Secretary of State applies to the appropriate judge for it to be extended, the judge may make an order accordingly; and this may happen on more than one occasion (s 99(4) as amended by para 19(3) of Sch 13 to the Police and Justice Act 2006).

8.40 The required period is the period of two months starting with the appropriate day (s 99(3)). The court considered how this operated in practice in *R (Zaporozhchenko and Redya) v Westminster Magistrates' Court and others*.[29] The judge sent the case to the Secretary of State on 3 September 2010. Section 99(3) means that the required period expired on 2 November 2010 (ie the eve of the corresponding date) and not 3 November 2010 (applying the corresponding date rule) as submitted by the defendant. The appropriate day is defined in detail in s 102.

---

27 *Mucelli v Government of the Republic of Albania and another* [2007] EWHC 2632 (Admin), paras 52–64.

28 This is important to take into account because it will affect the period within which an appeal must be lodged (see para 9.124). *Salazar-Duarte v United States* [2010] EWHC 3150 (Admin).

29 [2011] EWHC 34 (Admin).

D. Competing Extradition Claims and Deferral of Extradition

Where a defendant is being dealt with under Part 1, and a second Category 1 territory sends a Part 1 warrant to the UK for execution, then it is for the appropriate judge to decide which of the warrants is to take priority, in accordance with s 44. This provision is considered at para 5.144. **8.41**

However, where there are competing proceedings under Part 1 and Part 2, or two or more sets of proceedings under Part 2, the Secretary of State has power under the EA 2003 to regulate the proceedings to ensure their orderly processing and disposal. **8.42**

Also, where an extradition defendant is charged with a domestic offence then the appropriate judge (in Category 1 cases) or the Secretary of State (in Category 2 cases) has power to defer processing of the extradition case until after the domestic offence has been disposed of. **8.43**

These powers will be now be examined. **8.44**

Competing Part 1 warrant and an extradition request under Part 2

Section 179 applies if at the same time there is a Part 1 warrant in respect of a person, a certificate has been issued under s 2 in respect of the warrant, and the person has not been extradited in pursuance of the warrant or discharged, and there is a request for the same person's extradition, a certificate has been issued under s 70 in respect of the request, and the person has not been extradited in pursuance of the request or discharged. **8.45**

In this situation the Secretary of State may (s 179(2)): **8.46**

(a) order proceedings (or further proceedings) on one of them (the warrant or the request) to be deferred until the other one has been disposed of, if neither the warrant nor the request has been disposed of;
(b) order the defendant's extradition in pursuance of the warrant to be deferred until the request has been disposed of, if an order for his extradition in pursuance of the warrant has been made;
(c) order the defendant's extradition in pursuance of the request to be deferred until the warrant has been disposed of, if an order for his extradition in pursuance of the request has been made.

Section 179(3) prescribes the matters that the Secretary of State must take into account in taking his decision under s 179(2): **8.47**

(a) the relative seriousness of the offences concerned;
(b) the place where each offence was committed (or was alleged to have been committed);
(c) the date when the warrant was issued and the date when the request was received;
(d) whether, in the case of each offence, the person is accused of its commission (but not alleged to have been convicted) or is alleged to be unlawfully at large after conviction.

Section 179(5), inserted by para 2(7) of Sch 13 to the Police and Justice Act 2006, provides that for the purposes of s 179, a person is alleged to be unlawfully at large after conviction of an offence if he is alleged to have been convicted of it, and his extradition is sought for the purpose of his being sentenced for the offence or of his serving a sentence of imprisonment or another form of detention imposed in respect of the offence. **8.48**

Competing extradition requests under Part 2

Section 126 regulates competing requests for extradition under Part 2. It applies if the Secretary of State receives a valid request for the defendant's extradition to a Category 2 territory; the **8.49** person is in the UK; before the person is extradited in pursuance of the request or discharged, the Secretary of State receives another valid request for the defendant's extradition.

8.50 The Secretary of State may then do one of two things (s 126(2)):

(a) he may order proceedings (or further proceedings) on one of the requests to be deferred until the other one has been disposed of, if neither of the requests has been disposed of;
(b) he may order the defendant's extradition in pursuance of the request under consideration to be deferred until the other request has been disposed of, if an order for his extradition in pursuance of the request under consideration has been made.

8.51 In taking this decision the Secretary of State must take into account in particular the following (s 126(3)):

(a) the relative seriousness of the offences concerned;
(b) the place where each offence was committed (or was alleged to have been committed);
(c) the date when each request was received;
(d) whether, in the case of each offence, the defendant is accused of its commission (but not alleged to have been convicted) or is alleged to be unlawfully at large after conviction.

Resumption of deferred proceedings

8.52 Section 180 governs what is to happen where proceedings have been deferred under the EA 2003 because of a competing extradition claim. Section 180 applies if an order is made under the EA 2003 deferring proceedings on an extradition claim in respect of the defendant (the deferred claim) until another extradition claim in respect of the person has been disposed of; and the other extradition claim is disposed of.

8.53 In this context, an extradition claim is made in respect of a defendant if a Part 1 warrant is issued in respect of him or a request for his extradition is made (s 180(9)).

8.54 Section 180(2) provides that the judge may make an order for proceedings on the deferred claim to be resumed but, by s 180(3), no such order may be made after the end of the required period. The 'required period' is 21 days starting with the day on which the other extradition claim is disposed of (s 180(6)).

8.55 By s 180(4), the judge has a general discretion to order the defendant's discharge. However, s 180(5) provides that if the defendant applies to the appropriate judge to be discharged, the judge *must* order his discharge if the required period has ended, and the judge has not made an order under s 180(2) or already ordered the person's discharge.

8.56 If the proceedings on the deferred claim were under Part 1, s 67 applies for determining the appropriate judge (s 180(7)). If the proceedings on the deferred claim were under Part 2, s 139 applies for determining the appropriate judge (s 180(8)).

Proceedings where extradition has been deferred

8.57 Section 181 applies where a direction has been given deferring the defendant's extradition, rather than proceedings in respect of the extradition request. Section 181 applies if an order is made under the EA 2003 deferring the defendant's extradition in pursuance of an extradition claim (the deferred claim) until another extradition claim in respect of him has been disposed of; the other extradition claim is disposed of.

8.58 An extradition claim is made in respect of the defendant if a Part 1 warrant is issued in respect of him or a request for his extradition is made (s 181(9)).

By s 181(2), the judge may make an order for the defendant's extradition in pursuance of the deferred claim to cease to be deferred, however no order under subsection (2) may be made after the end of the required period (s 181(3)). The required period is 21 days starting with the day on which the other extradition claim is disposed of. **8.59**

Section 181(4) provides that if the defendant applies to the appropriate judge to be discharged, the judge may order his discharge. By s 181(5), if the defendant applies to the appropriate judge to be discharged, the judge *must* order his discharge if the required period has ended, and the judge has not made an order under subsection (2) or already ordered the defendant's discharge. **8.60**

If the defendant's extradition in pursuance of the deferred claim was ordered under Part 1, s 67 applies for determining the appropriate judge (s 181(7)). If the defendant's extradition in pursuance of the deferred claim was ordered under Part 2, s 139 applies for determining the appropriate judge (s 181(8)). **8.61**

Deferral of Part 2 extradition hearing because of domestic proceedings

The EA 2003 contains provisions governing how conflicting extradition and domestic criminal proceedings are to be dealt with. In Part 1 cases the power to defer is given to the appropriate judge rather than the Secretary of State by virtue of ss 22 and 23.[30] **8.62**

In Part 2 cases ss 97 and 98 are the relevant provisions. Section 97 applies if the appropriate judge has sent a case to the Secretary of State under Part 2 for his decision whether the defendant is to be extradited, and the defendant is then charged with an offence in the UK (s 97(1)). In this case the Secretary of State must not make his decision until the charge is disposed of; the charge is withdrawn; proceedings in respect of the charge are discontinued; or an order is made for the charge to lie on the file (or its Scottish equivalent) (s 97(2)). **8.63**

If a sentence of imprisonment or detention is imposed in respect of the offence the Secretary of State may defer making a decision on the extradition request until the person is released from detention pursuant to the sentence (whether on licence or otherwise) (s 97(3)). **8.64**

Where the appropriate judge sends a case to the Secretary of State for his decision whether the defendant is to be extradited, and the defendant is in custody serving a sentence of imprisonment or another form of detention in the UK, then the Secretary of State may defer making a decision with regard to the defendant's extradition until the person is released from detention pursuant to the sentence (whether on licence or otherwise) (s 98(2)). **8.65**

E. Asylum Claims

States which persecute minorities or other social groups frequently resort to the criminal law as a method of persecution.[31] The grounds for claiming asylum in the UK are contained in the Convention and Protocol relating to the Status of Refugees 1951[32] and 1967.[33] The extraneous considerations referred in ss 13 and 81 of the EA 2003 are similar in many respects to the **8.66**

---

30 See para 5.151.

31 *T v Immigration Officer* [1996] AC 742; *R v Governor of Brixton Prison ex p Kolczynski* [1955] 1 QB 540. For a modern example of political persecution masquerading as criminal due process, see *Government of Russian Federation v Temerko*, 23 December 2005 (Senior District Judge Workman, Bow Street Magistrates' Court).

32 Cmd 9171.

33 Cmd 3906.

provisions of the Convention.[34] It is not uncommon for an extradition defendant also to claim asylum in the UK either prior to arrest or following the commencement of extradition proceedings. If a person who is the subject of an extradition request from a Category 2 territory has been recognized as a refugee before any extradition proceedings have commenced then the Secretary of State may refuse to issue a certificate under section 70 (s 70(2)(b) discussed at para 4.38).

8.67 Under the EA 1989 the Secretary of State was generally reluctant to order deportation until the conclusion of extradition proceedings.[35] On the other hand, courts were reluctant to adjourn extradition proceedings pending the outcome of claims for asylum.[36] Thus the practice under the EA 1989 was for extradition proceedings to continue until the order for return stage under s 12 and for the Secretary of State then to determine the issues of whether to order return and whether to grant asylum at the same time. The Court of Appeal has given guidance to suggest that an outstanding asylum claim made by a person subject to an extradition request should normally lead to an adjournment of the extradition proceedings to allow a decision on the asylum claim.[37] The Administrative Court in *Kozlowski v District Court of Torun, Poland* [2012] EWHC 1706 (Admin) considered this guidance, finding that no adjournment was warranted on the facts of that case and expressing caution about the guidance at para 21.

8.68 The EA 2003 contains provisions to regulate the determination of a claim for asylum by an extradition defendant. These are ss 39 and 40 in Part 1 cases, and s 121 in Part 2 cases.

Asylum claims in Part 1 cases

8.69 Section 39 applies if a defendant in respect of whom a Part 1 warrant is issued makes an 'asylum claim' at any time in the 'relevant period', and an order is made under Part 1 for the person to be extradited in pursuance of the warrant.

8.70 An asylum claim has the meaning given by s 113(1) of the Nationality, Immigration and Asylum Act 2002,[38] namely, a claim made by a person that to remove him from or require him to leave the UK would breach the UK's obligations under the Refugee Convention.[39] However, this does not include a claim which, having regard to a former claim, falls to be disregarded in accordance with immigration rules.[40]

8.71 For the purposes of s 39, the 'relevant period' is the period starting when a certificate is issued under s 2 in respect of the warrant[41] and ending when the defendant is extradited in pursuance of the warrant (s 39(2)).[42]

8.72 Section 39(3) provides that the defendant must not be extradited in pursuance of the warrant before the asylum claim is finally determined, and ss 35, 36, 47, and 49 of the Act, which

---

34 See paras 5.38 and 6.25.

35 *Caddoux v Bow Street Magistrates' Court* [2004] EWHC 642 (Admin), para 11.

36 *R (Karpichkov) v Latvia and the Republic of South Africa*, 26 April 2001 (CO/2553/2000).

37 *R (Chichvarkin) v Secretary of State for the Home Department* [2011] EWCA Civ 91, para 61.

38 EA 2003, s 216(7).

39 That is the Convention relating to the Status of Refugees done at Geneva on 28 July 1951 and its Protocol (Cmd 9171 and Cmd 3906).

40 This proviso to the definition is inserted by the Immigration, Asylum and Nationality Act 2006, s 12, from a date to be appointed.

41 This section and s 121 are curiously drafted in that they do not apparently cover a situation where the defendant has applied for asylum before the certificate has been issued under s 2 or the request has been certified under s 70. See paras 8.86–8.87.

42 A curiosity of this section is that it does not specify what is to happen to the judge's extradition order if the Secretary of State allows the asylum claim. It is clear that the defendant cannot be lawfully extradited if the Secretary of State allows the asylum claim. One possibility for bringing the extradition case to an end would be for the defendant to apply to the appropriate judge for discharge under s 35 or 36.

govern the time for extradition, have effect subject to this stipulation. These are considered at paras 10.03, 11.14 and 11.21.

However, the right not to be extradited in s 39(3) is subject to s 40 (s 39(4)). Section 40(1) provides that s 39(3) does not apply in relation to a person if the Secretary of State has certified that the conditions in s 40(2) or the conditions in s 40(3) are satisfied in relation to him. **8.73**

The conditions in s 40(2) are that: **8.74**

(a) the Category 1 territory to which the person's extradition has been ordered has accepted that, under standing arrangements,[43] it is the responsible State in relation to the person's asylum claim;
(b) in the opinion of the Secretary of State, the person is not a national or citizen of the territory.

The conditions in s 40(3) are that, in the opinion of the Secretary of State: **8.75**

(a) the person is not a national or citizen of the Category 1 territory to which his extradition has been ordered;
(b) the person's life and liberty would not be threatened in that territory by reason of his race, religion, nationality, political opinion, or membership of a particular social group;
(c) the government of the territory would not send the person to another country otherwise than in accordance with the Refugee Convention.

Section 39(5) and (6) define when an asylum claim is finally determined for the purposes of s 39(3). If the Secretary of State allows the asylum claim, the claim is finally determined when he makes his decision on the claim (s 39(5)). **8.76**

However, if the Secretary of State rejects the asylum claim, the claim is finally determined (s 39(6)): **8.77**

(a) when the Secretary of State makes his decision on the claim, if there is no right to appeal against the Secretary of State's decision on the claim;
(b) when the period permitted for appealing against the Secretary of State's decision on the claim ends, if there is such a right but there is no such appeal;
(c) when the appeal against that decision is finally determined or is withdrawn or abandoned, if there is such an appeal.

An appeal against the Secretary of State's decision on an asylum claim is not finally determined for the purposes of s 39(6) at any time when a further appeal or an application for leave to bring a further appeal has been instituted and has not been finally determined or withdrawn or abandoned, or may be brought. By s 39(8), the remittal of an appeal is not a final determination for the purposes of s 39(7), and the possibility of an appeal out of time with leave must be ignored for the purposes of s 39(6) and (7). If an asylum claim is successful before an extradition order is made then if the extradition request is not withdrawn (see para 11.45) the court can stay proceedings as an abuse of process (see para 5.120 and *Government of the Russian Federation v Bourganov and Gorbachev*, 17 August 2005, Bow Street Magistrates' Court). **8.78**

[43] Defined in s 40(4) to be arrangements in force between the UK and the Category 1 territory for determining which State is responsible for considering applications for asylum. The EU Regulation which sets out the current arrangements is Council Regulation (EC) No 343/2003 of 18 February 2003 establishing the criteria and mechanisms for determining the member State responsible for examining an asylum application lodged in one of the member States by a third-country national.

Asylum claims in Part 2 cases

8.79 Section 121 applies where the defendant whose extradition has been requested under Part 2 makes an asylum claim at any time in the 'relevant period' and an order is made under Part 2 for him to be extradited in pursuance of the request (s 121(1)).

8.80 The relevant period is the period starting when a certificate is issued under s 70 in respect of the request and ending when the person is extradited in pursuance of the request (s 121(2)).

8.81 By s 121(3), the defendant must not be extradited in pursuance of the request before the asylum claim is finally determined; and ss 117 and 118 have effect subject to this right.

8.82 Section 121(4) provides that if the Secretary of State allows the asylum claim, the claim is finally determined when he makes his decision on the claim.

8.83 If the Secretary of State rejects the asylum claim, the claim is finally determined (s 121(5)):

(a) when the Secretary of State makes his decision on the claim, if there is no right to appeal against his decision on the claim;
(b) when the period permitted for appealing against the Secretary of State's decision on the claim ends, if there is such a right but there is no such appeal;
(c) when the appeal against that decision is finally determined or is withdrawn or abandoned, if there is such an appeal.

8.84 An appeal against the Secretary of State's decision on an asylum claim is not finally determined for the purposes of s 121(5) at any time when a further appeal or an application for leave to bring a further appeal has been instituted and has not been finally determined or withdrawn or abandoned, or may be brought.

8.85 By s 121(7) the remittal of an appeal is not a final determination for the purposes of s 121(6), and the possibility of an appeal out of time with leave must be ignored for the purposes of s 121(5) and (6). Para 8.78 considers the consequences if an asylum claim is successful before an extradition order is made.

Asylum claims which are made and not decided before extradition proceedings start[44]

8.86 There is no provision which deals expressly with an asylum claim which has been made before extradition proceedings are started. In light of the specific sections dealing with cases where asylum is claimed following the commencement of extradition proceedings, this omission is surprising.[45] It is clear that the protection against return for refugees extends to an asylum seeker.[46] Therefore, this protection should apply to a defendant who has claimed asylum and is then the subject of an extradition request made by their country of nationality.[47]

---

[44] See paras 8.69–8.85 which consider the position if an asylum claim is made after extradition proceedings have commenced. See para 4.38 which considers the situation where a successful asylum claim has been made in Part 2 cases before the Secretary of State has issued his certificate under s 70.

[45] The 2011 Extradition Review recommends that the protections afforded by ss 39 and 121 should be extended to asylum claims made before extradition proceedings have commenced (see paras 9.52–9.55 of the 2011 Extradition Review for the detailed recommendation). The Government has indicated that it agrees with this recommendation but the 2003 Act has not been amended to reflect this at the time of writing.

[46] In *R (European Roma Rights Centre) v Immigration Officer* [2005] 2 AC 1, the House of Lords confirmed that there was a general principle that a person who left the state of his nationality and applied to the authorities of another state for asylum, whether at the frontier of the second state or from within it, should not be rejected or returned to the first state without appropriate inquiry into the persecution of which he claimed to have a well-founded fear.

[47] *R (Dos Santos) v Judge Margarida Isabel Pereira De Almeida of the Cascais Court, 2nd Criminal Chamber, Portugal* [2010] EWHC 1815 (Admin), para 17.

The position is more complicated if the asylum claim relates to a state other than the requesting territory. If the defendant submits that they will face unfair treatment in the requesting territory on one of the Refugee Convention grounds they can seek to rely on the extraneous considerations bar to extradition.[48] If the defendant submits that there is a risk that they might be sent from the requesting territory to the state from which they are seeking refuge then the court will determine whether this is a real risk. For example, it might be argued that the requesting territory would not properly honour its obligations pursuant to the Refugee Convention if an asylum claim was made after extradition had taken place.[49] If the court finds a real risk exists then it could decide that extradition should not be allowed to take place until the asylum claim has been finally determined and the court can use its case-management powers to achieve this.[50] If the court finds that there is a real risk that the defendant would be sent be sent to the country from which they are seeking refuge and this would involve or lead to a breach of their Convention Rights then extradition would be barred. **8.87**

[48] Sections 13 and 81; see paras 5.38 and 6.25.

[49] *Ignaoua v Italy* [2008] EWHC 2619 (Admin); *Hilali v Secretary of State for the Home Department* [2008] EWHC 905 (Admin),

[50] *R (Dos Santos) v Judge Margarida Isabel Pereira De Almeida of the Cascais Court, 2nd Criminal Chamber, Portugal* [2010] EWHC 1815 (Admin); *R (Chichvarkin) v Secretary of State for the Home Department* [2011] EWCA Civ 91, para 61.

9

APPEALS

A. Introduction

One of the Government's principal criticisms of the EA 1989 was that it afforded the defendant multiple opportunities to challenge the magistrate's decision to commit him.[1] The Government blamed extradition defendants' appeals for what it saw as unnecessary delays in the extradition process. During the debate on the Bill's Second Reading, the Minister of State set out the government's case:[2] **9.01**

> Our extradition arrangements are in urgent need of reform. On average, it takes 18 months to extradite someone from the UK and, in many cases, much longer. The system allows the fugitive to raise the same—arguably, often spurious—points time and again, and to mount numerous legal challenges. Even when—as has happened many times—an individual appeals all the way to the House of Lords following the committal hearing, he can, once the Secretary of State has considered the case, appeal all the way again on exactly the same grounds.

The EA 2003 provides a single statutory right of appeal to the High Court for both the defendant and the requesting state against decisions made by the appropriate judge and the Secretary **9.02**

[1] See the first edition of this work at Chs 8 and 10.
[2] Hansard Vol 396 col 39.

of State.[3] Before considering this right of appeal in detail it is helpful to provide a historical overview of appeals in extradition cases.

Habeas corpus and extradition

9.03 The writ of *habeas corpus ad subjiciendum*, commonly known as *habeas corpus*, is a process for securing the liberty of the subject by affording an effective means of immediate release from unlawful or unjustifiable detention.[4] Generally regarded as one of the common law's greatest achievements,[5] *habeas corpus* is a prerogative writ by which the Sovereign has a right to inquire into the causes for which any of her subjects are deprived of his or her liberty.[6] By it, the High Court, at the instance of the aggrieved subject, commands the production of that subject, and inquires into the cause of his or her imprisonment. If there is no legal justification for the detention, the subject is ordered to be released.

9.04 From the nineteenth century onwards the method by which an extradition defendant challenged the magistrate's decision to commit him was by way of an application for a writ of *habeas corpus*.[7] In *Nikonovs v Governor of Brixton Prison* [2006] 1 All ER 927 Scott Baker LJ commented at para 19:

> In *Linnett v Coles* [1987] QB 555 at 561 Lawton LJ said that a writ of *habeas corpus* was probably the most cherished sacred cow in the British constitution; but the law had never allowed it to graze in all legal pastures. However, the one legal pasture in which it has grazed freely for many years is extradition ...

9.05 Section 11 of the EA 1870 and s 11(1) of the EA 1989 required the committing magistrate to inform the defendant of his right to apply for a writ of *habeas corpus*, and the defendant was protected from return for a period of 15 days to allow him to apply to the High Court and, thereafter, until his application was disposed of.

9.06 Although the original purpose of a writ of *habeas corpus* was to bring the body of a detained person before the court so that the legality of the gaoler's justification for his detention (known as the return to the writ) could be examined, over time the scope of review in extradition cases expanded so that the court could review not just the return, but the case as it appeared before the magistrate, that is, to look at the evidence which was before him, and to consider whether any magistrate, properly applying his mind to the question, could reasonably have come to the conclusion that there was a prima facie case.[8]

9.07 Section 10 of the Fugitive Offenders Act 1881, s 8(3) of the Fugitive Offenders Act 1967, and s 11(3) and Sch 1, para 8(1) of the EA 1989, provided statutory grounds for applying for a writ of *habeas corpus*.[9] The compass of *habeas corpus* was also extended in the cases to include those

---

3 For a discussion of some of the structural problems introduced by the EA 2003, see Spencer, 'Implementing the European arrest warrant: a tale of how not to do it' Stat LR [2009] 184.

4 See generally, Farbey, Sharpe and Atrill, *The Law of Habeas Corpus* (3rd edn, Oxford, 2011).

5 'The provisions made by the law for the liberty of the subject have been found for ages effectual to an extent never known in any other country through the medium of the summary right to the writ of *habeas corpus*': *R v Batcheldor* (1839) 1 Per and Dav 516 at 567 per Lord Denman CJ.

6 See *Crowley's Case* (1818) 2 Swan 1 at 48 per Lord Eldon LC; *R v Cowle* (1759) 2 Burr 834 at 856 per Lord Mansfield CJ; Corner's Crown Practice 110. 'If any man be imprisoned by another a *corpus cum causa* (*ie habeas corpus*) can be granted to those who imprison him, for the King ought to have an account rendered to him concerning the liberty of his subjects, and the restraint thereof': 2 Roll Abr 69. Detention in the context of extradition can include remand on bail: *R v Secretary of State for the Home Department ex p Launder* (No 2) [1998] QB 944, 1011.

7 *R v Oldham Justices ex p Cawley* [1997] QB 1, 17; *Re Tivnan* (1864) 5 B and S 645; *Re Windsor* (1865) 6 B and S 522.

8 *Armah v Government of Ghana* [1968] AC 1982.

9 cf *Knowles v Government of the United States of America* [2007] 1 WLR 47, PC.

who had been released on bail but were subject to an extradition request, who for all purposes were treated as if they were in custody.[10] *Habeas corpus* remains the principal means by which extradition decisions are challenged in the United States.

If the Secretary of State ordered extradition then the case was not at an end. In cases under Part III of the EA 1989 the defendant also had a statutory right to seek judicial review of the Secretary of State's decision to return him,[11] and this remedy was also available in Sch 1 cases. **9.08**

So far as the requesting state was concerned, in cases dealt with under Part III of the EA 1989, it had the right to appeal to the High Court by way of case stated under s 10 if the district judge refused to make an order of committal. In Sch 1 cases its remedy was to seek a judicial review of the judge's decision to discharge the defendant.[12] **9.09**

Appeals under the EA 2003

The EA 2003 simplified the appeals process by creating a unified statutory right of appeal to the High Court against the appropriate judge's decision following the extradition hearing and (in Category 2 cases) against the Secretary of State's decision to order or refuse extradition. The right of appeal is granted to both the defendant and the requesting state, and the defendant cannot be returned whilst such an appeal is outstanding. The EA 2003 also introduced time limits for the hearing of appeals in an effort to speed up the extradition process. **9.10**

The EA 2003 also provides for a right of appeal to the Supreme Court with leave where the case involves a point of law of general public importance. **9.11**

Appeals, *habeas corpus*, and judicial review

Section 34 of the EA 2003 provides that a decision of the judge under Part 1 may be questioned in legal proceedings only by means of an appeal under Part 1, while s 116 provides that decisions of the judge or the Secretary of State under Part 2 may be questioned in legal proceedings only by means of an appeal under Part 2. As will be seen later, ss 26, 103, and 108 limit the defendant's right of statutory appeal to decisions made in the course of the extradition hearing and to the Secretary of State's decision to order extradition. The question thus arises as to the extent to which ss 34 and 116 oust the defendant's ability to apply for *habeas corpus* or judicial review of other decisions under Part 1 or Part 2, against which no right of statutory appeal lies. **9.12**

On one view, read literally, the meaning of ss 34 and 116 is clear. It is that all decisions under Parts 1 and 2 made by a judge or the Secretary of State cannot be questioned except on an appeal. Where no right of appeal is provided for by the Act, for example, decisions taken at an initial hearing, the decision must stand whether it is right or wrong. An alternative and narrower construction is that ss 34 and 116 are only intended to relate to appeals that are provided for in Parts 1 and 2. In other words, they only 'bite' in circumstances where a statutory right of appeal is provided for and operate so as to preclude interlocutory challenges to decisions made by the judge. If this construction is correct then *habeas corpus* and judicial review remain available in the ordinary way to challenge all other decisions under Parts 1 and 2 as well as matters such as the validity of the Part 1 certificate issued by SOCA. **9.13**

[10] EA 1989, s 11; *R v Secretary of State for the Home Department ex p Launder (No. 2)* [1998] QB 994, 1011.

[11] EA 1989, s 13(6)–(8).

[12] *Atkinson v Government of the United States of America* [1971] AC 197, 235.

9.14 It is clear that in enacting ss 34 and 116 Parliament did not intend to remove the general right of a defendant to apply for *habeas corpus*.[13] On 26 June 2003[14] Baroness Anelay of St Johns, before the Grand Committee, quoted the Minister in the House of Commons:

> The common law right of habeas corpus goes back many centuries and there is nothing in the Bill that affects it ... It is always open to a fugitive to raise *habeas corpus* issues. At every stage, the district judge is required to consider whether remanding in custody or granting bail is appropriate, and to ensure that custody issues are properly taken into account.

9.15 On the same occasion Baroness Scotland of Asthal said:[15]

> Let me make clear from the start that there is certainly no attempt to remove *habeas corpus* by the measures in the Bill. The provisions seek to abolish the statutory *habeas corpus*, which was first introduced in 1967 and then consolidated through the Extradition Act 1989, and replace it with a different appeal system. *Habeas corpus*, as we know and love it, which was given birth to by the Magna Carta, remains.
>
> During the Bill's passage in the other place, various assertions were made that we might be abolishing *habeas corpus*. I want to make it absolutely clear that any such concerns are quite wrong. The common law right of *habeas corpus* remains; anyone who is subject to extradition can bring a common-law *habeas corpus* claim. Whether it will succeed is obviously an entirely different matter ... I hope that Members of the Committee will accept that the procedures which the Bill puts in place comply fully with the principles of *habeas corpus*. And although, as I said, there would be nothing to prevent a person bringing a *habeas corpus* claim, it is hard to see how it could possibly succeed, the principles having already been satisfied by the scheme created in the statute. For that reason I cannot see why we need to include a special provision requiring the High Court to consider *habeas corpus* factors.

9.16 In light of these assurances Baroness Anelay withdrew her amendment to include in the Extradition Bill an express right to apply for *habeas corpus*.

9.17 In *Nikonovs v Governor of Brixton Prison* [2006] 1 All ER 927 the defendant was arrested under Part 1 of the EA 2003 but was not brought before the district judge as soon as practicable as required by s 4(3). His application for discharge under s 4(5) was refused by the judge and he applied for *habeas corpus*. The government argued as a preliminary point that the application was precluded by s 34.[16] In rejecting this submission, Scott Baker LJ said at paras 18–19:

> *Habeas corpus* is directed to the lawfulness of a person's detention. Section 34 is silent as to the right to challenge by *habeas corpus* the lawfulness of continuing detention resulting from a erroneous decision of a judge under subsection 4(5) not to discharge the claimant. True by subsection 4(6) a person is to be treated as continuing in legal custody until he is discharged under subsection 4(5) but I would not regard lawful custody as continuing after a decision is taken not to discharge him when he should have been discharged. Absent a right of appeal, did Parliament really intend *habeas corpus* should not be available? Did Parliament really intend that a person who ought to have been discharged because he should have been brought before the appropriate judge sooner, but nevertheless remains in custody, should have no remedy? In my view the passages from Hansard that I have cited make the answer clear beyond a peradventure. It would in my judgment require the strongest words in a provision such as section 34 to remove the ancient remedy of *habeas corpus* ... In my judgment the remedy is available in this case and the court has jurisdiction to entertain the claimant's application.

[13] See for example *Nikonovs v Governor of Brixton Prison* [2006] 1 All ER 927 DC.

[14] 650 HL Official Report (5th series) col GC162.

[15] Ibid. at GC163.

[16] In *Pinto v Governor of HM Prison Brixton* [2004] EWHC 2986 (Admin) the jurisdiction to apply for *habeas corpus* had previously been conceded.

The High Court in *Nikonovs* therefore adopted the narrow construction of s 34 referred to above. Thus, challenges to decisions made by the appropriate judge and the Secretary of State under Parts 1 and 2, other than those which may be challenged by way of statutory appeal,[17] may be brought by way of judicial review or *habeas corpus* proceedings. That section 34 does not oust the general supervisory jurisdiction of the High Court was confirmed by the High Court of Northern Ireland in *Re An Application by Liam Campbell for a writ of habeas corpus ad subjiciendum* [2009] NIQB 82. **9.18**

Habeas corpus has, so far as the defendant is concerned, obvious procedural advantages. Unlike an application for judicial review, there is no requirement that he obtain permission to apply for *habeas corpus* and his ability to take the case beyond the High Court to the Supreme Court does not depend on the need to obtain certification of a point of law of general public importance. Applying the principles established in *Nikonovs v Governor of Brixton Prison* [2006] 1 All ER 927, *habeas corpus* applications have been entertained under the EA 2003 in respect of failures to bring the defendant before the court for the initial hearing as soon as practicable (s 4 of the EA 2003);[18] failure to serve a copy of the EAW upon arrest (s 4 of the EA 2003);[19] refusals to adjourn;[20] decisions to remand in custody taken without jurisdiction;[21] applications for discharge under s 113 following failure to comply with CPR Part 52 time limits for the hearing of appeals;[22] refusal to discharge following failure to comply with the required period for surrender (ss 36 and 117 of the EA 2003);[23] and (at one time) to material changes in circumstances occurring after the conclusion of the statutory appeals process.[24] **9.19**

However, *habeas corpus* does not exist as a means by which to seek to litigate issues that are outwith the jurisdiction of the appropriate judge to consider in extradition proceedings.[25] In **9.20**

---

17 In *Pinto v Governor of HM Prison Brixton* [2004] EWHC 2986 (Admin) *habeas corpus* was granted on grounds of non-compliance with the conditions in s 2 of the EA 2003. However, it is now established that the appropriate judge is required to determine compliance with s 2 validity at the extradition hearing, and thus that a statutory appeal lies in respect of such issues: *Boudhiba v Central Examining Court No 5 of the National Court of Justice Madrid, Spain* [2007] 1 WLR 124.

18 *Atlinski v Her Majesty's Prison Wandsworth* [2009] EWHC 2713 (Admin); *Nikonovs v Governor of Brixton Prison* [2006] 1 All ER 927 DC.

19 *Stanczyk v Circuit Court in Katowice, Poland* [2010] EWHC 3651 (Admin).

20 *Slator v Bow Street Magistrates' Court* [2006] EWHC 2628 (Admin); *R (Handa) v Bow Street Magistrates' Court* [2004] EWHC 3116. However, it is now accepted that the appropriate remedy by which to challenge adjournment decisions is judicial review. In *Raffile v Government of the United States of America* [2005] 1 All ER 889, para 35, the possibility was contemplated of a challenge to an adjournment decision as being within the scope of the statutory appeals procedure. However, subsequent cases did not support that view and appellate challenges to refusals to adjourn have been repeatedly rejected on the basis that the appropriate remedy is judicial review: *Ras v City of Westminster Magistrates' Court* [2011] EWHC 562 (Admin); *R (Slavik) v District Court of Nitra, Slovak Republic* [2011] EWHC 265 (Admin); *R (Koniak) v Regional Court for Warsaw, Poland* [2010] EWHC 3501 (Admin); *Kaminski and Others v Judicial Authority of Poland* [2010] EWHC 2772 (Admin); *R (Roszas) v Baranya County Court, Hungary* [2010] EWHC 1265 (Admin); *Olah v Regional Court in Plzen, Czech Republic* [2008] EWHC 2701 (Admin).

21 *Asliturk v HMP Wandsworth* [2010] EWHC 1720 (Admin).

22 *Wright v City of Westminster Magistrates' Court* [2011] EWHC 515 (Admin).

23 *Owens v City of Westminster Magistrates' Court* [2010] 1 WLR 17, although at para 13 the court indicated that judicial review is arguably the preferable procedural route.

24 *Hilali v Governor of HMP Whitemoor and Others* [2007] 3 WLR 621 DC. However, in *Ignaoua, Khemiri and Chehidi v The Judicial Authority of the Courts of Milan* [2008] EWHC 2619 (Admin) the court suggested that the appropriate remedy in such circumstances would be to apply to re-open the final appeal pursuant to CPR 52.17. Where there has been no statutory appeal, *habeas corpus* remains unavailable; *R (Mann) v City of Westminster Magistrates' Court* [2010] EWHC 48 (Admin).

25 The same principles apply to judicial review: *R (Atkinson) v Commissioner of the Metropolitan Police Force* [2009] EWHC 2661 (Admin), where the issue on judicial review was the refusal of the Secretary of State to attempt to obtain the agreement of the requesting state for the defendant to serve his service sentence in UK, in circumstances where the EA 2003 does not incorporate Article 4(6) of the EAW Framework Decision.

R (Hilali) v Governor of Whitemoor Prison [2008] 1 AC 805, the House of Lords confirmed that an application for *habeas corpus* on the grounds that there was no case to answer in the requested state must always be rejected as having been excluded by the provisions of the EA 2003. The application for *habeas corpus* there was based on a post-appeal change of circumstances in the requesting state, namely the acquittal in Spain of another suspect and the declared inadmissibility of telephone intercept evidence which had been relied on in support of the European arrest warrant. An inquiry into that question was held to be contrary to the principle of mutual recognition.

9.21 In many cases where a decision is made within the EA 2003, but where no statutory right of appeal exists, judicial review rather than *habeas corpus* may, applying conventional public law principles, be the most appropriate remedy.[26] In *Re An Application by Liam Campbell for a writ of habeas corpus ad subjiciendum* [2009] NIQB 82, on an application for *habeas corpus* arising from a preliminary ruling on abuse of process, against which no statutory appeal lay,[27] the High Court of Northern Ireland held that *habeas corpus* is a remedy of last resort and thus generally inappropriate where judicial review was available as an alternative remedy.[28]

9.22 The High Court has yet to lay down clear guidance as to when judicial review, rather than *habeas corpus*, is the appropriate remedy in extradition cases under the EA 2003.[29] Therefore, alongside *habeas corpus*, judicial review applications have been entertained or indicated as appropriate under the EA 2003 in respect of challenges to SOCA certification of an EAW under s 2(7);[30] the Secretary of State's certification of a request under s 70;[31] refusal by the Secretary of State

---

Similarly, judicial review does not lie against a refusal of the district judge, post-surrender, to order a defendant's repatriation where the EA 2003 provides no such power; *R (Hilali) v Secretary of State for the Home Department* [2010] 1 WLR 241 DC.

[26] In *Re An Application by Liam Campbell for a writ of habeas corpus ad subjiciendum* [2009] NIQB 82, the High Court of Northern Ireland observed that the distinctions between these two forms of legal challenge are not merely technical. They include, most importantly, differences in procedure, parties, and available remedies. Judicial review has the merit of identifying the real respondent and putting such respondent on notice of the challenge at the outset. This, in turn, enhances the court's prospects of being fully informed, receiving all material evidence, and hearing argument from both parties at the earliest possible stage. Historically, challenges to the legality of a person's detention in extradition cases have, conventionally, been brought by applications for the writ of *habeas corpus*. This is exemplified in *R v Governor of Brixton Prison, ex p Mehmet* [1962] 2 QB 1. In *R v Oldham Justices and Another ex p Cawley* [1997] QB 1, Simon Brown LJ was disposed to accept that in extradition cases, *habeas corpus* had become 'the accepted remedy' (at p 17). Notably, however, in the passage in this text there is a strong emphasis on the nature of the decision under challenge as a pointer to the appropriate remedy: '... Perhaps the most important factor in any given case is to consider the nature of the decision or proceeding to be reviewed ... Where the decision is one in respect of which there really is no other form of redress, or is one concerning which *habeas corpus* has become the accepted remedy, the courts will wield whatever powers of review are necessary to give relief where it is thought that something has gone wrong ... The significant matter for consideration is the nature of the decision to be reviewed rather than the nature of the error alleged ...'. While this passage suggests that there should be some flexibility in the court's approach, having regard doubtless to the hallowed importance of the liberty of the citizen, it nonetheless supports the view that the writ of *habeas corpus* is a remedy of last resort. The appropriate remedy in a case under the EA 2003 will ultimately depend on the particular decision under challenge. In cases of genuine doubt, the challenging party may wish to initiate both forms of proceeding.

[27] Abuse of process being outwith the statutory scheme; *Bermingham v Director of the Serious Fraud Office* [2007] QB 727.

[28] See also *Central Examining Court of the National Court of Madrid v City of Westminster Magistrates' Court* [2007] EWHC 2059 (Admin) concerning judicial review of decisions on abuse of process.

[29] cf *Gronostajski v Government of Poland* [2007] EWHC 3314 (Admin), para 8; *Owens v City of Westminster Magistrates' Court* [2010] 1 WLR 17, paras 12–14.

[30] *Dhar v National Office of the Public Prosecution Service, the Netherlands* [2012] EWHC 697 (Admin); *Harmatos v Office of the King's Prosecutor in Dendermonde, Belgium* [2011] EWHC 1598 (Admin).

[31] *Akaroglu v The Government of Romania and Others* [2008] 1 All ER 27 DC; *R (Bleta) v Secretary of State for the Home Department* [2005] 1 WLR 3194 DC.

to de-designate a Part 1 territory;[32] rulings on identity (s 7);[33] refusals to adjourn;[34] failure to commence the extradition hearing within the required time limits (ss 8 and 75);[35] proceeding in the involuntary absence of the defendant;[36] failure to provide adequate translation facilities during an extradition hearing;[37] failure to consider submissions;[38] refusal to issue witness summons;[39] defects in an extradition order;[40] conflicting domestic and extradition orders;[41] refusal of a High Court officer to refer an application to a judge;[42] wrongful extension of the required period for surrender (s 35);[43] refusal to discharge following a failure to comply with the required period for surrender (ss 36 and 117 of the EA 2003);[44] breaches of diplomatic assurances;[45] granting of post-surrender consent to prosecute for additional offences (ss 54 and 55);[46] and arguably even decisions under s 91 EA 2003 (physical and mental health).[47]

B. Time Limits for Instituting a Statutory Appeal

Common to all statutory appeal provisions under Parts 1 and 2 of the EA 2003 is a requirement that 'notice of an appeal' be 'given in accordance with rules of court' before the end of 'the permitted period', which is seven days starting with the day on which the extradition order or order for discharge is made in Part 1 cases (ss 26(4)[48] and 28(5)), and in Part 2 cases 14 days starting with the day on which discharge is ordered (s 105(5)),[49] or notification of the Secretary **9.23**

[32] *Oliver v Secretary of State for the Home Department* [2006] CMLR 46.

[33] *Hilali v The National Court, Madrid and Another* [2007] 1 WLR 768.

[34] *Marusinski v Regional Court of Piatrkow, Poland* [2011] EWHC 1296 (Admin); *R (Griffin) v City of Westminster Magistrates' Court* [2012] 1 WLR 270; *Ras v City of Westminster Magistrates' Court* [2011] EWHC 562 (Admin); *R (Slavik) v District Court of Nitra, Slovak Republic* [2011] EWHC 265 (Admin); *R (Koniak) v Regional Court for Warsaw, Poland* [2010] EWHC 3501 (Admin); *Kaminski v Judicial Authority of Poland* [2010] EWHC 2772 (Admin); *Herdman v City of Westminster Magistrates' Court* [2010] EWHC 1533 (Admin); *R (Roszas) v Baranya County Court, Hungary* [2010] EWHC 1265 (Admin); *Olah v Regional Court in Plzen, Czech Republic* [2008] EWHC 2701 (Admin).

[35] *Asliturk v The City of Westminster Magistrates' Court* [2011] 1 WLR 1139 DC; *Gronostajski v Government of Poland* [2007] EWHC 3314 (Admin). Note however that, in *Kozluk v Circuit Court Lublin* [2009] EWHC 3523 (Admin) and in *R (Jeziorowski) v District Court in Torun, Poland* [2010] EWHC 2112 (Admin), the High Court entertained statutory appeals against refusals to discharge under s 8.

[36] *R (Pasquetti) v Westminster Magistrates' Court* [2010] EWHC 3139 (Admin).

[37] *Cimieri v Court of Florence* [2010] EWHC 1471 (Admin).

[38] *R (Berners) v Council of the Criminal Matters Court Regional Court of Riga Latvia* [2010] EWHC 1010 (Admin).

[39] *Kaupaitis v Prosecutor General, Republic of Lithuania* [2006] EWHC 1745 (Admin).

[40] *R (Koniak) v Regional Court for Warsaw, Poland* [2010] EWHC 3501 (Admin).

[41] *Governor of HMP Wandsworth v Kinderis* [2008] QB 347.

[42] *Arunthavaraja v Administrative Court Office and Another* [2009] EWHC 1921 (Admin).

[43] *Szklanny v City of Westminster Magistrates' Court* [2008] 1 WLR 789. cf *Kasprzak v Warsaw Regional Court, Poland* [2011] EWHC 100 (Admin), where the High Court held it had no power to set aside orders made by it under s 36 of the EA 2003.

[44] *Kolanowski v City of Westminster Magistrates' Court* [2011] EWHC 2557 (Admin); *Kasprzak v Warsaw Regional Court, Poland* [2011] EWHC 100 (Admin); *Wood v City of Westminster Magistrates' Court* [2007] EWHC 2058 (Admin).

[45] *R (Gomes) v Secretary of State for the Home Department* [2010] EWHC 168 (Admin).

[46] *Chyba v District Court in Strakonice* [2008] EWHC 3292 (Admin).

[47] *Asliturk v The City of Westminster Magistrates' Court* [2011] 1 WLR 1139. This obiter observation cannot be correct because decisions under ss 25 and 91 are clearly susceptible to a statutory appeal.

[48] Section 26(4) provides: 'Notice of an appeal under this section must be given in accordance with rules of court before the end of the permitted period, which is 7 days starting with the day on which the order is made.' Section 28(5) is in a similar form.

[49] Section 105(5) provides: 'Notice of an appeal under this section must be given in accordance with rules of court before the end of the permitted period, which is 14 days starting with the day on which the order for the person's discharge is made.' Sections 103(9), 108(4), and 110(5) are in a similar form.

of State's order for extradition or discharge (ss 103(9), 108(4) and 110(5)). The rules of court are those contained in para 22.6A of the Practice Direction to CPR Part 52.[50]

9.24 These provisions have proved amongst the most controversial of the EA 2003. Difficulties have arisen because the time limits in the EA 2003 are short and take no account of weekends or public holidays.[51] Also, the day on which the order appealed against is made is always included in the calculation.[52] The EA 2003 makes no distinction between defendants on bail and in custody.[53] Often, a failure to comply with the time limits for appeal will not necessarily be the result of fault on the part of the defendant (or the requesting state). For example, the defendant's legal representative may be negligent, the defendant may be unrepresented and not speak English (a common occurrence in extradition cases for obvious reasons), or the court may be unexpectedly closed. Following the entry into force of the EA 2003 it rapidly became apparent that these inflexible statutory requirements for giving notice of appeal had the potential to work considerable injustice in individual cases. For example, in *R (Bergman) v District Court in Kladno, Czech Republic* [2011] EWHC 267 (Admin), a notice of appeal was prepared by an unrepresented defendant who had been remanded in custody and was faxed in draft to the judicial authority and filed, all within the seven-day period, but no stamped copy was served, because the High Court did not provide it to him until much later. The High Court held that failure to serve a sealed notice of appeal upon the respondent was fatal. Irwin J, at para 10, recorded his 'concern that unrepresented litigants who are in custody will often find it very hard to comply with the necessary requirements, despite every effort on the part of the court staff'.

9.25 *R (Mann) v City of Westminster Magistrates' Court* [2010] EWHC 48 (Admin) illustrates how important it is to comply with these strict time limits for giving notice of appeal.[54] Mr Mann's lawyer had filed his notice of appeal with the court on time but served it on the CPS one day late. The High Court held (applying *Mucelli v Government of Albania* and *Moulai v Deputy Public Prosecutor in Cretiel, France* [2009] 1 WLR 276 as discussed below) that there was no power to extend the time for service; no power to apply for judicial review or *habeas corpus*; no power to

---

[50] Para 22.6A(3) provides that in appeals under s 26 or 28: '(a) the appellant's notice must be filed and served before the expiry of 7 days, starting with the day on which the order is made'. Para 22.6A(5) provides that: 'Where an appeal is brought under section 103 of the Act, the appellant's notice must be filed and served before the expiry of 14 days, starting with the day on which the Secretary of State informs the person under section 100(1) or (4) of the Act of the order he has made in respect of the person.' There are similar rules in para 22.6A(3) for other appeals under Part 2. See para 9.98.

[51] Other than those that fall on the final day, as to which see para 9.28; *Lukaszewski v The District Court in Torun, Poland* [2012] UKSC 20, para 20.

[52] However late in the day service of the triggering order is made; *R (Amoako) v Director of Public Prosecutions* [2006] EWHC 1572 (Admin). The provisions of the CPR regarding deemed service cannot operate to delay the commencement of the required period until the following day; *Lukaszewski and Others v The District Court in Torun, Poland and Others* [2012] UKSC 20, para. 20. Delivery amounts to communication. It does not matter that the solicitor may not read the communication until later; *Salazar-Duarte v The Government of the United States of America* [2010] EWHC 3150 (Admin). In *Chodan v United States* [2010] EWHC 2207 (Admin), the court confirmed that s 103(9) identifies the starting point by reference to a particular day rather than a particular time and does not allow for 14 periods of 24 hours running consecutively from the time when a person was informed of an order.

[53] *R (Pigas) v District Court of Jelena Gora, Poland* [2010] EWHC 1763 (Admin).

[54] See also *Henderson v Court of Appeal of Aix En Provence* [2009] EWHC 1701 (Admin) where the High Court held it had no jurisdiction to entertain an appeal against an extradition order where the notice of appeal was served outside the statutory time limit. The High Court observed that there is nothing in the EAW Framework Decision, EU law, or the European Convention on Human Rights that precluded the application of time limits to extradition appeals or required an appeal to be considered where there had been a failure to comply with them. See also *R (Preiss) v Dobele District Court, Latvia* [2011] EWHC 316 (Admin) confirming that the position is not altered by the EU Charter on Fundamental Rights.

re-open the extradition hearing under the 'slip rule' in s 142 of Magistrates' Courts Act 1980; and no power to judicially review the decision of SOCA to enforce the extradition order.

Following a number of conflicting cases from the High Court, the issue of what constituted 'giving' notice of appeal under the EA 2003 ultimately came before the House of Lords in the conjoined Part 1 and Part 2 cases of *Mucelli v Government of Albania* and *Moulai v Deputy Public Prosecutor in Cretiel, France* [2009] 1 WLR 276. The defendants had filed their notices of appeal with the High Court within the specified times, namely seven days under s 26(4) and 14 days under s 103(9). However, in both cases, the requesting state argued that the notice had not been served upon the CPS within the specified time. *Moulai*'s case was governed by s 26(4) and he had served his notice by fax on the sixth day after the making of the extradition order. The fax transmission was completed a few minutes after 4.00 p.m. *Mucelli*'s case was governed by s 103(9), and he had filed his notice of appeal with the High Court within the 14 day period but not served it on the CPS until well outside that period. **9.26**

The House of Lords held by a majority (Lord Rodger dissenting) that 'giving' of notice of appeal means both filing at court *and* serving on all respondents within the seven- and 14-day periods respectively, as provided for in para 22.6A of the Practice Direction to CPR Part 52.[55] The majority held that where the EA 2003, as primary legislation, fixes a time limit for the giving of notice of an appeal, the appeal court has no power to extend it under CPR 3.1(2)(a) or any other CPR rule, unless the statute itself so provides. Subject to one exception, the required filing *and* service must be achieved before the end of the seventh day in Part 1 cases or the fourteenth day in Part 2 cases. However, the House of Lords held that just as the CPR contains no power to extend the statutory period, neither may it cut it down. CPR 6.7 provided (at the relevant time) that any document served after 4.00 p.m. should be deemed to be served on the next day. The House of Lords held that was incapable of rendering out of time the notice of appeal served by Moulai after 4.00 p.m. on the last day of the permitted period. It held that service at any time before midnight on the final day would have sufficed, for example by fax or posting through the door.[56] **9.27**

The majority of the House of Lords held that the only exception to these largely inflexible statutory time limits is where the requisite recipient's office is closed during the whole of the last day of the required period. In such a case the notice of appeal will be validly filed or served if it is given at any time during the first succeeding day on which the office is open (ie, the next business day).[57] Where, however, the recipient's office is open during normal office hours on the final day, but closed before midnight, time is not thereby similarly to be extended to the next business day.[58] **9.28**

In *Lukaszewski v The District Court in Torun, Poland* [2012] UKSC 20 the Supreme Court was invited, but declined by a majority, to revisit the correctness of the decision in *Mucelli v Government of Albania* and *Moulai v Deputy Public Prosecutor in Cretiel, France* [2009] 1 WLR 276. However, in its decision the Supreme Court did go some way towards mitigating **9.29**

55 But not interested parties. The Secretary of State is not a party to an appeal against the decision of the district judge under EA 2003, s 103. Whilst service on the Secretary of State is required by the Practice Direction to CPR Part 52, it is not a statutory requirement and failure does not deprive the court of jurisdiction under s 103(9); *Aldhouse v Royal Government of Thailand* [2012] EWHC 191 (Admin).

56 *Mucelli v Government of Albania* and *Moulai v Deputy Public Prosecutor in Cretiel, France* [2009] 1 WLR 276, paras 39, 81–82.

57 *Mucelli v Government of Albania* and *Moulai v Deputy Public Prosecutor in Cretiel, France* [2009] 1 WLR 276, para 84.

58 *Mucelli v Government of Albania* and *Moulai v Deputy Public Prosecutor in Cretiel, France* [2009] 1 WLR 276, para 85.

the inflexibility of the statutory time limits of the EA 2003. The Supreme Court held that, in cases where the defendant is a UK national, he or she possesses a civil right to remain in the UK which is subject to the procedural rights in Article 6 of the European Convention on Human Rights. Hence, proceedings under the EA 2003 operate so as to determine his Article 6 rights because an extradition order can determine whether or not he can remain in the UK.[59] Insofar as a right of appeal exists, Article 6(1) requires that any restriction on the right of appeal must not impair 'the very essence' of the right; any such restriction must pursue a legitimate aim and must involve a 'reasonable relationship of proportionality between the means employed and the aim sought to be achieved'.[60] The Supreme Court held that the statutory time limits governing the giving of notice of appeal under the EA 2003 offend this principle. Accordingly, the Supreme Court held that they fell to be 'read down' in accordance with s 3 of the Human Rights Act 1998 so as to permit of discretionary extension in exceptional circumstances, namely, where the litigant has done all he can to bring and notify an appeal timeously. Thus a UK national may, in exceptional circumstances, apply for an extension of the required period for giving notice of appeal.

9.30 By contrast, the same legal reasoning cannot avail foreign nationals (who enjoy no comparable civil right to remain in the UK)[61] or requesting states (who enjoy no Convention rights).[62] Thus, neither a foreign national (appealing under ss 26, 103, or 108) nor a requesting state (appealing under ss 28, 105, or 110) may apply for an extension of time. Lady Hale commented upon the obviously discriminatory nature of this result.[63]

9.31 The Supreme Court in *Lukaszewski v The District Court in Torun, Poland* [2012] UKSC 20 also introduced a degree of flexibility as to the required content of a notice of appeal:

> a generous view can and should be taken of this, bearing in mind the shortness of the permitted period and the fact that what really matters is that an appeal should have been filed and all respondents should be on notice of this, sufficient to warn them that they should not proceed with extradition pending an appeal.[64]

---

59 The European Court of Human Rights has consistently held that extradition proceedings do not concern a dispute ('*contestation*') over an applicant's civil rights and obligations, or the 'determination of a criminal charge', which under Article 6(1) relates to the full process of examining an individual's guilt or innocence in respect of a criminal offence, and not merely, as is the case in extradition proceedings, to the process of determining whether or not a person may be extradited to a foreign country: *Toliono v San Marino and Italy* (2012) Application No 44853/10, para 59; *Muminov v The Russian Federation* (2011) 52 EHRR 23, para 126; *Garayev v Azerbaijan* (2010) Application No 53688/08 at para 109; *AB v. Poland* (2007) App No 33878/96; *Mamatkulov and Askarov v. Turkey* (2005) 41 EHRR 25, para 82; *RAF v Spain* (2003) Application No 53652/00, para 1; *Salgado v Spain* (2002) Application No 65964/01, para 1; *Maaouia v France* (2001) 33 EHRR 32, para 40; *Raidl v Austria* (1995) Application No 25342/94; *EGM v Luxembourg* (1994) DR 144, p148; *Farmakopoulos v Belgium* (1990) 64 DR 52, p 69; *Kirkwood v United Kingdom* (1984) 37 DR 158, p175; *H. v Spain* (1983) DR 93, p94. These decisions have, however, always been made in the context of cases concerning extradition of foreign nationals. The European Court of Human Rights has not yet dealt with an extradition case concerning a national of the extraditing state in which Article 6(1) has been argued by reference to the conduct of the extradition proceedings in the requested state (as opposed to prospective treatment in the requesting state). In the absence of any direct Strasbourg authority applying these principles to a case concerning an own-national of an extraditing state, the Supreme Court was able to suggest that the principles apply *only* to the extradition of aliens.

60 *Tolstoy Miloslavsky v United Kingdom* (1995) 20 EHRR 442; *Stone Court Shipping SA v Spain* (2005) 40 EHRR 749. For a prior rejection of this argument, see the discussion in *Szepsel v District Court of Krakow, Poland* [2011] EWHC 3347 (Admin).

61 Although it may be argued that EU nationals enjoy such a right under EU law concerning free movement of persons under Directive 2004/38/EC on the right of citizens of the Union and their family members to move and reside freely within the territory of the member States, which are transposed into UK law by the Immigration (European Economic Area) Regulations 2006, as amended by SI 2009/1117 and SI 2011/1247.

62 *R v Wier* [2001] 1 WLR 421.

63 *Lukaszewski v The District Court in Torun, Poland* [2012] UKSC 20, para 52.

64 *Lukaszewski v The District Court in Torun, Poland* [2012] UKSC 20, para 18.

Although in *Mucelli v Government of Albania* and *Moulai v Deputy Public Prosecutor in Cretiel, France* [2009] 1 WLR 276 the House of Lords held that a failure to comply with the mandatory statutory time limits for filing and serving a notice of appeal is fatal to the appeal, by contrast, a failure to comply with procedural rules can be cured in appropriate cases by the court in the exercise of its discretion under (in England) CPR 3.9 and 3.10. For example, in *Office of Public Prosecutor of Hamburg, Germany v Hughes* [2009] EWHC 279 (Admin), the High Court treated as a mere procedural error, which could be corrected, the endorsement in a notice of appeal of a wrong date of arrest (the effect of such endorsement being that, on the face of the notice, the 40-day period allowed for the court to begin to hear the substance of the appeal would have expired a month early). **9.32**

In a series of cases, the High Court has held that service of an unsealed (ie, draft) notice of appeal is, at most, a procedural error.[65] It has held that service of a sealed notice would require, as a matter of fact, filing to occur before close of court business on the final day, and thus operate to cut down the full seven-day period to which the appellant is entitled. Sealing is not a requirement of valid filing. Filing means delivering and is a unilateral act. Therefore, leaving with court staff is sufficient. This line of authority was cited with apparent approval by the Supreme Court in *Lukaszewski v The District Court in Torun, Poland* [2012] UKSC 20. **9.33**

Service of the sealed front sheet of a notice of appeal only may suffice. In *Lukaszewski v The District Court in Torun, Poland* [2012] UKSC 20 unrepresented defendants in custody faxed the notices of appeals to the Administrative Court for filing and stamping. The Administrative Court faxed a copy of the sealed front page back to the prison legal services department which then faxed to the CPS (as the legal representatives of the judicial authority of the state requesting surrender) a copy of the sealed front page together with a cover sheet. The Supreme Court held at para 19 that: **9.34**

> The front page of the notices of appeal returned by the court and served by fax ... showed the relevant High Court references and stamps with the dates of filing as well as the names and addresses of the appellants and the respondent Polish court. The subsequent pages which were not returned or served identified matters such as the decision appealed (though in current extradition practice this would be a decision of the Westminster Magistrates' Court), its date, the grounds and a statement of belief. The irregularity involved in their absence was capable of cure, and on the present facts certainly merited this. The Crown Prosecution Service can have had no difficulty in identifying the decision being appealed, and it would be disproportionate if the practice followed by the court and the prison Legal Services Department should lead to these appellants losing any right of appeal.[66]

Service of a document which merely states an intention to appeal may also suffice: **9.35**

> In terms of the rules, this was a highly irregular notice of any appeal, and, although it was dated the same date as his solicitors in fact filed notice of appeal with the court on his behalf, it was framed as 'notice of my intent to appeal', rather than as notice of an actual appeal. Nonetheless, the statute is capable of embracing the Scottish practice, whereby a draft note of an appeal is served before being lodged with the court. It follows that notice of an intent to appeal must be within the statutory language. I would regard [the] letter as notice to the Secretary of State of an appeal within the statute, albeit that the letter was highly irregular in

---

65 *Sciezka v Court in Sad Okregowy, Poland* [2009] EWHC 2259 (Admin); *Dunne v High Court Dublin* [2009] EWHC 2003 (Admin); *Arunthavaraga v Administrative Court Office* [2009] EWHC 18921 (Admin); *R (Kane) v Trial Court No 5 Marbella, Spain* [2012] 1 WLR 375; *Regional Court in Konin, Poland v Walerianczyk* [2012] 1 WLR 363 DC; *R (Bergman) v District Court in Kladno, Czech Republic* [2011] EWHC 267 (Admin).

66 Service of an unsealed front sheet was not specifically addressed by the Supreme Court in *Lukaszewski*, but *R (Kane) v Trial Court No 5 Marbella, Spain* [2012] 1 WLR 375 (which was cited with apparent approval at para 6) suggests that this constitutes a valid, albeit irregular, notice of appeal.

terms of the rules. Provided it counts as a notice within the statute, the court is able to cure the irregularity if it thinks fit.[67]

9.36 Likewise, a notice of appeal which articulates no grounds of appeal will be valid, although irregular and in need of an application to amend. Resolving conflicting High Court authority,[68] in *Lukaszewski v The District Court in Torun, Poland* [2012] UKSC, para 19, the Supreme Court held that:

> to have any prospect of success an appeal must at some point be supported by grounds. Rules may provide that such grounds must be stated or summarised in the appeal notice, and do in fact do so: CPR 52.4, read with note 52.4.4, prescribed form N161 section 6 and Practice Direction – Appeal, para 3.2 at 52PD.5. *Non constat* however that a purported notice of appeal is a nullity unless accompanied from the outset by grounds. If, contrary to rules of court, it is not, that is an irregularity, but one which can in an appropriate case be cured under CPR 3.9 and 3.10. This is the position in principle. As a matter of practice also, there is no attraction in a conclusion whereby a notice without any grounds would be a nullity incapable of grounding any appeal, whereas a notice with palpably inadequate grounds would be merely irregular and capable of cure by amendment.

C. Appeals in Category 1 Cases

9.37 The relevant provisions are EA 2003, ss 26–34.

9.38 By s 34, a decision of the judge under Part 1 may be questioned in legal proceedings only by means of an appeal under Part 1.[69]

Rules of court

9.39 Paragraph 22.6A of the Practice Direction to CPR Part 52 contains the rules of court for appeals under ss 26(4) (appeals by the defendant)[70] and 28(5) (appeals by the requesting state).[71] In summary this paragraph provides that:

(a) Appeals to the High Court under the EA 2003 must be brought in the Administrative Court of the Queen's Bench Division.
(b) Where an appeal is brought under section 26 or 28 of the Act:
  (i) the appellant's notice must be filed and served before the expiry of seven days, starting with the day on which the order is made. As discussed above, this seven-day period is derived from statute rather than the CPR and is thus generally non-extendable. A notice of appeal lodged or served out of time will generally not be accepted and is fatal to the appeal;

---

[67] *Lukaszewski v The District Court in Torun, Poland* [2012] UKSC, para 20. cf *Szelagowski v The Regional Court of Piotrkow Trybunalski, Poland* [2011] EWHC 1033 (Admin).

[68] The Supreme Court upheld the approach adopted in *Polkowski v District Court in Kalisz, Poland* [2011] EWHC 3649 (Admin); *Filipek v Lublin Provincial Court, Poland* [2011] EWHC 1961 (Admin); *Radvilavicious v District Court of Alytus, Lithuania* [2011] EWHC 1795 (Admin); *Kaminski and Lukaszuk and Ciarach and Ziolkowski v Judicial Authority of Poland and Others* [2010] EWHC 2772 (Admin). Compare the approach adopted in *Koziel v District Court of Kielce, Poland* [2011] EWHC 3781 (Admin); *Urbonas v Prosecutor General's Office, Republic of Lithuania* [2011] EWHC 3124 (Admin); *R (Prahl) v District Court in Kwldzynie, Poland* [2011] EWHC 3050 (Admin); *Pomiechowski v District Court of Legunica 59-220, Poland* [2012] 1 WLR 391.

[69] See para 9.12 for a discussion of the extent to which this curtails the defendant's right to apply for judicial review and *habeas corpus*.

[70] See para 9.44.

[71] See para 9.64.

(ii) the appellant must endorse the appellant's notice with the date of the defendant's arrest;[72]

(iii) the appellant must serve a copy of the appellant's notice on the CPS, if they are not a party to the appeal, in addition to the persons to be served under rule 52.4(3) and in accordance with that rule;[73]

(iv) the High Court must begin to hear the substantive appeal within 40 days of the person's arrest, although the High Court may extend this period of 40 days if it believes it to be in the interests of justice to do so.[74]

Appeal by defendant against an order for extradition (s 26)

If the appropriate judge orders the defendant's extradition under Part 1, the defendant may appeal to the High Court against the order unless he consented to his extradition (s 26(1)). The appeal may be brought on a question of law or fact (s 26(3)).[75] **9.40**

Insofar as an appeal may be brought on a question of fact, the High Court will ordinarily pay respect to judicial findings of fact, made by designated judges with particular experience of extradition proceedings.[76] Many of the bars to extradition in Part 1 (and Part 2) depend upon finding that extradition, in particular circumstances, will be unjust or oppressive.[77] Where such bars are in play on an appeal, the High Court has been willing to show more flexibility rather than look for some error of reasoning. The High Court will form its own view of whether any bars to extradition are made out, and the court is not limited to a *Wednesbury* review of the judge's conclusions on this issue. In *Union of India v Narang* [1978] AC 247, 279, Lord Morris of Borth-y-Guest said: **9.41**

> No contrary opinion will lightly be formed. But if after due consideration a contrary opinion is in fact formed, those upon whom devolves the duty of considering the matter cannot in my view be absolved or inhibited from expressing their opinion. If they were, there would be little purpose in having an appeal.

In *Government of United States v Tollman* [2008] 3 All ER 350, para 95, Moses LJ commented that: **9.42**

> There is ample authority demonstrating differing views as to justice and injustice in which either the district judge or the Divisional Court or the House of Lords has reached a contrary view.

---

[72] Failure to comply with this provision is not fatal to an appeal; see *Office of Public Prosecutor of Hamburg, Germany v Hughes* [2009] EWHC 279 (Admin) discussed at para 9.32.

[73] Failure to comply with this provision is not fatal to an appeal. Whilst service on interested parties is required by the Practice Direction to CPR part 52, it is not a statutory requirement and failure does not deprive the court of jurisdiction to hear an appeal; *Aldhouse v Royal Government of Thailand* [2012] EWHC 191 (Admin).

[74] See s 31 discussed at para 9.72.

[75] Insofar as an appeal may be brought on a question of fact, the High Court will ordinarily pay respect to judicial findings of fact, made by designated judges with particular experience of extradition proceedings; *S v The Court of Bologna* [2010] EWHC 1184 (Admin); *Sinani v The Republic of Albania* [2009] EWHC 2773 (Admin); *Sciezka v The Court in Sad Okregowy, Kielce, Poland* [2009] EWHC 2748 (Admin); *Von Der Pahlen v Leoben High Court, Austria* [2009] EWHC 383 (Admin); *Wiejak v Olsztyn Circuit Court of Poland* [2007] EWHC 2123 (Admin).

[76] *S v The Court of Bologna* [2010] EWHC 1184 (Admin); *Sinani v The Republic of Albania* [2009] EWHC 2773 (Admin); *Sciezka v The Court in Sad Okregowy, Kielce, Poland* [2009] EWHC 2748 (Admin); *Von Der Pahlen v Leoben High Court, Austria* [2009] EWHC 383 (Admin); *Wiejak v Olsztyn Circuit Court of Poland* [2007] EWHC 2123 (Admin).

[77] Bars to extradition are discussed in Ch 5.

9.43 In *Howes v Her Majesty's Advocate* [2009] SCL 341 Lord Reed said in relation to s 91 giving the opinion of the court:

> A judgment as to whether it would be unjust or oppressive to extradite a requested person is not ... a technical issue of law, but requires the court to form an overall judgment upon the facts of the particular case: a judgment which ... is likely to reflect shades of grey rather than black or white. Previous cases are therefore illustrative of the court's approach rather than definitive of the circumstances in which an order for discharge may or may not be appropriate.

Procedure for appealing

9.44 Notice of an appeal under s 26 must be given in accordance with rules of court[78] before the end of the permitted period, which is seven days starting with the day on which the order is made (s 26(4)). This provision is discussed in detail at paras 9.23–9.36.

Powers on the appeal

9.45 Section 27(1) provides that on an appeal under s 26 the High Court may either allow the appeal or dismiss the appeal. There is no power under s 26 to remit the matter back to the district judge for reconsideration. If the High Court allows the appeal it must order the defendant's discharge and quash the order for his extradition (s 27(5)).

9.46 The court may allow the appeal only if the conditions in s 27(3) or (4) are satisfied (s 27(2)). The conditions in s 27(3) are that:

(a) the appropriate judge ought to have decided a question before him at the extradition hearing differently;
(b) if he had decided the question in the way he ought to have done, he would have been required to order the person's discharge.

9.47 The conditions in s 27(4) are that:

(a) an issue is raised that was not raised at the extradition hearing or evidence is available that was not available at the extradition hearing;
(b) the issue or evidence would have resulted in the appropriate judge deciding a question before him at the extradition hearing differently;
(c) if he had decided the question in that way, he would have been required to order the person's discharge.

Fresh evidence

9.48 Section 27(4) allows the High Court to receive fresh evidence on an appeal. In *Miklis v Deputy Prosecutor General of Lithuania* [2006] 4 All ER 808 the Administrative Court gave guidance where an appellant seeks to rely on fresh evidence under s 27(4). The defendant appealed under s 26 against an extradition order made in relation to offences of dishonesty. He submitted that the judge should not have made the order because, on the evidence before him, he should not have been satisfied that extradition would be compatible with his Convention rights within the meaning of the Human Rights Act 1998 (s 21(1)), and that it would be unjust or oppressive to extradite him by reason of his mental condition so as to have required his discharge pursuant to s 25 of the EA 2003.

9.49 Alternatively, the defendant submitted that the judge would have come to a different decision on these two issues if he had before him the fresh evidence put before the Administrative Court

[78] See para 9.39.

by the defendant, first as to treatment of offenders in Lithuania, and second as to the appellant's health, pursuant to s 27(2) and (4)(a). At para 3 Latham LJ said:

> It should be remembered that section 27(4) of the Act, dealing with new evidence, refers to evidence at the appeal 'that was not available at the extradition hearing'. The word 'available' makes it plain that, whilst I would not consider that the requirements of *Ladd v Marshall* [1954] 1 WLR 1489, had to be met where not only the liberty of the individual, but also matters relating to human rights are in issue, nonetheless the court will require to be persuaded that there is some good reason for the material not having been made available to the District Judge. And where there could be any suggestion of the Appellant 'keeping his powder dry' he must expect the court to view any application to rely on such evidence with some scepticism.

The question of when the Adminstrative Court will admit fresh evidence was considered in *Szombathely City Court v Fenyvesi* [2009] 4 All ER 324. This related to an appeal by the requesting state under s 29(4)(a), but the same test will apply under s 27(4).[79] In *Fenyvesi* the respondents were ethnic Roma who had challenged the EAW issued to secure their return on the grounds that it had been issued for the purpose of prosecuting or punishing them on account of their race (s 13(a)). They also argued that, if they were extradited, they might be prejudiced at their trial or punished or detained by reason of their race (s 13(b)). The evidence to support this argument was advanced at first instance and went unchallenged by the Hungarian issuing judicial authority. The judge at first instance was not persuaded that the arrest warrants were issued because they were of Roma origin but did conclude that they might be prejudiced at their trial or punished, detained, or restricted in their personal liberty by reason of their race and so discharged the arrest warrants. The Hungarian issuing judicial authority appealed and sought to adduce before the court fresh evidence not adduced before the district judge. The High Court concluded that: **9.50**

> In our judgment, evidence which was 'not available at the extradition hearing' means evidence which either did not exist at the time of the extradition hearing, or which was not at the disposal of the party wishing to adduce it and which he could not with reasonable diligence have obtained. If it was at the party's disposal or could have been so obtained, it was available. It may on occasions be material to consider whether or when the party knew the case he had to meet. But a party taken by surprise is able to ask for an adjournment. In addition, the court needs to decide that, if the evidence had been adduced, the result would have been different, resulting in the person's discharge. This is a strict test, consonant with the parliamentary intent and that of the Framework Decision, that extradition cases should be dealt with speedily and should not generally be held up by an attempt to introduce equivocal fresh evidence which was available to a diligent party at the extradition hearing. A party seeking to persuade the court that proposed evidence was not available should normally serve a witness statement explaining why it was not available. The appellants did not do this in the present appeal.[80]

Insofar as they are inconsistent with the approach taken in cases previously, the principles in *Fenyvesi* prevail.[81] The approach in *Fenyvesi* has been confirmed in a number of cases. Few of these cases expound any discrete principles of law, and most are fact-specific. However, some general principles emerge from the post-*Fenyvesi* case law. The test is a strict one.[82] There is no exception for foreign law.[83] A more lenient approach may be adopted on applications by defendants, where the liberty of the subject is at stake, as compared with requesting states.[84] **9.51**

---

79 *Kalniets v District Court of Ogre* [2009] EWHC 534 (Admin).
80 *Szombathely City Court and Ors v Fenyvesi and Another* [2009] 4 All ER 324 DC, para 32.
81 *Khan v Government of the United States of America* [2010] EWHC 1127 (Admin).
82 *R (Sidorowicz) v The Circuit Court of Zielona Gora, Poland* [2012] EWHC 206 (Admin).
83 *Beretki v Harghita Law Court, Romania* [2012] EWHC 336 (Admin).
84 *R (Hamodi) v Circuit Court in Gliwice, Poland* [2011] EWHC 620 (Admin).

Unrepresented defendants may be granted greater latitude.[85] Fresh evidence in draft form only and based on unconfirmed information and limited procedural documentation is inadmissible.[86] Unsigned evidence with no statement of truth is inadmissible.[87] Assertions of fault on the part of legal advisors below will require a waiver of privilege.[88] In all cases, a witness statement from the solicitor below is required explaining why the evidence was not adduced.[89] Failure of the duty solicitor to make appropriate enquiries is not an adequate reason.[90] A changed account is inadmissible without an explanation of the reason for the change.[91] Experts generally have the opportunity to address issues in evidence at first instance.[92] Accordingly, fresh medical opinion is inadmissible where no explanation is adduced for the doctor changing his opinion without an intervening examination.[93] A requesting state is expected to predict defence arguments.[94] Evidence is inadmissible where a defendant deliberately chose not to adduce evidence below after application for an adjournment was refused.[95] Evidence deliberately abandoned or not deployed below is not admissible.[96] Refusal of a district judge below to grant an adjournment to enable evidence to be obtained may be relevant.[97] It is artificial not to admit fresh evidence when the correctness of a refusal to adjourn (to obtain the evidence) is in issue.[98] Procedures for obtaining evidence from abroad are known to be cumbersome and time consuming.[99] Availability of evidence on the internet does not mean that it was available where diligence was exercised.[100] It is unfair to exclude evidence demonstrating a factual error by the appropriate judge.[101]

9.52 *Szombathely City Court v Fenyvesi* [2009] 4 All ER 324, paras 34-35, recognizes that the High Court's obligation to receive and consider fresh evidence may be stronger in a case concerning human rights:

> ... [the EA] is not expressed in terms which appear to give the court a discretion; although a degree of latitude may need to be introduced from elsewhere. As Latham LJ said in *Miklis*, there may occasionally be cases where what might otherwise be a breach of the European Convention on Human Rights may be avoided by admitting fresh evidence, tendered on behalf of a defendant, which a

---

85 *Nowicki v Military Court of Gydnia Poland* [2011] EWHC 1962 (Admin); *Kloska v Circuit Court in Katowice, Poland* [2011] EWHC 1647 (Admin).

86 *R (Advejevs) v Jekabplis District Court of the Republic of Latvia* [2011] EWHC 3049 (Admin).

87 *Jalocha v Judicial Authority of Poland* [2011] EWHC 3006 (Admin).

88 *Kis v District Court in Sokolov, Czech Republic* [2012] EWHC 938 (Admin); *R (Halahan) v Audiencia Provincial de Gupuzkoa, Spain* [2011] EWHC 621 (Admin); *R (Koniak) v Regional Court for Warsaw, Poland* [2010] EWHC 3501 (Admin); *Agundbiade v Court of Munich* [2010] EWHC 2116 (Admin); *Sondy v The Crown Prosecution Service* [2010] EWHC 108 (Admin).

89 *Krzyzak v Regional Court of Tarnow, Poland*; *Fugas v Circuit Court of Katowice, Poland* [2012] EWHC 810 (Admin).

90 *Chrzescijanski v Circuit Court of Olsztyn, Poland* [2012] EWHC 701 (Admin).

91 *R (Gaikis) v District Court of Cesis, Latvia* [2011] EWHC 3633 (Admin).

92 *Jones v District Court of Kaunus* [2010] EWHC 1684 (Admin).

93 *Hewitt and Woodward v First Instance and Magistrates' Court No 1 of Denia, Spain* [2009] EWHC 2158 (Admin).

94 *Olszewksi v Circuit Court in Katowice and Regional Court in Bialystok, Poland* [2011] EWHC 186 (Admin).

95 *Herdman, Taylor, Hollands, Branton and Bell v City of Westminster Magistrates' Court and Others* [2010] EWHC 1533 (Admin).

96 *Sondy v The Crown Prosecution Service* [2010] EWHC 108 (Admin). In *Jones v Government of the United States of America* [2012] EWHC 2332 (Admin), para 20, the High Court said that it was impermissible to raise on appeal a point abandoned in the lower court unless good reasons are put forward for so doing and explained in a witness statement.

97 *R (Sobczak) v Judicial Authority in Poland* [2011] EWHC 284 (Admin).

98 *Usti Nad Labem Regional Court, Czech Republic v Janiga* [2010] EWHC 463 (Admin).

99 *Usti Nad Labem Regional Court, Czech Republic v Janiga* [2010] EWHC 463 (Admin).

100 *Mihociu v Central Court of the District of Pest, Hungary* [2010] EWHC 708 (Admin).

101 *Mihociu v Central Court of the District of Pest, Hungary* [2010] EWHC 708 (Admin).

> strict application of the section would not permit. The justification for this would be a modulation of section 29(4) with reference to section 3 of the Human Rights Act 1998 ... This apparent imbalance between defendants and judicial authorities arises from the fact that a defendant may have the benefit of Human Rights considerations which the judicial authorities do not.[102]
>
> [However] even for defendants, the court will not readily admit fresh evidence which they should have adduced before the District Judge, and which is tendered to try to repair holes which should have been plugged before the District Judge, simply because it has a human rights label attached to it. The threshold remains high. The court must still be satisfied that the evidence would have resulted in the judge deciding the relevant question differently, so that he would not have ordered the defendant's discharge. In short, the fresh evidence must be decisive.[103]

It is now widely recognized that human rights cases represent an exception to the general rigour with which s 27(4) is applied. In *R (Gorczowska) v District Court in Torun Poland* [2012] EWHC 378 (Admin), para 7, Collins J said: **9.53**

> This court is a public body and, in accordance with the terms of the Human Rights Act, has to take account of a party's human rights in deciding any case. That seems to me to mean that it is more likely that the court should take account of evidence which goes directly to human rights, even if that evidence was not, but could have been, produced below. It does not mean that in every case it would be appropriate to take it into account, but it seems to me that it would not normally be right to ignore it.

However, even in human rights cases, the fresh evidence must be decisive.[104] **9.54**

Fresh issues

Section 27(4) also allows the court to consider fresh legal issues on an appeal. On one reading of s 27(4)(a) the ability to raise a fresh legal issue on appeal is not constrained in any way. That is the construction which initially prevailed in Scotland. In *Trajer v Lord Advocate* (2009) JC 108 the High Court of Justiciary took the view that the language of the EA 2003 permitted it to hear an appeal based on a new issue without any form of constraint or need for justification of the course taken below. However, subsequent cases have taken a more nuanced approach. Many cases raising a fresh issue will almost invariably require the admission of fresh evidence to substantiate them. Where fresh evidence is required to make good the fresh legal issue, the court will apply the principles applicable to fresh evidence (discussed at para 9.48).[105] **9.55**

It is only where the fresh legal issue can be argued and determined upon the evidence already adduced below that different considerations may come into play. This was the approach in *Hoholm v The Government of Norway* [2009] EWHC 1513 (Admin), where, noting that the EA 2003 distinguishes between new issues and new evidence, the High Court held that if the issue was available to be raised on the evidence adduced at the hearing then a defendant is in general, if not always, entitled to raise it on appeal.[106] **9.56**

However, in *Khan v Government of the United States of America* [2010] EWHC 1127 (Admin), the correctness of this approach was doubted. *Khan* was a case where the fresh issue sought to be raised required the admission of fresh evidence. The Court observed that the distinction drawn in *Hoholm* was 'difficult to follow' and that the same principles should govern the admission **9.57**

---

[102] *Szombathely City Court v Fenyvesi* [2009] 4 All ER 324, para 34.
[103] *Szombathely City Court v Fenyvesi* [2009] 4 All ER 324, para 35.
[104] *Beretki v Harghita Law Court, Romania* [2012] EWHC 336 (Admin).
[105] *Engler v Her Majesty's Advocate* [2010] HCJAC 42; *Kapri v The Lord Advocate, for and on behalf of the Republic of Albania* [2012] HCJAC 17.
[106] Per Stanley Burnton LJ at para 19.

of fresh issues and fresh evidence in all cases. In *Khan* the Court said that there was no good reason why the issue of forum had not been raised below (previous representatives had taken the view that the issue was unarguable) and special circumstances were required to depart from the EA 2003 (there, s 104(4)).

9.58 The difference of approach in *Hoholm v The Government of Norway* [2009] EWHC 1513 (Admin) and *Khan v Government of the United States of America* [2010] EWHC 1127 was revisited in *Herdman, Taylor, Hollands, Branton and Bell v City of Westminster Magistrates' Court* [2010] EWHC 1533 (Admin), para 26. The Court said that the *Hoholm* approach was applicable where the issue was available to be raised on the evidence adduced at the hearing. In *R (Soltysiak) v Judicial Authority of Poland* [2011] EWHC 1338 (Admin), a case concerning a fresh issue not dependent upon fresh evidence, *Hoholm* was approved and observations to the contrary in *Khan* were held to have been made *obiter*. The *Hoholm* approach may now be regarded as settled law and has been approved and applied regularly since.[107]

9.59 Section 2 'validity' issues may be raised on appeal regardless of the course taken below. In *Boudhiba v Central Examining Court No 5 of the National Court of Justice, Madrid* [2007] 1 WLR 124 DC the defendant's extradition was ordered by the judge under Part 1 of the EA 2003 and he appealed under s 26. At the extradition hearing no point had been taken about the validity of the Part 1 warrant and he sought to raise the issue before the Administrative Court that the warrant did not comply with s 2(3)(a).[108]

9.60 The respondent took a preliminary point on this ground of appeal. It submitted that this argument had not been raised before the district judge and submitted that it could not therefore be raised on appeal. It was submitted that s 27(2) and (4) provide that an appeal may be allowed where a new issue is raised or new evidence is presented at an appeal but only if that new issue or evidence would have resulted in the district judge deciding a question before him at the extradition hearing differently. It was thus argued that new issues can be raised and new evidence presented but the Administrative Court cannot be asked to decide questions that were not before the district judge, the word 'question' having a specific meaning under the EA 2003, namely, the questions which begin at s 10 which the appropriate judge has to decide before ordering extradition or discharge. It was argued that these are the only questions for the judge at the extradition hearing.

9.61 The Government's contention was that it was open to an appellant to argue a new issue but not to raise a question which had not been raised before. The Government accepted that it was at least arguable that, under s 11, the district judge had to decide the question raised by each potential bar to extradition, whether or not he received submissions about it. The Government therefore accepted that it would be open to an appellant to raise any bar to extradition on appeal, even though it had not been raised below. But, it submitted, the argument under s 2(3)(a) of the 2003 Act was not a question that could ever arise for the district judge at the extradition hearing.

9.62 In rejecting this submission Smith LJ said at para 15:

> The structure of the 2003 Act purports to set out exhaustively the procedure to be followed. Certain questions are to be considered at the initial hearing; then others at the extradition hearing. On the face of it, the adequacy of the warrant and compliance with the requirements

---

107 *Voros v The District Courts of Sopron, Gyor and Zalaegerszeg, Hungary* [2012] EWHC 518 (Admin); *Sypnieswska v Regional Court of Poznan, Poland* [2012] EWHC 899 (Admin); *Polkowski v District Court in Kalisz, Poland* [2011] EWHC 3649 (Admin); *Zgudka v Regional Court in Kielce, Poland* [2011] EWHC 1258 (Admin); *Krajewski v Circuit Court of Torun, Poland and Another* [2011] EWHC 1068 (Admin).

108 See para 2.09.

of s 2 are not questions to be considered at either hearing. From their position in the 2003 Act, it appears that they are preliminary matters which should be considered before the warrant is given a certificate by the designated authority in this country pursuant to s 2(7). However, we were told that, prior to certification, the warrant is scrutinised by the Crown Prosecution Service, who may seek the advice of counsel. This is necessarily a one-sided process. If the warrant is certificated, the arrest is authorised. If the person arrested considers that the warrant is inadequate and his arrest unlawful, he can apply for *habeas corpus*. But, if he does not do that and the case proceeds against him, must it be taken that he has waived any objection to the validity of the warrant? On reflection, I think not. The warrant founds the jurisdiction of the appropriate judge. Even if no objection is taken to the validity of the warrant, it must be assumed that the court has considered and been satisfied as to its validity. Otherwise it could not have accepted jurisdiction. So, even though validity is not expressly mentioned in the 2003 Act as a question which must be determined, it must be treated as a question which has been answered. If, at any stage of the proceedings, the question of validity is raised, it calls jurisdiction into question. For that reason, despite the absence of an express power to consider compliance with s 2(3) or (4), I am satisfied that the appropriate judge is entitled to consider and determine whether, as the result of non-compliance with those provisions, he does not have jurisdiction. Further, the jurisdiction of this court is also dependent on the validity of the warrant. So, although s 27 permits this court to allow an appeal only if it is satisfied that the appropriate judge ought to have decided a question before him at the extradition hearing differently or would have decided it differently if he or she had considered the new issues or evidence raised on appeal, this court can still examine the validity of the warrant. If this court were to hold that the warrant did not comply with s 2, the proceedings would have been a nullity.

Appeal by the requesting state against an order for discharge (s 28)

If the judge orders a person's discharge at the extradition hearing the authority which issued the Part 1 warrant may appeal to the High Court against the relevant decision, that is the decision which resulted in the order for the person's discharge (s 28(3)), unless the order for discharge was under s 41 (withdrawal of warrant) (s 28(1) and (2)). An appeal under s 28 may be brought on a question of law or fact (s 28(4)).[109] **9.63**

Procedure for appealing

Notice of an appeal must be given in accordance with rules of court[110] before the end of the permitted period, which is seven days starting with the day on which the order for the person's discharge is made (s 28(5)). This provision is governed by the principles discussed at paras 9.23–9.36. **9.64**

Powers on the appeal

On an appeal under s 28 the High Court may either allow the appeal or dismiss the appeal (s 29(1)). **9.65**

The court may allow the appeal only if the conditions in s 29(3) or (4) are satisfied (s 29(2)). The conditions in s 29(3) are that: **9.66**

(a) the judge ought to have decided the relevant question differently;

[109] Insofar as an appeal may be brought on a question of fact, the High Court will ordinarily pay respect to judicial findings of fact, made by designated judges with particular experience of extradition proceedings; *S v The Court of Bologna* [2010] EWHC 1184 (Admin); *Sinani v The Republic of Albania* [2009] EWHC 2773 (Admin); *Sciezka v The Court in Sad Okregowy, Kielce, Poland* [2009] EWHC 2748 (Admin); *Von Der Pahlen v Leoben High Court, Austria* [2009] EWHC 383 (Admin); *Wiejak v Olsztyn Circuit Court of Poland* [2007] EWHC 2123 (Admin).

[110] See para 9.39.

(b) if he had decided the question in the way he ought to have done, he would not have been required to order the person's discharge.

9.67 The conditions in s 29(4) are that:

(a) an issue is raised that was not raised at the extradition hearing or evidence is available that was not available at the extradition hearing;[111]
(b) the issue or evidence would have resulted in the judge deciding the relevant question differently;
(c) if he had decided the question in that way, he would not have been required to order the person's discharge.

9.68 If the court allows the appeal it must (s 29(5)):

(a) quash the order discharging the person;
(b) remit the case to the judge;
(c) direct him to proceed as he would have been required to do if he had decided the relevant question differently at the extradition hearing. By s 29(6), a question is the relevant question if the judge's decision on it resulted in the order for the person's discharge. Once remitted, the extradition proceeding re-commences, and the district judge is required by statute to determine all outstanding issues and either order extradition or discharge the defendant again. In either case, the provisions of ss 26 and 28 are re-engaged. Of course, in parallel with this process, the case may proceed to the Supreme Court under s 32 against the decision on the appeal to the High Court.

9.69 Section 29(7) and (8), inserted by para 7 to Sch 13 to the Police and Justice Act 2006, provide that if the court allows the appeal it must remand the person in custody or on bail, and that if the court remands the person in custody it may later grant bail.

Detention pending an appeal under s 28 by the requesting state

9.70 Where a defendant is discharged and the requesting state successfully appeals there is an obvious risk that he will have absconded by the time of that decision, rendering it no more than a *brutum fulmen*.[112] Hence, where the judge orders the defendant's discharge, the requesting state has the right to have the defendant detained in custody or on bail pending an appeal to the High Court under s 28 provided that, immediately after the appropriate judge orders the defendant's discharge, the judge is informed by the authority which issued the Part 1 warrant that it intends to appeal under (s 30(1)). The judge must then remand the person in custody or on bail while the appeal is pending (s 30(2)), and if the judge remands the person in custody, he may later grant bail (s 30(3)).

9.71 An appeal under s 28 ceases to be pending at the earliest of these times (s 30(4)):

(a) when the proceedings on the appeal are discontinued;
(b) when the High Court allows the appeal, or dismisses the appeal, unless, where the appeal is dismissed, the authority immediately informs the court that it intends to apply for leave to appeal to the Supreme Court;[113]

---

[111] See paras 9.48–9.62.
[112] An 'innocuous thunderbolt'; Lord Diplock's memorable phrase in *Government of the United States of America v McCaffery* [1984] 1 WLR 867 HL, 873, where precisely that happened and the defendant disappeared after the High Court's decision in his favour.
[113] EA 2003, s 30(4)(b), as amended by para 8(2)(a) of Sch 13 to the Police and Justice Act 2006.

(c) at the end of the permitted period, which is 28 days starting with the day on which leave to appeal to the Supreme Court against the decision of the High Court on the appeal is granted if no appeal to the Supreme Court is brought before the end of that period;[114]
(d) when there is no further step that can be taken by the authority which issued the Part 1 warrant in relation to the appeal (ignoring any power of a court to grant leave to take a step out of time).

Time limit for start of hearing of appeal to High Court

In accordance with its overall purpose of speeding up the extradition process, and Article 17 of the EAW Framework Decision, the EA 2003 contains provisions which require that rules of court be made setting time limits for the hearing of appeals by the High Court against the appropriate judge's decision. However, these time limits are hardly ever adhered to in practice because of the work load of the High Court. **9.72**

Section 31(1) and (2) contains provisions relating to the making of rules of court regarding time limits for s 26 and s 28 appeals. The rules must prescribe the period (the relevant period) within which the High Court must begin to hear an appeal. They must also provide for the relevant period to start with the date on which the person in respect of whom a Part 1 warrant is issued: **9.73**

(a) was arrested under s 5, if he was arrested under that section;
(b) was arrested under the Part 1 warrant, if he was not arrested under s 5.

The High Court must begin[115] to hear the appeal before the end of the relevant period (s 31(3)). The High Court may extend the relevant period if it believes it to be in the interests of justice to do so (s 31(4)).[116] The power in s 31(4) may be exercised even after the end of the relevant period.[117] **9.74**

As explained above,[118] para 22.6A of the Practice Direction to CPR Part 52 prescribes 40 days as the relevant period. **9.75**

---

[114] EA 2003, s 30(4)(c), as amended by para 8(2)(b) of Sch 13 to the Police and Justice Act 2006.

[115] The point at which the High Court begins to hear an appeal may be difficult to ascertain. In *Moulai v Deputy Public Prosecutor of Creteil, France* [2009] EWHC 1030 (Admin), it was argued that a preliminary hearing, concerning whether notice of appeal had been properly given and thus whether the court had jurisdiction to entertain the appeal, did not commence the hearing of the appeal. The issue was ultimately not decided.

[116] The requirements of the interests of justice were considered in *Wright v City of Westminster Magistrates' Court* [2011] EWHC 515 (Admin), a Part 2 case. Whether an extension of time should be refused is matter of discretion. The time limits are important and oversight by the court, whilst not a complete answer, is a relevant consideration. Exceptionality is not required for the grant of an extension. Relevant considerations included, on the facts, that no realistic objection could have been raised at time, that delay in the hearing of the appeal was due to the appellant's requests for time, that neither party sought to have the case listed earlier, the seriousness of the offence, the absence of prejudice (relevant but not decisive), the fact that the defendant was on bail throughout, and the public interest in international extradition.

[117] The power to extend time can be exercised even after time has expired; *Office of the King's Prosecutor, Brussels v Cando Armas* [2005] 1 WLR 1389. In *Moulai v Deputy Public Prosecutor of Creteil, France* [2009] EWHC 1030 (Admin), the High Court held at paras 14–16 that the express wording of s 31(5) meant that the power to extend time can be exercised even after time has expired, and even if the application to extend is made after the expiry of the period, if the court believes it to be in the interests of justice to do so. The correctness of *Moulai* was affirmed in *Wright v City of Westminster Magistrates' Court* [2011] EWHC 515 (Admin), a decision under s 113, the materially identical provision in Part 2. In *Statkevicius v Prosecutor General Office, Lithuania* [2011] EWHC 2733 (Admin), it was held at paras 16–21 that an application to extend time under s 31(5) may be made and entertained even after a defendant has lodged, and as a response to, an application for relief under s 31(6).

[118] See para 9.39.

Disposal of appeal if time limit not complied with

9.76 If s 31(3) is not complied with, and the appeal is under s 26, the appeal must be taken to have been allowed by a decision of the High Court; the person whose extradition has been ordered must be taken to have been discharged by the High Court; and the order for the person's extradition must be taken to have been quashed by the High Court (s 31(6)). If s 31(3) is not complied with and the appeal is under s 28, the appeal must be taken to have been dismissed by a decision of the High Court (s 31(7)).

9.77 In *Statkevicius v Prosecutor General Office, Lithuania* [2011] EWHC 2733 (Admin), paras 16–21, it was held that an application to further extend time under s 31(5) may be made and entertained even after a party has lodged, and as a response to, an application for relief under s 31(6).

Appeals to the Supreme Court (s 32)

9.78 Under the EA 1989 the defendant and the requesting state could appeal, with leave, to the House of lords from a decision of the High Court dismissing or allowing an application for a writ of *habeas corpus ad subjiciendum.*[119] By s 15(3) of the Administration of Justice Act 1960, no certificate of a point of law of general public importance was required. The EA 2003 removes this indulgence and brings extradition appeals into line with other criminal appeals by requiring a certificate from the High Court, as well as the grant of leave to appeal.

9.79 Section 32(1) provides that an appeal lies to the Supreme Court from a decision of the High Court on an appeal under s 26 or 28. The appeal can be brought by the person in respect of whom the Part 1 warrant was issued and the authority which issued the Part 1 warrant.

9.80 An appeal lies only with the leave of the High Court or the Supreme Court (s 32(3)). Section 32(4) provides that leave to appeal must not be granted unless the High Court has certified that there is a point of law of general public importance involved in the decision,[120] and it appears to the court granting leave that the point is one which ought to be considered by the Supreme Court.

9.81 An application to the High Court for leave to appeal must be made before the end of the permitted period, which is 14 days starting with the day on which the court makes its decision on the appeal (s 32(5)).[121]

9.82 An application to the Supreme Court for leave to appeal under s 32 must be made before the end of the permitted period, which is 14 days starting with the day on which the High Court refuses leave to appeal (s 32(6)). It is to be observed that, on its face, this time limit is absolute

[119] Administration of Justice Act 1960, s 1.

[120] In *Pilecki v Circuit Court of Legnica, Poland* [2008] 1 WLR 325, it was noted that where a point of law of general public importance had been certified under s 32(4) of the EA 2003, with the result that an application for leave to appeal to the Supreme Court became competent, the proper procedure was for inquiries to be made with the Judicial Office as to what progress, if any, had been made with the application before it was concluded that a decision of the High Court had become final in terms of s 36(5).

[121] In relation to the expiry of this period, see *Owens v City of Westminster Magistrates' Court* [2010] 1 WLR 17. A refusal by the High Court to certify a point of law following an unsuccessful extradition appeal to the High Court does not of itself make the High Court's decision final or abridge the period of 14 days allowed for making an appeal against the High Court's decision. The High Court reasoned that the remainder of the 14-day period continued to run so as to permit the applicant to renew the application to certify, or to apply to certify additional points of law. Accordingly, the full period of 14 days had to have expired before a decision of the High Court became final and the period of ten days for surrender under s 36 could commence. Where, on the other hand, the decision on certification is taken by the High Court after the expiry of the 14 days, then a refusal to certify will render the High Court's decision final immediately; *Wood v City of Westminster Magistrates' Court* [2007] EWHC 2058 (Admin).

and, unlike s 2(3) of the Administration of Justice Act 1960, there is no power for the High Court or Supreme Court to grant an extension. This inflexibility has the potential to cause serious difficulties for an extradition defendant. Following the decision of the Supreme Court in *Lukaszewski v The District Court in Torun, Poland* [2012] UKSC 20 it is arguable that this provision must be read down under s 3 of the Human Rights Act 1998 so as to permit applications out of time by UK citizens.[122]

If leave to appeal is granted, the appeal must be brought[123] before the end of the permitted period, which is 28 days starting with the day on which leave is granted (s 32(7)). Section 32(8) provides that if s 32(7) is not complied with then the appeal must be taken to have been brought and it must be taken to have been dismissed by the Supreme Court immediately after the end of the period permitted under s 32(7). **9.83**

By s 32(9), any power of a court to extend the period permitted for bringing the appeal and any power of a court to grant leave to take a step out of time must be ignored for the purposes of s 32(8)(b). **9.84**

The High Court may grant bail to a person appealing under s 32, or applying for leave to appeal under s 32, against the dismissal of his appeal under s 26 (s 32(10)).[124] **9.85**

Section 32(11) and (12) contain provisions relating to the composition of the Supreme Court for the hearing and determination of appeals. **9.86**

By s 32(13), no right of appeal under the EA 2003 lies from a decision of the High Court of Justiciary in Scotland to the Supreme Court. However, in *BH v The Lord Advocate & Ors* [2012] 3 WLR 151, the Supreme Court held (in the context of the Part 2 provisions of s 114) that a right of appeal exists as a devolution issue under the Scotland Act 1998, Sch 6. This is the case despite the incompatibility of a devolution appeal with the operation of the required period for surrender in s 36. Moreover, such an appeal will, where brought by the requesting state against an order for discharge, suffer the obvious problem that the s 33A power to remand the defendant in custody pending appeal will not, as the law presently stands, be available. **9.87**

Powers of the Supreme Court on the appeal

Section 33 sets out the powers of the Supreme Court on an appeal under s 32 and provides that the Supreme Court may allow the appeal, or dismiss the appeal. **9.88**

Where the appeal is brought by the defendant (against an order upholding his extradition) and the appeal is allowed, the Supreme Court must order the person's discharge and quash the order for his extradition, if the appeal was against a decision of the High Court to dismiss an appeal under s 26 (s 33(3)). **9.89**

Where the appeal is brought by the requesting authority against the allowing of an appeal under s 26 brought by the defendant, and the Supreme Court allows the requesting authority's appeal, it must (s 33(5)): **9.90**

(a) quash the order of the High Court under s 27(5) discharging the person;
(b) order the person to be extradited to the Category 1 territory in which the warrant was issued.

122 See para 9.29.
123 The EA 2003 does not define when an appeal is 'brought' but it plainly cannot mean 'heard'. Under the Supreme Court's procedures, an appeal is brought when the Petition of Appeal is lodged.
124 Inserted by para 8(3) of Sch 13 to the Police and Justice Act 2006.

9.91 Where the appeal is brought by the requesting authority against the dismissal of an appeal under s 28 brought by the requesting authority, and the Supreme Court allows the requesting authority's appeal:

(a) if the judge would have been required to order the person in respect of whom the warrant was issued to be extradited had he decided the relevant question differently, the Supreme Court must (s 33(7)):
   (i) quash the order of the judge discharging the person;
   (ii) order the person to be extradited to the Category 1 territory in which the warrant was issued.
(b) in any other case, the Supreme Court must (s 33(8)):
   (i) quash the order of the judge discharging the person in respect of whom the warrant was issued;
   (ii) remit the case to the judge;
   (iii) direct him to proceed as he would have been required to do if he had decided the relevant question differently at the extradition hearing. By s 33(9), a question is the relevant question if the judge's decision on it resulted in the order for the person's discharge.

9.92 No provision is made for remission to the district judge for reconsideration of the issue that gave rise to the appeal. However, in *Norris v Government of the United States of America* [2008] 1 AC 920, at para 110, notwithstanding the existence of no express power to remit in s 115 EA (the corresponding Part 2 provision), it was held that:

> we have no doubt that the House has an inherent power to remit determination of an issue to an inferior tribunal where the interests of justice so require, and that is a power which nothing in the 2003 Act purports to abrogate.[125]

9.93 Sections 33(10) and (11), inserted by para 8(4) of Sch 13 to the Police and Justice Act 2006, provide that in a case where s 32(5), (7), or (8) applies, the Supreme Court must remand, in custody or on bail, the person in respect of whom the warrant was issued, and if the Supreme Court remands the person in custody the High Court may later grant bail.

Detention pending an appeal under s 32 by the requesting state

9.94 As originally drafted, the EA contained no provision for a defendant to be detained, or his bail continued, pending an appeal by the requesting state to the Supreme Court. Section 33A, inserted by para 8(5) of Sch 13 to the Police and Justice Act 2006, contains provisions concerning remand pending appeals under s 32. Section 33A mirrors, with appropriate modification, the provisions of s 30 discussed at para 9.70.

D. Appeals in Category 2 Cases

9.95 As has been noted at para 9.01, one of the Government's principal criticisms of the EA 1989 related to what it saw as the unnecessary multiplicity of defendant appeals. The EA 2003 addresses this issue by removing the Secretary of State's general discretion to refuse extradition,[126] severely curtailing the right of the defendant to make representations to the Secretary of State,

[125] There can be no doubt that the Supreme Court has the same power, both as part of the inherent jurisdiction transferred to it from the House of Lords, and pursuant to s 40(5) of the Constitutional Reform Act 2005, by which the Court has power 'to determine any question necessary to be determined for the purposes of doing justice' in an appeal to it under any enactment.

[126] cf EA 1989, s 12.

and by providing for a single combined statutory appeal to the High Court against both the appropriate judge's decision to send the case to the Secretary of State, and the Secretary of State's decision to order return.

The relevant provisions are ss 103–116. They provide for appeals against decisions made by the appropriate judge under Part 2 and also decisions made by the Secretary of State. **9.96**

By s 116, a decision of the judge or the Secretary of State under Part 2 may be questioned in legal proceedings only by means of an appeal under Part 2.[127] **9.97**

Rules of court

The rules of court governing appeals under Part 2 are contained in para 22.6A(5)–(12) of the Practice Direction to CPR Part 52. In summary: **9.98**

(a) Where an appeal is brought under s 103, the appellant's notice must be filed and served before the expiry of 14 days, starting with the day on which the Secretary of State informs the person under s 100(1) or (4) of the Act of the order he has made in respect of the person. As discussed above, this 14-day period is derived from statute rather than the CPR and therefore cannot generally be extended. Therefore if the notice of appeal is filed or served out of time there can generally be no valid appeal.[128]
(b) Where an appeal is brought under s 105 of the Act, the appellant's notice must be filed and served before the expiry of 14 days, starting with the day on which the order for discharge is made. As discussed above, this 14-day period can't be extended.
(c) Where an appeal is brought under s 108 of the Act the appellant's notice must be filed and served before the expiry of 14 days, starting with the day on which the Secretary of State informs the person that he has ordered his extradition. Again, this 14-day period is derived from statute rather than the CPR and generally cannot be extended.[129]
(d) Where an appeal is brought under s 110 of the Act the appellant's notice must be filed and served before the expiry of 14 days, starting with the day on which the Secretary of State informs the person acting on behalf of a Category 2 territory, as defined in s 69 of the Act, of the order for discharge. This period cannot be extended.[130]
(e) Subject to para 22.6A(10), where an appeal is brought under s 103, 105, 108, or 110, the High Court must begin to hear the substantive appeal within 76 days of the appellant's notice being filed.[131]
(f) Para 22.6A(10) provides that where an appeal is brought under s 103 before the Secretary of State has decided whether the person is to be extradited then the period of 76 days does not start until the day on which the Secretary of State informs the person of his decision; and the Secretary of State must, as soon as practicable after he informs the person of his decision, inform the High Court of his decision and of the date on which he informed the person of his decision.

[127] See para 9.12 for a discussion of s 34, the equivalent provision in Part 1 cases, and the extent to which it curtails the defendant' s right to apply for judicial review and *habeas corpus*.

[128] *Mucelli v Government of Albania* and *Moulai v Deputy Public Prosecutor in Cretiel, France* [2009] 1 WLR 276. See para 9.26.

[129] *Mucelli v Government of Albania* and *Moulai v Deputy Public Prosecutor in Cretiel, France* [2009] 1 WLR 276. See para 9.26.

[130] *Mucelli v Government of Albania* and *Moulai v Deputy Public Prosecutor in Cretiel, France* [2009] 1 WLR 276. See para 9.26

[131] See s 113 discussed at para 9.138.

(g) The High Court may extend the period of 76 days if it believes it to be in the interests of justice to do so.
(h) Where an appeal is brought under s 103, 105, 108, or 110 of the Act, the appellant must serve a copy of the appellant's notice on the CPS and the Home Office, if they are not a party to the appeal, in addition to the persons to be served under CPR 52.4(3) and in accordance with that rule.[132]

Appeal by the defendant against appropriate judge's decision (s 103)

9.99 If the appropriate judge sends a case to the Secretary of State under Part 2 for his decision whether the defendant is to be extradited, the defendant may appeal to the High Court against that (the relevant) decision (s 103(1)), unless he consented to his extradition under s 127 (s 103(2)). The relevant decision is the decision that resulted in the case being sent to the Secretary of State (s 103(3)). The appeal may be brought on a question of law or fact (s 103(4)).[133] No appeal can be brought under this section if the Secretary of State has already ordered the person's discharge (s 103(7)).

Procedure for appealing

9.100 Notice of the appeal must be given in accordance with rules of court[134] before the end of the permitted period, which is 14 days starting with the day on which the Secretary of State informs the defendant under s 100(1) or (4) of the order he has made in respect of him (s 103(9)). This provision is governed by the principles discussed at paras 9.23–9.36.

9.101 Importantly, s 103(5) provides that if the appeal is brought before the Secretary of State has decided whether the person is to be extradited, the appeal must not be heard until after the Secretary of State has made his decision. If the Secretary of State then orders the person's discharge the appeal must not be proceeded with (s 103(6)). However, where the Secretary of State discharges the defendant, and notice of an appeal under s 110 is given by the requesting state, s 103(6) and (7) do not apply, but no appeal may be brought under s 103 if the High Court has made its decision on the s 110 appeal (s 103(9)).

Powers on the appeal

9.102 On an appeal under s 103 the High Court may allow the appeal (s 104(1)(a)); direct the judge to decide again a question (or questions) which he decided at the extradition hearing (s 104(1)(b)); or dismiss the appeal (s 104(1)(c)).

9.103 The court may only allow the appeal if the conditions in s 104(3) or (4) are satisfied (s 104(2)). The conditions in s 104(3) are that:

(a) the judge ought to have decided a question before him at the extradition hearing differently;

---

[132] Failure to comply with this provision is not fatal to an appeal. Whilst service on interested parties is required by the Practice Direction to CPR Part 52, it is not a statutory requirement and so a failure to comply with it does not deprive the court of jurisdiction to hear an appeal; *Aldhouse v Royal Government of Thailand* [2012] EWHC 191 (Admin).

[133] Insofar as an appeal may be brought on a question of fact, the High Court will ordinarily pay respect to judicial findings of fact, made by designated judges with particular experience of extradition proceedings; *S v The Court of Bologna* [2010] EWHC 1184 (Admin); *Sinani v The Republic of Albania* [2009] EWHC 2773 (Admin); *Sciezka v The Court in Sad Okregowy, Kielce, Poland* [2009] EWHC 2748 (Admin); *Von Der Pahlen v Leoben High Court, Austria* [2009] EWHC 383 (Admin); *Wiejak v Olsztyn Circuit Court of Poland* [2007] EWHC 2123 (Admin).

[134] See para 9.98.

(b) if he had decided the question in the way he ought to have done, he would have been required to order the person's discharge.

The conditions in s 104(4) are that: **9.104**

(a) an issue is raised that was not raised at the extradition hearing or evidence is available that was not available at the extradition hearing;[135]
(b) the issue or evidence would have resulted in the judge deciding a question before him at the extradition hearing differently;
(c) if he had decided the question in that way, he would have been required to order the person's discharge.

If the court allows the appeal (under s 104(1)(a)) it must order the person's discharge and quash the order for his extradition (s 104(5)). **9.105**

Section 104(1)(b) remittal for reconsideration

Where the case is remitted to the appropriate judge for re-determination under s 104(1)(b), the hearing of the remitted question is not an 'extradition hearing' within the meaning of s 140; it is an appeal hearing as defined by s 104.[136] If the judge comes to the same decision as he did at the extradition hearing on the question that is (or all the questions that are) the subject of a direction under s 104(1)(b) the appeal must be taken to have been dismissed by a decision of the High Court (s 104(7)). **9.106**

In *R (Okandeji) v Bow Street Magistrates' Court* [2006] 1 WLR 674, the claimant's extradition was requested by the Government of Australia. The district judge sent the case to the Secretary of State for a decision as to whether the claimant should be extradited pursuant to s 87(3) of the EA 2003. The Secretary of State made an order for extradition and the claimant appealed to the High Court, pursuant to s 103. The High Court sent the case back to the district judge, pursuant to s 104(1)(b), with a direction that he should decide again a question in relation to drugs and bail offences upon receipt of further evidence from the Australian Government. Following further evidence, the district judge decided the question against the defendant again. By that decision, the original appeal stood dismissed (s 104(7)). The judge declined to send the case again to the Secretary of State, with the result that no appeal lay against this second decision. The claimant applied for judicial review of that refusal. Maurice Kay LJ held that judicial review was not available (s 116), and that s 104(7) was not to be properly characterized as a provision ousting the supervisory jurisdiction of the High Court and thus objectionable on that ground. The only avenue of appeal open to the defendant against the district judge's second decision was an appeal directly to the Supreme Court under s 114: **9.107**

> Where this court has remitted a question to the district judge under section 104(1)(b) but the district judge has come to the same conclusion as he did at the original extradition hearing, 'the appeal must be taken to have been dismissed by a decision of the High Court' [s 104(7)]. In these circumstances, judicial review of the second decision of the district judge is simply unavailable. This is made abundantly clear by section 116 which limits challenges to decisions of District Judges to the appeal procedure described by Part 2. Accordingly, a deemed decision of the High Court is not amenable to judicial review by the High Court nor to any route of appeal save that, in an appropriate case, the deemed decision may result in an appeal to the House of Lords under section 114 subject to certification and leave.[137]

135 This provision is governed by the principles discussed at paras 9.48–9.62.
136 *Chen and Mitoi v Government of Romania* [2009] 1 WLR 257 DC, para 58.
137 *R (Okandeji) v Bow Street Magistrates' Court* [2006] 1 WLR 674 was approved in *Chen and Mitoi v Government of Romania* [2009] 1 WLR 257 DC.

9.108 Where on the other hand the case is remitted to the appropriate judge for re-determination under s 104(1)(b), and the judge comes to a *different* decision on the question remitted, he must order the person's discharge (s 104(6)). The judge is limited, by s 104(1)(b), to deciding again the questions which he decided at the extradition hearing. He may not, having decided those questions differently, resume the extradition hearing.

9.109 In *Chen and Mitoi v Government of Romania* [2009] 1 WLR 257 the defendant raised an issue under s 85 following his conviction *in absentia*. The district judge found that he had deliberately absented himself from trial (s 85(3)) and, thus that he did not have to consider the remainder of s 85 (see s 85(4)), and so sent the defendant's case to the Secretary of State, who ordered extradition. On an appeal under s 103, the case was remitted to the district judge under s 104(1)(b) with a direction to 'reconsider the question under s 85(3)'. At the remitted hearing, the district judge decided again the question under s 85(1), this time finding that it had not been demonstrated to the criminal standard that the defendant had deliberately absented himself from trial. Having made that determination, the district judge went on to consider s 85(5) *et seq* and, answering them adversely to the defendant, sent his case against to the Secretary of State.

9.110 The defendant contended and the High Court agreed that, having answered the remitted question differently, the district judge was bound by s 104(6) to order the defendant's discharge. The decision to continue the extradition hearing, to answer questions not remitted, and to send the case again to the Secretary of State was *ultra vires* her powers under s 104.[138] In purporting to decide issues beyond those within the question remitted to her and in sending the case a second time to the Secretary of State, she was acting outwith the powers conferred upon her by the statute. Once she went beyond the four corners of the statute, the Court said that the judge was not making a decision under Part 2, and accordingly the prohibition in s 116 on questioning her decision other than by an appeal under Part 2 did not bite.[139] The High Court observed that:

> The difficulties that have arisen in this case illustrate that it is crucial when a question is remitted under s 104(1)(b) first that great care is taken in formulating the precise question the district judge is required to answer and second that the court's order should spell out precisely and accurately the court's decision.[140]
>
> With hindsight the question remitted should have been drawn so as to cover the whole of s 85. The question the judge should have been asked to decide was whether Mitoi was entitled to be discharged under s 85, thus bringing into the question s 85(5). The Divisional Court did not formulate the question in that way because the Romanian Government never made it clear to it that Mitoi could indeed be retried.[141]

Appeal by the requesting state against discharge at extradition hearing (s 105)

9.111 If at the extradition hearing the judge orders a person's discharge, an appeal to the High Court may be brought on behalf of the Category 2 territory under s 105 against the relevant decision (s 105(1)), namely, the decision which resulted in the order for the person's discharge (s 105(3)). The appeal may be brought on a question of law or fact.[142] However no appeal is possible if the discharge took place under s 122 (withdrawal of request).

---

[138] At paras 44–67.
[139] At para 62.
[140] At para 47.
[141] At para 67.
[142] Insofar as an appeal may be brought on a question of fact, the High Court will ordinarily pay respect to judicial findings of fact, made by designated judges with particular experience of extradition proceedings; *S v The Court of Bologna* [2010] EWHC 1184 (Admin); *Sinani v The Republic of Albania* [2009] EWHC 2773

Procedure for appealing

Notice of an appeal under s 105 must be given in accordance with rules of court[143] before the end of the permitted period, which is 14 days starting with the day on which the order for the defendant's discharge is made (s 105(5)). This provision is governed by the principles discussed at paras 9.23–9.36. **9.112**

Powers on the appeal

On an appeal under s 105 the High Court may (s 106(1)): **9.113**

(a) allow the appeal;
(b) direct the judge to decide the relevant question again;
(c) dismiss the appeal.

By s 106(2), a question is the relevant question if the judge's decision on it resulted in the order for the person's discharge. **9.114**

The court may only allow the appeal if the conditions in s 106(4) or (5) are satisfied (s 106(3)). The conditions in s 106(4) are that: **9.115**

(a) the judge ought to have decided the relevant question differently;
(b) if he had decided the question in the way he ought to have done, he would not have been required to order the person's discharge.

The conditions in s 106(5) are that: **9.116**

(a) an issue is raised that was not raised at the extradition hearing or evidence is available that was not available at the extradition hearing;[144]
(b) the issue or evidence would have resulted in the judge deciding the relevant question differently;
(c) if he had decided the question in that way, he would not have been required to order the person's discharge.

If the court allows the appeal it must quash the order discharging the defendant, remit the case to the judge, and direct him to proceed as he would have been required to do if he had decided the relevant question differently at the extradition hearing (s 106(6)). **9.117**

Section 106(1)(b) remittal for reconsideration

If the court makes a direction under s 106(1)(b) and the judge decides the relevant question differently he must proceed as he would have been required to do if he had decided that question differently at the extradition hearing (s 106(7)). The different wording of s 106(7) as compared with s 104(6) means that the issues that arose in *Chen and Mitoi v Government of Romania* [2009] 1 WLR 257 will not arise on a s 105 appeal. **9.118**

If the court makes a direction under s 106(1)(b) and the judge does not decide the relevant question differently the appeal must be taken to have been dismissed by a decision of the High Court (s 106(8)). The principles in *R (Okandeji) v Bow Street Magistrates' Court* [2006] 1 WLR 674, discussed at para 9.107, apply in this situation, and the only avenue for the requesting **9.119**

(Admin); *Sciezka v The Court in Sad Okregowy, Kielce, Poland* [2009] EWHC 2748 (Admin); *Von Der Pahlen v Leoben High Court, Austria* [2009] EWHC 383 (Admin); *Wiejak v Olsztyn Circuit Court of Poland* [2007] EWHC 2123 (Admin).

143 See para 9.98.

144 This provision is governed by the principles discussed above at paras 9.48–9.62.

state to appeal the substantive second decision of the district judge will be directly to the Supreme Court under s 114.

9.120 Sections 106(9) and 106(10), inserted by para 8(7) of Sch 13 to the Police and Justice Act 2006, provide that if the court allows the appeal, or makes a direction under s 106(1)(b), it must remand the person in custody or on bail. If the court remands the person in custody it may later grant bail.

Detention pending an appeal under s 105 by the requesting state

9.121 Under s 107, the requesting state has the right to ask the judge to remand the defendant in custody or on bail where it wishes to appeal under s 105 against an order for discharge. Section 107, as amended by para 8(8) of Sch 13 to the Police and Justice Act 2006, is in similar terms to s 30, discussed at para 9.70, with the addition that by s 107(4)(b)(ii), in a Part 2 case, the appeal also ceases to be pending when the High Court makes an order for remittal under s 106(1)(b).

Appeal by the defendant against Secretary of State's extradition order (s 108)

9.122 Sections 108 and 109 contain a right of appeal by the defendant where the Secretary of State orders his extradition under Part 2.

9.123 If the Secretary of State orders a person's extradition under Part 2, the person may appeal to the High Court against the order (s 108(1)), unless the defendant consented to his extradition under s 127. The appeal under s 108 may be brought on a question of law or fact (s 108(3)).[145]

Procedure for appealing

9.124 Notice of an appeal under s 108 must be given in accordance with rules of court[146] before the end of the permitted period, which is 14 days starting with the day on which (under s 100(1)) the Secretary of State informs the person of the order (s 108(4)). This provision is governed by the principles discussed at paras 9.23–9.36.

Powers on the appeal

9.125 On an appeal under s 108 the High Court may allow the appeal or dismiss the appeal (s 109(1)). If the court allows the appeal it must order the defendant's discharge and quash the order for his extradition (s 109(5)). There is no power under s 109 to remit the matter back to the Secretary of State for reconsideration.

9.126 The court may allow the appeal only if the conditions in s 109(3) or (4) are satisfied (s 109(2)). The conditions in s 109(3) are that:

(a) the Secretary of State ought to have decided a question before him differently;
(b) if he had decided the question in the way he ought to have done, he would not have ordered the person's extradition.

---

[145] Insofar as an appeal may be brought on a question of fact, the High Court will ordinarily pay respect to judicial findings of fact, made by designated judges with particular experience of extradition proceedings; *S v The Court of Bologna* [2010] EWHC 1184 (Admin); *Sinani v The Republic of Albania* [2009] EWHC 2773 (Admin); *Sciezka v The Court in Sad Okregowy, Kielce, Poland* [2009] EWHC 2748 (Admin); *Von Der Pahlen v Leoben High Court, Austria* [2009] EWHC 383 (Admin); *Wiejak v Olsztyn Circuit Court of Poland* [2007] EWHC 2123 (Admin).

[146] See para 9.98.

The conditions in s 109(4) are that: 9.127

(a) an issue is raised that was not raised when the case was being considered by the Secretary of State or information is available that was not available at that time;[147]
(b) the issue or information would have resulted in the Secretary of State deciding a question before him differently;
(c) if he had decided the question in that way, he would not have ordered the person's extradition.

Appeal by the requesting state against Secretary of State's order discharging the defendant (s 110)

The requesting Category 2 territory can appeal to the High Court under ss 110 and 111 against a decision by the Secretary of State to discharge the defendant (s 110(1)), unless the discharge took place under s 123 (withdrawal of request) (s 110(2)). An appeal under s 110 may be brought on a question of law or fact (s 110(4)).[148] 9.128

Procedure for appealing

Notice of an appeal under s 110 must be given in accordance with rules of court[149] before the end of the permitted period, which is 14 days starting with the day on which (under s 100(4)) the Secretary of State informs a person acting on behalf of the Category 2 territory of the order (s 110(5)). This provision is governed by the principles discussed at paras 9.23–9.36. 9.129

Powers on the appeal

On an appeal under s 110 the High Court may allow the appeal or dismiss the appeal (s 111(1)). If the court allows the appeal it must quash the order discharging the defendant and order his extradition (s 111(5)). There is no power under s 111 to remit the matter back to the Secretary of State for reconsideration. 9.130

The court may allow the appeal only if the conditions in s 111(3) or (4) are satisfied (s 111(2)). The conditions in s 111(3) are that: 9.131

(a) the Secretary of State ought to have decided a question before him differently;
(b) if he had decided the question in the way he ought to have done, he would have ordered the defendant's extradition.

The conditions in s 111(4) are that: 9.132

(a) an issue is raised that was not raised when the case was being considered by the Secretary of State or information is available that was not available at that time;[150]

---

[147] This provision is governed by the principles discussed above at paras 9.52–9.68. A contention that s109(4) of the 2003 Act implicitly prevents account being taken by the High Court of material provided by the Secretary of State after the Secretary of State's decision in order to *uphold* his decision where the appeal would otherwise have been successful was rejected by the High Court in *Welsh and Thrasher v Secretary of State for the Home Department and Another* [2007] 1 WLR 1281, para 151.

[148] Insofar as an appeal may be brought on a question of fact, the High Court will ordinarily pay respect to judicial findings of fact, made by designated judges with particular experience of extradition proceedings; *S v The Court of Bologna* [2010] EWHC 1184 (Admin); *Sinani v The Republic of Albania* [2009] EWHC 2773 (Admin); *Sciezka v The Court in Sad Okregowy, Kielce, Poland* [2009] EWHC 2748 (Admin); *Von Der Pahlen v Leoben High Court, Austria* [2009] EWHC 383 (Admin); *Wiejak v Olsztyn Circuit Court of Poland* [2007] EWHC 2123 (Admin).

[149] See para 9.98.

[150] This provision is governed by the principles discussed at paras 9.48–9.62.

(b) the issue or information would have resulted in the Secretary of State deciding a question before him differently;

(c) if he had decided the question in that way, he would have ordered the defendant's extradition.

9.133 Sections 111(6) and (7), inserted by para 8(9) of Sch 13 to the Police and Justice Act 2006, provide that if the court allows the appeal it must remand the person in custody or on bail, and if the court remands the person in custody it may later grant bail.

Detention pending an appeal under s 110 by the requesting state

9.134 Section 112, as substituted by para 8(10) of Sch 13 to the Police and Justice Act 2006, applies where the Secretary of State orders the person's discharge under Part 2.

9.135 Section 112(2) provides that, subject to s 112(3), the order made by the appropriate judge under s 92(4) (the remand order) remains in force until the end of the period of three days beginning with the day on which the person's discharge is ordered. If, within that period, the Secretary of State is informed in writing on behalf of the Category 2 territory of an intention to appeal under s 110, the remand order remains in force while the appeal is pending.

9.136 If the person is remanded in custody under s 92(4), the appropriate judge may grant bail (s 112(3)).

9.137 For the purposes of s 112(2)(b), s 112(4) provides that an appeal under s 110 ceases to be pending at the earliest of these times: when the proceedings on the appeal are discontinued; when the High Court allows the appeal, or dismisses the appeal, unless, where the appeal is dismissed, the court is immediately informed on behalf of the Category 2 territory of an intention to apply for leave to appeal to the Supreme Court; at the end of the permitted period, which is 28 days starting with the day on which leave to appeal to the Supreme Court against the decision of the High Court on the appeal is granted, if no appeal to the Supreme Court is brought before the end of that period; when there is no further step that can be taken on behalf of the Category 2 territory in relation to the appeal (ignoring any power of a court to grant leave to take a step out of time).

Time limits for appeals to the High Court

9.138 Section 113 contains provisions for the making of rules of court concerning the time within which appeals to the High Court must begin. Section 113 is in materially identical terms to s 31, discussed above at para 9.73. As explained above,[151] para 22.6A of the Practice Direction to CPR Part 52 prescribes 76 days as the relevant period under s 113.

Appeals to the Supreme Court (s 114)

9.139 An appeal lies to the Supreme Court under s 114 from a decision of the High Court on an appeal under ss 103, 105, 108, or 110 (s 114(1)) at the instance of the defendant or a person acting on behalf of the Category 2 territory (s 114(2)).

9.140 Section 114 is in similar terms to s 32, considered above.[152]

9.141 Section 114 is amended by para 8(11) of Sch 13 to the Police and Justice Act 2006 by the substitution of a new s 114(10) which provides that the High Court may grant bail to a person appealing under s 114, or applying for leave to appeal under s 114, against the dismissal of his appeal under s 103 or 108.

---

151 Para 9.98.
152 Para 9.78.

By s 114(13), no right of appeal under the EA 2003 lies from a decision of the High Court of Justiciary in Scotland to the Supreme Court. However, in *BH v The Lord Advocate* [2012] 3 WLR 151, the Supreme Court held that a right of appeal exists as a devolution issue under the Scotland Act 1998, Sch 6. This is the case despite the incompatibility of a devolution appeal with the operation of the required period for surrender in s 118. Moreover, such an appeal will, where brought by the requesting state against an order for discharge, suffer the obvious problem that the s 115A power to remand the defendant in custody pending appeal will not, as the law presently stands, be available. **9.142**

Powers of the Supreme Court on the appeal

The powers of the Supreme Court on appeal are contained in s 115, which is in terms similar to s 33, considered at para 9.88. **9.143**

As under s 33, no provision is made in s 115 for remission to the district judge for reconsideration of the issue that gave rise to the appeal. However, in *Norris v Government of the United States of America* [2008] 1 AC 920, para 110, notwithstanding the existence of no express power to remit in s 115, it was held that: **9.144**

> we have no doubt that the House has an inherent power to remit determination of an issue to an inferior tribunal where the interests of justice so require, and that is a power which nothing in the 2003 Act purports to abrogate.[153]

Sections 115(9) and (10), inserted by para 8(12) of Sch 13 to the Police and Justice Act 2006, provide that in a case where s 115(5) or (7) applies, the Supreme Court must remand, in custody or on bail, the person whose extradition is requested, and if the Supreme Court remands the person in custody the High Court may later grant bail. **9.145**

Detention pending an appeal under s 114 by the requesting state

As originally drafted, the EA 2003 contained no provision for a defendant to be detained, or his bail continued, pending an appeal by the requesting state to the Supreme Court. Section 115A, inserted by para 8(13) of Sch 13 to the Police and Justice Act 2006, provides that the section applies if on an appeal under s 103 or 108 the High Court orders the person's discharge; and immediately after it does so, the court is informed on behalf of the Category 2 territory of an intention to appeal under s 114. **9.146**

The High Court must remand the person in custody or on bail while the appeal is pending. If the court remands the person in custody it may later grant bail (s 115A(2)–(3)). **9.147**

By s 115A(4), an appeal under s 114 ceases to be pending at the earliest of these times: when the proceedings on the appeal are discontinued; at the end of the permitted period, which is 28 days starting with the day on which leave to appeal to the Supreme Court against the decision of the High Court on the appeal under s 103 or 108 is granted, if no appeal to the Supreme Court is brought before the end of that period; when there is no further step that can be taken on behalf of the Category 2 territory in relation to the appeal (ignoring any power of a court to grant leave to take a step out of time). **9.148**

[153] There can be no doubt that the Supreme Court has the same power, both as part of the inherent jurisdiction transferred to it from the House of Lords, and pursuant to s 40(5) of the Constitutional Reform Act 2005, by which the Court has power 'to determine any question necessary to be determined for the purposes of doing justice' in an appeal to it under any enactment.

E. Remedies After the Appeals Process Has Concluded

9.149 Post-appeal challenges by a defendant where there has been a significant change of circumstances after the conclusion of the statutory appeals process but before he has been actually extradited, have created particular procedural difficulties. The requirements of justice—as well the Human Rights Act 1998, which precludes a public authority from acting so as to violate an individual's Convention rights—would suggest that there should be some remedy. However the prescriptive statutory structure of the EA 2003 appears, on its face, to preclude a remedy. This has not prevented the courts from fashioning a remedy, and the law now appears to be as follows.

9.150 In Part 1 cases, where there has been an appeal, the appropriate remedy is to apply to re-open the final appeal rather than to apply for *habeas corpus* or judicial review.[154] In Part 1 cases where there has been no appeal, or no properly constituted appeal, judicial review does not exist as a means by which to circumvent the statutory appeal time limits.[155] However, an application for judicial review of SOCA's decision to affect surrender may be made.[156]

9.151 In Part 2 cases, the position is complicated by the involvement of the Secretary of State. The appropriate course is to seek judicial review of the refusal of the Secretary of State to withdraw the extradition order (following representations as to why the order should be withdrawn).[157]

9.152 However, in all cases, the basis of the High Court's jurisdiction to intervene post-exhaustion of the statutory appeals process is the Human Rights Act 1998, and the court may therefore not act on any supervening event that does not constitute a human rights event, of a nature and degree to undermine the efficacy of the original decision to extradite.[158] Abuse of process constitutes no exception to this principle.[159]

---

[154] *R (Greer aka Bailey) v The Serious Organised Crime Agency [2011] EWHC 446 (Admin); Ignaoua, Khemiri and Chehidi v The Judicial Authority of the Courts of Milan and Others* [2008] EWHC 2619 (Admin).

[155] *R (Wawrzniak) v District Court in Poznan, Poland* [2010] EWHC 2794 (Admin); *R (Mann) v City of Westminster Magistrates' Court and Others* [2010] EWHC 48 (Admin).

[156] *R (Mann) v Serious Organised Crime Agency* [2010] EWHC 1760 (Admin); *Atkinson v Commissioner of the Metropolitan Police Force* [2009] EWHC 2661 (Admin); *Navadunskis v The Serious Organised Crime Agency* [2009] EWHC 1292 (Admin).

[157] *R (Vatoci) v Secretary of State for the Home Department and Another* [2012] EWHC 1356 (Admin); *Mucelli (No 2), Hoxhaj and Gjoka v Government of Albania* [2012] EWHC 95 (Admin); *Taylor v HMP Wandsworth* [2009] EWHC 1020 (Admin); *R (McKinnon) v Secretary of State for Home Affairs* [2009] EWHC 2021 (Admin).

[158] *R (Vatoci) v Secretary of State for the Home Department* [2012] EWHC 1356 (Admin); *Mucelli (No 2), Hoxhaj and Gjoka v Government of Albania* [2012] EWHC 95 (Admin); *R (Greer aka Bailey) v The Serious Organised Crime Agency* [2011] EWHC 446 (Admin); *R (Mann) v The Serious Organised Crime Agency* [2010] EWHC 1760 (Admin); *R (Mann) v City of Westminster Magistrates' Court* [2010] EWHC 48 (Admin); *Atkinson v Commissioner of the Metropolitan Police Force* [2009] EWHC 2661 (Admin); *R (McKinnon) v Secretary of State for Home Affairs* [2009] EWHC 2021 (Admin); *McKinnon v Government of the United States* [2007] EWHC 762 (Admin).

[159] *Salazar-Duarte v The Government of the United States of America* [2010] EWHC 3150 (Admin).

10

TIME FOR EXTRADITION

A. Introduction

Extradition legislation from the EA 1870 onwards generally required the defendant's return to take place as quickly as possible after the Secretary of State ordered it. Section 16 and para 10 of Sch 1 to the EA 1989 gave the defendant the right to apply for discharge if he was not extradited within a certain period following the making of an order for his return, which application, unless there was a 'sufficient cause' for not ordering discharge,[1] the court was obliged to grant.[2] **10.01**

This policy is continued in the EA 2003. The EA 2003 lays down time limits within which extradition must take place following the conclusion of proceedings, in default of which the defendant must be discharged unless 'reasonable cause'[3] is shown for the delay. **10.02**

B. Time for Extradition in Part 1 Cases

Sections 35 and 36 specify the period within which extradition must take place in cases where there is no appeal, and where there has been an appeal, respectively. **10.03**

[1] For the principles applicable to the exercise of these provisions, and similarly worded provisions in the EA 1870, the Fugitive Offenders Act 1881 and the Fugitive Offenders Act 1967, which required 'sufficient cause' to be shown for not ordering discharge: see *In re Shuter* [1960] 1 QB 142 (sufficient cause may include difficulties arranging a suitable escort; sufficient cause does not only relate to something outside the control of the relevant authorities but includes general considerations of reasonableness; but if sufficient cause is not shown discharge is mandatory); *R v Governor of Brixton Prison ex p Enahoro* [1963] 2 QB 455 (sufficient cause may include delay at the defendant's own request or in the defendant's own interests; including delay to facilitate pending parliamentary consideration of the case); *Re Oskar*, 29 February 1988, CO/190/88 (delay caused by misunderstanding of the relevant time limits by the United Kingdom authorities not sufficient cause); *In re Akbar*, 29 October 1996, CO/3690/96 (delay caused in the conduct of other procedural steps by the United Kingdom authorities not sufficient cause).

[2] Use of the word 'may' in conjunction with this phrase meant 'shall' order discharge: see *In re Shuter* [1960] 1 QB 142.

[3] 'Reasonable cause' and 'sufficient cause' mean the same thing: *Re Lindley*, 29 October 1997, CO/1183/97.

Time for extradition where there is no appeal

10.04 Section 35 applies where the appropriate judge has ordered the defendant's extradition to a Category 1 territory and no notice of appeal has been given under s 26 before the end of the period permitted under that section. For these purposes, any power of a court to extend the period permitted for giving notice of appeal and any power of a court to grant leave to take a step out of time has to be ignored (s 35(6)). However s 35 does not apply if the judge's order is made under s 46 or 48 (consent to extradition).

10.05 Where s 35 applies, the defendant must be extradited before the end of the 'required period' (s 35(3)). This period is 10 days starting with the first day after the period permitted under s 26(4) for giving notice of appeal against the judge's order; or, if the judge and the authority which issued the Part 1 warrant agree a later date, 10 days starting with that later date.[4]

Agreement of a later date

10.06 Applications to agree a later date for surrender under s 35(4)(b) are made by the CPS on behalf of the issuing judicial authority to the appropriate judge and are made *ex parte*. There is no requirement for the CPS to serve on the defendant copies of the written request and supporting material submitted to the relevant court.[5]

10.07 Because the request is not made in the context of a claim or *inter partes* litigation, whether actual or prospective, and does not seek a court order *against* anyone, no formal application is required, and there are no requirements to file or serve any application.[6]

10.08 Whilst the court has power to hear representations from the requested person, there is no statutory entitlement to a requested person to be notified of a request for an extension and to be heard in opposition to it. The court will decide whether there is a need for such representations in the interest of fairness. In assessing the validity of the reasons given by the CPS for the request for an agreement to extension of time, if the court feels that there are possible reasons to question it or that representations could assist, it may direct that the necessary arrangements be made. Otherwise, it is open to the court to decide whether to make the order without hearing the person concerned.[7]

10.09 There is no duty upon the court to give reasons.[8] Whilst the agreement is generally recorded in a formal order, that is a matter of convenience and good sense rather than a legal necessity.[9] Although the defendant has no *entitlement* to be notified of the request or to be heard in relation to it, fairness and good administration require that the defendant should be informed of any extension agreed by the relevant court, since it bears directly on his right to apply for discharge under s 35(5) if extradition has not been effected before the end of the required period. It is wasteful and undesirable for a person to be informed for the first time of an extension only by way of defence to an application under s 35(5). The existing practice is for the court to send a copy of the court's order recording the extension to the extraditee as well as to the CPS.

---

4 EA 2003, s 35, as amended by para 9(1) of Sch 13 to the Police and Justice Act 2006.

5 *Kasprzak v Warsaw Regional Court, Poland*; *Bingham v Trial Court No 4 of Marbella, Spain*; *Wilson-Campbell v Court of Instruction No 4 of Orihuela, Alicante, Spain* [2011] EWHC 100 (Admin), para 50.

6 Ibid, para 45.

7 Ibid, paras 48–49; *Kolanowski v City of Westminster Magistrates' Court & Another* [2011] EWHC 2557 (Admin), para 21.

8 *Kasprzak v Warsaw Regional Court, Poland*; *Bingham v Trial Court No 4 of Marbella, Spain*; *Wilson-Campbell v Court of Instruction No 4 of Orihuela, Alicante, Spain* [2011] EWHC 100 (Admin), para 40.

9 Ibid, para 45.

Successive agreements to extend time for surrender are permissible under s 35(4)(b). **10.10**

An agreement may be made even after the original extended (or re-extended) period has expired. So long as a valid extension is currently in place, no application for discharge may be made or granted.[10] Where a required period expires and an application for discharge under s 35(5) is lodged before it is further extended, a later extension will preclude the right of the requested person to argue before the magistrates' court that there had been a failure to extradite him before the end of the original period, that reasonable cause had not been shown for the delay, and that discharge should therefore be ordered retrospectively.[11] **10.11**

In what factual circumstances should the powers given by s 35(4)(b) be exercised? Ordinarily, cases in which an extension of time is sought are those in which the mechanics of removal have not been activated during the relevant period; usually due to problems with arranging flights. These cases present little difficulty as they are plainly within the contemplation of Article 23 of the EAW Framework Decision. But are the circumstances of application of s 35(4)(b) confined to those stated in Article 23? The English courts have so far answered that question in the negative and held that s 35(4)(b), and other mirror provisions in the EA 2003, confer the 'widest possible discretion', although one to be exercised with due regard for the wording and purpose of the Framework Decision.[12] Therefore, for example, an agreement was upheld in *R (Bartlett) v Court of First Instance of Hasselt, Belgium* [2011] EWHC 1407 (Admin) so as to enable the courts in the requesting state to permit the trial of co-defendants not to have to be re-commenced. **10.12**

However, this approach is out of line with that taken in other jurisdictions. In *Rimsa v Governor of Cloverhill Prison & Another* [2010] IESC 47 it was held by the Supreme Court of Ireland that s 16(5)(b) of the Irish European Arrest Warrant Act 2003,[13] in materially identical terms to s 35(4)(b) of the EA 2003, was 'clearly intended to give effect to Article 23'. It would follow that the circumstances in which a s35(4)(b) agreement may be made should therefore be limited to 'circumstances beyond the control of any of the Member States' such as cancelled flights, limited transport on public holidays, or adverse weather conditions (Article 23(3)) and 'serious humanitarian reasons' (Article 23(4)). **10.13**

The High Court has no power to order a requested person's discharge for non-compliance with the procedural or substantive requirements of s 35(4)(b), whether under CPR Part 23 or CPR Part 40, or by way of judicial review; the legality of any agreement must be challenged on an application under s 35(5),[14] considered at para 10.15. **10.14**

---

[10] *R (Bingham) v City of Westminster Magistrates' Court* [2011] EWHC 1348 (Admin).

[11] *R (Bingham) v City of Westminster Magistrates' Court* [2011] EWHC 1348 (Admin). cf *Kasprzak v Warsaw Regional Court, Poland*; *Bingham v Trial Court No 4 of Marbella, Spain*; *Wilson-Campbell v Court of Instruction No 4 of Orihuela, Alicante, Spain* [2011] EWHC 100 (Admin), paras 55–56; see also *Kolanowski v City of Westminster Magistrates' Court & Another* [2011] EWHC 2557 (Admin) at paras 22–23.

[12] *Szklanny v City of Westminster Magistrates' Court & Another* [2008] 1 WLR 789, paras 16–18; see also *R (Bartlett) v Court of First Instance of Hasselt, Belgium* [2011] EWHC 1407 (Admin), para 8.

[13] Section 16(5)(b) of the Irish European Arrest Warrant Act 2003 is in materially identical terms to s 35(4)(b) save that the issuing judicial authority's agreement is there made with the Irish Central Authority (the Department of Justice, Equality & Law Reform) rather than the Irish court. In *Rimsa v Governor of Cloverhill Prison & Another* [2010] IESC 47, the Irish Supreme Court further held that s 16(5)(b) was not unconstitutional on the basis that (despite Article 23 of the Framework Decision) it does not involve an Irish court. An agreement made between the Irish Central Authority and another non-judicial authority in the issuing state was however found to be outwith s 16(5)(b).

[14] *Kasprzak v Warsaw Regional Court, Poland*; *Bingham v Trial Court No 4 of Marbella, Spain*; *Wilson-Campbell v Court of Instruction No 4 of Orihuela, Alicante, Spain* [2011] EWHC 100 (Admin), para 51.

Failure to extradite within the required period and application for discharge

10.15 Although there is a positive duty under s 35(3) to extradite the defendant before the end of the required period, the section does not prohibit the person's removal after the expiry of the required period, which may nonetheless be carried out; subject only to an application for discharge under s 35(5) being made.[15] If s 35(3) is not complied with and the person applies to the appropriate judge for discharge the judge must order the defendant's discharge unless 'reasonable cause is shown *for the delay*' (s 35(5)).[16] The origins of this phrase are important. As seen above, earlier extradition legislation required the court to order discharge unless sufficient cause were shown *for not ordering discharge*. This was a wide discretionary power which permitted the court to have regard to general considerations of reasonableness.[17] By contrast, the different scheme contained within the Backing of Warrants (Republic of Ireland) Act 1965, s 6, provided that discharge 'may' be ordered unless 'reasonable cause is shown *for the delay*'. This scheme was considered in *Re Lindley*, 29 October 1997, CO/1183/97, and the phrase was held to warrant a 'markedly different' approach to that which prevailed under other extradition legislation. The wording required that the 'reasonable cause' be referable to the delay. However, because the 1965 Act conferred a discretionary power upon the court, by the use of the word 'may', the court also had an overriding general discretionary power (as wide as under the alternative scheme), the exercise of which was constrained only in those cases where reasonable cause was shown for the delay; where that discretion could only be exercised so as not to order discharge.

10.16 Section 35(5) of the EA 2003 requires that 'the judge *must* order his discharge, unless reasonable cause is shown *for the delay*'. This is comparable to the wording in the Backing of Warrants (Republic of Ireland) Act 1965 ('reasonable cause is shown *for the delay*') but without the overriding discretionary power. The EA 2003 therefore deliberately narrows the circumstances in which the court may decline to order discharge; to those where reasonable cause is shown *for the delay*. General considerations of comity or reasonableness (eg, it is only a short delay, or there has been an oversight) ought not come into play. Under the EA 2003, the court is concerned, and only concerned, with whether there is reasonable cause for the delay. Under Part 1 of the EA 2003, decisions under previous legislation ought therefore to be of little direct assistance.

10.17 Section 35(5) additionally differs in other ways from earlier extradition legislation, in that Part 1 of the EA 2003 is intended to give effect to the EAW Framework Decision. The High Court thus initially[18] subscribed to the view that the application of the concept of 'reasonable cause' was additionally constrained by Article 23 of the EAW Framework Decision which provides that:

> ...
>
> 1. The person requested shall be surrendered as soon as possible on a date agreed between the authorities concerned.

---

[15] An order granting *habeas corpus* directs a person's release from custody not the quashing of the order for extradition. Technically, the EAW and the order for extradition remain extant. However, such an EAW will not continue to attract the provisions of s 35 (or s 36). Where, therefore, a subsequent EAW is issued, a defendant is not able to assert that surrender upon the subsequent EAW is precluded by section 35(5); *Minister of Justice Equality and Law Reform v Koncis* [2011] IESC 37, para 36.

[16] cf s 16(7) of the Irish European Arrest Warrant Act 2003 which provides for mandatory discharge if extradition is not affected within the 10-day period (or such other period as is agreed under s 16(5)(b)).

[17] *In re Shuter* [1960] 1 QB 142.

[18] *Governor of HMP Wandsworth v Kinderis* [2008] QB 347, para 29; *Szklanny v City of Westminster Magistrates' Court & Another* [2008] 1 WLR 789, paras 17–18.

2. He or she shall be surrendered no later than 10 days after the final decision on the execution of the European arrest warrant.
3. If the surrender of the requested person within the period laid down in paragraph 2 is prevented by circumstances beyond the control of any of the Member States, the executing and issuing judicial authorities shall immediately contact each other and agree on a new surrender date. In that event, the surrender shall take place within 10 days of the new date thus agreed.
4. The surrender may exceptionally be temporarily postponed for serious humanitarian reasons, for example if there are substantial grounds for believing that it would manifestly endanger the requested person's life or health. The execution of the European arrest warrant shall take place as soon as these grounds have ceased to exist. The executing judicial authority shall immediately inform the issuing judicial authority and agree on a new surrender date. In that event, the surrender shall take place within 10 days of the new date thus agreed ...

'Circumstances beyond the control of any of the Member States' (Article 23(3)) is intended to cover cases of *force majeure*. Thus, if extradition is to be effected by air, a strike by airline or air traffic control staff over a period during which the extradition is set to take place might well fall within this category.[19] So too will the requested person deliberately evading surrender.[20] **10.18**

'Serious humanitarian reasons' (Article 23(4)) plainly overlaps with the power in s 25(3)(b) to adjourn extradition proceedings pending recovery from physical or mental ill-health, but is potentially wider in scope and not limited by considerations of oppression or injustice.[21] **10.19**

However, more recently, the High Court has observed that s 35(5) provides a degree of flexibility that is not necessarily constrained by Article 23.[22] Therefore, the High Court has also applied s 35(5) (or s 36(8)) to circumstances beyond those contemplated by Article 23, where to do so is deemed to further the overall purpose and intent of the EAW Framework Decision. Accordingly, the existence of extant proceedings upon other EAWs issued by the same Category 1 territory, not being competing EAWs within the meaning of s 44, may be a reasonable cause for delay.[23] Similarly, administrative error or misconstruction of the applicable period has been held to be capable of constituting reasonable cause for the delay.[24] The concept of 'reasonableness' of the delay has thus re-emerged.[25] Despite this, a defence application for surrender to be delayed due to an outstanding challenge before the European Court of Human Rights, where no Rule 39 interim measures have been granted, has been held to 'straightforwardly undermine' the operation of s 35.[26] **10.20**

By what procedure should a challenge to a decision under s 35(5) be made? In *Gronastajski v Government of Poland* [2007] EWHC 3314 (Admin), para 8, a case concerned with the different, **10.21**

---

[19] *Governor of HMP Wandsworth v Kinderis* [2008] QB 347, para 29.

[20] *Kolanowski v City of Westminster Magistrates' Court & Another* [2011] EWHC 2557 (Admin).

[21] As to the narrow application of which (in the context of delay), see *Gomes and Goodyer v Government of Trinidad & Tobago* [2009] 1 WLR 1038; cf *Dewani v Government of the Republic of South Africa* [2012] EWHC 842 (Admin).

[22] *Owens v City of Westminster Magistrates' Court* [2010] 1 WLR 17, paras 51–52; *R (Bartlett) v Court of First Instance of Hasselt, Belgium* [2011] EWHC 1407 (Admin), para 12.

[23] *R (Caldarelli) v City of Westminster Magistrates' Court* [2009] EWHC 107 (Admin), para 48; *Kolanowski v City of Westminster Magistrates' Court & Another* [2011] EWHC 2557 (Admin), paras 24–26.

[24] *Owens v City of Westminster Magistrates' Court* [2010] 1 WLR 17, paras 48–50.

[25] Ibid, para 53.

[26] *R (Mann) v Serious Organised Crime Agency* [2010] EWHC 1760 (Admin), para 29.

but similarly worded, provisions of EA 2003, s 8(8), the High Court held that a challenge to a refusal to discharge should be brought by way of application for judicial review. Of course, in comparison to *habeas corpus*, a judicial review challenge requires permission, involves a different standard of review, and requires certification of a point of law as a pre-condition to further appeal. The EA 2003 provides for no statutory appeal against a refusal to discharge under s 35(5). Therefore, the principles established in *Nikonovs v The Governor of HM Prison Brixton* [2006] 1 WLR 1518, suggest that *habeas corpus* ought to be an available route of challenge. The issue was ultimately left undecided in *Owens v City of Westminster Magistrates' Court* [2010] 1 WLR 17, paras 11–14.

Time for extradition where the defendant appeals

10.22 Section 36 applies where the defendant has appealed to the High Court under s 26 and the effect of the High Court's decision (or that of the Supreme Court) is that the person is to be extradited.

10.23 Where a defendant has failed to comply with the mandatory provisions of s 26(4), such that the High Court has no jurisdiction to entertain the appeal,[27] has the defendant ... 'appealed' to the High Court under s 26? If not, then s 35 applies and the required period under s 35(4) will invariably have expired. Therefore, the High Court has consistently held, 'notwithstanding the apparent theoretical illogicality of the position', that a finding that there was no valid appeal constitutes an order on the appeal (ie a dismissal of the appeal);[28] once an appeal notice is filed, the High Court is seized of the appeal and dismisses it within the meaning of s 27, for want of jurisdiction.[29] Therefore, s 36 rather than s 35 applies.

10.24 Section 36 provides that the defendant must be extradited to the Category 1 territory before the end of the 'required period' (s 36(2)). By s 36(3), this period is:

(a) 10 days starting with the day on which the decision of the relevant court (ie the High Court or Supreme Court) on the appeal becomes final or proceedings on the appeal are discontinued, or
(b) if the relevant court and the authority which issued the Part 1 warrant agree a later date, 10 days starting with that later date.[30]

10.25 'Finality' is defined in s 36(5). The decision of the High Court on the appeal becomes final:

(a) when the period permitted for applying to the High Court for leave to appeal to the Supreme Court ends, if there is no such application;

[27] *Mucelli v Government of Albania; Moulai v Deputy Public Prosecutor in Cretiel, France* [2009] 1 WLR 276.

[28] *Marsh v Prague 6 District Court, Czech Republic* [2010] EWHC 3810 (Admin). Striking out of the list for failure to comply with an 'Unless Order' also constitutes a dismissal of the appeal for the purposes of s 36: *Osieniecki v Regional Court in Radom, Poland* [2012] EWHC 1096 (Admin).

[29] *Greer v The Judicial Authority of Ireland* [2010] EWHC 3510 (Admin). This must also be implicit in the fact that *Mucelli v Government of Albania; Moulai v Deputy Public Prosecutor in Cretiel, France* [2009] 1 WLR 276 itself was permitted to proceed to the House of Lords under ss 32 and 114.

[30] 'Relevant court' is defined by s 36(4) and the principles described at paras 10.06–10.14 in relation to s 35(4)(b) will apply. A request for extension of time may be made during the currency of the appeal proceedings but does not have to be made at that point and is much more likely in practice to arise at a later date, when the proceedings are at an end and some difficulty has arisen in effecting removal; at a time when the decision of the High Court had become final and the Part 1 warrant has been 'disposed of' (see EA 2003, s 213(1)(c)). Such a request cannot therefore be accommodated within the procedures governing extradition appeals. It has a *sui generis* character, independent of any extant legal proceedings: *Kasprzak v Warsaw Regional Court, Poland*; *Bingham v Trial Court No 4 of Marbella, Spain*; *Wilson-Campbell v Court of Instruction No 4 of Orihuela, Alicante, Spain* [2011] EWHC 100 (Admin), para 43.

(b) when the period permitted for applying to the Supreme Court for leave to appeal to it ends, if the High Court refuses leave to appeal and there is no application to the Supreme Court for leave to appeal;
(c) when the Supreme Court refuses leave to appeal to it;
(d) at the end of the permitted period, which is 28 days starting with the day on which leave to appeal to appeal to the Supreme Court is granted, if no such appeal is brought before the end of that period.

For these purposes, any power of a court to extend the period permitted for giving notice of appeal and any power of a court to grant leave to take a step out of time has to be ignored (s 36(6)). **10.26**

Determining the point at which a High Court decision on appeal becomes 'final' within the meaning of s 36(5)(a) has proved problematic. Section 32(5) provides for a 14-day period within which an application to the High Court for leave to appeal to the Supreme Court must be made. Section 32(4)(a) further provides that leave to appeal may not be granted unless the High Court has certified a point of law of general public importance. It might be thought therefore that once the High Court refuses to certify, its powers to grant leave become academic and its decision becomes final. However, in a 'remarkable'[31] omission, s 36 does not mention the certification process. It has therefore been held that, even where the High Court hears and refuses an application to certify within that 14-day period, the decision of the High Court on the appeal has not become final; because a repeat or further application to certify could theoretically be made.[32] The 14-day period contemplated in s 35(5)(a) cannot therefore be abridged. The same would be true of a case where the putative appellant informs the court immediately that he does not intend to seek to apply for certification or leave. The period for applying to the High Court for leave to appeal does not thereby end, and the decision of the High Court on the appeal does not become final, when the High Court refuses to certify a point of law of general public importance. In all cases, the full 14-day period for applying for leave must run its course before the decision of the High Court is capable of becoming final (and the s 36 duty to extradite commences). Of course, once the 14-day period has ended, if the High Court then refuses to certify, its decision will have become final immediately; because no further application to certify can then be made and no possibility of further appeal can arise.[33] **10.27**

The decision of the Supreme Court on the appeal becomes final when it is made (s 36(7)). **10.28**

If s 36(2) is not complied with and the person applies to the appropriate judge to be discharged the judge must order his discharge unless reasonable cause is shown for the delay (s 36(8)), and the principles considered at paras 10.15–10.21 in relation to s 35(5) will apply. **10.29**

Undertaking from Part 1 territory concerning person serving sentence

As explained at para 5.154, s 23[34] confers a discretion on the appropriate judge to postpone a Part 1 extradition hearing until after a defendant who is in custody serving a sentence of imprisonment in the UK has completed his sentence. The judge may adjourn the extradition hearing until the person is released from detention pursuant to the sentence (whether on licence or otherwise). However, under s 37, as amended by paras 9–10 of Sch 13 to the Police and Justice Act 2006, the judge also has the power to order extradition provided that an appropriate **10.30**

---

31 *Wood v City of Westminster Magistrates' Court* [2007] EWHC 2058 (Admin), para 5.
32 *Owens v City of Westminster Magistrates' Court* [2010] 1 WLR 17, paras 21–32.
33 *Wood v City of Westminster Magistrates' Court* [2007] EWHC 2058 (Admin).
34 As amended by the Police and Justice Act 2006, Sch 13(1), para 7, and by the Policing and Crime Act 2009, s 71(3).

undertaking is received from the Category 1 territory that the defendant will be returned to the UK at the conclusion of his sentence; so as to serve the outstanding UK sentence.

10.31 Section 37 applies if the appropriate judge orders the defendant's extradition to a Category 1 territory (other than under s 46 or 48 (consent)); and the defendant is serving a sentence of imprisonment or another form of detention in the UK either in custody or on licence.

10.32 Section 37(3) provides that the judge may make the order for extradition subject to the condition that extradition is not to take place before he receives an undertaking given on behalf of the Category 1 territory in terms specified by him. If the judge makes such an order then s 37(7) and (8) apply:

(a) Section 37(7) provides that if the judge does not receive the undertaking before the end of the period of 21 days starting with the day on which he makes the order and the defendant applies for discharge then the judge must order his discharge.
(b) Section 37(8)(a) provides that in a case where s 35 applies, the required period for the purpose of s 35(3) is 10 days starting with the day on which the judge receives the undertaking (if the day is later than the day mentioned in s 35(4)(a)).[35] Section 37(8)(b) states that where s 36 applies, the required period for the purposes of s 36(2) is 10 days starting with the day on which the decision of the relevant court on the appeal becomes final within the meaning of s 36 or (if later) the day on which the judge receives the undertaking.

10.33 Section 37(4) specifies the terms of the undertaking which the judge can seek from the requesting state in relation to a person who is within s 37(1)(b)(i) (ie in custody). Where the person is accused of an offence in the Category 1 territory they include:

(a) that the defendant be kept in custody until the conclusion of the proceedings against him for the offence and any offence in respect of which he is permitted to be dealt with in the Category 1 territory;
(b) that the defendant be returned to the UK to serve the remainder of his sentence on the conclusion of those proceedings.

10.34 Section 37(4A) provides that the terms which may be specified by the judge in relation to a person within s 37(1)(b)(ii) (ie on licence) who is accused in a Category 1 territory of the commission of an offence include terms that the person be returned to the UK to serve the remainder of his sentence after serving any sentence imposed on him in the Category 1 territory for the offence, and any other offence in respect of which he is permitted to be dealt with in the Category 1 territory.

10.35 If the defendant is alleged to be unlawfully at large after conviction in the Category 1 territory the terms which the judge can seek in the form of an undertaking include that the defendant be returned to the UK to serve the remainder of his sentence after serving any sentence imposed on him in the Category 1 territory (s 37(5)).

10.36 In *R (Handa) v Bow Street Magistrates' Court* [2004] EWHC 2986 (Admin) the Administrative Court pointed out that the operation of s 37 was undermined by the absence of any corresponding power to interrupt a sentence of domestic imprisonment to allow for extradition. Tuckey LJ said at para 30:[36]

> I would observe that the absence of any provision in UK law permitting the interruption of domestic custody is something that Parliament seems to have overlooked when enacting the 2003 Act. Sections 259 and 260 of the Criminal Justice Act 2003 allow for the removal of

[35] Inserted by para 9(2) of Sch 13 to the Police and Justice Act 2006.
[36] cf *R (Slator) v Bow Street Magistrates' Court* [2006] EWHC 2628 (Admin).

> persons from the UK in asylum and immigration cases, but no provision is made in that Act, or anywhere else, for the removal in extradition cases of persons serving domestic sentences. The absence of such a provision entirely undermines s 37 ... and s 186 ... I need hardly say that the sooner Parliament fills this yawning gap the better.

The gap has been filled by the insertion of EA 2003, s 197A, by para 25 to Sch 13 of the Police and Justice Act 2006. Section 197A provides[37] that if an order is made under Part 1 or 2 for the extradition of a person who is in custody serving a sentence of imprisonment or another form of detention in the UK, the order is sufficient authority for the person to be removed from the prison or other institution where he is detained. **10.37**

Time for extradition where extradition has been deferred

The power of the appropriate judge under s 44 to defer extradition under Part 1 until the conclusion of other Part 1 proceedings was considered in para 5.144. The power of the Secretary of State to make such an order under s 179 in the face of a competing extradition request under Part 2 was considered in para 8.45. **10.38**

Section 38[38] specifies the time within which the defendant must be extradited where the appropriate judge subsequently makes an order under s 181(2) that the defendant be extradited following disposal of the competing claim. Section 38 applies if: **10.39**

(a) an order is made under Part 1 for the defendant to be extradited to a Category 1 territory in pursuance of a Part 1 warrant (except under s 46 or 48 (consent));
(b) before the defendant is extradited, an order is made under s 44(4)(b) or s 179(2)(b) for his extradition in pursuance of the warrant to be deferred;
(c) the appropriate judge makes an order under s 181(2) for the defendant's extradition in pursuance of the warrant to cease to be deferred.

In a case where s 35 applies, the required period for the purposes of s 35(3) is 10 days starting with the day on which the order under s 181(2) is made (if the day on which the order is made is later than the day mentioned in s 35(4)(a)). **10.40**

In a case where s 36 applies, the required period for the purposes of s 36(2) is 10 days starting with the day on which the decision of the relevant court on the appeal becomes final (within the meaning of s 36) or (if later) the day on which the order under s 181(2) is made. **10.41**

C. Time for Extradition in Part 2 Cases

Time for extradition where there is no appeal

Section 117 specifies the time within which the defendant must be extradited in a Part 2 case where he does not appeal against his extradition. Section 117 applies if: **10.42**

(a) the Secretary of State orders the defendant's extradition to a Category 2 territory under Part 2, and
(b) no notice of an appeal under s 103 or 108 is given before the end of the permitted period, which is 14 days starting with the day on which the Secretary of State informs the defendant under s 100(1) that he has ordered his extradition. For this purpose, any power of a court to extend the period permitted for giving notice of appeal and any power of a court to grant leave to take a step out of time must be ignored.

---

[37] As further amended by the Policing and Crime Act 2009, s 71(9).
[38] As amended by the Police and Justice Act 2006, Sch 13(1), para 9(3).

10.43 By s 117(2), the defendant must be extradited to the Category 2 territory before the end of the 'required period', which is 28 days starting with the day on which the Secretary of State makes the order.

10.44 If s 117(2) is not complied with and the defendant applies to the appropriate judge to be discharged the judge must order his discharge, unless reasonable cause is shown for the delay. The principles considered at paras 10.15–10.21 in relation to s 35(5) apply equally here, save that Part 2 is not constrained by Article 23 of the Framework Decision, and thus the concept of 'reasonable cause' may be wider in this context.

Time for extradition where there has been an appeal

10.45 The time period for extradition where the defendant has appealed to the High Court or Supreme Court is specified in s 118. The section applies if:

(a) there is an appeal to the High Court under s 103, 108 or 110 against a decision or order relating to the defendant's extradition to a Category 2 territory, and
(b) the effect of the decision of the relevant court on the appeal is that the defendant is to be extradited there.

10.46 By s 118(2), the defendant must be extradited to the requesting Category 2 territory before the end of the required period, which is 28 days starting with:

(a) the day on which the decision of the relevant court on the appeal becomes final, or
(b) the day on which proceedings on the appeal are discontinued.

10.47 The relevant court is the High Court if there is no appeal to the Supreme Court against the decision of the High Court on the appeal, or, if there is such an appeal, the Supreme Court (s 118(3)).

10.48 The decision of the High Court on the appeal becomes final (s 118(4)):

(a) when the period permitted for applying to the High Court for leave to appeal to the Supreme Court ends, if there is no such application;[39]
(b) when the period permitted for applying to the Supreme Court for leave to appeal to it ends, if the High Court refuses leave to appeal and there is no application to the Supreme Court for leave to appeal;
(c) when the Supreme Court refuses leave to appeal to it;
(d) at the end of the permitted period, which is 28 days starting with the day on which leave to appeal to the Supreme Court is granted, if no such appeal is brought before the end of that period.

10.49 The decision of the Supreme Court on the appeal becomes final when it is made (s 188(6)).

10.50 The power of a court to extend the period permitted for applying for leave to appeal and any power of a court to grant leave to take a step out of time must be ignored for the purposes of s 118(4).

10.51 If s 118(2) is not complied with and the defendant applies to the appropriate judge to be discharged the judge must order his discharge, unless reasonable cause is shown for the delay. The principles and case law discussed at paras 10.15–10.21 in relation to s 35(5) apply equally here, save that Part 2 is not constrained by Article 23 of the EAW Framework Decision and thus the concept of 'reasonable cause' may be wider in this context.

---

39 The issues and case law discussed above at para 10.27 apply equally here.

Time for extradition where undertakings sought from requesting state

Where the extradition is sought of a defendant serving a sentence of imprisonment in the UK, in parallel with the appropriate judge's powers under s 37 in a Part 1 case, the Secretary of State has the power in Part 2 cases to order extradition prior to completion of the sentence on condition that the requesting state gives appropriate undertakings to ensure the defendant returns to the UK to complete his sentence. In such a case, s 119 of the EA 2003 specifies the time within which such undertakings must be given and the time within which the defendant must be extradited. **10.52**

Section 119, as amended by para 13 of Sch 13 to the Police and Justice Act 2006, applies if the Secretary of State orders the defendant's extradition to a Category 2 territory under Part 2 and the defendant is serving a sentence of imprisonment or another form of detention in the UK in custody or on licence. As discussed at para 10.37, by s 197A of the EA 2003, the order for extradition is sufficient authority for the person to be removed from the prison or other institution where he is detained. **10.53**

The Secretary of State may make the order for extradition subject to the condition that extradition is not to take place before he receives an undertaking given on behalf of the Category 2 territory in terms specified by him (s 119(2)). **10.54**

The terms which may be specified by the Secretary of State in relation to a defendant accused in a Category 2 territory of the commission of an offence who is in custody in the UK (ie within s 119(1)(b)(i)) include terms: **10.55**

(a) that the defendant be kept in custody until the conclusion of the proceedings against him for the offence and any other offence in respect of which he is permitted to be dealt with in the Category 2 territory;
(b) that the defendant be returned to the UK to serve the remainder of his sentence on the conclusion of those proceedings.

Section 119(3A) provides that the terms which may be specified by the Secretary of State in relation to a person within s 119(1)(b)(ii) (ie a person on licence) who is accused in a Category 2 territory of the commission of an offence include terms that the person be returned to the UK to serve the remainder of his sentence after serving any sentence imposed on him in the Category 2 territory for the offence, and any other offence in respect of which he is permitted to be dealt with in the Category 2 territory. **10.56**

The terms which may be specified by the Secretary of State, in relation to a defendant alleged to be unlawfully at large after conviction of an offence by a court in a Category 2 territory, include terms that he be returned to the UK to serve the remainder of his sentence after serving any sentence imposed on him in the Category 2 territory for the offence, and any other offence in respect of which he is permitted to be dealt with in the Category 2 territory. **10.57**

Section 119(6) and (7) apply if the Secretary of State makes an order for extradition subject to a condition under s 119(2): **10.58**

(a) By s 119(6), if the Secretary of State does not receive the undertaking before the end of the period of 21 days starting with the day on which he makes the order and the person applies to the High Court to be discharged, the court must order his discharge.
(b) By s 119(7), if the Secretary of State receives the undertaking before the end of that period:
    (i) in a case where s 117 applies, the required period for the purposes of s 117(2) is 28 days starting with the day on which the Secretary of State receives the undertaking;

(ii) in a case where s 118 applies, the required period for the purposes of s 118(2) is 28 days starting with the day on which the decision of the relevant court on the appeal becomes final (within the meaning of s 118) or (if later) the day on which the Secretary of State receives the undertaking.

Time for extradition following deferral for a competing claim

10.59 In parallel with the appropriate judge's powers under s 44 in a Part 1 case, the Secretary of State has power under s 126 to defer extradition under Part 2 until the conclusion of other Part 2 proceedings. The Secretary of State also has power to make such an order under s 179 in the face of a competing Part 1 warrant. Section 120 specifies the time limit for extradition where the Secretary of State has deferred extradition under Part 2 because of a competing Part 1 warrant or Part 2 request and, for whatever reason, the order for deferral has been lifted under s 181.

10.60 Section 120 applies if:

(a) an order is made under Part 2 for the defendant to be extradited to a Category 2 territory in pursuance of a request for his extradition;
(b) before the defendant is extradited to the territory an order is made under s 126(2) or 179(2) for his extradition in pursuance of the request to be deferred;
(c) the appropriate judge makes an order under s 181(2) for the defendant's extradition in pursuance of the request to cease to be deferred.

10.61 Section 120(2) provides that in a case where s 117 applies, the required period for the purposes of s 117(2) is 28 days starting with the day on which the order under s 181(2) is made.

10.62 In a case where s 118 applies, the required period for the purposes of s 118(2) is 28 days starting with the day on which the decision of the relevant court on the appeal becomes final (within the meaning of s 118) or (if later) the day on which the order under s 181(2) is made.

11

CONSENT TO EXTRADITION; WITHDRAWAL OF CLAIMS FOR EXTRADITION

A. Introduction

Some defendants do not wish to contest the request for their extradition and want to return as quickly as possible to the requesting state. The EA 1870 did not provide any mechanism for expedited return. This was recognized as undesirable in 1982 by the Home Office Working Party on Extradition, and it made appropriate recommendations in its Report. **11.01**

In the EA 1989 Parliament introduced a simplified procedure in s 14 and para 9 of Sch 1 by which the defendant could waive his rights under the Act. Appropriate forms of consent were contained in the Schedule to the Magistrates' Court (Extradition) Rules 1989.[1] However, these provisions gave rise to some difficulties in their application,[2] and the European Union Extradition Regulations 2002[3] introduced significant changes to the procedure for consenting to return in EU cases. **11.02**

The EA 2003 introduces revised procedures by which the defendant can consent to extradition. These are considered in the first part of this chapter. **11.03**

The EA 2003 also sets out in detail the procedure to be followed where a Part 1 warrant or an extradition request is withdrawn by the requesting state. These provisions are considered later in this chapter. **11.04**

B. Consent to Extradition

Consent to extradition in Part 1 cases

Section 45(1) and (2) provide that a defendant arrested under a Part 1 warrant, or a person provisionally arrested under s 5, may consent to his extradition to the Category 1 territory in which the warrant was issued. Consent must be voluntary and it must be made in full awarenesss of its consequences, which includes the legal consequences under the 2003 Act.[4] **11.05**

> What then is involved in the notion of voluntariness in this context? Clearly, consent should involve the deliberate agreement or acquiescence by a person of full age, with requisite

[1] SI 1989/1527.
[2] *In the Matter of Akbar*, 31 July 1996, CO/1797/96.
[3] SI 2002/419.
[4] *Re Ballan's Application for Judicial Review* [2008] NIQB 140, paras 22 and 24.

> mental capacity who is not under duress or coercion. In my judgment it must also involve a decision taken on a properly informed basis. If a person consents to surrender when he has been caused to believe that he has no option but to do so and where there are, in fact, grounds on which legitimate objection could be made, his consent cannot be described as voluntary in any true sense. This does not mean that a person deciding whether to consent must be made aware of every possible ground, however arcane or esoteric, on which he might withhold consent. But if he gives his consent on an understanding of the facts or legal position which is incorrect and if, had he been in possession of the accurate information, he would not have done so, then I do not consider that his consent can be said to be voluntary.[5]

The appropriate judge should reconsider an order to extradite made after the defendant has consented if it is submitted that the defendant has not provided his consent voluntarily or with an understanding of the consequences. This does not involve considering whether the consent can be revoked as if it has not been validly given if it is not voluntary and with an understanding of the consequences.[6]

11.06 By s 45(3), if the defendant consents to his extradition under s 45 he must be taken to have waived any right he would have (apart from the consent) not to be dealt with in the Category 1 territory for an offence committed before his extradition. Accordingly, a defendant who consents to his return waives his specialty protection in the requesting state. Specialty has been considered in para 5.72 in the context of bars to extradition.

11.07 Section 45(4) is an important provision and contains a number of requirements to ensure that the defendant's consent to extradition is given fully and freely and with a proper understanding of the consequences. It provides that consent under s 45 must be given before the appropriate judge; must be recorded in writing; and is irrevocable.

11.08 Section 45(5) provides that the defendant may not give his consent under s 45 unless he is legally represented before the appropriate judge at the time he gives consent. However, by s 45(6), he need not be legally represented if he has been informed of his right to apply for legal aid and has had the opportunity to apply for legal aid, but he has refused or failed to apply; he has applied for legal aid but his application has been refused; or he was granted legal aid but the legal aid was withdrawn.

11.09 By s 45(8), a defendant is to be treated as legally represented before the appropriate judge if (and only if) he has the assistance of counsel or a solicitor to represent him in the proceedings before the appropriate judge.

11.10 Once the defendant has given his consent under s 45 then the procedure under s 46 applies. The judge must remand the defendant in custody or on bail (s 46(2)) although, if the person is remanded in custody, the appropriate judge may later grant bail (s 46(3)).

11.11 Section 46(4) disapplies the judge's duty under s 8 to fix a date for the start of the extradition hearing. Also, if the extradition hearing has begun, the judge is no longer required to proceed (or continue proceeding) under ss 10–25.

11.12 By s 46(6), the judge must order the defendant's extradition to the Category 1 territory within the period of 10 days starting with the day on which consent is given. This sub-section has effect subject to ss 48 and 51.

---

[5] Ibid, paras 23–24.
[6] Ibid, para 29.

Importantly, if s 46(6) is not complied with and the person applies to the judge to be discharged the judge must order his discharge. **11.13**

Once the order for extradition has been made by the appropriate judge under s 46(6) then s 47 applies. By s 47(2), the defendant must be extradited to the Category 1 territory before the end of the required period. This is 10 days starting with the day on which the order is made or, if the judge and the authority which issued the Part 1 warrant agree a later date, 10 days starting with the later date.[7] If s 47(2) is not complied with and the defendant applies to the judge to be discharged the judge must order his discharge, unless reasonable cause is shown for the delay. **11.14**

If before the defendant is extradited the judge is informed by the designated authority that the Part 1 warrant has been withdrawn then s 47(2) does not apply, and the judge must order the defendant's discharge. **11.15**

Other Part 1 warrant issued following consent to return to Category 1 territory

Where the defendant has consented to his extradition to a Category 1 territory and another Part 1 warrant is issued before he has been extradited then ss 48 and 49 apply. These sections require the judge to decide whether to order extradition pursuant to the consent or to defer proceedings to allow the second warrant to be disposed of. **11.16**

Section 48 applies if: **11.17**

(a) the defendant consents under s 45 to his extradition to a Category 1 territory, and
(b) the conditions in s 48(2) are satisfied before the judge orders his extradition under s 46(6).

The conditions in s 48(2) are that: **11.18**

(a) the judge is informed that another Part 1 warrant has been issued in respect of the defendant;
(b) the warrant falls to be dealt with by the judge or by a judge who is the appropriate judge in another part of the UK;
(c) the warrant has not been disposed of.

In such a case, the duty of the judge to order extradition under s 46(6) within 10 days of the defendant's consent does not apply, and the judge may either order the defendant's extradition pursuant to his consent, or order further proceedings on the warrant under consideration to be deferred until the other warrant has been disposed of (s 48(3)). **11.19**

In deciding under s 48(3) what order to make, the judge must take into account in particular (s 48(5)): **11.20**

(a) the relative seriousness of the offences concerned;
(b) the place where each offence was committed (or was alleged to have been committed);
(c) the date on which each warrant was issued;
(d) whether, in the case of each offence, the defendant is accused of its commission (but not alleged to have been convicted) or is alleged to be unlawfully at large after conviction.

---

[7] In *Governor of HMP Wandsworth v Kinderis* [2007] EWHC 998 (Admin) the court highlighted the failure of the 2003 Act to cater for the situation when a person has given consent before the extradition hearing starts, and so ss 46 and 47 apply, and the court is aware of a domestic prosecution—s 22 does not apply in these circumstances. This has now been addressed by ss 8A and 8B which apply before the extradition hearing commences.

11.21 If the judge makes an order under s 48(3)(a) for the defendant's extradition to a Category 1 territory pursuant to his consent then s 49 applies (s 49(1)). Section 49(2) requires that the defendant be extradited to the Category 1 territory before the end of the required period. The required period is 10 days starting with the day on which the order is made, or if the judge and the authority which issued the Part 1 warrant agree a later date, 10 days starting with the later date (s 49(3)).

11.22 If s 49(2) is not complied with and the defendant applies to the judge to be discharged the judge must order his discharge, unless reasonable cause is shown for the delay (s 49(4)). However, if before the defendant is extradited to the Category 1 territory the judge is informed by the designated authority (see s 2(9)) that the Part 1 warrant has been withdrawn then s 49(2) does not apply, and the judge must order the defendant's discharge (s 49(5)).

11.23 If, however, the judge makes an order under s 48(3)(b) for proceedings on the Part 1 warrant to be deferred until the other warrant has been disposed of then s 50 applies (s 50(1)). The judge must remand the person in respect of whom the warrant was issued in custody or on bail (s 50(2)) although if the person is remanded in custody the appropriate judge may later grant bail (s 50(3)).

11.24 If an order is made under s 180 for proceedings on the warrant to be resumed, the period specified in s 46(6) within which extradition has to take place must be taken to be 10 days starting with the day on which the order under s 180 is made (s 50(4)).

Extradition request made under Part 2 following consent to return to Category 1 territory

11.25 Section 51 governs the procedure where an extradition request is made by a Category 2 territory in respect of a defendant who has consented to his return to a Category 1 territory.

11.26 Section 51 applies if:

(a) a defendant in respect of whom a Part 1 warrant is issued consents under s 45 to his extradition, and
(b) the condition in s 51(2) is satisfied before the judge orders his extradition under s 46(6) or 48(3)(a). This condition is that a certificate has been issued by the Secretary of State under s 70 in respect of the extradition request, and the request has not been disposed of.

11.27 As explained at para 8.45, s 179 allows the Secretary of State to regulate competing extradition claims by making appropriate orders for deferral. Where s 51 applies, the judge must not make an order under s 46(6) or 48(3) until he has been informed what order has been made by the Secretary of State under s 179(2).

11.28 If the order under s 179(2) is for further proceedings on the warrant to be deferred until the request has been disposed of, the judge must remand the person in custody or on bail (s 51(4)). If the person is remanded in custody the appropriate judge may later grant bail (s 51(5)).

11.29 If the order under s 179(2) is for further proceedings on the warrant to be deferred until the request has been disposed of, and an order is made under s 180 for proceedings on the warrant to be resumed, the period specified in s 46(6) must be taken to be 10 days starting with the day on which the order under s 180 is made.

11.30 If the order under s 179(2) is for further proceedings on the request to be deferred until the warrant has been disposed of, the period specified in s 46(6) must be taken to be 10 days starting with the day on which the judge is informed of the order.

Undertaking in relation to defendant serving sentence who has consented to extradition

11.31 Section 52, as amended by para 11 of Sch 13 to the Police and Justice Act 2006, allows the appropriate judge to seek a suitable undertaking from the requesting territory that a defendant who is a serving prisoner in the UK who has consented to extradition will be returned to the UK at the conclusion of the foreign proceedings to serve the remainder of his sentence.

Section 52 applies if: **11.32**

(a) the appropriate judge makes an order under s 46(6) or 48(3)(a) for the defendant's extradition to a Category 1 territory;
(b) the defendant is serving a sentence of imprisonment or another form of detention in the UK either in custody or on licence.

The judge may make the order for extradition subject to the condition that extradition is not to take place before he receives an undertaking given on behalf of the Category 1 territory in terms specified by him (s 52(2)).

The terms which may be specified in relation to an accused person who is in custody in the UK include terms (s 52(3)): **11.33**

(a) that the defendant be kept in custody until the conclusion of the proceedings against him for the offence and any other offence in respect of which he is permitted to be dealt with in the Category 1 territory;
(b) that the defendant be returned to the UK to serve the remainder of his sentence on the conclusion of those proceedings.

By s 52(3A), the terms which may be specified by the judge in relation to a person within s 52(1)(b)(ii) (ie a prisoner on licence) who is accused in a Category 1 territory of the commission of an offence include terms that the person be returned to the UK to serve the remainder of his sentence after serving any sentence imposed on him in the Category 1 territory for the offence, and any other offence in respect of which he is permitted to be dealt with in the Category 1 territory. **11.34**

The terms which may be specified by the judge in relation to a defendant alleged to be unlawfully at large after conviction of an offence include terms that he be returned to the UK to serve the remainder of his sentence after serving any sentence imposed on him in the Category 1 territory for the offence and any other offence in respect of which he is permitted to be dealt with in the Category 1 territory (s 52(4)). **11.35**

If the judge makes an order for extradition subject to a condition under s 52(2) then the required period for the purposes of ss 47(2) and 49(2) is 10 days starting with the day on which the judge receives the undertaking (s 52(5)). **11.36**

Consent to extradition in Part 2 cases

The mode of giving consent to extradition in Part 2 cases is dealt with in ss 127 and 128. **11.37**

Section 127(1) provides that a defendant who has been arrested under a warrant issued under s 71 may consent to his extradition to the Category 2 territory to which his extradition is requested. Also, a defendant who has been arrested under a provisional warrant issued under s 73 may consent to his extradition to the Category 2 territory in which he is accused of the commission of an offence or is alleged to have been convicted of an offence (s 127(2)). By s 127(3), consent under s 127 must be given in writing and is irrevocable. Consent must be voluntary and it must be made in full awarenesss of its consequences, which includes the legal consequences under the 2003 Act.[8] **11.38**

[8] *Re Ballan's Application for Judicial Review* [2008] NIQB 140, paras 22 and 24. See para 11.05.

11.39 Where consent is given under s 127 before the defendant's case is sent to the Secretary of State for his decision whether the defendant is to be extradited, then the consent must be given before the appropriate judge (s 127(4)). In any other case, consent must be given to the Secretary of State (s 127(5)).

11.40 The defendant may not give his consent under s 127 before the appropriate judge unless he is legally represented before the appropriate judge at the time he gives consent, or he is a person to whom s 127(7) applies. This subsection applies to the defendant if he has been informed of his right to apply for legal aid and has had the opportunity to apply for legal aid, but he has refused or failed to apply; he has applied for legal aid but his application has been refused; or he was granted legal aid but the legal aid was withdrawn. Legal aid is defined in s 127(8).

11.41 For the purposes of s 127(6) the defendant is to be treated as legally represented before the appropriate judge if (and only if) he has the assistance of counsel or a solicitor to represent him in the proceedings before the appropriate judge.

11.42 Section 128 applies if a person gives his consent under s 127 to the appropriate judge. If the judge has not fixed a date under s 75 or 76 on which the extradition hearing is to begin he is not required to do so (s 128(2)). If the extradition hearing has begun, the judge is no longer required to proceed or continue proceeding under ss 78–91 (s 128(3)). The judge must send the case to the Secretary of State for his decision whether the person is to be extradited.[9]

11.43 By s 128(5), consent under Part 2 constitutes a waiver of the specialty protection to which the defendant would otherwise be entitled. The defendant must be taken to have waived any right he would have (apart from the consent) not to be dealt with in the Category 2 territory for an offence committed before his extradition. By s 95(2), the prohibition on return where there are no speciality arrangements with the requesting Category 2 territory does not apply where the defendant consented to return before his case was sent to the Secretary of State.

11.44 In a consent case the defendant loses any right to appeal to the High Court by s 100(2) and under s 117(2), the defendant must be extradited to the Category 2 territory before the end of the required period, which is 28 days starting with the day on which the Secretary of State makes the order.

C. Withdrawal of the Claim for Extradition

11.45 In some cases the requesting state withdraws its request for extradition before proceedings in the UK have concluded. This may happen for a number of reasons. For example, further investigation may reveal that there is insufficient evidence to secure a conviction, or the circumstances may change so that the defendant's continued prosecution is undesirable.

11.46 Whereas the EA 1989 did not specify what was to happen in such circumstances, the EA 2003 contains provisions to deal with this eventuality. There are separate sections dealing with Part 1 and Part 2 cases.

Withdrawal of Part 1 warrant

11.47 The operative provisions in relation to Part 1 cases are ss 41–43.

---

[9] In *Governor of HMP Wandsworth v Kinderis* [2007] EWHC 998 (Admin) the court highlighted the failure of the 2003 Act to cater for the situation when a person has given consent before the extradition hearing starts and the court is aware of a domestic prosecution. This has now been addressed by ss 76A and 76B which apply before the extradition hearing commences.

Section 41 applies if at any time in the relevant period the appropriate judge is informed by the designated authority that a Part 1 warrant issued in respect of the defendant has been withdrawn (s 41(1)). Section 41(3) provides that in such a case the judge must order the defendant's discharge. If the person is not before the judge at the time the judge orders his discharge, the judge must inform him of the order as soon as practicable. **11.48**

By s 41(2), the relevant period is the period starting when the person is first brought before the appropriate judge following his arrest under Part 1 and ending when the person is extradited in pursuance of the warrant, or discharged. **11.49**

Section 42 deals with withdrawal of the warrant while an appeal to the High Court under s 26 or 28 is pending. It applies if, at any time in the relevant period, the High Court is informed by the designated authority that a Part 1 warrant issued in respect of the defendant has been withdrawn (s 42(1)). In such a case, if the appeal is under s 26, the Court must order the defendant's discharge and quash the order for his extradition; if the appeal is under s 28, the Court must dismiss the appeal (s 42(3)). **11.50**

If the defendant is not before the Court at the time the court orders his discharge the Court must inform him of the order as soon as practicable (s 42(4)). **11.51**

In this case the relevant period is the period starting when notice of an appeal to the High Court is given by the person or the authority which issued the warrant and ending when proceedings on the appeal are discontinued or the High Court makes its decision on the appeal (s 42(2)). **11.52**

Section 43 provides for the discharge of the defendant whilst an appeal to the Supreme Court is pending. It applies if at any time in the 'relevant period' the Supreme Court is informed by the designated authority that a Part 1 warrant issued in respect of the defendant has been withdrawn (s 43(1)). If the appeal is brought by the defendant the Supreme Court must order the person's discharge and quash the order for his extradition, in a case where the appeal was against a decision of the High Court to dismiss an appeal under s 26 (s 43(3)). If the appeal is brought by the authority which issued the warrant, the Supreme Court must dismiss the appeal (s 43(4)). **11.53**

In this case the relevant period is the period starting when leave to appeal to the Supreme Court is granted to the defendant or the authority which issued the warrant, and ending when proceedings on the appeal are discontinued or the Supreme Court makes its decision on the appeal (s 43(2)). **11.54**

If the defendant is not before the Supreme Court at the time it orders his discharge, the Supreme Court must inform him of the order as soon as practicable (s 43(5)). **11.55**

Withdrawal of the extradition request in Part 2 cases

The relevant sections in Part 2 cases are ss 122–125. **11.56**

Section 122 applies if at any time in the relevant period the appropriate judge is informed by the Secretary of State that a request for the defendant's extradition has been withdrawn (s 122(1)). The judge must then order the defendant's discharge (s 122(3)). If the defendant is not before the judge at the time the judge orders his discharge, the judge must inform him of the order as soon as practicable (s 122(4)). **11.57**

By s 122(2) the relevant period is the period starting when the defendant first appears or is brought before the appropriate judge following his arrest under Part 2, and ending when the judge orders the defendant's discharge or sends the case to the Secretary of State for his decision whether the person is to be extradited. **11.58**

11.59 Section 123 applies if, during the relevant period, the Secretary of State is informed that a request for a person's extradition has been withdrawn. In that case, the Secretary of State must order the person's discharge (s 123(3)).

11.60 By s 123(2) the relevant period is the period starting when the judge sends the case to the Secretary of State for his decision whether the defendant is to be extradited, and ending when the person is extradited in pursuance of the request or discharged.

11.61 Section 124 deals with the situation where the extradition request is withdrawn while there is an appeal to the High Court by the defendant or the requesting state. It applies if, during the relevant period, the High Court is informed by the Secretary of State that a request for the defendant's extradition has been withdrawn (s 124(1)). If the appeal is under s 103 or 108, the court must order the defendant's discharge and quash the order for his extradition, if the Secretary of State has ordered his extradition (s 124(3)). If the appeal is under s 105 or 110, the Court must dismiss the appeal (s 124(4)). If the person is not before the court at the time the Court orders his discharge, the court must inform him of the order as soon as practicable (s 124(5)).

11.62 The relevant period is the period starting when notice of an appeal to the court is given by the defendant or by a person acting on behalf of the Category 2 territory to which his extradition is requested, and ending when proceedings on the appeal are discontinued or the Court makes its decision on the appeal.

11.63 Where the extradition request is withdrawn while an appeal to the Supreme Court is pending then s 125 applies. It applies if, at any time in the relevant period, the Supreme Court is informed by the Secretary of State that a request for a person's extradition has been withdrawn. In such a case, if the appeal is brought by the defendant, the Supreme Court must order his discharge and quash the order for his extradition, in a case where the appeal was against a decision of the High Court to dismiss an appeal under s 103 or 108 (s 125(3)).

11.64 If the appeal is brought by a person acting on behalf of the Category 2 territory the Supreme Court must dismiss the appeal (s 125(4)). If the person whose extradition is requested is not before the Supreme Court at the time it orders his discharge, the Supreme Court must inform him of the order as soon as practicable (s 125(5)).

11.65 For these purposes, the relevant period is the period starting when leave to appeal to the Supreme Court is granted to the defendant or a person acting on behalf of the requesting Category 2 territory, and ending when proceedings on the appeal are discontinued or the Supreme Court makes its decision on the appeal (s 125(2)).

12

RETURN TO THE UNITED KINGDOM

A. Introduction

The EA 1989 was primarily concerned with incoming extradition requests and outgoing defendants. The principal provisions applicable to outgoing extradition requests were Part IV and para 17 of Sch 1, which provided specialty protection for defendants extradited to the UK.[1] **12.01**

The EA 1989 did not provide statutory authority for the making of extradition requests by the UK (known as outgoing requests), which were made under the Royal Prerogative.[2] The arrest **12.02**

[1] *R v Corrigan* [1931] 1 KB 527; *R v Aubrey-Fletcher ex p Ross Munro* [1968] 1 QB 620; *Kerr and Smith* (1976) 62 Cr App R 210. Specialty is dealt with at paras 12.26, 12.58, 12.62 and 12.81. On occasion, rather than pursuing a legitimate extradition request, UK prosecuting authorities have resorted to illegal methods to obtain the return of a defendant for trial (see *R v Horseferry Road Magistrates' Court ex p Bennett* [1994] 2 AC 42; *R v Horseferry Road Magistrates' Court ex p Bennett (No. 3)* [1995] 1 Cr App R 147; *R v Mullen* [2000] QB 520). This is known as 'disguised extradition' and is dealt with below at para 12.69.

[2] *Barton v The Commonwealth of Australia* [1974] 131 CLR.

warrant and necessary supporting evidence was forwarded to the Home Office for certification, and was then forwarded to the Foreign and Commonwealth Office for service on the foreign state through diplomatic channels.

12.03 In contrast, Part 3 of the EA 2003, considered in the first part of this chapter, puts the making of outgoing requests on a statutory basis in cases where the requested territory is a Category 1 territory. Part 3 specifies how the arrest warrant is to be obtained, and it specifies the offences for which extradition can be requested by the UK.

12.04 Requests for extradition to Category 2 territories continue to be dealt with under the Royal Prerogative. The pre-2004 law concerning the limits of the powers of the UK courts to review the circumstances of their issuance, continue to apply.[3]

12.05 The second part of this chapter considers the return of extradited persons to the UK to serve the remainder of their sentences.

B. Extradition from Category 1 Territories

Offences for which extradition may be requested

12.06 Under Part 3 of the EA 2003 (ss 142–155A), the UK may seek the extradition of a defendant from a Category 1 territory in respect of 'extradition offences' as that term is defined in s 148.[4] It is therefore convenient to consider this definition before examining the mechanism for seeking the defendant's extradition.

12.07 Section 148(1) provides that, in an accusation case, conduct constitutes an extradition offence in relation to the UK if it occurs in the UK and is punishable under the law of the relevant part of the UK (as defined in s 142(6)) with imprisonment or another form of detention for a term of 12 months or a greater punishment. Part 3 requires no assessment of dual criminality which is a matter for the executing state.

12.08 Conduct also constitutes an extradition offence in relation to the UK if the conduct occurs outside the UK and the conduct constitutes an extra-territorial offence punishable under the law of the relevant part of the UK with imprisonment or another form of detention for a term of 12 months or a greater punishment (s 148(2)).

12.09 However s 148(1) and (2) do not apply in relation to the defendant's conduct if he has been convicted by a court in the UK and he has been sentenced for the offence (s 148(3), as amended by para 2(6) of Sch 13 to the Police and Justice Act 2006). In such a case s 148(4) and (5) apply. By s 148(4), conduct also constitutes an extradition offence in relation to the UK if the conduct occurs in the UK and a sentence of imprisonment or another form of detention for a term of four months or a greater punishment has been imposed in the UK in respect of the conduct.

12.10 By s 148(5), conduct also constitutes an extradition offence in relation to the UK if the conduct occurs outside the UK; the conduct constitutes an extra-territorial offence; and a sentence of imprisonment or another form of detention for a term of four months or a greater punishment has been imposed in the UK in respect of the conduct.

---

[3] *R v Secretary of State for the Home Department ex p Bagudu*, 8 September 2003 (CO/4208/2003); *R v Secretary of State for Trade and Industry ex p Levitt*, 16 January 1998 (CO/3811/97).

[4] 'Offences' means criminal offences; with the consequence that the UK cannot seek extradition for civil offences, including civil contempt, even where such proceedings have resulted, or may result, in punishment by way of committal to prison: *OB v The Director of the Serious Fraud Office* [2012] EWCA Crim 67.

The relevant part of the UK is the part of the UK in which the relevant proceedings are taking place (s 142(6)). The relevant proceedings are the proceedings in which it is necessary to decide whether conduct constitutes an extradition offence (s 142(7)). **12.11**

The definitions in s 148(1)–(5) apply for the purposes of ss 142–147 (issuance of Part 3 warrants, service of UK sentence abroad, specialty, and consent). **12.12**

Part 3 warrants

The first stage in seeking the extradition of a defendant from a Category 1 territory involves obtaining a Part 3 warrant from an appropriate judge (s 142(3)). By s 142(1), an appropriate judge[5] may issue a Part 3 warrant in respect of a person if a constable or an 'appropriate person' applies to him for a Part 3 warrant, and the conditions in s 142(2) or s 142(2A) are satisfied. **12.13**

Section 142(9) defines an 'appropriate person' to be a person of a description specified in an order made by the Secretary of State for the purposes of s 142. The Extradition Act 2003 (Part 3 Designation) Order 2003[6] has specified that the following are appropriate persons for these purposes: **12.14**

- the Director of the Revenue and Customs Prosecutions Office;
- any member of the Serious Fraud Office designated by the Director of the Serious Fraud Office under s 1(7) of the Criminal Justice Act 1987;
- the Director of Public Prosecutions, any Crown Prosecutor and any counsel or solicitor instructed by the Crown Prosecution Service for the purposes of the case concerned.

The condition in s 142(2), as substituted by para 21(2) of Sch 13 to the Police and Justice Act 2006, is that there are reasonable grounds for believing that the person has committed an extradition offence, and a domestic warrant has been issued in respect of the person. **12.15**

The condition in s 142(2A) is that there are reasonable grounds for believing that the person is 'unlawfully at large after conviction'[7] of an extradition offence by a court in the UK, and either a domestic warrant has been issued in respect of the person or the person may (if unlawfully at large as mentioned in s 142(2A)(a)) be arrested without a warrant. **12.16**

A domestic warrant is, in England and Wales, a warrant for the arrest or apprehension of a person which is issued under the provisions specified in s 142(8A).[8] **12.17**

A Part 3 warrant is defined by s 142(3) to be an arrest warrant which contains one of the statements referred to in s 142(4) or s 142(5), and the certificate referred to in s 142(6). **12.18**

---

[5] Defined in s 149 to be, in England and Wales, a district judge (Magistrates' Courts), a justice of the peace, or a judge entitled to exercise the jurisdiction of the Crown Court.

[6] SI 2003/3335, as amended by the Extradition Act 2003 (Part 3 Designation) (Amendment) Order 2005 (SI 2005/1127).

[7] By statutory omission, the term 'unlawfully at large after conviction' here does not bear the wider meaning ascribed to it elsewhere in the EA 2003. The re-definition of this term, introduced into Parts 1 and 2 of the 2003 Act (ss 68A and 140A) by Sch 13, paras 2(2) and 2(4) of the Police and Justice Act 2006, does not extend to all provisions of Part 3. The 2006 Act was intended to remove the difficulties that had arisen with the concept of 'unlawfully at large after conviction' in earlier legislation which the EA 2003 in its original form had not addressed (see, eg, *Urru v The Governor of HM Prison Brixton & The Government of Italy* (2000) CO/4009/99). So far as Part 3 was concerned, the 2006 Act replaced all existing references to 'unlawfully at large after conviction' (in ss 142(5)(a), 143(4), and 148(3)(a)) with 'been convicted'. However, the 2006 Act also added s 142(2A) without similar modification and thus re-introduced 'unlawfully at large' into Part 3 of the EA 2003 in its unmodified state.

[8] Namely, s 72 of the Criminal Justice Act 1967; s 7 of the Bail Act 1976; s 51 of the Judicature (Northern Ireland) Act 1978; s 1 of the Magistrates' Courts Act 1980; Arts 20 or 25 of the Magistrates' Courts (Northern Ireland) Order 1981 (SI 1981/1675 (NI 26)); or the Criminal Procedure (Scotland) Act 1995. Or, in the case of Northern Ireland, a warrant issued at common law by a Crown Court judge (s 142(8)).

12.19 The statement referred to in s 142(4) concerns defendants who are accused of offences. It is a statement that the person, in respect of whom the warrant is issued, is accused in the UK of the commission of an extradition offence specified in the warrant, and the warrant is issued with a view to his arrest and extradition to the UK for the purpose of being prosecuted for the offence.

12.20 The statement referred to in s 142(5) relates to persons convicted of extradition offences. As amended by para 1(3) of Sch 13 to the Police and Justice Act 2006, the statement referred to in s 142(5) is a statement that the person in respect of whom the warrant is issued has been convicted of an extradition offence specified in the warrant by a court in the UK, and the warrant is issued with a view to his arrest and extradition to the UK for the purpose of being sentenced for the offence or of serving a sentence of imprisonment or another form of detention imposed in respect of the offence.

12.21 The certificate referred to in s 142(6) is one certifying:

(a) whether the conduct constituting the extradition offence specified in the warrant falls within the European Framework List as defined in s 215;
(b) whether the offence is an extra-territorial offence; and
(c) the maximum punishment that may be imposed on conviction of the offence or (if the person has been sentenced for the offence) the sentence that has been imposed.

12.22 The conduct which falls within the European Framework List includes conduct which constitutes an attempt, conspiracy, or incitement to carry out conduct falling within the list, or aiding, abetting, counselling, or procuring the carrying out of conduct falling within the list (s 142(7)).

Category 1 countries not applying the EAW Framework Decision to offences committed before a specified date

12.23 Article 32 of the EAW Framework Decision permits member States to reserve the right to exclude from the operation of the EAW requests for extradition for offences committed before specified dates. Section 155A, inserted by para 24 of Sch 13 to the Police and Justice Act 2006, contains powers relating to requests for extradition for such offences from such countries.

12.24 Section 155A applies to a Category 1 territory that deals with European extradition requests (ie requests for extradition made by the UK or a Category 1 territory otherwise than in accordance with the system provided for in the EAW Framework Decision) if they relate to acts committed before a particular date ('the relevant date'). The Secretary of State may by order provide that, in the case of an extradition request which is made to a specified Category 1 territory to which s 155A applies, and relates to acts committed before the relevant date, Part 3 is to have effect as if that territory were a Category 2 territory (ie Part 3 will not apply), and with such modifications as may be specified.[9]

12.25 Where such an order is made, the Secretary of State has the same powers to request a person's extradition in relation to acts committed before the relevant date as he would have in the case of a Category 2 territory (ie pursuant to the Royal Prerogative).

---

[9] By the Extradition Act 2003 (Specification of Category 1 Territories) Order 2009 (SI 2009/2768), the following territories are designated as ones to which Part 3 of the EA 2003 has effect as if it were a Part 2 territory; Austria (for offences committed prior to 7 August 2002); the Czech Republic (for offences committed prior to 1 November 2004); France (for offences committed prior to 1 November 1993); Italy (for offences committed prior to 7 August 2002); Luxembourg (for offences committed prior to 7 August 2002); and Slovenia (for offences committed prior to 7 August 2002).

Specialty protection for defendants extradited to the UK

A defendant extradited to the UK from a Category 1 territory is entitled to the specialty protection contained in s 146. In other words, following his extradition, he may only be tried in respect of the offences specified in that section. The general principles by which a UK court will determine the claim of a defendant to the specialty protections of s 146 are discussed at para 12.81. **12.26**

Section 146 applies if the defendant is extradited[10] to the UK from a Category 1 territory in pursuance of a Part 3 warrant (s 146(1)). Section 146(2) provides that the defendant may be 'dealt with'[11] in the UK for an offence committed before his extradition only if the offence falls within s 146(3) or the condition in s 146(4) is satisfied. These exceptions are in some instances narrower and in others instances wider than Article 27 of the EAW Framework Decision, to which s 146 seeks to give effect. **12.27**

The offences specified in s 146(3) are as follows: **12.28**

(a) the offence in respect of which the defendant is extradited;[12]
(b) an offence disclosed by the information provided to the Category 1 territory in respect of that offence;[13]

---

[10] cf surrender by consent, which involves the waiver of specialty protection (Articles 13 & 27(3)(e) of the Framework Decision). Consent engages s 147 EA, as to which see below at para 12.32.

[11] Unlike under s 150(8) (extradition from Commonwealth countries) and s 151A(5) (extradition from other territories), s 146 contains no definition of 'dealing with'. The term is therefore to be construed in accordance with the wider definition under Article 27(2) of the EAW Framework Decision to which it gives effect ('prosecuted, sentenced or otherwise deprived of his or her liberty'). In *CPS Newcastle v D* [2011] EWCA Crim 1892, however, the Court of Appeal observed that there exists no material difference between s 146(2), Article 27(2) of the Framework Decision and ss 150–151 of the EA 2003. In all cases, the emphasis of is upon detention pending trial, the trial process, and sentence. Thus the Court held (disapproving *CPS Newcastle v D* [2009] EWCA Crim 1423) that the mere 'prior procedural step' of charging a defendant or obtaining the consent of the DPP to charge, does not constitute 'dealing with' a defendant. Hence, also the mere making of an application for permission (under Part 10 of the Criminal Justice Act 2003) to quash a prior acquittal, and for a retrial, did not amount to 'dealing with' a defendant within the meaning of s 146(2) EA 2003. Such an application could therefore lawfully be made prior to the obtaining of consent to that prosecution by the extraditing State (although the prosecution of the re-trial could not).

[12] See Article 27(2) of the EAW Framework Decision. It should be noted that 'the offence for which he or she was surrendered' has been afforded a very broad interpretation by the European Court of Justice in *In Criminal Proceedings Against Leymann and Pustarov* [2008] C-388/08 PPU. There, having been extradited for the offence of importing amphetamines, but prosecuted upon return for importing hashish, the Court ruled that a modification of the description of the offence concerning the kind of narcotics concerned is not such, of itself, as to define an 'offence other' than that for which the person was surrendered within the meaning of Article 27(2) of the Framework Decision (para 63). The offence concerned was still punishable by imprisonment for a maximum period of at least three years and came under the rubric 'illegal trafficking in narcotic drugs' in the Framework List in Article 2(2) of the EAW Framework Decision (para 62). The Court observed that the surrender request is based on information which reflects the state of investigations at the time of issue of the EAW. It is therefore possible that, in the course of the proceedings, the description of the offence will no longer correspond in all respects to the original description. The evidence which has been gathered can lead to a clarification or even a modification of the constituent elements of the offence which initially justified the issue of the EAW (para 53).

[13] As the Court of Appeal observed in *R v Seddon* [2009] 1 WLR 2342, this exception is not within the EAW Framework Decision and is arguably inconsistent with Article 27. It is wider than the 'lesser offence' exception that applies in some but not all Part 2 cases (see s 150(3)(b) and (4)). For a construction of the word 'sentence' so as to include sentence for a lesser offence, as being 'consistent with the concept of justice', see *Minister of Justice, Equality and Law Reform v Dundon* [2005] IESC 13, para 11. Mere reference in passing, within the EAW, to the facts that underlie the new offence will not satisfy s 146(3)(b): *R v Seddon* (supra); *R v Dey* [2010] EWCA Crim 1190. In *R v Seddon*, an EAW issued for surrender for prosecution for an offence of blackmail, contained no indication whatever that the defendant was required in relation to any Bail Act 1976 offence, nor any assertion that such an offence existed. What it did was to refer in passing, in the statement of facts, to the fact that the defendant had failed to answer his bail and was unlawfully at large after conviction. The Court of

(c) an extradition offence in respect of which consent to the defendant being dealt with is given on behalf of the territory in response to a request made by the appropriate judge;[14]
(d) an offence which is not punishable with imprisonment or another form of detention;[15]
(e) an offence in respect of which the person will not be detained in connection with his trial, sentence or appeal;[16]
(f) an offence in respect of which the person waives the right that he would have (but for s 146(6)(f)) not to be dealt with for the offence.[17]

12.29 The condition in s 146(4) is that the defendant has been given an opportunity to leave the UK and either he has not done so before the end of the 'permitted period', or he has done so before the end of the permitted period and has returned to the UK. The permitted period is 45 days starting with the day on which the defendant arrives in the UK (s 146(5)).[18]

12.30 The operation of the specialty principle in this context can be illustrated by an example, based on the facts of *Kerr and Smith* (1976) 62 Cr App R 210 (a case under the EA 1870). Suppose that a Part 3 warrant is submitted to Denmark for the return of D for an offence of robbery contrary to s 8(1) of the Theft Act 1968. The Part 3 warrant only specifies the offence of robbery, however the factual account of the offence provided by the UK to Denmark refers to D as having carried a sawn-off shotgun in the course of the robbery. This is an offence contrary to s 18 of the Firearms Act 1968. Extradition is granted.

12.31 D could be tried for robbery and for the s 18 offence because it was disclosed in the information provided to Denmark and s 146(3)(b) would therefore apply.[19] If, however, evidence came to light that prior to his extradition D had assaulted his wife, in circumstances where the UK has jurisdiction to prosecute that assault, then he could not be tried for this offence in the UK until after he had been given an opportunity to leave the UK after serving his sentence for the robbery, unless Denmark consented or he waived his rights. This is because the offence

---

Appeal held that s 146(3)(b) was intended to cover: (a) 'lesser included offences' within the extradition offence for which surrender had been sought, for example manslaughter where the extradition offence for which surrender is sought was murder or similar examples; and possibly also (although it was not necessary for the court to give a concluded view) (b) an 'ancillary offence' disclosed within the conduct complained of. An example of the second category would be an EAW which seeks surrender for an offence of robbery where the facts of the robbery disclosed in the warrant reveal that the robber was armed at the time.

14 As amended by para 23 of Sch 13 to the Police and Justice Act 2006. See Articles 27(1), 27(3)(g), and 27(4) of the EAW Framework Decision. It is not necessary for the receiving state to wait for consent to commence the prosecution so long as no deprivation of liberty is imposed (see further at n 16 regarding s 146(3)(e)).

15 See Article 27(3)(b) of the EAW Framework Decision. It should be noted that the EA 2003 does not enact Article 27(3)(d) of the Framework Decision which would permit prosecution as an exception to the specialty rule where the new offence is punishable by a non-custodial sentence but with imprisonment possible in *lieu* of that non-custodial sentence (ie imprisonment in default of payment of a confiscation order). As the EA 2003 stands, prosecution for any offence, other than that for which extradition is granted, which may attract such a default sentence is prohibited by s 146 (unless the extraditing state or the defendant consents).

16 See Article 27(3)(c) of the EAW Framework Decision. The interaction between Articles 27(3)(c) and 27(3)(g) were also examined in *In Criminal Proceedings Against Leymann and Pustarov* [2008] C-388/08 PPU. There, following surrender, the defendant was prosecuted for an offence requiring consent of the surrendering state. The Court held that, even though the offence gave rise to a penalty involving deprivation of liberty, Article 27(3)(c) permitted the receiving state to commence the prosecution prior to receipt of consent, provided that no such measures were applied during the proceedings. If however, after judgment has been given, that person is sentenced to a penalty or a measure restricting liberty, consent is required in order to enable that penalty to be executed (para 73).

17 See Article 27(3)(f) of the EAW Framework Decision.

18 See Article 27(3)(a) of the Framework Decision.

19 Although, as noted above, this is not a situation for which the EAW Framework Decision caters.

of assault did not form part of the information supplied in support of the application for his extradition.

Being 'extradited' to the UK is a term of art. It is to be distinguished from being surrendered to the UK by consent. Where the defendant consents to his extradition in the Category 1 state then s 147 applies. This section clarifies the uncertainty in the law under the EA 1989 discussed in *R v Secretary of State for the Home Department ex p Johnson* [1999] QB 1174, namely whether a defendant who had waived his rights in the foreign state nevertheless retained specialty protection in the UK. **12.32**

Section 147 applies if the defendant is extradited to the UK from a Category 1 territory in pursuance of a Part 3 warrant and he consented to his extradition to the UK in accordance with the law of the Category 1 territory. By s 147(2), s 146(2) (the rule of specialty) does not apply if the conditions in s 147(3) or (4) are satisfied. **12.33**

The conditions in s 147(3) are that under the law of the Category 1 territory, the effect of the defendant's consent is to waive his right to specialty and he has not revoked his consent in accordance with that law, if he is permitted to do so under that law. **12.34**

The conditions in s 147(4) are that: **12.35**

(a) under the law of the Category 1 territory, the effect of the defendant's consent is not to waive his right under s 146(2); [but]
(b) he has expressly waived his right under s 146(2) in accordance with that law;
(c) he has not revoked his consent in accordance with that law, if he is permitted to do so under that law; and
(d) he has not revoked the waiver of his right under s 146(2) in accordance with that law, if he is permitted to do so under that law.

Outstanding convictions and remission of punishment

As a corollary to the provisions of the EA 2003 concerning the rule of specialty, s 152 provides for all other outstanding sentences to be treated as served. Section 152, as amended by s 75 of the Policing and Crime Act 2009, applies if: **12.36**

(a) a person is extradited to the UK;
(b) before his extradition he has been convicted of an offence in the UK;
(c) he has not been extradited in respect of that offence.

By s 152(2), the sentence for the offence must be treated as served,[20] but the person's conviction for the offence must be treated as a conviction for all other purposes. **12.37**

Extradition of serving prisoners to the UK

The UK is able to grant extradition to Category 1 territories of serving prisoners subject to suitable undertakings that they will be returned to the UK at the conclusion of foreign proceedings (see s 37 discussed at para 10.30).[21] Conversely, the UK is also able to request the extradition to the UK of defendants serving sentences of imprisonment in Category 1 territories in exchange **12.38**

---

[20] Note that s 152 contains no provision equivalent to s 153C(6). Therefore, under s 152, all aspects of the sentence, not merely the term of imprisonment or other detention, are deemed served.

[21] The power to interrupt a sentence of imprisonment for the purpose of extradition is now contained in EA 2003, s 197A; cf *R (Handa) v Bow Street Magistrates' Court* [2004] EWHC 2986, para 30. Section 59 governs the treatment of such persons upon return and is discussed at para 12.95.

for suitable undertakings by the Secretary of State. This is the process of temporary surrender envisaged by Article 24 of the EAW Framework Decision.

12.39 Section 153A[22] applies if:

(a) the defendant is accused in the UK of the commission of, or has been convicted by or before a UK court of, an offence;
(b) a Part 3 warrant is issued in respect of the defendant;
(c) the defendant is serving a sentence of imprisonment or another form of detention in the Category 1 territory;
(d) the defendant's extradition to the UK from the Category 1 territory in pursuance of the Part 3 warrant is made subject to a condition that an undertaking is given by or on behalf of the UK with regard to his treatment in the UK or his return to the Category 1 territory (or both).

12.40 Section 153A(2) provides that the Secretary of State may, but is not obliged to, give an undertaking to a person acting on behalf of the Category 1 territory with regard to the treatment in the UK of the defendant and/or his return to the Category 1 territory. Nothing in s 153A requires the return of a person to a Category 1 territory if the Secretary of State is not satisfied that the return will be compatible with the person's Convention rights or with the UK's obligations under the 1951 Refugee Convention (s 153D).

12.41 The terms which may be included by the Secretary of State in an undertaking given under s 153A(2) in relation to a defendant accused in the UK of an offence include terms:

(a) that the defendant be kept in custody until the conclusion of the proceedings against him for the offence and any other offence in respect of which he is permitted to be dealt with in the UK;
(b) that the person be returned to the Category 1 territory to serve the remainder of his sentence on the conclusion of those proceedings.

12.42 The terms which may be included by the Secretary of State in an undertaking given under s 153A(2) in relation to a defendant who has been convicted of an offence by or before a court in the UK include terms that he will be returned to the Category 1 territory to serve the remainder of his sentence after he would otherwise be released in the UK, whether or not on licence (s 153A(4)).

12.43 A defendant who is returned to the Category 1 territory to serve the remainder of his sentence there pursuant to a s 153A undertaking, may ultimately be returned (or may himself voluntarily return) again to the UK following the completion of his sentence in the Category 1 territory. Such a person may not yet be wholly free from the consequences of his original UK sentence, or the risk of return to custody (eg because he may breach the terms of his licence or may be subject to a default sentence in lieu of payment of a confiscation order). Section 153B[23] governs the treatment of the defendant upon his return to the UK.

12.44 Section 153B(2) provides that the time spent by the defendant outside the UK pursuant to the s 153A undertaking will not count as time served as part of the original UK sentence.

12.45 If, upon return, the defendant is not entitled to be released from his UK sentence, he is to be treated as being unlawfully at large from that sentence and liable to be detained in pursuance of the sentence (s153B(3)).

[22] Which, under s 74(3) of the Policing and Crime Act 2009, replaced s 143 (so as to bring non-Category 1 territories within its scope).
[23] Inserted by s 74(3) of the Policing and Justice Act 2009.

If the defendant was returned to the Category 1 territory pursuant to the s 153A undertaking, because he had been released on licence from his UK sentence, and he remains entitled to be released under the terms of that licence, the licence is deemed to have been suspended pending his return to the UK (s 153B(4)) and will re-commence upon his return to the UK. **12.46**

If the defendant was returned to the Category 1 territory pursuant to the s 153A undertaking, otherwise than having been released on licence from his UK sentence, but is now entitled to be released on licence (pursuant to any of the statutory provisions listed in s 153B(10)(a)), he will be liable to be detained upon his return to the UK and must then be released on licence within five days (s 153B(4)(b) and 153B(5)–(9)). **12.47**

Return to Category 1 territory to serve sentence imposed in the UK

The EA 2003 also contains powers allowing sentences imposed in the UK on extradited defendants to be served in the Category 1 territory from where he was extradited, and for the defendant to be repatriated to the Category 1 territory for this purpose. This is the process envisaged by Article 5(3) of the EAW Framework Decision.[24] **12.48**

Section 153C[25] applies where a defendant is extradited to the UK from a Category 1 territory for the purposes of being prosecuted for an offence and his extradition was made subject to a condition that the UK undertakes that, if he is convicted of the offence and a sentence of imprisonment or another form of detention is imposed in respect of it, he is to be returned to the Category 1 territory to serve that sentence. **12.49**

In such circumstances, the Secretary of State may, but is not obliged, to give such an undertaking to the Category 1 territory (s 153C(2)). Nothing in s 153C requires the return of a person to a Category 1 territory if the Secretary of State is not satisfied that the return will be compatible with the person's Convention rights or with the UK's obligations under the 1951 Refugee Convention (s 153D). **12.50**

If such an undertaking has been given and the defendant is convicted of the offence and a sentence of imprisonment or another form of detention is imposed in respect of it in the UK, s 153C(4) provides that the person must be returned to the Category 1 territory to serve that sentence as soon as is reasonably practicable after the sentence is imposed (and any other proceedings in respect of the offence are concluded). If s 153C(4) is complied with the sentence of imprisonment or other form of detention[26] for the offence is treated as served but the person's conviction for the offence is treated as a conviction for all other purposes (s 153C(5)). If s 153C(4) is not complied with and the person applies to the UK court which imposed the sentence to be discharged, the court must order his discharge, unless reasonable cause is shown for the delay (s 153C(7)–(8)). **12.51**

Service of sentence in the requested Category 1 territory

The EA 2003 also allows sentences imposed in the UK upon which a Part 3 warrant is based to be served in the requested Category 1 territory (in lieu of extradition to the UK). **12.52**

Section 145 applies if a Part 3 warrant is issued in respect of a defendant; the certificate contained in the warrant certifies that a sentence has been imposed; an undertaking is given on **12.53**

[24] Note though that, unlike Article 5(3) of the EAW Framework Decision, the EA 2003 is not restricted in its potential application to own-nationals or residents of the executing member State.

[25] Which, under s 74(3) of the Policing and Crime Act 2009, replaced s 144 (so as to bring non-Category 1 territories within its scope).

[26] But not other aspects of the sentence, such as confiscation (s 153C(6)).

behalf of a Category 1 territory that the defendant will be required to serve the sentence in the territory; on the basis of the undertaking the person is not extradited to the UK from the Category 1 territory.

12.54 In such a case, so far as the UK is concerned, the sentence for the offence must be treated as served[27] but the person's conviction for the offence must be treated as a conviction for all other purposes (s 145(2); as amended by s 75(2) of the Policing and Crime Act 2009).

C. Extradition from Category 2 Territories

12.55 The provisions of the EA 2003 dealing with return to the UK from Category 2 territories are less elaborate than those governing return from Category 1 territories. In particular, there is no power, equivalent to s 145 discussed at para 12.53, to allow sentenced prisoners to be imprisoned in the requested state in lieu of extradition to the UK.

12.56 The content of the extradition request continues to be governed by relevant treaty provisions[28] and the request is made pursuant to the Royal Prerogative.

12.57 Sections 150 and 151A of the EA 2003 provide specialty protection for defendants returned from Category 2 territories.

Specialty protection for defendants extradited from Commonwealth countries, British overseas territories, and the Hong Kong SAR

12.58 Section 150 applies where a defendant is extradited to the UK from a Category 2 territory under the law of the territory corresponding to Part 2 of the EA 2003, and the territory is a Commonwealth country, a British overseas territory, or the Hong Kong SAR. The general principles by which a UK court will determine the claim of a defendant to the specialty protections of s 150 are discussed at para 12.81.

12.59 Section 150(2) provides that in such a case the defendant may be 'dealt with' in the UK for an offence committed before his extradition only if the offence is one falling within s 150(3) or the condition in s 150(6) is satisfied. By s 150(8), a person is 'dealt with' in the UK for an offence if he is tried there for it or he is detained with a view to trial there for it.[29]

---

27 Note that s 145 contains no provision equivalent to s 153C(6). Therefore, under s 145, all aspects of the sentence, not merely the term of imprisonment or other detention, are deemed served.

28 See, for example, Article 12 of the European Convention on Extradition 1957 and Article 8(2) of the Extradition Treaty concluded in 2003 between the UK and the United States of America (Cm 5821), the latter of which provides that all requests for extradition shall be supported by: '(a) as accurate a description as possible of the person sought, together with any other information that would help to establish identity and probable location; (b) a statement of the facts of the offense(s); (c) the relevant text of the law(s) describing the essential elements of the offense for which extradition is requested; (d) the relevant text of the law(s) prescribing punishment for the offense for which extradition is requested; and (e) documents, statements, or other types of information specified in paragraphs 3 or 4 of this Article, as applicable.'

29 cf the wider definition that appears to apply in Part 1 cases, discussed at para 12.27. However, in *CPS Newcastle v D* [2011] EWCA Crim 1892, the Court of Appeal observed that there exists no material difference between the definition of 'dealing with' in s 146(2), Article 27(2) of the EAW Framework Decision, and ss 150–151 of the EA 2003. In all cases, the emphasis is upon detention pending trial, the trial process, and sentence. Thus the Court held (disapproving *CPS Newcastle v D* [2009] EWCA Crim 1423) that the mere 'prior procedural step' of charging a defendant or obtaining the consent of the DPP to charge, does not constitute 'dealing with' a defendant. Hence also, the mere making of an application for permission (under Part 10 of the Criminal Justice Act 2003) to quash a prior acquittal, and for a retrial, did not amount to 'dealing with' the defendant.

The offences in s 150(3) are:[30] 12.60

(a) the offence in respect of which the defendant is extradited;
(b) a 'lesser offence' disclosed by the information provided to the Category 2 territory in respect of that offence. Section 150(4) defines 'lesser offences'. An offence is a lesser offence in relation to another offence if the maximum punishment for it is less severe than the maximum punishment for the other offence;[31]
(c) an offence in respect of which consent to the defendant being dealt with is given by or on behalf of the 'relevant authority.' By s 150(5), the relevant authority is:
    (i) if the person has been extradited from a Commonwealth country, the government of the country;
    (ii) if the person has been extradited from a British overseas territory, the person administering the territory;
    (iii) if the person has been extradited from the Hong Kong SAR, the government of the Region.

The condition in s 150(6) referred to in s 150(2)(b) is that the 'protected period' has ended. The protected period is 45 days starting with the first day after his extradition to the UK on which the defendant is given an opportunity to leave the UK.[32] 12.61

Specialty protection for defendants extradited from other Category 2 territories

Section 151A[33] provides specialty protection for defendants extradited to the UK from territories other than those covered by s 146 or s 150. The general principles by which a UK court will determine the claim of a defendant to the specialty protections of s 151A are discussed at para 12.81. 12.62

Where s 151A applies, the defendant may be dealt with in the UK for an offence committed before his extradition only if the offence is one falling within s 151A(3) or the condition in s 151A(4) is satisfied. By s 151A(5), a person is 'dealt with' in the UK for an offence if he is tried there for it or he is detained with a view to trial there for it.[34] 12.63

The offences in s 151A(3) are:[35] 12.64

(a) the offence in respect of which the person is extradited;
(b) an offence disclosed by the information provided to the Category 2 territory in respect of that offence;[36]

---

[30] Note that s 150, like s 151A below, does not include exceptions equivalent to those found in s 146(3)(d)–(f), and thus excludes, notably, the possibility of the defendant himself waiving specialty.

[31] This is a narrower exception than in Part 1 cases (under s 146(3)(b)) and in other Part 2 cases (under s 151A(3)(b)).

[32] This is the same as the 'permitted period' in s 146.

[33] Which, under s76(3) of the Policing and Justice Act 2009, replaced s 151 of the EA 2003.

[34] cf the wider definition that appears to apply in Part 1 cases, discussed at para 12.27. However, in *CPS Newcastle v D* [2011] EWCA Crim 1892, the Court of Appeal observed that there exists no material difference between the definition of 'dealing with' in s 146(2), Article 27(2) of the Framework Decision and ss 150–151 of the EA 2003. In all cases, the emphasis is upon detention pending trial, the trial process, and sentence. Thus the Court held (disapproving *CPS Newcastle v D* [2009] EWCA Crim 1423) that the mere 'prior procedural step' of charging a defendant or obtaining the consent of the DPP to charge, does not constitute 'dealing with' a defendant. Hence, also, the mere making of an application for permission (under Part 10 of the Criminal Justice Act 2003) to quash a prior acquittal, and for a retrial, did not amount to 'dealing with' the defendant.

[35] Note that s 151A, like s 150, does not include exceptions equivalent to those found in s 146(3)(d)–(f), and thus excludes, notably, the possibility of the defendant himself waiving specialty.

[36] Note that this is not restricted to 'lesser offences' and is therefore wider than s 150(3)(b) and mirrors instead s 146(3)(b) discussed at para 12.28. Thus, *R v Seddon* [2009] 1 WLR 2342 decided under s 146 was followed in *R v Jones* [2011] EWCA Crim 107, a case under s 151A.

(c) an offence in respect of which consent to the person being dealt with is given on behalf of the territory.

12.65 The condition in s 151A(4) is that the person has returned to the territory from which he was extradited, or the person has been given an opportunity to leave the UK. Note that there is here no 45-day 'permitted' or 'protected' period.[37]

Outstanding convictions and remission of punishment

12.66 Section 152, discussed at para 12.36, also applies to persons extradited from non-Category 1 territories.

Extradition of serving prisoners to the UK

12.67 Sections 153A and 153B, discussed at para 12.38, also apply to persons extradited from non-Category 1 territories.[38]

Return to Category 2 territory to serve sentence imposed in the UK

12.68 Section 153C, discussed at para 12.48, also applies to persons extradited from non-Category 1 territories.

D. Disguised Extradition[39]

12.69 Disguised extradition is the name given to the process whereby a defendant is returned to a country to face trial otherwise than through lawful extradition procedures. Where a defendant is returned to the UK for trial other than through regular extradition procedures then, if there has been bad faith on the part of UK authorities, or a deliberate flouting of domestic or international law, then the criminal proceedings against him are liable in exceptional circumstances to be stayed as an abuse of process.[40]

12.70 The development of this species of abuse of process in English law occurred comparatively recently. Before the decision of the House of Lords in *R v Horseferry Road Magistrates' Court ex p Bennett* [1994] 2 AC 42 there was a conflict of authority on the question of whether English courts had jurisdiction to inquire into the circumstances in which a defendant had been brought before them and jurisdiction to stay proceedings as an abuse of process.[41]

12.71 Bennett was a New Zealand citizen who was accused of offences of dishonesty in the UK. He was traced to South Africa by the English police and forcibly returned to the UK. There was no extradition treaty between the two countries, and although a special arrangement could

---

[37] cf ss 146 and 150.

[38] As under Part 1 (s 37), the UK is also able to *grant* extradition to Category 1 territories of serving prisoners subject to suitable undertakings that they will be returned to the UK at the conclusion of foreign proceedings (see s 119). The power to interrupt a sentence of imprisonment for the purpose of extradition is now contained in EA 2003, s 197A; cf *R (Handa) v Bow Street Magistrates' Court* [2004] EWHC 2986, para 30. Section 132 governs the treatment of such persons upon return and is discussed at para 12.100.

[39] See Choo, 'The Consequences of Illegal Extradition' [1992] Crim L 490. For a historical review of this subject, see O' Higgins, 'Unlawful Seizure and Irregular Extradition' BYIL XXXVI 1960; O' Higgins, 'Disguised Extradition; the Soblen Case' (1964) 27 MLR 52; Thornberry, 'Dr Soblen and the Alien Law of the United Kingdom' 12 ICLQ 414. For the American perspective on the issue of disguised extradition, see Bush, 'How did we get here? Foreign abduction after *Alverez-Machain*' (1993) 45 Stan Law Rev 939.

[40] *R v Horseferry Road Magistrates' Court ex p Bennett* [1994] 2 AC 42.

[41] *Ex p Susannah Scott* (1829) 9 B & C 446; *Marks* (1802) 3 East 157; *ex p Krans* (1823) 1 B & C 258; *Sinclair v HM Advocate* (1890) 17 R(J) 38; *R v Officer Commanding Depot Battalion, RASC Colchester ex p Elliott* [1949] 1 All ER 373; *R v Plymouth Justices ex p Driver* [1986] QB 95.

have made under s 15 of the EA 1989, no such arrangement had been made for political reasons, international sanctions against South Africa being in force at the time. The South African authorities decided that Bennett should be repatriated to New Zealand via London. When his flight arrived in London he was arrested and charged. When he appeared before the magistrates' court he alleged that there had been collusion between the UK and South African authorities to ensure his presence in London in defiance of extradition procedures. He argued that the proceedings against him were an abuse of process. His application was refused by the magistrate who held that he had no jurisdiction to inquire into the circumstances by which Bennett had come before him. Bennett sought judicial review of the magistrate's decision.

The Divisional Court refused the application and held that an English court had no power to inquire into the circumstances under which a person appearing before it had been brought within the jurisdiction. The defendant appealed to the House of Lords. Because the issue before the House of Lords was limited to the question of jurisdiction, the facts were still disputed. Lord Griffiths set out the assumed factual basis at pp 52–53: **12.72**

> it must be assumed that the English police took a deliberate decision not to pursue extradition procedures but to persuade the South African police to arrest and forcibly return the appellant to this country, under the pretext of deporting him to New Zealand via Heathrow so that he could be arrested at Heathrow and tried for the offences of dishonesty he is alleged to have committed in 1989. I shall also assume that the Crown Prosecution Service were consulted and approved of the behaviour of the police.

On the issue of principle Lord Griffiths concluded at pp 61–62: **12.73**

> In the present case there is no suggestion that the appellant cannot have a fair trial, nor could it be suggested that it would have been unfair to try him if he had been returned to this country through extradition procedures. If the court is to have the power to interfere with the prosecution in the present circumstances it must be because the judiciary accept a responsibility for the maintenance of the rule of law that embraces a willingness to oversee executive action and to refuse to countenance behaviour that threatens either basic human rights or the rule of law.
>
> My Lords, I have no doubt that the judiciary should accept this responsibility in the field of criminal law ... if it comes to the attention of the court that there has been a serious abuse of power it should, in my view, express its disapproval by refusing to act upon it.
>
> Let us consider the position in the context of extradition ... If a practice developed in which the police or prosecuting authorities of this country ignored extradition procedures and secured the return of an accused by a mere request to police colleagues in another country they would be flouting the extradition procedures and depriving the accused of the safeguards built into the extradition process for his benefit. It is to my mind unthinkable that in such circumstances the court should declare itself to be powerless and stand idly by; I echo the words of Lord Devlin in *Connelly v Director of Public Prosecutions* [1964] AC 1254, 1354: 'The courts cannot contemplate for a moment the transference to the Executive of the responsibility for seeing that the process of law is not abused.'
>
> ... In my view your Lordships should now declare that where process of law is available to return an accused to this country through extradition procedures our courts will refuse to try him if he has been forcibly brought within our jurisdiction in disregard of those procedures by a process to which our own police, prosecuting or other executive authorities have been a knowing party.

Whether criminal proceedings will be stayed against a defendant who has been the subject of a disguised extradition depends in part upon the seriousness of the offence he is charged with, and how the broader public interest is to be weighed against the illegality involved in bringing him into the UK. In *Mullen* [2000] QB 520 the Court of Appeal allowed M's appeal **12.74** against conviction because he had been deported from Zimbabwe to the UK instead of being extradited. Documents disclosed for the purposes of the appeal showed the UK Government to have acted in bad faith and to have violated the rule of law in procuring M's unlawful extradition from Zimbabwe.[42] In giving the judgment of the Court, Rose LJ referred to *Latif* [1996] 1 WLR 104 and the need to balance the seriousness of the offence against the conduct of the authorities in determining whether or not a stay should be ordered.

12.75 In *Latif* [1996] 1 WLR 104 the House of Lords upheld the decision of the trial judge who had declined to stay the proceedings. The defendant had been tricked into bringing a consignment of heroin into the UK by an undercover customs officer. Lord Steyn distinguished the decision in *R v Horseferry Road Magistrates' Court ex p Bennett* [1994] 2 AC 42 on the grounds that, in the circumstances, the conduct of the Customs officer was not so unworthy or shameful as to 'affront the public conscience'.

12.76 In *R v Jama*,[43] a decision at first instance, Simon J summarised the principles of law applicable to disguised extradition as follows: (i) the burden of proving an abuse of process lies on the defendant; (ii) the standard of proof is the balance of probabilities;[44] (iii) the court may stay on the grounds of abuse if it is satisfied that UK authorities acted unlawfully, or procured or connived in unlawful procedures or in violation of international law;[45] (iv) the involvement of UK authorities in illegal activities is a necessary component.[46] If the only proven illegality is conduct on the part of the foreign state in which the UK has not been involved then there can be no basis for a stay;[47] (v) if the court is satisfied that there has been wrongdoing by UK authorities, in deciding whether to stay proceedings, then it must weigh the countervailing considerations of policy and justice by considering whether there has been an abuse of process which amounts to such an affront to the public conscience that the proceedings should to be stayed;[48] (vi) the cases where it will be appropriate to order a stay will be rare.

12.77 A foreign state is entitled to deport a person to the UK even though he is wanted there for trial. There are likely to be no grounds for staying a prosecution as an abuse of process where a defendant is deported or returned to the UK instead of being extradited in circumstances where there has been no illegality or collusion between the foreign and UK authorities. As the Court of Appeal said in *R v Burns* [2002] EWCA (Crim) 1324, paras 28–30, the abuse of process jurisdiction in this context is concerned to ensure that the UK Executive observes the rule of law, and so in the absence of any wrongdoing by UK authorities there can be no basis for a stay of proceedings. In *R v Staines Magistrates' Court ex p Westfallen* [1998] 1 WLR 652, the Divisional Court said, at p 662, that:

> The question in each of these cases is whether it appears that the police or the prosecuting authorities have acted illegally or procured or connived at unlawful procedures or violated international law or the domestic law of foreign states or abused their powers in a way that should lead this court to stay the proceedings against the applicants.

---

42 cf *R v Horseferry Road Magistrates Court ex p Bennett (No 3)* [1995] 1 Cr App R147; *Gokal*, 11 March 1999 (CA 9704132/S2), in which the Court of Appeal upheld the trial judge's decision not to order disclosure of material relating to the circumstances in which the defendant had been brought into the UK.

43 Unreported, 14 July 2008, Woolwich Crown Court, where the defendant, who was accused of murder, had been returned from Somalia to the UK pursuant to a special arrangement. He claimed that he had been effectively kidnapped and put on a plane bound for the UK. cf *R v Ali* [2011] EWCA Crim 1653.

44 *R v Hounsham* [2005] EWCA Crim 1366.

45 *R v Staines Magistrates' Court ex p Westfallen* [1998] 1 WLR 652, 665.

46 *R v Staines Magistrates' Court ex p Westfallen* [1998] 1 WLR 652, 667.

47 *R v Burns* [2002] EWCA (Crim) 1324, paras 28–30.

48 *Latif* [1996] 1 WLR 104, 112; *Mullen* [2000] QB 520, 537.

> ... The Norwegians were entitled under their own law to deport these applicants. The propriety of the deportations is acknowledged and indeed could not be challenged. It is difficult to see why the Kingdom of Norway should be obliged to keep the applicants whilst the British applied for extradition if they wished to deport them. It was indeed a natural step for Norway to send the applicants back to where they had come from. There is in the material before us nothing to suggest that the British authorities procured or influenced that decision. It is true that they did not in any way resist it, and there is no reason why they should have resisted it. It is very probable that they welcomed the decision, but in my judgment they would have been failing in their duty as law enforcement agencies if they had not welcomed it. In my judgment there is nothing to suggest any impropriety such as would attract application of the ratio in *R v Horseferry Road Magistrates' Court ex p Bennett* [1994] 1 AC 42 in this case.

Thus, the question whether criminal proceedings against a person who has been deported to the UK rather than extradited are an abuse of process depends upon the foreign state's purpose in deporting the defendant, and whether the UK authorities have been knowingly involved in illegality. In *R v Governor of Brixton Prison ex p Soblen* [1963] 2 QB 243 the Home Secretary ordered the deportation to the United States of Soblen, who was wanted for trial there. He asserted that he should have been extradited. Lord Denning MR examined the relationship between deportation and extradition. Having set out the two conflicting principles, namely, that a man was not to be returned for trial except in accordance with the EA 1870, and that the Home Secretary can deport a person whose presence in the UK is not conducive to the public good, he said at p 302: **12.78**

> How are we to decide between these two principles? It seems to me that it depends on the purpose with which the act is done. If it was done for an authorised purpose, it was lawful. If it was done professedly for an authorised purpose, but in fact for a different purpose with an ulterior object, it was unlawful. If, therefore, the purpose of the Home Secretary in this case was to surrender the applicant as a fugitive criminal to the United States of America because they had asked for him, then it would be unlawful. But if the Home Secretary's purpose was to deport him to his own country because the Home Secretary considered his presence here to be not conducive to the public good, then the Home Secretary's action is lawful. It is open to these courts to inquire whether the purpose of the Home Secretary was a lawful or an unlawful purpose. Was there a misuse of the power or not? The courts can always go behind the face of the deportation order in order to see whether the powers entrusted by Parliament have been exercised lawfully or no.

In *Mohammed v President of the Republic of South Africa* 2001 (3) SALR 893 (CC), Mohammed had been deported from South Africa to the United States to face trial on capital charges instead of being extradited. The Court held he had been unlawfully deported and observed, at para 43, that:[49] **12.79**

> Deportation is usually a unilateral act while extradition is consensual. Different procedures are prescribed for deportation and extradition, and those differences may be material in specific cases, particularly where the legality of the expulsion is challenged. In the circumstances of the present case, however, the distinction is not relevant. The procedure followed in removing Mohammed to the United States of America was unlawful whether it is characterised as a deportation or an extradition. Moreover, an obligation on the South African government to secure an assurance that the death penalty will not be imposed on a person whom it causes to be removed from South Africa to another country cannot depend on whether the removal is by extradition or deportation. That obligation depends on the facts of the particular case and

[49] The South African Constitutional Court held that even if the government had behaved lawfully, its failure to obtain undertakings that the defendant would not be sentenced to death prior to deportation would still have rendered his deportation unconstitutional.

the provisions of the Constitution, not on the provisions of the empowering legislation or extradition treaty under which the 'deportation' or 'extradition' is carried out.

12.80 Detention for the purposes of disguised extradition may also violate Articles 5(1)(f) and 18 of the European Convention on Human Rights.[50] In *Bozano v France* (1987) 9 EHRR 297 the applicant's extradition from France to Italy was requested, however the request failed. France then delivered the applicant to Switzerland, who then extradited him to Italy. The European Court of Human Rights held that the return to Switzerland had been a disguised form of extradition, and accordingly that the applicant's detention had been arbitrary and therefore in breach of Article 5(1)(f).[51]

E. Claiming Specialty Protection in the UK

12.81 A defendant who believes that his trial will breach his specialty rights has a number of potential remedies, including applying to quash counts on the indictment pursuant to the relevant provisions of the EA 2003, or applying to have the case stayed as an abuse of process. Cases decided under the EA 1870 and the EA 1989 established a number of principles in the application of the specialty rule to those returned to the UK. Firstly, the onus is on the defendant to show that his trial or sentence breaches the rule of specialty.[52] In making this determination the court of trial may examine the documents in the extradition proceedings to determine whether the offence charged satisfies the rule of specialty.[53]

12.82 Whilst the prosecution is prevented from trying a defendant for offences other than those which comply with the rule, there is no bar to their obtaining and adducing additional evidence to support charges which do so comply. In *R v Aubrey-Fletcher ex p Ross-Munro* [1968] 1 QB 620 the defendant was extradited from France on a warrant containing six charges. At committal the magistrate indicated that in his view the evidence was insufficient and he granted the prosecution an adjournment. At the next hearing the prosecution sought to adduce the evidence of a witness whose evidence had not been used in the extradition. Objection was taken, but it was held that the only restriction was that the crime should be based on the same allegation as the crime in the warrant.[54]

12.83 Unless they amount to the determination of a fresh criminal charge within the meaning of Article 6 of the European Convention on Human Rights, the enforcement, even by way of imprisonment, of ancillary orders which form part of the sentence imposed for the offence

---

50 Article 5(1)(f) permits detention for the purposes of extradition or deportation: see para 7.43; cf *R v McDonald* [2005] EWCA 1970.

51 Different principles may operate when a defendant is unlawfully returned from a state which is not a party to the European Convention on Human Rights: *Sanchez Ramirez v France* (2006) 43 EHRR 54, but note that the breadth of the Commission's observations in that case appear not to be dependent upon the status of the surrendering state as a non-ECHR state party. See also *Samiev v Georgia* (2011) App. 9934/10, Nov 16, (ECtHR). For a case concerning unlawful return from a Convention state *to* a state which is not a party to the Convention, in which *Bozano v France* (1987) 9 EHRR 297 was applied, see *Iskandarov v Russia* (2010) App. 17185/05, September 23, ECtHR, para 149.

52 *R v Corrigan* [1931] 1 KB 527.

53 *R v Aubrey-Fletcher ex p Ross Munro* [1968] 1 QB 620.

54 cf *Welsh v Secretary of State for the Home Department* [2006] 3 All ER 204. See also *Beggs v Her Majesty's Advocate* [2010] ScotHCJAC 27 where extradition was sought for an offence of murder, the facts of which included (a) a sexual assault upon the victim and (b) dismemberment of the body. The assault could have been, but was not, charged as a separate offence. The dismemberment was charged as a separate offence (attempting to pervert the course of justice) in respect of which extradition was refused. Following extradition, the defendant was prosecuted only for murder (for which extradition had been granted), but with the acts of assault and dismemberment adduced in evidence in support of that charge. Specialty was held not to be violated thereby.

for which extradition was granted does not engage the rule of specialty. Thus imposition of a term of imprisonment in default of payment of a confiscation order (which formed part of the sentence imposed for the offence for which extradition was granted) was held in *R (Director of Revenue and Customs Prosecutions) v Birmingham Magistrates' Court and Woolley* [2010] EWHC 12 (Admin) not to violate specialty.[55] The enforcement of such orders, which do not amount to the determination of a fresh criminal charge within the meaning of Article 6 of the Convention, constitutes 'dealing with' the defendant, but for matters falling within the exceptions to the rule (there, in s 151A(a) of the EA 2003).

Restrictions imposed by foreign courts on the offences for which the defendant can be tried in the UK do not override the terms of domestic legislation. *R v Davidson* (1977) 64 Cr App R 209 concerned an extradition from West Germany. The German Court had entered a *caveat* that the defendant should only be tried in relation to the management of companies named in the warrant. The Court of Appeal took the view that neither the decision of the German Court nor the extradition Treaty were appropriate matters for enquiry in this country. The English courts should be concerned only to ensure compliance with the domestic extradition legislation. For an application of these principles, see *R (Director of Revenue & Customs Prosecutions) v Birmingham Magistrates' Court and Woolley* [2010] EWHC 12 (Admin) where the High Court held that an express reservation to the Swiss order for extradition did not, applying *R v Davidson*, bind the UK courts.[56] **12.84**

The rule of specialty does not extend to protect the defendant from civil proceedings, including contempt proceedings, even though they may result in imprisonment. In *Pooley v Whetham* [1880] 15 Ch D 435, P was arrested in France on a warrant in respect of bankruptcy offences. He was returned to the UK, tried and acquitted of the bankruptcy charges, then detained in custody as a result of outstanding contempt proceedings resulting from his having disobeyed a court order in a civil action. The Court of Appeal held that P was not entitled to be discharged until he had purged his contempt. It held that the word 'offence' in s 19 of the EA 1870 meant a criminal act triable in a criminal court.[57] It therefore did not cover contempt of court arising from the consequences of failing to comply with a court order; which 'offence' was civil not criminal in nature, notwithstanding that it could result in punishment by way of committal to prison.[58] In *OB v The Director of the Serious Fraud Office* [2012] EWCA Crim 67, the Court of Appeal held that contempt of court flowing from breach of a Proceeds of Crime Act 2002 restraint order made in criminal proceedings similarly constituted a civil not criminal contempt and was, applying *Pooley v Whetham* [1880] 15 Ch D 435 and *R v Seddon* [2009] 1 WLR 2342, accordingly outwith the scope of the principle of specialty and s 151A of the EA 2003 which 'bite and only bite on detention, trial and punishment for criminal offences'. **12.85**

---

[55] In *Woolley v United Kingdom* (2012) App. 28019/10, whilst accepting that violation of specialty constitutes, in principle, a breach of Articles 5 and 6 ECHR, the European Court of Human Rights upheld the decision of the High Court that the imposition of a term of imprisonment in default of payment of a confiscation order did not constitute the determination of a fresh criminal charge, within the meaning of Article 6 ECHR. cf *Phillips v United Kingdom* (2001) 11 BHRC 280; *Crowther v United Kingdom* (2005) App. 53741/00, February 11, ECHR.

[56] In *Woolley v United Kingdom* (2012) App. 28019/10, the European Court of Human Rights held, at para 84, that this approach entailed no violation of Article 5, in the absence of bad faith or intention to deceive on the part of the UK authorities in the making or drafting of the original extradition request.

[57] See also *R v Seddon* [2009] 1 WLR 2342, para 20.

[58] cf *Cobra Golf Inc v Rata* [1998] Ch 109, 139; *Daltel Europe Ltd v Makki* [2006 1 WLR 2704, para 51.

F. General Provisions Relating to Return to the UK

12.86 Sections 152–155 of Part 3 relate to return from both Category 1 and 2 territories, some of which have been discussed above.[59]

Grant of bail where undertaking given to requested state

12.87 As has been seen, in some cases extradition to the UK may be made subject to undertakings given by the Secretary of State. Section 154 applies where the Secretary of State has given such an undertaking and it includes terms that the defendant will be kept in custody until the conclusion of proceedings against him in the UK.

12.88 Section 154(2) provides that in such a case a court, judge, or justice of the peace may grant bail to the person in the proceedings only if the court, judge, or justice of the peace considers that there are exceptional circumstances which justify it.[60]

Return of persons who are acquitted or not tried

12.89 Of course, not all defendants who are extradited to the UK will be convicted of the offence for which their extradition was sought. They may be acquitted or they may not be proceeded against for any number of reasons. Such defendants are entitled under the EA 2003 to be returned to the territory from where they were extradited free of charge as quickly as possible after the conclusion of the proceedings against them.

12.90 Section 153[61] applies where the defendant is accused in the UK of the commission of an offence; he is extradited to the UK in respect of the offence; and the condition in s 153(2) or (3) is satisfied.

12.91 The condition in s 153(2) is that proceedings against the defendant are not begun before the end of the required period, which is six months starting with the day on which the person arrives in the UK, and before the end of the period of three months starting immediately after the end of the required period the person asks the Secretary of State to return him to the territory from which he was extradited.

12.92 The condition in s 153(3) is that at his trial for the offence the person is acquitted or is discharged under any of the provisions specified in s 153(4),[62] and before the end of the period of three months starting immediately after the date of his acquittal or discharge the person asks the Secretary of State to return him to the territory from which he was extradited.

12.93 Where a defendant requests return, the Secretary of State must arrange for him to be sent back, free of charge and with as little delay as possible, to the territory from which he was extradited to the UK in respect of the offence.

Service personnel

12.94 Section 155[63] confers power on the Secretary of State to make an order applying Part 3 to defendants whose extradition is sought or has been ordered under service law.[64]

---

[59] Paras 12.36–12.51 and 12.66–12.68.

[60] For a detailed discussion of the compatibility of such limiting provisions with Article 5 of the European Convention on Human Rights, see Emmerson, Ashworth, and Macdonald, *Human Rights and Criminal Justice* (3rd edn, 2012, Oxford), Ch 8.

[61] As amended by s 74(4) of the Policing and Crime Act 2009.

[62] These are s 12(1) of the Powers of Criminal Courts (Sentencing) Act 2000; s 246(1), (2), or (3) of the Criminal Procedure (Scotland) Act 1995; Art 4(1) of the Criminal Justice (Northern Ireland) Order 1996 (SI 1996/3160).

[63] As amended by the Sch 16, para 204 of the Armed Forces Act 2006.

[64] As defined by ss 367–369 of the Armed Forces Act 2006 and s 4(3)(a) (attached Commonwealth personnel) of the Visiting Forces (British Commonwealth) Act 1933 (see s 216(13A) of the EA 2003 and s 374 of the 2006 Act).

G. Return of Persons to the UK to Serve the Remainder of their Sentences

Return from Category 1 territory (s 59)

Section 59 of the EA 2003[65] applies where a person who is serving a sentence of imprisonment or another form of detention in the UK is extradited to a Category 1 territory in accordance with Part 1 and then returned to the UK to serve the remainder of his sentence (or otherwise returns to the UK). **12.95**

Section 59 mirrors the relevant provisions of s 153B discussed above.[66] Therefore, the time spent by the defendant outside the UK pursuant to his extradition will not count as time served as part of the original UK sentence (s 59(2)), unless he was extradited for the purpose of being prosecuted for the foreign offence and was not convicted of it (or any other offence which the Category 1 territory were permitted to deal with), in which case time spent in custody in the Category 1 territory in connection with the offence(s) will count (s 59(3)–(4)). **12.96**

If, upon return, the defendant is not entitled to be released from his UK sentence, he is to be treated as being unlawfully at large from that sentence and liable to be detained in pursuance of the sentence (s59(5)). **12.97**

If the defendant had been released on licence from his UK sentence, and he remains entitled to be released under the terms of that licence, the licence is deemed to have been suspended pending his return to the UK (s 59(6)(a)) and will re-commence upon his return to the UK. **12.98**

If the defendant was extradited otherwise than having been released on licence from his UK sentence, but is now entitled to be released on licence (pursuant to any of the statutory provisions listed in s 59(11)), he will be liable to be detained upon his return to the UK and must then be released on licence within five days (s 59(6)(b) and (7)–(10)). **12.99**

Return from Category 2 territory (s 132)

Section 132[67] is in identical terms to s 59 considered in para 12.95, with Category 2 territory replacing Category 1 where appropriate. **12.100**

H. Crediting Time Served in Custody Abroad Awaiting Extradition to the UK

Crediting time served in custody abroad awaiting extradition is not a requirement of the European Convention on Human Rights.[68] However, it is a requirement of many of the international instruments which underpin extradition to the UK. For example, Article 26 of the EAW Framework Decision provides that: **12.101**

> The issuing Member State *shall deduct all periods* of detention arising from the execution of a European arrest warrant from the total period of detention to be served in the issuing Member State as a result of a custodial sentence or detention being passed.

---

65 As substituted by s 72 of the Policing and Justice Act 2009.

66 Paras 12.43–12.47.

67 As substituted by s 73 of the Policing and Crime Act 2009.

68 See *Zandbergs v Sweden* (2011) App. 71092/01, December 20, ECtHR, para 63; *R (Murphy) v Secretary of State for the Home Department* [2005] EWHC 3116 (Admin); *A v United Kingdom* (1986) 8 EHRR CD90.

12.102 Whilst the European Convention on Extradition 1957 is silent on the issue of crediting time served, Resolution 75(12) of the Committee of Ministers on the Practical Application of the European Convention on Extradition provides that:

> the time spent in detention by an individual solely for the purposes of extradition in the territory of the requested state, or of a state of transit, *shall be taken into consideration* when deciding the penalty involving deprivation of liberty or detention which he has to serve for the offence for which he was extradited.[69]

12.103 However, UK domestic law does not always give effect to these international obligations.

Persons extradited to the UK for the purpose of trial or sentence

12.104 By virtue of s 243 of the Criminal Justice Act 2003, the crediting of time spent on remand abroad awaiting extradition by an accused person extradited to the UK is automatic.[70] A person returned to the UK in pursuance of extradition arrangements[71] who is tried for the offence in respect of which his sentence was imposed, without having first been restored or had an opportunity of leaving the UK, is deemed to be a fixed-term prisoner for the purposes of s 240 of the Criminal Justice Act 2003, and any period in which he was kept in custody while awaiting his extradition to the UK will be credited.

12.105 By amendments made by Sch 13(2) of the Police and Justice Act 2006, s 243 of the Criminal Justice Act 2003 now also encompasses the crediting of time spent on remand abroad awaiting extradition by persons unlawfully at large from the UK after trial but before sentence. A person returned to the UK who is subsequently sentenced for the offence in respect of which he was extradited, without having first been restored or having had an opportunity of leaving the UK, is also deemed to be a fixed-term prisoner for the purposes of s 240 of the Criminal Justice Act 2003, and any period in which he was kept in custody while awaiting his extradition to the UK will be credited.

12.106 These provisions give proper effect to the mandatory requirements of, for example, Article 26 of the Framework Decision in Part 1 cases, and the Recommendation of the Committee of Ministers in Part 2 cases governed by the European Convention on Extradition. However, s 243 applies to all persons tried or sentenced after return to the UK, from *any* foreign State.

Persons extradited to the UK for the purpose of serving a sentence already imposed

12.107 However, where a person is unlawfully at large from a sentence already imposed before flight from the UK, the position is reversed by s 49(2) of the Prisons Act 1952, which provides that, in such cases, time spent absent from the prison is not credited unless the Secretary of State orders otherwise.

12.108 In *R v Governor of Leeds Prison ex p Stafford* [1964] 2 WLR 731, the Divisional Court held that a person detained abroad pursuant to a UK extradition request made to enforce a sentence already imposed was 'unlawfully at large' from that sentence and was not, whilst detained abroad, 'detained in pursuance of the sentence' within the meaning of s 49. In 1956, Stafford was sentenced to seven years' imprisonment by a UK court. Later that year he escaped from prison and fled to Trinidad. A warrant for his arrest was issued in London and sent to Trinidad and in April 1957 he was arrested and committed to prison. He was returned to England in June

[69] Recommendation (86)13 of the Committee of Ministers also provides that '… time spent in custody pending extradition should be deducted from the sentence in the same manner as time spent in custody pending trial …'.

[70] Previously discretionary under s 47 of the Criminal Justice Act 1991.

[71] A definition which is broad enough to encompass consent to extradition.

1964, at a time when, if the days spent in detention in Trinidad were to be computed towards the service of his sentence that sentence would have been completed. The Divisional Court was called upon to consider two proposed interpretations of s 49. Stafford argued that 'unlawfully at large' meant that the person was at liberty (which Stafford was not). The Secretary of State argued that 'unlawfully at large' meant no more than that the defendant was away from the UK prison at which he was liable to be detained (which Stafford was). The Divisional Court agreed with the latter construction.

R v Governor of Leeds Prison ex p Stafford [1964] 2 WLR 731 was applied by the High Court in *R (Woolley) v Ministry of Justice* [2012] EWHC 295 (Admin). The High Court held that '... there is no or insufficient causal connection between the original [UK] sentence and an order of a foreign court providing for the detention of the absconder pending his extradition ... [the defendant is] detained in pursuance of the order of the [foreign] Court, not, save in a "but for" sense, in pursuance of the original sentence ...'. So far as the scope of application of s 49(2)(a) was concerned, the High Court held that s 49(2)(a) was 'still apt to cover *detention in the United Kingdom* pending the absconder's return to the place where he is required in law to be detained'. **12.109**

Under s 49 as presently applied, and para 7 of the Prison Service Order on Sentence Calculation (PSO 6650), it is only in 'exceptional circumstances' that the Secretary of State will allow a period spent in custody abroad awaiting extradition to the UK to be credited against the sentence to be served. **12.110**

Thus, s 49 of the Prisons Act 1952 as applied appears to be in conflict with the requirements of Article 26 of the EAW Framework Decision.[72] The Ministry of Justice's current solution to this problem is to operate a policy whereby the Secretary of State's discretion is, in all Part 1 cases, exercised in favour of crediting time, although it is difficult to see how such a policy is compatible with the High Court's construction of s 49 of the Prisons Act 1952. **12.111**

In cases under Part 2 of the EA 2003 to which the European Convention on Extradition 1957 is applicable, s 49 similarly operates in conflict with the Resolution and Recommendation of the Committee of Ministers referred to at para 12.102. However, the High Court in *R (Woolley) v Ministry of Justice* [2012] EWHC 295 (Admin) held that the Recommendation is of 'no compulsive legal force'.[73] **12.112**

[72] Caution should be exercised with respect to the observation of the High Court in *R (Woolley) v Ministry of Justice* [2012] EWHC 295 (Admin), para 31 that 'the rule in [*R v Governor of Leeds Prison ex p Stafford* [1964] 2 WLR 731] applies only to those who abscond after being sentenced and only outside the EAW territories'. That is not correct. Section 49 of the Prisons Act 1952 applies to all those extradited to the UK for the purposes of serving a sentence which has already imposed, including those extradited pursuant to the EAW Framework Decision.

[73] The High Court distinguished between Recommendations of the Council of Europe and Recommendations of the Council of the European Union, as to which, see *Grimaldi v Fonds de Maladies Professionnelles (Occupational Diseases Fund, Brussels)* [1991] 2 CMLR 265, para 9; *Alassini v Telecom Italia SpA* [2010] 3 CMLR 17, paras 39–40.

13

POLICE POWERS IN EXTRADITION CASES

A. Introduction

Part 4 of the EA 2003 is entitled 'Police Powers' and contains powers of entry, search, and seizure for use in extradition cases. It also contains provisions for dealing with extradition detainees who are in police custody following arrest. Part 4 should be read in conjunction with the Codes of Practice issued by the Secretary of State under s 173.[1] **13.01**

Before considering Part 4 in detail it is instructive to consider some of the difficulties created by the former law which Part 4 is intended to remedy. **13.02**

History of search and seizure in extradition cases

Extradition treaties commonly include provisions requiring the requested state to hand over property which might be relevant to the offence for which extradition is requested. For example, **13.03**

[1] Para 13.30.

Article 20 of the European Convention on Extradition requires the requested state '... so far as its law permits and at the request of the requesting party, seize and hand over property ...'. Article 29 of the EAW Framework Decision requires the executing judicial party, in accordance with national law, to seize and hand over evidence which may be required as evidence or which has been acquired by the defendant as a result of the offence. Treaty provisions such as this make clear that the power of search and seizure in extradition cases is to be governed by the requested state's domestic law.

13.04 Between 1881 and 1989 Parliament enacted various provisions which allowed magistrates to issue search warrants in relation to offences committed in Empire and Commonwealth countries. Section 24 of the Fugitive Offenders Act 1881 which, until its repeal by the Fugitive Offenders Act 1967, governed extradition within the Empire and Commonwealth,[2] permitted a magistrate to issue a warrant to search for any property alleged to be stolen or to be otherwise unlawfully taken or obtained by the defendant, or otherwise to be the subject of the offence for which extradition was requested. These powers were the same as the court or magistrate would have if the property had been stolen or otherwise unlawfully taken or obtained, or the offence had been committed, within the jurisdiction of the magistrate.

13.05 In contrast, the EA 1870 did not contain any provisions relating to search and seizure for the purposes of extradition to foreign states.

13.06 Section 6(5) of the Fugitive Offenders Act 1967 contained a special search provision where the defendant was accused of an offence of stealing or receiving stolen property. This provision was replicated in s 8(6) of the EA 1989 in relation to designated Commonwealth countries and colonies. Other than this section, the EA 1989 was silent as to search and seizure in extradition cases.

Part II of the Police and Criminal Evidence Act 1984

13.07 The principal legislation concerning entry, search, and seizure is Part 2 of the Police and Criminal Evidence Act 1984 (PACE), as amended. Sections 8–23 consolidate many but not all of the police's powers of entry, search, and seizure. Part 2 contains provisions on search warrants, various categories of sensitive or privileged material (ss 8–16), and powers of seizure (ss 19–20). In particular, s 8 creates a general power to obtain a search warrant in the case of an indictable offence, while s 9 and Sch 1 enable search warrants and production orders to be obtained for special procedure material and excluded material.[3] Common law powers of entry following arrest are also codified in Part 2.

The decision in *R (Rottman) v Commissioner of Police for the Metropolis*[4]

13.08 In *R v Southwark Crown Court ex p Sorsky Defries* [1996] Crim LR 195 the Divisional Court held that the word 'offence' in Part 2 of PACE refers to domestic offences and that it does not include foreign offences.[5] In *R (Rottman) v Commissioner of Police for the Metropolis* [2002] 2 AC 692 the principal question before the House of Lords was whether the powers of entry and search in Part 2 are applicable in extradition cases. Despite the decision in *R v Southwark Crown Court ex p Sorsky Defries* [1996] Crim LR 195 some police forces continued to rely on their Part II powers when carrying out extradition arrests in the belief that the statutory powers of entry and search contained in Part 2 applied to foreign offences.

---

[2] Para 1.17.

[3] As defined in PACE, ss 11 and 14.

[4] [2002] 2 AC 692.

[5] cf *Air-India v Wiggins* [1980] 1 WLR 815; *Cox v Army Council* [1963] AC 48.

In *R (Rottman) v Commissioner of Police for the Metropolis* [2002] 2 AC 692 an arrest warrant was issued in Germany for Rottman's arrest in connection with alleged fraud offences. A provisional warrant for Rottman's arrest was issued by the Bow Street Magistrates' Court under s 8(1)(b) of the EA 1989 while he was living in the UK. He was arrested in the driveway of his house by three police officers a few yards from his front door. The officers then entered and searched the house and removed items belonging to Rottman which they suspected might hold evidence of the alleged offences or proceeds of the offences, having acted in purported reliance on ss 18, 19, and 32 in Part 2 of PACE and in the belief that they had in any event power under the common law to search the premises of a suspect following his arrest on an extradition warrant. **13.09**

Before the House of Lords the Commissioner argued that the powers in Part II of PACE applied in extradition cases. The House of Lords rejected this argument. Lord Hutton said at para 66: **13.10**

> ... [counsel] also submitted that ... police had power under both section 18 and section 19 to search the respondent's house and to seize the articles. I would reject, as did the Divisional Court, the argument that the police had such a power under either section. Section 18 only applies to the premises of a person who is under arrest for an 'arrestable offence'. An 'arrestable offence' is defined in section 24(1) as an offence for which the sentence is fixed by law, an offence for which a person of 21 years or over (not previously convicted) may be sentenced to imprisonment for a term of five years (or might be so sentenced but for the restrictions imposed by section 33 of the Magistrates' Courts Act 1980) or a long list of domestic offences created by United Kingdom statutes. Therefore it is clear, in my opinion, that an 'arrestable offence' is a domestic offence and the extradition crime alleged to have been committed by the respondent in Germany cannot be regarded as an 'arrestable offence' within the meaning of section 24(1).
>
> Nor, in my opinion, can the appellant rely on section 19(3)(a). That section only applies to the seizure of evidence in relation to 'an offence which [the police officer] is investigating or any other offence'. In *R v Southwark Crown Court ex p Sorsky Defries* [1996] Crim LR 195 the Divisional Court held that the words in section 19(3)(a) 'any other offence' were confined to domestic offences because ... in the absence of an express provision to the contrary the word 'offence' in a statute meant a domestic offence.

In para 68 Lord Hutton also rejected the Commissioner's contention that s 32 conferred a power to enter and search R's house. **13.11**

However, by a majority,[6] the House of Lords held that the police had had a limited power at common law to enter and search Rottman's house following his arrest and that this power had survived the coming into force of PACE. The common law power relied upon by the majority was that identified by Lloyd LJ in *R v Governor of Pentonville Prison ex p Osman* [1990] 1 WLR 277, 311. There, documents had been seized following Osman's arrest on a provisional warrant issued under s 6 of the Fugitive Offenders Act 1967. Objection was taken that there was no common law power to search and seize documents in relation to a crime alleged to have been committed abroad. Rejecting this argument, Lloyd LJ held at p 311: **13.12**

> ... It is beyond dispute that, in relation to a domestic offence, a police officer entering a house in pursuance of a warrant of arrest, or otherwise lawfully arresting a defendant, is entitled to take any goods or documents which he reasonably believes to be material evidence in relation to the crime for which the defendant is being arrested: *Ghani v Jones* [1970] 1 QB 693, 706. Is there then any difference between a warrant of arrest in domestic proceedings and a provisional warrant under section 6 of the Fugitive Offenders Act 1967? We can see none. The

6 Lord Hope of Craighead dissented.

police powers of search and seizure consequent on a lawful arrest ought to be, and in our judgment are, the same in both cases.

13.13 The common law power identified *R (Rottman) v Commissioner of Police for the Metropolis* [2002] 2 AC 692 is relatively narrow. In *R (Hewitson) v Chief Constable of Dorset* [2003] EWHC 3296 (Admin) the Administrative Court held that the police had acted unlawfully in searching the house of man who had been arrested under a provisional warrant several hours earlier some distance away from the flat. The Court declined to extend the common law power of search further than the limits identified in *Rottman*, saying that do so would represent a substantial leap in—rather than an incremental development of—the common law.

13.14 Part 4 of the EA 2003 was enacted in order to reverse the decision in *R (Rottman) v Commissioner of Police for the Metropolis* [2002] 2 AC 692 and to give police powers in extradition cases a statutory basis.

13.15 Before considering these powers in detail it is useful to give an overview of Part 4's more important sections.

B. Outline of Part 4 of the EA 2003

Search and seizure under warrant

13.16 Section 156 of the EA 2003 permits a justice of the peace to issue a search and seizure warrant where a person's extradition is sought under Part 1 or Part 2 of the EA 2003. A search and seizure warrant is a warrant authorizing a constable to enter and search the premises specified in the application for the warrant and to seize and retain any material found there which falls within s 156(6) which is not legally privileged material, excluded material, or special procedure material as defined in ss 10, 11, and 14 of PACE.[7]

13.17 Section 157 empowers a circuit judge to make a production order in respect of material which is not legally privileged. A production order is an order either requiring the person in possession or control of special procedure material or excluded material to produce it to a constable for him to take away, or requiring that person to give a constable access to the special procedure material or excluded material within the period stated in the order. The period will be seven days unless the judge believes a longer period would be appropriate.

13.18 Section 160 allows a circuit judge to issue a warrant in respect of excluded material and special procedure material if he is satisfied that the requirements for the making of a production order are fulfilled, and the further requirements for the issue of a warrant under s 160(8) are fulfilled.

Search and seizure without warrant

13.19 Section 161 applies if a constable has power to arrest a person under an 'extradition arrest power'. Section 174(2) provides that each of the following is an extradition arrest power: a Part 1 warrant in respect of which a certificate under s 2 has been issued; s 5; a warrant issued under s 71; and a provisional warrant issued under s 73. By s 161(2), a constable may enter and search any premises for the purpose of exercising the power of arrest if he has reasonable grounds for believing that the person is on the premises.

13.20 By s 162, if a person has been arrested under an extradition arrest power at a place other than a police station a constable may enter and search any premises in which the person was at the

[7] EA 2003, s 174.

time of his arrest or immediately before his arrest if he has reasonable grounds for believing the matters set out in s 162(2).

Section 163 governs the search of the defendant after his arrest. A constable may search the defendant as provided for in s 163(2) and (3). **13.21**

Section 164 provides for entry and search of premises after arrest. It represents a codification of the *Osman/Rottman* common law power discussed above.[8] Section 164 applies if a person has been arrested under an extradition arrest power. In such a case a constable may enter and search any premises occupied or controlled by the person if the constable has the reasonable grounds specified in s 164(2). **13.22**

Treatment after arrest and delivery up of seized property

Sections 166–171 deal with treatment of the arrested person in the police station. Section 166 deals with fingerprints and samples; s 167 covers searches and examination for the purposes of establishing identity; and s 171 provides for other rights in PACE to be applied to extradition defendants by order. **13.23**

The Extradition Act 2003 (Police Powers) Order 2003[9] has been made under s 171. Article 2 provides that ss 55, 56, and 58 of PACE apply in the circumstances described in EA 2003, s 171(1), with the modifications specified in the Article. **13.24**

Section 172 deals with the delivery up of property to the requesting state that has been seized or produced under Part 4 or anything which has been seized under ss 50 or 51 of the Criminal Justice and Police Act 2001 in reliance on a power of seizure conferred by Part 4. **13.25**

Definitions

Section 174 is the definitions section for Part 4. **13.26**

Use of force in exercise of Part 4 powers

Section 209 provides that a person may use reasonable force, if necessary, in the exercise of a power conferred by the EA 2003.[10] **13.27**

Application of Part 4 to customs officers

The powers in Part 4 are exercisable by constables. However, s 175 states that the Treasury may by order provide for any provision of Part 4 which applies in relation to police officers or persons arrested by police officers to apply with specified modifications in relation to customs officers or persons arrested by customs officers. By s 216(8) a customs officer is a person commissioned by the Commissioners of Customs and Excise under s 6(3) of the Customs and Excise Management Act 1979. **13.28**

Meaning of 'premises'

The powers in Part 4 included the power to search 'premises'. By s 174(5)(a), in England and Wales, 'premises' has the meaning given by s 23 of PACE, namely:[11] **13.29**

> … 'premises' includes any place and, in particular, includes—(a) any vehicle, vessel, aircraft or hovercraft; (b) any offshore installation; (ba) any renewable energy installation; (c) any tent or movable structure; 'offshore installation' has the meaning given to it by section 1 of the

[8] Para 13.12.
[9] SI 2003/3106.
[10] cf s 117 of PACE.
[11] cf *Cowan v Condon* [2000] 1 WLR 254.

Mineral Workings (Offshore Installations) Act 1971; 'renewable energy installation' has the same meaning as in Chapter 2 of Part 2 of the Energy Act 2004.

C. Codes of Practice

13.30 In the same way that Codes of Practice have been issued under s 66 of PACE in order to regulate the conduct of persons charged with the duty of investigating offences under PACE, so s 173 of the EA 2003 requires the Secretary of State to issue Codes of Practice in connection with the police's powers under the EA 2003. The Codes of Practice made under the EA 2003 have already been referred to in the context of arrest.[12]

13.31 Section 173(1) requires the Secretary of State to issue Codes of Practice in connection with the following matters: the exercise of the powers conferred by Part 4; the retention, use, and return of anything seized or produced under Part 4; access to and the taking of photographs and copies of anything so seized or produced; and the retention, use, disclosure, and destruction of fingerprints, a sample, or a photograph taken under Part 4.

13.32 The first edition of the Codes was published on 18 December 2003 and they came into force on 1 January 2004.[13] The Codes can be obtained from the Home Office website.[14]

13.33 Three Codes of Practice have been published to date:

- Code B, which deals with searches, seizure, retention, use, and delivery of property
- Code C, which governs arrest and detention, and treatment of detained persons
- Code D, which deals with identification of persons

13.34 Guidance on the application of the Codes is set out in paras 1.5–1.6:

> 1.5 These Codes set out the police powers which may be relied upon in extradition cases, additional to the police's common law powers. The powers in the Act are modelled on those contained in PACE, but where necessary and appropriate, they supplement domestic provisions to enable officers to respond to extradition requests effectively.
>
> 1.6 Where these Codes are silent, officers should have regard to relevant domestic provisions set out in the revised edition of the PACE Codes of Practice (PACE Codes), effective from 1 April 2003. Where procedures in extradition cases are the same as those in domestic cases, these Codes refer officers to the relevant section in the PACE Codes.

13.35 Section 173(6) makes clear that a failure by a constable to comply with a provision of the Codes does not of itself make him liable to criminal or civil proceedings. Section 173(4) states that a Code issued under the section is admissible in evidence in proceedings under the Act and must be taken into account by a judge or court in determining any question to which it appears to the judge or the court to be relevant.

D. Search and Seizure Warrants and Production Orders

13.36 The following paragraphs consider the powers of search and seizure conferred by ss 156–160. These sections create three principal methods of obtaining documents: under a search and seizure warrant under s 156 if the material sought does not consist of or include excluded material

---

12 Para 4.62.

13 The Extradition Act 2003 (Police Powers: Codes of Practice) Order 2003, SI 2003/3336.

14 <http://www.homeoffice.gov.uk/publications/police/operational-policing/extradition-codes-of-practice>.

or special procedure material; under a production order issued under s 157 or a search warrant issued under s 160 if the material sought does consist of or include such items.

The terms 'excluded material' and 'special procedure material' bear the same meanings as in ss 11 and 14 of PACE respectively.[15] **13.37**

Documents subject to legal privilege can never lawfully be seized under Part 4.[16] In the EA 2003, 'legal privilege' bears the same meaning as in s 10 of PACE: s 174(4).[17] **13.38**

Code B makes clear that the police should not be drawn into investigating foreign offences when executing searches under Part 4. Para 1.3 states: **13.39**

> Searches conducted under powers in the Extradition Act 2003 may only be undertaken for the purpose of obtaining evidence of the extradition offence for use in the prosecution of the person accused of the extradition offence. Officers may not investigate crimes on behalf of the requesting authority or territory, other than to speak to persons for the purpose of assisting establishing ownership or connection to the property.

Search and seizure warrants (s 156)

Section 156 confers power on a justice of the peace to issue a search and seizure warrant on application by a constable provided the requirements in s 156(8) for the grant of such a warrant are met. **13.40**

A search and seizure warrant is defined by s 156(5) to be a warrant authorizing a constable to enter and search the premises specified in the application for the warrant, and to seize and retain any material found there which falls within s 156(6). **13.41**

Section 156 is the equivalent of s 8 of PACE in that it only permits a warrant to be issued in respect of material which does not consist of or include special procedure material, excluded material, or items subject to legal privilege.[18] **13.42**

Code of Practice, Code B, para 3, contains provisions relating to applications for search warrants under s 156. **13.43**

Material which can be sought under a search and seizure warrant

The material that can be sought under a search and seizure warrant is specified in s 156(6). Material may be seized if: **13.44**

(a) it would be likely to be admissible evidence at a trial in the relevant part of the UK for the offence specified in the application for the warrant (on the assumption that conduct constituting that offence would constitute an offence in that part of the UK), and
(b) it does not consist of or include items subject to legal privilege, excluded material, or special procedure material.

Sections 50 and 51 of the Criminal Justice and Police Act 2001 confer additional powers of seizure to deal with the 'sifting' problem identified in *R v Chesterfield Justices ex p Bramley* **13.45**

---

[15] EA 2003, s 174(3) and (6).

[16] The 'sifting' powers in Part 2 of the Criminal Justice and Police Act 2001 do, however, apply: see para 13.45.

[17] *R v Central Criminal Court ex p Francis & Francis (a Firm))* [1989] AC 346; *R (Miller Gardner Solicitors (a firm)) v Minshull Street Crown Court* [2002] EWHC 3077 (Admin); *R (Rogers) v Manchester Crown Court* [1999] 1 WLR 832.

[18] cf *Bates v Chief Constable of Avon and Somerset Constabulary* [2009] EWHC 942 (Admin); *Power-Hynes v Norwich Magistrates' Court* [2009] EWHC 1512 (Admin).

[2000] QB 576. In that case the Administrative Court held that an officer executing a search warrant issued under s 8 of PACE is only empowered to seize material falling within the scope of the warrant or within s 19 of PACE. Therefore, the Court held that there was no power for an officer to seize material for the purpose of sifting through it to determine whether it came within the scope of the warrant. Accordingly, if an officer seized items which when examined were found to be outside the scope of the warrant and not covered by s 19, even if the officer had acted in good faith, there was no defence in PACE to an action for trespass to goods based on the seizure.

13.46 Section 50 allows material to be seized from premises for the purpose of determining whether it is material which may be lawfully seized. Section 165(1) of the EA 2003 extends Sch 1 of the Criminal Justice and Police Act 2001 to include the powers of seizure in ss 156(5), 160(5), 161(4), 162(6) and (7) of the EA 2003 among the powers to which s 50 applies.

13.47 Section 20 of PACE as amended by s 70 of the Criminal Justice and Police Act 2001 extends the powers of seizure in the EA 2003 to include information stored in an electronic form.

Conditions for the grant of a search and seizure warrant

13.48 Section 156(8) sets out the conditions which have to be met before a search and seizure warrant can be issued. There must be reasonable grounds for believing that:

(a) the offence specified in the application has been committed by the person so specified;
(b) the person is in the UK or is on his way to the UK;
(c) the offence is an extradition offence within the meaning given by s 64 (if the person's extradition is sought by a Category 1 territory) or s 137 (if extradition is sought by a Category 2 territory);
(d) there is material on the premises specified in the application which falls within s 156(6);
(e) any of the conditions referred to in s 156(9) are satisfied.

13.49 The conditions in s 156(9) are:

(a) that it is not practicable to communicate with a person entitled to grant entry to the premises;
(b) that it is practicable to communicate with a person entitled to grant entry to the premises but it is not practicable to communicate with a person entitled to grant access to the material referred to in s 156(8)(d);
(c) that entry to the premises will not be granted unless a warrant is produced;
(d) that the purpose of a search may be frustrated or seriously prejudiced unless a constable arriving at the premises can secure immediate entry to them.

13.50 It is not a condition precedent to the grant of a warrant under s 156 that other methods of obtaining the material have been tried without success or have not been tried because they are bound to fail.[19]

13.51 A justice of the peace to whom application is made under s 156 must be careful to ensure that the applicant is entitled to the warrant.[20] If the police do not identify the conditions they rely upon then the warrant is invalid.[21] In particular, he must be personally satisfied on the material before him that the conditions in s 156(8) are satisfied. He is not entitled simply to accept

[19] cf *R v Billericay Justices ex p Frank Harris (Coaches) Ltd* [1991] Crim LR 472.
[20] *Williams v Summerfield* [1972] QB 512.
[21] cf *Redknapp v Commissioner of the City of London Police* [2008] EWHC 1177 (Admin), which considered a warrant issued under s 8 of PACE.

the assertions of the applicant for the warrant. In *R v Guildhall Magistrates Court ex p Primlaks Holdings (Panama) Limited* [1990] 1 QB 261, 272 Parker LJ said in relation to s 8 of PACE in words that are equally applicable to s 156 of the EA 2003:

> Before concluding this judgment I find it necessary to make certain observations with regard to applications under section 8 of the Act. It confers a draconian power and it is of vital importance that it should be clearly understood by all concerned that it is for the justice to satisfy himself that there are reasonable grounds for believing the various matters set out. The fact that a police officer, who has been investigating the matter, states in the information that he considers that there are reasonable grounds is not enough. The justice must himself be satisfied. In the present case Detective Inspector Keating did not even so state. He merely stated that the matters set out led to the belief that there were reasonable grounds for suspecting that the first of the conditions was satisfied. This would not be completely fatal, for a justice would be entitled to consider that the facts went further. But if the applicant goes no further than to speak of reasonable grounds for suspicion, a justice would in my judgment need to be very cautious indeed before he went further. In the present case he clearly could not have done so.

Contents of the application for a search and seizure warrant

Section 156(2), (3), and (4) specify the information that an application for a search and seizure warrant must contain. It must state that: **13.52**

(a) the extradition of a person specified in the application is sought under Part 1 or Part 2;
(b) the warrant is sought in relation to premises specified in the application;
(c) the warrant is sought in relation to material, or material of a description, specified in the application;
(d) that material, or material of that description, is believed to be on the premises.

If the application states that the extradition of the person is sought under Part 1, the application must also state that the person is accused in a Category 1 territory specified in the application of the commission of an offence which is specified in the application, and which is an extradition offence within the meaning given by s 64 (s 156(3)). **13.53**

If the application states that the extradition of the person is sought under Part 2, the application must also state that the person is accused in a Category 2 territory specified in the application of the commission of an offence which is specified in the application, and which is an extradition offence within the meaning given by s 137 (s 156(4)). **13.54**

Section 15 of PACE imposes additional requirements for the contents of the application for the warrant. These are considered at para 13.57. **13.55**

The applicant is under a duty to make full disclosure when applying for a warrant or order under s 156, 157, or 160.[22] In particular, it is the duty of the applicant to set out, either in the notice itself or in further documentation, a description of all that is sought.[23] **13.56**

Safeguards in the execution of search and seizure warrants

Warrants issued under s 156 are subject to the safeguards contained in ss 15 and 16 of PACE. Section 15(1) of PACE states: **13.57**

> This section and section 16 below have effect in relation to the issue to constables under any enactment, including an enactment contained in an Act passed after this Act, of warrants to

[22] *R v Lewes Crown Court ex p Hill* (1991) 93 Cr App R 60, 69; *R v Acton Crown Court ex p Layton* [1993] Crim LR 458.

[23] *R v Central Criminal Court ex p Adegbesan* 84 Cr App R 219; *R v Inner London Crown Court ex p Baines and Baines (a Firm)* [1988] QB 579.

enter and search premises; and an entry on or search of premises under a warrant is unlawful unless it complies with this section and section 16 below.

13.58 The protections in ss 15 and 16 are designed to protect the person whose premises are being searched and are stringent in their effect.[24] Failure to comply with any of the requirements of either section will render the entry, search, and seizure unlawful and leave the relevant police force exposed to an action for damages.[25]

13.59 Section 15 requires the warrant to contain essential information such as the name of the person who applies for it, the name of the enactment under which is was issued, the address of the premises to be searched, and the date on which it is issued (s 15(6)—see Van der Pijl and another v Kingston Crown Court [2012] All ER(D) 235 (Dec)). The warrant must also authorize entry on one occasion only unless it authorizes multiple entries (s 15(5)).

13.60 Section 16 contains procedural requirements for the conduct of searches. Section 16(1) provides that a warrant to enter and search premises may be executed by any constable. Such a warrant may authorize persons to accompany any constable who is executing it (s 16(2)). If a person not named on the warrant accompanies the constable in the execution of the warrant then the entry, search, and seizure will be unlawful.[26] Therefore, if foreign investigators wish to be present then this must be made clear in the application and they should be named on the warrant. They are not permitted to take part in the search itself, but merely to assist the officers in identifying relevant material.[27]

13.61 The entry and search must take place within three months of the date of the warrant (s 16(3)), and must take place at a reasonable hour unless the constable executing it considers that this would frustrate the purpose of the search (s 16(4)). The constable must identify himself to the occupier (or other person present), produce the warrant, and supply him with a copy of it (s 16(5) and (6)). If no-one is present then a copy of the warrant must be left at the premises (s 16(7)).

13.62 Section 16(8) provides that the search must be a search to the extent required for the purpose for which the warrant was issued. It follows that if items are seized which fall outside the terms of the warrant then their seizure will be unlawful unless the items seized can properly be described as de minimis.[28]

Production orders (s 157)

13.63 Section 156(6) makes clear that sensitive material relating to an extradition offence cannot be seized under a search and seizure warrant. In this context, sensitive material means 'excluded material' as defined by s 11 of PACE and 'special procedure material' as defined by s 14 of PACE.[29]

13.64 Where there are grounds for believing that the material to be sought includes such material, then a production order under s 157 or a warrant under s 160 must be obtained. These provisions contain powers analogous to those contained in s 9 and Sch 1 of PACE.

13.65 A production order is defined by s 157(5) to be an order either:

(a) requiring the person that the application for the order specifies as appearing to be in possession or control of special procedure material or excluded material to produce it to a constable (within the period stated in the order) for him to take away, or

---

24 *R v Central Criminal Court ex p AJD Holdings Ltd* [1992] Crim LR 669.

25 *R v Chief Constable of Warwickshire ex p Fitzpatrick* [1999] 1 WLR 564, 574; *R v Chief Constable of Lancashire ex p Parker* [1993] QB 577, 584.

26 *Gross v Southwark Crown Court*, 24 July 1998 (CO/1759/98).

27 cf *R v Reading Justices ex p Southwest Meats Ltd* [1992] Crim LR 672. But note s 16(2A).

28 *R v Chief Constable of Warwickshire ex p Fitzpatrick*, [1999] 1 WLR 564, 575; *R v Southwark Crown Court ex p Sorsky Defries* [1996] Crim LR 195; cf *R v Chesterfield Justices ex p Bramley* [2000] QB 576, 588.

29 These definitions apply in relation to the EA 2003 by virtue of s 174(3) and (6).

(b) requiring that person to give a constable access to the special procedure material or excluded material within the period stated in the order.

Production orders have effect as if they were orders of the court (s 157(7)). Hence it is a contempt of court to fail to comply with a production order. **13.66**

The period stated in a production order must be a period of seven days starting with the day on which the order is made, unless it appears to the judge by whom the order is made that a longer period would be appropriate (s 157(6)). **13.67**

Unlike a search and seizure warrant, which can be issued by a justice of the peace, a production order may only be issued by a judge (in England and Wales) (s 157(1) and (8)). **13.68**

For guidance on applying for a production order under s 157, see Code B, para 3. **13.69**

Requirements for making a production order

Because production orders provide access to material which by definition is sensitive and confidential, a number of decisions have emphasized the heavy responsibility borne by those who apply for them and by judges considering whether to grant them.[30] **13.70**

Sections 157(1) and 158(2) provide that a production order may be made if the judge has reasonable grounds for believing that: **13.71**

(a) the offence specified in the application has been committed by the person so specified;
(b) the person is in the UK or is on his way to the UK;
(c) the offence is an extradition offence within the meaning given by s 64 (if extradition is sought by a Category 1 territory) or s 137 (if extradition is sought by a Category 2 territory);
(d) there is material which consists of or includes special procedure material or excluded material on premises specified in the application;
(e) the material would be likely to be admissible evidence at a trial in the relevant part of the UK for the offence specified in the application (on the assumption that conduct constituting that offence would constitute an offence in that part of the UK). By s 158(3), the relevant part of the UK is the part of the UK where the judge exercises jurisdiction.

Section 158(4) is an important provision. It provides that it must appear that other methods of obtaining the material either have been tried without success or have not been tried because they were bound to fail. **13.72**

It is not sufficient for a constable simply to assert that the conditions in s 158 have been met. The judge should not make an order unless personally satisfied that the conditions are fulfilled.[31] In *R (Bright) v Central Criminal Court* [2000] 1 WLR 662, 677 Judge LJ said: **13.73**

> ... it is clear that the judge personally must be satisfied that the statutory requirements have been established. He is not simply asking himself whether the decision of the constable making the application was reasonable, nor whether it would be susceptible to judicial review on *Wednesbury* grounds ... This follows from the express wording of the statute, 'If ... a circuit judge is satisfied that one ... of the sets of access conditions is fulfilled'. The purpose of this provision is to interpose between the opinion of the police officer seeking the order and the consequences to the individual or organisation to whom the order is addressed the safeguard of a judgment and decision of a circuit judge.

30 *R v Lewes Crown Court ex p Hill* (1991) 93 Cr App R 60, 65.

31 cf *R v Crown Court at Lewes ex p Hill* 93 Cr App R 60; *R v Guildhall Magistrates' Court ex p Primlaks Holdings (Panama) Inc* [1990] 1 QB 261, 272.

13.74 Section 158(5) provides that it must be in the public interest that the material should be produced or that access to it should be given. This provision makes clear that the judge retains an overall discretion whether or not to grant a production order even if all the other conditions are fulfilled. However, if the offence to which the application relates is serious enough it is inconsistent to refuse an application for access to material by finding that it is not in the public interest that access should be given.[32]

13.75 In *R (Bright) v Central Criminal Court* [2000] 1 WLR 662 the Divisional Court held in a case under Sch 1 of PACE that the fact that compliance with the order by the person ordered to make production may involve him in incriminating himself is not per se a reason for not making an order.

13.76 The judge must give reasons for making an order under s 157.[33]

Contents of application for a production order

13.77 Section 157(2) requires an application for a production order to state that:

(a) the extradition of a person specified in the application is sought under Part 1 or Part 2;
(b) the order is sought in relation to premises specified in the application;
(c) the order is sought in relation to material, or material of a description, specified in the application;
(d) the material is special procedure material or excluded material;
(e) a person specified in the application appears to be in possession or control of the material.

13.78 If the application states that the extradition of the person is sought under Part 1, the application must also state that the person is accused in a Category 1 territory specified in the application of the commission of an offence which is specified in the application, and which is an extradition offence within the meaning given by s 64 (s 157(3)).

13.79 If the application states that the extradition of the person is sought under Part 2, the application must also state that the person is accused in a Category 2 territory specified in the application of the commission of an offence which is specified in the application, and which is an extradition offence within the meaning given by s 137 (s 157(4)).

13.80 As explained above at para 13.56, an applicant for a production order is under a duty to make full and frank disclosure of all relevant matters.

Information held electronically

13.81 Section 159 applies if any of the special procedure material or excluded material specified in an application for a production order consists of information stored in any electronic form (s 159(1)).

13.82 If the production order is an order requiring a person to produce the material to a constable for him to take away, it has effect as an order to produce the material in a form in which it can be taken away by him; or in a form in which it is visible and legible or from which it can readily be produced in a visible and legible form (s 159(2)).

---

32 *R v Crown Court at Northampton ex p Director of Public Prosecutions* 93 Cr App R 376.

33 cf *R v Central Criminal Court ex p Propend Finance Property Ltd* [1996] 2 Cr App R 26; *R v Lewes Crown Court ex p Nigel Weller & Co (a firm)*, 12 May 1999, CO/2890/98.

If the order is an order requiring a person to give a constable access to the material, it has effect as an order to give him access to the material in a form in which it is visible and legible, or from which it can readily be produced in a visible and legible form (s 159(3)). **13.83**

Search warrants under s 160 for special procedure material and excluded material

A warrant under s 160 authorizes a constable to enter and search the premises specified in the application for the warrant, and to seize and retain any material found there which falls within s 160(6) and which is special procedure material, if the application for the warrant states that the warrant is sought in relation to special procedure material; and to seize and retain any material found there which falls within s 160(6) and which is excluded material, if the application for the warrant states that the warrant is sought in relation to excluded material. **13.84**

Material falls within s 160(6) if it would be likely to be admissible evidence at a trial in the relevant part of the UK for the offence specified in the application for the warrant (on the assumption that conduct constituting that offence would constitute an offence in that part of the UK). **13.85**

The power to allow access to excluded and special procedure material under warrant is a draconian power which should only be used as a last resort where no other method of obtaining the material is available.[34] **13.86**

In *R v Central Criminal Court ex p AJD Holdings* [1992] Crim LR 669 the Court said in relation to the equivalent power in para 12 of Sch 1 of PACE that it was important before any search warrant was applied for that careful consideration was given to what material it is hoped a search might reveal, so as to be clear to anyone subsequently considering the lawfulness of the warrant. The application should make clear that the material sought related to the crime under investigation. A written note should be made of anything said in support of the application beyond what was set out in the written application. There should be careful briefing of the officers who were to execute the search, including how material to be searched for might be thought to relate to the crime under investigation. **13.87**

For guidance on applying for a warrant under s 160, see Code B, para 3. **13.88**

Requirements for the grant of a search warrant under s 160

Section 160 provides that a judge may, on an application made to him by a constable, issue a warrant under s 160 if he is satisfied: **13.89**

(a) that the requirements for the making of a production order contained in s 158 are fulfilled, and
(b) that the further requirement for the issue of a warrant under s 160, contained in s 160(8), is fulfilled.

The requirements for the making of a production order have been considered above.[35] The further requirement for the issue of a warrant under s 160(8) is that any of the following conditions is satisfied: **13.90**

(a) it is not practicable to communicate with a person entitled to grant entry to the premises;

---

[34] *R v Southwark Crown Court ex p Bowles* [1998] AC 641, 649.
[35] Para 13.70.

(b) it is practicable to communicate with a person entitled to grant entry to the premises but it is not practicable to communicate with a person entitled to grant access to the material referred to in s 158(2)(d);
(c) the material contains information which is subject to a restriction on disclosure or an obligation of secrecy contained in an enactment (including one passed after the EA 2003) and is likely to be disclosed in breach of the restriction or obligation if a warrant is not issued.

Contents of the application for a s 160 warrant

13.91 In addition to the information required by s 15 of PACE, an application for a warrant under s 160 must state that:

(a) the extradition of a person specified in the application is sought under Part 1 or Part 2 of the EA 2003;
(b) the warrant is sought in relation to premises specified in the application;
(c) the warrant is sought in relation to material, or material of a description, specified in the application;
(d) the material is special procedure material or excluded material.

13.92 If the application states that the extradition of the person is sought under Part 1, the application must also state that the person is accused in a Category 1 territory specified in the application of the commission of an offence which is specified in the application, and which is an extradition offence within the meaning given by s 64.

13.93 If the application states that the extradition of the person is sought under Part 2, the application must also state that the person is accused in a Category 2 territory specified in the application of the commission of an offence which is specified in the application, and which is an extradition offence within the meaning given by s 137.

13.94 As explained above, an applicant for a s 160 warrant is under a duty to make full and frank disclosure of all relevant matters.

Safeguards in the execution of s 160 warrants

13.95 The safeguards contained in ss 15 and 16 of PACE apply in relation to s 160 warrants by virtue of s 15(1). Sections 15 and 16 are considered at para 13.57.[36]

E. Search and Seizure Without a Warrant

13.96 This section considers the police's search powers under ss 161–164. There are four principal powers: the power to enter and search premises for the purposes of arrest (s 161); the power to enter and search premises in which the person was at time of arrest (s 162); the power to search a person on arrest (s 163); and the power to enter and search premises controlled by a person under arrest (s 164).

Entry and search of premises for purposes of making an arrest (s 161)

13.97 Section 161 applies if a constable has power to arrest a person under an extradition arrest power. Section 174(2) provides that each of the following is an extradition arrest power: a Part

[36] See also para 19.105.

1 warrant in respect of which a certificate under s 2 has been issued; s 5; a warrant issued under s 71; and a provisional warrant issued under s 73.

Section 161(2) provides that a constable may enter and search any premises for the purpose of exercising the power of arrest if he has reasonable grounds for believing that the person is on the premises. **13.98**

The power to search conferred by s 161(2) is exercisable only to the extent that is reasonably required for the purpose of exercising the power of arrest (s 161(3)). However, a constable who has entered premises in exercise of the power conferred by s 161(2) may seize and retain anything which is on the premises if he has reasonable grounds for believing that it has been obtained in consequence of the commission of an offence or it is evidence in relation to an offence, and that it is necessary to seize it in order to prevent it being concealed, lost, damaged, altered, or destroyed (s 161(4)). Here, an 'offence' includes an offence committed outside the UK (s 161(5)). **13.99**

If the premises contain two or more separate dwellings, the power conferred by s 161(2) is a power to enter and search only any parts of the premises which the occupiers of any dwelling comprised in the premises use in common with the occupiers of any other dwelling comprised in the premises, and any dwelling comprised in the premises in which the constable has reasonable grounds for believing that the person may be. **13.100**

Section 161 is analogous to s 17 of PACE. In *Riley v DPP* 91 Cr App R 14 the Divisional Court held that where police officers are invited onto premises by an occupier or other person authorized to do so, who had been told by them the reason for their entry, they are lawfully on the premises, and they do not have to comply with s 17, which applies to entry and search in the absence of consent. This reasoning is equally applicable to s 161. **13.101**

A police officer exercising his power to enter premises by the use of reasonable force, pursuant to ss 17 and 117 of PACE should, unless the circumstances make it impossible, impracticable, or undesirable, give any occupant present the reason for his exercising that power of entry.[37] Again, similar principles apply in the exercise of the power under s 161. **13.102**

For guidance on the exercise of the power under s 161, see Code B, para 4. **13.103**

Entry and search of premises on arrest (s 162)

Section 162 applies if a person has been arrested under an extradition arrest power at a place other than a police station. **13.104**

Section 162(2) provides that a constable may enter and search any premises in which the person was at the time of his arrest or immediately before his arrest if he has reasonable grounds for believing: **13.105**

(a) if the person has not been convicted of the 'relevant offence', that there is on the premises evidence (other than items subject to legal privilege) relating to the relevant offence;
(b) in any case, that there is on the premises evidence (other than items subject to legal privilege) relating to the identity of the person.

By s 162(3) the relevant offence is the offence: **13.106**

(a) referred to in the Part 1 warrant, if the arrest was under a Part 1 warrant;
(b) in respect of which the constable has reasonable grounds for believing that a Part 1 warrant has been or will be issued, if the arrest was under s 5;

[37] *O'Loughlin v Chief Constable of Essex* [1998] 1 WLR 374.

(c) in respect of which extradition is requested, if the arrest was under a warrant issued under s 71;
(d) of which the person is accused, if the arrest was under a provisional warrant.

13.107 The power to search conferred by s 162(2), if the person has not been convicted of the relevant offence, is a power to search for evidence (other than items subject to legal privilege) relating to the relevant offence, and in any case, is a power to search for evidence (other than items subject to legal privilege) relating to the identity of the person (s 162(4)).

13.108 The power to search conferred by s 162(2) is exercisable only to the extent that it is reasonably required for the purpose of discovering evidence in respect of which the power is available by virtue of s 162(4) (s 162(5)).

13.109 By s 162(6), a constable may seize and retain anything for which he may search by virtue of s 162(4) and (5).

13.110 A constable who has entered premises in exercise of the power conferred by s 162(2) may seize and retain anything which is on the premises if he has reasonable grounds for believing that it has been obtained in consequence of the commission of an offence or it is evidence in relation to an offence, and that it is necessary to seize it in order to prevent it being concealed, lost, damaged, altered, or destroyed. An offence includes an offence committed outside the UK (s 162(8)).

13.111 If the premises contain two or more separate dwellings, the power conferred by s 162(2) is a power to enter and search only any dwelling in which the arrest took place or in which the person was immediately before his arrest, and any parts of the premises which the occupier of any such dwelling uses in common with the occupiers of any other dwelling comprised in the premises (s 162(9)).

13.112 The power under s 162 is analogous to the power of entry and search conferred by s 32(2)(b) of PACE.[38]

13.113 For guidance on the exercise of the power under s 162, see Code B, para 4.

Search of person on arrest (s 163)

13.114 Section 163 applies if a person has been arrested under an extradition arrest power at a place other than a police station.

13.115 By s 163(2) a constable may search the person if he has reasonable grounds for believing that the person may present a danger to himself or others.

13.116 A constable may search the person under s 163(3) if he has reasonable grounds for believing that the person may have concealed on him anything which he might use to assist him to escape from lawful custody or anything which might be evidence relating to an offence or to the identity of the person.

13.117 The power to search conferred by s 163(3) is a power to search for anything falling within paragraph (a) or (b) of s 163(3) and is exercisable only to the extent that is reasonably required for the purpose of discovering such a thing (s 163(4)).

13.118 The powers conferred by s 163(2) and (3) do not authorize a constable to require a person to remove any of his clothing in public, other than an outer coat, jacket, or gloves, but they do authorize a search of a person's mouth (s 163(5)).

[38] cf *R (Hewitson) v Chief Constable of Dorset* [2003] EWHC 3296 (Admin).

A constable searching a person in exercise of the power conferred by s 163(2) may seize and retain anything he finds, if he has reasonable grounds for believing that the person searched might use it to cause physical injury to himself or to any other person (s 163(6)). **13.119**

A constable searching a person in exercise of the power conferred by s 163(3) may seize and retain anything he finds if he has reasonable grounds for believing that the person might use it to assist him to escape from lawful custody or that it is evidence of an offence or of the identity of the person or has been obtained in consequence of the commission of an offence (s 163(7)). **13.120**

Section 51 of the Criminal Justice and Police Act 2001 (see para 13.45) allows material to be seized from a person in order to determine whether it is material which may lawfully be seized. Section 165(1) of the EA 2003 extends Sch 1 of the Criminal Justice and Police Act 2001 to include the powers of seizure in s 163(6) and (7) among the powers to which s 51 applies. **13.121**

By s 163(8), an offence includes an offence committed outside the UK. **13.122**

Nothing in s 163 affects the power conferred by s 43 of the Terrorism Act 2000 to stop and search persons reasonably suspected of being terrorists. **13.123**

Section 163 is analogous to the powers of search contained in ss 32(1) and 32(2)(a) of PACE. **13.124**

For guidance on exercise of the power under s 163, see Code B, paras 4.3–4.11. **13.125**

Entry and search of premises after arrest (s 164)

Section 164 applies if a person has been arrested under an extradition arrest power. It represents a codification of the common law power recognized in *R (Rottman) v Commission of Police for the Metropolis* [2002] 2 AC 692 (see para 13.12). Code of Practice, Code B, paras 4.12–4.16, contains guidance on the exercise of the power under s 164. **13.126**

By s 164(2), a constable may enter and search any premises occupied or controlled by the person if the constable has reasonable grounds for suspecting, if the person has not been convicted of the relevant offence, that there is on the premises evidence (other than items subject to legal privilege) relating to the relevant offence and, in any case, that there is on the premises evidence (other than items subject to legal privilege) relating to the identity of the person. The premises must be occupied or controlled by the person under arrest as reasonable suspicion that the person occupies or controls them is not enough.[39] **13.127**

The relevant offence is defined by s 164(3) to be the offence: **13.128**

(a) referred to in the Part 1 warrant, if the arrest was under a Part 1 warrant;
(b) in respect of which the constable has reasonable grounds for believing that a Part 1 warrant has been or will be issued, if the arrest was under s 5;
(c) in respect of which extradition is requested, if the arrest was under a warrant issued under s 71;
(d) of which the person is accused, if the arrest was under a provisional warrant.

The power to search conferred by s 164(2), if the person has not been convicted of the relevant offence, is a power to search for evidence (other than items subject to legal privilege) relating to the relevant offence and, in any case, is a power to search for evidence (other than items subject to legal privilege) relating to the identity of the person. **13.129**

[39] cf *Khan v Commissioner of Police of the Metropolis* [2008] EWCA Civ 723, which considers s 18 of PACE.

13.130 The power to search conferred by s 164(2) is exercisable only to the extent that it is reasonably required for the purpose of discovering evidence in respect of which the power is available by virtue of s 164(4).

13.131 A constable may seize and retain anything for which he may search by virtue of s 164(4) and (5).

13.132 A constable who has entered premises in exercise of the power conferred by s 164(2) may seize and retain anything which is on the premises if he has reasonable grounds for believing that it has been obtained in consequence of the commission of an offence or it is evidence in relation to an offence, and that it is necessary to seize it in order to prevent it being concealed, lost, damaged, altered, or destroyed.

13.133 An offence includes an offence committed outside the UK (s 164(8)).

13.134 The powers conferred by s 164(2) and (6) may be exercised only if a police officer of the rank of inspector or above has given written authorization for their exercise (s 164(9)). But the power conferred by s 164(2) may be exercised without this authorization if it is exercised before the person arrested is taken to a police station, and the presence of the person at a place other than a police station is necessary for the effective exercise of the power to search (s 164(10)).

13.135 Section 164(9) and (10) do not apply to Scotland.

13.136 Section 164 is analogous to the power to search premises under s 18 of PACE, considered in *R (Rottman) v Commissioner of Police for the Metropolis* [2002] 2 AC 692. For guidance on the exercise of the power under s 164, see Code B, paras 4.12–4.16.

F. Treatment After Arrest

13.137 Code C, para 2.1 provides that an officer arresting a person wanted for extradition under the EA 2003 must caution the person in the following terms:

> You do not have to say anything, but anything you do say may be given in evidence.

and must give the person a copy of the warrant as soon as practicable after arrest. The detained person must then be taken to a police station, and treated in accordance with Code C.

13.138 Sections 166–168 and s 171 provide statutory authority for the fingerprinting and search of extradition defendants at police stations. Section 169 amends the analogous sections of PACE, namely ss 54A, 61, 63, and 64A so as to exclude persons arrested under extradition powers.

13.139 The terms 'appropriate consent', 'fingerprints', 'intimate search', and 'non-intimate sample' as used in these sections bear the same meaning as in s 65 of PACE: s 174(7), EA 2003.

Fingerprints and non-intimate samples (s 166)

13.140 Section 166 applies if a person has been arrested under an extradition arrest power and is detained at a police station.

13.141 Fingerprints may be taken from the person only if they are taken by a constable with the appropriate consent given in writing, or without that consent, under s 166(4) (s 166(2)).

13.142 A non-intimate sample may be taken from the person only if it is taken by a constable with the appropriate consent given in writing, or without that consent, under s 166(4) (s 166(3)).

13.143 Section 166(4) provides that fingerprints or a non-intimate sample may be taken from the person without the appropriate consent only if a police officer of at least the rank of inspector authorizes the fingerprints or sample to be taken.

For guidance on the exercise of these powers, see Code D, para 3. 13.144

Searches and examination for the purposes of ascertaining identity (s 167)

In extradition cases it is necessary to show that the person who has been arrested is the person whose extradition is sought by the requesting state.[40] Mistakes do sometimes occur. For example, in 2003 a British man, Derek Bond, was imprisoned in South Africa following a request for extradition by the United States for a different Derek Bond.[41] 13.145

Section 167 applies if a person has been arrested under an extradition arrest power and is detained at a police station and empowers the police to take steps to ascertain the identity of the arrested person. 13.146

Section 167(2) provides that if a police officer of at least the rank of inspector authorizes it, the person may be searched or examined, or both, for the purpose of facilitating the ascertainment of his identity. In this case, ascertaining a person's identity includes showing that he is not a particular person (s 167(7)). 13.147

An identifying mark found on a search or examination under s 167 may be photographed with the appropriate consent, or without the appropriate consent, if that consent is withheld or it is not practicable to obtain it (s 167(3)). 'Taking a photograph' includes using a process by means of which a visual image may be produced (s 167(8)). 'Mark' includes features and injuries and a mark is an identifying mark if its existence in a person's case facilitates the ascertainment of his identity (s 167(9)). 13.148

The only persons entitled to carry out a search or examination, or take a photograph, under s 167 are constables and persons designated for the purposes of s 167 by the appropriate police officer (s 167(4)). In England and Wales the appropriate police officer is the chief officer of police for the police area in which the police station in question is situated (s 167(10)). 13.149

Section 167 does not authorize a person either to carry out a search or examination of a person of the opposite sex, or to take a photograph of any part of the body (other than the face) of a person of the opposite sex (s 167(5)). Nor does it permit an intimate search to be carried out (s 167(6)). 13.150

Section 169 amends the sections dealing with of PACE. 13.151

Guidance of the exercise of the powers under s 167 is contained in Code D, para 4. 13.152

Photographing detainees

Section 168 applies if a person has been arrested under an extradition arrest power and is detained at a police station. The person may be photographed with the appropriate consent, or without the appropriate consent, if that consent is withheld or it is not practicable to obtain it (s 168(2)). 'Taking a photograph' includes using a process by means of which a visual image may be produced (s 168(5)). 13.153

A person proposing to take a photograph of a person under s 168 may, for the purpose of doing so, require the removal of any item or substance worn on or over the whole or any part of the head or face of the person to be photographed and, if the requirement is not complied with, may remove the item or substance himself (s 168(3)). 13.154

The only persons entitled to take a photograph under s 168 are constables and persons designated for the purposes of this section by the appropriate police officer (s 168(4)). In England 13.155

[40] *Re Anthony*, 27 June 1995 (CO/1657/94).

[41] The Times, 27 February 2003.

and Wales the appropriate police officer is the chief officer of police for the police area in which the police station in question is situated (s 168(6)).

Other treatment and rights of detained persons

13.156 PACE contains a number of provisions relating to detained persons which have no equivalents in the EA 2003. Section 171 enables subordinate legislation to be made to extend these PACE provisions to such persons.

13.157 Section 171 applies in relation to cases where a person:

(a) is arrested under an extradition arrest power at a police station;
(b) is taken to a police station after being arrested elsewhere under an extradition arrest power;
(c) is detained at a police station after being arrested under an extradition arrest power.[42]

13.158 In relation to those cases the Secretary of State may by order apply the following provisions of PACE (and the Northern Irish equivalents in s 171(4)) with specified modifications: s 54 (searches of detained persons); s 55 (intimate searches); s 56 (right to have someone informed when arrested); s 58 (access to legal advice). The Extradition Act 2003 (Police Powers) Order 2003 (SI 2003/3106) has been made under s 171. It provides that these sections of PACE shall apply in the circumstances described in s 171(1) with the modifications specified in Article 2(2), (3), and (4) of the Order.

G. Delivery of Seized Property to the Requesting State

13.159 As has been seen, many extradition treaties require property seized that is relevant to the extradition offence to be delivered up to the requesting state. The EA 2003 places the mechanism for doing on a statutory footing for the first time in s 172.

13.160 Section 172 applies to anything which has been seized or produced under Part 4, or anything which has been seized under s 50 or 51 of the Criminal Justice and Police Act 2001 in reliance on a power of seizure conferred by Part 4.

13.161 A constable may deliver any such thing to a person who is or is acting on behalf of an authority if the constable has reasonable grounds for believing that the authority is an authority of the 'relevant territory', and that it has functions such that it is appropriate for the thing to be delivered to it (s 172(2)).

13.162 'Relevant territory' is defined in s 172(3) and (4). If the relevant seizure power was a warrant issued under Part 4, or the thing was produced under an order made under Part 4, the relevant territory is the Category 1 or Category 2 territory specified in the application for the warrant or order.

13.163 If the relevant seizure power was s 161(4), 162(6) or (7), 163(6) or (7), or 164(6) or (7), the relevant territory is:

(a) the territory in which the Part 1 warrant was issued, in a case where the applicable extradition arrest power is a Part 1 warrant in respect of which a certificate under s 2 has been issued;

42 As defined in s 169(6).

(b) the territory in which a constable has reasonable grounds for believing that a Part 1 warrant has been or will be issued, in a case where the applicable extradition arrest power is s 5;
(c) the territory to which a person's extradition is requested, in a case where the applicable extradition arrest power is a warrant issued under s 71;
(d) the territory in which a person is accused of the commission of an offence or has been convicted of an offence, in a case where the applicable extradition arrest power is a provisional warrant under s 73.

The applicable extradition arrest power is defined by s 172(5) to be: **13.164**

(a) the extradition arrest power under which a constable had a power of arrest, if the relevant seizure power was s 161(4);
(b) the extradition arrest power under which a person was arrested, if the relevant seizure power was s 162(6) or (7), 163(6) or (7), or 164(6) or (7).

For these purposes, the 'relevant seizure power' is the power under which the thing was seized, or the power in reliance on which the thing was seized under s 50 or 51 of the Criminal Justice and Police Act 2001 (s 172(6)). **13.165**

Guidance on retention and delivery of property is contained in Code B, paras 7 and 8. **13.166**

14

POST-SURRENDER MATTERS

A. Introduction

The UK's involvement in the extradition process does not necessarily end with the defendant's surrender to the requesting territory. As explained at para 5.72, most extradition treaties incorporate the rule of specialty and the rule against re-extradition. These rules place restrictions on how an extradited defendant can be dealt with in the requesting state. If the state wishes to try the defendant for an offence other than one for which he was extradited, or if it wishes to extradite him to a third state, then it may be necessary for it to seek the consent of the UK. **14.01**

This chapter considers how such consent is to be given under the EA 2003. The EA 1989 provided that in all cases it was for the Secretary of State to grant or refuse consent. The EA 2003 divides responsibility for deciding whether or not to grant consent between the appropriate judge and the Secretary of State depending upon whether the requesting state is a Category 1 or Category 2 state. **14.02**

As explained at paras 10.30 and 10.52, the EA 2003 contains provisions which allow for a serving prisoner to be extradited from the UK, dealt with in the requesting territory, and then returned to the UK to complete his sentence before being re-extradited to serve the foreign sentence.[1] Sections 186–189 and Sch 1 provide for what is to happen in this situation once the defendant has served his sentence in the UK. These provisions are considered in the last section of this chapter. **14.03**

B. Consent to Prosecution for Further Offences

Consent following extradition to a Category 1 territory

This section considers the mechanism by which the UK grants consent for a Category 1 territory to try the defendant for additional offences. In essence, it is for the appropriate judge to grant or refuse consent in accordance with the procedure contained in ss 54 and 55. **14.04**

[1] EA 2003, ss 37 and 119.

14.05 Section 54 applies if a person is extradited to a Category 1 territory in respect of an offence in accordance with Part 1 of the EA 2003; the appropriate judge receives a request for consent to the person being dealt with in the Category 1 territory for another offence; and the request is certified under s 54 by the Part 1 designated authority.[2]

14.06 The designated authority may certify a request for consent if it believes that the authority making the request is a judicial authority of the Category 1 territory that has the function of making requests for the consent referred to in s 54(1)(b) in that territory. The certificate must contain the information specified in s 54(3).

14.07 The judge must serve notice on the person that he has received the request for consent unless he is satisfied that it would not be practicable to do so (s 54(4)).

14.08 The consent hearing must begin within 21 days of the request being received unless the period is extended under s 54(6) and it can be extended more than once (s 54(5)).

14.09 Section 55 specifies the questions which must be decided at the consent hearing. First, the judge must decide whether consent is, in fact, required (s 55(1)). Consent is not required to the person being dealt with in the territory for the offence if the person has been given an opportunity to leave the territory and he has not done so before the end of the permitted period, or if he did so before the end of the permitted period, and he has returned there (s 55(8)). The permitted period is 45 days starting with the day on which the person arrived in the territory following his extradition there in accordance with Part 1 (s 55(9)). If the judge decides that consent is not required then he must inform the requesting state accordingly (s 55(2)).

14.10 If consent is required, the judge must then decide whether the offence for which consent is requested is an extradition offence (s 55(3)). If it is not, then he must refuse consent (s 55(4)).

14.11 If the offence is an extradition offence, by virtue of s 55(5) the judge must decide whether he would order the person's extradition under ss 11–25 if the person were in the UK and the judge were required to proceed under s 11 in respect of the offence for which consent is requested. In effect, the judge is required to conduct an extradition hearing under Part 1.

14.12 If he decides in the affirmative he must grant consent, otherwise he must refuse consent (s 55(6) and (7)). If the judge grants consent then his decision can only be challenged by means of judicial review and not by bringing an appeal under s 26.[3]

Consent following extradition to a Category 2 territory

14.13 Where consent is sought from a Category 2 territory then it is for the Secretary of State to decide under s 129 whether consent should be given for the defendant to be dealt with in the territory for a further offence.

14.14 Section 129 applies if a person is extradited to a Category 2 territory in accordance with Part 2; and the Secretary of State receives a valid request for his consent to the person being dealt with in the territory for an offence other than the offence in respect of which he was extradited.

14.15 A request for consent is valid if it is made by an authority which is an authority of the territory and which the Secretary of State believes has the function of making requests for the consent referred to in s 129(1)(b) in that territory (s 129(2)).

---

[2] In England and Wales the Part 1 designated authority is SOCA: Extradition Act 2003 (Part 1 Designated Authorities) Order 2003 (SI 2003/3109), as amended. SOCA is due to be incorporated into the new National Crime Agency (NCA) in 2013.

[3] *Chyba v District Court in Strakonice, Czech Republic* [2008] All ER (D) 60 (Dec).

Following receipt of the request the Secretary of State must serve notice on the person that he has received the request for consent, unless he is satisfied that it would not be practicable to do so (s 129(3)). **14.16**

The Secretary of State must then decide whether the offence is an extradition offence (s 129(4)). If he decides this question negatively he must refuse his consent (s 129(5)). **14.17**

If, however, he decides that question in the affirmative he must decide whether the appropriate judge would send the case to him (for his decision whether the person was to be extradited) under ss 79–91 if the person were in the UK and the judge were required to proceed under s 79 in respect of the offence for which the Secretary of State's consent is requested (s 129(6)). **14.18**

If the Secretary of State decides this question negatively he must refuse his consent (s 129(7)). If the Secretary of State decides that question in the affirmative he must decide whether, if the person were in the UK, his extradition in respect of the offence would be prohibited under s 94, 95, or 96 (s 129(8)). **14.19**

If the Secretary of State decides the question in s 129(8) in the affirmative he must refuse his consent (s 129(9)). If, however, he decides that question in the negative he may give his consent (s 129(10)). **14.20**

C. Consent to Re-extradition

This section considers the process by which the UK can grant its consent for the re-extradition by a foreign state (State A) to another state (State B) of a defendant who was extradited from the UK to State A. **14.21**

Re-extradition to a Category 1 territory from a Category 1 territory

The appropriate judge has jurisdiction under ss 56 and 57 to grant consent on behalf of the UK for the defendant's re-extradition to a Category 1 territory from the Category 1 territory to which he was extradited from the UK under Part 1 of the EA 2003. **14.22**

Section 56 applies if a person is extradited to a Category 1 territory in accordance with Part 1; the appropriate judge receives a request for consent to the person's extradition to another Category 1 territory for an offence; and the request is certified under s 56 by the Part 1 designated authority (s 56(1)).[4] **14.23**

The designated authority may certify a request for consent under s 56 if it believes that the authority making the request is a judicial authority of the requesting territory, and that it has the function of making requests for the consent referred to in s 56(1)(b) in that territory (s 56(2)). The certificate under s 56(2) must contain the information required by s 56(3). **14.24**

The judge must serve notice on the person that he has received the request for consent, unless he is satisfied that it would not be practicable to do so (s 56(4)). **14.25**

Following receipt of the request the judge must hold a consent hearing. This must begin before the end of the required period, which is 21 days starting with the day on which the request for consent is received by the designated authority (s 56(5)). However, the judge may extend the required period if he believes it to be in the interests of justice to do so and it can be extended more than once (s 56(6)). **14.26**

[4] In England and Wales the Part 1 designated authority is SOCA: Extradition Act 2003 (Part 1 Designated Authorities) Order 2003 (SI 2003/3109), as amended. SOCA is due to be incorporated into the new National Crime Agency (NCA) in 2013.

14.27 If the consent hearing does not begin before the end of the required period and the judge does not exercise the power in s 56(6) to extend the period, which s 56(7) allows him to do even after the period has ended, the judge must refuse consent (s 56(8)).

14.28 The questions for decision at the consent hearing are specified in s 57.

14.29 First, the judge must decide whether consent is required to the person's extradition to the other Category 1 territory for the offence (s 57(1)). Section 57(10) provides that subject to s 57(8), the judge must decide whether consent is required to the person's extradition to the other territory for the offence by reference to what appears to him to be the arrangements made between the requesting territory and the UK. Section 57(8) provides that consent is not required to the person's extradition to the other territory for the offence if the person has been given an opportunity to leave the requesting territory and he has not done so before the end of the permitted period, or if he did so before the end of the permitted period, and he has returned there. The permitted period is 45 days starting with the day on which the person arrived in the requesting territory following his extradition there in accordance with Part 1 (s 57(9)).

14.30 If the judge decides that consent is not required he must inform the authority making the request of his decision (s 57(2)).

14.31 If the judge decides that consent is required he must decide whether the offence is an extradition offence in relation to the Category 1 territory referred to in s 57(1)(b). If the judge decides that it is not then he must refuse consent.

14.32 If the judge decides that the offence is an extradition offence he must decide whether he would order the person's extradition under ss 11–26 if the person were in the UK, and he were required to proceed under s 11 in respect of the offence for which consent is requested (s 58(5)).

14.33 If the judge decides the question in s 58(5) in the affirmative he must give consent, otherwise he must refuse consent.

Re-extradition to a Category 2 territory from a Category 1 territory

14.34 Section 58 applies where a person has been extradited to a Category 1 territory and a request is received by the Secretary of State for consent to the person's extradition to a Category 2 territory, and the request has been certificated by the designated Part 1 authority under s 58(2).[5]

14.35 The designated authority may certify a request for consent under s 58(2) if it believes that the authority making the request is a judicial authority of the requesting territory, and has the function of making requests for the consent referred to in s 58(1)(b) in that territory. A certificate under s 58(2) must contain the information required by s 58(3).

14.36 By s 58(4), the Secretary of State must serve notice on the person that he has received the request for consent, unless he is satisfied that it would not be practicable to do so.

14.37 The Secretary of State must then decide whether the offence is an extradition offence within the meaning given by s 137 in relation to the Category 2 territory (s 58(5)). If the Secretary of State decides this question negatively he must refuse consent (s 58(6)).

14.38 If the Secretary of State decides that the offence is an extradition offence he must decide whether the appropriate judge would send the case to him for his decision whether the person was to be extradited under ss 79–91 if the person were in the UK, and the judge were required

[5] In England and Wales the Part 1 designated authority is SOCA: Extradition Act 2003 (Part 1 Designated Authorities) Order 2003 (SI 2003/3109), as amended.

to proceed under s 80 in respect of the offence for which the Secretary of State's consent is requested (s 58(7)).

If the Secretary of State decides this question in the negative he must refuse his consent (s 58(8)). **14.39**

If he decides the question affirmatively he must decide whether, if the person were in the UK, his extradition to the Category 2 territory in respect of the offence would be prohibited under s 94, 95, or 96 (s 58(9)). If the Secretary of State decides this question negatively he may give consent. If the Secretary of State decides that question in the affirmative he must refuse consent. **14.40**

Re-extradition to a Category 1 territory from a Category 2 territory

It is for the Secretary of State to decide under s 131 whether consent should be given for re-extradition to a Category 1 territory from the Category 2 territory to which the defendant was extradited. **14.41**

Section 131 applies if the defendant is extradited to a Category 2 territory (the requesting territory) in accordance with Part 2 and the Secretary of State receives a valid request for his consent to his extradition to a Category 1 territory for an offence other than the offence in respect of which he was extradited. **14.42**

A request for consent is valid if it is made by an authority which is an authority of the requesting territory and which the Secretary of State believes has the function of making requests for the consent referred to in s 131(1)(b) in that territory (s 131(2)). **14.43**

The Secretary of State must serve notice on the person that he has received the request for consent, unless he is satisfied that it would not be practicable to do so (s 131(3)). **14.44**

The Secretary of State must decide whether the offence is an extradition offence within the meaning given by s 64 in relation to the Category 1 territory (s 131(4)). **14.45**

If the Secretary of State decides the question in s 131(4) in the negative he must refuse his consent (s 131(5)). **14.46**

If the Secretary of State decides that question in the affirmative he must decide whether the appropriate judge would order the person's extradition under ss 11–25 if the person were in the UK, and the judge were required to proceed under s 11 in respect of the offence for which the Secretary of State's consent is requested (s 131(6)). **14.47**

If the Secretary of State decides the question in s 131(6) in the affirmative he must give his consent (s 131(7)). If, however, he decides that question in the negative he must refuse his consent (s 131(8)). **14.48**

Re-extradition to a Category 2 territory from a Category 2 territory

It is for the Secretary of State to decide under s 130 whether consent should be given for re-extradition to a Category 2 territory from the Category 2 territory to which the defendant was extradited by the UK. **14.49**

Section 130 applies if the defendant is extradited to a Category 2 territory (the requesting territory) in accordance with Part 2 and the Secretary of State receives a valid request for his consent to the person's extradition to another Category 2 territory for an offence other than the offence in respect of which he was extradited. **14.50**

A request for consent is valid if it is made by an authority which is an authority of the requesting territory and which the Secretary of State believes has the function of making requests for the consent referred to in s 130(1)(b) in that territory (s 130(2)). **14.51**

14.52 The Secretary of State must serve notice on the person that he has received the request for consent, unless he is satisfied that it would not be practicable to do so (s 130(3)).

14.53 The Secretary of State must then decide whether the offence is an extradition offence in relation to the Category 2 territory referred to in s 130(1)(b) (s 130(4)).

14.54 If the Secretary of State decides this in the negative he must refuse his consent (s 130(5)). If he decides that question in the affirmative he must decide whether the appropriate judge would send the case to him (for his decision whether the person was to be extradited) under ss 79–91 if the person were in the UK, and the judge were required to proceed under s 79 in respect of the offence for which the Secretary of State's consent is requested.

14.55 If the Secretary of State decides the question in s 130(6) in the negative he must refuse his consent (s 130(7)). If the Secretary of State decides that question in the affirmative he must decide whether, if the person were in the UK, his extradition in respect of the offence would be prohibited under s 94, 95, or 96 (s 130(8)).

14.56 If the Secretary of State decides the question in s 130(8) in the affirmative he must refuse his consent. If, however, he decides that question in the negative he may give his consent (s 130(9)).

D. Re-extradition of Prisoners Who Have Served their Sentence

14.57 Sections 186–189 and Sch 1 of the EA 2003 contain elaborate provisions governing how serving UK prisoners who were extradited, sentenced, but then returned to the UK to serve out their UK sentences are to be dealt with at the conclusion of their sentences. The operation of these provisions is not free from difficulty. In *R (Handa) v Bow Street Magistrates' Court* [2004] EWHC 2986, para 30, Tuckey LJ pointed out:[6]

> ... I would observe that the absence of any provision in UK law permitting the interruption of domestic custody is something that Parliament seems to have overlooked when enacting the 2003 Act. Sections 259 and 260 of the Criminal Justice Act 2003 allow for the removal of persons from the UK in asylum and immigration cases, but no provision is made in that Act, or anywhere else, for the removal in extradition cases of persons serving domestic sentences. The absence of such a provision entirely undermines ... s 186 ... I need hardly say that the sooner Parliament fills this yawning gap the better.

14.58 Section 186 provides that s 187 applies in relation to a person if the following conditions in s 186(2)–(6) are satisfied:

(a) The first condition is that the person was extradited to a territory in accordance with Part 1 or Part 2.
(b) The second condition is that the person was serving a sentence of imprisonment or another form of detention in the UK (the UK sentence) before he was extradited.
(c) The third condition is that, if the person was extradited in accordance with Part 1, the Part 1 warrant in pursuance of which he was extradited contained a statement that it was issued with a view to his extradition for the purpose of being prosecuted for an offence; or, if the person was extradited in accordance with Part 2, the request in pursuance of which the person was extradited contained a statement that the person was accused of the commission of an offence.

[6] cf *R (Slator) v Bow Street Magistrates' Court* [2006] EWHC 2628 (Admin). See now EA 2003, s 197A.

(d) The fourth condition is that a certificate issued by a judicial authority of the territory shows that:
   (i) a sentence of imprisonment or another form of detention for a term of four months or a greater punishment (the overseas sentence) was imposed on the person in the territory; and
   (ii) the overseas sentence was imposed on him in respect of the offence specified in the warrant or request, or any other offence committed before his extradition in respect of which he was permitted to be dealt with in the territory.
(e) The fifth condition is that before serving the overseas sentence the person was returned to the UK to serve the remainder of the UK sentence.

If s 187 applies in relation to a person, as soon as practicable after the relevant time the person must be brought before the appropriate judge for the judge to decide whether the person is to be extradited again to the territory in which the overseas sentence was imposed (s 187(1)). **14.59**

The relevant time is the time at which the person would otherwise be released from detention pursuant to the UK sentence (whether or not on licence) (s 187(2)). **14.60**

If s 187(1) is not complied with and the person applies to the judge to be discharged, the judge must order his discharge. **14.61**

By s 187(4) the person must be treated as continuing in legal custody until he is brought before the appropriate judge under s 187(1) or he is discharged under s 187(3). **14.62**

Section 187(5) provides that if the person is brought before the appropriate judge under s 187(1), the judge must decide whether the territory in which the overseas sentence was imposed is a Category 1 territory, a Category 2 territory, or neither a Category 1 territory nor a Category 2 territory. **14.63**

If the judge decides that the territory is a Category 1 territory, s 188 applies (s 187(6)). **14.64**

If the judge decides that the territory is a Category 2 territory, s 189 applies (s 187(7)). If the judge decides that the territory is neither a Category 1 territory nor a Category 2 territory, he must order the person's discharge (s 187(8)). **14.65**

A person's discharge as a result of s 187, 188, or 189 does not affect any conditions on which he is released from detention pursuant to the UK sentence. **14.66**

Section 139 applies for determining the appropriate judge for the purposes of s 187. **14.67**

Re-extradition to Category 1 territories

If s 188 applies, the EA 2003 applies as it would if: **14.68**

(a) a Part 1 warrant had been issued in respect of the person;
(b) the warrant contained a statement that the person had been convicted of the relevant offence,[7] and the warrant was issued with a view to the person's arrest and extradition to the territory for the purpose of serving a sentence imposed in respect of the relevant offence;
(c) the warrant were issued by the authority of the territory which issued the certificate referred to in s 186(5);
(d) the relevant offence were specified in the warrant;
(e) the judge were the appropriate judge for the purposes of Part 1;

[7] As amended by para 2(8) of Sch 13 to the Police and Justice Act 2006.

(f) the hearing at which the judge is to make the decision referred to in s 187(1) were the extradition hearing;
(g) the proceedings before the judge were under Part 1.

14.69 As applied by s 188(1) the EA 2003 has effect with the modifications set out in Part 1 of Sch 1.

14.70 The relevant offence is the offence in respect of which the overseas sentence is imposed.

Re-extradition to Category 2 territories

14.71 If s 189 applies, the Act applies as it would if:

(a) a valid request for the person's extradition to the territory had been made;
(b) the request contained a statement that the person had been convicted of the relevant offence;[8]
(c) the relevant offence were specified in the request;
(d) the hearing at which the appropriate judge is to make the decision referred to in s 187(1) were the extradition hearing;
(e) the proceedings before the judge were under Part 2.

14.72 As applied by s 189(1) the EA 2003 has effect with the modifications set out in Part 2 of Sch 1.

14.73 The relevant offence is the offence in respect of which the overseas sentence is imposed (s 189(3)).

[8] As amended by para 2(9) of Sch 13 to the Police and Justice Act 2006.

15

THE EUROPEAN ARREST WARRANT

A. Introduction

This chapter examines the operation of the European arrest warrant (EAW) scheme within the EU.[1] The EAW deserves special attention because of its political importance and because it makes a number of significant changes to the way in which extradition requests within the EU are processed.[2] The focus of this chapter is the way in which the EAW has been implemented in states outside the UK. Part 1 of the EA 2003, which implements the EAW in the UK, is considered in detail elsewhere.[3] **15.01**

[1] See 2011 Extradition Review, Part 4.

[2] Although the scheme established by the Council Framework Decision of 13 June 2002 on the European arrest warrant and the surrender procedures between member States (the EAW Framework Decision) uses the term 'surrender' rather than 'extradition', the latter term will be used for consistency; cf the comments of Lord Phillips in *Assange v The Swedish Prosecuting Authority* [2012] 2 AC 471, para 74; *Advocaten voor de Wereld* [2007] ECR I-3633, para 28 (ECJ).

[3] See, in particular, Chapter 2 and Chapter 5. However in this chapter the UK's implementation of specific aspects of the EAW Framework Decision is noted where necessary.

15.02 The EAW was established by the EAW Framework Decision. Article 1 defines the EAW and imposes an obligation on member States to execute it:

> 1. The European arrest warrant is a judicial decision issued by a Member State with a view to the arrest and surrender by another Member State of a requested person, for the purposes of conducting a criminal prosecution or executing a custodial sentence or detention order.
>
> 2. Member States shall execute any European arrest warrant on the basis of the principle of mutual recognition and in accordance with the provisions of this Framework Decision.

15.03 The EAW Framework Decision prescribes a common form of arrest warrant which, after issue in one state, can be executed in any other member State of the EU (subject to local certification procedures) in order to secure the defendant's rapid return to the requesting state.

15.04 Statistics compiled by the European Commission[4] report that, between 2005 and 2009, 54,689 EAWs were issued and 11,630 EAWs executed. During the same period, between 51% and 62% of requested persons consented to their surrender, on average within 14–17 days. The average surrender time for those who did not consent was 48 days. This contrasts with the pre-EAW position of a 12-month average for the extradition of requested persons.

15.05 The EAW scheme has however been the subject of criticism by member States, European and national parliamentarians, groups from civil society, and individual citizens. There has, in particular, been consistent criticism of the indiscriminate use of EAWs to effect the return of persons who may have committed trivial offences or offences that by reason of the lapse of time should not be prosecuted. The EU has resisted the calls for substantive amendments to the EAW Framework Decision and has instead, recognizing the need to ensure that the EAW is used proportionately, called on judicial authorities in EU countries to apply a 'proportionality check' by considering the seriousness of the offence, the length of sentence, and the costs and benefits of executing an EAW.[5]

15.06 The courts in certain member States have also sought to curb disproportionate EAW requests by reference to Article 49(3) of the Charter of Fundamental Rights of the EU (laying down the principle of proportionality in connection with criminal offences and penalties) as a basis for refusing to surrender a person to an EU Member upon an EAW.[6] In the UK, the Government has announced it will take the opportunity of the 2014 JHA opt-out decision to work with the European Commission, and with other member States, to reform the EAW so that it provides the protections against both the disproportionate use of the EAW for trivial offences and the risk of lengthy pre-trial detention.[7]

15.07 Another area of criticism of the EAW scheme has concerned the procedural rights of suspects, including the need for an explicit national entitlement to legal representation. The absence of representation has in many cases been exacerbated by difficulties in obtaining information or accessing translation services and restrictions on pre-trial release. The

---

[4] See COM(2011) 175 Final, p 3.

[5] <http://ec.europa.eu/justice/criminal/recognition-decision/european-arrest-warrant/index_en.htm>. The 2011 Extradition Review considered the issue of proportionality at para 5.120 et seq.

[6] See, for example, in Germany *Oberlandesgericht Stuttgart* 25-2-2010 (NJW 2010, 1617-1619) and *Oberlandesgericht Hamm* 25-2-2010 (Az: (2) 4 Ausl A 163/08 and 89/09), and in the UK *HH v Deputy Prosecutor of the Italian Republic Genoa* [2012] UKSC 25.

[7] The Government Response to Sir Scott Baker's Review of the United Kingdom's Extradition Arrangements 2012 Cm 8458.

publication by the European Commission of the so-called 'roadmap' in 2009[8] was intended to lead to progress in improving the protection of procedural rights of the individual. However, other than rights to interpretation and basic information about rights, progress has been slow.

On 23 October 2009 the Council of the EU adopted a Framework Decision 2009/829/JHA[9] on the application, between member States of the EU, of the principle of mutual recognition to decisions on supervision measures as an alternative to provisional detention. This Framework Decision is due to be implemented on 1 December 2012 and introduces the possibility of transferring non-custodial supervision measures from the member State where a non-resident is suspected of having committed an offence to the member State where he/she is normally resident. This may allow a suspected person to be subject to a supervision measure in his or her normal environment pending trial in the foreign member State. It remains to be seen whether this will be effective to reduce the very high numbers of non nationals in pre-trial detention across the EU. It will require legislation in order to be implemented in the UK. **15.08**

In addition, Council Framework Decision 2009/948/JHA of 30 November 2009[10] on prevention and settlement of conflicts of exercise of jurisdiction in criminal proceedings seeks to provide a mechanism for consultation and co-operation between judicial authorities when a person is the subject of parallel criminal proceedings in different member States in respect of the same facts.[11] It entered into force on 15 December 2009 and had an implementation date of 15 June 2012. It is intended that this procedure should avoid the persistent violation of the principle of *ne bis in idem* or double jeopardy that is now a directly enforceable right under Article 50 of the EU Charter of Fundamental Rights.[12] The concept of 'same acts' in Article 3(2) of the EAW constitutes an autonomous concept of EU law that is to be interpreted in the light of the decisions on Article 54 of the Convention Implementing the Schengen Agreement and Article 50 of the EU Charter of Fundamental Rights. **15.09**

There has however been one area of criticism that has led to legislative action. Persistent difficulties have been experienced in relation to proceedings in absence. A Council Framework Decision of 26 February 2009[13] amended the EAW Framework Decision with the intention of enhancing the procedural rights of persons and fostering the application of the principle of mutual recognition to decisions rendered in the absence of the person concerned at the trial. The 2009 Framework Decision inserts a new Article 4(a) in relation to decisions rendered in the absence of the requested person into the EAW Framework Decision, deletes Article 5(1), and amends the EAW form of arrest warrant. It aims to provide clear and common grounds for non-recognition of decisions rendered following a trial at which the person concerned did not appear in person. It entered into force on 28 March 2009. **15.10**

---

[8] Resolution of the Council of 30 November 2009. OJ C 295, 4.12.2009, p.1.

[9] OJ L 294, 11.11.2009, p. 20.

[10] OJ L 328, 15.12.2009, p 42.

[11] For a discussion of how forum conflicts within the EU should be addressed, including an analysis of the Council Framework Decision of 30 November 2009 on the prevention and settlement of conflicts of exercise of jurisdiction in criminal proceedings, 2009/948/JHA, (L 328/42, 15 December 2009), see *Williams v Public Prosecutor – Lille Court Of First Instance, France* [2012] EWHC 2128 (Admin); cf *R (Bermingham) v Director of the Serious Fraud Office* [2006] EWHC 200 (Admin), paras 57–78.

[12] See *Assange v The Swedish Prosecuting Authority* [2012] 2 AC 471, paras 198–200; *Gozutok and Brugge* (Joined cases) C187/01 and C385/01, *Miraglia* C469/03, *Van Esbroeck* C436/04, *Gasparini* C467/04, *Van Straaten* C150/05, *Kretzinger* C288/05, *Kraaijenbrink* C67/05, *Borquain* C297/07, *Turansky* C491/07, and *Mantello* C261/09.

[13] 2002/584/JHA. The deadline for transposition was March 2011.

Background to the enactment of the EAW Framework Decision

15.11 The Treaty on European Union[14] identified areas relating to criminal justice, including judicial co-operation in criminal matters, as matters of common interest to be pursued for the purposes of achieving the objectives of the Union, in particular the free movement of persons.

15.12 This led to proposals intended to produce a simpler and quicker procedure for extradition within the EU, founded on member States' confidence in the integrity of each other's legal and judicial systems. The legal foundation of this movement was contained in Articles 31(a) and (b) and 34(2)(b) of the Treaty of Amsterdam,[15] which provided for judicial co-operation in criminal matters, the facilitation of extradition and the adoption of framework decisions. Framework decisions had the purpose of approximating the laws and regulations of the member States. They were binding upon the member States as to the result to be achieved, but left to the national authorities the choice of form and methods.[16]

15.13 The interpretative obligation attached to this method of legislation was the subject of consideration in *Criminal proceedings against Pupino* (Case-105/03) [2006] QB 83. The legal duty of conforming interpretation was set out in two passages in the judgment:[17]

> ... 43 In the light of all the above considerations, the court concludes that the principle of interpretation in conformity with Community law is binding in relation to framework decisions adopted in the context of Title VI of the Treaty on European Union. When applying national law, the national court that is called on to interpret it must do so as far as possible in the light of the wording and purpose of the framework decision in order to attain the result which it pursues and thus comply with Article 34.2(b) EU.
>
> ... 47 The obligation on the national court to refer to the content of a framework decision when interpreting the relevant rules of its national law ceases when the latter cannot receive an application which would lead to a result compatible with that envisaged by that framework decision. In other words, the principle of interpretation in conformity with Community law cannot serve as the basis for an interpretation of national law contra legem.

15.14 The abolition of the pillar division in the Treaty of Lisbon[18] also abolished this method of legislation for the purposes of future European criminal justice measures. In accordance with the Treaty of Lisbon, whenever a pre-Lisbon instrument such as the EAW Framework Decision is amended, the Commission's power to take infringement proceedings and the jurisdiction of the European Court of Justice become applicable to the amended measure. In any event, those powers will apply after 1 December 2014 at the end of the transitional period laid down in the Treaty of Lisbon.[19]

15.15 In addition, any future amendment of the EAW Framework Decision will mean that the rules introduced by the Treaty of Lisbon for the adoption of legislative measures in relation to the area of criminal justice will apply. These rules include co-decision between the European Parliament and Council and the possibility of the non-participation of some member States.

---

[14] Maastricht, 7 February 1992, OJ 1992 C191, p 1.

[15] OJ C 340, 10 November 1997.

[16] Article 34(2)(b), Treaty of Amsterdam. The Crime (International Cooperation) Act 2003 gives effect to a number of framework decisions in the field of mutual legal assistance: see Chapter 17.

[17] The duty does not apply in the UK for the reasons explained in *Assange v The Swedish Prosecuting Authority* [2012] 2 AC 471, paras 201–218.

[18] 2007/C 306/01.

[19] Subject to the so-called 'opt-out' for the UK and Poland: see *Assange v The Swedish Prosecuting Authority* [2012] 2 AC 471, paras 198–200.

Detailed background to the EAW

At a meeting of the European Council at Tampere, Finland, in October 1999 it was resolved that formal extradition procedures should be abolished among member States as far as persons who were fleeing from justice after having been finally sentenced were concerned, and replaced by a simple transfer of such persons. The Council and the Commission were invited to adopt a programme of measures. On 30 November 2000 the Council duly adopted a number of measures, one of the objects of these measures being the transfer of persons intent on fleeing justice after they have been finally sentenced.[20] **15.16**

On 27 November 2001, the Commission put forward detailed proposals for a Council Framework Decision on a European arrest warrant.[21] This was then the subject of parliamentary review.[22] Following discussions in the Council of Ministers, a further draft was produced in December 2001 that was to form the basis of the final Framework Decision approved by the Council and considered by the European Parliament in early 2002.[23] The form of the EAW is set out in the Annex to the EAW Framework Decision.[24] **15.17**

The EAW and Part 1 of the EA 2003

The key features of the EAW as implemented in the EA 2003 are as follows:[25] **15.18**

- EAW partners are designated as Part 1 territories pursuant to an order made by the Secretary of State.[26]
- There are simplified procedures for authentication,[27] transmission,[28] and arrest.[29]
- Removal of the dual criminality requirement for 32 framework offences.[30] In pre- conviction cases, these offences carry a maximum sentence of three years' imprisonment or more and, in conviction cases, a sentence of four months or more must have been imposed. The list of framework offences is set out in Sch 2 to the EA 2003.
- Removal of the role of the executive in the extradition process so that it becomes exclusively a judicial procedure.[31]
- Inclusion in s 11 of a number of mandatory grounds for refusing extradition.
- Abolition of the political offence exception to extradition.[32]
- Imposition of time limits to try and ensure rapid surrender.[33]
- EU countries may no longer refuse to surrender their own citizens to another EU country.

---

[20] Programme of measures to implement the principle of mutual recognition of decisions in criminal matters, OJ 2001 C12, p 10.

[21] COM/2001/0522 final-CNS 2001/0215.

[22] A detailed history of the process of drafting and scrutiny may be accessed at <http://ec.europa.eu/prelex/detail_dossier_real.cfm?CL=en&DosId=167840>.

[23] A5-0003/2002, 9 January 2002.

[24] 2002/584/JHA.

[25] For criticisms of the way in which the EAW scheme was implemented by Parliament in Part 1 of the EA 2003, see *Assange v The Swedish Prosecuting Authority* [2012] 2 AC 471, para 77; Spencer, 'Implementing the European Arrest Warrant: A Tale of How Not to Do It' (2009) 30(3) *Statute Law Review* 184.

[26] Extradition Act 2003 (Designation of Part 1 Territories) Order 2003 (SI 2003/3333); *R (Oliver) v Secretary of State for the Home Department* [2006] EWHC 1847 (Admin) (designation of Germany as a Part 1 territory lawful despite decision of German Federal Constitutional Court that EAW scheme unconstitutional under German Constitution).

[27] EA 2003, s 202.

[28] EA 2003, ss 203–204.

[29] EA 2003, ss 3–6. Part 1 introduces for the first time a power of arrest without a warrant in extradition cases.

[30] EA 2003, ss 64(2) and 65(2).

[31] EA 2003, s 2.

[32] cf EA 2003, s 13, which preserves political discrimination as a bar to extradition.

[33] EA 2003, ss 8(4) and 31.

B. The EAW Scheme

The purpose of the EAW

15.19 In *Office of the King's Prosecutor v Cando Armas* [2006] 2 AC 1, para 2, Lord Bingham said:

> It is not unusual for those facing prosecution or imprisonment in one country to take refuge in another in the hope of evading trial or punishment as the case may be. Procedures have long existed enabling the first country to seek the surrender of the fugitive by the second. But the procedures established by bilateral treaty have in the past been characterised by technicality and delay so great as to impede or even frustrate the efficacy of the process. There has accordingly been a movement among the member states of the European Union, gaining strength in recent years, to establish, as between themselves, a simpler, quicker, more effective procedure, founded on member states' confidence in the integrity of each other's legal and judicial systems.

15.20 The purpose of the EAW is outlined in recitals (5), (6), (10), and (11) of the Preamble to the EAW Framework Decision:

> (5) The objective set for the Union to become an area of freedom, security and justice leads to abolishing extradition between Member States and replacing it by a system of surrender between judicial authorities. Further, the introduction of a new simplified system of surrender of sentenced or suspected persons for the purposes of execution or prosecution of criminal sentences makes it possible to remove the complexity and potential for delay inherent in the present extradition procedures. Traditional cooperation relations which have prevailed up till now between Member States should be replaced by a system of free movement of judicial decisions in criminal matters, covering both pre-sentence and final decisions, within an area of freedom, security and justice.
>
> (6) The European arrest warrant provided for in this Framework Decision is the first concrete measure in the field of criminal law implementing the principle of mutual recognition which the European Council referred to as the 'cornerstone' of judicial cooperation... .
>
> (10) The mechanism of the European arrest warrant is based on a high level of confidence between Member States. Its implementation may be suspended only in the event of a serious and persistent breach by one of the member states of the principles set out in Article 6(1) of the Treaty on European Union, determined by the Council pursuant to Article 7(1) of the said Treaty with the consequences set out in Article 7(2) thereof.
>
> (11) In relations between Member States, the European arrest warrant should replace all the previous instruments concerning extradition, including the provisions of Title III of the Convention implementing the Schengen Agreement which concern extradition.

15.21 Thus it is clear that the principal purpose of the EAW Framework Decision was to reduce the level of formality in intra-EU extradition procedures and to speed up the process of extradition. Paragraphs 5 and 6 of the Preamble identify the EAW scheme as being the first step towards the more ambitious goal of intra-community mutual recognition of all criminal judgments and warrants and the abolition of extradition. A number of EU states including Spain, Latvia, Austria, Portugal, Slovenia, and Slovakia make reference to this objective in their domestic implementing legislation.

15.22 The European Court of Justice[34] has confirmed that the most significant objective pursued by the Framework Decision is that of facilitating and accelerating judicial co-operation.[35] The

[34] The ECJ. Following the entrance into force of the Treaty of Lisbon on 1 December 2009, the ECJ's official name was changed from the 'Court of Justice of the European Communities' to the 'Court of Justice' although in English it is still commonly referred to as the European Court of Justice. The Court of First Instance was renamed as the 'General Court', and the term 'Court of Justice of the European Union' officially designates the two courts, as along with its specialized tribunals, taken together. The Court's website is <http://curia.europa.eu/>.

[35] See Case C-303/05 *Advocaten voor de Wereld* [2007] ECR I-3633, para 31; Case C-296/08 PPU *Santesteban Goicoechea* [2008] ECR I-6307, paras 51, 55, and 76; and *Leymann and Pustovarov* [2008] ECR I-8983, para 42.

ECJ has also pointed out, as is clear from recitals (5) and (7), that the Framework Decision was intended to replace the multilateral systems of extradition between member States with a system of surrender, as between judicial authorities, of convicted persons or suspects for the purpose of enforcing judgments or of criminal proceedings, that system of surrender being based on the principle of mutual recognition.[36] That principle, which constitutes the 'cornerstone' of judicial co-operation, means that, pursuant to Article 1(2) of the Framework Decision, EU states are in principle obliged to give effect to a European arrest warrant. They are thus either obliged to execute, or may not refuse to execute, such a warrant, and they may make its execution subject to conditions only in the cases listed in Articles 3 to 5 of that Framework Decision. Equally, according to Article 28(3) of the Framework Decision, consent to a subsequent surrender may be refused only in those same cases.[37]

Definition and implementation of the EAW

The EAW Framework Decision required the implementation of national schemes of extradition so as to achieve a common form of intra-EU extradition. Member states were required to take the necessary measures (ie enact legislation if necessary) to comply with the provisions of the Framework Decision by 31 December 2003.[38] **15.23**

Member states were not obliged to implement the EAW Framework Decision by adopting its precise language and were free to use an appropriate existing measure (such as a national extradition law) if it satisfied the requirements of the EAW Framework Decision. However, given the obligation to ensure that the application of the EAW Framework Decision was achieved in a clear and precise manner and had binding force, most member States adopted new national measures to fulfil their obligations.[39] **15.24**

Not all the member States complied with the December 2003 deadline, however, by the time of the adoption of the relevant Italian law in April 2005, all member States had transposed the EAW Framework Decision into their national law via specific legislation. Several states had to revise their constitutions in order to do this. **15.25**

In the case of Germany the implementing law was struck down as unconstitutional in 2005 and was redrafted in its entirety in a law of 20 July 2006. **15.26**

In addition, since 2003, 14 states have amended their legislation to take account of periodic reports and recommendations made by the Council and the Commission. However, a number of states have declined to make recommended amendments notwithstanding criticism by the Commission.[40] The states criticized include the UK as well as Belgium, Denmark, Germany, Spain, and Italy. **15.27**

The text of the national laws

Member states are required to forward to the General Secretariat of the Council and to the Commission the text of the provisions transposing into their national law the obligations imposed on them by the EAW Framework Decision. The European Judicial Network contains extensive information on the relevant national law and practice.[41] Further national information **15.28**

[36] *Advocaten voor de Wereld* [2007] ECR I-3633, para 28; Case C-66/08; *Kozłowski* [2008] ECR I-6041, paras 31 and 43; Case C-123/08 *Wolzenburg* [2009] ECR I-9621, para 56; and Case C-261/09 *Mantello* [2010] ECR I-11477, para 35.

[37] See, to that effect, *Leymann and Pustovarov* [2008] ECR I-8983, paras 49 and 51; *Wolzenburg* [2009] ECR I-9621, para 57; and *Mantello*, [2010] ECR I-11477 paras 36 and 37.

[38] EAW Framework Decision, Article 34(1).

[39] See, for example, European Arrest Warrant Act 2003 (Republic of Ireland).

[40] COM(2011) 175 final, p 5.

[41] <http://www.ejn-crimjust.europa.eu/ejn/EJN_StaticPage.aspx?Bread=12>.

can be found on the website of the EAW Project.[42] The EAW Project site is designed to provide practical information on the operation of the EAW scheme in each EU country.

Other sources of information concerning the EAW

15.29 Information about extradition from EU states can be gleaned from the periodic reviews carried out by the European Commission and published in the form of working papers.[43] There is also a European Handbook on how to issue an EAW that provides guidelines for the adoption of good practice in the light of experience, and specific information on how EAW forms should be filled in.[44]

Dates in force

15.30 Since 14 May 2005 the EAW Framework Decision has been in force throughout member States.[45] New members have implemented the provisions on accession. The only exception is within the Nordic states: Denmark, Finland, and Sweden continue to rely on the existing reciprocal legislation in force between them in the context of intra-Nordic extradition.[46]

The retrospective effect of the EAW

15.31 Under Article 32 of the EAW Framework Decision, extradition requests received by member States before 1 January 2004 continue to be governed by the pre-existing laws relating to extradition. However, all requests received on or after 1 January 2004 were required under Article 31 to be dealt with under the EAW scheme unless the member State reserved the right to deal with requests relating to acts committed before 7 August 2002 under its pre-existing laws.

15.32 Most member States applied the EAW to all offences, whenever they are alleged to have been committed, if a request is received on or after 1 January 2004. However Austria, Czech Republic, France, Italy, Lithuania, and Slovenia[47] entered reservations in respect of old offences committed before certain dates which are dealt with by them under the extradition arrangements previously in force.[48]

15.33 In C-296/08, *Santesteban Goicoechea* [2008] ECR I-6307, the ECJ held that Article 31 of the Framework Decision was to be interpreted as referring only to situations in which the EAW system is applicable, which was not the case in that case where a request for extradition had been made to France in relation to acts committed before the date specified by France. The ECJ held that Article 32 did not preclude the application by France of the Convention relating to extradition between the member States of the EU drawn up by the Council Act of 27 September 1996 and signed on that date by all the member States, (the 1996 EU Convention) even though the 1996 EU Convention became applicable in France only after 1 January 2004. Making conventions such as the 1996 EU Convention on Extradition applicable was held not to interfere with the EAW system, since, in accordance with Article 31(1), the 1996 EU Convention could be used only where the European arrest warrant system did not apply.

---

42 <http://www.eurowarrant.net/> or <http://www.asser.nl/Default.aspx?site_id=8&level1=10789>.
43 See the third report SEC(2011) 430 final.
44 17195/1/10 REV 1 COPEN 275 EJN 72 EUROJUST 139.
45 Other than in Germany between July 2005 and 2006.
46 OJ L 246 of 29.9.2003.
47 Slovenia has since abandoned its reservation in its national laws.
48 The countries and dates are: Austria: acts committed after 7 August 2002; Czech Republic: acts by Czech nationals before 1 November 2004; France: acts committed after 1 November 1993; Italy: acts committed after 7 August 2002. Italy will also not execute EAWs issued before 14 May 2005; Lithuania: 7 August 2002. The Czech Republic and Lithuania will not issue EAWs for offences committed before the dates specified.

In the case of Cyprus and Luxembourg, no reservation was entered under Article 32 but each country has restrictions on surrender that are relevant. In Cyprus, the Supreme Court has held that surrender of Cypriot nationals for offences committed before 1 May 2004 may only take place under the pre-existing law. In Luxembourg the transitional arrangements in the national legislation were such that it may not surrender on an EAW persons wanted for offences committed prior to 7 August 2002 and may not issue EAWs for such offences. **15.34**

Geographical extent

The EAW scheme applies to all EU member States. At the time of writing, September 2012, these were: **15.35**

> Austria, Belgium, Bulgaria, Cyprus, the Czech Republic, Denmark, Estonia, Finland, France, Germany, Greece, Hungary, Ireland, Italy, Latvia, Lithuania, Luxembourg, Malta, the Netherlands, Poland, Portugal, Romania, Slovakia, Slovenia, Spain, Sweden, the UK.[49]

In most member States the geographical extent of the EAW is defined by reference to that state's membership of the EU. However in Malta, as in Ireland and the UK,[50] the transposing legislation applies only to those states which have been listed by Decree or Order. **15.36**

C. Offences Covered by the EAW Scheme

An EAW may, by Article 2 of the EAW Framework Decision, be issued for acts punishable by the law of the requesting state by a custodial sentence or detention order[51] for a maximum period of at least 12 months or, where a sentence has been passed or detention order made, for sentences of at least four months.[52] **15.37**

Article 2(2) of the EAW Framework Decision sets out a list of offences that are often referred to as 'framework list offences'. These are not so much specific offences as kinds of criminal conduct, described in very general terms. Some of these, such as murder and armed robbery, are likely to feature, expressed in rather similar terms, in any developed system of criminal law. Others, such as corruption, racism, xenophobia, swindling, and extortion, are often expressed differently in different criminal justice systems.[53] **15.38**

Underlying the list is an unstated assumption that offences of this character will feature in the criminal codes of all EU member States. Article 2(2) accordingly provides that these framework list offences, if punishable in the member State issuing the EAW by a custodial sentence or detention order for a maximum period of at least three years, and as defined by the law of that state, shall give rise to surrender pursuant to the warrant without verification of the double criminality of the act. This dispensation with the requirement of double criminality is the feature which distinguishes these framework list offences from others. The assumption is that double criminality need not be established in relation to these offences because it can, in effect, **15.39**

---

[49] The EAW also applies to Gibraltar: EAW Framework Decision, Article 33(2).

[50] Extradition Act 2003 (Designation of Part 1 Territories) Order 2003 (SI 2003/3333).

[51] Not all countries make reference to detention orders in their implementing legislation. It is not clear whether such member States are liable to refuse to execute an EAW if the punishment consists of a detention order.

[52] Although the EAW Framework Decision defines extraditable and framework list offences by reference to their punishment either in the form of a custodial sentence or a detention order, in Italy, the identification of offences that pass the punishability thresholds in the EAW is complicated by the fact that aggravating circumstances (that may increase the possible maximum sentence) must be excluded when calculating the threshold.

[53] *Office of the King's Prosecutor v Cando Armas* [2006] 2 AC 1, para 5.

be taken for granted.[54] As was explained in Chapter 1,[55] dual criminality has been a feature of the UK's extradition arrangements from the earliest times and its removal was therefore a significant change.

15.40 The operation of the European arrest warrant is not, however, confined to framework offences. Article 4(2) provides:

> For offences other than those covered by paragraph (2), surrender may be subject to the condition that the acts for which the European arrest warrant has been issued constitute an offence under the law of the executing [ie, the requested] Member State, whatever the constituent elements or however it is described.

15.41 Thus, while member States may not require proof of double criminality where framework list offences are in question, they may do so in relation to any offence not covered by that list.

The framework list in the EAW Framework Decision

15.42 The 32 categories of offences on the framework list are:

> Participation in a criminal organisation; terrorism; trafficking in human beings; sexual exploitation of children and child pornography; illicit trafficking in narcotic drugs and psychotropic substances; illicit trafficking in weapons, munitions and explosives; corruption; fraud, including that affecting the financial interests of the European Communities within the meaning of the Convention of 26 July 1995 on the protection of the European Communities' financial interests; laundering of the proceeds of crime; counterfeiting currency, including of the euro; computer-related crime; environmental crime, including illicit trafficking in endangered animal species and in endangered plant species and varieties; facilitation of unauthorised entry and residence; murder, grievous bodily injury; illicit trade in human organs and tissue; kidnapping, illegal restraint and hostage-taking; racism and xenophobia; organised or armed robbery; illicit trafficking in cultural goods, including antiques and works of art; swindling; racketeering and extortion; counterfeiting and piracy of products; forgery of administrative documents and trafficking therein; forgery of means of payment; illicit trafficking in hormonal substances and other growth promoters; illicit trafficking in nuclear or radioactive materials; trafficking in stolen vehicles; rape; arson; crimes within the jurisdiction of the International Criminal Court; unlawful seizure of aircraft/ships; and sabotage.

15.43 The following countries have have implemented the list as contemplated by Article 2(2): Austria; Bulgaria; Cyprus; the Czech Republic; Denmark; Finland; Germany; Hungary; Ireland; Latvia; Lithuania; Luxembourg; Malta; the Netherlands; Portugal; Romania; Slovakia; Slovenia; Spain; Sweden; and the UK.[56] In contrast, Italy has disregarded the list contained in Article 2(2) and replaced it with its own list of corresponding offences found in its national criminal law. The effect of this is to reintroduce the principle of dual criminality since the conduct has to be capable of being analysed in terms of Italian criminal law in order to fall within the Italian list.

15.44 There is significant variation within the member States as to the treatment of accessory liability and attempts to commit framework list offences. The Polish Penal Code treats both as equivalent to the commission of the offence and thus within the framework list. Nineteen member States (Belgium, Estonia, Greece, France, Italy, Cyprus, Latvia, Lithuania, Luxembourg, Hungary, Malta, the Netherlands, Austria, Portugal, Slovenia, Slovakia, Spain, Finland, Sweden) have indicated to the Commission that they consider double criminality to be abolished in relation to attempt and complicity in the listed offences, although their national legislation is silent on the point. By contrast Ireland has stated it will apply the double criminality principle to such acts.

---

[54] *Office of the King's Prosecutor, Brussels v Cando Armas* [2006] AC 1, para 5.
[55] Para 1.6.
[56] EA 2003, ss 64(2), 65(2), 215 and Sch 2.

The scope for the examination of the legal classification of an offence as part of the framework list by the requesting state is strictly limited in the legislation of all the member States, bar Italy. Either no check may be carried out, or there is only a prima facie examination of the classification in the issuing state. However, Belgian legislation specifies that abortion and euthanasia are not covered by 'murder or grievous bodily harm'. **15.45**

The punishability threshold of three years specified in Article 2(2) has been applied in all member States (with the possible exception of Italy). Finland and Sweden have, however, legislated that in relation to a custodial sentence passed for a framework list offence it must be for a length of at least four months as required by Article 2(1). Austria allows the length of any sentence under four months to be accumulated provided at least one of the offences is punishable by one year's imprisonment. **15.46**

The legality of the creation of the framework list was considered by the ECJ in C-303/05 *Advocaten voor de Wereld* [2007] ECR I-3633. The ECJ held that the listing of offences in Article 2(2) did not infringe the principle of legality since the definition of the offences and of the penalties continued to be matters determined by the laws of the issuing member State, in accordance with fundamental rights and fundamental legal principles. No breach of the principle of equality and non-discrimination arose since, in making the choice of the 32 categories of offences listed, the Council was able to form the view that, whether by reason of their inherent nature or by reason of the punishment incurred, the categories of offences listed featured among those the seriousness of which in terms of adversely affecting public order and public safety justified dispensing with the verification of double criminality. The ECJ observed that any lack of precision in the definition of the categories of offences in question giving rise to the possibility of disparate implementation of the EAW Framework Decision within the various national legal orders was not a matter of fundamental concern. The Court pointed out that it was not the objective of the EAW Framework Decision to harmonize the substantive criminal law of the member States and that nothing in Title VI of the EU Treaty makes the application of the EAW conditional on harmonization of the criminal laws of the member States within the area of the offences in question. **15.47**

Non-framework list offences

Under Article 2(1) of the EAW Framework Decision non-framework list offences are extraditable if either they are potentially punishable by 12 months or more custody or detention or if a sentence of four months or more has been imposed. This means that in most member States, where a person has already been sentenced and that sentence is four months or more, it is irrelevant that the maximum possible sentence may have been less than 12 months. **15.48**

However, both the Netherlands' and Austria's legislation require not only that the sentence be for at least four months but also that the related offence be punishable by at least 12 months. Austria also accumulates the length of the sentences or the punishments if more than one offence is committed by the same person. Poland has set a minimum threshold for sentences before extradition can be granted. **15.49**

D. Limitations on Surrender

The EAW Framework Decision limits the grounds for refusing surrender between member States. There are three mandatory grounds in Article 3 (amnesty; double jeopardy; and age) and seven optional grounds in Article 4. The purpose of these restrictions is to prevent extradition being refused on general or political grounds. However, they have not prevented member States for providing other grounds for refusal of extradition. **15.50**

15.51 All member States have transposed the three mandatory grounds with minor exceptions that are identified below. The optional grounds have led to considerable variations between member States. Many member States have interpreted the optional grounds in Article 4 as meaning that the state may choose whether a judge is required to refuse surrender where one of the Article 4 grounds exists or whether the judge has discretion in the matter. As a consequence, many states have made these mandatory grounds for refusal. At the same time, since this Article is optional, some member States have not transposed them into their national law at all. These member States are therefore not mentioned below.

15.52 In addition, explicit restrictions on surrender have been included in some member States' legislation in relation to fundamental human rights in reliance on paras 12 and 13 of the Preamble to the Framework Decision and Article 1(3).[57] These domestic provisions emphasize that the EAW Framework Decision was not intended to undermine such rights.

15.53 Restrictions on surrender have also been adopted in relation to the matters that may be the subject of a special guarantee under Article 5.

Mandatory ground: amnesty

15.54 The EAW Framework Decision allows extradition to be refused where there is amnesty in the executing member State (Article 3(1)). This has been adopted in Belgium, Bulgaria, the Czech Republic, Germany, Estonia, Greece, Spain, France, Italy, Cyprus, Latvia, Lithuania, Luxembourg, Hungary, Malta, Austria, Poland, Portugal, Slovenia, Slovakia, Finland, and Sweden. The Netherlands has not transposed this paragraph since there is no possibility of amnesty in that country. Denmark allows extradition to be refused only where there has been a pardon rather than amnesty. Ireland has transposed this paragraph to allow for immunity by virtue of amnesty or pardon in the issuing member State rather than the executing member State. This could have resulted in Ireland requiring additional information, not foreseen in the EAW form, in order to determine liability to surrender. However, as a matter of practice this has not happened. The UK has not adopted this ground.

Mandatory ground: restrictions on second prosecutions[58]

15.55 Belgium, the Czech Republic, Denmark, Germany, Estonia, Greece, Spain, France, Italy, Cyprus, Latvia, Lithuania, Luxembourg, Hungary, Malta, the Netherlands, Austria, Poland, Portugal, Slovenia, Slovakia, and Sweden have all reproduced the provisions in Article 3(2), which restrict extradition when:

> ... the requested person has been finally judged by a Member State in respect of the same acts provided that, where there has been sentence, the sentence has been served or is currently being served or may no longer be executed under the law of the sentencing Member State.

15.56 An additional ground of refusal based on this principle in relation to the International Criminal Court has been introduced in the majority of states.

15.57 This mandatory ground has been implemented in UK law in s 12 of the EA 2003.[59] In *Connelly v Director of Public Prosecutions* [1964] AC 125 and *Director of Public Prosecutions v Humphreys* [1977] AC 1 the House of Lords held that a prosecution would only be barred on the grounds of double jeopardy where precisely the same offence is charged in the later proceedings. This narrow formulation was adopted in relation to Part 2 cases[60] in *Bohning v Government of the*

---

57 cf EA 2003, s 21.
58 Sometimes referred to as *non bis in idem*; cf EA 2003, s 12.
59 Para 5.33.
60 EA 2003, s 80 bars extradition on the grounds of double jeopardy in Part 2 cases.

United States of America [2005] EWHC 2613. However, in *Fofana v Deputy Prosecutor Thubin Tribunal de Grande Instance de Meaux, France* [2006] EWHC 744 the Court adopted a broader interpretation of the double jeopardy bar to extradition, and the Court held that extradition was barred for offences which had a significant factual overlap with offences for which the defendant had been prosecuted in the UK.

A narrow formulation of the double jeopardy principle in UK law would not reflect the approach adopted by other member States or that of the European Court of Justice to the application of this bar on extradition. The ECJ confirmed in C261/09 *Mantello* [2010] ECR I-11477 that, for the purposes of the issue and execution of an EAW, the concept of 'same acts' in Article 3(2) of the Framework Decision is an autonomous concept of EU law and requires the national court to determine whether the material acts at issue constitute a set of facts or concrete circumstances which are inextricably linked together in time, in space, and by their subject matter with acts that have been finally disposed of by time bar,[61] by court decision on the merits of the case[62] (even one made prior to the EAW scheme coming into effect),[63] and even where the judgment is one rendered in absence,[64] or by a agreement with a prosecutor to pay a penalty that is effective under national law to bring a definitive end to a prosecution.[65] **15.58**

Mandatory ground: age of defendant

All member States have prohibited extradition in accordance with Article 3(3) if the person who is the subject of the EAW may not, owing to his age, be held criminally responsible for the acts on which the arrest warrant is based under the law of the executing state.[66] **15.59**

Optional ground: dual criminality and fiscal offences

Article 4(1) provides that it shall be an optional ground to refuse extradition if, in a non-framework list case, the act on which the EAW is based does not constitute an offence under the law of the executing member State. In other words, this ground allows member States to preserve the dual criminality requirement for non-framework offences. This optional ground does not apply to framework list offences. **15.60**

This optional ground is also subject to the proviso that, in relation to taxes or duties, customs and exchange, execution of the EAW is not to be refused on the ground that the law of the executing member State does not impose the same kind of tax or duty or does not contain the same type of rules as regards taxes, duties and customs, and exchange regulations as the law of the issuing member State. **15.61**

A total of 17 states have transposed Article 4(1) as a mandatory ground for refusing extradition, namely Belgium, the Czech Republic, France, Ireland, Italy, Cyprus, Lithuania, Luxembourg, Hungary, Malta, the Netherlands, Austria, Slovenia, Slovakia, Finland, Sweden, and the UK. Denmark, Germany, Greece, Spain, Poland, and Portugal maintain it as an optional ground. Estonia and Latvia have not transposed this paragraph but Estonia has stated it will apply it in practice. **15.62**

Belgium, Bulgaria, Czech Republic, Germany, Greece, Spain, France, Ireland, Cyprus, Latvia, Luxembourg, Hungary, Malta, Austria, Poland, Portugal, Romania, Slovenia, Slovakia, and the UK refer to the tax proviso in their legislation in line with the EAW Framework Decision.[67] **15.63**

---

61 *Gasparini* C467/04.
62 *Miraglia* C469/03.
63 *Van Esbroeck* C436/04.
64 *Borquain* C297/07.
65 *Gozutok and Brugge* (Joined cases) C187/01 and C385/01 cf *Turansky* C491/07.
66 EA 2003, s 15.
67 EA 2003, s 64(8).

15.64 The remaining states have not mentioned the proviso although Denmark, Lithuania, Sweden, and the Netherlands have stated they will follow the Framework Decision.

Optional ground: concurrent prosecution in the executing state

15.65 Article 4(2) provides that an optional ground for refusal exists where the person who is the subject of the EAW is being prosecuted in the executing member State for the same act as that on which the EAW is based.

15.66 Article 4(3) provides that extradition may also be refused where the judicial authorities of the executing member State have decided either not to prosecute for the offence on which the EAW is based or to halt proceedings, or where a final judgment has been passed upon the requested person in a member State, in respect of the same acts, which prevents further proceedings.

15.67 In relation to the optional ground in Article 4(2), some member States have implemented it as a mandatory ground: the Czech Republic, Greece (for Greek nationals), Italy, Hungary, Malta, the Netherlands, Austria, Slovenia (where offence committed against a Slovenian or the state), Slovakia, and Sweden.

15.68 Most states have implemented Article 4(2) as an optional ground for refusal (Belgium, Bulgaria, Denmark, Germany, Estonia, Greece (for others), Spain, France, Cyprus, Latvia, Lithuania, Luxembourg, Poland, Portugal, Slovenia (in all other cases), Finland, Romania, and the UK. The Republic of Ireland allows for mandatory refusal where prosecution is being considered but has not yet been decided.

15.69 Transposition of Article 4(3) requires a distinction to be drawn between Part 1 (where the executing judicial authorities decide not to prosecute); Part 2 (where it is decided to halt prosecution); and Part 3 (where a final judgment has been passed which prevents further proceedings).

15.70 Part 1 is mandatory for six member States: Ireland, Hungary, the Netherlands, Austria (with some exceptions for foreigners), Sweden, and Slovakia. It is optional for 17 member States: Belgium, Bulgaria, Denmark, Germany, Estonia, Greece, Spain, France, Cyprus, Latvia, Lithuania, Luxembourg, Poland, Portugal, Romania, Slovenia, and Finland.

15.71 Part 2 is mandatory for six member States: the Czech Republic, Ireland, Hungary, the Netherlands, Austria (with some exceptions for foreigners), and Slovenia. It is optional for 17 member States: Belgium, Bulgaria, Denmark, Germany, Estonia, Greece, Spain, France, Cyprus, Latvia, Lithuania, Luxembourg, Poland, Portugal, Romania, Slovakia, and Finland.

15.72 Part 3 is mandatory for ten member States: Belgium, the Czech Republic, Ireland, Italy, Hungary, the Netherlands, Austria (with some exceptions for foreigners), Slovenia (only in relation to a final judgment passed by Slovenia), Slovakia, and Sweden. It is optional for 11 member States: Bulgaria, Germany, Estonia, Greece, Spain, Cyprus, Luxembourg, Portugal, Slovakia, Finland, and Romania. Poland's legislation is not clear in this matter and could allow for refusal where a final judgment has been passed in any other state, including third states. However, given the jurisprudence of the European Court of Justice it is likely that refusal to execute an EAW will be treated as mandatory.[68]

Optional ground: time-barred prosecutions

15.73 Where the criminal prosecution or punishment of the requested person is statute-barred according to the law of the executing member State and the acts fall within the jurisdiction of

[68] See para 15.50.

that member State under its own criminal law, then there is an optional ground for refusal of extradition under Article 4(4).

This ground has been transposed as a mandatory ground by Belgium, the Czech Republic, Greece, France, Ireland, Italy, Latvia, Lithuania, Hungary, Malta, the Netherlands, Austria, Slovenia, Slovakia, and Sweden, and as an optional ground by Bulgaria, Denmark, Germany, Estonia, Spain, Cyprus, Luxembourg, Poland, Portugal, and Finland. **15.74**

Optional ground: sentence served in a third state

If the requested person has been finally judged by a third state in respect of the same acts identified in the warrant, then provided that, where there has been a sentence passed, the sentence has been served or is currently being served or may no longer be executed under the law of the sentencing country, this is an optional ground for refusal under Article 4(5). **15.75**

This has been transposed as a mandatory ground by the Czech Republic, France, Ireland, Lithuania, Hungary, Malta, the Netherlands, Austria, Poland, Slovenia, Slovakia, and Sweden, and as an optional ground by Belgium, Bulgaria, Denmark, Estonia, Greece, Spain, Cyprus, Luxembourg, Romania, and Finland. **15.76**

Optional ground: undertaking to impose sentence in the executing state

Article 4(6) provides that extradition may be refused if the EAW has been issued for the purposes of execution of a custodial sentence or a detention order and the requested person is staying in, or is a national or a resident of the executing member State, and that state undertakes to execute the sentence or detention order in accordance with its domestic law. **15.77**

This optional ground has been transposed as a mandatory ground by 14 states: Estonia (for nationals), Greece (for nationals), Italy (for nationals), Cyprus (for nationals), Germany (for nationals and residents), Hungary, Lithuania, Austria (for nationals), Latvia, the Netherlands, Poland (for nationals, residents, and those with asylum), Finland (for nationals), and Sweden; and as an optional ground by 14 states: Belgium (for residents and nationals), Bulgaria (for residents and nationals), Denmark (for residents and nationals), Greece (for residents), Spain, France (for nationals), Cyprus (for residents), Italy (for residents), Luxembourg, Poland (for residents), Portugal (for residents and nationals), Romania (for residents and nationals), Slovenia, and Finland. **15.78**

It seems likely that the High Court in Ireland could refuse to surrender a person on the basis of Article 4(6) even though this provision has not been transposed into Irish law. Although, as a general rule, a Framework Decision has no direct effect in Irish law, the Irish legislation prohibits surrender if the High Court assesses that the surrender is prohibited under the EAW Framework Decision (including the recitals thereto).[69] **15.79**

The Czech Republic and the Netherlands have also made this a mandatory ground for refusal for nationals and long-term residents. However, in such a case they do not undertake to execute the sentence but rather to convert it in line with the convention on sentenced persons. The practical result is that, contrary to the EAW Framework Decision's provision, execution of the sentence is subject to the double criminality principle for nationals and permanent residents. Furthermore, it is to be noted that in the Czech Republic, the executing judicial authority is bound by the decision of the person requested. The Czech Republic also applies reciprocity towards other member States in order to surrender its nationals. **15.80**

[69] European Arrest Warrant Act 2003, s 16(2)(d).

15.81 In Latvia this is a mandatory ground but there is no provision in the legislation requiring an undertaking to execute the sentence. Nevertheless, Latvia has stated that such an undertaking would be given.

15.82 In C-66/08 *Kozlowski* the ECJ held that the terms 'staying' and 'resident' that determine the scope of Article 4(6), were to be defined uniformly, since they concerned autonomous concepts of EU law. The Court held that in any national law transposing Article 4(6), member States were not entitled to give those terms a broader meaning than that which derived from such a uniform interpretation. In order to ascertain, when interpreting Article 4(6), whether there are connections between the requested person and the executing member State which lead to the conclusion that that person was covered by the term 'staying' within the meaning of that provision, it was for the executing judicial authority to make an overall assessment of various objective factors characterizing the situation of that person, including, in particular, the length, nature, and conditions of his presence and the family and economic connections which that person had with the executing member State.

15.83 It is clear that the ECJ will interpret Article 4(6) widely having regard to its objective of enabling weight to be given to the possibility of increasing a person's chances of reintegrating into society following upon a sentence of imprisonment.[70]

15.84 In relation to the protection afforded to residents, the ECJ accepted in Case C-123/08 *Wolzenburg* [2009] ECR I-9621 that Article 4(6) allows a margin of discretion to states in extending protection to residents. However, it held that, in the case of a citizen of the EU, the member State of execution could not, in addition to a condition as to the duration of residence in that state, make the application of the ground for optional non-execution of a European arrest warrant laid down in that provision subject to any supplementary administrative requirements, such as possession of a residence permit of indefinite duration.

15.85 In Case C-42/11 *Da Silva Jorge*, the ECJ held that Article 4(6) and Article 18 TFEU must be interpreted as meaning that, although a member State may, in transposing Article 4(6), purport to limit the protection to its own nationals, it cannot exclude automatically and absolutely from its scope the nationals of other member States staying or resident in its territory irrespective of their connections with it. Even in the face of a limitation that purports to cover only own nationals, national courts are required, taking into consideration the whole body of domestic law and applying the interpretative methods recognized by it, to interpret that law, so far as possible, in the light of the wording and the purpose of Article 4(6) which is intended to increase the chances of reintegrating into society a person sentenced to a custodial sentence in another member State, without any distinction between own nationals and a requested person who, without being a national of the executing member State, has been staying or been resident in the executing state for a sufficient period of time so as to have established connections with that state which enables him to invoke this ground for non-execution.

15.86 The ECJ held in *IB* C-306/09 that the Article 4(6) protection should apply even if the relevant sentence was passed *in absentia*, there being nothing to indicate that the EU legislator wished to exclude persons requested on the basis of a sentence imposed *in absentia* from the reintegration objective.

Optional ground: extra-territorial offences

15.87 Article 4(7) provides that extradition may be refused:

> ... where the EAW relates to offences which: (a) are regarded by the law of the executing Member State as having been committed in whole or in part in the territory of the executing

[70] See, in particular, Case C-123/08 *Wolzenburg* [2009] ECR I-9621, para 62.

Member State or in a place treated as such; or (b) have been committed outside the territory of the issuing Member State and the law of the executing Member State does not allow prosecution for the same offences when committed outside its territory.

Article 4(7)(a) has been transposed as an optional ground by 15 States: Belgium, Bulgaria, Spain, France, Cyprus, Latvia, Lithuania, Luxembourg, Hungary, the Netherlands, Poland, Portugal, Romania, Slovenia, and Finland, and as a mandatory ground by Greece, Ireland (only if proceedings have been brought in Ireland against the person concerned), Italy, Malta, Austria (only in respect of nationals), Slovakia, and also partly in Denmark and Sweden (where the act has been committed in these last two countries, even partly, but is not punishable therein). **15.88**

Article 4(7)(b) has been transposed as an optional ground by 13 states: Belgium, Bulgaria, Estonia, Spain, France, Cyprus, Latvia, Luxembourg, the Netherlands, Portugal, Romania, Slovenia, and Finland, and as a mandatory ground by nine states: Denmark, Greece, Ireland, Italy, Lithuania, Malta, the Netherlands, Austria (only in respect of nationals), and Slovakia. In the Netherlands, at the public prosecutor's request and only in terms of Dutch legislation, a refusal of surrender will be waived, unless, in the opinion of the court, the public prosecutor could not reasonably make such a request. **15.89**

For the reasons set out in relation to Article 4(6), it seems likely that the High Court in the Republic of Ireland could refuse to surrender a person on the basis of Article 4(7). **15.90**

Fundamental human rights

Two thirds of the member States chose to introduce expressly in various forms explicit grounds for refusing extradition based on the violation of fundamental rights (Article 1(3)) or discrimination (recitals 12 and 13). **15.91**

This was so even though it was never intended to make the general condition of respect for fundamental rights an explicit ground for refusal in the event of infringement under the EAW since any member State would always be entitled to refuse to execute an arrest warrant, if it found that the proceedings have been vitiated by infringement of Article 6 of the Treaty on European Union, the Charter of Fundamental Rights, and/or the constitutional principles common to the member States, such as rights of asylum.[71] This is the view taken by the Czech Republic, Estonia, Spain, Luxembourg, Hungary, and Slovakia who have not specifically referred to any of these rights, taking the view that they exist independently of the EAW Framework Decision. **15.92**

Belgium, Germany, Greece, Ireland, Italy, Cyprus, Lithuania, the Netherlands, Austria, Sweden, and the UK[72] have explicitly transposed Article 1(3) or referred to the ECHR and have made a breach of the rights contained within it a mandatory ground for refusal. **15.93**

Ireland and Italy, in addition to referring to the ECHR, require refusal where surrender would breach their national constitutions. **15.94**

Denmark, Germany, Greece, France, Ireland, Italy, Cyprus, Latvia, Malta, Austria, Slovenia, Finland, and the UK have completely or partially transposed recital 12 of the Preamble to **15.95**

---

[71] cf the observations in *IB* C-306/09 to the effect that Protocol No 24 annexed to the Treaty on European Union provides that, given the level of protection of fundamental rights and freedoms by the member States of the EU, member States are to be regarded as constituting safe countries of origin in respect of each other for all legal and practical purposes in relation to asylum matters.

[72] EA 2003, s 21.

the EAW Framework Decision into their law as a basis for refusing extradition. Recital 12 provides:

> This Framework Decision respects fundamental rights and observes the principles recognised by Article 6 of the Treaty on European Union and reflected in the Charter of Fundamental Rights of the European Union, in particular Chapter VI thereof. Nothing in this Framework Decision may be interpreted as prohibiting refusal to surrender a person for whom a EAW has been issued when there are reasons to believe, on the basis of objective elements, that the said arrest warrant has been issued for the purpose of prosecuting or punishing a person on the grounds of his or her sex, race, religion, ethnic origin, nationality, language, political opinions or sexual orientation, or that that person's position may be prejudiced for any of these reasons. This Framework Decision does not prevent a Member State from applying its constitutional rules relating to due process, freedom of association, freedom of the press and freedom of expression in other media.

15.96 Denmark, Germany, Greece, Ireland, Italy, Cyprus, Latvia, Malta, Austria, Portugal, and Finland have either partly or fully transposed recital 13.[73] Breach of this recital, which incorporates the requirements of Article 3 of the ECHR as well as the Sixth Protocol and Protocol No 13 to the ECHR,[74] is a mandatory ground for refusing extradition in these countries.

Article 5 special guarantees

15.97 Not all member States have opted to enforce the three guarantees provided for in Article 5. These are the guarantee that a re-trial may be required where a sentence or a detention order has been imposed, without notice, in the absence of the defendant (Article 5(1)); the guarantee that there will be a parole style review of any life sentence that has been imposed (Article 5(2)); and, where the person who is the subject of an EAW for the purposes of prosecution is a national or resident of the executing member State, the guarantee that the surrender will be subject to the condition that the person is returned to the executing member State in order to serve any custodial sentence or detention order (Article 5(3)).

Guaranteed re-trial

15.98 All member States except Spain and Latvia require the Article 5(1) guarantee.[75] Ireland requires a guarantee that the person will be notified of the time when and place where any re-trial in respect of the offence concerned will take place and that her or she will be permitted to be present when any such re-trial takes place.

Guaranteed review of a life sentence

15.99 Fourteen member States require this Article 5(2) guarantee: Bulgaria, Germany (as an optional ground for refusal), Estonia, Greece, Spain, Italy, Cyprus, Lithuania, the Netherlands, Poland, Portugal, Slovenia, Finland (the guarantee only requires the possibility of amending the sentence or clemency), and Romania, whilst Belgium, the Czech Republic, Denmark, France, Ireland, Latvia, Luxembourg, Hungary, Malta, Austria, Slovakia, and Sweden do not impose this condition.

Guaranteed transfer of sentence

15.100 In relation to the Article 5(3) guarantee, 22 states have this requirement (Belgium (optional for nationals and residents), Bulgaria (optional for nationals and residents), Denmark, Germany

---

[73] This provides: 'No person should be removed, expelled or extradited to a State where there is a serious risk that he or she would be subjected to the death penalty, torture or other inhuman or degrading treatment or punishment.'

[74] Paras 7.28 and 7.82.

[75] cf EA 2003, s 20.

(this is a mandatory requirement in relation to Germany nationals/residents), Estonia, Greece, Spain (optional), France (optional), Italy (mandatory in relation to nationals/residents), Cyprus (mandatory for nationals and optional for residents), Latvia (for nationals), Lithuania, Luxembourg (optional), Hungary (mandatory where the person requests it), Austria (mandatory for nationals), Poland (for nationals and those with asylum), Portugal (optional for nationals and residents), Romania (mandatory for nationals and optional for residents), Slovakia (on request for nationals and residents), Finland (for nationals when requested or residents with strong ties), Sweden (unless the person has resided for more than two years in the issuing member State) and the Netherlands (mandatory) whilst Ireland, Malta, and Slovakia do not impose this condition.

Dutch legislation states that surrender of a Dutch person may be allowed where requested **15.101** because of a criminal investigation against that person if, in the opinion of the Executing Judicial Authority, it is guaranteed that, if he is given a non-suspended custodial sentence in the issuing member State for acts for which surrender can be allowed, he will be able to serve that sentence in the Netherlands. The Netherlands has stated that it will not extradite a national for the prosecution of an offence that is not an offence under Dutch law, because it is impossible under the relevant treaties and the national law to transfer a person where the requirement of double criminality has not been met.

The majority of member States rely on the Council of Europe Convention on the Transfer of **15.102** Sentenced Persons 1983[76] and its Protocol[77] as their mechanism for the transfer of a sentenced person pursuant to Article 5(3). Like the UK, the Republic of Ireland has a specific domestic provision based on the Framework Decision. Only Finland has pending legislation implementing the Framework Decision on the application of the principle of mutual recognition to judgments in criminal matters imposing custodial sentences or measures involving deprivation of liberty for the purpose of their enforcement in the EU,[78] which makes specific provision for the enforcement of sentences in cases under Articles 4(6) and 5(3) of the EAW and that has an implementation date of 5 December 2011. Under the new scheme the consent of the sentenced person to transfer will no longer be a prerequisite in all cases.

Non-framework limitations on surrender

Many countries have introduced grounds for refusing extradition other than those provided **15.103** for in the EAW Framework Decision. Denmark, Italy, Malta, the Netherlands, and the UK have introduced additional reasons for refusal, such as delay, political discrimination, and national security, while other states have enacted grounds for refusal connected with the merits of the case, such as its special circumstances or the personal or family situation of the individual in question.

Italy will refuse to surrender on an EAW on a series of grounds beyond those identified in the **15.104** EAW Framework Decision. For example, an executing authority in Italy may refuse to execute an EAW where, according to Italian law, the facts constituting the offence relate to the exercise of a right or a duty or if the offence was committed under '*caso fortuito*' or '*forza maggiore*'; where the victim gave his consent to the act; where the requested person is pregnant or is the mother of a child less than three years old, except in circumstances of an exceptional gravity; where the requested person is an Italian citizen who did not know that the conduct was prohibited; where the law of the issuing member State does not provide for limits to pre-trial detention; where the

[76] CETS No 112

[77] CETS No 167.

[78] 2008/909/JHA.

offence is a political one (provided that terrorism cannot be considered as a political offence); and where the evidence or grounds on which the EAW is based are insufficient.

15.105 So far as the last restriction is concerned however, the Italian Supreme Court on 23 September 2005, in the case no 34355 (*Ilie Petre*), declared that the assessment of evidence by Italian judges does not imply the direct evaluation of the existence and relevance of elements of fact against the requested person, but only consists of the verification that the warrant was issued on the basis of evidence that the requesting judicial authorities itself had considered sufficient to provide the charges with a proper basis. The Italian Court of Appeal, therefore, can only assess whether the issuing authority had adopted the warrant having gathered sufficient evidence, without directly evaluating the evidence itself.

15.106 In relation to EAWs against Austrian nationals, Austria may require verification of the stated suspicion if there are doubts in this context, in particular if evidence is available or can be offered, which would dispel the suspicion immediately.

15.107 Denmark may refuse surrender on the ground of possible threat with torture, degrading treatment, or violation of due process as well as if the surrender appears to be unreasonable on humanitarian grounds.

15.108 In Malta, surrender must be refused where it would be unjust or oppressive to surrender the requested person to a member State, where that person has been extradited to Malta from a third state.

15.109 The Netherlands will refuse surrender if the Dutch executing judicial authority finds that there is no doubt that the requested person is innocent. The Netherlands has stated this will only occur if 'it is has become crystal clear to the executing judicial authority that the person could not have committed the offence'.

15.110 In Portugal, surrender will be refused if the arrest warrant is issued on account of political reasons, while in Denmark refusal will occur where there is a danger that, after extradition, the requested person will suffer persecution for political reasons.

15.111 In Poland the list of obligatory grounds for refusal includes cases where execution of an EAW would breach the freedoms and rights of a person, when the EAW concerns: (i) an offence committed without violence for political reasons; (ii) an offence committed by a national on the territory of Poland or on board of a Polish aircraft or ship; and (iii) an act committed by a national abroad, which does not constitute an offence according to Polish law.

The surrender of nationals

15.112 Although the fact that the defendant holds British citizenship has never been a ground for refusing extradition from the UK, prior to the implementation of the EAW Framework Decision, many continental states declined to surrender their own nationals. However, with the exception of Austria (which applied for exemption under Article 33), at the time of implementation of the EAW all member States purported to permit the surrender of their own nationals in their enabling legislation. Some imposed additional requirements. The Netherlands requires a systematic check on double criminality and has made the surrender of nationals contingent on an assurance that it would be able to convert their sentences. The Czech Republic has introduced a reciprocity clause and required the conversion of sentences imposed on its nationals. Most member States have also chosen to apply the condition that, in the case of their nationals, any sentence should be served on their territory (Articles 4(6) and 5(3)).

15.113 Since implementation of the EAW, the constitutionality of the implementing legislation in relation to the extradition of nationals has been challenged in a number of countries.

On 27 April 2005, the Constitutional Tribunal of the Republic of Poland held in case No P 1/05 on the application of the EAW to Polish citizens that Article 607(1) of the Criminal Procedure Code, insofar as it purported to permit the surrender of a Polish citizen to another member State of the EU on the basis of the EAW, did not conform with Article 55(1) of the Polish Constitution. The effect of this judgment was suspended for 18 months to allow time for a constitutional amendment to be made. **15.114**

On 18 July 2005 in Germany, the Federal Constitutional Court held the extradition of German nationals was unconstitutional. In that case the Constitutional Court struck down the whole of the implementation law.[79] **15.115**

On 7 November 2005, the Supreme Court of Cyprus upheld the decision of a District Court that the arrest of a Cypriot national and his surrender to the UK on the basis of an EAW could not be effected because the national law transposing the Framework Decision into the domestic legal order was unconstitutional. The Court rejected arguments that the EAW procedures did not amount to extradition and that the law of the EU overrode the domestic legislation of Cyprus. The Constitution has since been amended, however only in respect of acts committed after 1 May 2004. **15.116**

The Spanish Constitutional Court in Case No 292/2005, on 10 November 2005, held that Spain should not extradite its own nationals in the absence of reciprocity. In contrast the Portuguese Supreme Court, in applying Article 33(5) of the Portuguese Constitution, in Case No 4783/2004 on 4 October 2005, ruled that lack of reciprocity was not an obstacle to cooperation in the EU and therefore decided to surrender a Portuguese national to Spain. **15.117**

In Decision No 591/2005, the Greek Supreme Court (in Council), held that execution of an EAW in relation to a Greek national was not unconstitutional. **15.118**

Ireland and Slovakia are the only countries (other than the UK) who have made no special provisions in relation to their own nationals. **15.119**

Where surrender for the execution of a sentence is refused pursuant to Article 4(6) on the grounds that the person has nationality or is a resident of the executing state, four member States (Austria, Luxembourg, Slovenia, and Sweden) allow for the possibility of executing a sentence even where there is no dual criminality. In six other member States (Hungary, Latvia, the Netherlands, Poland, Portugal, and Romania) this is not possible. **15.120**

Procedure—speed

The EAW scheme was intended to operate swiftly. The provisions relating to the use of a judicial procedure, using a single form for the EAW, alternative means of transmission, and rules for procedural time limits, were all intended to achieve this policy goal. **15.121**

It has been estimated that, as a result of the entry into force of the EAW Framework Decision, the average time taken to execute a warrant in intra-EU extradition has fallen from more than nine months to 45 days. The 90-day limit requested by the EAW was respected in almost all cases. In cases where the person consents to his surrender the average time taken is 16 days. In practice, there are consents to surrender in more than half the cases reported. **15.122**

Documentation

Although all member States have adopted the use of a single EAW form as prescribed in Article 8, the requirements vary considerably in detail as to the language to be used and the time limits for the receipt of warrants following an arrest (from two to 40 days). **15.123**

[79] *R (Oliver) v Secretary of State for the Home Department* [2006] EWHC 1847.

15.124 The languages for the EAW accepted by each country pursuant to Article 8(2) are as follows:

Austria	German or other language if reciprocally receives Austrian requests in German.
Belgium	Dutch, French, or German.
Bulgaria	Bulgarian.
Czech Republic	Czech. In relation to the Slovak Republic, the Czech Republic shall accept an EAW produced in the Slovak language or accompanied by translation into the Slovak language The Ministry of Justice shall specify by Decree the model for the EAW and the language other than the official language(s) in which, curiously, the member States will accept an EAW.
Cyprus	Greek, Turkish, English.
Denmark	Danish, Swedish, English. If the case is urgent they will translate the warrant but generally they ask for translation.
Estonia	Estonian or English.
Finland	Finnish, Swedish, English.
France	French.
Germany	Any official language of any issuing member State which recognizes EAWs in German issued by German judicial authorities.
Greece	Greek.
Hungary	Hungarian or a translation of the warrant into Hungarian. In relation to member States which do not exclusively accept the EAW in their own official language or in one of their official languages, Hungary accepts the EAW in English, French, or German, or accompanied by a translation in one of those languages.
Ireland	Gaelic or English or a language that the Ministry of Justice may by order prescribe, or the EAW with a translation into Irish/English.
Italy	Italian.
Latvia	Latvian and English.
Lithuania	Lithuanian and English.
Luxembourg	French, German, or English.
Malta	Maltese or English.
The Netherlands	Dutch or English, or any another official language of the EU provided that an English translation is submitted at the same time.
Poland	Polish.
Portugal	Portuguese.
Romania	Romanian, French, or English.
Slovenia	Slovenian and English.
Slovakia	Slovakian or any other language based on reciprocity.
Spain	Spanish. Where an EAW is issued through a Schengen alert, the Executing Judicial Authority will ensure translation if it is not in Spanish.
Sweden	Swedish, Danish, Norwegian, English, or a translation to one of these languages.

15.125 Some member States impose requirements not provided for in the EAW Framework Decision, such as the obligation to attach items or documents not stipulated on the form. The Czech Republic requests additional items if the person was sentenced *in absentia* or, as regards time limitation, if a period of more than three years has lapsed between the commission of the offence and the issuing of the EAW.

15.126 In Italy, the legislation provides that the EAW shall be accompanied by additional documents. These include: a copy of the applicable provisions; the initial decision of the issuing judicial authority on which the EAW is based; information regarding the sources of evidence; all personal identification data available; and any other documents considered necessary according to the Italian issuing judicial authority to verify all additional grounds for refusal.

In Malta legislation seems to require additional certificates on the nature of the offence from the issuing judicial authority. **15.127**

Irish legislation requires that an incoming warrant be endorsed by the High Court before execution. **15.128**

At least 13 member States have set time limits for the provision of additional information or a translation of relevant documents (Denmark, Germany, Spain, France, Italy, Latvia, Lithuania, the Netherlands, Hungary, Austria, Poland, Portugal, Sweden). Of these countries, at least seven will either refuse the warrant or release the defendant if the information is not received in time or if the warrant is not complete (Germany, Spain, Italy, Lithuania, Portugal, Slovakia, Sweden). In contrast, some states such as Cyprus will send back an incomplete form and require it to be re-submitted. **15.129**

The means of authentication varies between member States from the requirement for the original, to a simple fax. Some member States will accept a copy of the EAW initially, though most of them require the original at a later date. **15.130**

Time limits for the receipt of documentation

The time limits after arrest for the receipt of the EAW are as follows: **15.131**

Austria	40 days.
Belgium	10 days.
Bulgaria	7 days from the beginning of detention.
Cyprus	3 days provided that the EAW has been issued before the arrest of the person sought.
Czech Republic	40 days.
Denmark	10 days. Danish executing authorities do not need to receive the EAW insofar as the information resulting from the Schengen Information System (SIS) alert is sufficient.
Estonia	3 working days.
Finland	As soon as possible. SIS alert sufficient.
Germany	40 days.
Greece	15 days, can be extended to 30 days.
Hungary	40 days.
France	6 working days.
Ireland	The person sought is arrested after the EAW has been received and endorsed by the High Court. (A time limit of 7 days will apply when the SIS will be applicable to Ireland.)
Italy	10 days. Italian executing authorities do not need to receive the EAW insofar as the information resulting from the SIS alert is sufficient.
Latvia	72 hours.
Lithuania	48 hours after the arrest of the person.
Luxembourg	6 working days.
Malta	The 48-hour limit applies only in cases where a provisional arrest has been effected in the absence of an EAW. It is only in exceptional circumstances that provisional arrests will be made.
Netherlands	In relation to member States who participate in the SIS: at latest on 23rd day from the arrest if based on a SIS alert. In relation to member States who do not participate in the SIS, the EAW has to be received as soon as possible.

Poland	48 hours.
Portugal	Left to discretion of courts, usually 10 days.
Romania	48 hours after arrest.
Slovenia	20 days.
Slovakia	18 days from the arrest of a person for the receipt of the original EAW and the original document containing the translation of the EAW into the Slovak language. If the mentioned documents are not received within 18 days, a prosecutor can make a motion to the judge for the release of a person from custody, where applicable; if the documents are not received within 40 days, the release of the person is mandatory.
Spain	The Spanish legislation does not provide for a deadline for the receipt of the original of the EAW. However, the Executing Judicial Authorities ask to receive the EAW as soon as possible and, in any case, within 10 days after the arrest of the person.
Sweden	As soon as possible (a few days, decided by the prosecutor).

Interpol alerts

15.132 The issue of an EAW does not operate to effect an automatic Interpol alert equivalent to a request for provisional arrest, unlike a Schengen Information System (SIS) alert.[80] Pending the application of the second Schengen Information System (SIS II), each member State may remedy this with a national provision.

15.133 The EAW statistical data indicate that in 2009 82.5% of the 12,111 EAWs issued by Schengen-participating states were transmitted via the SIS.

Time limits from receipt of documentation to final decision

15.134 Precise time limits are laid down in Articles 17 and 23 of the EAW Framework Decision. In a consent case a final decision should be taken within ten days. In other cases a final decision should be made within 60 days although in specific cases this limit may be extended by a further 30 days. On the whole most surrenders take place within the time limits laid down.

15.135 Other than Belgium and Ireland (and the UK), the remaining member States have transposed a deadline of ten days or less for taking a decision on surrender by consent. Belgian legislation does not provide for a formal deadline though it has been stated that the decision should in practice be taken within five days. At the same time consent is revocable until effective surrender and so a change in plea will result in a full hearing occurring. The Republic of Ireland does not provide a deadline for the taking of the decision following consent.

15.136 In France, the decision to surrender must be made within seven days of consent. In Lithuania, the judge must make his decision on surrender within three days of the defendant giving his consent.

15.137 Where there is no consented surrender, 17 member States, Austria, Bulgaria, Cyprus, Denmark, Estonia, Finland, Germany, Greece, Hungary, Ireland, Latvia, Lithuania, Luxembourg, Poland, Slovenia, Spain, and Sweden have transposed the Framework Decision of a 60-day deadline with a maximum extension of 30 days.

15.138 Belgian legislation provides that the initial decision on surrender must be taken within 15 days of arrest. However, there are two possibilities of appeal, which will, if taken, mean that the deadline of 60 days cannot be met (with appeals, the deadline is 64 days).

[80] EAW Framework Decision, Article 9(3).

French legislation provides that a final decision must be taken within 30 days of arrest. However, where an appeal in cassation is lodged, which France considers as an exceptional case, the deadline may total more than 90 days. 15.139

In the case of Italy, if there is no appeal the deadline is compliant with the EAW Framework Decision. Where the Court of Cassation sends the case back to the Court of Appeal, the length of the whole procedure may exceed 90 days. 15.140

Dutch legislation has transposed the provision and set the required deadlines. However, if the deadlines cannot be met, the court may extend the term indefinitely. 15.141

For the Czech Republic, Malta, Portugal, and Slovakia no limit is provided for the duration of the highest appeal (respectively before the Czech Republic Constitutional Court, the Malta Court of Criminal Appeal, the Portugal Constitutional Court, or the Slovakia Supreme Court). Thus, both the 60- and 90-day deadlines could in principle be exceeded. The Czech Republic has also specified that when two competing EAWs are served, the time limits provided in Article 17 shall only start to run from the date on which the last one was served. 15.142

Time limits from final decision to surrender

Article 23 provides for surrender no later than ten days after the final decision on the execution of the EAW. If the surrender is unavoidably delayed then a new surrender date must be set within ten days of any new date agreed. This provision has been implemented in all member States other than those mentioned in the following paragraphs. 15.143

Belgium, Denmark, Estonia, and Spain have introduced an additional deadline whereby surrender in exceptional circumstances can be postponed by a further ten days, that is surrender must occur at the most within 20 days of the final decision. This contrasts with the Framework Decision which requires that surrender occurs within ten days of the newly agreed surrender date whilst not specifying the time limit for that new date. 15.144

Postponement of surrender for serious humanitarian reasons is permitted under Article 23(4), however this provision has not been fully transposed in the Czech Republic, Denmark, Lithuania, and Poland. In particular, in the Czech Republic and Denmark there is no provision requiring the issuing judicial authority to be informed or for arranging a new date for surrender when the 'serious humanitarian reasons' foreseen in Article 23(4) have ceased to exist. 15.145

Postponed or conditional surrender

Postponed or conditional surrender is permitted under Article 24 if the person is being prosecuted in the executing member State or has already been sentenced there. Belgium, Bulgaria, the Czech Republic, Greece, Spain, France, Ireland, Italy, Cyprus, Lithuania, Luxembourg, Hungary, Austria, Portugal, Romania, Slovenia, Finland, and Sweden have transposed this provision. 15.146

Moreover, in Spain, the Spanish executing judicial authority is required to temporarily surrender the person on the request of the issuing judicial authority whilst in Malta the competent national authorities have no discretion but to postpone surrender where the requested person is to be prosecuted or sentenced in these countries. 15.147

Denmark has no binding transposition for Article 24 and has stated that the Ministry of Justice will consider what is the best option on a case-by-case basis. The Czech Republic, Latvia, and Slovakia have transposed only Article 24(1) and do not provide for temporary surrender pursuant to Article 24(2). Contrary to Article 24(1), postponement is possible before the final decision on surrender and not 'after deciding to execute the EAW' in Malta. 15.148

Prosecution for other offences (specialty)

15.149 Article 27 of the Framework decision provides that:

> 1. Each Member State may notify the General Secretariat of the Council that, in its relations with other Member States that have given the same notification, consent is presumed to have been given for the prosecution, sentencing or detention with a view to the carrying out of a custodial sentence or detention order for an offence committed prior to his or her surrender, other than that for which he or she was surrendered, unless in a particular case the executing judicial authority states otherwise in its decision on surrender.
>
> 2. Except in the cases referred to in paragraphs 1 and 3, a person surrendered may not be prosecuted, sentenced or otherwise deprived of his or her liberty for an offence committed prior to his or her surrender other than that for which he or she was surrendered.
>
> 3. Paragraph 2 does not apply in the following cases:
>
> (a) when the person having had an opportunity to leave the territory of the Member State to which he or she has been surrendered has not done so within 45 days of his or her final discharge, or has returned to that territory after leaving it;
>
> (b) the offence is not punishable by a custodial sentence or detention order;
>
> (c) the criminal proceedings do not give rise to the application of a measure restricting personal liberty;
>
> (d) when the person could be liable to a penalty or a measure not involving the deprivation of liberty, in particular a financial penalty or a measure in lieu thereof, even if the penalty or measure may give rise to a restriction of his or her personal liberty;
>
> (e) when the person consented to be surrendered, where appropriate at the same time as he or she renounced the speciality rule, in accordance with Article 13;
>
> (f) when the person, after his/her surrender, has expressly renounced entitlement to the speciality rule with regard to specific offences preceding his/her surrender. Renunciation shall be given before the competent judicial authorities of the issuing Member State and shall be recorded in accordance with that State's domestic law. The renunciation shall be drawn up in such a way as to make clear that the person has given it voluntarily and in full awareness of the consequences. To that end, the person shall have the right to legal counsel;
>
> (g) where the executing judicial authority which surrendered the person gives its consent in accordance with paragraph 4.
>
> 4. A request for consent shall be submitted to the executing judicial authority, accompanied by the information mentioned in Article 8(1) and a translation as referred to in Article 8(2). Consent shall be given when the offence for which it is requested is itself subject to surrender in accordance with the provisions of this Framework Decision. Consent shall be refused on the grounds referred to in Article 3 and otherwise may be refused only on the grounds referred to in Article 4. The decision shall be taken no later than 30 days after receipt of the request. For the situations mentioned in Article 5 the issuing Member State must give the guarantees provided for therein.

15.150 Only Estonia and Austria have notified the General Secretariat that, in their mutual relations, renunciation to the speciality rule under the conditions of Article 27(1) is presumed to have been given. The remaining member States have transposed the speciality rule pursuant to Article 27(2).

15.151 The transposition of the series of exceptions to the specialty rule laid down in Article 27(3)(a)–(g) varies among member States. All member States have transposed exception (a). Latvia has not transposed exception (b) whilst Poland has only partially transposed it. Five states have either not transposed exception (c) (Denmark, France, Latvia, Lithuania) or not fully transposed it (Poland). Denmark, Latvia, and Lithuania have not transposed exception (d). Denmark and Latvia have not transposed exception (e). Estonia has only partially transposed exception (f) and in the transposition of this exception by Italy reference is made to renunciation according to similar forms to those of the Italian law. The Republic of Ireland has not explicitly transposed exception (g) and has made a declaration that consent can only be provided by its central authority.

Lastly, in six member States the provisions on requests for consent under Article 27(4) have not (Latvia and Ireland) or not fully (Denmark, Estonia, the UK, and Malta) been transposed; the main difficulty with these last four countries being in respect of the 30-day deadline for making a decision on consent. **15.152**

In C-388/08 *Leymann and Pustovarov* [2008] ECR I-8983 the ECJ held that the concept of an 'offence other than' that for which the person was surrendered must be assessed with regard to the different stages of the proceedings and in the light of any procedural document capable of altering the legal classification of the offence. In order to assess, in the light of the consent requirement contained in Article 27(3)(g) of the Framework Decision, whether it is possible to infer from a procedural document an 'offence other' than that referred to in the European arrest warrant, the description of the offence in the European arrest warrant must be compared with that in the later procedural document. To require the consent of the executing member State for every modification of the description of the offence would go beyond what is implied by the specialty rule and interfere with the objective of speeding up and simplifying judicial co-operation of the kind referred to in the Framework Decision between the member States. In order to establish whether the offence under consideration is an 'offence other' than that for which the person was surrendered within the meaning of Article 27(2) of Framework Decision 2002/584, requiring the implementation of the consent procedure referred to in Article 27(3)(g) and 27(4) of that Framework Decision, it must be ascertained whether the constituent elements of the offence, according to the legal description given by the issuing state, are those in respect of which the person was surrendered and whether there is a sufficient correspondence between the information given in the arrest warrant and that contained in the later procedural document. Modifications concerning the time or place of the offence are allowed, in so far as they derive from evidence gathered in the course of the proceedings conducted in the issuing state concerning the conduct described in the arrest warrant, do not alter the nature of the offence, and do not lead to grounds for non-execution under Articles 3 and 4 of the Framework Decision. **15.153**

In the case of *Leymann and Pustovarov* [2008] ECR I-8983 it was held that a modification of the description of the offence, concerning only the kind of narcotics in question and not changing the legal classification of the offence, was not such, of itself, as to define an 'offence other' than that for which the person was surrendered within the meaning of Article 27(2) since it remained an offence still punishable according to the same scale of penalties and comes under the rubric 'illegal trafficking in narcotic drugs'. **15.154**

The ECJ observed that the exception in Article 27(3)(c), according to which the specialty rule provided for in Article 27(2) does not apply where the criminal proceedings do not give rise to the application of a measure restricting personal liberty, must be interpreted as meaning that, where there is an 'offence other' than that for which the person was surrendered, consent must be requested, in accordance with Article 27(4) and obtained if a penalty or a measure involving the deprivation of liberty is to be executed. The person surrendered can be prosecuted and sentenced for such an offence before that consent has been obtained, provided that no measure restricting liberty is applied during the prosecution or when judgment is given for that offence. The exception in Article 27(3)(c) does not, however, preclude a measure restricting liberty from being imposed on the person surrendered before consent has been obtained, where that restriction is lawful on the basis of other charges which appear in the European arrest warrant. **15.155**

15.156 In the case of multiple sequential surrenders within the EU on the basis of EAWs, the ECJ in *West* C-192/12 confirmed that the concept of the 'executing' member State or judicial authority in Article 27(4) refers to the state or authority which carried out the last surrender of the person to the member State which, as executing member State, is called upon to surrender that person to another state pursuant to an EAW.

Handing over of property

15.157 Article 29(1) of the EAW Framework Decision requires executing judicial authorities, in accordance with their national laws, either at the request of the judicial authority issuing the EAW or on their own initiative, to seize and hand over property which may be required as evidence, or has been acquired by the requested person as a result of the offence even if the EAW cannot be carried out.

15.158 If the property referred is liable to seizure or confiscation in the territory of the executing member State, it may be temporarily handed over and may be liable to be returned as soon as the criminal proceedings have been terminated.

15.159 Article 29 has been only partly transposed in four member States (Finland, Latvia, Slovenia, and Sweden), is limited to property found in the possession of the requested person upon arrest in the Netherlands, and reliant on mutual legal assistance provisions in Luxembourg and Slovakia.

Transit

15.160 All member States allow the transit of non-nationals in conformity with Article 25(1). Portugal has, however, excluded the possibility of transit of non-nationals where surrender is for the purposes of prosecution, whereas the Framework Decision foresees this possibility only in relation to nationals.

15.161 Sixteen member States (Belgium, the Czech Republic, Germany, Greece, France, Italy, Cyprus, Latvia, Luxembourg, Hungary, the Netherlands, Austria, Poland, Portugal, Slovenia, and Finland) permit the refusal of transit of their own nationals. The exception in Article 25(1) applies to residents of the above countries with the exclusion of Germany, France, Latvia, Lithuania, the Netherlands, and Poland.

15.162 Some member States (Bulgaria, Germany, Denmark, Germany, Estonia, Spain, France, Ireland, Cyprus, Luxembourg, Austria, Portugal, Romania, Slovenia, and Sweden) will also allow transit where the warrant is based on an act that is not an offence under the law of the transit state. This is in contrast to Latvia, Hungary, and the Netherlands who check the double criminality of the offence where it is not found in the Article 2(2) list.

16

EXTRADITION TO INTERNATIONAL CRIMINAL TRIBUNALS

A. Introduction

The conflicts in the Former Yugoslavia and the genocide in Rwanda in the 1990s led the United Nations to set up International Criminal Tribunals to try those accused of committing offences during the conflicts. Since the tribunals were established they have tried and convicted a large number of defendants of extremely serious crimes including murder, rape, and torture. **16.01**

This chapter considers the UK domestic law which allows for the return to these tribunals of those found within the UK who are wanted for trial by the tribunals or who have been convicted of an offence by them. This chapter also considers the provisions of the International Criminal Court Act 2001 which permit return to the International Criminal Court. **16.02**

International Criminal Tribunals[1]

The war in the Former Yugoslavia was an armed conflict that took place between March 1992 and November 1995. The war involved several ethnically defined factions within Yugoslavia including Bosnians, Serbs, and Croats. During the war there were serious and widespread violations of international humanitarian law. **16.03**

United Nations Security Council Resolution 827 of 1993 established the Tribunal for the Prosecution of Persons Responsible for Serious Violations of International Humanitarian Law Committed in the Territory of the Former Yugoslavia since 1991.[2] **16.04**

1 See also Archbold, *International Criminal Courts: Practice Procedure and Evidence* (2009).

2 The 'ICTY'. The Tribunal sits in The Hague, the Netherlands. The Tribunal's website is at http://www.un.org/icty. On the Tribunal and its work, see *Individual Criminal Responsibility Before the International Criminal Court – A Comparison with the Ad Hoc Tribunals*, International Criminal Law Review Volume 12, (2012) 1–70; *The Influence of the European Court of Human Rights' Case Law on International Criminal Law*, J Int Criminal Justice (2011) 9 (3): 571; *Critical Notes on a 'Success Story'*, J Int Criminal Justice (2011) 9 (3):

16.05 The ICTY was the first tribunal established under Chapter VII of the UN Charter as a measure to maintain international peace and security. It was the first international criminal court to enforce the existing body of international humanitarian law and, in particular, the first to judicially determine its customary law aspects. Decisions of the tribunal have made a valuable contribution to international criminal jurisprudence and are regularly cited by the House of Lords.[3]

16.06 The ICTY has indicted more than 150 defendants. Slobodan Milošević was the first sitting head of state indicted for war crimes. Other high-level indictees include Milan Babić, Croatian Serb Prime Minister of Republika Srpska Krajina; Ramush Haradinaj, Albanian Prime Minister of Kosovo; Radovan Karadžić, Montenegrin former President of Republika Srpska; and Ratko Mladić, the Bosnian Serb army commander.

16.07 The final indictments were issued in December 2004, the last of which were confirmed and unsealed in the spring of 2005. The ICTY aims to complete all trials by the end of 2012 and all appeals by 2015, with the exception of Radovan Karadžić whose trial is expected to end in 2014, and the recently arrested Ratko Mladić and Goran Hadžić. In due course the ICTY will transfer its responsibilities to the International Residual Mechanism for Criminal Tribunals,which is planned to begin functioning for the ICTY branch on 1 July 2013.[4]

16.08 The genocide in Rwanda also led to the establishment of an International Criminal Tribunal. Between April and July 1994 more than 800,000 people were murdered in Rwanda by militia groups organized along tribal lines. The perpetrators were from the Hutu tribe and the victims mainly from the Tutsi tribe. In 1994 the Security Council passed a Resolution[5] which established the International Criminal Tribunal for the prosecution of those responsible.[6]

16.09 The ICTR has finished a significant number of trials and convicted a number of defendants. According to the ICTR's Completion Strategy, in accordance with the UN, all first-instance cases were to have completed trial by the end of 2008. The United Nations Security Council has since called upon the Tribunal to finish its work by 31 December 2014 to prepare for its closure and transfer of its responsibilities to the International Residual Mechanism for Criminal Tribunals which will begin functioning for the ICTR branch on 1 July 2012.[7]

547; *The International Criminal Tribunal for the Former Yugoslavia: Paving the Way for Modern International Humanitarian Law Enforcement* (2011) Northern Ireland Legal Quarterly 62(1): 119–136; *On the Admissibility of Statements Made by the Defendant Prior to Trial* (2010) ICJ 8 1 (221); *Protecting Prisoners of War* (2010) ICJ 8 1 (199); *National Prosecution of International Crimes: Cases and Legislation* (2010) ICJ 8 1 (237); *Customary International Law in the 21st Century: Old Challenges and New Debates*, EJIL (2010) 21 (173); *The Requirement of 'Belonging' under International Humanitarian Law*, EJIL (2010) 21 (105); *The Interplay of Human Rights and Humanitarian Law: The Approach of the ICTY*, Conflict and Security Law 2009 14 (511); *The Contribution of the ICTY to the Grave Breaches Regime* (2009) ICJ 7 4 (743); *The Impact of the ICTY Trials on Public Opinion in the Former Yugoslavia* (2009) ICJ 7 1 (89); *Ensuring fair and expeditious trials at the International Criminal Tribunal for the Former Yugoslavia* (2000) 11 EJIL 569; *International judicial intervention: the International Criminal Tribunal for the Former Yugoslavia* (2000) 15 Int Rel 17; *The development of the law of armed conflict through the jurisprudence of the International Criminal Tribunal for the Former Yugoslavia* (1998) 3 JACL 198; *The International Criminal Tribunal for the Former Yugoslavia and the reluctant witness* (1998) 47 ICLQ 50; *Enforcement of sanctions imposed by the International Criminal Tribunals for Rwanda and the Former Yugoslavia* (1997) 5 Eur J Crime Cr L Cr J144.

[3] See for example *A v Secretary of State for the Home Department (No 2)* [2005] UKHL 71, para 33.

[4] The International Residual Mechanism for Criminal Tribunals is a mechanism established by UN Security Council Resolution 1966 (2010) to complete the work begun by the ICTY and the International Criminal Tribunal for Rwanda. It will be subdivided into two branches corresponding to the current two Tribunals: see <http://www.un.org/News/Press/docs/2010/sc10141.doc.htm>.

[5] No 955 of 1994.

[6] The ICTR: the Tribunal's main seat is in Arusha, Tanzania. The Tribunal's website is at http://www.ictr.org.

[7] <http://www.un.org/News/Press/docs/2010/sc10141.doc.htm>.

The UK has enacted special legislation under the provisions of the United Nations Act 1946 to give effect to these Resolutions and, in particular, to allow the extradition to the jurisdiction of the tribunals those accused or convicted of crimes over which the tribunals have jurisdiction. In these cases extradition is to the tribunal and *not* to the state in which the tribunal happens to be situated. Responsibility for the preparation of the extradition request rests with the prosecuting staff of the tribunal and the request is sent to the Secretary of State for processing under the domestic legislation. **16.10**

The International Criminal Court[8]

In 1948 the United Nations first recognized the need to establish a permanent international criminal court to try serious crimes such as war crimes and genocide. A draft statute for such a court was prepared in 1951 and a revised draft statute was completed in 1953. The General Assembly, however, decided to postpone consideration of the draft statute pending the adoption of a definition of aggression.[9] **16.11**

Between 1953 and 1989 the question of the establishment of an international criminal court was considered periodically. Further impetus was given in the 1990s by the conflict in Yugoslavia and the genocide in Rwanda which led to the establishment of the two ad hoc tribunals referred to above. Shortly afterwards, the International Law Commission completed its work on the draft statute for an international criminal court and in 1994 submitted the draft statute to the General Assembly. The statute was finalized at a conference in Rome in 1998 and the Statute of the International Criminal Court (ICC) was opened for signature later that year. In 1998, 120 states adopted the Rome statute, the legal basis for establishing the ICC. The statute entered into force four years later, when it was ratified by 60 countries. Only the US, Israel, China, Iraq, Libya, Qatar, and Yemen voted against the founding of the ICC. However, following the coming into office of President Barack Obama in 2009 the US tempered its opposition to the Court and supported the ICC's investigation and prosecution in Sudan. **16.12**

The first arrest warrants issued by the ICC in The Hague were aimed at Joseph Kony and the commanders of the Lord's Resistance Army for crimes against humanity and war crimes. The 2005 indictments include charges of murder, rape, the sexual enslavement of women and girls, and forcing children to fight. **16.13**

To date, the Court has opened investigations into seven situations in Africa: the Democratic Republic of the Congo; Uganda; the Central African Republic; Darfur, Sudan; the Republic of Kenya; the Libyan Arab Jamahiriya; and the Republic of Côte d'Ivoire. Of these seven, three were referred to the Court by the states parties (Uganda, Democratic Republic of the Congo, and the Central African Republic), two were referred by the UN Security Council (Darfur and Libya) and two were begun *proprio motu* by the Prosecutor (Kenya and Côte d'Ivoire). **16.14**

The ICC has 28 people, proceedings against 22 of whom are ongoing at the time of writing.[10] The ICC has issued arrest warrants for 19 individuals and summonses to nine others. Five individuals are in custody; one of them has been found guilty (with an appeal possible) while four of them are being tried. Nine individuals remain at large as fugitives. Additionally, two individuals have been arrested by national authorities, but have not yet been transferred to the Court. Proceedings against six individuals have finished following the death of two and the dismissal of charges against the other four. **16.15**

---

[8] The ICC's website is at <http://www.icc-cpi.int/Menus/ICC/>. See generally, Schabas, *An Introduction to the International Criminal Court* (4th edn, Cambridge, 2011).

[9] cf *R v Jones* [2006] UKHL 16.

[10] June 2012.

16.16 As of June 2012, the Court's first trial, the trial in the situation of the Democratic Republic of the Congo, has ended with the accused found guilty on 14 March 2012. Sentencing and reparations will be dealt with at a later stage. The trial regarding the Congo was concluded in May 2012; the judgment is pending. The trial regarding the Central African Republic is ongoing. A fourth trial chamber, for the trial in the situation of Darfur, Sudan, has been established. There are two trials upcoming in the Kenya situation, namely the *Ruto-Sang* and the *Muthaura-Kenyatta* trials for which a single Trial Chamber is responsible. The confirmation of charges hearing in the case in the Côte d'Ivoire situation is scheduled to start on 13 August 2012.

16.15 The Court's most recent arrest warrant, issued in November 2011, targeted former Ivory Coast President Laurent Gbagbo. Gbagbo is alleged to have organized, along with members of his inner circle, systematic attacks against civilians during the violence that followed the November 2010 election, a poll that precipitated the end of his decade-long presidential tenure.

16.18 The only serving head of state sought by the court is Sudan's president, Omar al-Bashir, who is wanted for alleged crimes against humanity (murder, torture, and rape), war crimes (attacks against civilians), and genocide. The case against Muammar Gaddafi, the Libyan leader, who was accused of crimes against humanity during the Libyan uprising, was dropped after his death.

16.19 The first defendant was convicted by the Court in March 2012. Thomas Lubanga, a Congolese warlord, was convicted of recruiting child soldiers.

16.20 In September 2001 the International Criminal Court Act 2001 came into force in the UK to give effect to the Statute of the ICC in domestic law. The 2001 Act's long title is:

> An Act to give effect to the Statute of the International Criminal Court; to provide for offences under the law of England and Wales and Northern Ireland corresponding to offences within the jurisdiction of that Court; and for connected purposes.

16.21 Part 2 of the International Criminal Court Act 2001 Act (ss 2–26) makes provision for the arrest and delivery up of persons to the ICC, where such persons are accused of a crime falling under the jurisdiction of the ICC or have been convicted of such a crime.

The Special Court for Sierra Leone

16.22 Although it is not an International Criminal Tribunal, the Special Court for Sierra Leone also deserves mention. On 12 June 2000, Sierra Leonean President Alhaji Ahmad Tejan Kabbah wrote to the Secretary-General of the United Nations asking the international community to try those responsible for crimes committed during the country's violent conflict. President Kabbah said that he believed the crimes were so grave as to be 'of concern to all persons in the world'.

16.23 Following this request the UN Security Council adopted Resolution 1315 of 2000 on 14 August 2000 requesting that the UN Secretary General start negotiations to create the Special Court. On 16 January 2002 an agreement establishing the Court was signed between the Government of Sierra Leone and the United Nations.[11] The first staff to work at the Special Court arrived in Freetown in July 2002.

16.24 The Special Court is part of the domestic court structure of Sierra Leone. Those wanted for trial by the Special Court are liable to be extradited from the UK to Sierra Leone in the ordinary way pursuant to a request from the Government of Sierra Leone. Sierra Leone has been designated as a Category 2 state for the purposes of the EA 2003.[12]

---

[11] The Court's website is at <http://www.sc-sl.org>.

[12] Extradition Act 2003 (Designation of Part 2 Territories) Order 2003 (SI 2003/3334).

In April 2012 the former President of Liberia, Charles Taylor, was convicted of crimes against humanity and war crimes, and subsequently sentenced to 50 years' imprisonment. **16.25**

The Special Tribunal for Lebanon[13]

The Special Tribunal for Lebanon also deserves mention as a tribunal of international character created by UN action. Inaugurated on 1 March 2009, the Tribunal's primary mandate is to hold trials for the people accused of carrying out the attack of 14 February 2005, which killed 23 people, including the former prime minister of Lebanon, Rafiq Hariri, and injured many others. The Tribunal also has jurisdiction over other attacks in Lebanon between 1 October 2004 and 12 December 2005 if it is proven that they are connected to the events of 14 February and are of similar nature and gravity. The mandate also allows the Tribunal to have jurisdiction over crimes carried out on any later date, decided by the parties and with the consent of the UN Security Council, if they are connected to the 14 February 2005 attack. **16.26**

The Tribunal was established following a request by the government of Lebanon to the United Nations, which passed creating the Tribunal as an independent, judicial organization composed of Lebanese and international judges. It is neither a UN court nor part of the Lebanese judicial system. It does, however, apply Lebanese criminal law. The Tribunal is also the first of its kind to deal with terrorism as a discrete crime. **16.27**

B. Extradition to the ICTY

Extradition to the ICTY is governed by the United Nations (International Tribunal) (Former Yugoslavia) Order 1996.[14] The Order is a self-contained code and operates independently of the EA 2003, although the procedure for seeking extradition has some similarity with the scheme established by the EA 2003. **16.28**

The 1996 Order only extends to the UK, however similar Orders have been made to allow return to the ICTY from the Channel Islands,[15] the Isle of Man,[16] and British overseas territories.[17] **16.29**

Endorsement of ICTY arrest warrants

Return to the ICTY operates under a backing of warrants system. Article 4(1) of the 1996 Order provides that where the Secretary of State receives from the ICTY a warrant of arrest issued by it, he must transmit the warrant to an appropriate judicial officer who must, subject to Article 4(2), endorse the warrant for execution in any part of the UK. **16.30**

Article 4(2) provides that where the warrant is for the arrest of a person convicted by the ICTY the warrant must not be endorsed unless the purpose of the warrant is to bring the defendant before the ICTY or be taken to a place where he is to undergo imprisonment under a sentence of the ICTY. **16.31**

---

[13] The Tribunal's website is at <http://www.stl-tsl.org>. The Tribunal's headquarters is on the outskirts of The Hague, the Netherlands, and it also has an office in Beirut, Lebanon.

[14] SI 1996/716 (referred to in this chapter as the 1996 Order), as amended.

[15] United Nations (International Tribunals) (Former Yugoslavia and Rwanda) (Jersey) Order 1997 (SI 1997/283); United Nations (International Tribunals) (Former Yugoslavia and Rwanda) (Guernsey) Order 1997 (SI 1997/281).

[16] United Nations (International Tribunals) (Former Yugoslavia and Rwanda) (Isle of Man) Order 1997 (SI 1997/282).

[17] United Nations (International Tribunals) (Former Yugoslavia and Rwanda) (British Overseas Territories) Order 1997 (SI 1997/1753).

16.32 Article 2 defines an appropriate judicial officer in England and Wales to be the Senior District Judge (Chief Magistrate) or a District Judge (Magistrates' Courts) designated by the Senior District Judge (Chief Magistrate) for the purposes of the 1996 Order.

Provisional arrest

16.33 Article 5(1) governs provisional arrest for the purposes of extradition to the ICTY. Where the Secretary of State receives a request from the ICTY for the arrest of a person who is suspected or accused of having committed an International Tribunal crime[18] or who has been convicted by the ICTY, and the request is not accompanied by a warrant but is made on the grounds of urgency, the Secretary of State must transmit the request to a constable and direct the constable to apply for a warrant for the arrest of that person.

16.34 By Article 5(1) an appropriate judicial officer may issue a warrant, referred to as a provisional warrant, for the arrest of a person on an application by a constable stating on oath that he has reason to believe that a request has been made on grounds of urgency by the ICTY for the arrest of a person who is suspected or accused of having committed an International Tribunal crime or who has been convicted by the ICTY of such an offence; that the person concerned is in or on his way to the UK, and that the purpose of the arrest is to enable the person concerned to be brought before the ICTY or to be taken to a place where he is to undergo imprisonment under a sentence of the ICTY.[19]

16.35 Where the judicial authority issues a warrant he is required by Article 5(2) to notify the Secretary of State that he has done so.

16.36 Article 5(4) requires a person arrested under a provisional warrant to be brought before a competent court[20] as soon as is practicable, and if an endorsed warrant[21] in respect of that person is produced to the court, the court proceeds as if he had been arrested under that warrant, and Article 6 thereafter applies. However, if no such warrant is produced, the court may, pending the production of the warrant, remand him for not more than 18 days at a time, however the total period of remand may not exceed 40 days in all.

16.37 Article 5(5) provides that if at any time an endorsed warrant relating to a person remanded under Article 5(4)(b) is produced to the court which remanded him, the court shall determine the period of remand and the person shall thereafter be treated as if arrested at that time under the endorsed warrant.

16.38 However, if an endorsed warrant relating to a defendant remanded under Article 5(4)(b) is not produced within the period of the remand (including any extension of that period) to the court which remanded him, then he must be discharged by the court.[22]

Bail; powers of competent court

16.39 Article 12 provides that where a court has power to remand a defendant in proceedings under the 1996 Order, the proceedings shall for the purposes of s 4 of the Bail Act 1976 (general right to bail) be treated as proceedings against a defendant in extradition proceedings as defined in s 2(2) of that Act.

---

[18] Defined by Art 2 to be one of the crimes specified in Arts 2, 3, 4, and 5 of the ICTY's Statute. The Statute is annexed to the 1996 Order as a Schedule.

[19] The warrant may be executed anywhere in the UK (Art 23(2)) and is to be treated for the purposes of any enactment relating to arrest warrants as if it were a warrant for a domestic offence: Art 23(1).

[20] Defined by Art 2 to be a court consisting of an appropriate judicial officer.

[21] In Arts 5 and 6 endorsed warrant means a warrant of arrest issued by the ICTY endorsed in accordance with Art 4: Art 5(6).

[22] Art 5(6).

Article 24 provides that for the purposes of proceedings under Art 6, 9 or 10, a competent court in England and Wales shall have like powers, including power to adjourn the case and meanwhile to remand the person arrested, as if the proceedings were the summary trial of an information against that person. It also provides that: s 16(1)(c) of the Prosecution of Offences Act 1985 (defence costs on dismissal) applies to the proceedings, reading the reference to the dismissal of the information as a reference to the discharge of the person arrested, and Part V of the Legal Aid Act 1988 (criminal legal aid) applies to the proceedings if the proceedings were proceedings for dealing with an offender as a defendant in extradition proceedings. **16.40**

Proceedings before a competent court under Article 6

Once the arrest stage has been completed, either by the endorsement of an ICTY warrant or arrest under a domestic provisional warrant followed by receipt of an ICTY warrant, the case moves to the substantive hearing before the competent court. This hearing is governed by Article 6 of the 1996 Order, and the court's powers are regulated by Article 24 of the Order. **16.41**

Appropriate orders

As soon as is practicable after a person is arrested under an endorsed warrant, he must be brought before a competent court.[23] Once before the court, subject to the provisions of Article 6, the court must make the appropriate order and remand him until it is executed.[24] **16.42**

Where the purpose of the arrest is to enable the defendant to be brought before the ICTY, the appropriate order is that the defendant be delivered up into the custody of the ICTY in accordance with arrangements made by the Secretary of State with the Registrar.[25] Where the purpose of the arrest is to enable the defendant to be taken to a place where he is to undergo imprisonment under a sentence of the ICTY, the appropriate order is that he be delivered up into the custody of the state where that place is situated in accordance with arrangements made by the Secretary of State with that state.[26] **16.43**

Grounds for not making the appropriate order

Article 6 effectively creates a presumption in favour of making an appropriate order, in that the grounds for not doing so are extremely limited. Proceedings under Article 6 do not require an evidential inquiry. Article 6(7) provides that nothing in the 1996 Order is to be construed as requiring a competent court to be satisfied that there is evidence sufficient to warrant the trial of an accused person by the ICTY. **16.44**

If it is shown to the satisfaction of the competent court that other criminal proceedings (not being proceedings under the Extradition Act 1989 or the Backing of Warrants (Republic of Ireland) Act 1965)[27] have been instituted in respect of the arrested person in a national court and that those proceedings: **16.45**

(a) have not been finally determined so far as they relate to conduct which would not constitute an International Tribunal crime, or
(b) have not been discontinued (whether in pursuance of the 1996 Order or otherwise) so far as they relate to conduct which would constitute an International Tribunal crime,

---

[23] Art 6(1).
[24] Art 6(1).
[25] Art 6(2).
[26] Art 6(3).
[27] The 1996 Order has apparently not been amended following the coming into force of the EA 2003 and the repeal of the Backing of Warrants (Republic of Ireland) Act 1965.

the proceedings under Article 6 must be adjourned and the competent court may remand the arrested person until the other criminal proceedings have been finally determined or have been discontinued, as the case may be.[28]

16.46 Article 6(5) provides an order shall not be made under Article 6(1) if it is shown to the satisfaction of the competent court:

(a) that the document purporting to be a warrant issued by the ICTY is not such a warrant or that it has not been endorsed in accordance with Article 4; or
(b) that the person brought before the court is not the person named or described in the warrant; or
(c) where the person has not been convicted by the ICTY of the offence specified in the warrant or any accompanying document, that the offence is not an International Tribunal crime, or
(d) notwithstanding that the offence is an International Tribunal crime, that the person would if he were charged with it in the UK be entitled to be discharged under any rule of law relating to previous acquittal or conviction.[29]

16.47 If the competent court refuses to make an order under Article 6(1), it must make an order remanding the person arrested until the Secretary of State has been notified of its decision and the grounds for not making an order. Having been notified, if the Secretary of State immediately informs the court that he intends to question the decision on the ground that it is wrong in law, the order remanding the person arrested continues to have effect (except as otherwise provided by the 1996 Order), so long as the case is pending.[30] If the court is not so informed, the person arrested must be discharged.[31]

16.48 Article 6(8) governs the situation where the person before the court is also subject to some form of final court order.[32] In effect, it allows the court to give precedence to the ICTY proceedings. It provides that where a competent court makes an order under Article 6(1) in respect of a defendant whose extradition has been ordered[33] or in respect of whom an order, other than a sentence of imprisonment or detention, has been made in criminal proceedings which have been finally determined, the court may make such other order as is necessary to give effect to the endorsed warrant, and an order may suspend or revoke a warrant, sentence (not being a sentence of imprisonment or detention), or other order made by that or any other court or any magistrate or other judicial officer in respect of the person.[34]

---

[28] Art 6(4).

[29] cf EA 2003, ss 12 and 80.

[30] Art 6(6)(a). The procedure for appealing to the High Court is set out in Art 7. The Secretary of State can, within 21 days of the decision (or longer, if the court allows) it, request the competent court to state a case for the opinion of the High Court. The application must state the question of law involved. If the High Court dismisses the appeal then the Secretary of State can appeal to the House of Lords (with permission) and s 1 of the Administration of Justice Act 1960 applies to the appeal.

[31] Art 6(6)(b).

[32] Art 14 governs pending criminal proceedings. Where the conditions in Art 14 are satisfied, domestic courts before whom there are relevant proceedings (as defined in Art 14(5)) against a defendant whose return is sought by the ICTY are required to discontinue them in order that the ICTY proceedings can take precedence. Discontinuance does not, however, prevent the re-institution of the proceedings later: Art 14(6).

[33] The 1996 Order does not appear to have been amended to take account of the enactment of the EA 2003.

[34] This Article requires amendment to reflect the enactment of the EA 2003 and the repeal of the EA 1989 and the Backing of Warrants (Republic of Ireland) Act 1965.

Habeas corpus; consent to delivery up

The defendant has the right to apply for *habeas corpus* under Article 11 of the 1996 Order. **16.49**

Article 11(1) provides that where a delivery order is made by a competent court in respect of the defendant, he shall not be delivered up under the order until the expiration of the period of 15 days beginning with the date on which the order is made, unless he gives notice in accordance with para (4) that he consents to his earlier delivery up. If within that period an application is made by him or on his behalf for a writ of *habeas corpus* he shall not be delivered up while proceedings on the application are pending. **16.50**

The competent court must inform the defendant that he will not be delivered up under the order during this period of 15 days unless he gives notice that he consents to earlier delivery, and that he has the right to apply for a writ of *habeas corpus*. **16.51**

Proceedings on an application for a writ of *habeas corpus* are treated as pending until any appeal in those proceedings is disposed of. An appeal shall be treated as disposed of at the expiration of the time within which the appeal may be brought or, where leave to appeal is required, within which the application for leave may be made, if not brought or made within that time. **16.52**

Where a defendant wishes to consent to his delivery up, he must sign a notice in the presence of a justice of the peace. A notice given by a person in custody must be delivered to the governor of the prison, and a notice given by a person on bail shall be delivered to the police officer in charge of the police station specified in his recognizance. **16.53**

The person receiving any such notice must ensure that the notice is attached to the order for the defendant's delivery up. **16.54**

Discharge of persons not delivered up

Where the International Tribunal informs the Secretary of State that a person arrested in pursuance of the 1996 Order is no longer required to be delivered up into its custody or into the custody of a state for imprisonment there, the Secretary of State must notify an appropriate judicial officer; and the appropriate judicial officer must, on receipt of such notification, make an order for the discharge of the person arrested.[35] **16.55**

If a person in respect of whom a delivery order has been made is not delivered up under the order within 40 days after it was made, a superior court exercising jurisdiction in the part of the UK within which it was made, upon application by or on behalf of that person, may, unless reasonable cause is shown for the delay, order him to be discharged. **16.56**

Authentication of ICTY documents

Article 27 governs authentication of ICTY documents. For the purposes of the 1996 Order and any connected proceedings, an International Tribunal document[36] may be taken to be such a document and to have been duly issued or made if either: **16.57**

(a) it purports to have been issued or made in accordance with the ICTY's Statute or Rules[37] or, in the case of a request to the Secretary of State, for the purposes of the 1996 Order, or

---

[35] Art 13(1).

[36] Defined by Art 27(2) to be a warrant, order, summons, or other process of the ICTY or a copy of such a document, or a request to the Secretary of State by the ICTY.

[37] Of which (along with the ICTY's seal) judicial notice must be taken: Art 27(3).

(b) it is verified by a certificate purporting to be signed by the President of the ICTY, the Registrar or the Prosecutor certifying that the document is an International Tribunal document or, as the case may be, a true copy of such a document.[38]

16.58 Where a facsimile transmission is used for the making of a request by the ICTY or the transmission of any supporting documents, or for the transmission of any document in consequence of such a request, the Order applies as if any documents so sent were the originals of the documents so transmitted.[39]

16.59 A document which is authenticated in accordance with Articles 27(1) or 2 is receivable in evidence.[40]

C. Extradition to the ICTR

16.60 Extradition to the ICTR is governed by the United Nations (International Tribunal) (Rwanda) Order 1996.[41] The Order is in similar terms to the United Nations (International Tribunal) (Former Yugoslavia) Order 1996,[42] considered in detail above at para 16.28.[43]

D. Extradition to the ICC

16.61 Part 2 of the International Criminal Court Act 2001 (ICC Act 2001) governs the arrest and surrender of persons accused or convicted of an International Criminal Court crime[44] who are wanted for trial before the ICC or are wanted for enforcement of sentence.

16.62 The procedure contained in Part 2 is very similar to the schemes for return to the ICTY and ICTR which have already been examined. Part 2 establishes a backing of warrants scheme, and the principal stages of the scheme are as follows.

Arrest for the purposes of return

16.63 Arrest for the purposes of return to the ICC can take place either following receipt and endorsement of a warrant of arrest directly from it,[45] or, in urgent cases, following the execution of a domestic provisional warrant.[46] In the case of provisional arrest, a warrant must be received from the ICC within the period specified in s 4(4) following which it must be endorsed.

---

38 Art 27(1).

39 Art 27(1A).

40 Art 27(1B).

41 SI 1996/1296, as amended.

42 SI 1996/716, as amended.

43 Return to the ICTR from British overseas territories, the Isle of Man, and the Channel Islands is governed by the United Nations (International Tribunals) (Former Yugoslavia and Rwanda) (British Overseas Territories) Order 1997 (SI 1997/1753), United Nations (International Tribunals) (Former Yugoslavia and Rwanda) (Isle of Man) Order 1997 (SI 1997/282), the United Nations (International Tribunals) (Former Yugoslavia and Rwanda) (Jersey) Order 1997 (SI 1997/283), and United Nations (International Tribunals) (Former Yugoslavia and Rwanda) (Guernsey) Order 1997 (SI 1997/281) respectively.

44 Defined in ICC Act 2001, s 1, to be a crime (other than the crime of aggression) over which the ICC has jurisdiction in accordance with the ICC Statute.

45 ICC Act 2001, s 2. The authentication provisions are contained in s 25.

46 ICC Act 2001, s 3.

Proceedings before competent court

The substantive proceedings take place before a competent court, ie before a magistrates court consisting of an appropriate judicial officer, that is, the Senior District Judge (Chief Magistrate) or a designated district judge.[47] **16.64**

If the competent court is satisfied that the warrant is a warrant of the ICC and that it has been duly endorsed under ICC Act 2001, s 2(3), or has been duly issued under s 2(4), and that the person brought before the court is the person named or described in the warrant, it must make an order that the defendant be delivered up into the custody of the ICC, or if the ICC so directs in the case of a person convicted by the ICC, into the custody of the state of enforcement. **16.65**

The court is enjoined from inquiring into whether the ICC warrant was properly issued, or whether there is sufficient evidence to warrant the defendant's trial.[48] **16.66**

The defendant can consent to his surrender, under s 7. **16.67**

A court proceeding under s 5 has similar powers, including the power to remand, as a court of summary jurisdiction hearing a trial of an information.[49] **16.68**

Where the court refuses to make an order for delivery up the Secretary of State can appeal (without permission) to the High Court, which conducts an appeal by way of re-hearing.[50] **16.69**

Habeas corpus and delivery up

The defendant has the right to seek *habeas corpus* under s 12, however the grounds upon which he can do so are limited, given that the competent court is only required to be satisfied of the matters in s 5(2). He is protected from return for a period of 15 days so that any application can be made. He can also waive the right to seek a review under s 13.[51] **16.70**

The defendant is entitled to be discharged if not delivered up within 40 days of the order for delivery being made without reasonable cause.[52] **16.71**

---

[47] ICC Act 2001, ss 4 and 5. Appropriate judicial officer and competent court are defined in s 26.

[48] ICC Act 2001, s 5(5).

[49] ICC Act 2001, s 6(2). There are detailed bail provisions in ss 16, 17, and 18. Section 18(1) requires that the ICC be consulted before the defendant can be granted bail, and the recommendations of the ICC must be taken into account before bail can be granted.

[50] ICC Act 2001, s 10.

[51] Magistrates' Court (International Criminal Court) (Forms) Rules 2001 (SI 2001/2600) specify the forms to be used.

[52] ICC Act 2001, s 19(1).

Part II

MUTUAL ASSISTANCE

17

INTRODUCTION TO INTERNATIONAL COOPERATION IN CRIMINAL MATTERS

A. Introduction

Mutual legal assistance ('MLA')[1] is the provision of assistance by one to state to another in the investigation and prosecution of crime. Although extradition can be regarded as one facet of MLA, in this Part, unless specifically noted, the term MLA should be understood as excluding extradition. MLA is an essential tool in the global fight against national and transnational crime. It is increasingly the case that states engaged in the investigation, prosecution, and suppression of criminal activity must rely on one another in order to successfully bring alleged offenders to justice, to prevent the commission of serious offences, and to confiscate offenders' proceeds of crime. The growth in technology and ease of travel during the twentieth century has led to the globalization of crime, particularly serious crimes such as organized crime, terrorism, and corruption, and reinforced the need for states to work efficiently together to achieve the mutual objective of combating criminal activity. In *United States of America v Cotroni* (1989) 48 CCC (3d) 193, 215, La Forest J of the Supreme Court of Canada said: **17.01**

> The investigation, prosecution and suppression of crime for the protection of the citizen and the maintenance of peace and public order is an important goal of all organized societies. The pursuit of that goal cannot realistically be confined within national boundaries. That has long been the case, but it is increasingly evident today.

This Part examines the means by which the UK gives effect to these important policy principles. It considers the law governing MLA in criminal matters, that is to say, the means by which **17.02**

[1] Usually abbreviated to 'mutual assistance'.

the UK can assist and seek the assistance of foreign states[2] in the investigation and prosecution of criminal offences.[3]

17.03 MLA in the UK is principally governed by the Crime (International Co-operation) Act 2003 (CICA 2003) and the Proceeds of Crime Act 2002 (External Requests and Orders) Order 2005 (the POCA Order).[4] CICA 2003 contains provisions allowing the UK to seek and provide assistance in a number of ways, including the service of process; the provision of evidence and information; the enforcement of foreign driving disqualifications; and other related matters.[5] The POCA Order enables the UK to restrain assets at the request of foreign states and also to enforce external confiscation orders.[6]

17.04 The UK Central Authority, which is part of the Home Office, is responsible for handling the majority of MLA matters in England, Wales, and Northern Ireland,[7] although, as explained at para 17.110, some areas of MLA can be dealt with directly between foreign and domestic law enforcement agencies. The Home Office's webpage <http://www.homeoffice.gov.uk/police/mutual-legal-assistance/> contains a variety of useful links and information about the UK Central Authority's work. The UK Border Agency,[8] which is also part of the Home Office, may deal with MLA requests concerning the smuggling of drugs; firearms and offensive weapons; chemical, biological, radiological, and nuclear hazards; products of animal origin; plant health; cash at the border; and the Convention on International Trade in Endangered Species of Wild Fauna and Flora.[9] Mutual legal assistance matters for England, Wales, and Northern Ireland relating to certain fiscal matters, such as the smuggling of tobacco and alcohol, intellectual

---

2 In this Part the term 'foreign state' includes the Channel Islands, the Isle of Man, and British overseas territories, which are responsible themselves for providing mutual assistance in response to requests from other countries (including the UK). The UK can also provide assistance to the International Criminal Court under Part 3 of the International Criminal Court Act 2001, and to the UN Tribunals for the Former Yugoslavia and Rwanda under the United Nations (International Tribunal) (Former Yugoslavia) Order 1996 (SI 1996/716) and the United Nations (International Tribunal) (Rwanda) Order 1996, SI 1996/1296, as amended, respectively.

3 But note that CICA 2003 also permits the UK to provide assistance in relation to administrative proceedings (defined in s 51 as proceedings outside the UK to which Article 3(1) of the Convention on Mutual Assistance in Criminal Matters applies (proceedings brought by administrative authorities in respect of administrative offences where a decision in the proceedings may be the subject of an appeal before a court)) and clemency proceedings (defined in s 51 as proceedings in a country outside the UK, not being proceedings before a court exercising criminal jurisdiction, for the removal or reduction of a penalty imposed on conviction of an offence in foreign states): para 19.21. There are also statutory provisions which enable foreign states to seek assistance from the UK in relation to financial and regulatory matters under the Companies Act 1989 and the Financial Services and Markets Act 2000. Part 1 of the Regulation of Investigatory Powers Act 2000 contains provisions relating to mutual assistance in the interception of communications. Section 1(4) provides that where the UK is a party to an international agreement which (a) relates to the provision of mutual assistance in connection with, or in the form of, the interception of communications; (b) requires the issue of a warrant, order, or equivalent instrument in cases in which assistance is given; and (c) is designated for the purposes of s 1(4) by an order made by the Secretary of State, it shall be the duty of the Secretary of State to secure that no request for assistance in accordance with the agreement is made on behalf of a person in the UK to the competent authorities of a country or territory outside the UK except with lawful authority. The relevant order is the Regulation of Investigatory Powers (Designation of an International Agreement) Order 2004 (SI 2004/158), which designates the Convention on Mutual Assistance in Criminal Matters.

4 SI 2005/3181, made under the Proceeds of Crime Act 2002.

5 CICA 2003 repealed the Criminal Justice (International Co-operation) Act 1990, however ss 5, 6, 9, and 10 of the 1990 Act remain in force.

6 Criminal Justice (International Co-operation) Act 1990 (Enforcement of Overseas Forfeiture Orders) Order 2005 (SI 2005/3180) contains powers enabling forfeiture of the instrumentalities of crime at the request of foreign states: para 25.80.

7 In practice, in relation to Northern Ireland, MLA matters are referred to the Northern Ireland Office. In Scotland, MLA matters are dealt with by the International Co-operation Unit of the Crown Office.

8 <http://www.ukba.homeoffice.gov.uk>.

9 <http://www.cites.org>.

property rights, strategic exports and indirect taxes (including VAT missing trader intra-community fraud) and related money laundering, may be dealt with by HM Revenue and Customs.[10]

B. The History of Cooperation in Criminal Matters[11]

Origins

Until the second half of the twentieth century, criminal MLA was limited to informal cooperation based upon principles of comity. Prior to the Second World War, it was rare to find legal provisions (such as a treaty) which required countries to assist each other in the investigation of crime. Countries primarily exercised (and were only interested in exercising) jurisdiction in relation to crimes committed within their own borders, particularly in common law countries. Although some countries also asserted jurisdiction over extra-territorial crimes, for example, those committed by their nationals abroad or those which threatened their national security, these extensions of jurisdiction were based on the enforcement of their own national laws, and in general were not borne of a concern to address conduct regarded as injurious to the international community as a whole. Crime was still regarded as a local matter, and states were not especially concerned with assisting other states, except on an uncertain and ad hoc basis.[12] **17.05**

The post-war years saw the international community embark upon the process of multilateral treaty making in the area of extradition and international criminal law, including MLA. The Council of Europe[13] was the primary international body leading the way in the field. The Council of Europe's European Convention on Mutual Assistance in Criminal Matters[14] opened for signature in 1959 and was one of the first multilateral MLA Conventions. Since then, there have been numerous regional instruments in the area of MLA. These include: Inter-American Convention on Mutual Assistance in Criminal Matters (1992);[15] Economic Community of West African States (ECOWAS) Convention on Mutual Assistance in Criminal Matters;[16] Caribbean Treaty of Mutual Legal Assistance in Serious Criminal Matters;[17] Arab **17.06**

[10] Para 19.06.

[11] See generally, Gilmore, *Mutual Assistance in Criminal and Business Regulatory Matters* (Cambridge, 2005); 'Symposium: International Law Enforcement, extradition, and mutual legal assistance in the 21st century' (2000) 23 Fordham Intl LJ 1235.

[12] D McClean, *International Cooperation in Civil and Criminal Matters* (Oxford, 2002), p 154; H Woltring, 'International Legal and Judicial Assistance – Past, Present and Future' (International Society for the Reform of the Criminal Law, 15th Annual Conference, <http://www.isrcl.org/papers>).

[13] The Council of Europe (not to be confused with the EU) was founded on 5 May 1949 by the Treaty of London (the Statute of the Council of Europe) (ETS No 001). Article 1 provides that the aim of the Council of Europe is to achieve a greater unity between its members for the purpose of safeguarding and realizing the ideals and principles which are their common heritage, and facilitating their economic and social progress. This aim is to be pursued through the organs of the Council by discussion of questions of common concern, and by agreements and common action in economic, social, cultural, scientific, legal, and administrative matters, and in the maintenance and further realization of human rights and fundamental freedoms. Article 4 provides that membership is open to any 'European' state. The term 'European' is construed liberally, and so countries such as Turkey and Russia are members of the Council of Europe. At the time of writing (August 2012) the only European countries which are not members are Belarus, Kazakhstan, and Vatican City. The Council of Europe works mainly through conventions. Several conventions have been opened for signature to non-member States. Important examples are the Convention on Cybercrime, signed by Canada, Japan, South Africa, and the United States. See generally, <http://www.coe.int>.

[14] ETS No 030. See also the First Additional Protocol to the Convention (ETS No 99). There is a Second Additional Protocol (ETS No 182), which the UK ratified in 2010.

[15] OAS Treaty Series No 75.

[16] 1992, A/P.1/7/92.

[17] 2000, available through <http://www.caricom.org>.

League Convention on Mutual Assistance in Criminal Matters 1983; and the South East Asia Treaty on Mutual Legal Assistance in Criminal Matters.[18] The United Nations has also published a Model Treaty on Mutual Assistance in Criminal Matters.[19]

17.07 In the later part of the twentieth century, and particularly following the Treaty on European Union in 1992,[20] there have a number of important developments within the EU relating to MLA, including the Schengen Convention[21] and the Convention on Mutual Assistance in Criminal Matters and its Protocol.[22] These are considered at para 17.22.

International MLA agreements[23]

17.08 The UK was comparatively slow to ratify international instruments relating to MLA. It did not sign and ratify the European Convention on Mutual Legal Assistance in Criminal Matters until 1991, more than 30 years after it opened for signature. Since then, the UK has ratified a number of instruments including the European Convention on Laundering, Search, Seizure and Confiscation of the Proceeds from Crime 1990;[24] the UN Convention Against Illicit Traffic in Narcotic Drugs and Psychotropic Substances 1988;[25] the Commonwealth Scheme;[26] Convention implementing the Schengen Agreement;[27] Convention on Mutual Assistance in Criminal Matters between Member States of the European Union 2000 and its Protocol;[28] United Nations Convention against Transnational Organised Crime 2000;[29] United Nations Convention against Corruption 2003.[30]

17.09 The UK is also signatory to a number of bilateral mutual legal assistance treaties ('MLATs'). These include:[31] Malaysia (2010);[32] the Philippines (2009);[33] Vietnam (2009);[34] Libya (2008);[35] United Arab Emirates (2006);[36] Algeria (2006);[37] Brazil (2005);[38] Hong Kong SAR

[18] 2004, available through <http://www.asean.org>.

[19] 1990, available through <http://www.unodc.org>.

[20] Official Journal 1992 C191.

[21] Official Journal L 239, 22 September 2000, p 19.

[22] Official Journal C 197, 12 July 2000, p 3.

[23] The bilateral and multilateral MLA agreements to which the UK is party are summarized in the MLA Guidelines, p 781 (Appendix M3).

[24] ETS No 141. There is also a Council of Europe Convention on the Laundering, Search, Seizure and Confiscation of the Proceeds from Crime and on the Financing of Terrorism (CETS No 198). At the time of writing (August 2012) the UK has neither signed nor ratified this Convention, although it has ratified its predecessor, the Convention on Laundering, Search, Seizure and Confiscation of the Proceeds from Crime, which opened for signature in 1990 (CETS No 141) and which was ratified by the UK in 1993.

[25] UNTS No 27627.

[26] Scheme Relating to Mutual Assistance in Criminal Matters within the Commonwealth, Commonwealth Secretariat, London, LMN (86) 13. The UK has also ratified the UN Convention against Transnational Organised Crime 2000 and the UN Convention Against Corruption 2003.

[27] Official Journal L 239, 22 September 2000, p 19. As explained at para 17.25, the UK does not participate in all parts of the Schengen Agreement. The parts of the Schengen Agreement in which the UK participates are listed in the Council Decision of 29 May 2000 (2000/365/EC).

[28] Official Journal L 181, 19 July 2003, p 34.

[29] United Nations Treaty Series, Vol 2225, p 209.

[30] United Nations Treaty Series, Vol 2349, p 51.

[31] A full list of MLATs, including those dealing with only certain offences, for example, drug trafficking, is available through <http://www.fco.gov.uk>.

[32] Cm 8266.

[33] Cm 8398.

[34] Cm 7879.

[35] Cm 7549.

[36] Cm 7282.

[37] Cm 6929.

[38] Cm 8087.

(1998);[39] Bolivia (1994); United States (1994);[40] Panama (1993);[41] (Nigeria) (1994);[42] and Canada (1993).[43]

European Convention on Mutual Legal Assistance in Criminal Matters 1959[44]

The 1959 Convention was borne out of the Council of Europe's work on the European Convention on Extradition 1957.[45] In 1953 the Committee of Ministers of the Council of Europe instructed the Secretary General to convene a Committee of Governmental Experts to examine the possibility of establishing principles of extradition which could be embodied in a European Convention on Extradition. The Committee of Experts mentioned in its report accompanying the draft Convention that it had discussed the question of mutual assistance in criminal proceedings and concluded that there should be such a Convention, a number of member States of the Council of Europe having by then concluded bilateral MLATs. During their 41st meeting in September 1956, the Ministers' Deputies decided at the request of the experts to widen their terms of reference, instructing them to prepare a draft Convention on Mutual Assistance in Criminal Matters. The Committee of Experts on Mutual Assistance in Criminal Matters met at the Council of Europe, Strasbourg, on a number of occasions in 1957 and 1958. The European Convention on Mutual Assistance was, by a decision taken by the Committee of Ministers sitting at Deputy level at its 71st meeting (April 1959), opened for signature by the member States of the Council of Europe on 20 April 1959. **17.10**

Article 1 of the Convention provides that Contracting States undertake:[46] **17.11**

> … to afford each other … the widest measure of mutual assistance in proceedings in respect of offences the punishment of which, at the time of the request for assistance, falls within the jurisdiction of the judicial authorities of the requesting Party.

Article 3(1) of the Convention provides that: **17.12**

> The requested Party shall execute in the manner provided for by its law any letters rogatory[47] relating to a criminal matter and addressed to it by the judicial authorities of the requesting Party for the purpose of procuring evidence or transmitting articles to be produced in evidence, records or documents.

Articles 7–9 contain detailed provisions concerning the service of writs and other records of judicial verdicts. Article 11 deals with the temporary transfer of prisoners for the purposes of giving evidence. **17.13**

---

[39] Cm 5199.

[40] Cm 2612. For a discussion of United States treaty practice in the mutual assistance field, see generally Ellis and Pisani, 'The United States Treaties on Mutual Assistance in Criminal Matters: A Comparative Analysis' (1985) 19 *J of Intl L* 189; Knapp, 'Mutual Legal Assistance Treaties as a Way to Pierce Bank Secrecy' (1988) 20 *J of Intl L* 405, 434; Nadelmann, 'Negotiations on Criminal Law Assistance Treaties' (1985) 33 *AJCL* 467; Nash, *Cumulative Digest of United States Practice in International Law, 1981–1988* (US Department of State: 1994 vol II) 1449, 1488; Ristau and Abbell, *International Judicial Assistance (Criminal)*, ss 12-4-1 *et seq*. For a list of United States MLATS see <http://www.travel.state.gov/law/info/judicial/judicial 690.html>.

[41] Cm 2620.

[42] Cm 901.

[43] (1993) Canada Gazette Part I, p 3458 (Vol 127, No 46).

[44] The Explanatory Report to the European Convention on Extradition 1959 is available at <http://conventions.coe.int/Treaty/EN/Reports/Html/030.htm>.

[45] ETS No 024.

[46] For a commentary on the Convention, see <http://conventions.coe.int/Treaty/EN/Reports/Html/030.htm>.

[47] Defined in the Convention's Explanatory Report <http://conventions.coe.int/Treaty/EN/Reports/Html/030.htm> as 'a mandate given by a judicial authority of one country to a foreign judicial authority to perform in its place one or more specified actions': see para 17.117.

17.14 Article 2 provides that assistance may be refused if the request concerns an offence which the requested party considers a political offence, an offence connected with a political offence, or a fiscal offence.[48] Assistance may also be refused if the requested party considers that execution of the request is likely to prejudice the sovereignty, security, *ordre public*, or other essential interests of its country.

17.15 Article 5 deals with dual criminality and allows any contracting party to:

> ... reserve the right to make the execution of letters rogatory for search or seizure of property dependent on one or more of the following conditions: (*a*) that the offence motivating the letters rogatory is punishable under both the law of the requesting party and the law of the requested party ...

17.16 The UK reserved the right provided for in Article 5, and s 7 of the Criminal Justice (International Co-operation) Act 1990 in relation to search and seizure provided that the offence in question must 'constitute a serious arrestable offence if it had occurred in any part of the United Kingdom'.[49] However, the requirement of dual criminality as a precondition for providing assistance has been removed to a large extent by the CICA 2003.[50]

17.17 The First Additional Protocol to the Convention,[51] which opened for signature in 1978, contains provisions intended to relax the Convention's restrictions on assistance in relation to fiscal offences. Article 1 provides that the contracting parties shall not exercise the right provided for in Article 2(a) of the Convention to refuse assistance *solely* on the ground that the request concerns an offence which the requested party considers a fiscal offence. Article 2 provides that in the case where a contracting party has made the execution of letters rogatory for search or seizure of property dependent on the condition that the offence motivating the letters rogatory is punishable under both the law of the requesting party and the law of the requested party, this condition shall be fulfilled, as regards fiscal offences, if the offence is punishable under the law of the requesting party and corresponds to an offence of the same nature under the law of the requested party. Article 2(2) provides that the request may not be refused on the ground that the law of the requested party does not impose the same kind of tax or duty or does not contain a tax, duty, customs and exchange regulation of the same kind as the law of the requesting party.

17.18 The Second Additional Protocol to the Convention[52] is intended to improve state parties' ability to react to cross-border crime in the light of political and social developments in Europe and technological developments throughout the world. It is intended to supplement the Convention and the First Additional Protocol by broadening the range of situations in which mutual assistance may be requested and by making the provision of assistance easier, quicker, and more flexible. It also takes account of the need to protect individual rights in the processing of personal data. Thus, in many provisions it follows very closely, often literally, the Convention on Mutual Assistance in Criminal Matters and the Schengen Convention.[53]

17.19 The European Convention on Mutual Assistance in Criminal Matters was an important achievement for its time in its recognition of the necessity for specific instruments for cooperation in evidence gathering. However, like all new instruments, it had limitations. Perhaps the

48 *R v Secretary of State for the Home Department ex p Fininvest Spa* [1997] 1 WLR 743, 758.
49 s 7(1) and (2)(b).
50 Para 19.02.
51 CETS No 099.
52 CETS No 182. It was ratified by the UK in 2010.
53 See the Explanatory Report to the Second Additional Protocol, para 9 <http://www.conventions.coe.int/Treaty/en/Reports/Html/182.htm>.

most notable in this instance was that the Convention was designed to operate amongst states of like legal tradition, namely the civil law states of Europe, and it was geared towards legal systems where criminal prosecutions were under the control of an investigating judge. It was not until the entry into force of Part 1 of the Criminal Justice (International Co-operation) Act 1990 in 1991 that the UK was able to ratify the Convention.

Commonwealth Scheme Relating to Mutual Assistance in Criminal Matters 1986

The Commonwealth Scheme was adopted by Commonwealth Law Ministers in Harare, Zimbabwe, in August 1986.[54] It is not treaty based and depends for its effective operation on the passage, by all members of the Commonwealth, of domestic legislation, including legislation to enable the exercise of powers and functions by their law enforcement and curial bodies on behalf of other Commonwealth countries. **17.20**

The Commonwealth Scheme provides for a wider range of assistance than its European counterpart, and recognizes the common law independence of the police in conducting investigations, as well as a non-judicial prosecutor exercising a prosecutorial discretion. The types of assistance envisaged by the Scheme include: **17.21**

- locating persons;
- serving judicial documents;
- obtaining and taking of evidence;
- making available records and other documents;
- facilitating the appearance of witnesses (including persons in custody) provided such persons consent, and
- issuing of process for compulsory measures including search and seizure.

EU developments in the field of MLA

Originally the EU (formerly, the European Economic Community and, subsequently, the European Community) focused on economic integration and the establishment of a Common Market. The Common Market is based on the principle that persons, products, services, and capital should be allowed to move freely from one country to the next. Such freedom of movement obviously benefits the European economy, but it also opens up new opportunities for crime, and new possibilities for offenders to move from one country to another, trying to evade justice. This concern led to the EU becoming active in the area of criminal justice. **17.22**

The EU came into being in 1993 with the coming into force of the Treaty on European Union. Between November 1993 and 2009, the EU legally comprised three pillars. These were: (a) the European Communities pillar, which handled economic, social, and environmental policies. This was the only pillar with a legal personality, consisting of the EC, the European Coal and Steel Community (ECSC, until its expiry in 2002), and the European Atomic Energy Community (EURATOM); (b) the Common Foreign and Security Policy (CFSP) pillar took care of foreign policy and military matters; (c) the Policy and Judicial Cooperation in Criminal Matters (PJCC) brought together cooperation in the fight against crime. This pillar was originally named Justice and Home Affairs (JHA). This structure lasted until 1 December 2009 and the entry into force of the Treaty of Lisbon, when the EU obtained a consolidated legal personality. **17.23**

---

54 Scheme Relating to Mutual Assistance in Criminal Matters within the Commonwealth, Commonwealth Secretariat, London, LMN (86) 13 ('the Harare Scheme'). The text of the Harare Scheme is available at <http://www.thecommonwealth.org>. At the time of writing (August 2012) a new Scheme is under consideration. See generally, D McClean, *International Cooperation in Civil and Criminal Matters* (2002), p 196.

17.24 In October 1999 the Tampere European Council adopted a comprehensive approach to put into practice the new political framework established by the Treaty of Amsterdam[55] in the area of justice and home affairs.[56] The European Council set ambitious objectives and deadlines for action by the EU in a number of areas including asylum and immigration, police and judicial cooperation, and the fight against crime. The result has been a number of EU initiatives, including Framework decisions,[57] in the area of criminal mutual assistance that have had an

---

[55] 1997 Official Journal C/340/1. Articles 31(a), (b), and 34(2)(b), which provided for judicial cooperation in criminal matters, the facilitation of extradition, and the adoption of Framework decisions. Framework decisions had the purpose of approximating the laws and regulations of the member States. They were binding upon the member States as to the result to be achieved, but left to the national authorities the choice of form and methods. The Treaty of Lisbon abolished Framework decisions and the EU can now enact directives and regulations in the area of criminal justice by means of the ordinary legislative process. For the complex transitional provisions relating to existing Framework decisions, see *Assange v Swedish Prosecuting Authority* [2012] 2 WLR 1275, paras 198–200. In October 2012 the Government announced its intention to opt out of pre-Lisbon EU criminal justices measures. The announcement has proved controversial and the House of Lords EU Sub-Committee on Justice, Institutions and Consumer Protection and the EU Sub-Committee on Home Affairs, Health and Education have launched a joint inquiry into the decision to opt out. See Alicia Hinarejos, JR Spencer and Steve Peers, 'Opting out of EU Criminal law: What is actually involved?', September 2012 (University of Cambridge Faculty of Law Research Paper No 25/2012), para 20.

[56] Para 15.11.

[57] These include the following: Council Framework Decision 2000/383/JHA of 29 May 2000 on increasing protection by criminal penalties and other sanctions against counterfeiting in connection with the introduction of the euro (OJ L 140, 14.6.2000, pp 1–3); Council Framework Decision 2001/220/JHA of 15 March 2001 on the standing of victims in criminal proceedings (OJ L 82, 22.3.2001, pp 1–4; Council Framework Decision 2001/413/JHA of 28 May 2001 combating fraud and counterfeiting of non-cash means of payment (OJ L 149, 2.6.2001, pp 1–4); Council Framework Decision 2001/500/JHA of 26 June 2001 on money laundering, the identification, tracing, freezing, seizing and confiscation of instrumentalities and the proceeds of crime (OJ L 182, 5.7.2001, pp 1–2); Council Framework Decision 2001/888/JHA of 6 December 2001 amending Framework Decision 2000/383/JHA on increasing protection by criminal penalties and other sanctions against counterfeiting in connection with the introduction of the euro (OJ L 329, 14.12.2001, pp 3–3); Council Framework Decision 2002/584/JHA of 13 June 2002 on the European arrest warrant and the surrender procedures between Member States – Statements made by certain Member States on the adoption of the Framework Decision (OJ L 190, 18.7.2002, pp 1–20); Council Framework Decision 2002/475/JHA of 13 June 2002 on combating terrorism (OJ L 164, 22.6.2002, pp 3–7); Council Framework Decision 2002/465/JHA of 13 June 2002 on joint investigation teams (OJ L 162, 20.6.2002, pp 1–3); Council Framework Decision 2002/629/JHA of 19 July 2002 on combating trafficking in human beings (OJ L 203, 1.8.2002, pp 1–4); Council Framework Decision 2002/946/JHA of 28 November 2002 on the strengthening of the penal framework to prevent the facilitation of unauthorised entry, transit and residence (OJ L 328, 5.12.2002, pp 1–3); Council Framework Decision 2003/80/JHA of 7 January 2003 on the protection of the environment through criminal law (OJ L 29, 5.2.2003, pp 55–58); Council Framework Decision 2003/568/JHA of 22 July 2003 on combating corruption in the private sector (OJ L 192, 31.7.2003, pp 54–56); Council Framework Decision 2003/577/JHA of 22 July 2003 on the execution in the European Union of orders freezing property or evidence (OJ L 196, 2.8.2003, pp 45–55); Council Framework Decision 2004/68/JHA of 22 December 2003 on combating the sexual exploitation of children and child pornography (OJ L 13, 20.1.2004, pp 44–48); Council Framework Decision 2004/757/JHA of 25 October 2004 laying down minimum provisions on the constituent elements of criminal acts and penalties in the field of illicit drug trafficking (OJ L 335, 11.11.2004, pp 8–11); Council Framework Decision 2005/212/JHA of 24 February 2005 on Confiscation of Crime-Related Proceeds, Instrumentalities and Property (OJ L 68, 15.3.2005, pp 49–51); Council Framework Decision 2005/214/JHA of 24 February 2005 on the application of the principle of mutual recognition to financial penalties (OJ L 76, 22.3.2005, pp 16–30); Council Framework Decision 2005/222/JHA of 24 February 2005 on attacks against information systems (OJ L 69, 16.3.2005, pp 67–71); Council Framework Decision 2005/667/JHA of 12 July 2005 to strengthen the criminal-law framework for the enforcement of the law against ship-source pollution (OJ L 255, 30.9.2005, pp 164–167); Council Framework Decision 2006/783/JHA of 6 October 2006 on the application of the principle of mutual recognition to confiscation orders (OJ L 328, 24.11.2006, pp 59–78); Council Framework Decision 2006/960/JHA of 18 December 2006 on simplifying the exchange of information and intelligence between law enforcement authorities of the Member States of the European Union (OJ L 386, 29.12.2006, pp 89–100); Council Framework Decision 2008/675/JHA of 24 July 2008 on taking account of convictions in the Member States of the European Union in the course of new criminal proceedings (OJ L 220, 15.8.2008, pp 32–34); Council Framework Decision 2008/841/JHA of 24 October 2008 on the fight

important impact on the UK's domestic legislation, including CICA 2003. However, even before Tampere, the EU had enacted legislation in the area of mutual assistance, which prepared the ground for post-Tampere developments.

The Schengen Convention[58]

France, Germany, Belgium, Luxembourg, and the Netherlands agreed on 14 June 1985 to sign an agreement on the gradual abolition of checks at their common borders. This became known as the Schengen Agreement, after the name of the town in Luxembourg where it was signed.[59] **17.25**

The Schengen Convention was signed in June 1990 and came into effect in March 1995.[60] By that time, other EU member states had joined the initial signatories of this inter-governmental agreement, which was signed outside the EU framework. The Convention abolished the checks at internal borders of the signatory states and created a single external frontier, where checks for all the Schengen signatories were to be carried out in accordance with a common set of rules. The Convention has 142 Articles providing measures for creating a common area of justice and security, following abolition of common borders. Its key aims are to facilitate free movement within participating states; to improve police cooperation; extend the provision of mutual legal assistance between EU states; and to improve access to the Schengen Information System (SIS).[61] **17.26**

The 1985 Schengen Agreement and the Schengen Convention, and the decisions and declarations adopted by the Schengen bodies are known collectively as the Schengen *acquis*. The texts are available on the Europa website.[62] **17.27**

against organised crime (OJ L 300, 11.11.2008, pp 42–45); Council Framework Decision 2008/909/JHA of 27 November 2008 on the application of the principle of mutual recognition to judgments in criminal matters imposing custodial sentences or measures involving deprivation of liberty for the purpose of their enforcement in the European Union (OJ L 327, 5.12.2008, pp 27–46); Council Framework Decision 2008/947/JHA of 27 November 2008 on the application of the principle of mutual recognition to judgments and probation decisions with a view to the supervision of probation measures and alternative sanctions (OJ L 337, 16.12.2008, pp 102–122); Council Framework Decision 2008/977/JHA of 27 November 2008 on the protection of personal data processed in the framework of police and judicial cooperation in criminal matters (OJ L 350, 30.12.2008, pp 60–71); Council Framework Decision 2008/913/JHA of 28 November 2008 on combating certain forms and expressions of racism and xenophobia by means of criminal law (OJ L 328, 6.12.2008, pp 55–58); Council Framework Decision 2008/919/JHA of 28 November 2008 amending Framework Decision 2002/475/JHA on combating terrorism (OJ L 330, 9.12.2008, pp 21–23); Council Framework Decision 2008/978/JHA of 18 December 2008 on the European evidence warrant for the purpose of obtaining objects, documents and data for use in proceedings in criminal matters (OJ L 350, 30.12.2008, pp 72–92); Council Framework Decision 2009/299/JHA of 26 February 2009 amending Framework Decisions 2002/584/JHA, 2005/214/JHA, 2006/783/JHA, 2008/909/JHA and 2008/947/JHA, thereby enhancing the procedural rights of persons and fostering the application of the principle of mutual recognition to decisions rendered in the absence of the person concerned at the trial (OJ L 81, 27.3.2009, pp 24–36); Council Framework Decision 2009/315/JHA of 26 February 2009 on the organisation and content of the exchange of information extracted from the criminal record between Member States (OJ L 93, 7.4.2009, pp 23–32); Council Framework Decision 2009/829/JHA of 23 October 2009 on the application, between Member States of the European Union, of the principle of mutual recognition to decisions on supervision measures as an alternative to provisional detention (OJ L 294, 11.11.2009, pp 20–40); Council Framework Decision 2009/905/JHA of 30 November 2009 on accreditation of forensic service providers carrying out laboratory activities (OJ L 322, 9.12.2009, pp 14–16); Council Framework Decision 2009/948/JHA of 30 November 2009 on prevention and settlement of conflicts of exercise of jurisdiction in criminal proceedings (OJ L 328, 15.12.2009, pp 42–47).

58 See generally, D McClean, *International Cooperation in Civil and Criminal Matters* (2002), p 168.

59 See Joubert and Bevers, *Schengen Investigated: A Comparative Interpretation of the Schengen Provisions on International Police Cooperation in the Light of the European Convention on Human Rights* (Martinus Nijhoff, 1996).

60 Official Journal L 239, 22 September 2000, p 19.

61 See Karanja, *Transparency and Proportionality in the Schengen Information System and Border Control Cooperation* (Martinus Nijhoff, 2008); 2011 Extradition Review, para 4.7.

62 <http://www.ec.europa.eu/justice_home/fsj/freetravel/frontiers/wai/fsj_freetravel_schengen_en.htm>.

17.28 The UK and Ireland have not fully signed up to the Schengen Convention and have not ended border controls with other EU member States. For this reason, EU citizens, as well as third-country nationals, still have to show their passports when travelling between the UK or Ireland and the rest of the EU (although not between Ireland and the UK which, together with the Channel Islands and the Isle of Man, constitute a common travel area for which passports are not needed).

17.29 In 1999 the UK asked to take part in some aspects of the Schengen *acquis*, namely police and judicial cooperation in criminal matters and the SIS. A Council Decision approving the UK's request was adopted on 29 May 2000 and, after evaluating the conditions that must precede implementation of the provisions governing police and judicial cooperation, the Council decided on 22 December 2004, that this part of the Schengen *acquis* could be implemented by the UK.[63] Parts of the Schengen *acquis* were then put into effect by the UK.

17.30 The purpose of the SIS is to facilitate law enforcement cooperation within the EU. The use of the SIS is a response to the abolition of border controls with the result that nationals may move freely within the Schengen area. This has made member States collectively responsible for detecting and deterring criminal conduct. According to the European Council, it has proved to be useful in locating and facilitating the arrest of persons who are the subject of a European arrest warrant: in 2009 82.5% (10,012) of the 12,111 warrants issued by Schengen participating states were transmitted via the SIS.[64]

17.31 At the time of writing (August 2012), 22 member States plus Iceland and Norway are connected to it. The SIS contains a database used by authorities of the Schengen member countries to exchange data on certain categories of people and objects, including persons wanted for arrest and extradition; aliens for whom an alert has been issued for the purposes of refusing entry; missing persons or persons needing temporary police protection (eg minors); witnesses and persons summoned to appear before judicial authorities; persons to be submitted to discreet surveillance or specific checks for the purposes of prosecuting criminal offences or for the prevention of threats to public security.

17.32 Member States supply information (which becomes an 'alert') from their national systems to the central system via a common secure network. Searches in SIS produce a 'hit' when details of a person or object match those of an existing alert. The data on the SIS is managed by a national system known as SIRENE.[65] Information is not forwarded on to the central section of the SIS by the national SIRENE bureau unless it is satisfied that Schengen rules have been applied correctly. It is only when the information is forwarded to the central section of the SIS that the data can be accessed by other SIS member States.

17.33 The Commission has been developing a successor to the SIS (SIS II) which will enable more member States to connect to it, increase the volume of data that it can hold, and expand the categories of data that may be included (eg, fingerprints and photographs). The UK is not connected to the current system, but will be connected to SIS II. However, its participation in SIS II will be limited to those elements of the Schengen *acquis* in which the UK takes part and which mainly concern police and judicial cooperation in criminal matters. Thus, when SIS II becomes operational (possibly around 2013), the UK will have access to the database which will include alerts for arrest and extradition.[66]

---

63 Council Decision 2004/926/EC [2004], OJ L 395/70.

64 2011 Extradition Review, para 4.9.

65 The acronym stands for Supplementary Information Request at National Entry.

66 Parliamentary European Scrutiny Committee – Tenth Report, Section 14 (17 July 2012), available through <http://www.publications.parliament.uk>.

A number of key provisions of the Schengen Convention are implemented by the UK through CICA 2003. These include: 17.34

- the continuation of surveillance by law enforcement officers if the subject crosses into another member State ('hot surveillance');[67]
- the extended provision of mutual legal assistance to include, in addition to ordinary criminal proceedings, clemency proceedings and administrative proceedings;[68]
- the sending of procedural documents directly by post rather than via central authorities;[69]
- the designation of a supervisory authority to carry out independent supervision of national data files from the SIS.[70]

Convention on Driving Disqualifications

The Convention on Driving Disqualifications[71] establishes a mandatory legal framework between EU member States so that drivers disqualified in a member State other than the one where they have their principal residence cannot circumvent the disqualification when they leave the state where the offence was committed. The measures adopted by the 1998 Convention include: 17.35

- requiring states in which the offence took place to notify the state of the offender's residence of any driving disqualification imposed on its nationals without delay;[72]
- requiring the state of residence to give effect to a decision to disqualify;[73]
- requiring member States to create powers to penalize drivers in their territory when they are disqualified in their state of residence.[74]

The provisions of this Convention are implemented in Part 3 of CICA 2003.[75] 17.36

Convention on Mutual Assistance in Criminal Matters and its Protocol

On 29 May 2000 the EU Council of Ministers adopted the Convention on Mutual Assistance in Criminal Matters.[76] Article 1 of the Convention explains that its purpose is to supplement the provisions between member States of inter alia the European Convention on Mutual Assistance in Criminal Matters and its Additional Protocol, and the mutual assistance provisions of the Schengen Convention. The Convention does not affect the application of more favourable provisions in bilateral or multilateral agreements between member States or criminal mutual assistance arrangements agreed[77] on the basis of uniform legislation or other special arrangements. 17.37

Thus, the Convention aims to encourage and modernize cooperation between judicial, police, and customs authorities within the EU, as well as with Norway and Iceland, by supplementing provisions in existing legal instruments and facilitating their application. The state receiving 17.38

---

[67] Art 40: see Ch 20.
[68] Art 49: see para 19.21.
[69] Art 52: see Ch 22.
[70] Art 114: see para 21.54.
[71] Official Journal C 216, 10/7/1998. For the Convention's Explanatory Report see the Official Journal C 211, 23 July 1999.
[72] Art 3.
[73] Art 4.
[74] Art 12.
[75] Ch 23.
[76] Official Journal 197, 12 July 2000, p 3. See Explanatory Report on the Convention of 29 May 2000 on Mutual Assistance in Criminal Matters between the Member States of the European Union, Official Journal C 379, 29 December 2000, p 7.
[77] As provided for in the European Convention on Mutual Assistance in Criminal Matters, Art 26(4).

a request must, in principle, comply with the formalities and procedures indicated by the requesting state.

17.39 Forms of assistance provided for by the Convention include:

- the handing of objects that have been stolen or obtained by other criminal means and that are found in another member State;
- the temporary transfer to the territory of a member State where an investigation is being carried out a person held on the territory of another member State;
- hearings by videoconference;
- hearings by telephone conference;
- permitting controlled deliveries on the territory of a member State in the framework of criminal investigations into offences that may give rise to extradition. These are to be directed and monitored by the authorities of the requested member State;
- the setting up of a joint investigation team by two or more EU member States for a specific purpose and for a limited period of time;
- covert investigations carried out by officers of another member State (as well as by officers of the home member State) acting under covert or false identity;
- requests for the interception of telecommunications. These may either be intercepted and transmitted directly to the requesting state or recorded for subsequent transmission.

17.40 The 2001 Protocol to the Convention[78] deals with requests for banking information and is implemented by Part 1, Chapter 4 of CICA 2003. It requires member States to ascertain whether persons subject to criminal investigation for serious crime hold bank accounts in the requested state's territory; to provide historical information on transactions carried out on a specific bank account over a specified period; to monitor transactions; and to impose a duty on banks not to inform the customer of an investigation.

17.41 CICA 2003 implements many of the provisions of the Convention on Mutual Assistance in Criminal Matters.

Council Framework Decision on the execution in the European Union of orders freezing property or evidence[79]

17.42 This Framework Decision was adopted by the EU Council of Ministers on 22 July 2003 on an initiative by Belgium, France, and Sweden. Its purpose is to establish the rules under which a member State is to recognize and execute in its territory a freezing order issued by a judicial authority of another member State in the framework of criminal proceedings.

17.43 A 'freezing order' means any measure taken by a judicial authority in a member State to prevent the destruction, transformation, displacement, and so on, of property. The evidence to which the Framework Decision applies includes objects, documents, or data which could be produced as evidence in criminal proceedings.

17.44 The Framework Decision is given effect to in Part 1 of CICA 2003.[80]

---

[78] Official Journal C 326, 21 November 2001, p 1. See Explanatory Report to the Protocol to the 2000 Convention on Mutual Assistance in Criminal Matters between the Member States of the European Union, Official Journal C 257, 24 October 2002, p 1.

[79] 2003/577/JHA, 22 July 2003; Official Journal L 196, 2 August 2003.

[80] CICA 2003, ss 10–12 and ss 20–27: see para 18.41 and para 19.140. See also the amendments to Sch 4 of the Terrorism Act 2000 made by Sch 4 of CICA 2003. These provisions are dealt with at para 25.103.

Council Framework Decision 2002/475/JHA of 13 June 2002 on combating terrorism[81]

Terrorism very often stems from the activities of networks operating at an international level. The profound changes in the nature of modern terrorism exemplified by the events of 11 September 2001 highlighted, in the opinion of the EU, the inadequacy of traditional forms of judicial and police cooperation in combating it. Because there are no borders within most of the EU, and because the right of free movements of people is guaranteed, in September 2001 the EU decided that new measures in the fight against terrorism had to be taken. The EU's concern was that terrorists might otherwise take advantage of any differences in legal treatment in different member States.[82] **17.45**

The overriding objective of the Framework Decision is to require member States to classify as 'terrorist offences' the conduct listed in Article 1, which includes attacks upon a person's life which may cause death, attacks upon the physical integrity of a person, and kidnapping or hostage taking. **17.46**

The Framework Decision also defines and penalizes 'terrorist groups' by requiring member States to ensure that offences such as directing a terrorist group are punishable.[83] Member states are also required to take extra-territorial jurisdiction in respect of the offences listed in Article 9 which is headed 'Jurisdiction and prosecution'. It provides: **17.47**

> 1. Each Member State shall take the necessary measures to establish its jurisdiction over the offences referred to in Articles 1 to 4 where:
>
> the offence is committed in whole or in part in its territory. Each Member State may extend its jurisdiction if the offence is committed in the territory of a Member State;
>
> the offence is committed on board a vessel flying its flag or an aircraft registered there;
>
> the offender is one of its nationals or residents;
>
> the offence is committed for the benefit of a legal person established in its territory;
>
> the offence is committed against the institutions or people of the Member State in question or against an institution of the European Union or body set up in accordance with the Treaty establishing the European Community or the Treaty on European Union and based in that Member State.

The UK's detailed domestic terrorist[84] laws contain many the provisions required by the Framework Decision,[85] however Part 2 of CICA 2003 contains additional provisions implementing Article 9. **17.48**

The Terrorism Act 2000 created a number of terrorist offences including membership of a proscribed organization (s 11); fundraising for the purposes of terrorism (s 15); possession of property for the purposes of terrorism (s 16); funding arrangements for the purposes of terrorism (s 17); and money laundering (s 18). Sections 62 and 63 of the Terrorism Act 2000 created extra-territorial jurisdiction over terrorist bombing offences and the financing and property offences in ss 15–18. **17.49**

---

[81] Official Journal L 164, 22 June 2002, p 3.

[82] Proposal for a Council Framework Decision on combating terrorism (2001/0217 (CNS)).

[83] Arts 2 and 5.

[84] The Terrorism Act 2000, s1 defines terrorism as the use or threat of action involving serious violence against a person or serious damage to property; action which endangers a person's life other than that of the person committing the action; action which creates a serious risk to the health or safety of the public or a section of the public; and action is designed seriously to interfere with or seriously to disrupt an electronic system, provided that the use or threat is designed to influence the government or an international governmental organization or to intimidate the public or a section of the public.

[85] See generally C Walker, *Blackstone's Guide to the Anti-terrorism Legislation* (2nd Edn, Oxford, 2009).

17.50 Part 2 of CICA 2003 is entitled 'Terrorist Act and Threats: Jurisdiction' and creates extra-territorial jurisdiction over a range of offences in the Terrorism Act 2000. It gives effect to Article 9 of the Framework Decision by ensuring that the UK has jurisdiction to try terrorist offences committed by UK nationals and residents regardless of where the conduct takes place. Section 52 of the CICA 2003 is headed 'Jurisdiction for terrorist offences' and inserts ss 63A, 63B, 63C, 63D, and 63E into the Terrorism Act 2000.

17.51 Section 63A provides that if a UK national or a UK resident does anything outside the UK, and his action, if done in any part of the UK would have constituted an offence under s 54 or any of ss 56–61 of the Terrorism Act 2000, he shall be guilty in that part of the UK of the offence.

17.52 Section 63B provides that if a UK national or a UK resident does anything outside the UK as an act of terrorism or for the purposes of terrorism, and his action, if done in any part of the UK, would have constituted an offence listed in s 63B(2), he shall be guilty in that part of the UK of the offence.[86]

17.53 Section 63C is headed 'Terrorist attacks abroad on UK nationals, residents and diplomatic staff etc: jurisdiction'. It provides that if a person does anything outside the UK as an act of terrorism or for the purposes of terrorism, and his action is done to, or in relation to, a UK national, a UK resident, or a protected person, and his action, if done in any part of the UK, would have constituted an offence listed in s 63C(2), he shall be guilty in that part of the UK of the offence.[87]

17.54 Section 63D is headed 'Terrorist attacks or threats abroad in connection with UK diplomatic premises etc: jurisdiction'. Section 63D(1) provides that if a person does anything outside the UK as an act of terrorism or for the purposes of terrorism, his action is done in connection with an attack on relevant premises or on a vehicle ordinarily used by a protected person, the attack is made when a protected person is on or in the premises or vehicle, and his action, if done in any part of the UK, would have constituted an offence listed in s 63D(2), he shall be guilty in that part of the UK of the offence.[88]

17.55 Section 63D(3) provides that if a person does anything outside the UK as an act of terrorism or for the purposes of terrorism, his action consists of a threat of an attack on relevant premises or on a vehicle ordinarily used by a protected person, the attack is threatened to be made when a protected person is, or is likely to be, on or in the premises or vehicle, an his action, if done in any part of the UK, would have constituted an offence listed in s 63D(4), he shall be guilty in that part of the UK of the offence.[89]

[86] The offences in s 63B(2) are murder, manslaughter, culpable homicide, rape, assault causing injury, assault to injury, kidnapping, abduction, false imprisonment, the offences under s 4, 16, 18, 20, 21, 22, 23, 24, 28, 29, 30, or 64 of the Offences against the Person Act 1861, an offence under any of ss 1–5 of the Forgery and Counterfeiting Act 1981, the uttering of a forged document or an offence under s 46A of the Criminal Law (Consolidation) (Scotland) Act 1995, an offence under s 1 or 2 of the Criminal Damage Act 1971, an offence under Art 3 or 4 of the Criminal Damage (Northern Ireland) Order 1977, malicious mischief, wilful fire-raising.

[87] The offences in s 63C(2) are murder, manslaughter, culpable homicide, rape, assault causing injury, assault to injury, kidnapping, abduction, false imprisonment, offences under s 4, 16, 18, 20, 21, 22, 23, 24, 28, 29, 30, or 64 of the Offences against the Person Act 1861, offences under s 1, 2, 3, 4, or 5(1) or (3) of the Forgery and Counterfeiting Act 1981, the uttering of a forged document or an offence under s 46A(1) of the Criminal Law (Consolidation) (Scotland) Act 1995.

[88] The offences in s 63D(2) are an offence under s 1 of the Criminal Damage Act 1971, an offence under Art 3 of the Criminal Damage (Northern Ireland) Order 1977, malicious mischief, wilful fire-raising.

[89] The offences in s 63D(4) are an offence under s 2 of the Criminal Damage Act 1971, an offence under Art 4 of the Criminal Damage (Northern Ireland) Order 1977, breach of the peace (in relation to Scotland only).

Section 63D(5) provides that 'relevant premises' means premises at which a protected person resides or is staying; or premises which a protected person uses for the purpose of carrying out his functions as such a person. **17.56**

For the purposes of ss 63A, 63B, and 63C a 'UK national' means an individual who is a British citizen; a British overseas territories citizen; a British National (Overseas); a British Overseas citizen; a person who under the British Nationality Act 1981 is a British subject; a British protected person within the meaning of the British Nationality Act 1981. A 'UK resident' means an individual who is resident in the UK. **17.57**

For the purposes of ss 63C and 63D a person is a protected person if he is a member of a UK diplomatic mission within the meaning of Article 1(b) of the Vienna Convention on Diplomatic Relations signed in 1961[90] (as that Article has effect in the UK by virtue of s 2 of and Sch 1 to the Diplomatic Privileges Act 1964); he is a member of a UK consular post within the meaning of Article 1(g) of the Vienna Convention on Consular Relations signed in 1963[91] (as that Article has effect in the UK by virtue of s 1 of and Sch 1 to the Consular Relations Act 1968); he carries out any functions for the purposes of the European Agency for the Evaluation of Medicinal Products, or he carries out any functions for the purposes of a body specified in an order made by the Secretary of State.[92] If, in any proceedings, a question arises as to whether a person is or was a protected person, a certificate issued by or under the authority of the Secretary of State, and stating any fact relating to the question, is to be conclusive evidence of that fact. **17.58**

Council Framework Decision 2001/413/JHA of 28 May 2001 on Combating Fraud and Counterfeiting non-cash means of Payment[93]

The aim of this Framework Decision is to ensure that all fraud involving non-cash means of payment is recognized as a criminal offence punishable by effective sanctions in all member States, and that mechanisms are put in place for cooperation between member States and between public and private departments or agencies to prosecute these offences efficiently. **17.59**

The Framework Decision requires member States to criminalize the misuse of specified 'payment instruments'.[94] Misuse includes theft, counterfeiting, receiving, fraudulent use, and possession. The UK's existing criminal law implements most of the Framework Decision, but ss 87 and 88 of CICA 2003 provide full compliance by incorporating the provisions of Article 2. **17.60**

European Evidence Warrant

On 19 January 2009 Council Framework Decision 2008/978/JHA of 18 December 2008 on the European evidence warrant for the purpose of obtaining objects, documents, and data for use in proceedings in criminal matters came into force ('EEW Framework Decision').[95] The EEW Framework Decision followed proposals put forward in 2003 by the European Commission to establish a mechanism to facilitate the obtaining of evidence in cross-border EU cases based on mutual recognition principles.[96] The EEW is obviously closely analogous to the EAW, considered in detail in Ch 15. **17.61**

---

90 United Nations Treaty Series, vol 500, p 95.

91 United Nations Treaty Series, vol 596, p 261.

92 s 63C(4) provides that the Secretary of State may specify a body under subs (3)(d) only if (a) it is established by or under the Treaty establishing the European Community or the Treaty on European Union, and (b) the principal place in which its functions are carried out is a place in the UK.

93 Official Journal L 140, 2 June 2001, p 1.

94 Art 2.

95 L 350/72, 30 December 2008.

96 2003/0270 (CNS), available at <http://www.eur-lex.europa.eu/LexUriServ/site/en/com/2003/com2003_0688en01.pdf>.

17.62 Article 1(1) of the EEW Framework Decision provides that an EEW is a judicial decision issued by a competent authority of a member State with a view to obtaining objects, documents, and data from another member State for the purposes of the proceedings specified in Article 5. Authorities competent to issue EEWs are a judge, a court, an investigating magistrate, a public prosecutor; or any other judicial authority as defined by the issuing state and, in the specific case, acting in its capacity as an investigating authority in criminal proceedings with competence to order the obtaining of evidence in cross-border cases in accordance with national law.[97] The competent authorities must be designated by the member States.[98] Member States must also designate the competent authorities for recognizing and executing the EEW.

17.63 Article 5 provides that the EEW may be issued for the following types of proceedings: criminal proceedings brought by or to be brought before a judicial authority for criminal offences under the national law of the issuing state; proceedings brought by administrative authorities for acts that are punishable under the law of the issuing state where the decision may give rise to court proceedings; proceedings brought by judicial authorities for acts that are punishable under the law of the issuing state where the decision may give rise to further court proceedings; all of these above, for offences for which the issuing state may punish or hold liable a legal person.

17.64 Article 4 provides that the EEW may not be issued with a view to requiring the executing authority to conduct interviews, take statements or initiate other types of hearings involving suspects, witnesses, experts, or any other party; carry out bodily examinations or obtain bodily material or biometric data directly from the body of any person, including DNA samples or fingerprints; obtain information in real time such as through the interception of communications, covert surveillance, or monitoring of bank accounts; conduct analysis of existing objects, documents, or data; and obtain communications data retained by providers of publicly available electronic communications service or a public communications network.

17.65 The issuing state must ensure that the evidence requested is necessary and proportionate for the proceedings. In addition, the acquisition of such evidence under similar circumstances in the issuing state must be provided for in its national law. Only once these conditions are met may the EEW be issued.[99]

17.66 When the competent authority of an issuing state has reasonable grounds to believe that relevant evidence is located on the territory of another member State, it may transmit the EEW to the competent authority of that state. The EEW must be transmitted directly from the issuing to the executing authority and in a manner that leaves a written record. To this end, member States may designate one or more central authorities that will assist the competent authorities. Member States may also take advantage of the secure telecommunications system of the European Judicial Network[100] for the transmission of EEWs.[101]

17.67 It is intended that the EEW be recognized by the executing authority without any further formality.[102] It is for the executing authority to choose and execute the necessary (and

---

[97] EEW Framework Decision, Article 2(c) and Article 2(d).

[98] EEW Framework Decision, Article 3.

[99] EEW Framework Decision, Article 7.

[100] The European Judicial Network (EJN) is a network of national contact points for the facilitation of judicial cooperation in criminal matters. The network was created by the Joint Action 98/428 JHA of 29 June 1998 in order to fulfil recommendation No 21 of the Action Plan to Combat Organised Crime adopted by the Council on 28 April 1997. From 24 December 2008, a new legal basis for the EJN came into force, namely Council Decision 2008/976/JHA of 16 December 2008 on the European Judicial Network. The EJN's website is <http://www.ejn-crimjust.europa.eu/ejn/>.

[101] EEW Framework Decision, Article 8.

[102] EEW Framework Decision, Article 11(1).

appropriate) measures under its law to execute the EEW,[103] unless it decides to invoke a ground for non-recognition, non-execution, or postponement. When the EEW has not been issued or validated by a judge, court, investigating magistrate, or public prosecutor, the executing authority may decide not to carry out a search or seizure to execute the warrant. However, it must consult the competent authority of the issuing state before taking such a decision. Member states may declare that they require such validation when the executing measures in a similar domestic case must be ordered or supervised by a judge, court, investigating magistrate, or public prosecutor under its law.

If not stipulated otherwise in the EEW Framework Decision, the executing authority shall comply with the formalities indicated by the issuing authority. However, these formalities may not contradict the fundamental principles of law of the executing state.[104] **17.68**

Articles 13 and 16 of the EEW Framework Decision provide for a number of grounds for non-execution or postponement of execution of an EEW. For example, the executing state may refuse to recognize or execute the EEW within 30 days of receiving it if: execution would breach the *ne bis in idem* principle; in certain cases specified in the EEW Framework Decision, the act is not an offence under its national law; execution is not possible with the measures available to the executing authority in the specific case; there is an immunity or privilege under the law of the executing state that makes its execution impossible; it has not been validated by a judge, court, investigative magistrate, or public prosecutor in the issuing state when so required; the offence was committed on the territory of the executing state or outside the issuing state where the law of the executing state does not allow for legal proceedings; it would harm national security interests; the form is incomplete or incorrectly completed. **17.69**

The recognition or execution of an EEW may only be subject to verification of double criminality if a search or seizure is required for its execution and if it is not related to the list of offences set out in Article 14(2) of the EEW Framework Decision.[105] If the EEW is not related to any of the offences set out in Article 14(2) and its execution would require a search or seizure, recognition, or execution of the EEW may be subject to the condition of double criminality.[106] In relation to offences in connection with taxes or duties, customs, and exchange, recognition or execution may not be opposed on the ground that the law of the executing state does not impose the same kind of tax or duty or does not contain a tax, duty, customs and exchange regulation of the same kind as the law of the issuing state.[107] **17.70**

---

[103] EEW Framework Decision, Article 11(2).

[104] EEW Framework Decision, Article 12.

[105] EEW Framework Decision, Article 14. These are: participation in a criminal organization; terrorism; trafficking in human beings; sexual exploitation of children and child pornography; illicit trafficking in narcotic drugs and psychotropic substances; illicit trafficking in weapons, munitions, and explosives; corruption; fraud, including that affecting the financial interests of the European Communities within the meaning of the Convention of 26 July 1995 on the protection of the European Communities' financial interests; laundering of the proceeds of crime; counterfeiting currency, including of the euro; computer-related crime; environmental crime, including illicit trafficking in endangered animal species and in endangered plant species and varieties; facilitation of unauthorized entry and residence; murder, grievous bodily injury, illicit trade in human organs and tissue; kidnapping, illegal restraint and hostage-taking; racism and xenophobia; organized or armed robbery; illicit trafficking in cultural goods, including antiques and works of art; swindling, racketeering, and extortion; counterfeiting and piracy of products; forgery of administrative documents and trafficking therein; forgery of means of payment; illicit trafficking in hormonal substances and other growth promoters; illicit trafficking in nuclear or radioactive materials; trafficking in stolen vehicles; rape; arson; crimes within the jurisdiction of the International Criminal Court; unlawful seizure of aircraft/ships; sabotage.

[106] EEW Framework Decision, Article 14(3).

[107] EEW Framework Decision, Article 14(3).

17.71 The executing state is required to take possession of the evidence within 60 days from receiving the EEW, unless there are grounds for postponement.[108]

17.72 Member states must ensure that all interested parties have access to legal remedies against the recognition and execution of an EEW. These remedies may be limited to cases where coercive measures are used. The actions are to be brought before a court in the executing state; however, the substantive reasons for issuing the EEW may only be brought before a court in the issuing state.[109]

17.73 The EEW Framework Decision excludes from the scope of the EEW evidence obtained from criminal suspects including interviews, bodily samples, DNA evidence, and the like. It also excludes procedural investigative measures which involve obtaining evidence in real time, such as interception of communications and monitoring of bank accounts. In its 2003 Proposal the Commission indicated that in due course it would put forward proposals for a second instrument to cover this type of evidence with the aim, eventually, of replacing the existing regime of mutual assistance within the EU by a single body of law based on the mutual recognition of judicial decisions and subject to minimum safeguards.[110]

17.74 Implementation of the EEW in the UK requires legislation. Although the deadline for implementation set by the EEW Framework Decision was 19 January 2011, at the time of writing (August 2012) there is no such legislation for England, Wales, or Northern Ireland. In relation to Scotland, the Criminal Justice and Licensing (Scotland) Act 2010, s 92, contains provisions enabling the EEW Framework Decision to be brought into force in Scotland by order of the Scottish Ministers. Section 92 is not currently in force.

17.75 Member states are currently discussing proposals for a new form of instrument, the European Investigation Order, because they believe that the existing framework for the gathering of evidence is too fragmented and complicated, and that a new approach is necessary.[111] The UK Government has signalled its intention to implement the EIO and consequently has suspended implementation of the EEW.[112] At the time of writing[113] the EIO is currently under discussion within the EU bodies.

Council Framework Decision 2005/214/JHA of 24 February 2005 on the application of the principle of mutual recognition to financial penalties

17.76 The Framework Decision on the application of the principle of mutual recognition to financial penalties will allow a competent authority to send, for execution, a financial penalty issued against a natural or legal person to a member State where the person has property, income, or is normally resident (or registered). Execution of the decision will occur without further formality unless one of the grounds for non-recognition is invoked. These grounds are: where the certificate accompanying the decision is incomplete; where a decision has already been made against the person for the same acts (*ne bis in idem*); where the principle of dual criminality applies; where execution is statute barred; where territoriality is an issue; where there is

---

108 EEW Framework Decision, Article 15(3).

109 EEW Framework Decision, Article 18.

110 2003/0270 (CNS), para 2.

111 Initiative of the Kingdom of Belgium, the Republic of Bulgaria, the Republic of Estonia, the Kingdom of Spain, the Republic of Austria, the Republic of Slovenia and the Kingdom of Sweden for a Directive of the European Parliament and of the Council regarding the European Investigation Order in criminal matters (COPEN 369, EUROJUST 217, EJN 185, CODEC 2509), 21 December 2011.

112 Hansard, 27 July 2010, cols 881–882.

113 September 2012.

immunity; where the person is under the age of criminal liability; where a decision was made *in absentia*; and where the fine is below €70.

A financial penalty in the context of the Framework Decision must be a final decision taken by either a judicial or administrative authority, provided there has been the possibility of appeal to a court. It covers both criminal offences and infringements of law and thus road traffic and health and safety offences, both of which have evidenced low levels of cross border enforcement, will be subject to mutual recognition. A list of offences, including infringements of road traffic regulations, has been drawn up for which the dual criminality rule does not apply. Finally, where the executing state is unable to enforce the penalty it may apply an alternative sanction to that requested, where the issuing state allows it. **17.77**

Agreement on Mutual Legal Assistance between the EU and the United States of America

On 20 September 2001, in the aftermath of the terrorist attacks in New York and Washington DC, the EU's Justice and Home Affairs Council called for the adoption of measures aimed at enhancing cooperation in criminal matters including mutual assistance arrangements between the EU and the United States of America. **17.78**

The Agreement on Mutual Legal Assistance between the EU and the United States was signed on 25 June 2003[114] and enters into force three months after contracting parties have exchanged instruments of ratification.[115] The basis in EU law for the Agreement is Articles 24 and 38 of the Treaty on European Union,[116] which enables the negotiation of international agreements in third pillar matters by the Council on a recommendation by the Presidency.[117] **17.79**

Although initial impetus for the Agreement was the events of 11 September 2001, it goes further than addressing mutual legal assistance merely in relation to terrorism and organized crime.[118] **17.80**

In summary, the Agreement gives United States law enforcement authorities access to bank accounts throughout the EU (and vice versa) in the context of investigations into serious crimes, including terrorism, organized crime, and financial crime. It is intended to improve practical cooperation by reducing delays in mutual legal assistance and also allows for the creation of joint investigative teams and the possibility of videoconferencing. It also contains extensive provisions in relation to data protection and the provision of evidence and information. **17.81**

The Agreement is not intended to be a substitute for existing bilateral arrangements between the United States and member States but is intended to supplement them.[119] Thus, the Agreement does not preclude the conclusion of bilateral Agreements between a member State and the United States provided they are consistent with the Agreement.[120] However, those member States which do not have bilateral mutual assistances treaties with the United States must apply **17.82**

---

114 Official Journal L 181, 19 July 2003, p 34, referred to in this section as 'the Agreement'. cf the Agreement on Extradition between the EU and the United States of America, Official Journal L181, 19 July 2003, p 27.

115 Art 18. Instruments of ratification were exchanged in October 2009 and the Agreement came into force in February 2010.

116 Art 24 is contained in Title V 'Provisions on a common foreign and security policy' and Art 38 is contained in Title VI 'Provisions on police and judicial co-operation in criminal matters'. Both articles are entitled 'Conclusion of agreements with non-member states and international bodies' and enable the EU to negotiate treaties with foreign states.

117 In 2009 the EU and Japan signed the Agreement between the EU and Japan on mutual legal assistance in criminal matters, Official Journal, L39/20, 12 February 2010.

118 See, for example, Art 4(4)(a).

119 Art 3(1).

120 Art 14.

the provisions of the Agreement as between themselves and the United States.[121] It is drafted to allow member States to continue to apply their grounds for refusal under the bilateral MLA treaties or legal principles of domestic law. Also, member States that at present do not have a MLA treaty with the United States may rely on their *ordre public* (security, sovereignty, or their other essential interests) in order to refuse to communicate information in certain cases.

17.83 The contracting parties to the Agreement are the EU and the United States.[122] The Agreement applies to the United States and member States.[123] States which accede to the EU after the Agreement comes into force are under an obligation to give effect to it.[124]

17.84 The Agreement applies to all offences irrespective of when they were committed and, in particular, whether they were committed before or after the Agreement entered into force.[125] The Agreement only applies to requests for assistance made after its entry into force. However, Articles 6 and 7 (videoconferencing and expedition) apply to requests pending in a requested State at the time the Agreement enters into force.[126]

17.85 Article 3 provides that the EU and the United States shall ensure that the provisions of the Agreement are applied in relation to bilateral MLA treaties between the member States and the United States, in force at the time of the entry into force of the Agreement. In particular:

- Article 4 is to be applied to provide for identification of financial accounts and transactions in addition to any authority already provided under bilateral treaty provisions;
- Article 5 is to be applied to authorize the formation and activities of joint investigative teams in addition to any authority already provided under bilateral treaty provisions;
- Article 6 is to be applied to authorize the taking of testimony of a person located in the requested state by use of videotechnology, in addition to any authority already provided under bilateral treaty provisions;
- Article 7 shall be applied to provide for the use of expedited means of communication in addition to any authority already provided under bilateral treaty provisions;
- Article 8 shall be applied to authorize the providing of MLA to the administrative authorities concerned, in addition to any authority already provided under bilateral treaty provisions;
- Article 9 shall, subject to Article 9(4) and (5), be applied in place of, or in the absence of bilateral treaty provisions governing limitations on use of information or evidence provided to the requesting state, and governing the conditioning or refusal of assistance on data protection grounds;
- Article 10 shall be applied in the absence of bilateral treaty provisions pertaining to the circumstances under which a requesting state may seek the confidentiality of its request.

17.86 Under Article 4 (a) and (b) a request for assistance may be made to identify whether a person identified in the request and suspected of, or charged with, a criminal offence holds bank accounts in the requested country's territory; to identify information regarding natural or legal persons convicted of or otherwise involved in a criminal offence; to identify information in the possession of non-bank financial institutions; or to identify financial transactions unrelated to accounts.

---

121 Art 3(3)(a).

122 Art 2(1).

123 Including territories for whose external relations a member State has responsibility, or countries that are not member States for whom a member State has other duties with respect to external relations, where agreed upon by exchange of diplomatic note between the contracting parties, duly confirmed by the relevant member State: Art 16(1).

124 Art 3(2)(b) and (c).

125 Art 12(1).

126 Art 12(2).

The scope of information covered in the Agreement is broader than offences relating to terrorism and organized crime, and could cover a wide range of information about genuine legitimate everyday transactions of innocent third parties.[127] The term 'otherwise involved in a criminal offence' in Article 4 does not specify whether a person must be under criminal investigation before information about him can be transmitted. For example, an innocent third party who is the victim of money laundering without their knowledge could be described as 'involved in a criminal offence' and his everyday account transaction information transmitted for the purpose of a US request.[128] **17.87**

Article 5 provides for joint investigative teams from the United States and a member State. These can be established and operated for the purpose of facilitating criminal investigations or prosecutions involving one or more member State and the United States. The procedure under which the team is to operate, such as its composition, duration, location, organization, functions, purpose, and terms of participation are to be agreed between the competent authorities responsible for the investigation or prosecution of criminal offences, as determined by the respective states concerned. **17.88**

Article 6 of the Agreement requires parties to enable the use of video technology for taking the testimony of a witness in proceedings for which MLA is available. The cost of establishing and servicing the transmission is borne by the requesting state. **17.89**

Article 8 of the Agreement provides that MLA shall be afforded 'to a national administrative authority, investigating conduct with a view to a criminal prosecution of the conduct, or referral of the conduct to criminal investigation or prosecution authorities, pursuant to its specific administrative or regulatory authority to undertake such investigation'. The government confirmed that assistance will not be provided if the requesting authority does not have proper competence in criminal matters.[129] **17.90**

The Group of Eight

The Group of Eight (G8) is a forum for the governments of eight of the world's largest economies.[130] The forum originated with a 1975 summit hosted by France that brought together representatives of six governments: France; Germany; Italy; Japan; the UK; and the United States, thus leading to the name Group of Six or G6. The summit became known as the Group of Seven or G7 the following year with the addition of Canada. In 1997, Russia was added to group which then became known as the G8. The EU is represented within the G8 but cannot host or chair summits. **17.91**

In 2011 the UN published *Requesting mutual legal assistance in criminal matters from G8 countries: A step-by-step guide.*[131] Insofar as the guide provides a practical outline of each G8 country's MLA requirements, it is complementary to existing, and more comprehensive, tools on MLA, namely the functional *Mutual Legal Assistance Writer Tool* of the UN Office on Drugs and Crime[132] and the G8's *Judicial Cooperation Handbook*. The UN Office on Drugs and **17.92**

---

[127] Session 2002–2003, 38th Report of the House of Lords Select Committee on the European Union, HL Paper 153.

[128] In Parliament the Minister of State indicated that the Government would require 'some assurance that there was an actual investigation going on': see the Session 2002–2003, 38th Report of the House of Lords Select Committee on the European Union, HL Paper 153.

[129] Session 2002–2003, 38th Report of the House of Lords Select Committee on the European Union, HL Paper 153, p 14.

[130] Although it actually excludes two of the actual eight largest economies by nominal GDP, namely China (2nd) and Brazil (6th).

[131] Published as a UN document: E/CN.15/2011/CRP.6.

[132] Available to registered users through <http://www.unodc.org>.

Crime has also published the *Manual on International Cooperation in Criminal Matters related to Terrorism*.[133]

Relationship between international agreements on mutual assistance and domestic legislation

17.93 In the UK, the provision of assistance to other states initially developed in connection with civil and commercial matters. The Foreign Tribunals Evidence Act 1856[134] allowed for the examination of witnesses in Great Britain and the production of 'writings or other documents' for civil matters pending before a foreign tribunal. The Act required the diplomatic agent of the foreign state to certify an application for assistance, which was then sent to the foreign court or judge having authority as provided for in s 6 of the Act. A person subject to an order made under the Act had the right to refuse to answer questions where to do so might incriminate him.[135] He also had the right not to produce documents that he could not be compelled to produce in ordinary domestic litigation.[136]

17.94 A rare example (for the time) of a provision dealing with assistance in criminal cases was s 24 of the Extradition Act 1870, which applied the Foreign Tribunals Evidence Act 1856 to criminal cases. Section 24 provided:

> … all the provisions of [the Foreign Tribunals Evidence Act 1856] shall be construed as if the term civil matter included a criminal matter, and the term cause included a proceeding against a criminal: provided that nothing in this section shall apply in the case of any criminal matter of a political character.

17.95 Domestic legislation in the field of mutual assistance in criminal matters has developed considerably from these rudimentary beginnings. To a large extent this development has been driven by MLA treaties and other international agreements described above. These instruments required the UK to amend its laws so to enable it to honour its international obligations.

17.96 Unlike in respect of extradition, where a treaty or other international arrangement is generally required,[137] the UK is able to entertain requests for mutual assistance even in the absence of a treaty arrangement.[138] Thus, domestic mutual assistance legislation does not require the existence of a treaty as a pre-condition for the granting of mutual assistance. The UK is able, in general, to offer assistance to any state irrespective of whether or not an international agreement or treaty is in place.

17.97 Mutual legal assistance treaties have a dual role to play in the mutual assistance process. First, they can be used as an aid to the interpretation of relevant legislation. In particular, parts of the CICA 2003 give effect to international agreements and Framework decisions, and this domestic law giving effect to them.[139] Secondly, the Secretary of State and the court may take into account treaty provisions when considering the extent to which assistance should be granted under the CICA 2003 or other legislation.[140]

[133] Available through <http://www.unodc.org>.

[134] 19 and 20 Vic c 113; repealed by Evidence (Proceedings in Other Jurisdictions) Act 1975.

[135] s 4(1).

[136] s 4(2).

[137] Para 1.04.

[138] MLA Guidelines, pp 761–762 (Appendix M3).

[139] *Assange v Swedish Prosecution Authority* [2012] 2 WLR 1275.

[140] *R v Secretary of State ex p Fininvest Spa* [1997] 1 WLR 743, 758; cf *R (Corner House Research) v Director of the Serious Fraud Office [2009]* 1 AC 756, paras 59–62.

C. UK Mutual Assistance Legislation in Outline

Crime (International Co-operation) Act 2003

The long title of the CICA 2003 is: **17.98**

> An Act to make provision for furthering co-operation with other countries in respect of criminal proceedings and investigations; to extend jurisdiction to deal with terrorist acts or threats outside the United Kingdom; to amend section 5 of the Forgery and Counterfeiting Act 1981 and make corresponding provision in relation to Scotland; and for connected purposes.

Part 1 of CICA 2003 largely replaces the UK's MLA legislation, contained in Part 1 of the Criminal Justice (International Co-operation) Act 1990, which enabled the UK to request and provide assistance to all countries. The 1990 Act came into force in 1991 and enabled the UK to ratify the European Convention on Mutual Assistance in Criminal Matters. It contained new powers which enabled the UK to assist, and seek assistance from, foreign states in relation to criminal law matters in a number of ways. These included the service of process; the taking of evidence in the UK before a nominated court; the use of search and seizure powers at the request of foreign states; and the transfer of prisoners for the purposes of giving evidence. **17.99**

The greater part of the Criminal Justice (International Co-operation) Act 1990 was repealed by CICA 2003. Sections 5 and 6 (transfer of prisoners) of the 1990 Act remain in force. **17.100**

The structure of CICA 2003 is as follows: **17.101**

Part 1 is entitled 'Mutual Assistance in Criminal Matters'. It re-enacts the mutual assistance provisions of the Criminal Justice (International Co-operation) Act 1990. It also implements the mutual legal assistance provisions of the Schengen Convention;[141] the Convention on Mutual Assistance in Criminal Matters 2000;[142] and the evidence-freezing provisions of the Council Framework Decision 2003/577/JHA of 22 July 2003.[143] Chapter 4 of Part 1 implements the 2001 Protocol to the Convention on Mutual Assistance in Criminal Matters[144] which creates obligations for participating countries to respond to requests for assistance with locating banking accounts and to provide banking information relating to criminal investigations.

Sections 1–6 deal with the service of domestic and overseas process (for example, a witness summons or a summons to attend as a defendant).[145] Sections 7–9 enable UK prosecuting authorities to send letters of request seeking assistance in obtaining evidence abroad.[146] Sections 10–12 deal with domestic freezing orders for protecting evidence in a participating country pending its transfer to the UK.[147] Sections 13–19 contain powers allowing evidence located in the UK to be obtained at the request of a foreign state.[148] Sections 20–28 deal with overseas freezing orders relating to evidence located in the UK.[149] Sections 29–31 govern evidence by television link.[150] Sections 32–46 contain powers allowing foreign states to request information about UK banking

[141] Para 17.25.
[142] Para 17.37.
[143] Para 17.42.
[144] Para 17.37.
[145] Ch 22.
[146] Ch 18.
[147] Para 18.41.
[148] Ch 19.
[149] Para 19.140.
[150] Paras 18.37 and 19.127.

transactions and for the UK to make requests for information about overseas banking transactions to be transmitted to the UK.[151] Sections 47 and 48 govern the transfer of UK prisoners abroad to assist UK investigations and deals with requests from abroad to the same effect.

Part 2 is entitled 'Terrorist Acts and Threats: Jurisdiction'. It implements the Framework Decision on Combating Terrorism, including the provisions relating to extra-territorial jurisdiction in respect of listed offences, in ss 52 and 53.[152]

Part 3 is entitled 'Road Traffic' and it contains new provisions implementing the Convention on Driving Disqualifications (ss 54–75) and provides for the mutual recognition of driving disqualifications within the UK (ss 76–79).[153]

Part 4 contains miscellaneous provisions.

There are also a number of Schedules.

Commencement

17.102 Different parts of CICA 2003 have come into force at different times, and parts of it are not in force at the time of writing (August 2012).[154] The Crime (International Co-operation) Act 2003 (Savings) Order 2004[155] contains detailed savings and transitional provisions.

Proceeds of Crime 2002 (External Requests and Orders) Order 2005[156]

17.103 The Proceeds of Crime Act 2002 (External Requests and Orders) Order 2005 (the POCA Order) has been made under the Proceeds of Crime Act 2002. It enables the UK to restrain assets at the request of foreign states and also to enforce external confiscation orders. It also provides the machinery whereby foreign states can utilize civil restraint powers akin to those contained in Part 5 of the Proceeds of Crime Act 2002.

17.104 The POCA Order is considered in detail in Chapter 25.

D. The UK Central Authority

17.105 The term 'central authority' refers to the department or body within a jurisdiction which acts as a central point for the transmission of incoming and outgoing requests for MLA in criminal matters and also the product of those requests. This form of transmission of requests between central authorities is known as 'indirect transmission' and is the method of transmission adopted by the UK to deal with requests from overseas authorities for assistance obtaining evidence located in the UK.[157] CICA 2003 also allows for the direct transmission of requests and evidence from the UK directly to the foreign judicial authority in certain situations.[158]

17.106 Responsibility for mutual assistance in criminal matters in England, Wales, and Northern Ireland lies with the Secretary of State for the Home Department. His/her functions under the

151 Paras 18.54 and 19.159.

152 Para 17.45.

153 Ch 23.

154 Crime (International Co-operation) Act 2003 (Commencement No 1) Order 2004 (SI 2004/786); Crime (International Co-operation) Act 2003 (Commencement No 2) Order 2004 (SI 2004/2624); Crime (International Co-operation) Act 2003 (Commencement No 3) Order 2006 (SI 2006/2811); Crime (International Co-operation) Act 2003 (Commencement No 4) Order 2008 (SI 2008/3009); Crime (International Co-operation) Act 2003 (Commencement No 5) Order 2009 (SI 2009/2605).

155 SI 2004/787.

156 SI 2005/3181.

157 CICA 2003, s 13.

158 CICA 2003, ss 7 and 8.

legislation are, in practice, exercised by the UK Central Authority, which is part of the Home Office's Judicial Cooperation Unit. The address of the UK Central Authority is:

United Kingdom Central Authority
Judicial Cooperation Unit
Home Office
5th Floor, Fry Building
2 Marsham Street
London SW1P 4DF
Tel: +44 207 035 4040
Fax: +44 207 035 6985 (urgent cases only)

The UK Central Authority's role in the MLA process includes: **17.107**

- ensuring that requests for legal assistance conform with the requirements of law in the relevant part of the UK and the UK's international obligations;
- ensuring that execution of requests is not inappropriate on public policy grounds (for example, requests involving double jeopardy will not be executed);
- deciding how requests might most appropriately be executed (for example, some requests asking for search and seizure of evidence may be executed effectively by a witness producing the evidence to a court);
- maintaining confidentiality of requests where necessary;
- ensuring, so far as possible, that assistance is provided within an appropriate time scale (for example, taking account of trial dates);
- drawing to the attention of the courts, the police, and other UK authorities or agencies requests for evidence to be obtained in the presence of foreign law enforcement officers, prosecutors or defence lawyers;
- seeking requesting authorities' agreement to meet extraordinary costs of executing requests and for services such as interpreters or stenographers or for duplication of documents. (Ordinarily, the UK authorities, in accordance with established international practice will meet costs, with the exception of TV/video link evidence);
- transmitting evidence received to the requesting authorities when it is not returned directly (and checking whether any part of the request remains outstanding).

The UK Central Authority also publishes the Mutual Legal Assistance Guidelines for the United Kingdom ('the MLA Guidelines').[159] The MLA Guidelines are essential reading for anyone wishing to seek MLA to or from the UK. The MLA Guidelines are contained at Appendix M3. Home Office Circular 023/2004, *Mutual Legal Assistance: Part 1 of the Crime (International Co-operation) Act 2003*, also contains a useful summary of some of the practical aspects of MLA in the UK. **17.108**

The UK Central Authority does not have responsibility for judicial cooperation with Scotland, the Channel Islands, the Isle of Man, or the British overseas territories. Relevant contact points for these countries and territories are listed in the MLA Guidelines. **17.109**

E. The Serious Organised Crime Agency[160]

Not all mutual cooperation in the investigation of crime requires the involvement of the UK Central Authority or other central authority. Although requests which require the UK **17.110**

[159] 10th edn, Home Office, September 2012 ('the MLA Guidelines'), Appendix M3. The MLA Guidelines are also available at <http://www.homeoffice.gov.uk/police/mutual-legal-assistance/>.

[160] Part 1 of the Crime and Courts Bill, introduced into Parliament in May 2012, will, if enacted, abolish SOCA and replace it by a new agency, the National Crime Agency.

to provide formal legal assistance in the form of search warrants, and so on, must in general be sent to the UK Central Authority for processing in accordance with the CICA 2003 or other legislation, where more informal investigative assistance is required then the authorities of the foreign state may approach the UK directly via Interpol with a request to provide assistance.[161]

17.111 The Serious Organised Crime and Police Act 2005 (SOCPA) created new law enforcement powers and established a new agency, the Serious Organised Crime Agency (SOCA).[162] SOCA commenced work on 1 April 2006 and replaced the National Criminal Intelligence Service and the National Crime Squad.[163] It also takes over the investigative work formerly undertaken by the Revenue and Customs in so far as it relates to revenue fraud, subject to the agreement of the Commissioners for Her Majesty's Revenue and Customs.[164]

17.112 At present, SOCA oversees the investigation of serious crime including drug-trafficking; organized immigration crime; money laundering; identity fraud; and revenue fraud. SOCA gathers, stores, analyses, and disseminates information relevant to the prevention, detection, investigation, or prosecution of offences, or the reduction of crime in other ways or the mitigation of its consequences.[165] SOCA can disseminate information to law enforcement agencies,[166] and such other persons as it considers appropriate in connection with its functions in relation to serious crime.[167]

17.113 SOCA has a number of wide-ranging new powers including the power to compel individuals to answer questions in interviews with prosecutors and produce documents on demand; and the power to plea-bargain with informants and convicted offenders. It also has enhanced confiscation powers in respect of proceeds of crime investigations.

17.114 SOCA also has an important role to play in mutual assistance matters. It is the UK National Central Bureau of Interpol[168] and the UK Liaison Bureau for Europol.[169] It has primary responsibility for processing requests for investigative help from overseas. Section 5(5) of the Serious Organised Crime and Police Act 2005 provides:

> SOCA may furnish such assistance as it considers appropriate in response to requests made by any government or other body exercising functions of a public nature in any country or territory outside the United Kingdom.[170]

---

[161] Eg, the Convention on Mutual Assistance in Criminal Matters, Art 7, which is headed 'Spontaneous exchange of information' provides: 'Within the limits of their national law, the competent authorities of the Member States may exchange information, without a request to that effect, relating to criminal offences and the infringements of rules of law referred to in Article 3(1), the punishment or handling of which falls within the competence of the receiving authority at the time the information is provided.'

[162] SOCPA, s 1(1).

[163] SOCPA, s 1(3); NCIS and NCS (Abolition) Order 2006 (SI 2006/540).

[164] SOCPA, s 2(4).

[165] SOCPA, s 3(1)(a) and (b).

[166] Defined by SOCPA, s 3(2)(d), to include 'any other person who is engaged outside the United Kingdom in the carrying on of activities similar to any carried on by SOCA or a police force'.

[167] SOCPA, s 3(2)(d).

[168] MLA Guidelines, App M3, p 785. See para 21.60.

[169] Para 21.60.

[170] Note, however, CICA 2003, s 5(6), which provides that s 5(5) does not apply to any request for assistance which could be made under s 13 (requests by overseas authorities to obtain evidence), and which is not a request in relation to which SOCA has functions under s 13 by virtue of an order under s 27(2) (general power of Secretary of State to delegate his functions to a designated body).

Examples of requests that may be submitted directly to SOCA without involving the UK Central Authority include requests for:[171] **17.115**

- interviewing witnesses or suspects in criminal investigations where the person to be interviewed is willing to cooperate without appearing or needing to appear before a judicial authority in the UK;
- sharing of information and intelligence concerning investigations into offences which have been committed in the UK (provided that the information or intelligence is not being requested for use in proceedings);
- asset tracing enquiries;
- providing details of previous convictions;
- providing, for investigative purposes, details of UK telephone subscribers;
- providing details of keepers of motor vehicles registered in the UK and of driving licences issued in the UK;
- obtaining medical or dental statements or records where the patient has given written consent;
- obtaining information from publicly available sources, such as, for example, the Land Register in relation to ownership of properties.

Requests of this nature for investigative assistance do not have to be sent to the UK Central Authority unless it is a requirement of the foreign authority making the request. Requests for both legal assistance and for investigative assistance can be sent both to the UK Central Authority and SOCA. They will jointly coordinate the execution of the request. Any such requests should be clearly marked to show the request had been submitted to both authorities. **17.116**

F. Letters of Request and *Commissions Rogatoires*

The terms 'letter of request' and 'letters rogatory' (or *commissions rogatoires*) both refer to the formal document sent from one state to another in order to seek MLA. Strictly speaking, a *commission rogatoire* is a document issued by a judicial authority of one state to a foreign judicial authority seeking its assistance in a specified manner, however in the UK the two terms have acquired a virtually synonymous meaning.[172] Although the term 'letters rogatory' is used in Chapter II of the European Convention on Mutual Assistance in Criminal Matters 1959[173] later instruments simply refer to a 'request' or 'letter of request', and those are the terms which will be used in this book. **17.117**

However, whilst they perform the same essential function, there is a practical distinction between a letter of request and a *commission rogatoire*. An earlier edition of the MLA Guidelines gave the following guidance in relation to requests from the UK under the heading '*Commission rogatoire* or Letter of Request'.[174] **17.118**

> The two documents are the same but it is important to use the correct title. *Commissions Rogatoires* are used for Civil Code jurisdictions and Letters of Request are appropriate for Common law jurisdictions. It is important in relation to *Commissions Rogatoires* that

[171] MLA Guidelines, App M3, p 776–777.
[172] D McClean, *International Cooperation in Civil and Criminal Matters* (2002), p 176.
[173] ETS No 030.
[174] See the 2nd edn of this work, App M3, p757.

'International' is left in the title as in some jurisdictions Magistrates within the same state send each other *Commissions Rogatoires* for evidence. The Civil Code system is normally based on territorial jurisdiction eg a Magistrate in the 1st arrondissement in Paris has no jurisdiction to collect evidence in Lyon and would therefore have to transmit a *commission rogatoire* to his colleague there to request the collection of relevant evidence. Letters of request are appropriate for Common law jurisdictions.

18

UK REQUESTS TO FOREIGN STATES FOR ASSISTANCE

This chapter examines the means by which UK prosecuting authorities and criminal defendants can seek the assistance of foreign authorities in relation to criminal investigations and proceedings in the UK. The majority of the relevant powers are contained in Part 1 of CICA 2003. **18.01**

A. Requests to Foreign States for Assistance in Obtaining Evidence

CICA 2003, ss 7–9, deal with requests to obtain evidence from abroad in relation to a prosecution or investigation taking place in the UK. These provisions develop and expand on s 3 of the Criminal Justice (International Co-operation) Act 1990, which they replace.[1] **18.02**

[1] On 18 December 2008 the Council of the EU adopted Council Framework Decision 2008/978/JHA on the European Evidence Warrant for the purpose of obtaining objects, documents, and data for use in proceedings in criminal matters (L350/72, 30 December 2008). The EEW will in due course be replaced by the European Investigation Order. The text of the EIO is Council of Europe document COPEN 117, EUROJUST 49, EJN 13, PARLNAT 13, CODEC 384. The goal of this measure, which was an initiative of seven member States presented in April 2010, is to allow member States to carry out investigative measures at the request of another member State on the basis of mutual recognition. The investigative measures would, for example, include interviewing of witnesses, searches and seizures, and (with additional safeguards) interception of telecommunications, observation, infiltration, and monitoring of bank accounts. The UK Government has signalled its intention to implement the EIO (Hansard, 27 July 2010, cols 881–882) and consequently has suspended implementation of the EEW. The EIO is currently (September 2012) under discussion within the EU bodies. See generally, Cian C Murphy, *The European Evidence Warrant: Mutual Recognition and Mutual (Dis)Trust? Crime within the area of Freedom, Security and Justice: A European Public Order*, Eckes, Konstadinides (eds), Cambridge University Press, 2011.

Persons able to request assistance

Requests by a judicial authority on the application of a prosecuting authority or the defendant

18.03 Both prosecutors and defendants may ask a court to make a request to a foreign state for assistance in obtaining evidence. Section 7(1) provides that if it appears to a judicial authority[2] in the UK on an application made by a person mentioned in s 7(3) that an offence has been committed or that there are reasonable grounds for suspecting that an offence has been committed, and that proceedings in respect of the offence have been instituted or that the offence is being investigated, the judicial authority may request assistance under s 7. The assistance that may be requested is assistance in obtaining outside the UK any evidence specified in the request for use in the proceedings or investigation (s 7(2)).

18.04 Section 7(3) provides that the application may be made in relation to England and Wales and Northern Ireland, by a prosecuting authority[3] and, where proceedings have been instituted, by the person charged in those proceedings.[4]

18.05 It is important to emphasize that by virtue of s 7(3)(c) the defendant may apply to a judicial authority for a request for assistance only if proceedings have been instituted. Therefore it is not possible for a person charged to seek discovery from a foreign country in the hope of dissuading the prosecuting authority in the UK from instituting proceedings. If proceedings have been instituted, and the person charged applies for a request for assistance, the court should exercise its discretion in favour of issuing the letter unless there are good reasons for not doing so.[5]

Direct requests for assistance by prosecuting authorities

18.06 Prosecuting agencies are also able to make requests for assistance directly to the foreign state if they have been designated in an order by the Secretary of State. Section 7(5) provides that in relation to England and Wales or Northern Ireland, a designated prosecuting authority may itself request assistance under s 7 if it appears to the authority that an offence has been committed or that there are reasonable grounds for suspecting that an offence has been committed, and the authority has instituted proceedings in respect of the offence in question or it is being investigated.

18.07 The following prosecuting authorities have been designated in the Crime (International Co-operation) Act 2003 (Designation of Prosecuting Authorities) Order 2004[6] for the purposes of s 7 and are thus able to make requests for assistance directly to foreign authorities:

> The Attorney General for England and Wales; the Attorney General for Northern Ireland; the Financial Services Authority; the Director of Public Prosecutions and any Crown Prosecutor; the Director of Public Prosecutions for Northern Ireland; the Director of Revenue and Customs Prosecutions and any person designated under s 37(1) of the Commissioners for Revenue and Customs Act 2005; the Director of the Serious Fraud

---

[2] s 7(4) defines judicial authority, in relation to England and Wales, to be any judge or justice of the peace; in relation to Scotland, any judge of the High Court or sheriff; in relation to Northern Ireland, any judge or resident magistrate.

[3] In relation to Scotland, by the Lord Advocate or a procurator fiscal (s 7(3)(b)).

[4] In relation to confidentiality, the UK Central Authority does not disclose letters of request to the prosecution. However, the possibility that the foreign authority will do so, or will supply any evidence gathered pursuant to the request to the prosecution, cannot be ruled out. Defence letters of request should always make clear that the material sought is confidential to the defence.

[5] *R v Forsyth (Elizabeth)* [1997] 2 Cr App R 299, 231.

[6] SI 2004/1034, as amended.

Office and any person designated under s 1(7) of the Criminal Justice Act 1987; the Environment Agency; the Secretary of State for Business, Innovation and Skills; the Secretary of State for Health; the Secretary of State for Transport; and the Secretary of State for Work and Pensions.

Section 7(7) provides that if a request for assistance under s 7 is made in reliance on Article 2 of the 2001 Protocol[7] to the Convention on Mutual Legal Assistance[8] (requests for information on banking transactions) in connection with the investigation of an offence, the request must state the grounds on which the person making the request considers the evidence specified in it to be relevant for the purposes of the investigation.[9] **18.08**

Meaning of 'evidence'

Section 7(2) refers to the request being for 'evidence ... for use in the proceedings or investigation'. Section 51(1) provides that 'evidence' includes 'information in any form and articles, and giving evidence includes answering a question or producing any information or article'. Thus the request for assistance need not be for admissible evidence. In *R v Secretary of State ex p Fininvest Spa* [1997] 1 WLR 743, 752 Simon Brown LJ considered the meaning of 'evidence' in s 4 of the Criminal Justice (International Co-operation) Act 1990 and his reasoning is consistent with the broad definition in s 51 of CICA 2003: **18.09**

> Inevitably there is some flexibility in the whole concept of evidence ... When, therefore, one is speaking of 'evidence' in the context of a criminal investigation, the permissible area of search must inevitably be wider than once that investigation is complete and the prosecution's concern is rather to prove an already investigated and 'instituted' offence.[10]

Letters of request in extradition proceedings

The wording of s 7(1) leaves open the question of whether a court can issue a letter of request in extradition proceedings. Whilst, obviously, it would be open to a prosecution agency to issue a letter of request if, as sometimes happens, a domestic investigation into the offence has been commenced, on occasion the defendant in extradition proceedings wishes to seek material from abroad to assist in his defence. There is, as yet, no authority directly on point, however it is probable that the court will incline to the view that s 7 does not extend to extradition proceedings. **18.10**

The court's power to issue a letter of request under s 7 depends upon reading the word 'proceedings' in s 7(3)(c) as including extradition proceedings, and the word 'offence' in s 7(1) as including a foreign offence, and regarding a defendant in extradition as having been 'charged' under foreign law. Whilst it is possible to read 'proceedings' as including extradition proceedings because extradition proceedings are criminal in nature,[11] a number of cases have held that **18.11**

---

7 Official Journal C 326, 21 November 2001, p 1; para 17.37. Art 2(1) provides: 'On request by the requesting State, the requested State shall provide the particulars of specified bank accounts and of banking operations which have been carried out during a specified period through one or more accounts specified in the request, including the particulars of any sending or recipient account.'

8 Official Journal 197, 12 July 2000, p 3.

9 cf Art 2(4) of the 2001 Protocol.

10 *R (JP Morgan Chase Bank National Association) v Director of the Serious Fraud Office* [2012] EWHC 1674 (Admin), para 29.

11 *R (Government of the United States of America v Senior District Judge*, Bow Street Magistrates' Court [2006] EWHC 2256 (Admin), para 76; *R v Governor of Brixton Prison ex p Levin* [1997] AC 741, 746. s 51(1) provides that 'criminal proceedings' in CICA 2003 'include criminal proceedings outside the United Kingdom in which a civil order may be made'.

where a statute uses the word 'offence' in an offence-creating section it is not to be interpreted as criminalizing conduct taking place outside the territory of the UK.[12] Whilst s 7 is not an offence-creating section, these authorities were applied in the context of the Criminal Justice (International Co-operation) Act 1990 to limit the meaning of 'offence' in that Act to domestic offences.[13]

18.12 The point was raised but not determined in *Cuoghi v Governor of Brixton Prison*.[14] Forbes J issued a letter of request under s 3 of the Criminal Justice (International Co-operation) Act 1990 at C's request because he wanted to use the evidence in *habeas corpus* proceedings under the Extradition Act 1989. Carnwath J set aside the letter of request on the application of the Government of Switzerland on the grounds that there was no jurisdiction to issue a letter of request in relation to a foreign offence. Hirst LJ granted leave to appeal, saying that the defendant's contentions were 'just arguable',[15] however the appeal was ultimately dismissed by Court of Appeal for want of jurisdiction and so the point was not determined.[16]

Procedure for obtaining a letter of request from a judicial authority[17]

18.13 The application for a letter of request should be made to the court seized of the matter. Therefore once the case has been committed, transferred, or sent to the Crown Court the application should be made to that court.

18.14 The application should contain particulars of the offence which it is alleged has been committed or the grounds upon which it is suspected that an offence has been committed; a statement of whether proceedings in respect of the offence have been instituted or the offence is being investigated; and particulars of the assistance requested in the form of a draft letter of request.

Contents of the letter of request[18]

18.15 There are no statutory provisions prescribing the contents of a letter of request,[19] but in order to be effective the letter of request must be as specific as possible about the circumstances of the case and the assistance required. The requested state will almost certainly know little about the case save what is contained in the letter of request and it is therefore necessary to explain as much about the case as possible and to indicate precisely what assistance is required.

18.16 The MLA Guidelines[20] contain detailed guidance on the contents of the letter of request for incoming and outgoing requests. All relevant information must be included, and this will vary

---

[12] *Cox v Army Council* [1963] AC 48, 67; *Air India v Wiggins* [1980] 1 WLR 815, 819.

[13] *R v Southwark Crown Court ex p Sorsky Defries* [1996] Crim L Rev 195; *R (Rottman) v Commissioner of Police for the Metropolis* [2002] 2 AC 692.

[14] *Cuoghi v Governor of Brixton Prison* [1997] 1 WLR 1346.

[15] *Cuoghi v Governor of Brixton Prison*, 26 March 1997.

[16] Where the proceedings are in the High Court, the Court has power to issue letters of request under CPR 34.13.

[17] MLA Guidelines, App M3, p 775.

[18] The UN's publication, *Requesting mutual legal assistance in criminal matters from G8 countries: A step-by-step guide*, April 2011 (E/CN.15/2011/CRP.6) is a useful guide to obtaining MLA from the G8 group of countries, namely: Canada, France, Germany, Italy, Japan, Russia, the UK, the United States.

[19] However, Art 14 of the European Convention on Mutual Assistance provides that every request must contain details of: (i) the authority making the request; (ii) the object of and the reason for the request; (iii) where possible, the identity and nationality of the person concerned; (iv) the name and address of the person to be served; (v) the offence involved and a summary of the facts. The content of some requests for specialized assistance are prescribed in CICA 2003, see for example s 43(6).

[20] MLA Guidelines, App M3, pp 763–764.

according to the nature of the assistance required. Letters of request must include the following details:

- Details and the address of the judicial or prosecuting authority conducting the investigation or proceedings to which the request relates, and the name, telephone, and fax details of the responsible official(s) there.
- Full name(s) of the subject(s) of the investigation or proceedings.
- A summary of the facts of the offence(s) and details of the offence(s) committed or alleged. Where evidence is required, the request should make clear that there are reasonable grounds for suspecting that the offence has been committed and that proceedings have been instituted in relation to the offence or, if proceedings have not been instituted, that the offence is being investigated.
- A description of the evidence or material or other assistance required, clearly stating whether original evidence or certified copies are required.
- The purpose for which the evidence or material or other assistance is required and the relevance of the assistance to the investigation or proceedings.

Requests should also state, to the extent necessary and possible: **18.17**

- The date of the trial or hearing and any other dates relevant for the purposes of executing the request; and any reasons why the request is urgent, for example because the accused person or suspect is in detention.
- The full name, date of birth, and location of any person from whom evidence is required making clear whether they are a witness or an actual or potential accused.
- Available information on the identity and whereabouts of any person to be located.
- Details, including the telephone number, of any British law enforcement officer who is familiar with the investigation.
- The request should also say whether and why the presence of officers or officials of the requesting authorities is required during the execution of the request. The names of such persons should be provided (in general, such officers or officials may observe, but may not participate in, the execution of requests).

Further specific information may also be required depending on the form of assistance sought.[21] **18.18**

Article 16(2) of the European Convention on Mutual Assistance allows states to require letters of request to be translated into their own language or another Council of Europe language, and most do so. Even in states where this is not a formal requirement a failure to supply a translation will generally delay execution of the request. **18.19**

Transmission of the request under s 8[22]

Section 8(1) provides that a request for assistance under s 7 may be sent directly to a court exercising jurisdiction in the place where the evidence is situated or to any authority recognized by the government of the country in question as the appropriate authority for receiving requests of that kind.[23] **18.20**

---

[21] See Section 3 of the MLA Guidelines (App M3). The UK Central Authority can advise where necessary.

[22] s 8 implements Art 6 of the Convention on Mutual Assistance in Criminal Matters. This provides that requests for mutual assistance may be transmitted directly between judicial authorities of member States concerned, rather than through central authorities. Art 6(2) allows for transmission via central authorities to continue in specific cases, and Art 6(3) allows for the UK and Ireland to continue to route requests through a central authority.

[23] Under the Criminal Justice (International Co-operation) Act 1990 direct transmission was only permissible in urgent cases.

18.21 Rule 32.3 of the Criminal Procedure Rules provides that where a request for assistance under s 7 is made by a justice of the peace or a judge exercising the jurisdiction of the Crown Court and is sent in accordance with s 8(1), the justices' clerk or the Crown Court officer must send a copy of the letter of request to the Secretary of State as soon as practicable after the request has been made.

18.22 Section 8(2) provides that if it is a request by a judicial authority or a designated prosecuting authority it may be sent to the Secretary of State[24] for forwarding to the court or authority mentioned in s 8(1). Indirect transmission via the Secretary of State[25] under s 8(2) is necessary if the requested country is not a member State, if the executing authority is unknown, or if Article 8 of the Convention on Mutual Assistance in Criminal Matters requires transmission via the central authority.[26] Direct transmission from designated prosecution agencies is permissible in certain cases for EU states and state parties to the Schengen Convention.[27] Article 8 requires that certain types of request for assistance including requests for the temporary transfer of prisoners and notices of information from judicial records[28] be made through member states' central authorities.

18.23 Annex E to the MLA Guidelines[29] lists the countries which permit direct transmissions for certain forms of assistance.

18.24 Section 8(3) implements Article 6(4) of the Convention on Mutual Assistance in Criminal Matters and provides that in cases of urgency, a request for assistance may be sent to the International Criminal Police Organisation (Interpol),[30] or any body or person competent to receive it under any provisions adopted under the Treaty on European Union, for forwarding to any court or authority mentioned in s 8(1).[31]

Execution of the request and transmission of the evidence to the UK

18.25 Once the letter has been transmitted, responsibility for its execution lies with the relevant authorities in the requested state in accordance with their domestic law. Mutual legal assistance treaties place obligations on signatories to comply with requests for assistance. For example, Article 1 of the European Convention on Mutual Assistance requires signatories to provide 'the widest measure of mutual assistance', and Article 3 requires signatories to execute any letter of request 'in the manner provided for by its law'.[32]

18.26 Mutual assistance treaties generally provide discretionary grounds for refusing to provide assistance. For example, Article 2 of the European Convention on Mutual Assistance permits a requested state to refuse assistance if the request concerns an offence which it considers to be a political offence, an offence connected with a political offence,[33] or a fiscal offence; or where execution of the request is likely to prejudice the sovereignty, security, *ordre public*, or other

---

24 In Scotland, the Lord Advocate.

25 In practice, the UK Central Authority.

26 See the Explanatory Notes to CICA 2003, para 40.

27 Schengen Convention, Art 53; Convention on Mutual Assistance in Criminal Matters, Art 6(1); MLA Guidelines, App M3, p 787.

28 cf European Convention on Mutual Legal Assistance in Criminal Matters, Art 22.

29 App M3, p 787.

30 SOCA is the UK's National Bureau of Interpol.

31 That is Eurojust, established under Part VI of the Treaty on European Union. Eurojust is described in more detail in para 21.17.

32 Para 6(1) of the Harare Scheme provides that 'the requested country shall grant the assistance requested as expeditiously as possible'; cf *R v I* [2008] EWCA Crim 3062 in relation to the MLAT between the UK and Nigeria.

33 *R v Secretary of State for the Home Department ex p Fininvest Spa* [1997] 1 WLR 743, 758–764.

essential interests of the requested state. Article 7 of the Commonwealth Scheme provides that a request may be refused inter alia if the conduct would not constitute an offence in the requested state; the offence in question is of a political or military character; the person accused has already been convicted or acquitted of the offence; where compliance would be contrary to the interests of the requested state; or where to provide assistance would facilitate the punishment of a person on the grounds of his race, religion, nationality, or political opinions.

Where assistance is refused then mutual assistance treaties generally require reasons to be given.[34] Article 4(3) of the Convention on Mutual Assistance in Criminal Matters provides that if the request cannot, or cannot fully, be executed in accordance with the requirements set by the requesting member State, the authorities of the requested member State must inform the requesting member State and indicate the conditions under which it might be possible to execute the request. **18.27**

Permitted use, admissibility, and return of the evidence

Restrictions on collateral use

CICA 2003, s 9, applies to evidence obtained pursuant to a request for assistance under s 7. Section 9(2) limits the use to which the evidence can be put in the UK.[35] The evidence may not without the consent of the 'appropriate overseas authority' be used for any purpose other than that specified in the request.[36] The appropriate overseas authority means the authority recognized by the government of the country in question as the appropriate authority for receiving requests of the kind in question (s 9(6)). **18.28**

The effect of this provision is to render inadmissible in evidence material obtained under s 7 in any criminal or civil[37] proceedings other than those explicitly specified in the letter of request. In *Gooch* [1999] 1 Cr App R (S) 283 evidence obtained for use at trial was used by the prosecution at the confiscation inquiry under the Drug Trafficking Offences Act 1996. The Court of Appeal held that because the letters of request plainly only sought evidence for use at trial the evidence was inadmissible by virtue of s 3 of the Criminal Justice (International Co-operation) Act 1990[38] in the confiscation inquiry because the consent of the requested state had not been obtained. **18.29**

In *BOC Ltd v Instrument Technology Limited* [2002] 1 QB 537 the Court of Appeal held that the restriction in s 3 of the Criminal Justice (International Co-operation) Act 1990 (in similar terms to s 9 of CICA 2003) was not directed at the use of evidence in civil proceedings. The width of the prohibition was said by the Court of Appeal to be implicitly restricted to the use of information by the prosecuting authority or the defendant in criminal investigations and proceedings. **18.30**

However, in *Crown Prosecution Service v Gohil* [2012] EWCA Civ 1550 the Court of Appeal held that *BOC Ltd v Instrument Technology Limited* [2002] 1 QB 537 was wrongly decided, and that s 9(2) of CICA 2003 precludes the use of MLA material in any other proceedings, whether civil or criminal.[39] **18.31**

---

34 For example Art 19, European Convention on Mutual Assistance; Art 4(3), Convention on Mutual Assistance in Criminal Matters; Commonwealth Scheme, para 6(3).

35 *R v I* [2008] EWCA Crim 3062, para 19.

36 This rule is analogous to the specialty rule in extradition law: see para 5.72. cf Art 11 of the Harare Commonwealth Scheme.

37 *Crown Prosecution Service v Gohil* [2012] EWCA Civ 1550.

38 In similar terms to s 9 of CICA 2003.

39 *XYZ (Liquidator of ABC Ltd) v HM Revenue and Customs* [2010] EWHC 1645 (Ch); *Megantic Services Ltd v Revenue and Customs Commissioners* [2010] UKUT 464 (TCC).

Admissibility

18.32 The fact that evidence has been obtained pursuant to a request under s 7 does not *per se* render it admissible at trial. Evidence which has been obtained in breach of any relevant MLAT may be inadmissible.[40] Also, the normal criminal rules of evidence apply to material obtained under a letter of request. Therefore hearsay evidence will be inadmissible unless one of the exceptions to the hearsay rule is applicable.[41] In relation to England and Wales, Chapter 2 of Part 11 of the Criminal Justice Act 2003 contains a number of provisions relating to hearsay.[42] Section 117 governs the admissibility of statements made in business documents. Section 117(1) provides that in criminal proceedings a statement contained in a document is admissible as evidence of any matter stated if oral evidence given in the proceedings would be admissible as evidence of that matter; the requirements of s 117(2) are satisfied, and the requirements of s 117(5) are satisfied, in a case where s 117(4) requires them to be.

18.33 The requirements of s 117(2) are satisfied if the document or the part containing the statement was created or received by a person in the course of a trade, business, profession, or other occupation, or as the holder of a paid or unpaid office; the person who supplied the information contained in the statement (the relevant person) had or may reasonably be supposed to have had personal knowledge of the matters dealt with, and each person (if any) through whom the information was supplied from the relevant person to the person mentioned in s 117(2)(a) received the information in the course of a trade, business, profession, or other occupation, or as the holder of a paid or unpaid office.

18.34 Section 117(4) requires that the additional conditions in s 117(5) (absence of the relevant person, etc) must be satisfied if the statement was prepared for the purposes of pending or contemplated criminal proceedings, or for a criminal investigation. However, if the statement was obtained pursuant to a request for assistance under s 7 of CICA 2003 then, by virtue of s 117(4)(b), the conditions in s 117(5) do not need to be satisfied.

Return of evidence to the requested state

18.35 When the evidence is no longer required for that purpose specified in the request (or for any other purpose for which such consent has been obtained), it must be returned to the appropriate overseas authority, unless that authority indicates that it need not be returned (s 9(3)).[43]

Defence requests for assistance to the United States

18.36 The MLA Guidelines quoted in the 2nd edition of this work,[44] explain that the UK–US Mutual Legal Assistance Treaty[45] cannot be used by a UK court as a legal base to seek the execution of

[40] In *R v I* [2008] EWCA Crim 3062 the Court of Appeal upheld the trial judge's preliminary ruling that evidence obtained from Nigeria in breach of the UK/Nigeria MLAT was inadmissible. The prosecution reserved the right to argue at trial that the evidence was nonetheless admissible pursuant to *Sang* [1980] AC 402.

[41] *Radak* [1999] 1 Cr App R 187.

[42] *Xhabri* [2005] 20 BHRC 233. In relation to Northern Ireland, s 9(4) provides that in exercising the discretion conferred by Art 5 of the Criminal Justice (Evidence, Etc.) (Northern Ireland) Order 1988 in relation to a statement contained in the evidence, the court must have regard to whether it was possible to challenge the statement by questioning the person who made it, and if proceedings have been instituted, to whether the local law allowed the parties to the proceedings to be legally represented when the evidence was being obtained. In Scotland, by s 9(5), the evidence may be received in evidence without being sworn to by witnesses, so far as that may be done without unfairness to either party.

[43] cf European Convention on Mutual Assistance in Criminal Matters, Art 6(2); Commonwealth Scheme, para 21(2).

[44] App M3, p 758.

[45] Mutual Legal Assistance Treaty with the United States of America, which entered into force on 12 February 1996.

a request in the United States on behalf of a defendant. The Guidelines provide the following information:

> Initially, a defendant seeking assistance from within the United States should ascertain whether a US person or entity in a position to assist will do so voluntarily. A defendant or his counsel may contact the US person or entity (eg, by letter, telephone) for this purpose. A US person or entity may agree to provide assistance by, for example, travelling here to appear in proceedings, providing an affidavit for use in the proceeding, or appearing before an authorised consular officer to give an oral statement for use in the proceeding. However, a US person or entity is under no obligation to provide voluntary assistance.
>
> When a defendant is unable to secure assistance on a voluntary basis, he may formally request assistance pursuant to the US international assistance statute, Title 28, section 1782, of the United States Code, which is available for use in connection with both civil and criminal proceedings in foreign jurisdictions.[46] A defendant may transmit a formal request either indirectly through the US Department of State or directly to a US federal district court or the US government agency or officer responsible for or having control over the information at issue. The request must be addressed to a court if court orders are required to secure assistance (eg, for testimony from a witness who is unwilling to testify or give a statement voluntarily, for records from a bank or Internet service provider that cannot produce its records without a court order). The request should be addressed to a government agency or officer for the production of government records, statements of government employees, and the like.
>
> Whether a defendant transmits a request directly or indirectly, he must identify the particular court, agency, or officer to receive the request and specify the location (mailing address) in the United States.
>
> Transmitting a request directly to a court, agency, or officer is quicker than transmitting it indirectly through the Department of State. The most effective means of transmitting a request to a court is to retain private legal counsel licensed to practice before that court and have counsel present the request to the court.
>
> A court receiving a request will determine whether to use its authority to execute it. When a court exercises its discretion in favor of execution, it will normally appoint a commissioner to collect the evidence (eg, take testimony, procure documents). A defendant is strongly advised to obtain private legal counsel licensed to practice before the court not only to present the matter to the court, but also to serve as commissioner for the court if or to the extent that the court orders execution.
>
> A British consular officer or other representative at the British Embassy may be able to aid the defendant in identifying the following: (1) means for obtaining assistance on a voluntary basis; (2) the appropriate court, agency, or officer in the United States to whom a request for assistance should be addressed; and (3) private legal counsel (whether pro bono or paid legal counsel) to present the request to the court and/or serve as commissioner to the court in executing it.

---

[46] USC 28 section 1782 is entitled 'Assistance to foreign and international tribunals and to litigants before such tribunals' and provides: (a) The district court of the district in which a person resides or is found may order him to give his testimony or statement or to produce a document or other thing for use in a proceeding in a foreign or international tribunal, including criminal investigations conducted before formal accusation. The order may be made pursuant to a letter rogatory issued, or request made, by a foreign or international tribunal or upon the application of any interested person and may direct that the testimony or statement be given, or the document or other thing be produced, before a person appointed by the court. By virtue of his appointment, the person appointed has power to administer any necessary oath and take the testimony or statement. The order may prescribe the practice and procedure, which may be in whole or part the practice and procedure of the foreign country or the international tribunal, for taking the testimony or statement or producing the document or other thing. To the extent that the order does not prescribe otherwise, the testimony or statement shall be taken, and the document or other thing produced, in accordance with the Federal Rules of Civil Procedure. A person may not be compelled to give his testimony or statement or to produce a document or other thing in violation of any legally applicable privilege. (b) This chapter does not preclude a person within the United States from voluntarily giving his testimony or statement, or producing a document or other thing, for use in a proceeding in a foreign or international tribunal before any person and in any manner acceptable to him.

B. Hearing Witnesses Abroad by Television Link

18.37 A television link may be used as a means of enabling a witness who is abroad to give evidence.[47] Outgoing requests from the UK are currently covered by the provisions contained in s 32 of the Criminal Justice Act 1988,[48] which allow the use of television links in limited circumstances. Section 32(1)(a) provides that a person other than the accused may give evidence through a live television link in proceedings to which s 32(1A) applies if the witness is outside the UK. These proceedings are trials on indictment; appeals to the Court of Appeal (Criminal Division); hearings of references under s 9 of the Criminal Appeal Act 1995; proceedings in youth courts; appeals to the Crown Court arising out of such proceedings; and hearings of references under s 11 of the Criminal Appeal Act 1995 so arising.

18.38 CICA 2003, s 29(1) provides that the Secretary of State may by order provide for s 32(1A) of the Criminal Justice Act 1988[49] (proceedings in which evidence may be given through a television link) to apply to any further description of criminal proceedings, or to all criminal proceedings. Thus, the section makes provision for the Secretary of State to extend the use of television links to other types of proceeding.[50]

18.39 Where such evidence is given under oath, the evidence is treated for the purposes of s 1 of the Perjury Act 1911 as if it had been given in the proceedings in the UK.[51] In *Forsyth (Elizabeth)* [1997] 2 Cr App R 299 the trial judge refused a defence application that he issue a letter of request to Northern Cyprus to allow Asil Nadir to give evidence via television link on the grounds that there was no extradition treaty between the UK and Northern Cyprus and therefore the penalties for perjury were, in effect, unenforceable. The Court of Appeal held that the judge erred in refusing the request and said that trial judges should, in general, look favourably on such applications.[52]

18.40 Where a decision to use a television link has been made, a letter of request can be sent to the foreign state under s 7 requesting that the witness be brought to a place where there are the appropriate facilities.

C. Requests to Foreign States to Freeze Evidence

18.41 The paragraphs that follow examine CICA 2003, ss 10–12, which provide for the making, transmission, and varying of domestic freezing orders made in the UK and sent abroad for execution.[53] These sections implement the Council Framework Decision on the execution

[47] cf Art 10(1) of the Convention on Mutual Assistance in Criminal Matters, which provides: 'If a person is in one Member State's territory and has to be heard as a witness or expert by the judicial authorities of another Member State, the latter may, where it is not desirable or possible for the person to be heard to appear in its territory in person, request that the hearing take place by videoconference …' This general provision is subject to the limitations and restrictions in Art 10(2)–(8).

[48] In Scotland, s 273 of the Criminal Procedure (Scotland) Act 1995.

[49] Or Art 81(1A) of the Police and Criminal Evidence (Northern Ireland) Order 1989 (SI 1989/1341). See s 29(2) in relation to Scotland.

[50] At the Committee stage of the debate on the Crime (International Co-operation) Bill in the House of Lords the Minister of State said that the Government had no present intention to use the power conferred by s 29 to seek evidence from abroad in a wider rage of cases than is currently permitted and that extensive consultation would be carried out before any changes were made: HL Deb, 23 January 2003, GC100.

[51] Criminal Justice Act 1988, s 32(3).

[52] cf *R v DPP* [2009] NICC 20.

[53] By s 51(1), 'evidence' includes 'information in any form and articles, and giving evidence includes answering a question or producing any information or article'.

in the EU of orders freezing property or evidence (referred to in this section as the Freezing Framework Decision).[54]

A domestic freezing order is an order for protecting evidence[55] which is in a 'participating country' pending its transfer to the UK (s 10(2)). A participating country is a country other than the UK which is a member State, and any other country designated by an order made by the Secretary of State (s 51(2)).[56] **18.42**

Schedule 4 of CICA 2003 contains amendments to Sch 4 of the Terrorism Act 2000 which provide for mutual recognition of freezing orders in relation to terrorist property. These are dealt with at para 25.107. **18.43**

Conditions for issuing a domestic freezing order

If it appears to a judicial authority in the UK,[57] on an application made by a person mentioned in s 10(4), that proceedings in respect of a listed offence have been instituted or such an offence is being investigated; that there are reasonable grounds to believe that there is evidence in a participating country which satisfies the requirements of s 10(3); and that a request has been made, or will be made, under s 7 for the evidence to be sent to the authority making the request, the judicial authority may make a domestic freezing order in respect of the evidence. **18.44**

Section 10(4) provides that the application may be made in relation to England and Wales and Northern Ireland, by a constable,[58] and in relation to Scotland, by the Lord Advocate or a procurator fiscal. **18.45**

A listed offence means an offence described in Article 3(2) of the Freezing Framework Decision, or an offence prescribed or of a description prescribed by an order made by the Secretary of State (s 28(5)). The offences described in Article 3(2) are those which are punishable by imprisonment for more than three years and are among the list of offences, namely: **18.46**

> Participation in a criminal organisation; terrorism; trafficking in human beings; sexual exploitation of children and child pornography; illicit trafficking in narcotic drugs and psychotropic substances; illicit trafficking in weapons, munitions and explosives; corruption; fraud, including that affecting the financial interests of the European Communities within the meaning of the Convention of 26 July 1995 on the Protection of the European Communities' Financial Interests; laundering of the proceeds of crime; counterfeiting

---

[54] 2003/577/JHA, 22 July 2003; Official Journal L 196, 2 August 2003.

[55] Sch 4 to CICA 2003 deals with orders to freeze terrorist assets, but orders to freeze property are not otherwise covered by the Act.

[56] Crime (International Co-operation) Act 2003 (Designation of Participating Countries) (England, Wales and Northern Ireland) Order 2008 (SI 2008/2156); Crime (International Co-operation) Act 2003 (Designation of Participating Countries) (England, Wales and Northern Ireland) Order 2009 (SI 2009/613); Crime (International Co-operation) Act 2003 (Designation of Participating Countries) (England, Wales and Northern Ireland) (No 2) Order 2009 (SI 2009/1764); Crime (International Co-operation) Act 2003 (Designation of Participating Countries) (England, Wales and Northern Ireland) Order 2010 (SI 2010/36); Crime (International Co-operation) Act 2003 (Designation of Participating Countries) (England, Wales and Northern Ireland) (No 2) Order 2011 (SI 2011/229).

[57] The judicial authorities are, in relation to England and Wales, any judge or justice of the peace; in relation to Scotland, any judge of the High Court or sheriff; in relation to Northern Ireland, any judge or resident magistrate (s 10(5)).

[58] s 27(1)(b) provides that the Treasury may make an order in relation to England and Wales and Northern Ireland for any function conferred on a constable under various provisions including s 10 to be exercisable instead in prescribed circumstances by a customs officer or a person acting under his direction. The Crime (International Co-operation) Act 2003 (Exercise of Functions) Order 2005 (SI 2005/425) has been made under s 27, however the power to apply for a domestic freezing order was not included within it.

currency, including of the euro; computer-related crime; environmental crime, including illicit trafficking in endangered animal species and in endangered plant species and varieties; facilitation of unauthorised entry and residence; murder, grievous bodily injury, illicit trade in human organs and tissue; kidnapping, illegal restraint and hostage-taking; racism and xenophobia; organised or armed robbery; illicit trafficking in cultural goods, including antiques and works of art; swindling; racketeering and extortion; counterfeiting and piracy of products; forgery of administrative documents and trafficking therein; forgery of means of payment; illicit trafficking in hormonal substances and other growth promoters; illicit trafficking in nuclear or radioactive materials; trafficking in stolen vehicles; rape; arson; crimes within the jurisdiction of the International Criminal Tribunal; unlawful seizure of aircraft/ships; sabotage.

18.47 The requirements of s 10(3) are that the evidence is on premises specified in the application in the participating country; that it is likely to be of substantial value (whether by itself or together with other evidence) to the proceedings or investigation; that it is likely to be admissible in evidence at a trial for the offence, and that it does not consist of or include items subject to legal privilege.

18.48 Section 10 does not prejudice the generality of the power to make a request for assistance under s 7 (s 10(6)).

Transmission of the domestic freezing order

18.49 Section 11 is headed 'Sending freezing orders'. A domestic freezing order made in England and Wales or Northern Ireland must be sent by the judicial authority which made it within 14 days[59] to the Secretary of State[60] for forwarding to a court exercising jurisdiction in the place where the evidence is situated, or any authority recognized by the government of the country in question as the appropriate authority for receiving orders of that kind (s 11(1)).

18.50 The order must be accompanied by a certificate giving the specified information and, unless the certificate indicates when the judicial authority expects such a request to be made, by a request under s 7 for the evidence to be sent to the authority making the request (s 10(4)).

18.51 Section 28(4) defines 'specified information' to be any information required to be given by the form of certificate annexed to the Freezing Framework Decision, or any information prescribed by an order made by the Secretary of State. The Annex to the Freezing Framework Decision specifies a standard form for the certificate. It includes details of the judicial authority issuing the freezing order, the transmitting central authority, and the executing authority; a precise description of the location of the evidence; details of the person suspected of having committed the offence; the action to be taken by the executing state after the freezing order has been executed; a summary of the grounds for issuing the order and the facts; and identification of the category which the offence falls into and a statement that is punishable by custodial sentence for at least three years.

18.52 The certificate must include a translation of it into an appropriate language of the participating country (if that language is not English) (s 10(5)). The certificate must be signed by or on behalf of the judicial authority who made the order and must include a statement as to the accuracy of the information given in it (s 10(6)). The signature may be an electronic signature.

---

59 s 11(3).

60 In Scotland, the order must be sent to the Lord Advocate (s 10(2)).

Amending or revoking a freezing order

Section 12 provides that the judicial authority that made a domestic freezing order may vary or revoke it on an application by the person who applied for the order; in relation to England and Wales and Northern Ireland, a prosecuting authority; in relation to Scotland, the Lord Advocate; and any other person affected by the order. **18.53**

D. Requests for Foreign Bank Information[61]

Part 1, Chapter 4 of CICA 2003 deals with disclosure of banking information in connection with criminal investigations. It implements the 2001 Protocol to the Convention on Mutual Assistance in Criminal Matters.[62] Requests for bank transaction information can generally relate to one of two things: (i) foreign bank account information; or (ii) the monitoring of banking transactions. This section examines how, and when, requests for overseas banking information can be made by the UK to foreign countries. **18.54**

Requests for information about a person's bank account (s 43)

Section 43 sets out the circumstances in which a request for information about an individual's bank account can be made to a foreign state. **18.55**

Section 43(1) provides that if it appears to a judicial authority[63] in the UK, on an application made by a prosecuting authority, that a person is subject to an investigation in the UK into serious criminal conduct;[64] that the person holds, or may hold, an account at a bank which is situated in a participating country;[65] and the information which the applicant seeks to obtain is likely to be of substantial value for the purposes of the investigation, the judicial authority may request assistance under this section. **18.56**

If it appears to a prosecuting authority mentioned in s 43(4) that the conditions in s 43(1)(a)–(c) are met, the authority may itself request assistance under s 43. The prosecuting authorities mentioned in s 43(4) are in relation to England and Wales and Northern Ireland, a prosecuting authority designated by an order made by the Secretary of State, and in relation to Scotland, the Lord Advocate or a procurator fiscal. **18.57**

---

[61] ss 42–46 of CICA 2003, discussed in this section, came into force on 1 November 2006: Crime (International Co-operation) Act 2003 (Commencement No 3) Order 2006 (SI 2006/2811).

[62] Official Journal C 326, 21 November 2001, p 1. See also the Explanatory Report to the Protocol to the 2000 Convention on Mutual Assistance in Criminal Matters between the Member States of the European Union, Official Journal C 257, 24 October 2002, p 1.

[63] The judicial authorities are, in relation to England and Wales, any judge or justice of the peace; in relation to Scotland, any sheriff; in relation to Northern Ireland, any judge or resident magistrate (s 43(2)).

[64] 'Serious criminal conduct' is defined by s 46(3) to be conduct which constitutes an offence to which Article 1(3) of the 2001 Protocol applies, or an offence specified in an order made by the Secretary of State or, in relation to Scotland, the Scottish ministers for the purpose of giving effect to any decision of the Council of the European Union under Art 1(6).

[65] For the meaning of 'participating country', see s 51(2). See Crime (International Co-operation) Act 2003 (Designation of Participating Countries) (England, Wales and Northern Ireland) Order 2008 (SI 2008/2156); Crime (International Co-operation) Act 2003 (Designation of Participating Countries) (England, Wales and Northern Ireland) Order 2009 (SI 2009/613); Crime (International Co-operation) Act 2003 (Designation of Participating Countries) (England, Wales and Northern Ireland) (No 2) Order 2009 (SI 2009/1764); Crime (International Co-operation) Act 2003 (Designation of Participating Countries) (England, Wales and Northern Ireland) Order 2010 (SI 2010/36); Crime (International Co-operation) Act 2003 (Designation of Participating Countries) (England, Wales and Northern Ireland) (No 2) Order 2011 (SI 2011/229).

18.58 The assistance that may be requested under s 43 is any assistance in obtaining from a participating country one or more of the following (s 43(5)):

- information as to whether the person in question holds any accounts at any banks situated in the participating country;
- details of any such accounts;
- details of transactions carried out in any period specified in the request in respect of any such accounts.

18.59 Section 43(6) provides that a request for assistance under s 43 must state the grounds on which the authority making the request thinks that the person in question may hold any account at a bank which is situated in a participating country and (if possible) specify the bank or banks in question; state the grounds on which the authority making the request considers that the information sought to be obtained is likely to be of substantial value for the purposes of the investigation, and include any information which may facilitate compliance with the request.

18.60 For the purposes of s 43, a person holds an account if the account is in his name or is held for his benefit, or he has a power of attorney in respect of the account (s 43(7)).

Monitoring banking transactions (s 44)

18.61 Section 44 governs requests for the monitoring of banking transactions. It implements Article 3 of the 2001 Protocol for the purpose of outgoing requests from the UK to other participating countries to monitor transactions conducted on a specified account or accounts.

18.62 Section 44(1) provides that if it appears to a judicial authority[66] in the UK on an application made by a prosecuting authority, that the information which the applicant seeks to obtain is relevant to an investigation in the UK into criminal conduct, the judicial authority may request assistance (s 44).

18.63 Section 44(3) and s 44(4) are identical to s 43(3) and s 43(4), and permit designated prosecuting authorities to make requests for assistance directly.

18.64 The assistance that may be requested under s 44 is any assistance in obtaining from a participating country[67] details of transactions to be carried out in any period specified in the request in respect of any accounts at banks situated in that country.

Sending requests under ss 43 and 44

18.65 Requests for assistance under s 43 or 44[68] are to be sent to the Secretary of State for forwarding to a court specified in the request and exercising jurisdiction in the place where the information is to be obtained, or to any authority recognized by the participating country in question as the appropriate authority for receiving requests for assistance of the kind to which this section applies (s 45(1)). In cases of urgency the request may be sent directly to the court (s 45(2)).

---

[66] The judicial authorities are, in relation to England and Wales, any judge or justice of the peace; in relation to Scotland, any sheriff; in relation to Northern Ireland, any judge or resident magistrate (s 44(2)).

[67] Section 51(2). See Crime (International Co-operation) Act 2003 (Designation of Participating Countries) (England, Wales and Northern Ireland) Order 2008 (SI 2008/2156); Crime (International Co-operation) Act 2003 (Designation of Participating Countries) (England, Wales and Northern Ireland) Order 2009 (SI 2009/613); Crime (International Co-operation) Act 2003 (Designation of Participating Countries) (England, Wales and Northern Ireland) (No 2) Order 2009 (SI 2009/1764); Crime (International Co-operation) Act 2003 (Designation of Participating Countries) (England, Wales and Northern Ireland) Order 2010 (SI 2010/36); Crime (International Co-operation) Act 2003 (Designation of Participating Countries) (England, Wales and Northern Ireland) (No 2) Order 2011 (SI 2011/229).

[68] Other than Scottish requests: see s 45(3) and (4).

19

REQUESTS BY FOREIGN STATES TO THE UK FOR ASSISTANCE IN PROVIDING EVIDENCE

A. Introduction

The provisions containing the UK's powers to grant mutual assistance to foreign states are complex. This chapter considers the relevant principles where the assistance requested involves the provision of evidence and information, including banking information, pursuant to a letter of request. Other forms of assistance relating to the service of process,[1] the transfer of prisoners,[2] the mutual recognition of driving disqualifications,[3] and restraint and confiscation matters[4] are considered in other chapters.[5] **19.01**

---

[1] Ch 22.

[2] Ch 24.

[3] Ch 23.

[4] Ch 25.

[5] This chapter does not include police-to-police assistance, sometimes referred to as police cooperation or mutual administrative assistance. This process entails police and other law enforcement officers in a foreign state asking for the assistance of law enforcement agencies in the UK to gather intelligence for an investigation. This can be an easier and quicker way to obtain information, as it does not require a letter of request, and in many countries intelligence collected by UK law enforcement agencies will constitute admissible evidence in criminal trials. Countries which do not require evidence to be sworn by witnesses in a court under their domestic law can consider using intelligence routes to request information, rather than submitting a letter of request to the UK Central Authority. The following agencies can receive intelligence enquiries directly from law enforcement officers in foreign jurisdictions: Europol and Interpol (via SOCA); UK Border Agency (where there is a data sharing agreement or memorandum of understanding between the UK and the requesting state); HMRC; and police forces: see para 17.110 and MLA Guidelines, App M3, PP 776–777.

B. Requests from Foreign States for Assistance in Obtaining Evidence

19.02 This section examines the methods by which the UK can grant assistance at the request of a foreign state in obtaining evidence for use in a range of foreign proceedings,[6] namely, criminal proceedings, administrative proceedings,[7] and clemency proceedings,[8] as well as in relation to foreign investigations.

Following its submission to the appropriate territorial authority in the UK,[9] processing such a request for assistance involves essentially three stages:

- assessment of the request and determination of the most appropriate method of giving effect to it;
- execution of the request; and
- transmission of the evidence.

19.03 The principal provisions are contained in Part 1, Chapter 2 of CICA 2003. Unless otherwise noted, all references to section numbers in this chapter refer to CICA 2003.

Incoming requests for assistance: initial steps

19.04 Section 13 provides that where a request for assistance in obtaining evidence in a part of the UK is received by the 'territorial authority' for that part of the UK, the authority may:

- If the conditions in s 14 are met, arrange for the evidence to be obtained under s 15. Section 15 empowers the territorial authority to nominate a court to receive the evidence sought, or in a case of serious and complex fraud, refer the matter to the Director of the SFO.
- Direct that a search warrant be applied for under or by virtue of s 16 or 17.[10]

Territorial authorities

19.05 Section 28(9) provides that the territorial authority in relation to evidence in England and Wales or Northern Ireland is the Secretary of State, and in relation to Scotland is the Lord Advocate.[11] In practice, the Secretary of State's functions in relation to England and Wales are

---

[6] The Schengen Convention and the Convention on Mutual Assistance in Criminal Matters extend mutual legal assistance to a range of proceedings and this is reflected in the range of assistance that can be provided under CICA 2003. It should be noted that requests *from* the UK can only relate to criminal proceedings because administrative proceedings and clemency proceedings do not exist under UK law: see Ch 18.

[7] Administrative proceedings are proceedings outside the UK to which Article 3(1) of the Convention on Mutual Assistance in Criminal Matters applies (proceedings brought by administrative authorities in respect of administrative offences where a decision in the proceedings may be the subject of an appeal before a court): CICA 2003, s 51(1).

[8] Clemency proceedings are proceedings in a country outside the UK, not being proceedings before a court exercising criminal jurisdiction, for the removal or reduction of a penalty imposed on conviction of an offence: CICA 2003, s 51(1).

[9] Para 19.05. For the avoidance of doubt, this chapter deals only with England, Scotland, Wales, and Northern Ireland. The Crown Dependencies, namely the Channel Islands (Guernsey and Jersey) and the Isle of Man, and the UK Overseas Territories (Anguilla, Bermuda, British Virgin Islands, Cayman Islands, Falklands, Gibraltar, Montserrat, St Helena, and the Turks and Caicos Islands) are not part of the UK. The Crown Dependencies and the Overseas Territories are wholly responsible for executing requests within their own jurisdictions according (usually) to their own domestic MLA laws. Requests for assistance should usually be sent to the Attorney General of the Crown Dependency or Overseas Territory from where the assistance is required. The contact details for these jurisdictions can be found at Annex B of the MLA Guidelines, App M3, p 782.

[10] Or, in relation to evidence in Scotland, s 18.

[11] International MLA treaties use the term 'central authorities'. Although the Convention on Mutual Assistance in Criminal Matters allows for direct transmission of requests (see Art 6(3)) the Explanatory Notes to CICA 2003, para 53, explain why the UK decided to opt out of direct transmission for incoming requests:

exercised by the UK Central Authority, which is part of the Home Office, and by the Northern Ireland Office in relation to Northern Ireland. The Lord Advocate's MLA functions in Scotland are exercised by the Crown Office.

HMRC may also act as a territorial authority for some purposes. Section 27(1)(a) states that the Treasury may by order provide, in relation to England and Wales or Northern Ireland, that the territorial authority's functions under various sections of CICA 2003, including ss 13–15, are to be exercisable instead in prescribed circumstances by the Commissioners of Customs and Excise. In exercise of this power the Treasury has made the Crime (International Co-operation) Act 2003 (Exercise of Functions) Order 2005.[12] Article 3 of the Order provides that any of the functions conferred on the Secretary of State (including functions conferred on him as the territorial authority in relation to evidence in England and Wales or Northern Ireland) under ss 13–15 of CICA 2003 may be exercised by the Commissioners instead of the Secretary of State where the circumstances mentioned in Articles 4–8 of the Order apply; and for the purposes of the Order a reference to the Secretary of State in those sections include the Commissioners.[13] Thus, where a request for assistance is received which relates to an offence of the type that is generally investigated and prosecuted by the Commissioners, for example, drug importation or VAT fraud, the request for assistance can be passed to them for processing. For the purpose of making a decision about a request for assistance the Commissioners must exercise the functions in s 14.[14] **19.06**

Who may make a request for assistance

Section 13(2) provides that the request for assistance may be made only by a court exercising criminal jurisdiction, or a prosecuting authority, in a country outside the UK; any other authority in such a country which appears to the territorial authority to have the function of making such requests for assistance;[15] or any international authority mentioned in s 13(3), namely, the International Criminal Police Organization (Interpol), or any other body or person competent to make a request of the kind to which the section applies under any provisions adopted under the Treaty on European Union (ie Eurojust).[16] **19.07**

In order to determine whether a foreign prosecuting authority falls within s 13, the territorial authority is not required to determine whether the foreign authority has the power under its domestic law to make the request.[17] However, whether or not it has the power is relevant to **19.08**

'Direct transmission is difficult to apply in our domestic system where jurisdiction is based largely on function rather than geography, and where the same authorities are not necessarily competent to both issue and execute letters of request. Misdirection of requests sent directly to the wrong authority would create delays, defeating the purpose of direct transmission which is to speed up the process.'

12 SI 2005/425.

13 Article 4 of the Order provides that the Commissioners may exercise the function under s 13 of arranging for evidence in England and Wales or Northern Ireland to be obtained under s 15 where a request for assistance has been made in connection with criminal proceedings or a criminal investigation mentioned in s 14(1)(a); and those proceedings or that investigation relate wholly or mainly to a 'relevant offence'. A relevant offence is defined in Article 2(1) of the Order to be conduct constituting an offence under the law of a country outside the UK which, if it occurred in England and Wales or Northern Ireland, would be an offence contrary to an enactment relating to an 'assigned matter'. An assigned matter means any matter in relation to which the Commissioners are for the time being required in pursuance of any enactment to perform any duties. These include indirect tax matters, alcohol and tobacco smuggling, and excise fraud.

14 Para 19.20.

15 For example, examining magistrates, see Explanatory Notes to CICA 2003, para 51.

16 Explanatory Notes to CICA 2003, para 51. Eurojust is considered at para 21.17.

17 *R (JP Morgan Chase National Association) v Director of the Serious Fraud Office* [2012] EWHC 1674 (Admin), para 56.

the Secretary of State's exercise of discretion whether to grant assistance, and to the form of assistance to be provided.[18]

The territorial authority's decision whether to grant assistance

19.09 In all cases the territorial authority must be satisfied that the request for assistance can properly be described as a request for obtaining 'evidence' and thus that it falls within s 13(1). Having regard to the broad definition of evidence in s 51(1), it is unlikely that a request for assistance will fail for this reason.[19] However, in *R v Secretary of State for the Home Department ex p Fininvest Spa* [1997] 1 WLR 743, 753 where the applicants complained that the request was a fishing expedition[20] rather than a request for evidence, the court indicated that as a general requirement a request for assistance should be 'as precise and focussed' as possible, although in a large investigation the request would inevitably be wide in scope.[21] The MLA Guidelines[22] require the requesting state to ensure that its request is proportionate (ie, proportionate to the level of crime being investigated), particularly for intrusive and time-consuming measures, such as search warrants, surveillance, and other court-ordered assistance. Requesting states are discouraged from making requests for assistance in relation to trivial offences.

19.10 Once a request has been received, the territorial authority has discretion whether to grant assistance.[23] There is a presumption that the UK will provide assistance, especially where there is a treaty relationship with the requesting state.[24] CICA 2003 does not circumscribe the limits

[18] *R (JP Morgan Chase National Association) v Director of the Serious Fraud Office* [2012] EWHC 1674 (Admin), paras 57–72.

[19] Section 51(1) provides that evidence 'includes information in any form and articles, and giving evidence includes answering a question or producing any information or article'; cf *R (JP Morgan Chase National Association) v Director of the Serious Fraud Office* [2012] EWHC 1674 (Admin), para 29.

[20] In the sense used by Kerr LJ in *In re State of Norway's Application* [1987] QB 433, 482: '[Fishing] arises in cases where what is sought is not evidence as such, but information which may lead to a line of inquiry which would disclose evidence. It is the search for material in the hope of being able to raise allegations of fact, as opposed to the elicitation of evidence to support allegations of fact, which have been raised *bona fide* with adequate particularization.'

[21] Concerns were expressed during the debates on the Crime (International Co-operation) Bill about the risk of 'fishing expeditions' which might arise as a result of the absence of statutory provisions limiting the use that requesting states can make of evidence supplied to them under ss 14–19 of the Act (unlike s 9, which restricts the use that can be made in the UK of requested evidence to the purpose specified purpose). The Attorney General answered concerns that were put to him in the House of Lords (HL Deb 25 February 2003, col 166):

> The general position in relation to mutual legal assistance—and the general position under the Bill and the 1990 Act—is, as I think I heard the noble Lord say, a matter for the discretion of the state that receives the request. I am told—something of which I was not aware when I responded previously, and which may be helpful—that on occasion, by relying on that general discretion, conditions are imposed in relation to particular requests where there is concern that a fishing expedition may be being conducted. There are examples where that has taken place.
>
> There is therefore a general ability to impose a condition in certain cases. We would not want as a matter of policy and practicality to establish a general power to do so in relation to incoming requests. Indeed, in certain cases that would be impossible. The noble Lord rightly referred to the bilateral treaty with the United States, which contains restrictions, but there are international obligations that, in a sense, go the other way. Article 23 of [the Convention on Mutual Legal Assistance in Criminal Matters] states that certain personal data communicated under the convention can be used for specific purposes that go beyond the proceedings to which the particular request applies. So there would be a problem with the provision contained in the amendment.

[22] App M3, p 762.

[23] CICA 2003, s 13, provides that where a request for assistance in obtaining evidence in a part of the UK is received by the territorial authority for that part, the authority 'may' grant the specified forms of assistance.

[24] *R (JP Morgan Chase National Association) v Director of the Serious Fraud Office* [2012] EWHC 1674 (Admin), para 52. The MLA Guidelines, App M3, p 760, state:

of this discretion, and the courts have been reluctant to do so. The expectation is that requests for assistance will be acted upon, unless there are compelling reasons for not doing so.[25] In *R (JP Morgan Chase National Association) v Director of the Serious Fraud Office* [2012] EWHC 1674 (Admin), para 53, Gross LJ said:

> What then might those 'compelling reasons' encompass? Here, as elsewhere, discretionary powers are to be exercised having regard to the facts of the individual case. For this reason and, more generally, because it would be unwise and inappropriate to do so, I do not think that there can be any exhaustive categories or list of cases where the SSHD[26] would be entitled or obliged to exercise her discretion against acting on a request for assistance. As already observed, statutory discretions should not readily be fettered. That said, first, the existence of cases where the SSHD may or should exercise her discretion to refuse to accede to a request underlines that her role is not that of a 'rubber stamp'. Mutual assistance should not be equated to a blank cheque. Secondly, cases of refusal to accede to a request must be rare or exceptional, for reasons already canvassed and if international mutual assistance is to function. Thirdly, I do not think that the SSHD's discretion to refuse to act on a request is confined to those instances enumerated in the Convention;[27] as will be recollected, the Convention does not have direct effect in English domestic law. Fourthly and confining myself to the context of the present case, I see much force in the approach advocated by [counsel for the SSHD]: namely, that it would (at least generally) be wrong for the SSHD to exercise her discretion in favour of answering a request when it was obviously unlawful—thus where it was undisputed or incapable of being properly disputed that the request was made unlawfully. For my part, I do not think it is necessary to demonstrate that the requesting authority was acting in bad faith and, indeed, a debate of such a nature might well be invidious; if, however, it was obvious that a requesting authority was acting in bad faith there would plainly be a most powerful case for the SSHD refusing to exercise her discretion.

In *R v Central Criminal Court ex p Propend Finance Property Limited* [1996] 2 Cr App R 26, 33 **19.11**
Laws LJ said that national security considerations could justify a refusal of assistance. Violation of the principles of *ne bis in idem* might also provide a basis for refusing assistance,[28] as might a request which is an abuse of process.[29]

> Due to the increasingly global nature of crime MLA is critical to criminal proceedings and ensuring justice for victims of crime. The UK is committed to assisting investigative, prosecuting and judicial authorities in combating international crime and is able to provide a wide range of MLA.

25 An earlier edition of the MLA Guidelines, quoted in the 2nd edition of this work at p755, stated:

> Experience so far has shown that requests to the Central Authorities for legal assistance are rarely declined. However, the UK may delay the execution of requests, which may prejudice ongoing UK investigations, or proceedings, and we may decline requests that affect our national security or other essential interests. No request will be declined without stating the reason or reasons why the request cannot be executed or without consulting the requesting authority and, where appropriate, inviting it to modify the request so that assistance may be provided. The UK will also decline to execute requests where a trial in the requesting country would involve double jeopardy (*ne bis in idem*). If the subject of a request has been convicted or acquitted in the UK or a third country of an offence arising from the conduct described in the request, the UK will not assist the gathering of evidence for another trial of the same person for the same conduct.

26 Secretary of State for the Home Department.

27 European Convention on Mutual Assistance, Article 2(a), provides that assistance may be refused if the request concerns an offence which the requested party considers a political offence, an offence connected with a political offence, or a fiscal offence: *R v Secretary of State for the Home Department ex p Fininvest Spa* [1997] 1 WLR 743, 758. Article 2(b) also provides that assistance may be refused if the requested party considers that execution of the request is likely to prejudice the sovereignty, security, *ordre public*, or its other essential interests.

28 Harare Scheme, Article 8(1)(d)

29 *R v Bow Street Magistrates' Court ex p Zardari*, 29 April 1998 (CO/1593/98).

19.12 The ambit of the territorial authority's discretion is informed by the policy of mutual assistance underlying CICA 2003, together with the reality of what the territorial authority is equipped and resourced to do.[30] Hence, where a person affected by a request raises issues of foreign law (eg whether the requesting authority has the power under its law to make the request) then the territorial authority is not, in general, required to resolve disputed issues of foreign law but may properly leave them for resolution by the foreign court.[31] Where, however, the letter of request is 'obviously unlawful' under the law of the requesting state then this may provide a basis for declining to give assistance.[32]

19.13 In exercising its discretion the territorial authority is not entitled to ignore any relevant treaty grounds for refusing assistance. MLATs and other international MLA instruments differ in their approach to restrictions on assistance. Some contain no expression restrictions,[33] whilst others contain extensive grounds on which assistance may be refused.[34] In *R v Secretary of State for the Home Department ex p Fininvest Spa* [1997] 1 WLR 743 the applicants argued that the Secretary of State had erred in granting assistance in respect of what they argued were political offences. Article 2 of the European Convention on Mutual Assistance permits states to refuse assistance in such cases. The Secretary of State argued that he was not bound to take such matters into account but retained a free and unfettered discretion. At p 758 this argument was rejected by Simon Brown LJ:[35]

> It seems to me quite impossible to contend that in exercising this general discretionary power the Secretary of State is entitled to ignore the express discretion arising under Article 2. The Secretary of State would in my judgment plainly be overlooking a material consideration if, for example, he simply forgot the existence of Article 2(a).

19.14 In taking the decision whether to grant assistance the territorial authority is under a duty to act lawfully, rationally,[36] and in a procedurally fair way. However, the requirements of procedural fairness in this context are to be determined having regard to the expectation that the territorial authority will provide assistance expeditiously to the requesting state.[37] The territorial authority is a public authority for the purposes of s 6(1) of the Human Rights Act 1998 and so must act compatibly with the Convention rights of any person likely to be affected by the grant of assistance. A grant of assistance may, for example, involve the infringement of a person's privacy rights under Article 8(1) and so need to be justified under Article 8(2).[38] It may also raise issues about the fairness of any trial in the requesting state.[39] The territorial authority is not bound to give effect to the whole of the request, nor is he required to grant the form of assistance requested by the foreign state.[40] Where, however, the requesting state is a party to the ECHR then the territorial authority is entitled to assume that an interested party's Convention rights will be protected in the courts of the requesting state.[41]

---

[30] *R (JP Morgan Chase National Association) v Director of the Serious Fraud Office* [2012] EWHC 1674 (Admin), paras 49–50.

[31] *R (Abacha) v Secretary of State for the Home Department* [2001] EWHC (Admin) 787, para 18.

[32] *R (JP Morgan Chase National Association) v Director of the Serious Fraud Office* [2012] EWHC 1674 (Admin), paras 62–72; *R v Secretary of State for the Home Department, ex p Abacha* [2001] EWHC Admin 787, para 18.

[33] For example, Convention on Mutual Assistance in Criminal Matters.

[34] For example, Harare Scheme, Article 8.

[35] cf *R (Corner House Research) v Director of the Serious Fraud Office* [2009] 1 AC 756, paras 60–62.

[36] *R (JP Morgan Chase National Association) v Director of the Serious Fraud Office* [2012] EWHC 1674 (Admin), para 67.

[37] *R (Abacha) v Secretary of State for the Home Department* [2001] EWHC (Admin) 787, para 18.

[38] *R (Hafner) v City of Westminster Magistrates' Court* [2010] 1 WLR 1005.

[39] *Government of United States of America v Montgomery (No 2)* [2004] 1 WLR 2241.

[40] *R v Central Criminal Court ex p Propend Finance Property Ltd* [1996] 2 Cr App R 26, 35–36.

[41] *R (JP Morgan Chase National Association) v Director of the Serious Fraud Office* [2012] EWHC 1674 (Admin), para 54.

A person affected by a decision to grant assistance can challenge it by way of judicial review and if appropriate, the court can order a stay pending the hearing.[42] **19.15**

Disclosure of the letter of request

Territorial authorities in the UK treat letters of request confidentially in accordance with relevant treaty provisions and general international practice.[43] Their practice is to neither confirm nor deny the existence of an MLA request, nor to disclose any of its content outside government departments, agencies, the courts, or enforcement agencies in the UK. Requests are not disclosed further than is necessary to obtain the co-operation of the witness or other person concerned. Where public statements are made by an overseas authority about the assistance it is requesting from the UK, the relevant territorial authority in the UK should be notified so that it can respond appropriately to any media or public enquiries. The MLA Guidelines[44] provide that requests will not be shown or copied to any witness or other person, nor are witnesses informed of the identity of any other witness. In the event that confidentiality requirements make execution of a request difficult or impossible, the territorial authority will consult the requesting authorities. In cases where disclosure of a request or part thereof is required by UK domestic law in order to execute the request, the requesting authority is given the opportunity to withdraw the request before disclosure to third parties is made. **19.16**

Thus, while territorial authorities strive to keep requests for assistance confidential, the wishes of the requesting state cannot be relied upon to keep a request confidential if to do so would result in unfairness. The fact that the requesting state may have an expectation that the request will be kept confidential cannot outweigh the territorial authority's duty to act fairly. In *R v Secretary of State for the Home Department ex p Zadari*, 11 March 1998, CO/345/98, Lord Bingham CJ said: **19.17**

> It appears clear that the Home Secretary is not bound—certainly not bound to the extent of allowing English procedures to be used unjustly to a suspect—to abide by the wishes of the foreign state, but it seems to me to be entirely proper that he should have regard to those wishes.

A person affected by a letter of request is generally entitled to know the gist of the letter in order that he can take advice as to whether to comply with any process resulting from it. In *R (Evans) v Director of the Serious Fraud Office* [2003] 1 WLR 299, the United States authorities sent a letter of request to the Secretary of State for mutual assistance in the investigation of a serious fraud. The Secretary of State, acting under s 4(2A) of the Criminal Justice (International Co-operation) Act 1990, requested the Director of the Serious Fraud Office to exercise the power under s 2(2) of the Criminal Justice Act 1987 to issue notices requiring the claimants to provide information in connection with the investigation. The claimants asked for disclosure of the letter of request so they could be satisfied that the information required was within its terms. That request was refused and the claimants sought judicial review of the refusal. In dismissing the claim, Kennedy LJ said at paras 11–12: **19.18**

> ... the requesting state may have a perfectly proper interest in ensuring that there is no early disclosure of some of the material contained in the letter of the request ... In my judgment

---

42 *R (Abacha) v Secretary of State for the Home Department* [2001] EWHC (Admin) 424.

43 *R (Abacha) v Secretary of State for the Home Department* [2001] EWHC (Admin) 787, para 14; MLA Guidelines, App M3, p 762. For examples of treaty provisions dealing with confidentiality, see Art 10 of the Harare Scheme and Art 7 of the UK/United States MLAT (1994) which provides: 'The requested party shall, upon request, keep confidential any information which might indicate that a request has been made or responded to. If the request cannot be executed without breaching confidentiality, the requested party shall so inform the requesting party which shall then determine the extent to which it wishes the request to be executed.'

44 App M3, p 762.

> ... having regard to the Treaty obligations it is right to start from the position that the letter of request is not a disclosable document, but justice must be done to those who are the subject of a section 2 notice pursuant to a letter of request and the consequential request from the Secretary of State to the Director of the Serious Fraud Office pursuant to section 4(2A) of the 1990 Act. The needs of justice can normally be met, as in this case, if when a request is made for disclosure of the letter of request, information is given as to the nature of the criminal investigation, but in some cases the requirements of justice may require more.[45]

19.19 There is no statutory right to make representations either upon receipt of a request or at the transmission stage,[46] and the UK Central Authority does not generally invite representations from parties potentially affected by a request. Nevertheless, in some cases fairness may require that a party affected should be permitted to make representations either as to why assistance should not be given or evidence should not be transmitted,[47] and in practice the UK Central Authority will entertain representations.[48]

Section 14 requirements and fiscal offences

19.20 Once a proper request has been received the territorial authority must decide whether the conditions in s 14 are satisfied and, if they are, which form of assistance under s 15 to provides or alternatively, whether to direct that a search warrant be applied for under s 17 (or s 18, in Scotland).

19.21 Section 14 provides that the territorial authority may arrange for evidence to be obtained under s 15 if the request for assistance in obtaining the evidence is made in connection with criminal proceedings or a criminal investigation, being carried on outside the UK; administrative proceedings, or an investigation into an act punishable in such proceedings, being carried on there;[49] clemency proceedings,[50] or proceedings on an appeal before a court against a decision in administrative proceedings, being carried on, or intended to be carried on, there.

19.22 In a case within s 14(1)(a) or (b) (criminal and administrative proceedings), the authority may arrange for the evidence to be so obtained only if the authority is satisfied (a) that an offence under the law of the country in question has been committed or that there are reasonable grounds for suspecting that such an offence has been committed, and (b) that proceedings in respect of the offence have been instituted in that country or that an investigation into the offence is being carried on there. An offence includes an act punishable in administrative proceedings. The territorial authority will be assisted in determining that these conditions are satisfied by an appropriate certificate from the requesting state. Where such a certificate is provided, s 14(3) provides that the territorial authority is to regard as conclusive a certificate as to the matters mentioned in s 14(2)(a) and (b) issued by any authority in the country in question which appears to him to be the appropriate authority to do so.[51]

19.23 At one time countries were wary about providing assistance in relation to fiscal offences, that is, offences in connection with taxes, duties, customs, and exchange.[52] For example, the European Convention on Mutual Assistance, Article 2(a), provides that assistance may be refused in

---

[45] *R (Energy Financing Team Ltd) v Director of the Serious Fraud Office* [2005] EWHC 1626 (Admin), para 17.

[46] cf EA 1989, s 13, which provided a right to make representations in extradition cases.

[47] cf *R (Abacha) v Secretary of State for the Home Department* [2001] EWHC (Admin) 787, para 17.

[48] *R (JP Morgan Chase National Association) v Director of the Serious Fraud Office* [2012] EWHC 1674 (Admin).

[49] As defined in s 51(1).

[50] As defined in s 51(1); cf Schengen Convention, Art 49.

[51] cf *R (Abacha) v Secretary of State for the Home Department* [2001] EWHC (Admin) 787, para 23.

[52] *R v Chief Metropolitan Stipendiary Magistrate ex p Government of Denmark* [1988] 1 WLR 1204.

relation to fiscal offences. This restriction was removed by the First Protocol to the Convention, Article 1 of which provides that the Contracting Parties to the Protocol shall not exercise the right to refuse assistance in relation to fiscal offence.

CICA 2003 does not in general require double criminality in relation to the offence for which assistance is sought as a pre-condition for the grant of assistance under s 15. However, double criminality may be required in relation to fiscal offences. Section 14(4) provides that if it appears to the territorial authority that the request for assistance relates to a fiscal offence in respect of which proceedings have not yet been instituted, the authority may not arrange for the evidence to be so obtained unless the request is from a country which is a member of the Commonwealth or is made pursuant to a treaty to which the UK is a party, or the authority is satisfied that if the conduct constituting the offence were to occur in a part of the UK, it would constitute an offence in that part. Thus, dual criminality is required in relation to requests for pre-trial assistance for fiscal offences where the request is made by a requesting state which is neither a member of the Commonwealth and not a party to a relevant treaty with the UK. In *R v Secretary of State for the Home Department ex p a Private Family Trust*, 13 November 1998 (CO/4164/98), Collins J rejected a submission that s 4(3) of the Criminal Justice (International Co-operation) Act 1990 (the equivalent of s 14(4)) had to be read as requiring dual criminality where proceedings relating to fiscal offences had actually commenced, rather than just being at an investigatory stage. **19.24**

Proceedings before a nominated court

Where the conditions in s 14 are satisfied, the territorial authority may nominate a court under s 15 to receive evidence to give effect to the request, usually by taking evidence on oath. Either a magistrates' court or the Crown Court may be nominated.[53] **19.25**

Where the territorial authority nominates a court under s 15, a notice of nomination is sent to the court. Schedule 1 to CICA 2003 is headed 'Proceedings of a Nominated Court under s 15' and contains detailed provisions concerning these proceedings. Rules 32.4 and 32.5 of the Criminal Procedure Rules also apply to proceedings before the nominated court. **19.26**

Paragraph 1 of Sch 1 provides that the nominated court shall have the like powers for securing the attendance of a witness for the purpose of the proceedings as it has for the purpose of other proceedings before it. The court can therefore issue a witness summons to secure the witnesses' attendance in precisely the same manner as in domestic matters.[54] **19.27**

Usually a witness summons is only necessary if the witness refuses to come to court voluntarily. Once nominated, the court usually liaises with the police, who contact the witness to ask him if he is willing to give evidence voluntarily. If so, a witness statement is drawn up and the person merely attends court to adopt the contents of his statement on oath. Paragraph 3 of Sch 1 empowers the court to administer oaths in the normal manner. **19.28**

Rule 32.4 of the Criminal Procedure Rules provides that a court nominated under s 15(1) may determine who may appear or take part in the proceedings under Sch 1 before the court and whether a party to the proceedings is entitled to be legally represented; and may direct that the public be excluded from those proceedings if it thinks it necessary to do so in the interests of justice. Generally, the requesting state and the witness are entitled to be represented and, **19.29**

---

[53] Criminal Procedure Rules, Rule 32.5. Westminster Magistrates' Court is the court which is most frequently nominated. The Court's address is 181 Marylebone Road, London, NW1 5BR. The Court has a dedicated International Jurisdiction Office: tel 020 3126 3010; fax 020 3126 3011.

[54] Magistrates Courts' Act 1980, s 97 (magistrates' courts); Criminal Procedure (Attendance of Witnesses) Act 1965, s 2 (Crown Court).

if he has notice of the nomination, the defendant in the foreign proceedings may also be represented.

19.30 Rule 32.5 provides that where a court is nominated under s 15(1) the justices' clerk or Crown Court officer shall enter in an overseas record details of the request in respect of which the notice under s 15(1) was given; the date on which, and place at which, the proceedings under Sch 1 took place; the name of any witness who gave evidence at the proceedings in question; the name of any person who took part in the proceedings as a legal representative or an interpreter; whether a witness was required to give evidence on oath or (by virtue of s 5 of the Oaths Act 1978) after making a solemn affirmation; and whether the opportunity to cross-examine any witness was refused.

19.31 The nominated court's task under s 15(1) is 'to receive any evidence to which the request relates which appears to the court to be appropriate for the purpose of giving effect to the request'. Because its jurisdiction and function are prescribed by statute, the court has no jurisdiction to inquire into whether the proceedings are an abuse of process, for example, because the requested state has acted in bad faith. However, these issues may be relevant to the territorial authority's decision to nominate a court and/or the decision to transmit the material. The territorial authority has power to retract a nomination.[55]

19.32 In *R v Secretary of State for the Home Department ex p Zadari*, 11 March 1998, CO/345/98, Lord Bingham said in relation to s 4 of the Criminal Justice (International Co-operation) Act 1990, which provided for proceedings before a nominated court:

> The 1990 Act provides for co-operation between different states in investigating and prosecuting serious international crime. Some of the suspects who are likely to be the subject of investigation and prosecution will be powerful, rich ruthless, sophisticated criminals ... It is ... quite plain that the process envisaged by section 4 is not a trial; it is the process of gathering evidence. The use to be made of the evidence so gathered is a matter for the requesting state. If the evidence taken in an English court is to be used as primary evidence in the requesting state, then one would ordinarily expect, if the requesting state's legal system is at all analogous to our own, that the requesting state would recognise the need for the suspect to have a full and fair opportunity to contest the evidence either here or in its own court. If the evidence taken in England was not to be used in evidence in the requesting state then the need for a full and fair opportunity to contest that evidence in this country would be much less and might not exist at all. It seems to me entirely appropriate for the United Kingdom, requested to act by a foreign state, to pay regard to the wishes of that state when responding to a request by someone in the position of the applicant for details of the case against him.

19.33 A letter of request seeking to have evidence taken on oath should state precisely what evidence is required. The MLA Guidelines require that a request for evidence to be taken on oath should contain the following: an express statement that the evidence is required to be taken on oath before a court and why this is necessary and why a statement taken by the police will not suffice; a list of questions to be asked; details of the requirements of the requesting state's procedure to be followed in taking the evidence, including any rules on privilege which a witness or suspect may be entitled to claim; any caution or formal notification of rights which should be given to the witness or suspect under the law of the requesting state.[56]

19.34 A request which is too widely drawn, or which is overly vague, may result in the court declining to give effect to it on the grounds of relevance, or because it would be oppressive to require the witness to produce large quantities of documents.[57]

---

55 *R v Bow Street Magistrates' Court ex p Zardari*, 29 April 1998 (CO/1593/98).

56 App M3, p 767.

57 *R v Bow Street Magistrates' Court ex p King*, 8 October 1997 (CO/3489/97).

Where the request seeks production of business or private documents then the Article 8 rights of the person affected may be engaged, and the nominated court must adopt a procedure to protect those rights. In so doing, the court will consider whether to give notice of the application to, and to hear submissions, from, any person whose Article 8 rights will be or may be infringed by giving effect to the application. In many cases it will be appropriate to give notice to parties whose Article 8 rights appear to be engaged. The court must be particularly careful to see that legal professional privilege is not infringed. As a general principle, privacy rights under Article 8(1) are unlikely to prevail in the face of Article 8(2), where disclosure of documents or information is necessary for the prevention of crime, but the court should protect documents or information that go beyond that which is necessary for this purpose.[58] **19.35**

Where the requesting state is unrepresented at the hearing the questions are usually asked by the magistrate or the legal adviser and the answers recorded in a deposition. If the requesting state is represented then cross-examination is permitted. It should be remembered, however, that the process envisaged by ss 14 and 15 is not a trial but a process of gathering evidence, and the court is undertaking an investigatory rather than an adjudicatory function.[59] **19.36**

Paragraph 5(1) provides that a person cannot be compelled to give any evidence which he could not be compelled to give in criminal proceedings in the part of the UK in which the nominated court exercises jurisdiction (para 5(1)(a)), or subject to para 5(2), in criminal proceedings in the country from which the request for the evidence has come (para 5(1)(b)). **19.37**

Thus, para 5 of Sch 1 applies the domestic rules regarding compellability of witnesses and the privilege against self-incrimination to proceedings before the nominated court under s 15(1). In applying para 5(1)(a) the court should transpose the foreign proceedings to the UK and consider the question of whether, if the foreign proceedings were English domestic criminal proceedings, and the foreign offence an English domestic offence, the witness would be entitled to refuse to answer.[60] This will be so where there is a real risk that the witness would incriminate himself by his evidence,[61] and also where he has been charged with an offence in the requesting state (and so would not be a compellable witness in equivalent circumstances in the UK).[62] The **19.38**

58 *R (Hafner) v City of Westminster Magistrates' Court* [2009] 1 WLR 1005, para 26.

59 *R v Secretary of State for the Home Department ex p Zardari*, 11 March 1998 (CO/6345/98) per Lord Bingham CJ.

60 In *R v Bow Street Magistrates' Court ex p King*, 8 October 1997 (CO/3489/97), Collins J held that Sch 1, para 4(1) to the Criminal Justice (International Co-operation) Act 1990 (in similar terms to para 5) also imposed a requirement that the evidence would be admissible in domestic proceedings and refused an application for leave to seek judicial review of the magistrate's refusal to give effect to a letter of request which sought the production of documents held by a third party on the ground that the documents would not themselves be admissible evidence (see *R v Derby Magistrates' Court ex p B* [1996] AC 487). On 1 April 1998 following a renewed application for leave May LJ and Scott Baker J granted leave on the grounds that it was reasonably arguable that the restrictions imposed by para 4(1) are limited to matters of privilege and do not encompass, as Collins J held they did, questions of admissibility in putative English proceedings. However, it appears that the case did not proceed to a full hearing and so the point remains open. The better view, however, is that a nominated court is not justified in declining to receive material solely on the grounds that it would be not be admissible as evidence. The word 'evidence' as used in s 15(1) does not mean admissible evidence (s 51(1) and *R v Secretary of State for the Home Department ex p Fininvest Spa* [1997] 1 WLR 734, 752) and none of the other methods of obtaining evidence in Part 1, Ch 2 of CICA 2003 are limited to admissible evidence. It would be curious if a nominated court alone were to be so restricted, especially since in some cases the Secretary of State may have a choice as to how to give assistance.

61 *C plc v P* [2009] 1 Ch 1; *Den Norske Bank ASA v Antonatos* [1999] QB 271; *Rio Tinto Zinc Corpn v Westinghouse Electric Corpn* [1978] AC 547; *Blunt v Park Lane Hotel* [1942] 2 KB 253. The right not to answer also applies where the risk relates to separate but ongoing domestic proceedings: *R (HM Commissioners for Customs and Excise) v Crown Court at Canterbury* [2002] EWHC 2584 (Admin), para 8.

62 MLA Guidelines, App M3, PP 767–778.

MLA Guidelines[63] enjoin requesting authorities to consider if it is worth making a request to compel a suspect to attend court if he is likely to remain silent.

19.39 A witness may also refuse to produce documentary evidence or give oral testimony on the grounds that the information sought is privileged. In respect of documents, he is protected from giving oral evidence as to their content, or as to his knowledge or belief founded on them.

19.40 Paragraph 5(1)(b) of Sch 1 allows a witness to claim the benefit of any equivalent rules on self-incrimination in the requesting state when giving evidence. It provides that a person cannot be compelled (subject to para 5(2)) when giving any evidence which he could not be compelled to give, in the country from which the request for the evidence has come. Paragraph 5(2) provides that para 5(1)(b) does not apply unless the claim of the person questioned to be exempt from giving the evidence is conceded by the court or authority which made the request.[64] Where the person's claim is not conceded, he may be required to give the evidence to which the claim relates (subject to the other provisions of para 5); but the evidence may not be forwarded to the court or authority which requested it if a court in the country in question, on the matter being referred to it, upholds the claim (para 5(3)).

19.41 If, on the other hand, the claim is not conceded then para 5(3) provides that the witness can be compelled to give evidence but that the evidence will not be transmitted if the claim to be exempt is upheld by the foreign court, tribunal, or authority upon the matter being referred to it.

19.42 A person cannot be compelled to give any evidence if his doing so would be prejudicial to the security of the UK (para 5(4)). A certificate signed by or on behalf of the Secretary of State or, where the court is in Scotland, the Lord Advocate, to the effect that it would be so prejudicial for that person to do so is conclusive evidence of that fact (para 5(5)). A person cannot be compelled to give any evidence in his capacity as an officer or servant of the Crown (para 5(6)). Paragraph 5(4) and (6) are without prejudice to the generality of para 5(1).

19.43 No order for costs can be made in proceedings under Sch 1 (para 8).

Forwarding the evidence to the foreign state

19.44 This is dealt with below.[65]

Referring a request to the SFO under s 15(2)

19.45 Where a request for evidence relates to a case of serious and complex fraud then it may be necessary to use the SFO's statutory powers and its expertise in order properly to give effect to the request. Section 15(2) permits the territorial authority to refer a case of serious and complex fraud to the SFO as an alternative to nominating a court under s 15(1).

19.46 Section 1(1) of the Criminal Justice Act 1987 constituted an SFO for England, Wales, and Northern Ireland. Section 1(2) required the Attorney General to appoint a person to be Director of the SFO, and s 1(3) empowers the Director to investigate 'any suspected offence which appears to him on reasonable grounds to involve serious or complex fraud'. Section 1(5) and (8) permits the Director to designate lawyers to exercise all of his functions under his direction.[66] Section 2A, inserted by the Criminal Justice and Immigration Act 2008, extends the SFO's powers to offences of bribery and corruption.

---

63 MLA Guidelines, App M3, p 768.

64 MLA Guidelines, App M3, p 768, require any relevant privilege to be specifically noted in the request.

65 Para 19.118.

66 The SFO's address is: The Officer In Charge, International Assistance, Serious Fraud Office, Elm House, 10–16 Elm Street, London, WC1X OBJ; Tel: (+44) (20) 7239 7367; Fax: (+44) (20) 7239 7102; <http://www.sfo.gov.uk>. The SFO also deals with restraint and confiscation matters in serious or complex fraud cases at the request of foreign states: see para 25.51.

CICA 2003, s 15(2) permits the Secretary of State to refer a letter of request to the Director of the SFO[67] as an alternative to nominating a court under s 15(1) where the offence to which the request relates appears to the Secretary of State to be an offence involving serious or complex fraud. A certificate under s 14(3) is conclusive and where there is a such a certificate the territorial authority is only required to be satisfied that the matters involves serious and complex fraud.[68] It is then for the Director to obtain any evidence to which the request relates which appears to him to be appropriate for the purpose of giving effect to the request. The Director has a duty to decide for himself how best to give effect to the request in furtherance of the overall investigation, and if that means going further than the letter of request he is entitled to do so.[69] **19.47**

It should be noted that it does not need to appear that the fraud is both serious *and* complex. It is sufficient if it is either serious *or* complex. The phrase 'serious or complex fraud' is not defined in either CICA 2003 or the Criminal Justice Act 1987. Whether or not a fraud is serious is a question of fact. The SFO uses as a rough guide the figure of £1 million being lost or at risk of being lost as a result of the fraud. However this figure is not determinative by itself. Other factors, apart from the amount of money involved, can make a fraud serious, for example, widespread public concern in the requesting state, or the involvement of prominent citizens. Whether a fraud is complex is also a question of fact. Factors which determine complexity include the number of transactions involved and the level of sophistication of the offence, for example, the use of corporate vehicles or trusts; and whether transactions have taken place in more than one country. **19.48**

Where a case has been referred to the Director of the SFO under s 15(2) he may use his investigatory powers under s 2 of the Criminal Justice Act 1987. Section 2(1) of that Act provides that the powers of the Director under s 2 shall be exercisable inter alia when he has been requested to do so by an authority entitled to make such a request in any case in which it appears to him that there is good reason to do so for the purpose of investigating the affairs, or any aspect of the affairs, of any person. By s 2(1A)(b), the Secretary of State acting under s 15(2) of CICA 2003 is an authority entitled to make such a request. **19.49**

If a request is sent to the Director under s 15(2) by the Secretary of State, the Director is entitled to decline to give effect to it if, upon examination, it does not concern serious or complex fraud. Section 2(1B) of the Criminal Justice Act 1987 provides that the Director shall not exercise his powers on a request from the Secretary of State acting in response to a request received from an overseas authority within s 2(1A)(b) unless it appears to the Director on reasonable grounds that the offence in respect of which he has been requested to obtain evidence involves serious or complex fraud. If the Director decides this condition is not satisfied then he will return the letter of request to the Secretary of State for execution by alternative means. **19.50**

Once a letter of request has been received and referred to the Director of the SFO under s 15(2) of CICA 2003, it is for the Director to decide how best to give effect to it.[70] **19.51**

The SFO's powers under s 2 of the Criminal Justice Act 1987

As an investigating authority, the SFO may conduct voluntary interviews and interviews under caution in the normal manner. However the SFO also has a range of coercive powers at its **19.52**

---

67 For Scotland, see s 15(3).

68 *(Abacha) v Secretary of State for the Home Department* [2001] EWHC (Admin) 787, para 23.

69 *R (Energy Financing Team Limited) v Director of SFO* [2005] EWHC 1626 (Admin), para 24(4).

70 *R (Energy Financing Team Ltd) v Director of the Serious Fraud Office* [2005] EWHC 1626 (Admin), para 24.

disposal under s 2 of the Criminal Justice Act 1987 in relation to interviews and the production of documents. They are coercive in the sense that a person who fails to answer questions or produce documents as required is liable to be prosecuted for a criminal offence under s 2(13), (14), or (16).[71]

19.53 In summary, the SFO's powers under s 2 of the Criminal Justice Act 1987 are as follows:

- Section 2(2) allows the SFO to require any person to answer any relevant questions, including questions about confidential matters, however s 2(9) entitles the person interviewed to refuse to answer on the grounds of legal professional privilege.
- Section 2(3) allows the SFO to require any person to produce to it any relevant documents,[72] including confidential documents, but not including documents subject to legal professional privilege.[73] It can also require the person producing them to provide an explanation[74] of them.
- Where the SFO considers that to require a person to produce relevant documents would be likely to result in their being destroyed, hidden, or moved from the jurisdiction, so as to frustrate any criminal investigation, s 2(4) allows it to apply to a court for a warrant to search that person's premises and seize the documents. Before granting a search warrant, s 2(4)(a) requires the justice of the peace to be satisfied either that the person concerned has failed to comply with a notice under s 2(3), that it is not practicable to serve such a notice, or that service would jeopardize the investigation.

19.54 Section 2(13) makes it an offence for a person to fail to comply without reasonable excuse with a requirement imposed on him under s 2.[75] Section 2(14) makes it an offence knowingly or recklessly to make a false statement in purported compliance with a requirement made under s 2. Section 2(16) makes it an offence to destroy or conceal, and so on, documents which the person knows or suspects are relevant to an investigation. These offences are punishable by fines and imprisonment. However, by s 2(9), s 2 cannot be used to obtain legally privileged material. A person may therefore refuse to answer questions or disclose documents on the grounds of legal professional privilege.[76]

Interviews under s 2(2)

19.55 These are commonly referred to as 's 2 interviews'. The power which they give the SFO is draconian. In *R v Director of the Serious Fraud Office ex p Johnson* [1993] COD 58 the applicant, who faced criminal charges, sought leave to apply for judicial review of a notice that had been served on his wife under s 2(2) requiring her to attend for interview. He contended that, by virtue of their marital relationship, his wife had a reasonable excuse within s 2(13) of the Act for refusing to comply with the notice. Auld J held that although s 80 of PACE prevents a person from being compelled to give evidence against his or her spouse, there is no analogous provision in the Criminal Justice Act 1987, it being a designedly draconian statute concerned with the investigation of fraud rather than the admissibility of evidence.

19.56 A s 2 interview differs from an interview under caution conducted by police officers in that the SFO is entitled to require the interviewee to answer on pain of prosecution under s 2(13) if he

71 *R v Director of Serious Fraud Office ex p Smith* [1993] (AC).
72 *Hamilton v Naviede* [1995] 2 AC 75.
73 Criminal Justice Act 1987, s 2(9).
74 For the meaning of 'explanation' in the similarly worded s 447(5)(a)(ii) of the Companies Act 1985, see *Attorney General's Reference (No. 2) of 1998* [2000] QB 412.
75 *R v Metropolitan Stipendiary Magistrate ex p Serious Fraud Office* [1995] COD 77.
76 *R v Central Criminal Court ex p Francis and Francis (a firm)* [1989] AC 346.

fails to do so.[77] They may also continue even after the interviewee has been charged,[78] although if a defendant refused to answer in such a case, a conviction for the offence under s 2(13) would likely violate Article 6 of the ECHR.[79]

A conviction based on material obtained from a defendant in a s 2 interview will be likely violate Article 6 of the ECHR.[80] **19.57**

The interview may be carried out by SFO investigators and/or police officers. If representatives of the foreign state have requested to be present then this is usually allowed, however they will not be permitted to conduct the interview or to take part in it.[81] However, they may consult with the SFO in relation to the interview. The interviewee is entitled to be legally represented during the interview, which is conducted in private and tape recorded. **19.58**

In *R v Serious Fraud Office ex p Maxwell (Kevin)*, The Times, 9 October 1992, the defendant sought an order to compel the SFO to comply with the common law duty of disclosure prior to his s 2 interview. It was held that, in accordance with s 1 of the Criminal Justice Act 1987, two concurrent forms of process were instigated by the Director of the SFO, namely, an investigative process and a judicial process; because the proposed interview with the defendant pursuant to s 2 was part of the investigative process, there was no obligation on the investigator to show to the person interviewed any information already available. The Court indicated that in some cases an investigator might find it fruitful or helpful to disclose such information, but in other cases it might be damaging; if the statutory investigator abused his powers, that could be corrected by judicial review. **19.59**

In *Marlwood Commercial Inc. v Kozeny* [2005] 1 WLR 104, the Court of Appeal dealt with an application made by a party to civil proceedings for permission to disclose to the SFO (in compliance with a notice given under s 2 of the Criminal Justice Act 1987 made as a result of a request pursuant to the Criminal Justice (International Co-operation) Act 1990), documents disclosed by another party pursuant to its obligations in the civil proceedings and which had been brought to England for that purpose. It was held that section 3(3) of the Criminal Justice Act 1987 did not override rule 31.22 of the Civil Procedure Rules 1998. However, the Court held that the public interest in the investigation or prosecution of a specific offence of serious or complex fraud took precedence over the merely general concern of the courts to control the collateral use of compulsorily disclosed documents. In the absence of other factors, the court's discretion should, as a matter of principle, prima facie be exercised in favour of compliance with a notice under s 2(3) of the 1987 Act; by itself the additional factor that the documents had been brought within the jurisdiction for the purposes of disclosure by a foreign litigant himself brought compulsorily before the English court should not be regarded as a reasonable excuse for non-compliance with the notice; and the courts should be prepared to grant permission under CPR 31.22 for their collateral use in production to the Director of the SFO. **19.60**

[77] Knowingly or recklessly making false statements is also an offence under s 2(14).

[78] *R v Director of the Serious Fraud Office ex p Smith* [1993] AC 1.

[79] *Shannon v United Kingdom* (2006) 42 EHRR 31; cf *R v Metropolitan Stipendiary Magistrate ex p Serious Fraud Office*, The Independent, 24 June 1994.

[80] *Saunders v United Kingdom* (1997) 23 EHRR 313. As a result of this decision, s 2(8AA) was inserted into the Criminal Justice Act 1987 to prohibit the use of such evidence except where it is raised by the defendant.

[81] Unless the Director has exercised his powers to designate a foreign investigator under s 2(11) of the Criminal Justice Act 1987.

A notice under s 2(3)

19.61 A s 2(3) notice is an order issued by the SFO which requires the person named (who may be the person under investigation or another person) to produce to the SFO any specified documents[82] which appear to the SFO to relate to any matter relevant to the investigation or any documents of a specified description which appear to him so to relate.[83] If the documents are produced the SFO can take copies or extracts from them,[84] or require the person producing them to provide an explanation of them.[85] If the documents are not produced the SFO can require the person to state where they are.[86] A failure without reasonable excuse to comply with a requirement issued under s 2(3) is an offence, as is intentionally or recklessly making a false statement.[87]

19.62 Section 2(3) is intended to be the primary method by which the SFO secures access to relevant documentation.[88] Although it also has the power to obtain a search warrant[89] it is not entitled to obtain a search warrant unless it considers that the use of a notice would seriously prejudice the investigation or there has previously been a failure to comply with such a notice. Especially where the SFO are seeking documents from professional advisers, the use of a s 2(3) notice should be the norm and not the exception.[90] The inappropriate use of a search warrant may be a disproportionate interference with the affected person's rights under Article 8 of the ECHR[91] rendering the search unlawful.

19.63 The power to require production of documents under s 2(3) remains exercisable even after the person under investigation has been charged.[92] However, the SFO's Operational Manual[93] states that they will not normally be used after the defendant has been charged.

19.64 Where the SFO exercises its power under s 2(3)(a)(ii) to require a person to provide an 'explanation' of documents which have been produced to it, it is not limited to asking syntactical questions about the contents of the documents. It is entitled to ask questions about the documents' contents designed not only to enable it to understand the context in which the documents came into existence but any transaction referred to in them and any other matters which would enable it to understand the significance of the documents for the purposes of its investigations. The SFO is therefore entitled to ask questions about subjects referred to in the documents and other matters arising out of and properly connected with those subjects, and

---

82 Defined in the Criminal Justice Act 1987, s 2(18), to include information recorded in any form. In relation to information recorded otherwise than in legible form, references in s 2 to its production include references to producing a copy of the information in legible form. Thus, the SFO can require the documents to be produced in legible form if they are held electronically. Computer hard drives are 'documents' for these purposes: *Kent Pharmaceuticals Ltd v Director of Serious Fraud Office* [2002] EWHC 3023 (Admin).

83 Criminal Justice Act 1987, s 2(3).

84 Criminal Justice Act 1987, s 2(3)(a)(i).

85 Criminal Justice Act 1987, s 2(3)(a)(ii).

86 Criminal Justice Act 1987, s 2(3)(b).

87 Criminal Justice Act 1987, s 2(13) and (14).

88 *R (Energy Financing Team Ltd) v Director of the Serious Fraud Office* [2005] EWHC 1626 (Admin), para 19; *R (Kent Pharmaceuticals Ltd) v Director of the Serious Fraud Office)* [2002] EWCA 3023, para 20.

89 Criminal Justice Act 1987, s 2(4), considered at para 19.67.

90 cf *Gross v Southwark Crown Court*, 24 July 1998 (CO/1759/98); *R v Leeds Crown Court ex p Switalski* [1991] Crim LR 559; *R v Maidstone Crown Court ex p Waitt* [1988] Crim LR 384.

91 *Niemietz v Germany* (1992) 16 EHRR 97; *R v Bow Street Magistrates' Court ex p Montgomery*, 25 February 1998 (CO/3263/97); cf *R v Secretary of State for the Home Department ex p Finnivest Spa* [1997] 1 WLR 743, 757, where Simon Brown LJ rejected the submission that the SFO's use of a search warrant was *Wednesbury* unreasonable.

92 *R v Director of Serious Fraud Office, ex p Saunders* [1988] Crim LR 837.

93 Available through <http://www.sfo.gov.uk>. See also *R (JP Morgan Chase Bank National Association) v Director of the Serious Fraud Office* [2012] EWHC 1674 (Admin), para 27.

these questions may include the purpose of the documents and their relationship with other documents produced.[94]

Section 2(3) notices are subject to the same requirements as to width and specificity as search warrants.[95] The specified documents, or the category of documents specified, must appear to the Director to 'relate to any matter relevant to the investigation'.[96] A notice which fails to satisfy this criterion will be unlawful and liable to be quashed on judicial review. Two factors in particular may result in a notice being unlawful. First, the notice may be so widely drawn that it includes documents or categories of documents which on any view could not be relevant to an inquiry.[97] Secondly, where the category of documents is specified by reference to a time period, the period may be wholly disproportionate to the period of the alleged offence.[98] **19.65**

Documents which would be protected from disclosure in the High Court by legal professional privilege do not have to be disclosed.[99] **19.66**

Search warrants under s 2(4)

In this section the law relating to search warrants under s 2(4) is analysed. Many of these principles are applicable to search warrants in general, including those issued under Part 2 and Sch 1 of (PACE). These warrants are considered below. **19.67**

Section 2(4) provides that on information laid on oath by a member of the SFO, a justice of the peace,[100] if satisfied, in relation to any documents that either: (a) there are reasonable grounds for believing that either a person has failed to comply with a s 2(3) notice (s 2(4)(a)); (b) that it is not practicable to serve a s 2(3) notice in relation to them (s 2(4)(b)); or (c) that the service of such a notice in relation to them might seriously prejudice the investigation s 2(4)(c)); and there are reasonable grounds for believing that there are such documents on the premises specified in the information, may issue a warrant as is mentioned in s 2(5). **19.68**

The warrant specified in s 2(5) is a warrant authorizing any constable to enter (using such force as is reasonably necessary for the purpose) and search the premises, and to take possession of any documents[101] appearing to be documents of the description specified in the information or to take in relation to such documents any other steps which may appear to be necessary for preserving them and preventing interference with them. **19.69**

An applicant for a search warrant (or any order sought on an ex parte basis) is under a duty of full and frank disclosure, that is, a duty to draw all material facts to the attention of the judge whether they weigh for or against the making of the order. The advocate must 'put on his defence hat' and ask himself, what, if he was representing the defendant or a party with a relevant interest, he would be saying to the judge.[102] The judge must be given all the information **19.70**

---

94 cf *Attorney General's Reference (No 2 of 1998)* [2000] QB 412, 426 (construing the analogous power in s 447 of the Companies Act 1985).

95 *R (Energy Financing Team Ltd) v Director of Serious Fraud Office* [2005] EWHC 1626 (Admin), para 24(5). Search warrants are considered at para 19.67.

96 Criminal Justice Act 1987, s 2(3).

97 *R v Secretary of State for the Home Department ex p Fininvest Spa* [1997] 1 WLR 743, 753 (although relief was refused as a matter of discretion); cf *R v Central Criminal Court ex p AJD Holdings Ltd*, The Times, 24 February 1992; *R v Southampton Crown Court ex p J & P* [1993] Crim LR 962.

98 *R v Southampton Crown Court ex p J & P* [1993] Crim LR 962; *Williams v Summerfield* [1972] QB 512; *R v Nottingham Justices ex p Lynn* (1984) 79 Cr App R 238.

99 s 2(9).

100 In Scotland, a sheriff.

101 As defined in s 2(18).

102 *R (Rawlinson & Hunter Trustees) v Central Criminal Court* [2012] EWHC (Admin) 2254, para 81; *Re Stanford* [2010] 1 WLR 941, para 191; *R (Mercury Tax Group) v HMRC* [2008] EWHC 2721, para 48; *R (Energy Financing Ltd) v Bow Street Magistrates' Court* [2006] 1 WLR 1316, para 24(3).

he needs to make an informed, balanced, and fair decision, and in particular must be given all the known material facts which indicate that the issue of a warrant might be inappropriate.[103]

19.71 A failure to comply with this obligation may result in the warrant being quashed, if the non-disclosure would (rather than merely may) have impacted on the decision to grant the warrant.[104] If the applicant was guilty of bad faith then the warrant may be quashed even if the non-disclosure was immaterial.[105]

19.72 In *R (Energy Financing Team Limited) v Director of the Serious Fraud Office* [2005] EWHC 1626 (Admin), para 24, Kennedy LJ summarized the relevant principles in relation to warrants under s 2(4) in the MLA context: (a) the grant and execution of a warrant to search and seize is a serious infringement of the liberty of the subject, which needs to be clearly justified, and before seeking or granting a warrant it is always necessary to consider whether some lesser measure, such as a notice under section 2(3) of the 1987 Act, will suffice; (b) if such a notice will not suffice, for example because the documents may be destroyed, consideration should be given to the possibility of obtaining the documents from an alternative untainted source, such as a bank, but where that would involve many enquiries of many institutions which might or might not be willing and able to produce the information required, the need to assist the investigating authority to make progress with its overall investigation may well, as in this case, render resort to alternative sources impracticable; (c) if an application is to be made for a warrant it is the duty of the applicant to give full assistance to the district judge, and that includes drawing to his or her attention anything that militates against the issue of a warrant;[106] (d) where the Director of the SFO is seeking a warrant pursuant to a request for mutual legal assistance the warrant does not need to reflect precisely the wording of the letter or letters of request. The Director has a duty to decide for himself how best to give effect to the request in furtherance of the overall investigation,[107] and if that means going further than the letter of request he is entitled to do so; (e) when there is an ongoing investigation into, for example, the affairs of a company which appears to have been at the centre of a fraud, it will always be difficult to say precisely what documentation of value to the inquiry may be recovered from those who are justifiably suspected of being in contact with the main target company, but nevertheless the warrant needs to be drafted with sufficient precision to enable both those who execute it and those whose property is affected by it to know whether any individual document or class of documents falls within it.[108] The specificity required will be no less than would be required for a notice under s 2(3) were it practicable to serve such a notice, and although the terms of

[103] *R (Rawlinson & Hunter Trustees) v Central Criminal Court* [2012] EWHC (Admin) 2254, para 82.

[104] In *R (Rawlinson & Hunter Trustees) v Central Criminal Court* [2012] EWHC (Admin) 2254, para 172, the High Court did not definitively decide whether the test for quashing a warrant was whether the non-disclosure *would* have made a difference to the judge's decision, or whether it was sufficient that it *might* have done so, though it inclined in favour of the former test; cf *R (Burgin) v Commissioner of Police for the Metropolis* [2011] EWHC 1385 (Admin), paras 66–71; paras 52–58; *R (Mercury Tax Group) v HMRC* [2008] EWHC 2721 (Admin), para 8; *R (Wood) v North Avon Magistrates' Court* [2009] EWHC 3614 (Admin), paras 34–37; *R (Faisaltex) v Crown Court at Preston* [2009 EWHC 1687 (Admin), para 81; *Jennings v CPS* [2006] 1 WLR 182.

[105] *R (Wood) v North Avon Magistrates' Court* [2009] EWHC 3614 (Admin), paras 35–37.

[106] Para 19.70

[107] *R v Secretary of State for the Home Department ex p Fininvest Spa* [1997] 1 WLR 743, 748, 750–753.

[108] A warrant which is so widely drawn that it authorizes the seizure of substantial material which is not relevant to the investigation is liable to be quashed: *R v Secretary of State for the Home Department ex p Fininvest Spa* [1997] 1 WLR 743; *R v Southampton Crown Court ex p J & P* [1993] Crim LR 96; *R v Central Criminal Court ex p AJD Holdings Ltd* [1992] Crim LR 669; *Williams v Summerfield* [1972] QB 512; *R v Nottingham Justices ex p Lynn* (1984) 70 Cr App R 238. A warrant which is so vague that the person searching cannot tell whether or not material falls within in it is also liable to be quashed: *R (Powers-Hynes) v Norwich Magistrates' Court* [2009] EWHC 1512 (Admin).

the warrant may be wide it will not simply be fishing if it is directed to support an investigation which has apparent merit; (f) the district judge from whom the warrant is being sought must have time to pre-read the material relied upon, namely the sworn information, usually supported by the letter(s) of request and the draft warrant; (g) the district judge has no power to set aside a warrant once granted; (h) the remedy which is available to a person or persons affected by a warrant is to seek judicial review; (i) often it may not be appropriate even after the warrant has been executed, to disclose to the person affected or his legal representatives all of the material laid before the district judge because to do so might alert others or frustrate the purposes of the overall enquiry, but the person affected has a right to be satisfied as to the legality of the procedure which led to the execution of the warrant, and if he or his representatives do ask to see what was laid before the district judge and to be told about what happened at the hearing, there should, so far as possible, be an accommodating response to that request. It is not sufficient to say that the applicant has been adequately protected because discretion has been exercised first by the Director of the SFO and then by the District Judge. In order to respond to the request of an applicant it may be that permission for disclosure has to be sought from an investigating authority abroad, and/or that what was produced or said to the district judge can only be disclosed in an edited form, but judicial control by way of judicial review cannot operate effectively unless the person or persons affected are put in a position to take meaningful advice, and if so advised to seek relief from the court.

The obtaining of a search warrant is never to be treated as a formality.[109] The judge must conduct a rigorous and critical scrutiny of the application.[110] The courts have consistently emphasized the importance of the issuing judge or magistrate giving reasons for the decision to issue a search warrant. This is because a search warrant constitutes an intrusion into the property and privacy of those affected, and the purpose of interposing a judge between those seeking a search warrant on the one hand and those whose rights are intruded into on the other is to ensure that the stringent requirement laid down by Parliament before warrants may lawfully be issued are in every case complied with. This is a matter of high constitutional principle.[111] In addition, it is important both for those affected and for a reviewing court to be able to identify the reasons for a decision to issue a warrant so that the legality of the decision can be assessed.[112] However, a failure to give reasons will not lead to a warrant being quashed if the reviewing court can discern for itself what the reasons must have been.[113] **19.73**

Warrants issued under s 2(4) are subject to the safeguards contained in ss 15 and 16 of PACE.[114] These are considered below.[115] **19.74**

Section 2(6) of the Criminal Justice Act 1987 provides that unless it is not practicable in the circumstances, a constable executing a warrant issued under s 2(4) shall be accompanied by an 'appropriate person'. Where an appropriate person accompanies a constable, he may exercise the powers conferred by s 2(5) but only in the company, and under the supervision, of **19.75**

---

109 *Redknapp v Commissioner of Police for City of London* [2009] 1 All ER 229, para 13; *R v Guildhall Magistrates' Court ex p Primlaks Holdings Co (Panama) Inc* [1990] 1 QB 261, 272.

110 *R (Rawlinson & Hunter Trustees) v Central Criminal Court* [2012] EWHC (Admin) 2254, para 89.

111 *Attorney General of Jamaica v Williams* [2008] AC 351, 358.

112 *R (Burgin) v Commissioner of Police for the Metropolis* [2011] EWHC 1835 (Admin), para 19; *R (Faisaltex Ltd) v The Crown Court at Preston* [2009] 1 WLR 1697, paras 29–30; *Williams v Summerfield* [1972] QB 512, 518.

113 *R (Burgin) v Commissioner of Police for the Metropolis* [2011] EWHC 1835 (Admin), para 34; *R (Glenn & Co Ltd) v Her Majesty's Commissioners for Revenue and Customs* [2011] EWHC 2998 (Admin), para 34; *R v Lewes Crown Court ex p Weller*, Unreported, 12 May 1999.

114 s 15(1) of the Police and Criminal Evidence Act 1984.

115 Para 19.105.

the constable (s 2(6A)). An 'appropriate person' means a member of the SFO or some person who is not a member of that Office but whom the Director has authorized to accompany the constable (s 2(7)).

19.76 Items which a constable has reasonable grounds to believe are subject to legal professional privilege may not be seized under any circumstances.[116] Difficulties may arise, however, where items subject to legal professional privilege are contained within a large number of other documents which can lawfully be seized. In such a case, Part 2 of the Criminal Justice and Police Act 2001 contains provisions allowing all the material to be seized for later examination and return of the privileged material.[117] The practice then is for the documents to be examined by independent counsel to determine which items, if any, are privileged in accordance with the procedure in Part 2.[118]

Privilege against self-incrimination in mutual assistance proceedings

19.77 Whilst a person giving evidence before a nominated court is entitled to rely on his common law privilege against self-incrimination,[119] evidence obtained from a suspect by the SFO under s 2 of the Criminal Justice Act 1987 overrides the privilege.[120] A suspect is not entitled to refuse to answer on the grounds that it might incriminate him. It follows that the use against the suspect at his trial in the UK of such material may violate his right to a fair trial under Article 6 of the ECHR.[121] However, s 2(8) restricts the use of compulsorily obtained material.

19.78 Consistently with this approach, before providing assistance using s 2 coercive powers, the SFO requires an undertaking from the requesting state that any evidence obtained from a person by use of compulsory questioning will not be used at that person's trial. The requesting authority is required to give an undertaking in the following form:[122]

> No statement made by any person to the Serious Fraud Office on foot of their coercive powers will be used against that person in a prosecution. Unless evidence relating to it is adduced, or a question relating to it is asked, in the proceedings, by or on behalf of that person.

19.79 This undertaking is intended to preserve the defendant's rights in the requesting state. If it is not given, the interviewee may have a reasonable excuse not to answer questions or produce documents and thus have a defence to a charge under s 2(13) of the Criminal Justice Act 1987. The undertaking does not prevent the requesting state using a witness's statutory interview in the trial if its law permits this; but it prevents it doing so if the interviewee is (or later becomes) a defendant in a criminal trial. The undertaking is not required in relation to the voluntary interviews of witnesses. It is only necessary when the SFO uses its statutory powers to obtain testimony.

Use of search warrants to give assistance to a foreign state

19.80 Section 13(1)(b) of CICA 2003 provides that where there is a request for assistance in obtaining evidence in a part of the UK the territorial authority may direct that a search warrant be applied

---

[116] s 26 of CICA 2003; s 19(6) of the Police and Criminal Evidence Act 1984; cf *R v Chesterfield Justices ex p Bramley* [2000] QB 576.

[117] *El Curd v Winchester Crown Court* [2011] EWHC 1853; *Windsor v Bristol Crown Court* [2011] EWHC 1899 (Admin).

[118] See also the amendments to Sch 1 to the Criminal Justice and Police Act 2001 made by s 26(3) of CICA 2003; cf *R v Customs and Excise Commissioners ex p Popely* [1999] STC 1016.

[119] Sch 1, para 5 to CICA 2003; para 19.38.

[120] *R v Director of the Serious Fraud Office ex p Smith* [1993] AC 1.

[121] *Lyons* [2003] 1 AC 976; *IJL v United Kingdom* (2000) BHRC 222; *Saunders v United Kingdom* (1996) 23 EHRR 313.

[122] See <http://www.sfo.gov.uk>.

for under or by virtue of s 16 or 17.[123] In relation to customs matters, the Commissioners may give a direction under s 13.[124]

Section 16 provides for the extension of the statutory search powers in Part 2 of the Police and Criminal Evidence Act 1984 (PACE) to cover overseas conduct. Section 17 provides a new free-standing power for a justice of the peace to grant a search warrant. **19.81**

Although ss 16 and 17 and the provisions of PACE refer to 'constables', customs officers may also apply for warrants under these provisions.[125] **19.82**

In order to understand the operation of s 16 it is first necessary to consider the powers in Part 2 of PACE. **19.83**

Warrants under s 8 of the Police and Criminal Evidence Act 1984

Section 8(1) of PACE permits a justice of the peace to issue a search warrant where there are reasonable grounds for believing (i) an indictable offence has been committed; (ii) there is material on the premises mentioned in s 8(1A) which is likely to be of substantial value to the investigation and likely to be relevant evidence;[126] (iii) the material does not consist of or include items subject to legal professional privilege,[127] excluded material,[128] or special procedure material;[129] and (iv) any of the conditions in s 8(3) is satisfied in relation to each set of premises specified in the application.[130] There is no statutory requirement for the magistrate to give reasons why he is satisfied that the conditions in s 8(1)(a)–(e) are made out and in some cases it may be unnecessary to do so, for example where the written information is compelling as to the grounds for belief, and clearly addresses the specific matters which are required to be addressed in s 8(1).[131] **19.84**

---

123 Or, in relation to evidence in Scotland, s 18.

124 Article 5 of the Crime (International Co-operation) Act 2003 (Exercise of Functions) Order 2005 (SI 2005/425) provides that the Commissioners may exercise the function under s 13 of directing that a search warrant be applied for under or by virtue of s 16 or 17 where a request for assistance has been made wholly or mainly in connection with a relevant offence (as defined in Art 2).

125 In relation to s 16, the Crime (International Co-operation) Act 2003 (Exercise of Functions) Order 2005 (SI 2005/425), Art 9, provides that any function conferred on a constable by virtue of s 16 in relation to a warrant or order under s 8 of, or Sch 1 to PACE may be exercised by a customs officer instead of a constable where the Commissioners have given a direction under s 13, or any such function is to be exercised by a customs officer for the purposes of an investigation relating wholly or mainly to a relevant offence (defined in Art 2) by an international joint investigation team of which he is a member, as defined in s 88(7) of the Police Act 1996. In relation to s 17, the Crime (International Co-operation) Act 2003 (Exercise of Functions) Order 2005 (SI 2005/425), Art 10, provides that any function conferred on a constable under s 17 may be exercised by a customs officer instead of a constable where the Commissioners have given a direction under s 13 that an application be made for a search warrant. The Crime (International Co-operation) Act 2003 (Exercise of Functions) Order 2009 (SI 2009/3021), Art 4, provides that the functions conferred on a constable under ss 17 and 19 of the Crime (International Co-operation) Act 2003 may be exercised by (a) a general customs official in relation to an offence, or to offences, which if committed in the UK would relate to a general customs matter; or (b) a customs revenue official in relation to an offence, or to offences, which if committed in the UK would relate to a customs revenue matter, those terms being defined in Art 3.

126 That is, anything that would be admissible in evidence at a trial for the offence: PACE, s 8(4). 'Material' in s 8(1) includes a computer hard disk: *R (Faisaltex Ltd) v The Crown Court at Preston* [2009] 1 WLR 1697, para 74.

127 As defined in s 10 of PACE: see *R v Central Criminal Court ex p Francis and Francis (a firm)* [1989] AC 346; *R v Guildhall Magistrates Court ex p Primlaks Holdings (Panama) Inc* [1990] 1 QB 261.

128 As defined in s 11 of PACE.

129 As defined in s 14 of PACE.

130 It is not a condition precedent to the grant of a warrant under s 8 that other methods of obtaining the material have been tried without success or not been tried because they were bound to fail: *R v Billericay Justices ex p Frank Harris (Coaches) Limited* [1991] Crim LR 472.

131 *R (Glenn & Co Ltd) v Her Majesty's Commissioners for Revenue and Customs* [2011] EWHC 2998 (Admin), para 29; *R (Cronin) v Sheffield Justices* [2003] 1 WLR 752, para 15.

19.85 The premises mentioned in s 8(1A) are one or more sets of premises specified in the application (in which case the application is for a 'specific premises warrant'); or any premises occupied or controlled by a person specified in the application, including such sets of premises as are so specified (in which case the application is for an 'all premises warrant').

19.86 Section 8(1B) provides that if the application is for an all premises warrant, the justice of the peace must also be satisfied that because of the particulars of the offence referred to in s 8(1)(a), there are reasonable grounds for believing that it is necessary to search premises occupied or controlled by the person in question which are not specified in the application in order to find the material referred to in para 8(1)(b); and that it is not reasonably practicable to specify in the application all the premises which he occupies or controls and which might need to be searched.

19.87 The conditions in s 8(3) are that it is not practicable to communicate with any person entitled to grant entry to the premises; that it is practicable to communicate with a person entitled to grant entry to the premises but it is not practicable to communicate with any person entitled to grant access to the evidence; that entry to the premises will not be granted unless a warrant is produced; that the purpose of a search may be frustrated or seriously prejudiced unless a constable arriving at the premises can secure immediate entry to them.

19.88 Where a warrant is issued, s 8(2) permits a constable to seize and retain anything for which a search has been authorised under s 8(1).

19.89 Section 8 warrants are the most common type of search warrant, nevertheless the courts have repeatedly emphasized that a justice of the peace to whom application is made under s 8 must be careful to ensure that the applicant is entitled to the warrant. He must be personally satisfied on the material before him that the conditions are satisfied. He is not entitled simply to accept the assertions of the applicant for the warrant.[132] In *R v Guildhall Magistrates' Court ex p Primlaks Holdings (Panama) Limited* [1990] 1 QB 261, 272–3 Parker LJ said:

> Before concluding this judgment I find it necessary to make certain observations with regard to applications under section 8 of the Act. It confers a draconian power and it is of vital importance that it should be clearly understood by all concerned that it is for the justice to satisfy himself that there are reasonable grounds for believing the various matters set out. The fact that a police officer, who has been investigating the matter, states in the information that he considers that there are reasonable grounds is not enough. The justice must himself be satisfied. In the present case Detective Inspector Keating did not even so state. He merely stated that the matters set out led to the belief that there were reasonable grounds for suspecting that the first of the conditions was satisfied. This would not be completely fatal, for a justice would be entitled to consider that the facts went further. But if the applicant goes no further than to speak of reasonable grounds for suspicion, a justice would in my judgment need to be very cautious indeed before he went further. In the present case he clearly could not have done so.

19.90 In *R (Redknapp) v Commissioner of the City of London Police* [2009] 1 WLR 209 it was said that obtaining a search warrant is never a formality, and that all the material necessary to justify the warrant's grant should be contained in the information provided on the application form. If the magistrate (or judge in the case of an application under s 9 of PACE) requires any further information to satisfy himself that the warrant is justified, a note should be made of the additional information so that there is a proper record of the full basis upon which the warrant has been granted; where the required information is not contained in the application form or in such a note, the warrant is unlawfully issued.

19.91 In *R (Wood) v North Avon Magistrates' Court* [2009] EWHC 3614, the observations in *R (Redknapp) v Commissioner of the City of London Police* [2009] 1 WLR 209 were approved.

---

[132] Para 19.97.

It was said also that, as a matter of good practice, a police officer applying for a search warrant under s 8 should, save in exceptional circumstances, be an officer directly involved in the investigation; and, in making the application, the police should make full and frank disclosure of any earlier search of the premises, because that would be material as to whether evidence of substantial value or relevance would still be on the premises (s 8(1)(b), (c)), and also as to whether the purposes of a search would be frustrated or seriously prejudiced if advance warning were to be given (s 8(3)(d)), which would depend on whether or not the defendant had cooperated with the earlier search.

Before issuing a warrant under s 8, a justice has to be satisfied that the material to be seized does not prima facie consist of material subject to legal privilege, excluded material, or special procedure material.[133] That the application may include such material may be obvious from the nature of the material sought or the occupation of the person affected. For example, in *R (Bates) v Chief Constable of Avon and Somerset* [2009] EWHC 942 (Admin) the High Court quashed a s 8 warrant which had authorized the seizure of computers of an expert witness, which were bound to include privileged material. In *R (Power-Hynes) v Norwich Magistrates' Court* [2009] EWHC 1512 (Admin), the warrant was quashed because the claimant was an accountant and company secretary for several companies, some of which not under investigation, and the warrant authorized the seizure of material which was special procedure material. **19.92**

If an item is seized as apparently falling within the scope of the warrant and it subsequently transpires to be subject to LPP, its seizure does not thereby become unlawful unless the officer had reasonable grounds to believe it to be subject to legal privilege at the time of seizure.[134] Where it is not practicable to separate out privileged material from non-privileged at the time of search (eg where both are contained on a computer) then Part 2 of the Criminal Justice and Police Act 2001 contains provisions allowing all the material to be seized for later examination and return of the privileged material.[135] **19.93**

Production orders and search warrants under s 9 and Sch 1

Where a constable wishes to obtain excluded material or special procedure material[136] then s 9 provides that an application to a judge under Sch 1 of PACE may be made.[137] Schedule 1 permits a judge to issue production orders and search warrants for material which cannot be obtained using a s 8 warrant. Applications under Sch 1 are often made in relation to material held by banks and media organizations.[138] **19.94**

---

133 *R v Guildhall Magistrates' Court ex p Primlaks Holdings Co (Panama) Inc* [1990] 1 QB 261, 270.

134 PACE, s 19(6); *R v Chesterfield Justices ex p Bramley* [2000] QB 576; cf *R v Customs and Excise Commissioners ex p Popely* [1999] STC 1016. Part 2 of the Criminal Justice and Police Act 2001 contains provisions allowing all the material to be seized for later examination and return of the privileged material. Section 19(6) of PACE is disapplied in relation to the extended powers of seizure provided for in ss 50 and 51 of the Criminal Justice and Police Act 2001.

135 *El Curd v Winchester Crown Court* [2011] EWHC 1853; *Windsor v Bristol Crown Court* [2011] EWHC 1899 (Admin).

136 In *R v Preston Crown Court ex p McGrath*, The Times, 27 October 1992, the Divisional Court held that where the material of the subject of the application is mixed in that it consists of special procedure material and other material, all of the material can be the subject of a special procedure order under Sch 1. Mann LJ said that Parliament could not have intended sequential applications under Sch 1 and s 8; see also *R v Snaresbrook Crown Court ex p Director of Public Prosecutions* (1988) 86 Cr App R 227.

137 The judge has discretion to hear an application for access to excluded material or special procedure material under Sch 1 in chambers: *R v Central Criminal Court ex p Director of Public Prosecutions*, The Times, 1 April 1988.

138 *R (Malik) v Manchester Crown Court* [2008] 4 All ER 403; *R (Bright) v Central Criminal Court* [2000] 1 WLR 662; *R v Bristol Crown Court, ex p Bristol Press and Picture Agency Ltd* 85 Cr App R 190; *R v Middlesex Guildhall Crown Court ex p Salinger* [1993] QB 564.

19.95 The provisions of Sch 1 are complicated and have been the subject of a considerable number of cases. Because these provisions permit the seizure of material which is confidential or which may relate to sensitive matters, the case law emphasizes the heavy responsibility on those applying for such orders and on judges considering applications under Sch 1. In *R v Lewes Crown Court ex p Hill* (1991) 93 Cr App R 60, 65 Bingham LJ said:

> The Police and Criminal Evidence Act governs a field in which there are two very obvious public interests. There is, first of all, a public interest in the effective investigation and prosecution of crime. Secondly, there is a public interest in protecting the personal and property rights of citizens against infringement and invasion. There is an obvious tension between these two public interests because crime could be most effectively investigated and prosecuted if the personal and property rights of citizens could be freely overridden and total protection of the personal and property rights of citizens would make investigation and prosecution of many crimes impossible or virtually so. The 1984 Act seeks to effect a carefully judged balance between these interests and that is why it is a detailed and complex Act. If the scheme intended by Parliament is to be implemented, it is important that the provisions laid down in the Act should be fully and fairly enforced. It would be quite wrong to approach the Act with any preconception as to how these provisions should be operated save in so far as such preconception is derived from the legislation itself. It is, in my judgment, clear that the courts must try to avoid any interpretation which would distort the parliamentary scheme and so upset the intended balance. In the present field, the primary duty to give effect to the parliamentary scheme rests on circuit judges. It seems plain that they are required to exercise those powers with great care and caution.

19.96 The applicant is under a duty to make full disclosure when applying under Sch 1.[139] In particular, it is the duty of the applicant to set out, either in the notice itself or in further documentation, a description of all that is sought to be produced.[140] The judge must also give reasons for making an order or granting a warrant under Sch 1.[141] Because of the complex access conditions in Sch 1, reasons are particularly important so that any reviewing court can see which conditions the warrant was granted under. In the absence of reasons this may be incapable of determination and the warrant is likely to be quashed as a consequence.[142]

19.97 A number of decisions have emphasized that it is not sufficient for a constable simply to assert that the conditions in Sch 1 have been met. The judge should not make an order unless personally satisfied after a full inquiry[143] that one or other of the sets of access conditions is fulfilled.[144] In *R (Bright) v Central Criminal Court* [2000] 1 WLR 662, 677 Judge LJ said:

> .... it is clear that the judge personally must be satisfied that the statutory requirements have been established. He is not simply asking himself whether the decision of the constable making the application was reasonable, nor whether it would be susceptible to judicial review on *Wednesbury* grounds ... This follows from the express wording of the statute, 'If ... a circuit judge is satisfied that one ... of the sets of access conditions is fulfilled'. The purpose of this provision is to interpose between the opinion of the police officer seeking the order and the consequences to the individual or organisation to whom the order is addressed the safeguard of a judgment and decision of a circuit judge.

---

[139] *R v Lewes Crown Court ex p Hill* (1991) 93 Cr App R 60, 69; *R v Acton Crown Court ex p Layton* [1993] Crim LR 458. See para 19.70.

[140] Para 19.70; *R v Central Criminal Court ex p Adegbesan* 84 Cr App R 219; *R v Inner London Crown Court ex p Baines and Baines (a Firm)* [1988] QB 579.

[141] *R v Central Criminal Court ex p Propend Finance Property Ltd [1996]* 2 Cr App R 26; *R v Lewes Crown Court ex p Nigel Weller & Co (a firm)* 12 May 1999 (CO/2890/98).

[142] Para 19.73.

[143] *R v Leeds Crown Court ex p Switalski* [1991] COD 199.

[144] *R v Crown Court at Lewes ex p Hill* (1991) 93 Cr App R 60; *R v Guildhall Magistrates' Court ex p Primlaks Holdings (Panama) Inc* [1990] 1 QB 261, 272; *R v Southampton Crown Court ex p J & P* [1993] Crim LR 962.

As to production orders, para 4 of Sch 1 permits[145] a judge to issue a production order provided that either of the sets of access conditions in para 2 is satisfied. A production order requires the person to whom it is addressed to produce the material to a constable for him to take away or give him access to it within seven days from the date of the order (para 4). **19.98**

An application for a production order must be made inter partes and a notice served on the person concerned under para 7.[146] Where such a notice has been served the person must not destroy, alter, or dispose of the material without the leave of the judge or a constable (para 11). **19.99**

In relation to search warrants, para 12 permits a judge to issue a search warrant where (i) either of the sets of access conditions in paras 2 or 3 and the conditions in para 14 are fulfilled in relation to each set of premises specified in the application;[147] or (ii) the access conditions in para 3 are fulfilled and an order under para 4 has not been complied with.[148] **19.100**

One of the conditions in para 14 (para 14(d)) is that the service of a notice under para 4 would seriously prejudice the investigation. This condition means that a warrant under Sch 1 should only be granted as a measure of last resort.[149] In *(Faisaltex Ltd) v Crown Court at Preston* [2009] 1 WLR 1697 it was held that there was no basis for issuing a warrant under Sch 1 in relation to material located in the offices of a firm of solicitors, where the solicitors were reputable and not under investigation. There was no reason to think that they would not comply with a production order, so the condition in para 14(d) was not satisfied.[150] **19.101**

A warrant under para 12 authorizes a constable to enter and search the premises or (as the case may be) all the premises occupied or controlled by the person referred to in para 2(a)(ii) or 3(a), including such sets of premises as are specified in the application (an 'all premises warrant'). **19.102**

In *R v Central Criminal Court ex p AJD Holdings* [1992] Crim LR 669 the court said that it was important, before any search warrant was applied for, that careful consideration was given to what material it is hoped a search might reveal, so as to be clear to anyone subsequently considering the lawfulness of the warrant. The application should make clear that the material sought related to the crime under investigation. A written note should be made of anything said in support of the application beyond what was set out in the written application. There should be careful briefing of the officers who were to execute the search, including how material to be **19.103**

---

145 Even where the access conditions are satisfied the judge retains a discretion whether or not to make an order or issue a warrant under para 12: *R (Bright) v Central Criminal Court* [2000] 1 WLR 662, 678. However once a judge has concluded under para (2)(a)(i) of Sch 1 that a serious offence has been committed, it is inconsistent to refuse an application for access to material by finding under para 2(c) that it is not in the public interest that access should be given: *R v Crown Court at Northampton ex p Director of Public Prosecutions* 93 Cr App R 376.

146 There is, however, no requirement to give notice of the proceedings to the accused or suspected person. Para 7 of Sch 1 applies as between the applicant and the person or institution in whose custody special procedure material is believed to be held: *R v Crown Court at Leicester ex p Director of Public Prosecutions* 86 Cr App R 254.

147 Para 12(a).

148 Para 12(b).

149 *R v Southwark Crown Court ex p Bowles* [1998] AC 641, 649. In *R v Central Criminal Court ex p AJD Holdings* [1992] Crim LR 669, Nolan LJ observed that the scheme of Sch 1 is that applications should normally be made *inter partes* save for certain exceptions. The fact that a solicitor is under investigation does not of itself justify intruding *ex parte* into his affairs and those of his clients. All the circumstances must be considered, including the seriousness of the matter being investigated, evidence already available to the police, and the extent to which the solicitor already knows of the interest in his affairs such as might cause him to destroy or interfere with documents; cf *R v Maidstone Crown Court, ex p Waitt* [1988] Crim LR 384 (*ex p* applications should never become a matter of common form); *R v Leeds Crown Court ex p Switalski* [1991] COD 199 where the court said that where a search was to be made of solicitors' premises one would expect the application to be *inter partes*, but not where the firm itself was under investigation.

150 cf *R (Miller Gardner Solicitors) v Minshull Street Crown Court* [2002] EWHC 3077 (Admin).

searched for might be thought to relate to the crime under investigation. The warrant in that case was quashed because it permitted the officers to search for material which could not have been relevant to their investigation. The court also quashed the warrants on two other grounds, namely that they wrongly included material subject to legal privilege, and that in any event they should have been applied for *inter partes*.[151]

19.104 Once a judge has made an *ex parte* order issuing a warrant pursuant to para 12, he has no power to review or rescind the order, even if it can be shown that he made it on an erroneous basis, having been given inaccurate or incomplete information. Instead, the aggrieved party should apply directly for judicial review.[152] In *Barclays Bank plc (Trading as Barclaycard) v Taylor* [1989] 1 WLR 1066 the Court of Appeal held that, irrespective of whether a notice under Sch 1 of PACE is defective, an access order, once made, being valid on its face, is fully effective until set aside by due process; and that since a banker's duty of confidentiality to his client is qualified by the exception of disclosure under compulsion of law, a bank which complies with an access order is not thereby in breach of its duty to its client.[153]

19.105 All search warrants, including those issued under s 2 of the Criminal Justice Act 1987 and Part 2 and Sch 1 of PACE are subject to the protections in ss 15 and 16 of PACE. These protections are designed to protect the person whose premises are being searched and are stringent in their effect.[154] A failure to comply with any of the requirements of either s 15 or 16 will render the entry, search and seizure unlawful and render the SFO and the relevant police force liable to an action for damages.[155]

19.106 Section 15 requires the warrant to contain essential information such as the name of the person who applies for it, the name of the enactment under which is was issued, the address of the premises to be searched, and the date on which it is issued.[156] The warrant must also authorize entry on one occasion only unless it expressly authorizes multiple entries.[157] Section 15(6)(b) requires the warrant to identify, so far as is practicable, the articles or persons to be sought. A warrant may fail this test because it is too wide,[158] or too vague,[159] and so liable to be quashed. The warrant should be sufficiently clear and precise for those interested in its execution to know precisely what are the limits of the power it grants.[160]

---

[151] *R (Redknapp) v Commissioner of the City of London Police* [2009] 1 WLR 209.

[152] *R (Energy Financing Team Ltd) v Director of the Serious Fraud Office* [2005] EWHC 1626 (Admin), para 24(8)–(9); *R v Liverpool Crown Court ex p Wimpey plc* [1991] COD 370; cf *R v Lewes Crown Court ex p Hill* (1991) 93 Cr App R 60, where the judge did entertain an application to set aside the warrant and no adverse comment was made by the Divisional Court.

[153] The Court went on to say that since such an order could not be made by consent and the responsibility for deciding whether the access conditions were satisfied rested with the judge making the order, and since the public interest in assisting the police investigation of crime might be frustrated if the account holder knew of the application, it is not necessary for the purpose of giving business efficacy to the banker–client relationship to imply an obligation that the bank, in the absence of special circumstances known only to itself, should either oppose or probe the application or supporting evidence, or that it should inform its client of the application.

[154] *R v Central Criminal Court ex p AJD Holdings Ltd* [1992] Crim LR 669.

[155] *Bhatti v Croydon Magistrates' Court* [2011] 1 WLR 948, paras 23–29; *R v Chesterfield Justices ex p Bramley* [2000] QB 576, 589; *R v Chief Constable of Warwickshire ex p Fitzpatrick* [1999] 1 WLR 564, 574; *R v Chief Constable of Lancashire ex p Parker* [1993] QB 577, 584.

[156] s 15(6).

[157] s 15(5).

[158] *R v Central Criminal Court ex p AJD Holdings Ltd* [1992] Crim LR 669; *R v Southampton Crown Court ex p J & P* [1993] Crim LR 962.

[159] *R (Powers-Hynes) v Norwich Magistrates' Court* [2009] EWHC 1512 (Admin).

[160] *R (Glenn & Co Ltd) v Her Majesty's Commissioners for Revenue and Customs* [2011] EWHC 2998 (Admin), para 58; *McGrath v Chief Constable of the Royal Ulster Constabulary* [2001] 2 AC 731, 738.

Section 16 contains procedural requirements for the conduct of searches.[161] Section 16(2) provides that a warrant to enter and search premises may authorize persons to accompany any constable who is executing it.[162] Section 16(2A) and (2B) provide that a person authorized to accompany the constable has the same powers as the constable whom he accompanies in respect of the execution of the warrant, and the seizure of anything to which the warrant relates, but he may exercise those powers only in the company, and under the supervision, of a constable.[163] The entry and search must take place within three months of the date of the warrant,[164] and must take place at a reasonable hour unless the constable executing it considers that this would frustrate the purpose of the search.[165] If the warrant is an all premises warrant, no premises which are not specified in it may be entered or searched unless a police officer of at least the rank of inspector has in writing authorized them to be entered.[166] No premises may be entered or searched for the second or any subsequent time under a warrant which authorizes multiple entries unless a police officer of at least the rank of inspector has in writing authorized that entry to those premises.[167] The constable must identify himself to the occupier (or other person present), produce the warrant, and supply him with a copy it.[168] If no-one is present then a copy of the warrant, must be left at the premises.[169] Section 16(8) provides that the search must be a search to the extent required for the purpose for which the warrant was issued. It follows that if items are seized which fall outside the terms of the warrant then their seizure will be unlawful unless the items seized can properly be described as *de minimis*.[170] If there is an ulterior improper motive for the search then it will be unlawful under s 16(8).[171] **19.107**

Use of the powers in Part 2 of the Police and Criminal Evidence Act 1984 following a request for mutual assistance

Having considered their operation in the domestic context, the use of the Part 2 procedures in the mutual assistance context can now be examined. In summary, CICA 2003, s 13(1)(b) provides that the territorial authority may direct that a search warrant be applied for under s 16. Section 16 provides that search warrants under Part 2 of PACE may be issued in respect of overseas criminal conduct provided that the condition of dual criminality is satisfied. **19.108**

Section 16(1) states that Part 2 of PACE is to have effect as if references to indictable offences in s 8 of and Sch 1 to PACE included any conduct which constitutes an offence under the law of a country outside the UK, and would, if it occurred in England and Wales, constitute an indictable offence.[172] **19.109**

---

161 See also Code B, issued under s 66 of PACE.

162 s 16(2). If a person not named on the warrant accompanies the constable in the execution of the warrant then the entry, search, and seizure will be unlawful: *Gross v Southwark Crown Court* [1999] QB 538 (presence of American investigator not named on the warrant unlawful). Therefore, if foreign investigators wish to be present then this must be made clear in the request and they should be named on the warrant.

163 *R (Van Der Pijl) v Kingston Upon Thames Crown Court* [2012] EWHC 1846 (Admin), paras 17–18.

164 s 16(3).

165 s 16(4).

166 s 16(3A). An 'all premises warrant' is defined in s 8(1A)(b) of PACE.

167 s 16(3B).

168 s 16(5) and (6). See *Bhatti v Croydon Magistrates' Court* [2011] 1 WLR 948; *R (Redknapp) v Commissioner of the City of London Police* [2009] 1 WLR 2091.

169 s 16(7).

170 *R v Chief Constable of Warwickshire ex p Fitzpatrick* [1999] 1 WLR 564, 575; *R v Southwark Crown Court ex p Sorsky Defries* [1996] Crim LR 195; but cf *R v Chesterfield Justices ex p Bramley* [2000] QB 576 at 588 where these decisions were doubted on this point.

171 *R (Paul Da Costa & Co) v Thames Magistrates' Court* [2002] STC 267.

172 See s 16(3) in relation to Northern Ireland.

19.110 An application for a warrant or order by virtue of s 16(1) may be made only in pursuance of a direction given under s 13 (s 16(2)(a)), or if it is an application for a warrant or order under s 8 of, or Sch 1 to, PACE by a constable[173] for the purposes of an investigation by an international joint investigation team of which he is a member (s 16(2)(b)).

19.111 An 'international joint investigation team' has the meaning given by s 88(7) of the Police Act 1996.[174] Thus, where the application has been made by the member of such a team, a direction by the territorial authority need not have been given. Section 16(2)(b) thus allows joint investigation teams to conduct investigations in the UK of serious criminal activity with links to one or more Member State.[175]

Warrants under s 17 of CICA 2003[176]

19.112 Section 17(1) provides that a justice of the peace may issue a warrant under s 17 if he is satisfied, on an application made by a constable,[177] that criminal proceedings have been instituted against a person in a country outside the UK or a person has been arrested in the course of a criminal investigation carried on there; the conduct constituting the offence which is the subject of the proceedings or investigation would, if it occurred in England and Wales constitute an indictable offence;[178] there are reasonable grounds for suspecting that there is on premises in England and Wales[179] occupied or controlled by that person evidence relating to the offence. Section 17 is broadly analogous to the power to issue a warrant under s 8 of PACE, however s 8 does not require criminal proceedings to have been instituted or that a person has been arrested.

19.113 A warrant under s 17 may authorize a constable to enter the premises in question and search the premises to the extent reasonably required for the purpose of discovering any evidence relating to the offence, and to seize and retain any evidence for which he is authorized to search.

19.114 By virtue of s 26(1) a court in England and Wales or Northern Ireland, or a justice of the peace, may not issue a warrant under s 17 in respect of any evidence unless the court or justice has reasonable grounds for believing that it does not consist of or include items subject to legal privilege.[180]

---

173 Or customs officer: para 19.82.

174 That is any investigation team formed in accordance with any Framework Decision on joint investigation teams adopted under Art 34 of the Treaty on European Union; the Convention on Mutual Assistance in Criminal Matters and its Protocol; or any international agreement to which the UK is a party and which is specified for the purposes of this section in an order made by the Secretary of State.

175 This provision implements Art 13 of the Convention on Mutual Assistance in Criminal Matters (entitled 'Joint investigation teams') which provides, amongst other things: '1. By mutual agreement, the competent authorities of two or more Member States may set up a joint investigation team for a specific purpose and a limited period, which may be extended by mutual consent, to carry out criminal investigations in one or more of the Member States setting up the team …'. Their purpose is to carry out joint investigations into crimes with cross-border elements, with a view to improving and speeding up the investigation of such crimes. Teams will be set up by two or more member States for a specific purpose and for specific investigations, which may be carried in any of the participating member States. All team members must act under the direction of the team leader, who must be provided by the competent authorities of the member State where the team carries out its investigation. If the investigation moves into another member State's territory, the team leader will change.

176 For Scotland, see s 18.

177 Or a customs officer: para 19.82.

178 In Northern Ireland, an arrestable offence.

179 Or Northern Ireland.

180 Para 19.84.

A warrant issued under s 17 is subject to the safeguards in ss 15 and 16 of PACE.[181] An application for a warrant under s 17(1) may be made only in pursuance of a direction given under s 13.[182] **19.115**

Giving the direction under s 13

Where the Secretary of State or the Commissioners have made a direction under s 13(1)(b) following a request for mutual assistance, one of four[183] forms of application may be made by either a constable or a customs officer:[184] **19.116**

- an application for a search warrant under s 8; an application for a production order under Sch 1 of PACE; or an application for a search warrant under Sch 1 of PACE, in each case, with the term indictable offence being read as including any conduct which is an offence under the law of a country or territory outside the UK and would constitute such an offence if it had occurred in the UK; or
- an application for a warrant under s 17.

In *R v Central Criminal Court ex p Propend Finance Property Ltd* [1996] 2 Cr App R 26 the Divisional Court considered whether the Secretary of State was required under the equivalent provision to s 16 in the Criminal Justice (International Co-operation) Act 1990 to specify in his direction what form of warrant or order should be obtained. The Secretary of State had given a direction to the Commissioner of the Metropolitan Police (under what was the equivalent of s 17 in the 1990 Act) which left the decision to him. The High Court held that the direction was unlawful and that the Secretary of State was required to specify the form of assistance to be given in the following form. This decision was, however doubted by Brooke LJ in *R v Southwark Crown Court ex p Gross*, 24 July 1998 (CO 1759/98).[185] **19.117**

Transmission of the evidence

Once the request has been executed and the evidence been obtained either in proceedings under s 15 before a nominated court, by the SFO, or using the powers in ss 16 and 17, the evidence may be transmitted to the requesting state either directly or indirectly. **19.118**

In relation to proceedings before a nominated court, para 6(1) of Sch 1 provides that the evidence received by the court is to be given to the court or authority that made the request or to the territorial authority for forwarding to the court or authority that made the request. So far as may be necessary in order to comply with the request where the evidence consists of a document, the original or a copy is to be provided, and where it consists of any other Article, the Article itself, or a description, photograph, or other representation of it, is to be provided (para 6(2)). **19.119**

By s 2(8A) of the Criminal Justice Act 1987, any evidence obtained by the Director for use by an overseas authority must be given to the overseas authority which requested it or given to the Secretary of State for forwarding to that overseas authority. If the Director makes a direct transmission he will normally require the provision of an undertaking that the document or **19.120**

---

181 Para 19.106 and para 19.107.

182 CICA 2003, s 17(2).

183 cf *R v Central Criminal Court ex p Propend Finance Property Ltd* [1996] 2 Cr App R 26, 32.

184 Crime (International Co-operation) Act 2003 (Exercise of Functions) Order 2005 (SI 2005/425).

185 Brooke LJ's comments were obiter dicta. Moreover, his views appear to have been predicated upon the false assumption that the Secretary of State is bound to direct the police to obtain a search warrant if that is the only form of assistance requested by the foreign state. However the Secretary of State is not under any such obligation. It is for him to decide on what form of assistance should be given and, indeed, whether to provide any assistance at all.

other information obtained will not be used other than in criminal prosecutions arising from the investigation set out in this letter of request, without the prior consent of the Secretary of State for the Home Department.

19.121 Section 19(1) of CICA 2003 allows any evidence seized under ss 16–18 to be sent directly by a constable to the requesting court or authority, unless the requesting territory is not a party to the Convention on Mutual Assistance on Criminal Matters, in which case the evidence will be sent to the territorial authority for forwarding to the requesting court or authority.[186]

19.122 Article 11 of the Crime (International Co-operation) Act 2003 (Exercise of Functions) Order 2005[187] provides that any function conferred under s 19 on a constable in England and Wales or Northern Ireland must be exercised by a customs officer instead of a constable where the evidence has been seized by a customs officer under a search warrant or production order issued by virtue of s 16, or a search warrant issued under s 17. Article 7 provides that the Commissioners may exercise the function under s 19 of forwarding evidence to the court or authority which made a request for assistance where that evidence has been sent to them by a customs officer under s 17 for such forwarding.

19.123 Whilst the point is not free from doubt, it would appear that the Secretary of State or other territorial authority retains a discretion to transmit the evidence and that it could decline to do so if it would not be appropriate. Whilst in the absence of any objection from the persons affected the Secretary of State is entitled to forward the material received from the executing authority to the requesting state, where an objection is raised the Secretary of State should not forward the material until the question has been resolved.[188]

19.124 The representatives of the foreign state are permitted to have some limited access to the documentation prior to its transmission for bona fide purposes connected with the execution of the request and no unlawful transmission takes place if they are permitted to see the documents or to take notes about them.[189]

Use of the evidence in the requesting state

19.125 CICA 2003 does not on its face limit the use of the evidence to the reasons it is needed as listed in the letter of request. However, before transmission takes place, the UK Central Authority generally requires the requesting authority to provide an undertaking that the evidence will only be used for the purposes for which assistance was granted, that is, that no document or other information obtained will be used other than in the criminal prosecutions arising from the investigation set out in the letter of request without the prior consent of the relevant UK authority.[190]

19.126 This form of undertaking provides a form of 'specialty protection' analogous to that which exists for extradition defendants.[191] However, if the undertaking is incapable of being observed

[186] See Government Explanatory Notes to CICA 2003, para 65. See App M3, p 776.

[187] SI 2005/425.

[188] *Gross v Southwark Crown Court*, 24 July 1998 (CO/1759/98).

[189] *R v Secretary of State for the Home Department ex p Fininvest Spa* [1997] 1 WLR 743, 757–758; *R v Central Criminal Court ex p Propend Property Ltd* [1996] 2 Cr App R 26, 32–33; *R v Southwark Crown Court ex p Sorsky Defries* [1996] COD 117.

[190] Para 11 of the Harare Scheme contains a specific restriction to this effect. Some countries, for example Switzerland, have entered reservations to Art 2(b) of the European Convention on Mutual Assistance 1959 requiring such an undertaking before assistance will be given. The UK did not enter a reservation but does require an undertaking; cf CICA 2003, s 9 which provides a statutory limitation in respect of evidence obtained from abroad for use in the UK. Whether an undertaking is required as a matter of law was doubted in *R (Abacha) v Secretary of State for the Home Department* [2001] EWHC Admin 787, para 44.

[191] Para 5.72.

by the requesting state because of the provisions of its domestic law (which might, as in Italy, permit civil parties to the criminal proceedings to obtain and use evidence obtained for the purposes of the criminal trial) then it may nevertheless be a proper exercise of the territorial authority's discretion to transmit material or offer assistance.[192]

Hearing evidence from the UK by television or telephone link[193]

Sections 30 and 31 of CICA 2003 introduce new measures to allow evidence to be taken in the UK and transmitted by television or telephone to criminal proceedings being conducted abroad. **19.127**

Television links

Section 30 applies where the Secretary of State receives a request from an authority mentioned in s 30(2) ('the external authority'), for a person in the UK to give evidence through a live television link in criminal proceedings before a court in a country outside the UK. For these purposes, criminal proceedings include any proceedings on an appeal before a court against a decision in administrative proceedings.[194] **19.128**

The authority referred to in s 30(2) is the authority in that country which appears to the Secretary of State to have the function of making requests of the kind to which this section applies. **19.129**

Unless he considers it inappropriate to do so, the Secretary of State must by notice in writing nominate a court in the UK where the witness may be heard in the proceedings in question through a live television link (s 30(3)). **19.130**

By s 30(4) anything done by the witness in the presence of the nominated court which, if it were done in proceedings before the court, would constitute contempt of court is to be treated for that purpose as done in proceedings before the court. Any statement made on oath by a witness giving evidence in pursuance of s 30 is to be treated for the purposes of s 1 of the Perjury Act 1911 as made in proceedings before the nominated court. **19.131**

Part 1 of Sch 2 (evidence given by television link) is to have effect to contain detailed provisions concerning evidence by television link. Subject to s 30(4) and (5) and the provisions of that Schedule, evidence given pursuant to s 30 is not to be treated for any purpose as evidence given in proceedings in the UK. **19.132**

Telephone links

Section 31 applies where the Secretary of State receives a request, from an authority mentioned in s 31(2) ('the external authority') in a participating country, for a person in the UK to give evidence by telephone in criminal proceedings before a court in that country. Criminal proceedings include any proceedings on an appeal before a court against a decision in administrative proceedings. **19.133**

The authority mentioned in s 31(2) is the authority in that country which appears to the Secretary of State to have the function of making requests of the kind to which this section applies. **19.134**

---

[192] *R (JP Morgan Chase Bank National Association) v Director of the Serious Fraud Office* [2012] EWHC 1674 (Admin), para 58.

[193] MLA Guidelines, App M3, p 769.

[194] Section 51(1).

19.135 A request under s 31(1) must specify the court in the participating country; give the name and address of the witness; state that the witness is willing to give evidence by telephone in the proceedings before that court.

19.136 By s 31(4), unless he considers it inappropriate to do so, the Secretary of State must by notice in writing nominate a court in the UK where the witness may be heard in the proceedings in question by telephone.

19.137 Anything done by the witness in the presence of the nominated court which, if it were done in proceedings before the court, would constitute contempt of court is to be treated for that purpose as done in proceedings before the court. Any statement made on oath by a witness giving evidence in pursuance of this section is to be treated for the purposes of s 1 of the Perjury Act 1911 as made in proceedings before the nominated court.

19.138 Part 2 of Sch 2 contains detailed provisions concerning telephone link evidence.

19.139 Subject to s 31(5) and (6) and the provisions of Sch 2, evidence given in pursuance of s 31 is not to be treated for any purpose as evidence given in proceedings in the UK.

C. Overseas Requests to Freeze Evidence in the UK[195]

19.140 This section examines the way in which overseas orders to freeze evidence located in the UK can be received and executed in the UK. Sections 20–27 give effect to the principle of mutual recognition of overseas freezing orders and implements in part the Council Framework Decision on the execution in the EU of orders freezing property or evidence (referred to in this section as the Freezing Framework Decision).[196] Section 66 of the Explanatory Notes to CICA 2003 explains:

> This section [s 20] implements one of the key measures set out in the 2003 Framework Decision: the requirement to execute an overseas order to freeze evidence for its subsequent use in any proceedings or investigation in a participating country, where the order is made by a court or other authority in that country. The UK is already able to consider requests for mutual legal assistance in similar circumstances, but the 2003 Framework Decision is based on the principle of mutual recognition, and requires the UK to recognise the validity of an overseas order from a participating country, subject to certain conditions, rather than consider it as a request for mutual legal assistance.

19.141 Schedule 4 of CICA 2003 contains amendments to Sch 4 of the Terrorism Act 2000 which provide for mutual recognition of freezing orders in relation to terrorist property. These are dealt with at para 25.104.

Receiving an overseas freezing order

19.142 Section 20 sets out the conditions that must be met before the territorial authority in the UK, namely the Secretary of State or the Lord Advocate, sends the overseas freezing order to a court to be considered for execution under s 21.

19.143 Section 20(1) provides that s 21 applies where an overseas freezing order made by a court or authority in a 'participating country'[197] is received from the court or authority which made or

[195] The relevant provisions of CICA 2003 came into force on 19 October 2009.

[196] 2003/577/JHA, 22 July 2003; Official Journal L 196, 2 August 2003.

[197] By s 51(2), a participating country is a country other than the UK which is a member State on a day appointed for the commencement of that provision, and any other country designated by an order made by the

confirmed the order by the territorial authority for the part of the UK in which the evidence to which the order relates is situated.

An overseas freezing order is an order for protecting, pending its transfer to the participating country, evidence which is in the UK and may be used in any proceedings or investigation in the participating country, and in respect of which the following requirements are met. 19.144

- The order must have been made by a court exercising criminal jurisdiction in the country; a prosecuting authority in the country; or any other authority in the country which appears to the territorial authority to have the function of making such orders.[198]
- The order must relate to criminal proceedings instituted in the participating country in respect of a listed offence,[199] or a criminal investigation being carried on there into such an offence.
- The order must be accompanied by a certificate which gives the specified information;[200] but a certificate may be treated as giving any specified information which is not given in it if the

Secretary of State. See Crime (International Co-operation) Act 2003 (Designation of Participating Countries) (England, Wales and Northern Ireland) Order 2008 (SI 2008/2156); Crime (International Co-operation) Act 2003 (Designation of Participating Countries) (England, Wales and Northern Ireland) Order 2009 (SI 2009/613); Crime (International Co-operation) Act 2003 (Designation of Participating Countries) (England, Wales and Northern Ireland) (No 2) Order 2009 (SI 2009/1764); Crime (International Co-operation) Act 2003 (Designation of Participating Countries) (England, Wales and Northern Ireland) Order 2010 (SI 2010/36); Crime (International Co-operation) Act 2003 (Designation of Participating Countries) (England, Wales and Northern Ireland) (No 2) Order 2011 (SI 2011/229).

[198] In relation to clause 20(3)(c) of the Bill (now s 20(3)(c)) the Attorney General said during the Committee stage in the House of Lords (see HL Deb 23 January 2003, GC84 and 85):

> ... the purpose of Clause 20(3)(c) is to cover all judicial authorities in other EU countries. I say 'other EU countries' because that is the limit on the application of this provision. EU judicial authorities are designated under the 1959 Council of Europe convention, so they are clearly identified ... For many years, we have been able to execute requests for mutual legal assistance, including for search and seizure, by authorities of this type. Section 7(4)(b) of the 1990 Act includes that type of person. That is re-enacted by Clause 13(2)(b) of the Bill. So the provision merely applies to the new concept of the freezing order the same approach that has already been adopted in relation to mutual legal assistance. It has not caused any difficulties in practice. It must be available for the enforcement of overseas freezing orders.

[199] A listed offence means an offence described in Art 3(2) of the Council Framework Decision, or an offence prescribed or of a description prescribed by an order made by the Secretary of State (s 28(5)). The offences described in Art 3(2) are those which are punishable by imprisonment for more than three years and are among the list of offences:

> Participation in a criminal organisation; terrorism; trafficking in human beings; sexual exploitation of children and child pornography; illicit trafficking in narcotic drugs and psychotropic substances; illicit trafficking in weapons, munitions and explosives; corruption; fraud, including that affecting the financial interests of the European Communities within the meaning of the Convention of 26 July 1995 on the Protection of the European Communities' Financial Interests; laundering of the proceeds of crime; counterfeiting currency, including of the euro; computer-related crime; environmental crime, including illicit trafficking in endangered animal species and in endangered plant species and varieties; facilitation of unauthorised entry and residence; murder, grievous bodily injury, illicit trade in human organs and tissue; kidnapping, illegal restraint and hostage-taking; racism and xenophobia; organised or armed robbery; illicit trafficking in cultural goods, including antiques and works of art; swindling; racketeering and extortion; counterfeiting and piracy of products; forgery of administrative documents and trafficking therein; forgery of means of payment; illicit trafficking in hormonal substances and other growth promoters; illicit trafficking in nuclear or radioactive materials; trafficking in stolen vehicles; rape; arson; crimes within the jurisdiction of the International Criminal Tribunal; unlawful seizure of aircraft/ships; sabotage.

[200] By s 28(7), this is any information required to be given by the form of certificate annexed to the Council Framework Decision, or any information prescribed by an order made by the Secretary of State. The standard form of certificate annexed to the Council Framework Decision includes: details of the issuing judicial authority; details of the authority competent to enforce the freezing order in the issuing state; details of the central

territorial authority has the information in question. References in Chapter 2 of Part 1 of CICA 2003 to an overseas freezing order include its accompanying certificate.

- The certificate must be signed by or on behalf of the court or authority which made or confirmed the order; include a statement as to the accuracy of the information given in it; if it is not in English, include a translation of it into English (or, if appropriate, Welsh).
- The order must be accompanied by a request for the evidence to be sent to a court or authority mentioned in s 13(2), unless the certificate indicates when such a request is expected to be made.

Nominating a court

19.145 Section s 21(1)(a) provides that if the conditions of s 20 are met the territorial authority must nominate a court in England and Wales or (as the case may be) Northern Ireland to give effect to the overseas freezing order; send a copy of the overseas freezing order to the nominated court and to the chief officer of police for the area in which the evidence is situated; and tell the chief officer which court has been nominated.

19.146 The nominated court is to consider the overseas freezing order on its own initiative within a period prescribed by rules of court (s 21(3)). Before giving effect to the overseas freezing order, the nominated court must give the chief officer of police an opportunity to be heard (s 21(4)).

19.147 The court may decide not to give effect to the overseas freezing order only if, in its opinion, one of the following conditions is met. The first condition is that, if the person whose conduct is in question were charged in the participating country with the offence to which the overseas freezing order relates or in the UK with a corresponding offence, he would be entitled to be discharged under any rule of law relating to previous acquittal or conviction. The second condition is that giving effect to the overseas freezing order would be incompatible with any of the Convention rights within the meaning of the Human Rights Act 1998.

Giving effect to the overseas freezing order

19.148 Section 22 provides the mechanism whereby the nominated court gives effect to the overseas freezing order.

19.149 Section 22(1) provides that the nominated court is to give effect to the overseas freezing order by issuing a warrant authorizing a constable to enter the premises to which the overseas freezing order relates and search the premises to the extent reasonably required for the purpose of discovering any evidence to which the order relates, and to seize and retain any evidence for which he is authorized to search. But, in relation to England and Wales and Northern Ireland, so far as the overseas freezing order relates to excluded material or special procedure material[201] the court is to give effect to the order by making a production order (s 22(2)).

19.150 Section 26(1) provides that the court may not issue a warrant under s 22 in respect of any evidence unless the court has reasonable grounds for believing that it does not consist of or include

---

authority responsible for transmission and reception of the freezing order (UK and Ireland only); details about the freezing order itself (date, purpose, executing procedure, for example); information about the evidence subject to the overseas freezing order (a precise description of the property and its last known location); details about the identity of the natural or legal person suspected of the offence (or convicted thereof); details as to whether the executing state should confiscate, secure, and/or transfer the evidence to the issuing state; a description of the relevant grounds for the freezing order and a summary of facts as known to the issuing judicial authority as well as the legal remedies against the freezing order for interested parties, including bona fide third parties, available in the issuing state.

[201] As defined in s 28(3).

items subject to legal privilege, excluded material, or special procedure material. Section 26(1) does not prevent a warrant under s 22(5) being issued for special procedure material or excluded material.

A production order is an order for the person who appears to the court to be in possession of the material to produce it to a constable before the end of the period of seven days beginning with the date of the production order or such longer period as the production order may specify. The constable may take away any material produced to him under a production order; and the material is to be treated for the purposes of s 21 of PACE as if it had been seized by the constable (s 22(3)). **19.151**

If a person fails to comply with a production order, the court may (whether or not it deals with the matter as a contempt of court) issue a warrant under s 22(1) in respect of the material to which the production order relates (s 22(4)). **19.152**

Section 23 provides that the nominated court may postpone giving effect to an overseas freezing order in respect of any evidence in order to avoid prejudicing a criminal investigation which is taking place in the UK or if under an order made by a court in criminal proceedings in the UK, the evidence may not be removed from the UK. **19.153**

Evidence seized under the order

Section 24(1) provides that any evidence seized by or produced to the constable under s 22 is to be retained by him until he is given a notice under s 24(2) or authorized to release it under s 25(2). **19.154**

By s 24(2), if the overseas freezing order was accompanied by a request for the evidence to be sent to a court or authority mentioned in s 13(2), or the territorial authority subsequently receives such a request, the territorial authority may by notice require the constable to send the evidence to the court or authority that made the request. **19.155**

Release of evidence held under the order

On an application made by a person mentioned in s 25(2), the nominated court may authorize the release of any evidence retained by a constable under s 24 if, in its opinion the condition in s 21(6) or (7) is met (double jeopardy and human rights), or the overseas freezing order has ceased to have effect in the participating country. **19.156**

In relation to England and Wales and Northern Ireland, the persons who may make such an application are the chief officer of police to whom a copy of the order was sent; the constable; any other person affected by the order (s 25(2)). **19.157**

If the territorial authority decides not to give a notice under s 24(2) in respect of any evidence retained by a constable under that section, the authority must give the constable a notice authorizing him to release the evidence. **19.158**

D. Requests for UK Bank Transaction Information[202]

Part 1, Chapter 4 of CICA 2003 provides for the disclosure of banking information in connection with criminal investigations in EU member States or other designated states.[203] Chapter 4 **19.159**

---

[202] MLA Guidelines, App M3, p 769.
[203] ss 37–41 apply to Scotland.

implements the 2001 Protocol to the Convention on Mutual Assistance in Criminal Matters.[204] The purpose of the Protocol is to tackle serious crime, in particular economic crime and money laundering. Countries participating in the 2001 Protocol are obliged to identify, provide information about, and monitor bank accounts at the request of other participating countries, subject to certain restrictions and conditions which are explained in more detail below. The 2001 Protocol obliges participating countries to establish mechanisms whereby they can provide the stipulated information. The manner in which they do so is left to individual participating countries.

Request for customer information from a UK financial institution

Receipt of request

19.160 Section 32 applies where the Secretary of State receives a request from an authority mentioned in s 32(2) for customer information to be obtained in relation to a person who appears to him to be subject to an investigation in a participating country[205] into serious criminal conduct.

19.161 The authority mentioned in s 32(2) is the authority in a participating country which appears to the Secretary of State to have the function of making requests of the kind to which s 32 applies.

19.162 After receiving a request the Secretary of State may direct a senior police officer[206] to apply, or arrange for a constable to apply, for a customer information order; or direct a senior customs officer[207] to apply, or arrange for a customs officer to apply, for such an order (s 32(3)).[208]

19.163 Section 32(4) defines a customer information order to be an order made by a judge[209] that a financial institution[210] specified in the application for the order must, on being required to do so by notice in writing given by the applicant for the order, provide any such customer information as it has relating to the person specified in the application.

---

[204] Official Journal C 326, 21 November 2001, p 1. See also the Explanatory Report to the Protocol to the 2000 Convention on Mutual Assistance in Criminal Matters between the Member States of the European Union, Official Journal C 257, 24 October 2002, p 1.

[205] A participating country means a country other than the UK which is a member State and any other country designated by an order made by the Secretary of State: s 51(2). See Crime (International Co-operation) Act 2003 (Designation of Participating Countries) (England, Wales and Northern Ireland) Order 2008 (SI 2008/2156); Crime (International Co-operation) Act 2003 (Designation of Participating Countries) (England, Wales and Northern Ireland) Order 2009 (SI 2009/613); Crime (International Co-operation) Act 2003 (Designation of Participating Countries) (England, Wales and Northern Ireland) (No 2) Order 2009 (SI 2009/1764); Crime (International Co-operation) Act 2003 (Designation of Participating Countries) (England, Wales and Northern Ireland) Order 2010 (SI 2010/36); Crime (International Co-operation) Act 2003 (Designation of Participating Countries) (England, Wales and Northern Ireland) (No 2) Order 2011 (SI 2011/229).

[206] That is a police officer who is not below the rank of superintendent: s 46(1).

[207] That is a customs officer who is not below the grade designated by the Commissioners of Customs and Excise as equivalent to the rank of superintendent: s 46(1).

[208] During the debate on the Crime (International Co-operation) Bill the Minister said (HL Deb 27 January 2003, cc 128GC):

> One of the matters that the Secretary of State will take into account will be whether the request contains the information specified in Article 1 of the Protocol, in particular the conditions in Article 1(4). That includes, for example, the requirement that the requesting authority state why it is considered that the requested information is likely to be of substantial value to the investigation. If that information is not given, refusal may follow. The test is the same as one of the tests under domestic law in PACE. We are confident, therefore, that we will not be allowing fishing expeditions.

[209] That is in England and Wales, a judge entitled to exercise the jurisdiction of the Crown Court: s 46(5)(a).

[210] s 46(4) defines a 'financial institution' to be a person who is carrying on business in the regulated sector, and in relation to a customer information order or an account monitoring order, includes a person who was

A financial institution which is required to provide information under a customer information order must provide the information to the applicant for the order in such manner, and at or by such time, as the applicant requires (s 32(5)). A customer information order has effect in spite of any restriction on the disclosure of information (however imposed) (s 32(6)). Thus a financial institution may lawfully disclose information under a customer information order in spite of the duty of confidentiality it owes to the account holder. **19.164**

'Customer information' is defined in s 32(6) by reference to the definition of that term in the Proceeds of Crime Act 2002. Section 32(6) provides that s 364 of the Proceeds of Crime Act 2002 (meaning of customer information), except s 364(2)(f) and s 364(3)(i), has effect for the purposes of s 32 as if it were included in Chapter 2 of Part 8 of the Proceeds of Crime Act 2002. Section 364(1) provides that 'customer information', in relation to a person and a financial institution, is information whether the person holds, or has held, an account or accounts or any safe deposit box at the financial institution (whether solely or jointly with another) and (if so) information as to the matters specified in s 364(2) if the person is an individual; and the matters specified in s 364(3) if the person is a company or limited liability partnership or a similar body incorporated or otherwise established outside the UK. **19.165**

Customer information obtained in pursuance of a customer information order is to be given to the Secretary of State and sent by him to the authority which made the request (s 32(8)). **19.166**

It is an offence for a financial institution to fail to comply with a customer information order. Section 36(1) provides that a financial institution is guilty of an offence if without reasonable excuse it fails to comply with a requirement imposed on it under a customer information order. A financial institution guilty of an offence under s 36(1) is liable on summary conviction to a fine not exceeding level 5 on the standard scale. **19.167**

A financial institution is also guilty of an offence if, in purported compliance with a customer information order, it makes a statement which it knows to be false or misleading in a material particular, or recklessly makes a statement which is false or misleading in a material particular. A financial institution guilty of an offence under s 36(3) is liable on summary conviction, to a fine not exceeding the statutory maximum, or on conviction on indictment, to a fine. **19.168**

Making, varying, or discharging a customer information order

A judge may make a customer information order, on an application made to him pursuant to a direction under s 32(3), if he is satisfied that the person specified in the application is subject to an investigation in the country in question; the investigation concerns conduct which is serious criminal conduct;[211] the conduct constitutes an offence in England and Wales or (as the case may be) Northern Ireland, or would do were it to occur there; and the order is sought for the purposes of the investigation (s 33(1)). **19.169**

The application may be made *ex parte* to a judge in chambers (s 33(2)). The application may specify: all financial institutions; a description, or particular descriptions, of financial institutions; or a particular financial institution or particular financial institutions (s 33(3)). **19.170**

---

carrying on business in the regulated sector at a time which is the time to which any requirement for him to provide information under the order is to relate. 'Business in the regulated sector' is to be interpreted in accordance with Sch 9 to the Proceeds of Crime Act 2002.

[211] s 46(3) provides that serious criminal conduct means conduct which constitutes an offence to which Art 1(3) of the 2001 Protocol applies, or an offence specified in an order made by the Secretary of State or, in relation to Scotland, the Scottish Ministers for the purpose of giving effect to any decision of the Council of the EU under Art 1(6). Art 1(3) of the Protocol includes inter alia offences which are punishable by a maximum term of imprisonment of at least four years in the requesting member State and two years in the requested state.

19.171 The court may discharge or vary a customer information order on an application made by the person who applied for the order; a senior police officer; a constable authorized by a senior police officer to make the application; a senior customs officer; a customs officer authorized by a senior customs officer to make the application (s 33(4)).

Requests to the UK to monitor bank accounts

19.172 Sections 35 and 36 implement Article 3 of the 2001 Protocol in relation to incoming requests for account monitoring orders. Article 3 provides for requests to be made for a specified bank account to be monitored during a specified period of time. Such a request might be made subsequent to an Article 1 request for bank details or in cases where the investigator already has the details of the relevant account. Account monitoring procedures were introduced in the UK under the Proceeds of Crime Act 2002,[212] but separate provision is required in this Act to ensure that the UK can respond to all requests that meet the requirements of the 2001 Protocol, which has a wider scope than the Proceeds of Crime Act 2002.

Request for an account monitoring order

19.173 Section 35 applies where the Secretary of State receives a request from an authority mentioned in s 35(2) for account information to be obtained in relation to an investigation in a participating country[213] into criminal conduct.

19.174 The authority referred to in s 35(2) is the authority in that country which appears to the Secretary of State to have the function of making requests of the kind to which this section applies.

19.175 The Secretary of State may direct a senior police officer[214] to apply, or arrange for a constable to apply, for an account monitoring order; or direct a senior customs officer[215] to apply, or arrange for a customs officer to apply, for such an order.

19.176 An account monitoring order is an order made by a judge that a financial institution[216] specified in the application for the order must, for the period stated in the order,[217] provide account information of the description specified in the order to the applicant in the manner, and at or by the time or times, stated in the order (s 35(4)). An account monitoring order has effect in spite of any restriction on the disclosure of information (however imposed) and so overrides the institution's duties of confidentiality (s 35(6)).

[212] See s 370 of the Proceeds of Crime Act 2002.

[213] A participating country means a country other than the UK which is a member State and any other country designated by an order made by the Secretary of State: s 51(2).

[214] That is a police officer who is not below the rank of superintendent: s 46(1).

[215] That is a customs officer who is not below the grade designated by the Commissioners of Customs and Excise as equivalent to the rank of superintendent: s 46(1).

[216] s 46(4) defines a 'financial institution' to be a person who is carrying on business in the regulated sector, and in relation to a customer information order or an account monitoring order, includes a person who was carrying on business in the regulated sector at a time which is the time to which any requirement for him to provide information under the order is to relate. 'Business in the regulated sector' is to be interpreted in accordance with Sch 9 to the Proceeds of Crime Act 2002.

[217] In relation to this period the Government's Explanatory Notes to CICA 2003, para 98 comment: 'Article 3(3) of the 2001 Protocol provides that the order shall be made with due regard for the national law of the requested Member State. Under the Proceeds of Crime Act 2002, account monitoring orders may be made for a period of up to 90 days and the same restriction will apply to requests under the 2001 Protocol. No limit is stated because the arrangements will be made between the relevant authorities on a case by case basis, as provided for in Article 3(4) of the 2001 Protocol.'

Account information is information relating to an account or accounts held at the financial institution specified in the application by the person so specified (whether solely or jointly with another) (s 35(5)). **19.177**

Account information obtained in pursuance of an account monitoring order is to be given to the Secretary of State and sent by him to the authority which made the request (s 35(7)). **19.178**

Making, varying, or discharging an account monitoring order

Section 36(1) provides that a judge may make an account monitoring order, on an application made to him in pursuance of a direction under s 35(3), if he is satisfied that there is an investigation in the country in question into criminal conduct, and the order is sought for the purposes of the investigation. **19.179**

The application may be made *ex parte* to a judge in chambers (s 36(2)). **19.180**

The application may specify information relating to all accounts held by the person specified in the application for the order at the financial institution so specified; a particular description, or particular descriptions, of accounts so held, or a particular account, or particular accounts, so held (s 36(3)). **19.181**

The court may discharge or vary an account monitoring order on an application made by the person who applied for the order; a senior police officer; a constable authorized by a senior police officer to make the application; a senior customs officer; a customs officer authorized by a senior customs officer to make the application (s 36(4)). **19.182**

Account monitoring orders have effect as if they were orders of the court (s 36(5)). **19.183**

The offence of disclosure in relation to customer information orders and account monitoring orders

In order to be effective it is obvious that customer information orders and account monitoring orders must remain confidential. Section 42 makes it an offence for a financial institution or its employees to disclose information about these orders. **19.184**

Section 42 applies where a financial institution is specified in a customer information order or account monitoring order made in any part of the UK, or the Secretary of State or the Lord Advocate receives a request under s 13 for evidence to be obtained from a financial institution in connection with the investigation of an offence in reliance on Article 2 (requests for information on banking transactions) of the 2001 Protocol. **19.185**

If the institution, or an employee of the institution, discloses any of the following information, the institution or (as the case may be) the employee is guilty of an offence (s 42(2)). That information is that the request to obtain customer information or account information, or the request mentioned in s 42(1)(b), has been received; that the investigation to which the request relates is being carried out; or that, in pursuance of the request, information has been given to the authority which made the request. **19.186**

An institution guilty of an offence under s 42 is liable on summary conviction, to a fine not exceeding the statutory maximum, and on conviction on indictment, to a fine. **19.187**

Any other person guilty of an offence under this section is liable on summary conviction, to imprisonment for a term not exceeding six months or to a fine not exceeding the statutory maximum, or to both, and on conviction on indictment, to imprisonment for a term not exceeding five years or to a fine, or to both. **19.188**

20

CROSS-BORDER SURVEILLANCE

A. Introduction

20.01 This chapter examines the provisions of the Regulation of Investigatory Powers Act 2000[1] and CICA 2003 which allow surveillance operations to be carried out in the UK by foreign police officers.

20.02 Article 40 of the Schengen Convention[2] provides that police officers keeping a person under surveillance in their own country because he is suspected of having committed an extraditable offence, may require neighbouring Schengen countries to assist in keeping the person under surveillance if he crosses the border into their territory. In the vast majority of cases such assistance will be requested in advance and, when the subject enters the UK, UK officers will take over the surveillance. These UK officers need to be properly authorized to conduct such surveillance under RIPA.[3]

20.03 However, on occasions it will not be possible for a request to be made sufficiently far in advance for a UK team to take over the surveillance at the point of entry to the UK. Section 83 of

[1] Referred to in this chapter as 'RIPA'. RIPA also provides for mutual assistance in the interception of communications. Section 1(4) provides that where the UK is a party to an international agreement which (a) relates to the provision of mutual assistance in connection with, or in the form of, the interception of communications; (b) requires the issue of a warrant, order or equivalent instrument in cases in which assistance is given; and (c) is designated for the purposes of s 1(4) by an order made by the Secretary of State, it shall be the duty of the Secretary of State to secure that no request for assistance in accordance with the agreement is made on behalf of a person in the UK to the competent authorities of a country or territory outside the UK except with lawful authority. The Convention on Mutual Assistance in Criminal Matters between the Member States of the EU (C197/1, 12 July 2000), contains provisions relating to requests for cooperation in relation to interception (see Articles 17–22) and is designated by the Regulation of Investigatory Powers (Designation of an International Agreement) Order 2004 (SI 2004/158).

[2] Official Journal L 239, 22 September 2000, p 19. Article 40(1) provides that officers of one of the Schengen Contracting Parties who, as part of a criminal investigation, are keeping under surveillance in their country a person who is presumed to have participated in an extraditable criminal offence shall be authorized to continue their surveillance in the territory of another Contracting Party where the latter has authorized cross-border surveillance in response to a request for assistance made in advance. Conditions may be attached to the authorization.On request, the surveillance will be entrusted to officers of the Contracting Party in whose territory this is carried out. The request for assistance must be sent to an authority designated by each of the Contracting Parties and empowered to grant or to pass on the requested authorization. Article 40(2) provides that where, for particularly urgent reasons, prior authorization cannot be requested from the other Contracting Party, the officers carrying out the surveillance shall be authorized to continue beyond the border the surveillance of a person presumed to have committed criminal offences listed in Article 40(7), provided that the conditions specified in Article 40 are met.

[3] In Scotland the relevant Act is the Regulation of Investigatory Powers (Scotland) Act 2000.

CICA 2003 implements Article 40(2) of the Schengen Convention, which covers such cases, by making provision for a foreign surveillance operation which was initiated in one participating country but which has had to travel unexpectedly to the UK, to continue lawfully to keep an individual under surveillance for a period of up to five hours. Home Office Circular 3/2005 contains operational guidance concerning cross-border surveillance under the powers discussed below.

B. Surveillance in the UK by Foreign Officers

20.04 Section 83 of CICA 2003 amends RIPA by inserting a new section (s 76A) to allow police or customs officers from other member States to continue surveillance on UK territory for a period of up to five hours.

20.05 Section 76A(1) provides that s 76A applies where a foreign police or customs officer is carrying out 'relevant surveillance' outside the UK which is lawful under the law of the country or territory in which it is being carried out; circumstances arise by virtue of which the surveillance can for the time being be carried out only in the UK and it is not reasonably practicable in those circumstances for a UK officer[4] to carry out the surveillance in the UK in accordance with an authorization under Part 2 of RIPA.

20.06 Section 76A(10) defines a foreign police or customs officer to be a police or customs officer who, in relation to a country or territory other than the UK, is an officer for the purposes of Article 40 of the Schengen Convention or any other international agreement to which the UK is a party and which is specified for the purposes of the section in an order made by the Secretary of State with the consent of the Scottish Ministers.

20.07 Section 76A(2) defines 'relevant surveillance' to be surveillance which is carried out in relation to a person who is suspected of having committed a 'relevant crime'; and is, for the purposes of Part 2 of RIPA, directed surveillance[5] or intrusive surveillance.[6]

20.08 Section 76A(3) defines a 'relevant crime' to be a crime which falls within Article 40(7) of the Schengen Convention; or is a crime for the purposes of any other international agreement to which the UK is a party and which is specified for the purposes of s 76A in an order made by the Secretary of State with the consent of the Scottish Ministers.[7] The crimes listed in Article 40(7) of the Schengen Convention are:

> Murder; manslaughter; rape; arson; forgery of money; aggravated burglary and robbery and receiving stolen goods; extortion; kidnapping and hostage taking; trafficking in human beings;

---

[4] That is a member of a police force; a member of the staff of the Serious Organized Crime Agency; or a customs officer (or their Scottish equivalents): s 76A(11).

[5] s 26(2) of RIPA defines directed surveillance (subject to s 26(6)) to be surveillance which is covert but not intrusive and is undertaken (a) for the purposes of a specific investigation or a specific operation; (b) in such a manner as is likely to result in the obtaining of private information about a person (whether or not one specifically identified for the purposes of the investigation or operation); and (c) otherwise than by way of an immediate response to events or circumstances the nature of which is such that it would not be reasonably practicable for an authorization under Part 2 of RIPA to be sought for the carrying out of the surveillance.

[6] s 26(3) of RIPA provides that, subject to s 26(4)–(6), surveillance is intrusive for the purposes of this Part if, and only if, it is covert surveillance that (a) is carried out in relation to anything taking place on any residential premises or in any private vehicle; and (b) involves the presence of an individual on the premises or in the vehicle or is carried out by means of a surveillance device.

[7] The sorts of crimes the Government indicated it would designate will be 'very similar to those covered by Article 40 of Schengen. They would be serious crimes ... We ... would not, as a matter of policy, agree to that kind of arrangement in respect of petty offences': HL Deb 3 March 2003 col 644, per Lord Filkin.

illicit trafficking in narcotic drugs and psychotropic substances; breach of the laws on arms and explosives; wilful damage through the use of explosives; illicit transportation of toxic and hazardous waste.

Section 76A(4) provides that relevant surveillance carried out by the foreign police or customs officer in the UK during the permitted period[8] is to be lawful for all purposes if the condition mentioned in s 76A(6) is satisfied; the officer carries out the surveillance only in places to which members of the public have or are permitted to have access, whether on payment or otherwise; and conditions specified in any order made by the Secretary of State with the consent of the Scottish ministers are satisfied in relation to its carrying out. However, no surveillance is lawful by virtue of this subsection if the officer subsequently seeks to stop and question the person in the UK in relation to the relevant crime. Also, a person designated by an order made by the Secretary of State may notify the officer that the surveillance is to cease being lawful by virtue of s 76A(4) when he gives the notification (s 76A(8)). The Director General of SOCA has been designated for these purposes by the Regulation of Investigatory Powers (Foreign Surveillance Operations) Order 2004.[9] **20.09**

The condition in s 76A(6) is satisfied if, immediately after the officer enters the UK, he notifies a person designated by the Director General of the Serious Organized Crime Agency of that fact; and (if the officer has not done so before) he requests an application to be made for an authorization under Part 2 of RIPA for the carrying out of the surveillance. **20.10**

Section 76A(5) provides that the officer is not to be subject to any civil liability in respect of any conduct of his which is incidental to any surveillance that is lawful by virtue of s 76A(4). **20.11**

Section 84 provides protection for foreign officers whilst they are carrying out their duties in the UK. Section 84(1) provides that for the purposes of s 89 of the Police Act 1996 (assaults on constables) any person who is carrying out surveillance in England and Wales under s 76A of RIPA is to be treated as if he were acting as a constable in the execution of his duty. **20.12**

---

[8] The 'permitted period' means the period of five hours beginning with the time when the officer enters the UK: s 76A(7), unless pursuant to s 76(8) a person designated by an order made by the Secretary of State orders the surveillance to cease. The Director General of SOCA has been designated for this purpose by the Regulation of Investigatory Powers (Foreign Surveillance Operations) Order 2004 (SI 2004/1128), as amended.

[9] SI 2004/1128.

21

INTERNATIONAL INFORMATION SYSTEMS AND MUTUAL LEGAL ASSISTANCE INSTITUTIONS

A. Introduction

Since the 1990s the EU has been increasingly active in criminal justice matters.[1] This chapter examines the EU bodies and systems that have developed to enable the police, judiciary, and customs within the EU to exchange information concerning crime and those suspected of having committed criminal offences. The principal bodies and systems are Europol and the Europol Information System; Eurojust; the Schengen Information System (SIS); the Customs Information System; and the European Justice Network (EJN). They are the primary means by which information can be exchanged across borders within the EU in an effort to combat cross-border crime. **21.01**

This chapter also looks at the work of Interpol, which is the best-known international body working in the field of mutual legal assistance. **21.02**

B. European Information Systems

The European Police Office (Europol)

The European Police Office (Europol) is the EU law enforcement organization that handles criminal intelligence with the aim of combating serious international organized crime. It is based in The Hague and its current (2012) Director is a former British civil servant, Robert Wainwright.[2] **21.03**

---

1 Para 15.11, para 17.22.

2 See <https://www.europol.europa.eu/>.

21.04 The establishment of Europol was agreed in the Treaty of Amsterdam, which inserted a new Title VI in the Treaty on European Union. Article K.1 declared a number of areas as matters of common interest, including, in Article K.1(9), police cooperation for the purposes of preventing and combating terrorism, unlawful drug trafficking, and other serious forms of international crime, including if necessary certain aspects of customs cooperation, in connection with the organization of a Union-wide system for exchanging information within a European Police Office.

21.05 The Council Act of 26 July 1995 drew up the Convention on the establishment of a European Police Office (the Europol Convention).[3] The Europol Convention was ratified by all member States and came into force on 1 October 1998. Europol began operating on 1 July 1999, replacing the Europol Drugs Unit, which had been set up on a temporary basis in 1995. On 1 January 2002 Europol's mandate was extended to deal with the serious forms of international crime listed in the Annex to the Europol Convention. Europol is accountable to the Council of Ministers for Justice and Home Affairs.

21.06 In 2009 the Council enacted Council Decision of 6 April 2009 establishing the European Police Office (the Europol Decision).[4] The Europol Decision provided a new legal basis within the EU for Europol and created a 'new' Europol in place of the existing organization with effect from 1 January 2010.

21.07 Europol's objective is set out in Article 3 of the Europol Decision:

> The objective of Europol shall be to support and strengthen action by the competent authorities of the Member States and their mutual cooperation in preventing and combating organized crime, terrorism and other forms of serious crime affecting two or more Member States.

21.08 Article 4 specifies the crimes which fall within Europol's competence. Europol's remit covers organized crime, terrorism, and the other forms of serious crime as listed in the Annex to the Europol Decision affecting two or more member States in such a way as to require a common approach by the member States owing to the scale, significance, and consequences of the offences, as well as related offences.[5]

21.09 Article 5 of the Europol Decision sets out Europol's principal tasks. These include (a) collecting, storing, processing, analysing, and exchanging information and intelligence; (b) notifying member States' competent authorities of information concerning them and of any connections identified between criminal offences; (c) aiding investigations in the member States, in particular by forwarding all relevant information to the national units;[6] (d) asking the competent

---

[3] Official Journal C 316, 27 November 1995.

[4] 2009/371/JHA, Official Journal L 121/37, 15 May 2009.

[5] The crimes listed in the Annex are: unlawful drug trafficking; illegal money-laundering activities; crime connected with nuclear and radioactive substances; illegal immigrant smuggling; trafficking in human beings; motor vehicle crime; murder; grievous bodily injury; illicit trade in human organs and tissue; kidnapping, illegal restraint and hostage taking; racism and xenophobia; organized robbery; illicit trafficking in cultural goods, including antiquities and works of art; swindling and fraud; racketeering and extortion; counterfeiting and product piracy; forgery of administrative documents and trafficking therein; forgery of money and means of payment; computer crime; corruption; illicit trafficking in arms, ammunition, and explosives; illicit trafficking in endangered animal species; illicit trafficking in endangered plant species and varieties; environmental crime; illicit trafficking in hormonal substances and other growth promoters.

[6] Pursuant to Articles 8 and 9 of the Decision, each member State has a designated Europol National Unit which is the liaison body between Europol and the competent authorities of that State. The heads of national units meet on a regular basis to assist Europol on operational matters, on their own initiative or at the request of the Management Board or Director. Each national unit seconds at least one ELO to Europol, who is hosted at Europol headquarters in their own liaison bureau. They represent the interests of their national unit at Europol in accordance with their national law. SOCA is the UK's Europol National Unit.

authorities of the member States concerned to initiate, conduct, or coordinate investigations and to suggest the setting up of joint investigation teams[7] in specific cases; (e) providing intelligence and analytical support to member States in connection with major international events; (f) preparing threat assessments, strategic analyses, and general situation reports relating to its objective, including organized crime threat assessments.

Europol has no executive powers and is a support service for the law enforcement agencies of member States. Europol officials are not entitled to arrest suspects or to act without the approval of national authorities. However, the support provided by Europol can contribute to the executive measures carried out by national authorities. **21.10**

Europol has negotiated bilateral operational or strategic agreements with other states and international organizations including: Bulgaria; Canada; Colombia; Eurojust; European Central Bank; European Commission; European Monitoring Centre for Drugs and Drug Addiction; Iceland; Interpol; Norway; Romania; Russia; Switzerland; Turkey, United Nations Office on Drugs and Crime; the United States of America; and the World Customs Organization. **21.11**

Europol Information System (EIS)

The Europol Information System (EIS) was established by Title II of the Europol Convention, and is now provided for in Articles 11–13 of the Europol Decision. **21.12**

Article 11(1) provides that Europol shall maintain the EIS. Article 12(1) provides that the EIS can only be used to process such data as are necessary for the performance of Europol's tasks. The data input shall relate to: (a) persons who, in accordance with the national law of the member State concerned, are suspected of having committed or having taken part in a criminal offence in respect of which Europol is competent or who have been convicted of such an offence; (b) persons regarding whom there are factual indications or reasonable grounds under the national law of the member state concerned to believe that they will commit criminal offences in respect of which Europol is competent. **21.13**

Only certain information relating to suspects can be held on the EIS. Article 12(2) provides that the data relating to the persons referred to in Article 12(1) may include only the following particulars: surname, maiden name, given names, and any alias or assumed name; date and place of birth; nationality; sex; place of residence, profession, and whereabouts of the person concerned; social security numbers, driving licences, identification documents, and passport data; and where necessary, other characteristics likely to assist in identification, including any specific objective physical characteristics not subject to change such as dactyloscopic data[8] and DNA profile (established from the non-coding part of DNA). Article 12(3) permits data relating to (inter alia) previous convictions and *modus operandi* also to be processed by the EIS. **21.14**

Article 12(5) requires the deletion of data relating to a case from the EIS if those proceedings against the person concerned are definitively dropped or if that person is definitively acquitted. **21.15**

Article 13(1) governs use of the EIS. National units, liaison officers, the Director, Deputy Directors, and duly empowered Europol staff have the right to input data directly into the EIS and to retrieve them from it. Data may be retrieved by Europol where it is necessary for the performance of its tasks in a particular case. Retrieval by the national units and liaison officers shall be effected in accordance with the laws, regulations, administrative provisions, and **21.16**

[7] See Article 6, and see also CICA 2003, s 16(5) and the Police Act 1996, s 88(7).

[8] That is, fingerprints.

procedures of the accessing party, and subject to any additional provisions laid down in the Europol Decision.

Eurojust

21.17 In order to reinforce the fight against serious organized crime, in October 1999 the Tampere European Council agreed that a unit should be set up to improve the coordination of prosecutions and investigations within member States.

21.18 Eurojust was the first permanent network of judicial authorities to be established anywhere in the world. Eurojust hosts meetings between investigators and prosecutors from different states dealing with individual cases and at a strategic level and specific types of criminality. Its mission is to enhance the development of Europe-wide cooperation in criminal justice matters.

21.19 Eurojust was established by Council Decision of 28 February 2002[9] (the Eurojust Decision). It is a body with legal personality and is financed by the general budget of the EU. It is based in The Hague.[10] The Eurojust Decision was amended by a further Decision in 2003[11] and was further amended in 2008 when the Council's Decision on the Strengthening of Eurojust was ratified.[12] The 2008 Decision's purpose was to enhance the operational capabilities of Eurojust, increase the exchange of information between the interested parties, facilitate and strengthen cooperation between national authorities and Eurojust, and strengthen and establish relationships with partners and third states.

21.20 Article 2 of the Eurojust Decision provides that it shall be composed of members seconded by each member State, being either a prosecutor, judge, or police officer. Article 3 sets out Eurojust's objectives. It provides that in the context of investigations and prosecutions of the crimes referred to in Article 4, concerning two or more member States, particularly when it is organized, the objectives of Eurojust are to stimulate and improve the coordination, between the competent authorities of the member States, of investigations and prosecutions in the member States; to improve cooperation between the competent authorities of the member States, in particular by facilitating the execution of international mutual legal assistance and the implementation of extradition requests; and to otherwise support the competent authorities of the member States in order to render their investigations and prosecutions more effective.

21.21 Article 4(1) specifies that Eurojust is competent to act in relation to the types of crime and the offences in respect of which Europol is at all times competent to act, and related offences. These are described in para 21.08. For types of offences other than those referred to in Article 4(1), Eurojust may in addition, in accordance with its objectives, assist in investigations and prosecutions at the request of a competent authority of a member state.

21.22 Article 6 provides that Eurojust may, among other things, ask the competent authorities of the member States concerned to consider undertaking an investigation or prosecution of specific acts. It can set up a joint investigation team in keeping with the relevant cooperation instruments and provide it with any information that is necessary for it to carry out its tasks. Eurojust is also responsible for ensuring that the competent authorities of the member States concerned inform each other on investigations and prosecutions of which it has been informed. It can also assist the competent authorities of the member States, at their request, in ensuring the best possible coordination of investigations and prosecutions, and give assistance in order to improve cooperation between the competent national authorities.

---

[9] 2002/187/JHA.
[10] <http://www.eurojust.europa.eu>.
[11] 2003/659/JHA.
[12] 2009/486/JHA.

Eurojust is also referred to in the Treaty of Lisbon, Chapter 4, Articles 85 and 86. Article 85 mentions Eurojust and defines its mission, namely, to support and strengthen coordination and cooperation between national investigating and prosecuting authorities in relation to serious crime affecting two or more member States. Article 86 provides that, in order to combat crimes affecting the financial interests of the EU, the Council, by means of regulations adopted in accordance with a special legislative procedure, may establish a European Public Prosecutor's Office from Eurojust.[13] **21.23**

Schengen Information System

The Schengen Aquis

In 1985 the Schengen Agreement between Belgium, the Netherlands, Luxembourg, France, and Germany was signed with the aim of abolishing checks at their common borders and facilitating the movement and transport of goods.[14] **21.24**

The Schengen Agreement was signed outside the EU framework, and in 1990 a number of member States signed the Convention implementing the Schengen Agreement (the Schengen Convention).[15] The Schengen Convention came into effect in 1995. The Convention abolished the checks at internal borders of the signatory states and created a single external frontier, where checks for all the Schengen signatories were to be carried out in accordance with a common set of rules. Signatories to the Schengen Convention are referred to as 'Schengen Group Member States'. **21.25**

Among the main measures adopted by Schengen countries in the Convention are: the removal of checks at common borders, replacing them with external border checks; a common definition of the rules for crossing external borders and uniform rules and procedures for controls there; separation in air terminals and ports of people travelling within the Schengen area from those arriving from countries outside the area; harmonization of the rules regarding conditions of entry and visas for short stays; coordination between administrations on surveillance of borders (liaison officers and harmonization of instructions and staff training); the definition of the role of carriers in measures to combat illegal immigration; the requirement for all non-EU nationals moving from one country to another to lodge a declaration; the drawing up of rules for asylum seekers; the introduction of cross-border rights of surveillance and hot pursuit for police forces in the Schengen states; the strengthening of legal cooperation through a faster extradition system and faster distribution of information about the implementation of criminal judgments; and the creation of the SIS. **21.26**

Protocol 4 to the Treaty of Amsterdam incorporates the developments brought about by the Schengen Agreement into the EU framework. **21.27**

One of the Council's most important tasks in incorporating the Schengen area was to choose from among the provisions and measures taken by the signatory states those which formed a genuine *acquis*, that is a body of law which could serve as a basis for further cooperation. A list of the elements which make up the *acquis*, setting out the corresponding legal basis for each of them in the EC Treaty and the Treaty on European Union was adopted on 20 May 1999.[16] **21.28**

---

[13] See Green Paper on criminal-law protection of the financial interests of the Community and the establishment of a European Prosecutor, Brussels, 11 December 2001 COM (2001) 715 final; Follow-up Report on the Green Paper on the criminal-law protection of the financial interests of the Community and the establishment of a European Prosecutor, Brussels, 19 March 2003, COM(2003) 128 final.

[14] Para 17.25.

[15] Official Journal L 239, 22 September 2000, p 19.

[16] Official Journal L 176, 10 July 1999; *corrigendum*: Official Journal L 9, 13 January 2000.

21.29 The UK and Ireland have not signed the Schengen Convention. However, in accordance with Article 4 to the Protocol in the Annex to the Treaty of Amsterdam, the UK and Ireland can take part in all or some of the Schengen arrangements if the 13 Schengen Group Member States and the government representative of the country in question vote unanimously in favour within the Council.

21.30 In March 1999 the UK asked to take part in some aspects of Schengen, namely police and judicial cooperation in criminal matters, the fight against drugs and the SIS. A Council Decision approving the request by the UK was adopted on 29 May 2000.[17] CICA 2003 integrates into domestic law the provisions of the Schengen Convention relating to police and legal cooperation in criminal matters, the fight against drugs, and incorporates the SIS into domestic law.

21.31 After evaluating the conditions that must precede implementation of the provisions governing police and judicial cooperation, the Council decided on 22 December 2004 that this part of the Schengen *acquis* could be implemented by the UK.[18]

21.32 Ireland also asked to take part in some aspects of Schengen, roughly corresponding to the aspects covered by the UK's request, in June 2000. The Council adopted a decision approving Ireland's request on 28 February 2002.[19]

21.33 The member States that joined the EU on 1 May 2004 are bound by the entire Schengen *acquis*, but certain provisions will apply to them only after border controls have been abolished. They will be abolished by the Council when SIS II is operational[20] and when those member States have passed a test to show that they meet all the conditions required for the application of compensatory measure enabling internal border controls to be abolished.

The Schengen Information System (SIS)

21.34 The SIS was established by Title IV of the Schengen Convention. In essence, the SIS is a computer database of information on specific individuals, vehicles, or objects which are lost or stolen, that can be accessed by all police stations and consular agents from participating states. Article 92 provides:

> 1. The Contracting Parties shall set up and maintain a joint information system, hereinafter referred to as 'the Schengen Information System', consisting of a national section in each of the Contracting Parties and a technical support function. The Schengen Information System shall enable the authorities designated by the Contracting Parties, by means of an automated search procedure, to have access to alerts on persons and property for the purposes of border checks and other police and customs checks carried out within the country in accordance with national law and, in the case of the specific category of alerts referred to in Article 96, for the purposes of issuing visas, residence permits and the administration of legislation on aliens in the context of the application of the provisions of this Convention relating to the movement of persons.

---

[17] Official Journal L 131, 1 June 2000.

[18] Official Journal, L 395, 21 December 2004. Other EU and non-EU states are involved in the Schengen *acquis*. Although Denmark has signed the Schengen Agreement, it can choose within the EU framework whether or not to apply any new decisions taken under Title IV of the EC Treaty, even those that constitute a development of the Schengen *acquis*. But Denmark is bound by certain measures under the common visa policy. Sweden, Finland, Denmark, Iceland, and Norway belong to the Nordic passport union, which has abolished internal border checks. On 1 December 2000 the Council decided that, as from 25 March 2001, the Schengen *acquis* arrangements would apply to these five countries (Official Journal L 309, 9 December 2000). In addition, SIS arrangements were put into effect as from 1 January 2000.

[19] Official Journal L 64, 7 March 2002.

[20] Para 21.44.

2. Each Contracting Party shall set up and maintain, for its own account and at its own risk, its national section of the Schengen Information System, the data file of which shall be made materially identical to the data files of the national sections of each of the other Contracting Parties by means of the technical support function. To ensure the rapid and effective transmission of data as referred to in paragraph 3, each Contracting Party shall observe, when setting up its national section, the protocols and procedures which the Contracting Parties have jointly established for the technical support function. Each national section's data file shall be available for the purposes of carrying out automated searches in the territory of each of the Contracting Parties. It shall not be possible to search the data files of other Contracting Parties' national sections.

Article 93 provides that the purpose of the SIS is to maintain public policy and public security, including national security, in the territories of participating states and to apply the provisions of the Schengen Convention relating to the movement of persons in those territories, using information communicated via the system. **21.35**

Article 94 provides that the SIS is to contain only those categories of data which are supplied by each participating state, as required for the purposes laid down in Articles 95–100. The categories of data specified in Article 94(2) are: persons for whom an alert has been issued; objects referred to in Article 100 and vehicles referred to in Article 99. For persons, the information shall be no more than the following: surname and forenames, any aliases possibly entered separately; any specific objective physical characteristics not subject to change; first letter of second forename; date and place of birth; sex; nationality; whether the persons concerned are armed; whether the persons concerned are violent; reason for the alert; action to be taken. **21.36**

Article 95 provides that data on persons wanted for arrest for the purposes of extradition shall be entered at the request of the judicial authority of the requesting party. Before issuing an alert, the party concerned must check whether the arrest is authorized under the national law of the requested party. The party issuing the alert shall send the requested party by the quickest means possible both the alert and the information specified in Article 95(2).[21] **21.37**

Article 96 provides that data on aliens for whom an alert has been issued for the purposes of refusing entry shall be entered on the basis of a national alert resulting from decisions taken by the competent administrative authorities or courts in accordance with the rules of procedure laid down by national law. Decisions may be based on a threat to public policy or public security or to national security which the presence of an alien in national territory may pose. **21.38**

Article 97 deals with missing persons and other vulnerable individuals. It provides that data on missing persons or persons who, for their own protection or in order to prevent threats, need temporarily to be placed under police protection at the request of the competent authority or the competent judicial authority of the party issuing the alert shall be entered into the SIS, so that the police authorities may communicate their whereabouts to the party issuing the alert or may move the persons to a safe place in order to prevent them from continuing their journey, if so authorized by national law. **21.39**

Article 98 provides that data on witnesses, persons summoned to appear in connection with criminal proceedings, or persons who are to be served with a criminal judgment or a summons to report in order to serve a penalty involving deprivation of liberty shall be entered, at the request of the competent judicial authorities, for the purposes of communicating their place of residence or domicile. Information requested is to be communicated to the requesting party **21.40**

[21] cf EA 2003, s 212; EAW Framework Decision, Art 9.

in accordance with national law and the conventions in force on mutual assistance in criminal matters.

21.41 Article 99 allows data on persons or vehicles to be entered in accordance with the national law of the party issuing the alert, for the purposes of discreet surveillance or of specific checks in accordance with Article 99(5).

21.42 Article 100 provides that data on objects sought for the purposes of seizure or use as evidence in criminal proceedings shall be entered in the SIS. If a search brings to light an alert for an object which has been found, the authority which matched the two items of data shall contact the authority which issued the alert in order to agree on the measures to be taken. For this purpose, personal data may also be communicated in accordance with this Convention. The measures to be taken by the party which found the object must be in accordance with its national law.

21.43 Member States supply information (which becomes an 'alert') from their national systems to the central system via a common secure network. Searches in SIS produce a 'hit' when details of a person or object match those of an existing alert. The data on the SIS is managed by a national system known as SIRENE.[22] Information is not forwarded on to the central section of the SIS by the national SIRENE bureau unless it is satisfied that Schengen rules have been applied correctly. It is only when the information is forwarded to the central section of the SIS that the data can be accessed by other SIS member States.

21.44 The UK is not part of the SIS. However, expansion of the EU led to concerns that the SIS will not be able to cope with EU enlargement. Therefore, SIS II is currently under development and is anticipated to 'go live' in 2013.[23]

The Customs Information System

21.45 The formation of the European Single Market in 1993 and the subsequent abolition of border controls drove customs administrations in member States to create a means of combating smuggling on a European level. As a result, the Customs Information System (CIS) was established under the Convention on the use of information technology for customs purposes[24] (the Customs Convention) and Council Regulation (EC) No 515/97 of 13 March 1997 on mutual assistance between the administrative authorities of the member States and cooperation between the latter and the Commission to ensure the correct application of the law on customs or agricultural matters.[25] The CIS is located in Brussels. The CIS was a development of the principles of the 1967 Naples Convention which dealt with mutual assistance between Customs administrations in member States.[26]

21.46 The aim of the CIS is to enable national customs services to exchange and disseminate information on smuggling activities and requests for action. It will assist in preventing, investigating, and prosecuting serious contraventions of national laws by increasing the effectiveness of

---

22 The acronym stands for Supplementary Information Request at National Entry.

23 Proposal for Council Decision on the establishment, operation and use of the second generation Schengen information system (SIS II) COM (2005) 230 Final 31 May 2005 Council Doc 9942/05; Proposal for a Regulation of the European Parliament and of the Council on the establishment, operation and use of the second generation Schengen information system (SIS II) COM (2005) 236 Final 31 May 2005 Council Doc 9943/05; Parliamentary European Scrutiny Committee – Tenth Report, Section 14 (17 July 2012), available through <http://www.publications.parliament.uk>.

24 Official Journal C 136, 27 November 1995, p 34.

25 Official Journal L 082, 22 March 1997, p 1.

26 Replaced by Council Act 98/C 24/01 of 18 December 1997 drawing up, on the basis of Article K3 of the Treaty on European Union, the Convention on mutual assistance and cooperation between customs administrations, Official Journal C 24 of 23 January 1998 ('Naples II').

cooperation and control procedures of the customs administrations of the member States. The information system offers immediate access to relevant customs information to all member States, without communication barriers. Since information can be accessed quickly, legitimate trade will be facilitated while officers can act effectively, on the basis of information regarding possible illegal activities.

The CIS consists of two databases, one falling within the framework of European Community actions, and the other falling under intergovernmental action. The Customs Convention sets out the procedures to be adopted in the use of information technology for customs purposes. It outlines the broad parameters of information that may be stored, the manner in which information can be amended, security systems, and data-protection provisions. **21.47**

The main categories of information collected relate to commodities; means of transport; businesses; persons; fraud trends; availability of expertise. **21.48**

European Judicial Network

The European Judicial Network (EJN)[27] is a network of national contact points for the facilitation of judicial cooperation in criminal matters. The network was created by the Joint Action 98/428 JHA of 29 June 1998[28] in order to fulfil recommendation No 21 of the Action Plan to Combat Organised Crime adopted by the Council on 28 April 1997.[29] **21.49**

A new legal basis for the EJN entered into force on 24 December 2008, namely the Council Decision 2008/976/JHA of 16 December 2008 on the European Judicial Network. **21.50**

The EJN is composed of contact points in member States and at the European Commission. Its Secretariat is based in The Hague. **21.51**

National contact points are designated by each member State among central authorities in charge of international judicial cooperation, judicial authorities, and other competent authorities with specific responsibilities in the field of international judicial cooperation, both in general and for certain forms of serious crime, such as organized crime, corruption, drug trafficking, or terrorism. In the UK, the CPS and the SFO have EJN contact points.[30] **21.52**

EJN provides assistance by acting as active intermediaries to facilitate judicial cooperation; by providing legal and practical information to competent local authorities; by providing support with requests for judicial cooperation; by creating an EU judicial culture; and by cooperating with other judicial networks, third countries, and judicial partners. **21.53**

Data protection issues

The storage and use of personal information by prosecuting authorities carries with it the risk of abuse either by them or by ill-intentioned individuals or organizations. Article 114[31] of the Schengen Convention requires member States to designate a supervisory authority to carry out independent supervision of the data. Article 114 provides: **21.54**

> Each contracting Party shall designate a supervisory authority responsible, in compliance with national law, for carrying out independent supervision of the data file of the national section of the Schengen Information System and for checking that the processing ad utilization of

---

27 <http://www.ejn-crimjust.europa.eu>.

28 Official Journal L 191, 7 July 1998, p 4.

29 Official Journal C 251, 15 August 1997, p 1.

30 <http://www.homeoffice.gov.uk/police/mutual-legal-assistance/assistance-from-overseas/>.

31 In Ch 3 of Title IV which is entitled 'Protection of personal data and security of data under the Schengen Information System'.

> data included in the [SIS] are not in violation of the rights of the person concerned. For this purpose the supervisory authority shall have access to the data file of the national section of the [SIS] ... Any person shall have the right to ask the supervisory authorities to check the data concerning him which are included in the [SIS], and the use which is made of such data. That right shall be governed by the national law of the Contracting Party to which the request is made. If the data have been included by another Contracting Party, the check shall be carried out in close co-ordination with that Contracting Party's supervisory authority.

21.55 In the UK the supervisory authority is the Information Commissioner.[32] CICA 2003, s 81, creates a power of independent inspection for the Information Commissioner in respect of the SIS, the Europol Information System,[33] and the CIS,[34] by inserting a new s 54A into the Data Protection Act 1998. The section confers inspection rights in connection with data held in the three systems for the purpose of ensuring that it is being processed in accordance with the Data Protection Act 1998.

C. Provisions of CICA 2003 Relating to European Information Systems

21.56 In order to give effect to the European information systems in domestic law, laws regulating the use and disclosure of information have been amended so that disclosure for the purposes of these information systems is not unlawful.

Disclosure of information by the SFO

21.57 Section 3 of the Criminal Justice Act 1987 restricts the disclosure of information obtained by the SFO in the course of its investigations.[35] Section 80 of CICA 2003 amends s 3 to allow disclosure for the purposes of the European information systems.

21.58 Section 3(5) provides that subject to s 3(1) and (3), and to any provision of an agreement for the supply of information which restricts the disclosure of the information supplied, information obtained by any person in his capacity as a member of the SFO may be disclosed by any member of the SFO designated by the Director for the purposes of s 3(5). Section 3(5) and (6) are amended by CICA 2003, s 80, and allow information to be disclosed for the purposes of a criminal investigation or criminal proceedings in the UK or elsewhere, and for it to be disclosed inter alia to any person or body having, under the Treaty on European Union or any other treaty to which the UK is a party, the function of receiving information of the kind in question, and any person or body having, under the law of any country or territory outside the UK, the function of receiving information relating to the proceeds of crime.

Driver licensing information

21.59 Section 82 of CICA 2003 provides that information held in any form by the Secretary of State under Part 3 of the Road Traffic Act 1988 (licensing of drivers of vehicles) may be disclosed for the purposes of the Schengen information system (within the meaning of CICA 2003, s 81).

---

[32] The office established by Data Protection Act 1998, s 6(1): see <http://www.ico.gov.uk/what_we_cover/international_duties.aspx>.

[33] Para 21.12.

[34] Para 21.45.

[35] *R (Kent Pharmaceuticals Ltd) v Director of the Serious Fraud Office* [2005] 1 WLR 1302.

D. The International Criminal Police Organization (Interpol)[36]

Introduction

The aims, activities, forms of assistance, structure, and functioning of Interpol are examined in this section. **21.60**

During the First International Criminal Police Congress held in Monaco in 1914, 14 countries and states discussed the possibility of establishing an international criminal records office and harmonizing extradition procedures. In 1923, Dr Johannes Schober, Chief of Police in Vienna, Austria, organized the second International Criminal Police Congress that set up the International Criminal Police Commission (ICPC), with its headquarters in Vienna. The ICPC was Interpol's predecessor.[37] **21.61**

Today, the International Criminal Police Organization (Interpol)[38] has 190 member countries, and is the largest and best-known international police organization in the world. As an intergovernmental organization, Interpol is second in size only to the UN, where it has observer status.[39] Its headquarters are in Lyon, France.[40] **21.62**

Interpol is represented in member States by National Central Bureaux (NCBs). SOCA is the UK National Central Bureau of Interpol.[41] Its address is: **21.63**

UK National Central Bureau of Interpol
PO Box 8000
London
SE11 5EN
Tel: +44 20 7238 8115
Fax: +44 20 7238 8112

Structure

Interpol is comprised of a General Assembly, an Executive Committee, a General Secretariat, the National Central Bureau of each member country, and Advisers.[42] **21.64**

The General Assembly is the 'body of supreme authority' in the organization.[43] Each member country is represented by a government-appointed delegate(s) at the General Assembly and has one vote. Delegates meet once a year to take all major decisions affecting general policy. **21.65**

In accordance with Article 17 of the Interpol's General Regulations, the General Assembly takes its decisions in plenary session, usually by adopting resolutions which vary in legal status depending on whether the resolution relates to Interpol's functioning or to international law enforcement. Resolutions relating to the functioning of the organization are binding on its organs. Resolutions relating to law enforcement do not have a mandatory character for the member countries. In this area Interpol is restricted by the national laws and sovereignty of member countries and so can do no more than ask, urge, or encourage a particular course of action. **21.66**

---

36 <http://www.interpol.int>.

37 D McClean, *International Cooperation in Civil and Criminal Matters* (2002), p 161.

38 The official name of Interpol since its Constitution came into force on 13 June 1956: see Art 1.

39 Resolution A/RES/51/1, 15 October 1996.

40 Interpol General Secretariat, 200 quai Charles de Gaulle, 69006 Lyon, France; Fax: +33 (0)4 72 44 71 63.

41 SOCA will be abolished and replaced by the National Crime Agency if Part 1 of the Crime and Courts Bill is enacted.

42 Art 5 of the Constitution.

43 Art 6 of the Constitution.

21.67 The Executive Committee is comprised of 13 members: the President of the Organization, the three Vice-Presidents, and nine Delegates. The functions of the Executive Committee are to: supervise the execution of the decisions of the General Assembly; prepare the agenda for sessions of the General Assembly; submit to the General Assembly any programme of work or project which it considers useful; supervise the administration and work of the Secretary General; exercise all the powers delegated to it by the Assembly.[44]

21.68 The General Secretariat is made up of Interpol's permanent departments[45] and consists of the General Secretary and a technical and administrative staff.[46] The appointment of the Secretary-General is proposed by the Executive Committee and approved by the General Assembly for a period of five years.[47] The Secretary-General engages and directs the staff, administers the budget, and directs permanent departments according to the directives decided upon by the General Assembly or Executive Committee to whom he is responsible. The exercise of the Secretary-General's duties are carried out on behalf of Interpol and not any particular country. The General Secretariat's functions are specified in Article 26 of the Constitution and include putting in application the decisions of the General Assembly and the Executive Committee and serving as an international centre in the fight against ordinary crime.

21.69 In the exercise of their duties, the Constitution prohibits either the Secretary General or the staff from soliciting or accepting instructions from any government or authority outside the organization.[48] However, with the approval of the General Assembly, the Executive Committee or, in urgent cases, the Secretary-General may accept duties within the scope of its activities and competence either from other international institutions or in application of international conventions.[49]

21.70 As noted at para 21.63, each member country has an Interpol contact point called the National Central Bureau (NCB) which foreign governments requiring assistance contact directly. Each NCB is made up of national officers operating in accordance with their national laws.

The aims and scope of Interpol's activities

21.71 Interpol's Constitution is the principal document governing the organization. Article 2 of the Constitution provides that Interpol's aims are:

> (1) To ensure and promote the widest possible mutual assistance between all criminal police authorities within the limits of the laws existing in the different countries and in the spirit of the Universal Declaration of Human Rights;
>
> (2) To establish and develop all institutions likely to contribute effectively to the prevention and suppression of ordinary law crimes.

21.72 To carry out this mission, Interpol provides four principal services, referred to as its core functions:[50] (a) secure global police communications services. The fundamental condition for international police cooperation is for police forces to be able to communicate with each other securely throughout the world; (b) operational data services and databases for police. Once police can communicate internationally, they need access to information to assist in their

---

44 Art 22 of the Constitution.
45 Art 25 of the Constitution.
46 Art 27 of the Constitution.
47 Art 28 of the Constitution.
48 Art 30 of the Constitution.
49 Art 41 of the Constitution.
50 See Kersten, 'Enhancing International Law Enforcement Cooperation: A Global Overview by Interpol', in Aromaa and Viljanen, *Enhancing International Law Enforcement Cooperation, including Extradition Measures* (Monsey, New York, 2005), pp 40–50.

investigations or help them to prevent crime. Interpol has therefore developed and maintains a range of global databases, covering key data such as names of individuals, wanted persons, fingerprints, photographs, DNA, stolen and lost identification and travel documents, and Interpol notices.[51] Other projects deal with the sexual exploitation of children on the Internet, stolen vehicles and stolen works of art, bioterrorism, police training, victim identification, and cooperation with other international organizations; (c) operational police support services. Interpol currently prioritizes crime-fighting programmes on fugitives, terrorism, drugs and organized crime, trafficking in human beings, financial and high-tech crime, and corruption; (d) training.

Interpol's activities extend only to ordinary law crimes, that is to say, crimes which are not prohibited by Article 3 of the Constitution. This forbids the organization to undertake any 'intervention or activities of a political, military, religious or racial character'.[52] If an offence that is the subject of a request would compromise Interpol's neutrality, Interpol may refuse to process a request on the basis of Article 3. **21.73**

In order to determine whether a request relates to an ordinary law crime or a prohibited Article 3 topic, Interpol distinguishes (i) requests for assistance based on offences that are by their nature political, religious, or racial and are prohibited; and (ii) requests which are not by their nature political, religious, or racial but which may nonetheless be prohibited. Examples of offences which are by their nature prohibited are membership of a political organization; the expression of certain prohibited opinions; offences involving the press; insulting the authorities; offences against the internal or external security of the state; desertion from the armed forces; and recruitment or propaganda for particular religions and membership of a racial group.[53] Article 3 also covers any acts committed by politicians in connection with their political activities, even if those concerned are prosecuted after their fall from power and, in some cases, after they have fled abroad.[54] **21.74**

Offences that do not intrinsically violate Article 3 are assessed on a case-by-case basis to determine whether the political or the ordinary law element is predominant.[55] **21.75**

Offences involving terrorism, whilst often politically motivated, do not always come within the scope of Article 3. Resolution AGN/53/RES/7 (Luxembourg, 1984) gives guidance as to how Article 3 should be interpreted in relation to terrorist offences: **21.76**

> When offences are committed by persons with definite political motives but when the offences committed have no direct connection with the political life of the offenders' country or the cause for which they are fighting, the crime may no longer be deemed to come within the scope of Article 3. This is particularly true when offences are committed in countries which are not directly involved (ie outside the 'conflict area') and when the offences constitute a serious threat to personal freedom, life or property.

The restrictions contained in Article 3 are (or should be) enforced initially by Interpol's National Central Bureaux. All requests that are received, and circulate on Interpol's network of requests, must comply with the Constitution. If a request violates the Constitution then the request (in theory, at least) will not be recorded on Interpol's database of requests. **21.77**

---

51 Para 21.78.

52 This is a position that has been adopted by Interpol since 1946 when the International Criminal Police Commission decided to adopt a position of neutrality in the post-war period to gain the respect of the administrative and judicial authorities in all member countries.

53 Resolution AGN/53/RES/7 (Luxembourg, 1984).

54 Resolution AGN/53/RES/7 (Luxembourg, 1984).

55 Resolution AGN/20/RES/11 (Lisbon, 1951).

Interpol may consider that a request does not violate Article 3, but member States still have the sovereign right to determine whether an offence is political, particularly in the context of extradition proceedings.[56] Conversely, if Interpol refuses to put a request on its database, the requesting country can forward the request through a channel other than Interpol, for example, by informal assistance from other states.

Interpol Notices[57]

21.78 Interpol's Notices system principally consists of a set of colour-coded notices (Red, Blue, Green, Yellow, Black, Purple, and Orange) published for specific purposes. Special Notices may also be published within the framework of specific cooperation which are not covered by the colour categories of Notice. The rules governing Interpol's Notices are contained in its Rules on the Processing of Data, Title 3, Chapter II, which came into force on 1 July 2012. In summary:

- Red Notices (Article 82) are published at the request of an NCB or an international entity with powers of investigation and prosecution in criminal matters in order to seek the location of a wanted person and his/her detention, arrest, or restriction of movement for the purpose of extradition, surrender, or similar lawful action. The alleged offence must meet the criteria set out in Interpol's Rules on the Processing of Data, and in particular a red notice may not be published for the following categories of offences (Article 83): (i) offences that in various countries raise controversial issues relating to behavioural or cultural norms; (ii) offences relating to family/private matters; (iii) offences originating from a violation of laws or regulations of an administrative nature or deriving from private disputes, unless the criminal activity is aimed at facilitating a serious crime or is suspected of being connected to organized crime. Article 86 requires the General Secretariat to conduct a legal review of all Red Notices prior to their publication to ensure compliance with Interpol's Constitution and Rules, in particular with Articles 2 and 3 of the Constitution.
- Blue Notices (Article 88) are published in order to obtain information on a person of interest in a criminal investigation, and/or to locate a person of interest in a criminal investigation, and/or identify a person.
- Green Notices (Article 89) are published to warn about a person's criminal activities where that person is considered to be a possible threat to public safety.
- Yellow Notices (Article 90) are published to locate a missing person or to identify a person unable to identify himself/herself.
- Black Notices (Article 91) are published to identify dead bodies that have been discovered by the police.
- Purple Notices (Article 92) are published in order to warn about modi operandi, objects, devices, or concealment methods used by offenders, and/or to request information on offences to resolve them or assist in their investigation.
- Orange Notices (Article 93) are published to warn of an event, a person, an object, a process, or a modus operandi representing an imminent threat to public safety and likely to cause serious damage to property or injury to persons.

21.79 Interpol also publishes stolen works of art notices (Article 94) and Interpol/United Nations Security Council Special Notices (Article 95), which are notifications that a person or entity is subject to UN Sanctions.

21.80 Similar to the Notice is another alert mechanism known as a 'diffusion'. This is less formal than a Notice but is also used to request the arrest or location of an individual or additional informa-

[56] cf EA 2003, ss 13 and 81.
[57] <http://www.interpol.int/INTERPOL-expertise/Notices>.

tion in relation to a police investigation. A diffusion is circulated directly by an NCB to the member countries of its choice or to the entire Interpol membership (Article 97).

Challenging Interpol

Interpol's procedures are open to abuse by repressive or unscrupulous regimes, who may seek to use Interpol's systems to harass those whom it regards as undesirable, irrespective of whether or not there are *bona fide* grounds to suspect they have committed a criminal offence.[58] The availability of Interpol's files and notices to police of 190 countries around the world means that anyone whose personal information is processed by Interpol is likely to be stopped and checked at control points; be refused entry or a visa; be deported; or even be arrested and extradited. Seeking relief against Interpol in the relevent local court is problematical for aggrieved individuals.[59] However, it is possible to invoke Interpol's internal rules in order to have a Red Notice revoked, or to seek the amendment or deletion of information held by Interpol, by making an application to the Commission for the Control of Interpol's Files (CCF). **21.81**

The CCF is an independent monitoring body established under Articles 36 and 37 of Interpol's Constitution. It operates in accordance with the Operating Rules of the Commission for the Control of Interpol's Files and the Rules on the Control of Information and Access to Interpol's Files.[60] It has three main functions: (i) monitoring the application of Interpol's data protection rules to personal data processed by Interpol; (ii) advising Interpol with regard to any operations or projects concerning the processing of personal information; (iii) processing requests for access to Interpol's files. Individuals have the right to ask the CCF to examine any material held by Interpol about them (eg an accusation of crime) and to request that it be deleted if, for example, it is politically motivated and so incompatible with Article 3 of Interpol's Constitution, or to seek its amendment if it is inaccurate.[61] **21.82**

UK requests to Interpol

CICA 2003, s 8, makes provision for the transmission of UK requests for assistance in obtaining evidence from abroad.[62] It provides that a request for assistance may be sent by a judicial authority in the UK to either a court exercising jurisdiction in the place where the evidence is situated, or to any authority recognized by the government of the requesting country as the appropriate authority for receiving requests of that kind. Requests by judicial authorities or designated prosecuting authorities can also be made via the Secretary of State, who forwards the request on. Section 8(3) implements Article 6(4) of the Mutual Convention on Mutual Assistance in Criminal Matters so that in cases of urgency, a request for assistance may be sent via Interpol. **21.83**

Interpol's global communications system: I-24/7

A global communications system called I-24/7 ('Interpol-24 hours a day/7 days a week') allows Interpol's National Central Bureaux to access each other's national police databases. I-24/7 **21.84**

---

58 See <http://www.rednoticelawjournal.com>.

59 Attempts by aggrieved individuals in local courts to force Interpol to take action have in general proved to be unsuccessful: Martha, 'Challenging Acts of Interpol in Domestic Courts', in Reinisch, *Challenging Acts of International Organisations Before National Courts* (Oxford, 2011); Slomanson, 'Civil Actions Against Interpol – A field compass', 55(3) *Temple Law Review* 567–599.

60 <http://www.interpol.int/About-INTERPOL/Structure-and-governance/CCF/Access-to-INTERPOL's-files>.

61 The CCF's approach is described in 'Remedies Against Interpol: role and practice of defence lawyers', a speech delivered by Interpol's then General Counsel to the European Criminal Bar Association Conference in 2007, text available through <http://www.ecba.org>.

62 Para 18.20.

provides for the storing, exchange, and processing of police information including databases of information on Interpol notices; stolen car vehicles; stolen/lost travel and ID documents; stolen works of art; payment cards; a terrorism watch list; names, fingerprints, DNA; photographs; identification documents; international weapons trafficking and trafficking in human beings-related material.

21.85 The accessibility of this much information to as many national police forces as there are members of Interpol is intended to enhance international police cooperation. Interpol gives the following example of how I-24/7 is intended to operate:[63]

> A clandestine print shop is raided in Bulgaria, where counterfeit currency is found and a fingerprint discovered. The fingerprint is linked with one found on a firearm at a murder scene in Australia and belongs to an individual wanted by Interpol London for homicide. The suspect is stopped at Amsterdam's international airport, about to board a plane to Tokyo using a forged travel document stolen in Belgium. A search on I-24/7 would reveal where and when the document was stolen, that the individual is wanted in the UK and is linked with serious crimes in Australia and Bulgaria. Telephone numbers in his possession would link him with drug seizures in Japan.

63 <http://www.interpol.int/Public/ICPO/FactSheets/FS200301.asp>. I-Link is a related dynamic web application that allows officers in member countries to manage their data directly, and standardizes the format of the data exchanged.

22

MUTUAL ASSISTANCE IN THE SERVICE OF PROCESS

This chapter examines the statutory provisions governing the service of UK process overseas and the service of foreign procedural documents in the UK. These are contained in Part 1, Chapter 1 of CICA 2003. **22.01**

A. Service of UK Process Overseas

The principal provisions relating to the service of process overseas are CICA 2003, ss 3 and 4. In summary, ss 3 and 4 allow for process to be served directly by post or other means rather than through central authorities. **22.02**

Section 51(3) provides that in relation to England, Wales, and Northern Ireland[1] 'process' means: **22.03**

> any summons or order issued or made by a court and includes—(a) any other document issued or made by a court for service on parties or witnesses, (b) any document issued by a prosecuting authority outside the UK for the purposes of criminal proceedings.

Section 3 applies to any process issued or made for the purposes of criminal proceedings by a court in England and Wales or Northern Ireland. The process may be issued or made in spite of the fact that the person on whom it is to be served is outside the UK (s 3(2)). Where the process is to be served outside the UK and the person at whose request it is issued or made believes that the person on whom it is to be served does not understand English, he must inform the court of that fact, and provide the court with a copy of the process, or of so much of it as is material, translated into an appropriate language (s 3(3)).[2] **22.04**

Process served outside the UK requiring a person to appear as a party or attend as a witness must *not* include notice of a penalty and must be accompanied by a notice giving any information required to be given by rules of court (s 3(4)). Rule 32.1 of the Criminal Procedure Rules 2012[3] provides that the notice must state that the person required by the process to appear as a party or attend as a witness can obtain information about his rights in connection with the **22.05**

---

1 See s 51(4) in relation to Scotland.

2 This provision gives effect to Art 52(3) of the Schengen Convention, which protects a person who does not respond to process received by post from punishment. The Schengen Convention is described at para 17.25.

3 SI 2012/1726.

notice from the relevant authority. The relevant authority where the process is served at the request of the prosecuting authority, is that authority. The relevant authority where the notice is served at the request of the defendant or the prosecutor in the case of a private prosecution, is the court by which the process is served (rule 32.1(3)). The notice must also contain particulars about the relevant authority, namely, its name and address, telephone and fax number and e-mail address; and the name of a person who can provide the necessary information together with their contact details. Rule 32.1(5) requires the justices' clerk or Crown Court officer to send together with any process served outside the UK any translation which is provided under s 3(3)(b), and any translation of the information required to be given under rule 32.

22.06 Section 3(5) provides that if process requiring a person to appear as a party or attend as a witness is served outside the UK, no obligation to comply with the process under the law of the part of the UK in which the process is issued or made is imposed by virtue of the service. Accordingly, failure to comply with the process does not constitute contempt of court and is not a ground for issuing a warrant to secure the attendance of the person in question (s 3(6)). However, by s 3(7), the process may subsequently be served on the person in question in the UK (with the usual consequences for non-compliance).

22.07 Section 4 governs service of process otherwise than by post. Process to which s 4 applies may, instead of being served by post, be served on a person outside the UK in accordance with arrangements made by the Secretary of State (s 4(1)). In these cases, process may be sent via the Secretary of State to the central authority of the other country, which will transmit the process to the recipient. But where the person is in a 'participating country', the process may be served in accordance with those arrangements only if one of the following conditions is met, namely, that the correct address of the person is unknown; that it has not been possible to serve the process by post; or that there are good reasons for thinking that service by post will not be effective or is inappropriate (s 4(3)). A participating country means a country other than the UK which is a member State, and any other country designated by an order made by the Secretary of State (s 51(2)).

22.08 Rule 32.2 of the Criminal Procedure Rules 2012[4] provides that a statement in a certificate given by or on behalf of the Secretary of State that process has been served on any person under s 4(1); of the manner in which service was effected; and of the date on which process was served, shall be admissible as evidence of any facts so stated.

22.09 Article 12 of the European Convention on Mutual Assistance requires a witness summoned from abroad to be given immunity from arrest or prosecution for a period of 15 days after the date when he could have left the country. However, the UK has entered a reservation to this provision to the effect that it will only grant immunity if requested to do so by the witness or the authorities of the requested state, and it will not do so where it is not in the public interest. A witness returning from abroad who wishes to claim immunity should therefore do so in advance by making arrangements with the UK Central Authority.[5]

Service of written charge and requisition

22.10 Section 29 of the Criminal Justice Act 2003 introduced a new method of commencing criminal proceedings in England and Wales, namely the written charge.[6] Section 29(1) provides that

[4] SI 2012/1726.

[5] Breach of such an undertaking not to prosecute could give rise to an abuse of process: cf *R v Bloomfield* [1997] 1 Cr App R 135; *R v Croydon Justices ex p Dean* [1993] QB 739; *R v Abu Hamza* [2007] QB 659, paras 50–54.

[6] Pursuant to various Commencement Orders made under the Criminal Justice Act 2003, s 29 came into effect in different parts of the country and for different purposes on different dates: see Criminal Justice Act 2003 (Commencement No 16) Order 2007; Criminal Justice Act 2003 (Commencement No 21) Order 2008;

a public prosecutor[7] may institute criminal proceedings against a person by issuing a document (a 'written charge') which charges the person with an offence. Where a public prosecutor issues a written charge, it must at the same time issue a document (a 'requisition') which requires the person to appear before a magistrates' court to answer the written charge. By s 29(3), the written charge and requisition must be served on the person concerned, and a copy of both must be served on the court named in the requisition.

Section 4A of CICA 2003, contains provisions concerning service of these documents on a person who is overseas. Section 4A(2) provides that the written charge or requisition may be issued in spite of the fact that the person on whom it is to be served is outside the UK. By s 4A(3), where the written charge or requisition is to be served outside the UK and the prosecutor believes that the person on whom it is to be served does not understand English, the written charge or requisition must be accompanied by a translation of it in an appropriate language. A written charge or requisition served outside the UK must be accompanied by a notice giving any information required to be given by rules of court (s 4A(4)). If a requisition is served outside the UK, no obligation under the law of England and Wales to comply with the requisition is imposed by virtue of the service (s 4A(5)). Accordingly, failure to comply with the requisition is not a ground for issuing a warrant to secure the attendance of the person in question (s 4A(6)). However, by s 4A(7), the requisition may subsequently be served on the person in question in the UK (with the usual consequences for non-compliance). **22.11**

By s 4B(1) a written charge or requisition to which s 4A applies may, instead of being served by post, be served on a person outside the UK in accordance with arrangements made by the Secretary of State. But where the person is in a participating country,[8] the written charge or requisition may be served in accordance with those arrangements only if one of the following conditions is met. The conditions are that the correct address of the person is unknown; that it has not been possible to serve the written charge or requisition by post; or that there are good reasons for thinking that service by post will not be effective or is inappropriate. **22.12**

B. Service of Overseas Process in the UK

CICA 2003, ss 1 and 2 contain the procedure by which overseas process[9] and other procedural documents may be served in the UK. It is not a requirement that the document be sent first to the Secretary of State. Documents may be sent directly to the person to whom they are addressed. The provisions of CICA 2003 only apply where the documents have been sent to the Secretary of State for service. **22.13**

Section 1 provides for the service of overseas procedural legal documents in the UK when received by the Secretary of State.[10] The Secretary of State has a discretion in deciding whether to cause service to take place and the discretion of the Secretary of State in CICA 2003 when **22.14**

Criminal Justice Act 2003 (Commencement No 23) Order 2009; Criminal Justice Act 2003 (Commencement No 25) Order 2010; Criminal Justice Act 2003 (Commencement No 26) Order 2011; Criminal Justice Act 2003 (Commencement No 27) Order 2012.

[7] Defined in Criminal Justice Act 2003, s 29(5) and Criminal Justice Act 2003 (New Method of Instituting Proceedings) (Public Prosecutor Specification) Order 2011 (SI 2011/2224) to be a police force, the Director of the SFO, the DPP, the Director of Revenue and Customs Prosecutions or a person authorized by him to institute criminal proceedings, the Director General of the Serious Organised Crime Agency or a person authorized by him to institute criminal proceedings, and other prosecuting bodies.

[8] As defined in CICA 2003, s 51(2).

[9] 'Process' is defined in s 51(3).

[10] Or the Lord Advocate in Scotland.

deciding whether to accede to a request to gather evidence was considered by the Administrative Court in *JP Morgan Chase Bank National Association and others v Director of the Serious Fraud Office and another* [2012] EWHC 1674 (Admin) (see also *Drozd and Janousek v France and Spain* (1992) 14 EHRR 745 in which the European Court of Human Rights considered how mutual legal assistance requests might violate the European Convention on Human Rights). The request may be for service by post, in which case the Secretary of State may cause the process or document to be so served, or it may be for personal service, in which case the Secretary of State may direct the chief of police of the area where the person appears to be, to effect personal service.[11] In practice, service under s 1 will almost always be by post directly from the UK Central Authority unless the whereabouts of the person concerned is not known or if it is a procedural requirement of the state making the request that personal service is effected of the document.

22.15 There is no requirement under UK law to comply with an overseas procedural document which requires a person to attend as a party to proceedings or a witness in them. Section 2(1) provides that s 2(2) and (3) apply to any process served in a part of the UK by virtue of s 1 requiring a person to appear as a party or attend as a witness.

22.16 Section 2(2) provides that there is no obligation *under the law of that part of the UK* to comply with the process imposed by virtue of its service.

22.17 Section 2(3) states that the process must be accompanied by a notice stating the effect of s 2(2); indicating that the person on whom it is served may wish to seek advice as to the possible consequences of his failing to comply with the process under the law of the country where it was issued or made; and indicating that under that law he may not be accorded the same rights and privileges as a party or as a witness as would be accorded to him in proceedings in the part of the UK in which the process is served.

22.18 Section 2(4) provides that where a chief officer of police causes any process or document to be served under s 1, he must at once tell the Secretary of State when and how it was served, and (if possible) provide him with a receipt signed by the person on whom it was served. By s 2(5), where the chief officer of police is unable to cause any process or document to be served as directed, he must at once inform the Secretary of State of that fact and of the reason.

22.19 Section 2 deals only with the situation in the UK. Of course, there may be penalties or other serious consequences in the requesting state or in subsequent extradition proceedings if the person on whom the document is served fails to respond to it. In *Re Durkin*,[12] a judgment convicting the defendant in his absence in France was served on him in the UK under the equivalent provision of s 1 of the Criminal Justice (International Co-operation) Act 1990. Under French law, the judgment could be set aside provided that objection was taken within a certain period after the date of service. The defendant failed to object and his conviction became final. The High Court held that it would not be unjust or oppressive to extradite him even though he would no longer be able to obtain a trial in his presence and would be liable to serve his sentence. In *Atkinson v Supreme Court of the Republic of Cyprus* [2010] 1 WLR 570 one of the defendants had been served with notice of a prosecution appeal by the Secretary of State. Therefore, the High Court found that he had been aware of the appeal and deliberately chosen not to attend. This meant that s 20 of the EA 2003 did not operate so as to require the judge to consider whether he was entitled to a re-trial.

[11] CICA 2003, s 1(3).

[12] *Re Durkin*, 16 March 2001 (CO/1378/1999).

The MLA Guidelines[13] give the following guidance to foreign states seeking the service of documents in the UK. Requesting authorities should give the UK Central Authority at least six weeks to serve any process where there are court hearings involved, otherwise there is a possibility that responses will not be received in time to be of use to the requesting authority. Original documents must be provided with a translation or, if the originals cannot be provided, a translation certified as a true copy of the original. The request should include the identity, date of birth, and location of any person on whom a summons or judgment is to be served; details of that person's connection with the proceedings and details of any particular way in which the summons or judgment should be served. Details of any allowances and expenses to which a person asked to appear in proceedings abroad is entitled should be provided. The address of the court where the proceedings are to take place should be provided, together with the name and telephone number of an official of the court from whom the person asked to appear can seek further information if necessary. **22.20**

[13] MLA Guidelines, App M3. Service of process is dealt with in Section 3, and Annex D provides a draft letter of request to the UK for the service of process.

23

MUTUAL RECOGNITION OF DRIVING DISQUALIFICATIONS WITHIN THE EUROPEAN UNION

A. Introduction

Part 3 of CICA 2003 is entitled 'Road Traffic'. Chapter 1 of Part 3 implements the Convention on Driving Disqualifications 1998.[1] Chapter 2 deals with the mutual recognition between Great Britain and Northern Ireland of driving licences and the powers of the Secretary of State to revoke licences.[2] **23.01**

The Convention on Driving Disqualifications was drawn up in 1998 on the basis of Article K.3 of the Treaty on European Union. The Explanatory Report to the Convention[3] explains the mischief which the Convention is designed to address. The growth of road traffic across the EU has been encouraged by the single market and the removal of internal frontier controls between most of the member States. The EU concluded that this made it necessary to ensure that decisions on driving disqualifications are no longer enforced only in the territory of a single member State, but also throughout the EU. The Convention reflects a collective effort by EU states to improve road safety. **23.02**

It has been recognized that there is a disparity of treatment between drivers who are disqualified in their own country from driving and those who are disqualified in a country other than the one in which they are normally resident. In the first case, removing the right to drive prevents the licence holder from driving in any country where the licence previously allowed him to drive. However, in the second case, the disqualification applies only within the country where it was imposed and only for as long as the person is in that country; indeed, the licence, if it has been taken by the authorities of that state, must be returned to the driver when he leaves that country. So whereas in the first case, the driver's actions lead to his being banned from driving in other countries, as well as in his own country of residence where the disqualification was **23.03**

---

1 Official Journal C 216/1, 10 July 1998, p 2, referred to in this chapter as 'the Convention'.

2 At the time of writing (April 2012), Ch 1 was only in force in relation to offenders who are normally resident in Ireland: para 23.19.

3 Official Journal C 211, 23 July 1999, p 1.

imposed, in the second case it does not; moreover, the driver can immediately drive legally in any other country where the driving licence is accepted.

23.04 The EU concluded that this difference in treatment was not only contrary to the interests of road safety in the EU but was also inequitable. Thus, in 1989, the subject was raised by the Dutch Presidency in the Judicial Cooperation Working Group with a view to finding a solution. The subject remained under discussion until 1998, when the text of the Convention was finalized.

23.05 The Convention will come into effect when it has been ratified by all member States[4] but there is also provision for the Convention to be implemented on a bilateral basis between participating member States.[5]

B. The Convention on Driving Disqualifications in Outline

23.06 In essence, the Convention provides a mechanism whereby a disqualification in respect of the most serious road traffic offences imposed on a driver in a member State other than his state of residence can be applied in all member States.

23.07 Article 1 defines the terms 'driving disqualification' and other key terms used in the Convention. A driving disqualification means:

> ... any measure related to the commission of a road traffic offence which results in withdrawal or suspension of the right to drive of a driver of a motor vehicle and which is no longer subject to a right of appeal. The measure may constitute either a primary, secondary or supplementary penalty or a safety measure and may have been taken either by a judicial authority or by an administrative authority.

23.08 This definition recognizes the diversity of laws and systems relating to disqualification which are in operation in the member States. In some countries, a driving disqualification is imposed as a primary measure, for example as part of a criminal penalty; in other states, it is a secondary or supplementary measure, perhaps imposed as a consequence of a conviction; in yet others, it may be imposed quite independently of a criminal conviction—even by a completely separate administrative authority purely as a safety measure. For the purposes of the Convention, the term 'driving disqualification' is intended to cover any measure linked to the commission of a road traffic offence which results in the withdrawal or suspension of the driving licence or the right to drive. This excludes the removal of a licence as a result of, for example, exclusively a medical condition or solely on the basis of a points system.[6]

23.09 Article 1 defines the 'State of the offence' to be the member State within the territory of which the road traffic offence that has given rise to a driving disqualification was committed. The driver's 'State of residence' is defined to be the member State within the territory of which the person who has been disqualified from driving is normally resident within the meaning of Article 9 of Directive 91/439/EEC.[7]

23.10 Under Article 2, member States undertake to cooperate in accordance with the provisions of the Convention so as to achieve the objective that drivers who are disqualified in a member State

4 Art 15(3).
5 Art 15(4).
6 Explanatory Report, para 4.
7 Official Journal L 237, 24 August 1991, p 1 as amended by Directive 97/26/EC, Official Journal L 150, 7 June 1997, p 41.

other than their state of residence should not be able to escape the effects of their disqualification simply by leaving the state of the offence.

Article 3 establishes the mechanism which triggers the enforcement process which the Convention provides. This is a compulsory notification under Article 3(1) from the state of the offence to the state of residence of the disqualification it has imposed in respect of offences listed in the Annex to the Convention. Article 6(2)(a) provides that the state of residence may refuse to give effect to the driving disqualification if the conduct for which a disqualification has been imposed in the state of the offence does not constitute an offence under the law of the state of residence, that is there is no dual criminality. Article 3(2) allows member States to agree with each other that notifications pursuant to Article 3(1) shall not be made in certain cases in which Article 6(2)(a) would apply. **23.11**

Directive 91/439/EEC[8] introduced Community driving licences. Article 8 of the Directive provides that a holder of a valid national driving licence issued by a member State who has taken up normal residence in another member State may request that his driving licence be exchanged for an equivalent licence. Article 8(2) provides that the member State in which the driver resides may apply its national provisions on the restriction, suspension, withdrawal, or cancellation of the right to drive to the holder of a driving licence issued by another member State. As a consequence, the member State to be notified pursuant to Article 3 of the Convention may be a member State other than that which issued the driving licence concerned. It was therefore understood at the adoption of the Convention that in such cases the member State which issued the licence would be informed of the situation by the state of residence.[9] **23.12**

Article 4(1) sets out three possible ways in which member States, when acting as a state of residence, can give effect to decisions imposing disqualification. The first is by direct execution of the decision imposing the disqualification (Article 4(1)(a)). In effect, the state of residence recognizes the decision taken in the state of the offence and gives effect to it with a minimum of formality and without the need for the decision to be endorsed or confirmed in any way by a court in the state of residence. The second possible method of enforcing disqualifications is indirect execution of the decision imposing disqualification via a judicial or administrative decision (Article 4(1)(b)). This method of enforcement allows the decisions of the state of the offence to be endorsed or confirmed by a judicial or administrative authority in the state of residence. **23.13**

Precisely how this result is to be achieved is left to each member State to decide and is likely to vary, according to different domestic systems. The third method of enforcement (Article 4(1)(c)) is by conversion of the decision imposing disqualification into a judicial or administrative decision of its own, thereby in effect replacing the decision of the state of the offence by a new decision of the state of residence. Enforcement under Article 4(1)(b) or (c) is subject to a number of conditions which are laid down in Article 4(2) and (3). These are designed, for the most part, to give flexibility to cater for differences in laws in the member States. **23.14**

The purpose of Article 5 is to make it clear that a state of residence, having given effect to a disqualification imposed on one of its own residents by a state of offence, is not debarred from taking any additional road safety measures that it considers appropriate and that are permitted under its own legislation. **23.15**

8 Official Journal L 237, 24 August 1991, p 1 as amended by Directive 97/26/EC, Official Journal L 150, 7 June 1997, p 41, given effect to in the UK by Part 3 of the Road Traffic Act 1988.

9 Explanatory Report, para 4.

23.16 Article 6 sets out the only reasons which justify a refusal by a state of residence to give effect to a notification sent by a state of offence. Article 6(1) sets out the circumstances in which the state of residence *must* refuse to give effect to a driving disqualification which is notified to it. Article 6(2) sets out circumstances where the state of residence *may* refuse to do so.

23.17 The mandatory conditions for refusal mentioned in Article 6(1) include where the driving disqualification has already been fully enforced in the state of the offence; where the person who is the subject of a notification has already had a disqualification imposed on him in the state of residence for the same acts and that disqualification has been or is being enforced; and where the period of limitation for the measure would have expired under its own legislation. The circumstances referred to in Article 6(2), where a state of residence has discretion under the Convention to refuse to give effect to a disqualification notified to it, include where there is no dual criminality; where the period of disqualification left unserved by the time the state of residence has received the notification and is in the position to enforce it is less than one month; and where the acts giving rise to the disqualification, through offences in both states, are not offences for which disqualification can be imposed under the law of the state of residence.

23.18 Articles 7–20 contain the procedural provisions for handling notifications given under Article 3 and the other matters in the Convention.

C. The Implementation of the Convention in UK Law

23.19 This section examines the provisions of Chapter 1, Part 3, of CICA 2003, which implement the Convention. Sections 54 and 55 enable the Secretary of State to give notice to other member States of driving disqualifications imposed on non-UK residents. Sections 56 and 57 stipulate the conditions under which a driving disqualification imposed by another member State on a person normally resident in the UK will be enforced in the UK. Sections 59–71 deal with appeals against disqualifications and their suspension and the endorsement of licences.

23.20 At the time of writing,[10] Chapter 1 of Part 3 was only in force in relation to offenders who are normally resident in Ireland. Chapter 1 and the Mutual Recognition of Driving Disqualifications (Great Britain and Ireland) Regulations 2008 (SI 2008/3010) came into force on 28 January 2010.[11] The CPS's helpful guidance on these provisions, 'Mutual Recognition of Driving Disqualifications', is available at <http://www.cps.gov.uk>.

Notification to EU states of disqualifications imposed on their nationals in the UK

23.21 Where s 55 applies, the 'appropriate Minister' must give the central authority of the member State in which the offender is normally resident a notice of disqualification. The appropriate minister means, in relation to Great Britain, the Secretary of State and, in relation to Northern Ireland, the Department of the Environment.

23.22 Section 54(1) provides that s 55 applies where an offender who is normally resident in a member State other than the UK is convicted of an offence mentioned in Sch 3; no appeal is outstanding in relation to the offence,[12] and the 'driving disqualification condition' is met in relation to the offence.

---

[10] April 2012.

[11] Crime (International Co-operation) Act 2003 (Commencement No 4) Order 2008 (SI 2008/3009), article 2, and the London, Edinburgh and Belfast Gazette, 26 January 2010.

[12] No appeal is outstanding in relation to an offence in the circumstances specified in s 54(5).

The offences in Part 1 of Sch 3 are:[13] **23.23**

> Manslaughter or culpable homicide by the driver of a motor vehicle; an offence under s 89(1) of the Road Traffic Regulation Act 1984 (exceeding speed limit); an offence under any of the following sections of the Road Traffic Act 1988: s 1 (causing death by dangerous driving); s 2 (dangerous driving); s 3 (careless, and inconsiderate, driving); s 3A (causing death by careless driving when under influence of drink or drugs); s 4 (driving, or being in charge, when under influence of drink or drugs); s 5 (driving, or being in charge, of a motor vehicle with alcohol concentration above prescribed limit); s 6 (failing to provide a specimen of breath for a breath test); s 7 (failing to provide specimen for analysis or laboratory test); an offence under s 12 of the Road Traffic Act 1988 (motor racing and speed trials on public ways); an offence under s 103(1)(b) of the Road Traffic Act 1988; an offence under s 170(4) of the Road Traffic Act 1988.

The offences in Part 2 of Sch 3 are those offences mentioned in Part 1 of Sch 2 to the Road Traffic Offenders Act 1988 which are not mentioned in Part 1 of Sch 3. **23.24**

The driving disqualification condition is met in relation to an offence mentioned in Part 1 of Sch 3 if an order of disqualification is made in respect of the offence. In relation to an offence mentioned in Part 2 of Sch 3, the condition is met if an order of disqualification for a period not less than the minimum period is made in respect of the offence (s 54(2)). The minimum period is six months, or where the state in which the offender normally resides is a prescribed state,[14] a shorter period equal to the period prescribed in relation to the state (s 54(3)). When determining whether the period of disqualification is not less than the minimum period, any extension period imposed pursuant to any of the provisions in s 54(3A)[15] is to be disregarded. **23.25**

Section 54(5) provides that s 55 does not apply in prescribed circumstances, that is circumstances prescribed by regulations made by the appropriate minister.[16] The Explanatory Notes to CICA 2003,[17] para 121, explain that where another member State has declared that it will apply, in full or in part, the discretionary conditions to the recognition of disqualifications described in Article 6(2) of the Convention, the regulations will state when notification is not required in respect of that state. **23.26**

Section 55 is headed 'Duty to give notice to foreign authorities of driving disqualification of a non-UK resident' and is the means by which the UK gives effect to its obligation under Article 3(1) of the Convention. **23.27**

A notice under s 55 must give the particulars and information specified in s 55(2) and (3) including the offender's name, address, and date of birth; particulars of the offence; state that no appeal is outstanding in relation to it; give particulars of the disqualification; state whether or not the offender took part in the proceedings in which the disqualification was imposed; state that the offender has been informed that any decision made for the purposes of the Convention will have no effect on the disqualification. **23.28**

The notice under s 55 must be accompanied by the original or a certified copy of the order of disqualification (s 55(4)). Where the offender did not take part in the proceedings which led to the disqualification, the notice must be accompanied by evidence that the **23.29**

---

13 The Northern Irish equivalent offences are specified in Sch 3 but omitted in this list.

14 That is prescribed by regulations made by the appropriate minister: s 74(1).

15 Article 8A of the Criminal Justice (Northern Ireland) Order 1980; s 35A or s 35C of the Road Traffic Offenders Act 1988; s 248D of the Criminal Procedure (Scotland) Act 1995; Article 40A of the Road Traffic Offenders (Northern Ireland) Order 1996; s 147A of the Powers of Criminal Courts (Sentencing) Act 2000; Article 91A of the Criminal Justice (Northern Ireland) Order 2008.

16 s 74(1).

17 <http://www.opsi.gov.uk/ACTS/en2003/2003en32.htm>.

offender was duly notified of those proceedings (s 55(5)). Where the offender is the holder of a Community licence, the notice must also be accompanied by the licence unless it has been returned to the driver under s 91A(7)(b)(ii) of the Road Traffic Offenders Act 1988 (s 55(6)).

23.30 Where the period of disqualification is reduced by virtue of s 34A of the Road Traffic Offenders Act 1988, the appropriate minister must give the central authority particulars of the reduction (s 55(7)). Where the disqualification is removed by an order under s 42 of that Act, the appropriate minister must give the central authority particulars of the removal (s 55(8)).

Recognition in the UK of driving disqualifications imposed in member States

23.31 Sections 56–58 contain the provisions which allow driving disqualifications imposed in member States to be implemented in the UK on offenders who are normally resident there.

23.32 Where s 57 applies, the appropriate minister must give the offender a notice the effect of which is to disqualify the offender from driving in accordance with the terms of the notice.

23.33 Section 56(1) provides that s 57 applies where an individual ('the offender') who is normally resident in the UK is convicted in another member State of an offence falling within s 56(5); no appeal is outstanding in relation to the offence; the driving disqualification condition is met in relation to the offence; and the offender was duly notified of the proceedings ('the relevant proceedings') in which the disqualification was imposed and was entitled to take part in them.

23.34 An offence falls within s 56(5) if it is constituted by conduct falling within any of paras 1–5 of the Annex to the Convention (s 56(5)(a)), or other conduct which constitutes a road traffic offence for the purposes of the Convention (s 56(5)(b)).

23.35 The Annex to the Convention is headed 'Conduct covered by Article 3 of the Convention' and paras 1–5 list the following offences:

1. Reckless or dangerous driving (whether or not resulting in death, injury or serious risk).
2. Wilful failure to carry out the obligations placed on drivers after being involved in road accidents (hit-and-run driving).
3. Driving a vehicle while under the influence of alcohol or other substances affecting or diminishing the mental and physical abilities of a driver.

   Refusal to submit to alcohol and drug tests.
4. Driving a vehicle faster than the permitted speed.
5. Driving a vehicle whilst disqualified.

23.36 The driving disqualification condition is met in relation to an offence falling within s 56(5)(a), if, as a result of the offence, the offender is disqualified in the state in which the conviction is made. In relation to an offence falling within s 56(5)(b) the condition is met if, as a result of the offence, the offender is disqualified in that state for a period not less than the minimum period (s 56(2)). For the purposes of s 56 an offender is disqualified in a state if he is disqualified in that state for holding or obtaining a licence to drive a motor vehicle granted under the law of that state (however the disqualification is described under that law) (s 56(3)).

23.37 The minimum period referred to in s 56(2) is a period of six months, or where the state in which the conviction is made is a prescribed state,[18] a shorter period equal to the period prescribed in relation to that state.

[18] That is prescribed in regulations made by the appropriate minister: s 74(1).

Section 56(6) provides that s 57 does not apply if the relevant proceedings were brought later than the time at which summary proceedings for any corresponding offence under the law of the part of the UK in which the offender is normally resident could have been brought.[19] Section 56(7) defines corresponding offences. An offence is a corresponding offence if the conduct constituting the offence outside the UK took place in any part of the UK, and that conduct is, or corresponds to, conduct which would constitute an offence under the law of that part. **23.38**

The appropriate minister may make regulations treating offences under the law of a part of the UK as corresponding to offences under the law of a member State other than the UK (s 56(8)). **23.39**

For the purposes of s 56 no appeal is outstanding in relation to an offence if no appeal is brought against an offender's conviction of the offence, or any decision made as a result of his conviction, within the time allowed for making such appeals, or such an appeal is brought and the proceedings on appeal are finally concluded. **23.40**

Recognition in the UK of foreign driving disqualifications

Section 57 contains the machinery for giving effect in the UK to foreign driving disqualifications. Where s 57 applies (ie where the conditions in s 56 are met) the appropriate minister *must* give the offender a notice under the section if the unexpired period of the foreign disqualification is not less than one month, and *may* give him a notice if that period is less than one month (s 57(1)).[20] The notice may be given to the offender by delivering it to him, leaving it at his proper address, or sending it to him by post.[21] **23.41**

The unexpired period of the foreign disqualification is the period of the foreign disqualification, less any period of that disqualification which is treated by regulations made by the appropriate minister as having been served in the state in which the offender was convicted (s 57(2)).[22] In relation to Ireland, article 2(1) of the Mutual Recognition of Driving Disqualifications (Great Britain and Northern Ireland) Regulations 2008 (SI 2008/3010) provides that for the purpose of calculating the unexpired period of foreign disqualification pursuant to s 57(2), the period to be treated as having been served in Ireland (a) commences on the day the disqualification came into operation in Ireland; and (b) ends on the day immediately before the beginning of the relevant period of disqualification specified in s 57(5)(a). This is subject to article 2(2), which provides that in determining the period to be treated as having been served in Ireland, any time during which the operation of the disqualification imposed in Ireland is suspended is to be disregarded. **23.42**

Once the offender has received a notice under s 57 he is then disqualified from driving. Section 57(4) provides that if the appropriate minister gives the offender a notice under this section, the offender is disqualified in each part of the UK for the relevant period, and if the **23.43**

---

[19] This accords with Art 6(1)(d) of the Convention which precludes enforcement of a disqualification where the period of limitation would have expired under the state of residence's legislation.

[20] By s 70, if the appropriate minister gives a notice under s 57 to a person, he must give the 'competent authority' particulars of the disqualification which arises by virtue of that section. If the appropriate minister does not give such a notice, he must give his reasons to the competent authority. Competent authority, in relation to a state, means an authority which is a competent authority in relation to the state for the purposes of the Convention: s 74(1).

[21] s 71(1).

[22] s 57(3) provides that the provision which may be made by regulations under s 57(2)(b) includes provision for treating any period during which a central authority or competent authority of a state has seized a licence without returning it as a period which has been served in that state.

foreign disqualification is also effective until a condition is satisfied, until the condition or a corresponding prescribed condition is satisfied.

23.44 Where the holder of a Great Britain licence or Northern Ireland licence is disqualified by virtue of s 57, the licence is to be treated as revoked with effect from the beginning of the period of disqualification (s 66).

23.45 Section 57(5) provides that the relevant period in s 57(4) is the period which begins at the end of the period of 21 days[23] beginning with the day on which the notice is given, and is equal to the unexpired period of the foreign disqualification. However, if the foreign disqualification is at any time removed otherwise than in prescribed circumstances, the offender ceases to be disqualified in each part of the UK from that time (s 57(6)).

23.46 In determining the expiration of the period for which a person is disqualified by virtue of s 57, any time during which the disqualification is suspended,[24] or he is not disqualified, is to be disregarded (s 67).

23.47 Where the foreign disqualification is for life then the condition in s 57(1)(a) is to be treated as satisfied, and the other references in ss 57 and 58 to the unexpired period of the foreign disqualification are to be read as references to a disqualification for life (s 57(8)).

Contents of the s 57 notice and obligations on the driver

23.48 Section 58 prescribes the contents of the s 57 notice. The notice must be in writing[25] and give particulars of the offence in respect of which the foreign disqualification was imposed and the period of that disqualification; state that the offender is disqualified in each part of the UK for a period equal to the unexpired period of the foreign disqualification; state the date from which, and period for which, he is disqualified; give particulars of any relevant condition mentioned in s 57(4)(b); and give details of the offender's right to appeal under s 59.

23.49 Section 63(1) provides that a person in Great Britain[26] who receives a s 57 notice and is the holder of a licence, must deliver his licence and its counterpart[27] to the Secretary of State before the end of the period of 21 days[28] beginning with the day on which the notice is given. Section 63 contains detailed provisions relating to the production of the licence to the Secretary of State.

23.50 Section 65 concerns the production of Community licences under s 63 or 64. Section 65 applies where the holder of a Community licence is disqualified by virtue of s 57, and the licence is sent to the Secretary of State or the Department under s 63 or 64. The Secretary of State or (as the case may be) the Department of the Environment in Northern Ireland must send the holder's name and address, and particulars of the disqualification, to the licensing authority in the EEA state in respect of which the licence was issued (s 65(2)). However this need not be done if the EEA state is the same as the state in which the offence in relation to which the holder is disqualified was committed (s 65(3)).

---

23 The appropriate minister may make regulations substituting a longer period: s 57(7).

24 For example pending an appeal under s 60.

25 s 58(2). The notice may also contain such other information as the appropriate minister may deem appropriate: s 58(3).

26 s 64 contains analogous provisions for Northern Ireland.

27 This has the same meaning as in Part 3 of the Road Traffic Act 1988: s 74(1).

28 The appropriate minister may make regulations substituting a longer period: s 63(2).

Sections 68[29] and 69[30] (as amended by the Road Safety Act 2006 from a date to be appointed) contain provisions requiring particulars of the disqualification to be endorsed on the offender's driving licence by the Secretary of State or the Department of the Environment. **23.51**

Appeal against a s 57 notice

A person who is disqualified from driving having received a s 57 notice may appeal against the disqualification. Section 59(1) provides that a person who is disqualified by virtue of s 57 may, after giving notice to the appropriate minister of his intention to do so, appeal to the appropriate court against the disqualification. **23.52**

The appropriate court is, in relation to England and Wales, a magistrates' court acting for the petty sessions area in which the applicant resides; in relation to Scotland, the sheriff within whose jurisdiction the applicant resides; in relation to Northern Ireland, a court of summary jurisdiction acting for the petty sessions district in which the applicant resides (s 59(2)). **23.53**

The appeal must be made before the end of the period of 21 days[31] beginning with the day on which the s 57 notice is given to the applicant (s 59(3)). **23.54**

If the appropriate court is satisfied that s 57 does not apply to the applicant's case, it must allow the appeal (s 59(5)), otherwise it must dismiss the appeal (s 59(6)). Thus the right of appeal provided for in s 60 permits the offender to appeal on the grounds that s 57 does not apply to him because the criteria in s 56 are not made out, for example, because he was not notified of the proceedings as required by s 56(1)(d). It does permit an appeal against the underlying decision to disqualify him taken in the member State. **23.55**

Where on an appeal against the disqualification the appeal is allowed, the court by which the appeal is allowed must send notice of that fact to the appropriate minister (s 59(7)).[32] **23.56**

Suspension of disqualification pending appeal

Section 60 contains powers allowing appellate courts in England and Wales[33] to suspend the disqualification pending the offender's appeal. Section 60 applies where a person is disqualified by virtue of s 57. **23.57**

Where an offender appeals to a magistrates' court against the disqualification, the court may, if it thinks fit, suspend the disqualification (s 60(2)). **23.58**

Where the offender makes an application for a statement of case in respect of the decision of the court under s 111 of the Magistrates' Courts Act 1980, the High Court may, if it thinks fit, suspend the disqualification. **23.59**

Where the offender has appealed, or applied for leave to appeal, to the Supreme Court under s 1 of the Administration of Justice Act 1960 from any decision of the High Court which is material to the disqualification, the High Court may, if it thinks fit, suspend the disqualification. **23.60**

Any power of a court under s 60 to suspend the disqualification is a power to do so on such terms as the court thinks fit (s 60(5)). Where a court suspends the disqualification, it must send notice of the suspension to the Secretary of State (s 60(6)). The notice must be sent in **23.61**

---

29 Great Britain.

30 Northern Ireland.

31 The appropriate minister may make regulations substituting a longer period: s 59(4).

32 The notice must be sent in such manner and to such address, and contain such particulars, as the appropriate minister may determine: s 59(8).

33 ss 61 and 62 contain analogous powers for Scotland and Northern Ireland.

such manner and to such address, and contain such particulars, as the Secretary of State may determine (s 60(7)).

D. Mutual Recognition of Disqualifications within the UK

23.62 Chapter 2 of Part 3 of CICA 2003 contains provisions relating to the mutual recognition of driving disqualifications as between Great Britain, Northern Ireland, the Channel Islands, and so on.

Disqualification in Great Britain if disqualified in Northern Ireland, and so on

23.63 Section 76 inserts new s 102A into the Road Traffic Act 1988. Section 102A(1) provides that a person is disqualified from holding or obtaining a licence to drive a motor vehicle of any class so long as he is subject to a relevant disqualification imposed outside Great Britain. For the purposes of s 102A a person is subject to a relevant disqualification imposed outside Great Britain if, in respect of any offence a court in Northern Ireland disqualifies him for holding or obtaining a Northern Ireland licence; a court in the Isle of Man or any of the Channel Islands disqualifies him for holding or obtaining a British external licence; or a court in Gibraltar disqualifies him for holding or obtaining a licence to drive a motor vehicle granted under the law of Gibraltar (s 102A(2)).

23.64 A certificate signed by the Secretary of State which states, in respect of a person, any matter relating to the question whether he is subject to a relevant disqualification imposed outside Great Britain shall be evidence of the matter so stated (s 102A(3)). A certificate stating that matter and purporting to be so signed shall be deemed to be so signed unless the contrary is proved (s 102A(4)).

24

TRANSFER OF PRISONERS TO AND FROM THE UK FOR THE PURPOSE OF GIVING EVIDENCE AND ASSISTING INVESTIGATIONS

A. Introduction

The Criminal Justice (International Co-operation) Act 1990 contains provisions allowing UK prisoners (ie those who are serving sentences imposed in the UK or who are remanded in the UK for a domestic offence)[1] to be taken overseas to give evidence in foreign criminal proceedings or to assist with foreign criminal investigations.[2] It also enables requests to be made to foreign states that prisoners held there be transferred to the UK to give evidence in criminal proceedings there or assist in criminal investigations.[3] These measures give effect to the UK's international obligations under Article 11 of the European Convention on Mutual Assistance in Criminal Matters. **24.01**

Modern technology means that it is often easier (and cheaper) for prisoners to give evidence via television links than it is to transfer them abroad,[4] and overseas investigators may submit a letter of request for evidence to be taken on oath in the UK under Sch 1 of CICA 2003. The provisions in the Criminal Justice (International Co-operation) Act 1990 are therefore used fairly infrequently. **24.02**

Sections 47 and 48 of CICA 2003 give effect to Article 9 of the Convention on Mutual Assistance in Criminal Matters and allow for the transfer of domestic prisoners overseas to assist in investigations being carried on there in relation to offences which were or may have been committed in the UK, and the transfer of overseas prisoners to the UK for similar purposes. **24.03**

---

1 Criminal Justice (International Co-operation) Act 1990, s 5(9). It is not permissible to extradite an individual merely for the purposes of assisting with a criminal investigation: *Assange v Swedish Prosecution Authority* [2011] EWHC 2849 (Admin), para 152.

2 Criminal Justice (International Co-operation) Act 1990, s 5(1). Prisoners may be transferred within the UK and Channel Islands for the purposes of giving evidence under the Crime (Sentences) Act 1997, Sch 1, para 3.

3 Criminal Justice (International Co-operation) Act 1990, s 6.

4 Criminal Justice Act 1988, s 32.

B. Transfer of UK Prisoners Overseas

24.04 Section 5 of the Criminal Justice (International Co-operation) Act 1990 is entitled 'Transfer of United Kingdom prisoner to give evidence or assist investigation overseas'.[5] Section 5(1) provides that the Secretary of State may, if he thinks fit, issue a warrant providing for a prisoner serving a sentence in a prison or other institution to which the Prison Act 1952 applies to be transferred to a country or territory outside the UK for the purpose of giving evidence in criminal proceedings there; or of being identified in, or otherwise by his presence assisting, such proceedings or the investigation of an offence (s 5(1)). By s 5(9), s 5 applies to a person in custody awaiting trial or sentence and a person committed to prison for default in paying a fine as it applies to a prisoner.

24.05 No warrant can be issued under s 5(1) unless the prisoner consents. Section 5(2) provides that no warrant shall be issued under s 5 in respect of any prisoner unless he has consented to being transferred under s 5(1). That consent may be given either by the prisoner himself, or where his mental condition makes this inappropriate, by an appropriate person. Once consent has been given it cannot be withdrawn.

24.06 A warrant under s 5 authorizes the taking of the prisoner to a place in the UK and his delivery at a place of departure from the UK into the custody of a person representing the appropriate authority of the country or territory to which the prisoner is to be transferred; and the bringing of the prisoner back to the UK and his transfer in custody to the place where he is liable to be detained under the sentence to which he is subject (s 5(3)).

24.07 By s 5(4), where a warrant has been issued in respect of a prisoner under s 5 he shall be deemed to be in legal custody at any time when, being in the UK or on board a British ship, British aircraft, or British hovercraft, he is being taken under the warrant to or from any place or being kept in custody under the warrant.

24.08 The person authorized on the warrant to transport the prisoner has all the powers, authority, protection, and privileges of a constable in the part of the UK in which that person is for the time being and, when the prisoner is outside the UK, of a constable in the part of the UK to or from which the prisoner is to be taken under the warrant.[6]

24.09 Where a foreign state or territory wishes to have a prisoner transferred then it should send a letter of request to the UK Central Authority. This should contain the following information:[7] the dates on which the presence abroad of the prisoner is required, including the dates on which the court or other proceedings for which the prisoner is required will commence and are likely to be concluded; information for the purpose of obtaining the prisoner's consent to the transfer and satisfying the UK authorities that arrangements will be made to keep the prisoner in secure custody. This should include information relating to whether the prisoner will have immunity from prosecution for previous offences; details of proposed arrangements for collecting the prisoner from and returning the prisoner to the UK; details of the type of secure accommodation in which the prisoner will be held in the requesting state; details of the type of escort available abroad to and from the secure accommodation.

Transfer abroad to assist with a UK investigation

24.10 Article 11 of the European Convention on Mutual Legal Assistance in Criminal Matters provides that a person in custody in one state whose presence is required to assist with an investigation

[5] cf European Convention on Mutual Legal Assistance in Criminal Matters, Art 11.
[6] Criminal Justice (International Co-operation) Act 1990, s 5(5).
[7] MLA Guidelines, App M3, p 773.

in another state can be transferred to that member State. Article 9 of the Convention on Mutual Assistance in Criminal Matters contains further provisions which enable a member State, which is conducting an investigation in another member State, to transfer a prisoner in its custody to that second member State in order to assist the investigation.

Section 47 of CICA 2003 gives effect to Article 9 in domestic law. This section provides for prisoners from the UK to be transferred to another participating country to assist with an investigation. This differs from s 5 of the Criminal Justice (International Co-operation) Act 1990, which covers the transfer of UK prisoners to other countries at the request of the authorities of that country to assist their investigations. This new power might be used, for example, where a prisoner assisting a UK investigation could identify a site or participate in an identification parade in another participating country. **24.11**

Section 47 is entitled 'Transfer of UK prisoner to assist investigation abroad'. Section 47(1) provides that the Secretary of State may, pursuant to an agreement with the competent authority of a participating country, issue a warrant providing for any person to whom s 47 applies (a prisoner) to be transferred to that country for the purpose of assisting there in the investigation of an offence. The offence must be one which was or may have been committed in the UK. **24.12**

Section 47 applies to a person serving a sentence in a prison; in custody awaiting trial or sentence, or committed to prison for default in paying a fine (s 47(2)). **24.13**

A warrant may be issued in respect of a prisoner under s 47(1) only if the prisoner, or in the circumstances mentioned in s 47(5), a person appearing to the Secretary of State to be an appropriate person to act on the prisoner's behalf, has made a written statement consenting to his being transferred for the purpose mentioned in s 47(1). These circumstances are those in which it appears to the Secretary of State to be inappropriate for the prisoner to act for himself, by reason of his physical or mental condition or his youth. **24.14**

By s 47(6), once consent has been given then it is irrevocable. **24.15**

Section 47(7) provides that a warrant under s 47 authorizes the taking of the prisoner to a place in the UK and his delivery at a place of departure from the UK into the custody of a person representing the appropriate authority of the participating country to which the prisoner is to be transferred, and the bringing of the prisoner back to the UK and his transfer in custody to the place where he is liable to be detained under the sentence or order to which he is subject. **24.16**

Section 47(9) provides that s 5(3A)–(8) of the Criminal Justice (International Co-operation) Act 1990 Act have effect in relation to a warrant issued under s 47 section as they have effect in relation to a warrant issued under s 5 of the 1990 Act. **24.17**

C. Transfer of Prisoners from Abroad to the UK

The Criminal Justice (International Co-operation) Act 1990, s 6, is entitled 'Transfer of overseas prisoner to give evidence or assist investigation in the UK'. **24.18**

Section 6 applies where the presence in the UK of a prisoner who is detained overseas is necessary either for criminal proceedings there, or to assist with a criminal investigation. The Secretary of State, having satisfied himself that the requested state is likely to consent, and once the prisoner has consented,[8] can issue a warrant to the requested state. **24.19**

[8] Criminal Justice (International Co-operation) Act 1990, s 6(3).

24.20 The warrant has the effect of authorizing the bringing of the prisoner to the UK, the taking of the prisoner to, and his detention in custody at, the place or places in the UK as are specified in the warrant; and the returning of the prisoner to the country or territory from which he has come. Section 5(4)–(8) have effect in relation to a warrant issued under s 6 as they have effect in relation to a warrant issued under s 5.[9]

24.21 Article 12 of the European Convention on Mutual Assistance 1959 requires states to grant immunity from prosecution to a person who appears on a summons issued by a judicial authority in a requesting state for a period of 15 days from the date when his presence is no longer required. However, the UK has entered a reservation which requires the immunity to be specifically claimed by the person or the authorities of the requesting state, and reserves the UK's right not to grant immunity where it would not be in the public interest to do so.

Transfer of an overseas prisoner to the UK to assist in an investigation

24.22 Section 48 of CICA 2003 provides for the transfer of a prisoner from a participating country[10] to the UK in order to assist with that country's investigation.

24.23 Section 48(1) provides that the Secretary of State may, pursuant to an agreement with the competent authority of a participating country, issue a warrant providing for any person to whom this section applies ('the overseas prisoner') to be transferred to the UK for the purpose of assisting in the investigation of an offence. The offence must be one which was or may have been committed in the participating country.

24.24 Section 48 applies to a person who is detained in custody in a participating country by virtue of a sentence or order of a court exercising criminal jurisdiction there, or in consequence of having been transferred there from the UK under the Repatriation of Prisoners Act 1984 or under any similar provision or arrangement from any other country.

24.25 A warrant may be issued in respect of an overseas prisoner under s 48(1) only if the competent authority provides a written statement made by the prisoner consenting to his being transferred for the purpose mentioned in that subsection (s 48(4)). Such consent cannot be withdrawn after the issue of the warrant (s 48(5)).

24.26 A warrant under s 48 authorizes the bringing of the prisoner to the UK, the taking of the prisoner to, and his detention in custody at, any place or places in the UK specified in the warrant, and the returning of the prisoner to the country from which he has come.

24.27 Section 48(7) provides that s 5(4)–(8) of the Criminal Justice (International Co-operation) Act 1990 have effect in relation to a warrant issued under s 48 as they have effect in relation to a warrant issued under that section.

---

[9] Criminal Justice (International Co-operation) Act 1990, s 6(5).

[10] Defined in CICA 2003, s 51(2), to be a country other than the UK which is a member State and any other country designated by an order made by the Secretary of State.

25

MUTUAL LEGAL ASSISTANCE IN RELATION TO CONFISCATION AND FORFEITURE

A. Introduction

The statutory provisions analysed in this chapter give effect to the UK's international obligations to assist other states in relation to restraint, confiscation, and forfeiture matters.[1] Specific powers relating to the gathering of evidence for use in confiscation matters are also considered in this chapter.[2] General powers relating to the gathering of evidence and information including banking information have been considered in earlier chapters in the context of mutual assistance in the provision of evidence.[3] **25.01**

This chapter also examines the provisions of Sch 4 of CICA 2003 which contain provisions amending Sch 4 of the Terrorism Act 2000 allowing for the mutual recognition of freezing orders in relation to terrorist property. **25.02**

The relevant statutory provisions are contained in both primary and secondary legislation. Part 2 of the Proceeds of Crime Act 2002 (POCA 2002) contains provisions which allow requests for assistance to be made to foreign states by prosecutors in relation to restraint and **25.03**

[1] See in particular the European Convention on Laundering, Search Seizure and Confiscation of the Proceeds of Crime (CETS 141); the UN Convention Against Illicit Traffic in Narcotic Drugs and Psychotropic Substances (UNTS No 27627); European Convention on Mutual Legal Assistance in Criminal Matters (CETS 30); the Convention on Mutual Assistance in Criminal Matters (2000/C197/01). See *Perry v Serious Organised Crime Agency* [2012] UKSC 22, paras 19–30.

[2] Para 25.22 and para 25.75.

[3] A number of general powers for requesting evidence from overseas are contained in Part 1, Ch 2 of CICA 2003. Sections 43–45 of CICA 2003 permit UK judicial authorities to make requests for banking information to foreign states at the request of designated prosecuting authorities in cases of serious criminal conduct: see para 18.02 and para 18.54.

confiscation.[4] Part 11 of POCA 2002 is entitled 'Co-operation' and contains enabling provisions for the making of subordinate legislation for the freezing and realization of the proceeds of crime at the request of foreign states[5] and for the enforcement of orders in the different parts of the UK.[6]

25.04 Three Orders have been made using the powers in Part 11 of POCA 2002 that are of particular relevance to this chapter:

- In relation to requests from foreign states, the Proceeds of Crime Act 2002 (External Requests and Orders) Order 2005[7] (referred to in this chapter as 'the POCA Order 2005') came into force on 1 January 2006.[8]
- Within the different parts of the UK, the relevant orders are the Proceeds of Crime Act 2002 (Enforcement in different parts of the United Kingdom) Order 2002[9] and the Proceeds of Crime Act 2002 (Investigations in different parts of the United Kingdom) Order 2003.[10]

B. Requests by the UK for Assistance in Relation to Restraint and Confiscation

25.05 This section considers the powers available to prosecuting authorities in the UK to seek the assistance of foreign states in relation to restraint and confiscation orders made in the UK.

Requests by the UK for assistance in restraining property and enforcing confiscation orders

25.06 The confiscation provisions of Part 2 of POCA 2002 permit an order to be made based upon the value of the defendant's property, wherever it is situated.[11] It follows that assistance may be required from foreign states in order to preserve the defendant's property to prevent it from being dissipated prior to confiscation. The High Court can also order the defendant to repatriate his assets held abroad[12] and assistance from the foreign state concerned may also be needed in order to facilitate this process.

25.07 Where the UK requires assistance from a foreign state then a letter of request may be sent under CICA 2003, s 7.[13] In addition, a prosecutor may make a request for assistance under POCA 2002, s 74. Assistance in investigations often also takes place informally between police forces via Interpol.[14] The extent to which the foreign state will be able to provide the assistance sought will depend upon its domestic law.

25.08 Part 2 of POCA 2002 is entitled 'Confiscation: England and Wales'. Section 74 is entitled 'Enforcement abroad' and sets out the conditions which must be satisfied before a request for assistance in the freezing and realization of property may be made by authorities in England and Wales to jurisdictions outside the UK.[15] It applies if: any of the conditions in s 40 is

4 POCA 2002, s 74; *Perry v Serious Organised Crime Agency* [2012] UKSC 22, para 38.
5 POCA 2002, s 444.
6 POCA 2002, s 443; *Perry v Serious Organised Crime Agency* [2012] UKSC 22, para 36.
7 SI 2005/3181.
8 Para 25.27.
9 SI 2002/3133.
10 SI 2003/425; see para 25.144.
11 POCA 2002, s 84(1); cf *Perry v Serious Organised Crime Agency* [2012] UKSC 22, paras 37–38.
12 *Director of Public Prosecutions v Scarlett* [2001] 1 WLR 515.
13 Para 18.02.
14 Para 21.60.
15 *Perry v Serious Organised Crime Agency* [2012] UKSC 22, para 38.

satisfied; the prosecutor believes that realizable property is situated in a country or territory outside the UK (the receiving country); and the prosecutor sends a 'request for assistance' to the Secretary of State with a view to it being forwarded under s 74.

In a case where no confiscation order has been made, a request for assistance is a request to the government of the receiving country to secure that any person is prohibited from dealing with realizable property (s 74(2)). In a case where a confiscation order has been made and has not been satisfied, discharged, or quashed, a request for assistance is a request to the government of the receiving country to secure that any person is prohibited from dealing with realizable property; that realizable property is realized; and that the proceeds are applied in accordance with the law of the receiving country (s 74(3)). **25.09**

Section 74(4) provides that no request for assistance may be made for the purposes of s 74 in a case where a confiscation order has been made and has been satisfied, discharged, or quashed. **25.10**

If the Secretary of State believes it is appropriate to do so then, under s 74(5), he may forward the request for assistance to the government of the receiving country. **25.11**

If property is realized in pursuance of a request under s 74(3) the amount ordered to be paid under the confiscation order must be taken to be reduced by an amount equal to the proceeds of realization. A certificate purporting to be issued by or on behalf of the requested government is admissible as evidence of the facts it states if it states: that property has been realized in pursuance of a request under s 74(3); the date of realization; and the proceeds of realization. **25.12**

The conditions in s 40

Section 40 of POCA 2002 sets out the conditions which need to be satisfied before a restraint order can be made by the Crown Court. If any of these conditions is satisfied then the prosecutor may seek the assistance of a foreign state under POCA 2002, s 74. Section 40(1) provides that the Crown Court may exercise the powers conferred by s 41 if any of the following conditions is satisfied. **25.13**

The first condition is that a criminal investigation has been started in England and Wales with regard to an offence, and there is reasonable cause to believe that the alleged offender has benefited from his criminal conduct (s 40(2)). **25.14**

The second condition is that proceedings for an offence have been started in England and Wales and not concluded, and there is reasonable cause to believe that the defendant has benefited from his criminal conduct (s 40(3)). The second condition is not satisfied if the court believes that there has been undue delay in continuing the proceedings, or the prosecutor does not intend to proceed (s 40(7)). **25.15**

The third condition is that an application by the prosecutor has been made under s 19, 20, 27, or 28 and not concluded, or the court believes that such an application is to be made, and there is reasonable cause to believe that the defendant has benefited from his criminal conduct (s 40(4)). **25.16**

The fourth condition is that an application by the prosecutor has been made under s 21 and not concluded, or the court believes that such an application is to be made, and there is reasonable cause to believe that the court will decide under that section that the amount found under the new calculation of the defendant's benefit exceeds the relevant amount (as defined in that section) (s 40(5)). **25.17**

The fifth condition is that an application by the prosecutor has been made under s 22 and not concluded, or the court believes that such an application is to be made, and there is reasonable cause to believe that the court will decide under that section that the amount found under **25.18** the new calculation of the available amount exceeds the relevant amount (as defined in that section) (s 40(6)).

25.19 If an application mentioned in the third, fourth, or fifth condition has been made the condition is not satisfied if the court believes that there has been undue delay in continuing the application, or the prosecutor does not intend to proceed (s 40(8)).

Temporal limitations in respect of requests for assistance

25.20 Article 5 of the Proceeds of Crime Act 2002 (Commencement No 5, Transitional Provisions, Savings and Amendment) Order 2003[16] provides that s 41 (restraint orders) and s 74 (enforcement abroad) of POCA 2002 shall not have effect where the powers in those sections would otherwise be exercisable by virtue of a condition in s 40(2) or s 40(3) of POCA 2002 being satisfied, and the offence mentioned in s 40(2)(a) or s 40(3)(a), as the case may be, was committed before 24 March 2003.[17]

Contents of the request

25.21 Letters of request for the restraint of property should include the following information:[18]

- the name, address, nationality, date, and place of birth and present location of the defendant(s) or person(s) concerned;
- details of the offence with which the defendant has been, or is about to be, charged;
- details of the law applicable to the charges and the evidence against the defendant;
- if relevant, particulars of the property which it is intended to restrain and details of the link between the defendant and the property;
- where applicable, details of any court orders already made in the UK against the defendant in respect of his or her property. If any court order has been made a duly authenticated copy should be included with the request.

Requests for assistance in evidence gathering in connection with restraint and confiscation

25.22 Section 7 of CICA 2003 allows prosecuting authorities to seek the assistance of foreign states in connection with the provision of evidence.[19] Requests to foreign states for banking information may also be made under CICA 2003, ss 43 and 44.[20]

C. Foreign Requests to the UK for Assistance with Restraint, Confiscation, and Forfeiture

Introduction

25.23 The UK can provide assistance in enforcing foreign forfeiture[21] and confiscation orders in respect of assets held in the UK or elsewhere. The UK is also able to restrain assets at the request of foreign states. The principal legislation is the POCA Order 2005, made under s 444 of POCA 2002. This gives effect to the UK's obligations under (inter alia) Chapter III of the European Convention on Laundering, Search Seizure and Confiscation of the Proceeds of Crime.[22] Part 2

16 SI 2003/333.
17 *Revenue & Customs Prosecutions Office v Hill* [2005] EWCA Crim 3271.
18 MLA Guidelines, App M3, pp 770–771.
19 Para 18.02.
20 Para 18.54.
21 Forfeiture is considered at para 25.80.
22 CETS 141; *Perry v Serious Organised Crime Agency* [2012] UKSC 22, paras 19–30.

applies to England and Wales; Part 3 to Scotland; and Part 4 to Northern Ireland. This section deals only with England and Wales.

Prior to the coming into force of the POCA Order 2005, foreign requests for assistance in restraint and confiscation matters were dealt with by different statutory regimes depending upon whether the request related to a drugs offence or a non-drugs offence.[23] The POCA Order 2005 simplifies the law by providing a single scheme for the enforcement of foreign confiscation orders and the provision of assistance in obtaining restraint orders. **25.24**

Whereas under the previous statutory regimes applications for restraint orders at the request of foreign states and the enforcement or overseas confiscation orders were made to the High Court, under the POCA Order 2005 the application is made to the Crown Court. **25.25**

Definitions

The POCA Order 2005 uses the following terms: **25.26**

- *External request*: this is a request by an overseas authority to prohibit dealing with relevant property which is identified in the request.[24]
- *Overseas authority*: this is an authority which has responsibility in a country or territory outside the UK, for making a request to an authority in another country, including the UK, to prohibit dealing with relevant property.[25]
- *Relevant property*: property is relevant property if there are reasonable grounds to believe that it may be needed to satisfy an external order which has been or which may be made.[26]
- *External order*: this is an order which is made by an overseas court where property is found or believed to have been obtained as a result of or in connection with criminal conduct, and is for the recovery of specified property or a specified sum of money.[27]

Commencement and temporal scope of the POCA Order 2005

The POCA Order 2005 came into force on 1 January 2006. **25.27**

Article 8 of the POCA Order 2005 provides that the Crown Court may make a restraint order if either of the conditions in Article 7 is satisfied. Article 7(4) of the POCA Order 2005 provides that in determining whether these conditions are satisfied, the Court must have regard to the definitions in s 447(1), (4)–(8), and (11) of POCA 2002. Section 447(7) of POCA 2002 defines 'criminal conduct' to include conduct that is criminal in the UK, and conduct which would be criminal if it had been committed in the UK. **25.28**

It follows that the Crown Court can make a restraint order under the POCA Order 2005 at the request of a foreign state provided that the conduct alleged would have been criminal in the UK at the time it was committed. Unlike in the case of domestic restraint and confiscation orders made under Part 2 of POCA 2002, the POCA Order 2005 is not restricted to offences committed after 24 March 2003, or after the date it came into force, because it does not contain any equivalent of Articles 3 and 5 of the Proceeds of Crime Act 2002 (Commencement No 5, Transitional Provisions, Savings and Amendment) Order 2003,[28] and s 447(7) of POCA 2002 does not restrict the meaning of 'criminal conduct' to conduct occurring after any particular date. **25.29**

---

23 Drug Trafficking Act 1994 (Designated Countries and Territories) Order 1996, SI 1996/2880; Criminal Justice Act 1988 (Designated Countries and Territories) Order 1991, SI 1991/2873.
24 POCA 2002, s 447(1).
25 POCA 2002, s 447(11).
26 POCA 2002, s 447(4).
27 POCA 2002, s 447(2).
28 SI 2003/333.

25.30 Thus, the UK can grant assistance and the court can make a restraint order in relation to an offence whenever it was committed.[29]

Geographical extent of the POCA Order 2005

25.31 The POCA Order 2005 only applies to property situated in the UK and so orders made under it only apply in relation to property in the relevant part of the UK. In *King v Director of the Serious Fraud Office* [2009] 1 WLR 748 the applicant, a British national who was a long-term resident in South Africa, was charged there with numerous fraud offences. In 2006 the South African prosecuting authority made an external request to the UK for assistance in obtaining restraint and disclosure orders in respect of property belonging to the applicant and to specified companies of which he was alleged to be the alter ego. Pursuant to Article 6(2)(3) of the POCA Order 2005, the request was referred to the Director of the SFO, who applied to the Crown Court, without notice to the applicant, for both such orders under Article 8(1)(4) of the Order. The judge granted the orders in respect of all property held by the applicant and the specified companies, including property held outside England and Wales. He refused the applicant's subsequent application to discharge the orders and held, in reliance on the definition of 'property' in s 447(4) of POCA 2002 'all property wherever situated', that where the condition in Article 7(3) of the Order was satisfied, that relevant property in England and Wales was identified in the external request, the Crown Court had power under Article 8 of the Order also to restrain assets outside the jurisdiction. The Court of Appeal, allowing the applicant's appeal, held that the scope of the orders was restricted to relevant property located within England and Wales, and substituted orders to that effect.

25.32 The Director appealed to the House of Lords which dismissed the appeal. Lord Phillips held that Part 2 of the POCA Order 2005 amounts to a clear and coherent scheme whereby, under Articles 6, 7, and 8, jurisdiction to make a restraint order in response to an external request only arises where that request concerns relevant property in England or Wales which was identified in the request, and any restraint order made had to prohibit dealing with the relevant property which was so identified. Also, the seizure and enforcement provisions in the POCA Order 2005, pursuant to which disclosure orders could be made, applied the same territorial requirement and no machinery was provided for the powers so conferred to be exercised in relation to property outside England and Wales. Although 'property' was defined in s 447(4) of the 2002 Act as property wherever situated, Lord Phillips said that whether that word bore that meaning depended on its context, so that where the POCA Order 2005 Order expressly or by implication referred to property in England and Wales it referred only to property situated there; and that, accordingly, the Crown Court had no jurisdiction to make restraint or disclosure orders in respect of property located outside England and Wales, and the decision of the Court of Appeal as to the scope of the orders was to be upheld.

Reference of a letter of request by the Secretary of State

25.33 Article 6 of the POCA Order 2005 sets out the manner in which the Secretary of State is to deal with an incoming request concerning relevant property in England and Wales.

[29] Whilst it can be argued that this construction of the POCA Order 2005 offends against the presumption against the non-retroactive application of criminal statutes, there are difficulties with this argument. There is nothing in Article 7 to suggest that it does not apply to offences committed before it came into force. Moreover, in *Government of the United States of America v Montgomery* [2001] 1 WLR 196, para 30, a submission based upon retroactivity was rejected by the House of Lords in relation to one of the predecessors to the POCA Order 2005, namely, the Criminal Justice Act 1988 (Designated Countries and Territories) Order 1991 (the 1991 Order) (SI 1991/2873).

Article 6(1) provides that except where Article 6(2) applies (cases of serious and complex fraud), the Secretary of State may refer an external request in connection with criminal investigations or proceedings in the country from which the request was made and concerning relevant property in England or Wales to either the DPP or the Director of Revenue and Customs Prosecutions, to process it. **25.34**

Where the conditions in Article 6(2) are met, that is, it appears to the Secretary of State that the request is made in connection with criminal investigations or proceedings which relate to an offence involving serious or complex fraud, and it concerns relevant property in England or Wales, the Secretary of State may refer the request to the Director of the Serious Fraud Office to process it. Once the request has been referred by the Secretary of State it is for the relevant Director to arrange for an application to be made to the Crown Court under Article 7 for a restraint order, or to arrange for further inquiries. **25.35**

Article 6(5) provides that the relevant Director may ask the overseas authority which made the request for such further information as may be necessary to determine whether the request is likely to satisfy either of the conditions in Article 7. Where a request concerns relevant property which is in Scotland or Northern Ireland as well as England or Wales, so much of the request as concerns such property shall be dealt with under Part 3 or 4 of the POCA Order 2005, respectively. **25.36**

The Crown Court's power to make a restraint order and to enforce an external order at the request of a foreign state

Restraint orders

The Crown Court's powers to make a restraint order pursuant to an external request are contained in Chapter 1 of Part 2 of the POCA Order 2005. Article 8 provides that the Crown Court may make a restraint order if either condition in Article 7 is satisfied.[30] **25.37**

Article 7(4) provides that in determining whether the conditions in Article 7 are satisfied and whether the request is an external request within the meaning of POCA 2002, the Court must have regard to the definitions in s 447(1), (4)–(8), and (11). Evidence must not be excluded in restraint proceedings on the grounds that it is hearsay evidence.[31] **25.38**

The definitions in ss 447(1), (4)–(8), and (11) of POCA 2002 are as follows: **25.39**

- Section 447(1) provides that an external request is a request by an overseas authority to prohibit dealing with relevant property which is identified in the request.
- Section 447(4)–(8) provide as follows. Property is all property wherever situated and includes money; all forms of property, real or personal, heritable or moveable; things in action and other intangible or incorporeal property (s 447(4)). Property is obtained by a person if he obtains an interest in it (s 447(5)). References to an interest, in relation to property other than land, include references to a right (including a right to possession) (s 447(6)). Property is relevant property if there are reasonable grounds to believe that it may be needed to satisfy an external order which has been or which may be made (s 447(7)). Criminal conduct is conduct which constitutes an offence in any part of the UK, or would constitute an offence in any part of the UK if it occurred there (s 447(8)).
- Section 447(11) provides that an overseas authority is an authority which has responsibility in a country or territory outside the UK for making a request to an authority in another country or territory (including the UK) to prohibit dealing with relevant property; for carrying out

30 *Wastell v Stanford International Bank Ltd* [2010] EWCA Civ 137, paras 68–74.

31 POCA Order 2005, Art 13.

an investigation into whether property has been obtained as a result of or in connection with criminal conduct; or for carrying out an investigation into whether a money laundering offence has been committed.

The Article 7 conditions

25.40 Article 8 provides that the Crown Court may make a restraint order if either of the conditions in Article 7 is satisfied.

25.41 The first condition in Article 7 is that relevant property in England and Wales is identified in the external request; a criminal investigation has been started in the country from which the external request was made with regard to an offence; and there is reasonable cause to believe that the alleged offender named in the request has benefited from his criminal conduct.

25.42 The second condition in Article 7 is that relevant property in England and Wales is identified in the external request; proceedings for an offence have been started in the country from which the external request was made and not concluded; and there is reasonable cause to believe that the defendant named in the request has benefited from his criminal conduct.

Procedure

25.43 The procedure for applying for a restraint order is set out in Rule 57.15 and Part 59 of the Criminal Procedure Rules. The application must be in writing and be supported by a witness statement which must give the grounds for the application; give full details of the realizable property in respect of which the applicant is seeking the order and specify the person holding that realizable property; and give the grounds for, and full details of, any application for an ancillary order under Article 8(4) for the purposes of ensuring that the restraint order is effective.[32] The applicant is under a duty to make full and frank disclosure of all relevant matters weighing both in favour and against the granting of the order.[33] Non-disclosure may, but does not automatically, justify discharging the order.[34]

25.44 In considering an application for a restraint order the Court is required to have regard to the legislative steer contained in Article 46 which requires it to have regard to the need to preserve the value for the time being of realizable property or specified property so that it can be made available for satisfying an external order.[35] No account is to be taken of any obligation of a defendant or a recipient of a tainted gift if the obligation conflicts with the object of satisfying any external order against the defendant that has been or may be registered under Article 22.

25.45 However, the court's powers must be exercised with a view to allowing a person other than the defendant or a recipient of a tainted gift to retain or recover the value of any interest held by him. In the case of realizable property or specified property held by a recipient of a tainted gift, the powers must be exercised with a view to realizing no more than the value for the time being of the gift.

25.46 An application to discharge or vary a restraint order may be made under Article 9.

25.47 Articles 10 and 11 provide a right of appeal to the Court of Appeal and House of Lords against a refusal to grant a restraint order, an order made under Article 8(4), and a decision made on an application to vary or discharge the order under Article 9(2).

---

32 Para 25.67.

33 *Director of the Serious Fraud Office v A* [2007] EWCA Crim 1927, para 5.

34 Ibid, para 18; *Wastell v Stanford International Bank Ltd* [2010] EWCA Civ 137, para 83; cf para 19.70.

35 For the approach under POCA 2002, see *R v Windsor* [2011] 2 Cr App R (S) 7; *Re B (Restraint Order)* [2009] 1 Cr App R 14; *Director of the Serious Fraud Office v A* [2007] EWCA Crim 1927. In the latter case the Court of Appeal left open the question whether the fairness of the foreign judicial system (in that case, Iran) could provide a basis for not making a restraint order.

By Article 12, if a restraint order is in force a constable or a relevant officer of Revenue and Customs may seize any property which is specified in it to prevent its removal from England and Wales. Any property so seized must be dealt with in accordance with the Court's directions. **25.48**

The Court may appoint a management receiver under Article 15 who may then exercise the powers specified in Article 16 in relation to property specified in the order. **25.49**

Enforcement of external orders

The Crown Court's power to enforce an external order is contained in Part 2, Chapter 2 of the POCA Order 2005. There are three principal stages in the enforcement of such an order: **25.50**

- Reference to the Director of the appropriate prosecution agency by the Secretary of State.
- Application by the relevant Director to the Crown Court for the registration of the order.
- Enforcement of the order by the relevant Director. Article 27 also allows for the appointment of an enforcement receiver to manage the property and to realize it in satisfaction of the confiscation order in accordance with Article 28.

The first step in the enforcement of an external order following its receipt from a foreign state is its referral to the Director of the relevant prosecution agency. Except where Article 18(2) applies (cases of serious or complex fraud) the Secretary of State may refer an external order arising from a criminal conviction in the country from which the order was sent and concerning relevant property in England and Wales[36] to either the DPP or the Director of Revenue and Customs Prosecutions.[37] In a case falling under Article 18(2) the order may be referred to the Director of the SFO.[38] **25.51**

Following a reference by the Secretary of State, the relevant Director may apply to the Crown Court to give effect to the external order under Article 20(1). The request may be *ex parte* to a judge in chambers and must include a request that the relevant Director be appointed as the enforcement authority for the order. **25.52**

Conditions for giving effect to an external order

By Article 21, the Crown Court must decide to give effect to the external order by registering it where all of the following conditions are satisfied. **25.53**

The first condition is that the external order was made consequent on the conviction of the person named in the order and no appeal is outstanding in respect of that conviction. **25.54**

The second condition is that the external order is in force and no appeal is outstanding in respect of it. **25.55**

The third condition is that giving effect to the external order would not be incompatible with the Convention rights (within the meaning of the Human Rights Act 1998) of any person affected by it.[39] In *Government of the United States of America v Montgomery (No 2)* [2004] 1 WLR 2241, the House of Lords considered whether the enforcement of an external order would violate the defendants' Convention rights. Their Lordships held that it could do so, but **25.56**

---

[36] By Art 18(5), where an order concerns relevant property which is in Scotland or Northern Ireland as well as England or Wales, so much of the request as concerns such property shall be dealt with under Part 3 or 4 of the POCA Order 2005, respectively.

[37] POCA Order 2005, Art 18(1).

[38] For the powers of the SFO and the meaning of 'serious or complex fraud', see para 19.45.

[39] *Government of the United States of America v Montgomery (No 2)* [2004] 1 WLR 2241.

only in an exceptional case where there would be a flagrant denial of justice (which was not the case on the facts).[40] Lord Carswell said at para 24:

> The European Court has affirmed on a number of occasions the existence in principle of the possibility in a suitable case of invoking Article 6. The context has generally been that of extradition or expulsion of aliens seeking admission to the country concerned, but in my opinion it is capable of being applied to the enforcement in a Convention state of a judgment obtained in another state, whether or not the latter is an adherent to the Convention. No decision was cited to your Lordships in which the court went so far as to hold that an act of extradition or expulsion amounted to a breach of Article 6, and in all of the reported cases the European Court has strongly emphasised the exceptional nature of such a jurisdiction and the flagrant nature of the deprivation of an applicant's rights which would be required to trigger it.

25.57 The fourth condition applies only in respect of an external order which authorizes the confiscation of property other than money that is specified in the order. In such a case, the specified property must not be subject to a charge under the legislation specified in Article 21(6).

25.58 In determining whether the order is an external order within the meaning of the POCA 2002 the Court must have regard to the definitions in s 447(2), (4), (5), (6), (8), and (10).[41]

25.59 By Article 22, where the Crown Court decides to give effect to an external order it must register the order in that court; provide for the notice of the registration to be given to any person affected by it; and appoint the relevant Director as the enforcement authority for the order.

25.60 The Crown Court may cancel the registration of the external order, or vary the property to which it applies, on an application by the relevant Director or any person affected by it if or to the extent that the court is of the opinion that any of the conditions in Article 21 are not satisfied.[42] The court must cancel the registration of the external order on such an application if it appears that the order has been satisfied by payment of the amount due (where the order is for the payment of a sum of money), or the property has been surrendered (where the order is for the recovery of specified property), or by any other means.[43]

25.61 Articles 23 and 24 provide a right of appeal to the Court of Appeal and the House of Lords against a refusal to register an external confiscation order or a refusal to cancel or vary it.

25.62 Article 26 contains provisions for the time within which money specified in the external order must be paid.

Orders which may be made in addition to and in aid of restraint orders and external orders

25.63 By Article 8(4) of the POCA Order 2005 the Crown Court may make such orders as it believes are appropriate for the purpose of ensuring the restraint order is effective.[44] Examples of such orders that have been granted in domestic restraint cases include:

- an order requiring the defendant to swear an affidavit as to the whereabouts of his assets;[45]

---

[40] A flagrant denial of justice goes beyond mere irregularities or lack of safeguards in the trial procedures. Such a denial only exists where the breach of the principles of fair trial guaranteed by Article 6 is so fundamental as to amount to a nullification of the very essence of the right: *Othman v United Kingdom* [2012] ECHR 56, paras 258–260; *RB (Algeria) v Secretary of State* [2010] 2 AC 110, paras 133–142, 195–203, 243–249, 258–261; *Dudko v Government of the Russian Federation* [2010] EWHC 1125 (Admin), para 36. See para 7.64.

[41] Art 21(7).

[42] Art 22(3).

[43] Art 22(4).

[44] cf POCA 2002, s 41(7).

[45] *Re O (Disclosure Order)* [1991] 2 QB 520. Orders for disclosure may only be made in relation to property in the UK: *King v Director of the Serious Fraud Office* [2009] 1 WLR 748.

- an order for cross-examination on the defendant's disclosure affidavit.[46] This power should only be used in exceptional circumstances where there are justifiable concerns over whether the defendant has given full disclosure of his assets.[47] The only legitimate purpose of the cross-examination is to establish the extent of a defendant's assets and hence would be unnecessary if sufficient assets are known about to meet the claim;[48]
- an order requiring the defendant to repatriate his assets;[49]
- an order for the delivery up of the defendant's passport.[50]

The extent to which these orders can properly be made in respect of restraint orders made at the request of a foreign state remains to be considered. Some are more likely to be appropriate than others. It is unlikely that a UK court would order a defendant domiciled abroad to surrender his passport. However, there is no reason in principle why a court in the UK should not order the defendant to repatriate his assets to the UK so that they are available for restraint and subsequent confiscation. No doubt, however, before making such an order the court would require evidence as to whether a similar power exists under the law of the requesting state and whether or not the court had exercised it. **25.64**

As already noted, the Crown Court may also appoint a management receiver in aid of a restraint order under Article 15 of the POCA Order 2005. The receiver may exercise the powers in Article 16, which include the power to take possession of the property; the power to manage or otherwise deal with it; the power to start, carry on, or defend legal proceedings in connection with the property; and the power to realize the property to meet the receiver's expenses. **25.65**

Part 60 of the Criminal Procedure Rules contains rules relating to the appointment of management receivers. Part 2, Chapter 3 of the POCA Order 2005 contains procedural provisions concerning receivers. **25.66**

Confiscation orders: orders which may be made by a UK court[51]

Article 27 contains provisions allowing for the appointment of enforcement receivers by the Crown Court on the application of the relevant Director where (in the case of a monetary external order, that is an external order requiring payment of a sum of money) the time specified under Article 26 has expired. An enforcement receiver appointed under Article 27 has the powers contained in Articles 28 and 29. **25.67**

Chapter 3 of Part 2 contains procedural provisions concerning receivers. **25.68**

The procedure for enforcing foreign orders in the UK

Where a designated country wishes to enforce an external order in England, Wales, and Northern Ireland, the appropriate authority seeking assistance should send a letter of request including the order to the UK Central Authority. Requests in relation to Scotland should be sent to the Crown Office. Requests for the enforcement of an external order should include the original order or a duly authenticated copy of it and evidence showing that the confiscation order is in force and that neither the order nor any conviction to which it may relate is subject to appeal. The request ideally should also indicate that all or a certain amount of the sum payable **25.69**

---

46 *A J Bekhor & Co Ltd v Bilton* [1981] QB 923.

47 *Den Norske Bank ASA v Antonatos* [1999] QB 271.

48 *Great Future International Ltd v Sealand Housing Corporation* [2001] CPLR 293.

49 *Director of Public Prosecutions v Scarlett* [2000] 1 WLR 515. This was a repatriation order made in ordinary domestic criminal proceedings, however the reasoning is equally application to restraint proceedings brought at the instance of a foreign state.

50 *Bayer AG v Winter* [1986] 1 WLR 497; *B v B* [1997] 3 All ER 258.

51 POCA Order 2005, Arts 27–39 and Part 2, Ch 3 of POCA 2002.

under the order remains unpaid in the territory of the requesting state or that other property recoverable under the order remains unrecovered there.[52]

25.70 Once a letter of request containing the relevant information has been received by the UK Central Authority, and the Secretary of State has decided that it is appropriate to provide assistance, the letter is sent to the Director of an appropriate prosecuting authority[53] who will act on behalf of the designated state in proceedings in the UK.

25.71 The procedure for obtaining a restraint order in the Crown Court and for enforcing an external order is contained in Part 57.15 of the Criminal Procedure Rules.[54] Part 57.15 provides that the rules in Part 57 and in Parts 59–61 and 71 apply with the necessary modifications to proceedings under the POCA Order 2005 in the same way that they apply to corresponding proceedings under Part 2 of the Proceeds of Crime Act 2002.[55]

Remitting confiscated property to the requesting state

25.72 Property (or its equivalent in money) recovered under a foreign confiscation or forfeiture order in the UK is not automatically transmitted to the foreign enforcement authority or state. Property (or its equivalent in money) recovered under a foreign confiscation order is placed in the UK Government's Consolidated Fund.[56] There is no legal power which enables the UK court to remit the property to a foreign state or other recipient. Forfeited property, in England and Wales, is disposed of at the direction of the High Court, which must give persons holding any interest in the property in question a 'reasonable opportunity' to make representations to the court.

25.73 The UK has entered into agreements with Canada[57] and the United States of America[58] to determine the ultimate destination of property or sums of money confiscated (in the UK, as defined by UK law) or forfeited (in Canada or the United States of America). These agreements permit the UK to share property (or an equivalent amount of money) confiscated in the UK with the requesting state.

25.74 Where there is no such agreement the foreign state must request the remittance of property or sums of money on a diplomatic basis. If the requesting state is one which itself would remit property or sums of money, which it recovers in its own procedures, this is likely to give rise to a diplomatic expectation of reciprocal remittance from the UK. Where it is the case that remittance is requested by a foreign state on the basis that the property and or money, would, if remitted, be returned to a victim or paid as compensation to a victim of crime the request for

---

52 MLA Guidelines, App M3, p 771.

53 See POCA Order 2005, Arts 6 and 18.

54 SI 2005/384, inserted by the Criminal Procedure (Amendment) Rules 2006, SI 2006/385 with effect from 3 April 2006.

55 See T Moloney and D Atkinson, *Blackstone's Guide to the Criminal Procedure Rules* (2nd edn, Oxford 2011).

56 In the same way, where the UK seeks the assistance of a foreign state in enforcing a domestic confiscation order under POCA 2002, s 74, any property recovered in the foreign state falls to be dealt with under that state's law and is not automatically remitted to the UK: POCA 2002, s 74(3).

57 Agreement between the Government of the United Kingdom and the Government of Canada Regarding the Sharing of Forfeited or Confiscated Assets or their Equivalent Funds, signed in London on 21 February 2001, Treaty Series 028/2001, CM 5180. The Agreement provides for the sharing of assets forfeited in Canada or confiscated in the UK. An exchange of Notes between the United Kingdom and Canada to Extend the Agreement Regarding the Sharing of Forfeited or Confiscated Assets or their Equivalent Funds was signed on 21 January 2003.

58 Agreement between the Government of the United Kingdom and the Government of the United States of America Regarding the Sharing of Forfeited or Confiscated Assets or their Equivalent Funds, signed in Washington on 31 March 2003 and ratified by the UK on that date.

remittance has more force still. The UK Central Authority deals with these requests and may agree to remit a portion of funds recovered (after itself obtaining the approval of the Treasury). All other funds recovered are paid to the Consolidated Fund and are not remitted to other states or persons.

Foreign requests for assistance in gathering evidence in relation to confiscation

Investigations using powers in CICA 2003

The methods by which assistance may be provided by the UK to foreign states in relation to evidence gathering have been summarized in earlier chapters. These powers are available for use in relation to restraint and confiscation investigations. In summary, the powers available under CICA 2003 and other statutes include: **25.75**

- Search and seizure warrants: warrants authorizing an appropriate person to enter and search specified premises and to seize and retain any material found there which is likely to be of substantial value to the civil recovery investigation.[59]
- Production orders: orders requiring a specified person appearing to be in possession or control of material to produce it to an appropriate officer for him to take away, or requiring a specified person to give an appropriate officer access to the material.[60]
- Voluntary and compulsory interviews.[61]
- Proceedings before a nominated court.[62]
- Customer information orders: orders requiring financial institutions to provide certain information in relation to a specified customer of the institution.[63]
- Account monitoring orders: orders requiring financial institutions to provide certain account information in relation to an account held by the financial institution.[64]

Investigations using powers in POCA 2002

Prior to the enactment of POCA 2002 there were different statutory provisions dealing with investigations in drugs and non-drugs cases.[65] However, the investigatory powers contained in POCA 2002 apply to 'criminal conduct' and 'unlawful conduct' generally, and these expressions include any conduct that constitutes an offence or is unlawful in any part of the UK or would constitute an offence or be unlawful in any part of the UK if it occurred there.[66] **25.76**

Part 8 of POCA 2002 is entitled 'Investigations' and Chapter 2 contains an extensive range of investigatory powers including search warrants and production orders for use in tracing the proceeds of crime and money laundering investigations in England and Wales. Section 445(1) provides that Her Majesty may by Order in Council make provision to enable orders equivalent to those under Part 8 to be made, and warrants equivalent to those under Part 8 to be issued, for the purposes of an 'external investigation', and make provision creating offences in relation to external investigations which are equivalent to offences created by Part 8. **25.77**

An 'external investigation' is defined in s 447(3) to be an investigation by an overseas authority into whether property has been obtained as a result of or in connection with criminal conduct; **25.78**

[59] CICA 2003, ss 13(1)(b), 16, and 17; CICA 2003, s 15(2) and Criminal Justice Act 1987, s 2(4): paras 19.04, 19.67, and 19.80.

[60] CICA 2003, s 15(2) and Criminal Justice Act 1987, s 2(3): para 19.61.

[61] CICA 2003, s 15(2) and Criminal Justice Act 1987, s 2(2): para 19.55.

[62] CICA 2003, s 15 and Sch 1: para 19.25.

[63] CICA 2003, s 32: para 19.160.

[64] CICA 2003, ss 35 and 36: para 19.172.

[65] Criminal Justice Act 1988, ss 93I, 93H (non-drugs); Drug Trafficking Act 1994, ss 55 and 56 (drugs): see generally *R v Crown Court at Southwark ex p Bowles* [1998] AC 641.

[66] POCA 2002, ss 241(2), 413(1), 447(8).

the extent or whereabouts of property obtained as a result of or in connection with criminal conduct; or whether a money laundering offence has been committed.

25.79 No Order in Council had been made under s 445 at the time of writing (August 2012).

D. Mutual Assistance in Relation to Forfeiture

Forfeiture orders

25.80 Forfeiture orders are orders for the forfeiture, destruction, deprivation, or other disposal of property used (or intended to be used) in the commission of a criminal offence. Such properties are sometimes known as 'the instrumentalities of crime'. Instrumentalities of crime do not come within the scope of powers in respect of the proceeds of crime and therefore require separate provisions. These proceedings are civil rather than criminal in the UK and may have the same character in foreign jurisdictions. The UK forfeiture orders discussed here are not necessarily the same in character as forfeiture orders made in other jurisdictions where the terms may be used to include the removal of a person's proceeds of crime.

25.81 The Criminal Justice (International Co-operation) Act 1990, as amended by the Serious Organised Crime and Police Act 2005, s 95, confers the power to make an Order in Council to provide for the enforcement in the UK of an order made by a court in a country or territory outside the UK designated in the Order in Council which is for the forfeiture or destruction or the forfeiture or other disposal of anything in respect of which an offence to which s 9 applies has been committed or which was used or intended for use in connection with the commission of such an offence.

25.82 Section 95 of the Serious Organised Crime and Police Act 2005 extended the offences to which s 9 applies from primarily drug-related offences to cover any offence that corresponds to, or is similar to, an offence under the law of any part of the UK. By providing assistance in a greater range of circumstances, the UK is able to fulfil requirements to confiscate instrumentalities of crime under various international agreements. In particular, it fulfils the UK's obligations under the UN Convention against Transnational Organized Crime[67] and the UN Convention against Corruption, and allowed the UK to ratify these Conventions.[68]

25.83 The UN Convention against Transnational Organized Crime was signed by the UK on 14 December 2000 and ratified on 9 February 2006. It promotes international cooperation to address transnational organized crime and requires state parties to criminalize activities associated with organized crime. The Convention came into force on 29 September 2003. There are also three Protocols to the Convention dealing with the trafficking of persons, the smuggling of migrants, and the manufacture and trafficking of firearms. The UN Convention against Corruption was signed by the UK on 9 December 2003 and ratified on 9 February 2006. It will strengthen international cooperation against corruption and facilitate the recovery of stolen state assets. It came into force on 14 December 2005.

25.84 The Criminal Justice (International Co-operation) Act 1990 (Enforcement of Overseas Forfeiture Orders) Order 2005[69] (the CJ Order 2005) is a self-contained Order in Council made under the Criminal Justice (International Co-operation) Act 1990, s 9(1), which permits

[67] Doc A/55/383. The Convention was adopted by resolution A/RES/55/25 of 15 November 2000 at the fifty-fifth session of the General Assembly of the United Nations.

[68] Doc A/58/422. The Convention was adopted by the General Assembly of the UN on 31 October 2003 at UN Headquarters in New York.

[69] SI 2005/3180.

forfeiture orders made by foreign courts to be enforced in the UK. It also permits restraint orders to be made in support of forfeiture orders. It only applies to England and Wales. Separate Orders have been made in respect of Scotland and Northern Ireland.[70]

The CJ Order 2005 replaced the existing Order[71] made under s 9 of the Criminal Justice (International Co-operation) Act 1990 and brought the requirements for handling overseas requests for instrumentalities of crime into line with those in respect of assets under POCA 2002 and the POCA Order 2005. It applies to any offence that corresponds to or is similar to an offence under the law of England and Wales. **25.85**

The UK is able to provide assistance to those countries designated in Sch 2 to the CJ Order 2005. As at September 2012 these countries were: **25.86**

> Afghanistan, Albania, Algeria, Andorra, Angola, Antigua and Barbuda, Argentina, Armenia, Australia, Austria, Azerbaijan, Bahamas, Bahrain, Bangladesh, Barbados, Belarus, Belgium, Belize, Benin, Bhutan, Bolivia, Bosnia and Herzegovina, Botswana, Brazil, Brunei Darussalem, Bulgaria, Burkina Faso, Burundi, Cambodia, Cameroon, Canada, Cape Verde, Central African Republic, Chad, Chile, China, Colombia, Comoros, Congo, Cook Islands, Costa Rica, Côte D'Ivoire, Croatia, Cuba, Cyprus, Czech Republic, Denmark, Djibouti, Dominica, Dominican Republic, Ecuador, Egypt, El Salvador, Eritrea, Equatorial Guinea, Estonia, Ethiopia, Fiji, Finland, France, Gabon, Gambia, Georgia, Germany, Ghana, Greece, Grenada, Guatemala, Guinea, Guinea-Bissau, Guyana, Haiti, Honduras, Hungary, Iceland, India, Indonesia, Iran (Islamic Republic of), Iraq, Ireland, Israel, Italy, Jamaica, Japan, Jordan, Kazakhstan, Kenya, Kuwait, Kyrgyzstan, Lao's People's Democratic Republic, Latvia, Lebanon, Lesotho, Liberia, Libyan Arab Jamahiriya, Liechtenstein, Lithuania, Luxembourg, Madagascar, Malawi, Malaysia, Maldives, Mali, Malta, Mauritania, Mauritius, Mexico, Micronesia (Federal States of), Moldova, Monaco, Mongolia, Morocco, Mozambique, Myanmar, Namibia, Nauru, Nepal, Netherlands, New Zealand, Nicaragua, Niger, Nigeria, Norway, Oman, Pakistan, Panama, Paraguay, Peru, Philippines, Poland, Portugal, Qatar, Republic of Korea, Romania, Russian Federation, Rwanda, Saint Kitts & Nevis, Saint Lucia, Saint Vincent and the Grenadines, San Marino, San Tome & Principe, Saudi Arabia, Senegal, Serbia and Montenegro, Seychelles, Sierra Leone, Singapore, Slovakia, Slovenia, South Africa, Spain, Sri Lanka, Sudan, Suriname, Swaziland, Sweden, Switzerland, Syrian Arab Republic, Tajikistan, Thailand, the Former Yugoslav Republic of Macedonia, Togo, Tonga, Trinidad and Tobago, Tunisia, Turkey, Turkmenistan, Uganda, Ukraine, United Arab Emirates, United Republic of Tanzania, United States of America, Uruguay, Uzbekistan, Venezuela, Vietnam, Yemen, Zambia, Zimbabwe.

Restraint in aid of an external forfeiture order yet to be made

The Crown Court has power to grant a restraint order in aid of an external forfeiture order that is yet to be made under Part 2 of the CJ Order 2005. This is an order made by a court in a designated country for the forfeiture and destruction, or the forfeiture and other disposal, of anything in respect of which a relevant offence has been committed or which was used or intended for use in connection with the commission of such an offence.[72] **25.87**

Under Article 3, the Secretary of State may refer to the Director of Public Prosecutions, the Director of Revenue and Customs Prosecutions, or the Director of the SFO (in a case of serious or complex fraud) for processing a request for the restraint of property made by or on **25.88**

[70] Criminal Justice (International Co-operation) Act 1990 (Enforcement of Overseas Forfeiture Orders) (Scotland) Order 2005 (SSI 2005/581); Criminal Justice (International Co-operation) Act 1990 (Enforcement of Overseas Forfeiture Orders) (Northern Ireland) Order 2005 (SI 2005/3179).

[71] SI 1991/1463.

[72] Art 36(1).

behalf of an overseas authority in a designated country, and for the purpose of facilitating the enforcement of any external forfeiture order which has yet to be made.

25.89 By Article 4, on an application by a relevant Director, the Crown Court may exercise the powers conferred by Article 5 if the following conditions are satisfied: relevant property in England and Wales is identified in the request; a criminal investigation or proceedings for an offence have been started in the country from which the request was made, and it appears to the court that there are reasonable grounds for believing that as a result of that investigation or those proceedings an external forfeiture order may be made against the person named in the request.

25.90 Property is 'relevant property' if there are reasonable grounds to believe that it may be needed to satisfy an external forfeiture order which has been made or which may be made.[73]

25.91 Article 5 provides that the Crown Court may make a restraint order prohibiting any specified person from dealing with relevant property which is identified in the request and specified in the order. The Crown Court is also able to make such orders as it believes is appropriate for the purpose of ensuring that the restraint order is effective.[74]

25.92 Article 6 provides for the variation and discharge of an order made under Article 5. Articles 7 and 8 provide for an appeal to the Court of Appeal and the House of Lords against decisions taken by the Crown Court in relation to restraint orders. If a restraint order is in force a constable or a relevant officer of Revenue and Customs may seize any property which is specified in it to prevent its removal from England and Wales.[75]

25.93 Articles 12 and 13 permit the appointment of a management receiver in respect of any property which is specified in the restraint order.

Enforcement of an external forfeiture order

25.94 Part 3 contains provisions allowing for the enforcement of external forfeiture orders. These provisions are closely analogous to the equivalent provisions in the POCA Order 2005.

25.95 By Article 15, the Secretary of State may refer an external forfeiture order concerning relevant property in England or Wales to the Director of Public Prosecutions, the Director of Revenue and Customs Prosecutions or, in a case of serious and complex fraud, the Director of the Serious Fraud Office, for processing. The relevant Director may then apply to the Crown Court to give effect to the external forfeiture order.

25.96 The Crown Court must decide to give effect to an external forfeiture order if it is satisfied that all of the following conditions are met.

25.97 The first condition is that the external forfeiture order was made consequent on the conviction of the person named in the order and no appeal is outstanding in respect of that conviction.

25.98 The second condition is that the external forfeiture order is in force and no appeal is outstanding in respect of it.

25.99 The third condition is that giving effect to the external forfeiture order would not be incompatible with any of the Convention rights (within the meaning of the Human Rights Act 1998) of any person affected by it.

25.100 The fourth condition is that the property whose confiscation is specified in the external forfeiture order must not be subject to a charge under any of the provisions mentioned in Article 18(5).

---

[73] Art 38(3).
[74] Art 6(4).
[75] Art 9(1).

Where the Crown Court decides to give effect to an external forfeiture order, it must register the order in that court; provide for notice of the registration to be given to any person affected by it; and appoint the relevant Director as the enforcement authority for the order.[76] 25.101

Articles 20 and 21 provide for a right of appeal to the Court of Appeal and the House of Lords. 25.102

Articles 22 and 23 provide for the appointment of enforcement receivers. Part 4 contains further provisions concerning receivers. 25.103

E. Freezing Orders in Relation to Terrorist Property

The UK can restrain and forfeit terrorist property at the request of foreign states. Before considering the provisions concerning MLA, it is necessary to consider the relevant domestic law. 25.104

Restraint and forfeiture in terrorist cases

Section 15(1), (2), and (3) of the Terrorism Act 2000 make it an offence to solicit, receive, or provide funds or other property for the purposes of terrorism.[77] Section 16(1) and (2) make it an offence to use money or other property for the purposes of terrorism. Section 17 concerns funding arrangements, and provides that it is an offence for a person to become involved in an arrangement as a result of which money or other property is made available to another person, and he knows or suspects that it will be used for the purposes of terrorism. Section 18 criminalizes the laundering of 'terrorist property'.[78] 25.105

Section 23[79] and Sch 4 of the Terrorism Act 2000 provides for powers of restraint and forfeiture in relation to terrorist property where a defendant has been convicted of one or more of the offences under ss 15–18 of the Act. 25.106

Section 23(1) provides that the court by or before which a person is convicted of an offence under any of ss 15–18 of the Terrorism Act 2000 may make a forfeiture order in accordance with the provisions of s 23. 25.107

Where a person is convicted of an offence under s 15(1) or (2) or 16, the court may order the forfeiture of any money or other property which, at the time of the offence, the person had in their possession or under their control and which (a) had been used for the purposes of terrorism; or (b) they intended should be used, or had reasonable cause to suspect might be used, for those purposes. 25.108

Where a person is convicted of an offence under s 15(3) the court may order the forfeiture of any money or other property which, at the time of the offence, the person had in their possession or under their control and (a) which had been used for the purposes of terrorism; or (b) which, at that time, they knew or had reasonable cause to suspect would or might be used for those purposes (s 23(3)). 25.109

Section 23(4) provides that where a person is convicted of an offence under s 17 or 18 the court may order the forfeiture of any money or other property which, at the time of the offence, the person had in their possession or under their control and which (a) had been used for the purposes of terrorism; or (b) was, at that time, intended by them to be used for those purposes. 25.110

---

[76] Art 19(1).
[77] *R v Saleem* [2009] EWCA Crim 920. Terrorism is defined in s 1 of the Terrorism Act 2000.
[78] Terrorist property is defined in s 14 of the Terrorism Act 2000.
[79] Inserted by the Counter-Terrorism Act 2008, s 34.

25.111 Where a person is convicted of an offence under s 17 the court may order the forfeiture of the money or other property to which the arrangement in question related, and which (a) had been used for the purposes of terrorism; or (b) at the time of the offence, the person knew or had reasonable cause to suspect would or might be used for those purposes (s 23(5)).

25.112 Where a person is convicted of an offence under s 18 the court may order the forfeiture of the money or other property to which the arrangement in question related (s 23(6)).

25.113 Where a person is convicted of an offence under any of ss 15–18, the court may order the forfeiture of any money or other property which wholly or partly, and directly or indirectly, is received by any person as a payment or other reward in connection with the commission of the offence (s 23(7)).

25.114 Sections 23A and 23B contain additional and supplementary provisions.

Sch 4 of the Terrorism Act 2000

25.115 Schedule 4 of the Terrorism Act 2000 contains procedural provisions relating to forfeiture orders under s 23. In particular, it confers powers on the High Court to make a restraint order to freeze terrorist property pre-trial.

25.116 Paragraph 2 of Sch 4 provides that where a court in England and Wales makes a forfeiture order it may make such other provision as appears to it to be necessary for giving effect to the order, and in particular it may require any of the forfeited property to be paid or handed over to the proper officer or to a constable designated for the purpose by the chief officer of police of a police force specified in the order; direct any of the forfeited property other than money or land to be sold or otherwise disposed of in such manner as the court may direct and the proceeds (if any) to be paid to the proper officer; appoint a receiver to take possession, subject to such conditions and exceptions as may be specified by the court, of any of the forfeited property; to realize it in such manner as the court may direct and to pay the proceeds to the proper officer; direct a specified part of any forfeited money, or of the proceeds of the sale, disposal, or realization of any forfeited property, to be paid by the proper officer to a specified person.

25.117 Para 4A permits the court to make an award to victims in the circumstances specified.

25.118 Paragraph 5 allows the High Court to make a restraint order in respect of terrorist property. The High Court may make a restraint order under para 5 where proceedings have been instituted in England and Wales for an offence under any of ss 15–18; the proceedings have not been concluded; an application for a restraint order is made to the High Court by the prosecutor; and a forfeiture order has been made, or it appears to the High Court that a forfeiture order may be made, in the proceedings for the offence.

25.119 The High Court may also make a restraint order under para 5 where a criminal investigation has been started in England and Wales with regard to an offence under any of ss 15–18; an application for a restraint order is made to the High Court by the person who the High Court is satisfied will have the conduct of any proceedings for the offence; and it appears to the High Court that a forfeiture order may be made in any proceedings for the offence.

25.120 A restraint order under para 5 prohibits a person to whom notice of it is given, subject to any conditions and exceptions specified in the order, from dealing with property in respect of which a forfeiture order has been or could be made in any proceedings referred to in para 5(1) and (2).

UK requests to foreign states to freeze terrorist assets

Schedule 4 of CICA 2003 amends Sch 4 of the Terrorism Act 2000 to provide for mutual recognition of orders freezing terrorist assets.[80] The purpose of the amendments is to limit the capacity of terrorist organizations by destabilizing them and preventing groups from profiting from terrorist activity.[81] 25.121

Definitions

Schedule 4 of CICA 2003 inserts new paras 11A–11G into Sch 4 of the Terrorism Act 2000. References in these paragraphs to 'the relevant Framework Decision' means the Framework Decision on the execution in the European Union of orders freezing property or evidence adopted by the Council of the European Union on 22 July 2003.[82] A 'listed offence' in these paragraphs means an offence described in Article 3(2) of the relevant Framework Decision, or a prescribed offence[83] or an offence of a prescribed description (para 11A(3)).[84] 25.122

Specified information, in relation to a certificate under para 11B or 11D, means any information required to be given by the form of certificate annexed to the relevant Framework Decision, or any prescribed information (para 11A(5)). 25.123

A participating country means a country other than the UK which is a member State on a day appointed for the commencement of Sch 4 to CICA 2003 and any other member State designated by an order made by the Secretary of State. 25.124

Certification by the High Court

Paragraph 11B of Sch 4 provides that if any of the property to which an application for a restraint order relates is property in a participating country, the applicant may ask the High Court to make a certificate under para 11B. 25.125

The High Court may give a certificate under para 11B if it makes a restraint order in relation to property in the participating country, and it is satisfied that there is a good arguable case that the property is likely to be used for the purposes of a listed offence, or is the proceeds of the commission of a listed offence. 25.126

The 'good arguable case' test in para 11B(2)(b) is based on the test for an interim receiving order pending civil recovery under Part 5 of the Proceeds of Crime Act 2002, s 246(5).[85] 25.127

A certificate under para 11B is a certificate which is made for the purposes of the relevant Framework Decision, and gives the specified information. 25.128

If the High Court makes a certificate under para 11B the restraint order must provide for notice of the certificate to be given to the person affected by it, and para 6(2)–(4) of Sch 4 applies to the certificate as it applies to the restraint order. 25.129

Sending domestic freezing orders

Paragraph 11C provides that if a certificate is made under para 11B, the restraint order and the certificate are to be sent to the Secretary of State for forwarding to a court exercising jurisdiction 25.130

80 The amendments were not in force at the time of writing (September 2012).

81 See the Joint Committee on Human Rights Third Report, Session 2002–03.

82 2003/577/JHA.

83 'Prescribed' means prescribed in an order by the Secretary of State (para 11A(6)).

84 An order under para 11A(3)(b) which, for the purposes of para 11D, prescribes an offence or a description of offences may require that the conduct which constitutes the offence or offences would, if it occurred in a part of the UK, constitute an offence in that part.

85 HL Deb 3 February 2003, c GC26.

in the place where the property is situated, or any authority recognized by the government of the participating country as the appropriate authority for receiving orders of that kind.[86]

25.131 The restraint order and the certificate must be accompanied by a forfeiture order, unless the certificate indicates when the court expects a forfeiture order to be sent. The certificate must include a translation of it into an appropriate language of the participating country (if that language is not English). The certificate must be signed by or on behalf of the court and must include a statement as to the accuracy of the information given in it. The signature may be an electronic signature. If the restraint order and the certificate are not accompanied by a forfeiture order, but a forfeiture order is subsequently made, it is to be sent to the Secretary of State for forwarding.

Freezing terrorist assets in the UK at the request of foreign states

Overseas freezing orders

25.132 Paragraph 11D of Sch 4 provides that para 11E applies where an overseas freezing order made by an appropriate court or authority in a participating country is received by the Secretary of State from the court or authority which made or confirmed the order.

25.133 An overseas freezing order is an order prohibiting dealing with property which is in the UK, and which the appropriate court or authority considers is likely to be used for the purposes of a listed offence or is the proceeds of the commission of such an offence, and in respect of which an order has been or may be made by a court exercising criminal jurisdiction in the participating country for the forfeiture of the property, and in respect of which the other requirements of para 11D are met.

25.134 The first condition is that the action which the appropriate court or authority considered would constitute or, as the case may be, constituted the listed offence is action done as an act of terrorism or for the purposes of terrorism.

25.135 Also, the order must relate to criminal proceedings instituted in the participating country, or a criminal investigation being carried on there. The order must be accompanied by a certificate which gives the specified information; but a certificate may be treated as giving any specified information which is not given in it if the Secretary of State has the information in question. The certificate must be signed by or on behalf of the court or authority which made or confirmed the order, include a statement as to the accuracy of the information given in it, and if it is not in English, include a translation of it into English. The signature may be an electronic signature. The order must be accompanied by an order made by a court exercising criminal jurisdiction in that country for the forfeiture of the property, unless the certificate indicates when such an order is expected to be sent.

25.136 An appropriate court or authority in a participating country in relation to an overseas freezing order is a court exercising criminal jurisdiction in the country; a prosecuting authority in the country; or any other authority in the country which appears to the Secretary of State to have the function of making such orders.

Enforcement of overseas freezing orders

25.137 Where para 11E applies the Secretary of State must send a copy of the overseas freezing order to the High Court and to the Director of Public Prosecutions.

---

[86] Art 4 of the Freezing Framework Decision provides for direct transmission of freezing orders between judicial authorities, however the UK and Ireland have retained the right for requests to be sent via central authorities.

The High Court is to consider the overseas freezing order on its own initiative within a period prescribed by rules of court. Before giving effect to the overseas freezing order, the court must give the Director an opportunity to be heard. **25.138**

The court may decide not to give effect to the overseas freezing order only if, in its opinion, giving effect to it would be incompatible with any of the Convention rights within the meaning of the Human Rights Act 1998. **25.139**

The Court may postpone giving effect to an overseas freezing order in respect of any property in order to avoid prejudicing a criminal investigation which is taking place in the UK or if, under an order made by a court in criminal proceedings in the UK, the property may not be dealt with (para 11F). **25.140**

By para 11G, where the High Court decides to give effect to an overseas freezing order, it must register the order in that court, and provide for notice of the registration to be given to any person affected by it. For the purpose of enforcing an overseas freezing order registered in the High Court, the order is to have effect as if it were an order made by that court. **25.141**

Paragraph 11G(3) provides that para 7 (powers of seizure) applies to an overseas freezing order registered in the High Court as it applies to a domestic restraint order made under para 5. **25.142**

The High Court may cancel the registration of the order, or vary the property to which the order applies, on an application by the Director of Public Prosecutions or any other person affected by it, if or to the extent that the court is of the opinion mentioned in para 11E(4) (the order violates a person's Convention rights), or the court is of the opinion that the order has ceased to have effect in the participating country. **25.143**

F. Mutual Enforcement within the UK

This section provides an overview of the law relating to the mutual enforcement within the UK of restraint orders and other orders under POCA 2002. **25.144**

Section 443 of POCA 2002 contains enabling provisions which allow Orders in Council to be made to allow for the mutual enforcement of restraint and confiscation in the different parts of the UK. **25.145**

The Proceeds of Crime Act 2002 (Enforcement in different parts of the United Kingdom) Order 2002[87] has been made under s 443. This makes provision for orders relating to restraint and receivership made under POCA 2002 in one part of the UK to be enforced in another part. Part I is introductory and contains an extensive set of definitions. Part II deals with the enforcement of Scottish and Northern Ireland orders in England and Wales. Part III deals with the enforcement of English or Welsh orders and Northern Ireland orders in Scotland. Part IV deals with the enforcement of English or Welsh orders and Scottish orders in Northern Ireland. **25.146**

The same model is used for each jurisdiction. The Order in Council provides that orders automatically have effect throughout the UK. However, proceedings for their enforcement may only be brought if the orders are registered in the Crown Court for England and Wales, the Court of Session for Scotland, and the High Court for Northern Ireland.[88] The court in which **25.147**

---

[87] SI 2002/3133.

[88] For example, Art 3 provides: '(1) Any Northern Ireland restraint order or Scottish restraint order has effect in England and Wales. (2) Proceedings for or with respect to the enforcement or contravention of a Northern Ireland restraint order or a Scottish restraint order may only be taken if the order is registered in accordance with article 6.'

the order is registered then has the same powers to enforce the order as if it had made the order itself. Supplementary provision is made about land registration and admissibility of evidence. For Scotland, the Order in Council makes supplementary provisions about inhibition, arrestment, and deeds relating to heritable property.

25.148 The Proceeds of Crime Act 2002 (Investigations in different parts of the United Kingdom) Order 2003[89] has also been made, under ss 443(1)(d) and (e), (3) and (4), and 459(2) of POCA 2002.

25.149 Part 8 of POCA 2002 provides for various orders and warrants to be issued in relation to confiscation investigations, money laundering investigations, and civil recovery investigations. This Order makes provision for orders and warrants made or issued under Part 8 of POCA 2002 in one part of the UK to be enforced in another part of the UK.

25.150 Articles 3 and 4 make provision for the enforcement in England and Wales of production orders made in Scotland or Northern Ireland for the purposes of a confiscation investigation or money laundering investigation. The effect is that the order may be enforced by the authorities in England and Wales, or the authorities of the jurisdiction which made the order, or by the authorities of both jurisdictions acting together. The rules for England and Wales as to material which does not need to be produced in relation to production orders apply. The order has effect as an order of the Crown Court in England and Wales so that contempt proceedings can be brought for non-compliance.

25.151 Articles 5 and 6 make provision for the enforcement in England and Wales of search and seizure warrants issued in Scotland or Northern Ireland for the purposes of a confiscation investigation or money laundering investigation. The warrant may be enforced by the authorities in England and Wales, or the authorities of the jurisdiction which made the order, or by the authorities of both jurisdictions acting together. The rules for England and Wales as to material which cannot be seized apply. The provisions of English law apply to the execution of the warrant but the law of the jurisdiction which made the order applies in relation to retention and copying of material seized under the warrant.

25.152 Articles 7 and 8 make provision for the enforcement in England and Wales of disclosure orders made in Scotland or Northern Ireland for the purposes of a confiscation investigation. Two regimes apply. The first regime deals with the situation where an officer travels to England and Wales to execute the disclosure order. In this case, the English law as to exclusions from the disclosure order applies, if the disclosure order is breached then the offender commits an offence under English law. The second regime deals with the situation where an officer requires a person in England and Wales to travel to the jurisdiction in which he is situated in order to execute a disclosure order. In this case, the law of the jurisdiction in which the officer is situated applies but a person who fails to comply commits an offence under English law, as well as the law of that jurisdiction.

25.153 Articles 9 and 10 make provision for the enforcement in England and Wales of customer information orders made in Scotland or Northern Ireland for the purposes of a confiscation investigation or money laundering investigation. The English law as to exclusions applies and if the customer information order is breached then the offender commits an offence under English law, as well as the law of the jurisdiction in which the order was made.

25.154 Articles 11 and 12 make provision for the enforcement in England and Wales of account monitoring orders made in Scotland or Northern Ireland for the purposes of a confiscation

[89] SI 2003/425, as amended by Proceeds of Crime 2002 (Investigations in different parts of the United Kingdom) (Amendment) Order 2008 (SI 2008/298).

investigation or money laundering investigation. The order may be enforced by the authorities in England and Wales, or the authorities of the jurisdiction which made the order, or by the authorities of both jurisdictions acting together. The English law as to exclusions applies. The order has effect as an order of the Crown Court in England and Wales so that contempt proceedings can be brought for non-compliance.

Part 3 makes corresponding provision for orders and warrants made or issued in England and Wales or Scotland to be enforced in Northern Ireland. **25.155**

Part 4 makes corresponding provision for orders and warrants made or issued in England and Wales or Northern Ireland to be enforced in Scotland. **25.156**

Article 33 makes it clear that an order or warrant to which Parts 2–4 apply can only be discharged or varied in the jurisdiction in which it was made or issued. It also deals with the application of the two Codes of Practice which Part 8 of the Act provides for (one for England, Wales, and Northern Ireland and one for Scotland) where Parts 2–4 apply. **25.157**

Article 34 amends the Civil Jurisdiction and Judgments Act 1982 so that orders and warrants made or issued under Part 8 of POCA 2002 for the purposes of a civil recovery investigation fall within the provisions of that Act as to enforcement in different parts of the UK. **25.158**

APPENDICES

APPENDIX E1

The Extradition Act 1870

(33 & 34 Vict., c.52)

An Act for amending the Law relating to the Extradition of Criminals
[9th August 1870][1]

PRELIMINARY

1. Short title

This Act may be cited as 'The Extradition Act, 1870'.

2. Where arrangements for surrender of criminals made, Order in Council to apply

Where an arrangement has been made with any foreign state with respect to the surrender to such state of any fugitive criminals, Her Majesty may, by Order in Council, direct that this Act shall apply in the case of such a foreign state.

Her Majesty may, by the same or any subsequent order, limit the operation of the order, and restrict the same to fugitive criminals who are in or suspected of being in part of Her Majesty's dominions specified in the order, and render the operation thereof subject to such conditions, exceptions, and qualifications as may be deemed expedient.

Every such order shell recite or embody the term of the arrangement, and shall not remain in force for any longer period than the arrangement.

Every such order shall be laid before both Houses of Parliament within six weeks after it is made, or, if Parliament be not then sitting, within six weeks after the then next meeting of Parliament, and shall also be published in the London Gazette.

3. Restrictions on surrender of criminals

The following restrictions shall be observed with respect to the surrender of fugitive criminals:

(1) A fugitive criminal shall not be surrendered if the offence in respect of which his surrender is demanded is one of a political character, or of he prove to the satisfaction of the police magistrate or the court before whom he is brought on habeas corpus, or to the Secretary of State, that the requisition for his surrender has in fact been made with a view to try or punish him for an offence of political character;

(2) A fugitive criminal shall not be surrendered to a foreign state unless provision is made by the law of that state, or by arrangement, that the fugitive criminal shall not, until he has been restored or had an opportunity of returning to Her Majesty's dominions, be detained or tried in that foreign state for any offence committed prior to his surrender other than the extradition crime proved by the facts on which the surrender is grounded;

(3) A fugitive criminal who has been accused of some other offence within English jurisdiction not being the same offence for which his surrender is asked, or is undergoing sentence under any conviction in the United Kingdom, shall not be surrendered until after he has been discharged, whether by acquittal or on expiration of his sentence or otherwise [, or unless an order is made for the charge in respect of the offence to lie on the file];[2]

(4) A fugitive criminal shall not be surrendered until the expiration of fifteen days from the date of his being committed to prison to await his surrender.

---

[1] Preamble repealed by the SLR (No 2) Act 1893.

[2] The words in square brackets were inserted by the Criminal Justice Act 1988, s 1, Sch 1, para 1.

4. Provisions for arrangement of surrender

An Order in Council for applying this Act in the case of any foreign state shall not be made unless the arrangement—

(1) provides for the determination of it by either party to it after the expiration of a notice not exceeding one year; and
(2) is in conformity with the provisions of this Act, and in particular with the restrictions on the surrender of fugitive criminals contained in this Act.

5. Publication and effect of order

When an order applying this Act in the case of any foreign state has been published in the London Gazette, this Act (after the date specified in the order, or if no date is specified in the order, after the date of publication,) shall, so long as the order remains in force, but subject to limitations, restrictions, conditions, exceptions, and qualifications, if any, contained in the order, apply in the case of such a foreign state. An Order in Council shall be conclusive evidence that the arrangement therein referred to complies with the requisitions of this Act, and that this Act applies in the case of the foreign state mentioned in the order, and the validity of such order shall not be questioned in any legal proceedings whatsoever.

6. Liability of criminal to surrender

Where this Act applies in the case of any foreign state, every fugitive criminal of that state who is in or suspected of being in any part of Her Majesty's dominions, or that part which is specified in the order applying this Act (as the case may be), shall be liable to be apprehended and surrendered in manner provided by this Act, whether the crime in respect of which the surrender is sought was committed before or after the date of the order, and whether there is or is not any concurrent jurisdiction in any court of Her Majesty's dominions over that crime.

7. Order of Secretary of State for issue of warrant in United Kingdom if crime is not of a political character

A requisition for the surrender of a fugitive criminal of any foreign state, who is in or suspected of being in the United Kingdom, shall be made to a Secretary of State by some person recognised by the Secretary of State as a diplomatic representative of that foreign state. A Secretary of State may, by order under his hand and seal, signify to a police magistrate that such requisition has been made, and require him to issue his warrant for the apprehension of the fugitive criminal.

If the Secretary of State is of the opinion that the offence is one of a political character, he may if he think fit, refuse to send any such order, and may also at any time order a fugitive criminal accused or convicted of such offence to be discharged from custody.

8. Issue of warrant by police, magistrate, justice, &c

A warrant for the apprehension of a fugitive criminal, whether accused or convicted of a crime, who is in or suspected of being in the United Kingdom, may be issued —

(1) by a police magistrate on receipt of the said order of the Secretary of State, and on such evidence as would in his opinion justify the warrant if the crime had been committed or the criminal convicted in England; and
(2) by a police magistrate or any justice of the peace in any part of the united Kingdom, on such information or complaint and such evidence or after such proceedings as would in then opinion of the person issuing the warrant justify the issue of a warrant if the crime had been committed or the criminal convicted in that part of the United Kingdom in which he exercises jurisdiction.

Any person issuing a warrant under this section without an order from a Secretary of State shall forthwith send a report of the fact of such issue, together with the evidence and information or complaint, or certified copies thereof, to a Secretary of State, who may if he think fit order the warrant to be cancelled, and the person who has been apprehended on the warrant to be discharged.

A fugitive criminal, when apprehended on a warrant issued without the order of a Secretary of State, shall be brought before some person having power to issue a warrant under this section, who shall by warrant order him to be brought and the prisoner shall accordingly be brought before a police magistrate.

A fugitive criminal apprehended on a warrant issued without the order of a Secretary of State shall be discharged by the police magistrate, unless the police magistrate, within such reasonable time as, with reference to the circumstances of the case, he may fix, receives from a Secretary of State an order signifying that a requisition has been made for the surrender of such criminal.

9. Hearing of case and evidence of political character of crime

When a fugitive criminal is brought before the police magistrate, the police magistrate shall hear the case in the same manner, and have the same jurisdiction and powers, as near as may be, as if the prisoner where brought before him charged with an indictable offence committed in England.

The police magistrate shall receive any evidence which may be tendered to show that the crime of which the prisoner is accused or alleged to have been convicted is an offence of political character or is not an extradition crime.

10. Committal or discharge of prisoner

In the case of a fugitive criminal accused of an extradition crime, if the foreign warrant authorising the arrest of such criminal is duly authenticated, and such evidence is produced as (subject to the provisions of this Act) would, according to the law of England, justify the committal for trial of the prisoner if the crime of which he is accused had been committed in England, the police magistrate shall commit him to prison, but otherwise shall order him to be discharged.

In the case of a fugitive criminal alleged to have been convicted of an extradition crimes, if such evidence is produced as (subject to the provisions of this Act) would, according to the law of England, prove that that the prisoner was convicted of such crime, then police magistrate shall commit him to prison, but otherwise shall order him to be discharged.

If he commits such criminal to prison, he shall commit him ...,[3] there to await the warrant of a Secretary of State for his surrender, and shall forthwith send to a Secretary of State a certificate of his committal, and such report on the case as he may think fit.

11. Surrender of fugitive to foreign state by warrant of Secretary of State

If the police magistrate commits a fugitive criminal to prison, he shall inform such criminal that he will not have to be surrendered until after the expiration of fifteen days, and that he has the right to apply for a writ of Habeas corpus.

Upon the expiration of the said fifteen days, or, if a writ of Habeas corpus is issued, after the decision of the court upon the return to the writ, as the case may be, or after such further period as may be allowed in either case by a Secretary of State, it shall be lawful for a Secretary of State, by warrant under his hand and seal, to order the fugitive criminal (if not delivered on the decision of the court) to be surrendered to such person as may in his opinion be duly authorised to receive the fugitive criminal by the foreign state from which the requisition for the surrender proceeded, and such fugitive criminal shall be surrendered accordingly.

It shall he lawful for any person to whom such warrant is directed and for the person so authorised as aforesaid to receive, hold in custody, and convey within the jurisdiction of such foreign state the criminal mentioned in the warrant; and if the criminal escapes out of any custody to which he may he delivered on or in pursuance of such warrant, it shall be lawful to retake him in the same manner as any person accused of any crime against the laws of that part if Her Majesty's dominions to which he escapes to be retaken upon an escape.

11A. Simplified procedure

(1) A person may give notice that he waives the rights conferred on him by section 11 above.

(2) A notice under this section shall be given in England and Wales in the manner prescribed by rules under section 144 of the Magistrates' Courts Act 1980 and, without prejudice to the generality of subsection (1) of that section, the power to make such rules shall include power to make provision for a magistrate to order the committal for return of a person with his consent at any time after his arrest.

(3) A notice under this section shall be given in Scotland in the manner prescribed by the High Court of Justiciary by Act of Adjournal and the sheriff may order the committal for return of a person with his consent at any time after his arrest.

---

[3] The words omitted, which provided for committal to the Middlesex House of Detention, or to some other prison in Middlesex, were repealed by the Administration of Justice Act 1964, ss 39(2), 41(8), Sch 3, para 9, Sch 5.

(4) Where an order is made under this section, this Act shall cease to apply to the person in respect of whom it is made, except that if, within one month after the order is made, he is not surrendered to the foreign state to which he is to be returned, the High Court, upon application by or on behalf of that person, may, unless reasonable cause is shown for the delay, order him to be discharged.][4]

12. Discharge of persons apprehended if not conveyed out of the United Kingdom within two months

If the fugitive criminal who has been committed to prison is not surrendered and conveyed out of the United Kingdom within two months after such committal, or, if a writ of Habeas corpus is issued, after the decision of the court upon the return of the writ, it shall be lawful for any judge of one of Her Majesty's Superior Courts at Westminster, upon application made to him by or on behalf of the criminal, and upon proof that reasonable notice of the intention to make such application has been given to a Secretary of State, to order the criminal to be discharged out of custody, unless sufficient cause is shown to the contrary.

13. Execution of warrant of police magistrate

The warrant of the police magistrate issued in pursuance of this Act may be executed in any part of the United Kingdom in the same manner as if the same had been originally issued or subsequently endorsed by a justice of the peace having jurisdiction in the place where the same is executed.

14. Depositions to be evidence

Depositions of statements taken on oath, taken in a foreign state, and copies of such original depositions or statements, and foreign certificates of or judicial documents stating the fact of conviction, may if duly authenticated, be received in evidence in proceedings under this Act.

15. Authentication of depositions and warrants

Foreign warrants and depositions or statements on oath, and copies thereof, and certificates of or judicial documents stating the fact of a conviction, shall be deemed duly authenticated for the purposes of this Act if authenticated in manner provided for the time being by law or authenticated as follows:

(1) If the warrant purports to be signed by a judge, magistrate, or officer of the foreign state where the same was issued;

(2) If the depositions or statements or the copies thereof purport to be certified under the hand of a judge, magistrate, or officer of the foreign state where the same where taken to be the original depositions or statements, or to be true copies thereof, as the case may require; and

(3) If the certificate or judicial document stating the fact of a conviction purports to be certified by a judge, magistrate, or officer of the foreign state where the conviction took place; and

if in every case the warrants, depositions, statements, copies, certificates, and judicial documents (as the case may be) are authenticated by the oath of some witness or by being sealed with the official seal of the minister of justice or some other minister of state; and all courts of justice, justices, and magistrates shall take judicial notice of such official seal, and shall admit the documents so authenticated by it to be received in evidence without further proof.

Crimes committed at sea

16. Jurisdiction as to crimes committed at sea

Where the crime in respect of which the surrender of a fugitive criminal is sought was committed on board any vessel on the high seas which comes into any port of the United Kingdom, the following provisions shall have effect:

(1) This Act shall be construed as if any stipendiary magistrate in England or Ireland, and any [sheriff principal] or [sheriff][5] in Scotland, were substituted for the police magistrate throughout this Act, except the part relating to the execution of the warrant of the police magistrate:

---

[4] The section in square brackets was inserted by the Criminal Justice Act 1988, s 1, Sch 1, para 2.

[5] The words in square brackets were substituted by the Sheriff Courts (Scotland) Act 1971, s 4.

(2) The criminal may be committed to any prison to which the person committing him has power to commit persons accused of the like crime:
(3) If the fugitive criminal is apprehended on a warrant issued without the order of a Secretary of State, he shall be brought before the stipendiary magistrate, [sheriff principal] or [sheriff] who issued the warrant, or who has jurisdiction in the port where the vessel lies, or in the place nearest to that port.

Fugitive criminals in British possessions

17. Proceedings as to fugitive criminals in British possessions

This Act, when applied by Order in Council, shall, unless it is otherwise provided by such order, extend to every British possession in the same manner as if throughout this Act the British possession were substituted for the United Kingdom or England, as the case may require, but with the following modifications: namely,

(1) The requisition for the surrender of a fugitive criminal who is in or suspected of being in a British possession may be made to the governor of that British possession by any person recognised by that governor as a consul general, consul, or vice-consul, or (if the fugitive criminal has escaped from a colony or dependency of the foreign state on behalf of which the requisition is made) as the governor of such colony or dependency;
(2) No warrant of a Secretary of State shall be required, and all powers vested in or acts authorised or required to be done under this Act by the police magistrate and the Secretary of State, or either of them, in relation to the surrender of a fugitive criminal, may be done by the governor of the British possession alone;
(3) Any prison in the British possession may be substituted for a prison in Middlesex;
(4) A judge of any court exercising in the British possession the like powers as the Court of Queen's Bench exercises in England may exercise the power of discharging a criminal when not conveyed within two months out of such British possession.

18. Saving of laws of British possessions

If by any law or ordinance, made before or after the passing of this Act by the Legislature of any British possession, provision is made for carrying into effect within such possession the surrender of fugitive criminals who are in or suspected of being in such British possession, Her Majesty may, by Order in Council applying this Act in the case of any foreign state, or by any subsequent order, either suspend the operation within any such British possession of this Act, or any part thereof, so far as it relates to such foreign state, and so long as such law or ordinance continues in force there, and no longer; or direct that such law or ordinance, or any part thereof, shall have effect in such British possession, with or without modifications and alterations, as if it were part of this Act.

General provisions

19. Criminal surrendered by foreign state not triable for previous crime

Where, in pursuance of any arrangement with a foreign state, any person accused or convicted of any crime, which, if committed in England, would be one of the crimes described in the first schedule to this Act is surrendered by that foreign state, such person shall not, until he has been restored or had an opportunity of returning to such foreign state, be triable or tried for any offence committed prior to the surrender in any part of Her Majesty's dominions other than such of the said crimes as may be proved on the facts on which the surrender is grounded.

20. As to use of forms in second schedule

The forms set forth in the second schedule to this Act, or forms as nearto as circumstances admit, may be used in all matters to which such forms refer, and in the case of a British possession may be so used, mutatis mutandis, and when used shall be deemed valid and sufficient in law.

21. Revocation, &c of Order in Council

Her Majesty may, by Order in Council, revoke or alter, subject to the restrictions in this Act, any Order in Council made in pursuance of this Act, and all the provisions of this Act with respect to the original order shall (so far as applicable) apply, mutatis mutandis, to any such new order.

22. Application in Channel Islands and Isle of Man

This Act (except so far as relates to the execution of warrants in the Channel Islands) shall extend to the Channel Islands and Isle of Man in the same manner as if they were part of the United Kingdom; and the royal courts of the Channel Islands are hereby respectively authorised and required to register this Act.

23. Saving for Indian treaties

Nothing in this Act shall affect the lawful powers of Her Majesty or of the Governor General of India in Council to make treaties for the extradition of criminals with Indian native states, or with any other Asiatic states coterminous with British India, or to carry into execution the provisions of any such treaties made either before or after the passing of this Act.

24. Power of foreign state to obtain evidence in United Kingdom

The testimony of any witness may be obtained in relation to any criminal matter pending in any court or tribunal in a foreign state in like manner as it may be obtained in relation to any civil matter under the Act of the session of the nineteenth and twentieth years of the reign of Her present Majesty, chapter one hundred and thirteen, intituled 'An Act to provide for taking evidence in Her Majesty's Dominions in relation to civil and commercial matters pending before foreign tribunals'; and all the provisions of that Act shall be construed as if the term civil matter included criminal matter, and the term cause included a proceeding against a criminal: Provided that nothing in this section shall apply in the case of a criminal matter of a political character.

25. Foreign state includes dependencies

For the purposes of this Act, every colony, dependency, and constituent part of a foreign state, and every vessel of that state, shall (except where expressly mentioned as distinct in this Act) be deemed to be within the jurisdiction of and to be part of such foreign state.

26. Definition of terms

In this Act, unless the context otherwise requires,—

The Term 'British possession' means any colony, plantation, island, territory, or settlement within Her Majesty's dominions, and not within the United Kingdom, the Channel Islands, and Isle of Man; and all colonies, plantations, territories, and settlements under one legislature, as herein-after defined, are deemed to be one British possession;

The term 'legislature' means any person or persons who can exercise legislative authority in a British possession, and where there are local legislatures as well as one central legislature, means the central legislature only;

The term 'governor' means any person or persons administering the government of a British possession,. . .;[6]

The term 'extradition crime' means a crime which, if committed in England or within English jurisdiction, would be one of the crimes described in the first schedule to this Act;

The term 'conviction' and 'convicted' do not include or refer to a conviction which under foreign law is a conviction for contumacy, but the term 'accused person' includes a person so convicted for contumacy;

The term 'fugitive criminal' means any person accused or convicted of an extradition crime committed within the jurisdiction of any foreign state who is in or is suspected of being in some part of Her Majesty's dominions; and the term 'fugitive criminal of a foreign state' means a fugitive criminal accused or convicted of an extradition crime committed within the jurisdiction of that state;

..........[7]

The term 'police magistrate' means [the chief metropolitan stipendiary magistrate or a metropolitan stipendiary magistrate designated by the Lord Chancellor for the purposes of this Act and the Acts that may be cited together with it as the Extradition Acts 1870 to 1935];[8]

---

[6] The words omitted from the definition of 'governor' were repealed by the Government of India (Adaptation of Acts of Parliament) Order 1937, SR & O 1937/230.

[7] The definition omitted was repealed by the SLR (No 2) Act 1893.

[8] The words in square brackets were substituted by the Criminal Justice Act 1988, s 1, Sch 1, para 3.

The term 'justice of the peace' includes in Scotland any [sheriff principal, sheriff],[9] or magistrate;

The term 'warrant', in the case of any foreign state, includes any judicial document authorising the arrest of a person accused or convicted of crime.

Repeal of acts

27. Repeal of Acts in third schedule

The Acts specified in the third schedule to this Act are hereby repealed as to the whole of Her Majesty's dominions; and this Act (with the exception of anything contained within it which is inconsistent with the treaties referred to in the Acts so repealed) shall apply (as regards crimes committed either before or after the passing of this Act), in the case of foreign states with which those treaties are made, in the same manner as if an Order in Council referring to such treaties had been made in pursuance of this Act, and as if such order had directed that every law and ordinance which is in force in any British possession with respect to such treaties should have effect as part of this Act ...[10]

Schedules

First Schedule

List of Crimes (as amended and supplemented)

The following list of crimes is to be construed according to the law existing in England, or in a British possession, (as the case may be), at the date of the alleged crime, whether by common law or by statute made before or after the passing of this Act:

Murder, ...[11] and conspiracy to murder.

Manslaughter.

Counterfeiting and altering money and uttering counterfeit or altered money. Forgery, counterfeiting, and altering, and uttering what is forged or counterfeited or altered.

....

Crimes by bankrupts against bankruptcy law.

....

Rape.

Abduction.

....

Piracy by law of nations.

Sinking or destroying a vessel at sea, ... or conspiring to do so.

Assaults on board a ship on the high seas with intent to destroy life or to do grievous bodily harm.

Revolt or conspiracy to revolt by two or more persons on board a ship on the high seas against the authority of the master.

Kidnapping or false imprisonment.[12]

Perjury or subornation of perjury, whether under common or statute law.[13]

Any indictable offence under the Theft Act 1968, or the Theft Act 1978, or any Act amending or substituted for either, which is not included in the first Schedule to the principle Act;[14]

---

[9] The words in square brackets were substituted by the Sheriff Courts (Scotland) Act 1971, s 4.

[10] The words omitted were repealed by the SLR Act 1883.

[11] The words omitted in the Schedule were repealed respectively by the Theft Act 1968, s 33(3), (4), Sch 3, Pt III; the Criminal Damage Act 1971, s 11(8), Sch, Pt III; the Suppression of Terrorism Act 1978, s 9(2), Sch 2; and the Child Abduction Act 1984, s 11(5)(*b*).

[12] Added by Extradition Act 1873.

[13] Added by Extradition Act 1873.

[14] Originally added by the Extradition Act 1873, now as amended by the Theft Act 1968, Sch 2, Pt II and the Theft Act 1978, s 5(3).

Any indictable offence under the Criminal Damage Act 1971 or the unrepealed provisions of the Malicious Damage Act 1861, or any Act amending or substituted for either, which is not included in the first Schedule to the principal Act.[15]

Any indictable offence under the Forgery Act 1861 or any Act amending or substituted for it, which is not included in the first Schedule to the principal Act.[16]

Any indictable offence under the Coinage Offences Act 1861 or any act amending or substituted for it, which is not included in the first Schedule to the principal Act.[17]

Any indictable offence under the Offences against the Person Act 1861 or any Act amending or substituted for it, which is not included in the first Schedule to the principal Act.[18]

Any indictable offence under the law for the time being in force in relation to bankruptcy, which is not included in the first Schedule to the principal Act.[19]

Any indictable offence under the Sexual Offences Act 1956, or any act amending or substituted for it, which is not included in the first Schedule to the principal Act, and in the case of sections 2, 5 to 12, 22 and 23 of the Sexual Offences Act 1956, any attempt to commit the offence.[20]

Offences committed against the Slave Trade Acts 1824 and 1873 and any enactments amending them.[21]

Bribery.[22]

Offences against any enactment for the time being in force relating to dangerous drugs, and attempts to commit such offences.[23]

Attempts to commit offences in connection with counterfeit currency.[24]

Aiding, abetting, counselling or procuring suicide.[25]

Impeding the apprehension or prosecution of persons having committed extradition crimes.[26]

Genocide, any conspiracy to commit genocide, and any direct and public incitement to commit genocide.[27]

Cruelty to children or young persons under sixteen years of age by persons having their custody, charge or care.[28]

Indecent conduct with or towards children under the age of fourteen.[29]

Conspiring to commit any offence against any enactment for the time being in force in relation to dangerous drugs.[30]

Offences and attempts to commit offences against the Hijacking Act 1971 and the Protection of Aircraft Act 1973.

Indecent photographs of children.[31]

Any offence under the Explosive Substances Act, 1883, including conspiracy to cause explosions.[32]

Any indictable offence under the Firearms Act, 1968.[33]

15 Added by the Extradition Act 1873.
16 Added by the Extradition Act 1873.
17 Added by the Extradition Act 1873.
18 Added by the Extradition Act 1873.
19 Added by the Extradition Act 1873.
20 Added by the Extradition Act 1873.
21 Added by the Slave Trade Act 1873, s 27.
22 Added by the Extradition Act 1906, s 1.
23 Added by the Extradition Act 1932, s 1.
24 Added by the Counterfeit Currency (Convention) Act 1953, s 4.
25 Added by the Suicides Act 1961, Sch 1, Pt II.
26 Added by the Criminal Law Act 1967, s 4(6).
27 Added by the Genocide Act 1969, s 2(1)(a).
28 Added by the Children and Young Persons Act 1969, s 60(1)(a).
29 Added by the Children and Young Persons Act 1969, s 60(1)(a).
30 Added by the Misuse of Drugs Act 1971, s 33.
31 Added by the Protection of Children Act 1978, s 1.
32 Added by the Suppression of Terrorism Act 1978, s 3(1).
33 Added by the Suppression of Terrorism Act 1978, s 3(1).

Any attempt to commit any of the crimes listed in Schedule 1 to this Act, including crimes added to this list after 1978.[34]

The taking of hostages.[35]

Any offence under the Prohibition of Female Circumcision Act,1985, s 1.[36]

Torture.[37]

Any offence under the Companies (Insider Dealing) Act, 1985.[38]

Offences under the s 24 of the Drug Trafficking Offences Act 1986 (assisting another to retain the benefit of drug trafficking).[39]

Any offence under s 1(3)(2) of the Internationally Protected Persons Act, 1978.

Any offence under s 2 of the Nuclear Material (Offences) Act, 1983.

Any offence under ss 1–4 of the Aviation Security Act, 1982.

Any offence under ss 2 or 3 of the Computer Misuse Act, 1990, including conspiracy to commit such an offence or attempt to commit an offence under s 3.[40]

Offences under sections 1 and 9–13 of the Aviation and Maritime Security Act 1990 including attempts to commit such offences;[41]

Drug trafficking.[42]

Threats of attack on UN workers.[43]

Second Schedule

Form of Order of Secretary of State to the Police Magistrate.

To the chief magistrate of the metropolitan police courts *or* other magistrate of the metropolitan police court in Bow Street [*or* the stipendiary magistrate at].

WHEREAS, in pursuance of an arrangement with|, referred to in
an Order of Her Majesty in Council dated the|day of|, a
requisition has been made to me,|, one of Her Majesty's
Principal Secretaries of State, by|, the diplomatic
representative of|, for the surrender of|,
late of|, accused [*or* convicted] of the commission of the crime of
within the jurisdiction of|:

Now I hereby, by this order under my hand and seal, signify to you that such requisition has been made, and require you to issue a warrant for the apprehension of such fugitive, provided that the conditions of The Extradition Act, 1870, relating to the issue of such warrant, are in your judgement complied with.

Given under the hand and seal of the undersigned, one of Her Majesty's Principal Secretaries of State, this day of|.

Form of Warrant of Apprehension by Order of Secretary of State.

Metropolitan|}
police district,|}|To all and each of the constables of the metropolitan
police
[*or* county *or*|}|police force [*or* of the county *or* borough of|].
borough of|]|}

34 Added by the Suppression of Terrorism Act 1978, s 3(1).

35 Added by the Taking of Hostages Act 1982, s 3.

36 Added by the Prohibition of Female Circumcision Act 1985, s 3.

37 Added by virtue of the Criminal Justice Act 1988, s 126(1).

38 Added by virtue of the Criminal Justice Act 1988, Sch1, para 4.

39 Added by virtue of the Criminal Justice Act 1988, Sch1, para 4.

40 Computer Misuse Act 1990, s 15; statutory amendment in accordance with s 37(3) of the 1989 Act to Orders in Council made under s 2 of the 1870 Act.

41 Aviation and Maritime Security Act 1990, s 49; as n 30.

42 Criminal Justice (International Co-operation Act 1990, s 22(1); as n 30.

43 United Nations Personnel Act 1997, s 6; as n 30.

to wit.|}
WHEREAS the Right Honourable|one of Her Majesty's Principal
Secretaries of State, by order under his hand and seal, hath signified to me that
requisition hath been duly made to him for the surrender of|late
of|, accused [*or* convicted] of the commission of the crime of
within the jurisdiction of|: This is therefore to command
you in Her Majesty's name forthwith to apprehend the said
pursuant to The Extradition Act, 1870, wherever he may be found in the United
Kingdom or Isle of Man, and bring him before me or some other [*magistrate
sitting in this court], to show cause why he should not be surrendered in pursuance
of the said Extradition Act, for which this shall be your warrant.
Given under my hand and seal at [*Bow Street, one of the police courts of
the metropolis] this|day of|18|.|J.P.
***
* Note. - Alter as required.
***
Form of warrant of Apprehension without Order of Secretary of State.
Metropolitan|}
police district,|}|To all and each of the constables of the metropolitan
police
[*or* the county *or*|}|police force [*or* of the county *or* borough of|].
borough of|]|}
to wit.|}
WHEREAS it has been shown to the undersigned, one of Her Majesty's justices
of the peace in and for the metropolitan police district [*or* the said county *or* borough
of|] that|late of|is accused [*or* convicted]
of the commission of the crime of|within the jurisdiction of
: This is therefore to command you in Her Majesty's name to forthwith apprehend
the said|and to bring him before me or some other magistrate
sitting at this court [*or* one of Her Majesty's justices of the peace in and for the
county [*or* borough] of|] to be further dealt with according to
law, for which this shall be your warrant.
Given under my hand and seal at Bow Street, one of the police courts of the
metropolis, [*or*|in the county *or* borough aforesaid] this|day
of|18|.|J.P.
Form of warrant for bringing Prisoner before the Police Magistrate.
County [*or*|}|To|constable of the police force
borough of|]|}|of|and to all other peace officers in the said
county
to wit.|}|[*or* borough] of
WHEREAS|late of|accused [*or* alleged to be convicted
of] the commission of the crime of|within the jurisdiction of
has been apprehended and brought before the undersigned, one of Her Majesty's
justices of the peace in and for the said county [*or* borough] of
And whereas by The Extradition Act, 1870, he is required to be brought before
the chief magistrate of the metropolitan police court, or one of the police magistrates
of the metropolis sitting in Bow Street, within the metropolitan police district
[*or* the stipendiary magistrate for|]: This is therefore to
command you the said constable in Her Majesty's name forthwith to take and
convey the said|to the metropolitan police district [*or* the said
] and there carry before the said chief magistrate or one of the police magistrates
of the metropolis sitting at Bow Street within the said district [*or* before a stipendiary
magistrate sitting in the said|] to show cause why he should
not be surrendered in pursuance of The Extradition Act, 1870, and otherwise be
dealt with in accordance with law, for which this shall be your warrant.
Given under my hand and seal at|in the county [*or* borough]
aforesaid, this|day of|18|.| J.P.

Form of Warrant of Committal.

Metropolitan|}|To|one of the constables of the
police district,|}|metropolitan police force, [*or* of the police force of
the county
[*or* the county *or*|}|*or* borough of|], and to the keeper of
borough of|]|}|the|.
to wit.|}

BE it remembered, that on this|day of|in the year of our Lord
late of|is brought before me|the chief
magistrate of the metropolitan police courts [*or* one of the police magistrates of
the metropolis] sitting at the police court in Bow Street, within the metropolitan
police district, [*or* a stipendiary magistrate for|], to show cause why
he should not be surrendered in pursuance of The Extradition Act, 1870, on the
ground of his being accused [*or* convicted] of the commission of the crime of
within the jurisdiction of|, and forasmuch as no sufficient cause has
been shown to me why he should not be surrendered in pursuance of the said
Act:

This is therefore to command you the said constable in Her Majesty's name forthwith
to convey and deliver the body of the said|into the custody
of said keeper of the|at|, and you the said keeper to receive
the said|into your custody, and him there safely to keep until he is thence
delivered pursuant to the provisions of the said Extradition Act, for which this
shall be your warrant.

Given under my hand and seal at Bow Street, one of the police courts of the
metropolis, [*or* at the said|] this day of|18|. J.P.

Form of the Warrant of Secretary of State for Surrender of Fugitive.

To the keeper of|and to

WHEREAS|late of|accused [*or* convicted]
of the commission of the crime of|within the jurisdiction of
, was delivered into the custody of you|the keeper of
by warrant dated|pursuant to The Extradition Act, 1870:

Now do I hereby, in pursuance of the said Act, order you the said keeper to deliver
the body of the said|into the custody of the said|,
and I command you the said|to receive the said|into
your custody, and to convey him within the jurisdiction of the said|,
and there place him in the custody of any person or persons appointed by the
said|to receive him, for which this shall be your warrant.

Given under the hand and seal of the undersigned, one of Her Majesty's Principal
Secretaries of State, this day of

Third Schedule

Provides details of Acts repealed.

APPENDIX E2

Extradition Act 1989 as amended before its repeal by the Extradition Act 2003 on 1st of January 2004

Extradition Act 1989

(c. 33)

An Act to consolidate enactments relating to extradition under the Criminal Justice Act 1988, the Fugitive Offenders Act 1967 and the Extradition Acts 1870 to 1935, with amendments to give effect to recommendations of the Law Commission and the Scottish Law Commission.

[27th July1 1989]

BE IT ENACTED by the Queen's most Excellent Majesty, by and with the advice and consent of the Lords Spiritual and Temporal, and Commons, in this present Parliament assembled, and by the authority of the same, as follows:—

Part I
Introductory

General

1. Liability to extradition

(1) Where extradition procedures under Part III of this Act are available as between the United Kingdom and a foreign state, a person in the United Kingdom who—
   (a) is accused in that state of the commission of an extradition crime; or
   (b) is alleged to be unlawfully at large after conviction of an extradition crime by a court in that state,

may be arrested and returned to that state in accordance with those procedures.

(2) Subject to the provisions of this Act, a person in the United Kingdom who is accused of an extradition crime—
   (a) in a Commonwealth country designated for the purposes of this subsection under section 5(1) below; or
   (b) in a colony,

or who is alleged to be unlawfully at large after conviction of such an offence in any such country or in a colony, may be arrested and returned to that country or colony in accordance with extradition procedures under Part III of this Act.

[(2A) Subject to the provisions of this Act, a person in the United Kingdom who—
   (a) is accused in the Hong Kong Special Administrative Region of an extradition crime, or
   (b) is alleged to be unlawfully at large after conviction for such an offence in that Region, may be arrested and returned to that Region in accordance with extradition procedures under Part III of this Act.][1]

(3) Where an Order in Council under section 2 of the Extradition Act 1870 is in force in relation to a foreign state, Schedule 1 to this Act (the provisions of which derive from that Act and certain associated enactments) shall have effect in relation to that state, but subject to the limitations, restrictions, conditions, exceptions and qualifications, if any, contained in the Order.

Extradition crimes

2. Meaning of 'extradition crime'

(1) In this Act, except in Schedule 1, 'extradition crime' means—

---

[1] Amended by SI 1997/1178.

(a) conduct in the territory of a foreign state, a designated Commonwealth country[, a colony or the Hong Kong Special Administrative Region][2] which, if it occurred in the United Kingdom, would constitute an offence punishable with imprisonment for a term of 12 months, or any greater punishment, and which, however described in the law of the foreign state, Commonwealth country or colony [or of the Hong Kong Special Administrative Region],[3] is so punishable under that law;

(b) an extra-territorial offence against the law of a foreign state, designated Commonwealth country or colony[, or of the Hong Kong Special Administrative Region,][4] which is punishable under that law with imprisonment for a term of 12 months, or any greater punishment, and which satisfies—

(i) the condition specified in subsection (2) below; or

(ii) all the conditions specified in subsection (3) below[, or

(iii) the condition specified in subsection (3A) below].[5]

(2) The condition mentioned in subsection (1)(b)(i) above is that in corresponding circumstances equivalent conduct would constitute an extra-territorial offence against the law of the United Kingdom punishable with imprisonment for a term of 12 months, or any greater punishment.

(3) The conditions mentioned in subsection (1)(b)(ii) above are—

(a) that the foreign state, Commonwealth country or colony [or the Hong Kong Special Administrative Region][6] bases its jurisdiction on the nationality of the offender;

(b) that the conduct constituting the offence occurred outside the United Kingdom; and

(c) that, if it occurred in the United Kingdom, it would constitute an offence under the law of the United Kingdom punishable with imprisonment for a term of 12 months, or any greater punishment.

[(3A) The condition mentioned in subsection (1)(b)(iii) above is that the conduct constituting the offence constitutes or, if committed in the United Kingdom would constitute—

(a) an offence under section 51 or 58 of the International Criminal Court Act 2001 (genocide, crimes against humanity and war crimes),

(b) an offence under section 52 or 59 of that Act (conduct ancillary to genocide etc committed outside the jurisdiction), or

(c) an ancillary offence, as defined in section 55 or 62 of that Act, in relation to any such offence.][7]

(4) For the purposes of [this Act, except Schedule 1][8]—

(a) the law of a foreign state, designated Commonwealth country or colony includes the law of any part of it and the law of the United Kingdom includes the law of any part of the United Kingdom;

(b) conduct in a colony or dependency of a foreign state or of a designated Commonwealth country, or a vessel, aircraft or hovercraft of a foreign state or of such a country, shall be treated as if it were conduct in the territory of that state or country; [...][9]

(c) conduct in a vessel, aircraft or hovercraft of a colony of the United Kingdom shall be treated as if it were conduct in that colony[; but—

(d) reference shall be made to the law of the colony or dependency of a foreign state or of a designated Commonwealth country, and not (where different) to the law of the foreign state or Commonwealth country, to determine the level of punishment applicable to conduct in that colony or dependency[; and

(d) conduct in a vessel, aircraft or hovercraft of the Hong Kong Special Administrative Region shall be treated as if it were conduct in that Region].[10]][11]

---

2 Amended by SI 1997/1178.
3 Amended by SI 1997/1178.
4 Amended by SI 1997/1178.
5 Amended by the International Criminal Court Act 2001.
6 Amended by SI 1997/1178.
7 Amended by the International Criminal Court Act 2001.
8 Amended by the Criminal Justice and Public Order Act 1994.
9 Repealed by SI 1997/1178.
10 Amended by SI 1997/1178.
11 Amended by the Criminal Justice and Public Order Act 1994.

[(5) References in this section to an offence under any provision of the International Criminal Court Act 2001, or to an offence ancillary to such an offence, include any corresponding offence under the law of Scotland.][12]

Return to foreign states

3. Arrangements for availability of Part III procedure

(1) In this Act 'extradition arrangements' means arrangements made with a foreign state under which extradition procedures under Part III of this Act will be available as between the United Kingdom and that state.

(2) For this purpose 'foreign state' means any state other than—
- (i) the United Kingdom;
- (ii) a country mentioned in Schedule 3 to the British Nationality Act 1981 (countries whose citizens are Commonwealth citizens);
- (iii) a colony; [...][13]
- (iv) the Republic of Ireland[; or
- (v) the Hong Kong Special Administrative Region],[14]

but a state which is a party to the European Convention on Extradition done at Paris on 13th December 1957 may be treated as a foreign state.

(3) Extradition arrangements may be—
- (a) arrangements of a general nature made with one or more states and relating to the operation of extradition procedures under Part III of this Act (in this Act referred to as 'general extradition arrangements'); or
- (b) arrangements relating to the operation of those procedures in particular cases (in this Act referred to as 'special extradition arrangements') made with a state with which there are no general extradition arrangements.

4. Orders in Council as to extradition

(1) Where general extradition arrangements have been made, her Majesty may, by Order in Council reciting or embodying their terms, direct that this Act, so far as it relates to extradition procedures under Part III of this Act, shall apply as between the United Kingdom and the foreign state, or any foreign state, with which they have been made, subject to the limitations, restrictions, exceptions and qualifications, if any, contained in the Order.

(2) An Order in Council under this section shall not be made unless the general extradition arrangements to which it relates—
- (a) provide for their determination after the expiration of a notice given by a party to them and not exceeding one year or for their denunciation by means of such a notice; and
- (b) are in conformity with the provisions of this Act, and in particular with the restrictions on return contained in Part II of this Act.

(3) An Order in Council under this section shall be conclusive evidence that the arrangements therein referred to comply with this Act and that this Act, so far as it relates to extradition procedures under Part III of this Act, applies in the case of the foreign state, or any foreign state, mentioned in the Order.

(4) An Order in Council under this section shall be laid before Parliament after being made.

(5) An Order in Council under this section which does not provide that a person may only be returned to the foreign state requesting his return if the court of committal is satisfied that the evidence would be sufficient to [make a case requiring an answer by that person if the proceedings were a summary trial of an information against him and][15] the extradition crime had taken place within the jurisdiction of the court shall be subject to annulment in pursuance of a resolution of either House of Parliament.

---

[12] Amended by the International Criminal Court Act 2001.
[13] Repealed by SI 1997/1178.
[14] Amended by SI 1997/1178.
[15] Amended by the Criminal Justice and Public Order Act 1994.

RETURN TO COMMONWEALTH COUNTRIES AND COLONIES

5. Procedure for designation etc

(1) Her Majesty may by Order in Council designate for the purposes of section 1(2) above any country for the time being mentioned in Schedule 3 to the British Nationality Act 1981 (countries whose citizens are Commonwealth citizens); and any country so designated is in this Act referred to as a 'designated Commonwealth country'.
(2) This Act has effect in relation to all colonies.
(3) Her Majesty may by Order in Council direct that this Act shall have effect in relation to the return of persons to, or in relation to persons returned from, any designated Commonwealth country or any colony subject to such exceptions, adaptations or modifications as may be specified in the Order.
(4) Any Order under this section may contain such transitional or other incidental and supplementary provisions as may appear to Her Majesty to be necessary or expedient.
(5) For the purposes of any Order in Council under subsection (1) above, any territory for the external relations of which a Commonwealth country is responsible may be treated as part of that country or, if the Government of that country so requests, as a separate country.
(6) Any Order in Council under this section, other than an Order to which subsection (7) below applies, shall be subject to annulment in pursuance of a resolution of either House of Parliament.
(7) No recommendation shall be made to Her Majesty in Council to make an Order in Council to make an Order containing any such directions as is authorised by subsection (3) above unless a draft of the Order has been laid before Parliament and approved by resolution of each House of Parliament.

PART II
Restrictions on return

6. General restrictions on return

(1) A person shall not be returned under Part III of this Act, or committed or kept in custody for the purposes of return, if it appears to an appropriate authority—
  (a) that the offence of which that person is accused or was convicted is an offence of a political character;
  (b) that it is an offence under military law which is not also an offence under the general criminal law;
  (c) that the request for his return (though purporting to be made on account of an extradition crime) is in fact made for the purpose of prosecuting or punishing him on account of his race, religion, nationality or political opinions; or
  (d) that he might, if returned, be prejudiced at his trial or punished, detained or restricted in his personal liberty by reason of his race, religion, nationality or political opinions.
(2) A person who is alleged to be unlawfully at large after conviction of an extradition crime shall not be returned to a foreign state [or to the Hong Kong Special Administrative Region],[16] or committed or kept in custody for the purposes of return to a foreign state [or to that Region],[17] if it appears to an appropriate authority—
  (a) that the conviction was obtained in his absence; and
  (b) that it would not be in the interests of justice to return him on the ground of that conviction.
(3) A person accused of an offence shall not be returned, or committed or kept in custody for the purposes of return, if it appears to an appropriate authority that if charged with that offence in the United Kingdom he would be entitled to be discharged under any rule of law relating to previous acquittal or conviction.
(4) A person shall not be returned, or committed or kept in custody for the purposes of such return, unless provision is made by the relevant law, or by an arrangement made with the relevant foreign state, Commonwealth country or colony [or with the Hong Kong Special Administrative Region],[18]

[16] Amended by SI 1997/1178.
[17] Amended by SI 1997/1178.
[18] Amended by SI 1997/1178.

for securing that he will not, unless he has first had an opportunity to leave it, be dealt with there for or in respect of any offence committed before his return to it other than—

(a) the offence in respect of which his return is ordered;

(b) an offence, other than an offence excluded by subsection (5) below, which is disclosed by the facts in respect of which his return was ordered; or

(c) subject to subsection (6) below, any other offence being an extradition crime in respect of which the Secretary of State [or the Scottish Ministers][19] may consent to his being dealt with.

(5) The offences excluded from paragraph (b) of subsection (4) above are offences in relation to which an order for the return of the person concerned could not lawfully be made.

(6) The Secretary of State [or the Scottish Ministers][20] may not give consent under paragraph (c) of that subsection in respect of an offence in relation to which it appears to him [or them][21] that an order for the return of the person concerned could not lawfully be made, or would not in fact be made.

(7) Any such arrangement as is mentioned in subsection (4) above which is made with a designated Commonwealth country or a colony may be an arrangement made for the particular case or an arrangement of a more general nature; and for the purposes of that subsection a certificate issued by or under the authority of the Secretary of State [or the Scottish Ministers][22] confirming the existence of an arrangement with a Commonwealth country or a colony and stating its terms shall be conclusive evidence of the matters contained in the certificate.

(8) In relation to a Commonwealth country or a colony the reference in subsection (1) above to an offence of a political character does not include an offence against the life or person of the Head of the Commonwealth or attempting or conspiring to commit, or assisting, counselling or procuring the commission of or being accessory before or after the fact to such an offence, or of impeding the apprehension or prosecution of persons guilty of such an offence.

(9) In this Act 'appropriate authority' means—

[(a) the Secretary of State, or, except in section 25(1), in the case of a function that is exercisable in or as regards Scotland, the Scottish Ministers;][23]

(b) the court of committal;

(c) the High Court or High Court of Justiciary on an application for habeas corpus or for review of the order of committal.

(10) In this section, in relation to Commonwealth countries and colonies, 'race' includes tribe.

Part III
Procedure

General

7. Extradition request and authority to proceed

(1) Subject to the provisions of this Act relating to provisional warrants, a person shall not be dealt with under this Part of this Act except in pursuance of an order of the Secretary of State [or the Scottish Ministers][24] (in this Act referred to as an 'authority to proceed') issued in pursuance of a request (in this Act referred to as an 'extradition request') for the surrender of a person under this Act made [to the Secretary of State][25]—

[(a) by—

(i) an authority in a foreign state which appears to the Secretary of State to have the function of making extradition requests in that foreign state, or

(ii) some person recognised by the Secretary of State as a diplomatic or consular representative of a foreign state; or][26]

---

[19] Amended by SI 1999/1750.
[20] Amended by SI 1999/1750.
[21] Amended by SI 1999/1750.
[22] Amended by SI 1999/1750.
[23] Amended by SI 1999/1750.
[24] Amended by SI 1999/1750.
[25] Amended by the Criminal Justice and Public Order Act 1994.
[26] Amended by the Criminal Justice and Public Order Act 1994.

(b) by or on behalf of the Government of a designated Commonwealth country, or the Governor of a colony[; or

(c) by or on behalf of the Government of the Hong Kong Special Administrative Region],[27]

[and an extradition request may be made by facsimile transmission and an authority to proceed issued without waiting to receive the original].[28]

(2) There shall be furnished with any such request—

(a) particulars of the person whose return is requested;

(b) particulars of the offence of which he is accused or was convicted (including evidence [or, in a case falling within subsection (2A) below, information][29] sufficient to justify the issue of a warrant for his arrest under this Act);

(c) in the case of a person accused of an offence, a warrant [or a duly authenticated copy of a warrant][30] for his arrest issued in the foreign state, Commonwealth country or colony [or in the Hong Kong Special Administrative Region];[31] and

(d) in the case of a person unlawfully at large after conviction of an offence, a certificate [or a duly authenticated copy of a certificate][32] of the conviction and sentence,

and copies of them shall be served on the person whose return is requested before he is brought before the court of committal.

[(2A) Where—

(a) the extradition request is made by a foreign state; and

(b) an Order in Council falling within section 4(5) above is in force in relation to that state,

it shall be a sufficient compliance with subsection (2)(b) above to furnish information sufficient to justify the issue of a warrant for his arrest under this Act.][33]

(3) Rules under section 144 of the Magistrates' Courts Act 1980 may make provision as to the procedure for service under subsection (2) above in England and Wales and the High Court of Justiciary may, by Act of Adjournal, make rules as to such procedure in Scotland.

(4) On receipt of any such request the Secretary of State [or the Scottish Ministers][34] may issue an authority to proceed unless it appears to him [or them][35] that an order for the return of the person concerned could not lawfully be made, or would not in fact be made, in accordance with the provisions of this Act.

(5) An authority to proceed shall specify the offence or offences under the law of the United Kingdom which it appears to the Secretary of State [or the Scottish Ministers][36] would be constituted by equivalent conduct in the United Kingdom.

(6) In this section 'warrant', in the case of any foreign state, includes any judicial document authorising the arrest of a person accused of a crime.

[(7) Where an extradition request is made by facsimile transmission this Act (including subsection (2) above) shall have effect as if the foreign documents so sent were the originals used to make the transmission and receivable in evidence accordingly.][37]

8. Arrest for purposes of committal

(1) For the purposes of this Part of this Act a warrant for the arrest of a person may be issued—

(a) on receipt of an authority to proceed—

(i) by the [Senior District Judge (Chief Magistrate) or another District Judge (Magistrates' Courts) designated by him];[38]

(ii) by the sheriff of Lothian and Borders;

---

27 Amended by SI 1997/1178.
28 Amended by the Criminal Justice and Public Order Act 1994.
29 Amended by the Criminal Justice and Public Order Act 1994.
30 Amended by the Criminal Justice and Public Order Act 1994.
31 Amended by SI 1997/1178.
32 Amended by the Criminal Justice and Public Order Act 1994.
33 Amended by the Criminal Justice and Public Order Act 1994.
34 Amended by SI 1999/1750.
35 Amended by SI 1999/1750.
36 Amended by SI 1999/1750.
37 Amended by the Criminal Justice and Public Order Act 1994.
38 Amended by the Access to Justice Act 1999.

(b) without such an authority—
(i) [...][39]
(ii) by a justice of the peace in any part of the United Kingdom; and
(iii) in Scotland, by a sheriff;
upon information that the said person is or is believed to be in or on his way to the United Kingdom; and any warrant issued by virtue of paragraph (b) above is in this Act referred to as a 'provisional warrant'.

(2) [...][40]

(3) A person empowered to issue warrants of arrest under this section may issue such a warrant if he is supplied with such evidence [or, in a case falling within subsection (3A) below, information][41] as would in his opinion justify the issue of a warrant for the arrest of a person accused or, as the case may be, convicted within his jurisdiction and it appears to him that the conduct alleged would constitute an extradition crime.

[(3A) Where—
(a) the extradition request or, where a provisional warrant is applied for, the request for the person's arrest is made by a foreign state; and
(b) an Order in Council falling within section 4(5) above is in force in relation to that state,
it shall be sufficient for the purposes of subsection (3) above to supply such information as would, in the opinion of the person so empowered, justify the issue of a warrant of arrest.][42]

(4) Where a provisional warrant is issued under this section, the authority by whom it is issued shall forthwith give notice to the Secretary of State [or the Scottish Ministers],[43] and transmit to him [or them][44] the information and evidence, or certified copies of the information and evidence, upon which it was issued; and the Secretary of State [or the Scottish Ministers][45] may in any case, and shall if he decides [or, they decide][46] not to issue an authority to proceed in respect of the person to whom the warrant relates, by order cancel the warrant and, if that person has been arrested under it, discharge him from custody.

(5) A warrant of arrest issued under this section may, without being backed, be executed in any part of the United Kingdom and may be so executed by any person to whom it is directed or by any constable.

(6) Where a warrant is issued under this section for the arrest of a person accused of an offence of stealing or receiving stolen property in a designated Commonwealth country or a colony or any other offence committed in such a country or in a colony in respect of property, a justice of the peace in any part of the United Kingdom and in Scotland a sheriff shall have the like power to issue a warrant to search for the property as if the offence had been committed within his jurisdiction.

9. Proceedings for committal

(1) A person arrested in pursuance of a warrant under section 8 above shall (unless previously discharged under subsection (4) of that section) be brought as soon as practicable before a court (in this Act referred to as 'the court of committal') [...].[47]

(2) For the purposes of proceedings under this section a court of committal in England and Wales [shall consist of the Senior District Judge (Chief Magistrate) or another District Judge (Magistrates' Courts) designated by him and][48] shall have the like [powers, as nearly as may be, including powers to adjourn the case and meanwhile to remand the person arrested under the warrant either in custody or on bail, as if the proceedings were the summary trial of an information against him; and section 16(1)(c) of the Prosecution of Offences Act 1985 (costs on dismissal) shall apply accordingly reading the reference to the dismissal of the information as a reference to the discharge of the person arrested.][49]

[39] Repealed by the Access to Justice Act 1999.
[40] Repealed by the Access to Justice Act 1999.
[41] Amended by the Criminal Justice and Public Order Act 1994.
[42] Amended by the Criminal Justice and Public Order Act 1994.
[43] Amended by SI 1999/1750.
[44] Amended by SI 1999/1750.
[45] Amended by SI 1999/1750.
[46] Amended by SI 1999/1750.
[47] Repealed by the Access to Justice Act 1999.
[48] Amended by the Access to Justice Act 1999.
[49] Amended by the Criminal Justice and Public Order Act 1994.

[(2A) If a court of committal in England and Wales exercises its power to adjourn the case it shall on so doing remand the person arrested in custody or on bail.][50]

(3) For the purposes of proceedings under this section a court of committal in Scotland [shall consist of the sheriff of Lothian and Borders and][51] shall have the like powers, including power to adjourn the case and meanwhile to remand the person arrested under the warrant either in custody or on bail, and the proceedings shall be conducted as nearly as may be in the like manner, as if the proceedings were summary proceedings in respect of an offence alleged to have been committed by that person; and the provisions of the Legal Aid (Scotland) Act 1986 relating to such proceedings or any appellate proceedings following thereon shall apply accordingly to that person.

(4) Where—

(a) the extradition request is made by a foreign state; and

(b) an Order in Council such as is mentioned in subsection (8) below is in force in relation to that state,

there is no need to furnish the court of committal with evidence sufficient to [make a case requiring an answer by the arrested person if the proceedings were the summary trial of an information against him.][52]

(5) Where the person arrested is in custody by virtue of a provisional warrant and no authority to proceed has been received in respect of him, the court of committal may fix a period (of which the court shall give notice to the Secretary of State [or the Scottish Ministers][53]) after which he will be discharged from custody unless such an authority has been received.

(6) In exercising the power conferred by subsection (5) above in a case where the extradition request is made under general extradition arrangements as the court shall have regard to any period specified for the purpose in the Order in Council relating to the arrangements.

(7) Where—

(a) the extradition request is made under general extradition arrangements but no period is so specified; or

(b) the application is made under special extradition arrangements,

the court of committal may fix a reasonable period.

[(7A) In exercising the power conferred by subsection (5) above in a case where the extradition request is made by or on behalf of the Government of the Hong Kong Special Administrative Region the court shall not fix a period ending more than 60 days after the day of the person's arrest, unless the exceptional circumstances of the case justify a longer period.][54]

(8) Where an authority to proceed has been issued in respect of the person arrested and the court of committal is satisfied, after hearing any representations made in support of the extradition request or on behalf of that person, that the offence to which the authority relates is an extradition crime, and is further satisfied—

(a) where that person is accused of the offence, unless an Order in Council giving effect to general extradition arrangements under which the extradition request was made otherwise provides, that the evidence would be sufficient to [make a case requiring an answer by that person if the proceedings were the summary trial of an information against him.][55]

(b) where that person is alleged to be unlawfully at large after conviction of the offence, that he has been so convicted and appears to be so at large,

the court, unless his committal is prohibited by any other provision of this Act, shall commit him to custody or on bail—

(i) to await the Secretary of State's [or the Scottish Ministers'][56] decision as to his return; and

(ii) if the Secretary of State decides [or the Scottish Ministers decide][57] that he shall be returned, to await his return.

---

50 Amended by the Criminal Justice and Public Order Act 1994.
51 Amended by the Access to Justice Act 1999.
52 Amended by the Criminal Justice and Public Order Act 1994.
53 Amended by SI 1999/1750.
54 Amended by SI 1997/1178.
55 Amended by the Criminal Justice and Public Order Act 1994.
56 Amended by SI 1999/1750.
57 Amended by SI 1999/1750.

(9) If the court commits a person under subsection (8) above, it shall issue a certificate of the offence against the law of the United Kingdom which would be constituted by his conduct.

(10) If the court commits a person to custody in the exercise of that power, it may subsequently grant bail if it considers it appropriate to do so.

(11) If—

(a) the court is not satisfied as mentioned in subsection (8) above in relation to the person arrested; or

(b) his committal is prohibited by a provision of this Act,

it shall discharge him.

10. Statement of case by court

(1) If the court of committal refuses to make an order in relation to a person under section 9 above in respect of the offence or, as the case may be, any of the offences to which the authority to proceed relates, the foreign state, Commonwealth country or colony seeking the surrender of that person to it may question the proceeding on the ground that it is wrong in law by applying to the court to state a case for the opinion of the High Court or, in Scotland, the High Court of Justiciary on the question of law involved.

(2) If the state, country or colony seeking return immediately informs the court of committal that it intends to make such an application, the court shall make an order providing for the detention of the person to whom the authority to proceed relates, or directing that he shall not be released except on bail.

(3) Rules of Court may specify—

(a) a period within which such an application must be made unless the court grants a longer period; and

(b) a period within which the court of committal must comply with such an application.

(4) Where the court of committal fails to comply with an application under subsection (1) above within the period specified by Rules of Court, the High Court or, in Scotland, the High Court of Justiciary may, on the application of the state, country or colony that applied for the case to be stated, make an order requiring the court to state a case.

(5) The High Court or High Court of Justiciary shall have power—

(a) to remit the case to the court of committal to decide it according to the opinion of the High Court or High Court of Justiciary on the question of law; or

(b) to dismiss the appeal.

(6) Where the court dismisses an appeal relating to an offence, it shall by order declare that that offence is not an offence in respect of which the Secretary of State has [or the Scottish Ministers have][58] power to make an order for return in respect of the person whose return was requested.

(7) An order made by a [District Judge (Magistrates' Courts)][59] under subsection (2) above shall cease to have effect if—

(a) the court dismisses the appeal in respect of the offence or all the offences to which it relates; and

(b) the foreign state, Commonwealth country or colony does not immediately—

(i) apply for leave to appeal to the House of Lords; or

(ii) inform the court that it intends to apply for leave.

(8) An order made by the sheriff of Lothian and Borders under subsection (2) above shall cease to have effect if the court dismisses the appeal in respect of the offence or all the offences to which it relates.

(9) In relation to a decision of a court on an appeal under this section, section 1 of the Administration of Justice Act 1960 (right of appeal to the House of Lords) shall have effect as if so much of subsection (2) as restricts the grant of leave to appeal were omitted.

(10) The House of Lords may exercise any powers of the High Court under subsection (5) above and subsection (6) above shall apply to them as it applies to that Court.

[58] Amended by SI 1999/1750.

[59] Amended by the Access to Justice Act 1999.

(11) Subject to subsections (7) and (8) above, an order under subsection (2) above shall have effect so long as the case is pending.

(12) For the purposes of this section a case is pending (unless proceedings are discontinued) until (disregarding any power of a court to grant leave to take any step out of time) there is no step that the state, country or colony can take.

(13) In the application of this section to Scotland subsections (9) and (10) above shall be omitted and in relation to an appeal under this section in Scotland the court may make an order providing for the detention of the person to whom it relates or it may grant bail; and [section 177(2) and (3) of the Criminal Procedure (Scotland) Act 1995][60] shall apply for the purpose of such an appeal as it applies for the purpose of an appeal such as is mentioned in [section 176][61] of that Act.

[(14) This section shall apply to the Hong Kong Special Administrative Region in the same way as it applies to any foreign state, Commonwealth country or colony.][62]

11. Application for habeas corpus etc.

(1) Where a person is committed under section 9 above, the court shall inform him in ordinary language of his right to make an application for habeas corpus, and shall forthwith give notice of the committal to the Secretary of State [or the Scottish Ministers].[63]

(2) A person committed shall not be returned—

(a) in any case, until the expiration of the period of 15 days beginning with the day on which the order for his committal is made;

(b) if an application for habeas corpus is made in his case, so long as proceedings on that application are pending.

(3) Without prejudice to any jurisdiction of the High Court apart from this section, the court shall order the applicant's discharge if it appears to the court in relation to the offence, or each of the offences, in respect of which the applicant's return is sought, that—

(a) by reason of the trivial nature of the offence; or

(b) by reason of the passage of time since he is alleged to have committed it or to have become unlawfully at large, as the case may be; or

(c) because the accusation against him is not made in good faith in the interests of justice,

it would, having regard to all the circumstances, be unjust or oppressive to return him.

(4) On any such application the court may receive additional evidence relevant to the exercise of its jurisdiction under section 6 above or subsection (3) above.

(5) Proceedings on an application for habeas corpus shall be treated for the purposes of this section as pending (unless they are discontinued) until (disregarding any power of a court to grant leave to appeal out of time) there is no further possibility of an appeal.

(6) In the application of this section to Scotland references to an application for habeas corpus shall be construed as references to an application for review of the order of committal and references to the High Court shall be construed as references to the High Court of Justiciary.

12. Order for return

(1) Where a person is committed under section 9 above and is not discharged by order of the High Court or the High Court of Justiciary, the Secretary of State [or the Scottish Ministers][64] may by warrant order him to be returned unless his return is prohibited, or prohibited for the time being, by this Act, or the Secretary of State decides [or the Scottish Ministers decide][65] under this section to make no such order in his case.

(2) Without prejudice to his general discretion as to the making of an order for the return of a person to a foreign state, Commonwealth country or colony [or to the Hong Kong Special Administrative Region][66]—

[60] Amended by the Criminal Procedure (Consequential Provisions) (Scotland) Act 1995.
[61] Amended by the Criminal Procedure (Consequential Provisions) (Scotland) Act 1995.
[62] Amended by SI 1997/1178.
[63] Amended by SI 1999/1750.
[64] Amended by SI 1999/1750.
[65] Amended by SI 1999/1750.
[66] Amended by SI 1997/1178.

(a) the Secretary of State [or the Scottish Ministers][67] shall not make an order in the case of any person if it appears to the Secretary of State [or the Scottish Ministers][68] in relation to the offence, or each of the offences, in respect of which his return is sought, that—
(i) by reason of its trivial nature; or
(ii) by reason of the passage of time since he is alleged to have committed it or to have become unlawfully at large, as the case may be; or
(iii) because the accusation against him is not made in good faith in the interests of justice,
it would, having regard to all the circumstances, be unjust or oppressive to return him; and
(b) the Secretary of State [or the Scottish Ministers][69] may decide to make no order for the return of a person accused or convicted of an offence not punishable with death in Great Britain if that person could be or has been sentenced to death for that offence in the country by which the request for his return is made.

(3) An order for return shall not be made in the case of a person who is serving a sentence of imprisonment or detention, or is charged with an offence, in the United Kingdom—
(a) in the case of a person serving such a sentence, until the sentence has been served;
(b) in the case of a person charged with an offence, until the charge is disposed of or withdrawn or unless an order is made for it to lie on the file and, if it results in his serving a term of imprisonment or detention, until the sentence has been served.

(4) In the application of this section to Scotland, the reference in subsection (3) above to an order being made for the charge to lie on the file shall be construed as a reference to the diet being deserted pro loco et tempore.

(5) The Secretary of State [or the Scottish Ministers][70] may decide to make no order under this section for the return of a person committed in consequence of an extradition request if another extradition request or a requisition under Schedule 1 to this Act has been made in respect of him and it appears to the Secretary of State [or the Scottish Ministers],[71] having regard to all the circumstances of the case and in particular—
(a) the relevant seriousness of the offences in question;
(b) the date on which each such request was made; and
(c) the nationality or citizenship of the person concerned and his ordinary residence,
that preference should be given to that other request or requisition.

(6) Notice of the issue of a warrant under this section for the return of a person to a Commonwealth country or colony shall forthwith be given to the person to be returned.

13. Return to foreign states—supplementary

(1) The Secretary of State [or the Scottish Ministers][72] shall give the person to whom an order under section 12(1) above for return to a foreign state [or to the Hong Kong Special Administrative Region][73] would relate notice in writing that he is contemplating making such an order.

(2) The person to whom such an order would relate shall have a right to make representations, at any time before the expiration of the period of 15 days commencing with the date on which the notice is given, as to why he should not be returned to the foreign state, and unless he waives that right, no such order shall be made in relation to him before the end of that period.

(3) A notice under subsection (1) above shall explain in ordinary language the right conferred by subsection (2) above.

(4) It shall be the duty of the Secretary of State [or the Scottish Ministers][74] to consider any representations made in the exercise of that right.

(5) Unless the person to whom it relates waives the right conferred on him by subsection (6) below, he shall not be returned to the foreign state [or to the Hong Kong Special Administrative Region][75]

---

67 Amended by SI 1999/1750.
68 Amended by SI 1999/1750.
69 Amended by SI 1999/1750.
70 Amended by SI 1999/1750.
71 Amended by SI 1999/1750.
72 Amended by SI 1999/1750.
73 Amended by SI 1997/1178.
74 Amended by SI 1999/1750.
75 Amended by SI 1997/1178.

until the expiration of the period of 7 days commencing with the date on which the warrant is issued or such longer period as—

(a) in England and Wales, rules under section 84 of the Supreme Court Act 1981 may provide; or

(b) in Scotland, the High Court of Justiciary may provide by Act of Adjournal.

(6) At any time within that period he may apply for leave to seek judicial review of the Secretary of State's [or the Scottish Ministers'][76] decision to make the order.

(7) If he applies for judicial review, he may not be returned so long as the proceedings for judicial review are pending.

(8) Proceedings for judicial review shall be treated for the purposes of this section as pending (unless they are discontinued) until (disregarding any power of a court to grant leave to appeal out of time) there is no further possibility of an appeal.

(9) A warrant under section 12 above—

(a) shall state in ordinary language that the Secretary of State has [or the Scottish Ministers have][77] considered any representations made in the exercise of the right conferred by subsection (2) above; and

(b) shall explain in ordinary language the rights conferred by this section on a person whose return to a foreign state [or to the Hong Kong Special Administrative Region][78] has been ordered under section 12 above,

and a copy shall be given to the person to whom it relates as soon as the order for his return is made.

14. Simplified procedure

(1) A person may give notice that he waives the rights conferred on him by section 11 above.

(2) A notice under this section shall be given in England and Wales in the manner prescribed by rules under section 144 of the Magistrates' Courts Act 1980, and without prejudice to the generality of subsection (1) of that section, the power to make such rules shall include power to make provision for a magistrate to order the committal for return of a person with his consent at any time after his arrest.

(3) A notice under this section shall be given in Scotland in the manner prescribed by the High Court of Justiciary by Act of Adjournal and the sheriff may order the committal for return of a person with his consent at any time after his arrest.

(4) Where an order is made by virtue of this section, this Act shall cease to apply to the person in respect of whom it is made, except that, if he is not surrendered within one month after the order is made, the High Court or, in Scotland, the High Court of Justiciary, upon application by or on behalf of that person, may, unless reasonable cause is shown for the delay, order him to be discharged.

Special extradition arrangements

15. Special extradition arrangements

(1) Where special extradition arrangements have been made in respect of a person, extradition procedures shall be available in the case of that person, as between the United Kingdom and the foreign state with which the arrangements have been made, subject to the limitations, restrictions, exceptions and qualifications, if any, contained in the arrangements.

(2) If the Secretary of State issues a certificate of special extradition arrangements, it shall be conclusive evidence of all matters stated in it.

(3) In subsection (2) above 'certificate of special extradition arrangements' means a certificate—

(a) that special extradition arrangements have been made in respect of a person as between the United Kingdom and a foreign state specified in the certificate; and

(b) that extradition procedures are available in the case of that person as between the United Kingdom and the foreign state to the extent specified in the certificate.

---

[76] Amended by SI 1999/1750.

[77] Amended by SI 1999/1750.

[78] Amended by SI 1997/1178.

Effect of delay

16. Discharge in case of delay

(1) If a person committed under section 9 above is still in the United Kingdom after the expiration of the relevant period, he may apply to the High Court or the High Court of Justiciary for his discharge.
(2) Unless he has instituted proceedings for judicial review of the Secretary of State's decision to order his return, the relevant period is—
  (a) the period of two months beginning with the first day on which, having regard to section 11(2) above, he could have been returned;
  (b) where a warrant for his return has been issued under section 12 above, the period of one month beginning with the day on which that warrant was issued.
(3) If he has instituted such proceedings, the relevant period is the period expiring one month after they end.
(4) Proceedings for judicial review end for the purposes of this section—
  (a) if they are discontinued, on the day of discontinuance; and
  (b) if they are determined, on the day on which (disregarding any power of a court to grant leave to appeal out of time) there is no further possibility of an appeal.
(5) If upon an application under this section the court is satisfied that reasonable notice of the proposed application has been given to the Secretary of State, the court may, unless sufficient cause is shown to the contrary, by order direct the application to be disregarded and, if a warrant for his return has been issued under section 12 above, quash that warrant.

Custody

17. Custody

(1) Any person remanded or committed to custody under this Part of this Act shall be committed to the like institution as a person charged with an offence before the court of committal.
(2) If any person who is in custody by virtue of a warrant under this Act escapes out of custody, he may be retaken in any part of the United Kingdom in like manner as a person escaping from custody under a warrant for his arrest issued in that part in respect of an offence committed in that part.
(3) Where a person, being in custody in any part of the United Kingdom whether under this Part of this Act or otherwise, is required to be removed in custody under this Act to another part of the United Kingdom and is so removed by sea or by air, he shall be deemed to continue in legal custody until he reaches the place to which he is required to be removed.
(4) A warrant for the return of any person shall be sufficient authority for all persons to whom it is directed and all constables to receive that person, keep him in custody and convey him into the jurisdiction to which he is to be returned.

Part IV
Treatment of Persons Returned

18. Restrictions upon proceedings for other offences in case of persons returned by foreign states

(1) Where any person is returned to the United Kingdom by a foreign state in pursuance of extradition arrangements, he shall not, unless he has first been restored or had an opportunity of leaving the United Kingdom, be triable or tried for any offence committed prior to the surrender in any part of the United Kingdom, other than—
  (a) an offence in respect of which he was returned; or
  (b) any offence disclosed by the particulars furnished to the foreign state on which his return is grounded; or
  (c) any other offence in respect of which the foreign state may consent to his being tried.
(2) Where any person returned to the United Kingdom in pursuance of extradition arrangements has been convicted before his return of an offence for which his return was not granted, any punishment for that offence shall by operation of this section be remitted; but his conviction for it shall be treated as a conviction for all other purposes.

19. Restrictions upon proceedings for other offences in case of persons returned by designated Commonwealth countries or colonies

(1) This section applies to any person accused or convicted of an offence under the law of or of any part of the United Kingdom who is returned to the United Kingdom—
   (a) from any designated Commonwealth country, under any law of that country corresponding with this Act;
   (b) from any colony, under this Act as extended to that colony or under any corresponding law of that colony.

(2) A person to whom this section applies shall not, during the period described in subsection (3) below, be dealt with in the United Kingdom for or in respect of any offence committed before he was returned to the United Kingdom other than—
   (i) the offence in respect of which he was returned;
   (ii) any lesser offence disclosed by the particulars furnished to the Commonwealth country or colony on which his return is grounded; or
   (iii) any other offence in respect of which the Government of the Commonwealth country or Governor of the colony from which he was returned may consent to his being dealt with.

(3) The period referred to in subsection (2) above in relation to a person to whom this section applies is the period beginning with the day of his arrival in the United Kingdom on his return as mentioned in subsection (1) above and ending 45 days after the first subsequent day on which he has the opportunity to leave the United Kingdom.

(4) Where a person to whom this section applies has been convicted before his return to the United Kingdom of an offence for which his return was not granted, any punishment for that offence shall by operation of this section be remitted; but his conviction for it shall be treated as a conviction for all other purposes.

(5) In this section 'dealt with' means tried or returned or surrendered to any country or colony or detained with a view to trial or with a view to such return or surrender.

[19A. Restrictions upon proceedings for other offences in case of persons returned by the Hong Kong Special Administrative Region

(1) This section applies to any person accused or convicted of an offence under the law of or any part of the United Kingdom who is returned to the United Kingdom from the Hong Kong Special Administrative Region under any law of that Region corresponding to this Act.

(2) A person to whom this section applies shall not, during the period described in subsection (3) below, be dealt with in the United Kingdom for or in respect of any offence committed before he was returned to the United Kingdom other than—
   (i) the offence in respect of which he was returned;
   (ii) any lesser offence disclosed by the particulars furnished to the Hong Kong Special Administrative Region on which his return is grounded; or
   (iii) any other offence in respect of which the Government of the Hong Kong Special Administrative Region may consent to his being dealt with.

(3) The period referred to in subsection (2) above, in relation to a person to whom this section applies, is the period beginning with the day of his arrival in the United Kingdom on his return as mentioned in subsection (1) above and ending 40 days after the first subsequent day on which he has the opportunity to leave the United Kingdom.

(4) Where a person to whom this section applies has been convicted before his return to the United Kingdom of an offence for which his return was not granted, any punishment for that conviction shall by operation of this section be remitted; but his conviction for it shall be treated as a conviction for all other purposes.

(5) In this section 'dealt with' has the same meaning as in section 19.][79]

20. Restoration of persons not tried or acquitted

(1) This section applies to any person accused of an offence under the law of the United Kingdom who is returned to the United Kingdom in pursuance of extradition arrangements or as mentioned in section 19(1) [or section 19A(1)][80] above.

[79] Inserted by SI 1997/1178.
[80] Amended by SI 1997/1178.

(2) If in the case of a person to whom this section applies either—
  (a) proceedings against him for the offence for which he was returned are not begun within the period of six months beginning with the day of his arrival in the United Kingdom on being returned; or
  (b) on his trial for that offence, he is acquitted or discharged under any of the following provisions—
    (i) [section 12(1) of the Powers of Criminal Courts (Sentencing) Act 2000];[81]
    (ii) section 182 or 383 of the Criminal Procedure (Scotland) Act 1975;
    (iii) section 5(1) of the Probation Act (Northern Ireland) 1950,

  the Secretary of State may, if he thinks fit [or the Scottish Ministers may if they think fit],[82] on the request of that person, arrange for him to be sent back free of charge and with as little delay as possible to the jurisdiction of the foreign state, Commonwealth country or colony[, or of the Hong Kong Special Administrative Region,][83] from which he was returned.

Part V
Special Cases

Repatriation Cases

21. Persons serving sentences outside country of conviction

(1) This section applies where—
  (a) a request is made—
    (i) by some person recognised as a diplomatic or consular representative of a foreign state in the case of which an Order in Council under section 2 of the Extradition Act 1870 applies or as between which and the United Kingdom extradition procedures under Part III of this Act are available; or
    (ii) by or on behalf of the Government of a designated Commonwealth country or the Governor of a colony[; or
    (iii) by or on behalf of the Government of the Hong Kong Special Administrative Region],[84]

  for the arrest and return of a person in the United Kingdom who is alleged to be unlawfully at large from a prison in which he was serving a sentence in pursuance of international arrangements for the repatriation of prisoners sentenced in one country ('the country of conviction') to serve their sentences in another ('the country of imprisonment'); and
  (b) there are furnished with the request—
    (i) particulars of the person whose return is requested;
    (ii) particulars of the offence of which he was convicted (including evidence sufficient to justify the issue of a warrant for his arrest under the relevant legislation);
    (iii) a certificate of the conviction and sentence; and
    (iv) a certificate of the international arrangements for repatriation under which he was held.

(2) Where this section applies, the relevant legislation shall have effect—
  (a) if the request is from the country of conviction, as if the person to whom the request relates were alleged to be unlawfully at large from a prison in that country; and
  (b) if it is from the country of imprisonment, as if he were alleged to have been convicted of a corresponding offence under the law of that country committed there,

  and the question whether the person to whom the request relates is to be returned shall be determined, subject to subsection (3) below, in accordance with that legislation.

(3) A person shall not be returned under subsection (2)(b) above unless—
  (a) the offence was committed in the country of conviction; or
  (b) the offence was not committed there but was committed in circumstances in which he might be returned on a request made by the country of conviction.

---

81 Amended by the Powers of Criminal Courts (Sentencing) Act 2000.
82 Amended by SI 1999/1750.
83 Amended by SI 1997/1178.
84 Amended by SI 1997/1178.

(4) In this section 'the relevant legislation' means the provisions of this Act that are relevant—
  (a) if the case falls within paragraph (a) of subsection (2) above, to extradition to the country of conviction; and
  (b) if it falls within paragraph (b), to extradition to the country of imprisonment.

International Convention cases

22. Extension of purposes of extradition for offences under Acts giving effect to international Conventions

(1) Except as provided by subsection (6) below, this section has effect where—
  (a) general extradition arrangements have not been made with a state which is a party to a Convention to which this section applies; and
  (b) no Order in Council under section 2 of the Extradition Act 1870 is in force in relation to that state.

(2) The Conventions to which this section applies are—
  (a) the Convention on Offences and certain other Acts committed on board Aircraft, which was signed at Tokyo on 14th September 1963 ('the Tokyo Convention');
  (b) the Convention for the Suppression of Unlawful Seizure of Aircraft, which was signed at the Hague on 16th December 1970 ('the Hague Convention');
  (c) the Convention for the Suppression of Unlawful Acts against the Safety of Civil Aviation, which was signed at Montreal on 23rd September 1971 ('the Montreal Convention');
  (d) the Convention on the Prevention and Punishment of Crimes against Internationally Protected Persons adopted by the United Nations General Assembly in 1973 ('the Internationally Protected Persons Convention');
  (e) the International Convention against the Taking of Hostages opened for signature at New York on 18th December 1979 ('the Hostages Convention');
  (f) the Convention on the Physical Protection of Nuclear Material opened for signature at Vienna and New York on 3rd March 1980 ('the Nuclear Material Convention');
  (g) the United Nations Convention Against Torture and other Cruel, Inhuman or Degrading Treatment or Punishment adopted by the United Nations General Assembly on 10th December 1984 ('the Torture Convention');
  [(h) the United Nations Convention against Illicit Traffic in Narcotic Drugs and Psychotropic Substances which was signed in Vienna on 20th December 1988 ('the Vienna Convention')];[85]
  [(i) the Protocol for the Suppression of Unlawful Acts of Violence at Airports Serving International Civil Aviation, supplementary to the Montreal Convention, which was signed at Montreal on 24th February 1988 ('the Montreal Protocol');
  (j) the Convention for the Suppression of Unlawful Acts against the Safety of Maritime Navigation, which was signed at Rome on 10th March 1988 ('the Rome Convention');
  (k) the Protocol for the Suppression of Unlawful Acts against the Safety of Fixed Platforms Located on the Continental Shelf, which was also signed at Rome on 10th March 1988 ('the Rome Protocol');][86]
  [(l) the Convention on the Safety of United Nations and Associated Personnel adopted by the General Assembly of the United Nations on 9th December 1994 ('the UN Personnel Convention');][87]
  [(m) the Convention for the Suppression of Terrorist Bombings, which was opened for signature at New York on 12th January 1998 ('the Terrorist Bombings Convention');
  (n) the Convention for the Suppression of the Financing of Terrorism which was opened for signature at New York on 10th January 2000 ('the Terrorist Finance Convention').][88]

(3) Where this section has effect, an Order in Council applying this Act may be made under section 4 above as if a Convention to which this section applies that is specified in the order constituted general

---

[85] Amended by the Criminal Justice (International Co-operation) Act 1990.
[86] Amended by the Aviation and Maritime Security Act 1990.
[87] Amended by the United Nations Personnel Act 1997.
[88] Amended by the Terrorism Act 2000.

extradition arrangements between the United Kingdom and the foreign state, or any foreign state, party to the Convention; but where this Act is so applied, it shall have effect only in respect—

(a) of the relevant offences;

(b) of an attempt to commit a relevant offence;

(c) of counselling, procuring, commanding, aiding or abetting a relevant offence; and

(d) of being accessory before or after the fact to a relevant offence.

(4) The relevant offences are—

(a) in relation to the Tokyo Convention, any offence committed on board an aircraft in flight;

(b) in relation to the Hague Convention, any offence under or by virtue of section 1 or 6(1) or (2)(a) of the Aviation Security Act 1982;

(c) in relation to the Montreal Convention, any offence under or by virtue of section 2, 3 or 6(2)(b) or (c) of that Act;

(d) in relation to the Internationally Protected Persons Convention—

(i) an offence mentioned in paragraph (a) of subsection (1) of section 1 of the Internationally Protected Persons Act 1978 which is committed against a protected person within the meaning of that section;

(ii) an offence mentioned in paragraph (b) of that subsection which is committed in connection with such an attack as is so mentioned; and

(iii) an offence under section 1(3) of that Act;

(e) in relation to the Hostages Convention, an offence under the Taking of Hostages Act 1982;

(f) in relation to the Nuclear Material Convention—

(i) an offence mentioned in paragraph (a), (b), (c) or (d) of subsection (1) of section 1 of the Nuclear Material (Offences) Act 1983 which is committed by doing an act in relation to or by means of nuclear material; and

(ii) an offence under section 2 of that Act; [...][89]

(g) in relation to the Torture Convention, torture [[...][90]

(h) in relation to the Vienna Convention—

[(i) any offence which is specified in—

(a) paragraph 1 of Schedule 2 to the Proceeds of Crime Act 2002 (drug trafficking offences), or

(b) so far as it relates to that paragraph, paragraph 10 of that Schedule;

(ia) any offence which by virtue of section 415 of the Proceeds of Crime Act 2002 is a money laundering offence for the purposes of Part 8 of that Act;][91]

[(ii) any offence which is specified in—

(a) paragraph 2 of Schedule 4 to the Proceeds of Crime Act 2002, or

(b) so far as it relates to that paragraph, paragraph 10 of that Schedule;

(iia) any offence which by virtue of section 415 of the Proceeds of Crime Act 2002 is a money laundering offence for the purposes of Part 8 of that Act;][92] [[...][93]

[(iii) any offence which is specified in—

(a) paragraph 1 of Schedule 5 to the Proceeds of Crime Act 2002 (drug trafficking offences), or

(b) so far as it relates to that paragraph, paragraph 10 of that Schedule; and][94]

(iv) any offence which by virtue of section 415 of the Proceeds of Crime Act 2002 is a money laundering offence for the purposes of Part 8 of that Act;][95]][96]

[(i) in relation to the Montreal Protocol, an offence under section 1 of the Aviation and Maritime Security Act 1990;

---

89 Repealed by the Criminal Justice (International Co-operation) Act 1990.
90 Repealed by the Aviation and Maritime Security Act 1990.
91 Amended by the Proceeds of Crime Act 2002.
92 Amended by the Proceeds of Crime Act 2002.
93 Repealed by the Proceeds of Crime Act 2002.
94 Amended by SI 1990/2588.
95 Amended by the Proceeds of Crime Act 2002.
96 Amended by the Criminal Justice (International Co-operation) Act 1990.

(j) in relation to the Rome Convention, an offence under section 9 or 12 of that Act or an offence under section 11 or 13 of that Act committed in relation to a ship (within the meaning of Part II of that Act); and

(k) in relation to the Rome Protocol, an offence under section 10 of that Act or an offence under section 11 or 13 of that Act committed in relation to a fixed platform (within the meaning of Part II of that Act);][97]

[(l) in relation to the UN Personnel Convention—

(i) an offence mentioned in section 1(2) of the United Nations Personnel Act 1997 which is committed against a UN worker within the meaning of that Act;

(ii) an offence mentioned in subsection (2) of section 2 of that Act which is committed in connection with such an attack as is mentioned in subsection (1) of that section; and

(iii) an offence under section 3 of that Act;][98]

[(m) in relation to the Terrorist Bombings Convention, an offence, committed as an act of terrorism or for the purposes of terrorism, under—

(i) section 2, 3 or 5 of the Explosive Substances Act 1883 (causing explosions, &c),

(ii) section 1 of the Biological Weapons Act 1974 (biological weapons), or

(iii) section 2 of the Chemical Weapons Act 1996 (chemical weapons);

(n) in relation to the Terrorist Finance Convention, an offence under any of sections 15 to 18 of the Terrorism Act 2000 (terrorist property: offences).][99]

(5) An Order in Council such as is mentioned in subsection (3) above may not provide that a court dealing with a person arrested for an offence shall not be under a duty to determine whether the evidence would be sufficient to [make a case requiring an answer by that person if the proceedings were the summary trial of an information against him].[100]

(6) For the purposes of general extradition procedures under Part III of this Act, in their application (whether or not by virtue of such an Order in Council) as between the United Kingdom and any other state, any act or omission, wherever it takes place, which constitutes—

(a) an offence mentioned in this section; and

(b) an offence against the law of that state,

shall be deemed to be an offence committed within the territory of that state.

(7) Subsections (4) and (5) of section 92 of the Civil Aviation Act 1982 shall apply for the purposes of this section as they apply for the purposes of that section.

(8) Section 98 of that Act shall have effect as if the reference to sections 92 to 95 included a reference to this section.

[23. Genocide, crimes against humanity and war crimes

(1) This section applies to—

(a) any offence that if committed in the United Kingdom would be punishable as—

(i) an offence under section 51 or 58 of the International Criminal Court Act 2001 (genocide, crimes against humanity and war crimes),

(ii) an offence under section 52 or 59 of that Act (conduct ancillary to genocide, etc committed outside the jurisdiction), or

(iii) an ancillary offence, as defined in section 55 or 62 of that Act, in relation to any such offence as is mentioned in sub-paragraph (i) or (ii); and

(b) any offence punishable in the United Kingdom under section 1 of the Geneva Conventions Act 1957 (grave breach of scheduled conventions).

(2) For the purposes of this Act—

(a) an offence to which this section applies shall not be regarded as an offence of a political character, and

(b) no proceedings in respect of such an offence shall be regarded as a criminal matter of a political character.

---

[97] Amended by the Aviation and Maritime Security Act 1990.

[98] Amended by the United Nations Personnel Act 1997.

[99] Amended by the Terrorism Act 2000.

[100] Amended by the Criminal Justice and Public Order Act 1994.

(3) It is not an objection to proceedings against a person in respect of an offence to which this section applies that under the law in force at the time when and in the place where he is alleged to have committed the act of which he is accused, or of which he was convicted, he could not have been punished for it.

(4) References in this section to an offence under any provision of the International Criminal Court Act 2001, or to an offence ancillary to such an offence, include any corresponding offence under the law of Scotland.][101]

24. Suppression of terrorism

(1) For the purposes mentioned in subsection (2) below—
  (a) no offence to which section 1 of the Suppression of Terrorism Act 1978 applies shall be regarded as an offence of a political character; and
  (b) no proceedings in respect of an offence to which that section applies shall be regarded as a criminal matter of a political character or as criminal proceedings of a political character.

(2) Those purposes are the purposes—
  (a) of a request for the return of a person in accordance with extradition procedures under Part III of this Act made by a country to which this subsection applies; and
  (b) of a requisition under Schedule 1 to this Act which is made by such a country.

(3) Subsection (2) above applies—
  (a) to a country for the time being designated in an order made by the Secretary of State as a party to the European Convention on the Suppression of Terrorism signed at Strasbourg on 27th January 1977[, other than a country that is a party to the 1996 Convention];[102] and
  (b) to a country in relation to which the Secretary of State has made an order under section 5 of the Suppression of Terrorism Act 1978 applying that subsection.

(4) In relation to a requisition under Schedule 1 to this Act which is made by a country to which subsection (2) above applies that Schedule shall have effect as if at the end of paragraph 1(2)(b) there were added—

'or
  (c) he proves to the satisfaction of the [District Judge (Magistrates' Courts)][103] or the court before whom he is brought on habeas corpus, or to the Secretary of State—
    (i) that the requisition for his surrender has in fact been made with a view to try or punish him on account of his race, religion, nationality or political opinions; or
    (ii) that he might, if surrendered, be prejudiced at his trial or punished, detained or restricted in his personal liberty by reason of his race, religion, nationality or political opinions.'.

[(5) Subsections (1) and (2) above shall have effect in relation to an offence to which section 22(4)(m) or (n) above applies as they have effect in relation to an offence to which section 1 of the Suppression of Terrorism Act 1978 applies.

(6) For that purpose subsection (2) applies to a country which is a party to—
  (a) the Convention for the Suppression of Terrorist Bombings mentioned in section 22(2)(m) above, or
  (b) the Convention for the Suppression of the Financing of Terrorism mentioned in section 22(2)(n) above.][104]

25. Hostage-taking

(1) A person shall not be returned under this Act to a designated Commonwealth country which is party to the Convention referred to in subsection (3) below, or committed or kept in custody for the purposes of such return, if it appears to the appropriate authority—
  (a) that he might, if returned, be prejudiced at his trial by reason of the impossibility of effecting communications between him and the appropriate authorities of the state entitled to exercise rights of protection in relation to him; and

---

[101] Substituted by the International Criminal Court Act 2001.
[102] Amended by SI 2002/419.
[103] Amended by the Access to Justice Act 1999.
[104] Amended by the Terrorism Act 2000.

(b) that the act or omission constituting the offence of which he has been accused or convicted also constituted an offence under section 1 of the Taking of Hostages Act 1982 or an attempt to commit such an offence.

(2) Where the Secretary of State certifies that a country is a party to the Convention, the certificate shall, in any proceedings under this Act, be conclusive evidence of that fact.

(3) The Convention mentioned in subsections (1) and (2) above is the International Convention against the Taking of Hostages opened for signature at New York on 18th December 1979.

Part VI
Miscellaneous and Supplementary

Evidence

26. Authentication of foreign documents

(1) In extradition proceedings in relation to a person whose return has been requested by a foreign state foreign documents may be authenticated by the oath of a witness, but shall in any case be deemed duly authenticated—

(a) if they purport to be signed by a judge, magistrate or officer of the foreign state where they were issued; and

(b) if they purport to be certified by being sealed with the official seal of the Minister of Justice, or some other Minister of State, of the foreign state.

[(1A) In extradition proceedings in relation to a person whose return has been requested by or on behalf of the Government of the Hong Kong Special Administrative Region documents from that Region may be authenticated by the oath of a witness, but shall in any case be deemed duly authenticated—

(a) if they purport to be signed by a judge, magistrate or officer of the Hong Kong Special Administrative Region; and

(b) if they purport to be certified by being sealed—

(i) with an official or public seal of the Hong Kong Special Administrative Region, or

(ii) by an officer of that Region.][105]

(2) Judicial notice shall be taken of such certification as is mentioned in subsection (1)(b) [or (1A)(b)][106] above, and documents authenticated by such certification shall be received in evidence without further proof.

27. Evidence—Commonwealth countries and colonies

(1) In any proceedings under this Act in relation to a person whose return has been requested by a designated Commonwealth country or a colony, including proceedings on an application for habeas corpus in respect of a person in custody under this Act—

(a) a document, duly authenticated, which purports to set out evidence given on oath in a designated Commonwealth country or a colony shall be admissible as evidence of the matters stated in it;

(b) a document, duly authenticated, which purports to have been received in evidence, or to be a copy of a document so received, in any proceeding in any designated Commonwealth country or any colony shall be admissible in evidence;

(c) a document, duly authenticated, which certifies that a person was convicted on a date specified in the document of an offence against the law of, or of a part of, any such country or any colony shall be admissible as evidence of the fact and date of the conviction.

(2) A document shall be deemed to be duly authenticated for the purposes of this section—

(a) in the case of a document purporting to set out evidence given as mentioned in subsection (1)(a) above, if the document purports to be certified by a judge or magistrate or officer in or of the country or colony in question to be the original document containing or recording that evidence or a true copy of such a document;

[105] Amended by SI 1997/1178.
[106] Amended by SI 1997/1178.

(b) in the case of a document which purports to have been received in evidence as mentioned in subsection (1)(b) above or to be a copy of a document so received, if the document purports to be certified as mentioned in paragraph (a) above to have been, or to be a true copy of a document which has been, so received;

(c) in the case of a document which certifies that a person was convicted as mentioned in subsection (1)(c) above, if the document purports to be certified as mentioned in paragraph (a) above,

and in any such case the document is authenticated either by the oath of a witness or by the official seal of a Minister of the designated Commonwealth country or of the Governor or a Minister, secretary or other officer administering a department of the government of the colony, as the case may be.

(3) Nothing in this section shall prejudice the admission in evidence of any document which is admissible in evidence apart from this section.

(4) In the application of this section to Scotland, for the words 'admissible as evidence' in both places where they occur, there shall be substituted the words 'sufficient evidence'.

Warrants and orders

28. Form of warrants and orders

(1) Any warrant or order to be issued or made by the Secretary of State under this Act shall be given under the hand of the Secretary of State, a Minister of State or an Under-Secretary of State.

[(1A) Any warrant or order to be issued or made by the Scottish Ministers under this Act shall be given under the hand of a member of the Scottish Executive.][107]

(2) The Secretary of State may by regulations made by statutory instrument prescribe the form of any document required for the purposes of this Act in its application to return to foreign states (except a notice under section 14 above) and the form of any warrant or order to be issued or made under this Act in its application to return to Commonwealth countries[, colonies and the Hong Kong Special Administrative Region].[108]

Channel islands and isle of man

29. Application to Channel Islands and Isle of Man

(1) Subject to the provisions of this section, Parts I to V of this Act shall extend to the Channel Islands and the Isle of Man, and shall have effect as if each of them were part of the United Kingdom.

(2) Her Majesty may by Order in Council direct that any provision contained in those Parts shall, in its application to any of the said Islands, have effect subject to such exceptions, adaptations or modifications as may be specified in the Order.

(3) An Order in Council under this section relating to any provision of this Act as it has effect in relation to Commonwealth countries or colonies may contain such transitional or other incidental and supplementary provisions as may appear to Her Majesty to be necessary or expedient.

(4) Paragraph 18 of Schedule 1 to this Act has effect as to the application of that Schedule to the Channel Islands and the Isle of Man.

Extradition between colonies and foreign states

30. General extradition arrangements

(1) Upon the making of an Order in Council under section 4 above—

(a) the provisions of this Act relating to general extradition arrangements; and

(b) section 21 above,

shall, unless the Order otherwise provides, extend to every colony, as regards the extradition arrangements to which the Order refers, but subject—

(a) to the modifications set out in subsections (2) to (5) below;

(b) to any further modifications as to procedure prescribed by the law of the colony; and

---

107 Amended by SI 1999/1750.

108 Amended by SI 1997/1178.

(c) to the limitations, restrictions, exceptions and qualifications, if any, contained in the Order.

(2) A reference to the colony shall be substituted for any reference to the United Kingdom.

(3) An extradition request may be made to the Governor and the Governor may exercise the powers of the Secretary of State.

(4) An extradition request may be made by a consular representative recognised by the Governor.

(5) Any reference to a magistrate, judge or court shall be construed as a reference to such judicial authority as the law of the colony may provide.

31. Special extradition arrangements

(1) Her Majesty may by Order in Council direct that this section shall extend to any colony specified in the Order in the case of foreign states with whom there are no general extradition arrangements, subject to the limitations, restrictions, exceptions and qualifications, if any, contained in the Order.

(2) Where arrangements have been made in respect of a person under which extradition procedures under Part III of this Act or section 21 above will be available as between a colony to which this section applies and a foreign state, such extradition procedures shall be available in the case of that person, as between the colony and the state with whom the arrangements have been made, subject—

(a) to the modifications of this Act set out in section 30(2) to (5) above;

(b) to any further modifications as to procedure prescribed by the law of the colony; and

(c) to the limitations, restrictions, exceptions and qualifications, if any, contained in the arrangements.

(3) If the Governor or the Secretary of State issues a certificate—

(a) that such arrangements have been made; and

(b) that such extradition procedures are available in the case of the person named in the certificate as between the colony and the foreign state to the extent specified in the certificate,

it shall be conclusive evidence of all matters stated in it.

ORDERS IN COUNCIL RELATING TO COLONIES ETC

32. Application of provisions of Act by Order in Council

(1) Her Majesty may by Order in Council make provision for extending all or any of the provisions of this Act relating to return to Commonwealth countries (other than this section) to any colony, with the substitution of a reference to that colony for any reference to the United Kingdom, and with such other exceptions, adaptations or modifications as may be specified in the Order.

(2) Without prejudice to the generality of subsection (1) above, an Order in Council under this section may—

(a) so far as it extends to any colony provisions of this Act relating to the return of persons to and the treatment of persons returned from designated Commonwealth countries, apply those provisions in relation to the Republic of Ireland as they apply in relation to a designated Commonwealth country;

(b) so far as it extends to any colony provisions of this Act relating to the return of persons to and the treatment of persons returned from colonies, apply those provisions in relation to the United Kingdom as they apply in relation to a colony.

[(2A) An Order in Council under this section may make such provision as appears to Her Majesty to be necessary or expedient in consequence of or in connection with the provisions of section 1(1) of the Hong Kong Act 1985 for the purposes of the surrender of persons from a British overseas territory to the Hong Kong Special Administrative Region of the People's Republic of China and the treatment of persons surrendered to a British overseas territory from that Region.][109]

(3) Any Order in Council under this section shall be subject to annulment in pursuance of a resolution of either House of Parliament.

---

[109] Amended by SI 2002/1824.

33. Alternative arrangements for colonies

(1) Without prejudice to the powers exercisable by virtue of section 32 above, Her Majesty may by Order in Council make, for any colony, such special provision as appears to Her to be appropriate as between that colony and any other country being either a designated Commonwealth country or a colony—
   (a) for authorising and regulating the return to that other country of persons accused or convicted in it of offences;
   (b) for regulating the treatment in the colony for which the Order makes provision of persons returned to it from that other country pursuant to this Act or any Order in Council under this Act or any corresponding law of that other country.
(2) The legislature of any colony shall have power to make provision, not inconsistent with any Order in Council under this section or section 32 above which extends to that colony, for any purpose for which provision could be made by such an Order in Council.
(3) Any Order in Council under this section shall be subject to annulment in pursuance of a resolution of either House of Parliament.

34. Colonies—supplementary

(1) Her Majesty may by Order in Council direct that any provision to which this section applies shall have effect in any colony.
(2) This section applies—
   (a) to any provision of this Act that corresponds to a provision of the Extradition Act 1870 with amendments made by the Criminal Justice Act 1988; and
   (b) to any provision of this Act that corresponds to a provision of the Fugitive Offenders Act 1967 with amendments and repeals made by the Criminal Justice Act 1988.
(3) The repeal by this Act of the Fugitive Offenders Act 1967 does not affect an Order in Council made under section 16 or 17 of that Act or the power to revoke or amend such an Order.

[1995 and 1996 Convention cases

34A. Application of Act in 1995 and 1996 Convention cases

Schedule 1A provides for the application of this Act as between—
(a) the United Kingdom and states other than the Republic of Ireland that are parties to the 1995 Convention;
(b) the United Kingdom and states other than the Republic of Ireland that are parties to the 1996 Convention.][110]

General

35. Interpretation

(1) In this Act—

'appropriate authority' has the meaning assigned to it by section 6(9) above;
'authority to proceed' has the meaning assigned to it by section 7(1) above;
'court of committal' has the meaning assigned to it by section 9(1) above;
'designated Commonwealth country' has the meaning assigned to it by section 5(1) above,
[...][111]
'extradition crime', subject to paragraph 20 of Schedule 1 to this Act, is to be construed in accordance with section 2 above;
'extradition arrangements', 'general extradition arrangements' and 'special extradition arrangements' have the meanings assigned to them by section 3 above;
'extradition request' has the meaning assigned to it by section 7(1) above;

---

110 Inserted by SI 2002/419.
111 Repealed by the Access to Justice Act 1999.

['Hong Kong Special Administrative Region' means the Hong Kong Special Administrative Region of the People's Republic of China;][112]

['the 1995 Convention' means the Convention drawn up on the basis of Article K3 of the Treaty on European Union on Simplified Extradition Procedure between the Member States of the European Union;][113]

['the 1996 Convention' means the Convention drawn up on the basis of Article K3 of the Treaty on European Union relating to Extradition between the Member States of the European Union;][114]

['party to the 1995 Convention' means a state in respect of which the 1995 Convention is in force either generally or between it and the United Kingdom;][115]

['party to the 1996 Convention' means a state in respect of which the 1996 Convention is in force either generally or between it and the United Kingdom;][116]

[...];[117] and

'provisional warrant' has the meaning assigned to it by section 8(1) above.

(2) For the purposes of this Act a person convicted in his absence in a designated Commonwealth country or a colony shall be treated as a person accused of the offence of which he is convicted.

[(3) For the purposes of the application of this Act by virtue of any Order in Council in force under it or section 2 of the Extradition Act 1870, any reference in this Act to evidence making a case requiring an answer by an accused person shall be taken to indicate a determination of the same question as is indicated by a reference (however expressed) in any such Order (or arrangements embodied or recited in it) to evidence warranting or justifying the committal for trial of an accused person.][118]

Supplementary

36. Amendments

(1) In paragraph 4 of Schedule 3 to the Parliamentary Commissioner Act 1967 (matters not subject to investigation by Commissioner) for the words from 'or' to the end there shall be substituted the words, 'the Fugitive Offenders Act 1967 or the Extradition Act 1989'.

(2) The following subsection shall be substituted for subsection (1) of section 3 of the Genocide Act 1969 (application to Channel Islands, Isle of Man and colonies)—

'(1) Section 12 of the Backing of Warrants (Republic of Ireland) Act 1965 shall extend to the provisions of this Act amending that Act'.

(3) In section 2(2) of the Bail Act 1976 in the definition of 'proceedings against a fugitive offender' for the words from 'section', in the first place where it occurs, to '1967' there shall be substituted the words 'the Extradition Act 1989'.

(4) In paragraph (a) of subsection (1) of section 5 of the Suppression of Terrorism Act 1978 (power to apply provisions of Act to countries that are not parties to the European Convention on the Suppression of Terrorism) for the words 'Fugitive Offenders Act 1967' there shall be substituted the words 'Extradition Act 1989'.

(5) In paragraph (b) of that subsection after '1870' there shall be inserted the words 'or in the Extradition Act 1989'.

(6) The following paragraph shall be substituted for paragraph (c) of that subsection—

'(c) a colony.'.

(7) In paragraph (i) of that subsection for the words 'of this Act which would, apart from this section, apply only in relation to convention countries' there shall be substituted the words 'to which this paragraph applies'.

(8) The following subsection shall be inserted after that subsection—

'(1A) Subsection (1)(i) above applies—

(a) to the provisions of this Act which would, apart from this section, apply only in relation to convention countries; and

---

112 Amended by SI 1997/1178.
113 Amended by SI 2002/419.
114 Amended by SI 2002/419.
115 Amended by SI 2002/419.
116 Amended by SI 2002/419.
117 Repealed by the Access to Justice Act 1999.
118 Amended by the Criminal Justice and Public Order Act 1994.

(b) to section 24(1) and (2) of the Extradition Act 1989.'.

(9) The following subsection shall be added at the end of section 6 of the Nuclear Material (Offences) Act 1983—

'(5) In this section 'the Convention' means the Convention on the Physical Protection of Nuclear Material opened for signature at Vienna and New York on 3rd March 1980.'

37. Repeals etc.

(1) The enactments mentioned in Schedule 2 to this Act (which this Act replaces) are repealed to the extent specified in the third column of that Schedule.

(2) The Extradition Act 1895 is repealed as of no practical utility.

(3) The repeal by this Act of the Extradition Act 1870 does not affect an Order in Council made under section 2 of that Act or the power to revoke or alter such an Order.

(4) Notwithstanding the repeal any forms that might have been used by virtue of section 20 of the Act may continue to be used and shall be deemed to be valid and sufficient in law.

(5) Section 2A of the Backing of Warrants (Republic of Ireland) Act 1965 shall continue to have effect notwithstanding the repeal of section 1(9) of the Criminal Justice Act 1988 (which introduced Schedule 1 to the Act, Part II of which inserted section 2A in the Act of 1965) and the repeal of Schedule 1.

(6) The repeal of an enactment relating to a Convention to which section 22 above applies does not affect an Order in Council made under any provision whose effect is reproduced in that section or in section 29 above or any power to revoke, amend or re-enact such an Order.

38. Short title, commencement and extent

(1) This Act may be cited as the Extradition Act 1989.

(2) The provisions of this Act other than any provision to which subsection (3) below applies shall come into force at the end of the period of two months beginning with the day on which it is passed.

(3) The provisions of this Act to which this subsection applies are sections 7(3), 10(3) and 14(2) and (3) above, this section and paragraph 9(2) of Schedule 1.

(4) Section 136(1) of the Criminal Justice Act 1988 (which provided that torture should be deemed to be included in the list of extradition crimes contained in Schedule 1 to the Extradition Act 1870) and paragraph 4 of Schedule 1 to that Act (which provided that any offence under the Company Securities (Insider Dealing) Act 1985 and offences under section 24 of the Drug Trafficking Offences Act 1986 should be deemed to be so included) shall come into force immediately before this Act comes into force.

(5) This Act extends to Northern Ireland.

SCHEDULE 1
Provisions deriving from Extradition Act 1870 and associated enactments

Section 1

Restrictions On Surrender

1.

(1) The following restrictions shall be observed with respect to the surrender of fugitive criminals.

(2) A fugitive criminal shall not be surrendered—

(a) if the offence in respect of which his surrender is demanded is one of a political character, or

(b) if he proves to the satisfaction of the [District Judge (Magistrates' Courts)][119] or the court before whom he is brought on habeas corpus, or `to the Secretary of State, that the requisition for his surrender has in fact been made with a view to try or punish him for an offence of a political character.

(3) A fugitive criminal shall not be surrendered to a foreign state unless provision is made by the law of that state, or by arrangement, that the fugitive criminal shall not, until he has been restored or had an opportunity of returning to Her Majesty's dominions, be detained or tried in that foreign state

[119] Amended by the Access to Justice Act 1999.

for any offence committed prior to his surrender other than the extradition crime proved by the facts on which the surrender is grounded.

(4) A fugitive criminal who has been accused of some offence within United Kingdom jurisdiction not being the offence for which his surrender is asked, or is undergoing sentence under any conviction in the United Kingdom, shall not be surrendered until after he has been discharged, whether by acquittal or on expiration of his sentence or otherwise, or unless an order is made for the charge in respect of the offence to lie on the file.

(5) A fugitive criminal shall not be surrendered until the expiration of fifteen days from the date of his being committed to prison to await his surrender.

Effect of order

2. An Order in Council under section 2 of the Extradition Act 1870 shall be conclusive evidence that the arrangement referred to in it complies with this Schedule and that this Schedule applies in the case of the foreign state mentioned in the Order.

Liability of criminal to surrender

3. Where this Schedule has effect in the case of any foreign state, every fugitive criminal of that state who is in or suspected of being in any part of Her Majesty's dominions, or that part which is specified in the Order in Council relating to that state (as the case may be), shall be liable to be apprehended and surrendered in manner provided by this Schedule, whether the crime in respect of which the surrender is sought was committed before or after the date of the Order, and whether there is or is not any concurrent jurisdiction in any court of Her Majesty's dominions over that crime.

Order of Secretary of State for issue of warrant in United Kingdom if crime is not of political character

4.

(1) A requisition for the surrender of a fugitive criminal of any foreign state, who is in or suspected of being in the United Kingdom, shall be made to the Secretary of State by some person recognised by the Secretary of State as a diplomatic or consular representative of that foreign state.

(2) The Secretary of State may by order signify to [the Senior District Judge (Chief Magistrate) or another District Judge (Magistrates' Courts) designated by him][120] that such a requisition has been made, and require him to issue his warrant for the apprehension of the fugitive criminal.

(3) If the Secretary of State is of opinion that the offence is one of a political character, he may, if he thinks fit, refuse to send any such order as is mentioned in sub-paragraph (2) above, and may also at any time order a fugitive criminal accused or convicted of such offence to be discharged from custody.

Issue of warrant by metropolitan magistrate, justice etc

5.

(1) A warrant for the apprehension of a fugitive criminal, whether accused or convicted of crime, who is in or suspected of being in the United Kingdom, may be issued—

- (a) by [the Senior District Judge (Chief Magistrate), or another District Judge (Magistrates' Courts) designated by him,][121] on receipt of the order of the Secretary of State, and on such evidence as would in his opinion justify the issue of the warrant if the crime had been committed or the criminal convicted in England or Wales; and
- (b) by [...][122] any justice of the peace in any part of the United Kingdom, on such information or complaint and such evidence or after such proceedings as would in the opinion of the person issuing the warrant justify the issue of a warrant if the crime had been committed or the criminal convicted in that part of the United Kingdom in which he exercises jurisdiction.

---

120 Amended by the Access to Justice Act 1999.
121 Amended by the Access to Justice Act 1999.
122 Repealed by the Access to Justice Act 1999.

(2) Any person issuing a warrant under this paragraph without an order of the Secretary of State shall forthwith send a report of the fact of such issue, together with the evidence and information or complaint, or certified copies thereof, to the Secretary of State, who may if he thinks fit order the warrant to be cancelled, and the person who has been apprehended on the warrant to be discharged.

(3) A fugitive criminal, when apprehended on a warrant issued without the order of the Secretary of State, shall be brought before some person having power to issue a warrant under this paragraph, who shall by warrant order him to be brought and the prisoner shall accordingly be brought before [the Senior District Judge (Chief Magistrate), or another District Judge (Magistrates' Courts) designated by him].[123]

(4) A fugitive criminal apprehended on a warrant issued without the order of the Secretary of State shall be discharged by the [District Judge (Magistrates' Courts) unless he],[124] within such reasonable time as, with reference to the circumstances of the case, he may fix, receives from the Secretary of State an order signifying that a requisition has been made for the surrender of such criminal.

Hearing of case and evidence of political character of crime

6.

(1) When a fugitive criminal is brought before the [District Judge (Magistrates' Courts) he][125] shall [have the same powers, as near as may be, including power to adjourn the case and meanwhile to remand the prisoner either in custody or on bail, as if the proceedings were the summary trial of an information against him for an offence committed in England and Wales; and section 16(1)(c) of the Prosecution of Offences Act 1985 (costs on dismissal) shall apply accordingly reading the reference to the dismissal of the information as a reference to the discharge of the prisoner.][126]

[(1A) If the metropolitan magistrate exercises his power to adjourn the case he shall on so doing remand the prisoner either in custody or on bail.][127]

(2) The [District Judge (Magistrates' Courts)][128] shall receive any evidence which may be tendered to show that the crime of which the prisoner is accused or alleged to have been convicted is an offence of a political character or is not an extradition crime.

Committal or discharge of prisoner

7.

(1) In the case of a fugitive criminal accused of an extradition crime, if the foreign warrant authorising the arrest of such criminal is duly authenticated, and such evidence is produced as (subject to the provisions of this Schedule) would, according to the law of England and Wales, [make a case requiring an answer by the prisoner if the proceedings were for the trial in England and Wales of an information for the crime,][129] the [District Judge (Magistrates' Courts)][130] shall commit him to prison, but otherwise shall order him to be discharged.

(2) In the case of a fugitive criminal alleged to have been convicted of an extradition crime, if such evidence is produced as (subject to the provisions of this Schedule) would, according to the law of England and Wales, prove that the prisoner was convicted of such crime, the [District Judge (Magistrates' Courts)][131] shall commit him to prison, but otherwise shall order him to be discharged.

(3) If he commits such criminal to prison, he shall commit him there to await the warrant of the Secretary of State for his surrender, and shall forthwith send to the Secretary of State a certificate of the committal, and such report upon the case as he may think fit.

---

[123] Amended by the Access to Justice Act 1999.
[124] Amended by the Access to Justice Act 1999.
[125] Amended by the Access to Justice Act 1999.
[126] Amended by the Criminal Justice and Public Order Act 1994.
[127] Amended by the Criminal Justice and Public Order Act 1994.
[128] Amended by the Access to Justice Act 1999.
[129] Amended by the Criminal Justice and Public Order Act 1994.
[130] Amended by the Access to Justice Act 1999.
[131] Amended by the Access to Justice Act 1999.

Surrender of fugitive to foreign state by warrant of Secretary of State

8.

(1) If the [District Judge (Magistrates' Courts)][132] commits a fugitive criminal to prison, he shall inform such criminal that he will not be surrendered until after the expiration of fifteen days, and that he has a right to apply for a writ of habeas corpus.

(2) Upon the expiration of the said fifteen days, or, if a writ of habeas corpus is issued, after the decision of the court upon the return to the writ, as the case may be, or after such further period as may be allowed in either case by the Secretary of State, the Secretary of State may by warrant order the fugitive criminal (if not delivered on the decision of the court) to be surrendered to such person as may in his opinion be duly authorised to receive the fugitive criminal by the foreign state from which the requisition for the surrender proceeded, and such fugitive criminal shall be surrendered accordingly.

(3) It shall be lawful for any person to whom such warrant is directed and for the person so authorised as aforesaid to receive, hold in custody, and convey within the jurisdiction of such foreign state the criminal mentioned in the warrant; and if the criminal escapes out of any custody to which he may be delivered on or in pursuance of such warrant, it shall be lawful to retake him in the same manner as any person accused of any crime against the laws of that part of Her Majesty's dominions to which he escapes may be retaken upon an escape.

Simplified procedure

9.

(1) A person may give notice that he waives the rights conferred on him by paragraph 8 above.

(2) A notice under this paragraph shall be given in England and Wales in the manner prescribed by rules under section 144 of the Magistrates' Courts Act 1980 and, without prejudice to the generality of subsection (1) of that section, the power to make such rules shall include power to make provision for a magistrate to order the committal for return of a person with his consent at any time after his arrest.

(3) A notice under this paragraph shall be given in Scotland in the manner prescribed by the High Court of Justiciary by Act of Adjournal and the sheriff may order the committal for return of a person with his consent at any time after his arrest.

(4) Where an order is made under this paragraph, this Schedule shall cease to apply to the person in respect of whom it is made, except that if, within one month after the order is made, he is not surrendered to the foreign state to which he is to be returned, the High Court, upon application by or on behalf of that person, may, unless reasonable cause is shown for the delay, order him to be discharged.

Discharge of persons apprehended if not conveyed out of United Kingdom within 2 months

10. If the fugitive criminal who has been committed to prison is not surrendered and conveyed out of the United Kingdom within two months after such committal, or, if a writ of habeas corpus is issued, after the decision of the court upon the return to the writ, it shall be lawful for any judge of the High Court, upon application made to him by or on behalf of the criminal, and upon proof that reasonable notice of the intention to make such application has been given to the Secretary of State, to order the criminal to be discharged out of custody, unless sufficient cause is shown to the contrary.

Execution of Warrant of [District Judge (Magistrates' Courts)][133]

11. The warrant of the [District Judge (Magistrates' Courts)][134] issued in pursuance of this Schedule may be executed in any part of the United Kingdom in the same manner as if it had been

132 Amended by the Access to Justice Act 1999.
133 Amended by the Access to Justice Act 1999.
134 Amended by the Access to Justice Act 1999.

originally issued or subsequently endorsed by a justice of the peace having jurisdiction in the place where the same is executed.

Depositions etc to be evidence

12. Depositions and statements on oath taken in a foreign state, and copies of such original depositions or statements and foreign certificates of or judicial documents stating the fact of conviction, may, if duly authenticated, be received in evidence in proceedings under this Schedule.

Crimes committed at sea

13.

(1) Where the crime in respect of which the surrender of a fugitive criminal is sought was committed on board any vessel or hovercraft on the high seas which comes into any port of the United Kingdom, the following provisions shall have effect—
  (a) this Schedule shall be construed as if [the references to the Senior District Judge (Chief Magistrate) or another District Judge (Magistrates' Courts) designated by him were to any District Judge (Magistrates' Courts) and those references and the references to a District Judge (Magistrates' Courts) (apart from that in paragraph 11) included any sheriff in Scotland and any resident magistrate in Northern Ireland];[135]
  (b) the criminal may be committed to any prison to which the person committing him has power to commit persons accused of the like crime;
  (c) if the fugitive criminal is apprehended on a warrant issued without the order of the Secretary of State, he shall be brought before [any District Judge (Magistrates' Courts), or the][136] sheriff or resident magistrate who issued the warrant, or who has jurisdiction in the port where the vessel lies, or in the place nearest to that port.

(2) [...][137]

Aircraft

14.

(1) For the purposes of the application of this Schedule to crimes committed on board an aircraft in flight, any aircraft registered in a country which is for the time being certified to be a country specified in an Order in Council made by virtue of section 105 of the Civil Aviation Act 1982 to be a Convention country as defined in section 105(1) of that Act shall at any time while that aircraft is in flight be deemed to be within the jurisdiction of that country, whether or not it is for the time being also within the jurisdiction of any other country.

(2) Paragraph 13 above shall have effect where a person's surrender is sought in respect of a crime committed on board an aircraft in flight which lands in the United Kingdom, but as if for references to the port where the vessel lies there were substituted references to the place at which the person whose surrender is sought is disembarked.

(3) Subsections (4) and (5) of section 92 of the Civil Aviation Act 1982 shall apply for the purposes of this paragraph as they apply for the purposes of that section.

(4) For the purposes of this Schedule any act, wherever committed, which—
  (a) is an offence under any of the provisions of Part I of the Aviation Security Act 1982 (other than sections 4 and 7) or an attempt to commit such an offence, or would be such an offence or attempt but for section 1(2), 2(4), or 3(5) or (6) of that Act; and
  (b) is an offence against the law of any state in relation to which this Schedule has effect,

shall be deemed to be an offence committed within the jurisdiction of that state.

[135] Amended by the Access to Justice Act 1999.
[136] Amended by the Access to Justice Act 1999.
[137] Repealed by the Access to Justice Act 1999.

DEEMED EXTENSION OF JURISDICTION OF FOREIGN STATES

15. For the purposes of this Schedule any act, wherever committed, which is any of the following offences—

(a) an offence mentioned in paragraph (a) of subsection (1) of section 1 of the Internationally Protected Persons Act 1978 which is committed against a protected person within the meaning of that section;

(b) an offence mentioned in paragraph (b) of that subsection which is committed in connection with such an attack as is so mentioned;

(c) an attempt to commit an offence mentioned in the preceding paragraphs;

(d) an offence under section 1(3) of the Internationally Protected Persons Act 1978;

(e) an offence under the Taking of Hostages Act 1982 or an attempt to commit such an offence;

(f) an offence mentioned in paragraphs (a) to (d) of subsection (1) of section 1 of the Nuclear Material (Offences) Act 1983 which is committed by doing an act in relation to or by means of nuclear material, as defined in that Act;

(g) an offence under section 2 of that Act;

(h) an attempt to commit an offence mentioned in paragraphs (f) or (g) above; [...][138]

(i) torture,

[[(j) any offence which is specified in—

(i) paragraph 1 of Schedule 2 to the Proceeds of Crime Act 2002 (drug trafficking offences), or

(ii) so far as it relates to that paragraph, paragraph 10 of that Schedule;

(ja) any offence which by virtue of section 415 of the Proceeds of Crime Act 2002 is a money laundering offence for the purposes of Part 8 of that Act;][139]

[(k) any offence which is specified in—

(i) paragraph 2 of Schedule 4 to the Proceeds of Crime Act 2002, or

(ii) so far as it relates to that paragraph, paragraph 10 of that Schedule;][140]

(ka) any offence which by virtue of section 415 of the Proceeds of Crime Act 2002 is a money laundering offence for the purposes of Part 8 of that Act;][141] [or

(l) an offence under section 1, 9, 10, 11, 12 or 13 of the Aviation and Maritime Security Act 1990 or an attempt to commit such an offence;][142] [or

[(m) any offence which is specified in—

(i) paragraph 1 of Schedule 5 to the Proceeds of Crime Act 2002 (drug trafficking offences), or

(ii) so far as it relates to that paragraph, paragraph 10 of that Schedule;

(ma) any offence which by virtue of section 415 of the Proceeds of Crime Act 2002 is a money laundering offence for the purposes of Part 8 of that Act];[143]][144] [or

(n) an offence mentioned in section 1(2) of the United Nations Personnel Act 1997 which is committed against a UN worker within the meaning of that Act; or

(o) an offence mentioned in subsection (2) of section 2 of that Act which is committed in connection with such an attack as is mentioned in subsection (1) of that section;

(p) an offence under section 3 of that Act;]

(q) an attempt to commit an offence mentioned in paragraph (n), (o) or (p);][145] and an offence against the law of any state in relation to which this Schedule has effect shall be deemed to be an offence committed within the jurisdiction of that state.

---

138 Repealed by the Criminal Justice (International Co-operation) Act 1990.
139 Amended by the Proceeds of Crime Act 2002.
140 Amended by the Criminal Justice (International Co-operation) Act 1990.
141 Amended by the Proceeds of Crime Act 2002.
142 Amended by the Aviation and Maritime Security Act 1990.
143 Amended by the Proceeds of Crime Act 2002.
144 Amended by SI 1990/2588.
145 Amended by the United Nations Personnel Act 1997.

Fugitive criminals in colonies

16. This Schedule, when applied by Order in Council, shall, unless it is otherwise provided by such Order, extend to every colony in the same manner as if throughout this Schedule a reference to the colony were substituted for the United Kingdom or England and Wales, as the case may require, but with the following modifications, namely—

(a) the requisition for the surrender of a fugitive criminal who is in or suspected of being in a colony may be made to the governor of that colony by any person recognised by that governor as a consular representative, or (if the fugitive criminal has escaped from a colony or dependency of the foreign state on behalf of which the requisition is made) as the governor of such colony or dependency;

(b) no warrant of the Secretary of State shall be required, and all powers vested in or acts authorised or required to be done under this Schedule by the metropolitan magistrate and the Secretary of State, or either of them, in relation to the surrender of a fugitive criminal, may be done by the governor of the colony alone;

(c) a judge of any court exercising in the colony the like powers as the High Court exercises in England and Wales may exercise the power of discharging a criminal when not conveyed within two months out of such British possession.

Criminal surrendered by foreign state not triable for previous crime

17. Where in pursuance of any arrangement with a foreign state, any person accused or convicted of an extradition crime is surrendered by that foreign state, such person shall not until he has been restored or had an opportunity of returning to such foreign state, be triable or tried for any offence committed prior to the surrender in any part of Her Majesty's dominions other than such of the said crimes as may be proved by the facts on which the surrender is grounded.

Application of schedule in Channel Islands and Isle of Man

18. This Schedule (except so far as relates to the execution of warrants in the Channel Islands) shall extend to the Channel Islands and Isle of Man in the same manner as if they were part of the United Kingdom; and the royal courts of the Channel Islands are hereby respectively authorised and required to register this Schedule.

Dependencies of foreign states

19. For the purposes of this Schedule, every colony, dependency, and constituent part of a foreign state, and every vessel of that state, shall (except where expressly mentioned as distinct in this Schedule) be deemed to be within the jurisdiction of and to be part of such foreign state.

Interpretation

20. In this Schedule, unless the context otherwise requires—

'colony' includes colonies under one legislature;

'conviction' and 'convicted' do not include or refer to a conviction which under foreign law is a conviction for contumacy, but 'accused person' includes a person so convicted for contumacy;

'extradition crime', in relation to any foreign state, is to be construed by reference to the Order in Council under section 2 of the Extradition Act 1870 applying to that state as it had effect immediately before the coming into force of this Act and to any amendments thereafter made to that Order;

'fugitive criminal' means any person accused or convicted of an extradition crime committed within the jurisdiction of any foreign state who is in or is suspected of being in some part of Her Majesty's dominions;

'fugitive criminal of a foreign state' means a fugitive criminal accused or convicted of an extradition crime committed within the jurisdiction of that state;

'justice of the peace' includes in Scotland a sheriff;

'legislature' means any person or persons who can exercise legislative authority in a colony, and where there are local legislatures as well as a central legislature, means the central legislature only;

'warrant', in the case of any foreign state, includes any judicial document authorising the arrest of a person accused of crime.

[SCHEDULE 1A
The 1995 Convention and the 1996 Convention

PART 1
THE 1995 CONVENTION

1. Application of Act

This Act applies as if the terms of the 1995 Convention were general extradition arrangements made between the United Kingdom and the states other than the Republic of Ireland that are parties to it.

2. Adaptations of Act

As applied by paragraph 1 above, this Act has effect as between the United Kingdom and the states other than the Republic of Ireland that are parties to the 1995 Convention with the following adaptations.

3. In section 6 after subsection (6) insert—

'(6A) Subsection (4) above does not apply if the person has consented to his return to the relevant foreign state under section 14A below.'.

4. In section 9 after subsection (3) insert—

'(3A) The Court of committal shall, as soon as practicable and in any event before committing the person arrested under subsection (8) below—

(a) inform him that he may consent to his return to the foreign state that made the extradition request; and

(b) explain the effect of any such consent and the procedure that will apply if he gives any such consent.

(3B) The court of committal shall also inform the person arrested that—

(a) any such consent is to be given in writing and is irrevocable;

(b) any such consent is to be given to the court, if it is given before an order for committal under subsection (8) below has been made;

(c) any such consent is to be given to the Secretary of State or the Scottish Ministers, if it is given after an order for committal under subsection (8) below has been made.'.

5. After section 14 insert—

'14A Consent to return

(1) A person arrested in pursuance of a warrant under section 8 above may consent to his return to the foreign state that made the extradition request.

(2) Any consent under this section is irrevocable.

(3) If the person has not been committed under section 9 above, any consent under this section must be given by notice in writing to the court of committal.

(4) In England and Wales, the notice is to be given in the manner prescribed by rules under section 144 of the Magistrates' Courts Act 1980.

(5) Without prejudice to the generality of section 144(1) of that Act, the power to make rules under that section includes power to make provision for a [Senior District Judge (Chief Magistrate) or another District Judge (Magistrates' Courts) designated by him for the purposes of this Act][146] to order the committal for return of a person if he gives consent under this section before he is committed under section 9 above.

(6) In Scotland, the notice is to be given in the manner prescribed by the High Court of Justiciary by Act of Adjournal and the sheriff may order the committal for return of a person if he gives consent under this section before he is committed under section 9 above.

(7) Where an order is made by virtue of subsection (5) or (6) above, this Act shall cease to apply to the person in respect of whom the order is made, subject to subsection (8) below.

(8) If the person is not returned within 20 days after the order is made, the High Court or in Scotland the High Court of Justiciary may, on application by him or on his behalf, order him to be discharged unless reasonable cause is shown for the delay.

[146] Amended by SI 2002/1662.

(9) If the person has been committed under section 9 above, any consent under this section must be given to the Secretary of State or the Scottish Ministers.

(10) The Secretary of State or the Scottish Ministers may, by warrant, order his return at any time under this section.'.

6. In section 18 after subsection (1) insert—

'(1A) In a case where the foreign state by which the person is returned has made a declaration under Article 9(a) of the 1995 Convention, subsection (1) above does not apply if—

(a) the person has consented to his return, and

(b) where the state has made a declaration under Article 7(4) of that Convention, he has not revoked his consent.

(1B) In a case where the foreign state by which the person is returned has made a declaration under Article 9(b) of the 1995 Convention, subsection (1) above does not apply if—

(a) the person has consented to his return and has renounced the benefit of subsection (1) above, and

(b) where the state has made a declaration under Article 7(4) of that Convention, he has not revoked his consent or renunciation.'.

Part 2
The 1996 Convention

7. **Application of Act**

This Act applies as if the terms of the 1996 Convention were general extradition arrangements made between the United Kingdom and the other states other than the Republic of Ireland that are parties to it.

8. **Adaptations of Act**

As applied by paragraph 7 above, this Act has effect as between the United Kingdom and the states other than the Republic of Ireland that are parties to the 1996 Convention with the following adaptations.

9.

(1) Section 2 is amended as follows.

(2) In subsection (1)(a)—

(a) for '12 months' substitute '6 months';

(b) for 'so punishable under that law' substitute 'punishable under that law with imprisonment, or any form of detention wherever served, for a term of 12 months, or any greater punishment'.

(3) In subsection (1)(b) after 'imprisonment' insert ', or any form of detention wherever served,'.

(4) In subsections (2) and (3) for '12 months' substitute '6 months'.

10.

(1) Section 6 is amended as follows.

(2) In subsection (1), omit paragraph (a).

(3) In subsection (4) after paragraph (a) insert—

'(aa) an offence which is not punishable with imprisonment or any other form of detention;

(ab) an offence in respect of which he will not be detained in connection with his trial, sentence or appeal;

(ac) an offence in respect of which an appropriate authority is satisfied that a sentence of imprisonment or any other form of detention will be imposed only if he has specifically waived the right which (but for this paragraph) he would have not to be dealt with for the offence;'.

(4) [...][147]

(5) After subsection (6) insert—

'(6A) Subsection (4) above does not apply if

(a) the relevant foreign state has made a declaration under Article 11 of the 1996 Convention, and

(b) no indication has been given by the Secretary of State or the Scottish Ministers that consent should not be deemed to have been given in the person's case.'.

11.

(1) Section 18 is amended as follows.

[147] Repealed by SI 2002/1662.

(2) In subsection (1) after paragraph (b) insert—
'(ba) an offence which is not punishable with imprisonment; or
(bb) an offence in respect of which no custodial sentence will be imposed; or
(bc) an offence in connection with which the person returned will not be detained in custody; or
(bd) an offence in respect of which he has notified the court in writing that he waives the right which (but for this paragraph) he would have not to be tried for the offence; or'.

(3) After subsection (1) insert—
'(1A) Subsection (1) above does not apply if—
(a) the foreign state has made a declaration under Article 11 of the 1996 Convention, and
(b) no indication has been given by the foreign state that consent should not be deemed to have been given in the person's case.
[(1B) Where the foreign state has made a declaration under Article 6(3) of the 1996 Convention, fiscal offences, other than those connected with excise, value added tax or customs, are excluded from paragraph (ba) to (bd) of subsection (1) above.]'.[148]

12.

(1) Section 26 is amended as follows.

(2) For subsection (1) substitute—

'(1) In extradition proceedings in relation to a person whose return has been requested by a foreign state, a copy of an arrest warrant or certificate of conviction issued in the foreign state shall be deemed duly authenticated if it purports to be certified as a true copy of the original by a judicial or other authority of the state.'.

(3) In subsection (2) for '(1)(b)' substitute '(1)'.][149]

SCHEDULE 2
Repeals

SECTION 37

Chapter	Short title	Extent of repeal
33 & 34 Vict c 52.	Extradition Act 1870.	The whole Act.
36 & 37 Vict c 60.	Extradition Act 1873.	In section 1, the words from the beginning to 'and', in the fourth place where it occurs and the word 'alone'.
		Sections 3 and 4.
		Sections 6 to 8.
		The Schedule.
36 & 37 Vict c 88.	Slave Trade Act 1873.	Section 27.
58 & 59 Vict c 33.	Extradition Act 1895.	The whole Act.
6 Edw 7 c 15.	Extradition Act 1906.	The whole Act.
22 & 23 Geo 5 c 39.	Extradition Act 1932.	The whole Act.
25 & 26 Geo 5 c 25.	Counterfeit Currency (Convention) Act 1935.	Section 6(4).
4 & 5 Eliz 2 c 69.	Sexual Offences Act 1956.	In Schedule 3, the entry relating to the Extradition Act 1873.
9 & 10 Eliz 2 c 60.	Suicide Act 1961.	In Schedule 1, in Part II, the entry relating to the Extradition Act 1870.
1967 c 58.	Criminal Law Act 1967.	Section 4(6).
		Section 11(2)(a)(i).
1967 c 68.	Fugitive Offenders Act 1967.	The whole Act.

148 Amended by SI 2002/1662.
149 Inserted by SI 2002/419.

1968 c 60.	Theft Act 1968.	In Part II of Schedule 2, the entry relating to the Extradition Act 1873.
1969 c 12.	Genocide Act 1969.	In section 2, subsection (1), and in subsection (2), the words 'the Acts mentioned in subsection (1) of this section, the Extradition Act 1873 and'.
1969 c 54.	Children and Young Persons Act 1969.	Section 60.
1971 c 38.	Misuse of Drugs Act 1971.	Section 33.
1971 c 48.	Criminal Damage Act 1971.	Section 11(4).
1973 c 62.	Powers of Criminal Courts Act 1973.	In Schedule 5, paragraph 15.
1978 c 17.	Internationally Protected Persons Act 1978.	Section 3.
		Section 4(1).
1978 c 26.	Suppression of Terrorism Act 1978.	Section 1(3)(a) and (b).
		Section 2(1).
		Section 3.
1978 c 31.	Theft Act 1978.	Section 5(3).
1978 c 37.	Protection of Children Act 1978.	Section 1(6).
1981 c 61.	British Nationality Act 1981.	In Schedule 7, the entry relating to the Fugitive Offenders Act 1967.
1982 c 16.	Civil Aviation Act 1982.	Section 93.
1982 c 28.	Taking of Hostages Act 1982.	Sections 3(1) and (4).
		Section 4.
		Section 5(1).
1982 c 36.	Aviation Security Act 1982.	Section 9.
		Section 39(1).
1983 c 18.	Nuclear Material (Offences) Act 1983.	Section 5.
		Section 7(1).
1985 c 38.	Prohibition of Female Circumcision Act 1985.	Section 3(1).
1988 c 33.	Criminal Justice Act 1988.	Sections 1 to 21.
		Sections 136 and 137.
		Section 138(2) and (3).
		Schedule 1.
		In Schedule 15, paragraphs 34, 54, 55, 57, 81, 83 to 88 and 95 and 96.
1989 c 4.	Prevention of Terrorism (Temporary Provisions) Act 1989.	In Schedule 8, paragraph 1.

APPENDIX E3

Extradition Act 2003

(c. 41)

An Act to make provision about extradition.

[20th November 2003]

BE IT ENACTED by the Queen's most Excellent Majesty, by and with the advice and consent of the Lords Spiritual and Temporal, and Commons, in this present Parliament assembled, and by the authority of the same, as follows:—

CONTENTS

Part 1
Extradition to Category 1 Territories

Introduction

Arrest

The initial hearing

The extradition hearing

MATTERS ARISING BEFORE END OF EXTRADITION HEARING

APPEALS

TIME FOR EXTRADITION

WITHDRAWAL OF PART 1 WARRANT

COMPETING PART 1 WARRANTS

CONSENT TO EXTRADITION

POST-EXTRADITION MATTERS

Post-extradition matters

Costs

Repatriation cases

Interpretation

Part 3
Extradition to the United Kingdom

Extradition from category 1 territories

Extradition from category 2 territories

General

Part 4
Police Powers

Warrants And Orders

Search and seizure without warrant

Treatment following arrest

Delivery of seized property

Codes of practice

General

Part 5
Miscellaneous and General

British overseas territories

Competing extradition claims

Legal aid

Re-extradition

Conduct of extradition proceedings

Parties to international conventions

Special extradition arrangements

Human rights

Genocide etc

Custody and bail

Evidence

Other miscellaneous provisions

Part 1
Extradition to Category 1 territories

INTRODUCTION

1. Extradition to category 1 territories

(1) This Part deals with extradition from the United Kingdom to the territories designated for the purposes of this Part by order made by the Secretary of State.
(2) In this Act references to category 1 territories are to the territories designated for the purposes of this Part.
(3) A territory may not be designated for the purposes of this Part if a person found guilty in the territory of a criminal offence may be sentenced to death for the offence under the general criminal law of the territory.

2. Part 1 warrant and certificate

(1) This section applies if the designated authority receives a Part 1 warrant in respect of a person.
(2) A Part 1 warrant is an arrest warrant which is issued by a judicial authority of a category 1 territory and which contains—
   (a) the statement referred to in subsection (3) and the information referred to in subsection (4), or
   (b) the statement referred to in subsection (5) and the information referred to in subsection (6).
(3) The statement is one that—

(a) the person in respect of whom the Part 1 warrant is issued is accused in the category 1 territory of the commission of an offence specified in the warrant, and
(b) the Part 1 warrant is issued with a view to his arrest and extradition to the category 1 territory for the purpose of being prosecuted for the offence.

(4) The information is—
(a) particulars of the person's identity;
(b) particulars of any other warrant issued in the category 1 territory for the person's arrest in respect of the offence;
(c) particulars of the circumstances in which the person is alleged to have committed the offence, including the conduct alleged to constitute the offence, the time and place at which he is alleged to have committed the offence and any provision of the law of the category 1 territory under which the conduct is alleged to constitute an offence;
(d) particulars of the sentence which may be imposed under the law of the category 1 territory in respect of the offence if the person is convicted of it.

(5) The statement is one that—
(a) the person in respect of whom the Part 1 warrant is issued [has been convicted][1] of an offence specified in the warrant by a court in the category 1 territory, and
(b) the Part 1 warrant is issued with a view to his arrest and extradition to the category 1 territory for the purpose of being sentenced for the offence or of serving a sentence of imprisonment or another form of detention imposed in respect of the offence.

(6) The information is—
(a) particulars of the person's identity;
(b) particulars of the conviction;
(c) particulars of any other warrant issued in the category 1 territory for the person's arrest in respect of the offence;
(d) particulars of the sentence which may be imposed under the law of the category 1 territory in respect of the offence, if the person has not been sentenced for the offence;
(e) particulars of the sentence which has been imposed under the law of the category 1 territory in respect of the offence, if the person has been sentenced for the offence.

(7) The designated authority may issue a certificate under this section if it believes that the authority which issued the Part 1 warrant has the function of issuing arrest warrants in the category 1 territory.

(8) A certificate under this section must certify that the authority which issued the Part 1 warrant has the function of issuing arrest warrants in the category 1 territory.

(9) The designated authority is the authority designated for the purposes of this Part by order made by the Secretary of State.

(10) An order made under subsection (9) may—
(a) designate more than one authority;
(b) designate different authorities for different parts of the United Kingdom.

Arrest

3. Arrest under certified Part 1 warrant

(1) This section applies if a certificate is issued under section 2 in respect of a Part 1 warrant issued in respect of a person.

(2) The warrant may be executed by a constable or a customs officer in any part of the United Kingdom.

[(3) The warrant may be executed by a service policeman anywhere, but only if the person is subject to service law or is a civilian subject to service discipline.][2]

(5) The warrant may be executed even if neither the warrant nor a copy of it is in the possession of the person executing it at the time of the arrest.

(6) ...[3]

[1] Amended by the Police and Justice Act 2006.
[2] Amended by the Armed Forces Act 2006.
[3] Amended by the Armed Forces Act 2006.

4. Person arrested under Part 1 warrant

(1) This section applies if a person is arrested under a Part 1 warrant.
(2) A copy of the warrant must be given to the person as soon as practicable after his arrest.
(3) The person must be brought as soon as practicable before the appropriate judge.
(4) If subsection (2) is not complied with and the person applies to the judge to be discharged, the judge may order his discharge.
(5) If subsection (3) is not complied with and the person applies to the judge to be discharged, the judge must order his discharge.
(6) A person arrested under the warrant must be treated as continuing in legal custody until he is brought before the appropriate judge under subsection (3) or he is discharged under subsection (4) or (5).

5. Provisional arrest

(1) A constable, a customs officer or a service policeman may arrest a person without a warrant if he has reasonable grounds for believing—
  (a) that a Part 1 warrant has been or will be issued in respect of the person by an authority of a category 1 territory, and
  (b) that the authority has the function of issuing arrest warrants in the category 1 territory.
(2) A constable or a customs officer may arrest a person under subsection (1) in any part of the United Kingdom.
[(3) A service policeman may arrest a person under subsection (1) only if the person is subject to service law or is a civilian subject to service discipline.
(4) If a service policeman has power to arrest a person under subsection (1) he may exercise the power anywhere.][4]

6. Person arrested under section 5

(1) This section applies if a person is arrested under section 5.
[(2) The person must be brought before the appropriate judge within 48 hours starting with the time when the person is arrested.
(2A) The documents specified in subsection (4) must be produced to the judge within 48 hours starting with the time when the person is arrested but this is subject to any extension under subsection (3B).
(2B) Subsection (3) applies if—
  (a) the person has been brought before the judge in compliance with subsection (2); but
  (b) documents have not been produced to the judge in compliance with subsection (2A).
(3) The person must be brought before the judge when the documents are produced to the judge.
(3A) While the person is before the judge in pursuance of subsection (2), the authority of the category 1 territory may apply to the judge for an extension of the 48 hour period mentioned in subsection (2A) by a further 48 hours.
(3B) The judge may grant an extension if the judge decides that subsection (2A) could not reasonably be complied with within the initial 48 hour period.
(3C) The judge must decide whether that subsection could reasonably be so complied with on a balance of probabilities.
(3D) Notice of an application under subsection (3A) must be given in accordance with rules of court.][5]
(4) The documents are—
  (a) a Part 1 warrant in respect of the person;
  (b) a certificate under section 2 in respect of the warrant.
(5) A copy of the warrant must be given to the person as soon as practicable after his arrest.
[(5A) Subsection (5B) applies if—
  (a) the person is before the judge in pursuance of subsection (2); and
  (b) the documents specified in subsection (4) have not been produced to the judge.

---

[4] Amended by the Armed Forces Act 2006.
[5] Amended by the Policing and Crime Act 2009.

(5B) The judge must remand the person in custody or on bail (subject to subsection (6)).][6]

(6) If subsection (2)[, (2A) or (3)][7] is not complied with and the person applies to the judge to be discharged, the judge must order his discharge.

(7) If subsection (5) is not complied with and the person applies to the judge to be discharged, the judge may order his discharge.

(8) The person must be treated as continuing in legal custody until he is brought before the appropriate judge under subsection (2) or he is discharged under subsection (6) or (7).

[(8A) In calculating a period of 48 hours for the purposes of this section no account is to be taken of—

(a) any Saturday or Sunday;

(b) Christmas Day;

(c) Good Friday; or

(d) any day falling within subsection (8B).

(8B) The following days fall within this subsection—

(a) in Scotland, any day prescribed under section 8(2) of the Criminal Procedure (Scotland) Act 1995 as a court holiday in the court of the appropriate judge;

(b) in any part of the United Kingdom, any day that is a bank holiday under the Banking and Financial Dealings Act 1971 in that part of the United Kingdom.][8]

(9) Subsection (10) applies if—

(a) a person is arrested under section 5 on the basis of a belief that a Part 1 warrant has been or will be issued in respect of him;

(b) the person is discharged under subsection (6) or (7).

(10) The person must not be arrested again under section 5 on the basis of a belief relating to the same Part 1 warrant.

The initial hearing

7. Identity of person arrested

(1) This section applies if—

(a) a person arrested under a Part 1 warrant is brought before the appropriate judge under section 4(3), or

(b) a person [arrested under section 5 is brought before the appropriate judge under section 6 and section 6(2A)][9] is complied with in relation to him.

(2) The judge must decide whether the person brought before him is the person in respect of whom—

(a) the warrant referred to in subsection (1)(a) was issued, or

(b) the warrant referred to in section 6(4) was issued.

(3) The judge must decide the question in subsection (2) on a balance of probabilities.

(4) If the judge decides the question in subsection (2) in the negative he must order the person's discharge.

(5) If the judge decides that question in the affirmative he must proceed under section 8.

(6) In England and Wales, the judge has the same powers (as nearly as may be) as a magistrates' court would have if the proceedings were the summary trial of an information against the person.

(7) In Scotland—

(a) the judge has the same powers (as nearly as may be) as if the proceedings were summary proceedings in respect of an offence alleged to have been committed by the person; but

(b) in his making any decision under subsection (2) evidence from a single source shall be sufficient.

(8) In Northern Ireland, the judge has the same powers (as nearly as may be) as a magistrates' court would have if the proceedings were the hearing and determination of a complaint against the person.

(9) If the judge exercises his power to adjourn the proceedings he must remand the person in custody or on bail.

(10) [If the person is remanded in custody, the appropriate judge may][10] later grant bail.

---

[6] Amended by the Policing and Crime Act 2009.

[7] Amended by the Policing and Crime Act 2009.

[8] Amended by the Policing and Crime Act 2009.

[9] Amended by the Policing and Crime Act 2009.

[10] Amended by the Police and Justice Act 2006.

8. Remand etc.

(1) If the judge is required to proceed under this section he must—
  (a) fix a date on which the extradition hearing is to begin;
  (b) inform the person of the contents of the Part 1 warrant;
  (c) give the person the required information about consent;
  (d) remand the person in custody or on bail.
(2) [If the person is remanded in custody, the appropriate judge may][11] later grant bail.
(3) The required information about consent is—
  (a) that the person may consent to his extradition to the category 1 territory in which the Part 1 warrant was issued;
  (b) an explanation of the effect of consent and the procedure that will apply if he gives consent;
  (c) that consent must be given before the judge and is irrevocable.
(4) The date fixed under subsection (1) must not be later than the end of the permitted period, which is 21 days starting with the date of the arrest referred to in section 7(1)(a) or (b).
(5) If before the date fixed under subsection (1) (or this subsection) a party to the proceedings applies to the judge for a later date to be fixed and the judge believes it to be in the interests of justice to do so, he may fix a later date; and this subsection may apply more than once.
(6) Subsections (7) and (8) apply if the extradition hearing does not begin on or before the date fixed under this section.
(7) If the person applies to the judge to be discharged the judge must order his discharge, unless reasonable cause is shown for the delay.
(8) If no application is made under subsection (7) the judge must order the person's discharge on the first occasion after the date fixed under this section when the person appears or is brought before the judge, unless reasonable cause is shown for the delay.

[8A. Person charged with offence in United Kingdom before extradition hearing

(1) This section applies if—
  (a) a person has been brought before the appropriate judge under section 4(3) or 6(2) but the extradition hearing has not begun; and
  (b) the judge is informed that the person is charged with an offence in the United Kingdom.
(2) The judge must order further proceedings in respect of the extradition to be adjourned until one of these occurs—
  (a) the charge is disposed of;
  (b) the charge is withdrawn;
  (c) proceedings in respect of the charge are discontinued;
  (d) an order is made for the charge to lie on the file, or in relation to Scotland, the diet is deserted *pro loco et tempore.*
(3) If a sentence of imprisonment or another form of detention is imposed in respect of the offence charged, the judge may order further proceedings in respect of the extradition to be adjourned until the person is released from detention pursuant to the sentence (whether on licence or otherwise).][12]

[8B. Person serving sentence in United Kingdom before extradition hearing

(1) This section applies if—
  (a) a person has been brought before the appropriate judge under section 4(3) or 6(2) but the extradition hearing has not begun; and
  (b) the judge is informed that the person is in custody serving a sentence of imprisonment or another form of detention in the United Kingdom.
(2) The judge may order further proceedings in respect of the extradition to be adjourned until the person is released from detention pursuant to the sentence (whether on licence or otherwise).
(3) In a case where further proceedings in respect of the extradition are adjourned under subsection (2)—

[11] Amended by the Police and Justice Act 2006.
[12] Amended by the Policing and Crime Act 2009.

(a) section 131 of the Magistrates' Courts Act 1980 (remand of accused already in custody) has effect as if a reference to 28 clear days in subsection (1) or (2) of that section were a reference to six months;
(b) Article 47(2) of the Magistrates' Courts (Northern Ireland) Order 1981 (period of remand in custody) has effect as if a reference to 28 days in—
   (i) sub-paragraph (a)(iii), or
   (ii) the words after sub-paragraph (b),
   were a reference to six months.][13]

The extradition hearing

9. Judge's powers at extradition hearing

(1) In England and Wales, at the extradition hearing the appropriate judge has the same powers (as nearly as may be) as a magistrates' court would have if the proceedings were the summary trial of an information against the person in respect of whom the Part 1 warrant was issued.
(2) In Scotland, at the extradition hearing the appropriate judge has the same powers (as nearly as may be) as if the proceedings were summary proceedings in respect of an offence alleged to have been committed by the person in respect of whom the Part 1 warrant was issued.
(3) In Northern Ireland, at the extradition hearing the appropriate judge has the same powers (as nearly as may be) as a magistrates' court would have if the proceedings were the hearing and determination of a complaint against the person in respect of whom the Part 1 warrant was issued.
(4) If the judge adjourns the extradition hearing he must remand the person in custody or on bail.
(5) [If the person is remanded in custody, the appropriate judge may][14] later grant bail.

10. Initial stage of extradition hearing

(1) This section applies if a person in respect of whom a Part 1 warrant is issued appears or is brought before the appropriate judge for the extradition hearing.
(2) The judge must decide whether the offence specified in the Part 1 warrant is an extradition offence.
(3) If the judge decides the question in subsection (2) in the negative he must order the person's discharge.
(4) If the judge decides that question in the affirmative he must proceed under section 11.

11. Bars to extradition

(1) If the judge is required to proceed under this section he must decide whether the person's extradition to the category 1 territory is barred by reason of—
   (a) the rule against double jeopardy;
   (b) extraneous considerations;
   (c) the passage of time;
   (d) the person's age;
   (e) hostage-taking considerations;
   (f) speciality;
   (g) the person's earlier extradition to the United Kingdom from another category 1 territory;
   (h) the person's earlier extradition to the United Kingdom from a non-category 1 territory.
   [(i) the person's earlier transfer to the United Kingdom by the International Criminal Court.][15]
(2) [Sections 12 to 19A][16] apply for the interpretation of subsection (1).
(3) If the judge decides any of the questions in subsection (1) in the affirmative he must order the person's discharge.
(4) If the judge decides those questions in the negative and the person is alleged to be unlawfully at large after conviction of the extradition offence, the judge must proceed under section 20.
(5) If the judge decides those questions in the negative and the person is accused of the commission of the extradition offence but is not alleged to be unlawfully at large after conviction of it, the judge must proceed under section 21.

---

[13] Amended by the Policing and Crime Act 2009.
[14] Amended by the Police and Justice Act 2006.
[15] Amended by the Police and Justice Act 2006.
[16] Amended by the Police and Justice Act 2006.

12. Rule against double jeopardy

A person's extradition to a category 1 territory is barred by reason of the rule against double jeopardy if (and only if) it appears that he would be entitled to be discharged under any rule of law relating to previous acquittal or conviction on the assumption—

(a) that the conduct constituting the extradition offence constituted an offence in the part of the United Kingdom where the judge exercises jurisdiction;
(b) that the person were charged with the extradition offence in that part of the United Kingdom.

13. Extraneous considerations

A person's extradition to a category 1 territory is barred by reason of extraneous considerations if (and only if) it appears that—

(a) the Part 1 warrant issued in respect of him (though purporting to be issued on account of the extradition offence) is in fact issued for the purpose of prosecuting or punishing him on account of his race, religion, nationality, gender, sexual orientation or political opinions, or
(b) if extradited he might be prejudiced at his trial or punished, detained or restricted in his personal liberty by reason of his race, religion, nationality, gender, sexual orientation or political opinions.

14. Passage of time

A person's extradition to a category 1 territory is barred by reason of the passage of time if (and only if) it appears that it would be unjust or oppressive to extradite him by reason of the passage of time since he is alleged to have committed the extradition offence or [since he is alleged to have—

(a) committed the extradition offence (where he is accused of its commission), or
(b) become unlawfully at large (where he is alleged to have been convicted of it)].[17]

15. Age

A person's extradition to a category 1 territory is barred by reason of his age if (and only if) it would be conclusively presumed because of his age that he could not be guilty of the extradition offence on the assumption—

(a) that the conduct constituting the extradition offence constituted an offence in the part of the United Kingdom where the judge exercises jurisdiction;
(b) that the person carried out the conduct when the extradition offence was committed (or alleged to be committed);
(c) that the person carried out the conduct in the part of the United Kingdom where the judge exercises jurisdiction.

16. Hostage-taking considerations

(1) A person's extradition to a category 1 territory is barred by reason of hostage-taking considerations if (and only if) the territory is a party to the Hostage-taking Convention and it appears that—
  (a) if extradited he might be prejudiced at his trial because communication between him and the appropriate authorities would not be possible, and
  (b) the act or omission constituting the extradition offence also constitutes an offence under section 1 of the Taking of Hostages Act 1982 (c. 28) or an attempt to commit such an offence.
(2) The appropriate authorities are the authorities of the territory which are entitled to exercise rights of protection in relation to him.
(3) A certificate issued by the Secretary of State that a territory is a party to the Hostage-taking Convention is conclusive evidence of that fact for the purposes of subsection (1).
(4) The Hostage-taking Convention is the International Convention against the Taking of Hostages opened for signature at New York on 18 December 1979.

[17] Amended by the Police and Justice Act 2006.

17. Speciality

(1) A person's extradition to a category 1 territory is barred by reason of speciality if (and only if) there are no speciality arrangements with the category 1 territory.

(2) There are speciality arrangements with a category 1 territory if, under the law of that territory or arrangements made between it and the United Kingdom, a person who is extradited to the territory from the United Kingdom may be dealt with in the territory for an offence committed before his extradition only if—

(a) the offence is one falling within subsection (3), or

(b) the condition in subsection (4) is satisfied.

(3) The offences are—

(a) the offence in respect of which the person is extradited;

(b) an extradition offence disclosed by the same facts as that offence;

(c) an extradition offence in respect of which the appropriate judge gives his consent under section 55 to the person being dealt with;

(d) an offence which is not punishable with imprisonment or another form of detention;

(e) an offence in respect of which the person will not be detained in connection with his trial, sentence or appeal;

(f) an offence in respect of which the person waives the right that he would have (but for this paragraph) not to be dealt with for the offence.

(4) The condition is that the person is given an opportunity to leave the category 1 territory and—

(a) he does not do so before the end of the permitted period, or

(b) if he does so before the end of the permitted period, he returns there.

(5) The permitted period is 45 days starting with the day on which the person arrives in the category 1 territory.

(6) Arrangements made with a category 1 territory which is a Commonwealth country or a British overseas territory may be made for a particular case or more generally.

(7) A certificate issued by or under the authority of the Secretary of State confirming the existence of arrangements with a category 1 territory which is a Commonwealth country or a British overseas territory and stating the terms of the arrangements is conclusive evidence of those matters.

18. Earlier extradition to United Kingdom from category 1 territory

A person's extradition to a category 1 territory is barred by reason of his earlier extradition to the United Kingdom from another category 1 territory if (and only if)—

(a) the person was extradited to the United Kingdom from another category 1 territory (the extraditing territory);

(b) under arrangements between the United Kingdom and the extraditing territory, that territory's consent is required to the person's extradition from the United Kingdom to the category 1 territory in respect of the extradition offence under consideration;

(c) that consent has not been given on behalf of the extraditing territory.

19. Earlier extradition to United Kingdom from non-category 1 territory

A person's extradition to a category 1 territory is barred by reason of his earlier extradition to the United Kingdom from a non-category 1 territory if (and only if)—

(a) the person was extradited to the United Kingdom from a territory that is not a category 1 territory (the extraditing territory);

(b) under arrangements between the United Kingdom and the extraditing territory, that territory's consent is required to the person's being dealt with in the United Kingdom in respect of the extradition offence under consideration;

(c) consent has not been given on behalf of the extraditing territory to the person's extradition from the United Kingdom to the category 1 territory in respect of the extradition offence under consideration.

[19A. Earlier transfer to United Kingdom by International Criminal Court

(1) A person's extradition to a category 1 territory is barred by reason of his earlier transfer by the International Criminal Court if (and only if)—

(a) the person was transferred to the United Kingdom to serve a sentence imposed by the Court;
(b) under arrangements between the United Kingdom and the Court, the consent of the Presidency of the Court is required to the person's extradition from the United Kingdom to the category 1 territory in respect of the extradition offence under consideration;
(c) that consent has not been given.

(2) Subsection (1) does not apply if the person has served the sentence imposed by the Court and has subsequently—
(a) remained voluntarily in the United Kingdom for more than 30 days, or
(b) left the United Kingdom and returned to it.][18]

20. Case where person has been convicted

(1) If the judge is required to proceed under this section (by virtue of section 11) he must decide whether the person was convicted in his presence.
(2) If the judge decides the question in subsection (1) in the affirmative he must proceed under section 21.
(3) If the judge decides that question in the negative he must decide whether the person deliberately absented himself from his trial.
(4) If the judge decides the question in subsection (3) in the affirmative he must proceed under section 21.
(5) If the judge decides that question in the negative he must decide whether the person would be entitled to a retrial or (on appeal) to a review amounting to a retrial.
(6) If the judge decides the question in subsection (5) in the affirmative he must proceed under section 21.
(7) If the judge decides that question in the negative he must order the person's discharge.
(8) The judge must not decide the question in subsection (5) in the affirmative unless, in any proceedings that it is alleged would constitute a retrial or a review amounting to a retrial, the person would have these rights—
(a) the right to defend himself in person or through legal assistance of his own choosing or, if he had not sufficient means to pay for legal assistance, to be given it free when the interests of justice so required;
(b) the right to examine or have examined witnesses against him and to obtain the attendance and examination of witnesses on his behalf under the same conditions as witnesses against him.

21. Human rights

(1) If the judge is required to proceed under this section (by virtue of section 11 or 20) he must decide whether the person's extradition would be compatible with the Convention rights within the meaning of the Human Rights Act 1998 (c. 42).
(2) If the judge decides the question in subsection (1) in the negative he must order the person's discharge.
(3) If the judge decides that question in the affirmative he must order the person to be extradited to the category 1 territory in which the warrant was issued.
(4) If the judge makes an order under subsection (3) he must remand the person in custody or on bail to wait for his extradition to the category 1 territory.
(5) [If the person is remanded in custody, the appropriate judge may][19] later grant bail.

Matters arising before end of extradition hearing

22. Person charged with offence in United Kingdom

(1) This section applies if at any time in the extradition hearing the judge is informed that the person in respect of whom the Part 1 warrant is issued is charged with an offence in the United Kingdom.
(2) The judge must adjourn the extradition hearing until one of these occurs—
(a) the charge is disposed of;

[18] Amended by the Police and Justice Act 2006.
[19] Amended by the Police and Justice Act 2006.

(b) the charge is withdrawn;
(c) proceedings in respect of the charge are discontinued;
(d) an order is made for the charge to lie on the file, or in relation to Scotland, the diet is deserted *pro loco et tempore*.

(3) If a sentence of imprisonment or another form of detention is imposed in respect of the offence charged, the judge may adjourn the extradition hearing until [the person is released from detention pursuant to the sentence (whether on licence or otherwise)].[20]

(4) If before he adjourns the extradition hearing under subsection (2) the judge has decided under section 11 whether the person's extradition is barred by reason of the rule against double jeopardy, the judge must decide that question again after the resumption of the hearing.

23. Person serving sentence in United Kingdom

(1) This section applies if at any time in the extradition hearing the judge is informed that the person in respect of whom the Part 1 warrant is issued is [in custody][21] serving a sentence of imprisonment or another form of detention in the United Kingdom.

(2) The judge may adjourn the extradition hearing until [the person is released from detention pursuant to the sentence (whether on licence or otherwise)].[22]

[(3) In a case where an extradition hearing is adjourned under subsection (2)—
(a) section 131 of the Magistrates' Courts Act 1980 (remand of accused already in custody) has effect as if a reference to 28 clear days in subsection (1) or (2) of that section were a reference to six months;
(b) Article 47(2) of the Magistrates' Courts (Northern Ireland) Order 1981 (S.I. 1981/1675 (N.I. 26)) (period of remand in custody) has effect as if a reference to 28 days in—
(i) paragraph (a)(iii), or
(ii) the words after paragraph (b),
were a reference to six months.][23]

24. Extradition request

(1) This section applies if at any time in the extradition hearing the judge is informed that—
(a) a certificate has been issued under section 70 in respect of a request for the person's extradition;
(b) the request has not been disposed of;
(c) an order has been made under section 179(2) for further proceedings on the warrant to be deferred until the request has been disposed of.

(2) The judge must remand the person in custody or on bail.

(3) [If the person is remanded in custody, the appropriate judge may][24] later grant bail.

25. Physical or mental condition

(1) This section applies if at any time in the extradition hearing it appears to the judge that the condition in subsection (2) is satisfied.

(2) The condition is that the physical or mental condition of the person in respect of whom the Part 1 warrant is issued is such that it would be unjust or oppressive to extradite him.

(3) The judge must—
(a) order the person's discharge, or
(b) adjourn the extradition hearing until it appears to him that the condition in subsection (2) is no longer satisfied.

Appeals

26. Appeal against extradition order

(1) If the appropriate judge orders a person's extradition under this Part, the person may appeal to the High Court against the order.

---

[20] Amended by the Policing and Crime Act 2009.
[21] Amended by the Policing and Crime Act 2009.
[22] Amended by the Policing and Crime Act 2009.
[23] Amended by the Police and Justice Act 2006.
[24] Amended by the Police and Justice Act 2006.

(2) But subsection (1) does not apply if the order is made under section 46 or 48.
(3) An appeal under this section may be brought on a question of law or fact.
(4) Notice of an appeal under this section must be given in accordance with rules of court before the end of the permitted period, which is 7 days starting with the day on which the order is made.

27. Court's powers on appeal under section 26

(1) On an appeal under section 26 the High Court may—
  (a) allow the appeal;
  (b) dismiss the appeal.
(2) The court may allow the appeal only if the conditions in subsection (3) or the conditions in subsection (4) are satisfied.
(3) The conditions are that—
  (a) the appropriate judge ought to have decided a question before him at the extradition hearing differently;
  (b) if he had decided the question in the way he ought to have done, he would have been required to order the person's discharge.
(4) The conditions are that—
  (a) an issue is raised that was not raised at the extradition hearing or evidence is available that was not available at the extradition hearing;
  (b) the issue or evidence would have resulted in the appropriate judge deciding a question before him at the extradition hearing differently;
  (c) if he had decided the question in that way, he would have been required to order the person's discharge.
(5) If the court allows the appeal it must—
  (a) order the person's discharge;
  (b) quash the order for his extradition.

28. Appeal against discharge at extradition hearing

(1) If the judge orders a person's discharge at the extradition hearing the authority which issued the Part 1 warrant may appeal to the High Court against the relevant decision.
(2) But subsection (1) does not apply if the order for the person's discharge was under section 41.
(3) The relevant decision is the decision which resulted in the order for the person's discharge.
(4) An appeal under this section may be brought on a question of law or fact.
(5) Notice of an appeal under this section must be given in accordance with rules of court before the end of the permitted period, which is 7 days starting with the day on which the order for the person's discharge is made.

29. Court's powers on appeal under section 28

(1) On an appeal under section 28 the High Court may—
  (a) allow the appeal;
  (b) dismiss the appeal.
(2) The court may allow the appeal only if the conditions in subsection (3) or the conditions in subsection (4) are satisfied.
(3) The conditions are that—
  (a) the judge ought to have decided the relevant question differently;
  (b) if he had decided the question in the way he ought to have done, he would not have been required to order the person's discharge.
(4) The conditions are that—
  (a) an issue is raised that was not raised at the extradition hearing or evidence is available that was not available at the extradition hearing;
  (b) the issue or evidence would have resulted in the judge deciding the relevant question differently;
  (c) if he had decided the question in that way, he would not have been required to order the person's discharge.
(5) If the court allows the appeal it must—
  (a) quash the order discharging the person;

(b) remit the case to the judge;

(c) direct him to proceed as he would have been required to do if he had decided the relevant question differently at the extradition hearing.

(6) A question is the relevant question if the judge's decision on it resulted in the order for the person's discharge.

[(7) If the court allows the appeal it must remand the person in custody or on bail.

(8) If the court remands the person in custody it may later grant bail.][25]

30. Detention pending conclusion of appeal under section 28

(1) This section applies if immediately after the judge orders the person's discharge the judge is informed by the authority which issued the Part 1 warrant that it intends to appeal under section 28.

(2) The judge must remand the person in custody or on bail while the appeal is pending.

(3) [If the person is remanded in custody, the appropriate judge may][26] later grant bail.

(4) An appeal under section 28 ceases to be pending at the earliest of these times—

(a) when the proceedings on the appeal are discontinued;

[(b) when the High Court—

(i) allows the appeal, or

(ii) dismisses the appeal,

unless, where the appeal is dismissed, the authority immediately informs the court that it intends to apply for leave to appeal to the [Supreme Court];[27]][28]

(c) at the end of the permitted period, which is 28 days starting with the day on which leave to appeal to the [Supreme Court][29] against the decision of the High Court on the appeal is granted[, if no appeal to the [Supreme Court][30] is brought before the end of that period];[31]

(d) when there is no further step that can be taken by the authority which issued the Part 1 warrant in relation to the appeal (ignoring any power of a court to grant leave to take a step out of time).

(5) The preceding provisions of this section apply to Scotland with these modifications—

(a) in subsection (4)(b) omit the words from '[unless]'[32] to the end;

(b) omit subsection (4)(c).

31. Appeal to High Court: time limit for start of hearing

(1) Rules of court must prescribe the period (the relevant period) within which the High Court must begin to hear an appeal under section 26 or 28.

(2) Rules of court must provide for the relevant period to start with the date on which the person in respect of whom a Part 1 warrant is issued—

(a) was arrested under section 5, if he was arrested under that section;

(b) was arrested under the Part 1 warrant, if he was not arrested under section 5.

(3) The High Court must begin to hear the appeal before the end of the relevant period.

(4) The High Court may extend the relevant period if it believes it to be in the interests of justice to do so; and this subsection may apply more than once.

(5) The power in subsection (4) may be exercised even after the end of the relevant period.

(6) If subsection (3) is not complied with and the appeal is under section 26—

(a) the appeal must be taken to have been allowed by a decision of the High Court;

(b) the person whose extradition has been ordered must be taken to have been discharged by the High Court;

(c) the order for the person's extradition must be taken to have been quashed by the High Court.

(7) If subsection (3) is not complied with and the appeal is under section 28 the appeal must be taken to have been dismissed by a decision of the High Court.

---

25 Amended by the Police and Justice Act 2006.

26 Amended by the Police and Justice Act 2006.

27 Amended by the Constitutional Reform Act 2005.

28 Amended by the Police and Justice Act 2006.

29 Amended by the Constitutional Reform Act 2005.

30 Amended by the Constitutional Reform Act 2005.

31 Amended by the Police and Justice Act 2006.

32 Amended by the Police and Justice Act 2006.

32. Appeal to [Supreme Court][33]

(1) An appeal lies to the [Supreme Court][34] from a decision of the High Court on an appeal under section 26 or 28.
(2) An appeal under this section lies at the instance of—
  (a) the person in respect of whom the Part 1 warrant was issued;
  (b) the authority which issued the Part 1 warrant.
(3) An appeal under this section lies only with the leave of the High Court or the [Supreme Court].[35]
(4) Leave to appeal under this section must not be granted unless—
  (a) the High Court has certified that there is a point of law of general public importance involved in the decision, and
  (b) it appears to the court granting leave that the point is one which ought to be considered by the [Supreme Court].[36]
(5) An application to the High Court for leave to appeal under this section must be made before the end of the permitted period, which is 14 days starting with the day on which the court makes its decision on the appeal to it.
(6) An application to the [Supreme Court][37] for leave to appeal under this section must be made before the end of the permitted period, which is 14 days starting with the day on which the High Court refuses leave to appeal.
(7) If leave to appeal under this section is granted, the appeal must be brought before the end of the permitted period, which is 28 days starting with the day on which leave is granted.
(8) If subsection (7) is not complied with—
  (a) the appeal must be taken to have been brought;
  (b) the appeal must be taken to have been dismissed by the [Supreme Court][38] immediately after the end of the period permitted under that subsection.
(9) These must be ignored for the purposes of subsection (8)(b)—
  (a) any power of a court to extend the period permitted for bringing the appeal;
  (b) any power of a court to grant leave to take a step out of time.
[(10) The High Court may grant bail to a person appealing under this section, or applying for leave to appeal under this section, against the dismissal of his appeal under section 26.][39]
(11) Section 5 of the Appellate Jurisdiction Act 1876 (c. 59) (composition of House of Lords for hearing and determination of appeals) applies in relation to an appeal under this section or an application for leave to appeal under this section as it applies in relation to an appeal under that Act.
(12) An order of the House of Lords which provides for an application for leave to appeal under this section to be determined by a committee constituted in accordance with section 5 of the Appellate Jurisdiction Act 1876 may direct that the decision of the committee is taken on behalf of the House.
(13) The preceding provisions of this section do not apply to Scotland.

33. Powers of [Supreme Court][40] on appeal under section 32

(1) On an appeal under section 32 the [Supreme Court][41] may—
  (a) allow the appeal;
  (b) dismiss the appeal.
(2) Subsection (3) applies if—
  (a) the person in respect of whom the Part 1 warrant was issued brings an appeal under section 32, and
  (b) the [Supreme Court][42] allows the appeal.

---

33 Amended by the Constitutional Reform Act 2005.
34 Amended by the Constitutional Reform Act 2005.
35 Amended by the Constitutional Reform Act 2005.
36 Amended by the Constitutional Reform Act 2005.
37 Amended by the Constitutional Reform Act 2005.
38 Amended by the Constitutional Reform Act 2005.
39 Amended by the Police and Justice Act 2006.
40 Amended by the Constitutional Reform Act 2005.
41 Amended by the Constitutional Reform Act 2005.
42 Amended by the Constitutional Reform Act 2005.

(3) The [Supreme Court][43] must—
  (a) order the person's discharge;
  (b) quash the order for his extradition, if the appeal was against a decision of the High Court to dismiss an appeal under section 26.

(4) Subsection (5) applies if—
  (a) the High Court allows an appeal under section 26 by the person in respect of whom the Part 1 warrant was issued,
  (b) the authority which issued the warrant brings an appeal under section 32 against the decision of the High Court, and
  (c) the [Supreme Court][44] allows the appeal.

(5) The [Supreme Court][45] must—
  (a) quash the order of the High Court under section 27(5) discharging the person;
  (b) order the person to be extradited to the category 1 territory in which the warrant was issued.

(6) Subsections (7) and (8) apply if—
  (a) the High Court dismisses an appeal under section 28 against a decision made by the judge at the extradition hearing,
  (b) the authority which issued the Part 1 warrant brings an appeal under section 32 against the decision of the High Court, and
  (c) the [Supreme Court][46] allows the appeal.

(7) If the judge would have been required to order the person in respect of whom the warrant was issued to be extradited had he decided the relevant question differently, the [Supreme Court][47] must—
  (a) quash the order of the judge discharging the person;
  (b) order the person to be extradited to the category 1 territory in which the warrant was issued.

(8) In any other case, the [Supreme Court][48] must—
  (a) quash the order of the judge discharging the person in respect of whom the warrant was issued;
  (b) remit the case to the judge;
  (c) direct him to proceed as he would have been required to do if he had decided the relevant question differently at the extradition hearing.

(9) A question is the relevant question if the judge's decision on it resulted in the order for the person's discharge.

[(10) In a case where—
  (a) subsection (5) applies, or
  (b) subsections (7) and (8) apply,the [Supreme Court][49] must remand, in custody or on bail, the person in respect of whom the warrant was issued.

(11) If the [Supreme Court][50] remands the person in custody the High Court may later grant bail.][51]

[33A. Detention pending conclusion of certain appeals under section 32

(1) This section applies if immediately after the High Court orders the person's discharge the court is informed by the authority which issued the Part 1 warrant that it intends to appeal under section 32.

(2) The court must remand the person in custody or on bail while the appeal under section 32 is pending.

(3) If the court remands the person in custody it may later grant bail.

(4) An appeal under section 32 ceases to be pending at the earliest of these times—
  (a) when the proceedings on the appeal are discontinued;

[43] Amended by the Constitutional Reform Act 2005.
[44] Amended by the Constitutional Reform Act 2005.
[45] Amended by the Constitutional Reform Act 2005.
[46] Amended by the Constitutional Reform Act 2005.
[47] Amended by the Constitutional Reform Act 2005.
[48] Amended by the Constitutional Reform Act 2005.
[49] Amended by the Constitutional Reform Act 2005.
[50] Amended by the Constitutional Reform Act 2005.
[51] Amended by the Police and Justice Act 2006.

(b) at the end of the permitted period, which is 28 days starting with the day on which leave to appeal to the [Supreme Court][52] against the decision of the High Court on the appeal under section 26 is granted, if no appeal to the [Supreme Court][53] is brought before the end of that period;

(c) when there is no further step that can be taken by the authority which issued the Part 1 warrant in relation to the appeal (ignoring any power of a court to grant leave to take a step out of time).

(5) The preceding provisions of this section do not apply to Scotland.][54]

34. Appeals: general

A decision of the judge under this Part may be questioned in legal proceedings only by means of an appeal under this Part.

Time for extradition

35. Extradition where no appeal

(1) This section applies if—

(a) the appropriate judge orders a person's extradition to a category 1 territory under this Part, and

(b) no notice of an appeal under section 26 is given before the end of the period permitted under that section.

(2) But this section does not apply if the order is made under section 46 or 48.

(3) The person must be extradited to the category 1 territory before the end of the required period.

(4) The required period is—

(a) 10 days starting with [the first day after the period permitted under section 26 for giving notice of appeal against the judge's order],[55] or

(b) if the judge and the authority which issued the Part 1 warrant agree a later date, 10 days starting with the later date.

(5) If subsection (3) is not complied with and the person applies to the appropriate judge to be discharged the judge must order his discharge, unless reasonable cause is shown for the delay.

(6) These must be ignored for the purposes of subsection (1)(b)—

(a) any power of a court to extend the period permitted for giving notice of appeal;

(b) any power of a court to grant leave to take a step out of time.

36. Extradition following appeal

(1) This section applies if—

(a) there is an appeal to the High Court under section 26 against an order for a person's extradition to a category 1 territory, and

(b) the effect of the decision of the relevant court on the appeal is that the person is to be extradited there.

(2) The person must be extradited to the category 1 territory before the end of the required period.

(3) The required period is—

(a) 10 days starting with the day on which the decision of the relevant court on the appeal becomes final or proceedings on the appeal are discontinued, or

(b) if the relevant court and the authority which issued the Part 1 warrant agree a later date, 10 days starting with the later date.

(4) The relevant court is—

(a) the High Court, if there is no appeal to the [Supreme Court][56] against the decision of the High Court on the appeal;

(b) the [Supreme Court],[57] if there is such an appeal.

---

52 Amended by the Constitutional Reform Act 2005.

53 Amended by the Constitutional Reform Act 2005.

54 Amended by the Police and Justice Act 2006.

55 Amended by the Police and Justice Act 2006.

56 Amended by the Constitutional Reform Act 2005.

57 Amended by the Constitutional Reform Act 2005.

(5) The decision of the High Court on the appeal becomes final—
   (a) when the period permitted for applying to the High Court for leave to appeal to the [Supreme Court][58] ends, if there is no such application;
   (b) when the period permitted for applying to the [Supreme Court][59] for leave to appeal to it ends, if the High Court refuses leave to appeal and there is no application to the [Supreme Court][60] for leave to appeal;
   (c) when the [Supreme Court][61] refuses leave to appeal to it;
   (d) at the end of the permitted period, which is 28 days starting with the day on which leave to appeal to the [Supreme Court][62] is granted, if no such appeal is brought before the end of that period.

(6) These must be ignored for the purposes of subsection (5)—
   (a) any power of a court to extend the period permitted for applying for leave to appeal;
   (b) any power of a court to grant leave to take a step out of time.

(7) The decision of the [Supreme Court][63] on the appeal becomes final when it is made.

(8) If subsection (2) is not complied with and the person applies to the appropriate judge to be discharged the judge must order his discharge, unless reasonable cause is shown for the delay.

(9) The preceding provisions of this section apply to Scotland with these modifications—
   (a) in subsections (1) and (3) for 'relevant court' substitute 'High Court';
   (b) omit subsections (4) to (7).

37. Undertaking in relation to person serving sentence in United Kingdom

(1) This section applies if—
   (a) the appropriate judge orders a person's extradition to a category 1 territory under this Part;
   (b) the person is serving a sentence of imprisonment or another form of detention in the United Kingdom[, either—
      (i) in custody, or
      (ii) on licence].[64]

(2) But this section does not apply if the order is made under section 46 or 48.

(3) The judge may make the order for extradition subject to the condition that extradition is not to take place before he receives an undertaking given on behalf of the category 1 territory in terms specified by him.

(4) The terms which may be specified by the judge in relation to a person [within subsection (1)(b)(i) who is][65] accused in a category 1 territory of the commission of an offence include terms—
   (a) that the person be kept in custody until the conclusion of the proceedings against him for the offence and any other offence in respect of which he is permitted to be dealt with in the category 1 territory;
   (b) that the person be returned to the United Kingdom to serve the remainder of his sentence on the conclusion of those proceedings.

[(4A) The terms which may be specified by the judge in relation to a person within subsection (1)(b)(ii) who is accused in a category 1 territory of the commission of an offence include terms that the person be returned to the United Kingdom to serve the remainder of his sentence after serving any sentence imposed on him in the category 1 territory for—
   (a) the offence, and
   (b) any other offence in respect of which he is permitted to be dealt with in the category 1 territory.][66]

---

58 Amended by the Constitutional Reform Act 2005.
59 Amended by the Constitutional Reform Act 2005.
60 Amended by the Constitutional Reform Act 2005.
61 Amended by the Constitutional Reform Act 2005.
62 Amended by the Constitutional Reform Act 2005.
63 Amended by the Constitutional Reform Act 2005.
64 Amended by the Police and Justice Act 2006.
65 Amended by the Police and Justice Act 2006.
66 Amended by the Police and Justice Act 2006.

(5) The terms which may be specified by the judge in relation to a person alleged to be unlawfully at large after conviction of an offence by a court in a category 1 territory include terms that the person be returned to the United Kingdom to serve the remainder of his sentence after serving any sentence imposed on him in the category 1 territory for—
   (a) the offence, and
   (b) any other offence in respect of which he is permitted to be dealt with in the category 1 territory.
(6) Subsections (7) and (8) apply if the judge makes an order for extradition subject to a condition under subsection (3).
(7) If the judge does not receive the undertaking before the end of the period of 21 days starting with the day on which he makes the order and the person applies to the appropriate judge to be discharged, the judge must order his discharge.
(8) If the judge receives the undertaking before the end of that period—
   (a) in a case where section 35 applies, the required period for the purposes of section 35(3) is 10 days starting with the day on which the judge receives the undertaking;
   (b) in a case where section 36 applies, the required period for the purposes of section 36(2) is 10 days starting with the day on which the decision of the relevant court on the appeal becomes final (within the meaning of that section) or (if later) the day on which the judge receives the undertaking.
   [Paragraph (a) applies only if the day mentioned in that paragraph is later than the day mentioned in section 35(4)(a).][67]

38. Extradition following deferral for competing claim

(1) This section applies if—
   (a) an order is made under this Part for a person to be extradited to a category 1 territory in pursuance of a Part 1 warrant;
   (b) before the person is extradited to the territory an order is made under section 44(4)(b) or 179(2)(b) for the person's extradition in pursuance of the warrant to be deferred;
   (c) the appropriate judge makes an order under section 181(2) for the person's extradition in pursuance of the warrant to cease to be deferred.
(2) But this section does not apply if the order for the person's extradition is made under section 46 or 48.
(3) In a case where section 35 applies, the required period for the purposes of section 35(3) is 10 days starting with the day on which the order under section 181(2) is made.
   [This subsection applies only if the day on which the order is made is later than the day mentioned in section 35(4)(a).][68]
(4) In a case where section 36 applies, the required period for the purposes of section 36(2) is 10 days starting with the day on which the decision of the relevant court on the appeal becomes final (within the meaning of that section) or (if later) the day on which the order under section 181(2) is made.

39. Asylum claim

(1) This section applies if—
   (a) a person in respect of whom a Part 1 warrant is issued makes an asylum claim at any time in the relevant period;
   (b) an order is made under this Part for the person to be extradited in pursuance of the warrant.
(2) The relevant period is the period—
   (a) starting when a certificate is issued under section 2 in respect of the warrant;
   (b) ending when the person is extradited in pursuance of the warrant.
(3) The person must not be extradited in pursuance of the warrant before the asylum claim is finally determined; and sections 35, 36, 47 and 49 have effect subject to this.
(4) Subsection (3) is subject to section 40.
(5) If the Secretary of State allows the asylum claim, the claim is finally determined when he makes his decision on the claim.

---

[67] Amended by the Police and Justice Act 2006.
[68] Amended by the Police and Justice Act 2006.

(6) If the Secretary of State rejects the asylum claim, the claim is finally determined—
 (a) when the Secretary of State makes his decision on the claim, if there is no right to appeal against the Secretary of State's decision on the claim;
 (b) when the period permitted for appealing against the Secretary of State's decision on the claim ends, if there is such a right but there is no such appeal;
 (c) when the appeal against that decision is finally determined or is withdrawn or abandoned, if there is such an appeal.

(7) An appeal against the Secretary of State's decision on an asylum claim is not finally determined for the purposes of subsection (6) at any time when a further appeal or an application for leave to bring a further appeal—
 (a) has been instituted and has not been finally determined or withdrawn or abandoned, or
 (b) may be brought.

(8) The remittal of an appeal is not a final determination for the purposes of subsection (7).

(9) The possibility of an appeal out of time with leave must be ignored for the purposes of subsections (6) and (7).

40. Certificate in respect of asylum claimant

(1) Section 39(3) does not apply in relation to a person if the Secretary of State has certified that the conditions in subsection (2) or the conditions in subsection (3) are satisfied in relation to him.

(2) The conditions are that—
 (a) the category 1 territory to which the person's extradition has been ordered has accepted that, under standing arrangements, it is the responsible State in relation to the person's asylum claim;
 (b) in the opinion of the Secretary of State, the person is not a national or citizen of the territory.

(3) The conditions are that, in the opinion of the Secretary of State—
 (a) the person is not a national or citizen of the category 1 territory to which his extradition has been ordered;
 (b) the person's life and liberty would not be threatened in that territory by reason of his race, religion, nationality, political opinion or membership of a particular social group;
 (c) the government of the territory would not send the person to another country otherwise than in accordance with the Refugee Convention.

(4) In this section—
'the Refugee Convention' has the meaning given by section 167(1) of the Immigration and Asylum Act 1999 (c. 33);
'standing arrangements' means arrangements in force between the United Kingdom and the category 1 territory for determining which State is responsible for considering applications for asylum.

Withdrawal of Part 1 Warrant

41. Withdrawal of warrant before extradition

(1) This section applies if at any time in the relevant period the appropriate judge is informed by the designated authority that a Part 1 warrant issued in respect of a person has been withdrawn.

(2) The relevant period is the period—
 (a) starting when the person is first brought before the appropriate judge following his arrest under this Part;
 (b) ending when the person is extradited in pursuance of the warrant or discharged.

(3) The judge must order the person's discharge.

(4) If the person is not before the judge at the time the judge orders his discharge, the judge must inform him of the order as soon as practicable.

42. Withdrawal of warrant while appeal to High Court pending

(1) This section applies if at any time in the relevant period the High Court is informed by the designated authority that a Part 1 warrant issued in respect of a person has been withdrawn.

(2) The relevant period is the period—
 (a) starting when notice of an appeal to the court is given by the person or the authority which issued the warrant;

(b) ending when proceedings on the appeal are discontinued or the court makes its decision on the appeal.

(3) The court must—

(a) if the appeal is under section 26, order the person's discharge and quash the order for his extradition;

(b) if the appeal is under section 28, dismiss the appeal.

(4) If the person is not before the court at the time the court orders his discharge, the court must inform him of the order as soon as practicable.

43. Withdrawal of warrant while appeal to [Supreme Court][69] pending

(1) This section applies if at any time in the relevant period the [Supreme Court][70] is informed by the designated authority that a Part 1 warrant issued in respect of a person has been withdrawn.

(2) The relevant period is the period—

(a) starting when leave to appeal to the [Supreme Court][71] is granted to the person or the authority which issued the warrant;

(b) ending when proceedings on the appeal are discontinued or the [Supreme Court][72] makes its decision on the appeal.

(3) If the appeal is brought by the person in respect of whom the warrant was issued the [Supreme Court][73] must—

(a) order the person's discharge;

(b) quash the order for his extradition, in a case where the appeal was against a decision of the High Court to dismiss an appeal under section 26.

(4) If the appeal is brought by the authority which issued the warrant the [Supreme Court][74] must dismiss the appeal.

(5) If the person is not before the [Supreme Court][75] at the time it orders his discharge, the [Supreme Court][76] must inform him of the order as soon as practicable.

Competing part 1 warrants

44. Competing Part 1 warrants

(1) This section applies if at any time in the relevant period the conditions in subsection (3) are satisfied in relation to a person in respect of whom a Part 1 warrant has been issued.

(2) The relevant period is the period—

(a) starting when the person is first brought before the appropriate judge following his arrest under this Part;

(b) ending when the person is extradited in pursuance of the warrant or discharged.

(3) The conditions are that—

(a) the judge is informed that another Part 1 warrant has been issued in respect of the person;

(b) the other warrant falls to be dealt with by the judge or by a judge who is the appropriate judge in another part of the United Kingdom;

(c) the other warrant has not been disposed of.

(4) The judge may—

(a) order further proceedings on the warrant under consideration to be deferred until the other warrant has been disposed of, if the warrant under consideration has not been disposed of;

(b) order the person's extradition in pursuance of the warrant under consideration to be deferred until the other warrant has been disposed of, if an order for his extradition in pursuance of the warrant under consideration has been made.

---

69 Amended by the Constitutional Reform Act 2005.
70 Amended by the Constitutional Reform Act 2005.
71 Amended by the Constitutional Reform Act 2005.
72 Amended by the Constitutional Reform Act 2005.
73 Amended by the Constitutional Reform Act 2005.
74 Amended by the Constitutional Reform Act 2005.
75 Amended by the Constitutional Reform Act 2005.
76 Amended by the Constitutional Reform Act 2005.

(5) If the judge makes an order under subsection (4) and the person is not already remanded in custody or on bail, the judge must remand the person in custody or on bail.
(6) [If the person is remanded in custody, the appropriate judge may][77] later grant bail.
(7) In applying subsection (4) the judge must take account in particular of these matters—
 (a) the relative seriousness of the offences concerned;
 (b) the place where each offence was committed (or was alleged to have been committed);
 (c) the date on which each warrant was issued;
 (d) whether, in the case of each offence, the person is accused of its commission (but not alleged to have been convicted) or is alleged to be unlawfully at large after conviction.

Consent to extradition

45. Consent to extradition

(1) A person arrested under a Part 1 warrant may consent to his extradition to the category 1 territory in which the warrant was issued.
(2) A person arrested under section 5 may consent to his extradition to the category 1 territory referred to in subsection (1) of that section.
(3) If a person consents to his extradition under this section he must be taken to have waived any right he would have (apart from the consent) not to be dealt with in the category 1 territory for an offence committed before his extradition.
(4) Consent under this section—
 (a) must be given before the appropriate judge;
 (b) must be recorded in writing;
 (c) is irrevocable.
(5) A person may not give his consent under this section unless—
 (a) he is legally represented before the appropriate judge at the time he gives consent, or
 (b) he is a person to whom subsection (6) applies.
(6) This subsection applies to a person if—
 (a) he has been informed of his right to apply for legal aid and has had the opportunity to apply for legal aid, but he has refused or failed to apply;
 (b) he has applied for legal aid but his application has been refused;
 (c) he was granted legal aid but the legal aid was withdrawn.
(7) In subsection (6) 'legal aid' means—
 (a) in England and Wales, a right to representation funded by the Legal Services Commission as part of the Criminal Defence Service;
 (b) in Scotland, such legal aid as is available by virtue of section 183(a) of this Act;
 (c) in Northern Ireland, such free legal aid as is available by virtue of sections 184 and 185 of this Act.
(8) For the purposes of subsection (5) a person is to be treated as legally represented before the appropriate judge if (and only if) he has the assistance of counsel or a solicitor to represent him in the proceedings before the appropriate judge.

46. Extradition order following consent

(1) This section applies if a person consents to his extradition under section 45.
(2) The judge must remand the person in custody or on bail.
(3) [If the person is remanded in custody, the appropriate judge may][78] later grant bail.
(4) If the judge has not fixed a date under section 8 on which the extradition hearing is to begin he is not required to do so.
(5) If the extradition hearing has begun the judge is no longer required to proceed or continue proceeding under sections 10 to 25.
(6) The judge must within the period of 10 days starting with the day on which consent is given order the person's extradition to the category 1 territory.

---

77 Amended by the Police and Justice Act 2006.
78 Amended by the Police and Justice Act 2006.

(7) Subsection (6) has effect subject to sections 48 and 51.
(8) If subsection (6) is not complied with and the person applies to the judge to be discharged the judge must order his discharge.

47. Extradition to category 1 territory following consent

(1) This section applies if the appropriate judge makes an order under section 46(6) for a person's extradition to a category 1 territory.
(2) The person must be extradited to the category 1 territory before the end of the required period.
(3) The required period is—
 (a) 10 days starting with the day on which the order is made, or
 (b) if the judge and the authority which issued the Part 1 warrant agree a later date, 10 days starting with the later date.
(4) If subsection (2) is not complied with and the person applies to the judge to be discharged the judge must order his discharge, unless reasonable cause is shown for the delay.
(5) If before the person is extradited to the category 1 territory the judge is informed by the designated authority that the Part 1 warrant has been withdrawn—
 (a) subsection (2) does not apply, and
 (b) the judge must order the person's discharge.

48. Other warrant issued following consent

(1) This section applies if—
 (a) a person consents under section 45 to his extradition to a category 1 territory, and
 (b) the conditions in subsection (2) are satisfied before the judge orders his extradition under section 46(6).
(2) The conditions are that—
 (a) the judge is informed that another Part 1 warrant has been issued in respect of the person;
 (b) the warrant falls to be dealt with by the judge or by a judge who is the appropriate judge in another part of the United Kingdom;
 (c) the warrant has not been disposed of.
(3) Section 46(6) does not apply but the judge may—
 (a) order the person's extradition in pursuance of his consent, or
 (b) order further proceedings on the warrant under consideration to be deferred until the other warrant has been disposed of.
(4) Subsection (3) is subject to section 51.
(5) In applying subsection (3) the judge must take account in particular of these matters—
 (a) the relative seriousness of the offences concerned;
 (b) the place where each offence was committed (or was alleged to have been committed);
 (c) the date on which each warrant was issued;
 (d) whether, in the case of each offence, the person is accused of its commission (but not alleged to have been convicted) or is alleged to be unlawfully at large after conviction.

49. Other warrant issued: extradition to category 1 territory

(1) This section applies if the appropriate judge makes an order under section 48(3)(a) for a person's extradition to a category 1 territory.
(2) The person must be extradited to the category 1 territory before the end of the required period.
(3) The required period is—
 (a) 10 days starting with the day on which the order is made, or
 (b) if the judge and the authority which issued the Part 1 warrant agree a later date, 10 days starting with the later date.
(4) If subsection (2) is not complied with and the person applies to the judge to be discharged the judge must order his discharge, unless reasonable cause is shown for the delay.
(5) If before the person is extradited to the category 1 territory the judge is informed by the designated authority that the Part 1 warrant has been withdrawn—
 (a) subsection (2) does not apply, and
 (b) the judge must order the person's discharge.

50. Other warrant issued: proceedings deferred

(1) This section applies if the appropriate judge makes an order under section 48(3)(b) for further proceedings on a Part 1 warrant to be deferred.
(2) The judge must remand the person in respect of whom the warrant was issued in custody or on bail.
(3) [If the person is remanded in custody, the appropriate judge may][79] later grant bail.
(4) If an order is made under section 180 for proceedings on the warrant to be resumed, the period specified in section 46(6) must be taken to be 10 days starting with the day on which the order under section 180 is made.

51. Extradition request following consent

(1) This section applies if—
  (a) a person in respect of whom a Part 1 warrant is issued consents under section 45 to his extradition to the category 1 territory in which the warrant was issued, and
  (b) the condition in subsection (2) is satisfied before the judge orders his extradition under section 46(6) or 48(3)(a).
(2) The condition is that the judge is informed that—
  (a) a certificate has been issued under section 70 in respect of a request for the person's extradition;
  (b) the request has not been disposed of.
(3) The judge must not make an order under section 46(6) or 48(3) until he is informed what order has been made under section 179(2).
(4) If the order under section 179(2) is for further proceedings on the warrant to be deferred until the request has been disposed of, the judge must remand the person in custody or on bail.
(5) [If the person is remanded in custody, the appropriate judge may][80] later grant bail.
(6) If—
  (a) the order under section 179(2) is for further proceedings on the warrant to be deferred until the request has been disposed of, and
  (b) an order is made under section 180 for proceedings on the warrant to be resumed, the period specified in section 46(6) must be taken to be 10 days starting with the day on which the order under section 180 is made.
(7) If the order under section 179(2) is for further proceedings on the request to be deferred until the warrant has been disposed of, the period specified in section 46(6) must be taken to be 10 days starting with the day on which the judge is informed of the order.

52. Undertaking in relation to person serving sentence

(1) This section applies if—
  (a) the appropriate judge makes an order under section 46(6) or 48(3)(a) for a person's extradition to a category 1 territory;
  (b) the person is serving a sentence of imprisonment or another form of detention in the United Kingdom[, either—
    (i) in custody, or
    (ii) on licence].[81]
(2) The judge may make the order for extradition subject to the condition that extradition is not to take place before he receives an undertaking given on behalf of the category 1 territory in terms specified by him.
(3) The terms which may be specified by the judge in relation to a person [within subsection (1)(b)(i) who is][82] accused in a category 1 territory of the commission of an offence include terms—
  (a) that the person be kept in custody until the conclusion of the proceedings against him for the offence and any other offence in respect of which he is permitted to be dealt with in the category 1 territory;

---

[79] Amended by the Police and Justice Act 2006.
[80] Amended by the Police and Justice Act 2006.
[81] Amended by the Police and Justice Act 2006.
[82] Amended by the Police and Justice Act 2006.

(b) that the person be returned to the United Kingdom to serve the remainder of his sentence on the conclusion of those proceedings.

[(3A) The terms which may be specified by the judge in relation to a person within subsection (1)(b)(ii) who is accused in a category 1 territory of the commission of an offence include terms that the person be returned to the United Kingdom to serve the remainder of his sentence after serving any sentence imposed on him in the category 1 territory for—

(a) the offence, and

(b) any other offence in respect of which he is permitted to be dealt with in the category 1 territory.][83]

(4) The terms which may be specified by the judge in relation to a person alleged to be unlawfully at large after conviction of an offence by a court in a category 1 territory include terms that the person be returned to the United Kingdom to serve the remainder of his sentence after serving any sentence imposed on him in the category 1 territory for—

(a) the offence, and

(b) any other offence in respect of which he is permitted to be dealt with in the category 1 territory.

(5) If the judge makes an order for extradition subject to a condition under subsection (2) the required period for the purposes of sections 47(2) and 49(2) is 10 days starting with the day on which the judge receives the undertaking.

53. Extradition following deferral for competing claim

(1) This section applies if—

(a) an order is made under section 46(6) or 48(3)(a) for a person to be extradited to a category 1 territory in pursuance of a Part 1 warrant;

(b) before the person is extradited to the territory an order is made under section 44(4)(b) or 179(2)(b) for the person's extradition in pursuance of the warrant to be deferred;

(c) the appropriate judge makes an order under section 181(2) for the person's extradition in pursuance of the warrant to cease to be deferred.

(2) The required period for the purposes of sections 47(2) and 49(2) is 10 days starting with the day on which the order under section 181(2) is made.

Post-extradition matters

54. Request for consent to other offence being dealt with

(1) This section applies if—

(a) a person is extradited to a category 1 territory in respect of an offence in accordance with this Part;

(b) the appropriate judge receives a request for consent to the person being dealt with in the territory for another offence;

(c) the request is certified under this section by the designated authority.

(2) The designated authority may certify a request for consent under this section if it believes that the authority making the request—

(a) is a judicial authority of the territory, and

(b) has the function of making requests for the consent referred to in subsection (1)(b) in that territory.

(3) A certificate under subsection (2) must certify that the authority making the request falls within paragraphs (a) and (b) of that subsection.

(4) The judge must serve notice on the person that he has received the request for consent, unless he is satisfied that it would not be practicable to do so.

(5) The consent hearing must begin before the end of the required period, which is 21 days starting with the day on which the request for consent is received by the designated authority.

(6) The judge may extend the required period if he believes it to be in the interests of justice to do so; and this subsection may apply more than once.

---

[83] Amended by the Police and Justice Act 2006.

(7) The power in subsection (6) may be exercised even after the end of the required period.

(8) If the consent hearing does not begin before the end of the required period and the judge does not exercise the power in subsection (6) to extend the period, he must refuse consent.

(9) The judge may at any time adjourn the consent hearing.

(10) The consent hearing is the hearing at which the judge is to consider the request for consent.

55. Questions for decision at consent hearing

(1) At the consent hearing under section 54 the judge must decide whether consent is required to the person being dealt with in the territory for the offence for which consent is requested.

(2) If the judge decides the question in subsection (1) in the negative he must inform the authority making the request of his decision.

(3) If the judge decides that question in the affirmative he must decide whether the offence for which consent is requested is an extradition offence.

(4) If the judge decides the question in subsection (3) in the negative he must refuse consent.

(5) If the judge decides that question in the affirmative he must decide whether he would order the person's extradition under sections 11 to 25 if—

- (a) the person were in the United Kingdom, and
- (b) the judge were required to proceed under section 11 in respect of the offence for which consent is requested.

(6) If the judge decides the question in subsection (5) in the affirmative he must give consent.

(7) If the judge decides that question in the negative he must refuse consent.

(8) Consent is not required to the person being dealt with in the territory for the offence if the person has been given an opportunity to leave the territory and—

- (a) he has not done so before the end of the permitted period, or
- (b) if he did so before the end of the permitted period, he has returned there.

(9) The permitted period is 45 days starting with the day on which the person arrived in the territory following his extradition there in accordance with this Part.

(10) Subject to subsection (8), the judge must decide whether consent is required to the person being dealt with in the territory for the offence by reference to what appears to him to be the law of the territory or arrangements made between the territory and the United Kingdom.

56. Request for consent to further extradition to category 1 territory

(1) This section applies if—

- (a) a person is extradited to a category 1 territory (the requesting territory) in accordance with this Part;
- (b) the appropriate judge receives a request for consent to the person's extradition to another category 1 territory for an offence;
- (c) the request is certified under this section by the designated authority.

(2) The designated authority may certify a request for consent under this section if it believes that the authority making the request—

- (a) is a judicial authority of the requesting territory, and
- (b) has the function of making requests for the consent referred to in subsection (1)(b) in that territory.

(3) A certificate under subsection (2) must certify that the authority making the request falls within paragraphs (a) and (b) of that subsection.

(4) The judge must serve notice on the person that he has received the request for consent, unless he is satisfied that it would not be practicable to do so.

(5) The consent hearing must begin before the end of the required period, which is 21 days starting with the day on which the request for consent is received by the designated authority.

(6) The judge may extend the required period if he believes it to be in the interests of justice to do so; and this subsection may apply more than once.

(7) The power in subsection (6) may be exercised even after the end of the required period.

(8) If the consent hearing does not begin before the end of the required period and the judge does not exercise the power in subsection (6) to extend the period, he must refuse consent.

(9) The judge may at any time adjourn the consent hearing.

(10) The consent hearing is the hearing at which the judge is to consider the request for consent.

57. Questions for decision at consent hearing

(1) At the consent hearing under section 56 the judge must decide whether consent is required to the person's extradition to the other category 1 territory for the offence.
(2) If the judge decides the question in subsection (1) in the negative he must inform the authority making the request of his decision.
(3) If the judge decides that question in the affirmative he must decide whether the offence is an extradition offence in relation to the category 1 territory referred to in section 56(1)(b).
(4) If the judge decides the question in subsection (3) in the negative he must refuse consent.
(5) If the judge decides that question in the affirmative he must decide whether he would order the person's extradition under sections 11 to 25 if—
 (a) the person were in the United Kingdom, and
 (b) the judge were required to proceed under section 11 in respect of the offence for which consent is requested.
(6) If the judge decides the question in subsection (5) in the affirmative he must give consent.
(7) If the judge decides that question in the negative he must refuse consent.
(8) Consent is not required to the person's extradition to the other territory for the offence if the person has been given an opportunity to leave the requesting territory and—
 (a) he has not done so before the end of the permitted period, or
 (b) if he did so before the end of the permitted period, he has returned there.
(9) The permitted period is 45 days starting with the day on which the person arrived in the requesting territory following his extradition there in accordance with this Part.
(10) Subject to subsection (8), the judge must decide whether consent is required to the person's extradition to the other territory for the offence by reference to what appears to him to be the arrangements made between the requesting territory and the United Kingdom.

58. Consent to further extradition to category 2 territory

(1) This section applies if—
 (a) a person is extradited to a category 1 territory (the requesting territory) in accordance with this Part;
 (b) the Secretary of State receives a request for consent to the person's extradition to a category 2 territory for an offence;
 (c) the request is certified under this section by the designated authority.
(2) The designated authority may certify a request for consent under this section if it believes that the authority making the request—
 (a) is a judicial authority of the requesting territory, and
 (b) has the function of making requests for the consent referred to in subsection (1)(b) in that territory.
(3) A certificate under subsection (2) must certify that the authority making the request falls within paragraphs (a) and (b) of that subsection.
(4) The Secretary of State must serve notice on the person that he has received the request for consent, unless he is satisfied that it would not be practicable to do so.
(5) The Secretary of State must decide whether the offence is an extradition offence within the meaning given by section 137 in relation to the category 2 territory.
(6) If the Secretary of State decides the question in subsection (5) in the negative he must refuse consent.
(7) If the Secretary of State decides that question in the affirmative he must decide whether the appropriate judge would send the case to him (for his decision whether the person was to be extradited) under sections 79 to 91 if—
 (a) the person were in the United Kingdom, and
 (b) the judge were required to proceed under section 79 in respect of the offence for which the Secretary of State's consent is requested.
(8) If the Secretary of State decides the question in subsection (7) in the negative he must refuse his consent.
(9) If the Secretary of State decides that question in the affirmative he must decide whether, if the person were in the United Kingdom, his extradition to the category 2 territory in respect of the offence would be prohibited under section 94, 95 or 96.

(10) If the Secretary of State decides the question in subsection (9) in the negative he may give consent.
(11) If the Secretary of State decides that question in the affirmative he must refuse consent.
(12) This section applies in relation to any function which falls under this section to be exercised in relation to Scotland only as if the references in this section to the Secretary of State were to the Scottish Ministers.

[59. Return of person to serve remainder of sentence

(1) This section applies if—
 (a) a person who is serving a sentence of imprisonment or another form of detention in the United Kingdom is extradited to a category 1 territory in accordance with this Part;
 (b) the person is returned to the United Kingdom to serve the remainder of the sentence or the person otherwise returns to the United Kingdom.
(2) Time during which the person was outside the United Kingdom as a result of the extradition does not count as time served by the person as part of the sentence.
(3) But subsection (2) does not apply if—
 (a) the person was extradited for the purpose of being prosecuted for an offence, and
 (b) the person has not been convicted of the offence or of any other offence in respect of which the person was permitted to be dealt with in the category 1 territory.
(4) In a case falling within subsection (3), time during which the person was outside the United Kingdom as a result of the extradition counts as time served by the person as part of the sentence if (and only if) it was spent in custody in connection with the offence or any other offence in respect of which the person was permitted to be dealt with in the territory.
(5) In a case where the person is not entitled to be released from detention pursuant to the sentence—
 (a) the person is liable to be detained in pursuance of the sentence, and
 (b) if at large, the person must be treated as being unlawfully at large.
(6) In a case where the person is entitled to be released from detention on licence pursuant to the sentence—
 (a) if the person was released on licence at the time of extradition, the licence is suspended until the person's return;
 (b) if the person was not released on licence at that time, subsections (7) to (10) apply in relation to the person ("the offender").
(7) The offender is liable to be detained, on return, in any place in which the offender could have been detained pursuant to the sentence before the time of extradition.
(8) A constable or immigration officer may—
 (a) take the offender into custody, and
 (b) convey the offender to the place mentioned in subsection (7).
(9) The offender must be released on licence within the period of 5 days beginning when the offender is taken (or retaken) into custody under this section.
(10) In calculating a period of 5 days for the purposes of subsection (9) no account is to be taken of—
 (a) any Saturday or Sunday,
 (b) Christmas Day,
 (c) Good Friday, or
 (d) in any part of the United Kingdom, any day that is a bank holiday under the Banking and Financial Dealings Act 1971 in that part of the United Kingdom.
(11) A person is entitled to be released from detention if there is—
 (a) a duty to release the person under section 33(1), (1A) or (2) of the Criminal Justice Act 1991,
 (b) a duty to release the person under section 244 of the Criminal Justice Act 2003 (other than temporarily on licence pursuant to an intermittent custody order under section 183(1)(b) of the Criminal Justice Act 2003),
 (c) a duty to release the person under section 1, 1AA or 7(1) of the Prisoners and Criminal Proceedings (Scotland) Act 1993 or section 5, 11(2), 13, 19 or 23 of the Custodial Sentences and Weapons (Scotland) Act 2007, or
 (d) a duty to release the person under section 1 of the Northern Ireland (Remission of Sentences) Act 1995, Article 26 of the Criminal Justice (Northern Ireland) Order 1996 or Article 17 or 18(8) of the Criminal Justice (Northern Ireland) Order 2008.

(12) The powers conferred on a constable by subsection (8) are exercisable in any part of the United Kingdom.
(13) An immigration officer is a person who is an immigration officer within the meaning of the Immigration Act 1971.][84]

Costs

60. Costs where extradition ordered

(1) This section applies if any of the following occurs in relation to a person in respect of whom a Part 1 warrant is issued—
  (a) an order for the person's extradition is made under this Part;
  (b) the High Court dismisses an appeal under section 26;
  (c) the High Court or the [Supreme Court][85] dismisses an application for leave to appeal to the [Supreme Court][86] under section 32, if the application is made by the person;
  (d) the [Supreme Court][87] dismisses an appeal under section 32, if the appeal is brought by the person.
(2) In a case falling within subsection (1)(a), the appropriate judge may make such order as he considers just and reasonable with regard to the costs to be paid by the person.
(3) In a case falling within subsection (1)(b), (c) or (d), the court by which the application or appeal is dismissed may make such order as it considers just and reasonable with regard to the costs to be paid by the person.
(4) An order for costs under this section—
  (a) must specify their amount;
  (b) may name the person to whom they are to be paid.

61. Costs where discharge ordered

(1) This section applies if any of the following occurs in relation to a person in respect of whom a Part 1 warrant is issued—
  (a) an order for the person's discharge is made under this Part;
  (b) the person is taken to be discharged under this Part;
  (c) the High Court dismisses an appeal under section 28;
  (d) the High Court or the [Supreme Court][88] dismisses an application for leave to appeal to the [Supreme Court][89] under section 32, if the application is made by the authority which issued the warrant;
  (e) the [Supreme Court][90] dismisses an appeal under section 32, if the appeal is brought by the authority which issued the warrant.
(2) In a case falling within subsection (1)(a), an order under subsection (5) in favour of the person may be made by—
  (a) the appropriate judge, if the order for the person's discharge is made by him;
  (b) the High Court, if the order for the person's discharge is made by it;
  (c) the [Supreme Court][91], if the order for the person's discharge is made by it.
(3) In a case falling within subsection (1)(b), the appropriate judge may make an order under subsection (5) in favour of the person.
(4) In a case falling within subsection (1)(c), (d) or (e), the court by which the application or appeal is dismissed may make an order under subsection (5) in favour of the person.
(5) An order under this subsection in favour of a person is an order for a payment of the appropriate amount to be made to the person out of money provided by Parliament.

---

[84] Amended by the Policing and Crime Act 2009.
[85] Amended by the Constitutional Reform Act 2005.
[86] Amended by the Constitutional Reform Act 2005.
[87] Amended by the Constitutional Reform Act 2005.
[88] Amended by the Constitutional Reform Act 2005.
[89] Amended by the Constitutional Reform Act 2005.
[90] Amended by the Constitutional Reform Act 2005.
[91] Amended by the Constitutional Reform Act 2005.

[(5A) In England and Wales, an order under subsection (5) is to be made, and the appropriate amount is to be determined, in accordance with sections 62A and 62B.

(5B) In Scotland and Northern Ireland, an order under subsection (5) is to be made, and the appropriate amount is to be determined, in accordance with subsections (6) to (9).][92]

(6) The appropriate amount is such amount as the judge or court making the order under subsection (5) considers reasonably sufficient to compensate the person in whose favour the order is made for any expenses properly incurred by him in the proceedings under this Part.

(7) But if the judge or court making an order under subsection (5) is of the opinion that there are circumstances which make it inappropriate that the person in whose favour the order is made should recover the full amount mentioned in subsection (6), the judge or court must—
- (a) assess what amount would in his or its opinion be just and reasonable;
- (b) specify that amount in the order as the appropriate amount.

(8) Unless subsection (7) applies, the appropriate amount—
- (a) must be specified in the order, if the court considers it appropriate for it to be so specified and the person in whose favour the order is made agrees the amount;
- (b) must be determined in accordance with regulations made by the Lord Chancellor for the purposes of this section, in any other case.

[(9) In relation to proceedings in Northern Ireland (including proceedings in the Supreme Court on an appeal, or on an application for leave to appeal, from proceedings in Northern Ireland)—
- (a) subsection (5) has effect as if for "out of money provided by Parliament" there were substituted "by the Department of Justice in Northern Ireland";
- (b) the power to make regulations under subsection (8)(b) is exercisable by the Department of Justice in Northern Ireland (and not by the Lord Chancellor).][93]

62. Costs where discharge ordered: supplementary

(1) ...

(2) ...[94]

(3) In Northern Ireland, section 7 of the Costs in Criminal Cases Act (Northern Ireland) 1968 (c. 10) (rules relating to costs) applies in relation to section 61 as that section applies in relation to sections 2 to 5 of that Act.

[62A Appropriate amount: England and Wales

(1) For the purposes of an order under section 61(5), the appropriate amount is such amount as the judge or court making the order considers reasonably sufficient to compensate the person in whose favour the order is made for any expenses properly incurred by the person in the proceedings under this Part.

(2) But if the judge or court considers that there are circumstances that make it inappropriate for the person to recover the full amount mentioned in subsection (1), the order under section 61(5) must be for the payment out of money provided by Parliament of such lesser amount as the judge or court considers just and reasonable.

(3) Subsections (1) and (2) have effect subject to—
- (a) section 62B, and
- (b) regulations under section 20(1A)(d) of the Prosecution of Offences Act 1985 (as applied by this section).

(4) When making an order under section 61(5), the judge or court must fix the amount to be paid out of money provided by Parliament in the order if the judge or court considers it appropriate to do so and—
- (a) the person in whose favour the order is made agrees the amount, or
- (b) subsection (2) applies.

(5) Where the judge or court does not fix the amount to be paid out of money provided by Parliament in the order—
- (a) the judge or court must describe in the order any reduction required under subsection (2), and

---

92 Amended by Legal Aid, Sentencing and Punishment of Offenders Act 2012

93 Amended by SI 2010/976.

94 Repealed by Legal Aid, Sentencing and Punishment of Offenders Act 2012

(b) the amount must be fixed by means of a determination made by or on behalf of the judge or court in accordance with procedures specified in regulations made by the Lord Chancellor.

(6) Subsections (1A) to (1C) and (3) of section 20 of the Prosecution of Offences Act 1985 (regulations as to amounts ordered to be paid out of central funds) apply in relation to amounts payable out of money provided by Parliament in pursuance of an order under section 61 as they apply in relation to amounts payable out of central funds in pursuance of costs orders made under section 16 of that Act.

(7) This section extends to England and Wales only.][95]

[62B Legal costs: England and Wales

(1) An order under section 61(5) may not require the payment out of money provided by Parliament of an amount that includes an amount in respect of legal costs incurred by the person in whose favour the order is made, subject to the following provisions of this section.

(2) Subsection (1) does not apply in relation to legal costs incurred in—

(a) proceedings in a magistrates' court, or

(b) proceedings in the Supreme Court.

(3) The Lord Chancellor may by regulations make provision about exceptions from the prohibition in subsection (1), including—

(a) provision amending this section by adding, modifying or removing an exception, and

(b) provision for an exception to arise where a determination has been made by a person specified in the regulations.

(4) Regulations under subsection (3) may not remove or limit the exception provided by subsection (2)(b).

(5) Where a judge or court makes an order under section 61(5) requiring the payment out of money provided by Parliament of an amount that includes an amount in respect of legal costs, the order must include a statement to that effect.

(6) Where, in an order under section 61(5), a judge or court fixes an amount to be paid out of money provided by Parliament that includes an amount in respect of legal costs incurred in proceedings in a court other than the Supreme Court, the latter amount must not exceed an amount specified by regulations made by the Lord Chancellor.

(7) In this section—

"legal costs" means fees, charges, disbursements and other amounts payable in respect of advocacy services or litigation services including, in particular, expert witness costs;

"advocacy services" means any services which it would be reasonable to expect a person who is exercising, or contemplating exercising, a right of audience in relation to any proceedings, or contemplated proceedings, to provide;

"expert witness costs" means amounts payable in respect of the services of an expert witness, including amounts payable in connection with attendance by the witness at court or elsewhere;

"litigation services" means any services which it would be reasonable to expect a person who is exercising, or contemplating exercising, a right to conduct litigation in relation to proceedings, or contemplated proceedings, to provide.

(8) This section extends to England and Wales only.][96]

Repatriation cases

63. Persons serving sentences outside territory where convicted

(1) This section applies if an arrest warrant is issued in respect of a person by an authority of a category 1 territory and the warrant contains the statement referred to in subsection (2).

(2) The statement is one that—

(a) the person is alleged to be unlawfully at large from a prison in one territory (the imprisoning territory) in which he was serving a sentence after conviction of an offence specified in the warrant by a court in another territory (the convicting territory), and

[95] Inserted by Legal Aid, Sentencing and Punishment of Offenders Act 2012

[96] Inserted by Legal Aid, Sentencing and Punishment of Offenders Act 2012

(b) the person was serving the sentence in pursuance of international arrangements for prisoners sentenced in one territory to be repatriated to another territory in order to serve their sentence, and

(c) the warrant is issued with a view to his arrest and extradition to the category 1 territory for the purpose of serving a sentence or another form of detention imposed in respect of the offence.

(3) If the category 1 territory is either the imprisoning territory or the convicting territory, section 2(2)(b) has effect as if the reference to the statement referred to in subsection (5) of that section were a reference to the statement referred to in subsection (2) of this section.

(4) If the category 1 territory is the imprisoning territory—

(a) section 2(6)(e) has effect as if 'the category 1 territory' read 'the convicting territory';

(b) section 10(2) has effect as if 'an extradition offence' read 'an extradition offence in relation to the convicting territory';

(c) section 20(5) has effect as if after 'entitled' there were inserted 'in the convicting territory';

(d) section 37(5) has effect as if 'a category 1 territory' read 'the convicting territory' and as if 'the category 1 territory' in both places read 'the convicting territory';

(e) section 52(4) has effect as if 'a category 1 territory' read 'the convicting territory' and as if 'the category 1 territory' in both places read 'the convicting territory';

(f) section 65(1) has effect as if 'a category 1 territory' read 'the convicting territory';

(g) section 65(2) has effect as if 'the category 1 territory' in the opening words and paragraphs (a) and (c) read 'the convicting territory' and as if 'the category 1 territory' in paragraph (b) read 'the imprisoning territory';

(h) in section 65, subsections (3), (4), (5), (6) and (8) have effect as if 'the category 1 territory' in each place read 'the convicting territory'.

Interpretation

64. Extradition offences: person not sentenced for offence

(1) This section applies in relation to conduct of a person if—

(a) he is accused in a category 1 territory of the commission of an offence constituted by the conduct, or

(b) he is alleged to be unlawfully at large after conviction by a court in a category 1 territory of an offence constituted by the conduct and he has not been sentenced for the offence.

(2) The conduct constitutes an extradition offence in relation to the category 1 territory if these conditions are satisfied—

(a) the conduct occurs in the category 1 territory and no part of it occurs in the United Kingdom;

(b) a certificate issued by an appropriate authority of the category 1 territory shows that the conduct falls within the European framework list;

(c) the certificate shows that the conduct is punishable under the law of the category 1 territory with imprisonment or another form of detention for a term of 3 years or a greater punishment.

(3) The conduct also constitutes an extradition offence in relation to the category 1 territory if these conditions are satisfied—

(a) the conduct occurs in the category 1 territory;

(b) the conduct would constitute an offence under the law of the relevant part of the United Kingdom if it occurred in that part of the United Kingdom;

(c) the conduct is punishable under the law of the category 1 territory with imprisonment or another form of detention for a term of 12 months or a greater punishment (however it is described in that law).

(4) The conduct also constitutes an extradition offence in relation to the category 1 territory if these conditions are satisfied—

(a) the conduct occurs outside the category 1 territory;

(b) the conduct is punishable under the law of the category 1 territory with imprisonment or another form of detention for a term of 12 months or a greater punishment (however it is described in that law);

(c) in corresponding circumstances equivalent conduct would constitute an extra-territorial offence under the law of the relevant part of the United Kingdom punishable with imprisonment or another form of detention for a term of 12 months or a greater punishment.

(5) The conduct also constitutes an extradition offence in relation to the category 1 territory if these conditions are satisfied—
 (a) the conduct occurs outside the category 1 territory and no part of it occurs in the United Kingdom;
 (b) the conduct would constitute an offence under the law of the relevant part of the United Kingdom punishable with imprisonment or another form of detention for a term of 12 months or a greater punishment if it occurred in that part of the United Kingdom;
 (c) the conduct is so punishable under the law of the category 1 territory (however it is described in that law).

(6) The conduct also constitutes an extradition offence in relation to the category 1 territory if these conditions are satisfied—
 (a) the conduct occurs outside the category 1 territory and no part of it occurs in the United Kingdom;
 (b) the conduct is punishable under the law of the category 1 territory with imprisonment or another form of detention for a term of 12 months or a greater punishment (however it is described in that law);
 (c) the conduct constitutes or if committed in the United Kingdom would constitute an offence mentioned in subsection (7).

(7) The offences are—
 (a) an offence under section 51 or 58 of the International Criminal Court Act 2001 (c. 17) (genocide, crimes against humanity and war crimes);
 (b) an offence under section 52 or 59 of that Act (conduct ancillary to genocide etc. committed outside the jurisdiction);
 (c) an ancillary offence, as defined in section 55 or 62 of that Act, in relation to an offence falling within paragraph (a) or (b);
 (d) an offence under section 1 of the International Criminal Court (Scotland) Act 2001 (asp 13) (genocide, crimes against humanity and war crimes);
 (e) an offence under section 2 of that Act (conduct ancillary to genocide etc. committed outside the jurisdiction);
 (f) an ancillary offence, as defined in section 7 of that Act, in relation to an offence falling within paragraph (d) or (e).

(8) For the purposes of subsections (3)(b), (4)(c) and (5)(b)—
 (a) if the conduct relates to a tax or duty, it is immaterial that the law of the relevant part of the United Kingdom does not impose the same kind of tax or duty or does not contain rules of the same kind as those of the law of the category 1 territory;
 (b) if the conduct relates to customs or exchange, it is immaterial that the law of the relevant part of the United Kingdom does not contain rules of the same kind as those of the law of the category 1 territory.

(9) This section applies for the purposes of this Part.

65. Extradition offences: person sentenced for offence

(1) This section applies in relation to conduct of a person if—
 (a) he is alleged to be unlawfully at large after conviction by a court in a category 1 territory of an offence constituted by the conduct, and
 (b) he has been sentenced for the offence.

(2) The conduct constitutes an extradition offence in relation to the category 1 territory if these conditions are satisfied—
 (a) the conduct occurs in the category 1 territory and no part of it occurs in the United Kingdom;
 (b) a certificate issued by an appropriate authority of the category 1 territory shows that the conduct falls within the European framework list;
 (c) the certificate shows that a sentence of imprisonment or another form of detention for a term of 12 months or a greater punishment has been imposed in the category 1 territory in respect of the conduct.

(3) The conduct also constitutes an extradition offence in relation to the category 1 territory if these conditions are satisfied—
 (a) the conduct occurs in the category 1 territory;

(b) the conduct would constitute an offence under the law of the relevant part of the United Kingdom if it occurred in that part of the United Kingdom;
(c) a sentence of imprisonment or another form of detention for a term of 4 months or a greater punishment has been imposed in the category 1 territory in respect of the conduct.

(4) The conduct also constitutes an extradition offence in relation to the category 1 territory if these conditions are satisfied—
(a) the conduct occurs outside the category 1 territory;
(b) a sentence of imprisonment or another form of detention for a term of 4 months or a greater punishment has been imposed in the category 1 territory in respect of the conduct;
(c) in corresponding circumstances equivalent conduct would constitute an extra-territorial offence under the law of the relevant part of the United Kingdom punishable with imprisonment or another form of detention for a term of 12 months or a greater punishment.

(5) The conduct also constitutes an extradition offence in relation to the category 1 territory if these conditions are satisfied—
(a) the conduct occurs outside the category 1 territory and no part of it occurs in the United Kingdom;
(b) the conduct would constitute an offence under the law of the relevant part of the United Kingdom punishable with imprisonment or another form of detention for a term of 12 months or a greater punishment if it occurred in that part of the United Kingdom;
(c) a sentence of imprisonment or another form of detention for a term of 4 months or a greater punishment has been imposed in the category 1 territory in respect of the conduct.

(6) The conduct also constitutes an extradition offence in relation to the category 1 territory if these conditions are satisfied—
(a) the conduct occurs outside the category 1 territory and no part of it occurs in the United Kingdom;
(b) a sentence of imprisonment or another form of detention for a term of 4 months or a greater punishment has been imposed in the category 1 territory in respect of the conduct;
(c) the conduct constitutes or if committed in the United Kingdom would constitute an offence mentioned in subsection (7).

(7) The offences are—
(a) an offence under section 51 or 58 of the International Criminal Court Act 2001 (c. 17) (genocide, crimes against humanity and war crimes);
(b) an offence under section 52 or 59 of that Act (conduct ancillary to genocide etc. committed outside the jurisdiction);
(c) an ancillary offence, as defined in section 55 or 62 of that Act, in relation to an offence falling within paragraph (a) or (b);
(d) an offence under section 1 of the International Criminal Court (Scotland) Act 2001 (asp 13) (genocide, crimes against humanity and war crimes);
(e) an offence under section 2 of that Act (conduct ancillary to genocide etc. committed outside the jurisdiction);
(f) an ancillary offence, as defined in section 7 of that Act, in relation to an offence falling within paragraph (d) or (e).

(8) For the purposes of subsections (3)(b), (4)(c) and (5)(b)—
(a) if the conduct relates to a tax or duty, it is immaterial that the law of the relevant part of the United Kingdom does not impose the same kind of tax or duty or does not contain rules of the same kind as those of the law of the category 1 territory;
(b) if the conduct relates to customs or exchange, it is immaterial that the law of the relevant part of the United Kingdom does not contain rules of the same kind as those of the law of the category 1 territory.

(9) This section applies for the purposes of this Part.

66. Extradition offences: supplementary

(1) Subsections (2) to (4) apply for the purposes of sections 64 and 65.

(2) An appropriate authority of a category 1 territory is a judicial authority of the territory which the appropriate judge believes has the function of issuing arrest warrants in that territory.

(3) The law of a territory is the general criminal law of the territory.

(4) The relevant part of the United Kingdom is the part of the United Kingdom in which the relevant proceedings are taking place.
(5) The relevant proceedings are the proceedings in which it is necessary to decide whether conduct constitutes an extradition offence.

67. The appropriate judge

(1) The appropriate judge is—
(a) in England and Wales, a District Judge (Magistrates' Courts) designated for the purposes of this Part [by the Lord Chief Justice of England and Wales after consulting the Lord Chancellor];[97]
(b) in Scotland, the sheriff of Lothian and Borders;
(c) in Northern Ireland, such county court judge or resident magistrate as is designated for the purposes of this Part [by the Lord Chief Justice of Northern Ireland after consulting the [Department of Justice in Northern Ireland][98]].[99]
(2) A designation under subsection (1) may be made for all cases or for such cases (or cases of such description) as the designation stipulates.
(3) More than one designation may be made under subsection (1).
[(3A) The use of the expression 'the judge' in a section containing a previous reference to 'the appropriate judge' or 'the judge' does not in itself require both references to be read as referring to the same individual.][100]
(4) This section applies for the purposes of this Part.
[(5) The Lord Chief Justice of England and Wales may nominate a judicial office holder (as defined in section 109(4) of the Constitutional Reform Act 2005) to exercise his functions under subsection (1)(a).
(6) The Lord Chief Justice of Northern Ireland may nominate any of the following to exercise his functions under subsection (1)(c)—
(a) the holder of one of the offices listed in Schedule 1 to the Justice (Northern Ireland) Act 2002;
(b) a Lord Justice of Appeal (as defined in section 88 of that Act).][101]

68. The extradition hearing

(1) The extradition hearing is the hearing at which the appropriate judge is to decide whether a person in respect of whom a Part 1 warrant was issued is to be extradited to the category 1 territory in which it was issued.
(2) This section applies for the purposes of this Part.

[68A. Unlawfully at large

(1) A person is alleged to be unlawfully at large after conviction of an offence if—
(a) he is alleged to have been convicted of it, and
(b) his extradition is sought for the purpose of his being sentenced for the offence or of his serving a sentence of imprisonment or another form of detention imposed in respect of the offence.
(2) This section applies for the purposes of this Part, other than sections 14 and 63.][102]

[97] Amended by the Constitutional Reform Act 2005.
[98] Amended by SI 2010/976.
[99] Amended by the Constitutional Reform Act 2005.
[100] Amended by the Police and Justice Act 2006.
[101] Amended by the Constitutional Reform Act 2005.
[102] Amended by the Police and Justice Act 2006.

Part 2
Extradition to Category 2 Territories

Introduction

69. Extradition to category 2 territories

(1) This Part deals with extradition from the United Kingdom to the territories designated for the purposes of this Part by order made by the Secretary of State.
(2) In this Act references to category 2 territories are to the territories designated for the purposes of this Part.

70. Extradition request and certificate

(1) The Secretary of State must [(subject to subsection (2))][103] issue a certificate under this section if he receives a valid request for the extradition [of a person to a category 2 territory].[104]
[(2) The Secretary of State may refuse to issue a certificate under this section if—
(a) he has power under section 126 to order that proceedings on the request be deferred,
(b) the person whose extradition is requested has been recorded by the Secretary of State as a refugee within the meaning of the Refugee Convention, or
(c) the person whose extradition is requested has been granted leave to enter or remain in the United Kingdom on the ground that it would be a breach of Article 2 or 3 of the Human Rights Convention to remove him to the territory to which extradition is requested.
(2A) In subsection (2)—
'Refugee Convention' has the meaning given by section 167(1) of the Immigration and Asylum Act 1999;
'Human Rights Convention' has the meaning given to 'the Convention' by section 21(1) of the Human Rights Act 1998.][105]
(3) A request for a person's extradition is valid if—
(a) it contains the statement referred to in subsection (4) [or the statement referred to in subsection (4A)],[106] and
(b) it is made in the approved way.
[(4) The statement is one that—
(a) the person is accused in the category 2 territory of the commission of an offence specified in the request, and
(b) the request is made with a view to his arrest and extradition to the category 2 territory for the purpose of being prosecuted for the offence.
(4A) The statement is one that—
(a) the person has been convicted of an offence specified in the request by a court in the category 2 territory, and
(b) the request is made with a view to his arrest and extradition to the category 2 territory for the purpose of being sentenced for the offence or of serving a sentence of imprisonment or another form of detention imposed in respect of the offence.][107]
(5) A request for extradition to a category 2 territory which is a British overseas territory is made in the approved way if it is made by or on behalf of the person administering the territory.
(6) A request for extradition to a category 2 territory which is the Hong Kong Special Administrative Region of the People's Republic of China is made in the approved way if it is made by or on behalf of the government of the Region.
(7) A request for extradition to any other category 2 territory is made in the approved way if it is made—
(a) by an authority of the territory which the Secretary of State believes has the function of making requests for extradition in that territory, or

[103] Amended by the Police and Justice Act 2006.
[104] Amended by the Police and Justice Act 2006.
[105] Amended by the Police and Justice Act 2006.
[106] Amended by the Police and Justice Act 2006.
[107] Amended by the Police and Justice Act 2006.

(b) by a person recognised by the Secretary of State as a diplomatic or consular representative of the territory.

(8) A certificate under this section must—

[(a)] [108] certify that the request is made in the approved way[, and

(b) identify the order by which the territory in question is designated as a category 2 territory.][109]

(9) If a certificate is issued under this section the Secretary of State must send [the request and the certificate to the appropriate judge].[110]

Arrest

71. Arrest warrant following extradition request

(1) This section applies if the Secretary of State sends documents to the appropriate judge under section 70.

(2) The judge may issue a warrant for the arrest of the person whose extradition is requested if the judge has reasonable grounds for believing that—

(a) the offence in respect of which extradition is requested is an extradition offence, and

(b) there is evidence falling within subsection (3).

(3) The evidence is—

(a) evidence that would justify the issue of a warrant for the arrest of a person accused of the offence within the judge's jurisdiction, if the person whose extradition is requested is accused of the commission of the offence;

(b) evidence that would justify the issue of a warrant for the arrest of a person unlawfully at large after conviction of the offence within the judge's jurisdiction, if the person whose extradition is requested is alleged to be unlawfully at large after conviction of the offence.

(4) But if the category 2 territory to which extradition is requested is designated for the purposes of this section by order made by the Secretary of State, subsections (2) and (3) have effect as if 'evidence' read 'information'.

(5) A warrant issued under this section may—

(a) be executed by any person to whom it is directed or by any constable or customs officer;

(b) be executed even if neither the warrant nor a copy of it is in the possession of the person executing it at the time of the arrest.

[(6) If a warrant issued under this section—

(a) is directed to a service policeman, and

(b) is in respect of a person subject to service law or a civilian subject to service discipline,it may be executed anywhere.][111]

(7) In any other case, a warrant issued under this section may be executed in any part of the United Kingdom.

(8) ...[112]

72. Person arrested under section 71

(1) This section applies if a person is arrested under a warrant issued under section 71.

(2) A copy of the warrant must be given to the person as soon as practicable after his arrest.

(3) The person must be brought as soon as practicable before the appropriate judge.

(4) But subsection (3) does not apply if—

(a) the person is granted bail by a constable following his arrest, or

(b) the Secretary of State decides under section 126 that the request for the person's extradition is not to be proceeded with.

(5) If subsection (2) is not complied with and the person applies to the judge to be discharged, the judge may order his discharge.

---

[108] Amended by the Police and Justice Act 2006.
[109] Amended by the Police and Justice Act 2006.
[110] Amended by the Police and Justice Act 2006.
[111] Amended by the Armed Forces Act 2006.
[112] Amended by the Armed Forces Act 2006.

(6) If subsection (3) is not complied with and the person applies to the judge to be discharged, the judge must order his discharge.
(7) When the person first appears or is brought before the appropriate judge, the judge must—
  (a) inform him of the contents of the request for his extradition;
  (b) give him the required information about consent;
  (c) remand him in custody or on bail.
(8) The required information about consent is—
  (a) that the person may consent to his extradition to the category 2 territory to which his extradition is requested;
  (b) an explanation of the effect of consent and the procedure that will apply if he gives consent;
  (c) that consent must be given in writing and is irrevocable.
(9) [If the person is remanded in custody, the appropriate judge may][113] later grant bail.
(10) Subsection (4)(a) applies to Scotland with the omission of the words 'by a constable'.

73. Provisional warrant

(1) This section applies if a justice of the peace is satisfied on information in writing and on oath that a person within subsection (2)—
  (a) is or is believed to be in the United Kingdom, or
  (b) is or is believed to be on his way to the United Kingdom.
(2) A person is within this subsection if—
  (a) he is accused in a category 2 territory of the commission of an offence, or
  (b) he is alleged to be unlawfully at large after conviction of an offence by a court in a category 2 territory.
(3) The justice may issue a warrant for the arrest of the person (a provisional warrant) if he has reasonable grounds for believing that—
  (a) the offence of which the person is accused or has been convicted is an extradition offence, and
  (b) there is written evidence falling within subsection (4).
(4) The evidence is—
  (a) evidence that would justify the issue of a warrant for the arrest of a person accused of the offence within the justice's jurisdiction, if the person in respect of whom the warrant is sought is accused of the commission of the offence;
  (b) evidence that would justify the issue of a warrant for the arrest of a person unlawfully at large after conviction of the offence within the justice's jurisdiction, if the person in respect of whom the warrant is sought is alleged to be unlawfully at large after conviction of the offence.
(5) But if the category 2 territory is designated for the purposes of this section by order made by the Secretary of State, subsections (3) and (4) have effect as if 'evidence' read 'information'.
(6) A provisional warrant may—
  (a) be executed by any person to whom it is directed or by any constable or customs officer;
  (b) be executed even if neither the warrant nor a copy of it is in the possession of the person executing it at the time of the arrest.
[(7) If a warrant issued under this section—
  (a) is directed to a service policeman, and
  (b) is in respect of a person subject to service law or a civilian subject to service discipline,it may be executed anywhere.][114]
(8) In any other case, a warrant issued under this section may be executed in any part of the United Kingdom.
(9) ...[115]
(10) The preceding provisions of this section apply to Scotland with these modifications—
  (a) in subsection (1) for 'justice of the peace is satisfied on information in writing and on oath' substitute 'sheriff is satisfied, on an application by a procurator fiscal,';
  (b) in subsection (3) for 'justice' substitute 'sheriff';

---

113 Amended by the Police and Justice Act 2006.
114 Amended by the Armed Forces Act 2006.
115 Amended by the Armed Forces Act 2006.

(c) in subsection (4) for 'justice's', in paragraphs (a) and (b), substitute 'sheriff's'.

(11) Subsection (1) applies to Northern Ireland with the substitution of 'a complaint' for 'information'.

74. Person arrested under provisional warrant

(1) This section applies if a person is arrested under a provisional warrant.

(2) A copy of the warrant must be given to the person as soon as practicable after his arrest.

(3) The person must be brought as soon as practicable before the appropriate judge.

(4) But subsection (3) does not apply if—

(a) the person is granted bail by a constable following his arrest, or

(b) in a case where the Secretary of State has received a valid request for the person's extradition, the Secretary of State decides under section 126 that the request is not to be proceeded with.

(5) If subsection (2) is not complied with and the person applies to the judge to be discharged, the judge may order his discharge.

(6) If subsection (3) is not complied with and the person applies to the judge to be discharged, the judge must order his discharge.

(7) When the person first appears or is brought before the appropriate judge, the judge must—

(a) inform him that he is accused of the commission of an offence in a category 2 territory or that he is alleged to be unlawfully at large after conviction of an offence by a court in a category 2 territory;

(b) give him the required information about consent;

(c) remand him in custody or on bail.

(8) The required information about consent is—

(a) that the person may consent to his extradition to the category 2 territory in which he is accused of the commission of an offence or is alleged to have been convicted of an offence;

(b) an explanation of the effect of consent and the procedure that will apply if he gives consent;

(c) that consent must be given in writing and is irrevocable.

(9) [If the person is remanded in custody, the appropriate judge may][116] later grant bail.

(10) The judge must order the person's discharge if the documents referred to in section 70(9) are not received by the judge within the required period.

(11) The required period is—

(a) 45 days starting with the day on which the person was arrested, or

(b) if the category 2 territory is designated by order made by the Secretary of State for the purposes of this section, any longer period permitted by the order.

(12) Subsection (4)(a) applies to Scotland with the omission of the words 'by a constable'.

THE EXTRADITION HEARING

75. Date of extradition hearing: arrest under section 71

(1) When a person arrested under a warrant issued under section 71 first appears or is brought before the appropriate judge, the judge must fix a date on which the extradition hearing is to begin.

(2) The date fixed under subsection (1) must not be later than the end of the permitted period, which is 2 months starting with the date on which the person first appears or is brought before the judge.

(3) If before the date fixed under subsection (1) (or this subsection) a party to the proceedings applies to the judge for a later date to be fixed and the judge believes it to be in the interests of justice to do so, he may fix a later date; and this subsection may apply more than once.

(4) If the extradition hearing does not begin on or before the date fixed under this section and the person applies to the judge to be discharged, the judge must order his discharge.

76. Date of extradition hearing: arrest under provisional warrant

(1) Subsection (2) applies if—

(a) a person is arrested under a provisional warrant, and

[116] Amended by the Police and Justice Act 2006.

(b) the documents referred to in section 70(9) are received by the appropriate judge within the period required under section 74(10).

(2) The judge must fix a date on which the extradition hearing is to begin.

(3) The date fixed under subsection (2) must not be later than the end of the permitted period, which is 2 months starting with the date on which the judge receives the documents.

(4) If before the date fixed under subsection (2) (or this subsection) a party to the proceedings applies to the judge for a later date to be fixed and the judge believes it to be in the interests of justice to do so, he may fix a later date; and this subsection may apply more than once.

(5) If the extradition hearing does not begin on or before the date fixed under this section and the person applies to the judge to be discharged, the judge must order his discharge.

[76A. Person charged with offence in United Kingdom before extradition hearing

(1) This section applies if—

(a) a person has been brought before the appropriate judge under section 72(3) or 74(3) but the extradition hearing has not begun; and

(b) the judge is informed that the person is charged with an offence in the United Kingdom.

(2) The judge must order further proceedings in respect of the extradition to be adjourned until one of these occurs—

(a) the charge is disposed of;

(b) the charge is withdrawn;

(c) proceedings in respect of the charge are discontinued;

(d) an order is made for the charge to lie on the file, or in relation to Scotland, the diet is deserted *pro loco et tempore*.

(3) If a sentence of imprisonment or another form of detention is imposed in respect of the offence charged, the judge may order further proceedings in respect of the extradition to be adjourned until the person is released from detention pursuant to the sentence (whether on licence or otherwise).][117]

[76B. Person serving sentence in United Kingdom before extradition hearing

(1) This section applies if—

(a) a person has been brought before the appropriate judge under section 72(3) or 74(3) but the extradition hearing has not begun; and

(b) the judge is informed that the person is in custody serving a sentence of imprisonment or another form of detention in the United Kingdom.

(2) The judge may order further proceedings in respect of the extradition to be adjourned until the person is released from detention pursuant to the sentence (whether on licence or otherwise).

(3) In a case where further proceedings in respect of the extradition are adjourned under subsection (2)—

(a) section 131 of the Magistrates' Courts Act 1980 (remand of accused already in custody) has effect as if a reference to 28 clear days in subsection (1) or (2) of that section were a reference to six months;

(b) Article 47(2) of the Magistrates' Courts (Northern Ireland) Order 1981 (period of remand in custody) has effect as if a reference to 28 days in—

(i) sub-paragraph (a)(iii), or

(ii) the words after sub-paragraph (b),were a reference to six months.][118]

77. Judge's powers at extradition hearing

(1) In England and Wales, at the extradition hearing the appropriate judge has the same powers (as nearly as may be) as a magistrates' court would have if the proceedings were the summary trial of an information against the person whose extradition is requested.

[117] Amended by the Policing and Crime Act 2009.
[118] Amended by the Policing and Crime Act 2009.

(2) In Scotland—
 (a) at the extradition hearing the appropriate judge has the same powers (as nearly as may be) as if the proceedings were summary proceedings in respect of an offence alleged to have been committed by the person whose extradition is requested; but
 (b) in his making any decision under section 78(4)(a) evidence from a single source shall be sufficient.
(3) In Northern Ireland, at the extradition hearing the appropriate judge has the same powers (as nearly as may be) as a magistrates' court would have if the proceedings were the hearing and determination of a complaint against the person whose extradition is requested.
(4) If the judge adjourns the extradition hearing he must remand the person in custody or on bail.
(5) [If the person is remanded in custody, the appropriate judge may][119] later grant bail.

78. Initial stages of extradition hearing

(1) This section applies if a person alleged to be the person whose extradition is requested appears or is brought before the appropriate judge for the extradition hearing.
(2) The judge must decide whether the documents sent to him by the Secretary of State consist of (or include)—
 (a) the documents referred to in section 70(9);
 (b) particulars of the person whose extradition is requested;
 (c) particulars of the offence specified in the request;
 (d) in the case of a person accused of an offence, a warrant for his arrest issued in the category 2 territory;
 (e) in the case of a person alleged to be unlawfully at large after conviction of an offence, a certificate issued in the category 2 territory of the conviction and (if he has been sentenced) of the sentence.
(3) If the judge decides the question in subsection (2) in the negative he must order the person's discharge.
(4) If the judge decides that question in the affirmative he must decide whether—
 (a) the person appearing or brought before him is the person whose extradition is requested;
 (b) the offence specified in the request is an extradition offence;
 (c) copies of the documents sent to the judge by the Secretary of State have been served on the person.
(5) The judge must decide the question in subsection (4)(a) on a balance of probabilities.
(6) If the judge decides any of the questions in subsection (4) in the negative he must order the person's discharge.
(7) If the judge decides those questions in the affirmative he must proceed under section 79.
(8) The reference in subsection (2)(d) to a warrant for a person's arrest includes a reference to a judicial document authorising his arrest.

79. Bars to extradition

(1) If the judge is required to proceed under this section he must decide whether the person's extradition to the category 2 territory is barred by reason of—
 (a) the rule against double jeopardy;
 (b) extraneous considerations;
 (c) the passage of time;
 (d) hostage-taking considerations.
(2) Sections 80 to 83 apply for the interpretation of subsection (1).
(3) If the judge decides any of the questions in subsection (1) in the affirmative he must order the person's discharge.
(4) If the judge decides those questions in the negative and the person is accused of the commission of the extradition offence but is not alleged to be unlawfully at large after conviction of it, the judge must proceed under section 84.
(5) If the judge decides those questions in the negative and the person is alleged to be unlawfully at large after conviction of the extradition offence, the judge must proceed under section 85.

---

[119] Amended by the Police and Justice Act 2006.

80. Rule against double jeopardy

A person's extradition to a category 2 territory is barred by reason of the rule against double jeopardy if (and only if) it appears that he would be entitled to be discharged under any rule of law relating to previous acquittal or conviction if he were charged with the extradition offence in the part of the United Kingdom where the judge exercises his jurisdiction.

81. Extraneous considerations

A person's extradition to a category 2 territory is barred by reason of extraneous considerations if (and only if) it appears that—

(a) the request for his extradition (though purporting to be made on account of the extradition offence) is in fact made for the purpose of prosecuting or punishing him on account of his race, religion, nationality, gender, sexual orientation or political opinions, or

(b) if extradited he might be prejudiced at his trial or punished, detained or restricted in his personal liberty by reason of his race, religion, nationality, gender, sexual orientation or political opinions.

82. Passage of time

A person's extradition to a category 2 territory is barred by reason of the passage of time if (and only if) it appears that it would be unjust or oppressive to extradite him by reason of the passage of time since he is alleged to have committed the extradition offence or [since he is alleged to have—

(a) committed the extradition offence (where he is accused of its commission), or

(b) become unlawfully at large (where he is alleged to have been convicted of it)].[120]

83. Hostage-taking considerations

(1) A person's extradition to a category 2 territory is barred by reason of hostage-taking considerations if (and only if) the territory is a party to the Hostage-taking Convention and it appears that—

(a) if extradited he might be prejudiced at his trial because communication between him and the appropriate authorities would not be possible, and

(b) the act or omission constituting the extradition offence also constitutes an offence under section 1 of the Taking of Hostages Act 1982 (c. 28) or an attempt to commit such an offence.

(2) The appropriate authorities are the authorities of the territory which are entitled to exercise rights of protection in relation to him.

(3) A certificate issued by the Secretary of State that a territory is a party to the Hostage-taking Convention is conclusive evidence of that fact for the purposes of subsection (1).

(4) The Hostage-taking Convention is the International Convention against the Taking of Hostages opened for signature at New York on 18 December 1979.

84. Case where person has not been convicted

(1) If the judge is required to proceed under this section he must decide whether there is evidence which would be sufficient to make a case requiring an answer by the person if the proceedings were the summary trial of an information against him.

(2) In deciding the question in subsection (1) the judge may treat a statement made by a person in a document as admissible evidence of a fact if—

(a) the statement is made by the person to a police officer or another person charged with the duty of investigating offences or charging offenders, and

(b) direct oral evidence by the person of the fact would be admissible.

(3) In deciding whether to treat a statement made by a person in a document as admissible evidence of a fact, the judge must in particular have regard—

(a) to the nature and source of the document;

(b) to whether or not, having regard to the nature and source of the document and to any other circumstances that appear to the judge to be relevant, it is likely that the document is authentic;

---

120 Amended by the Police and Justice Act 2006.

(c) to the extent to which the statement appears to supply evidence which would not be readily available if the statement were not treated as being admissible evidence of the fact;
(d) to the relevance of the evidence that the statement appears to supply to any issue likely to have to be determined by the judge in deciding the question in subsection (1);
(e) to any risk that the admission or exclusion of the statement will result in unfairness to the person whose extradition is sought, having regard in particular to whether it is likely to be possible to controvert the statement if the person making it does not attend to give oral evidence in the proceedings.

(4) A summary in a document of a statement made by a person must be treated as a statement made by the person in the document for the purposes of subsection (2).
(5) If the judge decides the question in subsection (1) in the negative he must order the person's discharge.
(6) If the judge decides that question in the affirmative he must proceed under section 87.
(7) If the judge is required to proceed under this section and the category 2 territory to which extradition is requested is designated for the purposes of this section by order made by the Secretary of State—
(a) the judge must not decide under subsection (1), and
(b) he must proceed under section 87.

(8) Subsection (1) applies to Scotland with the substitution of 'summary proceedings in respect of an offence alleged to have been committed by the person (except that for this purpose evidence from a single source shall be sufficient)' for 'the summary trial of an information against him'.
(9) Subsection (1) applies to Northern Ireland with the substitution of 'the hearing and determination of a complaint' for 'the summary trial of an information'.

85. Case where person has been convicted

(1) If the judge is required to proceed under this section he must decide whether the person was convicted in his presence.
(2) If the judge decides the question in subsection (1) in the affirmative he must proceed under section 87.
(3) If the judge decides that question in the negative he must decide whether the person deliberately absented himself from his trial.
(4) If the judge decides the question in subsection (3) in the affirmative he must proceed under section 87.
(5) If the judge decides that question in the negative he must decide whether the person would be entitled to a retrial or (on appeal) to a review amounting to a retrial.
(6) If the judge decides the question in subsection (5) in the affirmative he must proceed under section 86.
(7) If the judge decides that question in the negative he must order the person's discharge.
(8) The judge must not decide the question in subsection (5) in the affirmative unless, in any proceedings that it is alleged would constitute a retrial or a review amounting to a retrial, the person would have these rights—
(a) the right to defend himself in person or through legal assistance of his own choosing or, if he had not sufficient means to pay for legal assistance, to be given it free when the interests of justice so required;
(b) the right to examine or have examined witnesses against him and to obtain the attendance and examination of witnesses on his behalf under the same conditions as witnesses against him.

86. Conviction in person's absence

(1) If the judge is required to proceed under this section he must decide whether there is evidence which would be sufficient to make a case requiring an answer by the person if the proceedings were the summary trial of an information against him.
(2) In deciding the question in subsection (1) the judge may treat a statement made by a person in a document as admissible evidence of a fact if—
(a) the statement is made by the person to a police officer or another person charged with the duty of investigating offences or charging offenders, and
(b) direct oral evidence by the person of the fact would be admissible.

(3) In deciding whether to treat a statement made by a person in a document as admissible evidence of a fact, the judge must in particular have regard—
  (a) to the nature and source of the document;
  (b) to whether or not, having regard to the nature and source of the document and to any other circumstances that appear to the judge to be relevant, it is likely that the document is authentic;
  (c) to the extent to which the statement appears to supply evidence which would not be readily available if the statement were not treated as being admissible evidence of the fact;
  (d) to the relevance of the evidence that the statement appears to supply to any issue likely to have to be determined by the judge in deciding the question in subsection (1);
  (e) to any risk that the admission or exclusion of the statement will result in unfairness to the person whose extradition is sought, having regard in particular to whether it is likely to be possible to controvert the statement if the person making it does not attend to give oral evidence in the proceedings.

(4) A summary in a document of a statement made by a person must be treated as a statement made by the person in the document for the purposes of subsection (2).

(5) If the judge decides the question in subsection (1) in the negative he must order the person's discharge.

(6) If the judge decides that question in the affirmative he must proceed under section 87.

(7) If the judge is required to proceed under this section and the category 2 territory to which extradition is requested is designated for the purposes of this section by order made by the Secretary of State—
  (a) the judge must not decide under subsection (1), and
  (b) he must proceed under section 87.

(8) Subsection (1) applies to Scotland with the substitution of 'summary proceedings in respect of an offence alleged to have been committed by the person (except that for this purpose evidence from a single source shall be sufficient)' for 'the summary trial of an information against him'.

(9) Subsection (1) applies to Northern Ireland with the substitution of 'the hearing and determination of a complaint' for 'the summary trial of an information'.

87. Human rights

(1) If the judge is required to proceed under this section (by virtue of section 84, 85 or 86) he must decide whether the person's extradition would be compatible with the Convention rights within the meaning of the Human Rights Act 1998 (c. 42).

(2) If the judge decides the question in subsection (1) in the negative he must order the person's discharge.

(3) If the judge decides that question in the affirmative he must send the case to the Secretary of State for his decision whether the person is to be extradited.

88. Person charged with offence in United Kingdom

(1) This section applies if at any time in the extradition hearing the judge is informed that the person is charged with an offence in the United Kingdom.

(2) The judge must adjourn the extradition hearing until one of these occurs—
  (a) the charge is disposed of;
  (b) the charge is withdrawn;
  (c) proceedings in respect of the charge are discontinued;
  (d) an order is made for the charge to lie on the file, or in relation to Scotland, the diet is deserted *pro loco et tempore*.

(3) If a sentence of imprisonment or another form of detention is imposed in respect of the offence charged, the judge may adjourn the extradition hearing until [the person is released from detention pursuant to the sentence (whether on licence or otherwise)].[121]

(4) If before he adjourns the extradition hearing under subsection (2) the judge has decided under section 79 whether the person's extradition is barred by reason of the rule against double jeopardy, the judge must decide that question again after the resumption of the hearing.

---

[121] Amended by the Policing and Crime Act 2009.

89. Person serving sentence in United Kingdom

(1) This section applies if at any time in the extradition hearing the judge is informed that the person is [in custody][122] serving a sentence of imprisonment or another form of detention in the United Kingdom.
(2) The judge may adjourn the extradition hearing until [the person is released from detention pursuant to the sentence (whether on licence or otherwise)].[123]
[(3) In a case where an extradition hearing is adjourned under subsection (2)—
(a) section 131 of the Magistrates' Courts Act 1980 (remand of accused already in custody) has effect as if a reference to 28 clear days in subsection (1) or (2) of that section were a reference to six months;
(b) Article 47(2) of the Magistrates' Courts (Northern Ireland) Order 1981 (S.I. 1981/1675 (N.I. 26)) (period of remand in custody) has effect as if a reference to 28 days in—
(i) paragraph (a)(iii), or
(ii) the words after paragraph (b),
were a reference to six months.][124]

90. Competing extradition claim

(1) This section applies if at any time in the extradition hearing the judge is informed that the conditions in subsection (2) or (3) are met.
(2) The conditions are that—
(a) the Secretary of State has received another valid request for the person's extradition to a category 2 territory;
(b) the other request has not been disposed of;
(c) the Secretary of State has made an order under section 126(2) for further proceedings on the request under consideration to be deferred until the other request has been disposed of.
(3) The conditions are that—
(a) a certificate has been issued under section 2 in respect of a Part 1 warrant issued in respect of the person;
(b) the warrant has not been disposed of;
(c) the Secretary of State has made an order under section 179(2) for further proceedings on the request to be deferred until the warrant has been disposed of.
(4) The judge must remand the person in custody or on bail.
(5) [If the person is remanded in custody, the appropriate judge may][125] later grant bail.

91. Physical or mental condition

(1) This section applies if at any time in the extradition hearing it appears to the judge that the condition in subsection (2) is satisfied.
(2) The condition is that the physical or mental condition of the person is such that it would be unjust or oppressive to extradite him.
(3) The judge must—
(a) order the person's discharge, or
(b) adjourn the extradition hearing until it appears to him that the condition in subsection (2) is no longer satisfied.

92. Case sent to Secretary of State

(1) This section applies if the appropriate judge sends a case to the Secretary of State under this Part for his decision whether a person is to be extradited.
(2) The judge must inform the person in ordinary language that—
(a) he has a right to appeal to the High Court;

[122] Amended by the Policing and Crime Act 2009.
[123] Amended by the Policing and Crime Act 2009.
[124] Amended by the Police and Justice Act 2006.
[125] Amended by the Police and Justice Act 2006.

(b) if he exercises the right the appeal will not be heard until the Secretary of State has made his decision.

(3) But subsection (2) does not apply if the person has consented to his extradition under section 127.

(4) The judge must remand the person in custody or on bail—

(a) to wait for the Secretary of State's decision, and

(b) to wait for his extradition to the territory to which extradition is requested (if the Secretary of State orders him to be extradited).

(5) [If the person is remanded in custody, the appropriate judge may][126] later grant bail.

Secretary of state's functions

93. Secretary of State's consideration of case

(1) This section applies if the appropriate judge sends a case to the Secretary of State under this Part for his decision whether a person is to be extradited.

(2) The Secretary of State must decide whether he is prohibited from ordering the person's extradition under any of these sections—

(a) section 94 (death penalty);

(b) section 95 (speciality);

(c) section 96 (earlier extradition to United Kingdom from other territory).

[(d) section 96A (earlier transfer to United Kingdom by International Criminal Court).][127]

(3) If the Secretary of State decides any of the questions in subsection (2) in the affirmative he must order the person's discharge.

(4) If the Secretary of State decides those questions in the negative he must order the person to be extradited to the territory to which his extradition is requested unless—

(a) he is informed that the request has been withdrawn,

(b) he makes an order under section 126(2) or 179(2) for further proceedings on the request to be deferred and the person is discharged under section 180, or

(c) he orders the person's discharge under section 208.

(5) In deciding the questions in subsection (2), the Secretary of State is not required to consider any representations received by him after the end of the permitted period.

(6) The permitted period is the period of [4 weeks][128] starting with the appropriate day.

[(7) In the case of a person who has consented under section 127 to his extradition, the Secretary of State is not required—

(a) to wait until the end of the permitted period before ordering the person's extradition, or

(b) to consider any representations received after the order is made.][129]

94. Death penalty

(1) The Secretary of State must not order a person's extradition to a category 2 territory if he could be, will be or has been sentenced to death for the offence concerned in the category 2 territory.

(2) Subsection (1) does not apply if the Secretary of State receives a written assurance which he considers adequate that a sentence of death—

(a) will not be imposed, or

(b) will not be carried out (if imposed).

95. Speciality

(1) The Secretary of State must not order a person's extradition to a category 2 territory if there are no speciality arrangements with the category 2 territory.

(2) But subsection (1) does not apply if the person consented to his extradition under section 127 before his case was sent to the Secretary of State.

(3) There are speciality arrangements with a category 2 territory if (and only if) under the law of that territory or arrangements made between it and the United Kingdom a person who is extradited to

[126] Amended by the Police and Justice Act 2006.
[127] Amended by the Police and Justice Act 2006.
[128] Amended by the Police and Justice Act 2006.
[129] Amended by the Police and Justice Act 2006.

the territory from the United Kingdom may be dealt with in the territory for an offence committed before his extradition only if—

(a) the offence is one falling within subsection (4), or
(b) he is first given an opportunity to leave the territory.

(4) The offences are—

(a) the offence in respect of which the person is extradited;
(b) an extradition offence disclosed by the same facts as that offence, other than one in respect of which a sentence of death could be imposed;
(c) an extradition offence in respect of which the Secretary of State consents to the person being dealt with;
(d) an offence in respect of which the person waives the right that he would have (but for this paragraph) not to be dealt with for the offence.

(5) Arrangements made with a category 2 territory which is a Commonwealth country or a British overseas territory may be made for a particular case or more generally.

(6) A certificate issued by or under the authority of the Secretary of State confirming the existence of arrangements with a category 2 territory which is a Commonwealth country or a British overseas territory and stating the terms of the arrangements is conclusive evidence of those matters.

96. Earlier extradition to United Kingdom from other territory

The Secretary of State must not order a person's extradition to a category 2 territory if—

(a) the person was extradited to the United Kingdom from another territory (the extraditing territory);
(b) under arrangements between the United Kingdom and the extraditing territory, that territory's consent is required to the person's extradition from the United Kingdom to the category 2 territory in respect of the extradition offence under consideration;
(c) that consent has not been given on behalf of the extraditing territory.

[96A. Earlier transfer to United Kingdom by International Criminal Court

(1) The Secretary of State must not order a person's extradition to a category 2 territory if—

(a) the person was transferred to the United Kingdom to serve a sentence imposed by the International Criminal Court;
(b) under arrangements between the United Kingdom and the Court, the consent of the Presidency of the Court is required to the person's extradition from the United Kingdom to the category 2 territory in respect of the extradition offence under consideration;
(c) that consent has not been given.

(2) Subsection (1) does not apply if the person has served the sentence imposed by the Court and has subsequently—

(a) remained voluntarily in the United Kingdom for more than 30 days, or
(b) left the United Kingdom and returned to it.][130]

97. Deferral: person charged with offence in United Kingdom

(1) This section applies if—

(a) the appropriate judge sends a case to the Secretary of State under this Part for his decision whether a person is to be extradited;
(b) the person is charged with an offence in the United Kingdom.

(2) The Secretary of State must not make a decision with regard to the person's extradition until one of these occurs—

(a) the charge is disposed of;
(b) the charge is withdrawn;
(c) proceedings in respect of the charge are discontinued;
(d) an order is made for the charge to lie on the file or, in relation to Scotland, the diet is deserted *pro loco et tempore*.

[130] Amended by the Police and Justice Act 2006.

(3) If a sentence of imprisonment or another form of detention is imposed in respect of the offence charged, the Secretary of State may defer making a decision with regard to the person's extradition until [the person is released from detention pursuant to the sentence (whether on licence or otherwise)].[131]

98. Deferral: person serving sentence in United Kingdom

(1) This section applies if—
 (a) the appropriate judge sends a case to the Secretary of State under this Part for his decision whether a person is to be extradited;
 (b) the person is [in custody][132] serving a sentence of imprisonment or another form of detention in the United Kingdom.
(2) The Secretary of State may defer making a decision with regard to the person's extradition until [the person is released from detention pursuant to the sentence (whether on licence or otherwise)].[133]

99. Time limit for order for extradition or discharge

(1) This section applies if—
 (a) the appropriate judge sends a case to the Secretary of State under this Part for his decision whether a person is to be extradited;
 (b) within the required period the Secretary of State does not make an order for the person's extradition or discharge.
(2) If the person applies to [the appropriate judge][134] to be discharged, [the judge][135] must order his discharge.
(3) The required period is the period of 2 months starting with the appropriate day.
(4) If before the required period ends the Secretary of State [applies to the appropriate judge][136] for it to be extended [the judge may][137] make an order accordingly; and this subsection may apply more than once.

100. Information

(1) If the Secretary of State orders a person's extradition under this Part he must—
 (a) inform the person of the order;
 (b) inform him in ordinary language that he has a right of appeal to the High Court;
 (c) inform a person acting on behalf of the category 2 territory of the order.
(2) But subsection (1)(b) does not apply if the person has consented to his extradition under section 127.
(3) If the Secretary of State orders a person's extradition under this Part and he has received an assurance such as is mentioned in section 94(2), he must give the person a copy of the assurance when he informs him under subsection (1) of the order.
(4) If the Secretary of State orders a person's discharge under this Part he must—
 (a) inform him of the order;
 (b) inform a person acting on behalf of the category 2 territory of the order.

101. Making of order for extradition or discharge

(1) An order to which this section applies must be made under the hand of one of these—
 (a) the Secretary of State;
 (b) a Minister of State;
 (c) a Parliamentary Under-Secretary of State;
 (d) a senior official.

---

[131] Amended by the Policing and Crime Act 2009.
[132] Amended by the Policing and Crime Act 2009.
[133] Amended by the Policing and Crime Act 2009.
[134] Amended by the Police and Justice Act 2006.
[135] Amended by the Police and Justice Act 2006.
[136] Amended by the Police and Justice Act 2006.
[137] Amended by the Police and Justice Act 2006.

(2) But, in relation to Scotland, an order to which this section applies must be made under the hand of one of these—
(a) a member of the Scottish Executive or a junior Scottish Minister;
(b) a senior official who is a member of the staff of the Scottish Administration.
(3) This section applies to—
(a) an order under section 93 for a person's extradition;
(b) an order under section 93 or 123 for a person's discharge.
(4) A senior official is—
(a) a member of the Senior Civil Service;
(b) a member of the Senior Management Structure of Her Majesty's Diplomatic Service.
(5) If it appears to the Secretary of State that it is necessary to do so in consequence of any changes to the structure or grading of the [statutory civil service (or any part of it)],[138] he may by order make such amendments to subsection (4) as appear to him appropriate to preserve (so far as practicable) the effect of that subsection.
[(6) In subsection (5) "the statutory civil service" means the civil service within the meaning of Chapter 1 of Part 1 of the Constitutional Reform and Governance Act 2010 (see section 1(4) of that Act).][139]

102. The appropriate day

(1) This section applies for the purposes of sections 93 and 99 if the appropriate judge sends a case to the Secretary of State under this Part for his decision whether a person is to be extradited.
(2) If the person is charged with an offence in the United Kingdom, the appropriate day is the day on which one of these occurs—
(a) the charge is disposed of;
(b) the charge is withdrawn;
(c) proceedings in respect of the charge are discontinued;
(d) an order is made for the charge to lie on the file, or in relation to Scotland, the diet is deserted *pro loco et tempore.*
(3) If under section 97(3) or 98(2) the Secretary of State defers making a decision[, the appropriate day is the day on which the person is released from detention pursuant to the sentence (whether on licence or otherwise)].[140]
(4) If section 126 applies in relation to the request for the person's extradition (the request concerned) the appropriate day is—
(a) the day on which the Secretary of State makes an order under that section, if the order is for proceedings on the other request to be deferred;
(b) the day on which an order under section 180 is made, if the order under section 126 is for proceedings on the request concerned to be deferred and the order under section 180 is for the proceedings to be resumed.
(5) If section 179 applies in relation to the request for the person's extradition, the appropriate day is—
(a) the day on which the Secretary of State makes an order under that section, if the order is for proceedings on the warrant to be deferred;
(b) the day on which an order under section 180 is made, if the order under section 179 is for proceedings on the request to be deferred and the order under section 180 is for the proceedings to be resumed.
(6) If more than one of subsections (2) to (5) applies, the appropriate day is the latest of the days found under the subsections which apply.
(7) In any other case, the appropriate day is the day on which the judge sends the case to the Secretary of State for his decision whether the person is to be extradited.

[138] Amended by the Constitutional Reform and Governance Act 2010.
[139] Amended by the Constitutional Reform and Governance Act 2010.
[140] Amended by the Policing and Crime Act 2009.

Appeals

103. Appeal where case sent to Secretary of State

(1) If the judge sends a case to the Secretary of State under this Part for his decision whether a person is to be extradited, the person may appeal to the High Court against the relevant decision.
(2) But subsection (1) does not apply if the person consented to his extradition under section 127 before his case was sent to the Secretary of State.
(3) The relevant decision is the decision that resulted in the case being sent to the Secretary of State.
(4) An appeal under this section may be brought on a question of law or fact.
(5) If an appeal is brought under this section before the Secretary of State has decided whether the person is to be extradited the appeal must not be heard until after the Secretary of State has made his decision.
(6) If the Secretary of State orders the person's discharge the appeal must not be proceeded with.
(7) No appeal may be brought under this section if the Secretary of State has ordered the person's discharge.
(8) If notice of an appeal under section 110 against the decision which resulted in the order for the person's discharge is given in accordance with subsection (5) of that section—
   (a) subsections (6) and (7) do not apply;
   (b) no appeal may be brought under this section if the High Court has made its decision on the appeal.
(9) Notice of an appeal under this section must be given in accordance with rules of court before the end of the permitted period, which is 14 days starting with the day on which the Secretary of State informs the person under section 100(1) or (4) of the order he has made in respect of the person.

104. Court's powers on appeal under section 103

(1) On an appeal under section 103 the High Court may—
   (a) allow the appeal;
   (b) direct the judge to decide again a question (or questions) which he decided at the extradition hearing;
   (c) dismiss the appeal.
(2) The court may allow the appeal only if the conditions in subsection (3) or the conditions in subsection (4) are satisfied.
(3) The conditions are that—
   (a) the judge ought to have decided a question before him at the extradition hearing differently;
   (b) if he had decided the question in the way he ought to have done, he would have been required to order the person's discharge.
(4) The conditions are that—
   (a) an issue is raised that was not raised at the extradition hearing or evidence is available that was not available at the extradition hearing;
   (b) the issue or evidence would have resulted in the judge deciding a question before him at the extradition hearing differently;
   (c) if he had decided the question in that way, he would have been required to order the person's discharge.
(5) If the court allows the appeal it must—
   (a) order the person's discharge;
   (b) quash the order for his extradition.
(6) If the judge comes to a different decision on any question that is the subject of a direction under subsection (1)(b) he must order the person's discharge.
(7) If the judge comes to the same decision as he did at the extradition hearing on the question that is (or all the questions that are) the subject of a direction under subsection (1)(b) the appeal must be taken to have been dismissed by a decision of the High Court.
[(8) If the court makes a direction under subsection (1)(b) it must remand the person in custody or on bail.
(9) If the court remands the person in custody it may later grant bail.][141]

[141] Amended by the Police and Justice Act 2006.

105. Appeal against discharge at extradition hearing

(1) If at the extradition hearing the judge orders a person's discharge, an appeal to the High Court may be brought on behalf of the category 2 territory against the relevant decision.
(2) But subsection (1) does not apply if the order for the person's discharge was under section 122.
(3) The relevant decision is the decision which resulted in the order for the person's discharge.
(4) An appeal under this section may be brought on a question of law or fact.
(5) Notice of an appeal under this section must be given in accordance with rules of court before the end of the permitted period, which is 14 days starting with the day on which the order for the person's discharge is made.

106. Court's powers on appeal under section 105

(1) On an appeal under section 105 the High Court may—
 (a) allow the appeal;
 (b) direct the judge to decide the relevant question again;
 (c) dismiss the appeal.
(2) A question is the relevant question if the judge's decision on it resulted in the order for the person's discharge.
(3) The court may allow the appeal only if the conditions in subsection (4) or the conditions in subsection (5) are satisfied.
(4) The conditions are that—
 (a) the judge ought to have decided the relevant question differently;
 (b) if he had decided the question in the way he ought to have done, he would not have been required to order the person's discharge.
(5) The conditions are that—
 (a) an issue is raised that was not raised at the extradition hearing or evidence is available that was not available at the extradition hearing;
 (b) the issue or evidence would have resulted in the judge deciding the relevant question differently;
 (c) if he had decided the question in that way, he would not have been required to order the person's discharge.
(6) If the court allows the appeal it must—
 (a) quash the order discharging the person;
 (b) remit the case to the judge;
 (c) direct him to proceed as he would have been required to do if he had decided the relevant question differently at the extradition hearing.
(7) If the court makes a direction under subsection (1)(b) and the judge decides the relevant question differently he must proceed as he would have been required to do if he had decided that question differently at the extradition hearing.
(8) If the court makes a direction under subsection (1)(b) and the judge does not decide the relevant question differently the appeal must be taken to have been dismissed by a decision of the High Court.
[(9) If the court—
 (a) allows the appeal, or
 (b) makes a direction under subsection (1)(b),
 it must remand the person in custody or on bail.
(10) If the court remands the person in custody it may later grant bail.][142]

107. Detention pending conclusion of appeal under section 105

(1) This section applies if immediately after the judge orders the person's discharge the judge is informed on behalf of the category 2 territory of an intention to appeal under section 105.
(2) The judge must remand the person in custody or on bail while the appeal is pending.
(3) [If the person is remanded in custody, the appropriate judge may][143] later grant bail.

[142] Amended by the Police and Justice Act 2006.
[143] Amended by the Police and Justice Act 2006.

(4) An appeal under section 105 ceases to be pending at the earliest of these times—
(a) when the proceedings on the appeal are discontinued;
[(b) when the High Court—
(i) allows the appeal,
(ii) makes a direction under section 106(1)(b), or
(iii) dismisses the appeal,
unless, where the appeal is dismissed, the court is immediately informed on behalf of the category 2 territory of an intention to apply for leave to appeal to the [Supreme Court];[144]][145]
(c) at the end of the permitted period, which is 28 days starting with the day on which leave to appeal to the [Supreme Court][146] against the decision of the High Court on the appeal is granted[, if no appeal to the [Supreme Court][147] is brought before the end of that period];[148]
(d) when there is no further step that can be taken on behalf of the category 2 territory in relation to the appeal (ignoring any power of a court to grant leave to take a step out of time).
(5) The preceding provisions of this section apply to Scotland with these modifications—
(a) in subsection (4)(b) omit the words from '[unless]'[149] to the end;
(b) omit subsection (4)(c).

108. Appeal against extradition order

(1) If the Secretary of State orders a person's extradition under this Part, the person may appeal to the High Court against the order.
(2) But subsection (1) does not apply if the person has consented to his extradition under section 127.
(3) An appeal under this section may be brought on a question of law or fact.
(4) Notice of an appeal under this section must be given in accordance with rules of court before the end of the permitted period, which is 14 days starting with the day on which the Secretary of State informs the person of the order under section 100(1).

109. Court's powers on appeal under section 108

(1) On an appeal under section 108 the High Court may—
(a) allow the appeal;
(b) dismiss the appeal.
(2) The court may allow the appeal only if the conditions in subsection (3) or the conditions in subsection (4) are satisfied.
(3) The conditions are that—
(a) the Secretary of State ought to have decided a question before him differently;
(b) if he had decided the question in the way he ought to have done, he would not have ordered the person's extradition.
(4) The conditions are that—
(a) an issue is raised that was not raised when the case was being considered by the Secretary of State or information is available that was not available at that time;
(b) the issue or information would have resulted in the Secretary of State deciding a question before him differently;
(c) if he had decided the question in that way, he would not have ordered the person's extradition.
(5) If the court allows the appeal it must—
(a) order the person's discharge;
(b) quash the order for his extradition.

110. Appeal against discharge by Secretary of State

(1) If the Secretary of State makes an order for a person's discharge under this Part, an appeal to the High Court may be brought on behalf of the category 2 territory against the relevant decision.

---

144 Amended by the Constitutional Reform Act 2005.
145 Amended by the Police and Justice Act 2006.
146 Amended by the Constitutional Reform Act 2005.
147 Amended by the Constitutional Reform Act 2005.
148 Amended by the Police and Justice Act 2006.
149 Amended by the Police and Justice Act 2006.

(2) But subsection (1) does not apply if the order for the person's discharge was under section 123.
(3) The relevant decision is the decision which resulted in the order for the person's discharge.
(4) An appeal under this section may be brought on a question of law or fact.
(5) Notice of an appeal under this section must be given in accordance with rules of court before the end of the permitted period, which is 14 days starting with the day on which (under section 100(4)) the Secretary of State informs a person acting on behalf of the category 2 territory of the order.

111. Court's powers on appeal under section 110

(1) On an appeal under section 110 the High Court may—
  (a) allow the appeal;
  (b) dismiss the appeal.
(2) The court may allow the appeal only if the conditions in subsection (3) or the conditions in subsection (4) are satisfied.
(3) The conditions are that—
  (a) the Secretary of State ought to have decided a question before him differently;
  (b) if he had decided the question in the way he ought to have done, he would have ordered the person's extradition.
(4) The conditions are that—
  (a) an issue is raised that was not raised when the case was being considered by the Secretary of State or information is available that was not available at that time;
  (b) the issue or information would have resulted in the Secretary of State deciding a question before him differently;
  (c) if he had decided the question in that way, he would have ordered the person's extradition.
(5) If the court allows the appeal it must—
  (a) quash the order discharging the person;
  (b) order the person's extradition.
[(6) If the court allows the appeal it must remand the person in custody or on bail.
(7) If the court remands the person in custody it may later grant bail.][150]

[112. Detention pending conclusion of appeal under section 110

(1) This section applies in a case where the Secretary of State orders the person's discharge under this Part.
(2) Subject to subsection (3)—
  (a) the order made by the appropriate judge under section 92(4) ('the remand order') remains in force until the end of the period of three days beginning with the day on which the person's discharge is ordered;
  (b) if within that period the Secretary of State is informed in writing on behalf of the category 2 territory of an intention to appeal under section 110, the remand order remains in force while the appeal is pending.
(3) If the person is remanded in custody under section 92(4), the appropriate judge may grant bail.
(4) An appeal under section 110 ceases to be pending at the earliest of these times—
  (a) when the proceedings on the appeal are discontinued;
  (b) when the High Court—
    (i) allows the appeal, or
    (ii) dismisses the appeal,
  unless, where the appeal is dismissed, the court is immediately informed on behalf of the category 2 territory of an intention to apply for leave to appeal to the [Supreme Court];[151]
  (c) at the end of the permitted period, which is 28 days starting with the day on which leave to appeal to the [Supreme Court][152] against the decision of the High Court on the appeal is granted, if no appeal to the [Supreme Court][153] is brought before the end of that period;

150 Amended by the Police and Justice Act 2006.
151 Amended by the Constitutional Reform Act 2005.
152 Amended by the Constitutional Reform Act 2005.
153 Amended by the Constitutional Reform Act 2005.

(d) when there is no further step that can be taken on behalf of the category 2 territory in relation to the appeal (ignoring any power of a court to grant leave to take a step out of time).

(5) The preceding provisions of this section apply to Scotland with these modifications—

(a) in subsection (4)(b) omit the words from 'unless' to the end;

(b) omit subsection (4)(c).][154]

113. Appeal to High Court: time limit for start of hearing

(1) Rules of court must prescribe the period (the relevant period) within which the High Court must begin to hear an appeal under section 103, 105, 108 or 110.

(2) The High Court must begin to hear the appeal before the end of the relevant period.

(3) The High Court may extend the relevant period if it believes it to be in the interests of justice to do so; and this subsection may apply more than once.

(4) The power in subsection (3) may be exercised even after the end of the relevant period.

(5) If subsection (2) is not complied with and the appeal is under section 103 or 108—

(a) the appeal must be taken to have been allowed by a decision of the High Court;

(b) the person whose extradition has been ordered must be taken to have been discharged by the High Court;

(c) the order for the person's extradition must be taken to have been quashed by the High Court.

(6) If subsection (2) is not complied with and the appeal is under section 105 or 110 the appeal must be taken to have been dismissed by a decision of the High Court.

114. Appeal to [Supreme Court][155]

(1) An appeal lies to the [Supreme Court][156] from a decision of the High Court on an appeal under section 103, 105, 108 or 110.

(2) An appeal under this section lies at the instance of—

(a) the person whose extradition is requested;

(b) a person acting on behalf of the category 2 territory.

(3) An appeal under this section lies only with the leave of the High Court or the [Supreme Court].[157]

(4) Leave to appeal under this section must not be granted unless—

(a) the High Court has certified that there is a point of law of general public importance involved in the decision, and

(b) it appears to the court granting leave that the point is one which ought to be considered by the [Supreme Court].[158]

(5) An application to the High Court for leave to appeal under this section must be made before the end of the permitted period, which is 14 days starting with the day on which the court makes its decision on the appeal to it.

(6) An application to the [Supreme Court][159] for leave to appeal under this section must be made before the end of the permitted period, which is 14 days starting with the day on which the High Court refuses leave to appeal.

(7) If leave to appeal under this section is granted, the appeal must be brought before the end of the permitted period, which is 28 days starting with the day on which leave is granted.

(8) If subsection (7) is not complied with—

(a) the appeal must be taken to have been brought;

(b) the appeal must be taken to have been dismissed by the [Supreme Court][160] immediately after the end of the period permitted under that subsection.

(9) These must be ignored for the purposes of subsection (8)(b)—

(a) any power of a court to extend the period permitted for bringing the appeal;

(b) any power of a court to grant leave to take a step out of time.

---

[154] Amended by the Police and Justice Act 2006.
[155] Amended by the Constitutional Reform Act 2005.
[156] Amended by the Constitutional Reform Act 2005.
[157] Amended by the Constitutional Reform Act 2005.
[158] Amended by the Constitutional Reform Act 2005.
[159] Amended by the Constitutional Reform Act 2005.
[160] Amended by the Constitutional Reform Act 2005.

[(10) The High Court may grant bail to a person appealing under this section, or applying for leave to appeal under this section, against the dismissal of his appeal under section 103 or 108.][161]

(11) Section 5 of the Appellate Jurisdiction Act 1876 (c. 59) (composition of House of Lords for hearing and determination of appeals) applies in relation to an appeal under this section or an application for leave to appeal under this section as it applies in relation to an appeal under that Act.

(12) An order of the House of Lords which provides for an application for leave to appeal under this section to be determined by a committee constituted in accordance with section 5 of the Appellate Jurisdiction Act 1876 may direct that the decision of the committee is taken on behalf of the House.

(13) The preceding provisions of this section do not apply to Scotland.

115. Powers of [Supreme Court][162] on appeal under section 114

(1) On an appeal under section 114 the [Supreme Court][163] may—
  (a) allow the appeal;
  (b) dismiss the appeal.

(2) Subsection (3) applies if—
  (a) the person whose extradition is requested brings an appeal under section 114, and
  (b) the [Supreme Court][164] allows the appeal.

(3) The [Supreme Court][165] must—
  (a) order the person's discharge;
  (b) quash the order for his extradition, if the appeal was against a decision of the High Court to dismiss an appeal under section 103 or 108 or to allow an appeal under section 110.

(4) Subsection (5) applies if—
  (a) the High Court allows an appeal under section 103 or 108 by the person whose extradition is requested or dismisses an appeal under section 110 by a person acting on behalf of the category 2 territory,
  (b) a person acting on behalf of the category 2 territory brings an appeal under section 114 against the decision of the High Court, and
  (c) the [Supreme Court][166] allows the appeal.

(5) The [Supreme Court][167] must—
  (a) quash the order discharging the person made by the High Court under section 104(5) or 109(5) or by the Secretary of State under this Part;
  (b) order the person to be extradited to the category 2 territory.

(6) Subsection (7) applies if—
  (a) the High Court dismisses an appeal under section 105 against a decision made by the judge at the extradition hearing,
  (b) a person acting on behalf of the category 2 territory brings an appeal under section 114 against the decision of the High Court, and
  (c) the [Supreme Court][168] allows the appeal.

(7) The [Supreme Court][169] must—
  (a) quash the order of the judge discharging the person whose extradition is requested;
  (b) remit the case to the judge;
  (c) direct him to proceed as he would have been required to do if he had decided the relevant question differently at the extradition hearing.

(8) A question is the relevant question if the judge's decision on it resulted in the order for the person's discharge.

161 Amended by the Police and Justice Act 2006.
162 Amended by the Constitutional Reform Act 2005.
163 Amended by the Constitutional Reform Act 2005.
164 Amended by the Constitutional Reform Act 2005.
165 Amended by the Constitutional Reform Act 2005.
166 Amended by the Constitutional Reform Act 2005.
167 Amended by the Constitutional Reform Act 2005.
168 Amended by the Constitutional Reform Act 2005.
169 Amended by the Constitutional Reform Act 2005.

[(9) In a case where subsection (5) or (7) applies, the [Supreme Court][170] must remand, in custody or on bail, the person whose extradition is requested.

(10) If the [Supreme Court][171] remands the person in custody the High Court may later grant bail.][172]

[115A. Detention pending conclusion of certain appeals under section 114

(1) This section applies if—
   (a) on an appeal under section 103 or 108 the High Court orders the person's discharge;
   (b) immediately after it does so, the court is informed on behalf of the category 2 territory of an intention to appeal under section 114.

(2) The court must remand the person in custody or on bail while the appeal is pending.

(3) If the court remands the person in custody it may later grant bail.

(4) An appeal under section 114 ceases to be pending at the earliest of these times—
   (a) when the proceedings on the appeal are discontinued;
   (b) at the end of the permitted period, which is 28 days starting with the day on which leave to appeal to the [Supreme Court][173] against the decision of the High Court on the appeal under section 103 or 108 is granted, if no appeal to the [Supreme Court][174] is brought before the end of that period;
   (c) when there is no further step that can be taken on behalf of the category 2 territory in relation to the appeal (ignoring any power of a court to grant leave to take a step out of time).

(5) The preceding provisions of this section do not apply to Scotland.][175]

116. Appeals: general

A decision under this Part of the judge or the Secretary of State may be questioned in legal proceedings only by means of an appeal under this Part.

TIME FOR EXTRADITION

117. Extradition where no appeal

(1) This section applies if—
   (a) the Secretary of State orders a person's extradition to a category 2 territory under this Part, and
   (b) no notice of an appeal under section 103 or 108 is given before the end of the permitted period, which is 14 days starting with the day on which the Secretary of State informs the person under section 100(1) that he has ordered his extradition.

(2) The person must be extradited to the category 2 territory before the end of the required period, which is 28 days starting with the day on which the Secretary of State makes the order.

(3) If subsection (2) is not complied with and the person applies to the appropriate judge to be discharged the judge must order his discharge, unless reasonable cause is shown for the delay.

(4) These must be ignored for the purposes of subsection (1)(b)—
   (a) any power of a court to extend the period permitted for giving notice of appeal;
   (b) any power of a court to grant leave to take a step out of time.

118. Extradition following appeal

(1) This section applies if—
   (a) there is an appeal to the High Court under section 103, 108 or 110 against a decision or order relating to a person's extradition to a category 2 territory, and
   (b) the effect of the decision of the relevant court on the appeal is that the person is to be extradited there.

---

170 Amended by the Constitutional Reform Act 2005.
171 Amended by the Constitutional Reform Act 2005.
172 Amended by the Police and Justice Act 2006.
173 Amended by the Constitutional Reform Act 2005.
174 Amended by the Constitutional Reform Act 2005.
175 Amended by the Police and Justice Act 2006.

(2) The person must be extradited to the category 2 territory before the end of the required period, which is 28 days starting with—
 (a) the day on which the decision of the relevant court on the appeal becomes final, or
 (b) the day on which proceedings on the appeal are discontinued.
(3) The relevant court is—
 (a) the High Court, if there is no appeal to the [Supreme Court][176] against the decision of the High Court on the appeal;
 (b) the [Supreme Court],[177] if there is such an appeal.
(4) The decision of the High Court on the appeal becomes final—
 (a) when the period permitted for applying to the High Court for leave to appeal to the [Supreme Court][178] ends, if there is no such application;
 (b) when the period permitted for applying to the [Supreme Court][179] for leave to appeal to it ends, if the High Court refuses leave to appeal and there is no application to the [Supreme Court][180] for leave to appeal;
 (c) when the [Supreme Court][181] refuses leave to appeal to it;
 (d) at the end of the permitted period, which is 28 days starting with the day on which leave to appeal to the [Supreme Court][182] is granted, if no such appeal is brought before the end of that period.
(5) These must be ignored for the purposes of subsection (4)—
 (a) any power of a court to extend the period permitted for applying for leave to appeal;
 (b) any power of a court to grant leave to take a step out of time.
(6) The decision of the [Supreme Court][183] on the appeal becomes final when it is made.
(7) If subsection (2) is not complied with and the person applies to the appropriate judge to be discharged the judge must order his discharge, unless reasonable cause is shown for the delay.
(8) The preceding provisions of this section apply to Scotland with these modifications—
 (a) in subsections (1) and (2) for 'relevant court' substitute 'High Court';
 (b) omit subsections (3) to (6).

119. Undertaking in relation to person serving sentence in United Kingdom

(1) This section applies if—
 (a) the Secretary of State orders a person's extradition to a category 2 territory under this Part;
 (b) the person is serving a sentence of imprisonment or another form of detention in the United Kingdom[, either—
  (i) in custody, or
  (ii) on licence].[184]
(2) The Secretary of State may make the order for extradition subject to the condition that extradition is not to take place before he receives an undertaking given on behalf of the category 2 territory in terms specified by him.
(3) The terms which may be specified by the Secretary of State in relation to a person [within subsection (1)(b)(i) who is][185] accused in a category 2 territory of the commission of an offence include terms—
 (a) that the person be kept in custody until the conclusion of the proceedings against him for the offence and any other offence in respect of which he is permitted to be dealt with in the category 2 territory;
 (b) that the person be returned to the United Kingdom to serve the remainder of his sentence on the conclusion of those proceedings.

[176] Amended by the Constitutional Reform Act 2005.
[177] Amended by the Constitutional Reform Act 2005.
[178] Amended by the Constitutional Reform Act 2005.
[179] Amended by the Constitutional Reform Act 2005.
[180] Amended by the Constitutional Reform Act 2005.
[181] Amended by the Constitutional Reform Act 2005.
[182] Amended by the Constitutional Reform Act 2005.
[183] Amended by the Constitutional Reform Act 2005.
[184] Amended by the Police and Justice Act 2006.
[185] Amended by the Police and Justice Act 2006.

[(3A) The terms which may be specified by the Secretary of State in relation to a person within subsection (1)(b)(ii) who is accused in a category 2 territory of the commission of an offence include terms that the person be returned to the United Kingdom to serve the remainder of his sentence after serving any sentence imposed on him in the category 2 territory for—

(a) the offence, and

(b) any other offence in respect of which he is permitted to be dealt with in the category 2 territory.][186]

(4) The terms which may be specified by the Secretary of State in relation to a person alleged to be unlawfully at large after conviction of an offence by a court in a category 2 territory include terms that the person be returned to the United Kingdom to serve the remainder of his sentence after serving any sentence imposed on him in the category 2 territory for—

(a) the offence, and

(b) any other offence in respect of which he is permitted to be dealt with in the category 2 territory.

(5) Subsections (6) and (7) apply if the Secretary of State makes an order for extradition subject to a condition under subsection (2).

(6) If the Secretary of State does not receive the undertaking before the end of the period of 21 days starting with the day on which he makes the order and the person applies to the High Court to be discharged, the court must order his discharge.

(7) If the Secretary of State receives the undertaking before the end of that period—

(a) in a case where section 117 applies, the required period for the purposes of section 117(2) is 28 days starting with the day on which the Secretary of State receives the undertaking;

(b) in a case where section 118 applies, the required period for the purposes of section 118(2) is 28 days starting with the day on which the decision of the relevant court on the appeal becomes final (within the meaning of that section) or (if later) the day on which the Secretary of State receives the undertaking.

120. Extradition following deferral for competing claim

(1) This section applies if—

(a) an order is made under this Part for a person to be extradited to a category 2 territory in pursuance of a request for his extradition;

(b) before the person is extradited to the territory an order is made under section 126(2) or 179(2) for the person's extradition in pursuance of the request to be deferred;

(c) the appropriate judge makes an order under section 181(2) for the person's extradition in pursuance of the request to cease to be deferred.

(2) In a case where section 117 applies, the required period for the purposes of section 117(2) is 28 days starting with the day on which the order under section 181(2) is made.

(3) In a case where section 118 applies, the required period for the purposes of section 118(2) is 28 days starting with the day on which the decision of the relevant court on the appeal becomes final (within the meaning of that section) or (if later) the day on which the order under section 181(2) is made.

121. Asylum claim

(1) This section applies if—

(a) a person whose extradition is requested makes an asylum claim at any time in the relevant period;

(b) an order is made under this Part for the person to be extradited in pursuance of the request.

(2) The relevant period is the period—

(a) starting when a certificate is issued under section 70 in respect of the request;

(b) ending when the person is extradited in pursuance of the request.

(3) The person must not be extradited in pursuance of the request before the asylum claim is finally determined; and sections 117 and 118 have effect subject to this.

(4) If the Secretary of State allows the asylum claim, the claim is finally determined when he makes his decision on the claim.

---

[186] Amended by the Police and Justice Act 2006.

(5) If the Secretary of State rejects the asylum claim, the claim is finally determined—
   (a) when the Secretary of State makes his decision on the claim, if there is no right to appeal against the Secretary of State's decision on the claim;
   (b) when the period permitted for appealing against the Secretary of State's decision on the claim ends, if there is such a right but there is no such appeal;
   (c) when the appeal against that decision is finally determined or is withdrawn or abandoned, if there is such an appeal.
(6) An appeal against the Secretary of State's decision on an asylum claim is not finally determined for the purposes of subsection (5) at any time when a further appeal or an application for leave to bring a further appeal—
   (a) has been instituted and has not been finally determined or withdrawn or abandoned, or
   (b) may be brought.
(7) The remittal of an appeal is not a final determination for the purposes of subsection (6).
(8) The possibility of an appeal out of time with leave must be ignored for the purposes of sub-sections(5) and (6).

Withdrawal of extradition request

122. Withdrawal of request before end of extradition hearing

(1) This section applies if at any time in the relevant period the appropriate judge is informed by the Secretary of State that a request for a person's extradition has been withdrawn.
(2) The relevant period is the period—
   (a) starting when the person first appears or is brought before the appropriate judge following his arrest under this Part;
   (b) ending when the judge orders the person's discharge or sends the case to the Secretary of State for his decision whether the person is to be extradited.
(3) The judge must order the person's discharge.
(4) If the person is not before the judge at the time the judge orders his discharge, the judge must inform him of the order as soon as practicable.

123. Withdrawal of request after case sent to Secretary of State

(1) This section applies if at any time in the relevant period the Secretary of State is informed that a request for a person's extradition has been withdrawn.
(2) The relevant period is the period—
   (a) starting when the judge sends the case to the Secretary of State for his decision whether the person is to be extradited;
   (b) ending when the person is extradited in pursuance of the request or discharged.
(3) The Secretary of State must order the person's discharge.

124. Withdrawal of request while appeal to High Court pending

(1) This section applies if at any time in the relevant period the High Court is informed by the Secretary of State that a request for a person's extradition has been withdrawn.
(2) The relevant period is the period—
   (a) starting when notice of an appeal to the court is given by the person whose extradition is requested or by a person acting on behalf of the category 2 territory to which his extradition is requested;
   (b) ending when proceedings on the appeal are discontinued or the court makes its decision on the appeal.
(3) If the appeal is under section 103 or 108, the court must—
   (a) order the person's discharge;
   (b) quash the order for his extradition, if the Secretary of State has ordered his extradition.
(4) If the appeal is under section 105 or 110, the court must dismiss the appeal.
(5) If the person is not before the court at the time the court orders his discharge, the court must inform him of the order as soon as practicable.

125. Withdrawal of request while appeal to [Supreme Court][187] pending

(1) This section applies if at any time in the relevant period the [Supreme Court][188] is informed by the Secretary of State that a request for a person's extradition has been withdrawn.

(2) The relevant period is the period—

(a) starting when leave to appeal to the [Supreme Court][189] is granted to the person whose extradition is requested or a person acting on behalf of the category 2 territory to which his extradition is requested;

(b) ending when proceedings on the appeal are discontinued or the [Supreme Court][190] makes its decision on the appeal.

(3) If the appeal is brought by the person whose extradition is requested the [Supreme Court][191] must—

(a) order the person's discharge;

(b) quash the order for his extradition, in a case where the appeal was against a decision of the High Court to dismiss an appeal under section 103 or 108.

(4) If the appeal is brought by a person acting on behalf of the category 2 territory the [Supreme Court][192] must dismiss the appeal.

(5) If the person whose extradition is requested is not before the [Supreme Court][193] at the time it orders his discharge, the [Supreme Court][194] must inform him of the order as soon as practicable.

Competing extradition requests

126. Competing extradition requests

(1) This section applies if—

(a) the Secretary of State receives a valid request for a person's extradition to a category 2 territory;

(b) the person is in the United Kingdom;

(c) before the person is extradited in pursuance of the request or discharged, the Secretary of State receives another valid request for the person's extradition.

(2) The Secretary of State may—

(a) order proceedings (or further proceedings) on one of the requests to be deferred until the other one has been disposed of, if neither of the requests has been disposed of;

(b) order the person's extradition in pursuance of the request under consideration to be deferred until the other request has been disposed of, if an order for his extradition in pursuance of the request under consideration has been made.

(3) In applying subsection (2) the Secretary of State must take account in particular of these matters—

(a) the relative seriousness of the offences concerned;

(b) the place where each offence was committed (or was alleged to have been committed);

(c) the date when each request was received;

(d) whether, in the case of each offence, the person is accused of its commission (but not alleged to have been convicted) or is alleged to be unlawfully at large after conviction.

Consent to extradition

127. Consent to extradition: general

(1) A person arrested under a warrant issued under section 71 may consent to his extradition to the category 2 territory to which his extradition is requested.

---

[187] Amended by the Constitutional Reform Act 2005.
[188] Amended by the Constitutional Reform Act 2005.
[189] Amended by the Constitutional Reform Act 2005.
[190] Amended by the Constitutional Reform Act 2005.
[191] Amended by the Constitutional Reform Act 2005.
[192] Amended by the Constitutional Reform Act 2005.
[193] Amended by the Constitutional Reform Act 2005.
[194] Amended by the Constitutional Reform Act 2005.

(2) A person arrested under a provisional warrant may consent to his extradition to the category 2 territory in which he is accused of the commission of an offence or is alleged to have been convicted of an offence.
(3) Consent under this section—
 (a) must be given in writing;
 (b) is irrevocable.
(4) Consent under this section which is given by a person before his case is sent to the Secretary of State for the Secretary of State's decision whether he is to be extradited must be given before the appropriate judge.
(5) Consent under this section which is given in any other case must be given to the Secretary of State.
(6) A person may not give his consent under this section before the appropriate judge unless—
 (a) he is legally represented before the appropriate judge at the time he gives consent, or
 (b) he is a person to whom subsection (7) applies.
(7) This subsection applies to a person if—
 (a) he has been informed of his right to apply for legal aid and has had the opportunity to apply for legal aid, but he has refused or failed to apply;
 (b) he has applied for legal aid but his application has been refused;
 (c) he was granted legal aid but the legal aid was withdrawn.
(8) In subsection (7) 'legal aid' means—
 (a) in England and Wales, a right to representation funded by the Legal Services Commission as part of the Criminal Defence Service;
 (b) in Scotland, such legal aid as is available by virtue of section 183(a) of this Act;
 (c) in Northern Ireland, such free legal aid as is available by virtue of sections 184 and 185 of this Act.
(9) For the purposes of subsection (6) a person is to be treated as legally represented before the appropriate judge if (and only if) he has the assistance of counsel or a solicitor to represent him in the proceedings before the appropriate judge.

128. Consent to extradition before case sent to Secretary of State

(1) This section applies if a person gives his consent under section 127 to the appropriate judge.
(2) If the judge has not fixed a date under section 75 or 76 on which the extradition hearing is to begin he is not required to do so.
(3) If the extradition hearing has begun the judge is no longer required to proceed or continue proceeding under sections 78 to 91.
(4) The judge must send the case to the Secretary of State for his decision whether the person is to be extradited.
(5) The person must be taken to have waived any right he would have (apart from the consent) not to be dealt with in the category 2 territory for an offence committed before his extradition.

Post-extradition matters

129. Consent to other offence being dealt with

(1) This section applies if—
 (a) a person is extradited to a category 2 territory in accordance with this Part;
 (b) the Secretary of State receives a valid request for his consent to the person being dealt with in the territory for an offence other than the offence in respect of which he was extradited.
(2) A request for consent is valid if it is made by an authority which is an authority of the territory and which the Secretary of State believes has the function of making requests for the consent referred to in subsection (1)(b) in that territory.
(3) The Secretary of State must serve notice on the person that he has received the request for consent, unless he is satisfied that it would not be practicable to do so.
(4) The Secretary of State must decide whether the offence is an extradition offence.
(5) If the Secretary of State decides the question in subsection (4) in the negative he must refuse his consent.

(6) If the Secretary of State decides that question in the affirmative he must decide whether the appropriate judge would send the case to him (for his decision whether the person was to be extradited) under sections 79 to 91 if—
   (a) the person were in the United Kingdom, and
   (b) the judge were required to proceed under section 79 in respect of the offence for which the Secretary of State's consent is requested.
(7) If the Secretary of State decides the question in subsection (6) in the negative he must refuse his consent.
(8) If the Secretary of State decides that question in the affirmative he must decide whether, if the person were in the United Kingdom, his extradition in respect of the offence would be prohibited under section 94, 95 or 96.
(9) If the Secretary of State decides the question in subsection (8) in the affirmative he must refuse his consent.
(10) If the Secretary of State decides that question in the negative he may give his consent.

130. Consent to further extradition to category 2 territory

(1) This section applies if—
   (a) a person is extradited to a category 2 territory (the requesting territory) in accordance with this Part;
   (b) the Secretary of State receives a valid request for his consent to the person's extradition to another category 2 territory for an offence other than the offence in respect of which he was extradited.
(2) A request for consent is valid if it is made by an authority which is an authority of the requesting territory and which the Secretary of State believes has the function of making requests for the consent referred to in subsection (1)(b) in that territory.
(3) The Secretary of State must serve notice on the person that he has received the request for consent, unless he is satisfied that it would not be practicable to do so.
(4) The Secretary of State must decide whether the offence is an extradition offence in relation to the category 2 territory referred to in subsection (1)(b).
(5) If the Secretary of State decides the question in subsection (4) in the negative he must refuse his consent.
(6) If the Secretary of State decides that question in the affirmative he must decide whether the appropriate judge would send the case to him (for his decision whether the person was to be extradited) under sections 79 to 91 if—
   (a) the person were in the United Kingdom, and
   (b) the judge were required to proceed under section 79 in respect of the offence for which the Secretary of State's consent is requested.
(7) If the Secretary of State decides the question in subsection (6) in the negative he must refuse his consent.
(8) If the Secretary of State decides that question in the affirmative he must decide whether, if the person were in the United Kingdom, his extradition in respect of the offence would be prohibited under section 94, 95 or 96.
(9) If the Secretary of State decides the question in subsection (8) in the affirmative he must refuse his consent.
(10) If the Secretary of State decides that question in the negative he may give his consent.

131. Consent to further extradition to category 1 territory

(1) This section applies if—
   (a) a person is extradited to a category 2 territory (the requesting territory) in accordance with this Part;
   (b) the Secretary of State receives a valid request for his consent to the person's extradition to a category 1 territory for an offence other than the offence in respect of which he was extradited.
(2) A request for consent is valid if it is made by an authority which is an authority of the requesting territory and which the Secretary of State believes has the function of making requests for the consent referred to in subsection (1)(b) in that territory.
(3) The Secretary of State must serve notice on the person that he has received the request for consent, unless he is satisfied that it would not be practicable to do so.

(4) The Secretary of State must decide whether the offence is an extradition offence within the meaning given by section 64 in relation to the category 1 territory.
(5) If the Secretary of State decides the question in subsection (4) in the negative he must refuse his consent.
(6) If the Secretary of State decides that question in the affirmative he must decide whether the appropriate judge would order the person's extradition under sections 11 to 25 if—
   (a) the person were in the United Kingdom, and
   (b) the judge were required to proceed under section 11 in respect of the offence for which the Secretary of State's consent is requested.
(7) If the Secretary of State decides the question in subsection (6) in the affirmative he must give his consent.
(8) If the Secretary of State decides that question in the negative he must refuse his consent.

[132. Return of person to serve remainder of sentence

(1) This section applies if—
   (a) a person who is serving a sentence of imprisonment or another form of detention in the United Kingdom is extradited to a category 2 territory in accordance with this Part;
   (b) the person is returned to the United Kingdom to serve the remainder of the sentence or the person otherwise returns to the United Kingdom.
(2) Time during which the person was outside the United Kingdom as a result of the extradition does not count as time served by the person as part of the sentence.
(3) But subsection (2) does not apply if—
   (a) the person was extradited for the purpose of being prosecuted for an offence, and
   (b) the person has not been convicted of the offence or of any other offence in respect of which the person was permitted to be dealt with in the category 2 territory.
(4) In a case falling within subsection (3), time during which the person was outside the United Kingdom as a result of the extradition counts as time served by the person as part of the sentence if (and only if) it was spent in custody in connection with the offence or any other offence in respect of which the person was permitted to be dealt with in the territory.
(5) In a case where the person is not entitled to be released from detention pursuant to the sentence—
   (a) the person is liable to be detained in pursuance of the sentence, and
   (b) if at large, the person must be treated as being unlawfully at large.
(6) In a case where the person is entitled to be released from detention on licence pursuant to the sentence—
   (a) if the person was released on licence at the time of extradition, the licence is suspended until the person's return,
   (b) if the person was not released on licence at that time, subsections (7) to (10) apply in relation to the person ("the offender").
(7) The offender is liable to be detained, on return, in any place in which the offender could have been detained pursuant to the sentence before the time of extradition.
(8) A constable or immigration officer may—
   (a) take the offender into custody, and
   (b) convey the offender to the place mentioned in subsection (7).
(9) The offender must be released on licence within the period of 5 days beginning when the offender is taken (or retaken) into custody under this section.
(10) In calculating a period of 5 days for the purposes of subsection (9) no account is to be taken of any day mentioned in any of paragraphs (a) to (d) of section 59(10).
(11) A person is entitled to be released from detention if there is—
   (a) a duty to release the person under section 33(1), (1A) or (2) of the Criminal Justice Act 1991,
   (b) a duty to release the person under section 244 of the Criminal Justice Act 2003 (other than temporarily on licence pursuant to an intermittent custody order under section 183(1)(b) of the Criminal Justice Act 2003),
   (c) a duty to release the person under section 1, 1AA or 7(1) of the Prisoners and Criminal Proceedings (Scotland) Act 1993 or section 5, 11(2), 13, 19 or 23 of the Custodial Sentences and Weapons (Scotland) Act 2007, or

(d) a duty to release the person under section 1 of the Northern Ireland (Remission of Sentences) Act 1995, Article 26 of the Criminal Justice (Northern Ireland) Order 1996 or Article 17 or 18(8) of the Criminal Justice (Northern Ireland) Order 2008.

(12) The powers conferred on a constable by subsection (8) are exercisable in any part of the United Kingdom.

(13) An immigration officer is a person who is an immigration officer within the meaning of the Immigration Act 1971.][195]

Costs

133. Costs where extradition ordered

(1) This section applies if any of the following occurs in relation to a person whose extradition is requested under this Part—
  (a) an order for the person's extradition is made under this Part;
  (b) the High Court dismisses an appeal under section 103 or 108;
  (c) the High Court or the [Supreme Court][196] dismisses an application for leave to appeal to the [Supreme Court][197] under section 114, if the application is made by the person;
  (d) the [Supreme Court][198] dismisses an appeal under section 114, if the appeal is brought by the person.

(2) In a case falling within subsection (1)(a), the appropriate judge may make such order as he considers just and reasonable with regard to the costs to be paid by the person.

(3) In a case falling within subsection (1)(b) by virtue of section 104(7), the judge who decides the question that is (or all the questions that are) the subject of a direction under section 104(1)(b) may make such order as he considers just and reasonable with regard to the costs to be paid by the person.

(4) In any other case falling within subsection (1)(b), the High Court may make such order as it considers just and reasonable with regard to the costs to be paid by the person.

(5) In a case falling within subsection (1)(c) or (d), the court by which the application or appeal is dismissed may make such order as it considers just and reasonable with regard to the costs to be paid by the person.

(6) An order for costs under this section—
  (a) must specify their amount;
  (b) may name the person to whom they are to be paid.

134. Costs where discharge ordered

(1) This section applies if any of the following occurs in relation to a person whose extradition to a category 2 territory is requested under this Part—
  (a) an order for the person's discharge is made under this Part;
  (b) the person is taken to be discharged under this Part;
  (c) the High Court dismisses an appeal under section 105 or 110;
  (d) the High Court or the [Supreme Court][199] dismisses an application for leave to appeal to the [Supreme Court][200] under section 114, if the application is made on behalf of the category 2 territory;
  (e) the [Supreme Court][201] dismisses an appeal under section 114, if the appeal is brought on behalf of the category 2 territory.

(2) In a case falling within subsection (1)(a), an order under subsection (5) in favour of the person may be made by—
  (a) the appropriate judge, if the order for the person's discharge is made by him or by the Secretary of State;

---

195 Amended by the Policing and Crime Act 2009.
196 Amended by the Constitutional Reform Act 2005.
197 Amended by the Constitutional Reform Act 2005.
198 Amended by the Constitutional Reform Act 2005.
199 Amended by the Constitutional Reform Act 2005.
200 Amended by the Constitutional Reform Act 2005.
201 Amended by the Constitutional Reform Act 2005.

(b) the High Court, if the order for the person's discharge is made by it;
(c) the [Supreme Court],[202] if the order for the person's discharge is made by it.

(3) In a case falling within subsection (1)(b), the appropriate judge may make an order under subsection (5) in favour of the person.

(4) In a case falling within subsection (1)(c), (d) or (e), the court by which the application or appeal is dismissed may make an order under subsection (5) in favour of the person.

(5) An order under this subsection in favour of a person is an order for a payment of the appropriate amount to be made to the person out of money provided by Parliament.

[(5A) In England and Wales, an order under subsection (5) is to be made, and the appropriate amount is to be determined, in accordance with sections 135A and 135B.

(5B) In Scotland and Northern Ireland, an order under subsection (5) is to be made, and the appropriate amount is to be determined, in accordance with subsections (6) to (9).][203]

(6) The appropriate amount is such amount as the judge or court making the order under subsection (5) considers reasonably sufficient to compensate the person in whose favour the order is made for any expenses properly incurred by him in the proceedings under this Part.

(7) But if the judge or court making an order under subsection (5) is of the opinion that there are circumstances which make it inappropriate that the person in whose favour the order is made should recover the full amount mentioned in subsection (6), the judge or court must—
(a) assess what amount would in his or its opinion be just and reasonable;
(b) specify that amount in the order as the appropriate amount.

(8) Unless subsection (7) applies, the appropriate amount—
(a) must be specified in the order, if the court considers it appropriate for it to be so specified and the person in whose favour the order is made agrees the amount;
(b) must be determined in accordance with regulations made by the Lord Chancellor for the purposes of this section, in any other case.

[(9) In relation to proceedings in Northern Ireland (including proceedings in the Supreme Court on an appeal, or on an application for leave to appeal, from proceedings in Northern Ireland)—
(a) subsection (5) has effect as if for "out of money provided by Parliament" there were substituted "by the Department of Justice in Northern Ireland";
(b) the power to make regulations under subsection (8)(b) is exercisable by the Department of Justice in Northern Ireland (and not by the Lord Chancellor).][204]

135. Costs where discharge ordered: supplementary

(1) ...
(2) ...[205]
(3) In Northern Ireland, section 7 of the Costs in Criminal Cases Act (Northern Ireland) 1968 (c. 10) (rules relating to costs) applies in relation to section 134 as that section applies in relation to sections 2 to 5 of that Act.

[135A Appropriate amount: England and Wales

(1) For the purposes of an order under section 134(5), the appropriate amount is such amount as the judge or court making the order considers reasonably sufficient to compensate the person in whose favour the order is made for any expenses properly incurred by the person in the proceedings under this Part.

(2) But if the judge or court considers that there are circumstances that make it inappropriate for the person to recover the full amount mentioned in subsection (1), the order under section 134(5) must be for the payment out of money provided by Parliament of such lesser amount as the judge or court considers just and reasonable.

(3) Subsections (1) and (2) have effect subject to—
(a) section 135B, and

202 Amended by the Constitutional Reform Act 2005.
203 Amended by the Legal Aid Sentencing and Punishment of Offenders Act 2012.
204 Amended by SI 2010/976.
205 Repealed by the Legal Aid Sentencing and Punishment of Offenders Act 2012.

(b) regulations under section 20(1A)(d) of the Prosecution of Offences Act 1985 (as applied by this section).

(4) When making an order under section 134(5), the judge or court must fix the amount to be paid out of money provided by Parliament in the order if the judge or court considers it appropriate to do so and—

(a) the person in whose favour the order is made agrees the amount, or

(b) subsection (2) applies.

(5) Where the judge or court does not fix the amount to be paid out of money provided by Parliament in the order—

(a) the judge or court must describe in the order any reduction required under subsection (2), and

(b) the amount must be fixed by means of a determination made by or on behalf of the court in accordance with procedures specified in regulations made by the Lord Chancellor.

(6) Subsections (1A) to (1C) and (3) of section 20 of the Prosecution of Offences Act 1985 (regulations as to amounts ordered to be paid out of central funds) apply in relation to amounts payable out of money provided by Parliament in pursuance of an order under section 134 as they apply in relation to amounts payable out of central funds in pursuance of costs orders made under section 16 of that Act.

(7) This section extends to England and Wales only.][206]

[135B Legal costs: England and Wales

(1) An order under section 134(5) may not require the payment out of money provided by Parliament of an amount that includes an amount in respect of legal costs incurred by the person in whose favour the order is made, subject to the following provisions of this section.

(2) Subsection (1) does not apply in relation to legal costs incurred in—

(a) proceedings in a magistrates' court, or

(b) proceedings in the Supreme Court.

(3) The Lord Chancellor may by regulations make provision about exceptions from the prohibition in subsection (1), including—

(a) provision amending this section by adding, modifying or removing an exception, and

(b) provision for an exception to arise where a determination has been made by a person specified in the regulations.

(4) Regulations under subsection (3) may not remove or limit the exception provided by subsection (2)(b).

(5) Where a judge or court makes an order under section 134(5) requiring the payment out of money provided by Parliament of an amount that includes an amount in respect of legal costs, the order must include a statement to that effect.

(6) Where, in an order under section 134(5), a judge or court fixes an amount to be paid out of money provided by Parliament that includes an amount in respect of legal costs incurred in proceedings in a court other than the Supreme Court, the latter amount must not exceed an amount specified by regulations made by the Lord Chancellor.

(7) In this section—

"legal costs" means fees, charges, disbursements and other amounts payable in respect of advocacy services or litigation services including, in particular, expert witness costs;

"advocacy services" means any services which it would be reasonable to expect a person who is exercising, or contemplating exercising, a right of audience in relation to any proceedings, or contemplated proceedings, to provide;

"expert witness costs" means amounts payable in respect of the services of an expert witness, including amounts payable in connection with attendance by the witness at court or elsewhere;

"litigation services" means any services which it would be reasonable to expect a person who is exercising, or contemplating exercising, a right to conduct litigation in relation to proceedings, or contemplated proceedings, to provide.

(8) This section extends to England and Wales only.][207]

---

[206] Inserted by the Legal Aid Sentencing and Punishment of Offenders Act 2012.

[207] Inserted by the Legal Aid Sentencing and Punishment of Offenders Act 2012.

Repatriation cases

136. Persons serving sentences outside territory where convicted

(1) This section applies if—
   (a) a request is made for a person's extradition to a category 2 territory and the request contains the statement referred to in subsection (2), or
   (b) a provisional warrant for a person's arrest is sought on behalf of a category 2 territory and the information laid before the justice contains the statement referred to in subsection (2).

(2) The statement is one that the person—
   (a) is alleged to be unlawfully at large from a prison in one territory (the imprisoning territory) in which he was serving a sentence after conviction of an offence specified in the request by a court in another territory (the convicting territory), and
   (b) was serving the sentence in pursuance of international arrangements for prisoners sentenced in one territory to be repatriated to another territory in order to serve their sentence.

(3) If the category 2 territory is either the imprisoning territory or the convicting territory—
   (a) section 70(3) has effect as if the reference to the statement referred to in subsection (4) of that section were a reference to the statement referred to in subsection (2) of this section;
   (b) section 73(1) has effect as if the reference to a person within subsection (2) of that section were a reference to the person referred to in subsection (1)(b) of this section.

(4) If the category 2 territory is the imprisoning territory—
   (a) sections 71(2)(a), 73(3)(a) and 78(4)(b) have effect as if 'an extradition offence' read 'an extradition offence in relation to the convicting territory';
   (b) sections 74(8)(a) and 127(2) have effect as if 'the category 2 territory in which he is accused of the commission of an offence or is alleged to have been convicted of an offence' read 'the imprisoning territory';
   (c) section 74(11)(b) has effect as if 'the category 2 territory' read 'the imprisoning territory';
   (d) section 78(2)(e) has effect as if 'the category 2 territory' read 'the convicting territory';
   (e) section 85(5) has effect as if after 'entitled' there were inserted 'in the convicting territory';
   (f) section 119(4) has effect as if 'a category 2 territory' read 'the convicting territory' and as if 'the category 2 territory' in both places read 'the convicting territory';
   (g) section 138(1) has effect as if 'a category 2 territory' read 'the convicting territory';
   (h) in section 138, subsections (2), (3), (4), (5) and (7) have effect as if 'the category 2 territory' read 'the convicting territory'.

(5) Subsection (1)(b) applies to Scotland with the substitution of 'application by the procurator fiscal sets out the matters referred to in paragraphs (a) and (b) of subsection (2)' for 'information laid by the justice contains the statement referred to in subsection (2)'.

(6) Subsection (1)(b) applies to Northern Ireland with the substitution of 'the complaint made to' for 'the information laid before'.

Interpretation

137. Extradition offences: person not sentenced for offence

(1) This section applies in relation to conduct of a person if—
   (a) he is accused in a category 2 territory of the commission of an offence constituted by the conduct, or
   (b) he is alleged to be unlawfully at large after conviction by a court in a category 2 territory of an offence constituted by the conduct and he has not been sentenced for the offence.

(2) The conduct constitutes an extradition offence in relation to the category 2 territory if these conditions are satisfied—
   (a) the conduct occurs in the category 2 territory;
   (b) the conduct would constitute an offence under the law of the relevant part of the United Kingdom punishable with imprisonment or another form of detention for a term of 12 months or a greater punishment if it occurred in that part of the United Kingdom;
   (c) the conduct is so punishable under the law of the category 2 territory (however it is described in that law).

(3) The conduct also constitutes an extradition offence in relation to the category 2 territory if these conditions are satisfied—
   (a) the conduct occurs outside the category 2 territory;
   (b) the conduct is punishable under the law of the category 2 territory with imprisonment or another form of detention for a term of 12 months or a greater punishment (however it is described in that law);
   (c) in corresponding circumstances equivalent conduct would constitute an extra-territorial offence under the law of the relevant part of the United Kingdom punishable with imprisonment or another form of detention for a term of 12 months or a greater punishment.

(4) The conduct also constitutes an extradition offence in relation to the category 2 territory if these conditions are satisfied—
   (a) the conduct occurs outside the category 2 territory and no part of it occurs in the United Kingdom;
   (b) the conduct would constitute an offence under the law of the relevant part of the United Kingdom punishable with imprisonment or another form of detention for a term of 12 months or a greater punishment if it occurred in that part of the United Kingdom;
   (c) the conduct is so punishable under the law of the category 2 territory (however it is described in that law).

(5) The conduct also constitutes an extradition offence in relation to the category 2 territory if these conditions are satisfied—
   (a) the conduct occurs outside the category 2 territory and no part of it occurs in the United Kingdom;
   (b) the conduct is punishable under the law of the category 2 territory with imprisonment for a term of 12 months or another form of detention or a greater punishment (however it is described in that law);
   (c) the conduct constitutes or if committed in the United Kingdom would constitute an offence mentioned in subsection (6).

(6) The offences are—
   (a) an offence under section 51 or 58 of the International Criminal Court Act 2001 (c. 17) (genocide, crimes against humanity and war crimes);
   (b) an offence under section 52 or 59 of that Act (conduct ancillary to genocide etc. committed outside the jurisdiction);
   (c) an ancillary offence, as defined in section 55 or 62 of that Act, in relation to an offence falling within paragraph (a) or (b);
   (d) an offence under section 1 of the International Criminal Court (Scotland) Act 2001 (asp 13) (genocide, crimes against humanity and war crimes);
   (e) an offence under section 2 of that Act (conduct ancillary to genocide etc. committed outside the jurisdiction);
   (f) an ancillary offence, as defined in section 7 of that Act, in relation to an offence falling within paragraph (d) or (e).

(7) If the conduct constitutes an offence under the military law of the category 2 territory but does not constitute an offence under the general criminal law of the relevant part of the United Kingdom it does not constitute an extradition offence; and subsections (1) to (6) have effect subject to this.

(8) The relevant part of the United Kingdom is the part of the United Kingdom in which—
   (a) the extradition hearing took place, if the question of whether conduct constitutes an extradition offence is to be decided by the Secretary of State;
   (b) proceedings in which it is necessary to decide that question are taking place, in any other case.

(9) Subsections (1) to (7) apply for the purposes of this Part.

138. Extradition offences: person sentenced for offence

(1) This section applies in relation to conduct of a person if—
   (a) he is alleged to be unlawfully at large after conviction by a court in a category 2 territory of an offence constituted by the conduct, and
   (b) he has been sentenced for the offence.

(2) The conduct constitutes an extradition offence in relation to the category 2 territory if these conditions are satisfied—
  (a) the conduct occurs in the category 2 territory;
  (b) the conduct would constitute an offence under the law of the relevant part of the United Kingdom punishable with imprisonment or another form of detention for a term of 12 months or a greater punishment if it occurred in that part of the United Kingdom;
  (c) a sentence of imprisonment or another form of detention for a term of 4 months or a greater punishment has been imposed in the category 2 territory in respect of the conduct.

(3) The conduct also constitutes an extradition offence in relation to the category 2 territory if these conditions are satisfied—
  (a) the conduct occurs outside the category 2 territory;
  (b) a sentence of imprisonment or another form of detention for a term of 4 months or a greater punishment has been imposed in the category 2 territory in respect of the conduct;
  (c) in corresponding circumstances equivalent conduct would constitute an extra-territorial offence under the law of the relevant part of the United Kingdom punishable with imprisonment or another form of detention for a term of 12 months or a greater punishment.

(4) The conduct also constitutes an extradition offence in relation to the category 2 territory if these conditions are satisfied—
  (a) the conduct occurs outside the category 2 territory and no part of it occurs in the United Kingdom;
  (b) the conduct would constitute an offence under the law of the relevant part of the United Kingdom punishable with imprisonment or another form of detention for a term of 12 months or a greater punishment if it occurred in that part of the United Kingdom;
  (c) a sentence of imprisonment or another form of detention for a term of 4 months or a greater punishment has been imposed in the category 2 territory in respect of the conduct.

(5) The conduct also constitutes an extradition offence in relation to the category 2 territory if these conditions are satisfied—
  (a) the conduct occurs outside the category 2 territory and no part of it occurs in the United Kingdom;
  (b) a sentence of imprisonment or another form of detention for a term of 4 months or a greater punishment has been imposed in the category 2 territory in respect of the conduct;
  (c) the conduct constitutes or if committed in the United Kingdom would constitute an offence mentioned in subsection (6).

(6) The offences are—
  (a) an offence under section 51 or 58 of the International Criminal Court Act 2001 (c. 17) (genocide, crimes against humanity and war crimes);
  (b) an offence under section 52 or 59 of that Act (conduct ancillary to genocide etc. committed outside the jurisdiction);
  (c) an ancillary offence, as defined in section 55 or 62 of that Act, in relation to an offence falling within paragraph (a) or (b);
  (d) an offence under section 1 of the International Criminal Court (Scotland) Act 2001 (asp 13) (genocide, crimes against humanity and war crimes);
  (e) an offence under section 2 of that Act (conduct ancillary to genocide etc. committed outside the jurisdiction);
  (f) an ancillary offence, as defined in section 7 of that Act, in relation to an offence falling within paragraph (d) or (e).

(7) If the conduct constitutes an offence under the military law of the category 2 territory but does not constitute an offence under the general criminal law of the relevant part of the United Kingdom it does not constitute an extradition offence; and subsections (1) to (6) have effect subject to this.

(8) The relevant part of the United Kingdom is the part of the United Kingdom in which—
  (a) the extradition hearing took place, if the question of whether conduct constitutes an extradition offence is to be decided by the Secretary of State;
  (b) proceedings in which it is necessary to decide that question are taking place, in any other case.

(9) Subsections (1) to (7) apply for the purposes of this Part.

139. The appropriate judge

(1) The appropriate judge is—
  (a) in England and Wales, a District Judge (Magistrates' Courts) designated for the purposes of this Part [by the Lord Chief Justice of England and Wales after consulting the Lord Chancellor];[208]
  (b) in Scotland, the sheriff of Lothian and Borders;
  (c) in Northern Ireland, such county court judge or resident magistrate as is designated for the purposes of this Part by the [Lord Chief Justice of Northern Ireland after consulting the [Department of Justice in Northern Ireland][209]].[210]
(2) A designation under subsection (1) may be made for all cases or for such cases (or cases of such description) as the designation stipulates.
(3) More than one designation may be made under subsection (1).
[(3A) The use of the expression 'the judge' in a section containing a previous reference to 'the appropriate judge' or 'the judge' does not in itself require both references to be read as referring to the same individual.][211]
(4) This section applies for the purposes of this Part.
[(5) The Lord Chief Justice of England and Wales may nominate a judicial office holder (as defined in section 109(4) of the Constitutional Reform Act 2005) to exercise his functions under subsection (1)(a).
(6) The Lord Chief Justice of Northern Ireland may nominate any of the following to exercise his functions under subsection (1)(c)—
  (a) the holder of one of the offices listed in Schedule 1 to the Justice (Northern Ireland) Act 2002;
  (b) a Lord Justice of Appeal (as defined in section 88 of that Act).][212]

140. The extradition hearing

(1) The extradition hearing is the hearing at which the appropriate judge is to deal with a request for extradition to a category 2 territory.
(2) This section applies for the purposes of this Part.

[140A. Unlawfully at large

(1) A person is alleged to be unlawfully at large after conviction of an offence if—
  (a) he is alleged to have been convicted of it, and
  (b) his extradition is sought for the purpose of his being sentenced for the offence or of his serving a sentence of imprisonment or another form of detention imposed in respect of the offence.
(2) This section applies for the purposes of this Part, other than sections 82 and 136.][213]

141. Scotland: references to Secretary of State

(1) This Part applies in relation to any function which falls under this Part to be exercised in relation to Scotland only as if references in this Part to the Secretary of State were to the Scottish Ministers.
(2) Subsection (1) does not apply to the references to the Secretary of State [in paragraph (b) of section 70(2), in paragraph (c) of section 93(4) and][214] in sections 83(3), 101(5) and 121.

---

208 Amended by the Constitutional Reform Act 2005.
209 Amended by SI 2010/976.
210 Amended by the Constitutional Reform Act 2005.
211 Amended by the Police and Justice Act 2006.
212 Amended by the Constitutional Reform Act 2005.
213 Amended by the Police and Justice Act 2006.
214 Amended by the Police and Justice Act 2006.

Part 3
Extradition to the United Kingdom

Extradition from category 1 territories

142. Issue of Part 3 warrant

(1) The appropriate judge may issue a Part 3 warrant in respect of a person if—
(a) a constable or an appropriate person applies to the judge for a Part 3 warrant, and
(b) the condition in subsection (2)[, or the condition in subsection (2A),][215] is satisfied.

[(2) The condition is that—
(a) there are reasonable grounds for believing that the person has committed an extradition offence, and
(b) a domestic warrant has been issued in respect of the person.

(2A) The condition is that—
(a) there are reasonable grounds for believing that the person is unlawfully at large after conviction of an extradition offence by a court in the United Kingdom, and
(b) either a domestic warrant has been issued in respect of the person or the person may (if unlawfully at large as mentioned in paragraph (a)) be arrested without a warrant.][216]

(3) A Part 3 warrant is an arrest warrant which contains—
(a) the statement referred to in subsection (4) or the statement referred to in subsection (5), and
(b) the certificate referred to in subsection (6).

(4) The statement is one that—
(a) the person in respect of whom the warrant is issued is accused in the United Kingdom of the commission of an extradition offence specified in the warrant, and
(b) the warrant is issued with a view to his arrest and extradition to the United Kingdom for the purpose of being prosecuted for the offence.

(5) The statement is one that—
(a) the person in respect of whom the warrant is issued [has been convicted][217] of an extradition offence specified in the warrant by a court in the United Kingdom, and
(b) the warrant is issued with a view to his arrest and extradition to the United Kingdom for the purpose of being sentenced for the offence or of serving a sentence of imprisonment or another form of detention imposed in respect of the offence.

(6) The certificate is one certifying—
(a) whether the conduct constituting the extradition offence specified in the warrant falls within the European framework list;
(b) whether the offence is an extra-territorial offence;
(c) what is the maximum punishment that may be imposed on conviction of the offence or (if the person has been sentenced for the offence) what sentence has been imposed.

(7) The conduct which falls within the European framework list must be taken for the purposes of subsection (6)(a) to include conduct which constitutes—
(a) an attempt, conspiracy or incitement to carry out conduct falling within the list, or
(b) aiding, abetting, counselling or procuring the carrying out of conduct falling within the list.

[(8) A domestic warrant is a warrant for the arrest or apprehension of a person which is issued under any of the provisions referred to in subsection (8A), or at common law by a Crown Court judge in Northern Ireland.

(8A) The provisions are—
(a) section 72 of the Criminal Justice Act 1967;
(b) section 7 of the Bail Act 1976;
(c) section 51 of the Judicature (Northern Ireland) Act 1978;
(d) section 1 of the Magistrates' Courts Act 1980;

---

215 Amended by the Police and Justice Act 2006.
216 Amended by the Police and Justice Act 2006.
217 Amended by the Police and Justice Act 2006.

(e) Article 20 or 25 of the Magistrates' Courts (Northern Ireland) Order 1981 (S.I. 1981/1675 (N.I. 26));
(f) the Criminal Procedure (Scotland) Act 1995.][218]

(9) An appropriate person is a person of a description specified in an order made by the Secretary of State for the purposes of this section.

(10) Subsection (1)(a) applies to Scotland with the substitution of 'a procurator fiscal' for 'a constable or an appropriate person'.

143, 144. ...[219]

145. Service of sentence in territory executing Part 3 warrant

(1) This section applies if—
(a) a Part 3 warrant is issued in respect of a person;
(b) the certificate contained in the warrant certifies that a sentence has been imposed;
(c) an undertaking is given on behalf of a category 1 territory that the person will be required to serve the sentence in the territory;
(d) on the basis of the undertaking the person is not extradited to the United Kingdom from the category 1 territory.

(2) The [sentence for the offence must be treated as served][220] but the person's conviction for the offence must be treated as a conviction for all other purposes.

146. Dealing with person for other offences

(1) This section applies if a person is extradited to the United Kingdom from a category 1 territory in pursuance of a Part 3 warrant.

(2) The person may be dealt with in the United Kingdom for an offence committed before his extradition only if—
(a) the offence is one falling within subsection (3), or
(b) the condition in subsection (4) is satisfied.

(3) The offences are—
(a) the offence in respect of which the person is extradited;
(b) an offence disclosed by the information provided to the category 1 territory in respect of that offence;
(c) an extradition offence in respect of which consent to the person being dealt with is given on behalf of the territory [in response to a request made by the appropriate judge];[221]
(d) an offence which is not punishable with imprisonment or another form of detention;
(e) an offence in respect of which the person will not be detained in connection with his trial, sentence or appeal;
(f) an offence in respect of which the person waives the right that he would have (but for this paragraph) not to be dealt with for the offence.

(4) The condition is that the person has been given an opportunity to leave the United Kingdom and—
(a) he has not done so before the end of the permitted period, or
(b) he has done so before the end of the permitted period and has returned to the United Kingdom.

(5) The permitted period is 45 days starting with the day on which the person arrives in the United Kingdom.

147. Effect of consent to extradition to the United Kingdom

(1) This section applies if—
(a) a person is extradited to the United Kingdom from a category 1 territory in pursuance of a Part 3 warrant;

[218] Amended by the Police and Justice Act 2006.
[219] Amended by the Policing and Crime Act 2009.
[220] Amended by the Policing and Crime Act 2009.
[221] Amended by the Police and Justice Act 2006.

(b) the person consented to his extradition to the United Kingdom in accordance with the law of the category 1 territory.

(2) Section 146(2) does not apply if the conditions in subsection (3) or the conditions in subsection (4) are satisfied.

(3) The conditions are that—

(a) under the law of the category 1 territory, the effect of the person's consent is to waive his right under section 146(2);

(b) the person has not revoked his consent in accordance with that law, if he is permitted to do so under that law.

(4) The conditions are that—

(a) under the law of the category 1 territory, the effect of the person's consent is not to waive his right under section 146(2);

(b) the person has expressly waived his right under section 146(2) in accordance with that law;

(c) the person has not revoked his consent in accordance with that law, if he is permitted to do so under that law;

(d) the person has not revoked the waiver of his right under section 146(2) in accordance with that law, if he is permitted to do so under that law.

148. Extradition offences

(1) Conduct constitutes an extradition offence in relation to the United Kingdom if these conditions are satisfied—

(a) the conduct occurs in the United Kingdom;

(b) the conduct is punishable under the law of the relevant part of the United Kingdom with imprisonment or another form of detention for a term of 12 months or a greater punishment.

(2) Conduct also constitutes an extradition offence in relation to the United Kingdom if these conditions are satisfied—

(a) the conduct occurs outside the United Kingdom;

(b) the conduct constitutes an extra-territorial offence punishable under the law of the relevant part of the United Kingdom with imprisonment or another form of detention for a term of 12 months or a greater punishment.

(3) But subsections (1) and (2) do not apply in relation to conduct of a person if—

(a) he [has been convicted][222] by a court in the United Kingdom of the offence constituted by the conduct, and

(b) he has been sentenced for the offence.

(4) Conduct also constitutes an extradition offence in relation to the United Kingdom if these conditions are satisfied—

(a) the conduct occurs in the United Kingdom;

(b) a sentence of imprisonment or another form of detention for a term of 4 months or a greater punishment has been imposed in the United Kingdom in respect of the conduct.

(5) Conduct also constitutes an extradition offence in relation to the United Kingdom if these conditions are satisfied—

(a) the conduct occurs outside the United Kingdom;

(b) the conduct constitutes an extra-territorial offence;

(c) a sentence of imprisonment or another form of detention for a term of 4 months or a greater punishment has been imposed in the United Kingdom in respect of the conduct.

(6) The relevant part of the United Kingdom is the part of the United Kingdom in which the relevant proceedings are taking place.

(7) The relevant proceedings are the proceedings in which it is necessary to decide whether conduct constitutes an extradition offence.

(8) Subsections (1) to (5) apply for the purposes of sections 142 to 147.

---

[222] Amended by the Police and Justice Act 2006.

149. The appropriate judge

(1) The appropriate judge is—
(a) in England and Wales, a District Judge (Magistrates' Courts), a justice of the peace or a judge entitled to exercise the jurisdiction of the Crown Court;
(b) in Scotland, a sheriff;
(c) in Northern Ireland, a justice of the peace, a resident magistrate or a Crown Court judge.
(2) This section applies for the purposes of sections 142 to 147.

Extradition from category 2 territories

150. Dealing with person for other offences: Commonwealth countries etc.

(1) This section applies if—
(a) a person is extradited to the United Kingdom from a category 2 territory under law of the territory corresponding to Part 2 of this Act, and
(b) the territory is a Commonwealth country, a British overseas territory or the Hong Kong Special Administrative Region of the People's Republic of China.
(2) The person may be dealt with in the United Kingdom for an offence committed before his extradition only if—
(a) the offence is one falling within subsection (3), or
(b) the condition in subsection (6) is satisfied.
(3) The offences are—
(a) the offence in respect of which the person is extradited;
(b) a lesser offence disclosed by the information provided to the category 2 territory in respect of that offence;
(c) an offence in respect of which consent to the person being dealt with is given by or on behalf of the relevant authority.
(4) An offence is a lesser offence in relation to another offence if the maximum punishment for it is less severe than the maximum punishment for the other offence.
(5) The relevant authority is—
(a) if the person has been extradited from a Commonwealth country, the government of the country;
(b) if the person has been extradited from a British overseas territory, the person administering the territory;
(c) if the person has been extradited from the Hong Kong Special Administrative Region of the People's Republic of China, the government of the Region.
(6) The condition is that the protected period has ended.
(7) The protected period is 45 days starting with the first day after his extradition to the United Kingdom on which the person is given an opportunity to leave the United Kingdom.
(8) A person is dealt with in the United Kingdom for an offence if—
(a) he is tried there for it;
(b) he is detained with a view to trial there for it.

151. ...[223]

General

[151A. Dealing with person for other offences

(1) This section applies if a person is extradited to the United Kingdom from a territory which is not—
(a) a category 1 territory, or
(b) a territory falling within section 150(1)(b).
(2) The person may be dealt with in the United Kingdom for an offence committed before the person's extradition only if—
(a) the offence is one falling within subsection (3), or

[223] Amended by the Policing and Crime Act 2009.

(b) the condition in subsection (4) is satisfied.

(3) The offences are—

(a) the offence in respect of which the person is extradited;

(b) an offence disclosed by the information provided to the territory in respect of that offence;

(c) an offence in respect of which consent to the person being dealt with is given on behalf of the territory.

(4) The condition is that—

(a) the person has returned to the territory from which the person was extradited, or

(b) the person has been given an opportunity to leave the United Kingdom.

(5) A person is dealt with in the United Kingdom for an offence if—

(a) the person is tried there for it;

(b) the person is detained with a view to trial there for it.][224]

152. Remission of punishment for other offences

(1) This section applies if—

(a) a person is extradited to the United Kingdom [from a territory];[225]

(b) before his extradition he has been convicted of an offence in the United Kingdom;

(c) he has not been extradited in respect of that offence.

(2) The [sentence for the offence must be treated as served][226] but the person's conviction for the offence must be treated as a conviction for all other purposes.

153. Return of person acquitted or not tried

(1) This section applies if—

(a) a person is accused in the United Kingdom of the commission of an offence;

(b) the person is extradited to the United Kingdom in respect of the offence [from a territory];[227]

(c) the condition in subsection (2) or the condition in subsection (3) is satisfied.

(2) The condition is that—

(a) proceedings against the person for the offence are not begun before the end of the required period, which is 6 months starting with the day on which the person arrives in the United Kingdom on his extradition, and

(b) before the end of the period of 3 months starting immediately after the end of the required period the person asks the Secretary of State to return him to the territory from which he was extradited.

(3) The condition is that—

(a) at his trial for the offence the person is acquitted or is discharged under any of the provisions specified in subsection (4), and

(b) before the end of the period of 3 months starting immediately after the date of his acquittal or discharge the person asks the Secretary of State to return him to the territory from which he was extradited.

(4) The provisions are—

(a) section 12(1) of the Powers of Criminal Courts (Sentencing) Act 2000 (c. 6);

(b) section 246(1), (2) or (3) of the Criminal Procedure (Scotland) Act 1995 (c. 46);

(c) Article 4(1) of the Criminal Justice (Northern Ireland) Order 1996 (S.I. 1996/3160 (N.I. 24)).

(5) The Secretary of State must arrange for him to be sent back, free of charge and with as little delay as possible, to the territory from which he was extradited to the United Kingdom in respect of the offence.

(6) If the accusation in subsection (1)(a) relates to the commission of an offence in Scotland, subsections (2)(b), (3)(b) and (5) apply as if the references to the Secretary of State were references to the Scottish Ministers.

---

224 Amended by the Policing and Crime Act 2009.

225 Amended by the Policing and Crime Act 2009.

226 Amended by the Policing and Crime Act 2009.

227 Amended by the Policing and Crime Act 2009.

[153A. Undertaking in relation to person serving sentence

(1) This section applies if—
  (a) a person is accused in the United Kingdom of the commission of an offence or has been convicted of an offence by or before a court in the United Kingdom;
  (b) a Part 3 warrant is issued in respect of the person or the Secretary of State makes a request for the extradition of the person;
  (c) the person is serving a sentence of imprisonment or another form of detention in a territory;
  (d) the person's extradition to the United Kingdom from the territory in pursuance of the warrant or request is made subject to a condition that an undertaking is given by or on behalf of the United Kingdom with regard to the person's treatment in the United Kingdom or return to the territory (or both).

(2) The Secretary of State may give an undertaking to a person acting on behalf of the territory with regard to either or both of these things—
  (a) the treatment in the United Kingdom of the person in respect of whom the warrant is issued or the request for extradition is made;
  (b) the return of that person to the territory.

(3) The terms which may be included by the Secretary of State in an undertaking given under subsection (2) in relation to a person accused in the United Kingdom of the commission of an offence include terms—
  (a) that the person be kept in custody until the conclusion of the proceedings against the person for the offence and any other offence in respect of which the person is permitted to be dealt with in the United Kingdom;
  (b) that the person be returned to the territory to serve the remainder of the sentence on the conclusion of those proceedings.

(4) The terms which may be included by the Secretary of State in an undertaking given under subsection (2) in relation to a person who has been convicted of an offence by or before a court in the United Kingdom include terms that the person be returned to the territory to serve the remainder of the sentence after the person would otherwise be released from detention pursuant to the sentence imposed in the United Kingdom (whether or not on licence).

(5) If a person is to be returned to a territory by virtue of an undertaking given under subsection (2), the undertaking is sufficient authority for a constable—
  (a) to remove the person from any prison or other institution where the person is detained;
  (b) to keep the person in custody until returned;
  (c) to convey the person to the territory.][228]

[153B. Return of person in pursuance of undertaking

(1) This section applies if—
  (a) an undertaking is given under section 153A(2) as to the return of a person to a territory;
  (b) the person is returned to the territory in pursuance of the undertaking;
  (c) the person is returned to the United Kingdom to serve the remainder of any sentence imposed in the United Kingdom or the person otherwise returns to the United Kingdom.

(2) Time during which the person was outside the United Kingdom as a result of the undertaking given under section 153A(2) does not count as time served by the person as part of the sentence.

(3) If the person is not entitled to be released from detention pursuant to the sentence—
  (a) the person is liable to be detained in pursuance of the sentence, and
  (b) if at large, the person must be treated as being unlawfully at large.

(4) If the person is entitled to be released from detention on licence pursuant to the sentence—
  (a) if the person was released on licence at the time of return to the territory, the licence is suspended until the person's return to the United Kingdom;
  (b) if the person was not released on licence at that time, subsections (5) to (8) apply in relation to the person ("the offender").

[228] Amended by the Policing and Crime Act 2009.

(5) The offender is liable to be detained, on return to the United Kingdom, in any place in which the offender could have been detained pursuant to the sentence before the time of return to the territory.
(6) A constable or immigration officer may—
(a) take the offender into custody, and
(b) convey the offender to the place mentioned in subsection (5).
(7) The offender must be released on licence within the period of 5 days beginning when the offender is taken (or retaken) into custody under this section.
(8) In calculating a period of 5 days for the purposes of subsection (7) no account is to be taken of any day mentioned in any of paragraphs (a) to (d) of section 59(10).
(9) The powers conferred on a constable by subsection (6) are exercisable in any part of the United Kingdom.
(10) For the purposes of this section—
(a) a person is entitled to be released from detention if there is—
(i) a duty to release the person under section 33(1), (1A) or (2) of the Criminal Justice Act 1991,
(ii) a duty to release the person under section 244 of the Criminal Justice Act 2003 (other than temporarily on licence pursuant to an intermittent custody order under section 183(1)(b) of the Criminal Justice Act 2003),
(iii) a duty to release the person under section 1, 1AA or 7(1) of the Prisoners and Criminal Proceedings (Scotland) Act 1993 or section 5, 11(2), 13, 19 or 23 of the Custodial Sentences and Weapons (Scotland) Act 2007, or
(iv) a duty to release the person under section 1 of the Northern Ireland (Remission of Sentences) Act 1995, Article 26 of the Criminal Justice (Northern Ireland) Order 1996 or Article 17 or 18(8) of the Criminal Justice (Northern Ireland) Order 2008;
(b) an immigration officer is a person who is an immigration officer within the meaning of the Immigration Act 1971.][229]

[153C. Return to extraditing territory to serve sentence

(1) This section applies if—
(a) a person is extradited to the United Kingdom from a territory for the purposes of being prosecuted for an offence;
(b) the person's extradition is made subject to a condition that an undertaking is given by or on behalf of the United Kingdom as to the person's return to the territory.
(2) The Secretary of State may give an undertaking to a person acting on behalf of the territory as to the person's return to the territory.
(3) The terms which may be included by the Secretary of State in an undertaking given under subsection (2) in relation to a person include terms that if the person is convicted of the offence and a sentence of imprisonment or another form of detention is imposed in respect of it, the person is to be returned to the territory to serve the sentence.
(4) A person who is to be returned to a territory by virtue of an undertaking given under subsection (2) must be returned as soon as is reasonably practicable after the sentence is imposed and any other proceedings in respect of the offence are concluded.
(5) If subsection (4) is complied with the sentence for the offence is treated as served but the person's conviction for the offence must be treated as a conviction for all other purposes.
(6) The sentence for the offence is treated as served under subsection (5) only in so far as it consists of the sentence of imprisonment or another form of detention mentioned in subsection (3).
(7) Subsection (8) applies if—
(a) subsection (4) is not complied with, and
(b) the person applies to the court which imposed the sentence to expedite return to the territory.
(8) The court must order return by such date as is specified in the order unless reasonable cause is shown for the delay.

[229] Amended by the Policing and Crime Act 2009.

(9) If a person is to be returned by virtue of an undertaking given under subsection (2), a constable may—
   (a) remove the person from any prison or other institution where the person is detained;
   (b) keep the person in custody until returned;
   (c) convey the person to the territory to which the person is to be returned.][230]

[153D. Sections 153A and 153C etc: supplementary

(1) Nothing in section 153A or 153C requires the return of a person to a territory in a case in which the Secretary of State is not satisfied that the return is compatible with the Convention rights within the meaning of the Human Rights Act 1998 or with the United Kingdom's obligations under the Refugee Convention.
(2) References in sections 153A and 153C and subsection (1) above to the Secretary of State are to be read as references to the Scottish Ministers in a case in which—
   (a) a Part 3 warrant was issued in respect of the person to be returned, and
   (b) the warrant was issued by a sheriff.
(3) The reference in subsection (1) to the Refugee Convention is to the Convention relating to the Status of Refugees done at Geneva on 28 July 1951 and the Protocol to the Convention.][231]

154. Restriction on bail where undertaking given by Secretary of State

(1) This section applies in relation to a person if—
   (a) the Secretary of State has given an undertaking in connection with the person's extradition to the United Kingdom, and
   (b) the undertaking includes terms that the person be kept in custody until the conclusion of any proceedings against him in the United Kingdom for an offence.
(2) A court, judge or justice of the peace may grant bail to the person in the proceedings only if the court, judge or justice of the peace considers that there are exceptional circumstances which justify it.

155. Service personnel

The Secretary of State may by order provide for the preceding provisions of this Part to have effect with specified modifications in relation to a case where the person whose extradition is sought or ordered is subject to [service law].[232]

[155A. Category 1 territories not applying framework decision to old cases

(1) This section applies to a category 1 territory that deals with European extradition requests otherwise than in accordance with the system provided for in the European framework decision if they relate to acts committed before a particular date ('the relevant date').
(2) In the case of a territory to which this section applies, the Secretary of State has the same powers to request a person's extradition in relation to acts committed before the relevant date as he would have in the case of a category 2 territory.
(3) The Secretary of State may by order provide that, in the case of an extradition request which—
   (a) is made to a specified category 1 territory to which this section applies, and
   (b) relates to acts committed before the relevant date,

   this Part is to have effect as if that territory were a category 2 territory, and with such modifications as may be specified.
(4) In this section—

   'European extradition request' means a request for extradition made by the United Kingdom or a category 1 territory;

   'European framework decision' means the framework decision of the Council of the European Union made on 13 June 2002 on the European arrest warrant and the surrender procedures between member states (2002/584/JHA);

   'specified', in relation to an order under this section, means specified in the order.][233]

---

230 Amended by the Policing and Crime Act 2009.
231 Amended by the Policing and Crime Act 2009.
232 Amended by the Armed Forces Act 2006.
233 Amended by the Police and Justice Act 2006.

Part 4
Police Powers

Warrants and orders

156. Search and seizure warrants

(1) A justice of the peace may, on an application made to him by a constable, issue a search and seizure warrant if he is satisfied that the requirements for the issue of a search and seizure warrant are fulfilled.

(2) The application for a search and seizure warrant must state that—
  (a) the extradition of a person specified in the application is sought under Part 1 or Part 2;
  (b) the warrant is sought in relation to premises specified in the application;
  (c) the warrant is sought in relation to material, or material of a description, specified in the application;
  (d) that material, or material of that description, is believed to be on the premises.

(3) If the application states that the extradition of the person is sought under Part 1, the application must also state that the person is accused in a category 1 territory specified in the application of the commission of an offence—
  (a) which is specified in the application, and
  (b) which is an extradition offence within the meaning given by section 64.

(4) If the application states that the extradition of the person is sought under Part 2, the application must also state that the person is accused in a category 2 territory specified in the application of the commission of an offence—
  (a) which is specified in the application, and
  (b) which is an extradition offence within the meaning given by section 137.

(5) A search and seizure warrant is a warrant authorising a constable—
  (a) to enter and search the premises specified in the application for the warrant, and
  (b) to seize and retain any material found there which falls within subsection (6).

(6) Material falls within this subsection if—
  (a) it would be likely to be admissible evidence at a trial in the relevant part of the United Kingdom for the offence specified in the application for the warrant (on the assumption that conduct constituting that offence would constitute an offence in that part of the United Kingdom), and
  (b) it does not consist of or include items subject to legal privilege, excluded material or special procedure material.

(7) The relevant part of the United Kingdom is the part of the United Kingdom where the justice of the peace exercises jurisdiction.

(8) The requirements for the issue of a search and seizure warrant are that there are reasonable grounds for believing that—
  (a) the offence specified in the application has been committed by the person so specified;
  (b) the person is in the United Kingdom or is on his way to the United Kingdom;
  (c) the offence is an extradition offence within the meaning given by section 64 (if subsection (3) applies) or section 137 (if subsection (4) applies);
  (d) there is material on premises specified in the application which falls within subsection (6);
  (e) any of the conditions referred to in subsection (9) is satisfied.

(9) The conditions are—
  (a) that it is not practicable to communicate with a person entitled to grant entry to the premises;
  (b) that it is practicable to communicate with a person entitled to grant entry to the premises but it is not practicable to communicate with a person entitled to grant access to the material referred to in subsection (8)(d);
  (c) that entry to the premises will not be granted unless a warrant is produced;
  (d) that the purpose of a search may be frustrated or seriously prejudiced unless a constable arriving at the premises can secure immediate entry to them.

(10) The preceding provisions of this section apply to Scotland with these modifications—
  (a) in subsections (1) and (7) for 'justice of the peace' substitute 'sheriff';
  (b) in subsection (1) for 'constable' substitute 'procurator fiscal';

(c) for 'search and seizure warrant' substitute 'warrant to search';
(d) in subsection (6)(b) omit the words ', excluded material or special procedure material';
(e) subsections (8)(e) and (9) are omitted.

157. Production orders

(1) A judge may, on an application made to him by a constable, make a production order if he is satisfied that the requirements for the making of a production order are fulfilled.
(2) The application for a production order must state that—
(a) the extradition of a person specified in the application is sought under Part 1 or Part 2;
(b) the order is sought in relation to premises specified in the application;
(c) the order is sought in relation to material, or material of a description, specified in the application;
(d) the material is special procedure material or excluded material;
(e) a person specified in the application appears to be in possession or control of the material.
(3) If the application states that the extradition of the person is sought under Part 1, the application must also state that the person is accused in a category 1 territory specified in the application of the commission of an offence—
(a) which is specified in the application, and
(b) which is an extradition offence within the meaning given by section 64.
(4) If the application states that the extradition of the person is sought under Part 2, the application must also state that the person is accused in a category 2 territory specified in the application of the commission of an offence—
(a) which is specified in the application, and
(b) which is an extradition offence within the meaning given by section 137.
(5) A production order is an order either—
(a) requiring the person the application for the order specifies as appearing to be in possession or control of special procedure material or excluded material to produce it to a constable (within the period stated in the order) for him to take away, or
(b) requiring that person to give a constable access to the special procedure material or excluded material within the period stated in the order.
(6) The period stated in a production order must be a period of 7 days starting with the day on which the order is made, unless it appears to the judge by whom the order is made that a longer period would be appropriate.
(7) Production orders have effect as if they were orders of the court.
(8) In this section 'judge'—
(a) in England and Wales, means a circuit judge;
(b) in Northern Ireland, means a Crown Court judge.

158. Requirements for making of production order

(1) These are the requirements for the making of a production order.
(2) There must be reasonable grounds for believing that—
(a) the offence specified in the application has been committed by the person so specified;
(b) the person is in the United Kingdom or is on his way to the United Kingdom;
(c) the offence is an extradition offence within the meaning given by section 64 (if section 157(3) applies) or section 137 (if section 157(4) applies);
(d) there is material which consists of or includes special procedure material or excluded material on premises specified in the application;
(e) the material would be likely to be admissible evidence at a trial in the relevant part of the United Kingdom for the offence specified in the application (on the assumption that conduct constituting that offence would constitute an offence in that part of the United Kingdom).
(3) The relevant part of the United Kingdom is the part of the United Kingdom where the judge exercises jurisdiction.
(4) It must appear that other methods of obtaining the material—
(a) have been tried without success, or
(b) have not been tried because they were bound to fail.

(5) It must be in the public interest that the material should be produced or that access to it should be given.

159. Computer information

(1) This section applies if any of the special procedure material or excluded material specified in an application for a production order consists of information stored in any electronic form.
(2) If the order is an order requiring a person to produce the material to a constable for him to take away, it has effect as an order to produce the material in a form—
   (a) in which it can be taken away by him;
   (b) in which it is visible and legible or from which it can readily be produced in a visible and legible form.
(3) If the order is an order requiring a person to give a constable access to the material, it has effect as an order to give him access to the material in a form—
   (a) in which it is visible and legible, or
   (b) from which it can readily be produced in a visible and legible form.

160. Warrants: special procedure material and excluded material

(1) A judge may, on an application made to him by a constable, issue a warrant under this section if he is satisfied that—
   (a) the requirements for the making of a production order are fulfilled, and
   (b) the further requirement for the issue of a warrant under this section is fulfilled.
(2) The application for a warrant under this section must state that—
   (a) the extradition of a person specified in the application is sought under Part 1 or Part 2;
   (b) the warrant is sought in relation to premises specified in the application;
   (c) the warrant is sought in relation to material, or material of a description, specified in the application;
   (d) the material is special procedure material or excluded material.
(3) If the application states that the extradition of the person is sought under Part 1, the application must also state that the person is accused in a category 1 territory specified in the application of the commission of an offence—
   (a) which is specified in the application, and
   (b) which is an extradition offence within the meaning given by section 64.
(4) If the application states that the extradition of the person is sought under Part 2, the application must also state that the person is accused in a category 2 territory specified in the application of the commission of an offence—
   (a) which is specified in the application, and
   (b) which is an extradition offence within the meaning given by section 137.
(5) A warrant under this section authorises a constable to enter and search the premises specified in the application for the warrant and—
   (a) to seize and retain any material found there which falls within subsection (6) and which is special procedure material, if the application for the warrant states that the warrant is sought in relation to special procedure material;
   (b) to seize and retain any material found there which falls within subsection (6) and which is excluded material, if the application for the warrant states that the warrant is sought in relation to excluded material.
(6) Material falls within this subsection if it would be likely to be admissible evidence at a trial in the relevant part of the United Kingdom for the offence specified in the application for the warrant (on the assumption that conduct constituting that offence would constitute an offence in that part of the United Kingdom).
(7) The relevant part of the United Kingdom is the part of the United Kingdom where the judge exercises jurisdiction.
(8) The further requirement for the issue of a warrant under this section is that any of these conditions is satisfied—
   (a) it is not practicable to communicate with a person entitled to grant entry to the premises;

(b) it is practicable to communicate with a person entitled to grant entry to the premises but it is not practicable to communicate with a person entitled to grant access to the material referred to in section 158(2)(d);

(c) the material contains information which is subject to a restriction on disclosure or an obligation of secrecy contained in an enactment (including one passed after this Act) and is likely to be disclosed in breach of the restriction or obligation if a warrant is not issued.

(9) In this section 'judge'—

(a) in England and Wales, means a circuit judge;

(b) in Northern Ireland, means a Crown Court judge.

Search and seizure without warrant

161. Entry and search of premises for purposes of arrest

(1) This section applies if a constable has power to arrest a person under an extradition arrest power.

(2) A constable may enter and search any premises for the purpose of exercising the power of arrest if he has reasonable grounds for believing that the person is on the premises.

(3) The power to search conferred by subsection (2) is exercisable only to the extent that is reasonably required for the purpose of exercising the power of arrest.

(4) A constable who has entered premises in exercise of the power conferred by subsection (2) may seize and retain anything which is on the premises if he has reasonable grounds for believing—

(a) that it has been obtained in consequence of the commission of an offence or it is evidence in relation to an offence, and

(b) that it is necessary to seize it in order to prevent it being concealed, lost, damaged, altered or destroyed.

(5) An offence includes an offence committed outside the United Kingdom.

(6) If the premises contain 2 or more separate dwellings, the power conferred by subsection (2) is a power to enter and search only—

(a) any parts of the premises which the occupiers of any dwelling comprised in the premises use in common with the occupiers of any other dwelling comprised in the premises, and

(b) any dwelling comprised in the premises in which the constable has reasonable grounds for believing that the person may be.

162. Entry and search of premises on arrest

(1) This section applies if a person has been arrested under an extradition arrest power at a place other than a police station.

(2) A constable may enter and search any premises in which the person was at the time of his arrest or immediately before his arrest if he has reasonable grounds for believing—

(a) if the person has not been convicted of the relevant offence, that there is on the premises evidence (other than items subject to legal privilege) relating to the relevant offence;

(b) in any case, that there is on the premises evidence (other than items subject to legal privilege) relating to the identity of the person.

(3) The relevant offence is the offence—

(a) referred to in the Part 1 warrant, if the arrest was under a Part 1 warrant;

(b) in respect of which the constable has reasonable grounds for believing that a Part 1 warrant has been or will be issued, if the arrest was under section 5;

(c) in respect of which extradition is requested, if the arrest was under a warrant issued under section 71;

(d) of which the person is accused, if the arrest was under a provisional warrant.

(4) The power to search conferred by subsection (2)—

(a) if the person has not been convicted of the relevant offence, is a power to search for evidence (other than items subject to legal privilege) relating to the relevant offence;

(b) in any case, is a power to search for evidence (other than items subject to legal privilege) relating to the identity of the person.

(5) The power to search conferred by subsection (2) is exercisable only to the extent that it is reasonably required for the purpose of discovering evidence in respect of which the power is available by virtue of subsection (4).

(6) A constable may seize and retain anything for which he may search by virtue of subsections (4) and (5).

(7) A constable who has entered premises in exercise of the power conferred by subsection (2) may seize and retain anything which is on the premises if he has reasonable grounds for believing—

(a) that it has been obtained in consequence of the commission of an offence or it is evidence in relation to an offence, and

(b) that it is necessary to seize it in order to prevent it being concealed, lost, damaged, altered or destroyed.

(8) An offence includes an offence committed outside the United Kingdom.

(9) If the premises contain 2 or more separate dwellings, the power conferred by subsection (2) is a power to enter and search only—

(a) any dwelling in which the arrest took place or in which the person was immediately before his arrest, and

(b) any parts of the premises which the occupier of any such dwelling uses in common with the occupiers of any other dwelling comprised in the premises.

163. Search of person on arrest

(1) This section applies if a person has been arrested under an extradition arrest power at a place other than a police station.

(2) A constable may search the person if he has reasonable grounds for believing that the person may present a danger to himself or others.

(3) A constable may search the person if he has reasonable grounds for believing that the person may have concealed on him anything—

(a) which he might use to assist him to escape from lawful custody;

(b) which might be evidence relating to an offence or to the identity of the person.

(4) The power to search conferred by subsection (3)—

(a) is a power to search for anything falling within paragraph (a) or (b) of that subsection;

(b) is exercisable only to the extent that is reasonably required for the purpose of discovering such a thing.

(5) The powers conferred by subsections (2) and (3)—

(a) do not authorise a constable to require a person to remove any of his clothing in public, other than an outer coat, jacket or gloves;

(b) authorise a search of a person's mouth.

(6) A constable searching a person in exercise of the power conferred by subsection (2) may seize and retain anything he finds, if he has reasonable grounds for believing that the person searched might use it to cause physical injury to himself or to any other person.

(7) A constable searching a person in exercise of the power conferred by subsection (3) may seize and retain anything he finds if he has reasonable grounds for believing—

(a) that the person might use it to assist him to escape from lawful custody;

(b) that it is evidence of an offence or of the identity of the person or has been obtained in consequence of the commission of an offence.

(8) An offence includes an offence committed outside the United Kingdom.

(9) Nothing in this section affects the power conferred by section 43 of the Terrorism Act 2000 (c. 11).

164. Entry and search of premises after arrest

(1) This section applies if a person has been arrested under an extradition arrest power.

(2) A constable may enter and search any premises occupied or controlled by the person if the constable has reasonable grounds for suspecting—

(a) if the person has not been convicted of the relevant offence, that there is on the premises evidence (other than items subject to legal privilege) relating to the relevant offence;

(b) in any case, that there is on the premises evidence (other than items subject to legal privilege) relating to the identity of the person.

(3) The relevant offence is the offence—

(a) referred to in the Part 1 warrant, if the arrest was under a Part 1 warrant;

(b) in respect of which the constable has reasonable grounds for believing that a Part 1 warrant has been or will be issued, if the arrest was under section 5;

(c) in respect of which extradition is requested, if the arrest was under a warrant issued under section 71;
(d) of which the person is accused, if the arrest was under a provisional warrant.

(4) The power to search conferred by subsection (2)—
(a) if the person has not been convicted of the relevant offence, is a power to search for evidence (other than items subject to legal privilege) relating to the relevant offence;
(b) in any case, is a power to search for evidence (other than items subject to legal privilege) relating to the identity of the person.

(5) The power to search conferred by subsection (2) is exercisable only to the extent that it is reasonably required for the purpose of discovering evidence in respect of which the power is available by virtue of subsection (4).

(6) A constable may seize and retain anything for which he may search by virtue of subsections (4) and (5).

(7) A constable who has entered premises in exercise of the power conferred by subsection (2) may seize and retain anything which is on the premises if he has reasonable grounds for believing—
(a) that it has been obtained in consequence of the commission of an offence or it is evidence in relation to an offence, and
(b) that it is necessary to seize it in order to prevent it being concealed, lost, damaged, altered or destroyed.

(8) An offence includes an offence committed outside the United Kingdom.

(9) The powers conferred by subsections (2) and (6) may be exercised only if a police officer of the rank of inspector or above has given written authorisation for their exercise.

(10) But the power conferred by subsection (2) may be exercised without authorisation under subsection (9) if—
(a) it is exercised before the person arrested is taken to a police station, and
(b) the presence of the person at a place other than a police station is necessary for the effective exercise of the power to search.

(11) Subsections (9) and (10) do not apply to Scotland.

165. Additional seizure powers

(1) The Criminal Justice and Police Act 2001 (c. 16) is amended as follows.

(2) In Part 1 of Schedule 1 (powers of seizure to which section 50 of that Act applies) at the end add—

'73D. Extradition Act 2003 (c. 41)

The powers of seizure conferred by sections 156(5), 160(5), 161(4), 162(6) and (7) and 164(6) and (7) of the Extradition Act 2003 (seizure in connection with extradition).'

(3) In Part 2 of Schedule 1 (powers of seizure to which section 51 of that Act applies) at the end add—

'83A. Extradition Act 2003 (c. 41)

The powers of seizure conferred by section 163(6) and (7) of the Extradition Act 2003 (seizure in connection with extradition).'

Treatment following arrest

166. Fingerprints and samples

(1) This section applies if a person has been arrested under an extradition arrest power and is detained at a police station.

(2) Fingerprints may be taken from the person only if they are taken by a constable—
(a) with the appropriate consent given in writing, or
(b) without that consent, under subsection (4).

(3) A non-intimate sample may be taken from the person only if it is taken by a constable—
(a) with the appropriate consent given in writing, or
(b) without that consent, under subsection (4).

(4) Fingerprints or a non-intimate sample may be taken from the person without the appropriate consent only if a police officer of at least the rank of inspector authorises the fingerprints or sample to be taken.

167. Searches and examination

(1) This section applies if a person has been arrested under an extradition arrest power and is detained at a police station.
(2) If a police officer of at least the rank of inspector authorises it, the person may be searched or examined, or both, for the purpose of facilitating the ascertainment of his identity.
(3) An identifying mark found on a search or examination under this section may be photographed—
 (a) with the appropriate consent, or
 (b) without the appropriate consent, if that consent is withheld or it is not practicable to obtain it.
(4) The only persons entitled to carry out a search or examination, or take a photograph, under this section are—
 (a) constables;
 (b) persons designated for the purposes of this section by the appropriate police officer.
(5) A person may not under this section—
 (a) carry out a search or examination of a person of the opposite sex;
 (b) take a photograph of any part of the body (other than the face) of a person of the opposite sex.
(6) An intimate search may not be carried out under this section.
(7) Ascertaining a person's identity includes showing that he is not a particular person.
(8) Taking a photograph includes using a process by means of which a visual image may be produced; and photographing a person must be construed accordingly.
(9) Mark includes features and injuries and a mark is an identifying mark if its existence in a person's case facilitates the ascertainment of his identity.
(10) The appropriate police officer is—
 (a) in England and Wales, the chief officer of police for the police area in which the police station in question is situated;
 (b) in Northern Ireland, the Chief Constable of the Police Service of Northern Ireland.

168. Photographs

(1) This section applies if a person has been arrested under an extradition arrest power and is detained at a police station.
(2) The person may be photographed—
 (a) with the appropriate consent, or
 (b) without the appropriate consent, if that consent is withheld or it is not practicable to obtain it.
(3) A person proposing to take a photograph of a person under this section—
 (a) may for the purpose of doing so require the removal of any item or substance worn on or over the whole or any part of the head or face of the person to be photographed, and
 (b) if the requirement is not complied with may remove the item or substance himself.
(4) The only persons entitled to take a photograph under this section are—
 (a) constables;
 (b) persons designated for the purposes of this section by the appropriate police officer.
(5) Taking a photograph includes using a process by means of which a visual image may be produced; and photographing a person must be construed accordingly.
(6) The appropriate police officer is—
 (a) in England and Wales, the chief officer of police for the police area in which the police station in question is situated;
 (b) in Northern Ireland, the Chief Constable of the Police Service of Northern Ireland.

169. Evidence of identity: England and Wales

(1) The Police and Criminal Evidence Act 1984 (c. 60) is amended as follows.
(2) In section 54A (searches and examination to ascertain identity) at the end insert—
 '(13) Nothing in this section applies to a person arrested under an extradition arrest power.'
(3) In section 61 (fingerprinting) at the end insert—
 '(10) Nothing in this section applies to a person arrested under an extradition arrest power.'
(4) In section 63 (non-intimate samples) at the end insert—
 '(11) Nothing in this section applies to a person arrested under an extradition arrest power.'
(5) In section 64A (photographing of suspects etc.) at the end insert—
 '(7) Nothing in this section applies to a person arrested under an extradition arrest power.'

(6) In section 65 (interpretation of Part 5) after the definition of 'drug trafficking' and 'drug trafficking offence' insert—'extradition arrest power' means any of the following—
  (a) a Part 1 warrant (within the meaning given by the Extradition Act 2003) in respect of which a certificate under section 2 of that Act has been issued;
  (b) section 5 of that Act;
  (c) a warrant issued under section 71 of that Act;
  (d) a provisional warrant (within the meaning given by that Act).'

170. Evidence of identity: Northern Ireland

(1) The Police and Criminal Evidence (Northern Ireland) Order 1989 (S.I. 1989/1341 (N.I. 12)) is amended as follows.
(2) In Article 55A (searches and examination to ascertain identity) at the end insert—
'(13) Nothing in this Article applies to a person arrested under an extradition arrest power.'
(3) In Article 61 (fingerprinting) at the end insert—
'(10) Nothing in this Article applies to a person arrested under an extradition arrest power.'
(4) In Article 63 (non-intimate samples) at the end insert—
'(12) Nothing in this Article applies to a person arrested under an extradition arrest power.'
(5) In Article 64A (photographing of suspects etc.) at the end insert—
'(7) Nothing in this Article applies to a person arrested under an extradition arrest power.'
(6) In Article 53 (interpretation) after the definition of 'drug trafficking' and 'drug trafficking offence' insert—
'extradition arrest power' means any of the following—
  (a) a Part 1 warrant (within the meaning given by the Extradition Act 2003) in respect of which a certificate under section 2 of that Act has been issued;
  (b) section 5 of that Act;
  (c) a warrant issued under section 71 of that Act;
  (d) a provisional warrant (within the meaning given by that Act).'

171. Other treatment and rights

(1) This section applies in relation to cases where a person—
  (a) is arrested under an extradition arrest power at a police station;
  (b) is taken to a police station after being arrested elsewhere under an extradition arrest power;
  (c) is detained at a police station after being arrested under an extradition arrest power.
(2) In relation to those cases the Secretary of State may by order apply the provisions mentioned in subsections (3) and (4) with specified modifications.
(3) The provisions are these provisions of the Police and Criminal Evidence Act 1984 (c. 60)—
  (a) section 54 (searches of detained persons);
  (b) section 55 (intimate searches);
  (c) section 56 (right to have someone informed when arrested);
  (d) section 58 (access to legal advice).
(4) The provisions are these provisions of the Police and Criminal Evidence (Northern Ireland) Order 1989 (S.I. 1989/1341 (N.I. 12))—
  (a) Article 55 (searches of detained persons);
  (b) Article 56 (intimate searches);
  (c) Article 57 (right to have someone informed when arrested);
  (d) Article 59 (access to legal advice).

Delivery of seized property

172. Delivery of seized property

(1) This section applies to—
  (a) anything which has been seized or produced under this Part, or
  (b) anything which has been seized under section 50 or 51 of the Criminal Justice and Police Act 2001 (c. 16) in reliance on a power of seizure conferred by this Part.
(2) A constable may deliver any such thing to a person who is or is acting on behalf of an authority if the constable has reasonable grounds for believing that the authority—

(a) is an authority of the relevant territory, and
(b) has functions such that it is appropriate for the thing to be delivered to it.

(3) If the relevant seizure power was a warrant issued under this Part, or the thing was produced under an order made under this Part, the relevant territory is the category 1 or category 2 territory specified in the application for the warrant or order.

(4) If the relevant seizure power was section 161(4), 162(6) or (7), 163(6) or (7) or 164(6) or (7), the relevant territory is—
(a) the territory in which the Part 1 warrant was issued, in a case where the applicable extradition arrest power is a Part 1 warrant in respect of which a certificate under section 2 has been issued;
(b) the territory in which a constable has reasonable grounds for believing that a Part 1 warrant has been or will be issued, in a case where the applicable extradition arrest power is section 5;
(c) the territory to which a person's extradition is requested, in a case where the applicable extradition arrest power is a warrant issued under section 71;
(d) the territory in which a person is accused of the commission of an offence or has been convicted of an offence, in a case where the applicable extradition arrest power is a provisional warrant.

(5) The applicable extradition arrest power is—
(a) the extradition arrest power under which a constable had a power of arrest, if the relevant seizure power was section 161(4);
(b) the extradition arrest power under which a person was arrested, if the relevant seizure power was section 162(6) or (7), 163(6) or (7) or 164(6) or (7).

(6) The relevant seizure power is—
(a) the power under which the thing was seized, or
(b) the power in reliance on which the thing was seized under section 50 or 51 of the Criminal Justice and Police Act 2001 (c. 16).

(7) Subsection (1)(a) applies to Scotland with the insertion after 'Part' of '(so far as it applies to Scotland) or for the purposes of this Act (as it so applies) by virtue of any enactment or rule of law'.

(8) Subsection (2) applies to Scotland with the substitution of 'procurator fiscal' for 'constable'.

(9) In subsection (7) 'enactment' includes an enactment comprised in, or in an instrument made under, an Act of the Scottish Parliament.

Codes of practice

173. Codes of practice

(1) The Secretary of State must issue codes of practice in connection with—
(a) the exercise of the powers conferred by this Part;
(b) the retention, use and return of anything seized or produced under this Part;
(c) access to and the taking of photographs and copies of anything so seized or produced;
(d) the retention, use, disclosure and destruction of fingerprints, a sample or a photograph taken under this Part.

(2) If the Secretary of State proposes to issue a code of practice under this section he must—
(a) publish a draft of the code;
(b) consider any representations made to him about the draft;
(c) if he thinks it appropriate, modify the draft in the light of any such representations.

(3) The Secretary of State must lay the code before Parliament.

(4) When he has done so he may bring the code into operation by order.

(5) The Secretary of State may revise the whole or any part of a code issued under this section and issue the code as revised; and subsections (2) to (4) apply to such a revised code as they apply to the original code.

(6) A failure by a constable to comply with a provision of a code issued under this section does not of itself make him liable to criminal or civil proceedings.

(7) A code issued under this section is admissible in evidence in proceedings under this Act and must be taken into account by a judge or court in determining any question to which it appears to the judge or the court to be relevant.

(8) If the Secretary of State publishes a draft code of practice in connection with a matter specified in subsection (1) before the date on which this section comes into force—
(a) the draft is as effective as one published under subsection (2) on or after that date;

(b) representations made to the Secretary of State about the draft before that date are as effective as representations made to him about it after that date;
(c) modifications made by the Secretary of State to the draft in the light of any such representations before that date are as effective as any such modifications made by him on or after that date.

General

174. Interpretation

(1) Subsections (2) to (8) apply for the purposes of this Part.
(2) Each of these is an extradition arrest power—
  (a) a Part 1 warrant in respect of which a certificate under section 2 has been issued;
  (b) section 5;
  (c) a warrant issued under section 71;
  (d) a provisional warrant.
(3) 'Excluded material'—
  (a) in England and Wales, has the meaning given by section 11 of the 1984 Act;
  (b) in Northern Ireland, has the meaning given by Article 13 of the 1989 Order.
(4) 'Items subject to legal privilege'—
  (a) in England and Wales, has the meaning given by section 10 of the 1984 Act;
  (b) in Scotland, has the meaning given by section 412 of the 2002 Act;
  (c) in Northern Ireland, has the meaning given by Article 12 of the 1989 Order.
(5) 'Premises'—
  (a) in England and Wales, has the meaning given by section 23 of the 1984 Act;
  (b) in Scotland, has the meaning given by section 412 of the 2002 Act;
  (c) in Northern Ireland, has the meaning given by Article 25 of the 1989 Order.
(6) 'Special procedure material'—
  (a) in England and Wales, has the meaning given by section 14 of the 1984 Act;
  (b) in Northern Ireland, has the meaning given by Article 16 of the 1989 Order.
(7) The expressions in subsection (8) have the meanings given—
  (a) in England and Wales, by section 65 of the 1984 Act;
  (b) in Northern Ireland, by Article 53 of the 1989 Order.
(8) The expressions are—
  (a) appropriate consent;
  (b) fingerprints;
  (c) intimate search;
  (d) non-intimate sample.
(9) The 1984 Act is the Police and Criminal Evidence Act 1984 (c. 60).
(10) The 1989 Order is the Police and Criminal Evidence (Northern Ireland) Order 1989 (S.I. 1989/1341 (N.I. 12)).
(11) The 2002 Act is the Proceeds of Crime Act 2002 (c. 29).

175. Customs officers

The Treasury may by order provide for any provision of this Part which applies in relation to police officers or persons arrested by police officers to apply with specified modifications in relation to customs officers or persons arrested by customs officers.

176. Service policemen

The Secretary of State may by order provide for any provision of this Part which applies in relation to police officers or persons arrested by police officers to apply with specified modifications in relation to service policemen or persons arrested by service policemen.

Part 5
Miscellaneous and General

British overseas territories

177. Extradition from British overseas territories

(1) This section applies in relation to extradition—
(a) from a British overseas territory to a category 1 territory;
(b) from a British overseas territory to the United Kingdom;
(c) from a British overseas territory to a category 2 territory;
(d) from a British overseas territory to any of the Channel Islands or the Isle of Man.
(2) An Order in Council may provide for any provision of this Act applicable to extradition from the United Kingdom to apply to extradition in a case falling within subsection (1)(a) or (b).
(3) An Order in Council may provide for any provision of this Act applicable to extradition from the United Kingdom to a category 2 territory to apply to extradition in a case falling within subsection (1)(c) or (d).
(4) An Order in Council under this section may provide that the provision applied has effect with specified modifications.

178. Extradition to British overseas territories

(1) This section applies in relation to extradition—
(a) to a British overseas territory from a category 1 territory;
(b) to a British overseas territory from the United Kingdom;
(c) to a British overseas territory from a category 2 territory;
(d) to a British overseas territory from any of the Channel Islands or the Isle of Man.
(2) An Order in Council may provide for any provision of this Act applicable to extradition to the United Kingdom to apply to extradition in a case falling within subsection (1)(a) or (b).
(3) An Order in Council may provide for any provision of this Act applicable to extradition to the United Kingdom from a category 2 territory to apply to extradition in a case falling within subsection (1)(c) or (d).
(4) An Order in Council under this section may provide that the provision applied has effect with specified modifications.

Competing extradition claims

179. Competing claims to extradition

(1) This section applies if at the same time—
(a) there is a Part 1 warrant in respect of a person, a certificate has been issued under section 2 in respect of the warrant, and the person has not been extradited in pursuance of the warrant or discharged, and
(b) there is a request for the same person's extradition, a certificate has been issued under section 70 in respect of the request, and the person has not been extradited in pursuance of the request or discharged.
(2) The Secretary of State may—
(a) order proceedings (or further proceedings) on one of them (the warrant or the request) to be deferred until the other one has been disposed of, if neither the warrant nor the request has been disposed of;
(b) order the person's extradition in pursuance of the warrant to be deferred until the request has been disposed of, if an order for his extradition in pursuance of the warrant has been made;
(c) order the person's extradition in pursuance of the request to be deferred until the warrant has been disposed of, if an order for his extradition in pursuance of the request has been made.
(3) In applying subsection (2) the Secretary of State must take account in particular of these matters—
(a) the relative seriousness of the offences concerned;
(b) the place where each offence was committed (or was alleged to have been committed);
(c) the date when the warrant was issued and the date when the request was received;

(d) whether, in the case of each offence, the person is accused of its commission (but not alleged to have been convicted) or is alleged to be unlawfully at large after conviction.

(4) If both the certificates referred to in subsection (1) are issued in Scotland, the preceding provisions of this section apply as if the references to the Secretary of State were to the Scottish Ministers.

[(5) For the purposes of this section a person is alleged to be unlawfully at large after conviction of an offence if—

(a) he is alleged to have been convicted of it, and

(b) his extradition is sought for the purpose of his being sentenced for the offence or of his serving a sentence of imprisonment or another form of detention imposed in respect of the offence.][234]

180. Proceedings on deferred warrant or request

(1) This section applies if—

(a) an order is made under this Act deferring proceedings on an extradition claim in respect of a person (the deferred claim) until another extradition claim in respect of the person has been disposed of, and

(b) the other extradition claim is disposed of.

(2) The judge may make an order for proceedings on the deferred claim to be resumed.

(3) No order under subsection (2) may be made after the end of the required period.

(4) If the person applies to the appropriate judge to be discharged, the judge may order his discharge.

(5) If the person applies to the appropriate judge to be discharged, the judge must order his discharge if—

(a) the required period has ended, and

(b) the judge has not made an order under subsection (2) or ordered the person's discharge.

(6) The required period is 21 days starting with the day on which the other extradition claim is disposed of.

(7) If the proceedings on the deferred claim were under Part 1, section 67 applies for determining the appropriate judge.

(8) If the proceedings on the deferred claim were under Part 2, section 139 applies for determining the appropriate judge.

(9) An extradition claim is made in respect of a person if—

(a) a Part 1 warrant is issued in respect of him;

(b) a request for his extradition is made.

181. Proceedings where extradition deferred

(1) This section applies if—

(a) an order is made under this Act deferring a person's extradition in pursuance of an extradition claim (the deferred claim) until another extradition claim in respect of him has been disposed of;

(b) the other extradition claim is disposed of.

(2) The judge may make an order for the person's extradition in pursuance of the deferred claim to cease to be deferred.

(3) No order under subsection (2) may be made after the end of the required period.

(4) If the person applies to the appropriate judge to be discharged, the judge may order his discharge.

(5) If the person applies to the appropriate judge to be discharged, the judge must order his discharge if—

(a) the required period has ended, and

(b) the judge has not made an order under subsection (2) or ordered the person's discharge.

(6) The required period is 21 days starting with the day on which the other extradition claim is disposed of.

(7) If the person's extradition in pursuance of the deferred claim was ordered under Part 1, section 67 applies for determining the appropriate judge.

(8) If the person's extradition in pursuance of the deferred claim was ordered under Part 2, section 139 applies for determining the appropriate judge.

---

[234] Amended by the Police and Justice Act 2006.

(9) An extradition claim is made in respect of a person if—
 (a) a Part 1 warrant is issued in respect of him;
 (b) a request for his extradition is made.

Legal aid

182. Legal advice, assistance and representation: England and Wales

In section 12(2) of the Access to Justice Act 1999 (c. 22) (meaning of 'criminal proceedings') for paragraph (c) substitute—

'(c) proceedings for dealing with an individual under the Extradition Act 2003,'.

183. Legal aid: Scotland

The provisions of the Legal Aid (Scotland) Act 1986 (c. 47) apply—
 (a) in relation to proceedings in Scotland before the appropriate judge under Part 1, 2 or 5 of this Act as those provisions apply in relation to summary proceedings;
 (b) in relation to any proceedings on appeal arising out of such proceedings before the appropriate judge as those provisions apply in relation to appeals in summary proceedings.

184. Grant of free legal aid: Northern Ireland

(1) The appropriate judge may grant free legal aid to a person in connection with proceedings under Part 1 or Part 2 before the judge or the High Court.
(2) A judge of the High Court may grant free legal aid to a person in connection with proceedings under Part 1 or Part 2 before the High Court or the [Supreme Court].[235]
(3) If the appropriate judge refuses to grant free legal aid under subsection (1) in connection with proceedings before the High Court the person may appeal to the High Court against the judge's decision.
(4) A judge of the High Court may grant free legal aid to a person in connection with proceedings on an appeal under subsection (3).
(5) Free legal aid may be granted to a person under subsection (1), (2) or (4) only if it appears to the judge that—
 (a) the person's means are insufficient to enable him to obtain legal aid, and
 (b) it is desirable in the interests of justice that the person should be granted free legal aid.
(6) On an appeal under subsection (3) the High Court may—
 (a) allow the appeal;
 (b) dismiss the appeal.
(7) The High Court may allow an appeal under subsection (3) only if it appears to the High Court that—
 (a) the person's means are insufficient to enable him to obtain legal aid, and
 (b) it is desirable in the interests of justice that the person should be granted free legal aid.
(8) If the High Court allows an appeal under subsection (3) it must grant free legal aid to the person in connection with the proceedings under Part 1 or Part 2 before it.
(9) If on a question of granting free legal aid under this section or of allowing an appeal under subsection (3) there is a doubt as to whether—
 (a) the person's means are insufficient to enable him to obtain legal aid, or
 (b) it is desirable in the interests of justice that the person should be granted free legal aid,the doubt must be resolved in favour of granting him free legal aid.
(10) References in this section to granting free legal aid to a person are to assigning to him—
 (a) a solicitor and counsel, or
 (b) a solicitor only, or
 (c) counsel only.

185. Free legal aid: supplementary

(1) The provisions of the Legal Aid, Advice and Assistance (Northern Ireland) Order 1981 (S.I. 1981/228 (N.I. 8)) listed in subsection (2) apply in relation to free legal aid under section 184 in connection

[235] Amended by the Constitutional Reform Act 2005.

with proceedings before the appropriate judge or the High Court as they apply in relation to free legal aid under Part III of the Order.

(2) The provisions are—
(a) Article 32 (statements of means);
(b) Article 36(1) (payment of legal aid);
(c) Article 36(3) and (4) (rules);
(d) Article 36A (solicitors excluded from legal aid work);
(e) Article 37 (remuneration of solicitors and counsel);
(f) Article 40 (stamp duty exemption).

(3) As so applied those Articles have effect as if—
(a) a person granted free legal aid under section 184 had been granted a criminal aid certificate under Part III of the Order;
(b) section 184 were contained in Part III of the Order.

(4) The fees of any counsel, and the expenses and fees of any solicitor, assigned to a person under section 184 in connection with proceedings before the [Supreme Court][236] must be paid by the [Department of Justice in Northern Ireland].[237]

(5) The fees and expenses paid under subsection (4) must not exceed the amount [allowed][238] [by the Supreme Court or under Supreme Court Rules].[239]

(6) For the purposes of section 184 and this section the appropriate judge is—
(a) such county court judge or resident magistrate as is designated for the purposes of Part 1 [under section 67],[240] if the proceedings are under Part 1;
(b) such county court judge or resident magistrate as is designated for the purposes of Part 2 [under section 139],[241] if the proceedings are under Part 2.

Re-extradition

186. Re-extradition: preliminary

(1) Section 187 applies in relation to a person if the conditions in subsections (2) to (6) are satisfied.

(2) The first condition is that the person was extradited to a territory in accordance with Part 1 or Part 2.

(3) The second condition is that the person was serving a sentence of imprisonment or another form of detention in the United Kingdom (the UK sentence) before he was extradited.

(4) The third condition is that—
(a) if the person was extradited in accordance with Part 1, the Part 1 warrant in pursuance of which he was extradited contained a statement that it was issued with a view to his extradition for the purpose of being prosecuted for an offence;
(b) if the person was extradited in accordance with Part 2, the request in pursuance of which the person was extradited contained a statement that the person was accused of the commission of an offence.

(5) The fourth condition is that a certificate issued by a judicial authority of the territory shows that—
(a) a sentence of imprisonment or another form of detention for a term of 4 months or a greater punishment (the overseas sentence) was imposed on the person in the territory;
(b) the overseas sentence was imposed on him in respect of—
(i) the offence specified in the warrant or request, or
(ii) any other offence committed before his extradition in respect of which he was permitted to be dealt with in the territory.

(6) The fifth condition is that before serving the overseas sentence the person was returned to the United Kingdom to serve the remainder of the UK sentence.

---

236 Amended by the Constitutional Reform Act 2005.
237 Amended by SI 2010/976.
238 Amended by the Policing and Crime Act 2009.
239 Amended by the Constitutional Reform Act 2005.
240 Amended by the Constitutional Reform Act 2005.
241 Amended by the Constitutional Reform Act 2005.

187. Re-extradition hearing

(1) If this section applies in relation to a person, as soon as practicable after the relevant time the person must be brought before the appropriate judge for the judge to decide whether the person is to be extradited again to the territory in which the overseas sentence was imposed.
(2) The relevant time is the time at which the person would otherwise be released from detention pursuant to the UK sentence (whether or not on licence).
(3) If subsection (1) is not complied with and the person applies to the judge to be discharged, the judge must order his discharge.
(4) The person must be treated as continuing in legal custody until he is brought before the appropriate judge under subsection (1) or he is discharged under subsection (3).
(5) If the person is brought before the appropriate judge under subsection (1) the judge must decide whether the territory in which the overseas sentence was imposed is—
 (a) a category 1 territory;
 (b) a category 2 territory;
 (c) neither a category 1 territory nor a category 2 territory.
(6) If the judge decides that the territory is a category 1 territory, section 188 applies.
(7) If the judge decides that the territory is a category 2 territory, section 189 applies.
(8) If the judge decides that the territory is neither a category 1 territory nor a category 2 territory, he must order the person's discharge.
(9) A person's discharge as a result of this section or section 188 or 189 does not affect any conditions on which he is released from detention pursuant to the UK sentence.
[(10) Section 139 applies for the purposes of this section as it applies for the purposes of Part 2.][242]

188. Re-extradition to category 1 territories

(1) If this section applies, this Act applies as it would if—
 (a) a Part 1 warrant had been issued in respect of the person;
 (b) the warrant contained a statement that—
  (i) the person [had been convicted][243] of the relevant offence, and
  (ii) the warrant was issued with a view to the person's arrest and extradition to the territory for the purpose of serving a sentence imposed in respect of the relevant offence;
 (c) the warrant were issued by the authority of the territory which issued the certificate referred to in section 186(5);
 (d) the relevant offence were specified in the warrant;
 (e) the judge were the appropriate judge for the purposes of Part 1;
 (f) the hearing at which the judge is to make the decision referred to in section 187(1) were the extradition hearing;
 (g) the proceedings before the judge were under Part 1.
(2) As applied by subsection (1) this Act has effect with the modifications set out in Part 1 of Schedule 1.
(3) The relevant offence is the offence in respect of which the overseas sentence is imposed.

189. Re-extradition to category 2 territories

(1) If this section applies, this Act applies as it would if—
 (a) a valid request for the person's extradition to the territory had been made;
 (b) the request contained a statement that the person [had been convicted][244] of the relevant offence;
 (c) the relevant offence were specified in the request;
 (d) the hearing at which the appropriate judge is to make the decision referred to in section 187(1) were the extradition hearing;
 (e) the proceedings before the judge were under Part 2.

---

242 Amended by the Police and Justice Act 2006.
243 Amended by the Police and Justice Act 2006.
244 Amended by the Police and Justice Act 2006.

(2) As applied by subsection (1) this Act has effect with the modifications set out in Part 2 of Schedule 1.
(3) The relevant offence is the offence in respect of which the overseas sentence is imposed.

Conduct of extradition proceedings

190. Crown Prosecution Service: role in extradition proceedings

(1) The Prosecution of Offences Act 1985 (c. 23) is amended as follows.
(2) In section 3 (functions of the Director) in subsection (2) after paragraph (e) insert—
'(ea) to have the conduct of any extradition proceedings;
(eb) to give, to such extent as he considers appropriate, and to such persons as he considers appropriate, advice on any matters relating to extradition proceedings or proposed extradition proceedings;'.
(3) In section 3 after subsection (2) insert—
'(2A) Subsection (2)(ea) above does not require the Director to have the conduct of any extradition proceedings in respect of a person if he has received a request not to do so and—
(a) in a case where the proceedings are under Part 1 of the Extradition Act 2003, the request is made by the authority which issued the Part 1 warrant in respect of the person;
(b) in a case where the proceedings are under Part 2 of that Act, the request is made on behalf of the territory to which the person's extradition has been requested.'
(4) In section 5(1) (conduct of prosecutions on behalf of Crown Prosecution Service) after 'criminal proceedings' insert 'or extradition proceedings'.
(5) In section 14 (control of fees and expenses etc paid by the Service) in subsection (1)(a) after 'criminal proceedings' insert 'or extradition proceedings'.
(6) In section 15(1) (interpretation of Part 1) in the appropriate place insert—'extradition proceedings' means 'proceedings under the Extradition Act 2003;'.

191. Lord Advocate: role in extradition proceedings

(1) The Lord Advocate must—
(a) conduct any extradition proceedings in Scotland;
(b) give, to such extent as he considers appropriate, and to such persons as he considers appropriate, advice on any matters relating to extradition proceedings or proposed extradition proceedings, in Scotland.
(2) Subsection (1)(a) does not require the Lord Advocate to conduct any extradition proceedings in respect of a person if he has received a request not to do so and—
(a) in a case where the proceedings are under Part 1, the request is made by the authority which issued the Part 1 warrant in respect of the person;
(b) in a case where the proceedings are under Part 2, the request is made on behalf of the territory to which the person's extradition has been requested.

192. Northern Ireland DPP and Crown Solicitor: role in extradition proceedings

(1) The Prosecution of Offences (Northern Ireland) Order 1972 (S.I. 1972/538 (N.I. 1)) is amended as set out in subsections (2) to (4).
(2) In article 2(2) (interpretation) in the appropriate place insert—'extradition proceedings' means proceedings under the Extradition Act 2003;'.
(3) In article 4(7) (conduct of prosecutions on behalf of DPP) after 'prosecution' insert 'or extradition proceedings'.
(4) In article 5 (functions of DPP) after paragraph (1) insert—
'(1A) The Director may—
(a) have the conduct of any extradition proceedings in Northern Ireland;
(b) give to such persons as appear to him appropriate such advice as appears to him appropriate on matters relating to extradition proceedings, or proposed extradition proceedings, in Northern Ireland.'
(5) The Justice (Northern Ireland) Act 2002 (c. 26) is amended as set out in subsections (6) to (8).
(6) After section 31 insert—

'31A. Conduct of extradition proceedings

(1) The Director may have the conduct of any extradition proceedings in Northern Ireland.
(2) The Director may give to such persons as appear to him appropriate such advice as appears to him appropriate on matters relating to extradition proceedings, or proposed extradition proceedings, in Northern Ireland.'
(7) In section 36(2) (conduct of criminal proceedings on behalf of DPP) after 'criminal proceedings' insert 'or extradition proceedings'.
(8) In section 44 (interpretation) after subsection (6) insert—'(7) For the purposes of this Part 'extradition proceedings' means proceedings under the Extradition Act 2003.'
(9) The Crown Solicitor for Northern Ireland may—
 (a) have the conduct of any proceedings under this Act in Northern Ireland;
 (b) give to such persons as appear to him appropriate such advice as appears to him appropriate on matters relating to proceedings under this Act, or proposed proceedings under this Act, in Northern Ireland.

Parties to international conventions

193. Parties to international Conventions

(1) A territory may be designated by order made by the Secretary of State if—
 (a) it is not a category 1 territory or a category 2 territory, and
 (b) it is a party to an international Convention to which the United Kingdom is a party.
(2) This Act applies in relation to a territory designated by order under subsection (1) as if the territory were a category 2 territory.
(3) As applied to a territory by subsection (2), this Act has effect as if—
 (a) sections 71(4), 73(5), 74(11)(b), 84(7), 86(7), 137 and 138 were omitted;
 (b) the conduct that constituted an extradition offence for the purposes of Part 2 were the conduct specified in relation to the territory in the order under subsection (1) designating the territory.
(4) Conduct may be specified in relation to a territory in an order under subsection (1) designating the territory only if it is conduct to which the relevant Convention applies.
(5) The relevant Convention is the Convention referred to in subsection (1)(b) which is specified in relation to the territory in the order under subsection (1) designating it.

Special extradition arrangements

194. Special extradition arrangements

(1) This section applies if the Secretary of State believes that—
 (a) arrangements have been made between the United Kingdom and another territory for the extradition of a person to the territory, and
 (b) the territory is not a category 1 territory or a category 2 territory.
(2) The Secretary of State may certify that the conditions in paragraphs (a) and (b) of subsection (1) are satisfied in relation to the extradition of the person.
(3) If the Secretary of State issues a certificate under subsection (2) this Act applies in respect of the person's extradition to the territory as if the territory were a category 2 territory.
(4) As applied by subsection (3), this Act has effect—
 (a) as if sections 71(4), 73(5), 74(11)(b), 84(7) and 86(7) were omitted;
 (b) with any other modifications specified in the certificate.
(5) A certificate under subsection (2) in relation to a person is conclusive evidence that the conditions in paragraphs (a) and (b) of subsection (1) are satisfied in relation to the person's extradition.

Human rights

195. Human rights: appropriate tribunal

(1) The appropriate judge is the only appropriate tribunal in relation to proceedings under section 7(1)(a) of the Human Rights Act 1998 (c. 42) (proceedings for acts incompatible with Convention rights) if the proceedings relate to extradition under Part 1 or Part 2 of this Act.

(2) If the proceedings relate to extradition under Part 1, section 67 applies for determining the appropriate judge.
(3) If the proceedings relate to extradition under Part 2, section 139 applies for determining the appropriate judge.

Genocide etc

196. Genocide, crimes against humanity and war crimes

(1) This section applies if—
  (a) a Part 1 warrant in respect of a person is issued in respect of an offence mentioned in subsection (2), or
  (b) a valid request for a person's extradition is made in respect of an offence mentioned in subsection (2).
(2) The offences are—
  (a) an offence that if committed in the United Kingdom would be punishable as an offence under section 51 or 58 of the International Criminal Court Act 2001 (c. 17) (genocide, crimes against humanity and war crimes);
  (b) an offence that if committed in the United Kingdom would be punishable as an offence under section 52 or 59 of that Act (conduct ancillary to genocide, etc. committed outside the jurisdiction);
  (c) an offence that if committed in the United Kingdom would be punishable as an ancillary offence, as defined in section 55 or 62 of that Act, in relation to an offence falling within paragraph (a) or (b);
  (d) an offence that if committed in the United Kingdom would be punishable as an offence under section 1 of the International Criminal Court (Scotland) Act 2001 (asp 13) (genocide, crimes against humanity and war crimes);
  (e) an offence that if committed in the United Kingdom would be punishable as an offence under section 2 of that Act (conduct ancillary to genocide etc. committed outside the jurisdiction);
  (f) an offence that if committed in the United Kingdom would be punishable as an ancillary offence, as defined in section 7 of that Act, in relation to an offence falling within paragraph (d) or (e);
  (g) any offence punishable in the United Kingdom under section 1 of the Geneva Conventions Act 1957 (c. 52) (grave breach of scheduled conventions).
(3) It is not an objection to extradition under this Act that the person could not have been punished for the offence under the law in force at the time when and in the place where he is alleged to have committed the act of which he is accused or of which he has been convicted.

Custody and bail

197. Custody

(1) If a judge remands a person in custody under this Act, the person must be committed to the institution to which he would have been committed if charged with an offence before the judge.
(2) If a person in custody following his arrest under Part 1 or Part 2[, or kept in custody by virtue of a power under Part 3,][245] escapes from custody, he may be retaken in any part of the United Kingdom in the same way as he could have been if he had been in custody following his arrest or apprehension under a relevant domestic warrant.
(3) A relevant domestic warrant is a warrant for his arrest or apprehension issued in the part of the United Kingdom in question in respect of an offence committed there.
(4) Subsection (5) applies if—
  (a) a person is in custody in one part of the United Kingdom (whether under this Act or otherwise);
  (b) he is required to be removed to another part of the United Kingdom after being remanded in custody under this Act;
  (c) he is so removed by sea or air.

[245] Amended by the Policing and Crime Act 2009.

(5) The person must be treated as continuing in legal custody until he reaches the place to which he is required to be removed.
(6) An order for a person's extradition under this Act is sufficient authority for an appropriate person—
 (a) to receive him;
 (b) to keep him in custody until he is extradited under this Act;
 (c) to convey him to the territory to which he is to be extradited under this Act.
(7) An appropriate person is—
 (a) a person to whom the order is directed;
 (b) a constable.

[197A. Extradition of serving prisoner

If an order is made under Part 1 or 2 for the extradition of a person who is [in custody][246] serving a sentence of imprisonment or another form of detention in the United Kingdom, the order is sufficient authority for the person to be removed from the prison or other institution where he is detained.][247]

198. Bail: England and Wales

(1) The Bail Act 1976 (c. 63) is amended as follows.
(2) In section 1(1) (meaning of 'bail in criminal proceedings') after paragraph (b) insert—
 ', or
 (c) bail grantable in connection with extradition proceedings in respect of an offence.'
(3) In section 2(2) (other definitions) omit the definition of 'proceedings against a fugitive offender' and in the appropriate places insert—
 'extradition proceedings' means proceedings under the Extradition Act 2003;';
 'prosecutor', in relation to extradition proceedings, means the person acting on behalf of the territory to which extradition is sought;'.
(4) In section 4 (general right to bail) in subsection (2) omit the words 'or proceedings against a fugitive offender for the offence'.
(5) In section 4 after subsection (2) insert—
 '(2A) This section also applies to a person whose extradition is sought in respect of an offence, when—
  (a) he appears or is brought before a court in the course of or in connection with extradition proceedings in respect of the offence, or
  (b) he applies to a court for bail or for a variation of the conditions of bail in connection with the proceedings.
 (2B) But subsection (2A) above does not apply if the person is alleged to be unlawfully at large after conviction of the offence.'
(6) In section 5B (reconsideration of decisions granting bail) for subsection (1) substitute—
 '(A1) This section applies in any of these cases—
  (a) a magistrates' court has granted bail in criminal proceedings in connection with an offence to which this section applies or proceedings for such an offence;
  (b) a constable has granted bail in criminal proceedings in connection with proceedings for such an offence;
  (c) a magistrates' court or a constable has granted bail in connection with extradition proceedings.
(1) The court or the appropriate court in relation to the constable may, on application by the prosecutor for the decision to be reconsidered—
  (a) vary the conditions of bail,
  (b) impose conditions in respect of bail which has been granted unconditionally, or
  (c) withhold bail.'
(7) In section 7 (liability to arrest for absconding or breaking conditions of bail) after subsection (1) insert—

[246] Amended by the Policing and Crime Act 2009.
[247] Amended by the Police and Justice Act 2006.

'(1A) Subsection (1B) applies if—
(a) a person has been released on bail in connection with extradition proceedings,
(b) the person is under a duty to surrender into the custody of a constable, and
(c) the person fails to surrender to custody at the time appointed for him to do so.
(1B) A magistrates' court may issue a warrant for the person's arrest.'

(8) In section 7(4) omit the words from 'In reckoning' to 'Sunday'.

(9) In section 7 after subsection (4) insert—
'(4A) A person who has been released on bail in connection with extradition proceedings and is under a duty to surrender into the custody of a constable may be arrested without warrant by a constable on any of the grounds set out in paragraphs (a) to (c) of subsection (3).
(4B) A person arrested in pursuance of subsection (4A) above shall be brought as soon as practicable and in any event within 24 hours after his arrest before a justice of the peace for the petty sessions area in which he was arrested.'

(10) In section 7(5) after 'subsection (4)' insert 'or (4B)'.

(11) In section 7 after subsection (6) insert—
'(7) In reckoning for the purposes of this section any period of 24 hours, no account shall be taken of Christmas Day, Good Friday or any Sunday.'

(12) In Part 1 of Schedule 1 (defendants accused or convicted of imprisonable offences) for paragraph 1 substitute—
'1
The following provisions of this Part of this Schedule apply to the defendant if—
(a) the offence or one of the offences of which he is accused or convicted in the proceedings is punishable with imprisonment, or
(b) his extradition is sought in respect of an offence.'

(13) In Part 1 of Schedule 1 after paragraph 2A insert—
'2B
The defendant need not be granted bail in connection with extradition proceedings if—
(a) the conduct constituting the offence would, if carried out by the defendant in England and Wales, constitute an indictable offence or an offence triable either way; and
(b) it appears to the court that the defendant was on bail on the date of the offence.'

(14) In Part 1 of Schedule 1 in paragraph 6 after 'the offence' insert 'or the extradition proceedings'.

199. Bail: Scotland

After section 24 of the Criminal Procedure (Scotland) Act 1995 (c. 46) (bail and bail conditions) insert—

'24A. Bail: extradition proceedings

(1) In the application of the provisions of this Part by virtue of section 9(2) or 77(2) of the Extradition Act 2003 (judge's powers at extradition hearing), those provisions apply with the modifications that—
(a) references to the prosecutor are to be read as references to a person acting on behalf of the territory to which extradition is sought;
(b) the right of the Lord Advocate mentioned in section 24(2) of this Act applies to a person subject to extradition proceedings as it applies to a person charged with any crime or offence;
(c) the following do not apply—
(i) paragraph (b) of section 24(3); and
(ii) subsection (3) of section 30; and
(d) sections 28(1) and 33 apply to a person subject to extradition proceedings as they apply to an accused.

(2) Section 32 of this Act applies in relation to a refusal of bail, the amount of bail or a decision to allow bail or ordain appearance in proceedings under this Part as the Part applies by virtue of the sections of that Act of 2003 mentioned in subsection (1) above.

(3) The Scottish Ministers may, by order, for the purposes of section 9(2) or 77(2) of the Extradition Act 2003 make such amendments to this Part as they consider necessary or expedient.

(4) The order making power in subsection (3) above shall be exercisable by statutory instrument subject to annulment in pursuance of a resolution of the Scottish Parliament.'

200. Appeal against grant of bail

(1) Section 1 of the Bail (Amendment) Act 1993 (c. 26) (prosecution right of appeal against grant of bail) is amended as follows.
(2) After subsection (1) insert—
'(1A) Where a magistrates' court grants bail to a person in connection with extradition proceedings, the prosecution may appeal to a judge of the Crown Court against the granting of bail.'
(3) In subsection (3) for 'Such an appeal' substitute 'An appeal under subsection (1) or (1A)'.
(4) In subsection (4)—
(a) after subsection (1) insert 'or (1A)';
(b) for 'magistrates' court' substitute 'court which has granted bail';
(c) omit 'such'.
(5) In subsection (5) for 'magistrates' court' substitute 'court which has granted bail'.
(6) In subsection (6) for 'magistrates' court' substitute 'court which has granted bail'.
(7) In subsection (8)—
(a) after 'subsection (1)' insert 'or (1A)';
(b) omit 'magistrates' '.
(8) In subsection (10)(b) for 'reference in subsection (5) above to remand in custody is' substitute 'references in subsections (6) and (9) above to remand in custody are'.
(9) After subsection (11) insert—
'(12) In this section—
'extradition proceedings' means proceedings under the Extradition Act 2003;
'magistrates' court' and 'court' in relation to extradition proceedings means a District Judge (Magistrates' Courts) designated for the purposes of Part 1 or Part 2 of the Extradition Act 2003 by the Lord Chancellor;
'prosecution' in relation to extradition proceedings means the person acting on behalf of the territory to which extradition is sought.'

201. Remand to local authority accommodation

(1) Section 23 of the Children and Young Persons Act 1969 (c. 54) (remand to local authority accommodation) is amended as set out in subsections (2) to (11).
(2) In subsection (1) after 'following provisions of this section' insert ' (except subsection (1A))'.
(3) After subsection (1) insert—
'(1A) Where a court remands a child or young person in connection with extradition proceedings and he is not released on bail the remand shall be to local authority accommodation.'
(4) In subsection (4) after 'subsections (5)' insert ', (5ZA)'.
(5) In subsection (5) after 'security requirement' insert 'in relation to a person remanded in accordance with subsection (1) above'.
(6) After subsection (5) insert—
'(5ZA) A court shall not impose a security requirement in relation to a person remanded in accordance with subsection (1A) above unless—
(a) he has attained the age of twelve and is of a prescribed description;
(b) one or both of the conditions set out in subsection (5ZB) below is satisfied; and
(c) the condition set out in subsection (5AA) below is satisfied.
(5ZB) The conditions mentioned in subsection (5ZA)(b) above are—
(a) that the conduct constituting the offence to which the extradition proceedings relate would if committed in the United Kingdom constitute an offence punishable in the case of an adult with imprisonment for a term of fourteen years or more;
(b) that the person has previously absconded from the extradition proceedings or from proceedings in the United Kingdom or the requesting territory which relate to the conduct constituting the offence to which the extradition proceedings relate.
(5ZC) For the purposes of subsection (5ZB) above a person has absconded from proceedings if in relation to those proceedings—
(a) he has been released subject to a requirement to surrender to custody at a particular time and he has failed to surrender to custody at that time, or
(b) he has surrendered into the custody of a court and he has at any time absented himself from the court without its leave.'

(7) In subsection (5AA) for 'subsection (5)' substitute 'subsections (5) and (5ZA)'.

(8) In subsection (12) for the definition of 'relevant court' substitute—
"relevant court'—
(a) in relation to a person remanded to local authority accommodation under subsection (1) above, means the court by which he was so remanded, or any magistrates' court having jurisdiction in the place where he is for the time being;
(b) in relation to a person remanded to local authority accommodation under subsection (1A) above, means the court by which he was so remanded.'

(9) In subsection (12) in the appropriate places insert—"extradition proceedings' means proceedings under the Extradition Act 2003;';"requesting territory' means the territory to which a person's extradition is sought in extradition proceedings;'.

(10) In section 98(1) of the Crime and Disorder Act 1998 (c. 37) (modifications of section 23 of the Children and Young Persons Act 1969 (c. 54) in relation to 15 and 16 year old boys) after paragraph
(b) insert '; and
(c) is not remanded in connection with proceedings under the Extradition Act 2003.'

Evidence

202. Receivable documents

(1) A Part 1 warrant may be received in evidence in proceedings under this Act.

(2) Any other document issued in a category 1 territory may be received in evidence in proceedings under this Act if it is duly authenticated.

(3) A document issued in a category 2 territory may be received in evidence in proceedings under this Act if it is duly authenticated.

(4) A document issued in a category 1 or category 2 territory is duly authenticated if (and only if) one of these applies—
(a) it purports to be signed by a judge, magistrate or [officer][248] of the territory;
[(aa) it purports to be certified, whether by seal or otherwise, by the Ministry or Department of the territory responsible for justice or for foreign affairs;][249]
(b) it purports to be authenticated by the oath or affirmation of a witness.

(5) Subsections (2) and (3) do not prevent a document that is not duly authenticated from being received in evidence in proceedings under this Act.

203. Documents sent by facsimile

(1) This section applies if a document to be sent in connection with proceedings under this Act is sent by facsimile transmission.

(2) This Act has effect as if the document received by facsimile transmission were the document used to make the transmission.

[204. Warrant issued by category 1 territory: transmission by other electronic means

(1) This section applies if—
(a) an arrest warrant is issued by an authority of a category 1 territory in a case in which an article 26 alert is issued,
(b) the information contained in the warrant and the alert are transmitted to the designated authority by electronic means, and
(c) that information is received by the designated authority in a qualifying form.

(2) This section also applies if—
(a) an arrest warrant is issued by an authority of a category 1 territory in a case in which no article 26 alert is issued,
(b) the information contained in the warrant is transmitted to the designated authority by electronic means, and
(c) that information is received by the designated authority in a qualifying form.

[248] Amended by the Police and Justice Act 2006.
[249] Amended by the Police and Justice Act 2006.

(3) The reference in section 2(2) to an arrest warrant issued by a judicial authority of a category 1 territory is to be read as if it were a reference to the information received by the designated authority.
(4) The references in section 63(1) to an arrest warrant are to be read as if they were references to the information received by the designated authority.
(5) For the purposes of subsection (1), a reference to the information contained in the article 26 alert includes a reference to any information sent with that information relating to the case in question.
(6) For the purposes of this section—
    (a) an article 26 alert is an alert issued pursuant to article 26 of the Council Decision on the establishment, operation and use of the second generation Schengen Information System of 12 June 2007,
    (b) references to information being transmitted by electronic means do not include facsimile transmission, and
    (c) information is received in a qualifying form if it is received in a form in which it is intelligible and which is capable of being used for subsequent reference.][250]

205. Written statements and admissions

(1) The provisions mentioned in subsection (2) apply in relation to proceedings under this Act as they apply in relation to proceedings for an offence.
(2) The provisions are—
    (a) section 9 of the Criminal Justice Act 1967 (c. 80) (proof by written statement in criminal proceedings);
    (b) section 10 of the Criminal Justice Act 1967 (proof by formal admission in criminal proceedings);
    (c) section 1 of the Criminal Justice (Miscellaneous Provisions) Act (Northern Ireland) 1968 (c. 28) (proof by written statement in criminal proceedings);
    (d) section 2 of the Criminal Justice (Miscellaneous Provisions) Act (Northern Ireland) 1968 (proof by formal admission in criminal proceedings).
(3) As applied by subsection (1) in relation to proceedings under this Act, section 10 of the Criminal Justice Act 1967 and section 2 of the Criminal Justice (Miscellaneous Provisions) Act (Northern Ireland) 1968 have effect as if—
    (a) references to the defendant were to the person whose extradition is sought (or who has been extradited);
    (b) references to the prosecutor were to the category 1 or category 2 territory concerned;
    (c) references to the trial were to the proceedings under this Act for the purposes of which the admission is made;
    (d) references to subsequent criminal proceedings were to subsequent proceedings under this Act.

206. Burden and standard of proof

(1) This section applies if, in proceedings under this Act, a question arises as to burden or standard of proof.
(2) The question must be decided by applying any enactment or rule of law that would apply if the proceedings were proceedings for an offence.
(3) Any enactment or rule of law applied under subsection (2) to proceedings under this Act must be applied as if—
    (a) the person whose extradition is sought (or who has been extradited) were accused of an offence;
    (b) the category 1 or category 2 territory concerned were the prosecution.
(4) Subsections (2) and (3) are subject to any express provision of this Act.
(5) In this section 'enactment' includes an enactment comprised in, or in an instrument made under, an Act of the Scottish Parliament.

---

[250] Amended by the Policing and Crime Act 2009.

[LIVE LINKS

206A. Use of live links at certain hearings

(1) This section applies in relation to—
  (a) a hearing before the appropriate judge in proceedings under Part 1, other than—
    (i) an extradition hearing within the meaning of that Part;
    (ii) a hearing under section 54 or 56, and
  (b) a hearing before the appropriate judge in proceedings under Part 2, other than an extradition hearing within the meaning of that Part.
(2) If satisfied that the person affected by an extradition claim is likely to be in custody during the hearing, the appropriate judge may give a live link direction at any time before the hearing.
(3) A live link direction is a direction that, if the person is being held in custody at the time of the hearing, any attendance at the hearing is to be through a live link from the place at which the person is held.
(4) Such a direction—
  (a) may be given on the appropriate judge's own motion or on the application of a party to the proceedings, and
  (b) may be given in relation to all subsequent hearings to which this section applies, or to such hearing or hearings to which this section applies as may be specified or described in the direction.
(5) The appropriate judge may give such a direction only if satisfied that it is not contrary to the interests of justice to give the direction.
(6) A person affected by an extradition claim is to be treated as present in court when, by virtue of a live link direction, the person attends a hearing through a live link.][251]

[206B. Live links: supplementary

(1) The appropriate judge may rescind a live link direction at any time before or during a hearing to which it relates.
(2) The appropriate judge must not give a live link direction or rescind such a direction unless the parties to the proceedings have been given the opportunity to make representations.
(3) If a hearing takes place in relation to the giving or rescinding of a live link direction, the appropriate judge may require or permit any party to the proceedings who wishes to make representations to do so through a live link.
(4) If in a case where an appropriate judge has power to give a live link direction but decides not to do so, the appropriate judge must—
  (a) state in open court the reasons for not doing so, and
  (b) cause those reasons to be entered in the register of proceedings.
(5) Subsection (7) applies if—
  (a) an application for a live link direction is made under section 206A(4) in relation to a qualifying hearing but the application is refused, or
  (b) a live link direction is given in relation to a qualifying hearing but the direction is rescinded before the hearing takes place.
(6) A hearing is a qualifying hearing—
  (a) in relation to proceedings under Part 1, if it is a hearing by virtue of which section 4(3) would be complied with;
  (b) in relation to proceedings under Part 2, if it is a hearing by virtue of which section 72(3) or 74(3) would be complied with.
(7) The requirement in section 4(3), 72(3) or 74(3) (as the case requires) to bring the person as soon as practicable before the appropriate judge is to be read as a requirement to bring the person before that judge as soon as practicable after the application is refused or the direction is rescinded.][252]

[251] Amended by the Policing and Crime Act 2009.
[252] Amended by the Policing and Crime Act 2009.

[206C. Live links: interpretation

(1) This section applies for the purposes of section 206A and subsections (2) and (3) also apply for the purposes of section 206B.
(2) In relation to proceedings under Part 1, section 67 applies for determining the appropriate judge.
(3) In relation to proceedings under Part 2, section 139 applies for determining the appropriate judge.
(4) A person is affected by an extradition claim if—
 (a) a Part 1 warrant is issued in respect of the person;
 (b) the person is arrested under section 5;
 (c) a request for the person's extradition is made; or
 (d) a warrant under section 73 is issued in respect of the person.
(5) References to being in custody include—
 (a) in England and Wales, references to being in police detention within the meaning of the Police and Criminal Evidence Act 1984;
 (b) in Northern Ireland, references to being in police detention within the meaning of the Police and Criminal Evidence (Northern Ireland) Order 1989;
 (c) in Scotland, references to detention under section 14 of the Criminal Procedure (Scotland) Act 1995.
(6) "Live link" means an arrangement by which a person, while absent from the place where the hearing is being held, is able—
 (a) to see and hear the appropriate judge, and other persons,
 (b) to be seen and heard by the judge, other persons,
 and for this purpose any impairment of eyesight or hearing is to be disregarded.][253]

Other miscellaneous provisions

207. Extradition for more than one offence

The Secretary of State may by order provide for this Act to have effect with specified modifications in relation to a case where—
 (a) a Part 1 warrant is issued in respect of more than one offence;
 (b) a request for extradition is made in respect of more than one offence.

208. National security

(1) This section applies if the Secretary of State believes that the conditions in subsections (2) to (4) are satisfied in relation to a person.
(2) The first condition is that the person's extradition is sought or will be sought under Part 1 or Part 2 in respect of an offence.
(3) The second condition is that—
 (a) in engaging in the conduct constituting (or alleged to constitute) the offence the person was acting for the purpose of assisting in the exercise of a function conferred or imposed by or under an enactment, or
 (b) as a result of an authorisation given by the Secretary of State the person is not liable under the criminal law of any part of the United Kingdom for the conduct constituting (or alleged to constitute) the offence.
(4) The third condition is that the person's extradition in respect of the offence would be against the interests of national security.
(5) The Secretary of State may certify that the conditions in subsections (2) to (4) are satisfied in relation to the person.
(6) If the Secretary of State issues a certificate under subsection (5) he may—
 (a) direct that a Part 1 warrant issued in respect of the person and in respect of the offence is not to be proceeded with, or
 (b) direct that a request for the person's extradition in respect of the offence is not to be proceeded with.

[253] Amended by the Policing and Crime Act 2009.

(7) If the Secretary of State issues a certificate under subsection (5) he may order the person's discharge (instead of or in addition to giving a direction under subsection (6)).

(8) These rules apply if the Secretary of State gives a direction under subsection (6)(a) in respect of a warrant—

(a) if the designated authority has not issued a certificate under section 2 in respect of the warrant it must not do so;

(b) if the person is arrested under the warrant or under section 5 there is no requirement for him to be brought before the appropriate judge and he must be discharged;

(c) if the person is brought before the appropriate judge under section 4 or 6 the judge is no longer required to proceed or continue proceeding under sections 7 and 8;

(d) if the extradition hearing has begun the judge is no longer required to proceed or continue proceeding under sections 10 to 25;

(e) if the person has consented to his extradition, the judge is no longer required to order his extradition;

(f) if an appeal to the High Court or [Supreme Court][254] has been brought, the court is no longer required to hear or continue hearing the appeal;

(g) if the person's extradition has been ordered there is no requirement for him to be extradited.

(9) These rules apply if the Secretary of State gives a direction under subsection (6)(b) in respect of a request—

(a) if he has not issued a certificate under section 70 in respect of the request he is no longer required to do so;

(b) if the person is arrested under a warrant issued under section 71 or under a provisional warrant there is no requirement for him to appear or be brought before the appropriate judge and he must be discharged;

(c) if the person appears or is brought before the appropriate judge the judge is no longer required to proceed or continue proceeding under sections 72, 74, 75 and 76;

(d) if the extradition hearing has begun the judge is no longer required to proceed or continue proceeding under sections 78 to 91;

(e) if the person has given his consent to his extradition to the appropriate judge, the judge is no longer required to send the case to the Secretary of State for his decision whether the person is to be extradited;

(f) if an appeal to the High Court or [Supreme Court][255] has been brought, the court is no longer required to hear or continue hearing the appeal;

(g) if the person's extradition has been ordered there is no requirement for him to be extradited.

(10) These must be made under the hand of the Secretary of State—

(a) a certificate under subsection (5);

(b) a direction under subsection (6);

(c) an order under subsection (7).

(11) The preceding provisions of this section apply to Scotland with these modifications—

(a) in subsection (9)(a) for 'he has' substitute 'the Scottish Ministers have' and for 'he is' substitute 'they are';

(b) in subsection (9)(e) for 'Secretary of State for his' substitute 'Scottish Ministers for their'.

(12) In subsection (3) the reference to an enactment includes an enactment comprised in, or in an instrument made under, an Act of the Scottish Parliament.

209. Reasonable force

A person may use reasonable force, if necessary, in the exercise of a power conferred by this Act.

210. Rules of court

(1) Rules of court may make provision as to the practice and procedure to be followed in connection with proceedings under this Act.

(2) In Scotland any rules of court under this Act are to be made by Act of Adjournal.

[254] Amended by the Constitutional Reform Act 2005.

[255] Amended by the Constitutional Reform Act 2005.

211. Service of notices

Service of a notice on a person under section 54, 56, 58, 129, 130 or 131 may be effected in any of these ways—

(a) by delivering the notice to the person;
(b) by leaving it for him with another person at his last known or usual place of abode;
(c) by sending it by post in a letter addressed to him at his last known or usual place of abode.

212. Article 95 alerts: transitional provision

[(1) This section applies in a case where an article 95 alert is issued at the request of an authority of a category 1 territory.

(2) The reference in section 2(2) to an arrest warrant issued by a judicial authority of a category 1 territory is to be read—

(a) as if it were a reference to the alert issued at the request of the authority, and
(b) as if the alert included any information sent with it which relates to the case.

(2A) The references in section 63(1) to an arrest warrant are to be read in accordance with paragraphs (a) and (b) of subsection (2) above.][256]

(3) [In consequence of][257] by subsection (2), this Act has effect with these modifications—

(a) in sections 2(7) and (8), 28(1), 30(1) and (4)(d), 32(2)(b), 33(6)(b), 35(4)(b), 36(3)(b), 47(3)(b), 49(3)(b), 190(3) and 191(2)(a) for 'authority which issued the Part 1 warrant' substitute 'authority at the request of which the alert was issued';
(b) omit section 5;
(c) in sections 33(4)(b), 42(2)(a), 43(2)(a) and (4) and 61(1)(d) and (e), for 'authority which issued the warrant' substitute 'authority at the request of which the alert was issued';
(d) in section 66(2), for the words from 'believes' to the end substitute 'believes is the authority at the request of which the alert was issued'.

(4) An article 95 alert is an alert issued pursuant to article 95 of the Convention implementing the Schengen agreement of 14th June 1985.

INTERPRETATION

213. Disposal of Part 1 warrant and extradition request

(1) A Part 1 warrant issued in respect of a person is disposed of—

(a) when an order is made for the person's discharge in respect of the warrant and there is no further possibility of an appeal;
(b) when the person is taken to be discharged in respect of the warrant;
(c) when an order is made for the person's extradition in pursuance of the warrant and there is no further possibility of an appeal.

(2) A request for a person's extradition is disposed of—

(a) when an order is made for the person's discharge in respect of the request and there is no further possibility of an appeal;
(b) when the person is taken to be discharged in respect of the request;
(c) when an order is made for the person's extradition in pursuance of the request and there is no further possibility of an appeal.

(3) There is no further possibility of an appeal against an order for a person's discharge or extradition—

(a) when the period permitted for giving notice of an appeal to the High Court ends, if notice is not given before the end of that period;
(b) when the decision of the High Court on an appeal becomes final, if there is no appeal to the [Supreme Court][258] against that decision;
(c) when the decision of the [Supreme Court][259] on an appeal is made, if there is such an appeal.

---

[256] Amended by the Policing and Crime Act 2009.
[257] Amended by the Policing and Crime Act 2009.
[258] Amended by the Constitutional Reform Act 2005.
[259] Amended by the Constitutional Reform Act 2005.

(4) The decision of the High Court on an appeal becomes final—
  (a) when the period permitted for applying to the High Court for leave to appeal to the [Supreme Court][260] ends, if there is no such application;
  (b) when the period permitted for applying to the [Supreme Court][261] for leave to appeal to it ends, if the High Court refuses leave to appeal and there is no application to the [Supreme Court][262] for leave to appeal;
  (c) when the [Supreme Court][263] refuses leave to appeal to it;
  (d) at the end of the permitted period, which is 28 days starting with the day on which leave to appeal to the [Supreme Court][264] is granted, if no such appeal is brought before the end of that period.
(5) These must be ignored for the purposes of subsections (3) and (4)—
  (a) any power of a court to extend the period permitted for giving notice of appeal or for applying for leave to appeal;
  (b) any power of a court to grant leave to take a step out of time.
(6) Subsections (3) to (5) do not apply to Scotland.

214. Disposal of charge

(1) A charge against a person is disposed of—
  (a) if the person is acquitted in respect of it, when he is acquitted;
  (b) if the person is convicted in respect of it, when there is no further possibility of an appeal against the conviction.
(2) There is no further possibility of an appeal against a conviction—
  (a) when the period permitted for giving notice of application for leave to appeal to the Court of Appeal against the conviction ends, if the leave of the Court of Appeal is required and no such notice is given before the end of that period;
  (b) when the Court of Appeal refuses leave to appeal against the conviction, if the leave of the Court of Appeal is required and notice of application for leave is given before the end of that period;
  (c) when the period permitted for giving notice of appeal to the Court of Appeal against the conviction ends, if notice is not given before the end of that period;
  (d) when the decision of the Court of Appeal on an appeal becomes final, if there is no appeal to the [Supreme Court][265] against that decision;
  (e) when the decision of the [Supreme Court][266] on an appeal is made, if there is such an appeal.
(3) The decision of the Court of Appeal on an appeal becomes final—
  (a) when the period permitted for applying to the Court of Appeal for leave to appeal to the [Supreme Court][267] ends, if there is no such application;
  (b) when the period permitted for applying to the [Supreme Court][268] for leave to appeal to it ends, if the Court of Appeal refuses leave to appeal and there is no application to the [Supreme Court][269] for leave to appeal;
  (c) when the [Supreme Court][270] refuses leave to appeal to it;
  (d) at the end of the permitted period, which is 28 days starting with the day on which leave to appeal to the [Supreme Court][271] is granted, if no such appeal is brought before the end of that period.
(4) These must be ignored for the purposes of subsections (2) and (3)—
  (a) any power of a court to extend the period permitted for giving notice of appeal or of application for leave to appeal or for applying for leave to appeal;

260 Amended by the Constitutional Reform Act 2005.
261 Amended by the Constitutional Reform Act 2005.
262 Amended by the Constitutional Reform Act 2005.
263 Amended by the Constitutional Reform Act 2005.
264 Amended by the Constitutional Reform Act 2005.
265 Amended by the Constitutional Reform Act 2005.
266 Amended by the Constitutional Reform Act 2005.
267 Amended by the Constitutional Reform Act 2005.
268 Amended by the Constitutional Reform Act 2005.
269 Amended by the Constitutional Reform Act 2005.
270 Amended by the Constitutional Reform Act 2005.
271 Amended by the Constitutional Reform Act 2005.

(b) any power of a court to grant leave to take a step out of time.

(5) Subsections (2) to (4) do not apply to Scotland.

215. European framework list

(1) The European framework list is the list of conduct set out in Schedule 2.

(2) The Secretary of State may by order amend Schedule 2 for the purpose of ensuring that the list of conduct set out in the Schedule corresponds to the list of conduct set out in article 2.2 of the European framework decision.

(3) The European framework decision is the framework decision of the Council of the European Union made on 13 June 2002 on the European arrest warrant and the surrender procedures between member states (2002/584/JHA).

216. Other interpretative provisions

(1) References to a category 1 territory must be read in accordance with section 1.

(2) References to a category 2 territory must be read in accordance with section 69.

(3) References to the designated authority must be read in accordance with section 2(9).

(4) References to a Part 1 warrant must be read in accordance with section 2.

(5) References to a Part 3 warrant must be read in accordance with section 142.

(6) References to a valid request for a person's extradition must be read in accordance with section 70.

[(6A) References to releasing a person from detention pursuant to a sentence do not include releasing a person temporarily on licence pursuant to an intermittent custody order under section 183(1)(b) of the Criminal Justice Act 2003.][272]

(7) 'Asylum claim' has the meaning given by section 113(1) of the Nationality, Immigration and Asylum Act 2002 (c. 41).

[(7A) "Civilian subject to service discipline" has the same meaning as in the Armed Forces Act 2006.][273]

(8) A customs officer is a person commissioned by the Commissioners of Customs and Excise under section 6(3) of the Customs and Excise Management Act 1979 (c. 2).

(9) 'High Court' in relation to Scotland means the High Court of Justiciary.

(10) In relation to Scotland, references to an appeal being discontinued are to be construed as references to its being abandoned.

(11) 'Police officer' in relation to Northern Ireland has the same meaning as in the Police (Northern Ireland) Act 2000 (c. 32).

(12) A provisional warrant is a warrant issued under section 73(3).

[(13) "Service policeman" [has the meaning given by section 375(1) of the Armed Forces Act 2006].[274]

(13A) "Subject to service law" has the same meaning as in that Act.][275]

(15) This section and sections 213 to 215 apply for the purposes of this Act.

General

217. Form of documents

The Secretary of State may by regulations prescribe the form of any document required for the purposes of this Act.

218. Existing legislation on extradition

These Acts shall cease to have effect—

(a) the Backing of Warrants (Republic of Ireland) Act 1965 (c. 45);

(b) the Extradition Act 1989 (c. 33).

[272] Amended by the Policing and Crime Act 2009.

[273] Amended by the Armed Forces Act 2006.

[274] Amended by the Armed Forces Act 2011.

[275] Amended by the Armed Forces Act 2006.

219. Amendments

(1) Schedule 3 contains miscellaneous and consequential amendments.
(2) The Secretary of State may by order make—
 (a) any supplementary, incidental or consequential provision, and
 (b) any transitory, transitional or saving provision,which he considers necessary or expedient for the purposes of, in consequence of, or for giving full effect to any provision of this Act.
(3) An order under subsection (2) may, in particular—
 (a) provide for any provision of this Act which comes into force before another such provision has come into force to have effect, until that other provision has come into force, with such modifications as are specified in the order, and
 (b) amend, repeal or revoke any enactment other than one contained in an Act passed in a Session after that in which this Act is passed.
(4) The amendments that may be made under subsection (3)(b) are in addition to those made by or under any other provision of this Act.

220. Repeals

Schedule 4 contains repeals.

221. Commencement

The preceding provisions of this Act come into force in accordance with provision made by the Secretary of State by order.

222. Channel Islands and Isle of Man

An Order in Council may provide for this Act to extend to any of the Channel Islands or the Isle of Man with the modifications (if any) specified in the Order.

223. Orders and regulations

(1) References in this section to subordinate legislation are to—
 (a) an order of the Secretary of State under this Act (other than an order within subsection (2));
 (b) an order of the Treasury under this Act;
 (c) regulations under this Act.
(2) The orders referred to in subsection (1)(a) are—
 (a) an order for a person's extradition or discharge;
 (b) an order deferring proceedings on a warrant or request;
 (c) an order deferring a person's extradition in pursuance of a warrant or request.
(3) Subordinate legislation—
 (a) may make different provision for different purposes;
 (b) may include supplementary, incidental, saving or transitional provisions.
(4) A power to make subordinate legislation is exercisable by statutory instrument [(subject to subsection (10))].[276]
(5) No order mentioned in subsection (6) may be made unless a draft of the order has been laid before Parliament and approved by a resolution of each House.
(6) The orders are—
 (a) an order under any of these provisions—
  section 1(1);
  [section 62B(3)];[277]
  section 69(1);
  section 71(4);
  section 73(5);
  section 74(11)(b);
  section 84(7);
  section 86(7);

[276] Amended by SI 2010/976.
[277] Amended by Legal Aid Sentencing and Punishment of Offenders Act 2012.

[section 135B(3)];[278]
section 142(9);
section 173(4);
section 215(2);

(b) an order under section 219(2) which contains any provision (whether alone or with other provisions) amending or repealing any Act or provision of an Act.

(7) A statutory instrument is subject to annulment in pursuance of a resolution of either House of Parliament if it contains subordinate legislation other than an order mentioned in subsection (6) or an order under section 221.

(8) A territory may be designated by being named in an order made by the Secretary of State under this Act or by falling within a description set out in such an order.

(9) An order made by the Secretary of State under section 1(1) or 69(1) may provide that this Act has effect in relation to a territory designated by the order with specified modifications.

[(10) The power of the Department of Justice in Northern Ireland to make regulations under section 61(8)(b) or 134(8)(b) is exercisable by statutory rule for the purposes of the Statutory Rules (Northern Ireland) Order 1979.

(11) Regulations made by the Department of Justice are subject to negative resolution (within the meaning of section 41(6) of the Interpretation Act (Northern Ireland) 1954).][279]

224. Orders in Council

(1) An Order in Council under section 177 or 178 is subject to annulment in pursuance of a resolution of either House of Parliament.

(2) An Order in Council under this Act—
(a) may make different provision for different purposes;
(b) may include supplementary, incidental, saving or transitional provisions.

225. Finance

The following are to be paid out of money provided by Parliament—
(a) any expenditure incurred by the Lord Chancellor under this Act;
(b) any increase attributable to this Act in the sums payable out of money provided by Parliament under any other enactment.

226. Extent

(1) Sections 157 to 160, 166 to 168, 171, 173 and 205 do not extend to Scotland.
(2) Sections 154, 198, 200 and 201 extend to England and Wales only.
(3) Sections 183 and 199 extend to Scotland only.
(4) Sections 184 and 185 extend to Northern Ireland only.

227. Short title

This Act may be cited as the Extradition Act 2003.

Schedule 1
Re-Extradition: Modifications

Sections 188 And 189

Part 1
Category 1 Territories

1. In section 11(1), omit paragraphs (c), (g) and (h).
2. Omit sections 14, 18 and 19.

[278] Amended by Legal Aid Sentencing and Punishment of Offenders Act 2012.
[279] Amended by SI 2010/976.

3. In section 21(3), for 'must' substitute 'may'.
4. In section 31(2), for paragraphs (a) and (b) substitute 'would (apart from section 187(1)) be released from detention pursuant to the UK sentence (whether or not on licence)'.
5. In section 39(2)(a), for 'a certificate is issued under section 2 in respect of the warrant' substitute 'the person would (apart from section 187(1)) be released from detention pursuant to the UK sentence (whether or not on licence)'.
6. In section 44(2)(a), for 'following his arrest under this Part' substitute 'under section 187(1)'.
7. In section 45(1), for the words from 'arrested' to 'issued' substitute 'brought before the appropriate judge under section 187(1) may consent to his extradition to the territory in which the overseas sentence was imposed'.

Part 2
Category 2 Territories

8. In section 78, omit subsections (2), (3), (5) and (8).
9. In section 78, for subsection (4) substitute—
'(4) The judge must decide whether the offence specified in the request is an extradition offence.'
10. In section 78(6), for 'any of the questions' substitute 'the question'.
11. In section 78(7), for 'those questions' substitute 'that question'.
12. In section 79(1), omit paragraph (c).
13. Omit section 82.
14. In section 87(3), for the words from 'must send the case' to 'extradited' substitute 'may order the person to be extradited to the category 2 territory'.
15. In section 87, after subsection (3) insert—
'(4) If the judge makes an order under subsection (3) he must remand the person in custody or on bail to wait for his extradition to the territory.
(5) [If the person is remanded in custody, the appropriate judge may][280] later grant bail.'
16. In section 103(1)—
(a) for the words from 'sends a case' to 'extradited' substitute 'orders a person's extradition under this Part'; and
(b) for 'the relevant decision' substitute 'the order'.
17. In section 103(2), for the words from 'the person' to 'the Secretary of State' substitute 'the order is made under section 128'.
18. In section 103, omit subsections (3), (5), (6), (7) and (8).
19. In section 103(9), for the words from 'the Secretary of State' to 'person' substitute 'the order is made'.
20. In section 104, omit subsections (1)(b), (6) and (7).
21. In section 106, omit subsections (1)(b), (7) and (8).
22. In section 117(1)(a), for 'the Secretary of State' substitute 'the appropriate judge'.
23. In section 117(1)(b), for the words from 'permitted period' to 'extradition' substitute 'period permitted under that section'.
24. In section 117, after subsection (1) insert—
'(1A) But this section does not apply if the order is made under section 128.'
25. In section 117(2), for 'the Secretary of State' substitute 'the judge'.
26. In section 119(1)(a), for 'the Secretary of State' substitute 'the appropriate judge'.
27. In section 119, in subsections (2) to (6) and in each place in subsection (7), for 'the Secretary of State' substitute 'the judge'.
28. In section 120, after subsection (1) insert—
'(1A) But this section does not apply if the order for the person's extradition is made under section 128.'
29. In section 121(2)(a), for 'a certificate is issued under section 70 in respect of the request' substitute 'the person would (apart from section 187(1)) be released from detention pursuant to the UK sentence (whether or not on licence)'.

280 Amended by the Police and Justice Act 2006.

30. In section 127(1), for the words from 'arrested' to 'requested' substitute 'brought before the appropriate judge under section 187(1) may consent to his extradition to the territory in which the overseas sentence was imposed'.

31. In section 127(3), before paragraph (a) insert—

'(aa) must be given before the appropriate judge;'.

32. In section 127, omit subsections (4) and (5).

33. In section 128, after subsection (1) insert—

'(1A) The judge must remand the person in custody or on bail.

(1B) [If the person is remanded in custody, the appropriate judge may][281] later grant bail.'

34. In section 128(4), for the words from 'send the case' to 'extradited' substitute 'within the period of 10 days starting with the day on which consent is given order the person's extradition to the category 2 territory'.

35. In section 128, after subsection (5) insert—

'(6) Subsection (4) has effect subject to section 128B.

(7) If subsection (4) is not complied with and the person applies to the judge to be discharged the judge must order his discharge.'

36. After section 128 insert—

'128A. Extradition to category 2 territory following consent

(1) This section applies if the appropriate judge makes an order under section 128(4) for a person's extradition to a category 2 territory.

(2) The person must be extradited to the category 2 territory before the end of the required period, which is 28 days starting with the day on which the order is made.

(3) If subsection (2) is not complied with and the person applies to the judge to be discharged the judge must order his discharge, unless reasonable cause is shown for the delay.

128B. Extradition claim following consent

(1) This section applies if—

(a) a person consents under section 127 to his extradition to a category 2 territory, and

(b) before the judge orders his extradition under section 128(4), the judge is informed that the conditions in subsection (2) or (3) are met.

(2) The conditions are that—

(a) the Secretary of State has received another valid request for the person's extradition to a category 2 territory;

(b) the other request has not been disposed of.

(3) The conditions are that—

(a) a certificate has been issued under section 2 in respect of a Part 1 warrant issued in respect of the person;

(b) the warrant has not been disposed of.

(4) The judge must not make an order under section 128(4) until he is informed what order has been made under section 126(2) or 179(2).

(5) If the order under section 126(2) or 179(2) is for further proceedings on the request under consideration to be deferred until the other request, or the warrant, has been disposed of, the judge must remand the person in custody or on bail.

(6) [If the person is remanded in custody, the appropriate judge may][282] later grant bail.

(7) If—

(a) the order under section 126(2) or 179(2) is for further proceedings on the request under consideration to be deferred until the other request, or the warrant, has been disposed of, and

(b) an order is made under section 180 for proceedings on the request under consideration to be resumed,

the period specified in section 128(4) must be taken to be 10 days starting with the day on which the order under section 180 is made.

---

281 Amended by the Police and Justice Act 2006.

282 Amended by the Police and Justice Act 2006.

(8) If the order under section 126(2) or 179(2) is for further proceedings on the other request, or the warrant, to be deferred until the request under consideration has been disposed of, the period specified in section 128(4) must be taken to be 10 days starting with the day on which the judge is informed of the order.

128C. Extradition following deferral for competing claim

(1) This section applies if—
  (a) an order is made under section 128(4) for a person to be extradited to a category 2 territory in pursuance of a request for his extradition;
  (b) before the person is extradited to the territory an order is made under section 126(2) or 179(2) for the person's extradition in pursuance of the request to be deferred;
  (c) the appropriate judge makes an order under section 181(2) for the person's extradition in pursuance of the request to cease to be deferred.

(2) The required period for the purposes of section 128A(2) is 28 days starting with the day on which the order under section 181(2) is made.'

Schedule 2
European Framework List

SECTION 215

1. Participation in a criminal organisation.
2. Terrorism.
3. Trafficking in human beings.
4. Sexual exploitation of children and child pornography.
5. Illicit trafficking in narcotic drugs and psychotropic substances.
6. Illicit trafficking in weapons, munitions and explosives.
7. Corruption.
8. Fraud, including that affecting the financial interests of the [European Union][283] within the meaning of the Convention of 26 July 1995 on the protection of the [European Union's][284] financial interests.
9. Laundering of the proceeds of crime.
10. Counterfeiting currency, including of the euro.
11. Computer-related crime.
12. Environmental crime, including illicit trafficking in endangered animal species and in endangered plant species and varieties.
13. Facilitation of unauthorised entry and residence.
14. Murder, grievous bodily injury.
15. Illicit trade in human organs and tissue.
16. Kidnapping, illegal restraint and hostage-taking.
17. Racism and xenophobia.
18. Organised or armed robbery.
19. Illicit trafficking in cultural goods, including antiques and works of art.
20. Swindling.
21. Racketeering and extortion.
22. Counterfeiting and piracy of products.
23. Forgery of administrative documents and trafficking therein.
24. Forgery of means of payment.
25. Illicit trafficking in hormonal substances and other growth promoters.
26. Illicit trafficking in nuclear or radioactive materials.
27. Trafficking in stolen vehicles.
28. Rape.

283 Amended by SI 2011/1043.
284 Amended by SI 2011/1043.

29. Arson.
30. Crimes within the jurisdiction of the International Criminal Court.
31. Unlawful seizure of aircraft/ships.
32. Sabotage.

Schedule 3
Amendments

Section 219

Introduction

1. The amendments specified in this Schedule shall have effect.

Parliamentary Commissioner Act 1967 (C. 13)

2. In Schedule 3 to the Parliamentary Commissioner Act 1967 (c. 13) (matters not subject to investigation) for paragraph 4 substitute—
'4. Action taken by the Secretary of State under the Extradition Act 2003.'

Criminal Justice Act 1967 (C. 80)

3. Section 34 of the Criminal Justice Act 1967 (c. 80) (committal of persons under twenty-one accused of extradition crimes) shall cease to have effect.

Suppression of Terrorism Act 1978 (C. 26)

4. Sections 1 (offences not to be regarded as of a political character) and 2 (restrictions on return of criminal under Extradition Act 1870 or to Republic of Ireland) of the Suppression of Terrorism Act 1978 (c. 26) shall cease to have effect.
5. For section 5 of the Suppression of Terrorism Act 1978 substitute—

'5. Power to apply section 4 to non-convention countries

(1) The Secretary of State may by order direct that section 4 above shall apply in relation to a country falling within subsection (2) below as it applies in relation to a convention country, subject to the exceptions (if any) specified in the order.
(2) A country falls within this subsection if—
(a) it is not a convention country; and
(b) it is a category 1 territory or a category 2 territory within the meaning of the Extradition Act 2003.'

Criminal Justice (International Co-Operation) Act 1990 (C. 5)

6. Section 22(1) of the Criminal Justice (International Co-operation) Act 1990 (c. 5) (offences to which an Order in Council under the Extradition Act 1870 can apply) shall cease to have effect.

Computer Misuse Act 1990 (C. 18)

7. Section 15 of the Computer Misuse Act 1990 (c. 18) (extradition where Schedule 1 to the Extradition Act 1989 applies) shall cease to have effect.

Aviation and Maritime Security Act 1990 (C. 31)

8. Section 49 of the Aviation and Maritime Security Act 1990 (c. 31) (extradition by virtue of Orders in Council under Extradition Act 1870) shall cease to have effect.

Criminal Justice Act 1991 (c. 53)

9. In section 47 of the Criminal Justice Act 1991 (c. 53) (persons extradited to the United Kingdom) subsection (4) shall cease to have effect.

United Nations Personnel Act 1997 (c. 13)

10. Section 6(1) of the United Nations Personnel Act 1997 (c. 13) (offences to which an Order in Council under section 2 of the Extradition Act 1870 can apply) shall cease to have effect.

Terrorism Act 2000 (c. 11)

11. Section 64(5) of the Terrorism Act 2000 (c. 11) (offences to which an Order in Council under section 2 of the Extradition Act 1870 can apply) shall cease to have effect.

International Criminal Court Act 2001 (c. 17)

12. Section 71 of the International Criminal Court Act 2001 (c. 17) (extradition: Orders in Council under the Extradition Act 1870) shall cease to have effect.

13.

(1) Part 2 of Schedule 2 to the International Criminal Court Act 2001 (delivery up to International Criminal Court of persons subject to extradition proceedings) is amended as follows.

(2) For paragraph 7 (meaning of 'extradition proceedings') substitute—

'7. In this Part of this Schedule 'extradition proceedings' means proceedings before a court or judge in the United Kingdom under the Extradition Act 2003.'

(3) In paragraph 8 (extradition proceedings in England and Wales or Northern Ireland) after sub-paragraph (5) add—

'(6) References in this paragraph to a court include references to a judge.'

(4) In paragraph 9 (extradition proceedings in Scotland) after sub-paragraph (3) add—

'(4) References in this paragraph to a court include references to a judge.'

(5) In paragraph 10 (power to suspend or revoke warrant or order) for sub-paragraph (1) substitute—

'(1) Where a court makes a delivery order in respect of a person whose extradition has been ordered under the Extradition Act 2003, it may make any such order as is necessary to enable the delivery order to be executed.'

(6) In paragraph 10(2) omit the words 'by a court or judicial officer'.

Enterprise Act 2002 (c. 40)

14. Section 191 of the Enterprise Act 2002 (c. 40) (offences to which an Order in Council under the Extradition Act 1870 can apply) shall cease to have effect.

Schedule 4
Repeals

Section 220

Short title and chapter	Extent of repeal
Backing of Warrants (Republic of Ireland) Act 1965 (c. 45)	The whole Act.
Criminal Justice Act 1967 (c. 80)	Section 34.
Criminal Jurisdiction Act 1975 (c. 59)	In Schedule 3, paragraph 1.
Bail Act 1976 (c. 63)	In section 2(2) the definition of 'proceedings against a fugitive offender'.
	In section 4(2) the words 'or proceedings against a fugitive offender for the offence'.

	In section 7(4) the words from 'In reckoning' to 'Sunday'.
	In Schedule 2, paragraph 33.
Criminal Law Act 1977 (c. 45)	In Schedule 12, in the entry for the Bail Act 1976, paragraph 4.
Suppression of Terrorism Act 1978 (c. 26)	Sections 1 and 2.
	In section 8—
	(a) subsection (5)(a);
	(b) in subsection (6) the words from 'an order made under section 1(4)' to 'or'.
Extradition Act 1989 (c. 33)	The whole Act.
Criminal Justice (International Co-operation) Act 1990 (c. 5)	Section 22.
Computer Misuse Act 1990 (c. 18)	Section 15.
Aviation and Maritime Security Act 1990 (c. 31)	Section 49.
Criminal Justice Act 1991 (c. 53)	Section 47(4).
Bail (Amendment) Act 1993 (c. 26)	In section 1—
	(a) in subsection (4), the word 'such';
	(b) in subsection (8), the word 'magistrates''.
Criminal Justice Act 1993 (c. 36)	Section 72.
	Section 79(7).
Criminal Justice and Public Order Act 1994 (c. 33)	Sections 158 and 159.
United Nations Personnel Act 1997 (c. 13)	Section 6.
Justices of the Peace Act 1997 (c. 25)	In Schedule 5, paragraph 9.
Access to Justice Act 1999 (c. 22)	In Schedule 11, paragraphs 18 and 31 to 36.
Powers of Criminal Courts (Sentencing) Act 2000 (c. 6)	In Schedule 9, paragraph 124.
Terrorism Act 2000 (c. 11)	Section 64.
International Criminal Court Act 2001 (c. 17)	Sections 71 to 73.
	In paragraph 10(2) of Schedule 2, the words 'by a court or judicial officer'.
Proceeds of Crime Act 2002 (c. 29)	In Schedule 11, paragraph 18.
Enterprise Act 2002 (c. 40)	Section 191.

APPENDIX E4

European Arrest Warrant (EAW) Framework Decision

(Acts adopted pursuant to Title VI of the Treaty on European Union)

COUNCIL FRAMEWORK DECISION

of 13 June 2002

on the European arrest warrant and the surrender procedures between Member States

(2002/584/JHA)

THE COUNCIL OF THE EUROPEAN UNION,

Having regard to the Treaty on European Union, and in particular Article 31(a) and (b) and Article 34(2)(b) thereof,

Having regard to the proposal from the Commission,[1]

Having regard to the opinion of the European Parliament,[2]

Whereas:

(1) According to the Conclusions of the Tampere European Council of 15 and 16 October 1999, and in particular point 35 thereof, the formal extradition procedure should be abolished among the Member States in respect of persons who are fleeing from justice after having been finally sentenced and extradition procedures should be speeded up in respect of persons suspected of having committed an offence.

(2) The programme of measures to implement the principle of mutual recognition of criminal decisions envisaged in point 37 of the Tampere European Council Conclusions and adopted by the Council on 30 November 2000,[3] addresses the matter of mutual enforcement of arrest warrants.

(3) All or some Member States are parties to a number of conventions in the field of extradition, including the European Convention on extradition of 13 December 1957 and the European Convention on the suppression of terrorism of 27 January 1977. The Nordic States have extradition laws with identical wording.

(4) In addition, the following three Conventions dealing in whole or in part with extradition have been agreed upon among Member States and form part of the Union acquis: the Convention of 19 June 1990 implementing the Schengen Agreement of 14 June 1985 on the gradual abolition of checks at their common borders[4] (regarding relations between the Member States which are parties to that Convention), the Convention of 10 March 1995 on simplified extradition procedure between the Member States of the European Union[5] and the Convention of 27 September 1996 relating to extradition between the Member States of the European Union.[6]

(5) The objective set for the Union to become an area of freedom, security and justice leads to abolishing extradition between Member States and replacing it by a system of surrender between judicial authorities. Further, the introduction of a new simplified system of surrender of sentenced or suspected persons for the purposes of execution or prosecution of criminal sentences makes it possible to remove the complexity and potential for delay inherent in the

---

[1] OJ C 332 E, 27.11.2001, p 305.
[2] Opinion delivered on 9 January 2002 (not yet published in the Official Journal).
[3] OJ C 12 E, 15.1.2001, p 10.
[4] OJ L 239, 22.9.2000, p 19.
[5] OJ C 78, 30.3.1995, p 2.
[6] OJ C 313, 13.10.1996, p 12.

present extradition procedures. Traditional cooperation relations which have prevailed up till now between Member States should be replaced by a system of free movement of judicial decisions in criminal matters, covering both pre-sentence and final decisions, within an area of freedom, security and justice.

(6) The European arrest warrant provided for in this Framework Decision is the first concrete measure in the field of criminal law implementing the principle of mutual recognition which the European Council referred to as the cornerstone of judicial cooperation.

(7) Since the aim of replacing the system of multilateral extradition built upon the European Convention on Extradition of 13 December 1957 cannot be sufficiently achieved by the Member States acting unilaterally and can therefore, by reason of its scale and effects, be better achieved at Union level, the Council may adopt measures in accordance with the principle of subsidiarity as referred to in Article 2 of the Treaty on European Union and Article 5 of the Treaty establishing the European Community. In accordance with the principle of proportionality, as set out in the latter Article, this Framework Decision does not go beyond what is necessary in order to achieve that objective.

(8) Decisions on the execution of the European arrest warrant must be subject to sufficient controls, which means that a judicial authority of the Member State where the requested person has been arrested will have to take the decision on his or her surrender.

(9) The role of central authorities in the execution of a European arrest warrant must be limited to practical and administrative assistance.

(10) The mechanism of the European arrest warrant is based on a high level of confidence between Member States. Its implementation may be suspended only in the event of a serious and persistent breach by one of the Member States of the principles set out in Article 6(1) of the Treaty on European Union, determined by the Council pursuant to Article 7(1) of the said Treaty with the consequences set out in Article 7(2) thereof.

(11) In relations between Member States, the European arrest warrant should replace all the previous instruments concerning extradition, including the provisions of Title III of the Convention implementing the Schengen Agreement which concern extradition.

(12) This Framework Decision respects fundamental rights and observes the principles recognised by Article 6 of the Treaty on European Union and reflected in the Charter of Fundamental Rights of the European Union,[7] in particular Chapter VI thereof. Nothing in this Framework Decision may be interpreted as prohibiting refusal to surrender a person for whom a European arrest warrant has been issued when there are reasons to believe, on the basis of objective elements, that the said arrest warrant has been issued for the purpose of prosecuting or punishing a person on the grounds of his or her sex, race, religion, ethnic origin, nationality, language, political opinions or sexual orientation, or that that person's position may be prejudiced for any of these reasons. This Framework Decision does not prevent a Member State from applying its constitutional rules relating to due process, freedom of association, freedom of the press and freedom of expression in other media.

(13) No person should be removed, expelled or extradited to a State where there is a serious risk that he or she would be subjected to the death penalty, torture or other inhuman or degrading treatment or punishment.

(14) Since all Member States have ratified the Council of Europe Convention of 28 January 1981 for the protection of individuals with regard to automatic processing of personal data, the personal data processed in the context of the implementation of this Framework Decision should be protected in accordance with the principles of the said Convention.

---

[7] OJ C364, 18.12.2000, p 1.

HAS ADOPTED THIS FRAMEWORK DECISION:

Chapter I
General Principles

Article 1

Definition of the European arrest warrant and obligation to execute it

1. The European arrest warrant is a judicial decision issued by a Member State with a view to the arrest and surrender by another Member State of a requested person, for the purposes of conducting a criminal prosecution or executing a custodial sentence or detention order.
2. Member States shall execute any European arrest warrant on the basis of the principle of mutual recognition and in accordance with the provisions of this Framework Decision.
3. This Framework Decision shall not have the effect of modifying the obligation to respect fundamental rights and fundamental legal principles as enshrined in Article 6 of the Treaty on European Union.

Article 2

Scope of the European arrest warrant

1. A European arrest warrant may be issued for acts punishable by the law of the issuing Member State by a custodial sentence or a detention order for a maximum period of at least 12 months or, where a sentence has been passed or a detention order has been made, for sentences of at least four months.
2. The following offences, if they are punishable in the issuing Member State by a custodial sentence or a detention order for a maximum period of at least three years and as they are defined by the law of the issuing Member State, shall, under the terms of this Framework Decision and without verification of the double criminality of the act, give rise to surrender pursuant to a European arrest warrant:
   - participation in a criminal organisation,
   - terrorism,
   - trafficking in human beings,
   - sexual exploitation of children and child pornography,
   - illicit trafficking in narcotic drugs and psychotropic substances,
   - illicit trafficking in weapons, munitions and explosives,
   - corruption,
   - fraud, including that affecting the financial interests of the European Communities within the meaning of the Convention of 26 July 1995 on the protection of the European Communities' financial interests,
   - laundering of the proceeds of crime,
   - counterfeiting currency, including of the euro,
   - computer-related crime,
   - environmental crime, including illicit trafficking in endangered animal species and in endangered plant species and varieties,
   - facilitation of unauthorised entry and residence,
   - murder, grievous bodily injury,
   - illicit trade in human organs and tissue,
   - kidnapping, illegal restraint and hostage-taking,
   - racism and xenophobia,
   - organised or armed robbery,
   - illicit trafficking in cultural goods, including antiques and works of art,
   - swindling,
   - racketeering and extortion,
   - counterfeiting and piracy of products,
   - forgery of administrative documents and trafficking therein,
   - forgery of means of payment,
   - illicit trafficking in hormonal substances and other growth promoters,
   - illicit trafficking in nuclear or radioactive materials,
   - trafficking in stolen vehicles,
   - rape,

— arson,
— crimes within the jurisdiction of the International Criminal Court,
— unlawful seizure of aircraft/ships,
— sabotage.

3. The Council may decide at any time, acting unanimously after consultation of the European Parliament under the conditions laid down in Article 39(1) of the Treaty on European Union (TEU), to add other categories of offence to the list contained in paragraph 2. The Council shall examine, in the light of the report submitted by the Commission pursuant to Article 34(3), whether the list should be extended or amended.
4. For offences other than those covered by paragraph 2, surrender may be subject to the condition that the acts for which the European arrest warrant has been issued constitute an offence under the law of the executing Member State, whatever the constituent elements or however it is described.

Article 3

Grounds for mandatory non-execution of the European arrest warrant

The judicial authority of the Member State of execution (hereinafter 'executing judicial authority') shall refuse to execute the European arrest warrant in the following cases:

1. if the offence on which the arrest warrant is based is covered by amnesty in the executing Member State, where that State had jurisdiction to prosecute the offence under its own criminal law;
2. if the executing judicial authority is informed that the requested person has been finally judged by a Member State in respect of the same acts provided that, where there has been sentence, the sentence has been served or is currently being served or may no longer be executed under the law of the sentencing Member State;
3. if the person who is the subject of the European arrest warrant may not, owing to his age, be held criminally responsible for the acts on which the arrest warrant is based under the law of the executing State.

Article 4

Grounds for optional non-execution of the European arrest warrant

The executing judicial authority may refuse to execute the European arrest warrant:

1. if, in one of the cases referred to in Article 2(4), the act on which the European arrest warrant is based does not constitute an offence under the law of the executing Member State; however, in relation to taxes or duties, customs and exchange, execution of the European arrest warrant shall not be refused on the ground that the law of the executing Member State does not impose the same kind of tax or duty or does not contain the same type of rules as regards taxes, duties and customs and exchange regulations as the law of the issuing Member State;
2. where the person who is the subject of the European arrest warrant is being prosecuted in the executing Member State for the same act as that on which the European arrest warrant is based;
3. where the judicial authorities of the executing Member State have decided either not to prosecute for the offence on which the European arrest warrant is based or to halt proceedings, or where a final judgment has been passed upon the requested person in a Member State, in respect of the same acts, which prevents further proceedings;
4. where the criminal prosecution or punishment of the requested person is statute-barred according to the law of the executing Member State and the acts fall within the jurisdiction of that Member State under its own criminal law;
5. if the executing judicial authority is informed that the requested person has been finally judged by a third State in respect of the same acts provided that, where there has been sentence, the sentence has been served or is currently being served or may no longer be executed under the law of the sentencing country;
6. if the European arrest warrant has been issued for the purposes of execution of a custodial sentence or detention order, where the requested person is staying in, or is a national or a resident of the executing Member State and that State undertakes to execute the sentence or detention order in accordance with its domestic law;
7. where the European arrest warrant relates to offences which:
   (a) are regarded by the law of the executing Member State as having been committed in whole or in part in the territory of the executing Member State or in a place treated as such; or

(b) have been committed outside the territory of the issuing Member State and the law of the executing Member State does not allow prosecution for the same offences when committed outside its territory.

Article 4a

Decisions rendered following a trial at which the person did not appear in person

1. The executing judicial authority may also refuse to execute the European arrest warrant issued for the purpose of executing a custodial sentence or a detention order if the person did not appear in person at the trial resulting in the decision, unless the European arrest warrant states that the person, in accordance with further procedural requirements defined in the national law of the issuing Member State:
   (a) in due time:
      (i) either was summoned in person and thereby informed of the scheduled date and place of the trial which resulted in the decision, or by other means actually received official information of the scheduled date and place of that trial in such a manner that it was unequivocally established that he or she was aware of the scheduled trial; and
      (ii) was informed that a decision may be handed down if he or she does not appear for the trial; or
   (b) being aware of the scheduled trial, had given a mandate to a legal counsellor, who was either appointed by the person concerned or by the State, to defend him or her at the trial, and was indeed defended by that counsellor at the trial; or
   (c) after being served with the decision and being expressly informed about the right to a retrial, or an appeal, in which the person has the right to participate and which allows the merits of the case, including fresh evidence, to be re-examined, and which may lead to the original decision being reversed:
      (i) expressly stated that he or she does not contest the decision; or
      (ii) did not request a retrial or appeal within the applicable time frame; or
   (d) was not personally served with the decision but:
      (i) will be personally served with it without delay after the surrender and will be expressly informed of his or her right to a retrial, or an appeal, in which the person has the right to participate and which allows the merits of the case, including fresh evidence, to be re-examined, and which may lead to the original decision being reversed; and
      (ii) will be informed of the time frame within which he or she has to request such a retrial or appeal, as mentioned in the relevant European arrest warrant.
2. In case the European arrest warrant is issued for the purpose of executing a custodial sentence or detention order under the conditions of paragraph 1(d) and the person concerned has not previously received any official information about the existence of the criminal proceedings against him or her, he or she may, when being informed about the content of the European arrest warrant, request to receive a copy of the judgment before being surrendered. Immediately after having been informed about the request, the issuing authority shall provide the copy of the judgment via the executing authority to the person sought. The request of the person sought shall neither delay the surrender procedure nor delay the decision to execute the European arrest warrant. The provision of the judgment to the person concerned is for information purposes only; it shall neither be regarded as a formal service of the judgment nor actuate any time limits applicable for requesting a retrial or appeal.
3. In case a person is surrendered under the conditions of paragraph (1)(d) and he or she has requested a retrial or appeal, the detention of that person awaiting such retrial or appeal shall, until these proceedings are finalised, be reviewed in accordance with the law of the issuing Member State, either on a regular basis or upon request of the person concerned. Such a review shall in particular include the possibility of suspension or interruption of the detention. The retrial or appeal shall begin within due time after the surrender.[8]

[8] Amended by Council Framework Decision 2009/299/JHA of 26 February 2009.

Article 5

Guarantees to be given by the issuing Member State in particular cases

The execution of the European arrest warrant by the executing judicial authority may, by the law of the executing Member State, be subject to the following conditions:

1. ....[9]
2. if the offence on the basis of which the European arrest warrant has been issued is punishable by custodial life sentence or life-time detention order, the execution of the said arrest warrant may be subject to the condition that the issuing Member State has provisions in its legal system for a review of the penalty or measure imposed, on request or at the latest after 20 years, or for the application of measures of clemency to which the person is entitled to apply for under the law or practice of the issuing Member State, aiming at a non-execution of such penalty or measure;
3. where a person who is the subject of a European arrest warrant for the purposes of prosecution is a national or resident of the executing Member State, surrender may be subject to the condition that the person, after being heard, is returned to the executing Member State in order to serve there the custodial sentence or detention order passed against him in the issuing Member State.

Article 6

Determination of the competent judicial authorities

1. The issuing judicial authority shall be the judicial authority of the issuing Member State which is competent to issue a European arrest warrant by virtue of the law of that State.
2. The executing judicial authority shall be the judicial authority of the executing Member State which is competent to execute the European arrest warrant by virtue of the law of that State.
3. Each Member State shall inform the General Secretariat of the Council of the competent judicial authority under its law.

Article 7

Recourse to the central authority

1. Each Member State may designate a central authority or, when its legal system so provides, more than one central authority to assist the competent judicial authorities.
2. A Member State may, if it is necessary as a result of the organisation of its internal judicial system, make its central authority(ies) responsible for the administrative transmission and reception of European arrest warrants as well as for all other official correspondence relating thereto. Member State wishing to make use of the possibilities referred to in this Article shall communicate to the General Secretariat of the Council information relating to the designated central authority or central authorities. These indications shall be binding upon all the authorities of the issuing Member State.

Article 8

Content and form of the European arrest warrant

1. The European arrest warrant shall contain the following information set out in accordance with the form contained in the Annex:
   (a) the identity and nationality of the requested person;
   (b) the name, address, telephone and fax numbers and e-mail address of the issuing judicial authority;
   (c) evidence of an enforceable judgment, an arrest warrant or any other enforceable judicial decision having the same effect, coming within the scope of Articles 1 and 2;
   (d) the nature and legal classification of the offence, particularly in respect of Article 2;
   (e) a description of the circumstances in which the offence was committed, including the time, place and degree of participation in the offence by the requested person;
   (f) the penalty imposed, if there is a final judgment, or the prescribed scale of penalties for the offence under the law of the issuing Member State;
   (g) if possible, other consequences of the offence.

[9] Amended by Council Framework Decision 2009/299/JHA of 26 February 2009.

2. The European arrest warrant must be translated into the official language or one of the official languages of the executing Member State. Any Member State may, when this Framework Decision is adopted or at a later date, state in a declaration deposited with the General Secretariat of the Council that it will accept a translation in one or more other official languages of the Institutions of the European Communities.

Chapter 2
Surrender Procedure

Article 9

Transmission of a European arrest warrant

1. When the location of the requested person is known, the issuing judicial authority may transmit the European arrest warrant directly to the executing judicial authority.
2. The issuing judicial authority may, in any event, decide to issue an alert for the requested person in the Schengen Information System (SIS).
3. Such an alert shall be effected in accordance with the provisions of Article 95 of the Convention of 19 June 1990 implementing the Schengen Agreement of 14 June 1985 on the gradual abolition of controls at common borders. An alert in the Schengen Information System shall be equivalent to a European arrest warrant accompanied by the information set out in Article 8(1).

For a transitional period, until the SIS is capable of transmitting all the information described in Article 8, the alert shall be equivalent to a European arrest warrant pending the receipt of the original in due and proper form by the executing judicial authority.

Article 10

Detailed procedures for transmitting a European arrest warrant

1. If the issuing judicial authority does not know the competent executing judicial authority, it shall make the requisite enquiries, including through the contact points of the European Judicial Network,[10] in order to obtain that information from the executing Member State.
2. If the issuing judicial authority so wishes, transmission may be effected via the secure telecommunications system of the European Judicial Network.
3. If it is not possible to call on the services of the SIS, the issuing judicial authority may call on Interpol to transmit a European arrest warrant.
4. The issuing judicial authority may forward the European arrest warrant by any secure means capable of producing written records under conditions allowing the executing Member State to establish its authenticity.
5. All difficulties concerning the transmission or the authenticity of any document needed for the execution of the European arrest warrant shall be dealt with by direct contacts between the judicial authorities involved, or, where appropriate, with the involvement of the central authorities of the Member States.
6. If the authority which receives a European arrest warrant is not competent to act upon it, it shall automatically forward the European arrest warrant to the competent authority in its Member State and shall inform the issuing judicial authority accordingly.

Article 11

Rights of a requested person

1. When a requested person is arrested, the executing competent judicial authority shall, in accordance with its national law, inform that person of the European arrest warrant and of its contents, and also of the possibility of consenting to surrender to the issuing judicial authority.
2. A requested person who is arrested for the purpose of the execution of a European arrest warrant shall have a right to be assisted by a legal counsel and by an interpreter in accordance with the national law of the executing Member State.

[10] Council Joint Action 98/428/JHA of 29 June 1998 on the creation of a European Judicial Network (OJ L 191, 7.7.1998, p 4).

Article 12

Keeping the person in detention

When a person is arrested on the basis of a European arrest warrant, the executing judicial authority shall take a decision on whether the requested person should remain in detention, in accordance with the law of the executing Member State.

The person may be released provisionally at any time in conformity with the domestic law of the executing Member State, provided that the competent authority of the said Member State takes all the measures it deems necessary to prevent the person absconding.

Article 13

Consent to surrender

1. If the arrested person indicates that he or she consents to surrender, that consent and, if appropriate, express renunciation of entitlement to the 'speciality rule', referred to in Article 27(2), shall be given before the executing judicial authority, in accordance with the domestic law of the executing Member State.
2. Each Member State shall adopt the measures necessary to ensure that consent and, where appropriate, renunciation, as referred to in paragraph 1, are established in such a way as to show that the person concerned has expressed them voluntarily and in full awareness of the consequences. To that end, the requested person shall have the right to legal counsel.
3. The consent and, where appropriate, renunciation, as referred to in paragraph 1, shall be formally recorded in accordance with the procedure laid down by the domestic law of the executing Member State.
4. In principle, consent may not be revoked. Each Member State may provide that consent and, if appropriate, renunciation may be revoked, in accordance with the rules applicable under its domestic law. In this case, the period between the date of consent and that of its revocation shall not be taken into consideration in establishing the time limits laid down in Article 17. A Member State which wishes to have recourse to this possibility shall inform the General Secretariat of the Council accordingly when this Framework Decision is adopted and shall specify the procedures whereby revocation of consent shall be possible and any amendment to them.

Article 14

Hearing of the requested person

Where the arrested person does not consent to his or her surrender as referred to in Article 13, he or she shall be entitled to be heard by the executing judicial authority, in accordance with the law of the executing Member State.

Article 15

Surrender decision

1. The executing judicial authority shall decide, within the time-limits and under the conditions defined in this Framework Decision, whether the person is to be surrendered.
2. If the executing judicial authority finds the information communicated by the issuing Member State to be insufficient to allow it to decide on surrender, it shall request that the necessary supplementary information, in particular with respect to Articles 3 to 5 and Article 8, be furnished as a matter of urgency and may fix a time limit for the receipt thereof, taking into account the need to observe the time limits set in Article 17.
3. The issuing judicial authority may at any time forward any additional useful information to the executing judicial authority.

Article 16

Decision in the event of multiple requests

1. If two or more Member States have issued European arrest warrants for the same person, the decision on which of the European arrest warrants shall be executed shall be taken by the executing judicial authority with due consideration of all the circumstances and especially the relative seriousness and place of the offences, the respective dates of the European arrest warrants and whether the warrant

has been issued for the purposes of prosecution or for execution of a custodial sentence or detention order.

2. The executing judicial authority may seek the advice of Eurojust[11] when making the choice referred to in paragraph 1.
3. In the event of a conflict between a European arrest warrant and a request for extradition presented by a third country, the decision on whether the European arrest warrant or the extradition request takes precedence shall be taken by the competent authority of the executing Member State with due consideration of all the circumstances, in particular those referred to in paragraph 1 and those mentioned in the applicable convention.
4. This Article shall be without prejudice to Member States' obligations under the Statute of the International Criminal Court.

Article 17

Time limits and procedures for the decision to execute the European arrest warrant

1. A European arrest warrant shall be dealt with and executed as a matter of urgency.
2. In cases where the requested person consents to his surrender, the final decision on the execution of the European arrest warrant should be taken within a period of 10 days after consent has been given.
3. In other cases, the final decision on the execution of the European arrest warrant should be taken within a period of 60 days after the arrest of the requested person.
4. Where in specific cases the European arrest warrant cannot be executed within the time limits laid down in paragraphs 2 or 3, the executing judicial authority shall immediately inform the issuing judicial authority thereof, giving the reasons for the delay. In such case, the time limits may be extended by a further 30 days.
5. As long as the executing judicial authority has not taken a final decision on the European arrest warrant, it shall ensure that the material conditions necessary for effective surrender of the person remain fulfilled.
6. Reasons must be given for any refusal to execute a European arrest warrant.
7. Where in exceptional circumstances a Member State cannot observe the time limits provided for in this Article, it shall inform Eurojust, giving the reasons for the delay. In addition, a Member State which has experienced repeated delays on the part of another Member State in the execution of European arrest warrants shall inform the Council with a view to evaluating the implementation of this Framework Decision at Member State level.

Article 18

Situation pending the decision

1. Where the European arrest warrant has been issued for the purpose of conducting a criminal prosecution, the executing judicial authority must:
   (a) either agree that the requested person should be heard according to Article 19;
   (b) or agree to the temporary transfer of the requested person.
2. The conditions and the duration of the temporary transfer shall be determined by mutual agreement between the issuing and executing judicial authorities.
3. In the case of temporary transfer, the person must be able to return to the executing Member State to attend hearings concerning him or her as part of the surrender procedure.

Article 19

Hearing the person pending the decision

1. The requested person shall be heard by a judicial authority, assisted by another person designated in accordance with the law of the Member State of the requesting court.
2. The requested person shall be heard in accordance with the law of the executing Member State and with the conditions determined by mutual agreement between the issuing and executing judicial authorities.

---

[11] Council Decision 2002/187/JHA of 28 February 2002 setting up Eurojust with a view to reinforcing the fight against serious crime (OJ L 63, 6.3.2002, p 1).

3. The competent executing judicial authority may assign another judicial authority of its Member State to take part in the hearing of the requested person in order to ensure the proper application of this Article and of the conditions laid down.

Article 20

Privileges and immunities

1. Where the requested person enjoys a privilege or immunity regarding jurisdiction or execution in the executing Member State, the time limits referred to in Article 17 shall not start running unless, and counting from the day when, the executing judicial authority is informed of the fact that the privilege or immunity has been waived.
   The executing Member State shall ensure that the material conditions necessary for effective surrender are fulfilled when the person no longer enjoys such privilege or immunity.
2. Where power to waive the privilege or immunity lies with an authority of the executing Member State, the executing judicial authority shall request it to exercise that power forthwith. Where power to waive the privilege or immunity lies with an authority of another State or international organisation, it shall be for the issuing judicial authority to request it to exercise that power.

Article 21

Competing international obligations

This Framework Decision shall not prejudice the obligations of the executing Member State where the requested person has been extradited to that Member State from a third State and where that person is protected by provisions of the arrangement under which he or she was extradited concerning speciality. The executing Member State shall take all necessary measures for requesting forthwith the consent of the State from which the requested person was extradited so that he or she can be surrendered to the Member State which issued the European arrest warrant. The time limits referred to in Article 17 shall not start running until the day on which these speciality rules cease to apply. Pending the decision of the State from which the requested person was extradited, the executing Member State will ensure that the material conditions necessary for effective surrender remain fulfilled.

Article 22

Notification of the decision

The executing judicial authority shall notify the issuing judicial authority immediately of the decision on the action to be taken on the European arrest warrant.

Article 23

Time limits for surrender of the person

1. The person requested shall be surrendered as soon as possible on a date agreed between the authorities concerned.
2. He or she shall be surrendered no later than 10 days after the final decision on the execution of the European arrest warrant.
3. If the surrender of the requested person within the period laid down in paragraph 2 is prevented by circumstances beyond the control of any of the Member States, the executing and issuing judicial authorities shall immediately contact each other and agree on a new surrender date. In that event, the surrender shall take place within 10 days of the new date thus agreed.
4. The surrender may exceptionally be temporarily postponed for serious humanitarian reasons, for example if there are substantial grounds for believing that it would manifestly endanger the requested person's life or health. The execution of the European arrest warrant shall take place as soon as these grounds have ceased to exist. The executing judicial authority shall immediately inform the issuing judicial authority and agree on a new surrender date. In that event, the surrender shall take place within 10 days of the new date thus agreed.
5. Upon expiry of the time limits referred to in paragraphs 2 to 4, if the person is still being held in custody he shall be released.

Article 24

Postponed or conditional surrender

1. The executing judicial authority may, after deciding to execute the European arrest warrant, postpone the surrender of the requested person so that he or she may be prosecuted in the executing Member State or, if he or she has already been sentenced, so that he or she may serve, in its territory, a sentence passed for an act other than that referred to in the European arrest warrant.
2. Instead of postponing the surrender, the executing judicial authority may temporarily surrender the requested person to the issuing Member State under conditions to be determined by mutual agreement between the executing and the issuing judicial authorities. The agreement shall be made in writing and the conditions shall be binding on all the authorities in the issuing Member State.

Article 25

Transit

1. Each Member State shall, except when it avails itself of the possibility of refusal when the transit of a national or a resident is requested for the purpose of the execution of a custodial sentence or detention order, permit the transit through its territory of a requested person who is being surrendered provided that it has been given information on:
   (a) the identity and nationality of the person subject to the European arrest warrant;
   (b) the existence of a European arrest warrant;
   (c) the nature and legal classification of the offence;
   (d) the description of the circumstances of the offence, including the date and place. Where a person who is the subject of a European arrest warrant for the purposes of prosecution is a national or resident of the Member State of transit, transit may be subject to the condition that the person, after being heard, is returned to the transit Member State to serve the custodial sentence or detention order passed against him in the issuing Member State.
2. Each Member State shall designate an authority responsible for receiving transit requests and the necessary documents, as well as any other official correspondence relating to transit requests. Member States shall communicate this designation to the General Secretariat of the Council.
3. The transit request and the information set out in paragraph 1 may be addressed to the authority designated pursuant to paragraph 2 by any means capable of producing a written record. The Member State of transit shall notify its decision by the same procedure.
4. This Framework Decision does not apply in the case of transport by air without a scheduled stopover. However, if an unscheduled landing occurs, the issuing Member State shall provide the authority designated pursuant to paragraph 2 with the information provided for in paragraph 1.
5. Where a transit concerns a person who is to be extradited from a third State to a Member State this Article will apply mutatis mutandis. In particular the expression 'European arrest warrant' shall be deemed to be replaced by extradition request.

Chapter 3
Effects of the Surrender

Article 26

Deduction of the period of detention served in the executing Member State

1. The issuing Member State shall deduct all periods of detention arising from the execution of a European arrest warrant from the total period of detention to be served in the issuing Member State as a result of a custodial sentence or detention order being passed.
2. To that end, all information concerning the duration of the detention of the requested person on the basis of the European arrest warrant shall be transmitted by the executing judicial authority or the central authority designated under Article 7 to the issuing judicial authority at the time of the surrender.

Article 27

Possible prosecution for other offences

1. Each Member State may notify the General Secretariat of the Council that, in its relations with other Member States that have given the same notification, consent is presumed to have been given for the prosecution, sentencing or detention with a view to the carrying out of a custodial sentence or detention order for an offence committed prior to his or her surrender, other than that for which he or she was surrendered, unless in a particular case the executing judicial authority states otherwise in its decision on surrender.
2. Except in the cases referred to in paragraphs 1 and 3, a person surrendered may not be prosecuted, sentenced or otherwise deprived of his or her liberty for an offence committed prior to his or her surrender other than that for which he or she was surrendered.
3. Paragraph 2 does not apply in the following cases:
   (a) when the person having had an opportunity to leave the territory of the Member State to which he or she has been surrendered has not done so within 45 days of his or her final discharge, or has returned to that territory after leaving it;
   (b) the offence is not punishable by a custodial sentence or detention order;
   (c) the criminal proceedings do not give rise to the application of a measure restricting personal liberty;
   (d) when the person could be liable to a penalty or a measure not involving the deprivation of liberty, in particular a financial penalty or a measure in lieu thereof, even if the penalty or measure may give rise to a restriction of his or her personal liberty;
   (e) when the person consented to be surrendered, where appropriate at the same time as he or she renounced the speciality rule, in accordance with Article 13;
   (f) when the person, after his/her surrender, has expressly renounced entitlement to the speciality rule with regard to specific offences preceding his/her surrender. Renunciation shall be given before the competent judicial authorities of the issuing Member State and shall be recorded in accordance with that State's domestic law. The renunciation shall be drawn up in such a way as to make clear that the person has given it voluntarily and in full awareness of the consequences. To that end, the person shall have the right to legal counsel;
   (g) where the executing judicial authority which surrendered the person gives its consent in accordance with paragraph 4.
4. A request for consent shall be submitted to the executing judicial authority, accompanied by the information mentioned in Article 8(1) and a translation as referred to in Article 8(2). Consent shall be given when the offence for which it is requested is itself subject to surrender in accordance with the provisions of this Framework Decision. Consent shall be refused on the grounds referred to in Article 3 and otherwise may be refused only on the grounds referred to in Article 4.

The decision shall be taken no later than 30 days after receipt of the request. For the situations mentioned in Article 5 the issuing Member State must give the guarantees provided for therein.

Article 28

Surrender or subsequent extradition

1. Each Member State may notify the General Secretariat of the Council that, in its relations with other Member States which have given the same notification, the consent for the surrender of a person to a Member State other than the executing Member State pursuant to a European arrest warrant issued for an offence committed prior to his or her surrender is presumed to have been given, unless in a particular case the executing judicial authority states otherwise in its decision on surrender.
2. In any case, a person who has been surrendered to the issuing Member State pursuant to a European arrest warrant may, without the consent of the executing Member State, be surrendered to a Member State other than the executing Member State pursuant to a European arrest warrant issued for any offence committed prior to his or her surrender in the following cases:
   (a) where the requested person, having had an opportunity to leave the territory of the Member State to which he or she has been surrendered, has not done so within 45 days of his final discharge, or has returned to that territory after leaving it;
   (b) where the requested person consents to be surrendered to a Member State other than the executing Member State pursuant to a European arrest warrant. Consent shall be given before the

competent judicial authorities of the issuing Member State and shall be recorded in accordance with that State's national law. It shall be drawn up in such a way as to make clear that the person concerned has given it voluntarily and in full awareness of the consequences. To that end, the requested person shall have the right to legal counsel;

(c) where the requested person is not subject to the speciality rule, in accordance with Article 27(3) (a), (e), (f) and (g).

3. The executing judicial authority consents to the surrender to another Member State according to the following rules:
   (a) the request for consent shall be submitted in accordance with Article 9, accompanied by the information mentioned in Article 8(1) and a translation as stated in Article 8(2);
   (b) consent shall be given when the offence for which it is requested is itself subject to surrender in accordance with the provisions of this Framework Decision;
   (c) the decision shall be taken no later than 30 days after receipt of the request;
   (d) consent shall be refused on the grounds referred to in Article 3 and otherwise may be refused only on the grounds referred to in Article 4.

   For the situations referred to in Article 5, the issuing Member State must give the guarantees provided for therein.
4. Notwithstanding paragraph 1, a person who has been surrendered pursuant to a European arrest warrant shall not be extradited to a third State without the consent of the competent authority of the Member State which surrendered the person. Such consent shall be given in accordance with the Conventions by which that Member State is bound, as well as with its domestic law.

Article 29

Handing over of property

1. At the request of the issuing judicial authority or on its own initiative, the executing judicial authority shall, in accordance with its national law, seize and hand over property which:
   (a) may be required as evidence, or
   (b) has been acquired by the requested person as a result of the offence.
2. The property referred to in paragraph 1 shall be handed over even if the European arrest warrant cannot be carried out owing to the death or escape of the requested person.
3. If the property referred to in paragraph 1 is liable to seizure or confiscation in the territory of the executing Member State, the latter may, if the property is needed in connection with pending criminal proceedings, temporarily retain it or hand it over to the issuing Member State, on condition that it is returned.
4. Any rights which the executing Member State or third parties may have acquired in the property referred to in paragraph 1 shall be preserved. Where such rights exist, the issuing Member State shall return the property without charge to the executing Member State as soon as the criminal proceedings have been terminated.

Article 30

Expenses

1. Expenses incurred in the territory of the executing Member State for the execution of a European arrest warrant shall be borne by that Member State.
2. All other expenses shall be borne by the issuing Member State.

Chapter 4

General and final provisions

Article 31

Relation to other legal instruments

1. Without prejudice to their application in relations between Member States and third States, this Framework Decision shall, from 1 January 2004, replace the corresponding provisions of the following conventions applicable in the field of extradition in relations between the Member States:

(a) the European Convention on Extradition of 13 December 1957, its additional protocol of 15 October 1975, its second additional protocol of 17 March 1978, and the European Convention on the suppression of terrorism of 27 January 1977 as far as extradition is concerned;
(b) the Agreement between the 12 Member States of the European Communities on the simplification and modernisation of methods of transmitting extradition requests of 26 May 1989;
(c) the Convention of 10 March 1995 on simplified extradition procedure between the Member States of the European Union;
(d) the Convention of 27 September 1996 relating to extradition between the Member States of the European Union;
(e) Title III, Chapter 4 of the Convention of 19 June 1990 implementing the Schengen Agreement of 14 June 1985 on the gradual abolition of checks at common borders.

2. Member States may continue to apply bilateral or multilateral agreements or arrangements in force when this Framework Decision is adopted in so far as such agreements or arrangements allow the objectives of this Framework Decision to be extended or enlarged and help to simplify or facilitate further the procedures for surrender of persons who are the subject of European arrest warrants.

Member States may conclude bilateral or multilateral agreements or arrangements after this Framework Decision has come into force in so far as such agreements or arrangements allow the prescriptions of this Framework Decision to be extended or enlarged and help to simplify or facilitate further the procedures for surrender of persons who are the subject of European arrest warrants, in particular by fixing time limits shorter than those fixed in Article 17, by extending the list of offences laid down in Article 2(2), by further limiting the grounds for refusal set out in Articles 3 and 4, or by lowering the threshold provided for in Article 2(1) or (2).

The agreements and arrangements referred to in the second subparagraph may in no case affect relations with Member States which are not parties to them.

Member States shall, within three months from the entry into force of this Framework Decision, notify the Council and the Commission of the existing agreements and arrangements referred to in the first subparagraph which they wish to continue applying.

Member States shall also notify the Council and the Commission of any new agreement or arrangement as referred to in the second subparagraph, within three months of signing it.

3. Where the conventions or agreements referred to in paragraph 1 apply to the territories of Member States or to territories for whose external relations a Member State is responsible to which this Framework Decision does not apply, these instruments shall continue to govern the relations existing between those territories and the other Members States.

Article 32

Transitional provision

1. Extradition requests received before 1 January 2004 will continue to be governed by existing instruments relating to extradition. Requests received after that date will be governed by the rules adopted by Member States pursuant to this Framework Decision. However, any Member State may, at the time of the adoption of this Framework Decision by the Council, make a statement indicating that as executing Member State it will continue to deal with requests relating to acts committed before a date which it specifies in accordance with the extradition system applicable before 1 January 2004. The date in question may not be later than 7 August 2002. The said statement will be published in the Official Journal of the European Communities. It may be withdrawn at any time.

Article 33

Provisions concerning Austria and Gibraltar

1. As long as Austria has not modified Article 12(1) of the Auslieferungs- und Rechtshilfegesetz and, at the latest, until 31 December 2008, it may allow its executing judicial authorities to refuse the enforcement of a European arrest warrant if the requested person is an Austrian citizen and if the act for which the European arrest warrant has been issued is not punishable under Austrian law.
2. This Framework Decision shall apply to Gibraltar.

Article 34

Implementation

1. Member States shall take the necessary measures to comply with the provisions of this Framework Decision by 31 December 2003.
2. Member States shall transmit to the General Secretariat of the Council and to the Commission the text of the provisions transposing into their national law the obligations imposed on them under this Framework Decision. When doing so, each Member State may indicate that it will apply immediately this Framework Decision in its relations with those Member States which have given the same notification. The General Secretariat of the Council shall communicate to the Member States and to the Commission the information received pursuant to Article 7(2), Article 8(2), Article 13(4) and Article 25(2). It shall also have the information published in the Official Journal of the European Communities.
3. On the basis of the information communicated by the General Secretariat of the Council, the Commission shall, by 31 December 2004 at the latest, submit a report to the European Parliament and to the Council on the operation of this Framework Decision, accompanied, where necessary, by legislative proposals.
4. The Council shall in the second half of 2003 conduct a review, in particular of the practical application, of the provisions of this Framework Decision by the Member States as well as the functioning of the Schengen Information System.

Article 35

Entry into force

This Framework Decision shall enter into force on the twentieth day following that of its publication in the *Official Journal of the European Communities.*

Done at Luxembourg, 13 June 2002.

For the Council
The President
M. RAJOY BREY

ANNEX

European arrest warrant[12]

This warrant has been issued by a competent judicial authority. I request that the person mentioned below be arrested and surrendered for the purposes of conducting a criminal prosecution or executing a custodial sentence or detention order.

(a)Information regarding the identity of the requested person:..........

Name: ....

Forename(s): ....

Maiden name, where applicable: ....

Aliases, where applicable: ....

Sex: ....

Nationality: ....

Date of birth: ....

Place of birth: ....

Residence and/or known address: ....

Language(s) which the requested person understands (if known): ....

Distinctive marks/description of the requested person: ....

[12] This warrant must be written in, or translated into, one of the official languages of the executing Member State, when that State is known, or any other language accepted by that State.

Photo and fingerprints of the requested person, if they are available and can be transmitted, or contact details of the person to be contacted in order to obtain such information or a DNA profile (where this evidence can be supplied but has not been included)

(b) Decision on which the warrant is based:

1. Arrest warrant or judicial decision having the same effect:..

Type: ....

2. Enforceable judgement: ....

....

Reference:...

(c) Indications on the length of the sentence:

1. Maximum length of the custodial sentence or detention order which may be imposed for the offence(s): ....

....

2. Length of the custodial sentence or detention order imposed: ....

Remaining sentence to be served: ....

....

....

[(d) Indicate if the person appeared in person at the trial resulting in the decision:

1. [ ] Yes, the person appeared in person at the trial resulting in the decision.
2. [ ] No, the person did not appear in person at the trial resulting in the decision.
3. If you have ticked the box under point 2, please confirm the existence of one of the following:

[ ] 3.1a. the person was summoned in person on .... (day/month/year) and thereby informed of the scheduled date and place of the trial which resulted in the decision and was informed that a decision may be handed down if he or she does not appear for the trial;

OR

[ ] 3.1b. the person was not summoned in person but by other means actually received official information of the scheduled date and place of the trial which resulted in the decision, in such a manner that it was unequivocally established that he or she was aware of the scheduled trial, and was informed that a decision may be handed down if he or she does not appear for the trial;

OR

[ ] 3.2. being aware of the scheduled trial, the person had given a mandate t a legal counselor, who was either appointed by the person concerned by the State, to defend him or her at the trial, and was indeed defended by that counselor at the trial;

OR

[ ] 3.3. the person was served with the decision on ....(day/month/year) and was expressly informed about the right to a retrial or appeal, in which he or she has the right to participate and which allows the merits of the case, including fresh evidence, to be re-examined, and which may lead to the original decision being reversed, and

[ ] the person expressly stated that he or she does not contest the decision,

OR

[ ] the person did not request a retrial or appeal within the applicable time frame;

OR

[ ] 3.4. the person was not personally served with the decision, but

— the person will be personally served with this decision without delay after the surrender, and

— when served with the decision, the person will be expressly informed of his or her right to a retrial or appeal, in which he or she has the right to participate and which allows the merits of the case, including fresh evidence, to be re-examined, and which may lead to the original decision being reversed, and

— the person will be informed of the time frame within which he or she has to request a retrial or appeal, which will be ....days.

4. If you have ticked the box under points 3.1b, 3.2 or 3.3 above, please provide information about how the relevant condition has been met: ....

....

....

][13]

(e) Offences:

This warrant relates to in total: ....offences.

Description of the circumstances in which the offence(s) was (were) committed, including the time, place and degree of participation in the offence(s) by the requested person:...

....

....

Nature and legal classification of the offence(s) and the applicable statutory provision/code:

....

....

....

....

....

I. If applicable, tick one or more of the following offences punishable in the issuing Member State by a custodial sentence or detention order of a maximum of at least 3 years as defined by the laws of the issuing Member State:

participation in a criminal organisation;

terrorism;

trafficking in human beings;

sexual exploitation of children and child pornography;

illicit trafficking in narcotic drugs and psychotropic substances;

illicit trafficking in weapons, munitions and explosives;

corruption;

fraud, including that affecting the financial interests of the European Communities within the meaning of the Convention of 26 July 1995 on the protection of European Communities' financial interests;

laundering of the proceeds of crime;

counterfeiting of currency, including the euro;

computer-related crime;

environmental crime, including illicit trafficking in endangered animal species and in endangered plant species and varieties;

facilitation of unauthorised entry and residence;

murder, grievous bodily injury;

illicit trade in human organs and tissue;

kidnapping, illegal restraint and hostage-taking;

racism and xenophobia;

organised or armed robbery;

illicit trafficking in cultural goods, including antiques and works of art;

[13] Amended by Council Framework Decision 2009/299/JHA of 26 February 2009.

swindling;

racketeering and extortion;

counterfeiting and piracy of products;

forgery of administrative documents and trafficking therein;

forgery of means of payment;

illicit trafficking in hormonal substances and other growth promoters;

illicit trafficking in nuclear or radioactive materials;

trafficking in stolen vehicles;

rape;

arson;

crimes within the jurisdiction of the International Criminal Court;

unlawful seizure of aircraft/ships;

sabotage.

II. Full descriptions of offence(s) not covered by section I above:

....

....

(f) Other circumstances relevant to the case (optional information):

(NB: This could cover remarks on extraterritoriality, interruption of periods of time limitation and other consequences of the offence)

....

....

(g) This warrant pertains also to the seizure and handing over of property which may be required as evidence:

This warrant pertains also to the seizure and handing over of property acquired by the requested person as a result of the offence:

Description of the property (and location) (if known):

(h) The offence(s) on the basis of which this warrant has been issued is(are) punishable by/has(have) led to a custodial life sentence or lifetime detention order:

— the legal system of the issuing Member State allows for a review of the penalty or measure imposed. on request or at least after 20 years. aiming at a non-execution of such penalty or measure,

and/or

— the legal system of the issuing Member State allows for the application of measures of clemency to which the person is entitled under the law or practice of the issuing Member State, aiming at non-execution of such penalty or measure.

(i) The judicial authority which issued the warrant:

Official name:

Name of its representative[14]: ....

....

Post held (title/grade):...

....

File reference: ....

Address:...

....

[14] In the different language versions a reference to the 'holder' of the judicial authority will be included.

Tel: (country code) (area/city code) (...)..
Fax: (country code) (area/city code) (...) ....
E-mail: ....
Contact details of the person to contact to make necessary practical arrangements for the surrender:

....

Where a central authority has been made responsible for the transmission and administrative reception of

European arrest warrants:

Name of the central authority:

....

Contact person, if applicable (title/grade and name): ....

....

Address:...

....

Tel: (country code) (area/city code) (...)..
Fax: (country code) (area/city code) (...) ....
E-mail: ....
Signature of the issuing judicial authority and/or its representative:

....

Name:
Post held (title/grade):...
Date: ....
Official stamp (if available)

APPENDIX E5

Category 1 and Category 2 territories: Territories designated for the purposes of the EA 2003

Extradition Act 2003 (Designation of Part 1 Territories) Order 2003

(S.I. 2003/3333)

Made 18th December 2003

Coming into force 1st January 2004

Whereas a draft of this Order has been approved by each House of Parliament;

Now, therefore, the Secretary of State, in exercise of the powers conferred on him by section 1 of the Extradition Act 2003, hereby makes the following Order:

1.

This Order may be cited as the Extradition Act 2003 (Designation of Part 1 Territories) Order 2003 and shall come into force on 1st January 2004.

2.

(1) The territories set out in paragraph (2) are hereby designated for the purposes of Part 1 of the Extradition Act 2003.

(2) Those territories are—

[Austria,][1]
Belgium,
[Bulgaria,][2]
[Cyprus,][3]
[Czech Republic,][4]
Denmark,
[Estonia,][5]
Finland,
[France,][6]
[Germany,][7]
[Gibraltar,][8]
[Greece,][9]
[Hungary],[10]
Ireland,
[Italy][11]
[Latvia],[12]
[Lithuania,][13]

---

1 Amended by SI 2004/1898.
2 Amended by SI 2006/3451.
3 Amended by SI 2004/1898.
4 Amended by SI 2005/365.
5 Amended by SI 2005/365.
6 Amended by SI 2004/1898.
7 Amended by SI 2005/365.
8 Amended by SI 2007/2238.
9 Amended by SI 2005/365.
10 Amended by SI 2004/1898.
11 Amended by SI 2005/2036.
12 Amended by SI 2004/1898.
13 Amended by SI 2004/1898.

[Luxembourg,][14]
[Malta,][15]
[The Netherlands,][16]
[Poland,][17]
Portugal,
[Romania,][18]
[Slovakia,][19]
[Slovenia,][20]
Spain,
Sweden.

Extradition Act 2003 (Designation of Part 2 Territories) Order 2003 (S.I. 2003/3334)

Made 18th December 2003

Coming into force 1st January 2004

Whereas a draft of this Order has been approved by each House of Parliament;

Now, therefore, the Secretary of State, in exercise of the powers conferred on him by sections 69(1), 71(4), 73(5), 74(11)(b), 84(7) and 86(7) of the Extradition Act 2003, hereby makes the following Order:

1.

(1) This Order may be cited as the Extradition Act 2003 (Designation of Part 2 Territories) Order 2003 and shall come into force on 1st January 2004.
(2) In this Order 'the Act' means the Extradition Act 2003.

2.

(1) The territories set out in paragraph (2) are hereby designated for the purposes of Part 2 of the Act.
(2) Those territories are—
Albania,
[Algeria,][21]
Andorra,
Antigua and Barbuda,
Argentina,
Armenia,
Australia,
[...][22]
Azerbaijan,
The Bahamas,
Bangladesh,
Barbados,
Belize,
Bolivia,
Bosnia and Herzegovina,
Botswana,
Brazil,
Brunei,

[14] Amended by SI 2004/1898.
[15] Amended by SI 2004/1898.
[16] Amended by SI 2004/1898.
[17] Amended by SI 2004/1898.
[18] Amended by SI 2006/3451.
[19] Amended by SI 2005/365.
[20] Amended by SI 2004/1898.
[21] Amended by SI 2007/2238.
[22] Repealed by SI 2004/1898.

[...][23]
Canada,
Chile,
Colombia,
Cook Islands,
Croatia,
Cuba,
[...][24]
[...][25]
Dominica,
Ecuador,
El Salvador,
[...][26]
Fiji,
[...][27]
The Gambia,
Georgia,
[...][28]
Ghana,
[...][29]
Grenada,
Guatemala,
Guyana,
Hong Kong Special Administrative Region,
Haiti,
[...][30]
Iceland,
India,
Iraq,
Israel,
[...][31]
Jamaica,
Kenya,
Kiribati,
[...][32]
Lesotho,
Liberia,
[Libya,][33]
Liechtenstein,
[...][34]
[...][35]
Macedonia, FYR,
Malawi,
Malaysia,

23 Repealed by SI 2006/3451.
24 Repealed by SI 2004/1898.
25 Repealed by SI 2005/365.
26 Repealed by SI 2005/365.
27 Repealed by SI 2004/1898.
28 Repealed by SI 2005/365.
29 Repealed by SI 2005/365.
30 Repealed by SI 2004/1898.
31 Repealed by SI 2005/2036.
32 Repealed by SI 2004/1898.
33 Amended by SI 2010/861.
34 Repealed by SI 2004/1898.
35 Repealed by SI 2004/1898.

Maldives,
[...][36]
Mauritius,
Mexico,
Moldova,
Monaco,
[Montenegro,][37]
Nauru,
[...][38]
New Zealand,
Nicaragua,
Nigeria,
Norway,
Panama,
Papua New Guinea,
Paraguay,
Peru,
[...][39]
[...][40]
Russian Federation,
Saint Christopher and Nevis,
Saint Lucia,
Saint Vincent and the Grenadines,
San Marino,
Serbia [...],[41]
Seychelles,
Sierra Leone,
Singapore,
[...][42]
[...][43]
Solomon Islands,
South Africa,
Sri Lanka,
Swaziland,
Switzerland,
Tanzania,
Thailand,
Tonga,
Trinidad and Tobago,
Turkey,
Tuvalu,
Uganda,
Ukraine,
Uruguay,
[The United Arab Emirates,][44]
The United States of America,
Vanuatu,

36 Repealed by SI 2004/1898.
37 Amended by SI 2006/3451.
38 Repealed by SI 2004/1898.
39 Repealed by SI 2004/1898.
40 Repealed by SI 2006/3451.
41 Repealed by SI 2006/3451.
42 Repealed by SI 2005/365.
43 Repealed by SI 2004/1898.
44 Amended by SI 2008/1589.

Western Samoa,
Zambia,
Zimbabwe.

3.

(1) The territories set out in paragraph (2) are hereby designated for the purposes of section 71(4), 73(5), 84(7) and 86(7) of the Act.

(2) Those territories are—
Albania,
Andorra,
Armenia,
Australia,
[...][45]
Azerbaijan,
[Bosnia and Herzegovina,][46]
[...][47]
Canada,
Croatia,
[...][48]
[...][49]
[...][50]
[...][51]
Georgia,
[...][52]
[...][53]
[...][54]
Iceland,
Israel,
[...][55]
[...][56]
Liechtenstein,
[...][57]
[...][58]
Macedonia, FYR,
[...][59]
Moldova,
[...][60]
New Zealand,
Norway,
[...][61]
[...][62]

45 Repealed by SI 2004/1898.
46 Amended by SI 2006/3451.
47 Repealed by SI 2006/3451.
48 Repealed by SI 2004/1898.
49 Repealed by SI 2005/365.
50 Repealed by SI 2005/365.
51 Repealed by SI 2004/1898.
52 Repealed by SI 2005/365.
53 Repealed by SI 2005/365.
54 Repealed by SI 2004/1898.
55 Repealed by SI 2005/2036.
56 Repealed by SI 2004/1898.
57 Repealed by SI 2004/1898.
58 Repealed by SI 2004/1898.
59 Repealed by SI 2004/1898.
60 Repealed by SI 2004/1898.
61 Repealed by SI 2004/1898.
62 Repealed by SI 2006/3451.

Russian Federation,
Serbia and Montenegro,
[...][63]
[...][64]
South Africa,
Switzerland,
Turkey,
Ukraine,
The United States of America.[64a]

[(3) The Hong Kong Special Administrative Region is hereby designated for the purposes of section 71(4) and 73(5) of the Act.][65]

4.

(1) The territories set out in paragraph (2) are hereby designated for the purposes of section 74(11)(b) with the relevant longer period for each territory following in brackets.

(2) Those territories and relevant periods are—
[Argentina (65 days)][66]
Bolivia (65 days)
[...][67]
[Brazil (65 days)][68]
Chile [(65 days)][69]
[Colombia (65 days)][70]
Cuba (65 days)
[El Salvador (65 days)][71]
[Guatemala (95 days)][72]
Haiti (65 days)
[Hong Kong Special Administrative Region (65 days)][73]
Iraq (65 days)
Liberia (95 days)
[Libya (65 days)][74]
[Mexico (65 days)][75]
Monaco (65 days)
Nicaragua (65 days)
Panama [(95 days)][76]
Paraguay [(95 days)][77]
Peru (95 days)
San Marino (65 days)
Thailand (65 days)
[The United Arab Emirates (65 days)][78]
The United States of America (65 days).

---

63 Repealed by SI 2005/365.
64 Repealed by SI 2004/1898.
64a Revoked by the Police and Justice Act 2006, s 43(1), from a date to be appointed: see s 43(2)-(6) thereof.
65 Amended by SI 2005/365.
66 Amended by SI 2005/365.
67 Amended by SI 2007/2238.
68 Amended by SI 2005/365.
69 Amended by SI 2005/365.
70 Amended by SI 2005/365.
71 Amended by SI 2005/365.
72 Amended by SI 2005/365.
73 Amended by SI 2005/365.
74 Amended by SI 2010/861.
75 Amended by SI 2005/365.
76 Amended by SI 2005/365.
77 Amended by SI 2005/365.
78 Amended by SI 2008/1589.

APPENDIX E6

COUNCIL OF EUROPE   CONSEIL DE L'EUROPE

European Treaty Series – No. 24

EUROPEAN CONVENTION ON EXTRADITION*

Paris, 13.XII.1957

The governments signatory hereto, being members of the Council of Europe,
Considering that the aim of the Council of Europe is to achieve a greater unity between its members;
Considering that this purpose can be attained by the conclusion of agreements and by common action in legal matters;
Considering that the acceptance of uniform rules with regard to extradition is likely to assist this work of unification,
Have agreed as follows:

Article 1

Obligation to extradite

The Contracting Parties undertake to surrender to each other, subject to the provisions and conditions laid down in this Convention, all persons against whom the competent authorities of the requesting Party are proceeding for an offence or who are wanted by the said authorities for the carrying out of a sentence or detention order.

Article 2

Extraditable offences

1. Extradition shall be granted in respect of offences punishable under the laws of the requesting Party and of the requested Party by deprivation of liberty or under a detention order for a maximum period of at least one year or by a more severe penalty. Where a conviction and prison sentence have occurred or a detention order has been made in the territory of the requesting Party, the punishment awarded must have been for a period of at least four months.
2. If the request for extradition includes several separate offences each of which is punishable under the laws of the requesting Party and the requested Party by deprivation of liberty or under a detention order, but of which some do not fulfil the condition with regard to the amount of punishment which may be awarded, the requested Party shall also have the right to grant extradition for the latter offences.
3. Any Contracting Party whose law does not allow extradition for certain of the offences referred to in paragraph 1 of this article may, in so far as it is concerned, exclude such offences from the application of this Convention.
4. Any Contracting Party which wishes to avail itself of the right provided for in paragraph 3 of this article shall, at the time of deposit of its instrument of ratification or accession, transmit to the Secretary General of the Council of Europe either a list of the offences for which extradition is allowed or a list of those

* The European Convention on Extradition (ETS No 024) is reproduced with the kind permission of the Council of Europe.

for which it is excluded and shall at the same time indicate the legal provisions which allow or exclude extradition. The Secretary General of the Council shall forward these lists to the other signatories.

5. If extradition is subsequently excluded in respect of other offences by the law of a Contracting Party, that Party shall notify the Secretary General. The Secretary General shall inform the other signatories. Such notification shall not take effect until three months from the date of its receipt by the Secretary General.
6. Any Party which avails itself of the right provided for in paragraphs 4 or 5 of this article may at any time apply this Convention to offences which have been excluded from it. It shall inform the Secretary General of the Council of such changes, and the Secretary General shall inform the other signatories.
7. Any Party may apply reciprocity in respect of any offences excluded from the application of the Convention under this article.

Article 3

Political offences

1. Extradition shall not be granted if the offence in respect of which it is requested is regarded by the requested Party as a political offence or as an offence connected with a political offence.
2. The same rule shall apply if the requested Party has substantial grounds for believing that a request for extradition for an ordinary criminal offence has been made for the purpose of prosecuting or punishing a person on account of his race, religion, nationality or political opinion, or that that person's position may be prejudiced for any of these reasons.
3. The taking or attempted taking of the life of a Head of State or a member of his family shall not be deemed to be a political offence for the purposes of this Convention.
4. This article shall not affect any obligations which the Contracting Parties may have undertaken or may undertake under any other international convention of a multilateral character.

Article 4

Military offences

Extradition for offences under military law which are not offences under ordinary criminal law is excluded from the application of this Convention.

Article 5

Fiscal offences

Extradition shall be granted, in accordance with the provisions of this Convention, for offences in connection with taxes, duties, customs and exchange only if the Contracting Parties have so decided in respect of any such offence or category of offences.

Article 6

Extradition of nationals

1.
   (a) A Contracting Party shall have the right to refuse extradition of its nationals.
   (b) Each Contracting Party may, by a declaration made at the time of signature or of deposit of its instrument of ratification or accession, define as far as it is concerned the term "nationals" within the meaning of this Convention.
   (c) Nationality shall be determined as at the time of the decision concerning extradition. If, however, the person claimed is first recognised as a national of the requested Party during the period between the time of the decision and the time contemplated for the surrender, the requested Party may avail itself of the provision contained in sub-paragraph a of this article.
2. If the requested Party does not extradite its national, it shall at the request of the requesting Party submit the case to its competent authorities in order that proceedings may be taken if they are considered appropriate. For this purpose, the files, information and exhibits relating to the offence shall be transmitted without charge by the means provided for in Article 12, paragraph 1. The requesting Party shall be informed of the result of its request.

Article 7

Place of commission

1. The requested Party may refuse to extradite a person claimed for an offence which is regarded by its law as having been committed in whole or in part in its territory or in a place treated as its territory.

2. When the offence for which extradition is requested has been committed outside the territory of the requesting Party, extradition may only be refused if the law of the requested Party does not allow prosecution for the same category of offence when committed outside the latter Party's territory or does not allow extradition for the offence concerned.

Article 8

Pending proceedings for the same offences

The requested Party may refuse to extradite the person claimed if the competent authorities of such Party are proceeding against him in respect of the offence or offences for which extradition is requested.

Article 9

Non bis in idem

Extradition shall not be granted if final judgment has been passed by the competent authorities of the requested Party upon the person claimed in respect of the offence or offences for which extradition is requested. Extradition may be refused if the competent authorities of the requested Party have decided either not to institute or to terminate proceedings in respect of the same offence or offences.

Article 10

Lapse of time

Extradition shall not be granted when the person claimed has, according to the law of either the requesting or the requested Party, become immune by reason of lapse of time from prosecution or punishment.

Article 11

Capital punishment

If the offence for which extradition is requested is punishable by death under the law of the requesting Party, and if in respect of such offence the death-penalty is not provided for by the law of the requested Party or is not normally carried out, extradition may be refused unless the requesting Party gives such assurance as the requested Party considers sufficient that the death-penalty will not be carried out.

Article 12

The request and supporting documents

1. The request shall be in writing and shall be communicated through the diplomatic channel. Other means of communication may be arranged by direct agreement between two or more Parties.
2. The request shall be supported by:
   (a) the original or an authenticated copy of the conviction and sentence or detention order immediately enforceable or of the warrant of arrest or other order having the same effect and issued in accordance with the procedure laid down in the law of the requesting Party;
   (b) a statement of the offences for which extradition is requested. The time and place of their commission, their legal descriptions and a reference to the relevant legal provisions shall be set out as accurately as possible; and
   (c) a copy of the relevant enactments or, where this is not possible, a statement of the relevant law and as accurate a description as possible of the person claimed, together with any other information which will help to establish his identity and nationality.

Article 13

Supplementary information

If the information communicated by the requesting Party is found to be insufficient to allow the requested Party to make a decision in pursuance of this Convention, the latter Party shall request the necessary supplementary information and may fix a time-limit for the receipt thereof.

Article 14

Rule of speciality

1. A person who has been extradited shall not be proceeded against, sentenced or detained with a view to the carrying out of a sentence or detention order for any offence committed prior to his surrender other than that for which he was extradited, nor shall he be for any other reason restricted in his personal freedom, except in the following cases:

(a) when the Party which surrendered him consents. A request for consent shall be submitted, accompanied by the documents mentioned in Article 12 and a legal record of any statement made by the extradited person in respect of the offence concerned. Consent shall be given when the offence for which it is requested is itself subject to extradition in accordance with the provisions of this Convention;

(b) when that person, having had an opportunity to leave the territory of the Party to which he has been surrendered, has not done so within 45 days of his final discharge, or has returned to that territory after leaving it.

2. The requesting Party may, however, take any measures necessary to remove the person from its territory, or any measures necessary under its law, including proceedings by default, to prevent any legal effects of lapse of time.
3. When the description of the offence charged is altered in the course of proceedings, the extradited person shall only be proceeded against or sentenced in so far as the offence under its new description is shown by its constituent elements to be an offence which would allow extradition.

Article 15

Re-extradition to a third state

Except as provided for in Article 14, paragraph 1.b, the requesting Party shall not, without the consent of the requested Party, surrender to another Party or to a third State a person surrendered to the requesting Party and sought by the said other Party or third State in respect of offences committed before his surrender. The requested Party may request the production of the documents mentioned in Article 12, paragraph 2.

Article 16

Provisional arrest

1. In case of urgency the competent authorities of the requesting Party may request the provisional arrest of the person sought. The competent authorities of the requested Party shall decide the matter in accordance with its law.
2. The request for provisional arrest shall state that one of the documents mentioned in Article 12, paragraph 2.a, exists and that it is intended to send a request for extradition. It shall also state for what offence extradition will be requested and when and where such offence was committed and shall so far as possible give a description of the person sought.
3. A request for provisional arrest shall be sent to the competent authorities of the requested Party either through the diplomatic channel or direct by post or telegraph or through the International Criminal Police Organisation (Interpol) or by any other means affording evidence in writing or accepted by the requested Party. The requesting authority shall be informed without delay of the result of its request.
4. Provisional arrest may be terminated if, within a period of 18 days after arrest, the requested Party has not received the request for extradition and the documents mentioned in Article 12. It shall not, in any event, exceed 40 days from the date of such arrest. The possibility of provisional release at any time is not excluded, but the requested Party shall take any measures which it considers necessary to prevent the escape of the person sought.
5. Release shall not prejudice re-arrest and extradition if a request for extradition is received subsequently.

Article 17

Conflicting requests

If extradition is requested concurrently by more than one State, either for the same offence or for different offences, the requested Party shall make its decision having regard to all the circumstances and especially the relative seriousness and place of commission of the offences, the respective dates of the requests, the nationality of the person claimed and the possibility of subsequent extradition to another State.

Article 18

Surrender of the person to be extradited

1. The requested Party shall inform the requesting Party by the means mentioned in Article 12, paragraph 1, of its decision with regard to the extradition.
2. Reasons shall be given for any complete or partial rejection.

3. If the request is agreed to, the requesting Party shall be informed of the place and date of surrender and of the length of time for which the person claimed was detained with a view to surrender.
4. Subject to the provisions of paragraph 5 of this article, if the person claimed has not been taken over on the appointed date, he may be released after the expiry of 15 days and shall in any case be released after the expiry of 30 days. The requested Party may refuse to extradite him for the same offence.
5. If circumstances beyond its control prevent a Party from surrendering or taking over the person to be extradited, it shall notify the other Party. The two Parties shall agree a new date for surrender and the provisions of paragraph 4 of this article shall apply.

Article 19

Postponed or conditional surrender

1. The requested Party may, after making its decision on the request for extradition, postpone the surrender of the person claimed in order that he may be proceeded against by that Party or, if he has already been convicted, in order that he may serve his sentence in the territory of that Party for an offence other than that for which extradition is requested.
2. The requested Party may, instead of postponing surrender, temporarily surrender the person claimed to the requesting Party in accordance with conditions to be determined by mutual agreement between the Parties.

Article 20

Handing over of property

1. The requested Party shall, in so far as its law permits and at the request of the requesting Party, seize and hand over property:
   (a) which may be required as evidence, or
   (b) which has been acquired as a result of the offence and which, at the time of the arrest, is found in the possession of the person claimed or is discovered subsequently.
2. The property mentioned in paragraph 1 of this article shall be handed over even if extradition, having been agreed to, cannot be carried out owing to the death or escape of the person claimed.
3. When the said property is liable to seizure or confiscation in the territory of the requested Party, the latter may, in connection with pending criminal proceedings, temporarily retain it or hand it over on condition that it is returned.
4. Any rights which the requested Party or third parties may have acquired in the said property shall be preserved. Where these rights exist, the property shall be returned without charge to the requested Party as soon as possible after the trial.

Article 21

Transit

1. Transit through the territory of one of the Contracting Parties shall be granted on submission of a request by the means mentioned in Article 12, paragraph 1, provided that the offence concerned is not considered by the Party requested to grant transit as an offence of a political or purely military character having regard to Articles 3 and 4 of this Convention.
2. Transit of a national, within the meaning of Article 6, of a country requested to grant transit may be refused.
3. Subject to the provisions of paragraph 4 of this article, it shall be necessary to produce the documents mentioned in Article 12, paragraph 2.
4. If air transport is used, the following provisions shall apply:
   (a) when it is not intended to land, the requesting Party shall notify the Party over whose territory the flight is to be made and shall certify that one of the documents mentioned in Article 12, paragraph 2.a exists. In the case of an unscheduled landing, such notification shall have the effect of a request for provisional arrest as provided for in Article 16, and the requesting Party shall submit a formal request for transit;
   (b) when it is intended to land, the requesting Party shall submit a formal request for transit.
5. A Party may, however, at the time of signature or of the deposit of its instrument of ratification of, or accession to, this Convention, declare that it will only grant transit of a person on some or all of the conditions on which it grants extradition. In that event, reciprocity may be applied.

6. The transit of the extradited person shall not be carried out through any territory where there is reason to believe that his life or his freedom may be threatened by reason of his race, religion, nationality or political opinion.

Article 22

Procedure

Except where this Convention otherwise provides, the procedure with regard to extradition and provisional arrest shall be governed solely by the law of the requested Party.

Article 23

Language to be used

The documents to be produced shall be in the language of the requesting or requested Party. The requested Party may require a translation into one of the official languages of the Council of Europe to be chosen by it.

Article 24

Expenses

1. Expenses incurred in the territory of the requested Party by reason of extradition shall be borne by that Party.
2. Expenses incurred by reason of transit through the territory of a Party requested to grant transit shall be borne by the requesting Party.
3. In the event of extradition from a non-metropolitan territory of the requested Party, the expenses occasioned by travel between that territory and the metropolitan territory of the requesting Party shall be borne by the latter. The same rule shall apply to expenses occasioned by travel between the non-metropolitan territory of the requested Party and its metropolitan territory.

Article 25

Definition of "detention order"

For the purposes of this Convention, the expression "detention order" means any order involving deprivation of liberty which has been made by a criminal court in addition to or instead of a prison sentence.

Article 26

Reservations

1. Any Contracting Party may, when signing this Convention or when depositing its instrument of ratification or accession, make a reservation in respect of any provision or provisions of the Convention.
2. Any Contracting Party which has made a reservation shall withdraw it as soon as circumstances permit. Such withdrawal shall be made by notification to the Secretary General of the Council of Europe.
3. A Contracting Party which has made a reservation in respect of a provision of the Convention may not claim application of the said provision by another Party save in so far as it has itself accepted the provision.

Article 27

Territorial application

1. This Convention shall apply to the metropolitan territories of the Contracting Parties.
2. In respect of France, it shall also apply to Algeria and to the overseas Departments and, inrespect of the United Kingdom of Great Britain and Northern Ireland, to the Channel Islands and to the Isle of Man.
3. The Federal Republic of Germany may extend the application of this Convention to the *Land* of Berlin by notice addressed to the Secretary General of the Council of Europe, who shall notify the other Parties of such declaration.
4. By direct arrangement between two or more Contracting Parties, the application of this Convention may be extended, subject to the conditions laid down in the arrangement, to any territory of such Parties, other than the territories mentioned in paragraphs 1, 2 and 3 of this article, for whose international relations any such Party is responsible.

Article 28

Relations between this Convention and bilateral Agreements

1. This Convention shall, in respect of those countries to which it applies, supersede the provisions of any bilateral treaties, conventions or agreements governing extradition between any two Contracting Parties.
2. The Contracting Parties may conclude between themselves bilateral or multilateral agreements only in order to supplement the provisions of this Convention or to facilitate the application of the principles contained therein.
3. Where, as between two or more Contracting Parties, extradition takes place on the basis of a uniform law, the Parties shall be free to regulate their mutual relations in respect of extradition exclusively in accordance with such a system notwithstanding the provisions of this Convention. The same principle shall apply as between two or more Contracting Parties each of which has in force a law providing for the execution in its territory of warrants of arrest issued in the territory of the other Party or Parties. Contracting Parties which exclude or may in the future exclude the application of this Convention as between themselves in accordance with this paragraph shall notify the Secretary General of the Council of Europe accordingly. The Secretary General shall inform the other Contracting Parties of any notification received in accordance with this paragraph.

Article 29

Signature, ratification and entry into force

1. This Convention shall be open to signature by the members of the Council of Europe. It shall be ratified. The instruments of ratification shall be deposited with the Secretary General of the Council.
2. The Convention shall come into force 90 days after the date of deposit of the third instrument of ratification.
3. As regards any signatory ratifying subsequently the Convention shall come into force 90 days after the date of the deposit of its instrument of ratification.

Article 30

Accession

1. The Committee of Ministers of the Council of Europe may invite any State not a member of the Council to accede to this Convention, provided that the resolution containing such invitation receives the unanimous agreement of the members of the Council who have ratified the Convention.
2. Accession shall be by deposit with the Secretary General of the Council of an instrument of accession, which shall take effect 90 days after the date of its deposit.

Article 31

Denunciation

Any Contracting Party may denounce this Convention in so far as it is concerned by giving notice to the Secretary General of the Council of Europe. Denunciation shall take effect six months after the date when the Secretary General of the Council received such notification.

Article 32

Notifications

The Secretary General of the Council of Europe shall notify the members of the Council and the government of any State which has acceded to this Convention of:

- (a) the deposit of any instrument of ratification or accession;
- (b) the date of entry into force of this Convention;
- (c) any declaration made in accordance with the provisions of Article 6, paragraph 1, and of Article 21, paragraph 5;
- (d) any reservation made in accordance with Article 26, paragraph 1;
- (e) the withdrawal of any reservation in accordance with Article 26, paragraph 2;

(f) any notification of denunciation received in accordance with the provisions of Article 31 and by the date on which such denunciation will take effect.

In witness whereof the undersigned, being duly authorised thereto, have signed this Convention.

Done at Paris, this 13th day of December 1957, in English and French, both texts being equally authentic, in a single copy which shall remain deposited in the archives of the Council of Europe. The Secretary General of the Council of Europe shall transmit certified copies to the signatory governments.

SECOND ADDITIONAL PROTOCOL TO THE EUROPEAN CONVENTION ON EXTRADITION

Strasbourg, 17.III.1978

The member States of the Council of Europe, signatory to this Protocol,
Desirous of facilitating the application of the European Convention on Extradition opened for signature in Paris on 13 December 1957 (hereinafter referred to as "the Convention") in the field of fiscal offences;
Considering it also desirable to supplement the Convention in certain other respects,
Have agreed as follows:

Chapter I

Article 1

Paragraph 2 of Article 2 of the Convention shall be supplemented by the following provision: This right shall also apply to offences which are subject only to pecuniary sanctions.

Chapter II

Article 2

Article 5 of the Convention shall be replaced by the following provisions: "Fiscal offences

1. For offences in connection with taxes, duties, customs and exchange extradition shall take place between the Contracting Parties in accordance with the provisions of the Convention if the offence, under the law of the requested Party, corresponds to an offence of the same nature.
2. Extradition may not be refused on the ground that the law of the requested Party does not impose the same kind of tax or duty or does not contain a tax, duty, custom or exchange regulation of the same kind as the law of the requesting Party".

Chapter III

Article 3

The Convention shall be supplemented by the following provisions: "Judgments *in absentia*

1. When a Contracting Party requests from another Contracting Party the extradition of a person for the purpose of carrying out a sentence or detention order imposed by a decision rendered against him *in absentia,* the requested Party may refuse to extradite for this purpose if, in its opinion, the proceedings leading to the judgment did not satisfy the minimum rights of defence recognised as due to everyone charged with criminal offence. However, extradition shall be granted if the requesting Party gives an assurance considered sufficient to guarantee to the person claimed the right to a retrial which safeguards the rights of defence. This decision will authorise the requesting Party either to enforce the judgment in question if the convicted person does not make an opposition or, if he does, to take proceedings against the person extradited.
2. When the requested Party informs the person whose extradition has been requested of the judgment rendered against him in absentia, the requesting Party shall not regard this communication as a formal notification for the purposes of the criminal procedure in that State".

Chapter IV

Article 4

The Convention shall be supplemented by the following provisions: Amnesty Extradition shall not be granted for an offence in respect of which an amnesty has been declared in the requested State and which that State had competence to prosecute under its own criminal law.

Chapter V

Article 5

Paragraph 1 of Article 12 of the Convention shall be replaced by the following provisions: "The request shall be in writing and shall be addressed by the Ministry of Justice of the requesting Party to the Ministry of Justice of the requested Party; however, use of the diplomatic channel is not excluded. Other means of communication may be arranged by direct agreement between two or more Parties."

Chapter VI

Article 6

1. This Protocol shall be open to signature by the member States of the Council of Europe which have signed the Convention. It shall be subject to ratification, acceptance or approval. Instruments of ratification, acceptance or approval shall be deposited with the Secretary General of the Council of Europe.
2. The Protocol shall enter into force 90 days after the date of the deposit of the third instrument of ratification, acceptance or approval.
3. In respect of a signatory State ratifying, accepting or approving subsequently, the Protocol shall enter into force 90 days after the date of the deposit of its instrument of ratification, acceptance or approval.
4. A member State of the Council of Europe may not ratify, accept or approve this Protocol without having, simultaneously or previously, ratified the Convention.

Article 7

1. Any State which has acceded to the Convention may accede to this Protocol after the Protocol has entered into force.
2. Such accession shall be effected by depositing with the Secretary General of the Council of Europe an instrument of accession which shall take effect 90 days after the date of its deposit.

Article 8

1. Any State may, at the time of signature or when depositing its instrument of ratification, acceptance, approval or accession, specify the territory or territories to which this Protocol shall apply.
2. Any State may, when depositing its instrument of ratification, acceptance, approval or accession or at any later date, by declaration addressed to the Secretary General of the Council of Europe, extend this Protocol to any other territory or territories specified in the declaration and for whose international relations it is responsible or on whose behalf it is authorised to give undertakings.
3. Any declaration made in pursuance of the preceding paragraph may, in respect of any territory mentioned in such declaration, be withdrawn by means of a notification addressed to the Secretary General of the Council of Europe. Such withdrawal shall take effect six months after the date of receipt by the Secretary General of the Council of Europe of the notification.

Article 9

1. Reservations made by a State to a provision of the Convention shall be applicable also to this Protocol, unless that State otherwise declares at the time of signature or when depositing its instrument of ratification, acceptance, approval or accession.
2. Any State may, at the time of signature or when depositing its instrument of ratification, acceptance, approval or accession, declare that it reserves the right:

(a) not to accept Chapter I;
(b) not to accept Chapter II, or to accept it only in respect of certain offences or certain categories of the offences referred to in Article 2;
(c) not to accept Chapter III, or to accept only paragraph 1 of Article 3;
(d) not to accept Chapter IV;
(e) not to accept Chapter V.

3. Any Contracting Party may withdraw a reservation it has made in accordance with the foregoing paragraph by means of declaration addressed to the Secretary General of the Council of Europe which shall become effective as from the date of its receipt.
4. A Contracting Party which has applied to this Protocol a reservation made in respect of a provision of the Convention or which has made a reservation in respect of a provision of this Protocol may not claim the application of that provision by another Contracting Party; it may, however, if its reservation is partial or conditional claim, the application of that provision in so far as it has itself accepted it.
5. No other reservation may be made to the provisions of this Protocol.

Article 10

The European Committee on Crime Problems of the Council of Europe shall be kept informed regarding the application of this Protocol and shall do whatever is needful to facilitate a friendly settlement of any difficulty which may arise out of its execution.

Article 11

1. Any Contracting Party may, in so far as it is concerned, denounce this Protocol by means of a notification addressed to the Secretary General of the Council of Europe.
2. Such denunciation shall take effect six months after the date of receipt by the Secretary General of such notification.
3. Denunciation of the Convention entails automatically denunciation of this Protocol.

Article 12

The Secretary General of the Council of Europe shall notify the member States of the Council and any State which has acceded to the Convention of:

(a) any signature of this Protocol;
(b) any deposit of an instrument of ratification, acceptance, approval or accession;
(c) any date of entry into force of this Protocol in accordance with Articles 6 and 7;
(d) any declaration received in pursuance of the provisions of paragraphs 2 and 3 of Article 8;
(e) any declaration received in pursuance of the provisions of paragraph 1 of Article 9;
(f) any reservation made in pursuance of the provisions of paragraph 2 of Article 9;
(g) the withdrawal of any reservation carried out in pursuance of the provisions of paragraph 3 of Article 9;
(h) any notification received in pursuance of the provisions of Article 11 and the date on which denunciation takes effect.

In witness whereof the undersigned, being duly authorised thereto, have signed this Protocol.

Done at Strasbourg, this 17th day of March 1978, in English and in French, both texts being equally authoritative, in a single copy which shall remain deposited in the archives of the Council of Europe. The Secretary General of the Council of Europe shall transmit certified copies to each of the signatory and acceding States.

THIRD ADDITIONAL PROTOCOL TO THE EUROPEAN CONVENTION ON EXTRADITION

Strasbourg, 10.XI.2010

The member States of the Council of Europe, signatory to this Protocol,
Considering that the aim of the Council of Europe is to achieve greater unity between its members;
Desirous of strengthening their individual and collective ability to respond to crime;
Having regard to the provisions of the European Convention on Extradition (ETS No. 24) opened for signature in Paris on 13 December 1957 (hereinafter referred to as "the Convention"), as well as the two Additional Protocols thereto (ETS Nos. 86 and 98), done at Strasbourg on 15 October 1975 and on 17 March 1978, respectively;

Considering it desirable to supplement the Convention in certain respects in order to simplify and accelerate the extradition procedure when the person sought consents to extradition,
Have agreed as follows:Article 1

Obligation to extradite under the simplified procedure

Contracting Parties undertake to extradite to each other under the simplified procedure as provided for by this Protocol persons sought in accordance with Article 1 of the Convention, subject to the consent of such persons and the agreement of the requested Party.

Article 2

Initiation of the procedure

1. When the person sought is the subject of a request for provisional arrest in accordance with Article 16 of the Convention, the extradition referred to in Article 1 of this Protocol shall not be subject to the submission of a request for extradition and supporting documents in accordance with Article 12 of the Convention. The following information provided by the requesting Party shall be regarded as adequate by the requested Party for the purpose of applying Articles 3 to 5 of this Protocol and for taking its final decision on extradition under the simplified procedure:
   (a) the identity of the person sought, including his or her nationality or nationalities when available;
   (b) the authority requesting the arrest;
   (c) the existence of an arrest warrant or other document having the same legal effect or of an enforceable judgment, as well as a confirmation that the person is sought in accordance with Article 1 of the Convention;
   (d) the nature and legal description of the offence, including the maximum penalty or the penalty imposed in the final judgment, including whether any part of the judgment has already been enforced;
   (e) information concerning lapse of time and its interruption;
   (f) a description of the circumstances in which the offence was committed, including the time, place and degree of involvement of the person sought;
   (g) in so far as possible, the consequences of the offence;
   (h) in cases where extradition is requested for the enforcement of a final judgment, whether the judgment was rendered *in absentia*.
2. Notwithstanding paragraph 1, supplementary information may be requested if the information provided for in the said paragraph is insufficient to allow the requested Party to decide on extradition.
3. In cases where the requested Party has received a request for extradition in accordance with Article 12 of the Convention, this Protocol shall apply *mutatis mutandis*.

Article 3

Obligation to inform the person

Where a person sought for the purpose of extradition is arrested in accordance with Article 16 of the Convention, the competent authority of the requested Party shall inform that person, in accordance with its law and without undue delay, of the request relating to him or her and of the possibility of applying the simplified extradition procedure in accordance with this Protocol.

Article 4

Consent to extradition

1. The consent of the person sought and, if appropriate, his or her express renunciation of entitlement to the rule of speciality shall be given before the competent judicial authority of the requested Party in accordance with the law of that Party.
2. Each Party shall adopt the measures necessary to ensure that consent and, where appropriate, renunciation, as referred to in paragraph 1, are established in such a way as to show that the person concerned has expressed them voluntarily and in full awareness of the legal consequences. To that end, the person sought shall have the right to legal counsel. If necessary, the requested Party shall ensure that the person sought has the assistance of an interpreter.
3. Consent and, where appropriate, renunciation, as referred to in paragraph 1, shall be recorded in accordance with the law of the requested Party.

4. Subject to paragraph 5, consent and, where appropriate, renunciation, as referred to in paragraph 1, shall not be revoked.
5. Any State may, at the time of signature or when depositing its instrument of ratification, acceptance, approval or accession, or at any later time, declare that consent and, where appropriate, renunciation of entitlement to the rule of speciality, may be revoked. The consent may be revoked until the requested Party takes its final decision on extradition under the simplified procedure. In this case, the period between the notification of consent and that of its revocation shall not be taken into consideration in establishing the periods provided for in Article 16, paragraph 4, of the Convention. Renunciation of entitlement to the rule of speciality may be revoked until the surrender of the person concerned. Any revocation of the consent to extradition or the renunciation of entitlement to the rule of speciality shall be recorded in accordance with the law of the requested Party and notified to the requesting Party immediately.

Article 5

Renunciation of entitlement to the rule of speciality

Each State may declare, at the time of signature or when depositing its instrument of ratification, acceptance, approval or accession, or at any later time, that the rules laid down in Article 14 of the Convention do not apply where the person extradited by this State, in accordance with Article 4 of this Protocol:

(a) consents to extradition; or
(b) consents to extradition and expressly renounces his or her entitlement to the rule of speciality.

Article 6

Notifications in case of provisional arrest

1. So that the requesting Party may submit, where applicable, a request for extradition in accordance with Article 12 of the Convention, the requested Party shall notify it, as soon as possible and no later than ten days after the date of provisional arrest, whether or not the person sought has given his or her consent to extradition.
2. In exceptional cases where the requested Party decides not to apply the simplified procedure in spite of the consent of the person sought, it shall notify this to the requesting Party sufficiently in advance so as to allow the latter to submit a request for extradition before the period of forty days established under Article 16 of the Convention expires.

Article 7

Notification of the decision

Where the person sought has given his or her consent to extradition, the requested Party shall notify the requesting Party of its decision with regard to the extradition under the simplified procedure within twenty days of the date on which the person consented.

Article 8

Means of communication

For the purpose of this Protocol, communications may be forwarded through electronic or any other means affording evidence in writing, under conditions which allow the Parties to ascertain their authenticity, as well as through the International Criminal Police Organisation (Interpol). In any case, the Party concerned shall, upon request and at any time, submit the originals or authenticated copies of documents.

Article 9

Surrender of the person to be extradited

Surrender shall take place as soon as possible, and preferably within ten days from the date of notification of the extradition decision.

Article 10

Consent given after expiry of the deadline laid down in Article 6

Where the person sought has given his or her consent after expiry of the deadline of ten days laid down in Article 6, paragraph 1, of this Protocol, the requested Party shall apply the simplified procedure as provided for in this Protocol if it has not yet received a request for extradition within the meaning of Article 12 of the Convention.

Article 11

Transit

In the event of transit under the conditions laid down in Article 21 of the Convention, where a person is to be extradited under a simplified procedure to the requesting Party, the following provisions shall apply:

(a) the request for transit shall contain the information required in Article 2, paragraph 1, of this Protocol;

(b) the Party requested to grant transit may request supplementary information if the information provided for in sub-paragraph a is insufficient for the said Party to decide on transit.

Article 12

Relationship with the Convention and other international instruments

1. The words and expressions used in this Protocol shall be interpreted within the meaning of the Convention. As regards the Parties to this Protocol, the provisions of the Convention shall apply, *mutatis mutandis*, to the extent that they are compatible with the provisions of this Protocol.
2. The provisions of this Protocol are without prejudice to the application of Article 28, paragraphs 2 and 3, of the Convention concerning the relations between the Convention and bilateral or multilateral agreements.

Article 13

Friendly settlement

The European Committee on Crime Problems of the Council of Europe shall be kept informed regarding the application of this Protocol and shall do whatever is necessary to facilitate a friendly settlement of any difficulty which may arise out of its interpretation and application.

Article 14

Signature and entry into force

1. This Protocol shall be open for signature by the member States of the Council of Europe which are a Party to or have signed the Convention. It shall be subject to ratification, acceptance or approval. A signatory may not ratify, accept or approve this Protocol unless it has previously ratified, accepted or approved the Convention, or does so simultaneously. Instruments of ratification, acceptance or approval shall be deposited with the Secretary General of the Council of Europe.
2. This Protocol shall enter into force on the first day of the month following the expiration of a period of three months after the deposit of the third instrument of ratification, acceptance or approval.
3. In respect of any signatory State which subsequently deposits its instrument of ratification, acceptance or approval, this Protocol shall enter into force on the first day of the month following the expiration of a period of three months after the date of deposit.

Article 15

Accession

1. Any non-member State which has acceded to the Convention may accede to this Protocol after it has entered into force.
2. Such accession shall be effected by depositing an instrument of accession with the Secretary General of the Council of Europe.
3. In respect of any acceding State, the Protocol shall enter into force on the first day of the month following the expiration of a period of three months after the date of the deposit of the instrument of accession.

Article 16

Territorial application

1. Any State may, at the time of signature or when depositing its instrument of ratification, acceptance, approval or accession, specify the territory or territories to which this Protocol shall apply.

2. Any State may, at any later time, by declaration addressed to the Secretary General of the Council of Europe, extend the application of this Protocol to any other territory specified in the declaration. In respect of such territory the Protocol shall enter into force on the first day of the month following the expiration of a period of three months after the date of receipt of such declaration by the Secretary General.
3. Any declaration made under the two preceding paragraphs may, in respect of any territory specified in such declaration, be withdrawn by a notification addressed to the Secretary General of the Council of Europe. The withdrawal shall become effective on the first day of the month following the expiration of a period of six months after the date or receipt of such notification by the Secretary General.

Article 17

Declarations and reservations

1. Reservations made by a State to any provision of the Convention or the two Additional Protocols thereto shall also be applicable to this Protocol, unless that State otherwise declares at the time of signature or when depositing its instrument of ratification, acceptance, approval or accession. The same shall apply to any declaration made in respect or by virtue of any provision of the Convention or the two Additional Protocols thereto.
2. Any State may, at the time of signature or when depositing its instrument of ratification, acceptance, approval or accession, declare that it avails itself of the right not to accept wholly or in part Article 2, paragraph 1, of this Protocol. No other reservation may be made.
3. Any State may, at the time of signature or when depositing its instrument of ratification, acceptance, approval or accession, or at any later time, make the declarations provided for in Article 4, paragraph 5, and in Article 5 of this Protocol.
4. Any State may wholly or partially withdraw a reservation or declaration it has made in accordance with this Protocol, by means of a declaration addressed to the Secretary General of the Council of Europe, which shall become effective as from the date of its receipt.
5. Any Party which has made a reservation to Article 2, paragraph 1, of this Protocol, in accordance with paragraph 2 of this article may not claim the application of that paragraph by another Party. It may, however, if its reservation is partial or conditional, claim the application of that paragraph in so far as it has itself accepted it.

Article 18

Denunciation

1. Any Party may, in so far as it is concerned, denounce this Protocol by means of a notification addressed to the Secretary General of the Council of Europe.
2. Such denunciation shall become effective on the first day of the month following the expiration of a period of six months after the date of receipt of the notification by the Secretary General of the Council of Europe.
3. Denunciation of the Convention automatically entails denunciation of this Protocol.

Article 19

Notifications

The Secretary General of the Council of Europe shall notify the member States of the Council of Europe and any State which has acceded to this Protocol of:

(a) any signature;
(b) the deposit of any instrument of ratification, acceptance, approval or accession;
(c) any date of entry into force of this Protocol in accordance with Articles 14 and 15;
(d) any declaration made in accordance with Article 4, paragraph 5, Article 5, Article 16 and Article 17, paragraph 1, and any withdrawal of such a declaration;
(e) any reservation made in accordance with Article 17, paragraph 2, and any withdrawal of such a reservation;
(f) any notification received in pursuance of the provisions of Article 18 and the date on which denunciation takes effect;
(g) any other act, declaration, notification or communication relating to this Protocol.

In witness whereof the undersigned, being duly authorised thereto, have signed this Protocol.

Done at Strasbourg, this 10th day of November 2010, in English and in French, both texts being equally authentic, in a single copy which shall be deposited in the archives of the Council of Europe. The Secretary General of the Council of Europe shall transmit certified copies to each member State of the Council of Europe and to the non-member States which have acceded to the Convention.

FOURTH ADDITIONAL PROTOCOL TO THE EUROPEAN CONVENTION ON EXTRADITION

Vienna, 20.IX.2012 Third Additional Protocol

The member States of the Council of Europe, signatory to this Protocol,
Considering that the aim of the Council of Europe is to achieve greater unity between its members;
Desirous of strengthening their individual and collective ability to respond to crime;
Having regard to the provisions of the European Convention on Extradition (ETS No. 24) opened for signature in Paris on 13 December 1957 (hereinafter referred to as "the Convention"), as well as the three Additional Protocols thereto (ETS Nos. 86 and 98, CETS No. 209), done at Strasbourg on 15 October 1975, on 17 March 1978 and on 10 November 2010, respectively;
Considering it desirable to modernise a number of provisions of the Convention and supplement it in certain respects, taking into account the evolution of international co-operation in criminal matters since the entry into force of the Convention and the Additional Protocols thereto;
Have agreed as follows:

Article 1

Lapse of time

Article 10 of the Convention shall be replaced by the following provisions:

"Lapse of time

1. Extradition shall not be granted when the prosecution or punishment of the person claimed has become statute-barred according to the law of the requesting Party.
2. Extradition shall not be refused on the ground that the prosecution or punishment of the person claimed would be statute-barred according to the law of the requested Party.
3. Any State may, at the time of signature or when depositing its instrument of ratification, acceptance, approval or accession, declare that it reserves the right not to apply paragraph 2:
   (a) when the request for extradition is based on offences for which that State has jurisdiction under its own criminal law; and/or
   (b) if its domestic legislation explicitly prohibits extradition when the prosecution or punishment of the person claimed would be statute-barred according to its law.
4. When determining whether prosecution or punishment of the person sought would be statute-barred according to its law, any Party having made a reservation pursuant to paragraph 3 of this article shall take into consideration, in accordance with its law, any acts or events that have occurred in the requesting Party, in so far as acts or events of the same nature have the effect of interrupting or suspending time-limitation in the requested Party."

Article 2

The request and supporting documents

1. Article 12 of the Convention shall be replaced by the following provisions:

"The request and supporting documents

1. The request shall be in writing. It shall be submitted by the Ministry of Justice or other competent authority of the requesting Party to the Ministry of Justice or other competent authority of the requested Party. A State wishing to designate another competent authority than the Ministry of Justice shall notify the Secretary General of the Council of Europe of its competent authority at the time of signature or when depositing its instrument of ratification, acceptance, approval or accession, as well as of any subsequent changes relating to its competent authority.
2. The request shall be supported by:

(a) a copy of the conviction and sentence or detention order immediately enforceable or of the warrant of arrest or other order having the same effect and issued in accordance with the procedure laid down in the law of the requesting Party;
(b) a statement of the offences for which extradition is requested. The time and place of their commission, their legal descriptions and a reference to the relevant legal provisions, including provisions relating to lapse of time, shall be set out as accurately as possible; and
(c) a copy of the relevant enactments or, where this is not possible, a statement of the relevant law and as accurate a description as possible of the person claimed, together with any other information which will help to establish his or her identity, nationality and location."

3. Article 5 of the Second Additional Protocol to the Convention shall not apply as between Parties to the present Protocol.

Article 3

Rule of speciality

Article 14 of the Convention shall be replaced by the following provisions:

"Rule of speciality

1. A person who has been extradited shall not be arrested, prosecuted, tried, sentenced or detained with a view to the carrying out of a sentence or detention order, nor shall he or she be for any other reason restricted in his or her personal freedom for any offence committed prior to his or her surrender other than that for which he or she was extradited, except in the following cases:
   (a) when the Party which surrendered him or her consents. A request for consent shall be submitted, accompanied by the documents mentioned in Article 12 and a legal record of any statement made by the extradited person in respect of the offence concerned. Consent shall be given when the offence for which it is requested is itself subject to extradition in accordance with the provisions of this Convention. The decision shall be taken as soon as possible and no later than 90 days after receipt of the request for consent. Where it is not possible for the requested Party to comply with the period provided for in this paragraph, it shall inform the requesting Party, providing the reasons for the delay and the estimated time needed for the decision to be taken;
   (b) when that person, having had an opportunity to leave the territory of the Party to which he or she has been surrendered, has not done so within 30 days of his or her final discharge, or has returned to that territory after leaving it.
2. The requesting Party may, however:
   (a) carry out pre-trial investigations, except for measures restricting the personal freedom of the person concerned;
   (b) take any measures necessary under its law, including proceedings by default, to prevent any legal effects of lapse of time;
   (c) take any measures necessary to remove the person from its territory.
3. Any State may, at the time of signature or when depositing its instrument of ratification, acceptance, approval or accession or at any later time, declare that, by derogation from paragraph 1, a requesting Party which has made the same declaration may, when a request for consent is submitted pursuant to paragraph 1.a, restrict the personal freedom of the extradited person, provided that:
   (a) the requesting Party notifies, either at the same time as the request for consent pursuant to paragraph 1.a, or later, the date on which it intends to apply such restriction; and
   (b) the competent authority of the requested Party explicitly acknowledges receipt of this notification.

   The requested Party may express its opposition to that restriction at any time, which shall entail the obligation for the requesting Party to end the restriction immediately, including, where applicable, by releasing the extradited person.
4. When the description of the offence charged is altered in the course of proceedings, the extradited person shall only be proceeded against or sentenced in so far as the offence under its new description is shown by its constituent elements to be an offence which would allow extradition."

Article 4

Re-extradition to a third State

The text of Article 15 of the Convention shall become paragraph 1 of that article and shall be supplemented by the following second paragraph:

"2. The requested Party shall take its decision on the consent referred to in paragraph 1 as soon as possible and no later than 90 days after receipt of the request for consent, and, where applicable, of the documents mentioned in Article 12, paragraph 2. Where it is not possible for the requested Party to comply with the period provided for in this paragraph, it shall inform the requesting Party, providing the reasons for the delay and the estimated time needed for the decision to be taken."

Article 5

Transit

Article 21 of the Convention shall be replaced by the following provisions:

"Transit

1. Transit through the territory of one of the Contracting Parties shall be granted on submission of a request for transit, provided that the offence concerned is not considered by the Party requested to grant transit as an offence of a political or purely military character having regard to Articles 3 and 4 of this Convention.
2. The request for transit shall contain the following information:
   (a) the identity of the person to be extradited, including his or her nationality or nationalities when available;
   (b) the authority requesting the transit;
   (c) the existence of an arrest warrant or other order having the same legal effect or of an enforceable judgment, as well as a confirmation that the person is to be extradited;
   (d) the nature and legal description of the offence, including the maximum penalty or the penalty imposed in the final judgment;
   (e) a description of the circumstances in which the offence was committed, including the time, place and degree of involvement of the person sought.
3. In the event of an unscheduled landing, the requesting Party shall immediately certify that one of the documents mentioned in Article 12, paragraph 2.a exists. This notification shall have the effect of a request for provisional arrest as provided for in Article 16, and the requesting Party shall submit a request for transit to the Party on whose territory this landing has occurred.
4. Transit of a national, within the meaning of Article 6, of a country requested to grant transit may be refused.
5. Any State may, at the time of signature or when depositing its instrument of ratification, acceptance, approval or accession, declare that it reserves the right to grant transit of a person only on some or all of the conditions on which it grants extradition.
6. The transit of the extradited person shall not be carried out through any territory where there is reason to believe that his or her life or freedom may be threatened by reason of his or her race, religion, nationality or political opinion."

Article 6

Channels and means of communication

The Convention shall be supplemented by the following provisions:

"Channels and means of communication

1. For the purpose of the Convention, communications may be forwarded by using electronic or any other means affording evidence in writing, under conditions which allow the Parties to ascertain their authenticity. In any case, the Party concerned shall, upon request and at any time, submit the originals or authenticated copies of documents.
2. The use of the International Criminal Police Organization (Interpol) or of diplomatic channels is not excluded.
3. Any State may, at the time of signature or when depositing its instrument of ratification, acceptance, approval or accession, declare that, for the purpose of Article 12 and Article 14, paragraph 1.a, of the Convention, it reserves the right to require the original or authenticated copy of the request and supporting documents."

Article 7

Relationship with the Convention and other international instruments

1. The words and expressions used in this Protocol shall be interpreted within the meaning of the Convention. As regards the Parties to this Protocol, the provisions of the Convention shall apply, *mutatis mutandis*, to the extent that they are compatible with the provisions of this Protocol.
2. The provisions of this Protocol are without prejudice to the application of Article 28, paragraphs 2 and 3, of the Convention concerning the relations between the Convention and bilateral or multilateral agreements.

Article 8

Friendly settlement

The Convention shall be supplemented by the following provisions:

"Friendly settlement

The European Committee on Crime Problems of the Council of Europe shall be kept informed regarding the application of the Convention and the Additional Protocols thereto and shall do whatever is necessary to facilitate a friendly settlement of any difficulty which may arise out of their interpretation and application."

Article 9

Signature and entry into force

1. This Protocol shall be open for signature by the member States of the Council of Europe which are Parties to or have signed the Convention. It shall be subject to ratification, acceptance or approval. A signatory may not ratify, accept or approve this Protocol unless it has previously ratified, accepted or approved the Convention, or does so simultaneously. Instruments of ratification, acceptance or approval shall be deposited with the Secretary General of the Council of Europe.
2. This Protocol shall enter into force on the first day of the month following the expiration of a period of three months after the deposit of the third instrument of ratification, acceptance or approval.
3. In respect of any signatory State which subsequently deposits its instrument of ratification, acceptance or approval, this Protocol shall enter into force on the first day of the month following the expiration of a period of three months after the date of deposit.

Article 10

Accession

1. Any non-member State which has acceded to the Convention may accede to this Protocol after it has entered into force.
2. Such accession shall be effected by depositing an instrument of accession with the Secretary General of the Council of Europe.
3. In respect of any acceding State, the Protocol shall enter into force on the first day of the month following the expiration of a period of three months after the date of the deposit of the instrument of accession.

Article 11

Temporal scope

This Protocol shall apply to requests received after the entry into force of the Protocol between the Parties concerned.

Article 12

Territorial application

1. Any State may, at the time of signature or when depositing its instrument of ratification, acceptance, approval or accession, specify the territory or territories to which this Protocol shall apply.
2. Any State may, at any later time, by declaration addressed to the Secretary General of the Council of Europe, extend the application of this Protocol to any other territory specified in the declaration. In respect of such territory the Protocol shall enter into force on the first day of the month following the expiration of a period of three months after the date of receipt of such declaration by the Secretary General.

3. Any declaration made under the two preceding paragraphs may, in respect of any territory specified in such declaration, be withdrawn by a notification addressed to the Secretary General of the Council of Europe. The withdrawal shall become effective on the first day of the month following the expiration of a period of six months after the date of receipt of such notification by the Secretary General.

Article 13

Declarations and reservations

1. Reservations made by a State to the provisions of the Convention and the Additional Protocols thereto which are not amended by this Protocol shall also be applicable to this Protocol, unless that State otherwise declares at the time of signature or when depositing its instrument of ratification, acceptance, approval or accession. The same shall apply to any declaration made in respect or by virtue of any provision of the Convention and the Additional Protocols thereto.
2. Reservations and declarations made by a State to any provision of the Convention which is amended by this Protocol shall not be applicable as between the Parties to this Protocol.
3. No reservation may be made in respect of the provisions of this Protocol, with the exception of the reservations provided for in Article 10, paragraph 3, and Article 21, paragraph 5, of the Convention as amended by this Protocol, and in Article 6, paragraph 3, of this Protocol. Reciprocity may be applied to any reservation made.
4. Any State may wholly or partially withdraw a reservation or declaration it has made in accordance with this Protocol, by means of a notification addressed to the Secretary General of the Council of Europe, which shall become effective as from the date of its receipt.

Article 14

Denunciation

1. Any Party may, in so far as it is concerned, denounce this Protocol by means of a notification addressed to the Secretary General of the Council of Europe.
2. Such denunciation shall become effective on the first day of the month following the expiration of a period of six months after the date of receipt of the notification by the Secretary General of the Council of Europe.
3. Denunciation of the Convention automatically entails denunciation of this Protocol.

Article 15

Notifications

The Secretary General of the Council of Europe shall notify the member States of the Council of Europe and any State which has acceded to this Protocol of:

(a) any signature;
(b) the deposit of any instrument of ratification, acceptance, approval or accession;
(c) any date of entry into force of this Protocol in accordance with Articles 9 and 10;
(d) any reservation made in accordance with Article 10, paragraph 3, and Article 21, paragraph 5, of the Convention as amended by this Protocol, as well as Article 6, paragraph 3, of this Protocol, and any withdrawal of such a reservation;
(e) any declaration made in accordance with Article 12, paragraph 1, and Article 14, paragraph 3, of the Convention as amended by this Protocol, as well as Article 12 of this Protocol, and any withdrawal of such a declaration;
(f) any notification received in pursuance of the provisions of Article 14 and the date on which denunciation takes effect;
(g) any other act, declaration, notification or communication relating to this Protocol.

In witness whereof the undersigned, being duly authorised thereto, have signed this Protocol.

Done at Vienna, this 20th day of September 2012, in English and in French, both texts being equally authentic, in a single copy which shall be deposited in the archives of the Council of Europe. The Secretary General of the Council of Europe shall transmit certified copies to each member State of the Council of Europe and to the non-member States which have acceded to the Convention.

APPENDIX M1

Crime (International Co-operation) Act 2003

(c. 32)

An Act to make provision for furthering co-operation with other countries in respect of criminal proceedings and investigations; to extend jurisdiction to deal with terrorist acts or threats outside the United Kingdom; to amend section 5 of the Forgery and Counterfeiting Act 1981 and make corresponding provision in relation to Scotland; and for connected purposes.

[30th October 2003]

BE IT ENACTED by the Queen's most Excellent Majesty, by and with the advice and consent of the Lords Spiritual and Temporal, and Commons, in this present Parliament assembled, and by the authority of the same, as follows:—

CONTENTS

17. Warrants in England and Wales or Northern Ireland
18. Warrants in Scotland
19. Seized evidence

OVERSEAS FREEZING ORDERS

20. Overseas freezing orders
21. Considering the order
22. Giving effect to the order
23. Postponed effect
24. Evidence seized under the order
25. Release of evidence held under the order

GENERAL

26. POWERS UNDER WARRANTS
27. Exercise of powers by others
28. Interpretation of Chapter 2

Chapter 3
Hearing Evidence Through Television Links or by Telephone

29. Hearing witnesses abroad through television links
30. Hearing witnesses in the UK through television links
31. Hearing witnesses in the UK by telephone

Chapter 4
Information about Banking Transactions

REQUESTS FOR INFORMATION ABOUT BANKING TRANSACTIONS IN ENGLAND AND WALES AND NORTHERN IRELAND FOR USE ABROAD

32. Customer information
33. Making, varying or discharging customer information orders
34. Offences
35. Account information
36. Making, varying or discharging account monitoring orders

REQUESTS FOR INFORMATION ABOUT BANKING TRANSACTIONS IN SCOTLAND FOR USE ABROAD

37. Customer information
38. Making, varying or discharging customer information orders
39. Offences
40. Account information
41. Making, varying or discharging account monitoring orders

DISCLOSURE OF INFORMATION

42. Offence of disclosure

REQUESTS FOR INFORMATION ABOUT BANKING TRANSACTIONS FOR USE IN UK

43. Information about a person's bank account
44. Monitoring banking transactions

Part 1
Mutual Assistance in Criminal Matters

Chapter 1
Mutual Service of Process etc.

SERVICE OF OVERSEAS PROCESS IN THE UK

1. Service of overseas process

(1) The power conferred by subsection (3) is exercisable where the Secretary of State receives any process or other document to which this section applies from the government of, or other authority in, a country outside the United Kingdom, together with a request for the process or document to be served on a person in the United Kingdom.

(2) This section applies—

- (a) to any process issued or made in that country for the purposes of criminal proceedings,
- (b) to any document issued or made by an administrative authority in that country in administrative proceedings,
- (c) to any process issued or made for the purposes of any proceedings on an appeal before a court in that country against a decision in administrative proceedings,
- (d) to any document issued or made by an authority in that country for the purposes of clemency proceedings.

(3) The Secretary of State may cause the process or document to be served by post or, if the request is for personal service, direct the chief officer of police for the area in which that person appears to be to cause it to be personally served on him.
(4) In relation to any process or document to be served in Scotland, references in this section to the Secretary of State are to be read as references to the Lord Advocate.

2. Service of overseas process: supplementary

(1) Subsections (2) and (3) apply to any process served in a part of the United Kingdom by virtue of section 1 requiring a person to appear as a party or attend as a witness.
(2) No obligation under the law of that part to comply with the process is imposed by virtue of its service.
(3) The process must be accompanied by a notice—
 (a) stating the effect of subsection (2),
 (b) indicating that the person on whom it is served may wish to seek advice as to the possible consequences of his failing to comply with the process under the law of the country where it was issued or made, and
 (c) indicating that under that law he may not be accorded the same rights and privileges as a party or as a witness as would be accorded to him in proceedings in the part of the United Kingdom in which the process is served.
(4) Where a chief officer of police causes any process or document to be served under section 1, he must at once—
 (a) tell the Secretary of State (or, as the case may be, the Lord Advocate) when and how it was served, and
 (b) (if possible) provide him with a receipt signed by the person on whom it was served.
(5) Where the chief officer of police is unable to cause any process or document to be served as directed, he must at once inform the Secretary of State (or, as the case may be, the Lord Advocate) of that fact and of the reason.

Service of UK process abroad

3. General requirements for service of process

(1) This section applies to any process issued or made for the purposes of criminal proceedings by a court in England and Wales or Northern Ireland.
(2) The process may be issued or made in spite of the fact that the person on whom it is to be served is outside the United Kingdom.
(3) Where the process is to be served outside the United Kingdom and the person at whose request it is issued or made believes that the person on whom it is to be served does not understand English, he must—
 (a) inform the court of that fact, and
 (b) provide the court with a copy of the process, or of so much of it as is material, translated into an appropriate language.
(4) Process served outside the United Kingdom requiring a person to appear as a party or attend as a witness—
 (a) must not include notice of a penalty,
 (b) must be accompanied by a notice giving any information required to be given by rules of court.
(5) If process requiring a person to appear as a party or attend as a witness is served outside the United Kingdom, no obligation to comply with the process under the law of the part of the United Kingdom in which the process is issued or made is imposed by virtue of the service.
(6) Accordingly, failure to comply with the process does not constitute contempt of court and is not a ground for issuing a warrant to secure the attendance of the person in question.
(7) But the process may subsequently be served on the person in question in the United Kingdom (with the usual consequences for non-compliance).

4. Service of process otherwise than by post

(1) Process to which section 3 applies may, instead of being served by post, be served on a person outside the United Kingdom in accordance with arrangements made by the Secretary of State.
(2) But where the person is in a participating country, the process may be served in accordance with those arrangements only if one of the following conditions is met.
(3) The conditions are—
  (a) that the correct address of the person is unknown,
  (b) that it has not been possible to serve the process by post,
  (c) that there are good reasons for thinking that service by post will not be effective or is inappropriate.

5. General requirements for effecting Scottish citation etc.

(1) This section applies to any citation for the purposes of criminal proceedings in Scotland and to any document issued there for such purposes by the prosecutor or by the court.
(2) The citation may proceed or document be issued in spite of the fact that the person against whom it is to be effected or on whom it is to be served is outside the United Kingdom.
(3) Where—
  (a) citation or issue is by the prosecutor,
  (b) the citation is to be effected or the document issued is to be served outside the United Kingdom, and
  (c) the prosecutor believes that the person against whom it is to be effected or on whom it is to be served does not understand English,the citation or document must be accompanied by a translation of it (or, in the case of a document, by a translation of so much of it as is material) in an appropriate language.
(4) Where—
  (a) citation or issue is by the court,
  (b) the citation is to be effected or the document issued is to be served outside the United Kingdom, and
  (c) the person at whose request that is to happen believes that the person against whom it is to be effected or on whom it is to be served does not understand English,he must inform the court of that fact, and provide the court with a copy of the citation or document (or, in the case of a document, so much of it as is material) translated into an appropriate language.
(5) A citation effected outside the United Kingdom—
  (a) must not include notice of a penalty,
  (b) must be accompanied by a notice giving any information required to be given by rules of court.
(6) If a citation is effected outside the United Kingdom, no obligation under the law of Scotland to comply with the citation is imposed by virtue of its being so effected.
(7) Accordingly, failure to comply with the citation does not constitute contempt of court and is not a ground for issuing a warrant to secure the attendance of the person in question or for imposing any penalty.
(8) But the citation may subsequently be effected against the person in question in the United Kingdom (with the usual consequences for non-compliance).

6. Effecting Scottish citation etc. otherwise than by post

(1) A citation or document to which section 5 applies may, instead of being effected or served by post, be effected against or served on a person outside the United Kingdom in accordance with arrangements made by the Lord Advocate.
(2) But where the person is in a participating country, the citation may be effected or document served in accordance with those arrangements only if one of the following conditions is met.
(3) The conditions are—
  (a) that the correct address of the person is unknown,
  (b) that it has not been possible to effect the citation or serve the document by post,
  (c) that there are good reasons for thinking that citation or (as the case may be) service by post will not be effective or is inappropriate.

Chapter 2
Mutual Provision of Evidence

Assistance in obtaining evidence abroad

7. Requests for assistance in obtaining evidence abroad

(1) If it appears to a judicial authority in the United Kingdom on an application made by a person mentioned in subsection (3)—
 (a) that an offence has been committed or that there are reasonable grounds for suspecting that an offence has been committed, and
 (b) that proceedings in respect of the offence have been instituted or that the offence is being investigated,

the judicial authority may request assistance under this section.

(2) The assistance that may be requested under this section is assistance in obtaining outside the United Kingdom any evidence specified in the request for use in the proceedings or investigation.

(3) The application may be made—
 (a) in relation to England and Wales and Northern Ireland, by a prosecuting authority,
 (b) in relation to Scotland, by the Lord Advocate or a procurator fiscal,
 (c) where proceedings have been instituted, by the person charged in those proceedings.

(4) The judicial authorities are—
 (a) in relation to England and Wales, any judge or justice of the peace,
 (b) in relation to Scotland, any judge of the High Court or sheriff,
 (c) in relation to Northern Ireland, any judge or resident magistrate.

(5) In relation to England and Wales or Northern Ireland, a designated prosecuting authority may itself request assistance under this section if—
 (a) it appears to the authority that an offence has been committed or that there are reasonable grounds for suspecting that an offence has been committed, and
 (b) the authority has instituted proceedings in respect of the offence in question or it is being investigated.

'Designated' means designated by an order made by the Secretary of State.

(6) In relation to Scotland, the Lord Advocate or a procurator fiscal may himself request assistance under this section if it appears to him—
 (a) that an offence has been committed or that there are reasonable grounds for suspecting that an offence has been committed, and
 (b) that proceedings in respect of the offence have been instituted or that the offence is being investigated.

(7) If a request for assistance under this section is made in reliance on Article 2 of the 2001 Protocol (requests for information on banking transactions) in connection with the investigation of an offence, the request must state the grounds on which the person making the request considers the evidence specified in it to be relevant for the purposes of the investigation.

8. Sending requests for assistance

(1) A request for assistance under section 7 may be sent—
 (a) to a court exercising jurisdiction in the place where the evidence is situated, or
 (b) to any authority recognised by the government of the country in question as the appropriate authority for receiving requests of that kind.

(2) Alternatively, if it is a request by a judicial authority or a designated prosecuting authority it may be sent to the Secretary of State (in Scotland, the Lord Advocate) for forwarding to a court or authority mentioned in subsection (1).

(3) In cases of urgency, a request for assistance may be sent to—
 (a) the International Criminal Police Organisation, or
 (b) any body or person competent to receive it under any provisions adopted under the Treaty on European Union, for forwarding to any court or authority mentioned in subsection (1).

9. Use of evidence obtained

(1) This section applies to evidence obtained pursuant to a request for assistance under section 7.

(2) The evidence may not without the consent of the appropriate overseas authority be used for any purpose other than that specified in the request.
(3) When the evidence is no longer required for that purpose (or for any other purpose for which such consent has been obtained), it must be returned to the appropriate overseas authority, unless that authority indicates that it need not be returned.
(4) In exercising the discretion conferred by [. . .][1] [. . .][2] (exclusion of evidence otherwise admissible) in relation to a statement contained in the evidence, the court must have regard—
 (a) to whether it was possible to challenge the statement by questioning the person who made it, and
 (b) if proceedings have been instituted, to whether the local law allowed the parties to the proceedings to be legally represented when the evidence was being obtained.
(5) In Scotland, the evidence may be received in evidence without being sworn to by witnesses, so far as that may be done without unfairness to either party.
(6) In this section, the appropriate overseas authority means the authority recognised by the government of the country in question as the appropriate authority for receiving requests of the kind in question.

10. Domestic freezing orders

(1) If it appears to a judicial authority in the United Kingdom, on an application made by a person mentioned in subsection (4)—
 (a) that proceedings in respect of a listed offence have been instituted or such an offence is being investigated,
 (b) that there are reasonable grounds to believe that there is evidence in a participating country which satisfies the requirements of subsection (3), and
 (c) that a request has been made, or will be made, under section 7 for the evidence to be sent to the authority making the request,

 the judicial authority may make a domestic freezing order in respect of the evidence.
(2) A domestic freezing order is an order for protecting evidence which is in the participating country pending its transfer to the United Kingdom.
(3) The requirements are that the evidence—
 (a) is on premises specified in the application in the participating country,
 (b) is likely to be of substantial value (whether by itself or together with other evidence) to the proceedings or investigation,
 (c) is likely to be admissible in evidence at a trial for the offence, and
 (d) does not consist of or include items subject to legal privilege.
(4) The application may be made—
 (a) in relation to England and Wales and Northern Ireland, by a constable,
 (b) in relation to Scotland, by the Lord Advocate or a procurator fiscal.
(5) The judicial authorities are—
 (a) in relation to England and Wales, any judge or justice of the peace,
 (b) in relation to Scotland, any judge of the High Court or sheriff,
 (c) in relation to Northern Ireland, any judge or resident magistrate.
(6) This section does not prejudice the generality of the power to make a request for assistance under section 7.

11. Sending freezing orders

(1) A domestic freezing order made in England and Wales or Northern Ireland is to be sent to the Secretary of State for forwarding to—
 (a) a court exercising jurisdiction in the place where the evidence is situated, or
 (b) any authority recognised by the government of the country in question as the appropriate authority for receiving orders of that kind.

[1] Repealed by the Criminal Justice Act 2003.
[2] Repealed by SI 2004/1501.

(2) A domestic freezing order made in Scotland is to be sent to the Lord Advocate for forwarding to such a court or authority.
(3) The judicial authority is to send the order to the Secretary of State or the Lord Advocate before the end of the period of 14 days beginning with its being made.
(4) The order must be accompanied by a certificate giving the specified information and, unless the certificate indicates when the judicial authority expects such a request to be made, by a request under section 7 for the evidence to be sent to the authority making the request.
(5) The certificate must include a translation of it into an appropriate language of the participating country (if that language is not English).
(6) The certificate must be signed by or on behalf of the judicial authority who made the order and must include a statement as to the accuracy of the information given in it.
The signature may be an electronic signature.

12. Variation or revocation of freezing orders

(1) The judicial authority that made a domestic freezing order may vary or revoke it on an application by a person mentioned below.
(2) The persons are—
  (a) the person who applied for the order,
  (b) in relation to England and Wales and Northern Ireland, a prosecuting authority,
  (c) in relation to Scotland, the Lord Advocate,
  (d) any other person affected by the order.

Assisting overseas authorities to obtain evidence in the UK

13. Requests for assistance from overseas authorities

(1) Where a request for assistance in obtaining evidence in a part of the United Kingdom is received by the territorial authority for that part, the authority may—
  (a) if the conditions in section 14 are met, arrange for the evidence to be obtained under section 15, or
  (b) direct that a search warrant be applied for under or by virtue of section 16 or 17 or, in relation to evidence in Scotland, 18.
(2) The request for assistance may be made only by—
  (a) a court exercising criminal jurisdiction, or a prosecuting authority, in a country outside the United Kingdom,
  (b) any other authority in such a country which appears to the territorial authority to have the function of making such requests for assistance,
  (c) any international authority mentioned in subsection (3).
(3) The international authorities are—
  (a) the International Criminal Police Organisation,
  (b) any other body or person competent to make a request of the kind to which this section applies under any provisions adopted under the Treaty on European Union.

14. Powers to arrange for evidence to be obtained

(1) The territorial authority may arrange for evidence to be obtained under section 15 if the request for assistance in obtaining the evidence is made in connection with—
  (a) criminal proceedings or a criminal investigation, being carried on outside the United Kingdom,
  (b) administrative proceedings, or an investigation into an act punishable in such proceedings, being carried on there,
  (c) clemency proceedings, or proceedings on an appeal before a court against a decision in administrative proceedings, being carried on, or intended to be carried on, there.
(2) In a case within subsection (1)(a) or (b), the authority may arrange for the evidence to be so obtained only if the authority is satisfied—
  (a) that an offence under the law of the country in question has been committed or that there are reasonable grounds for suspecting that such an offence has been committed, and

(b) that proceedings in respect of the offence have been instituted in that country or that an investigation into the offence is being carried on there.

An offence includes an act punishable in administrative proceedings.

(3) The territorial authority is to regard as conclusive a certificate as to the matters mentioned in subsection (2)(a) and (b) issued by any authority in the country in question which appears to him to be the appropriate authority to do so.

(4) If it appears to the territorial authority that the request for assistance relates to a fiscal offence in respect of which proceedings have not yet been instituted, the authority may not arrange for the evidence to be so obtained unless—

(a) the request is from a country which is a member of the Commonwealth or is made pursuant to a treaty to which the United Kingdom is a party, or

(b) the authority is satisfied that if the conduct constituting the offence were to occur in a part of the United Kingdom, it would constitute an offence in that part.

15. Nominating a court etc. to receive evidence

(1) Where the evidence is in England and Wales or Northern Ireland, the Secretary of State may by a notice nominate a court to receive any evidence to which the request relates which appears to the court to be appropriate for the purpose of giving effect to the request.

(2) But if it appears to the Secretary of State that the request relates to an offence involving serious or complex fraud, he may refer the request (or any part of it) to the Director of the Serious Fraud Office for the Director to obtain any evidence to which the request or part relates which appears to him to be appropriate for the purpose of giving effect to the request or part.

(3) Where the evidence is in Scotland, the Lord Advocate may by a notice nominate a court to receive any evidence to which the request relates which appears to the court to be appropriate for the purpose of giving effect to the request.

(4) But if it appears to the Lord Advocate that the request relates to an offence involving serious or complex fraud, he may give a direction under section 27 of the Criminal Law (Consolidation) (Scotland) Act 1995 (c. 39) (directions applying investigatory provisions).

(5) Schedule 1 is to have effect in relation to proceedings before a court nominated under this section.

16. Extension of statutory search powers in England and Wales and Northern Ireland

(1) Part 2 of the Police and Criminal Evidence Act 1984 (c. 60) (powers of entry, search and seizure) is to have effect as if references to [indictable offences][3] in section 8 of, and Schedule 1 to, that Act included any conduct which—

(a) constitutes an offence under the law of a country outside the United Kingdom, and

(b) would, if it occurred in England and Wales, constitute [an indictable offence].[4]

(2) But an application for a warrant or order by virtue of subsection (1) may be made only—

(a) in pursuance of a direction given under section 13, or

(b) if it is an application for a warrant or order under section 8 of, or Schedule 1 to, that Act by a constable for the purposes of an investigation by an international joint investigation team of which he is a member.

(3) Part 3 of the Police and Criminal Evidence (Northern Ireland) Order 1989 (S.I. 1989/1341 (N.I.12)) (powers of entry, search and seizure) is to have effect as if references to [indictable offences][5] in Article 10 of, and Schedule 1 to, that Order included any conduct which—

(a) constitutes an offence under the law of a country outside the United Kingdom, and

(b) would, if it occurred in Northern Ireland, constitute [an indictable offence].[6]

(4) But an application for a warrant or order by virtue of subsection (3) may be made only—

(a) in pursuance of a direction given under section 13, or

---

[3] Amended by the Serious Organized Crime and Police Act 2005.

[4] Amended by the Serious Organized Crime and Police Act 2005.

[5] Amended by SI 2007/288.

[6] Amended by SI 2007/288.

(b) if it is an application for a warrant or order under Article 10 of, or Schedule 1 to, that Order, by a constable for the purposes of an investigation by an international joint investigation team of which he is a member.

(5) In this section, 'international joint investigation team' has the meaning given by section 88(7) of the Police Act 1996 (c. 16).

17. Warrants in England and Wales or Northern Ireland

(1) A justice of the peace may issue a warrant under this section if he is satisfied, on an application made by a constable, that the following conditions are met.

(2) But an application for a warrant under subsection (1) may be made only in pursuance of a direction given under section 13.

(3) The conditions are that—

(a) criminal proceedings have been instituted against a person in a country outside the United Kingdom or a person has been arrested in the course of a criminal investigation carried on there,

[(b) the conduct constituting the offence which is the subject of the proceedings or investigation would (if it occurred in England and Wales [or Northern Ireland][7]) constitute an indictable offence . . .,[8] and][9]

(c) there are reasonable grounds for suspecting that there is on premises in England and Wales or (as the case may be) Northern Ireland occupied or controlled by that person evidence relating to the offence. . . .[10]

(4) A warrant under this section may authorise a constable—

(a) to enter the premises in question and search the premises to the extent reasonably required for the purpose of discovering any evidence relating to the offence,

(b) to seize and retain any evidence for which he is authorised to search.

18. Warrants in Scotland

(1) If, on an application made by the procurator fiscal, it appears to the sheriff—

(a) that there are reasonable grounds for suspecting that an offence under the law of a country outside the United Kingdom has been committed, and

(b) that the conduct constituting the offence would, if it occurred in Scotland, constitute an offence punishable by imprisonment,

the sheriff has the like power to grant warrant authorising entry, search and seizure by any constable or customs officer as he has under section 134 of the Criminal Procedure (Scotland) Act 1995 (c. 46) in respect of any offence punishable at common law in Scotland.

(2) But an application for a warrant by virtue of subsection (1) may be made only—

(a) in pursuance of a direction given under section 13, or

(b) if it is an application made at the request of an international joint investigation team for the purposes of their investigation.

'International joint investigation team' has the meaning given by section 39(6) of the Police (Scotland) Act 1967 (c. 77).

19. Seized evidence

(1) Any evidence seized by a constable under or by virtue of section 16, 17 or 18 is to be sent to the court or authority which made the request for assistance or to the territorial authority for forwarding to that court or authority.

(2) So far as may be necessary in order to comply with the request for assistance—

(a) where the evidence consists of a document, the original or a copy is to be sent, and

(b) where the evidence consists of any other article, the article itself or a description, photograph or other representation of it is to be sent.

---

[7] Amended by SI 2007/288.

[8] Amended by SI 2007/288.

[9] Amended by the Serious Organized Crime and Police Act 2005.

[10] Amended by SI 2007/288.

(3) This section does not apply to evidence seized under or by virtue of section 16(2)(b) or (4)(b) or 18(2)(b).

Overseas freezing orders

20. Overseas freezing orders

(1) Section 21 applies where an overseas freezing order made by a court or authority in a participating country is received from the court or authority which made or confirmed the order by the territorial authority for the part of the United Kingdom in which the evidence to which the order relates is situated.

(2) An overseas freezing order is an order—

(a) for protecting, pending its transfer to the participating country, evidence which is in the United Kingdom and may be used in any proceedings or investigation in the participating country, and

(b) in respect of which the following requirements of this section are met.

(3) The order must have been made by—

(a) a court exercising criminal jurisdiction in the country,

(b) a prosecuting authority in the country,

(c) any other authority in the country which appears to the territorial authority to have the function of making such orders.

(4) The order must relate to—

(a) criminal proceedings instituted in the participating country in respect of a listed offence, or

(b) a criminal investigation being carried on there into such an offence.

(5) The order must be accompanied by a certificate which gives the specified information; but a certificate may be treated as giving any specified information which is not given in it if the territorial authority has the information in question.

(6) The certificate must—

(a) be signed by or on behalf of the court or authority which made or confirmed the order,

(b) include a statement as to the accuracy of the information given in it,

(c) if it is not in English, include a translation of it into English (or, if appropriate, Welsh).The signature may be an electronic signature.

(7) The order must be accompanied by a request for the evidence to be sent to a court or authority mentioned in section 13(2), unless the certificate indicates when such a request is expected to be made.

(8) References below in this Chapter to an overseas freezing order include its accompanying certificate.

21. Considering the order

(1) In relation to England and Wales and Northern Ireland, where this section applies the Secretary of State must—

(a) by a notice nominate a court in England and Wales or (as the case may be) Northern Ireland to give effect to the overseas freezing order,

(b) send a copy of the overseas freezing order to the nominated court and to the chief officer of police for the area in which the evidence is situated,

(c) tell the chief officer which court has been nominated.

(2) In relation to Scotland, where this section applies the Lord Advocate must—

(a) by a notice nominate a sheriff to give effect to the overseas freezing order,

(b) send a copy of the overseas freezing order to the sheriff and to the procurator fiscal.

In relation to Scotland, references below in this section and in sections 22 to 25 to the nominated court are to be read as references to the nominated sheriff.

(3) The nominated court is to consider the overseas freezing order on its own initiative within a period prescribed by rules of court.

(4) Before giving effect to the overseas freezing order, the nominated court must give the chief officer of police or (as the case may be) the procurator fiscal an opportunity to be heard.

(5) The court may decide not to give effect to the overseas freezing order only if, in its opinion, one of the following conditions is met.

(6) The first condition is that, if the person whose conduct is in question were charged in the participating country with the offence to which the overseas freezing order relates or in the United Kingdom with a corresponding offence, he would be entitled to be discharged under any rule of law relating to previous acquittal or conviction.
(7) The second condition is that giving effect to the overseas freezing order would be incompatible with any of the Convention rights (within the meaning of the Human Rights Act 1998 (c. 42)).

22. Giving effect to the order

(1) The nominated court is to give effect to the overseas freezing order by issuing a warrant authorising a constable—
  (a) to enter the premises to which the overseas freezing order relates and search the premises to the extent reasonably required for the purpose of discovering any evidence to which the order relates, and
  (b) to seize and retain any evidence for which he is authorised to search.
(2) But, in relation to England and Wales and Northern Ireland, so far as the overseas freezing order relates to excluded material or special procedure material the court is to give effect to the order by making a production order.
(3) A production order is an order for the person who appears to the court to be in possession of the material to produce it to a constable before the end of the period of seven days beginning with the date of the production order or such longer period as the production order may specify.
(4) The constable may take away any material produced to him under a production order; and the material is to be treated for the purposes of section 21 of the Police and Criminal Evidence Act 1984 (c. 60) or (as the case may be) Article 23 of the Police and Criminal Evidence (Northern Ireland) Order 1989 (S.I. 1989/1341 (N.I. 12)) (access and copying) as if it had been seized by the constable.
(5) If a person fails to comply with a production order, the court may (whether or not it deals with the matter as a contempt of court) issue a warrant under subsection (1) in respect of the material to which the production order relates.
(6) Section 409 of the Proceeds of Crime Act 2002 (c. 29) (jurisdiction of sheriff) has effect for the purposes of subsection (1) as if that subsection were included in Chapter 3 of Part 8 of that Act.

23. Postponed effect

The nominated court may postpone giving effect to an overseas freezing order in respect of any evidence—
  (a) in order to avoid prejudicing a criminal investigation which is taking place in the United Kingdom, or
  (b) if, under an order made by a court in criminal proceedings in the United Kingdom, the evidence may not be removed from the United Kingdom.

24. Evidence seized under the order

(1) Any evidence seized by or produced to the constable under section 22 is to be retained by him until he is given a notice under subsection (2) or authorised to release it under section 25.
(2) If—
  (a) the overseas freezing order was accompanied by a request for the evidence to be sent to a court or authority mentioned in section 13(2), or
  (b) the territorial authority subsequently receives such a request,the territorial authority may by notice require the constable to send the evidence to the court or authority that made the request.

25. Release of evidence held under the order

(1) On an application made by a person mentioned below, the nominated court may authorise the release of any evidence retained by a constable under section 24 if, in its opinion—
  (a) the condition in section 21(6) or (7) is met, or
  (b) the overseas freezing order has ceased to have effect in the participating country.
(2) In relation to England and Wales and Northern Ireland, the persons are—
  (a) the chief officer of police to whom a copy of the order was sent,
  (b) the constable,

(c) any other person affected by the order.

(3) In relation to Scotland, the persons are—

(a) the procurator fiscal to whom a copy of the order was sent,

(b) any other person affected by the order.

(4) If the territorial authority decides not to give a notice under section 24(2) in respect of any evidence retained by a constable under that section, the authority must give the constable a notice authorising him to release the evidence.

General

26. Powers under warrants

(1) A court in England and Wales or Northern Ireland, or a justice of the peace, may not issue a warrant under section 17 or 22 in respect of any evidence unless the court or justice has reasonable grounds for believing that it does not consist of or include items subject to legal privilege, excluded material or special procedure material.

(2) Subsection (1) does not prevent a warrant being issued by virtue of section 22(5) in respect of excluded material or special procedure material.

(3) In Schedule 1 to the Criminal Justice and Police Act 2001 (c. 16) (powers of seizure), in Part 1 (powers to which the additional powers in section 50 apply)—

(a) paragraph 49 is omitted,

(b) after paragraph 73B there is inserted—

'Crime (International Co-operation) Act 2003

73C.

The power of seizure conferred by sections 17 and 22 of the Crime (International Co-operation) Act 2003 (seizure of evidence relevant to overseas investigation or offence).'

(4) References in this Chapter to evidence seized by a person by virtue of or under any provision of this Chapter include evidence seized by a person by virtue of section 50 of the Criminal Justice and Police Act 2001 (additional powers of seizure), if it is seized in the course of a search authorised by a warrant issued by virtue of or under the provision in question.

(5) Subsection (4) does not require any evidence to be sent to the territorial authority or to any court or authority—

(a) before it has been found, on the completion of any examination required to be made by arrangements under section 53(2) of the Criminal Justice and Police Act 2001, to be property within subsection (3) of that section (property which may be retained after examination), or

(b) at a time when it constitutes property in respect of which a person is required to ensure that arrangements such as are mentioned in section 61(1) of that Act (duty to secure) are in force.

27. Exercise of powers by others

(1) The Treasury may by order provide, in relation to England and Wales or Northern Ireland—

(a) for any function conferred on the Secretary of State (whether or not in terms) under sections 10, 11 and 13 to 26 to be exercisable instead in prescribed circumstances by the [Commissioners for Revenue and Customs],[11]

(b) for any function conferred on a constable under those sections to be exercisable instead in prescribed circumstances by [an officer of Revenue and Customs][12] or a person acting under the direction of such an officer.

'Prescribed' means prescribed by the order.

(2) The Secretary of State may by order provide, in relation to England and Wales or Northern Ireland—

[11] Amended by the Criminal Justice and Immigration Act 2008.
[12] Amended by the Criminal Justice and Immigration Act 2008.

(a) for any function conferred on him under sections 13 to 26 to be exercisable instead in prescribed circumstances by a prescribed person,

(b) for any function conferred on a constable under those sections to be exercisable instead in prescribed circumstances by a prescribed person. 'Prescribed' means prescribed by the order.

(3) Subsection (2)(b) does not apply to any powers exercisable by virtue of section 16(2)(b) or (4)(b).

28. Interpretation of Chapter 2

(1) In this Chapter—

'domestic freezing order' has the meaning given by section 10(2),

'notice' means a notice in writing,

'overseas freezing order' has the meaning given by section 20,

'premises' has the same meaning as in the Police and Criminal Evidence Act 1984 (c. 60), Chapter 3 of Part 8 of the Proceeds of Crime Act 2002 (c. 29) or the Police and Criminal Evidence (Northern Ireland) Order 1989 (S.I. 1989/1341 (N.I. 12)) (as the case may be),

'the relevant Framework Decision' means the Framework Decision on the execution in the European Union of orders freezing property or evidence adopted by the Council of the European Union on 22nd July 2003.

(2) The following provisions have effect for the purposes of this Chapter.

(3) In relation to England and Wales and Northern Ireland, 'items subject to legal privilege', 'excluded material' and 'special procedure material' have the same meaning as in the Police and Criminal Evidence Act 1984 or (as the case may be) the Police and Criminal Evidence (Northern Ireland) Order 1989.

(4) In relation to Scotland, 'items subject to legal privilege' has the same meaning as in Chapter 3 of Part 8 of the Proceeds of Crime Act 2002.

(5) A listed offence means—

(a) an offence described in Article 3(2) of the relevant Framework Decision, or

(b) an offence prescribed or of a description prescribed by an order made by the Secretary of State.

(6) An order prescribing an offence or a description of offences under subsection (5)(b) may require, in the case of an overseas freezing order, that the conduct which constitutes the offence or offences would, if it occurred in a part of the United Kingdom, constitute an offence in that part.

(7) Specified information, in relation to a certificate required by section 11(4) or 20(5), means—

(a) any information required to be given by the form of certificate annexed to the relevant Framework Decision, or

(b) any information prescribed by an order made by the Secretary of State.

(8) In relation to Scotland, references above in this section to the Secretary of State are to be read as references to the Scottish Ministers.

(9) The territorial authority—

(a) in relation to evidence in England and Wales or Northern Ireland, is the Secretary of State,

(b) in relation to evidence in Scotland, is the Lord Advocate.

Chapter 3
Hearing Evidence through Television Links or by Telephone

29. Hearing witnesses abroad through television links

(1) The Secretary of State may by order provide for section 32(1A) of the Criminal Justice Act 1988 (c. 33) . . .[13] (proceedings in which evidence may be given through television link) to apply to any further description of criminal proceedings, or to all criminal proceedings.

(2) The Scottish Ministers may by order provide for section 273(1) of the Criminal Procedure (Scotland) Act 1995 (c. 46) (proceedings in which evidence may be given through television link) to apply to any further description of criminal proceedings, or to all criminal proceedings.

[(3) The Department of Justice in Northern Ireland may by order provide for Article 80A(4) of the Police and Criminal Evidence (Northern Ireland) Order 1989 (proceedings in which evidence may

[13] Amended by SI 2010/976.

be given through television link) to apply to any further description of criminal proceedings, or to all criminal proceedings.][14]

30. Hearing witnesses in the UK through television links

(1) This section applies where the Secretary of State receives a request, from an authority mentioned in subsection (2) ('the external authority'), for a person in the United Kingdom to give evidence through a live television link in criminal proceedings before a court in a country outside the United Kingdom.

Criminal proceedings include any proceedings on an appeal before a court against a decision in administrative proceedings.

(2) The authority referred to in subsection (1) is the authority in that country which appears to the Secretary of State to have the function of making requests of the kind to which this section applies.

(3) Unless he considers it inappropriate to do so, the Secretary of State must by notice in writing nominate a court in the United Kingdom where the witness may be heard in the proceedings in question through a live television link.

(4) Anything done by the witness in the presence of the nominated court which, if it were done in proceedings before the court, would constitute contempt of court is to be treated for that purpose as done in proceedings before the court.

(5) Any statement made on oath by a witness giving evidence in pursuance of this section is to be treated for the purposes of—

- (a) section 1 of the Perjury Act 1911 (c. 6),
- (b) Article 3 of the Perjury (Northern Ireland) Order 1979 (S.I. 1979/1714 (N.I. 19)),
- (c) sections 44 to 46 of the Criminal Law (Consolidation) (Scotland) Act 1995 (c. 39) or, in relation to Scotland, any matter pertaining to the common law crime of perjury,

as made in proceedings before the nominated court.

(6) Part 1 of Schedule 2 (evidence given by television link) is to have effect.

(7) Subject to subsections (4) and (5) and the provisions of that Schedule, evidence given pursuant to this section is not to be treated for any purpose as evidence given in proceedings in the United Kingdom.

(8) In relation to Scotland, references in this section and Part 1 of Schedule 2 to the Secretary of State are to be read as references to the Lord Advocate.

31. Hearing witnesses in the UK by telephone

(1) This section applies where the Secretary of State receives a request, from an authority mentioned in subsection (2) ('the external authority') in a participating country, for a person in the United Kingdom to give evidence by telephone in criminal proceedings before a court in that country.

Criminal proceedings include any proceedings on an appeal before a court against a decision in administrative proceedings.

(2) The authority referred to in subsection (1) is the authority in that country which appears to the Secretary of State to have the function of making requests of the kind to which this section applies.

(3) A request under subsection (1) must—

- (a) specify the court in the participating country,
- (b) give the name and address of the witness,
- (c) state that the witness is willing to give evidence by telephone in the proceedings before that court.

(4) Unless he considers it inappropriate to do so, the Secretary of State must by notice in writing nominate a court in the United Kingdom where the witness may be heard in the proceedings in question by telephone.

(5) Anything done by the witness in the presence of the nominated court which, if it were done in proceedings before the court, would constitute contempt of court is to be treated for that purpose as done in proceedings before the court.

---

[14] Amended by SI 2010/976.

(6) Any statement made on oath by a witness giving evidence in pursuance of this section is to be treated for the purposes of—
 (a) section 1 of the Perjury Act 1911 (c. 6),
 (b) Article 3 of the Perjury (Northern Ireland) Order 1979 (S.I. 1979/1714 (N.I. 19)),
 (c) sections 44 to 46 of the Criminal Law (Consolidation) (Scotland) Act 1995 (c. 39) or, in relation to Scotland, any matter pertaining to the common law crime of perjury,

as made in proceedings before the nominated court.

(7) Part 2 of Schedule 2 (evidence given by telephone link) is to have effect.

(8) Subject to subsections (5) and (6) and the provisions of that Schedule, evidence given in pursuance of this section is not to be treated for any purpose as evidence given in proceedings in the United Kingdom.

(9) In relation to Scotland, references in this section to the Secretary of State are to be read as references to the Lord Advocate.

Chapter 4
Information about Banking Transactions

Requests for information about banking transactions in England and Wales and Northern Ireland for use abroad

32. Customer information

(1) This section applies where the Secretary of State receives a request from an authority mentioned in subsection (2) for customer information to be obtained in relation to a person who appears to him to be subject to an investigation in a participating country into serious criminal conduct.

(2) The authority referred to in subsection (1) is the authority in that country which appears to the Secretary of State to have the function of making requests of the kind to which this section applies.

(3) The Secretary of State may—
 (a) direct a senior police officer to apply, or arrange for a constable to apply, for a customer information order,
 (b) direct a senior customs officer to apply, or arrange for a customs officer to apply, for such an order.

(4) A customer information order is an order made by a judge that a financial institution specified in the application for the order must, on being required to do so by notice in writing given by the applicant for the order, provide any such customer information as it has relating to the person specified in the application.

(5) A financial institution which is required to provide information under a customer information order must provide the information to the applicant for the order in such manner, and at or by such time, as the applicant requires.

(6) Section 364 of the Proceeds of Crime Act 2002 (c. 29) (meaning of customer information), except subsections (2)(f) and (3)(i), has effect for the purposes of this section as if this section were included in Chapter 2 of Part 8 of that Act.

(7) A customer information order has effect in spite of any restriction on the disclosure of information (however imposed).

(8) Customer information obtained in pursuance of a customer information order is to be given to the Secretary of State and sent by him to the authority which made the request.

33. Making, varying or discharging customer information orders

(1) A judge may make a customer information order, on an application made to him pursuant to a direction under section 32(3), if he is satisfied that—
 (a) the person specified in the application is subject to an investigation in the country in question,
 (b) the investigation concerns conduct which is serious criminal conduct,
 (c) the conduct constitutes an offence in England and Wales or (as the case may be) Northern Ireland, or would do were it to occur there, and
 (d) the order is sought for the purposes of the investigation.

(2) The application may be made ex parte to a judge in chambers.

(3) The application may specify—
  (a) all financial institutions,
  (b) a particular description, or particular descriptions, of financial institutions, or
  (c) a particular financial institution or particular financial institutions.

(4) The court may discharge or vary a customer information order on an application made by—
  (a) the person who applied for the order,
  (b) a senior police officer,
  (c) a constable authorised by a senior police officer to make the application,
  (d) a senior customs officer,
  (e) a customs officer authorised by a senior customs officer to make the application.

34. Offences

(1) A financial institution is guilty of an offence if without reasonable excuse it fails to comply with a requirement imposed on it under a customer information order.

(2) A financial institution guilty of an offence under subsection (1) is liable on summary conviction to a fine not exceeding level 5 on the standard scale.

(3) A financial institution is guilty of an offence if, in purported compliance with a customer information order, it—
  (a) makes a statement which it knows to be false or misleading in a material particular, or
  (b) recklessly makes a statement which is false or misleading in a material particular.

(4) A financial institution guilty of an offence under subsection (3) is liable—
  (a) on summary conviction, to a fine not exceeding the statutory maximum, or
  (b) on conviction on indictment, to a fine.

35. Account information

(1) This section applies where the Secretary of State receives a request from an authority mentioned in subsection (2) for account information to be obtained in relation to an investigation in a participating country into criminal conduct.

(2) The authority referred to in subsection (1) is the authority in that country which appears to the Secretary of State to have the function of making requests of the kind to which this section applies.

(3) The Secretary of State may—
  (a) direct a senior police officer to apply, or arrange for a constable to apply, for an account monitoring order,
  (b) direct a senior customs officer to apply, or arrange for a customs officer to apply, for such an order.

(4) An account monitoring order is an order made by a judge that a financial institution specified in the application for the order must, for the period stated in the order, provide account information of the description specified in the order to the applicant in the manner, and at or by the time or times, stated in the order.

(5) Account information is information relating to an account or accounts held at the financial institution specified in the application by the person so specified (whether solely or jointly with another).

(6) An account monitoring order has effect in spite of any restriction on the disclosure of information (however imposed).

(7) Account information obtained in pursuance of an account monitoring order is to be given to the Secretary of State and sent by him to the authority which made the request.

36. Making, varying or discharging account monitoring orders

(1) A judge may make an account monitoring order, on an application made to him in pursuance of a direction under section 35(3), if he is satisfied that—
  (a) there is an investigation in the country in question into criminal conduct, and
  (b) the order is sought for the purposes of the investigation.

(2) The application may be made ex parte to a judge in chambers.

(3) The application may specify information relating to—
  (a) all accounts held by the person specified in the application for the order at the financial institution so specified,
  (b) a particular description, or particular descriptions, of accounts so held, or

(c) a particular account, or particular accounts, so held.

(4) The court may discharge or vary an account monitoring order on an application made by—

(a) the person who applied for the order,

(b) a senior police officer,

(c) a constable authorised by a senior police officer to make the application,

(d) a senior customs officer,

(e) a customs officer authorised by a senior customs officer to make the application.

(5) Account monitoring orders have effect as if they were orders of the court.

Requests for information about banking transactions in Scotland for use abroad

37. Customer information

(1) This section applies where the Lord Advocate receives a request from an authority mentioned in subsection (2) for customer information to be obtained in relation to a person who appears to him to be subject to an investigation in a participating country into serious criminal conduct.

(2) The authority referred to in subsection (1) is the authority in that country which appears to the Lord Advocate to have the function of making requests of the kind to which this section applies.

(3) The Lord Advocate may direct a procurator fiscal to apply for a customer information order.

(4) A customer information order is an order made by a sheriff that a financial institution specified in the application for the order must, on being required to do so by notice in writing given by the applicant for the order, provide any such customer information as it has relating to the person specified in the application.

(5) A financial institution which is required to provide information under a customer information order must provide the information to the applicant for the order in such manner, and at or by such time, as the applicant requires.

(6) Section 398 of the Proceeds of Crime Act 2002 (c. 29) (meaning of customer information), except subsections (2)(f) and (3)(i), has effect for the purposes of this section as if this section were included in Chapter 3 of Part 8 of that Act.

(7) A customer information order has effect in spite of any restriction on the disclosure of information (however imposed).

(8) Customer information obtained in pursuance of a customer information order is to be given to the Lord Advocate and sent by him to the authority which made the request.

38. Making, varying or discharging customer information orders

(1) A sheriff may make a customer information order, on an application made to him pursuant to a direction under section 37(3), if he is satisfied that—

(a) the person specified in the application is subject to an investigation in the country in question,

(b) the investigation concerns conduct which is serious criminal conduct,

(c) the conduct constitutes an offence in Scotland, or would do were it to occur in Scotland, and

(d) the order is sought for the purposes of the investigation.

(2) The application may be made ex parte to a sheriff in chambers.

(3) The application may specify—

(a) all financial institutions,

(b) a particular description, or particular descriptions, of financial institutions, or

(c) a particular financial institution or particular financial institutions.

(4) The court may discharge or vary a customer information order on an application made by the procurator fiscal.

(5) Section 409 of the Proceeds of Crime Act 2002 (jurisdiction of sheriff) has effect for the purposes of this section as if this section were included in Chapter 3 of Part 8 of that Act.

39. Offences

(1) A financial institution is guilty of an offence if without reasonable excuse it fails to comply with a requirement imposed on it under a customer information order.

(2) A financial institution guilty of an offence under subsection (1) is liable on summary conviction to a fine not exceeding level 5 on the standard scale.

(3) A financial institution is guilty of an offence if, in purported compliance with a customer information order, it—
  (a) makes a statement which it knows to be false or misleading in a material particular, or
  (b) recklessly makes a statement which is false or misleading in a material particular.
(4) A financial institution guilty of an offence under subsection (3) is liable—
  (a) on summary conviction, to a fine not exceeding the statutory maximum, or
  (b) on conviction on indictment, to a fine.

40. Account information

(1) This section applies where the Lord Advocate receives a request from an authority mentioned in subsection (2) for account information to be obtained in relation to an investigation in a participating country into criminal conduct.
(2) The authority referred to in subsection (1) is the authority in that country which appears to the Lord Advocate to have the function of making requests of the kind to which this section applies.
(3) The Lord Advocate may direct a procurator fiscal to apply for an account monitoring order.
(4) An account monitoring order is an order made by a sheriff that a financial institution specified in the application for the order must, for the period stated in the order, provide account information of the description specified in the order to the applicant in the manner, and at or by the time or times, stated in the order.
(5) Account information is information relating to an account or accounts held at the financial institution specified in the application by the person so specified (whether solely or jointly with another).
(6) An account monitoring order has effect in spite of any restriction on the disclosure of information (however imposed).
(7) Account information obtained in pursuance of an account monitoring order is to be given to the Lord Advocate and sent by him to the authority which made the request.

41. Making, varying or discharging account monitoring orders

(1) A sheriff may make an account monitoring order, on an application made to him in pursuance of a direction under section 40(3), if he is satisfied that—
  (a) there is an investigation in the country in question into criminal conduct, and
  (b) the order is sought for the purposes of the investigation.
(2) The application may be made ex parte to a sheriff in chambers.
(3) The application may specify information relating to—
  (a) all accounts held by the person specified in the application for the order at the financial institution so specified,
  (b) a particular description, or particular descriptions, of accounts so held, or
  (c) a particular account, or particular accounts, so held.
(4) The court may discharge or vary an account monitoring order on an application made by the procurator fiscal.
(5) Section 409 of the Proceeds of Crime Act 2002 (c. 29) (jurisdiction of sheriff) has effect for the purposes of this section as if this section were included in Chapter 3 of Part 8 of that Act.

Disclosure of information

42. Offence of disclosure

(1) This section applies where—
  (a) a financial institution is specified in a customer information order or account monitoring order made in any part of the United Kingdom, or
  (b) the Secretary of State or the Lord Advocate receives a request under section 13 for evidence to be obtained from a financial institution in connection with the investigation of an offence in reliance on Article 2 (requests for information on banking transactions) of the 2001 Protocol.
(2) If the institution, or an employee of the institution, discloses any of the following information, the institution or (as the case may be) the employee is guilty of an offence.
(3) That information is—
  (a) that the request to obtain customer information or account information, or the request mentioned in subsection (1)(b), has been received,

(b) that the investigation to which the request relates is being carried out, or
(c) that, in pursuance of the request, information has been given to the authority which made the request.

(4) An institution guilty of an offence under this section is liable—
(a) on summary conviction, to a fine not exceeding the statutory maximum,
(b) on conviction on indictment, to a fine.

(5) Any other person guilty of an offence under this section is liable—
(a) on summary conviction, to imprisonment for a term not exceeding six months or to a fine not exceeding the statutory maximum, or to both,
(b) on conviction on indictment, to imprisonment for a term not exceeding five years or to a fine, or to both.

Requests for information about banking transactions for use in UK

43. Information about a person's bank account

(1) If it appears to a judicial authority in the United Kingdom, on an application made by a prosecuting authority, that—
(a) a person is subject to an investigation in the United Kingdom into serious criminal conduct,
(b) the person holds, or may hold, an account at a bank which is situated in a participating country, and
(c) the information which the applicant seeks to obtain is likely to be of substantial value for the purposes of the investigation,

the judicial authority may request assistance under this section.

(2) The judicial authorities are—
(a) in relation to England and Wales, any judge or justice of the peace,
(b) in relation to Scotland, any sheriff,
(c) in relation to Northern Ireland, any judge or resident magistrate.

(3) If it appears to a prosecuting authority mentioned in subsection (4) that paragraphs (a) to (c) of subsection (1) are met, the authority may itself request assistance under this section.

(4) The prosecuting authorities are—
(a) in relation to England and Wales and Northern Ireland, a prosecuting authority designated by an order made by the Secretary of State,
(b) in relation to Scotland, the Lord Advocate or a procurator fiscal.

(5) The assistance that may be requested under this section is any assistance in obtaining from a participating country one or more of the following—
(a) information as to whether the person in question holds any accounts at any banks situated in the participating country,
(b) details of any such accounts,
(c) details of transactions carried out in any period specified in the request in respect of any such accounts.

(6) A request for assistance under this section must—
(a) state the grounds on which the authority making the request thinks that the person in question may hold any account at a bank which is situated in a participating country and (if possible) specify the bank or banks in question,
(b) state the grounds on which the authority making the request considers that the information sought to be obtained is likely to be of substantial value for the purposes of the investigation, and
(c) include any information which may facilitate compliance with the request.

(7) For the purposes of this section, a person holds an account if—
(a) the account is in his name or is held for his benefit, or
(b) he has a power of attorney in respect of the account.

In relation to Scotland, a power of attorney includes a factory and commission.

44. Monitoring banking transactions

(1) If it appears to a judicial authority in the United Kingdom, on an application made by a prosecuting authority, that the information which the applicant seeks to obtain is relevant to an investigation in the United Kingdom into criminal conduct, the judicial authority may request assistance under this section.

(2) The judicial authorities are—
  (a) in relation to England and Wales, any judge or justice of the peace,
  (b) in relation to Scotland, any sheriff,
  (c) in relation to Northern Ireland, any judge or resident magistrate.

(3) If it appears to a prosecuting authority mentioned in subsection (4) that the information which it seeks to obtain is relevant to an investigation into criminal conduct, the authority may itself request assistance under this section.

(4) The prosecuting authorities are—
  (a) in relation to England and Wales and Northern Ireland, a prosecuting authority designated by an order made by the Secretary of State,
  (b) in relation to Scotland, the Lord Advocate or a procurator fiscal.

(5) The assistance that may be requested under this section is any assistance in obtaining from a participating country details of transactions to be carried out in any period specified in the request in respect of any accounts at banks situated in that country.

45. Sending requests for assistance

(1) A request for assistance under section 43 or 44, other than one to which subsection (3) or (4) applies, is to be sent to the Secretary of State for forwarding—
  (a) to a court specified in the request and exercising jurisdiction in the place where the information is to be obtained, or
  (b) to any authority recognised by the participating country in question as the appropriate authority for receiving requests for assistance of the kind to which this section applies.

(2) But in cases of urgency the request may be sent to a court referred to in subsection (1)(a).

(3) Such a request for assistance by the Lord Advocate is to be sent to a court or authority mentioned in subsection (1)(a) or (b).

(4) Such a request for assistance by a sheriff or a procurator fiscal is to be sent to such a court or authority, or to the Lord Advocate for forwarding to such a court or authority.

General

46. Interpretation of Chapter 4

(1) In this Chapter—
'the court' means the Crown Court or, in Scotland, the sheriff,
'senior police officer' means a police officer who is not below the rank of superintendent and 'senior customs officer' means a customs officer who is not below the grade designated by the Commissioners of Customs and Excise as equivalent to that rank.

(2) The following provisions apply for the purposes of this Chapter.

(3) Serious criminal conduct means conduct which constitutes—
  (a) an offence to which paragraph 3 of Article 1 (request for information on bank accounts) of the 2001 Protocol applies, or
  (b) an offence specified in an order made by the Secretary of State or, in relation to Scotland, the Scottish Ministers for the purpose of giving effect to any decision of the Council of the European Union under paragraph 6 of that Article.

(4) A financial institution—
  (a) means a person who is carrying on business in the regulated sector, and
  (b) in relation to a customer information order or an account monitoring order, includes a person who was carrying on business in the regulated sector at a time which is the time to which any requirement for him to provide information under the order is to relate.

'Business in the regulated sector' is to be interpreted in accordance with Schedule 9 to the Proceeds of Crime Act 2002 (c. 29).

(5) A judge means—

(a) in relation to England and Wales, a judge entitled to exercise the jurisdiction of the Crown Court,

(b) in relation to Northern Ireland, a Crown Court judge.

Chapter 5
Transfer of Prisoners

47. Transfer of UK prisoner to assist investigation abroad

(1) The Secretary of State may pursuant to an agreement with the competent authority of a participating country issue a warrant providing for any person to whom this section applies ('a prisoner') to be transferred to that country for the purpose of assisting there in the investigation of an offence. The offence must be one which was or may have been committed in the United Kingdom.

(2) This section applies to a person—

(a) serving a sentence in a prison,

(b) in custody awaiting trial or sentence, or

(c) committed to prison for default in paying a fine.

(3) But, in relation to transfer from Scotland—

(a) this section applies to any person detained in custody,

(b) references in this section to the Secretary of State are to be read as references to the Scottish Ministers.

(4) A warrant may be issued in respect of a prisoner under subsection (1) only if—

(a) the prisoner, or

(b) in the circumstances mentioned in subsection (5), a person appearing to the Secretary of State to be an appropriate person to act on the prisoner's behalf,

has made a written statement consenting to his being transferred for the purpose mentioned in subsection (1).

(5) The circumstances are those in which it appears to the Secretary of State to be inappropriate for the prisoner to act for himself, by reason of his physical or mental condition or his youth.

(6) Such consent cannot be withdrawn after the issue of the warrant.

(7) A warrant under this section authorises—

(a) the taking of the prisoner to a place in the United Kingdom and his delivery at a place of departure from the United Kingdom into the custody of a person representing the appropriate authority of the participating country to which the prisoner is to be transferred, and

(b) the bringing of the prisoner back to the United Kingdom and his transfer in custody to the place where he is liable to be detained under the sentence or order to which he is subject.

(8) References to a prison in this section include any other institution to which the Prison Act 1952 (c. 52), the Prison Act (Northern Ireland) 1953 (c. 18 (N.I.)) or Article 45(1) of the Criminal Justice (Children) (Northern Ireland) Order 1998 (S.I. 1998/1504 (N.I. 9)) applies.

(9) Subsections [(4)][15] to (8) of section 5 of the 1990 Act (transfer of UK prisoner to give evidence or assist investigation overseas) have effect in relation to a warrant issued under this section as they have effect in relation to a warrant issued under that section.

48. Transfer of EU etc. prisoner to assist UK investigation

(1) The Secretary of State may pursuant to an agreement with the competent authority of a participating country issue a warrant providing for any person to whom this section applies ('the overseas prisoner') to be transferred to the United Kingdom for the purpose of assisting in the investigation of an offence.

The offence must be one which was or may have been committed in the participating country.

(2) This section applies to a person who is detained in custody in a participating country—

[15] Amended by the Armed Forces Act 2006.

(a) by virtue of a sentence or order of a court exercising criminal jurisdiction there, or
(b) in consequence of[—
(a) having been transferred there, or responsibility for his detention and release having been transferred there, from the United Kingdom under the Repatriation of Prisoners Act 1984;
(b) having been transferred there, or responsibility for his detention and release having been transferred there, under any similar provision or arrangement from any other country or territory].[16]

(3) But, in relation to transfer to Scotland—
(a) this section applies to any person who is detained in custody in a participating country,
(b) the reference in subsection (1) to the Secretary of State is to be read as a reference to the Scottish Ministers.

(4) A warrant may be issued in respect of an overseas prisoner under subsection (1) only if the competent authority provides a written statement made by the prisoner consenting to his being transferred for the purpose mentioned in that subsection.

(5) Such consent cannot be withdrawn after the issue of the warrant.

(6) A warrant under this section authorises—
(a) the bringing of the prisoner to the United Kingdom,
(b) the taking of the prisoner to, and his detention in custody at, any place or places in the United Kingdom specified in the warrant,
(c) the returning of the prisoner to the country from which he has come.

(7) Subsections (4) to (8) of section 5 of the 1990 Act have effect in relation to a warrant issued under this section as they have effect in relation to a warrant issued under that section.

(8) A person is not subject to the Immigration Act 1971 (c. 77) in respect of his entry into or presence in the United Kingdom pursuant to a warrant under this section; but if the warrant ceases to have effect while he is still in the United Kingdom—
(a) he is to be treated for the purposes of that Act as if he has then illegally entered the United Kingdom, and
(b) the provisions of Schedule 2 to that Act have effect accordingly except that paragraph 20(1) (liability of carrier for expenses of custody etc. of illegal entrant) does not have effect in relation to directions for his removal given by virtue of this subsection.

Chapter 6
Supplementary

49. Rules of court

(1) Provision may be made by rules of court as to the practice and procedure to be followed in connection with proceedings under this Part.

(2) Rules of court made under this section by the High Court in Scotland are to be made by Act of Adjournal.

(3) The power to make rules of court under this section does not prejudice any existing power to make rules.

50. Subordinate legislation

(1) Any power to make an order conferred by this Part on the Secretary of State, the Treasury or the Scottish Ministers is exercisable by statutory instrument.

[(1A) Any power to make an order conferred by this Part on the Department of Justice in Northern Ireland is exercisable by statutory rule for the purposes of the Statutory Rules (Northern Ireland) Order 1979.][17]

(2) [An order made under this Part by the Secretary of State, the Treasury, the Scottish Ministers or the Department of Justice][18] may make different provision for different purposes.

---

[16] Amended by the Criminal Justice and Immigration Act 2008.
[17] Amended by SI 2010/976.
[18] Amended by SI 2010/976.

(3) A statutory instrument (other than an instrument to which subsection (5) applies) containing an order made by the Secretary of State or the Treasury is to be subject to annulment in pursuance of a resolution of either House of Parliament.

(4) A statutory instrument (other than an instrument to which subsection (5) applies) containing an order made by the Scottish Ministers is to be subject to annulment in pursuance of a resolution of the Scottish Parliament.

(5) A statutory instrument containing an order under section 51(2)(b) designating a country other than a member State is not to be made unless—

(a) in the case of an order to be made by the Secretary of State, a draft of the instrument has been laid before, and approved by resolution of, each House of Parliament,

(b) in the case of an order to be made by the Scottish Ministers, a draft of the instrument has been laid before, and approved by resolution of, the Scottish Parliament.

[(6) An order made by the Department of Justice is to be subject to negative resolution (within the meaning of section 41(6) of the Interpretation Act (Northern Ireland) 1954).][19]

51. General interpretation

(1) In this Part—

'the 1990 Act' means the Criminal Justice (International Co-operation) Act 1990 (c. 5),

'the 2001 Protocol' means the Protocol to the Mutual Legal Assistance Convention, established by Council Act of 16th October 2001 (2001/C326/01),

'administrative proceedings' means proceedings outside the United Kingdom to which Article 3(1) of the Mutual Legal Assistance Convention applies (proceedings brought by administrative authorities in respect of administrative offences where a decision in the proceedings may be the subject of an appeal before a court),

'chief officer of police'—

(a) in relation to any area in Scotland, means the chief constable for the police force maintained for that area,

(b) in relation to any area in Northern Ireland, means the Chief Constable of the Police Service of Northern Ireland,

'clemency proceedings' means proceedings in a country outside the United Kingdom, not being proceedings before a court exercising criminal jurisdiction, for the removal or reduction of a penalty imposed on conviction of an offence,

'country' includes territory,

'court' includes a tribunal,

'criminal proceedings' include criminal proceedings outside the United Kingdom in which a civil order may be made,

'customs officer' means an officer commissioned by the Commissioners of Customs and Excise under section 6(3) of the Customs and Excise Management Act 1979 (c. 2),

'evidence' includes information in any form and articles, and giving evidence includes answering a question or producing any information or article,

'the Mutual Legal Assistance Convention' means the Convention on Mutual Assistance in Criminal Matters established by Council Act of 29th May 2000 (2000/C197/01),

'the Schengen Convention' means the Convention implementing the Schengen Agreement of 14th June 1985.

(2) A participating country, in relation to any provision of this Part, means—

(a) a country other than the United Kingdom which is a member State on a day appointed for the commencement of that provision, and

(b) any other country designated by an order made by the Secretary of State or, in relation to Scotland, the Scottish Ministers.

(3) In this Part, 'process', in relation to England and Wales and Northern Ireland, means any summons or order issued or made by a court and includes—

(a) any other document issued or made by a court for service on parties or witnesses,

(b) any document issued by a prosecuting authority outside the United Kingdom for the purposes of criminal proceedings.

---

[19] Amended by SI 2010/976.

(4) In this Part, 'process', in relation to service in Scotland, means a citation by a court or by a prosecuting authority, or an order made by a court, and includes any other document issued or made as mentioned in subsection (3)(a) or (b).

Part 2
Terrorist Acts and Threats: Jurisdiction

52. Jurisdiction for terrorist offences

After section 63 of the Terrorism Act 2000 (c. 11) there is inserted—

'EXTRA-TERRITORIAL JURISDICTION FOR OTHER TERRORIST OFFENCES ETC.

63A. Other terrorist offences under this Act: jurisdiction

(1) If—
   (a) a United Kingdom national or a United Kingdom resident does anything outside the United Kingdom, and
   (b) his action, if done in any part of the United Kingdom, would have constituted an offence under section 54 or any of sections 56 to 61,

   he shall be guilty in that part of the United Kingdom of the offence.

(2) For the purposes of this section and sections 63B and 63C a 'United Kingdom national' means an individual who is—
   (a) a British citizen, a British overseas territories citizen, a British National (Overseas) or a British Overseas citizen,
   (b) a person who under the British Nationality Act 1981 is a British subject, or
   (c) a British protected person within the meaning of that Act.

(3) For the purposes of this section and sections 63B and 63C a 'United Kingdom resident' means an individual who is resident in the United Kingdom.

63B. Terrorist attacks abroad by UK nationals or residents: jurisdiction

(1) If—
   (a) a United Kingdom national or a United Kingdom resident does anything outside the United Kingdom as an act of terrorism or for the purposes of terrorism, and
   (b) his action, if done in any part of the United Kingdom, would have constituted an offence listed in subsection (2),

   he shall be guilty in that part of the United Kingdom of the offence.

(2) These are the offences—
   (a) murder, manslaughter, culpable homicide, rape, assault causing injury, assault to injury, kidnapping, abduction or false imprisonment,
   (b) an offence under section 4, 16, 18, 20, 21, 22, 23, 24, 28, 29, 30 or 64 of the Offences against the Person Act 1861,
   (c) an offence under any of sections 1 to 5 of the Forgery and Counterfeiting Act 1981,
   (d) the uttering of a forged document or an offence under section 46A of the Criminal Law (Consolidation) (Scotland) Act 1995,
   (e) an offence under section 1 or 2 of the Criminal Damage Act 1971,
   (f) an offence under Article 3 or 4 of the Criminal Damage (Northern Ireland) Order 1977,
   (g) malicious mischief,
   (h) wilful fire-raising.

63C. Terrorist attacks abroad on UK nationals, residents and diplomatic staff etc. : jurisdiction

(1) If—
   (a) a person does anything outside the United Kingdom as an act of terrorism or for the purposes of terrorism,

(b) his action is done to, or in relation to, a United Kingdom national, a United Kingdom resident or a protected person, and
(c) his action, if done in any part of the United Kingdom, would have constituted an offence listed in subsection (2),

he shall be guilty in that part of the United Kingdom of the offence.

(2) These are the offences—
(a) murder, manslaughter, culpable homicide, rape, assault causing injury, assault to injury, kidnapping, abduction or false imprisonment,
(b) an offence under section 4, 16, 18, 20, 21, 22, 23, 24, 28, 29, 30 or 64 of the Offences against the Person Act 1861,
(c) an offence under section 1, 2, 3, 4 or 5(1) or (3) of the Forgery and Counterfeiting Act 1981,
(d) the uttering of a forged document or an offence under section 46A(1) of the Criminal Law (Consolidation) (Scotland) Act 1995.

(3) For the purposes of this section and section 63D a person is a protected person if—
(a) he is a member of a United Kingdom diplomatic mission within the meaning of Article 1(b) of the Vienna Convention on Diplomatic Relations signed in 1961 (as that Article has effect in the United Kingdom by virtue of section 2 of and Schedule 1 to the Diplomatic Privileges Act 1964),
(b) he is a member of a United Kingdom consular post within the meaning of Article 1(g) of the Vienna Convention on Consular Relations signed in 1963 (as that Article has effect in the United Kingdom by virtue of section 1 of and Schedule 1 to the Consular Relations Act 1968),
(c) he carries out any functions for the purposes of the European Agency for the Evaluation of Medicinal Products, or
(d) he carries out any functions for the purposes of a body specified in an order made by the Secretary of State.

(4) The Secretary of State may specify a body under subsection (3)(d) only if—
(a) it is established by or under the Treaty establishing the European Community or the Treaty on European Union, and
(b) the principal place in which its functions are carried out is a place in the United Kingdom.

(5) If in any proceedings a question arises as to whether a person is or was a protected person, a certificate—
(a) issued by or under the authority of the Secretary of State, and
(b) stating any fact relating to the question,

is to be conclusive evidence of that fact.

63D. Terrorist attacks or threats abroad in connection with UK diplomatic premises etc.: jurisdiction

(1) If—
(a) a person does anything outside the United Kingdom as an act of terrorism or for the purposes of terrorism,
(b) his action is done in connection with an attack on relevant premises or on a vehicle ordinarily used by a protected person,
(c) the attack is made when a protected person is on or in the premises or vehicle, and
(d) his action, if done in any part of the United Kingdom, would have constituted an offence listed in subsection (2),

he shall be guilty in that part of the United Kingdom of the offence.

(2) These are the offences—
(a) an offence under section 1 of the Criminal Damage Act 1971,
(b) an offence under Article 3 of the Criminal Damage (Northern Ireland) Order 1977,
(c) malicious mischief,
(d) wilful fire-raising.

(3) If—
(a) a person does anything outside the United Kingdom as an act of terrorism or for the purposes of terrorism,
(b) his action consists of a threat of an attack on relevant premises or on a vehicle ordinarily used by a protected person,

(c) the attack is threatened to be made when a protected person is, or is likely to be, on or in the premises or vehicle, and
(d) his action, if done in any part of the United Kingdom, would have constituted an offence listed in subsection (4),

he shall be guilty in that part of the United Kingdom of the offence.

(4) These are the offences—
(a) an offence under section 2 of the Criminal Damage Act 1971,
(b) an offence under Article 4 of the Criminal Damage (Northern Ireland) Order 1977,
(c) breach of the peace (in relation to Scotland only).

(5) 'Relevant premises' means—
(a) premises at which a protected person resides or is staying, or
(b) premises which a protected person uses for the purpose of carrying out his functions as such a person.

63E. Sections 63B to 63D: supplementary

(1) Proceedings for an offence which (disregarding the Acts listed in subsection (2)) would not be an offence apart from section 63B, 63C or 63D are not to be started—
(a) in England and Wales, except by or with the consent of the Attorney General,
(b) in Northern Ireland, except by or with the consent of the Advocate General for Northern Ireland.

(2) These are the Acts—
(a) the Internationally Protected Persons Act 1978,
(b) the Suppression of Terrorism Act 1978,
(c) the Nuclear Material (Offences) Act 1983,
(d) the United Nations Personnel Act 1997.

(3) For the purposes of sections 63C and 63D it is immaterial whether a person knows that another person is a United Kingdom national, a United Kingdom resident or a protected person.

(4) In relation to any time before the coming into force of section 27(1) of the Justice (Northern Ireland) Act 2002, the reference in subsection (1)(b) to the Advocate General for Northern Ireland is to be read as a reference to the Attorney General for Northern Ireland.'

53. Jurisdiction for offence under section 113 of the Anti-terrorism, Crime and Security Act 2001

After section 113 of the Anti-terrorism, Crime and Security Act 2001 (c. 24) (use of noxious substances or things to cause harm and intimidate) there is inserted—

'113A. Application of section 113

(1) Section 113 applies to conduct done—
(a) in the United Kingdom; or
(b) outside the United Kingdom which satisfies the following two conditions.

(2) The first condition is that the conduct is done for the purpose of advancing a political, religious or ideological cause.

(3) The second condition is that the conduct is—
(a) by a United Kingdom national or a United Kingdom resident;
(b) by any person done to, or in relation to, a United Kingdom national, a United Kingdom resident or a protected person; or
(c) by any person done in circumstances which fall within section 63D(1)(b) and (c) or (3)(b) and (c) of the Terrorism Act 2000.

(4) The following expressions have the same meaning as they have for the purposes of sections 63C and 63D of that Act—
(a) 'United Kingdom national';
(b) 'United Kingdom resident';
(c) 'protected person'.

(5) For the purposes of this section it is immaterial whether a person knows that another is a United Kingdom national, a United Kingdom resident or a protected person.

113B. Consent to prosecution for offence under section 113

(1) Proceedings for an offence committed under section 113 outside the United Kingdom are not to be started—
   (a) in England and Wales, except by or with the consent of the Attorney General;
   (b) in Northern Ireland, except by or with the consent of the Advocate General for Northern Ireland.
(2) Proceedings for an offence committed under section 113 outside the United Kingdom may be taken, and the offence may for incidental purposes be treated as having been committed, in any part of the United Kingdom.
(3) In relation to any time before the coming into force of section 27(1) of the Justice (Northern Ireland) Act 2002, the reference in subsection (1)(b) to the Advocate General for Northern Ireland is to be read as a reference to the Attorney General for Northern Ireland.'

Part 3
Road Traffic

Chapter 1
Convention on Driving Disqualifications

Road traffic offences in UK

54. Application of section 55

(1) Section 55 applies where—
   (a) an individual ('the offender') who is normally resident in a member State other than the United Kingdom is convicted of an offence mentioned in Schedule 3,
   (b) no appeal is outstanding in relation to the offence, and
   (c) the driving disqualification condition is met in relation to the offence.
(2) The driving disqualification condition is met—
   (a) in relation to an offence mentioned in Part 1 of Schedule 3, if an order of disqualification is made in respect of the offence,
   (b) in relation to an offence mentioned in Part 2 of that Schedule, if an order of disqualification for a period not less than the minimum period is made in respect of the offence.
(3) The minimum period is—
   (a) a period of six months, or
   (b) where the State in which the offender normally resides is a prescribed State, a shorter period equal to the period prescribed in relation to the State.
(4) Section 55 does not apply in prescribed circumstances.
(5) For the purposes of this section no appeal is outstanding in relation to an offence if—
   (a) no appeal is brought against an offender's conviction of the offence, or any order made on his conviction, within the time allowed for making such appeals, or
   (b) such an appeal is brought and the proceedings on appeal are finally concluded.

55. Duty to give notice to foreign authorities of driving disqualification of a non-UK resident

(1) Where this section applies, the appropriate Minister must give the central authority of the State in which the offender is normally resident a notice under this section.
(2) A notice under this section must—
   (a) give the name, address and date of birth of the offender,
   (b) give particulars of the offence,
   (c) state that no appeal is outstanding in relation to it,
   (d) give particulars of the disqualification,
   (e) state whether or not the offender took part in the proceedings in which the disqualification was imposed,

(f) state that the offender has been informed that any decision made for the purposes of the convention on driving disqualifications will have no effect on the disqualification.

(3) A notice under this section may contain such other information as the appropriate Minister considers appropriate.

(4) A notice under this section must be accompanied by the original or a certified copy of the order of disqualification.

(5) Where the offender did not take part in the proceedings mentioned in subsection (2)(e), a notice under this section must also be accompanied by evidence that the offender was duly notified of those proceedings.

(6) Where the offender is the holder of a Community licence, a notice under this section must also be accompanied by the licence unless it has been returned to the driver—

(a) under section 91A(7)(b)(ii) of the Road Traffic Offenders Act 1988 (c. 53), or

(b) under Article 92A(7)(b)(ii) of the Road Traffic Offenders (Northern Ireland) Order 1996 (S.I. 1996/1320 (N.I. 10)).

(7) Where the period of disqualification is reduced by virtue of section 34A of that Act or Article 36 of that Order, the appropriate Minister must give the central authority particulars of the reduction.

(8) Where the disqualification is removed by an order under section 42 of that Act or Article 47 of that Order, the appropriate Minister must give the central authority particulars of the removal.

(9) The appropriate Minister must provide—

(a) the central authority, or

(b) the competent authority of the State mentioned in subsection (1),

with any further information which it requires for the purposes of the convention on driving disqualifications.

Disqualification in respect of road traffic offences outside UK

56. Application of section 57

(1) Section 57 applies where—

(a) an individual ('the offender') who is normally resident in the United Kingdom is convicted in another member State of an offence falling within subsection (5),

(b) no appeal is outstanding in relation to the offence,

(c) the driving disqualification condition is met in relation to the offence, and

(d) the offender was duly notified of the proceedings ('the relevant proceedings') in which the disqualification was imposed and was entitled to take part in them.

(2) The driving disqualification condition is met—

(a) in relation to an offence falling within subsection (5)(a), if, as a result of the offence, the offender is disqualified in the State in which the conviction is made,

(b) in relation to an offence falling within subsection (5)(b), if, as a result of the offence, the offender is disqualified in that State for a period not less than the minimum period.

(3) For the purposes of this section an offender is disqualified in a State if he is disqualified in that State for holding or obtaining a licence to drive a motor vehicle granted under the law of that State (however the disqualification is described under that law).

(4) The minimum period is—

(a) a period of six months, or

(b) where the State in which the conviction is made is a prescribed State, a shorter period equal to the period prescribed in relation to that State.

(5) An offence falls within this subsection if it is constituted by—

(a) conduct falling within any of paragraphs 1 to 5 of the Annex to the convention on driving disqualifications, or

(b) other conduct which constitutes a road traffic offence for the purposes of that convention.

(6) Section 57 does not apply if the relevant proceedings were brought later than the time at which summary proceedings for any corresponding offence under the law of the part of the United Kingdom in which the offender is normally resident could have been brought.

(7) An offence is a corresponding offence if—

(a) the conduct constituting the offence outside the United Kingdom took place in any part of the United Kingdom, and

(b) that conduct is, or corresponds to, conduct which would constitute an offence under the law of that part.

(8) The appropriate Minister may make regulations treating offences under the law of a part of the United Kingdom as corresponding to offences under the law of a member State other than the United Kingdom.

(9) For the purposes of this section no appeal is outstanding in relation to an offence if—

(a) no appeal is brought against an offender's conviction of the offence, or any decision made as a result of his conviction, within the time allowed for making such appeals, or

(b) such an appeal is brought and the proceedings on appeal are finally concluded.

57. Recognition in United Kingdom of foreign driving disqualification

(1) Where this section applies, the appropriate Minister—

(a) must give the offender a notice under this section if the unexpired period of the foreign disqualification is not less than one month, and

(b) may give him a notice under this section if that period is less than one month.

(2) The unexpired period of the foreign disqualification is—

(a) the period of the foreign disqualification, less

(b) any period of that disqualification which is treated by regulations made by the appropriate Minister as having been served in the State in which the offender was convicted.

(3) The provision which may be made by regulations under subsection (2)(b) includes provision for treating any period during which a central authority or competent authority of a State has seized a licence without returning it as a period which has been served in that State.

(4) If the appropriate Minister gives the offender a notice under this section, the offender is disqualified in each part of the United Kingdom—

(a) for the relevant period, and

(b) if the foreign disqualification is also effective until a condition is satisfied, until the condition or a corresponding prescribed condition is satisfied.

(5) The relevant period is the period which—

(a) begins at the end of the period of 21 days beginning with the day on which the notice is given, and

(b) is equal to the unexpired period of the foreign disqualification.

(6) But if the foreign disqualification is at any time removed otherwise than in prescribed circumstances, the offender ceases to be disqualified in each part of the United Kingdom from that time.

(7) The appropriate Minister may make regulations substituting a longer period for the period for the time being mentioned in subsection (5)(a).

(8) Where the foreign disqualification is for life—

(a) the condition in subsection (1)(a) is to be treated as satisfied, and

(b) the other references in this section and section 58 to the unexpired period of the foreign disqualification are to be read as references to a disqualification for life.

58. Notice under section 57

(1) A notice under section 57 must—

(a) give particulars of the offence in respect of which the foreign disqualification was imposed and the period of that disqualification,

(b) state that the offender is disqualified in each part of the United Kingdom for a period equal to the unexpired period of the foreign disqualification,

(c) state the date from which, and period for which, he is disqualified,

(d) give particulars of any relevant condition mentioned in section 57(4)(b),

(e) give details of his right to appeal under section 59.

(2) A notice under section 57 must be in writing.

(3) A notice under section 57 may contain such other information as the appropriate Minister considers appropriate.

Appeals

59. Appeal against disqualification

(1) A person who is disqualified by virtue of section 57 may, after giving notice to the appropriate Minister of his intention to do so, appeal to the appropriate court against the disqualification.
(2) The appropriate court is—
 (a) in relation to England and Wales, a magistrates' court [. . .],[20]
 (b) in relation to Scotland, the sheriff within whose jurisdiction the applicant resides,
 (c) in relation to Northern Ireland, a court of summary jurisdiction acting for the petty sessions district in which the applicant resides.
(3) The appeal must be made before the end of the period of 21 days beginning with the day on which the notice under section 57 is given to the applicant.
(4) But the appropriate Minister may make regulations substituting a longer period for the period for the time being mentioned in subsection (3).
(5) If the appropriate court is satisfied that section 57 does not apply to the applicant's case, it must allow the appeal.
(6) Otherwise it must dismiss the appeal.
(7) Where on an appeal against the disqualification the appeal is allowed, the court by which the appeal is allowed must send notice of that fact to the appropriate Minister.
(8) The notice must—
 (a) be sent in such manner and to such address, and
 (b) contain such particulars,
 as the appropriate Minister may determine.

60. Power of appellate courts in England and Wales to suspend disqualification

(1) This section applies where a person is disqualified by virtue of section 57.
(2) Where the person appeals to a magistrates' court against the disqualification, the court may, if it thinks fit, suspend the disqualification.
(3) Where the person makes an application in respect of the decision of the court under section 111 of the Magistrates' Courts Act 1980 (c. 43) (statement of case), the High Court may, if it thinks fit, suspend the disqualification.
(4) Where the person has appealed, or applied for leave to appeal, to the [Supreme Court][21] under section 1 of the Administration of Justice Act 1960 (c. 65) from any decision of the High Court which is material to the disqualification, the High Court may, if it thinks fit, suspend the disqualification.
(5) Any power of a court under this section to suspend the disqualification is a power to do so on such terms as the court thinks fit.
(6) Where, by virtue of this section, a court suspends the disqualification, it must send notice of the suspension to the Secretary of State.
(7) The notice must—
 (a) be sent in such manner and to such address, and
 (b) contain such particulars,
 as the Secretary of State may determine.

61. Power of appellate courts in Scotland to suspend disqualification

(1) This section applies where a person is disqualified by virtue of section 57.
(2) Where the person appeals to the sheriff against the disqualification, the sheriff may, if he thinks fit, suspend the disqualification on such terms as he thinks fit.
(3) Where the person appeals to the High Court of Justiciary from any decision of the sheriff, the court may, if it thinks fit, suspend the disqualification on such terms as it thinks fit.
 The power conferred by this subsection may be exercised by a single judge of the court.

---

[20] Repealed by SI 2005/886.
[21] Amended by the Constitutional Reform Act 2005.

(4) Where, by virtue of this section, a court suspends the disqualification, it must send notice of the suspension to the Secretary of State.
(5) The notice must—
 (a) be sent in such manner and to such address, and
 (b) contain such particulars, as the Secretary of State may determine.

62. Power of appellate courts in Northern Ireland to suspend disqualification

(1) This section applies where a person is disqualified by virtue of section 57.
(2) Where the person appeals to a court of summary jurisdiction against the disqualification, the court may, if it thinks fit, suspend the disqualification.
(3) Where the person makes an application in respect of the decision of the court under Article 146 of the Magistrates' Courts (Northern Ireland) Order 1981 (S.I. 1981/1675 (N.I. 26)) (statement of case), the Court of Appeal may, if it thinks fit, suspend the disqualification.
(4) Where the person has appealed, or applied for leave to appeal, to the [Supreme Court][22] under section 41 of the Judicature (Northern Ireland) Act 1978 (c. 23) from any decision of the Court of Appeal which is material to the disqualification, the Court of Appeal may, if it thinks fit, suspend the disqualification.
(5) Any power of a court under this section to suspend the disqualification is a power to do so on such terms as the court thinks fit.
(6) Where, by virtue of this section, a court suspends the disqualification, it must send notice of the suspension to the Department.
(7) The notice must—
 (a) be sent in such manner and to such address, and
 (b) contain such particulars,
 as the Department may determine.

Production of licence

63. Production of licence: Great Britain

(1) A person who—
 (a) is given a notice under section 57 by the Secretary of State, and
 (b) is the holder of a licence,
 must deliver his licence and its counterpart to the Secretary of State before the end of the period of 21 days beginning with the day on which the notice is given.
(2) The Secretary of State may make regulations substituting a longer period for the period for the time being mentioned in subsection (1).
(3) If—
 (a) a person delivers a current receipt for his licence and its counterpart to the Secretary of State within the period for the time being mentioned in subsection (1), and
 (b) on the return of his licence and its counterpart immediately delivers them to the Secretary of State,
 the duty under subsection (1) is to be taken as satisfied.
 'Receipt' means a receipt issued under section 56 of the Road Traffic Offenders Act 1988 (c. 53).
(4) Subsection (1) does not apply if the competent authority of the relevant State—
 (a) has the licence and its counterpart, or
 (b) has delivered them to the Secretary of State.
(5) The relevant State is the State in which the offence in relation to which the notice was given was committed.
(6) If the holder of a licence does not deliver his licence and its counterpart to the Secretary of State as required by subsection (1), he is guilty of an offence.
(7) A person is not guilty of an offence under subsection (6) if he satisfies the court that he has applied for a new licence and has not received it.

---

[22] Amended by the Constitutional Reform Act 2005.

In relation to the holder of a Northern Ireland licence or Community licence, a new licence includes the counterpart of such a licence.

(8) A person guilty of an offence under subsection (6) is liable on summary conviction to a fine not exceeding level 3 on the standard scale.

(9) 'Licence' means a Great Britain licence, a Northern Ireland licence or a Community licence.

64. Production of licence: Northern Ireland

(1) A person who—

(a) is given a notice under section 57 by the Department, and

(b) is the holder of a licence,

must deliver his licence and its counterpart to the Department before the end of the period of 21 days beginning with the day on which the notice is given.

(2) The Department may make regulations substituting a longer period for the period for the time being mentioned in subsection (1).

(3) If—

(a) a person delivers a current receipt for his licence and its counterpart to the Department within the period for the time being mentioned in subsection (1), and

(b) on the return of his licence and its counterpart immediately delivers them to the Department,

the duty under subsection (1) is to be taken as satisfied.

'Receipt' means a receipt issued under Article 62 of the Road Traffic Offenders (Northern Ireland) Order 1996 (S.I. 1996/1320 (N.I. 10)).

(4) Subsection (1) does not apply if the competent authority of the relevant State—

(a) has the licence and its counterpart, or

(b) has delivered them to the Department.

(5) The relevant State is the State in which the offence in relation to which the notice was given was committed.

(6) If the holder of a licence does not deliver his licence and its counterpart to the Department as required by subsection (1), he is guilty of an offence.

(7) A person is not guilty of an offence under subsection (6) if he satisfies the court that he has applied for a new licence and has not received it.

In relation to the holder of a Great Britain licence or Community licence, a new licence includes the counterpart of such a licence.

(8) A person guilty of an offence under subsection (6) is liable on summary conviction to a fine not exceeding level 3 on the standard scale.

(9) 'Licence' means a Northern Ireland licence, a Great Britain licence or a Community licence.

65. Production of licence: Community licence holders

(1) This section applies where—

(a) the holder of a Community licence is disqualified by virtue of section 57, and

(b) the licence is sent to the Secretary of State or the Department under section 63 or 64.

(2) The Secretary of State or (as the case may be) the Department must send—

(a) the holder's name and address, and

(b) particulars of the disqualification,

to the licensing authority in the EEA State in respect of which the licence was issued.

(3) But subsection (2) does not apply if the EEA State is the same as the State in which the offence in relation to which the holder is disqualified was committed.

(4) The Secretary of State or (as the case may be) the Department must return the licence to the holder—

(a) on the expiry of the relevant period of the disqualification (within the meaning of section 57), or

(b) if earlier, on being satisfied that the holder has left Great Britain or (as the case may be) Northern Ireland and is no longer normally resident there.

(5) But subsection (4) does not apply at any time where—

(a) the Secretary of State or the Department would otherwise be under a duty under paragraph (a) of that subsection to return the licence, and

(b) the holder would not at that time be authorised by virtue of section 99A(1) of the Road Traffic Act 1988 (c. 52) or Article 15A(1) of the Road Traffic (Northern Ireland) Order 1981 (S.I. 1981/154 (N.I. 1)) to drive in Great Britain or Northern Ireland a motor vehicle of any class.

(6) In that case the Secretary of State or (as the case may be) the Department must—

(a) send the licence to the licensing authority in the EEA State in respect of which it was issued, and

(b) explain to that authority the reasons for so doing.

(7) 'EEA State' has the same meaning as in Part 3 of the Road Traffic Act 1988.

Disqualification

66. Effect of disqualification by virtue of section 57

Where the holder of a Great Britain licence or Northern Ireland licence is disqualified by virtue of section 57, the licence is to be treated as revoked with effect from the beginning of the period of disqualification.

67. Rule for determining end of period of disqualification

In determining the expiration of the period for which a person is disqualified by virtue of section 57, any time during which—

(a) the disqualification is suspended, or

(b) he is not disqualified,

is to be disregarded.

Endorsement

68. Endorsement of licence: Great Britain

(1) This section applies where a person who is normally resident in Great Britain is disqualified by virtue of section 57.

(2) The Secretary of State must secure that particulars of the disqualification are endorsed on the counterpart of any Great Britain licence or of any Northern Ireland licence or Community licence which the person—

(a) may then hold, or

(b) may subsequently obtain,

until he becomes entitled under subsection (4) or (5) to have a Great Britain licence and its counterpart, or a counterpart of his Northern Ireland licence or Community licence, issued to him free from those particulars.

(3) On the issue to the person of—

(a) a new Great Britain licence, or

(b) a new counterpart of a Northern Ireland licence or Community licence,

those particulars must be entered on the counterpart of the new licence or the new counterpart unless he has become so entitled.

(4) The person is entitled to have issued to him with effect from the end of the period for which the endorsement remains effective a new Great Britain licence with a counterpart free from the endorsement if he—

(a) applies for a new licence under section 97(1) of the Road Traffic Act 1988 (c. 52),

(b) surrenders any subsisting licence and its counterpart,

(c) pays the fee prescribed by regulations under Part 3 of that Act, and

(d) satisfies the other requirements of section 97(1).

(5) The person is entitled to have issued to him with effect from the end of that period a new counterpart of any Northern Ireland licence or Community licence then held by him free from the endorsement if he makes an application to the Secretary of State for that purpose in such manner as the Secretary of State may determine.

(6) The endorsement remains effective until four years have elapsed since he was convicted of the offence in relation to which he is disqualified by virtue of section 57.

(7) Where the person ceases to be disqualified by virtue of section 57(6), the Secretary of State must secure that the relevant particulars are endorsed on the counterpart of the Great Britain licence or of any Northern Ireland licence or Community licence previously held by him.

69. Endorsement of licence: Northern Ireland

(1) This section applies where a person who is normally resident in Northern Ireland is disqualified by virtue of section 57.
(2) The Department must secure that particulars of the disqualification are endorsed on the counterpart of any Northern Ireland licence or the counterpart of any Great Britain licence or Community licence which the person—
   (a) may then hold, or
   (b) may subsequently obtain, until he becomes entitled under subsection (4) or (5) to have a Northern Ireland licence and its counterpart, or a counterpart of his Great Britain licence or Community licence, issued to him free from those particulars.
(3) On the issue to the person of—
   (a) a new Northern Ireland licence, or
   (b) a new counterpart of a Great Britain licence or Community licence,
   those particulars must be entered on the counterpart of the new licence or the new counterpart unless he has become so entitled.
(4) The person is entitled to have issued to him with effect from the end of the period for which the endorsement remains effective a new Northern Ireland licence with a counterpart free from the endorsement if he—
   (a) applies for a new licence under Article 13(1) of the Road Traffic (Northern Ireland) Order 1981 (S.I. 1981/154 (N.I. 1)),
   (b) surrenders any subsisting licence and its counterpart,
   (c) pays the fee prescribed by regulations under Part 2 of that Order, and
   (d) satisfies the other requirements of Article 13(1).
(5) The person is entitled to have issued to him with effect from the end of that period a new counterpart of any Great Britain licence or Community licence then held by him free from the endorsement if he makes an application to the Department for that purpose in such manner as it may determine.
(6) The endorsement remains effective until four years have elapsed since he was convicted of the offence in relation to which he is disqualified by virtue of section 57.
(7) Where the person ceases to be disqualified by virtue of section 57(6), the Department must secure that the relevant particulars are endorsed on the counterpart of the Northern Ireland licence or the counterpart of any Great Britain licence or Community licence previously held by him.

General

70. Duty of appropriate Minister to inform competent authority

(1) This section applies where a competent authority of any State gives the appropriate Minister a notice under the convention on driving disqualifications in respect of any person.
(2) If the appropriate Minister gives a notice under section 57 to that person, he must give the competent authority particulars of the disqualification which arises by virtue of that section.
(3) If the appropriate Minister does not give such a notice, he must give his reasons to the competent authority.

71. Notices

(1) A notice authorised or required under this Chapter to be given by the appropriate Minister to an individual, or a Community licence required to be returned to its holder by section 65, may be given or returned to him by—
   (a) delivering it to him,
   (b) leaving it at his proper address, or
   (c) sending it to him by post.
(2) For the purposes of—
   (a) subsection (1), and
   (b) section 7 of the Interpretation Act 1978 (c. 30) in its application to that subsection,
   the proper address of any individual is his latest address as known to the appropriate Minister.

72. Regulations: Great Britain

(1) Any power to make regulations conferred by this Chapter on the Secretary of State is exercisable by statutory instrument.
(2) A statutory instrument containing any such regulations is subject to annulment in pursuance of a resolution of either House of Parliament.
(3) The regulations may make different provision for different purposes.

73. Regulations: Northern Ireland

(1) Any power to make regulations conferred by this Chapter on the Department is exercisable by statutory rule for the purposes of the Statutory Rules (Northern Ireland) Order 1979 (S.I. 1979/1573 (N.I. 12)).
(2) Any such regulations are subject to negative resolution (within the meaning of the Interpretation Act (Northern Ireland) 1954 (c. 33 (N.I.)).
(3) The regulations may make different provision for different purposes.

74. Interpretation

(1) In this Chapter—
'appropriate Minister' means—
(a) in relation to Great Britain, the Secretary of State,
(b) in relation to Northern Ireland, the Department,
'central authority', in relation to a State, means an authority designated by the State as a central authority for the purposes of the convention on driving disqualifications,
'Community licence'—
(a) in relation to Great Britain, has the same meaning as in Part 3 of the Road Traffic Act 1988 (c. 52),
(b) in relation to Northern Ireland, has the same meaning as in Part 2 of the Road Traffic (Northern Ireland) Order 1981 (S.I. 1981/154 (N.I. 1)),
'competent authority', in relation to a State, means an authority which is a competent authority in relation to the State for the purposes of the convention on driving disqualifications,
'the convention on driving disqualifications' means the Convention drawn up on the basis of Article K.3 of the Treaty on European Union on Driving Disqualifications signed on 17th June 1998,
'counterpart'—
(a) in relation to Great Britain, has the same meaning as in Part 3 of the Road Traffic Act 1988 (c. 52),
(b) in relation to Northern Ireland, has the same meaning as in Part 2 of the Road Traffic (Northern Ireland) Order 1981 (S.I. 1981/154 (N.I.1)),
'the Department' means the Department of the Environment,
'disqualified', except in section 56, means—
(a) in relation to Great Britain, disqualified for holding or obtaining a Great Britain licence,
(b) in relation to Northern Ireland, disqualified for holding or obtaining a Northern Ireland licence,
and 'disqualification' is to be interpreted accordingly,
'foreign disqualification' means the disqualification mentioned in section 56,
'Great Britain licence' means a licence to drive a motor vehicle granted under Part 3 of the Road Traffic Act 1988,
'motor vehicle'—
(a) in relation to Great Britain, has the same meaning as in the Road Traffic Act 1988,
(b) in relation to Northern Ireland, has the same meaning as in the Road Traffic (Northern Ireland) Order 1995 (S.I. 1995/2994 (N.I.18)),
'Northern Ireland licence' means a licence to drive a motor vehicle granted under Part 2 of the Road Traffic (Northern Ireland) Order 1981,
'prescribed' means prescribed by regulations made by the appropriate Minister.
(2) In this Chapter a disqualification, or foreign disqualification, for life is to be treated as being for a period of not less than six months.

75. Application to Crown

This Chapter applies to vehicles and persons in the public service of the Crown.

Chapter 2
Mutual Recognition within the United Kingdom etc.

76. Recognition in Great Britain of disqualifications in Northern Ireland etc.

After section 102 of the Road Traffic Act 1988 there is inserted—

'Disqualification if disqualified in Northern Ireland etc.

102A. Disqualification while disqualified in Northern Ireland, Isle of Man, Channel Islands or Gibraltar

(1) A person is disqualified for holding or obtaining a licence to drive a motor vehicle of any class so long as he is subject to a relevant disqualification imposed outside Great Britain.
(2) For the purposes of this section a person is subject to a relevant disqualification imposed outside Great Britain if, in respect of any offence—
  (a) a court in Northern Ireland disqualifies him for holding or obtaining a Northern Ireland licence,
  (b) a court in the Isle of Man or any of the Channel Islands disqualifies him for holding or obtaining a British external licence, or
  (c) a court in Gibraltar disqualifies him for holding or obtaining a licence to drive a motor vehicle granted under the law of Gibraltar.
(3) A certificate signed by the Secretary of State which states, in respect of a person, any matter relating to the question whether he is subject to a relevant disqualification imposed outside Great Britain shall be evidence (in Scotland, sufficient evidence) of the matter so stated.
(4) A certificate stating that matter and purporting to be so signed shall be deemed to be so signed unless the contrary is proved.'

77. Endorsement of counterparts issued to Northern Ireland licence holders

(1) After section 109 of the Road Traffic Act 1988 (c. 52) there is inserted—

'109A. Counterparts issued to Northern Ireland licence holders

(1) The Secretary of State may issue to any Northern Ireland licence holder who—
  (a) has delivered his Northern Ireland licence to the Secretary of State, and
  (b) has provided him with the information specified in, or required under, subsection (3) below (whether or not in pursuance of this section),

  a document (referred to in this Part of this Act in relation to a Northern Ireland licence as a 'counterpart').
(2) The counterpart must—
  (a) be in such form, and
  (b) contain such information,

  designed for the endorsement of particulars relating to the Northern Ireland licence as the Secretary of State may determine.
(3) The information referred to in subsection (1) above is—
  (a) the name and address (whether in Great Britain or Northern Ireland) of the Northern Ireland licence holder;
  (b) his date of birth;
  (c) the classes of vehicle which he is authorised by his Northern Ireland licence to drive;
  (d) the period of validity of the licence;
  (e) whether it was granted in exchange for a licence issued by a state other than an EEA State; and
  (f) such other information as the Secretary of State may require for the purposes of the proper exercise of any of his functions under this Part or Part 4 of this Act.

(4) The Secretary of State—
  (a) may endorse a Northern Ireland licence delivered to him (whether or not in pursuance of this section) in such manner as he may determine—
    (i) with any part of the information specified in, or required under, subsection (3) above; or
    (ii) with information providing a means of ascertaining that information or any part of it; and
  (b) must return the Northern Ireland licence to the holder.

(5) Subsections (6) to (9), (11) (with the omission of paragraph (a)) and (12) of section 99B of this Act apply for the purposes of this section as if the references to a Community licence were references to a Northern Ireland licence.'

(2) After section 91 of the Road Traffic Offenders Act 1988 (c. 53) there is inserted—

'91ZA. Application to Northern Ireland licence holders

(1) The references to a licence in the following provisions of this Act include references to a Northern Ireland licence—
  (a) section 7,
  (b) section 26(7) and (8) and (9)(b),
  (c) section 27,
  (d) section 29(1),
  (e) section 30,
  (f) section 31(1),
  (g) section 32,
  (h) section 42(5),
  (i) section 44(1),
  (j) section 46(2),
  (k) section 47(2) and (3),
  (l) section 48(1) and (2).

(2) Accordingly, the reference in section 27(3)(b) of this Act to the suspension of a licence is to be construed in relation to a Northern Ireland licence holder as a reference to his ceasing to be authorised by virtue of section 109(1) of the Road Traffic Act 1988 to drive in Great Britain a motor vehicle of any class.

(3) The references in sections 26(9)(a) and 27(3) of this Act to a new licence include references to a counterpart of a Northern Ireland licence.

(4) In relation to a Northern Ireland licence holder to whom a counterpart is issued under section 109A of the Road Traffic Act 1988, the references in Part 3 of this Act (except sections 75(12), 76(8) and 77(9)) to a licence include references to a Northern Ireland licence.

(5) Where a court orders the endorsement of the counterpart of any Northern Ireland licence held by a person, it must send notice of the endorsement to the Secretary of State.

(6) The notice must—
  (a) be sent in such manner and to such address, and
  (b) contain such particulars,

as the Secretary of State may determine.

(7) Where a court orders the holder of a Northern Ireland licence to be disqualified, it must send the Northern Ireland licence and its counterpart (if any), on their being produced to the court, to the Secretary of State.

(8) The licence and its counterpart must be sent to such address as the Secretary of State may determine.

(9) Where—
  (a) a notice is sent to the Secretary of State under subsection (5) above, and
  (b) the particulars contained in the notice include—
    (i) particulars of an offence in respect of which the holder of a Northern Ireland licence is disqualified by an order of a court, and
    (ii) particulars of the disqualification,

the Secretary of State must send a notice containing the particulars mentioned in paragraph (b)(i) and (ii) to the licensing authority in Northern Ireland.

91ZB. Effect of endorsement on Northern Ireland licence holders

Section 91B applies in relation to Northern Ireland licences as it applies in relation to Community licences.'

78. Prohibition on holding or obtaining Great Britain and Northern Ireland licences

(1) The Road Traffic Act 1988 (c. 52) is amended as follows.

(2) In section 97 (grant of licences)—

(a) in subsection (1)(c), after sub-paragraph (i) there is inserted—

'(ia) any Northern Ireland licence held by him together with its Northern Ireland counterpart and its counterpart (if any) issued to him under this Part of this Act,',

(b) after subsection (1A) there is inserted—

'(1AA) Where a licence under this Part of this Act is granted to a person who surrenders under sub-paragraph (ia) of subsection (1)(c) above his Northern Ireland licence together with the counterparts mentioned in that sub-paragraph to the Secretary of State—

(a) that person ceases to be authorised by virtue of section 109(1) of this Act to drive in Great Britain a motor vehicle of any class, and

(b) the Secretary of State must send the Northern Ireland licence and its Northern Ireland counterpart to the licensing authority in Northern Ireland together with particulars of the class of motor vehicles to which the licence granted under this Part of this Act relates.'

(3) In section 99 (duration of licences), after subsection (3) there is inserted—

'(3A) Where—

(a) the Secretary of State is sent under a provision of Northern Ireland law corresponding to section 97(1AA) of this Act a licence granted under this Part of this Act to a person to drive a motor vehicle of any class, and

(b) the Secretary of State is satisfied that a Northern Ireland licence to drive a motor vehicle of that or a corresponding class has been granted to that person,

the Secretary of State must serve notice in writing on that person revoking the licence granted under this Part of this Act.'

(4) In section 102 (disqualification to prevent duplication of licences), at the end there is inserted—

'(2) A person is also disqualified for holding or obtaining a licence authorising him to drive a motor vehicle of any class so long as he is authorised by virtue of section 109(1) of this Act to drive a motor vehicle of that or a corresponding class.'

79. Disability and prospective disability

(1) The Road Traffic Act 1988 (c. 52) is amended as follows.

(2) After section 109A (as inserted by section 77 of this Act) there is inserted—

'109B. Revocation of authorisation conferred by Northern Ireland licence because of disability or prospective disability

(1) If the Secretary of State is at any time satisfied on inquiry—

(a) that a Northern Ireland licence holder is suffering from a relevant disability, and

(b) that he would be required by virtue of section 92(3) of this Act to refuse an application made by the holder at that time for a licence authorising him to drive a vehicle of the class in respect of which his Northern Ireland licence was issued or a class corresponding to that class,

he may serve notice in writing requiring the licence holder to deliver immediately to the Secretary of State his Northern Ireland licence together with its Northern Ireland counterpart and its counterpart (if any) issued to him under this Part of this Act ('the relevant counterparts').

(2) If the Secretary of State is satisfied on inquiry that a Northern Ireland licence holder is suffering from a prospective disability, he may—

(a) serve notice in writing on the Northern Ireland licence holder requiring him to deliver immediately to the Secretary of State his Northern Ireland licence together with the relevant counterparts, and

(b) on receipt of the Northern Ireland licence and those counterparts and of an application made for the purposes of this subsection, grant to the Northern Ireland licence holder, free of charge, a licence for a period determined by the Secretary of State under section 99(1)(b) of this Act.

(3) The Secretary of State may require a person to provide—

(a) evidence of his name, address, sex and date and place of birth, and

(b) a photograph which is a current likeness of him,

before granting a licence to him on an application for the purposes of subsection (2) above.

(4) A person who—

(a) is required under, or by virtue of, this section to deliver to the Secretary of State his Northern Ireland licence and the relevant counterparts, but

(b) without reasonable excuse, fails to do so,

is guilty of an offence.

(5) Where a Northern Ireland licence holder to whom a counterpart is issued under section 109A of this Act—

(a) is required under, or by virtue of, this section to deliver his Northern Ireland licence and that counterpart to the Secretary of State, and

(b) is not in possession of them in consequence of the fact that he has surrendered them to a constable or authorised person (within the meaning of Part 3 of the Road Traffic Offenders Act 1988) on receiving a fixed penalty notice given to him under section 54 of that Act,

he does not fail to comply with any such requirement if he delivers them to the Secretary of State immediately on their return.

(6) Where a Northern Ireland licence holder is served with a notice in pursuance of this section, he shall cease to be authorised by virtue of section 109(1) of this Act to drive in Great Britain a motor vehicle of any class from such date as may be specified in the notice, not being earlier than the date of service of the notice.

(7) Where a Northern Ireland licence is delivered to the Secretary of State in pursuance of this section, he must—

(a) send the licence and its Northern Ireland counterpart to the licensing authority in Northern Ireland, and

(b) explain to them his reasons for so doing.

109C. Information relating to disabilities etc.

Section 94 of this Act shall apply to a Northern Ireland licence holder who is normally resident in Great Britain as if—

(a) in subsection (1), for the words from the beginning to 'aware' there were substituted 'If a Northern Ireland licence holder who is authorised by virtue of section 109(1) of this Act to drive in Great Britain a motor vehicle of any class, is aware immediately before the relevant date, or becomes aware on or after that date',

(b) after that subsection there were inserted—

'(1A) For the purposes of subsection (1) 'relevant date' means—

(a) in the case where the licence holder first became normally resident in Great Britain on or before the date on which section 79 of the Crime (International Co-operation) Act 2003 comes into force, that date; and

(b) in any other case, the date on which he first became so resident.',

(c) for subsection (3A) there were substituted—

'(3A) A person who—

(a) is authorised by virtue of section 109(1) of this Act to drive in Great Britain a motor vehicle of any class, and

(b) drives on a road a motor vehicle of that class,

is guilty of an offence if at any earlier time while he was so authorised he was required by subsection (1) above to notify the Secretary of State but has failed without reasonable excuse to do so.',

(d) in subsection (4), the words 'an applicant for, or' (in both places) were omitted,

(e) in subsection (5), the words 'applicant or' and the words from the beginning of paragraph (c) to 'provisional licence' were omitted,

(f) in subsection (6)(b), the words 'applicant or' (in both places) were omitted,

(g) in subsection (7), the words 'applicant or' were omitted, and

(h) in subsection (8)—

(i) for '93' there were substituted '109B', and
(ii) the words 'applicant or' (in both places) were omitted.'

(3) In section 93 (revocation of licence because of disability or prospective disability)—
(a) in subsection (2A), at the end there is inserted 'or subsection (6) below',
(b) at the end there is inserted—

'(5) Where the Secretary of State—
(a) is at any time sent by the licensing authority in Northern Ireland a licence under a provision of Northern Ireland law corresponding to section 109B of this Act, and
(b) by virtue of the reasons given by that authority for sending the licence is at that time satisfied as mentioned in subsection (1)(a) and (b) above or that the licence holder is suffering from a prospective disability,

the Secretary of State may serve notice in writing on the licence holder revoking the licence with effect from such date as may be specified in the notice, not being earlier than the date of service of the notice.

(6) Where the reasons given by the licensing authority in Northern Ireland for sending the licence relate to a prospective disability of the holder, the Secretary of State may, on an application made for the purposes of this subsection, grant to the holder, free of charge, a new licence for a period determined by the Secretary of State under section 99(1)(b) of this Act."

Part 4
Miscellaneous

Information

80. Disclosure of information by SFO

In section 3 of the Criminal Justice Act 1987 (c. 38) (disclosure of information)—
(a) in subsection (5), for paragraph (c) there is substituted—
'(c) for the purposes of any criminal investigation or criminal proceedings, whether in the United Kingdom or elsewhere',
(b) at the end of subsection (6) there is inserted—
'(n) any person or body having, under the Treaty on European Union or any other treaty to which the United Kingdom is a party, the function of receiving information of the kind in question,
(o) any person or body having, under the law of any country or territory outside the United Kingdom, the function of receiving information relating to the proceeds of crime',

and the 'and' preceding paragraph (m) is omitted.

81. Inspection of overseas information systems

After section 54 of the Data Protection Act 1998 (c. 29) there is inserted—

'54A. Inspection of overseas information systems

(1) The Commissioner may inspect any personal data recorded in—
(a) the Schengen information system,
(b) the Europol information system,
(c) the Customs information system.
(2) The power conferred by subsection (1) is exercisable only for the purpose of assessing whether or not any processing of the data has been or is being carried out in compliance with this Act.
(3) The power includes power to inspect, operate and test equipment which is used for the processing of personal data.
(4) Before exercising the power, the Commissioner must give notice in writing of his intention to do so to the data controller.
(5) But subsection (4) does not apply if the Commissioner considers that the case is one of urgency.
(6) Any person who—
(a) intentionally obstructs a person exercising the power conferred by subsection (1), or

(b) fails without reasonable excuse to give any person exercising the power any assistance he may reasonably require,

is guilty of an offence.

(7) In this section—

'the Customs information system' means the information system established under Chapter II of the Convention on the Use of Information Technology for Customs Purposes,

'the Europol information system' means the information system established under Title II of the Convention on the Establishment of a European Police Office,

'the Schengen information system' means the information system established under Title IV of the Convention implementing the Schengen Agreement of 14th June 1985, or any system established in its place in pursuance of any Community obligation.'

82. Driver licensing information

Information held in any form—

(a) by the Secretary of State under Part 3 of the Road Traffic Act 1988 (c. 52), or

(b) by the Department of the Environment under Part 2 of the Road Traffic (Northern Ireland) Order 1981 (S.I. 1981/154 (N.I. 1)),

(licensing of drivers of vehicles) may be disclosed for the purposes of the Schengen information system (within the meaning of section 81).

Cross-border surveillance

83. Foreign surveillance operations

After section 76 of the Regulation of Investigatory Powers Act 2000 (c. 23) there is inserted—

'76A. Foreign surveillance operations

(1) This section applies where—

(a) a foreign police or customs officer is carrying out relevant surveillance outside the United Kingdom which is lawful under the law of the country or territory in which it is being carried out;

(b) circumstances arise by virtue of which the surveillance can for the time being be carried out only in the United Kingdom; and

(c) it is not reasonably practicable in those circumstances for a United Kingdom officer to carry out the surveillance in the United Kingdom in accordance with an authorisation under Part 2 or the Regulation of Investigatory Powers (Scotland) Act 2000.

(2) 'Relevant surveillance' means surveillance which—

(a) is carried out in relation to a person who is suspected of having committed a relevant crime; and

(b) is, for the purposes of Part 2, directed surveillance or intrusive surveillance.

(3) 'Relevant crime' means crime which—

(a) falls within Article 40(7) of the Schengen Convention; or

(b) is crime for the purposes of any other international agreement to which the United Kingdom is a party and which is specified for the purposes of this section in an order made by the Secretary of State with the consent of the Scottish Ministers.

(4) Relevant surveillance carried out by the foreign police or customs officer in the United Kingdom during the permitted period is to be lawful for all purposes if—

(a) the condition mentioned in subsection (6) is satisfied;

(b) the officer carries out the surveillance only in places to which members of the public have or are permitted to have access, whether on payment or otherwise; and

(c) conditions specified in any order made by the Secretary of State with the consent of the Scottish Ministers are satisfied in relation to its carrying out;

but no surveillance is lawful by virtue of this subsection if the officer subsequently seeks to stop and question the person in the United Kingdom in relation to the relevant crime.

(5) The officer is not to be subject to any civil liability in respect of any conduct of his which is incidental to any surveillance that is lawful by virtue of subsection (4).

(6) The condition in this subsection is satisfied if, immediately after the officer enters the United Kingdom—
   (a) he notifies a person designated by the Director General of the National Criminal Intelligence Service of that fact; and
   (b) (if the officer has not done so before) he requests an application to be made for an authorisation under Part 2, or the Regulation of Investigatory Powers (Scotland) Act 2000, for the carrying out of the surveillance.

(7) 'The permitted period' means the period of five hours beginning with the time when the officer enters the United Kingdom.

(8) But a person designated by an order made by the Secretary of State may notify the officer that the surveillance is to cease being lawful by virtue of subsection (4) when he gives the notification.

(9) The Secretary of State is not to make an order under subsection (4) unless a draft of the order has been laid before Parliament and approved by a resolution of each House.

(10) In this section references to a foreign police or customs officer are to a police or customs officer who, in relation to a country or territory other than the United Kingdom, is an officer for the purposes of—
   (a) Article 40 of the Schengen Convention; or
   (b) any other international agreement to which the United Kingdom is a party and which is specified for the purposes of this section in an order made by the Secretary of State with the consent of the Scottish Ministers.

(11) In this section—
   'the Schengen Convention' means the Convention implementing the Schengen Agreement of 14th June 1985;
   'United Kingdom officer' means—
   (a) a member of a police force;
   (b) a member of the National Criminal Intelligence Service;
   (c) a member of the National Crime Squad or of the Scottish Crime Squad (within the meaning of the Regulation of Investigatory Powers (Scotland) Act 2000);
   (d) a customs officer.'

84. Assaults on foreign officers

(1) For the purposes of section 89 of the Police Act 1996 (c. 16) (assaults on constables) any person who is carrying out surveillance in England and Wales under section 76A of the Regulation of Investigatory Powers Act 2000 (c. 23) is to be treated as if he were acting as a constable in the execution of his duty.

(2) For the purposes of section 41 of the Police (Scotland) Act 1967 (c. 77) (assaults on constables) any person who is carrying out surveillance in Scotland under section 76A of that Act of 2000 is to be so treated.

(3) For the purposes of section 66 of the Police (Northern Ireland) Act 1998 (c. 32) (assaults on constables) any person who is carrying out surveillance in Northern Ireland under section 76A of that Act of 2000 is to be so treated.

85.

[. . .][23]

86, 87.

[. . .][24]

False monetary instruments

88. False monetary instruments: England and Wales and Northern Ireland

(1) Section 5 of the Forgery and Counterfeiting Act 1981 (c. 45) (offences relating to money orders, share certificates, passports, etc.) is amended as follows.

---

23 Repealed by the Serious Organised Crime and Police Act 2005.
24 Repealed by SI 2004/1897.

(2) In subsection (5)—
  (a) in paragraph (g), at the end there is inserted 'and other bills of exchange',
  (b) after paragraph (h) there is inserted—
    '(ha) bankers' drafts;
    (hb) promissory notes;',
  (c) after paragraph (j) there is inserted—
    '(ja) debit cards;'.
(3) After subsection (6) there is inserted—
  '(7) An instrument is also an instrument to which this section applies if it is a monetary instrument specified for the purposes of this section by an order made by the Secretary of State.
(8) The power under subsection (7) above is exercisable by statutory instrument subject to annulment in pursuance of a resolution of either House of Parliament.'

89. False monetary instruments: Scotland

After section 46 of the Criminal Law (Consolidation) (Scotland) Act 1995 (c. 39) there is inserted—

'False monetary instruments

46A. False monetary instruments

(1) A person who counterfeits or falsifies a specified monetary instrument with the intention that it be uttered as genuine is guilty of an offence.
(2) A person who has in his custody or under his control, without lawful authority or excuse—
  (a) anything which is, and which he knows or believes to be, a counterfeited or falsified specified monetary instrument; or
  (b) any machine, implement or computer programme, or any paper or other material, which to his knowledge is specially designed or adapted for the making of a specified monetary instrument,
  is guilty of an offence.
(3) For the purposes of subsections (1) and (2)(a) above, it is immaterial that the specified monetary instrument (or purported specified monetary instrument) is not in a fit state to be uttered or that the counterfeiting or falsifying of it has not been finished or perfected.
(4) A person guilty of an offence under this section is liable on summary conviction—
  (a) to a fine not exceeding the statutory maximum;
  (b) to imprisonment for a term not exceeding six months; or
  (c) both to a fine and to such imprisonment.
(5) A person guilty of an offence—
  (a) under subsection (1) above is liable on conviction on indictment—
    (i) to a fine;
    (ii) to imprisonment for a term not exceeding ten years; or
    (iii) both to a fine and to such imprisonment;
  (b) under subsection (2) above is liable on conviction on indictment—
    (i) to a fine;
    (ii) if it is proved that the offence was committed with the intention that the specified monetary instrument in question be uttered (or as the case may be that a specified monetary instrument be uttered), to imprisonment for a term not exceeding ten years and if it is not so proved, to imprisonment for a term not exceeding two years; or
    (iii) both to a fine and to imprisonment for a term not exceeding ten years, if it is proved as mentioned in sub-paragraph (ii) above, or both to a fine and to imprisonment for a term not exceeding two years if it is not so proved.
(6) Where an offence under this section which has been committed—
  (a) by a body corporate is proved to have been committed with the consent or connivance of, or to be attributable to any neglect on the part of, a director, manager, secretary or other similar officer of that body; or
  (b) by a Scottish partnership is proved to have been committed with the consent or connivance of, or to be attributable to any neglect on the part of, a member of that partnership,

or by any person who was purporting to act in any such capacity, he as well as the body corporate, or as the case may be the partnership, is guilty of that offence and is liable to be proceeded against and punished accordingly.

(7) Where the affairs of a body corporate are managed by its members, subsection (6) above applies in relation to the actings and defaults of a member in connection with his functions of management as if he were a director of the body corporate.

(8) In subsections (1) to (5) above, 'specified' means for the time being specified for the purposes of this section, by order made by the Scottish Ministers.

(9) The power to make an order under subsection (8) above—

(a) includes power to make such incidental, supplemental, transitional or transitory provision as the Scottish Ministers think necessary or expedient; and

(b) is exercisable by statutory instrument.

(10) A statutory instrument containing such an order is subject to annulment in pursuance of a resolution of the Scottish Parliament.'

Freezing of terrorist property

90. Freezing of terrorist property

Schedule 4 is to have effect.

Part 5
Final Provisions

Chapter 1
Amendments and Repeals

91. Amendments and repeals

(1) Schedule 5 (minor and consequential amendments) is to have effect.

(2) The enactments set out in Schedule 6 are repealed to the extent specified.

Chapter 2
Miscellaneous

92. Northern Ireland

An Order in Council under paragraph 1(1) of the Schedule to the Northern Ireland Act 2000 (c. 1) (legislation for Northern Ireland during suspension of devolved government) which contains a statement that it is made only for purposes corresponding to those of Chapter 2 of Part 3 of this Act—

(a) is not to be subject to paragraph 2 of that Schedule (affirmative resolution of both Houses of Parliament), but

(b) is to be subject to annulment in pursuance of a resolution of either House of Parliament.

93. Supplementary and consequential provision

(1) The appropriate Minister may by order made by statutory instrument make—

(a) any supplementary, incidental or consequential provision,

(b) any transitory, transitional or saving provision,

which he considers necessary or expedient for the purposes of, in consequence of or for giving full effect to any provision of this Act.

(2) The appropriate Minister means—

(a) in relation to any provision that would, if included in an Act of the Scottish Parliament, be within the legislative competence of that Parliament, the Scottish Ministers,

(b) in relation to any other provision, the Secretary of State.

(3) The provision which may be made under subsection (1) includes provision amending or repealing any enactment or instrument.
(4) An order under this section may make different provision for different purposes.
(5) A statutory instrument (other than an instrument to which subsection (6) applies) containing an order under this section made by the Secretary of State is subject to annulment in pursuance of a resolution of either House of Parliament.
(6) A statutory instrument containing such an order which adds to, replaces or omits any part of the text of an Act is not to be made unless a draft of the instrument has been laid before, and approved by a resolution of, each House of Parliament.
(7) A statutory instrument (other than an instrument to which subsection (8) applies) containing an order under this section made by the Scottish Ministers is subject to annulment in pursuance of a resolution of the Scottish Parliament.
(8) A statutory instrument containing such an order which adds to, replaces or omits any part of the text of an Act or of an Act of the Scottish Parliament is not to be made unless a draft of the instrument has been laid before, and approved by a resolution of, the Scottish Parliament.

94. Commencement

(1) This Act (except this Chapter and the provisions mentioned in subsection (3)) is to come into force on such day as the Secretary of State may by order made by statutory instrument appoint.
(2) Any day appointed for the purposes of Part 1 (other than sections 32 to 41), and the related amendments and repeals, is to be one decided by the Secretary of State and the Scottish Ministers.
(3) The following are to come into force on such day as the Scottish Ministers may by order made by statutory instrument appoint—
  (a) sections 37 to 41,
  (b) section 89.
(4) An order under this section may make different provision for different purposes.

95. Extent

(1) Sections 32 to 36 extend only to England and Wales and Northern Ireland.
(2) Sections 37 to 41 extend only to Scotland.

96. Short title

This Act may be cited as the Crime (International Co-operation) Act 2003.

Schedule 1
Proceedings of a Nominated Court Under Section 15

Section 15

Securing attendance of witnesses

1. The court has the like powers for securing the attendance of a witness as it has for the purposes of other proceedings before the court.
2. In Scotland the court has power to issue a warrant to officers of law to cite witnesses, and section 156 of the Criminal Procedure (Scotland) Act 1995 (c. 46) applies in relation to a witness so cited.

Power to administer oaths

3. The court may take evidence on oath.

Proceedings

4. Rules of court under section 49 may, in particular, make provision in respect of the persons entitled to appear or take part in the proceedings and for excluding the public from the proceedings.

Privilege of witnesses

5.

(1) A person cannot be compelled to give any evidence which he could not be compelled to give—
   (a) in criminal proceedings in the part of the United Kingdom in which the nominated court exercises jurisdiction, or
   (b) subject to sub-paragraph (2), in criminal proceedings in the country from which the request for the evidence has come.

(2) Sub-paragraph (1)(b) does not apply unless the claim of the person questioned to be exempt from giving the evidence is conceded by the court or authority which made the request.

(3) Where the person's claim is not conceded, he may be required to give the evidence to which the claim relates (subject to the other provisions of this paragraph); but the evidence may not be forwarded to the court or authority which requested it if a court in the country in question, on the matter being referred to it, upholds the claim.

(4) A person cannot be compelled to give any evidence if his doing so would be prejudicial to the security of the United Kingdom.

(5) A certificate signed by or on behalf of the Secretary of State or, where the court is in Scotland, the Lord Advocate to the effect that it would be so prejudicial for that person to do so is conclusive evidence of that fact.

(6) A person cannot be compelled to give any evidence in his capacity as an officer or servant of the Crown.

(7) Sub-paragraphs (4) and (6) are without prejudice to the generality of sub-paragraph (1).

Forwarding evidence

6.

(1) The evidence received by the court is to be given to the court or authority that made the request or to the territorial authority for forwarding to the court or authority that made the request.

(2) So far as may be necessary in order to comply with the request—
   (a) where the evidence consists of a document, the original or a copy is to be provided,
   (b) where it consists of any other article, the article itself, or a description, photograph or other representation of it, is to be provided.

Supplementary

7. The Bankers' Books Evidence Act 1879 (c. 11) applies to the proceedings as it applies to other proceedings before the court.

8. No order for costs may be made.

Schedule 2
Evidence Given by Television Link or Telephone

Sections 30 And 31

Part 1
Evidence Given by Television Link

Securing attendance of witnesses

1. The nominated court has the like powers for securing the attendance of the witness to give evidence through the link as it has for the purpose of proceedings before the court.

2. In Scotland the nominated court has power to issue a warrant to officers of law to cite the witness for the purpose of securing his attendance to give evidence through the link, and section 156 of the Criminal Procedure (Scotland) Act 1995 (c. 46) applies in relation to the witness if so cited.

Conduct of hearing

3. The witness is to give evidence in the presence of the nominated court.
4. The nominated court is to establish the identity of the witness.
5. The nominated court is to intervene where it considers it necessary to do so to safeguard the rights of the witness.
6. The evidence is to be given under the supervision of the court of the country concerned.
7. The evidence is to be given in accordance with the laws of that country and with any measures for the protection of the witness agreed between the Secretary of State and the authority in that country which appears to him to have the function of entering into agreements of that kind.
8. Rules of court under section 49 must make provision for the use of interpreters.

Privilege of witness

9.

(1) The witness cannot be compelled to give any evidence which he could not be compelled to give in criminal proceedings in the part of the United Kingdom in which the nominated court exercises jurisdiction.
(2) The witness cannot be compelled to give any evidence if his doing so would be prejudicial to the security of the United Kingdom.
(3) A certificate signed by or on behalf of the Secretary of State or, where the court is in Scotland, the Lord Advocate to the effect that it would be so prejudicial for that person to do so is to be conclusive evidence of that fact.
(4) The witness cannot be compelled to give any evidence in his capacity as an officer or servant of the Crown.
(5) Sub-paragraphs (2) and (4) are without prejudice to the generality of sub-paragraph (1).

Record of hearing

10. Rules of court under section 49 must make provision—
    (a) for the drawing up of a record of the hearing,
    (b) for sending the record to the external authority.

Part 2
Evidence Given by Telephone

Notification of witness

11. The nominated court must notify the witness of the time when and the place at which he is to give evidence by telephone.

Conduct of hearing

12. The nominated court must be satisfied that the witness is willingly giving evidence by telephone.
13. The witness is to give evidence in the presence of the nominated court.
14. The nominated court is to establish the identity of the witness.
15. The evidence is to be given under the supervision of the court of the participating country.
16. The evidence is to be given in accordance with the laws of that country.
17. Rules of court under section 49 must make provision for the use of interpreters.

Schedule 3
Offences for the Purposes of Section 54

SECTION 54

Part 1
Offences Where Order of Disqualification for a Minimum Period Unnecessary

1.

(1) Manslaughter or culpable homicide by the driver of a motor vehicle.

(2) 'Driver'—

(a) in relation to Great Britain, has the same meaning as in the Road Traffic Act 1988 (c. 52),

(b) in relation to Northern Ireland, has the same meaning as in Article 2(2) of the Road Traffic (Northern Ireland) Order 1995 (S.I. 1995/2994 (N.I. 18)).

2. An offence under section 89(1) of the Road Traffic Regulation Act 1984 (c. 27) or Article 43(1) of the Road Traffic Regulation (Northern Ireland) Order 1997 (S.I. 1997/276 (N.I. 2)) (exceeding speed limit).

3. An offence under any of the following sections of the Road Traffic Act 1988 or Articles of the Road Traffic (Northern Ireland) Order 1995—

(a) section 1 or Article 9 (causing death by dangerous driving),

(b) section 2 or Article 10 (dangerous driving),

[(ba) section 2B (causing death by careless, or inconsiderate, driving),][25]

(c) section 3 or Article 12 (careless, and inconsiderate, driving),

[(ca)section 3ZB (causing death by driving: unlicensed, disqualified or uninsured drivers),][26]

(d) section 3A or Article 14 (causing death by careless driving when under influence of drink or drugs),

(e) section 4 or Article 15 (driving, or being in charge, when under influence of drink or drugs),

(f) section 5 or Article 16 (driving, or being in charge, of a motor vehicle with alcohol concentration above prescribed limit),

(g) section 6 or Article 17 (failing to provide a specimen of breath for a breath test),

(h) section 7 or Article 18 (failing to provide specimen for analysis or laboratory test).

4. An offence under section 12 of the Road Traffic Act 1988 (motor racing and speed trials on public ways).

5. An offence under section 103(1)(b) of the Road Traffic Act 1988 or Article 167(1) of the Road Traffic (Northern Ireland) Order 1981 (S.I. 1981/154 (N.I. 1)) (driving while disqualified).

6. An offence under section 170(4) of the Road Traffic Act 1988 or Article 175(2) of the Road Traffic (Northern Ireland) Order 1981 (failing to stop after accident and give particulars or report of accident).

Part 2
Offences Where Order of Disqualification for Minimum Period Necessary

7. An offence which—

(a) is mentioned in Part 1 of Schedule 2 to the Road Traffic Offenders Act 1988 (c. 53) or Part 1 of Schedule 1 to the Road Traffic Offenders (Northern Ireland) Order 1996 (S.I. 1996/1320 (N.I. 10)), but

(b) is not an offence mentioned in Part 1 of this Schedule.

[25] Amended by the Road Safety Act 2006.
[26] Amended by the Road Safety Act 2006.

Schedule 4
Terrorist Property: Freezing Orders

Section 90

1. The Terrorism Act 2000 (c. 11) is amended as follows.
2. In section 123 (orders and regulations), in subsection (2)(i), for 'paragraph' there is substituted 'paragraphs 11A, 25A, 41A and'.
3. In Part 1 of Schedule 4 (forfeiture orders: England and Wales), after paragraph 11 there is inserted—

'Domestic and overseas freezing orders

11A.

(1) This paragraph has effect for the purposes of paragraphs 11B to 11G.
(2) The relevant Framework Decision means the Framework Decision on the execution in the European Union of orders freezing property or evidence adopted by the Council of the European Union on 22nd July 2003.
(3) A listed offence means—
    (a) an offence described in Article 3(2) of the relevant Framework Decision, or
    (b) a prescribed offence or an offence of a prescribed description.
(4) An order under sub-paragraph (3)(b) which, for the purposes of paragraph 11D, prescribes an offence or a description of offences may require that the conduct which constitutes the offence or offences would, if it occurred in a part of the United Kingdom, constitute an offence in that part.
(5) Specified information, in relation to a certificate under paragraph 11B or 11D, means—
    (a) any information required to be given by the form of certificate annexed to the relevant Framework Decision, or
    (b) any prescribed information.
(6) In this paragraph, 'prescribed' means prescribed by an order made by the Secretary of State.
(7) A participating country means—
    (a) a country other than the United Kingdom which is a member State on a day appointed for the commencement of Schedule 4 to the Crime (International Co-operation) Act 2003, and
    (b) any other member State designated by an order made by the Secretary of State.
(8) 'Country' includes territory.
(9) Section 14(2)(a) applies for the purposes of determining what are the proceeds of the commission of an offence.

Domestic freezing orders: certification

11B.

(1) If any of the property to which an application for a restraint order relates is property in a participating country, the applicant may ask the High Court to make a certificate under this paragraph.
(2) The High Court may make a certificate under this paragraph if—
    (a) it makes a restraint order in relation to property in the participating country, and
    (b) it is satisfied that there is a good arguable case that the property is likely to be used for the purposes of a listed offence or is the proceeds of the commission of a listed offence.
(3) A certificate under this paragraph is a certificate which—
    (a) is made for the purposes of the relevant Framework Decision, and
    (b) gives the specified information.
(4) If the High Court makes a certificate under this paragraph—
    (a) the restraint order must provide for notice of the certificate to be given to the person affected by it, and
    (b) paragraph 6(2) to (4) applies to the certificate as it applies to the restraint order.

Sending domestic freezing orders

11C.

(1) If a certificate is made under paragraph 11B, the restraint order and the certificate are to be sent to the Secretary of State for forwarding to—
   (a) a court exercising jurisdiction in the place where the property is situated, or
   (b) any authority recognised by the government of the participating country as the appropriate authority for receiving orders of that kind.

(2) The restraint order and the certificate must be accompanied by a forfeiture order, unless the certificate indicates when the court expects a forfeiture order to be sent.

(3) The certificate must include a translation of it into an appropriate language of the participating country (if that language is not English).

(4) The certificate must be signed by or on behalf of the court and must include a statement as to the accuracy of the information given in it.
   The signature may be an electronic signature.

(5) If the restraint order and the certificate are not accompanied by a forfeiture order, but a forfeiture order is subsequently made, it is to be sent to the Secretary of State for forwarding as mentioned in sub-paragraph (1).

Overseas freezing orders

11D.

(1) Paragraph 11E applies where an overseas freezing order made by an appropriate court or authority in a participating country is received by the Secretary of State from the court or authority which made or confirmed the order.

(2) An overseas freezing order is an order prohibiting dealing with property—
   (a) which is in the United Kingdom,
   (b) which the appropriate court or authority considers is likely to be used for the purposes of a listed offence or is the proceeds of the commission of such an offence, and
   (c) in respect of which an order has been or may be made by a court exercising criminal jurisdiction in the participating country for the forfeiture of the property, and in respect of which the following requirements of this paragraph are met.

(3) The action which the appropriate court or authority considered would constitute or, as the case may be, constituted the listed offence is action done as an act of terrorism or for the purposes of terrorism.

(4) The order must relate to—
   (a) criminal proceedings instituted in the participating country, or
   (b) a criminal investigation being carried on there.

(5) The order must be accompanied by a certificate which gives the specified information; but a certificate may be treated as giving any specified information which is not given in it if the Secretary of State has the information in question.

(6) The certificate must—
   (a) be signed by or on behalf of the court or authority which made or confirmed the order,
   (b) include a statement as to the accuracy of the information given in it,
   (c) if it is not in English, include a translation of it into English (or, if appropriate, Welsh).
   The signature may be an electronic signature.

(7) The order must be accompanied by an order made by a court exercising criminal jurisdiction in that country for the forfeiture of the property, unless the certificate indicates when such an order is expected to be sent.

(8) An appropriate court or authority in a participating country in relation to an overseas freezing order is—
   (a) a court exercising criminal jurisdiction in the country,
   (b) a prosecuting authority in the country,
   (c) any other authority in the country which appears to the Secretary of State to have the function of making such orders.

(9) References in paragraphs 11E to 11G to an overseas freezing order include its accompanying certificate.

ENFORCEMENT OF OVERSEAS FREEZING ORDERS

11E.

(1) Where this paragraph applies the Secretary of State must send a copy of the overseas freezing order to the High Court and to the Director of Public Prosecutions.

(2) The court is to consider the overseas freezing order on its own initiative within a period prescribed by rules of court.

(3) Before giving effect to the overseas freezing order, the court must give the Director an opportunity to be heard.

(4) The court may decide not to give effect to the overseas freezing order only if, in its opinion, giving effect to it would be incompatible with any of the Convention rights (within the meaning of the Human Rights Act 1998).

11F. The High Court may postpone giving effect to an overseas freezing order in respect of any property—

(a) in order to avoid prejudicing a criminal investigation which is taking place in the United Kingdom, or

(b) if, under an order made by a court in criminal proceedings in the United Kingdom, the property may not be dealt with.

11G.

(1) Where the High Court decides to give effect to an overseas freezing order, it must—

(a) register the order in that court,

(b) provide for notice of the registration to be given to any person affected by it.

(2) For the purpose of enforcing an overseas freezing order registered in the High Court, the order is to have effect as if it were an order made by that court.

(3) Paragraph 7 applies to an overseas freezing order registered in the High Court as it applies to a restraint order under paragraph 5.

(4) The High Court may cancel the registration of the order, or vary the property to which the order applies, on an application by the Director of Public Prosecutions or any other person affected by it, if or to the extent that—

(a) the court is of the opinion mentioned in paragraph 11E(4), or

(b) the court is of the opinion that the order has ceased to have effect in the participating country.

(5) Her Majesty may by Order in Council make further provision for the enforcement in England and Wales of registered overseas freezing orders.

(6) An Order in Council under this paragraph—

(a) may make different provision for different cases,

(b) is not to be made unless a draft of it has been laid before and approved by resolution of each House of Parliament.'

4. In paragraph 14 of that Schedule (enforcement of orders made in designated countries), in sub-paragraph (2), after the second 'order' there is inserted '(other than an overseas freezing order within the meaning of paragraph 11D)'.

5. In Part 2 of that Schedule (forfeiture orders: Scotland), after paragraph 25 there is inserted—

'DOMESTIC AND OVERSEAS FREEZING ORDERS

25A.

(1) This paragraph has effect for the purposes of paragraphs 25B to 25G.

(2) The relevant Framework Decision means the Framework Decision on the execution in the European Union of orders freezing property or evidence adopted by the Council of the European Union on 22nd July 2003.

(3) A listed offence means—

(a) an offence described in Article 3(2) of the relevant Framework Decision, or

(b) a prescribed offence or an offence of a prescribed description.

(4) An order under sub-paragraph (3)(b) which, for the purposes of paragraph 25D, prescribes an offence or a description of offences may require that the conduct which constitutes the offence or offences would, if it occurred in a part of the United Kingdom, constitute an offence in that part.

(5) Specified information, in relation to a certificate under paragraph 25B or 25D, means—

(a) any information required to be given by the form of certificate annexed to the relevant Framework Decision, or

(b) any prescribed information.

(6) In this paragraph, 'prescribed' means prescribed by an order made by the Secretary of State.

(7) A participating country means—

(a) a country other than the United Kingdom which is a member State on a day appointed for the commencement of Schedule 4 to the Crime (International Co-operation) Act 2003, and

(b) any other member State designated by an order made by the Secretary of State.

(8) 'Country' includes territory.

(9) Section 14(2)(a) applies for the purposes of determining what are the proceeds of the commission of an offence.

Domestic freezing orders: certification

25B.

(1) If any of the property to which an application for a restraint order relates is property in a participating country, the applicant may ask the Court of Session to make a certificate under this paragraph.

(2) The Court of Session may make a certificate under this paragraph if—

(a) it makes a restraint order in relation to property in the participating country, and

(b) it is satisfied that there is a good arguable case that the property is likely to be used for the purposes of a listed offence or is the proceeds of the commission of a listed offence.

(3) A certificate under this paragraph is a certificate which—

(a) is made for the purposes of the relevant Framework Decision, and

(b) gives the specified information.

(4) If the Court of Session makes a certificate under this paragraph—

(a) the restraint order must provide for notice of the certificate to be given to the person affected by it, and

(b) paragraph 19(2) to (4) applies to the certificate as it applies to the restraint order.

Sending domestic freezing orders

25C.

(1) If a certificate is made under paragraph 25B, the restraint order and the certificate are to be sent to the Lord Advocate for forwarding to—

(a) a court exercising jurisdiction in the place where the property is situated, or

(b) any authority recognised by the government of the participating country as the appropriate authority for receiving orders of that kind.

(2) The restraint order and the certificate must be accompanied by a forfeiture order, unless the certificate indicates when the court expects a forfeiture order to be sent.

(3) The certificate must include a translation of it into an appropriate language of the participating country (if that language is not English).

(4) The certificate must be signed by or on behalf of the court and must include a statement as to the accuracy of the information given in it.

The signature may be an electronic signature.

(5) If the restraint order and the certificate are not accompanied by a forfeiture order, but a forfeiture order is subsequently made, it is to be sent to the Lord Advocate for forwarding as mentioned in sub-paragraph (1).

Overseas freezing orders

25D.

(1) Paragraph 25E applies where an overseas freezing order made by an appropriate court or authority in a participating country is received by the Secretary of State from the court or authority which made or confirmed the order.

(2) An overseas freezing order is an order prohibiting dealing with property—

(a) which is in the United Kingdom,

(b) which the appropriate court or authority considers is likely to be used for the purposes of a listed offence or is the proceeds of the commission of such an offence, and

(c) in respect of which an order has been or may be made by a court exercising criminal jurisdiction in the participating country for the forfeiture of the property, and in respect of which the following requirements of this paragraph are met.

(3) The action which the appropriate court or authority considered would constitute or, as the case may be, constituted the listed offence is action done as an act of terrorism or for the purposes of terrorism.

(4) The order must relate to—

(a) criminal proceedings instituted in the participating country, or

(b) a criminal investigation being carried on there.

(5) The order must be accompanied by a certificate which gives the specified information; but a certificate may be treated as giving any specified information which is not given in it if the Secretary of State has the information in question.

(6) The certificate must—

(a) be signed by or on behalf of the court or authority which made or confirmed the order,

(b) include a statement as to the accuracy of the information given in it,

(c) if it is not in English, include a translation of it into English.

The signature may be an electronic signature.

(7) The order must be accompanied by an order made by a court exercising criminal jurisdiction in that country for the forfeiture of the property, unless the certificate indicates when such an order is expected to be sent.

(8) An appropriate court or authority in a participating country in relation to an overseas freezing order is—

(a) a court exercising criminal jurisdiction in the country,

(b) a prosecuting authority in the country,

(c) any other authority in the country which appears to the Secretary of State to have the function of making such orders.

(9) References in paragraphs 25E to 25G to an overseas freezing order include its accompanying certificate.

Enforcement of overseas freezing orders

25E.

(1) Where this paragraph applies the Secretary of State must send a copy of the overseas freezing order to the Court of Session and to the Lord Advocate.

(2) The court is to consider the overseas freezing order on its own initiative within a period prescribed by rules of court.

(3) Before giving effect to the overseas freezing order, the court must give the Lord Advocate an opportunity to be heard.

(4) The court may decide not to give effect to the overseas freezing order only if, in its opinion, giving effect to it would be incompatible with any of the Convention rights (within the meaning of the Human Rights Act 1998).

25F.

The Court of Session may postpone giving effect to an overseas freezing order in respect of any property—

(a) in order to avoid prejudicing a criminal investigation which is taking place in the United Kingdom, or

(b) if, under an order made by a court in criminal proceedings in the United Kingdom, the property may not be dealt with.

25G.

(1) Where the Court of Session decides to give effect to an overseas freezing order, the Deputy Principal Clerk of Session must—
  (a) register the order in the Books of Council and Session,
  (b) provide for notice of the registration to be given to any person affected by it.

(2) For the purpose of enforcing an overseas freezing order registered in the Books of Council and Session, the order is to have effect as if it were an order made by the Court of Session.

(3) Paragraphs 20 and 21 apply to an overseas freezing order registered in the Books of Council and Session as they apply to a restraint order under paragraph 18.

(4) The Court of Session may cancel the registration of the order, or vary the property to which the order applies, on an application by the Lord Advocate or any other person affected by it, if or to the extent that—
  (a) the court is of the opinion mentioned in paragraph 25E(4), or
  (b) the court is of the opinion that the order has ceased to have effect in the participating country.

(5) Her Majesty may by Order in Council make further provision for the enforcement in Scotland of registered overseas freezing orders.

(6) An Order in Council under this paragraph—
  (a) may make different provision for different cases,
  (b) is not to be made unless a draft of it has been laid before and approved by resolution of each House of Parliament.'

6. In paragraph 28 of that Schedule (enforcement of orders made in designated countries), in sub-paragraph (2), after the second 'order' there is inserted '(other than an overseas freezing order within the meaning of paragraph 25D)'.

7. In Part 3 of that Schedule (forfeiture orders: Northern Ireland), after paragraph 41 there is inserted—

'DOMESTIC AND OVERSEAS FREEZING ORDERS

41A.

(1) This paragraph has effect for the purposes of paragraphs 41B to 41G.

(2) The relevant Framework Decision means the Framework Decision on the execution in the European Union of orders freezing property or evidence adopted by the Council of the European Union on 22nd July 2003.

(3) A listed offence means—
  (a) an offence described in Article 3(2) of the relevant Framework Decision, or
  (b) a prescribed offence or an offence of a prescribed description.

(4) An order under sub-paragraph (3)(b) which, for the purposes of paragraph 41D, prescribes an offence or a description of offences may require that the conduct which constitutes the offence or offences would, if it occurred in a part of the United Kingdom, constitute an offence in that part.

(5) Specified information, in relation to a certificate under paragraph 41B or 41D, means—
  (a) any information required to be given by the form of certificate annexed to the relevant Framework Decision, or
  (b) any prescribed information.

(6) In this paragraph, 'prescribed' means prescribed by an order made by the Secretary of State.

(7) A participating country means—
  (a) a country other than the United Kingdom which is a member State on a day appointed for the commencement of Schedule 4 to the Crime (International Co-operation) Act 2003, and
  (b) any other member State designated by an order made by the Secretary of State.

(8) 'Country' includes territory.

(9) Section 14(2)(a) applies for the purposes of determining what are the proceeds of the commission of an offence.

Domestic freezing orders: certification

41B.

(1) If any of the property to which an application for a restraint order relates is property in a participating country, the applicant may ask the High Court to make a certificate under this paragraph.

(2) The High Court may make a certificate under this paragraph if—

(a) it makes a restraint order in relation to property in the participating country, and

(b) it is satisfied that there is a good arguable case that the property is likely to be used for the purposes of a listed offence or is the proceeds of the commission of a listed offence.

(3) A certificate under this paragraph is a certificate which—

(a) is made for the purposes of the relevant Framework Decision, and

(b) gives the specified information.

(4) If the High Court makes a certificate under this paragraph—

(a) the restraint order must provide for notice of the certificate to be given to the person affected by it, and

(b) paragraph 34(2) to (4) applies to the certificate as it applies to the restraint order.

Sending domestic freezing orders

41C.

(1) If a certificate is made under paragraph 41B, the restraint order and the certificate are to be sent to the Secretary of State for forwarding to—

(a) a court exercising jurisdiction in the place where the property is situated, or

(b) any authority recognised by the government of the participating country as the appropriate authority for receiving orders of that kind.

(2) The restraint order and the certificate must be accompanied by a forfeiture order, unless the certificate indicates when the court expects a forfeiture order to be sent.

(3) The certificate must include a translation of it into an appropriate language of the participating country (if that language is not English).

(4) The certificate must be signed by or on behalf of the court and must include a statement as to the accuracy of the information given in it.

The signature may be an electronic signature.

(5) If the restraint order and the certificate are not accompanied by a forfeiture order, but a forfeiture order is subsequently made, it is to be sent to the Secretary of State for forwarding as mentioned in sub-paragraph (1).

Overseas freezing orders

41D.

(1) Paragraph 41E applies where an overseas freezing order made by an appropriate court or authority in a participating country is received by the Secretary of State from the court or authority which made or confirmed the order.

(2) An overseas freezing order is an order prohibiting dealing with property—

(a) which is in the United Kingdom,

(b) which the appropriate court or authority considers is likely to be used for the purposes of a listed offence or is the proceeds of the commission of such an offence, and

(c) in respect of which an order has been or may be made by a court exercising criminal jurisdiction in the participating country for the forfeiture of the property, and in respect of which the following requirements of this paragraph are met.

(3) The action which the appropriate court or authority considered would constitute or, as the case may be, constituted the listed offence is action done as an act of terrorism or for the purposes of terrorism.

(4) The order must relate to—

(a) criminal proceedings instituted in the participating country, or

(b) a criminal investigation being carried on there.

(5) The order must be accompanied by a certificate which gives the specified information; but a certificate may be treated as giving any specified information which is not given in it if the Secretary of State has the information in question.

(6) The certificate must—

(a) be signed by or on behalf of the court or authority which made or confirmed the order,

(b) include a statement as to the accuracy of the information given in it,

(c) if it is not in English, include a translation of it into English.

The signature may be an electronic signature.

(7) The order must be accompanied by an order made by a court exercising criminal jurisdiction in that country for the forfeiture of the property, unless the certificate indicates when such an order is expected to be sent.

(8) An appropriate court or authority in a participating country in relation to an overseas freezing order is—

(a) a court exercising criminal jurisdiction in the country,

(b) a prosecuting authority in the country,

(c) any other authority in the country which appears to the Secretary of State to have the function of making such orders.

(9) References in paragraphs 41E to 41G to an overseas freezing order include its accompanying certificate.

Enforcement of overseas freezing orders

41E.

(1) Where this paragraph applies the Secretary of State must send a copy of the overseas freezing order to the High Court and to the Director of Public Prosecutions for Northern Ireland.

(2) The court is to consider the overseas freezing order on its own initiative within a period prescribed by rules of court.

(3) Before giving effect to the overseas freezing order, the court must give the Director an opportunity to be heard.

(4) The court may decide not to give effect to the overseas freezing order only if, in its opinion, giving effect to it would be incompatible with any of the Convention rights (within the meaning of the Human Rights Act 1998).

41F.

The High Court may postpone giving effect to an overseas freezing order in respect of any property—

(a) in order to avoid prejudicing a criminal investigation which is taking place in the United Kingdom, or

(b) if, under an order made by a court in criminal proceedings in the United Kingdom, the property may not be dealt with.

41G.

(1) Where the High Court decides to give effect to an overseas freezing order, it must—

(a) register the order in that court,

(b) provide for notice of the registration to be given to any person affected by it.

(2) For the purpose of enforcing an overseas freezing order registered in the High Court, the order is to have effect as if it were an order made by that court.

(3) Paragraph 35 applies to an overseas freezing order registered in the High Court as it applies to a restraint order under paragraph 33.

(4) The High Court may cancel the registration of the order, or vary the property to which the order applies, on an application by the Director of Public Prosecutions for Northern Ireland or any other person affected by it, if or to the extent that—

(a) the court is of the opinion mentioned in paragraph 41E(4), or

(b) the court is of the opinion that the order has ceased to have effect in the participating country.

(5) Her Majesty may by Order in Council make further provision for the enforcement in Northern Ireland of registered overseas freezing orders.

(6) An Order in Council under this paragraph—

(a) may make different provision for different cases,

(b) is not to be made unless a draft of it has been laid before and approved by resolution of each House of Parliament.'

8. In paragraph 44 of that Schedule (enforcement of orders made in designated countries), in sub-paragraph (2), after the second 'order' there is inserted '(other than an overseas freezing order within the meaning of paragraph 41D)'.
9. In Part 4 of that Schedule (insolvency), in paragraph 45, at the end of paragraph (c) of the definition of 'restraint order' there is inserted 'or an order which is enforceable in England and Wales, Scotland or Northern Ireland by virtue of paragraph 11G, 25G or 41G'.

Schedule 5
Minor and Consequential Amendments

Section 91
The Internationally Protected Persons Act 1978 (C. 17)

1. The Internationally Protected Persons Act 1978 is amended as follows.
2. In section 2 (supplementary provisions), in subsections (1) and (2), for 'and the United Nations Personnel Act 1997' there is substituted, 'the United Nations Personnel Act 1997 and the Terrorism Act 2000'.

The Suppression of Terrorism Act 1978 (C. 26)

3. The Suppression of Terrorism Act 1978 is amended as follows.
4. In section 4 (jurisdiction in respect of offences committed outside United Kingdom), in subsections (4) and (5), for 'and the United Nations Personnel Act 1997' there is substituted, 'the United Nations Personnel Act 1997 and the Terrorism Act 2000'.

The Road Traffic (Northern Ireland) Order 1981 (S.I. 1981/154 (N.I. 1))

5. The Road Traffic (Northern Ireland) Order 1981 is amended as follows.
6. In Article 4 (exceptions to offence under Article 3), in paragraph (3)(a), after 'Road Traffic Orders' there is inserted 'or Chapter 1 of Part 3 of the Crime (International Co-operation) Act 2003'.

The Nuclear Material (Offences) Act 1983 (C. 18)

7. The Nuclear Material (Offences) Act 1983 is amended as follows.
8. In section 3 (supplemental), in subsections (1) and (2), for 'and the United Nations Personnel Act 1997' there is substituted, 'the United Nations Personnel Act 1997 and the Terrorism Act 2000'.

The Child Abduction Act 1984 (C. 37)

9. The Child Abduction Act 1984 is amended as follows.
10. In section 11 (consequential amendments and repeals), in subsection (3), after 'the Internationally Protected Persons Act 1978' there is inserted 'and sections 63B(2) and 63C(2) of the Terrorism Act 2000'.

The Criminal Justice Act 1987 (C. 38)

11. The Criminal Justice Act 1987 is amended as follows.
12. In section 2 (investigation powers of Director of Serious Fraud Office)—

    (a) in subsection (1A), for paragraph (b) there is substituted—

    '(b) the Secretary of State acting under section 15(2) of the Crime (International Co-operation) Act 2003, in response to a request received by him from a person mentioned in section 13(2) of that Act (an 'overseas authority').',

(b) in subsection (8A), for the words from 'furnished' to the end there is substituted 'given to the overseas authority which requested it or given to the Secretary of State for forwarding to that overseas authority)',
(c) subsection (8B) is omitted,
(d) in subsection (8C), for 'transmitted' (in both places) there is substituted 'forwarded',
(e) in subsection (18), ' (8B)' is omitted.

The Criminal Justice Act 1988 (C. 33)

13. The Criminal Justice Act 1988 is amended as follows.
14. In section 24 (business etc. documents), in subsection (4), for 'section 3 of the Criminal Justice (International Co-operation) Act 1990' there is substituted 'section 7 of the Crime (International Co-operation) Act 2003'.
15. In section 26 (statements in documents that appear to have been prepared for the purposes of criminal proceedings or investigations), for 'section 3 of the Criminal Justice (International Co-operation) Act 1990' there is substituted 'section 7 of the Crime (International Co-operation) Act 2003'.
16. In paragraph 6 of Schedule 13 (evidence before courts-martial etc.)—
(a) in sub-paragraph (1)—
(i) for 'section 3 of the Criminal Justice (International Co-operation) Act 1990' there is substituted 'section 7 of the Crime (International Co-operation) Act 2003', and
(ii) for 'letters of request or corresponding documents' there is substituted 'requests for assistance in obtaining outside the United Kingdom evidence', and
(b) in sub-paragraph (4), for 'letters of request or corresponding documents' there is substituted 'requests for assistance in obtaining evidence'.

The Road Traffic Act 1988 (C. 52)

17. The Road Traffic Act 1988 is amended as follows.
18. In section 88 (exceptions to offence under section 87)—
(a) in subsection (1A)(b)(ii), for 'section 4(1) of or paragraph 6(1) or 9(1)' there is substituted 'section 4 of or paragraph 6 or 9',
(b) in subsection (1B)(a), after 'Road Traffic Acts' there is inserted 'or Chapter 1 of Part 3 of the Crime (International Co-operation) Act 2003'.
19. In section 92 (requirements as to physical fitness of drivers), in subsection (7D), after '99D' there is inserted 'or 109C'.
20. In section 94A (driving after refusal or revocation of licence), in subsection (1)—
(a) in paragraph (a)(ii), for 'section 93(1) or (2)' there is substituted 'section 93',
(b) in paragraph (a)(iii)—
(i) after 'section 99C(1) or (2)' there is inserted 'or 109B',
(ii) after 'Community licence' there is inserted 'or Northern Ireland licence',
(c) in paragraph (b)(ii), at the end there is inserted 'or Northern Ireland licence'.
21. In section 97 (grant of licences), in subsection (1)(d), for 'section 4(1) of or paragraph 6(1) or 9(1)' there is substituted 'section 4 of or paragraph 6 or 9'.
22. In section 100 (appeals relating to licences), in subsection (1)—
(a) in paragraph (c), after '99(3)' there is inserted 'or (3A)',
(b) for 'or 99C' there is substituted, '99C or 109B'.
23. In section 105 (regulations)—
(a) in subsection (2)—
(i) in paragraph (a), after 'this Act,' there is inserted 'Northern Ireland licences,',
(ii) in paragraph (b)(iii), after 'this Act' there is inserted ', of Northern Ireland licences',
(iii) in paragraph (ea), after 'counterparts' (in the first place) there is inserted 'of Northern Ireland licences or' and after 'counterparts' (in the second place) there is inserted 'of Northern Ireland licences or (as the case may be)',
(iv) in paragraph (f), before 'Community licences' there is inserted 'Northern Ireland licences or',
(b) in subsection (5), for ', 91A and' there is substituted 'and 91ZA to'.

24. In section 107 (service of notices), for '99B or 99E' there is substituted '99B, 99E or 109A'.
25. In section 108 (interpretation), in subsection (1)—
    (a) in the definition of 'counterpart', the 'and' at the end of paragraph (a) is omitted and after that paragraph there is inserted—
        '(aa) in relation to a Northern Ireland licence, has the meaning given by section 109A of this Act (except in the definition of 'Northern Ireland counterpart' below), and',
    (b) in the definition of 'Northern Ireland driving licence' and 'Northern Ireland licence', at the end there is inserted 'and 'Northern Ireland counterpart' means the document issued with the Northern Ireland licence as a counterpart under the law of Northern Ireland'.
26. In section 109 (provisions as to Northern Ireland drivers' licences)—
    (a) in subsection (1), after 'Great Britain,' there is inserted 'in accordance with that licence,',
    (b) in subsection (2), paragraph (b) and the 'and' preceding it are omitted,
    (c) subsections (3) to (5) are omitted.
27. In section 164 (power of constables to require production of driving licence etc.)—
    (a) in subsection (3)—
        (i) in paragraph (a), before 'the Secretary of State' there is inserted 'a person is required to deliver his licence and its counterpart to the Secretary of State under section 63 of the Crime (International Co-operation) Act 2003 or',
        (ii) in paragraph (a)(iii), after '99C' there is inserted ', 109B',
        (iii) in paragraph (b), after '99C' there is inserted ', 109B' and after 'or 118' there is inserted 'or section 63 of the Crime (International Co-operation) Act 2003',
    (b) in subsection (11)—
        (i) in the definition of 'licence', after 'this Act' there is inserted, 'a Northern Ireland licence',
        (ii) after "counterpart',' there is inserted "Northern Ireland licence',' .
28. In section 167 (power of arrest for constable in Scotland), before 'Community licence' there is inserted 'Northern Ireland licence or'.
29. In section 173 (forgery of documents, etc.)—
    (a) in subsection (2)(aa), after 'counterpart of a' there is inserted 'Northern Ireland licence or',
    (b) in subsection (4), for 'and 'Community licence' there is substituted, 'Community licence' and 'Northern Ireland licence'.
30. In section 176 (power to seize certain articles)—
    (a) in subsection (1A), before 'Community licence' (in both places) there is inserted 'Northern Ireland licence or',
    (b) in subsection (3A), after 'such licence or' there is inserted 'of a Northern Ireland licence or',
    (c) in subsection (8), for 'and 'Community licence' there is substituted, 'Community licence' and 'Northern Ireland licence'.
31. In section 193A (tramcars and trolley vehicles), in subsection (2)(b), for '91A,' there is substituted '91ZA to'.

The Road Traffic Offenders Act 1988 (C. 53)

32. The Road Traffic Offenders Act 1988 is amended as follows.
33. In section 3 (restriction on institution of proceedings for certain offences), in subsection (2A), after '99D' there is inserted 'or 109C'.
34. In section 26 (interim disqualification), in subsection (10), for the words from 'and 91A(5)' to 'licences)' there is substituted, '91ZA(7) and 91A(5) of this Act'.
35. In section 98 (general interpretation), in subsection (1)—
    (a) in the definition of 'the provisions connected with the licensing of drivers', for '91A,' there is substituted '91ZA to',
    (b) for 'and 'EEA State' there is substituted, 'EEA State' and 'Northern Ireland licence'.
36. In Schedule 1 (offences to which sections 1, 6, 11 and 12(1) of the Act apply)—
    (a) in the entry for section 94(3) of the Road Traffic Act 1988, in column 1, at the end there is inserted 'or 109C',
    (b) in the entry for section 94(3A) of that Act, in column 1, at the end there is inserted 'or 109C(c)',
    (c) in the entry for section 94A of that Act, in column 2, at the end there is inserted 'or 109B',
    (d) in the entry for section 99B(11) of that Act—

(i) in column 1, at the end there is inserted 'and that subsection as applied by RTA section 109A(5)',
(ii) in column 2, at the end there is inserted 'or a requirement under section 99B(6) or (7) as applied by section 109A(5)'.

37. In Schedule 2 (prosecution and punishment of offences)—
(a) in the entry for section 94(3) of the Road Traffic Act 1988, in column 2, at the end there is inserted 'or 109C',
(b) in the entry for section 94(3A) of that Act, in column 2, at the end there is inserted 'or 109C(c)',
(c) in the entry for section 94A of that Act, in column 2, at the end there is inserted 'or 109B',
(d) in the entry for section 99B(11) of that Act—
(i) in column 1, at the end there is inserted 'and that subsection as applied by RTA section 109A(5)',
(ii) in column 2, at the end there is inserted 'or a requirement under section 99B(6) or (7) as applied by section 109A(5)',
(e) the entry for section 109 of that Act is omitted,
(f) before the entry for section 114 of that Act there is inserted—

'RTA section 109B(4)	Failure to deliver Northern Ireland licence to Secretary of State when required by notice under section 109B.	Summarily	Level 3 on the standard scale'

The Criminal Justice (Evidence, Etc.) (Northern Ireland) Order 1988 (S.I. 1988/1847 (N.I. 17))

38. The Criminal Justice (Evidence, Etc.) (Northern Ireland) Order 1988 is amended as follows.
39. In Article 4 (business etc. documents), in paragraph (4), for 'section 3 of the Criminal Justice (International Co-operation) Act 1990' there is substituted 'section 7 of the Crime (International Co-operation) Act 2003'.
40. In Article 6 (statements in documents that appear to have been prepared for the purposes of criminal proceedings or investigations), for 'section 3 of the Criminal Justice (International Co-operation) Act 1990' there is substituted 'section 7 of the Crime (International Co-operation) Act 2003'.

The Criminal Justice (International Co-Operation) Act 1990 (C. 5)

41. The Criminal Justice (International Co-operation) Act 1990 is amended as follows.
42. Sections 1 to 4, 7, 8 and 11 (mutual service of process and provision of evidence) are omitted.
43. In section 5 (transfer of UK prisoner to give evidence or assist investigation overseas), after subsection (3) there is inserted—
'(3A) A warrant under this section has effect in spite of section 127(1) of the Army Act 1955, section 127(1) of the Air Force Act 1955 or section 82A(1) of the Naval Discipline Act 1957 (restriction on removing persons out of the United Kingdom who are serving military sentences).'
44. Schedule 1 (proceedings of nominated court) is omitted.

The Road Traffic (New Drivers) Act 1995 (C. 13)

45. The Road Traffic (New Drivers) Act 1995 is amended as follows.
46. In section 2 (surrender of licences), at the end there is inserted—
'(6) In this section and section 3 "licence" includes a Northern Ireland licence.'
47. In section 3 (revocation of licences)—
(a) after subsection (1) there is inserted—
'(1A) Where the Secretary of State serves on the holder of a Northern Ireland licence a notice under subsection (1), the Secretary of State must send to the licensing authority in Northern Ireland—

(a) particulars of the notice; and
(b) the Northern Ireland licence.

(1B) Where the Secretary of State is sent by that licensing authority particulars of a notice served on the holder of a licence under a provision of Northern Ireland law corresponding to subsection (1), he must by notice served on the holder revoke the licence.',

(b) . . .[27]

(c) at the end, there is inserted—

'(3) In this section references to the revocation of a person's Northern Ireland licence are references to its revocation as respects Great Britain; and, accordingly, the person ceases to be authorised by virtue of section 109(1) of the Road Traffic Act 1988 to drive in Great Britain a motor vehicle of any class.'

48. In section 4 (re-testing)—
(a) in subsection (1)—
(i) for 'section 3(1)' there is substituted 'section 3',
(ii) after 'full licence' (in the second place it occurs) there is inserted 'or (as the case may be) full Northern Ireland licence',
(b) after subsection (1) there is inserted—
'(1A) Subject to subsection (5), the Secretary of State may not under that Part grant a person whose Northern Ireland licence has been revoked under a provision of Northern Ireland law corresponding to section 3(1) a full licence to drive any class of vehicles in relation to which the revoked licence was issued as a full Northern Ireland licence unless he satisfies the Secretary of State as mentioned in subsection (1).',
(c) in subsections (2) and (3), at the end there is inserted 'or (as the case may be) full Northern Ireland licence',
(d) in subsection (5)—
(i) for 'Subsection (1) does' there is substituted 'Subsections (1) and (1A) do', and
(ii) for 'section 3(1)' there is substituted 'section 3 or whose Northern Ireland licence has been revoked under a provision of Northern Ireland law corresponding to section 3(1)'.

49. In section 5 (restoration of licence without re-testing in certain cases)—
(a) in subsections (1), (4) and (6), for 'section 3(1)' there is substituted 'section 3',
(b) in subsections (3)(a) and (4)(c), after 'section 2' there is inserted 'or (as the case may be) the provision of Northern Ireland law corresponding to that section',
(c) at the end there is inserted—
'(11) Nothing in this section applies in relation to a person whose Northern Ireland licence has been revoked under section 3(1).'

50. In section 7 (early termination of probationary period)—
(a) in paragraph (b), for 'section 3(1)' there is substituted 'section 3',
(b) in paragraph (c)—
(i) for 'paragraph 5(1)' there is substituted 'paragraph 5',
(ii) for 'paragraph 8(1)' there is substituted 'paragraph 8'.

51. In section 9 (interpretation), after subsection (2) there is inserted—
'(2A) In this Act—
'full Northern Ireland licence' means a Northern Ireland licence other than a Northern Ireland provisional licence,
'Northern Ireland provisional licence' means a Northern Ireland licence which corresponds to a provisional licence.'

52. Schedule 1 (newly qualified drivers holding test certificates) is amended as follows.

53. In paragraph 1, at the end there is inserted—
'(3) In this Schedule 'licence' includes a Northern Ireland licence, 'full licence' includes a full Northern Ireland licence and 'provisional licence' includes a Northern Ireland provisional licence.
(4) In relation to the holder of a Northern Ireland licence, the following sub-paragraphs have effect for the purposes of this Schedule.
(5) References to a test certificate are references to a certificate or other document (in this Schedule referred to as a 'Northern Ireland test certificate') which is evidence that he has not more than

[27] Amended by the Road Safety Act 2006.

two years previously passed a Northern Ireland test of competence to drive corresponding to the test mentioned in sub-paragraph (1).

(6) References to prescribed conditions are references to conditions subject to which the Northern Ireland provisional licence was granted.'

54. In paragraph 2, after sub-paragraph (4) there is inserted—

'(4A) In relation to the holder of a Northern Ireland licence, the reference in sub-paragraph (4)(b) to section 98(2) of the Road Traffic Act 1988 is a reference to the corresponding provision under the law of Northern Ireland.'

55. In paragraph 5—

(a) after sub-paragraph (1) there is inserted—

'(1A) Where the Secretary of State serves on the holder of a Northern Ireland licence a notice under sub-paragraph (1), the Secretary of State must send to the licensing authority in Northern Ireland particulars of the notice together with the Northern Ireland test certificate.

(1B) Where the Secretary of State is sent by that licensing authority particulars of a notice served on the holder of a licence under a provision of Northern Ireland law corresponding to sub-paragraph (1), he must by notice served on that person revoke his test certificate.',

(b) . . .[28]

(c) at the end there is inserted—

'(4) In this paragraph and paragraph 8 references to the revocation of a person's Northern Ireland test certificate are references to its revocation as respects Great Britain.

(5) The effect of the revocation of a person's Northern Ireland test certificate as respects Great Britain is that any prescribed conditions to which his Northern Ireland provisional licence ceased to be subject when he became a qualified driver shall again apply for the purposes of section 109(1) of the Road Traffic Act 1988.'

56. In paragraph 6, in sub-paragraph (1), for 'paragraph 5(1)' there is substituted 'paragraph 5, or whose Northern Ireland test certificate has been revoked under a provision of Northern Ireland law corresponding to paragraph 5(1),'.

57. In paragraph 8—

(a) after sub-paragraph (1) there is inserted—

'(1A) Where the Secretary of State serves on the holder of a Northern Ireland licence a notice under sub-paragraph (1), the Secretary of State must send to the licensing authority in Northern Ireland particulars of the notice together with the Northern Ireland licence and the Northern Ireland test certificate.

(1B) Where the Secretary of State is sent by that licensing authority particulars of a notice served on the holder of a licence under a provision of Northern Ireland law corresponding to sub-paragraph (1), he must by notice served on that person revoke his licence and test certificate.',

(b) . . .[29]

(c) at the end there is inserted—

'(3) In this paragraph references to the revocation of a person's Northern Ireland licence are references to its revocation as respects Great Britain; and, accordingly, the person ceases to be authorised by virtue of section 109(1) of the Road Traffic Act 1988 to drive in Great Britain a motor vehicle of any class.'

58. In paragraph 9—

(a) in sub-paragraph (1), for 'paragraph 8(1)' there is substituted 'paragraph 8, or whose Northern Ireland licence and Northern Ireland test certificate have been revoked under a provision of Northern Ireland law corresponding to paragraph 8(1),',

(b) in sub-paragraph (4)(b)(i), after '1988' there is inserted ', or under a provision of Northern Ireland law corresponding to that section,'.

59. In paragraph 10(a)—

(a) for 'paragraph 5(1)' there is substituted 'paragraph 5 (or a person's Northern Ireland test certificate has been revoked under a provision of Northern Ireland law corresponding to paragraph 5(1))',

28 Amended by the Road Safety Act 2006.

29 Amended by the Road Safety Act 2006.

(b) for 'paragraph 8(1)' there is substituted 'paragraph 8 (or a person's Northern Ireland licence and Northern Ireland test certificate have been revoked under a provision of Northern Ireland law corresponding to paragraph 8(1))'.

60. In paragraph 11—
   (a) in sub-paragraphs (1) and (2)(c), for 'paragraph 5(1)' and 'paragraph 8(1)' there is substituted 'paragraph 5' and 'paragraph 8' respectively,
   (b) in sub-paragraph (1)(d), after 'section 2' there is inserted 'or (as the case may be) the provision of Northern Ireland law corresponding to that section'.

The Criminal Law (Consolidation) (Scotland) Act 1995 (c. 39)

61. The Criminal Law (Consolidation) (Scotland) Act 1995 is amended as follows.
62. In section 27 (Lord Advocate's direction), in subsection (2), for 'section 4(2B) of the Criminal Justice (International Co-operation) Act 1990' there is substituted 'section 15(4) of the Crime (International Co-operation) Act 2003'.
63. In section 28 (powers of investigation)—
   (a) in subsection (8), for the words from 'by the' to the end there is substituted 'by virtue of section 27(2) of this Act shall be given to the overseas authority which requested it or to the Lord Advocate for forwarding to that authority',
   (b) subsection (9) is omitted,
   (c) in subsection (10), for 'transmitted' (in both places) there is substituted 'forwarded'.

The Criminal Procedure (Scotland) Act 1995 (c. 46)

64. The Criminal Procedure (Scotland) Act 1995 is amended as follows.
65. In section 210(1)(c) (consideration, in passing sentence of imprisonment or detention, of time spent in custody), at the end there is inserted 'so however that a period of time spent both in custody on remand and, by virtue of section 47(1) of the Crime (International Co-operation) Act 2003, abroad is not for any reason to be discounted in a determination under paragraph (a) above or specification under paragraph (b) above'.

The United Nations Personnel Act 1997 (c. 13)

66. The United Nations Personnel Act 1997 is amended as follows.
67. In section 5 (supplementary provisions), in subsections (1) and (2), for 'and the Nuclear Material (Offences) Act 1983' there is substituted, 'the Nuclear Material (Offences) Act 1983 and the Terrorism Act 2000'.

The Data Protection Act 1998 (c. 29)

68. The Data Protection Act 1998 is amended as follows.
69. In section 28(1) (national security), for 'section' there is substituted 'sections 54A and'.
70. In section 60(2) and (3) (prosecutions and penalties), before 'paragraph 12' there is inserted 'section 54A and'.
71. In section 63(5) (application to the Crown), for 'section' there is substituted 'sections 54A and'.

The Powers of Criminal Courts (Sentencing) Act 2000 (c. 6)

72. The Powers of Criminal Courts (Sentencing) Act 2000 is amended as follows.
73. In section 146 (driving disqualification for any offence)—
   (a) in subsection (4), the 'or' at the end of paragraph (a) is omitted and after that paragraph there is inserted—
      '(aa) in the case where he holds a Northern Ireland licence (within the meaning of Part 3 of the Road Traffic Act 1988), his Northern Ireland licence and its counterpart (if any); or',
   (b) . . .[30]

[30] Amended by the Road Safety Act 2006.

74. In section 147 (driving disqualification where vehicle used for purposes of crime), in subsection (5), the 'or' at the end of paragraph (a) is omitted and after that paragraph there is inserted—
 '(aa) in the case where he holds a Northern Ireland licence (within the meaning of Part 3 of the Road Traffic Act 1988), his Northern Ireland licence and its counterpart (if any); or'.

The Terrorism Act 2000 (c. 11)

75. The Terrorism Act 2000 is amended as follows.
76. In section 121 (interpretation), in the definition of 'premises', before 'includes' (in the first place) there is inserted, 'except in section 63D,'.
77. In section 123 (orders and regulations), in subsection (2), after paragraph (b) there is inserted—
 '(ba) section 63C(3)(d);'.

The Regulation of Investigatory Powers Act 2000 (c. 23)

78. The Regulation of Investigatory Powers Act 2000 is amended as follows.
79. In section 65 (investigatory powers tribunal)—
 (a) in subsection (5)—
  (i) after paragraph (c) there is inserted—
   '(ca) the carrying out of surveillance by a foreign police or customs officer (within the meaning of section 76A);',
  (ii) in paragraph (d), at the beginning there is inserted 'other',
 (b) after subsection (7), there is inserted—
  '(7A) For the purposes of this section conduct also takes place in challengeable circumstances if it takes place, or purports to take place, under section 76A.'
80. In section 78 (orders, regulations and rules), in subsection (3)(a), for 'or 71(9)' there is substituted, '71(9) or 76A(9)'.

The Armed Forces Act 2001 (c. 19)

81. In section 31 of the Armed Forces Act 2001 (power to make provision in consequence of enactments relating to criminal justice), in subsection (7)—
 (a) after 'section' there is inserted 'section 5 of the Criminal Justice (International Co-operation) Act 1990 and',
 (b) for 'is' there is substituted 'are'.

The Proceeds of Crime Act 2002 (C. 29)

82, 83. . . .[31]

Schedule 6
Repeals

Section 91

Short title and chapter	*Extent of repeal*
Criminal Justice Act 1987 (c. 38)	In section 2— subsection (8B), in subsection (18), the word ' (8B)'. In section 3(6), the 'and' preceding paragraph (m).

[31] Amended by the Serious Crime Act 2007.

Short title and chapter	*Extent of repeal*
Road Traffic Act 1988 (c. 52)	In section 108(1), in the definition of 'counterpart', the 'and' at the end of paragraph (a). In section 109— in subsection (2), paragraph (b) and the 'and' preceding it, subsections (3) to (5).
Road Traffic Offenders Act 1988 (c. 53)	In Schedule 2, the entry for section 109 of the Road Traffic Act 1988.
Criminal Justice (International Co-operation) Act 1990 (c. 5)	Sections 1 to 4, 7, 8 and 11. Schedule 1. In Schedule 4, paragraphs 6(2) and 8.
Criminal Justice and Public Order Act 1994 (c. 33)	Section 164(1).
Criminal Law (Consolidation) (Scotland) Act 1995 (c. 39)	Section 28(9).
Powers of Criminal Courts (Sentencing) Act 2000 (c. 6)	In section 146— in subsection (4), the 'or' at the end of paragraph (a), in subsection (5), in the definition of 'counterpart', the 'and' at the end of paragraph (a). In section 147(5), the 'or' at the end of paragraph (a).
Criminal Justice and Police Act 2001 (c. 16)	In Schedule 1, paragraph 49.
Proceeds of Crime Act 2002 (c. 29)	Section 376(5).

APPENDIX M2

Proceeds of Crime Act 2002 (External Requests and Orders) Order 2005 Part 1, 2, and Schedule 5

Proceeds Of Crime Act 2002 (External Requests And Orders) Order 2005

(S.I. 2005/3181)

Made 15th November 2005

Laid before Parliament 25th November 2005

Coming into force 1st January 2006

At the Court at Buckingham Palace, the 15th day of November 2005
Present,
The Queen's Most Excellent Majesty in Council
Her Majesty, in pursuance of sections 444 and 459(2) of the Proceeds of Crime Act 2002, is pleased, by and with the advice of Her Privy Council, to order, and it is ordered, as follows:—

Contents

Chapter 2
External Orders

18. Action on receipt of external order in connection with criminal convictions
19. Authentication by the overseas court
20. Applications to give effect to external orders
21. Conditions for Crown Court to give effect to external orders
22. Registration of external orders
23. Appeal to Court of Appeal about external orders
24. Appeal to [Supreme Court] about external orders
25. Sums in currency other than sterling
26. Time for payment
27. Appointment of enforcement receivers
28. Powers of enforcement receivers in respect of monetary external orders
29. Powers of enforcement receivers in respect of external orders for the recovery of specified property
30. Appointment of Director of Agency's receivers
31. Powers of Director of Agency's receivers in respect of monetary external orders
32. Powers of Director of Agency's receivers in respect of external orders for the recovery of specified property
33. Application of sums by enforcement receivers
34. Sums received by relevant Director
35. Application of sums by Director of Agency's receivers
36. Application of sums received by the Director of the Agency
37. Satisfaction of external order
38. Restrictions relating to enforcement receivers
39. Restrictions relating to Director of the Agency's receivers

Chapter 3
Receivers and Procedure

40. Protection of receiver appointed under articles 15, 27 and 30
41. Further applications by receivers
42. Discharge and variation of receiver orders
43. Management receivers: discharge
44. Appeal to Court of Appeal about receivers
45. Appeal to the [Supreme Court] about receivers
46. Powers of court and receiver
47. Procedure on appeal to Court of Appeal under Part 2
48. Procedure on appeal to [Supreme Court] under Part 2

Chapter 4
Interpretation

49. Property
50. Tainted gifts
51. Gifts and their recipients
52. Value: the basic rule
53. Value of tainted gifts
54. Meaning of 'defendant'
55. Other interpretation
61. Inhibition of property affected by order
62. Arrestment of property affected by order
63. Management administrators
64. Seizure in pursuance of restraint order
65. Restraint orders: restrictions on proceedings and remedies

Schedule 5—Prescribed Enactments—Property Which is not Recoverable Property

Part 1
General Provisions

1. Title and commencement

This Order may be cited as the Proceeds of Crime Act 2002 (External Requests and Orders) Order 2005 and shall come into force on 1st January 2006.

2. Interpretation

In this Order—

'the Act' means the Proceeds of Crime Act 2002;

. . .[1]

'country' includes territory;

'external order' has the meaning set out in section 447(2) of the Act;

'external request' has the meaning set out in section 447(1) of the Act;

'a relevant officer of Revenue and Customs' means such an officer exercising functions by virtue of section 6 of the Commissioners for Revenue and Customs Act 2005.

3. Insolvency practitioners

(1) Paragraphs (2) and (3) apply if a person acting as an insolvency practitioner seizes or disposes of any property in relation to which his functions are not exercisable because—

(a) it is for the time being subject to a restraint order made under article 8, 58 or 95; or

(b) it is for the time being subject to a property freezing order made under article 147, an interim receiving order made under article 151, a prohibitory property order made under article 161 or an interim administration order made under article 167,

and at the time of the seizure or disposal he believes on reasonable grounds that he is entitled (whether in pursuance of an order of a court or otherwise) to seize or dispose of the property.

(2) He is not liable to any person in respect of any loss or damage resulting from the seizure or disposal, except so far as the loss or damage is caused by his negligence.

(3) He has a lien on the property or the proceeds of its sale—

(a) for such of his expenses as were incurred in connection with the liquidation, bankruptcy, sequestration or other proceedings in relation to which he purported to make the seizure or disposal, and

(b) for so much of his remuneration as may reasonably be assigned to his acting in connection with those proceedings.

(4) Paragraph (2) does not prejudice the generality of any provision of the 1985 Act, the 1986 Act, the 1989 Order or any Act or Order which confers a protection from liability on him.

(5) Paragraph (7) applies if—

(a) property is subject to a restraint order made under article 8, 58 or 95,

(b) a person acting as an insolvency practitioner incurs expenses in respect of property subject to the restraint order, and

(c) he does not know (and has no reasonable grounds to believe) that the property is subject to the restraint order.

(6) Paragraph (7) also applies if—

(a) property is subject to a restraint order made under article 8, 58 or 95,

(b) a person acting as an insolvency practitioner incurs expenses which are not ones in respect of property subject to the restraint order, and

(c) the expenses are ones which (but for the effect of the restraint order) might have been met by taking possession of and realising property subject to it.

[1] Amended by SI 2008/302.

(7) Whether or not he has seized or disposed of any property, he is entitled to payment of the expenses under—

(a) article 33(2) [or 34(3)][2] if the restraint order was made under article 7,

(b) article 77(2) or 78(3) if the restraint order was made under article 58,

(c) article 119(2) [or 120(3)][3] if the restraint order was made under article 95.

(8) Paragraph (10) applies if—

(a) property is subject to a property freezing order made under article 147, an interim receiving order made under article 151, a prohibitory property order made under article 161 or an interim administration order made under article 167,

(b) a person acting as an insolvency practitioner incurs expenses in respect of property subject to the order, and

(c) he does not know (and has no reasonable grounds to believe) that the property is subject to the order.

(9) Paragraph (10) also applies if—

(a) property is subject to a property freezing order made under article 147, an interim receiving order made under article 151, a prohibitory property order made under article 161 or an interim administration order made under article 167,

(b) a person acting as an insolvency practitioner incurs expenses which are not ones in respect of property subject to the order, and

(c) the expenses are ones which (but for the effect of the order) might have been met by taking possession of and realising property subject to it.

(10) Whether or not he has seized or disposed of any property, he is entitled to payment of the expenses under article 191.

4. Insolvency practitioners: interpretation

(1) This article applies for the purposes of article 3.

(2) A person acts as an insolvency practitioner if he so acts within the meaning given by section 388 of the 1986 Act or Article 3 of the 1989 Order; but this is subject to paragraphs (3) to (5).

(3) The expression 'person acting as an insolvency practitioner' includes the official receiver acting as receiver or manager of the property concerned.

(4) In applying section 388 of the 1986 Act under paragraph (2) above—

(a) the reference in section 388(2)(a) to a permanent or interim trustee in sequestration must be taken to include a reference to a trustee in sequestration;

(b) section 388(5) (which includes provision that nothing in the section applies to anything done by the official receiver or the Accountant in Bankruptcy) must be ignored.

(5) In applying Article 3 of the 1989 Order under paragraph (2) above, paragraph (5) (which includes provision that nothing in the Article applies to anything done by the official receiver) must be ignored.

(6) The following sub-paragraphs apply to references to Acts or Orders—

(a) the 1913 Act is the Bankruptcy (Scotland) Act 1913;

(b) the 1914 Act is the Bankruptcy Act 1914;

(c) the 1985 Act is the Bankruptcy (Scotland) Act 1985;

(d) the 1986 Act is the Insolvency Act 1986;

(e) the 1989 Order is the Insolvency (Northern Ireland) Order 1989.

(7) An award of sequestration is made on the date of sequestration within the meaning of section 12(4) of the 1985 Act.

5. Orders and regulations

(1) References in this article to subordinate legislation are to—

(a) any order under this Order (other than one falling to be made by a court);

(b) any regulations under this Order.

(2) Subordinate legislation—

(a) may make different provision for different purposes;

---

[2] Amended by SI 2008/302.

[3] Amended by SI 2008/302.

(b) may include supplementary, incidental, saving or transitional provisions.

(3) Any power to make subordinate legislation is exercisable by statutory instrument and, subject to paragraph (4), is subject to annulment in pursuance of a resolution of either House of Parliament.

(4) A statutory instrument containing regulations made under paragraph 6(2) of Schedule 1 is subject to annulment in pursuance of a resolution of the Scottish Parliament.

Part 2
Giving Effect in England and Wales to External Requests in Connection with Criminal Investigations or Proceedings and to External Orders Arising from such Proceedings

Chapter 1
External Requests

6. Action on receipt of external request in connection with criminal investigations or proceedings

(1) Except where paragraph (2) applies, the Secretary of State may refer an external request in connection with criminal investigations or proceedings in the country from which the request was made and concerning relevant property in England or Wales to—

(a) ...[4]

(b) the Director of Public Prosecutions;

(c) the Director of Revenue and Customs Prosecutions, to process it.

(2) This paragraph applies where it appears to the Secretary of State that the request—

(a) is made in connection with criminal investigations or proceedings which relate to an offence involving serious or complex fraud, and

(b) concerns relevant property in England or Wales.

(3) Where paragraph (2) applies, the Secretary of State may refer the request to the Director of the Serious Fraud Office to process it.

(4) In this Chapter 'the relevant Director' means the Director to whom an external request is referred under paragraph (1) or (3).

(5) The relevant Director may ask the overseas authority which made the request for such further information as may be necessary to determine whether the request is likely to satisfy either of the conditions in article 7.

(6) A request under paragraph (5) may include a request for statements which may be used as evidence.

(7) Where a request concerns relevant property which is in Scotland or Northern Ireland as well as England or Wales, so much of the request as concerns such property shall be dealt with under Part 3 or 4, respectively.

7. Conditions for Crown Court to give effect to external request

(1) The Crown Court may exercise the powers conferred by article 8 if either of the following conditions is satisfied.

(2) The first condition is that—

(a) relevant property in England and Wales is identified in the external request;

(b) a criminal investigation has been started in the country from which the external request was made with regard to an offence, and

(c) there is reasonable cause to believe that the alleged offender named in the request has benefited from his criminal conduct.

(3) The second condition is that—

(a) relevant property in England and Wales is identified in the external request;

(b) proceedings for an offence have been started in the country from which the external request was made and not concluded, and

---

[4] Amended by SI 2008/302.

(c) there is reasonable cause to believe that the defendant named in the request has benefited from his criminal conduct.

(4) In determining whether the conditions are satisfied and whether the request is an external request within the meaning of the Act, the Court must have regard to the definitions in subsections (1), (4) to (8) and (11) of section 447 of the Act.

(5) If the first condition is satisfied, references in this Chapter to the defendant are to the alleged offender.

8. Restraint orders

(1) If either condition set out in article 7 is satisfied, the Crown Court may make an order ('a restraint order') prohibiting any specified person from dealing with relevant property which is identified in the external request and specified in the order.

(2) A restraint order may be made subject to exceptions, and an exception may in particular—
  (a) make provision for reasonable living expenses and reasonable legal expenses in connection with the proceedings seeking a restraint order or the registration of an external order;
  (b) make provision for the purpose of enabling any person to carry on any trade, business, profession or occupation;
  (c) be made subject to conditions.

(3) Paragraph (4) applies if—
  (a) a court makes a restraint order, and
  (b) the applicant for the order applies to the court to proceed under paragraph (4) (whether as part of the application for the restraint order or at any time afterwards).

(4) The court may make such order as it believes is appropriate for the purpose of ensuring that the restraint order is effective.

(5) A restraint order does not affect property for the time being subject to a charge under any of these provisions—
  (a) section 9 of the Drug Trafficking Offences Act 1986;
  (b) section 78 of the Criminal Justice Act 1988;
  (c) Article 14 of the Criminal Justice (Confiscation) (Northern Ireland) Order 1990;
  (d) section 27 of the Drug Trafficking Act 1994;
  (e) Article 32 of the Proceeds of Crime (Northern Ireland) Order 1996.

(6) Dealing with property includes removing it from England and Wales.

9. Application, discharge and variation of restraint orders

(1) A restraint order—
  (a) may be made only on an application by the relevant Director;
  (b) may be made on an ex parte application to a judge in chambers.

(2) An application to discharge or vary a restraint order or an order under article 8(4) may be made to the Crown Court by—
  (a) the relevant Director;
  (b) any person affected by the order.

(3) Paragraphs (4) to (7) apply to an application under paragraph (2).

(4) The court—
  (a) may discharge the order;
  (b) may vary the order.

(5) If the condition in article 7 which was satisfied was that proceedings were started, the court must discharge the order if, at the conclusion of the proceedings, no external order has been made.

(6) If the condition in article 7 which was satisfied was that proceedings were started, the court must discharge the order if within a reasonable time an external order has not been registered under Chapter 2 of this Part.

(7) If the condition in article 7 which was satisfied was that an investigation was started, the court must discharge the order if within a reasonable time proceedings for the offence are not started.

10. Appeal to Court of Appeal about restraint orders

(1) If on an application for a restraint order the Crown Court decides not to make one, the relevant Director may appeal to the Court of Appeal against the decision.

(2) If an application is made under article 9(2) in relation to a restraint order or an order under article 8(4), the following persons may appeal to the Court of Appeal in respect of the Crown Court's decision on the application—
   (a) the relevant Director;
   (b) any person affected by the order.
(3) On an appeal under paragraph (1) or (2) the Court of Appeal may—
   (a) confirm the decision, or
   (b) make such order as it believes is appropriate.

11. Appeal to [Supreme Court][5] about restraint orders

(1) An appeal lies to the [Supreme Court][6] from a decision of the Court of Appeal on an appeal under article 10.
(2) An appeal under this article lies at the instance of any person who was a party to the proceedings before the Court of Appeal.
(3) On an appeal under this article the [Supreme Court][7] may—
   (a) confirm the decision of the Court of Appeal, or
   (b) make such order as it believes is appropriate.

12. Seizure in pursuance of restraint order

(1) If a restraint order is in force a constable or a relevant officer of Revenue and Customs may seize any property which is specified in it to prevent its removal from England and Wales.
(2) Property seized under paragraph (1) must be dealt with in accordance with the directions of the court which made the order.

13. Hearsay evidence in restraint proceedings

(1) Evidence must not be excluded in restraint proceedings on the ground that it is hearsay (of whatever degree).
(2) Sections 2 to 4 of the Civil Evidence Act 1995 apply in relation to restraint proceedings as those sections apply in relation to civil proceedings.
(3) Restraint proceedings are proceedings—
   (a) for a restraint order;
   (b) for the discharge or variation of a restraint order;
   (c) on an appeal under article 10 or 11.
(4) Hearsay is a statement which is made otherwise than by a person while giving oral evidence in the proceedings and which is rendered as evidence of the matters stated.
(5) Nothing in this article affects the admissibility of evidence which is admissible apart from this article.

14. Supplementary (restraint orders)

(1) The registration Acts—
   (a) apply in relation to restraint orders as they apply in relation to orders which affect land and are made by the court for the purpose of enforcing judgments or recognisances;
   (b) apply in relation to applications for restraint orders as they apply in relation to other pending land actions.
(2) The registration Acts are—
   (a) the Land Charges Act 1972;
   (b) the Land Registration Act 2002.
(3) But no notice may be entered in the register of title under the Land Registration Act 2002 in respect of a restraint order.

---

[5] Amended by SI 2011/1242.
[6] Amended by SI 2011/1242.
[7] Amended by SI 2011/1242.

15. Appointment of management receivers

(1) Paragraph (2) applies if—
- (a) the Crown Court makes a restraint order, and
- (b) the relevant Director applies to the court to proceed under paragraph (2) (whether as part of the application for the restraint order or at any time afterwards).

(2) The Crown Court may by order appoint a receiver in respect of any property which is specified in the restraint order.

16. Powers of management receivers

(1) If the court appoints a receiver under article 15 it may act under this article on the application of the relevant Director.

(2) The court may by order confer on the receiver the following powers in relation to any property which is specified in the restraint order—
- (a) power to take possession of the property;
- (b) power to manage or otherwise deal with the property;
- (c) power to start, carry on or defend any legal proceedings in respect of the property;
- (d) power to realise so much of the property as is necessary to meet the receiver's remuneration and expenses.

(3) The court may by order confer on the receiver power to enter any premises in England and Wales and to do any of the following—
- (a) search for or inspect anything authorised by the court;
- (b) make or obtain a copy, photograph or other record of anything so authorised;
- (c) remove anything which the receiver is required or authorised to take possession of in pursuance of an order of the court.

(4) The court may by order authorise the receiver to do any of the following for the purpose of the exercise of his functions—
- (a) hold property;
- (b) enter into contracts;
- (c) sue and be sued;
- (d) employ agents;
- (e) execute powers of attorney, deeds or other instruments;
- (f) take any other steps the court thinks appropriate.

(5) The court may order any person who has possession of property which is specified in the restraint order to give possession of it to the receiver.

(6) The court—
- (a) may order a person holding an interest in property which is specified in the restraint order to make to the receiver such payment as the court specifies in respect of a beneficial interest held by the defendant or the recipient of a tainted gift;
- (b) may (on the payment being made) by order transfer, grant or extinguish any interest in the property.

(7) Paragraphs (2), (5) and (6) do not apply to property for the time being subject to a charge under any of these provisions—
- (a) section 9 of the Drug Trafficking Offences Act 1986;
- (b) section 78 of the Criminal Justice Act 1988;
- (c) Article 14 of the Criminal Justice (Confiscation) (Northern Ireland) Order 1990;
- (d) section 27 of the Drug Trafficking Act 1994;
- (e) Article 32 of the Proceeds of Crime (Northern Ireland) Order 1996.

(8) The court must not—
- (a) confer the power mentioned in paragraph (2)(b) or (d) in respect of property, or
- (b) exercise the power conferred on it by paragraph (6) in respect of property,

unless it gives persons holding interests in the property a reasonable opportunity to make representations to it.

[(8A) Paragraph (8), so far as relating to the power mentioned in paragraph (2)(b), does not apply to property which—
- (a) is perishable; or

(b) ought to be disposed of before its value diminishes.][8]

(9) The court may order that a power conferred by an order under this article is subject to such conditions and exceptions as it specifies.

(10) Managing or otherwise dealing with property includes—
(a) selling the property or any part of it or interest in it;
(b) carrying on or arranging for another person to carry on any trade or business the assets of which are or are part of the property;
(c) incurring capital expenditure in respect of the property.

17. Restrictions relating to restraint orders

(1) Paragraphs (2) to (4) apply if a court makes a restraint order.

(2) No distress may be levied against any property which is specified in the order except with the leave of the Crown Court and subject to any terms the Crown Court may impose.

(3) If the order applies to a tenancy of any premises, no landlord or other person to whom rent is payable may exercise a right within paragraph (4) except with the leave of the Crown Court and subject to any terms the Crown Court may impose.

(4) A right is within this paragraph if it is a right of forfeiture by peaceable re-entry in relation to the premises in respect of any failure by the tenant to comply with any term or condition of the tenancy.

(5) If a court in which proceedings are pending in respect of any property is satisfied that a restraint order has been applied for or made in respect of the property, the court may either stay the proceedings or allow them to continue on any terms it thinks fit.

(6) Before exercising any power conferred by paragraph (5), the court must give an opportunity to be heard to—
(a) the relevant Director, and
(b) any receiver appointed in respect of the property under article 15 [or 27].[9]

Chapter 2
External Orders

18. Action on receipt of external order in connection with criminal convictions

(1) Except where paragraph (2) applies, the Secretary of State may refer an external order arising from a criminal conviction in the country from which the order was sent and concerning relevant property in England or Wales to—
(a) ...[10]
(b) the Director of Public Prosecutions;
(c) the Director of Revenue and Customs Prosecutions,
to process it.

(2) This paragraph applies where it appears to the Secretary of State that—
(a) the property or sum of money specified in the order was found, or was believed, to have been obtained as a result of, or in connection with, criminal conduct involving serious or complex fraud, and
(b) the order concerns relevant property in England or Wales.

(3) Where paragraph (2) applies, the Secretary of State may refer the order to the Director of the Serious Fraud Office to process it.

(4) In this Chapter 'the relevant Director' means the Director to whom an external order is referred under paragraph (1) or (3).

(5) Where an order concerns relevant property which is in Scotland or Northern Ireland as well as England or Wales, so much of the request as concerns such property shall be dealt with under Part 3 or 4, respectively.

---

[8] Amended by SI 2008/302.
[9] Amended by SI 2008/302.
[10] Amended by SI 2008/302.

19. Authentication by the overseas court

(1) Paragraph (2) applies where an overseas court has authenticated its involvement in—
  (a) any judgment,
  (b) any order,
  (c) any other document concerned with such a judgment or order or proceedings relating to it.
(2) Where this paragraph applies, any statement in the judgment, order or document is admissible in evidence in proceedings under this Chapter.

20. Applications to give effect to external orders

(1) An application may be made by the relevant Director to the Crown Court to give effect to an external order.
(2) No application to give effect to such an order may be made otherwise than under paragraph (1).
(3) An application under paragraph (1)—
  (a) shall include a request to appoint the relevant Director as the enforcement authority for the order;
  (b) may be made on an ex parte application to a judge in chambers.

21. Conditions for Crown Court to give effect to external orders

(1) The Crown Court must decide to give effect to an external order by registering it where all of the following conditions are satisfied.
(2) The first condition is that the external order was made consequent on the conviction of the person named in the order and no appeal is outstanding in respect of that conviction.
(3) The second condition is that the external order is in force and no appeal is outstanding in respect of it.
(4) The third condition is that giving effect to the external order would not be incompatible with any of the Convention rights (within the meaning of the Human Rights Act 1998) of any person affected by it.
(5) The fourth condition applies only in respect of an external order which authorises the confiscation of property other than money that is specified in the order.
(6) That condition is that the specified property must not be subject to a charge under any of the following provisions—
  (a) section 9 of the Drug Trafficking Offences Act 1986;
  (b) section 78 of the Criminal Justice Act 1988;
  (c) Article 14 of the Criminal Justice (Confiscation) (Northern Ireland) Order 1990;
  (d) section 27 of the Drug Trafficking Act 1994;
  (e) Article 32 of the Proceeds of Crime (Northern Ireland) Order 1996.
(7) In determining whether the order is an external order within the meaning of the Act, the Court must have regard to the definitions in subsections (2), (4), (5), (6), (8) and (10) of section 447 of the Act.
(8) In paragraph (3) 'appeal' includes—
  (a) any proceedings by way of discharging or setting aside the order; and
  (b) an application for a new trial or stay of execution.

22. Registration of external orders

(1) Where the Crown Court decides to give effect to an external order, it must—
  (a) register the order in that court;
  (b) provide for notice of the registration to be given to any person affected by it; and
  (c) appoint the relevant Director as the enforcement authority for the order.
(2) Only an external order registered by the Crown Court may be implemented under this Chapter.
(3) The Crown Court may cancel the registration of the external order, or vary the property to which it applies, on an application by the relevant Director or any person affected by it if, or to the extent that, the court is of the opinion that any of the conditions in article 21 is not satisfied.
(4) The Crown Court must cancel the registration of the external order, on an application by the relevant Director or any person affected by it, if it appears to the court that the order has been satisfied—
  (a) in the case of an order for the recovery of a sum of money specified in it, by payment of the amount due under it, or

(b) in the case of an order for the recovery of specified property, by the surrender of the property, or

(c) by any other means.

(5) Where the registration of an external order is cancelled or varied under paragraph (3) or (4), the Crown Court must provide for notice of this to be given to the relevant Director and any person affected by it.

23. Appeal to Court of Appeal about external orders

(1) If on an application for the Crown Court to give effect to an external order by registering it, the court decides not to do so, the relevant Director may appeal to the Court of Appeal against the decision.

(2) If an application is made under article 22(3) or (4) in relation to the registration of an external order, the following persons may appeal to the Court of Appeal in respect of the Crown Court's decision on the application—

(a) the relevant Director;

(b) any person affected by the registration.

(3) On an appeal under paragraph (1) or (2) the Court of Appeal may—

(a) confirm or set aside the decision to register; or

(b) direct the Crown Court to register the external order (or so much of it as relates to property other than to which article 21(6) applies).

24. Appeal to [Supreme Court][11] about external orders

(1) An appeal lies to the [Supreme Court][12] from a decision of the Court of Appeal on an appeal under article 23.

(2) An appeal under this article lies at the instance of any person who was a party to the proceedings before the Court of Appeal.

(3) On an appeal under this article the [Supreme Court][13] may—

(a) confirm or set aside the decision of the Court of Appeal, or

(b) direct the Crown Court to register the external order (or so much of it as relates to property other than property to which article 21(6) applies).

25. Sums in currency other than sterling

(1) This article applies where the external order which is registered under article 22 specifies a sum of money.

(2) If the sum of money which is specified is expressed in a currency other than sterling, the sum of money to be recovered is to be taken to be the sterling equivalent calculated in accordance with the rate of exchange prevailing at the end of the working day immediately preceding the day when the Crown Court registered the external order under article 22.

(3) The sterling equivalent must be calculated by the relevant Director.

(4) The notice referred to in article 22(1)(b) and (5) must set out the amount in sterling which is to be paid.

(5) In this article 'working day' means any day other than—

(a) a Saturday or Sunday;

(b) Christmas Day;

(c) Good Friday;

(d) any day that is a bank holiday in England and Wales under the Banking and Financial Dealings Act 1971.

26. Time for payment

(1) This article applies where the external order is for the recovery of a specified sum of money.

(2) Subject to paragraphs (3) to (6), the amount ordered to be paid under—

---

[11] Amended by SI 2011/1242.
[12] Amended by SI 2011/1242.
[13] Amended by SI 2011/1242.

(a) an external order that has been registered under article 22, or
(b) where article 25(2) applies, the notice under article 22(1)(b),

must be paid on the date on which the notice under article 22(1)(b) is delivered to the person affected by it.

(3) Where there is an appeal under article 23 or 24 and a sum falls to be paid when the appeal has been determined or withdrawn, the duty to pay is delayed until the day on which the appeal is determined or withdrawn.

(4) If the person affected by an external order which has been registered shows that he needs time to pay the amount ordered to be paid, the Crown Court which registered the order may make an order allowing payment to be made in a specified period.

(5) The specified period—
(a) must start with the day on which the notice under article 22(1)(b) was delivered to the person affected by the order or the day referred to in paragraph (3), as the case may be, and
(b) must not exceed six months.

(6) If within the specified period the person affected by an external order applies to the Crown Court which registered the order for the period to be extended and the court believes that there are exceptional circumstances, it may make an order extending the period.

(7) The extended period—
(a) must start with the day on which the notice under article 22(1)(b) was delivered to the person affected by it or the day referred to in paragraph (3), as the case may be, and
(b) must not exceed 12 months.

(8) An order under paragraph (6)—
(a) may be made after the end of the specified period, but
(b) must not be made after the end of the extended period.

(9) The court must not make an order under paragraph (4) or (6) unless it gives the relevant Director an opportunity to make representations.

27. Appointment of enforcement receivers

(1) This article applies if—
(a) an external order is registered,
(b) it is not satisfied, and
(c) in the case of an external order for the recovery of a specified sum of money, any period specified by order under article 26 has expired.

(2) On the application of the relevant Director ...[14] the Crown Court may by order appoint a receiver in respect of—
(a) where the external order is for the recovery of a specified sum of money, realisable property;
(b) where the external order is for the recovery of specified property, that property.

28. Powers of enforcement receivers in respect of monetary external orders

(1) If the court appoints a receiver under article 27, it may act under this article on the application of the relevant Director ...[15] where the external order is for the recovery of a specified sum of money.

(2) The court may by order confer on the receiver the following powers in relation to any realisable property—
(a) power to take possession of the property;
(b) power to manage or otherwise deal with the property;
(c) power to realise the property, in such manner as the court may specify;
(d) power to start, carry on or defend any legal proceedings in respect of the property.

(3) The court may by order confer on the receiver power to enter any premises in England and Wales and to do any of the following—
(a) search for or inspect anything authorised by the court;
(b) make or obtain a copy, photograph or other record, of anything so authorised;

[14] Amended by SI 2008/302.
[15] Amended by SI 2008/302.

(c) remove anything which the receiver is required or authorised to take possession of in pursuance of an order of the court.

(4) The court may by order authorise the receiver to do any of the following for the purposes of the exercise of his functions—

(a) hold property;

(b) enter into contracts;

(c) sue and be sued;

(d) employ agents;

(e) execute powers of attorney, deeds or other instruments;

(f) take any other steps the court thinks appropriate.

(5) The court may order any person who has possession of realisable property to give possession of it to the receiver.

(6) The court—

(a) may order a person holding an interest in realisable property to make to the receiver such payment as the court specifies in respect of a beneficial interest held by the defendant or the recipient of a tainted gift;

(b) may (on payment being made) by order transfer, grant or extinguish any interest in the property.

(7) Paragraphs (2), (5) and (6) do not apply to property for the time being subject to a charge under any of these provisions—

(a) section 9 of the Drug Trafficking Offences Act 1986;

(b) section 78 of the Criminal Justice Act 1988;

(c) Article 14 of the Criminal Justice (Confiscation) (Northern Ireland) Order 1990;

(d) section 27 of the Drug Trafficking Act 1994;

(e) Article 32 of the Proceeds of Crime (Northern Ireland) Order 1996.

(8) The court must not—

(a) confer the power mentioned in paragraph (2)(b) or (c) in respect of property, or

(b) exercise the power conferred on it by paragraph (6) in respect of property,

unless it gives persons holding interests in the property a reasonable opportunity to make representations to it.

[(8A) Paragraph (8), so far as relating to the power mentioned in paragraph (2)(b), does not apply to property which—

(a) is perishable; or

(b) ought to be disposed of before its value diminishes.][16]

(9) The court may order that a power conferred by an order under this article is subject to such conditions and exceptions as it specifies.

(10) Managing or otherwise dealing with property includes—

(a) selling the property or any part of it or interest in it;

(b) carrying on or arranging for another person to carry on any trade or business the assets of which are or are part of the property;

(c) incurring capital expenditure in respect of the property.

29. Powers of enforcement receivers in respect of external orders for the recovery of specified property

(1) If the court appoints a receiver under article 27, it may act under this article on the application of the relevant Director ...[17] where the external order is for the recovery of property specified in the order ('the specified property').

(2) The court may by order confer on the receiver the following powers in relation to the specified property—

(a) power to take possession of the property;

(b) power to manage or otherwise deal with the property;

(c) power to realise the property, in such manner as the court may specify;

[16] Amended by SI 2008/302.

[17] Amended by SI 2008/302.

(d) power to start, carry on or defend any legal proceedings in respect of the property.

(3) The court may by order confer on the receiver power to enter any premises in England and Wales and to do any of the following—

(a) search for or inspect anything authorised by the court;

(b) make or obtain a copy, photograph or other record of anything so authorised;

(c) remove anything which the receiver is required or authorised to take possession of in pursuance of an order of the court.

(4) The court may by order authorise the receiver to do any of the following for the purposes of the exercise of his functions—

(a) hold property;

(b) enter into contracts;

(c) sue and be sued;

(d) employ agents;

(e) execute powers of attorney, deeds or other instruments;

(f) take any other steps the court thinks appropriate.

(5) The court may order any person who has possession of the specified property to give possession of it to the receiver.

(6) The court—

(a) may order a person holding an interest in the specified property to make to the receiver such payment as the court specifies in respect of a beneficial interest held by the defendant or the recipient of a tainted gift;

(b) may (on the payment being made) by order transfer, grant or extinguish any interest in the property.

(7) The court must not—

(a) confer the power mentioned in paragraph (2)(b) or (c) in respect of property, or

(b) exercise the power conferred on it by paragraph (6) in respect of property, unless it gives persons holding interests in the property a reasonable opportunity to make representations to it.

[(7A) Paragraph (7), so far as relating to the power mentioned in paragraph (2)(b), does not apply to property which—

(a) is perishable; or

(b) ought to be disposed of before its value diminishes.][18]

(8) The court may order that a power conferred by an order under this article is subject to such conditions and exceptions as it specifies.

(9) Managing or otherwise dealing with property includes—

(a) selling the property or any part of it or interest in it;

(b) carrying on or arranging for another person to carry on any trade or business the assets of which are or are part of the property;

(c) incurring capital expenditure in respect of the property.

30–32. …[19]

33. Application of sums by enforcement receivers

(1) This article applies to sums which are in the hands of a receiver appointed under article 27 if they are—

(a) the proceeds of the realisation of property under article 28 or 29;

(b) where article 28 applies, sums (other than those mentioned in sub-paragraph (a)) in which the defendant holds an interest.

(2) The sums must be applied as follows—

(a) first, they must be applied in payment of such expenses incurred by a person acting as an insolvency practitioner as are payable under this paragraph by virtue of article 3;

(b) second, they must be applied in making any payments directed by the Crown Court;

(c) third, they must be applied on the defendant's behalf towards satisfaction of the external order.

---

[18] Amended by SI 2008/302.

[19] Amended by SI 2008/302.

(3) If the amount payable under the external order has been fully paid and any sums remain in the receiver's hands he must distribute them—
   (a) among such persons who held (or hold) interests in the property concerned as the Crown Court directs; and
   (b) in such proportions as it directs.
(4) Before making a direction under paragraph (3) the court must give persons who held (or hold) interests in the property concerned a reasonable opportunity to make representations to it.
(5) For the purposes of paragraphs (3) and (4) the property concerned is—
   (a) the property represented by the proceeds mentioned in paragraph (1)(a);
   (b) the sums mentioned in paragraph (1)(b).
(6) The receiver applies sums as mentioned in paragraph (2)(c) by paying them to the relevant Director on account of the amount payable under the order.

34. Sums received by relevant Director

(1) This article applies if a relevant Director receives sums on account of the amount payable under a registered external order or the value of the property specified in the order.
(2) The relevant Director's receipt of the sums reduces the amount payable under the order, but he must apply the sums received as follows.
(3) First he must apply them in payment of such expenses incurred by a person acting as an insolvency practitioner as—
   (a) are payable under this paragraph by virtue of article 3, but
   (b) are not already paid under article 33(2)(a).
(4) He must next apply them—
   (a) first, in payment of the remuneration and expenses of a receiver appointed under article 15 to the extent that they have not been met by virtue of the exercise by that receiver of a power conferred under article 16(2)(d);
   (b) second, in payment of the remuneration and expenses of the receiver appointed under article 27.
(5) Any sums which remain after the relevant Director has made any payments required by the preceding provisions of this article must be paid into the Consolidated Fund.
(6) Paragraph (4) does not apply if the receiver is a member of the staff of the Crown Prosecution Service, the Serious Fraud Office or the Revenue and Customs Prosecution Office; and it is immaterial whether he is a permanent or temporary member or he is on secondment from elsewhere.

35, 36. ...[20]

37. Satisfaction of external order

(1) A registered external order is satisfied when no amount is due under it.
(2) Where such an order authorises the recovery of property specified in it, no further amount is due under the order when all of the specified property has been sold.

38. Restrictions relating to enforcement receivers

(1) Paragraphs (2) to (4) apply if a court makes an order under article 27 appointing a receiver in respect of any realisable property or specified property.
(2) No distress may be levied against the property except with the leave of the Crown Court and subject to any terms the Crown Court may impose.
(3) If the receiver is appointed in respect of a tenancy of any premises, no landlord or other person to whom rent is payable may exercise a right within paragraph (4) except with the leave of the Crown Court and subject to any terms the Crown Court may impose.
(4) A right is within this paragraph if it is a right of forfeiture by peaceable re-entry in relation to the premises in respect of any failure by the tenant to comply with any term or condition of the tenancy.

[20] Amended by SI 2008/302.

(5) If a court in which proceedings are pending in respect of any property is satisfied that an order under article 27 appointing a receiver in respect of the property has been applied for or made, the court may either stay the proceedings or allow them to continue on any terms it thinks fit.

(6) Before exercising any power conferred by paragraph (5), the court must give an opportunity to be heard to—

(a) the relevant Director ...,[21] and

(b) the receiver (if the order under article 27 has been made).

39. ...[22]

Chapter 3
Receivers and Procedure

40. Protection of receiver appointed under articles 15, 27 and 30

If a receiver appointed under article 15 [or 27][23]—

(a) takes action in relation to property which is not realisable property or, as the case may be, the specified property,

(b) would be entitled to take the action if it were realisable property or, as the case may be, the specified property, and

(c) believes on reasonable grounds that he is entitled to take the action,

he is not liable to any person in respect of any loss or damage resulting from the action, except so far as the loss or damage is caused by his negligence.

41. Further applications by receivers

(1) This article applies to a receiver appointed under article 15 [or 27].[24]

(2) The receiver may apply to the Crown Court for an order giving directions as to the exercise of his powers.

(3) The following persons may apply to the Crown Court—

(a) any person affected by action taken by the receiver;

(b) any person who may be affected by action the receiver proposes to take.

(4) On an application under this article the court may make such order as it believes is appropriate.

42. Discharge and variation of receiver orders

(1) The following persons may apply to the Crown Court to vary or discharge an order made under article 15, 16 or 27 to [to 29][25]—

(a) the receiver;

(b) the relevant Director;

(c) any person affected by the order.

(2) On an application under this article the court—

(a) may discharge the order;

(b) may vary the order.

(3) But in the case of an order under article 15 or 16—

(a) if the condition in article 7 which was satisfied was that proceedings were started, the court must discharge the order if at the conclusion of the proceedings no external order has been made;

(b) if the condition which was satisfied was that proceedings were started, the court must discharge the order if within a reasonable time an external order has not been registered under Chapter 2 of this Part;

(c) if the condition which was satisfied was that an investigation was started, the court must discharge the order if within a reasonable time proceedings for the offence are not started.

---

21 Amended by SI 2008/302.
22 Amended by SI 2008/302.
23 Amended by SI 2008/302.
24 Amended by SI 2008/302.
25 Amended by SI 2008/302.

43. Management receivers: discharge

(1) This article applies if—
  (a) a receiver stands appointed under article 15 in respect of property which is identified in the restraint order (the management receiver), and
  (b) the court appoints a receiver under article 27 ....[26]
(2) The court must order the management receiver to transfer to the other receiver all property held by the management receiver by virtue of the powers conferred on him by article 16.
(3) ...[27]
(4) Paragraph (2) does not apply to property which the management receiver holds by virtue of the exercise by him of his power under article 16(2)(d).
(5) If the management receiver complies with an order under paragraph (2) he is discharged—
  (a) from his appointment under article 15;
  (b) from any obligation under this Order arising from his appointment.
(6) If this article applies the court may make such a consequential or incidental order as it believes is appropriate.

44. Appeal to Court of Appeal about receivers

(1) If on an application for an order under any of articles 15, 16 [or 27 to 29][28] the court decides not to make one, the person who applied for the order may appeal to the Court of Appeal against the decision.
(2) If the court makes an order under any of articles 15, 16 [or 27 to 29],[29] the following persons may appeal to the Court of Appeal in respect of the court's decision—
  (a) the person who applied for the order;
  (b) any person affected by the order.
(3) If on an application for an order under article 41 the court decides not to make one, the person who applied for the order may appeal to the Court of Appeal against the decision.
(4) If the court makes an order under article 41 the following persons may appeal to the Court of Appeal in respect of the court's decision—
  (a) the person who applied for the order;
  (b) any person affected by the order;
  (c) the receiver.
(5) The following persons may appeal to the Court of Appeal against a decision of the court on an application under article 42—
  (a) the person who applied for the order in respect of which the application was made;[30]
  (b) any person affected by the court's decision;
  (c) the receiver.
(6) On an appeal under this article the Court of Appeal may—
  (a) confirm the decision, or
  (b) make such order as it believes is appropriate.

45. Appeal to the [Supreme Court][31] about receivers

(1) An appeal lies to the [Supreme Court][32] from a decision of the Court of Appeal on an appeal under article 44.
(2) An appeal under this article lies at the instance of any person who was a party to the proceedings before the Court of Appeal.
(3) On an appeal under this article the [Supreme Court][33] may—
  (a) confirm the decision of the Court Appeal, or

---

[26] Amended by SI 2008/302.
[27] Amended by SI 2008/302.
[28] Amended by SI 2008/302.
[29] Amended by SI 2008/302.
[30] Amended by SI 2008/302.
[31] Amended by SI 2011/1242.
[32] Amended by SI 2011/1242.
[33] Amended by SI 2011/1242.

(b) make such order as it believes is appropriate.

46. Powers of court and receiver

(1) This article applies to—
  (a) the powers conferred on a court by this Part;
  (b) the powers of a receiver appointed under article 15 [or 27].[34]
(2) The powers—
  (a) must be exercised with a view to the value for the time being of realisable property or specified property being made available (by the property's realisation) for satisfying an external order that has been or may be made against the defendant;
  (b) must be exercised, in a case where an external order has not been made, with a view to securing that there is no diminution in the value of the property identified in the external request;
  (c) must be exercised without taking account of any obligation of a defendant or a recipient of a tainted gift if the obligation conflicts with the object of satisfying any external order against the defendant that has been or may be registered under article 22;
  (d) may be exercised in respect of a debt owed by the Crown.
(3) Paragraph (2) has effect subject to the following rules—
  (a) the powers must be exercised with a view to allowing a person other than the defendant or a recipient of a tainted gift to retain or recover the value of any interest held by him;
  (b) in the case of realisable property or specified property held by a recipient of a tainted gift, the powers must be exercised with a view to realising no more than the value for the time being of the gift;
  (c) in a case where an external order has not been made against the defendant, property must not be sold if the court so orders under paragraph (4).
(4) If on an application by the defendant or the recipient of a tainted gift, the court decides that property cannot be replaced it may order that it must not be sold.
(5) An order under paragraph (4) may be revoked or varied.

47. Procedure on appeal to Court of Appeal under Part 2

(1) An appeal to the Court of Appeal under this Part lies only with the leave of that Court.
(2) Subject to rules of court made under section 53(1) of the [Senior Courts Act 1981][35] (distribution of business between civil and criminal divisions) the criminal division of the Court of Appeal is the division—
  (a) to which an appeal to that Court under this Part is to lie, and
  (b) which is to exercise that Court's jurisdiction under this Part.
(3) In relation to appeals to the Court of Appeal under this Part, the Secretary of State may make an order containing provision corresponding to any provision in the Criminal Appeal Act 1968, subject to any specified modifications.
(4) Subject to any rules of court, the costs of and incidental to all proceedings on an appeal to the criminal division of the Court of Appeal under article 10, 23 or 44 are in the discretion of the court.
(5) The court shall have full power to determine by whom and to what extent the costs are to be paid.
(6) In any proceedings mentioned in paragraph (4), the court may—
  (a) disallow, or
  (b) (as the case may be) order the legal or other representative concerned to meet, the whole of any wasted costs or such part of them as may be determined in accordance with rules of court.
(7) In paragraph (6) 'wasted costs' means any costs incurred by a party—
  (a) as a result of any improper, unreasonable or negligent act or omission on the part of any legal or other representative or any employee of such a representative, or
  (b) which, in the light of any such act or omission occurring after they were incurred, the court considers it unreasonable to expect that party to pay.
(8) 'Legal or other representative', in relation to a party to proceedings, means any person exercising a right of audience or right to conduct litigation on his behalf.

[34] Amended by SI 2008/302.
[35] Amended by the Constitutional Reform Act 2005.

48. Procedure on appeal to [Supreme Court][36] under Part 2

(1) Section 33(3) of the Criminal Appeal Act 1968 (limitation on appeal from criminal division of the Court of Appeal) does not prevent an appeal to the [Supreme Court][37] under this Part.

(2) In relation to appeals to the [Supreme Court][38] under this Part, the Secretary of State may make an order containing provision corresponding to any provision in the Criminal Appeal Act 1968, subject to any specified modifications.

Chapter 4
Interpretation

49. Property

(1) In this Part, 'realisable property' means in a case where the external order specifies a sum of money, any free property held by the defendant or by the recipient of a tainted gift.

(2) 'Free property' has the same meaning as in section 82 of the Act (free property).

(3) The rules in paragraphs (a) and (c) to (g) of section 84(2) of the Act (property: general provisions) apply in relation to property under this Order (in addition to section 447(4) to (6) of the Act (interpretation)) as they apply in relation to property under Part 2 of the Act.

50. Tainted gifts

(1) In this Part, a gift is tainted if it was made by the defendant at any time after—
  (a) the date on which the offence to which the external order or external request relates was committed, or
  (b) if his criminal conduct consists of two or more such offences and they were committed on different dates, the date of the earliest.

(2) For the purposes of paragraph (1), an offence which is a continuing offence is committed on the first occasion when it is committed.

(3) A gift may be a tainted gift whether it was made before or after the coming into force of this Order.

51. Gifts and their recipients

(1) In this Part, a defendant is to be treated as making a gift if he transfers property to another person for a consideration whose value is significantly less than the value of the property at the time of the transfer.

(2) If paragraph (1) applies, the property given is to be treated as such share in the property transferred as is represented by the fraction—
  (a) whose numerator is the difference between the two values mentioned in paragraph (1), and
  (b) whose denominator is the value of the property at the time of the transfer.

(3) In this Part references to a recipient of a tainted gift are to a person to whom the defendant has made the gift.

52. Value: the basic rule

(1) Subject to article 53, this article applies where it is necessary under this Part to decide the value at any time of property then held by a person.

(2) Its value is the market value of the property at that time.

(3) But if at that time another person holds an interest in the property its value, in relation to the person mentioned in paragraph (1), is the market value of his interest at that time, ignoring any charging order under a provision listed in paragraph (4).

(4) Those provisions are—
  (a) section 9 of the Drug Trafficking Offences Act 1986;

---

[36] Amended by SI 2011/1242.
[37] Amended by SI 2011/1242.
[38] Amended by SI 2011/1242.

(b) section 78 of the Criminal Justice Act 1988;
(c) Article 14 of the Criminal Justice (Confiscation) (Northern Ireland) Order 1990;
(d) section 27 of the Drug Trafficking Act 1994;
(e) Article 32 of the Proceeds of Crime (Northern Ireland) Order 1996.

53. Value of tainted gifts

(1) The value at any time (the material time) of a tainted gift is the greater of the following—
 (a) the value (at time of the gift) of the property given, adjusted to take account of later changes in the value of money;
 (b) the value (at the material time) of the property found under paragraph (2).
(2) The property found under this paragraph is as follows—
 (a) if the recipient holds the property given, the property found under this paragraph is that property;
 (b) if the recipient holds no part of the property given, the property found under this paragraph is any property which directly or indirectly represents it in his hands;
 (c) if the recipient holds part of the property given, the property found under this paragraph is that part and any property which directly or indirectly represents the other part in his hands.
(3) The references in paragraph (1)(a) and (b) to the value are to the value found in accordance with article 52.

54. Meaning of 'defendant'

In this Part 'defendant'—
 (a) in relation to a restraint order means—
  (i) in a case in which the first condition in article 7 is satisfied, the alleged offender;
  (ii) in a case in which the second condition in article 7 is satisfied, the person against whom proceedings for an offence have been started in a country outside the United Kingdom (whether or not he has been convicted);
 (b) in relation to an external order, the person convicted of criminal conduct.

55. Other interpretation

In this Part—
 'relevant Director' has the meaning—
  (a) in the context of an external request, set out in article 6(4);
  (b) in the context of an external order, set out in article 18(4);
 'relevant property' means property which satisfies the test in section 447(7) of the Act;
 'specified property' means property specified in an external order (other than an order that specifies a sum of money).

Schedule 5
Prescribed Enactments

Article 206

Section 31 of the Salmon Fisheries (Scotland) Act 1868 (forfeiture of articles found in possession of any offender).

Section 8 of the Diseases of Fish Act 1937 (penalties and legal proceedings).

Sections 19 and 20 of the Salmon and Freshwater Fisheries (Protection) (Scotland) Act 1951.

Section 138 of the Army Act 1955 (restitution or compensation for theft etc.) (including where it has effect by virtue of paragraph 17 of Schedule 3 to the Armed Forces Act 1976), in circumstances other than where the disposal is of money which is paid as or towards compensation under section 138(5) of that Act or the disposal is the restitution of property given in exchange under section 138(6) of that Act.

Section 138 of the Air Force Act 1955 (restitution or compensation for theft etc.) in circumstances other than where the disposal is of money is paid as or towards compensation under section 138(5) of that Act or the disposal is the restitution of property given in exchange under section 138(6) of that Act.

Section 76 of the Naval Discipline Act 1957 (restitution or compensation on conviction of larceny etc.), in circumstances other than where the disposal is the restitution of property given in exchange under section 76(2)(a) of that Act or the disposal is of money which is paid as or towards compensation under section 76(2)(b) or (3) of that Act.

Section 3 of the Obscene Publications Act 1959 (powers of search and seizure).

Section 11(2) of the Sea Fish (Conservation) Act 1967 (penalties for offences).

Section 46(4) of the Courts-Martial (Appeals) Act 1968 (restitution of property), in circumstances where if the order had been made by the court-martial or Defence Council this Order would have provided that the property was not recoverable or (as the case may be) associated property.

Section 52 of the Firearms Act 1968 (forfeiture and disposal of firearms).

Section 27 of the Misuse of Drugs Act 1971 (forfeiture).

Sections 7 and 24 of the Forgery and Counterfeiting Act 1981 (powers of search, forfeiture etc.).

Section 4(4) of the Inshore Fishing (Scotland) Act 1984.

Section 25 of the Public Order Act 1986 (power to order forfeiture).

Section 66 of the Criminal Justice and Public Order Act 1994 (power of court to forfeit sound equipment) in the circumstances where no order is made under section 66(5) by virtue of section 66(6) of that Act for the delivery of property to a person appearing to be the owner of the property.

Section 43 of the Drug Trafficking Act 1994 (forfeiture).

Section 22 of the Proceeds of Crime (Scotland) Act 1995 (forfeiture: district court).

Section 24 of the Proceeds of Crime (Scotland) Act 1995 (forfeiture of property subject to suspended forfeiture order), in the circumstances where no order is made under section 26 of that Act in relation to the property.

Paragraph 3 of the Schedule to the Noise Act 1996 (forfeiture), in the circumstances where no order is made under paragraph 4 of that Schedule for the delivery of the equipment to a person appearing to be the owner of the equipment.

Section 6 of the Knives Act 1997 (forfeiture of knives and publications), in the circumstances where no order is made under section 7 of that Act for the delivery of property to a person appearing to be the owner of the property.

Section 143 of the Powers of Criminal Courts (Sentencing) Act 2000 (powers to deprive offender of property used etc. for purposes of crime), in the circumstances where no order is made under the Police (Property) Act 1897, as applied by section 144 of the Powers of Criminal Courts (Sentencing) Act 2000, for the delivery of the property to a person appearing to be the owner of the property.

Section 23 of the Terrorism Act 2000 (forfeiture).

Section 6 of the Royal Parks (Trading) Act 2000 (seizure, retention, disposal and forfeiture of property).

Paragraph 6 of Schedule 1 to the Anti-terrorism, Crime and Security Act 2001 (forfeiture).

Regulations 15 (disposal of vehicles) and 17 (disposal of contents) of the Goods Vehicles (Enforcement Powers) Regulations 2001, in the circumstances where the proceeds of sale have not been applied in meeting a claim to the proceeds of sale established under regulation 18(2) of those Regulations.

[Regulations made under Section 94 of the Armed Forces Act 2006 (property in possession of service police or CO).][39]

[39] Amended by SI 2009/2054.

APPENDIX M3

Requests for Mutual Legal Assistance in Criminal Matters—Guidelines for Authorities Outside of the United Kingdom (10th edn, September 2012)

Judicial Co-operation Unit
Home Office
5th Floor Fry Buidling
2 Marsham Street
London
SW1P 4DF

14th September 2012

CONTENTS

Section 1
Introduction

Section 2
How to make a request for MLA

Section 3
Forms of MLA the UK can provide

Service of Process Documents
Direct Transmission of Procedural Documents
Requests for Service of Process/Procedural Documents
Witness and Suspect Evidence
Witness and suspect evidence NOT required to be given under oath
Witness and suspect evidence to be taken on oath
Witness/Suspect Privilege
Evidence taken in court without an oath
Appointment of a lawyer to represent the accused or witness
Third Party material held in confidence – Telecommunications
Telephone and address information
Third Party material held in confidence – Banking Evidence
Customer Information Orders/Account Monitoring Orders
Evidence via Video or Telephone Conference
Video Conference (Television Link)
Telephone Conference
Restraint and Confiscation of Assets
Search and Seizure
Execution of search and seizure requests in England, Wales and Northern Ireland
Execution of search and seizure requests in Scotland
Temporary Transfer of a Prisoner for purposes of investigation
Transfer of a Prisoner for the purpose of serving the remainder of a prison sentence (non-MLA prisoner transfer)
Passport Information and Immigration Status
Other Requests for Mutual Legal Assistance
Joint Investigation Teams
Interception of Telecommunications
Article 21 Convention on Mutual Assistance in Criminal Matters
Transfer of Proceedings
DNA
Spontaneous Exchange of Information
Permission to Use Evidence for Other Purposes

Section 4
Officers present from the requesting state and transmission of evidence

Officers from the Requesting State present at the execution of a MLA
Notifying the UK of law enforcement officers travelling to the UK
Transmission of evidence

Section 5
MLA requests from the UK

Who can send an MLA request *from* the UK?
Direct Transmission to EU/Schengen countries

Section 6
Requests for intelligence

UK law enforcement agencies which can assist in relation to intelligence
How to make requests for intelligence from a UK law enforcement agency Assistance which can be requested from the UK via Police to Police enquiries

Requests for Mutual Legal Assistance in Criminal Matters Guidelines for Authorities Outside of the United Kingdom (10th edn, September 2012)

Judicial Co-operation Unit
Home Office
5th Floor Fry Building
2 Marsham Street
London

SW1P 4DF
14th September 2012

Section 1
Introduction

Mutual Legal Assistance ("MLA") is the formal way in which countries request and provide assistance in obtaining evidence located in one country to assist in criminal investigations or proceedings in another country. Due to the increasingly global nature of crime MLA is critical to criminal proceedings and ensuring justice for victims of crime. The UK is committed to assisting investigative, prosecuting and judicial authorities in combating international crime and is able to provide a wide range of MLA.

These guidelines are to ensure that requests for MLA received by the UK can be executed quickly and efficiently. The guidelines include:

- Guidance to authorities who wish to make a formal request for MLA **to the UK** ("requesting authorities");
- Guidance to authorities on what can be requested **from the UK** without making a formal request for MLA;
- Guidance on which authorities **in the UK** can send a formal request for MLA abroad

Guidance for authorities **within the UK**, who wish to make a request for MLA to a foreign state, can be found on the Crown Prosecution Service ("CPS") website: International Enquiries

The role of central authorities in the UK

Central authorities have the function of receiving, acceding to and ensuring the execution of MLA requests. All formal requests for assistance must be sent to a UK central authority for processing. The UK has three central authorities:

- UK Central Authority ("UKCA"), for MLA requests in England, Wales and Northern Ireland
- Crown Office, for MLA requests in Scotland
- Her Majesty's Revenue and Customs ("HMRC")

The Crown Office deals with all MLA requests for Scotland. HMRC deals with requests in England, Wales and Northern Ireland relating to indirect taxes. UKCA deals with all other requests for England, Wales and Northern Ireland, including MLA requests relating to the smuggling of prohibited and restricted items and direct tax. Contact details for these central authorities are in Section 2.

UK law allows the requesting State to serve procedural documents on affected individuals directly by post. Please see further details on this in Section 3.

Requests for the Crown Dependencies and the UK Overseas Territories

The Crown Dependencies (Bailiwicks of Guernsey and Jersey, and the Isle of Man), and Falklands, Gibraltar[1], Montserrat, St Helena, Turks and Caicos Islands, and Pitcairn) are not part of the UK. The Crown Dependencies and the Overseas Territories are wholly responsible for executing requests within their own jurisdictions. Requests should usually be sent to the Attorney General of the Crown Dependency or Overseas Territory from where the assistance is required. The contact details for these jurisdictions can be found at Annex B.

When MLA requests to the UK are appropriate

A request for MLA in criminal matters is only appropriate if evidence (as opposed to intelligence) from the UK is required for a criminal matter.

It can be easier and quicker to obtain intelligence and in many countries this will constitute admissible evidence in criminal trials. Requesting countries will need to determine whether, in relation to their legislation, a request for evidence or intelligence is more appropriate.

Requests for intelligence can be made on a police to police basis and a different process for this is followed. Please refer to Section 6 of this guide for how to make a request for intelligence from the UK.

[1] Requests to and from EU/Schengen Member States for Gibraltar must be sent via the UK Government/Gibraltar Liaison Unit in the Foreign & Commonwealth Office. See Annex B for more details.

Requests for assistance in civil matters are dealt with via a different process, as explained in Section 8 of this guidance.

Types of MLA that can be provided

There is a wide range of MLA that can be provided by the UK conditional on the correct criteria being met. Please refer to Section 3 of this guide for information about each of the different types of MLA.

Countries which the UK can assist

The UK can assist any country or territory in the world, whether or not that country is able to assist the UK. The UK can provide most forms of legal assistance without bilateral or international agreements.

See Annex A for a list of the international agreements that the UK is party to.

However where a bilateral or international agreement imposes specific conditions or procedures on the provision or requesting of MLA, the UK expects such conditions or procedures to be adhered to.

Reciprocity

The UK does not generally require reciprocity but would expect assistance from countries which are parties to relevant bilateral or international agreements with the UK. The UK would also expect reciprocity from countries to which we give assistance without a treaty or international agreement. Reciprocity is required in all requests for assistance in indirect tax matters.

UK executing authorities

There are a number of other organisations that are involved in the execution of MLA requests. Please see Annex C for a glossary of different organisations in the UK and their role in MLA.

Confidentiality

In line with established international practice, the central authorities will neither confirm nor deny the existence of an MLA request, nor disclose any of its content outside government departments, agencies, the courts or enforcement agencies in the UK without the consent of the requesting authority. Requests are not disclosed further than is necessary to obtain the co-operation of the witness or other person concerned. However, a Letter of Request (LOR, see Section 2) can be disclosed in connected UK proceedings if the request has been fully executed.

Where public statements are made by an overseas authority about the assistance it is requesting from the UK, the central authority should be notified so that they may respond appropriately to any media or public enquiries.

In general, requests are not shown or copied to any witness or other person, nor is any witness informed of the identity of any other witness. In the event that confidentiality requirements make execution of a request difficult or impossible, the central authority will consult the requesting authorities. In cases where disclosure of a request or part thereof is required by UK domestic law in order to execute the request it will normally be the case that the requesting authority will be given the opportunity to withdraw the request before disclosure to third parties is made.

From time to time the UK central authorities release statistical data on the number of MLA requests sent and received. Such data is only released where to do so would not breach the confidentiality of any individual request.

To the extent permitted by UK law, evidence obtained from foreign jurisdictions pursuant to an MLA request will not be used in the UK for any other purpose other than that specified in the request without the consent of the foreign jurisdiction.

Section 2

How to make a request for MLA

Requests for MLA must be sent to one of the UK's central authorities. This section gives information on what should be contained within a Letter of Request (LOR) and where it should be sent. However, this should be read in conjunction with Section 3 as the contents of the LOR are dependent on the type of assistance required by the requesting authority.

Prior to making an MLA request

It is possible, and often desirable, for overseas authorities to use police to police enquiries (for intelligence) or other intelligence sharing networks prior to making an MLA request. This can help improve the quality of the MLA request and the subsequent service received. Please refer to Section 6 (Requests for Intelligence) for more information.

Proportionality/*de minimis* requests

Please ensure that the request is proportionate (i.e. the request for assistance is proportionate to the level of crime being investigated), particularly for intrusive and time-consuming measures (such as search warrants, surveillance and other court-ordered assistance). Police forces in the UK are operationally independent and prioritise the execution of MLA requests alongside domestic work. In Scotland the police may be directed by the Lord Advocate/Procurator Fiscal to carry out enquiries. Consequently, and given the limited resources available to UK law enforcement, *de minimis* cases (requests for minor or trivial offences), are unlikely to be prioritised and we would urge requesting countries to consider the need for the evidence in question.

Cases are evaluated in their entirety, but it is common for the UK to receive requests which are clearly *de minimis*, such as in relation to minor frauds or driving offences. Priority will instead be granted to requests that involve:

- Serious criminal offences (e.g. murder or other crimes of violence, organized crime, terrorism, corruption, or wide-scale fraud)
- Evidence that is at risk of being concealed or destroyed
- Ongoing offences or where the safety of witnesses or the public is at risk
- An imminent trial date

Who can send a Letter of Request (LOR)

Any competent body under the law of the requesting country may make a request to the UK, but this must comply with section 13 of the Crime (International Co-operation) Act 2003 ("CICA").

Format of a request

These must always be made in writing:

- LORs to the UKCA should be sent via the post / courier or fax in urgent cases;
- LORs to HMRC can be sent via post or email;
- LORs to the Crown Office can be sent via post or email;
- LORs can also be sent to Interpol in urgent cases under section 8 of CICA 2003.

Language of requests

All LORs should be in English[2]. Requests not in English must be accompanied by translated copies. If an English translation is not provided, the request will be sent back to the requesting authority.

What must be included in a LOR

Please observe the following conditions when sending a request to the UK:

- Headed notepaper of the issuing authority must be used
- The request must be signed by the issuing authority
- For requests made in the English language; one signed hard copy **and** one copy of this must be provided
- For requests not made in the English language; one signed hard version of the non-English request **and** one translation of the request into English.

The LOR must include the following (if applicable):

- Details of the authority making the request, including the name, telephone number and email address (where available) of a contact person;

---

[2] EU member states that have ratified the 2000 MLAC should note Article 5(3) in relation to translations.

- Purpose for which assistance is sought;
- The type of assistance being requested (for example, if this is a request for evidence, service of process or enforcement of restraint and confiscation, etc) and any additional information that is required for requests of this type of assistance (see Section 3 of these guidelines);
- A description of the offences charged or under investigation and sentence or penalty;
- A copy of the legislation that criminalises the conduct in the requesting country and gives information on the offence, penalty and rights a person may be afforded;
- A summary of the facts giving rise to the request and connection this case has to the UK;
- Details of the person or persons (including legal) named in the request including, where available, address, date of birth and nationality;
- Details of the location of a company / person evidence is needed from;
- If a person needs to be visited, state whether they are a witness or a suspect;
- The name of the suspect and what they are being charged with;
- The connection between the evidence requested and the offence under investigation or proceedings. A clear *nexus* (direct link) must be established between the facts of the case as detailed in the request and the evidence requested. This goes further than just stating that the requested material is relevant to the case and should specify how it is relevant and will assist the case;
- Relevant dates e.g. date of court hearing (reason for special urgency or attention should be included in the covering letter of request);
- Details, including the telephone number and e-mail address if available, of any British law enforcement agency or officers who are familiar with the investigation (including, if relevant, the names of any UK based operations which the requesting authority is aware of)
- The title of the relevant convention or bilateral treaty under which the request is being made (please see Annex A for conventions and treaties the UK is party to);
- If this is a request for evidence, specify exactly what evidence is required (e.g. not just "banking evidence" but what kind of banking evidence);
- Confidentiality - the extent to which confidentiality applies;
- Details of any media attention, sensitivities or reasons for high profile interest in the case in the Requesting State.

Failure to provide the fullest information possible may result in delays or in a request not being executed in whole or in part.

Please see Annex D for an example structure LORs.

Where to send MLA requests

England, Wales, and Northern Ireland should be directed to:

UK Central Authority
5th Floor Fry Building
2 Marsham Street
London
SW1P 4DF
Fax: +44 20 7035 6985
Telephone: +44 20 7035 4040

Scotland should be directed to:
International Co-operation Unit
Crown Office
25 Chambers Street
Edinburgh

[3] However, requests relating to the smuggling of prohibited and restricted items and matters related to direct tax (income tax, corporation tax and capital gains tax) should be sent to the UKCA (please see earlier section on the role of UKCA).

EH1 1LA
Tel: +44 131 243 8152
Fax: +44 131 243 8153
Email: coicu@copfs.gsi.gov.uk

Indirect tax matters in England, Wales and Northern Ireland (such as smuggling of dutiable goods or Value Added Tax fraud)[3] *should be directed to*:

HM Revenue and Customs
Criminal Law and Information Law Advisory Team
HM Revenue and Customs – Solicitor's Office
Room 2/74
100 Parliament Street
London
SW1A 2BQ
Fax: +44 207 147 0433
Email: mla@hmrc.gsi.gov.uk

For requests for assistance from a British Crown Dependency or British Overseas Territory can be sent directly to the relevant authority listed in Annex B.

Requesting more than one form of MLA where restraint or confiscation is involved

Consideration should be given as to whether it is appropriate to separate out requests for restraint and confiscation in the same case. In the UK it is often easier to prepare the court papers when the request for restraint or confiscation is separate from the other forms of MLA requested. However, if it is made as a separate request this should be sent at the same time as the initial request (if possible).

Timescales in executing a request

This will depend on the nature of the request. Central authorities will take into account any reasons for urgency such as statutory and/or custody time limits, pre-trial court appearances or trial dates which are clearly stated in the request. The requesting authority should also update the central authority on any changes to these which will impact on the request.

The UKCA, HMRC and the Crown Office in Scotland aim to take initial action as quickly as possible. Initial actions will include acknowledging receipt of the request and providing the requesting authority with the name of the executing authority, the central authority caseworker/Procurator Fiscal Depute and their contact details. Failure to adhere to the advice in these guidelines may also cause delay to the execution of the request.

Urgent requests for assistance

If a LOR is urgent the central authority will deal with the request as quickly as possible. Please adhere to the following when submitting an urgent request:

- Do not mark a request as urgent unless it is urgent
- Detail why a request is urgent. Examples of why a request may be urgent include: somebody is being detained in custody; somebody is due to be released from custody; there is an immediate risk to individuals; risk of dissipation of assets
- Clearly state any dates which need to be met
- Please inform the central authority if the assistance is no longer needed so the use of our resources can be prioritised

Costs for MLA requests

Ordinarily, the UK will meet the costs of executing an MLA request. Exceptions include:

- fees and reasonable expenses of expert witnesses;
- the costs of establishing and operating video-conferencing or television links in England, Wales and Northern Ireland (the Crown Office does not charge for television links), and the interpretation and transcription of such proceedings;
- the costs of transferring persons in custody;
- the costs of obtaining transcripts of proceedings and judges' sentencing remarks; and

- costs of an extraordinary nature agreed with the requesting authority (these will be agreed before costs are incurred).

Notification where assistance is no longer required

Should the requested assistance no longer be required, the central authority should be informed immediately, quoting the central authority reference number.

Transmission

The UK does not require requests to come via diplomatic channels and central authorities are happy to receive requests directly. However, the requesting authority will clearly need to comply with its own domestic laws relating to the transmission of requests.

UK law allows the requesting State to serve procedural documents on affected individuals directly by post. Please see further details on this in Section 3.

Supplementary requests

MLA requests which relate to a previous LOR can be sent to the central authority as a supplementary request. Any supplementary requests should include the following:

- a statement that this is a request for supplementary information
- the central authority's reference number for the previous request
- all the information relevant to a standard MLA request (see above), plus any further information relating to the specific type of request that it is.

Requesting authorities must include the original central authority reference number on all follow-up correspondence or supplementary documents.

Queries about requests

Once a central authority has received a request for MLA the request will be logged and given a reference number. In England, Wales and Northern Ireland a UKCA caseworker will be assigned to the case and the requesting authority will be written to with these details. HMRC handle these requests centrally within their team. In Scotland the case will be allocated to a Procurator Fiscal Depute (Scottish Prosecutor).

The requesting authority will be written to with the details of the person dealing with their case. Any subsequent correspondence relating to the MLA request should be sent to the correct caseworker/and should always quote the central authority's reference number. The UKCA caseworker/ HMRC team/ Procurator Fiscal Depute should be informed if a request for assistance is no longer required, or if the case has been concluded by the requesting authority.

Section 3
Forms of MLA the UK can provide

This section details the form of the assistance the UK can provide and the specific information which should be included in requests from foreign authorities according to the form of assistance sought.

Service of Process Documents

Direct Transmission of Procedural Documents

Procedural documents may be sent directly by the requesting authority to the persons in the UK to whom they are addressed. The UK strongly encourages direct transmission of procedural documents to persons by post, unless this is not legally possible under the domestic law of the requesting authority.

Requests for Service of Process/Procedural Documents

In line with section 1 and 2 of CICA, a request may be made to the UKCA and the Crown Office for the service of procedural documents (e.g. a summons or judgement) issued by a court or authority in that state in relation to criminal proceedings. HMRC is not a central authority for the purposes of the service of documents.

All procedural documents which are to be served must be received by the UKCA or the Crown Office at least six weeks prior to any deadlines which are in place in the requesting state.

Note: The UK reserves the right not to serve process or procedural documents where to do so could place a person's safety at risk (for example if the procedural documents reveal the address of a key witness in a murder trial). Requesting authorities should therefore always consider if it is necessary to include details relating to witnesses or victims in such documents.

ADDITIONAL INFORMATION TO INCLUDE IN AN MLA SERVICE OF PROCESS REQUEST

There are particular requirements which must be included in a request for service of process:

- Specific instructions as to whether the documents **must** be served by hand. If no such instruction is provided the documents will be served by post. Where personal service is specifically requested, the central authority may arrange for the document to be served by the police.
- The documents should be received by the central authority at least six weeks prior to court hearings or other deadlines involved; otherwise there is a possibility that responses will not be received in time to be of use to the requesting authority. If the documents are not received in a timely manner the request may be returned. All dates of hearings or other deadlines should be stated clearly within the request.
- Details of any allowances and expenses to which a person asked to appear in proceedings abroad is entitled.
- The address of the court where the proceedings are to take place.
- The name and telephone number of an official of the court from whom the person asked to appear can seek further information if necessary.
- Specific instructions as to whether an execution of service must be returned to the requesting authority.

The person on whom a summons or judgement is served is asked to sign a receipt and return it to the UKCA to send to the requesting authority. UKCA will advise the requesting authority whether the document has been delivered or whether it was not possible to serve the document. In Scotland, the summons or judgement shall be served upon the person by either a police officer or police employee. Said police officer or employee shall complete an execution of service which shall be returned to the requesting authority. The person shall be asked to sign a receipt, but is under no obligation to do so.

Witness and Suspect Evidence

Witness and suspect evidence NOT required to be given under oath

If the requesting authority's legal system does not require evidence to be taken on oath, the letter of request should ask for the evidence to be obtained by UK law enforcement agencies.

NOTE: The police or other law enforcement officers are not authorised to administer oaths in the UK. In the UK evidence can only be made subject to an oath before a court.

Unless a MLA request specifically requires that evidence be given on oath, testimony will be taken without an oath being administered. This is considerably quicker and less resource intensive.

Police interviews require the consent of a witness or suspect. In cases where a witness or suspect refuses to give a statement the requesting authority will be informed so that it can decide whether to ask for the witness / suspect to be summonsed before a court. Where possible, the original request should state whether a person who does not agree to provide a statement should subsequently be compelled to attend court.

Please refer to Section 6 (Requests for Intelligence) for information on contacting witnesses via police channels.

ADDITIONAL INFORMATION TO INCLUDE IN A REQUEST FOR WITNESS/SUSPECT EVIDENCE (TESTIMONY) TO BE TAKEN BY THE POLICE:

- A list of questions to be asked should be provided if possible.
- Details of the prerequisites of any procedure to be followed in taking the evidence, including any rules on privilege which a witness or suspect may be entitled to claim. This will be complied with as far as is possible under UK law.
- Any caution or formal notification of rights which should be given to the witness under the law of the requesting State. The giving of such caution or formal notification will be complied with as far as is possible under UK law.

Please note that police officers are not normally authorised to administer oaths in the UK.

Witness and suspect evidence to be taken on oath

Requests for evidence may need to be "sworn" or taken on oath by a court.

Both witnesses and suspects can be compelled to attend court for the purposes of MLA requests under section 15 of CICA. However, schedule 1 of CICA makes it clear that a person cannot be compelled to give any evidence before a nominated court which he could not be compelled to give in criminal proceedings in the UK or if the criminal proceedings were being conducted in the requesting state. Of particular relevance in this context are:

- The privilege against self-incrimination; and
- The provisions in UK domestic law that a person *charged* with an offence cannot be compelled to give evidence in his own trial.

Requesting authorities should consider if it is worth making a request to compel a suspect to attend court if they are likely to remain silent. Ultimately it is a decision for the UK central authority whether to nominate a court and the central authority will take into account all the circumstances when making this decision.

ADDITIONAL INFORMATION TO INCLUDE IN AN MLA REQUEST FOR EVIDENCE (TESTIMONY) TO BE TAKEN BEFORE A COURT:

- Expressly state that the evidence is required to be taken on oath before a court.
- Provide details of why it is necessary for the statement to be taken on oath, rather than by the police.
- A list of questions to be asked should be provided, if possible.
- Avoid expressions such as "*to hear*" or "*to examine*" which are only used in Scottish law and have no precise meaning in English law. Use of such terms will delay the execution of the request whilst clarification is sought as to whether a court needs to be nominated or not.
- Details of the requirements of the requesting authority's procedure to be followed in taking the evidence, including any rules on privilege which a witness or suspect may be entitled to claim. This will be complied with as far as is possible under UK law. A person cannot be compelled to give any evidence which he could not be compelled to give in the UK or in the requesting authority (where such privilege is conceded by the requesting authority or court).
- Any caution or formal notification of rights which should be given to the witness or suspect under the law of the requesting State. This will be complied with as far as is possible under UK law.

Witness/Suspect Privilege

Where a witness claims privilege under the law of the requesting country, evidence will not be taken if the requesting authority concedes the claim. Where the claim is not conceded, the evidence may be taken but will not be sent to the requesting authority until a court in the requesting State rules on the matter.

Evidence taken in court without an oath

In relation to section 15 of CICA, schedule 1 provides that "*the court may take evidence on oath*" *(paragraph 3)*. Should the requesting authority not require an oath to be taken, this enables evidence to be taken in court without it.

Appointment of a lawyer to represent the accused or witness

In line with schedule 1 of CICA, the court nominated to receive the evidence can determine who can appear or take part in the proceedings, and whether a party may be legally represented. The court can therefore allow lawyers to be present, but it cannot appoint one. If a requesting authority explicitly asks for a lawyer to be appointed when evidence is received, the court will not be able to positively appoint a lawyer to represent the accused if he does not require one. Moreover, the central authority will not be able to pay for a lawyer from its own funds, nor is there a mechanism whereby legal aid can be provided to cover the cost.

Third Party material held in confidence – Telecommunications

In line with sections 13-15 of CICA, requests for telecommunications data such as subscriber checks and telephone billing for use as evidence should be sent to the relevant central authority. The central authority will then nominate a court to receive the evidence.

Requesting authorities should be aware that telecommunications companies in the UK normally retain billing and IP data for between 30 days and 12 months. It is possible to request the preservation of telecommunications data via Interpol pending the execution of an MLA request.

ADDITIONAL INFORMATION TO INCLUDE IN A REQUEST FOR TELE COMMUNICATIONS DATA:

- information concerning the source of the telephone numbers;
- the exact date, time and place of the incident under investigation;
- full details of individuals involved in the incident and the roles they played;
- why it is necessary to obtain the data and what is sought to be achieved from so obtaining it;
- why the objectives of the investigation cannot be achieved by other means;
- information must also be available to allow for consideration of the possibility of intrusion into the privacy of third parties and allow for the detailing of plans to minimise this.

Telephone and address information

If authorities require telephone numbers for businesses or people for non-evidential purposes it may be possible to locate information on 192.com or the BT Phonebook. This can provide information on a person or business phone number or address across yellow and white pages directories.

Third Party material held in confidence – Banking Evidence

In line with sections 13–15 of CICA requests for banking evidence should be sent to the relevant central authority. As there is no central record of bank accounts held in the UK, as much identifying information as possible should be given to identify the financial institution believed to be in possession of information. Requesting authorities should be aware that the retention policies of banks vary at around 5 years.

In England, Wales and Northern Ireland, evidence from financial institutions will usually be obtained by means of testimony given before a nominated court by a member of that institution's staff (who will produce any relevant documents as exhibits to his or her statement).

In Scotland, a direction is sought from the Lord Advocate under section 13 of CICA to crave a search warrant for the banking evidence. The bank will then submit the relevant documentation and witness statements to the police in answer to the warrant which in turn will be forwarded to the requesting authority.

ADDITIONAL INFORMATION TO INCLUDE IN A REQUEST FOR BANKING EVIDENCE (IF KNOWN):

- Name of the account holder and number of the account
- The address and/or number ("sort code") of the branch of the bank where the account is held
- The time period over which the information is sought. (An explanation must be given for any period that falls outside the time framework for the investigation)
- What grounds they believe that banks in the UK holds account(s) and to the extent available, which banks may be involved
- Specific documents required (e.g. account opening information, bank statements, etc).

Customer Information Orders / Account Monitoring Orders

Requesting authorities should note that sections 32 and 35 of CICA *only* apply to an investigation into serious criminal conduct by a "participating country". Therefore, only "participating countries" should make requests for Customer Information Orders ("CIOs") and Account Monitoring Orders ("AMOs") under section 35 of CICA. A list of "participating countries" for the purposes of CICA is at Annex A.

Evidence via Video or Telephone Conference

Video Conference (Television Link)

The basis for hearing witnesses in the UK through video conferencing is section 30 of CICA.

The UK will not assist with requests to hear evidence from *suspects* via video conference (see declaration in regard to Article 10(9) of the Convention on Mutual Assistance in Criminal Matters between the Member States of the European Union ("MLAC")).

Requesting authorities will be charged for video conferencing by the UKCA and are therefore required to provide a UK billing address within the letter of request. Scotland does not invoice requesting authorities for the costs of the television link.

ADDITIONAL INFORMATION TO INCLUDE IN A REQUEST FOR EVIDENCE VIA VIDEO CONFERENCE (TELEVISION LINK):

- A minimum of eight weeks notice given prior to the date of the video conferencing hearing;
- Written confirmation of a UK billing address;
- Email address of someone in the requesting authority that can be contacted at short notice who will provide technical assistance;
- Sufficient information to enable the central authority to identify and contact the witness(es);
- A list of questions to be asked if possible;
- Details of the requirements of your procedure to be followed in taking the evidence, including any rules on privilege which a witness may be entitled to claim;
- Any caution or formal notification of rights which should be given to the witness under the law of the requesting State;
- Details (if known at the time) of the technical requirements for establishing the link to ensure compatibility.

Telephone Conference

The basis for hearing witnesses in the UK through telephone conferencing is section 31 and schedule 2 of CICA. This section only applies to relevant participating countries (see Annex A for list of participating countries).

ADDITIONAL INFORMATION TO INCLUDE IN A REQUEST FOR EVIDENCE VIA TELEPHONE CONFERENCE:

- A minimum of eight weeks notice given prior to the date of the telephone link hearing;
- Confirmation that the witness has expressly agreed to give evidence via telephone link (this is required by schedule 2 of CICA);
- The name and address of the witness to be questioned;
- A list of questions to be asked should be provided, if possible;
- Details of the procedure to be followed in taking the evidence, including any rules on privilege which a witness may be entitled to claim;
- Any caution or formal notification of rights which should be given to the witness or suspect under the law of the requesting State.

Restraint and Confiscation of Assets

Requests for the restraint and confiscation of assets require **dual criminality** and a full justification as to why it is necessary. Without this information a court will be unable to give an order to effectively freeze assets or register an order to confiscate assets to allow it to be enforced. Once the assets have been identified, the central authority will decide who will execute a request and will refer it to the relevant authority accordingly, in line with the Proceeds of Crime Act 2002 (External Requests and Orders) Order 2005.

The UK central authority dealing with the request will make the appropriate applications before the Court for the assets to be restrained and will inform the requesting authority as soon as this has been done. The requesting authority must serve a copy of the restraint order upon the suspect and any other person known to be affected by it once it receives it from the UK. The UK courts will require an acknowledgement that this has been completed otherwise the court may discharge the order.

The order to freeze assets can be obtained by a court on behalf of a foreign jurisdiction at the investigative stage of criminal proceedings. See Annex D for an example LOR in a restraint and confiscation case. If the LOR is translated from a foreign language, the translations must be certified.

ADDITIONAL INFORMATION TO INCLUDE IN A REQUEST FOR RESTRAINT OF PROPERTY:

- The name, address, nationality, date and place of birth and present location of the suspect(s) or defendants whose criminal conduct has given rise to anticipated confiscation or forfeiture proceedings.
- Details of the criminal investigation.

- Details of the law applicable to the investigation and current evidence against the suspects.
- Particulars of the property which it is intended to restrain in the UK, the persons holding it and details of the link between the suspect and the property (this is important if the property to be restrained is held in the name of a third party such as a company or another person).
- State clearly whether prior assistance in the case (including asset tracing assistance) has been provided and, if so, give particulars of the UK enforcement or other authority involved and details of the assistance already received. If assistance has not previously been sought or provided this should be clearly stated.
- Where applicable, details of any court orders already made in the requesting State against the suspect in respect of his or her property. If any court order has been made, a duly authenticated copy should be included with the request - that is a true copy of that order certified by a person in his or her capacity as a judge, magistrate or officer of the relevant court of the requesting State, or by an official of the requesting authority. If no court orders have been made, this should be clearly stated.
- If possible, brief details of all known property held by the suspect outside the UK.
- State clearly that property in England and Wales must be restrained because there are insufficient property/assets elsewhere. If there are property/assets located elsewhere but these cannot be restrained, this must be clearly stated by the requesting authority.
- A certificate or statement issued by or on behalf of the requesting authority, stating:
- that an investigation has been instituted in that country and has not concluded, or that proceedings have been instituted and are ongoing in the requesting State;
- that the order which it is expected the court of the requesting State will make will have the purpose of recovering property or has the purpose of ordering the forfeiture of instrumentalities of crime.
- that any future order that is made can be enforced outside the jurisdiction of the requesting State;
- an undertaking to serve a copy of the order once it has been made upon the suspect and other persons known to be affected by the order.

ADDITIONAL INFORMATION TO INCLUDE IN A REQUEST FOR CONFISCATION OR FORFEITURE OF PROPERTY:

- The information as outlined above for restraint applications.
- An original confiscation or forfeiture order or a duly authenticated copy of the order.
- Even if the benefit gained from the offending has not yet been determined at the restraint stage, this should be stated where possible, as the courts cannot confiscate more than this amount.
- A certificate or statement issued by or on behalf of the requesting authority stating:
- That the order was made consequent on the conviction of the person named in the order
- that the order is in force and that neither the order nor any conviction to which it may relate is subject to appeal;
- that all or a certain amount of the sum payable under the order remains unpaid in the territory of the requesting State or that other property recoverable under the order remains un-recovered there;
- that the confiscation order has the purpose of recovering property, or the value of property received in connection with the commission of crime, or in the case of a forfeiture order has the purpose of ordering the forfeiture of instrumentalities of crime;
- that the order made can be enforced outside the jurisdiction of the requesting State;
- that the order for registration is not incompatible with the European Convention on Human Rights ("ECHR").

Search and Seizure

Requests for search and seizure require **dual criminality** and a full justification as to why it is necessary (see sections 16 to 19 of CICA). Central and executing authorities do not have the authority to issue warrants themselves; they must be in a position to convince a court to issue a search warrant or production order. It is not sufficient that a request is accompanied by a search warrant issued by an authority in the requesting State. The UK reserves the right to execute requests which specifically request search warrants be issued in other ways such as via the nomination of a court to take testimony.

ADDITIONAL INFORMATION TO INCLUDE IN A REQUEST FOR SEARCH AND SEIZURE OF EVIDENCE:

- The full address or a precise description of any place to be searched.
- A full explanation as to where the specific material or type of material is expected to be recovered from, such as within the house, garage premises, garden premises
- Details of how the place to be searched is connected with the case or the suspected person.
- Any information available which indicates that the material requested may be held on computer.
- Full details of the specific material or type of material to be seized (it will not usually be sufficient to simply state "evidence relevant to the investigation").
- A full description of the criminal conduct concerned. (Requests for search and seizure are subject to a need for dual criminality).
- An explanation why the material requested is considered both relevant and important evidence to the investigation or proceedings.
- Why the evidence is thought to be on the particular premises or in the possession of the particular person concerned.
- Why the material would not be produced to a UK court if the natural or legal person holding the material were ordered to do so by means of a witnesses summons. (This is to help ensure that applications to the UK courts for search warrants are successful and less likely to fail or be subject to subsequent legal challenge.)
- Appropriate undertakings for the safekeeping and return of any seized evidence.
- If it is anticipated that law enforcement officers may come across special procedure materials[4] during the course of a search.
- Any other information which would be of operational use to the executing authority in connection with the execution of the request.

Please note the search template form at Annex D. This is of great use when completing a LOR for search and seizure of evidence as it shows all the information that the UK executing authority will require (please also refer to Section 4 on attendance of overseas law enforcement officers).

Execution of search and seizure requests in England, Wales and Northern Ireland

Where further information is required about the offence or the material to be seized, depending on the particular circumstances, the UK central authority will inform the requesting authorities without delay. Notification of interested parties is not required where an application is made for a search warrant.

Execution of search and seizure requests in Scotland

The Crown Office in Scotland may direct a Procurator Fiscal (prosecutor) to obtain a search warrant. With regard to the dual criminality test, the equivalent crime in Scotland must be an offence punishable by imprisonment (section 18(1)(b) of CICA). Neither the police nor HMRC can apply for a search warrant in Scotland. Interested parties are not notified of the application for a search warrant. The concept of legal privilege applies equally in Scotland. The Procurator Fiscal will instruct the police or HMRC to transmit the evidence obtained directly to the requesting authorities.

Temporary Transfer of a Prisoner for purposes of investigation

Under section 5 of the Criminal Justice (International Cooperation) Act 1990, a UK prisoner can be *temporarily* transferred abroad to assist with overseas criminal investigations and proceedings. Prisoners cannot be transferred from the UK without their consent. Requests for temporary transfer of prisoners must be sent to the appropriate central authority (note this type of assistance cannot be accepted by HMRC).

Before agreeing to the transfer the relevant central authority must be satisfied that the presence of the prisoner is not already required in that part of the UK for the purposes of investigations or proceedings and that the transfer would not prolong the prisoner's period of detention.

---

[4] Special procedure material or materials subject to "Legal and Professional Privilege" include three categories of material to which different rules apply:

"excluded material" which includes confidential journalistic records, medical records and samples, counselling records

"legally privileged" which includes material relating to advice provided by a solicitor to his client unless this material is held with the intention of furthering a criminal purpose

"special procedure material" which includes other confidential business records and non-confidential journalistic material

Where the transfer is agreed with the requesting authority, the central authority arranges for:

- the prisoner in custody to be taken to a departure point in the UK and to be delivered into the custody of a person representing the requesting authority;
- for the prisoner to be escorted back to the UK by the requesting authority;
- the subsequent transfer of the prisoner in custody from the arrival point in the UK to his or her place of detention.

The costs of escorting and accommodating prisoners from their point of departure from the UK to their point of return to the UK are met by the requesting authority.

The central authority will liaise with the National Offender Management Service (NOMS) to ensure that the prisoner is taken to a point of departure in the UK and then taken back into prison custody when the requesting authority has completed their process.

NOMS would expect a minimum of three weeks notice to arrange the transfer of a prisoner from an English prison to a point of departure. This time is to ensure that the necessary arrangements for the prisoner to be handed over are made and relevant information concerning the prisoner's security category and any medical information is conveyed to the requesting state prior to transfer. The contact details for the relevant part of NOMS who can deal with these requests are:

Cross Border Transfers Section
Offender Safety, Rights & Responsibilities Group
National Offender Management Services
Post Point 4.16
4th Floor, Clive House
70 Petty France
London
SW1H 9EX
Tel: +44 300 0 475691
Fax: +44 300 0 476857

ADDITIONAL INFORMATION TO INCLUDE IN A REQUEST FOR TEMPORARY TRANSFER OF PRISONERS TO THE REQUESTING STATE TO ASSIST IN THE REQUESTING STATE'S INVESTIGATION:

- Dates on which the presence abroad of the prisoner is required, including the dates on which the court or other proceedings for which the prisoner is required will commence and are likely to be concluded;
- Information for the purpose of obtaining the prisoner's consent to the transfer and satisfying the UK authorities that arrangements will be made to keep the prisoner in secure custody such as:
- whether the prisoner will have immunity from prosecution for previous offences;
- details of proposed arrangements for collecting the prisoner from and returning the prisoner to the UK;
- details of the type of secure accommodation in which the prisoner will be held in the requesting State;
- details of the type of escort available abroad to and from the secure accommodation.

Transfer of a Prisoner for the purpose of serving the remainder of a prison sentence (non-MLA prisoner transfer)

The UK central authorities do not deal with requests for the transfer of prisoners for purposes of ensuring they serve the remainder of a prison sentence *or any* other non-MLA basis. The UK authority for other types of requests relating to Prisoner Transfer is:

Cross Border Transfers Section
Offender Safety, Rights and Responsibilities Group
Post Point 4.16
4th Floor, Clive House
70 Petty France
London
SW1H 9EX
Tel: +44 300 0 475691
Fax: +44 300 0 476857

Passport Information and Immigration Status

Requests for this information can be sought through intelligence routes (please see Section 6). If this information is sought for evidential purposes an MLA request should be made to the relevant central authority. Both central authorities and agencies acting in an intelligence capacity will apply to the Identity and Passport Service ("IPS") for this information.

ADDITIONAL INFORMATION REQUIRED:

- Details of person (name, date of birth and place of birth if known);
- Passport number (current and previous);
- State whether the request relates to the prevention and detection of crime or apprehension of prosecution of an offender;
- How the data being sought links to the offence being investigated.

Other Requests for Mutual Legal Assistance

Joint Investigation Teams

A Joint Investigation Team ("JIT") is an investigation team set up for a set period, based on an agreement between two or more States and/or competent authorities, for a specific purpose. A JIT can be considered in cases where close and co-ordinated co-operation between countries is required to effectively and efficiently investigate crime.

A JIT can be set up under:

- Council Framework Decision on Joint Investigation Teams (2002/465/JHA);
- Convention on Mutual Assistance in Criminal Matters between the Member States of the European Union ("MLAC");
- Second Additional Protocol("Second Additional Protocol") to the 1959 European Convention on Mutual Assistance in Criminal Matters ("Convention on Mutual Assistance in Criminal Matters");
- Convention on Mutual Assistance and Cooperation between Customs Administrations ("Naples II Convention");
- A specific bilateral/multilateral agreement with the participants in the JIT

Interception of Telecommunications

Please see Section 6 (Requests for Intelligence).

Article 21 Convention on Mutual Assistance in Criminal Matters

The UK will consider information laid with a view for proceedings under Article 21 of the Convention on Mutual Assistance in Criminal Matters on a case by case basis. These requests will not be automatically accepted.

Transfer of Proceedings

The UK is not a signatory to the European Convention on the Transfer of Proceedings in Criminal Matters.

DNA

The UK can consider a MLA request for a DNA sample to be taken from an individual; however the UK has no power to compel an individual to provide a DNA sample.

In addition, if a DNA profile is already held by the UK it will generally not be transferred abroad as part of a MLA request for the purposes of matching it to a crime scene profile. If a request for DNA matching is made, the requesting authority should send the crime scene profile to the UK for matching. This enables it to be checked not just against the individual concerned but also other profiles held on the UK's National DNA database.

Spontaneous Exchange of Information

If a UK central authority has information relating to a criminal offence which may lead or relate to an MLA request by a country, the UK may exchange this information with a country without the need for a request. Spontaneous exchange of information is also possible via police cooperation routes and will be channelled through SOCA.

Permission to Use Evidence for Other Purposes

Evidence/information provided by a UK central authority pursuant to an MLA request should not be used for any purpose other than that outlined in the original request without the consent of the UK central authority. If a requesting State wishes to use evidence for different purposes, or to share the evidence with a third country, formal permission to do so must be submitted in writing by the original requesting State to the central authority that dealt with the original request. As a general rule, a UK central authority will not give consent for evidence to be used for any purpose that could not have been the subject of a separate MLA request, for example the use of evidence in civil proceedings. However, each case will be considered separately on its own facts.

ADDITIONAL INFORMATION TO INCLUDE IN A REQUEST TO USE EVIDENCE FOR OTHER PURPOSES:

- The central authority's reference number for the original request
- What evidence is to be used
- How this evidence will be used
- Why this evidence is needed in this investigation / court proceedings.

Section 4
Officers present from the requesting state and transmission of evidence

Officers from the Requesting State present at the execution of a MLA request

If officers from the requesting State wish to be present during the execution of a MLA request, for example to participate in a search or to be present during the interview of a witness, this must also be requested. The central authority, in conjunction with the authority executing the request in the UK, will determine whether this is appropriate.

The requesting authority must give reasons as to why someone from the requesting State should be present. For example, if it is a very complex case it may be beneficial to have the investigating officer present. However, if it is not justified for an officer of the requesting State to be present this request will be refused.

Notifying the UK of law enforcement officers travelling to the UK

The relevant local police force in the UK must be made aware in advance if officers for the requesting State are due to travel to the UK. However, if the requesting State is unable to contact / identify the local police force, then SOCA can assist and pass on notification.

The relevant local police force in the UK must also be notified in advance if foreign law enforcement officers are due to travel to the UK to conduct official business even if this is not pursuant to MLA.

Transmission of evidence

Evidence will not automatically be given to foreign officers who may have been present during the execution. However, it may on occasion be practical to transfer the evidence through accompanying officers. In this case UK police must seek authorisation from a central authority.

Section 5
MLA requests from the UK

Who can send an MLA request *from* the UK?

Authorities that have been designated as a prosecuting authority under section 7 of CICA can make MLA requests to other countries. As well as the central authorities described in section 2, this includes:

- Magistrates' Courts, the Crown Court and the High Court;
- the Attorney General for England and Wales;
- the Director of Public Prosecutions and any Crown Prosecutor;
- the Director and any designated member of the Serious Fraud Office;
- the Environment Agency

- Secretary of State for Business, Innovation & Skills in respect of his function of investigating and prosecuting offences;
- Secretary of State for Health;
- Secretary of State for Transport;
- Secretary of State for Work and Pensions;
- District Courts and Sheriff Courts and the High Court of Justiciary;
- the Lord Advocate of Scotland;
- any Procurator Fiscal (Prosecutor in Scotland);
- the Attorney General for Northern Ireland;
- the Director of Public Prosecutions in Northern Ireland;
- the Financial Services Authority

If an authority is not designated under CICA, a prosecutor / defence lawyer will draft a LOR and then send this to a court for approval. The court will then forward this to the foreign authority or to the appropriate central authority in the UK.

Direct Transmission to EU/Schengen countries

The authorities listed above are able to send MLA requests to EU/Schengen countries from the UK directly, without the request going via a central authority in the UK. However, direct transmission from the UK to EU/Schengen countries is not possible for:

- requests for restraint and confiscation
- requests for the transfer of a prisoner to appear in court or assist an investigation;
- requests for Account Monitoring Orders or Customer Information Order; and,
- States where domestic legislation does not allow for it.

See Annex E for a list of countries that accept direct transmission.

Section 6
Requests for intelligence

This form of assistance may be referred to as "Police to Police Cooperation", "Mutual Assistance" or "Mutual Administrative Assistance". It entails police and other law enforcement officers in a requesting State asking for the assistance of law enforcement agencies in the UK to gather intelligence for an investigation. Intelligence can be an easier and quicker way to obtain information, as it does not require an LOR. In many countries' legal systems, intelligence collected by UK law enforcement agencies is directly admissible as evidence in criminal trials. Countries which do not require evidence to be sworn by witnesses in a court under their domestic law can consider using intelligence routes to request information to be used as evidence.

UK law enforcement agencies which can assist in relation to intelligence requests

The following agencies can receive intelligence enquiries directly from law enforcement officers in foreign jurisdictions:

- Europol via SOCA
- Interpol via SOCA
- UK Border Agency[5]
- HMRC[6]
- Police Forces

Please see Annex C for contact details for the above authorities.

[5] Assisting foreign authorities on an intelligence basis will be dependent on whether UKBA has a data sharing agreement or memorandum of understanding with that country.

[6] Assisting foreign authorities on an intelligence basis will be dependent on whether HMRC has a data sharing agreement or memorandum of understanding with that country. The transmission of personal data outside the EU will depend on whether the receiving jurisdiction has equivalent protections on the processing of such data as can be found in the EU Data Protection Directive and the UK"s Data Protection Act.

How to make requests for intelligence from a UK law enforcement agency

If direct contact between a foreign police force and a UK police force has not already been established, SOCA should be contacted with the request. SOCA acts as the UK Interpol gateway for all incoming and outgoing police to police enquiries. SOCA will forward requests through the Interpol network to the relevant police force or other law enforcement agency who will then execute the request.

Assistance which can be requested from the UK via Police to Police enquiries

Examples of requests that may be submitted directly to SOCA without involving the central authorities include:

- interviewing witnesses in criminal investigations where the person to be interviewed is willing to co-operate without appearing or needing to appear before a judicial authority in the UK;
- sharing of information and intelligence concerning investigations into offences which have been committed in the UK (provided that the information or intelligence is not being requested for use in proceedings);
- asset tracing enquiries;
- providing details of previous convictions;
- providing details of UK telephone subscribers and telecommunications data for non-evidential purposes (under the Regulation of Investigatory Powers Act 2000 ("RIPA"), see Section 3 if required for evidential purposes);
- providing details of keepers of motor vehicles registered in the UK and of driving licences issued in the UK;
- obtaining medical or dental statements or records with a patient's written consent;
- obtaining information from publicly available sources, such as for example the Land Register in relation to ownership of properties.

Such requests do not need to be made via a formal LOR and sent to the central authorities unless it is a requirement of the domestic law of the judicial authority making the request.

Requests for Interception of Telecommunications

International requests for assistance in the interception of telecommunications are made under articles 17 to 22 of the Convention on Mutual Legal Assistance in Criminal Matters between Member States of the European Union 2000.

In the UK the Regulation of Investigatory Powers Act 2000 (RIPA) provides the legislative framework governing the interception of telecommunications. It will not always be possible to accede to requests for interception and interception warrants must be personally authorised by the Secretary of State. The information obtained by interception must be used for intelligence purposes only.

Assistance which cannot be requested from the UK via Police to Police enquiries

Most requests for coercive measures (for example, production of bank records, restraint of assets or search and seizure) require authorisation by the relevant central authority and a court order, so a formal LOR must be sent. SOCA will not serve summons.

Contacting witnesses in the UK

Subject to the provisions of relevant bilateral or other international instruments, contact may be made with witnesses directly by letter, fax or telephone without informing the central authorities. If the witness is willing to assist the enquiry voluntarily, an approach may be made through SOCA to record his or her statement or to the central authorities if testimony on oath is required.

Intelligence requests for the Crown Dependencies and the UK Overseas Territories

Requests for intelligence from the Crown Dependencies, Falklands, and St Helena should be submitted via SOCA. The other Overseas Territories host Interpol sub-bureaux.

Section 7

Requests for criminal records

Although requests for criminal records may form part of a wider formal MLA request, requesting authorities **should not** obtain criminal record information from the UKCA (England, Wales and Northern Ireland) or Crown Office (Scotland).

Requests from EU Member States

Requests for criminal records from EU Member States are handled by the Exchange of Criminal Records ("UKCA-ECR") team at the ACPO Criminal Records Office ("ACRO"). The basis for exchanging records between EU Member States is Framework Decision 2009/315/JHA, which built on the Convention on Mutual Assistance in Criminal Matters and Council Decision 2005/876/JHA. This is achieved through the European Criminal Record Information System (ECRIS).

The functions of the UKCA-ECR team are to notify EU Member States of any convictions imposed in the UK on a citizen from that EU Member State, to receive notifications of convictions of UK nationals in other EU Member States and to make and reply to requests for previous convictions in connection with criminal proceedings against an EU national in another EU member state.

EU Member States must contact the UKCA-ECR team to request criminal record information regarding a British citizen subject to criminal proceedings in the EU.

A requesting authority from an EU Member State should make a request for criminal records through their own central authority, as the request will then be transmitted to the UKCA-ECR.

If the MLA central authorities (UK Central Authority or Crown Office) receive a request for criminal records (from an EU Member State) which only includes the information below, the request will be redirected to UKCA-ECR by email. However the UKCA-ECR will only provide the information requested if there is no requirement from the requesting authority that a witness statement be provided by UKCA-ECR in support of the records provided.

In all circumstances it is preferred that requesting authorities from EU Member States make all requests for criminal records through their own criminal record central authorities. Failure to do so may delay a response to your request.

For more background information please visit the ACRO website.

Criminal record information provided by the UKCA-ECR

Where an EU Member State requests criminal record information in relation to criminal proceedings, the ECR team will provide (in English) the requesting state with the following information:

- PNC ID
- Case ID(s)
- Full name (and if applicable previous name(s))
- Aliases
- Date of birth
- Place of birth
- Gender
- Nationality
- Name of Court(s) of Conviction/Sentence
- Date of Conviction(s)/Sentence(s)
- Type and Extent of Punishment(s)
- Legal Classification of Offence(s)
- Supplementary Penalties
- Subsequent Decision(s) Modifying Conviction(s)/Sentence(s)

If *specifically* requested the UKCA-ECR team can also provide (if available on the PNC record):

- Place of the Offence
- Circumstances of the Offence
- The last known address
- Fingerprints

Please note that all information supplied by UKCA-ECR will be in English. It is strongly recommended that requesting authorities make requests for criminal records via their own criminal record central authority, as the criminal record information provided by ECRIS is transmitted through a standardised European format which facilitates automatic translation.

The UKCA-ECR team **cannot** provide a requesting state with:

- Certificate of Conviction *from the Court* (see below)
- Judge's Sentencing Remarks (see below)
- Convicted Person's Parents" Names
- Status of any appeal against Conviction(s)/Sentence(s)
- Status of ongoing criminal investigations
- Current location of an individual convicted in the UK
- Total period(s) spent in custody/detention
- Information on use of interpreter in the course of criminal proceeding and, if not used, reasons why (see below)

Information to include in a request to the UKCA-ECR team

All requests should include:

- Details of the requesting authority
- Reason for the request
- Details on the identity of the person concerned in the request (including their name, birth name, aliases, sex, nationality, date of birth, place of birth, parents' names, residence or known address, fingerprints where available, other identification data where available).

Format

Where applicable the form available on the EJN website should be used.

Where to send requests

Requests to the ECR team should be sent by post or email:
UKCA-ECR
ACRO
PO Box 481 Fareham Hampshire PO14 9FS
United Kingdom
Tel: + 44 1489 569 805
Email: international.requests@ACRO.pnn.police.uk

If requests for criminal records are sent to UKCA or Crown Office in error the request will be forwarded to the UKCA-ECR team, but this may delay a substantive response.

Requests from the Rest of the World

Requests for criminal records from the rest of the world (non-EU Member States) are forwarded by SOCA on a case by case basis.

Requests for Certificate of Conviction/Memorandum of Conviction

Where the name and date of the court of conviction/sentence is known, requests for a Certificate of Conviction (Crown Court) or Memorandum of Conviction (Magistrates' Court) must be made to the court of conviction/sentence directly. If a requesting authority does not know the name or date of the court of conviction/sentence, a request for criminal records should be made first (see above).

Requests for the following information should also be redirected to the relevant court, who may be able to provide:

- Information on the use of an interpreter in the course of criminal proceeding and, if not used, the reasons why
- The identity of defence counsel in the proceedings

Contact details for courts in England & Wales, Northern Ireland, or Scotland can be found on their respective websites.

If requests are sent to the UK Central Authority or Crown Office the request will be redirected to the relevant court (if the name of the court has been provided by the requesting state), but this may delay a substantive response.

Requests for a Certificate of Conviction or a Memorandum of Conviction which are sent to the UK Central Authority or Crown Office which do not provide the name of the court and date of the conviction/sentence court will be rejected. The requesting authority should request the criminal record from the UKCA-ECR / SOCA and the requesting authority must then send the request directly to the relevant court.

Requests made to UKCA-ECR through ECRIS for details of criminal convictions will be provided as an extract from the PNC and will not be certified by the court. As outlined above, court certificates must be obtained directly from the relevant court.

Requests for Transcripts/Sentencing Remarks

It is not usual practice in the UK for a transcript of the proceedings or the Judge's sentencing remarks to be used as evidence in a subsequent criminal matter. Moreover, transcription services are generally provided by private contractors who usually charge by the folio (72 words), making the cost of a transcript of proceedings expensive. As such the cost of obtaining this evidence is of a substantial or extraordinary nature.

Requests for transcripts or sentencing remarks must be sent to UKCA (England, Wales and Northern Ireland) or Crown Office (Scotland) and must include:

- written confirmation (in English) that such evidence **is** required; and
- confirmation that the requesting authority is willing to pay for the costs of acquiring such evidence.

If these confirmations are not received at the time of the request a substantive response is likely to be delayed.

Section 8
Information about companies

Information about a company that is not required as evidence can be found on the Companies House website. This website has a search engine called webCHeck.

Companies House also offer other services to help find information on companies, some of which is free.

If **evidence** is required, requesting countries must make an MLA request to the UK. For information on how to go about this, please see earlier sections of the guidance. In particular, please note Section 3 regarding witness evidence and whether it is necessary to be given on oath.

Section 9
Civil matters

Mutual legal assistance requests to the UK relating to civil matters are dealt with by different authorities than those dealing with MLA requests in criminal matters.

Under the Civil Procedure Rules Part 34, MLA requests to and from the UK relating to civil matters are dealt with separately from criminal requests. Obtaining evidence from other jurisdictions in respect to civil litigation (which encompasses commercial litigation) is included within the Evidence (Proceedings in Other Jurisdictions) Act 1975 and such requests are dealt with by the Foreign and Commonwealth Office (FCO).

Requests for assistance with international civil matters should be sent to:

The Legalisation Office
Foreign & Commonwealth Office
PO Box 6255
Milton Keynes
MK10 1XX

European Judicial Network in Civil and Commercial Matters

There is a European Judicial Network (EJN) for Civil and Commercial Matters website where a large quantity of information about the Member States, Community law, European law and various aspects of civil and commercial law can be found.

ANNEX A – MLA TREATIES THE UK IS PARTY TO INTERNATIONAL AGREEMENTS THE UK HAS RATIFIED *(AS OF AUGUST 2012)*

2000 Convention on Mutual Assistance in Criminal Matters between the Member States of the European Union ("MLAC") & Protocol – Implementation

1959 European Convention on Mutual Assistance in Criminal Matters – List of Signatories

1978 Additional Protocol to European Convention on Mutual Assistance in Criminal Matters – List of Signatories

2001 Second Additional Protocol to European Convention on Mutual Assistance in Criminal Matters – List of Signatories

1990 European Convention on Laundering, Search, Seizure and Confiscation of the Proceeds from Crime – List of Signatories

1988 United Nations Convention against Illicit Traffic in Narcotic Drugs and Psychotropic Substances ('Vienna Convention') – List of Signatories

2000 United Nations Convention against Transnational Organised Crime 2000 ('UNTOC') – List of Signatories

2003 United Nations Convention against Corruption ('UNCAC') – List of Signatories

Commonwealth Scheme Relating to Mutual Assistance in Criminal Matters ('Harare Scheme')

Countries/Territories with Bilateral MLA Treaty with UK *(as of August 2012)*

Algeria	Japan (EU)
Antigua & Barbuda*	Libya
Argentina*	Malaysia
Australia*	Mexico*
Bahamas*	Netherlands*
Bahrain*	Nigeria*
Barbados*	Norway (EU)
Brazil	Panama*
Canada	Paraguay*
Chile*	Philippines
Colombia	Romania*
Ecuador*	Saudi Arabia*
Grenada*	Spain*
Guyana*	Sweden*
Hong Kong SAR	Thailand
Iceland (EU)	Ukraine*
India	United Arab Emirates
Ireland	Uruguay*
Italy*	USA (EU)
Vietnam	

* *– Indicates Restraint & Confiscation or Drug Trafficking MLA treaty EU – Indicates EU MLA treaty or EU led bilateral instrument that UK is party to*

Countries Designated as Participating Countries under CICA *(as of August 2012)*	Which CICA Sections Designated
Japan, USA	section 32, 35, 43, 44 and 45
Iceland, and Norway	sections 31, 32, 35, 43, 44, 45, 47 and 48, and schedule 2 (paragraph 15)
Albania, Bosnia and Herzegovina, Former Yugoslav Republic of Macedonia, Israel, Montenegro, Serbia, Cyprus, Czech Republic, Estonia, Hungary, Latvia, Lithuania, Malta, Poland, Slovakia, and Slovenia	section 4, 4B, section 31, 47, 48, and schedule 2 (paragraph 15)
Austria, Belgium, Bulgaria, Denmark, Finland, France, Germany, Greece, Italy, Ireland, Luxembourg, Netherlands, Romania, Spain, Sweden and Switzerland	section 4, 4B, 31, 32, 35, 43, 44, 45, 47, 48, and schedule 2 (paragraph 15)

Treaties/Conventions Extended to Overseas Territories/Crown Dependencies

Dependency/Territory	1959 Convention	1st Protocol	UNCAC	UNTOC	Vienna	Bilateral Ext
Isle of Man	✓	-	09/11/09	-	02/12/93	Hong Kong Mexico Thailand Ukraine USA
Jersey	✓	✓	09/11/09	-	07/07/97	
Guernsey	✓	-	09/11/09	-	03/04/02	
Gibraltar	-	-	-	27/11/07	-	
British Virgin Islands	-	-	12/10/06	17/05/12	08/02/95	
Cayman Islands	-	-	-	17/05/12	08/02/95	
Bermuda	-	-	-	-	08/02/95	
Turks & Caicos Islands	-	-	-	-	08/02/95	
Anguilla	-	-	-	-	08/02/95	
St Helena, Ascension Island & Tristan de Cunha	-	-	-	-	-	
Montserrat	-	-	-	-	08/02/95	
Falkland Islands Islands	-	-	-	11/01/07	-	

ANNEX B – CONTACT DETAILS FOR CROWN DEPENDENCIES & BRITISH OVERSEAS TERRITORIES

Requests for Crown Dependencies

Isle of Man

Attorney General's Chambers
3rd Floor
St Mary's Court
Hill Street
Douglas
Isle of Man
IM1 1EU

Tel: +44 1624 685452
Fax: +44 1624 629162

Guernsey

HM Attorney General
Attorney General's Chambers
St James Chambers
St Peter Port
Guernsey
GY1 2PA
Tel: +44 1481 723355
Fax: +44 1481 725439

Jersey

HM Attorney General
Attorney General's Chambers
Morier House
St Helier
Jersey
JE1 1DD
Tel: +44 1534 502280
Fax: +44 1534 502299

Requests for British Overseas Territories

Anguilla

The Attorney-General
The Secretariat
The Valley
Anguilla
Tel: +1 264 497 3044
Fax: +1 264 497 3126

Bermuda

The Attorney-General's Chambers
Global House
43 Church Street
Hamilton
HM12 Bermuda
Tel: +1 441 292 2463
Fax: +1 441 292 3608

British Virgin Islands

The Attorney-General
The Attorney-General's Chambers
Government of the British Virgin Islands
PO Box 242
Road Town
Tortola
Tel: + 1 284 494 3701
Fax: + 1 284 494 6760

Cayman Islands

The Attorney-General
The Attorney-General's Chambers
Government Administration Building
George Town
Grand Cayman

Cayman Islands
Tel: +1 345 949 7900
Fax: +1 345 949 6079

Gibraltar – Requests from Non EU/Schengen States[7]

Attorney-General
Joshua Hassan House
Secretary's Lane
Gibraltar
Tel: +350 70723
Fax: +350 79891

Gibraltar – Requests from EU/Schengen Member States

These must be sent to the above address via:
UK Government Gibraltar Liaison Unit
King Charles St
London
SW1H 2AH
Tel: +44 207 008 2502
Fax: +44 207 008 3629

Montserrat

The Attorney-General
The Attorney-General's Chambers
3 Farara Plaza
Brades
Montserrat
Tel: +1 664 491 4686
Fax: +1 664 491 4687

Turks and Caicos Islands

The Governor
Government House
Grand Turk
Turks and Caicos Islands
Tel: +1 649 946 2308
Fax: +1 649 946 2903

ANNEX C – GLOSSARY OF THE ROLE OF DIFFERENT ORGANISATIONS IN MLA REQUESTS

Crown Office and Procurator Fiscal Service

See Section 2 for contact details.

Crown Prosecution Service (CPS)

The Crown Prosecution Service is the Government Department responsible for prosecuting criminal cases investigated by the police in England and Wales. As the principal prosecuting authority in England and Wales, they are responsible for:

- advising the police on cases for possible prosecution;
- reviewing cases submitted by the police;
- determining any charges in all but minor cases;

[7] Requests to Gibraltar must be addressed to the Competent Judicial Authority "in" or "at" or "of" Gibraltar" but NOT "for Gibraltar". If requests are addressed "for Gibraltar" it is likely they will need to be reissued.

- preparing cases for court;
- presenting cases at court.

The majority of outgoing MLA requests from the UK are sent from the CPS.

The Revenue and Customs Prosecution Office (RCPO) merged with the CPS in April 2009. RCPO prosecutes cases in England and Wales investigated by Her Majesty's Revenue and Customs (HMRC) and the Serious Organised Crime Agency (SOCA). Further details can be found on the CPS website.

CPS Head Offices: Rose Court
2 Southwark Bridge
London
SE1 9HS
Tel: 020 3357 0000

United House Piccadilly
York YO1 9PQ
Tel: 01904 545400

Financial Services Authority (FSA)

The FSA regulates the financial services industry in the UK. The FSA has statutory powers under the Financial Services and Markets Act 2000 ("FSMA") to obtain documents or information and conduct interviews on behalf of overseas regulators (as defined in section 195 of FSMA) including law enforcement authorities These powers can be exercised pursuant to an MLA request, or pursuant to a request made on an administrative basis. Information about the FSA can be found on their website.

Financial Services Authority
25 The North Colonnade Requests for Mutual Legal Assistance in Criminal Matters – Guidelines for authorities outside of the United Kingdom
Canary Wharf
London E14 5HS
Tel +44 20 7066 1000 (switchboard)

Her Majesty's Revenue and Customs (HMRC)

Criminal and Information Law Team
HM Revenue and Customs - Solicitor's Office
Room 2/74
100 Parliament Street
London
SW1A 2BQ
Fax: +44 20 7147 0433
Email: mla@hmrc.gsi.gov.uk

Interpol/Europol

Interpol is the world's largest international police organisation, with 188 member countries. It facilitates cross-border police co-operation, and supports and assists all organisations, authorities and services whose role is to prevent or combat international crime. Interpol aims to facilitate international police co-operation even where diplomatic relations do not exist between particular countries.

Europol is the EU law enforcement organisation that handles criminal intelligence. Its aim is to improve the effectiveness and cooperation between the competent authorities of the member states in preventing and combating serious international organised crime and terrorism. The mission of Europol is to make a significant contribution to the EU law enforcement action against organised crime and terrorism, with an emphasis on targeting criminal organisations.

Within MLA, Interpol and Europol's role is to improve the sharing of intelligence between law enforcement agencies across the EU and globally.
UK National Central Bureau of Interpol,
c/o Serious & Organised Crime Agency (SOCA)
PO Box 8000,
London SE11 5EN
Tel: +44 20 7238 8115

Metropolitan Police Service (Met Police)

The Met Police is the largest police force in the UK and is responsible for the execution of a large number of MLA requests. The Met Police is also plays a large role in the receipt and submissions of requests for information via police cooperation (intelligence) routes. Further information about the Met Police can be found on their website. Requests for Mutual Legal Assistance in Criminal Matters – Guidelines for authorities outside of the United Kingdom
Metropolitan Police Service New Scotland Yard Broadway London SW1H 0BG
Non-urgent telephone enquiries: 0300 123 1212

Organised and Financial Crime Unit (OFCU)

OFCU has responsibility for providing advice on organised and financial crime including drug trafficking, people smuggling, hi tech crime, fraud and money laundering. It also has responsibility for the Government's strategy on asset recovery, the Proceeds of Crime Act 2002, and acts as the sponsor unit for the SOCA.

Organised and Financial Crime Unit
5th Floor Fry Building
2 Marsham Street
London
SW1P 4DF
Tel: +44 20 7035 1567

Serious Fraud Office (SFO)

The SFO executes MLA requests, as referred to them by the UKCA. The SFO deals with cases relating to serious and complex fraud. This is defined as:

- Sums exceeding £1 million
- A significant international dimension
- Likelihood of widespread public concern
- A need for highly specialised market or commercial knowledge
- The request and assistance required brings accountancy, legal and investigative skills together
- The use of section 2 powers of the Criminal Justice Act 1987 is appropriate.

The SFO also have information about making MLA requests on their website.

Serious Fraud Office Elm House 10-16 Elm Street London WC1X 0BJ Requests for Mutual Legal Assistance in Criminal Matters - Guidelines for authorities outside of the United Kingdom
Tel: +44 20 7239 7272 (switchboard) Fax: +44 20 7837 1689

Serious Organised Crime Agency (SOCA)

SOCA is an Executive Non-Departmental Public Body sponsored by, but operationally independent from, the Home Office. SOCA is an intelligence-led agency with law enforcement powers and harm reduction responsibilities. In terms of MLA requests, SOCA is heavily involved in requests that involve operational policing matters, such as covert investigations and cross-border surveillance. SOCA hosts the Europol National Unit and Interpol National Central Bureau. SOCA is also the UK's Financial Intelligence Unit (FIU). In December 2013 SOCA will become part of the new National Crime Agency (NCA), which will be an internationally recognised agency. The NCA will maintain a network of liaison officers, be home to the Interpol and Europol Bureaux and provide the primary point of contact on organised crime matters for international partners.

Serious Organised Crime Agency (SOCA)
PO Box 8000,
London SE11 5EN
Tel: +44 20 7238 8115

UK Border Agency (UKBA)

UKBA is the Non Departmental Government Agency responsible for the detection and prosecution of cross border crime in the UK. UKBA deals with a high number of MLA requests as well as requests for intelligence. **MLA requests to UKBA must be sent via a central authority.** UKBA can receive intelligence requests directly, but only from countries with which they have a data sharing agreement or memorandum of understanding. UKBA deals with criminal investigations relating to cross border trafficking in:

- Drugs
- Immigration
- Weapons
- Indecent / Obscene material
- Money seizures.
- CITES
- Other Prohibitions and Restrictions (including drugs; firearms and offensive weapons; chemical, biological, radiological and nuclear hazards; products of animal origin; plant health; cash at the border and the Convention on International Trade in Endangered Species of Wild Fauna and Flora)

International Mutual Assistance
UK Border Agency
5th Floor
Becket House
60-68 St Thomas Street
LONDON
SE1 3QU
Fax: +44 20 3513 8350
bamat@homeoffice.gsi.gov.uk

ANNEX D – EXAMPLE LORS TO UK

- Request for Evidence
- Service of Process
- Restraint of Proceeds of Crime
- Search Warrant
- Back to Contents Requests for Mutual Legal Assistance in Criminal Matters - Guidelines for authorities outside of the United Kingdom

ANNEX E – METHOD OF TRANSMISSION OF LETTERS OF REQUEST TO DIFFERENT STATES

EU/Schengen States that will accept direct transmission of letters of request (i.e. they do not need to be sent via a central authority in the UK):

Austria	Hungary	Poland
Belgium	Iceland	Portugal
Bulgaria	Ireland*	Romania
Cyprus	Italy	Slovakia
Czech Republic	Latvia	Slovenia
Denmark	Lithuania	Spain
Estonia	Luxembourg	Sweden
Finland	Malta	Switzerland
France	Netherlands	
Germany	Norway	

* *except requests for search warrants and/or Restraint/Confiscation*

EU/Schengen States that require transmission via their central authority

Greece
UK (*except for service of process)*

Treaties requiring transmission via central authorities

- Harare Scheme
- The UK is a party to a number of MLA bilateral agreements which impose certain conditions on when MLA may be provided and set out procedures to be followed (see links to international and bilateral treaties above).

Types of requests which must be sent via the appropriate UK central authority, regardless of whether a State accepts direct transmission:

- Restraint and confiscation
- Transfer of a prisoner to appear in court or assist an investigation
- Account Monitoring Orders
- Customer Information Order

GLOSSARY AND LIST OF ABBREVIATIONS

Administrative proceedings	Proceedings outside the UK to which Article 3(1) of the Convention on Mutual Legal Assistance in Criminal Proceedings applies, that is, proceedings brought by administrative authorities in respect of administrative offences where a decision in the proceedings may be the subject of an appeal before a court (CICA 2003, s 51(1)).
Appropriate judge	Under Parts 1 and 2 of the EA 2003, the appropriate judge in England and Wales is a district judge (Magistrates' Courts) (EA 2003, ss 67 and 139). In Part 3 of the EA 2003, in England and Wales the appropriate judge is a district judge (Magistrates' Courts), a justice of the peace, or a judge entitled to exercise the jurisdiction of the Crown Court (EA 2003, s 149). In Parts 1 and 2 of the EA 2003 the use of the expression 'the judge' in a section containing a previous reference to 'the appropriate judge' or 'the judge' does not in itself require both references to be read as referring to the same individual (s 67(3A) and 139(3A), inserted by para 15 of Sch 13 to the Police and Justice Act 2006).
Asylum claim	This expression has the meaning given by s 113(1) of the Nationality, Immigration and Asylum Act 2002 (EA 2003, s 216(7)).
British Islands	The UK and the Channel Islands.
British overseas territories	These are the territories listed in Sch 6 to the British Nationality Act 1981 (British Overseas Territories Act 2002, s 1(1) and (3)), namely: Anguilla; Bermuda; British Antarctic Territory; British Indian Ocean Territory; Cayman Islands; Falkland Islands; Gibraltar; Montserrat; Pitcairn, Henderson, Ducie and Oeno Islands; St Helena, Ascension and Tristan da Cunha; South Georgia and the South Sandwich Islands, the Sovereign Base Areas of Akrotiri and Dhekelia (that is to say the areas mentioned in s 21 of the Cyprus Act 1960); Turks and Caicos Islands; British Virgin Islands.
Category 1 territory	A country designated by an order of the Secretary of State, with whom the UK operates extradition procedures in accordance with Part 1 of the Act (EA 2003, s 1(2)). The relevant order is the Extradition Act 2003 (Designation of Part 1 Territories) Order 2003 (SI 2003/3333), as amended. As at September 2012, the Category 1 territories were: Austria; Belgium; Bulgaria; Cyprus; Czech Republic; Denmark; Estonia; Finland; France; Germany; Gibraltar; Greece; Hungary; Ireland; Italy; Latvia; Lithuania; Luxembourg; Malta, the Netherlands; Poland; Portugal; Romania; Slovakia; Slovenia; Spain; Sweden. This list is liable to change, however, and the most up-to-date version of the Order should always be consulted. See Appendix E5.
Category 2 territory	A country designated by an order of the Secretary of State, with whom the UK operates extradition procedures in accordance with Part 2 of the EA 2003 (s 69(2)). The relevant order is the Extradition Act 2003 (Designation of Part 2 Territories) Order 2003 (SI 2003/3334). As at September 2012, Category 2 territories were:

	Albania, Algeria, Andorra, Antigua and Barbuda, Argentina, Armenia, Australia, Azerbaijan, the Bahamas, Bangladesh, Barbados, Belize, Bolivia, Bosnia and Herzegovina, Botswana, Brazil, Brunei, Canada, Chile, Colombia, Cook Islands, Croatia, Cuba, Dominica, Ecuador, El Salvador, Fiji, the Gambia, Georgia, Ghana, Grenada, Guatemala, Guyana, Hong Kong Special Administrative Region, Haiti, Iceland, India, Iraq, Israel, Jamaica, Kenya, Kiribati, Lesotho, Liberia, Libya, Liechtenstein, Macedonia, FYR, Malawi, Malaysia, Maldives, Mauritius, Mexico, Moldova, Monaco, Montenegro, Nauru, New Zealand, Nicaragua, Nigeria, Norway, Panama, Papua New Guinea, Paraguay, Peru, Russian Federation, Saint Christopher and Nevis, Saint Lucia, Saint Vincent and the Grenadines, San Marino, Serbia, Seychelles, Sierra Leone, Singapore, Solomon Islands, South Africa, Sri Lanka, Swaziland, Switzerland, Tanzania, Thailand, Tonga, Trinidad and Tobago, Turkey, Tuvalu, Uganda, Ukraine, Uruguay, the United Arab Emirates, the United States of America, Vanuatu, Western Samoa, Zambia, Zimbabwe. This list is liable to change, however, and the most up-to-date version of the Order should always be consulted. See Appendix E5.
Certification	The process by which either a Part 1 warrant is checked by the designated authority under s 2, or an extradition request is checked by the Secretary of State under s 70.
Channel Islands	The Bailiwick of Guernsey and the Bailiwick of Jersey, that is, Guernsey, Jersey, Alderney, Sark, Herm, Jethou, Brecqhou, and Lihou. They are Crown Dependencies, and are not part of the UK.
CICA 2003	Crime (International Co-operation) Act 2003 (Appendix M1).
CJ Order 2005	Criminal Justice (International Co-operation) Act 1990 (Enforcement of Overseas Forfeiture Orders) Order 2005 (SI 2005/3180).
Clemency proceedings	Clemency proceedings are proceedings in a country outside the UK, not being proceedings before a court exercising criminal jurisdiction, for the removal or reduction of a penalty imposed on conviction of an offence (CICA 2003, s 51(1)).
Codes of Practice	The Codes issued by the Secretary of State under EA 2003, s 173: see Extradition Act 2003 (Police Powers: Codes of Practice) Order 2003 (SI 2003/3336).
Commonwealth Scheme Relating to Mutual Assistance in Criminal Matters 1986	The Scheme adopted by Commonwealth Law Ministers in Harare, Zimbabwe, in August 1986, in relation to mutual legal assistance in criminal matters (Commonwealth Secretariat, London, LMN (86) 13). A new Scheme is currently (August 2012) under consideration by the Commonwealth.
Convention on Driving Disqualifications	An EU Convention (Official Journal C 216, 10 July 1998) establishing a mandatory legal framework between member States so that drivers disqualified in a state other than the one where they have their principal residence cannot circumvent the disqualification when they leave the state where the offence was committed. It is implemented in Part 3 of CICA 2003.
Convention on Mutual Assistance in Criminal Matters and its Protocol	An EU Convention which was adopted by the Council of Ministers on 29 May 2000 (Official Journal 197, 12 July 2000, p 3). The Protocol was adopted in 2001 (Official Journal C 326, 21 November 2001, p 1).
Convention rights	Those rights specified in HRA 1998, s 1, that are given further effect to in domestic law, namely: Articles 2–12 and 14 of the ECHR; Articles 1–3 of the First Protocol to the ECHR; and Article 1 of the Thirteenth Protocol to the ECHR; in each case read with Articles 16–18 of the ECHR.

CPS	Crown Prosecution Service, established by the Prosecution of Offences Act 1985.
Criminal Procedure Rules	The Criminal Procedure Rules 2012 (SI 2012/1726). Part 17 contains rules relating to extradition and Part 32 contains rules relating to international cooperation. The majority of the rules in Part 17 only apply in relation to requests received prior to 31 December 2003, that is, requests dealt with under the EA 1989.
Customs officer	A person commissioned by the Commissioners of Customs and Excise under s 6(3) of the Customs and Excise Management Act 1979 (s 216(8)).
Designated authority	The organizations designated by order with the function of certifying Part 1 warrants received from Category 1 territories prior to the person's arrest (s 2(9)). Under the Extradition Act 2003 (Part 1 Designated Authorities) Order 2003 (SI 2003/3190) the designated central authorities for the UK are SOCA and the Crown Agent of the Scottish Crown Office.
Domestic freezing order	An order for protecting evidence which is overseas pending its transfer to the UK (CICA 2003, s 10(2)).
Domestic warrant	A warrant for the arrest or apprehension of a person which is issued under the provisions specified in EA 2003, s 142(8).
DPP	Director of Public Prosecutions.
EA 1870	The Extradition Act 1870 (Appendix E1).
EA 1989	Extradition Act 1989 (Appendix E2).
EA 2003	Extradition Act 2003 (Appendix E3).
EAW	European arrest warrant. The form of the EAW is annexed to the EAW Framework Decision.
EAW Framework Decision	Council Framework Decision of 13 June 2002 on the European arrest warrant and the surrender procedures between Member States (2002/584/JHA) (Appendix E4).
ECHR	European Convention on Human Rights 1950 (CETS 005).
ECJ	European Court of Justice. Following the entry into force of the Treaty of Lisbon on 1 December 2009, the ECJ's official name was changed from the 'Court of Justice of the European Communities' to the 'Court of Justice' although in English it is still commonly referred to as the European Court of Justice. The Court of First Instance was renamed as the 'General Court', and the term 'Court of Justice of the European Union' officially designates the two courts, as along with its specialized tribunals, taken together. The Court's website is <http://curia.europa.eu/>.
EEW	European evidence warrant, created by the EEW Framework Decision.
EEW Framework Decision	Council Framework Decision of 18 December 2008 on the European evidence warrant for the purpose of obtaining objects, documents, and data for use in proceedings in criminal matters (2008/978/JHA).
EIS	Europol Information System, the computerized database maintained by Europol provided for in Articles 11–13 of the Europol Decision.
EU	European Union.
Eurojust	The body established by the Eurojust Decision is to enhance the development of Europe-wide cooperation between prosecutors in criminal justice matters.
Eurojust Decision	European Council Decision of 28 February 2002 (2002/187/JHA), as amended by Council Decisions 2003/659/JHA and 2009/486/JHA.

European Convention on Extradition	The Council of Europe Convention on Extradition which opened for signature in 1957 (CETS 024). The Additional Protocol opened for signature in 1975 (CETS 086) and the Second Additional Protocol opened for signature in 1978 (CETS 098). The UK has ratified the Convention and the Protocols.
European Convention on Mutual Legal Assistance in Criminal Matters	The Council of Europe Convention on Mutual Assistance in Criminal Matters which opened for signature in 1959 (ETS No 030). The Additional Protocol to the Convention opened for signature in 1978 (ETS No 99). There is a Second Additional Protocol (ETS No 182) which the UK ratified in 2010.
European framework list	*See* Framework offence.
EIO	European Investigation Order. The goal of this measure, an initiative of seven member states presented in April 2010, is to allow member states to carry out investigative measures at the request of another member state on the basis of mutual recognition. The investigative measures would, for example, include interviewing of witnesses, searches and seizures, and (with additional safeguards) interception of telecommunications, observation, infiltration, and monitoring of bank accounts. The UK has signalled its intention to implement the EIO. The measure is currently (September 2012) under discussion within the EU bodies.
EJN	The European Judicial Network is a network of national contact points for the facilitation of judicial cooperation in criminal matters. Its legal basis is the Council Decision 2008/976/JHA of 16 December 2008 on the European Judicial Network: see <http://www.ejn-crimjust.europa.eu/ejn/>.
Europol	European Police Office, established by Council Decision of 6 April 2009 establishing the European Police Office (2009/371/JHA): see <https://www.europol.europa.eu/>.
Europol Convention	The Council Act of 26 July 1995 (Official Journal C 316, 27 November 1995) which established Europol. It was replaced by the Europol Decision with effect from 1 January 2010.
Europol Decision	Council Decision of 6 April 2009 establishing the European Police Office (2009/371/JHA), which replaced the Europol Convention with effect from 1 January 2010.
Excluded material	In general terms, material, records, or substances held in confidence (see PACE, s 11).
External order	An order which is made by an overseas court where property is found or believed to have been obtained as a result of or in connection with criminal conduct, and is for the recovery of specified property or a specified sum of money (POCA 2002, s 447(2)).
External request	A request by an overseas authority to prohibit dealing with relevant property which is identified in the request (POCA 2002, s 447(1)).
Extradition arrest power	For the purposes of Part 4 of the EA 2003, an extradition arrest power means a Part 1 warrant in respect of which a certificate under s 2 has been issued; s 5; a warrant issued under s 71; and a provisional warrant issued under s 73 (EA 2003, s 174(2)).
Extradition hearing	The main part of the extradition process where the appropriate judge considers the request for extradition of the person against criteria laid out in the Act (EA 2003, ss 68 and 140).
Extradition offence	An offence over which another country has jurisdiction, for which the person has been requested to stand trial, be sentenced, or serve a sentence abroad and for which the UK will consider extradition (EA 2003, ss 64–66 and ss 137–8). Alternatively, an offence for which the UK seeks a person's extradition from another country (EA 2003, s 148).

Extradition request	The documentation transmitted on a government-to-government basis from a Category 2 territory which requests a person's arrest and extradition (EA 2003, s 70). To be valid, the extradition request must meet the criteria in EA 2003, s 70(3).
Framework decision	A type of EU legislation that had the purpose of approximating the laws and regulations of member States. Framework decisions were binding upon member States as to the result to be achieved, but left to the national authorities the choice of form and methods (Treaty of Amsterdam, Article 34(2)(b)). The Treaty of Lisbon abolished Framework decisions and the EU can now enact directives and regulations in the area of criminal justice by means of the ordinary legislative process. For the complex transitional provisions relating to existing Framework decisions, see *Assange v Swedish Prosecuting Authority* [2012] 2 WLR 1275, paras 198–200.
Framework (list) offence	The list of conduct set out in EA 2003, Sch 2 to the Act (EA 2003, s 215). These are the offences for which dual criminality is not required under Part 1. The list in Sch 2 mirrors the list of conduct in the EAW Framework Decision.
Freezing Framework Decision	Council Framework Decision on the execution in the EU of orders freezing property or evidence (2003/577/JHA, 22 July 2003; Official Journal L 196, 2 August 2003).
Habeas corpus ad subjiciendum	Commonly known as the writ of *habeas corpus*, this is a process for securing the liberty of the subject by affording an effective means of immediate release from unlawful or unjustifiable detention.
Harare Scheme	*See* Commonwealth Scheme Relating to Mutual Assistance in Criminal Matters 1986.
HMRC	Her Majesty's Revenue and Customs. A department of the UK Government responsible inter alia for the collection of direct and indirect taxation and the enforcement of the criminal law in relation to its areas of responsibility.
Hong Kong SAR	Hong Kong Special Administrative Region of the People's Republic of China.
HRA 1998	Human Rights Act 1998.
ICC	International Criminal Court (see <http://www.un.org/law/icc>).
ICC Act 2001	International Criminal Court Act 2001.
ICTR	International Criminal Tribunal for Rwanda (see <http://www.ictr.org>).
ICTY	International Criminal Tribunal for the Former Yugoslavia (see <http://www.un.org/icty>).
Initial hearing	The stage in the extradition process under Part 1 at which the defendant is first brought before a district judge (EA 2003, ss 7–8).
Interpol	International Criminal Police Organization (<http://www.interpol.int>). SOCA is the UK National Bureau of Interpol.
Items subject to legal privilege	Communications between a professional legal adviser and the client that is concerned with the proceedings. Anything held with the intention of furthering a criminal cause is not covered (EA 2003, s 174(4); PACE, s 10).
Judicial authority	The authority in a Category 1 territory which has the function of issuing a Part 1 warrant in that country. The expression is also used in various places in CICA 2003.
Member state	A member State of the EU.
MLA	Mutual legal assistance, or mutual assistance. The process by which countries assist each other in the investigation and prosecution of crime. Extradition is a form of MLA, but in Part II of this book it is used to denote forms of assistance other than extradition.

MLA Guidelines	Mutual Legal Assistance Guidelines for the United Kingdom (10th edn, Home Office, September 2012) (Appendix M3).
MLAT	Mutual legal assistance treaty.
Nominated court	A court nominated under CICA 2003, s 14, to give effect to a request by receiving evidence under s 15 and Sch 1.
Overseas freezing order	An order for protecting, pending its transfer to a foreign state, evidence which is in the UK and may be used in any proceedings or investigation in that country (CICA 2003, s 20).
PACE	Police and Criminal Evidence Act 1984.
Part 1 territory	*See* Category 1 territory.
Part 2 territory	*See* Category 2 territory.
Part 1 warrant	An arrest warrant issued by a judicial authority in a Category 1 territory containing the information required by s 2(2) (s 2(2)).
Part 3 warrant	A warrant obtained for the purposes of requesting extradition from a Category 1 territory under Part 3 (s 142(3)).
Participating country	See CICA 2003, s 51(2). A participating country, in relation to any provision of Part 1 of CICA 2003, means (a) a country other than the UK which is a member state on a day appointed for the commencement of that provision; and (b) any other country designated by an order made by the Secretary of State or, in relation to Scotland, the Scottish Ministers. The following orders have been made in relation to England Wales and Northern Ireland: Crime (International Co-operation) Act 2003 (Designation of Participating Countries) (England, Wales and Northern Ireland) Order 2008 (SI 2008/2156); Crime (International Co-operation) Act 2003 (Designation of Participating Countries) (England, Wales and Northern Ireland) Order 2009 (SI 2009/613); Crime (International Co-operation) Act 2003 (Designation of Participating Countries) (England, Wales and Northern Ireland) (No 2) Order 2009 (SI 2009/1764); Crime (International Co-operation) Act 2003 (Designation of Participating Countries) (England, Wales and Northern Ireland) Order 2010 (SI 2010/36); Crime (International Co-operation) Act 2003 (Designation of Participating Countries) (England, Wales and Northern Ireland) (No 2) Order 2011 (SI 2011/229).
POCA 2002	Proceeds of Crime Act 2002.
POCA Order 2005	Proceeds of Crime Act 2002 (External Requests and Orders) Order 2005 (SI 2005/3181) (Appendix M2).
Production order	An order made for the production of documents under pain of criminal penalty for non-compliance. Production orders can be made under various statutory provisions including EA 2003, s 157; Criminal Justice Act 1987, s 2; and s 9 and Sch 1 of PACE.
Provisional arrest	(1) Arrest under Part 1 pending receipt of a certified Part 1 warrant or certified EAW; or (2) arrest under Part 2 under a provisional arrest warrant issued by a UK magistrate, pending receipt of the necessary documents required under EA 2003 (EA 2003, ss 5 and 73).
Refugee Convention	Convention and Protocol relating to the Status of Refugees 1951(Cmd 9171) and 1967 (Cmd 3906).
Relevant property	Property is relevant property if there are reasonable grounds to believe that it may be needed to satisfy an external order which has been or which may be made (POCA 2002, s 447(4)).

Schengen Convention	The EU Convention signed in June 1990 which came into effect in March 1995 (Official Journal L 239, 22 September 2000, p 19). The Convention abolished the checks at internal borders of the signatory states and created a single external frontier, where checks for all the Schengen signatories were to be carried out in accordance with a common set of rules. The Convention has 142 articles providing measures for creating a common area of justice and security, following abolition of common borders. Its key aims are to facilitate free movement within participating states; to improve police cooperation; extend the provision of MLA between EU states; and to improve access to the SIS, a system for the exchange of data relevant to criminal investigations within the EU. The UK is not currently part of the SIS, but will be part of the updated system, SIS II, which is expected to become operational in 2013.
Search and seizure warrant	A warrant issued by a court for the search of premises and seizure of material. Search and seizure warrants can be issued under various statutory provisions including EA 2003, s 156; CICA 2003, ss 16 and 17; and Part 2 and Sch 1 of PACE.
Serious or complex fraud	Those frauds in relation to which the Director of the SFO may exercise his powers under CICA 2003 and the Criminal Justice Act 1987.
Service policeman	A member of the Royal Navy Regulating Branch, the Royal Marines Police, the Royal Military Police, or the Royal Air Force Police (EA 2003, s 216(13)).
SFO	Serious Fraud Office: see <http://www.sfo.gov.uk>.
SIRENE	SIRENE stands for **S**upplementary **I**nformation **Re**quest at the **N**ational **E**ntry. The main task of SIRENE Bureaux established in all Schengen states is the exchange of additional or supplementary information on SIS alerts between the states. SIRENE Bureaux provide supplementary information on alerts and coordinate measures in relation to alerts in the SIS, and ensure that appropriate action is taken if a wanted person is arrested, a person who has been refused entry to the Schengen area tries to re-enter, a missing person found, a stolen car or ID document seized, and so on. When SIS is replaced by SIS II in 2013, SOCA will contain the UK's SIRENE Bureau.
SIS	Schengen Information System. *See* Schengen Convention.
SOCA	Serious Organized Crime Agency: see <http://www.soca.gov.uk>. If enacted, Part 1 of the Crime and Courts Bill (before Parliament in August 2012) will abolish SOCA and replace it with the National Crime Agency.
SOCPA	Serious Organized Crime and Police Act 2005, s 1 of which establishes SOCA.
Special procedure material	Journalistic material or material held in confidence by someone in a professional or official capacity, other than excluded material or items subject to legal privilege (EA 2003, s 174(6); PACE, s 14).
Speciality	*See* Specialty.
Specialty	A rule of extradition law that is intended to ensure that an extradited defendant is not dealt with in the requesting state for any offence other than that for which he was extradited: see EA 2003, ss 17 and 95.
Standing arrangements	Arrangements in force between the UK and the Category 1 territory for determining which state is responsible for considering applications for asylum (EA 2003, s 40(4)).

Territorial authority	The authority responsible for receiving and processing incoming letters of request. CICA 2003, s 28(9) defines the territorial authority in relation to evidence in England and Wales or Northern Ireland as the Secretary of State and in relation to Scotland as being the Lord Advocate. In practice, the functions of the Secretary of State are exercised by the UK Central Authority. The Commissioners of Customs and Excise may also act as a territorial authority for certain purposes.
Transmission	The process of sending evidence obtained in the UK to the requesting state pursuant to a request for mutual assistance.
Treaty of Amsterdam	The EU Treaty signed at Amsterdam on 10 November 1997 (Official Journal 1997 C 340).
Treaty on European Union	The EU Treaty signed at Maastricht on 7 February 1992 (Official Journal 1992 C191).
Treaty of Lisbon	The EU Treaty signed at Lisbon on 13 December 2007 which entered into force on 1 December 2009 (2007/C 306/01). It amends the two treaties which form the constitutional basis of the EU, namely the Treaty of Rome and the Treaty on European Union.
UK	United Kingdom, that is, England, Scotland, Wales, and Northern Ireland.
UK Central Authority	The Home Office agency which exercises the functions of the Secretary of State in relation to criminal mutual legal assistance in England and Wales, and provides guidance in relation to such assistance. Its address is: United Kingdom Central Authority, Home Office, 2 Marsham Street, London SW1P 4DF; tel +44 207 035 4040; fax +44 207 035 1280; e-mail ukcentralauthority@homeoffice.gsi.gov.uk. There is also a UK Central Authority for the Exchange of Criminal Records (within the EU): UK Central Authority for the Exchange of Criminal Records, PO Box 481, Fareham PO14 9FS; tel +44 (0)1489 569805.
UN	United Nations.

INDEX